Casebook on
Contract Law

Seventh Edition

Jill Poole

LLB, LLM, FCI Arb, of Lincoln's Inn, Barrister

Professor of Commercial Law, Deputy Director of the Centre for Legal Research
Faculty of Law, University of the West of England, Bristol

OXFORD
UNIVERSITY PRESS

OXFORD

UNIVERSITY PRESS

Great Clarendon Street, Oxford OX2 6DP

Oxford University Press is a department of the University of Oxford.
It furthers the University's objective of excellence in research, scholarship,
and education by publishing worldwide in

Oxford New York

Auckland Cape Town Dar es Salaam Hong Kong Karachi
Kuala Lumpur Madrid Melbourne Mexico City Nairobi
New Delhi Shanghai Taipei Toronto

With offices in

Argentina Austria Brazil Chile Czech Republic France Greece
Guatemala Hungary Italy Japan Poland Portugal Singapore
South Korea Switzerland Thailand Turkey Ukraine Vietnam

Oxford is a registered trade mark of Oxford University Press
in the UK and in certain other countries

Published in the United States
by Oxford University Press Inc., New York

First edition 1992
Second edition 1995
Third edition 1997
Fourth edition 1999
Reprinted 1999, 2000, 2001
Fifth edition 2001
Reprinted 2002
Sixth edition 2003
Seventh edition 2005

British Library Cataloguing in Publication Data

A catalogue record for this book is available from the British Library

Typeset by RefineCatch Limited, Bungay, Suffolk
Printed in Great Britain by
Ashford Colour Press Ltd., Gosport, Hampshire

ISBN 0–19–927550–5   978–0–19–927550–2

3 5 7 9 10 8 6 4 2

OUTLINE CONTENTS

DETAILED CONTENTS

PREFACE

This edition continues my aim of providing a structured discussion of contract case law which is as up to date as possible. My intention is that this casebook should be equally useful for students whether they wish to read about individual case decisions or want to promote their understanding of a topic. Each chapter is therefore intended to provide a readable, detailed, and structured account of relevant principles as developed through the case law. The emphasis reflects the fact that contract law courses require students to develop skills of application through the use of hypothetical problem questions so that it is necessary to be familiar with a large number of cases as illustrations of the development of principle. As usual, I have selected case law on the basis of relevance to course content and the extracts are chosen to illustrate the reasoning processes of the court so that students are better able to understand the decisions and the development of legal principles. I have also raised questions concerning the impact and significance of many of the decisions. The notes and questions continue to generate e-mails and written questions from students throughout the UK and abroad. I have endeavoured to respond to these many questions and I am grateful for the many positive comments and feedback. The publication of *Textbook on Contract Law* has enabled me to provide further explanation than would be possible within the confines of a book devoted purely to case law and to provide suggestions for resolving some of the issues raised as questions in this casebook.

There is a companion web site to support the publication of *Casebook* and *Textbook on Contract Law*. This web site contains notes relating to the new case reading exercises contained in Chapter 1, some self-test questions and answers, advice on answering problem-style questions and summaries of decisions occurring post-publication. The companion web site also provides the ideal forum to answer specific short questions concerning substantive principles of contract law and study techniques.

This edition includes a number of very important recent decisions including the much-awaited decision of the House of Lords in *Shogun Finance Ltd v Hudson* (mistake as to identity), which has necessitated a major rewrite of Chapter 3. Many of the most significant and interesting cases have been first instance decisions such as *Nisshin Shipping Co Ltd v Cleaves & Co Ltd* (examining The Contracts (Rights of Third Parties) Act 1999, Chapter 10), *Rolls-Royce Power Engineering plc v Ricardo Consulting Engineers Ltd* (discussion of the 'narrow ground' and 'broad ground' in the *St Martin's Property* Appeal, Chapter 10), and *Hamilton-Jones v David & Snape (a firm)* (damages for distress, Chapter 9). There have been a number of important decisions on terms, particularly implied terms and entire agreement clauses, as well as a number of cases examining the Unfair Terms in Consumer Contracts Regulations 1999, namely *Bairstow Eves London Central Ltd v Smith*, *Bankers Insurance Co Ltd v South*, and *Westminster Building Co Ltd v Beckingham*. New case law examining the scope of *White & Carter (Councils) Ltd v McGregor* is discussed in Chapter 8 and I have added some post-*Great Peace* case law in the discussion on common mistake in Chapter 11. It may have been anticipated that *Royal Bank of Scotland v Etridge (No. 2)* (Chapter 13) would represent the definitive statement of principle governing allegations of undue influence so that the usual complete rewrite of this section would no longer be required. However, the position remains confused since the principles in *Etridge* have been subjected to some curious interpretations as the courts have attempted further 'clarification'. Although this is a casebook, I have taken some liberties and included an outline of the recommendations contained in the Law Commission Report on *Unfair Terms in Contracts*, which was published the week before my writing deadline. If the draft Bill is enacted it will transform the legislative regulation of this area–and will impact on the case law in due course.

I would like to thank my colleagues at UWE for their support and particularly Adrian Chandler and James Devenney of the Commercial Law Research Unit for finding the time to discuss contract case law. My research assistant, Stephen Thomas, has assisted with copying and filing case law and academic articles, thereby ensuring that my contract database remains as comprehensive and up to date as possible. I am also extremely grateful to Michael Furmston and Rob Merkin who have been generally supportive and helped throughout my academic career. The team at Oxford University Press, especially Sarah Hyland and Phil Dines, deserve a special mention and my thanks for putting up with me and providing support and advice at every stage of the writing and production process. Finally, my thanks to the many colleagues at institutions throughout England and Wales and overseas who continue to recommend *Casebook on Contract Law* to their students. It is particularly gratifying to know I am so (in)famous in the Far East and even, according to one former student, 'a legend'!

Single parenthood is not easily reconciled with a daily commute, a demanding full-time job, and the writing process. That I somehow manage to keep juggling my many and various activities is the direct result of the support of my amazing parents, Dewi and Margaret. I need to thank them for many things but particularly for ensuring that I don't return each evening to a house in the condition in which my children leave it in the mornings. My friends have provided the usual pleasant distractions and have convincingly feigned a generous level of interest in all of my writing projects.

No edition would be complete without an update on my children and I know from student emails that this is often regarded as a more interesting inclusion than the latest judicial reassessment of contractual principle. When the first edition of this book was published, Becci and Alex (ages now withheld to avoid causing them embarrassment), were five and two (so you can do the maths for yourselves) and this book has grown with them. They are now both over 5 ft 9 inches tall and look down on their 'little mum' (unless I wear my very highest heels or stand on a step). They are tremendous fun, untidiness notwithstanding, and our house is a place of much hilarity and little peace. They have become accustomed to talking to my back while I tap away in my study and I have become accustomed to answering their questions (usually with some degree of toleration) while trying to hold a crucial legal argument in my head. On the one occasion on which I was a little late in leaving my study to commence my evening duty as resident chef, Alex and his girlfriend decided to take matters into their own hands and after one aborted attempt which proved totally inedible, managed to set the alternative menu–and the kitchen–on fire. Alex announced with great glee that he had managed to put it out quite quickly, so what was I worried about? Since then he has been enduring a course of my cookery lessons. Fortunately, Becci isn't as ambitious in the kitchen but has graduated to providing the on-call taxi service for her brother and his girlfriend. Thankfully that is one duty from which I am usually now excused.

I hope that this is a book which all students of contract law will continue to find useful in promoting their understanding of what can be a complex and technical subject and that my enthusiasm for this subject will prove infectious.

Jill Poole
Llandaff, Cardiff
E-mail address: jill.poole@uwe.ac.uk

ACKNOWLEDGEMENTS

The publishers and author would like to thank the following for permission to reproduce extracts from reports of cases as listed below:

Canada Law Book Publishing—Extract from *London Drugs Ltd v Kuehne & Nagel International Ltd* (1993) 97 DLR (4th) 261, reproduced by kind permission of *Access Copyright*, The Canadian Copyright Licensing Agency.

DSP Publishing Ltd—Extracts from the Commercial Law Cases reproduced by kind permission of DSP Publishing Ltd.

The Estates Gazette Ltd—Extracts from The Estates Gazette Law Reports are reproduced by kind permission of The Estates Gazette Group. Copyright: Reed Business Information 2005.

The High Court of Australia—Extracts from cases reported in The Commonwealth Law Reports are reproduced by kind permission of the High Court of Australia.

The Incorporated Council of Law Reporting for England and Wales—The Law Reports, the Weekly Law Reports and the Industrial Cases Reports. The special permission to reproduce in Chapter 1 extracts from the headnotes of *Carlill v Carbolic Smoke Ball Company* [1893] 1 QB 256 and *Howard Marine and Dredging Co. Ltd v A. Ogden and Sons (Excavations) Ltd* [1978] QB 574, is gratefully acknowledged.

The Incorporated Council of Law Reporting for Ireland (Irish Reports) —Extract from *Schawel v Reade* [1913] 2 IR 81 is reproduced with kind permission of the Incorporated Council of Law Reporting for Ireland.

Informa Professional Extracts from Lloyd's Law Reports and The Building Law Reports published by Informa Professional, a trading division of Informa UK Ltd, Informa House, 30–32 Mortimer Street, London W1W 7RE, Tel: + 44 (0)20 7017 5215, Fax: + 44 (0)20 7017 5274.

LexisNexis Butterworths—Extracts from The All England Law Reports, The All England Law Reports Commercial Cases, Family Court Reports, Law Times Reports and *Shuey v US* (23 L.Ed. 697 (1875)), reproduced by kind permission of Reed Elsevier (UK) Limited trading as LexisNexis Butterworths.

New Zealand Council of Law Reporting—Extracts from *Antons Trawling Co Ltd v Smith* [2003] 2 NZLR 23 reproduced by kind permission of the New Zealand Council of Law Reporting

Sweet and Maxwell Limited—Extracts from *Centrovincial Estates plc v Merchant Investors Assurance Co. Ltd.* [1983] Com LR 158 and *R v Attorney General of England and Wales* [2003] UKPC 22, [2003] EMLR 24, are reproduced by kind permission of Sweet & Maxwell Ltd.

Times Newspapers Ltd—The Times Law Reports, extract from *King's Norton Metal Co. Ltd v Edridge, Merrett and Co. Ltd* (1897) 14 TLR 98, Times Newspapers Limited, London 1897.

West Group Publishing Corporation—*Hamer v Sidway* 27 NE 256 (1891) and *Petterson v Pattberg* 161 NE 428 (1928) reprinted from the North Eastern Reporter (West's National Reporter System) by kind permission of the Thomson-West Publishing Corporation.

TABLE OF CASES

TABLE OF STATUTES

European ... Legislation

International Conventions

Australia

New Zealand

Uganda

United States

TABLE OF STATUTORY INSTRUMENTS

1

Guidance on Reading Cases

SECTION 1: **A GUIDING PRINCIPLE**

It is essential to acquire case reading skills for the purposes of legal research, but there is very little point in reading a case if after reading it you do not understand how it relates to the legal principles you will have learnt in lectures. It is important, therefore, to know what issue you should find in the case and use this to give your case reading some direction and context.

Read a case with either a broad heading or a specific principle in mind. The principle or heading will be indicated on your lecture outline, in the lecture itself or in a text-book. If you need to read a recent case and have no indication of the issues involved, you will need to be guided by the catchwords and headnote at the top of the report. An individual case may well be concerned with many different issues which you are not currently studying, and while it is interesting to read about them, pressures of time mean that it is necessary to direct your reading.

Of course, if you have a casebook someone else will have provided the headings and decided what parts of which decisions and judgments are relevant to illustrate this principle. This saves time and can be very helpful indeed while you are still in the process of acquiring the skill of deciding what is relevant.

SECTION 2: **USEFUL NOTES**

It is not simply a matter of reading a case; you must understand it and will probably wish to keep a note of it. It is advisable to remember that your notes should not be longer than the case itself!

The notes also need to be helpful. Avoid copying too much material (with the exception of the facts and specific statements in the judgments that you may wish to use later) and try to explain the case in your own words. This will ensure that you understand what you are writing and will be able to use it later.

It is also a useful practice to use one side of the paper for lecture notes and to make notes on the relevant cases on the back of the preceding sheet. Some people prefer the use of small cards with an index system.

Check for any case notes or other critical assessments of the case in question and the issues it raises. Try to appreciate the significance of the case to the legal issue involved.

SECTION 3: THE BASICS OF READING A CASE

(a) Decide which case or cases to read

The more cases you read properly the better. Many lecturers indicate, sometimes by the use of an asterisk, the cases that they consider to be the most important or the best illustrations of the principle.

(b) Use the citation to find the report of the case

As from 11 January 2001, neutral citation was introduced for decisions of the Court of Appeal and House of Lords, e.g. [2001] EWCA Civ 12 (see *Practice Direction (Form of Judgments, Paragraph Marking and Neutral Citation)* [2001] 1 WLR 194). The Practice Direction (High Court Judgments; Neutral Citation) [2002] 1 WLR 346 extended neutral citation to all judgments given by the High Court in London, e.g., EWHC [number] (Ch) for the Chancery Division, EWHC [number] (QB) for the Queen's Bench Division, EWHC [number] (Comm) for the Commercial Court. These changes are designed to facilitate the publication of judgments on the World Wide Web but will also assist in identifying individual judgments of issues involving the same parties.

(c) Note the full case name and court

These are given at the top of the report (in older cases in the *English Reports* you may have to find the beginning of the reports of that particular reporter to find out the court). The court deciding the case can be significant, and you will need to be familiar with the court structure (civil for contract cases) and the doctrine of precedent.

Also note the reference of the case, since this will be needed for inclusion in the footnotes in any written work.

In accordance with the *Practice Direction (Forms of Judgments, Paragraph Marking and Neutral Citation)* [2001] 1 WLR 194, as from 11 January 2001 all judgments will need to be cited using the neutral citation before the citation of any law report series, e.g. *Watford Electronics Ltd* v *Sanderson CFL Ltd* [2001] EWCA Civ 317, [2001] 1 All ER (Comm) 696, [2001] BLR 143. For the neutral citation, paragraphs should be cited and not page numbers, e.g. [2001] EWCA Civ 317 at [31]–[34].

The *Practice Direction* also makes it clear that where a case has been reported in the official Law Reports published by the Incorporated Council of Law Reporting, that source must be used before the High Court and Court of Appeal. It would therefore be sensible to adopt this practice as a student. Only where a case is not reported in the official Law Reports should other citations be used.

(d) Presentation of case reports

This is fairly standardised.

(i) Catchwords

At the top of the headnote there is a section identifying the issues in the case (known as the 'catchwords'). These should correspond at some point with the legal issues given in the heading or principle in your lecture notes or outline. There is no need to note these catchwords.

(ii) Headnote facts

Sometimes these facts will be very brief indeed and too general. On other occasions there will be full case facts and details of the decision at first instance, or previous appeals if the case is now on appeal.

Make notes on whatever facts are relevant to the principle you are using as your guide. If the headnote facts are brief, then look for further facts in the judgments.

Remember that each case is a decision on its particular facts so that the facts are important.

(iii) Statement of the decision of the court

The headnote may not be detailed enough on the reasons for the decision, so that you will need to look at the judgments themselves to extract this information.

(iv) More detailed facts

A more detailed statement of the facts may follow the headnote. Some judgments will also contain details of the facts. Lord Denning's judgments are particularly good at setting out the facts in a readable form, and he also used headings to useful effect. More generally, it has become common practice to use headings and sub-headings within judgments in order to separate and identify both issues of fact and of law.

(v) Details of the grounds of any appeal and the arguments of each set of counsel

It can be particularly useful to read these arguments in the light of the actual decision given in the headnote. They are also helpful to those who are participating in moots.

(vi) A judgment or number of judgments

The headnote will be helpful in many cases in indicating the majority, the judgments which require particular attention and the principles that you will need to look for in reading the judgments. It should also indicate any dissenting judgments.

With appeal cases the headnote may indicate relevant page numbers in judgments, e.g., *Howard Marine & Dredging Company Ltd* v *A. Ogden & Sons (Excavations) Ltd* [1978] QB 574 (see *pages 14–15 below*). As from 2001 all judgments have paragraph numbers which must be cited in the context of neutral citation.

If there is any difference of opinion on the reasons for a decision or an actual dissent, then these judgments require examination to determine the reasons given for the differences and dissents.

Ensure that the judgments do in fact correspond with the stated decision in the headnote, and use the comments in the judgments to explain and illustrate the decision.

(vii) Case law applied and distinguished

The names of those cases, which the court is purporting to apply and to rely on as justification for part or all of the decision, should be given. If the court is purporting to distinguish any case authority this should also be stated.

SECTION 4: READING A CASE IN PRACTICE

Your Contract Law tutor has advised you to read *Carlill v Carbolic Smoke Ball Company* [1893] 1 QB 256, on offer and acceptance.

Find the report of the case in volume one of the *Law Reports* Queen's Bench Division for 1893, at p. 256. (There are numerous other reports of this case, e.g., at 62 LJQB 257 or 67 LT 837.)

Make a note of the full case name and the fact that this is a decision of the Court of Appeal. (It may be preferable to list the members of the Court when stating the decision.) Also remember to note the reference used.

[IN THE COURT OF APPEAL]

CARLILL v CARBOLIC SMOKE BALL COMPANY

Contract—Offer by Advertisement—Performance of Condition in Advertisement— Notification of Acceptance of Offer—Wager—Insurance—8 & 9 Vict. c. 109–14 Geo. 3, c. 48, s. 2.

The defendants, the proprietors of a medical preparation called 'The Carbolic Smoke Ball,' issued an advertisement in which they offered to pay 100*l.* to any person who contracted influenza after having used one of their smoke balls in a specified manner and for a specified period. The plaintiff on the faith of the advertisment bought one of the balls, and used it in the manner and for the period specified, but nevertheless contracted the influenza:—

Held, affirming the decision of Hawkins, J that the above facts established a contract by the defendants to pay the plaintiff 100*l.* in the event which had happened; that such contract was neither a contract by way of wagering within 8 & 9 Vict c. 109, nor a policy within 14 Geo 3, c. 48, s. 2; and that the plaintiff was entitled to recover.

(a) Catchwords

The catchwords are helpful in advising that this is a case about a contract and is concerned with an offer by advertisement. This is within your guiding principle of offer and acceptance.

This case is also about two other issues which are not within your guiding principle of offer and acceptance, namely wager and insurance. Do not worry about these for the present.

(b) Facts

The facts given in the headnote are very brief indeed. A more detailed statement of the facts follows the headnote.

(c) Decision

The facts are followed by a brief statement of what was decided.

We are told that the Court of Appeal affirmed the first instance decision of Hawkins J (the reference for this is given at the bottom of p. 256 in note (2) as [1892] 2 QB 484). If you are mooting, it is advisable to have full details of this first instance decision in order to know the arguments presented and those that were accepted on that occasion.

The headnote states that the Court of Appeal held that the defendants (the Smoke Ball Company) agreed to pay the plaintiff £100 in the event which happened (namely, contracting influenza after having used one of the smoke balls in the specified manner and for the specified period).

We are also told that it was decided that it was not a wagering contract or a policy of insurance, so that the plaintiff was entitled to recover the £100. Although under the Civil Procedure Rules 1998, the term 'claimant' is used in place of plaintiff, this case pre-dates this change so that the term 'plaintiff' remains appropriate in this specific context.

(d) Note the facts

At this point it is advisable to note the facts to make it easier to understand the judgments. Because the headnote facts are too brief for this purpose, the statement of facts on pp. 256–7 of the report is used:

Carlill v Carbolic Smoke Ball Company
[1893] 1 QB 256 (CA)

The defendants, who made and sold a medical preparation called 'The Carbolic Smoke Ball', issued an advertisement in a number of newspapers in the following terms:

> £100 reward will be paid by the Carbolic Smoke Ball Company to any person who contracts the increasing epidemic influenza, colds, or any disease caused by taking cold, after having used the ball three times daily for two weeks according to the printed directions supplied with each ball. £1,000 is deposited with the Alliance Bank, Regent Street, shewing our sincerity in the matter.

On the faith of this advertisement, the plaintiff bought one of the balls at a chemist's and used it as directed three times a day from 20 November 1891 to 17 January 1892, when she contracted influenza.

She sought payment of the £100 and the defendants refused.

(e) The decision at first instance

Hawkins J at first instance held that the plaintiff was entitled to recover, since the advertisement was intended to attract custom and was supported by the deposit with the Company's bank. The Company should not have been surprised if they were held to their promise. (The only way to find this information is to look at the report of the first instance decision.)

Since the Court of Appeal is purporting to affirm the first instance decision, there is no need in this instance to make detailed notes on it.

(f) The decision of the Court of Appeal

Making a note of the Court of Appeal's decision in this case is comparatively difficult since the headnote is a broad statement of result without giving reasons. It is therefore necessary to look at the judgments. (There is also no indication in the headnote of any dissent, so that the three judgments should be saying the same thing.)

On occasions it can be helpful to look at the arguments of counsel, and in this case the defendants put forward a number of arguments as to why there should be no binding contract. However, since the members of the Court of Appeal identify and answer these points in their judgments, there is no need to duplicate them by making notes on the arguments of counsel.

(g) The judgments

Read each judgment and make quick, rough notes.

(i) The judgment of Lindley LJ

(a) Lindley LJ rejects the two arguments which are outside the scope of our directing issue, namely that it was an unenforceable wagering contract and insurance policy.

(b) Lindley LJ considered that there was no doubt that the language used indicated that a binding promise was being made. To be enforceable the promise must have been intended to give rise to legal relations (*page 178*). One of the arguments put by counsel for the defendants was that this advertisement was not intended to create legal relations. It was a 'mere puff' or advertising gimmick which was not intended to be taken literally and which therefore could not be enforced by the plaintiff.

LINDLEY LJ: . . . Was it a mere puff? My answer to that question is No, and I base my answer upon this passage: '1000*l*. is deposited with the Alliance Bank, shewing our sincerity in the matter.' Now, for what was that money deposited or that statement made except to negative the suggestion that this was a mere puff and meant nothing at all? The deposit is called in aid by the advertiser as proof of his sincerity in the matter—that is, the sincerity of his promise to pay this 100*l*. in the event which he has specified. I say this for the purpose of giving point to the observation that we are not inferring a promise; there is the promise, as plain as words can make it.

(c) He then identified this advertisement as an offer to the world.

LINDLEY LJ: . . . Now that point is common to the words of this advertisement and to the words of all other advertisements offering rewards. They are offers to anybody who performs the conditions named in the advertisement, and anybody who does perform the condition accepts the offer. In point of law this advertisement is an offer to pay 100*l*. to anybody who will perform these conditions, and the performance of the conditions is the acceptance of the offer.

The advertisement is an offer to pay a reward to anybody who performs the stipulated act, and performance of that act constitutes the acceptance of the offer.

Lindley LJ is stating that this is a unilateral offer, i.e., a promise to pay money in exchange for an act.

(d) A further argument on behalf of the defendants was that any acceptance had to be communicated to the offeror, and Mrs Carlill did not notify the Company that she intended to use the smoke ball in response to their advertisement.

LINDLEY LJ: But then it is said, 'Supposing that the performance of the conditions is an acceptance of the offer, that acceptance ought to have been notified.' Unquestionably, as a general proposition, when an offer is made, it is necessary in order to make a binding contract, not only that it should be accepted, but that the acceptance should be notified. But is that so in cases of this kind? . . . [I] think that the true view, in a case of this kind, is that the person who makes the offer shews by his language and from the nature of the transaction that he does not expect and does not require notice of the acceptance apart from notice of the performance.

Thus Lindley LJ stated that the nature of the transaction indicated that the offeror had waived the normal requirement of communication of acceptance (although it was necessary, having performed, to notify the offeror of this fact in order to claim the reward).

(e) It was argued that the language of the advertisement was so vague that it could not amount to a promise at all.

LINDLEY LJ: . . . The language is vague and uncertain in some respects, and particularly in this, that the 100*l.* is to be paid to any person who contracts the increasing epidemic after having used the balls three times daily for two weeks. It is said, When are they to be used? According to the language of the advertisement no time is fixed, and, construing the offer most strongly against the person who has made it, one might infer that any time was meant. I do not think that was meant, and to hold the contrary would be pushing too far the doctrine of taking language most strongly against the person using it. I do not think that business people or reasonable people would understand the words as meaning that if you took a smoke ball and used it three times daily for two weeks you were to be guaranteed against influenza for the rest of your life, and I think it would be pushing the language of the advertisement too far to construe it as meaning that. But if it does not mean that, what does it mean? It is for the defendants to shew what it does mean; and it strikes me that there are two, and possibly three, reasonable constructions to be put on this advertisement, any one of which will answer the purpose of the plaintiff. Possibly it may be limited to persons catching the 'increasing epidemic' (that is, the then prevailing epidemic), or any colds or diseases caused by taking cold, during the prevalence of the increasing epidemic. That is one suggestion; but it does not commend itself to me. Another suggested meaning is that you are warranted free from catching this epidemic, or colds or other diseases caused by taking cold, whilst you are using this remedy after using it for two weeks. If that is the meaning, the plaintiff is right, for she used the remedy for two weeks and went on using it till she got the epidemic. Another meaning, and the one which I rather prefer, is that the reward is offered to any person who contracts the epidemic or other disease within a reasonable time after having used the smoke ball.

Lindley LJ considered that the offer could be construed to apply to any person who contracted influenza within a reasonable time of having used the smoke ball. Clearly this covered the plaintiff, who had contracted influenza while using the smoke ball.

(f) The promise by the Company had to be supported by consideration (*pages 119–73*) provided by Mrs Carlill (i.e., Mrs Carlill had to give something of value in exchange for the Company's promise). At the time of this decision, consideration was seen as being either a benefit to the offeror (the Smoke Ball Company) and/or a detriment to the offeree (Mrs Carlill). Lindley LJ considered that consideration was present in the sense of a benefit to the offeror company and/or a detriment to the offeree (Mrs Carlill).

LINDLEY LJ: . . . It has been argued that this is nudum pactum—that there is no consideration. We must apply to that argument the usual legal tests. Let us see whether there is no advantage to the defendants. It is said that the use of the ball is no advantage to them, and that what benefits them is the sale; and the case is put that a lot of these balls might be stolen, and that it would be no advantage to the defendants if the thief or other people used them. The answer to that, I think, is as follows. It is quite obvious that in the view of the advertisers a use by the public of their remedy, if they can only get the public to have confidence enough to use it, will react and produce a sale which is directly beneficial to them. Therefore, the advertisers get out of the use an advantage which is enough to constitute a consideration.

But there is another view. Does not the person who acts upon this advertisement and accepts the offer put himself to some inconvenience at the request of the defendants? Is it nothing to use this ball three times daily for two weeks according to the directions at the request of the advertiser? Is that to go for nothing? It appears to me that there is a distinct inconvenience, not to say a detriment, to any person who so uses the smoke ball. I am of opinion, therefore, that there is ample consideration for the promise.

Lindley LJ is stating that the performance of the conditions in the unilateral offer constitutes both the acceptance of the promise and the consideration for it.

(g) Lindley LJ concludes his judgment with the following statement:

LINDLEY LJ: It appears to me, therefore, that the defendants must perform their promise, and, if they have been so unwary as to expose themselves to a great many actions, so much the worse for them.

(ii) The judgment of Bowen LJ

This is the clearest of the judgments and the one most frequently cited. The order of presentation of the issues is also the most logical:

(a) Was the advertisement too vague to be enforced?

BOWEN LJ: . . . The defendants contend, that it is an offer the terms of which are too vague to be treated as a definite offer, inasmuch as there is no limit of time fixed for the catching of the influenza, and it cannot be supposed that the advertisers seriously meant to promise to pay money to every person who catches the influenza at any time after the inhaling of the smoke ball. . . . It seems to me that in order to arrive at a right conclusion we must read this advertisement in its plain meaning, as the public would understand it. It was intended to be issued to the public and to be read by the public. How would an ordinary person reading this document construe it? It was intended unquestionably to have some effect, and I think the effect which it was intended to have, was to make people use the smoke ball, because the suggestions and allegations which it contains are directed immediately to the use of the smoke ball as distinct from the purchase of it. It did not follow that the smoke ball was to be purchased from the defendants directly, or even from agents of theirs directly. The intention was that the circulation of the smoke ball should be promoted, and that the use of it should be increased. The advertisement begins by saying that a reward will be paid by the Carbolic Smoke Ball Company to any person who contracts the increasing epidemic after using the ball. It has been said that the words do not apply only to persons who contract the epidemic after the publication of the advertisement, but include persons who had previously contracted the influenza. I cannot so read the advertisement. It is written in colloquial and popular language, and I think that it is equivalent to this: '100*l*. will be paid to any person who shall contract the increasing epidemic after having used the carbolic smoke ball three times daily for two weeks.' And it seems to me that the way in which the public would read it would be this, that if anybody, after the advertisement was published, used three times daily for two weeks the carbolic smoke ball, and then caught cold, he would be entitled to the reward.

Bowen LJ adopted the correct approach of looking at the statement objectively to see what the reasonable man would consider was intended (see *pages 18–19*).

BOWEN LJ: . . . Then again it was said: 'How long is this protection to endure? Is it to go on for ever, or for what limit of time?' I think that there are two constructions of this document, each of which is good sense, and each of which seems to me to satisfy the exigencies of the present action. It may mean that the protection is warranted to last during the epidemic, and it was during the epidemic that the plaintiff contracted the disease. I think, more probably, it means that the smoke ball will be a protection while it is in use. That seems to me the way in which an ordinary person would understand an advertisement about medicine, and about a specific against influenza. It could not be supposed that after you have left off using it you are still to be protected for ever, as if there was to be a stamp set upon your forehead that you were never to catch influenza because you had once used the carbolic smoke ball. I think the immunity is to last during the use of the ball. . . . I therefore, have myself no hesitation in saying that I think, on the construction of this advertisement, the protection was to enure during the time that the carbolic smoke ball was being used. My brother, the Lord Justice who preceded me, thinks that the contract would be sufficiently definite if you were to read it in the sense that the protection was to be warranted during a reasonable period after use. I have some difficulty myself on that point; but it is not necessary for me to consider it further, because the disease here was contracted during the use of the carbolic smoke ball.

Bowen LJ differs from Lindley LJ on the question of the length of the immunity. Lindley LJ considered it should last for a reasonable time after use of the smoke ball, while Bowen LJ confined it to protection during the use of the smoke ball. It did not affect the decision on these facts, since Mrs Carlill had been using the smoke ball when she contracted influenza.

(b) Bowen LJ then addressed the contention that this was a 'mere puff' and that there was no intention to create legal relations.

BOWEN LJ: Was it intended that the 100*l.* should, if the conditions were fulfilled, be paid? The advertisement says that 1000*l.* is lodged at the bank for the purpose. Therefore, it cannot be said that the statement that 100*l.* would be paid was intended to be a mere puff. I think it was intended to be understood by the public as an offer which was to be acted upon.

(c) He then went on to address the argument that this would amount to a contract with the whole world, which was not possible.

BOWEN LJ: . . . It is not a contract made with all the world. There is the fallacy of the argument. It is an offer made to all the world; and why should not an offer be made to all the world which is to ripen into a contract with anybody who comes forward and performs the condition? It is an offer to become liable to any one who, before it is retracted, performs the condition, and, although the offer is made to the world, the contract is made with that limited portion of the public who come forward and perform the condition on the faith of the advertisement. It is not like cases in which you offer to negotiate, or you issue advertisements that you have got a stock of books to sell, or houses to let, in which case there is no offer to be bound by any contract. Such advertisements are offers to negotiate—offers to receive offers—offers to chaffer, as, I think, some learned judge in one of the cases has said. If this is an offer to be bound, then it is a contract the moment the person fulfils the condition.

Bowen LJ raises the fact that this advertisement was an offer, whereas advertisements are normally invitations to treat (*pages 25–6*). The unilateral contract is therefore an exception to the general rule in *Partridge* v *Crittenden* [1968] 1 WLR 1204 (*page 25*), since an advertisement which requests the performance of an act will be an offer. Had it been construed as an invitation to treat, such advertisements to pay rewards would have made little sense. The offeror would have the benefit of seeing the stipulated conditions performed and yet would not be bound to pay the reward.

(d) Was it necessary that the acceptance be notified?

BOWEN LJ: . . . One cannot doubt that, as an ordinary rule of law, an acceptance of an offer made ought to be notified to the person who makes the offer, in order that the two minds may come together. Unless this is done the two minds may be apart, and there is not that consensus which is necessary according to the English law—I say nothing about the laws of other countries—to make a contract. But there is this clear gloss to be made upon that doctrine, that as notification of acceptance is required for the benefit of the person who makes the offer, the person who makes the offer may dispense with notice to himself if he thinks it desirable to do so, and I suppose there can be no doubt that where a person in an offer made by him to another person, expressly or impliedly intimates a particular mode of acceptance as sufficient to make the bargain binding, it is only necessary for the other person to whom such offer is made to follow the indicated method of acceptance; and if the person making the offer, expressly or impliedly intimates in his offer that it will be sufficient to act on the proposal without communicating acceptance of it to himself, performance of the condition is a sufficient acceptance without notification. . . .

Now, if that is the law, how are we to find out whether the person who makes the offer does intimate that notification of acceptance will not be necessary in order to constitute a binding bargain? In many cases you look to the offer itself. In many cases you extract from the character of the transaction that notification is not required, and in the advertisement cases it seems to me to follow as an inference to be drawn from the transaction itself that a person is not to notify his acceptance of the offer before he performs the condition, but that if he performs the condition notification is dispensed with. It seems to me that from the point of view of common sense no other idea could be entertained. If I advertise to the world that my dog is lost, and that anybody who brings the dog to a particular place will be paid some money, are all the police or other persons whose business it is to find lost dogs to be expected to sit down and write me a note saying that they have accepted my proposal? Why, of course, they at once look after the dog, and as soon as they find the dog they have performed the condition. The essence of the transaction is that the dog should be found, and it is not necessary under such circumstances, as it seems to me, that in order to make the contract binding there should be any notification of acceptance. It follows from the nature of the thing that the performance of the condition is sufficient acceptance without the notification of it, and a person who makes an offer in an advertisement of that kind makes an offer which must be read by the light of that common sense reflection. He does, therefore, in his offer impliedly indicate that he does not require notification of the acceptance of the offer.

While it is normally necessary to communicate an acceptance, the offeror may waive this requirement, either expressly or impliedly. In unilateral contracts the offeror will in most instances be taken to have waived the requirement of communication of an intention to accept, so that all that is required is that the requested act is performed.

(e) Lastly, in answer to the argument that since catching influenza was only a condition, the Company's promise was not supported by any consideration from Mrs Carlill, Bowen LJ agreed with Lindley LJ that there was both a benefit to the Company and a detriment to Mrs Carlill.

BOWEN LJ: . . . Can it be said here that if the person who reads this advertisement applies thrice daily, for such time as may seem to him tolerable, the carbolic smoke ball to his nostrils for a whole fortnight, he is doing nothing at all—that it is a mere act which is not to count towards consideration to support a promise (for the law does not require us to measure the adequacy of the consideration). Inconvenience sustained by one party at the request of the other is enough to create a consideration. I think, therefore, that it is consideration enough that the plaintiff took the trouble of using the smoke ball. But I think also that the defendants received a benefit from this user, for the use of the smoke ball was contemplated by the defendants as being indirectly a benefit to them, because the use of the smoke balls would promote their sale.

(iii) The judgment of A. L. Smith LJ

This judgment is more general in its presentation of the issues:

A. L. SMITH LJ: . . . It comes to this: 'In consideration of your buying my smoke ball, and then using it as I prescribe, I promise that if you catch the influenza within a certain time I will pay you 100*l*.' It must not be forgotten that this advertisement states that as security for what is being offered, and as proof of the sincerity of the offer, 1000*l*. is actually lodged at the bank wherewith to satisfy any possible demands which might be made in the event of the conditions contained therein being fulfilled and a person catching the epidemic so as to entitle him to the 100*l*. How can it be said that such a statement as that embodied only a mere expression of confidence in the wares which the defendants had to sell? I cannot read the advertisement in any such way. In my judgment, the advertisement was an offer intended to be acted upon, and when accepted and the conditions performed constituted a binding promise on which an action would lie, assuming there was consideration for that promise. . . .

(a) A. L. Smith LJ examined the vagueness of the promise.

A. L. SMITH LJ: . . . [I]t was said that the promise was too wide, because there is no limit of time within which the person has to catch the epidemic. There are three possible limits of time to this contract. The first is, catching the epidemic during its continuance; the second is, catching the influenza during the time you are using the ball; the third is, catching the influenza within a reasonable time after the expiration of the two weeks during which you have used the ball three times daily. It is not necessary to say which is the correct construction of this contract, for no question arises thereon. Whichever is the true construction, there is sufficient limit of time so as not to make the contract too vague on that account.

A. L. Smith LJ neatly avoided having to choose whether he preferred the construction of Lindley LJ or that of Bowen LJ by stating that it was not necessary to do so. As a result there is no clear interpretation of the promise by the Court of Appeal.

(b) There was no express requirement that acceptance be notified.

A. L. SMITH LJ: Then it was argued, that if the advertisement constituted an offer which might culminate in a contract if it was accepted, and its conditions performed, yet it was not accepted by the plaintiff in the manner contemplated, and that the offer contemplated was such that notice of the acceptance had to be given by the party using the carbolic ball to the defendants before user, so that the defendants might be at liberty to superintend the experiment. All I can say is, that there is no such clause in the advertisement, and that, in my judgment, no such clause can be read into it; and I entirely agree with what has fallen from my Brothers, that this is one of those cases in which a performance of the condition by using these smoke balls for two weeks three times a day is an acceptance of the offer.

This is helpful since it indicates that if a unilateral offeror does wish to know who is attempting to accept his offer, he must include an express provision requiring this.

(c) A. L. Smith LJ also recognised that performance of the conditions specified constituted the acceptance, and concluded by agreeing that consideration had been provided since it was a detriment to the offeree to use the smoke ball as requested and a benefit to the Company.

A. L. SMITH LJ: Lastly, it was said that there was no consideration, and that it was nudum pactum. There are two considerations here. One is the consideration of the inconvenience of having to use this carbolic smoke ball for two weeks three times a day; and the other more important consideration is the money gain likely to accrue to the defendants by the enhanced sale of the smoke balls, by reason of the plaintiff's user of them. There is ample consideration to support this promise. . . .

Counsel for the defendants argued that the terms of the advertisement would enable someone who stole the smoke ball to claim the reward when clearly the actions of this thief had not benefited the defendants by way of increased sales. Lindley LJ and Bowen LJ considered that the benefit was the general increase in sales through improved public confidence (see *pages 7–8 and 10*) and that this was a sufficient consideration. This definition would allow a thief to claim the reward. Of course, a thief would suffer a detriment in using the smoke ball in the stipulated manner.

(h) Notes on the decision and the judgments

It is now necessary to use the judgments to state the decision and explain it:

The Court of Appeal (Lindley, Bowen and A. L. Smith LJJ) held that the defendants' promise in their advertisement was sufficiently certain and constituted a unilateral offer.

This offer was a promise to pay £100 to anyone who performed the stipulated conditions, namely using the smoke ball three times a day as directed for two weeks and still catching influenza.

The promise was intended to have legal effects, since the defendants had demonstrated their sincerity by depositing £1,000 with their bank.

The plaintiff had performed these conditions and therefore had accepted the offer. In a unilateral contract the offeror will normally have impliedly waived the requirement that the acceptance must be communicated in order to be effective so that notification of acceptance is not required.

The performance of the act also constituted the consideration to support the defendants' promise; it was a detriment to the plaintiff to have to use the smoke ball in accordance with these directions, and it was a benefit to the defendants since the plaintiff's use of the smoke ball would indirectly improve its sales through increased public confidence in the product.

Therefore, since there was a binding contract the plaintiff was entitled to be paid the £100.

NOTE: You may wish to add to these notes by including any important statements from the judgments and by filling out the notes on the law concerning unilateral contracts. For example, you may wish to record Bowen LJ's statement that this was an offer to the world (see *page 9*) and his statement (see *page 10*) discussing the fact that in a unilateral contract there is no requirement to notify the offeror that you are intending to accept. Bowen LJ's example of the lost dog is particularly famous and worth noting.

(i) General notes on the legal principles in the case

You should always assess how the case you are reading fits into the general body of case law principles. If it appears out of line with previous authority you need to question whether the court in question realised this and if not, why not. If the court did realise the inconsistency, you will need to examine in detail the explanation for the decision in each judgment. You should also ask whether the case adds to the development of principle and, if so, in what way. Is this development a broad one or is it very case-fact specific?

Carlill v *Carbolic Smoke Ball Company* has been valuable in explaining the unilateral contract. A unilateral contract is a contract whereby the offeror makes a promise (in this case to pay £100) in return for the performance of a stipulated act. Mrs Carlill makes no promise and can decide not to continue her use of the smoke ball at any time.

To summarise, there are a number of exceptional rules which apply to unilateral contracts for which *Carlill* v *Carbolic Smoke Ball* is authority:

(a) Whereas the general rule is that an advertisement is an invitation to treat (i.e., an invitation to make an offer), if the advertisement requests the performance of an act then the advertisement will be an offer. This means that on performance of the requested act the offer has been accepted and there is a binding contract. Generally, a response to an advertisement can at best be only an offer so that there is no binding contract at that stage.

(b) Whereas the general rule is that an acceptance must be communicated to the offeror, the offeror may impliedly waive this requirement, and will be taken to have done so when the offer is unilateral unless there has been an express indication of the fact that notification is required.

(c) In a unilateral contract the requested act is both the acceptance and the consideration for the promise.

There are other legal principles applicable to unilateral contracts which it is convenient to consider at this point:

(i) It is possible to accept a unilateral offer of a reward only if you know that it has been made and accept in response to it (*R* v *Clarke* (1927) 40 CLR 227, *page 41*). This means that the act which is the purported acceptance cannot have been performed before any promise of a reward was made.

(ii) Since the acceptance is the performance of the stipulated act and performing this act may be a continuing act (as in *Carlill* v *Carbolic Smoke Ball*), the general principle should be that the offer may be revoked at any time before the act is completely performed. However, it now appears that it may not be possible to revoke a unilateral offer once the offeree has started to perform (*Errington* v *Errington & Woods* [1952] 1 KB 290, *page 58*).

(iii) Although the general rule is that a revocation of an offer must be communicated to the offeree, this is not practical in the case of a unilateral offer to the whole world since it is not possible to identify the potential offerees. The American case of *Shuey* v *US* 23 L ed 697, (1875) 92 US 73 (*page 61*) is authority for the fact that it is sufficient if the revocation is communicated using the same channel used to communicate the original offer, and if this is done it is irrelevant if particular offerees did not see or know about the revocation.

■ QUESTIONS

1. What was the stipulated act in *Carlill* v *Carbolic Smoke Ball*? Was it merely using the smoke ball as specified so that catching influenza was only a condition of entitlement to enforce the promise? Or was it using the ball as specified *and* catching influenza? (See *pages 119–21*.)

2. What do you think the position would have been if at the time of using the smoke ball Mrs Carlill's only reason for doing so was to avoid catching influenza?

3. Did the smoke ball have to be purchased by Mrs Carlill?

4. What would the legal position be if, when Mrs Carlill had been using the smoke ball for one week, the Company had issued another advertisement withdrawing their offer but, as Mrs Carlill did not see this, she had carried on using the smoke ball for the full two weeks and caught influenza?

NOTES

1. For further discussion of the background to the decision in *Carlill*, see A. W. B. Simpson, 'Quackery and Contract Law: The Case of the Carbolic Smoke Ball' (1985) 14 JLS 345.

2. In *Bowerman* v *Association of British Travel Agents Ltd* [1996] CLC 451, *page 184*, the majority of the Court of Appeal, relying on *Carlill* v *Carbolic Smoke Ball Co.*, held that a notice would reasonably have been read by the public as an offer by ABTA to give protection to the customer if the ABTA member failed financially. This unilateral offer was accepted by the customer when he booked a holiday with the ABTA member.

3. It is increasingly common for the courts to 'imply' unilateral contracts. See, for example, *Blackpool & Fylde Aero Club Ltd* v *Blackpool Borough Council* [1990] 1 WLR 1195, *page 30* below.

EXERCISES

1. *Howard Marine and Dredging Co. Ltd* v *A. Ogden & Sons (Excavations) Ltd* [1978] QB 574 (CA) (for facts see *pages 582–3*). The catchwords and headnote facts are far more detailed than in *Carlill* v *Carbolic Smoke Ball Company*, and the headnote decision is divided into four distinct issues namely, collateral warranty, damages for misrepresentation, the exemption clause and the possibility of an action in negligence at common law:

Held, (1) that the contractors could not establish any claim in contract for there was nothing in the pre-contract negotiations which could amount to a collateral warranty.

(2) (*Per* Bridge and Shaw LJJ) That the plaintiff owners were liable in tort for damages under section 2(1) of the Misrepresentation Act 1967, for the misrepresentation by their marine manager at the pre-contract meeting on July 11, 1974, as the deadweight capacity of the barges was a most material matter on which the contractors had relied in concluding the contract, and was one in respect of which the representor would have been liable had it been made fraudulently; that to avoid liability under the statutory terms the owners had to prove that their marine manager had had reasonable ground to believe and did believe up to the time the contract was made that the facts he represented were true; that on an analysis of the evidence that burden had not been discharged for the marine manager had not shown any objectively reasonable ground for disregarding the figure of deadweight capacity in the ship's documents and for preferring the Lloyd's Register incorrect figure; and accordingly the contractors' appeal should be allowed.

Per Bridge LJ. In the course of negotiations leading to a contract the Act of 1967 imposes an absolute obligation not to state facts which the representor cannot prove he had reasonable ground to believe (post, p. 596F).

(3) (*Per* Bridge and Shaw LJJ) That the owners could not escape liability by reliance on the exception clause, for, as the judge had held, it was a provision in an agreement which would exclude or restrict any liability to which a party to a contract might be subject by reason of any misrepresentation made by him within section 3 of the Act of 1967, and should therefore be of no effect unless the court in its discretion allowed reliance on it as being 'fair and reasonable in the circumstances of the case'; and accordingly, as it was not 'fair and reasonable' to allow the owners to rely on it, the owners' cross appeal should be dismissed.

Per Shaw LJ. The contractors also have a cause of action in negligence at common law, for in a business transaction whose nature made clear the importance and influence of the answer to the question as to the vessel's carrying capacity, the owners were under a duty of care in giving information on matters peculiarly within their knowledge (post, pp. 600F–601D).

Per Lord Denning MR. The trial judge's decision that the misrepresentation at the July 11 meeting was not negligent showed that he was satisfied that the representor had discharged the burden of proof imposed by section 2(1) and there was no reason for disturbing that decision (post, p. 593C G). Nor was there any reason why the court should not allow the owners to rely on the exception clause as 'fair and reasonable' under section 3 of the Act of 1967, since the parties to the contract were of equal bargaining power and the contractors could easily have obtained advice that the barges were not fit for the use for which they were intended before concluding the contract (post, p. 594B–F). Further, there was no special relationship between the parties which gave rise to the duty of care at common law; the only duty of the owners' marine manager was to be honest when asked about the dead-weight capacity; he had answered as best he could from memory and the contractors should not have acted on his oral answers without further inquiry (post, pp. 591H–592C).

Decision of Bristow J reversed in part.

The first part of the Court of Appeal's judgment relates to the contention that the pre-contractual statement was a collateral warranty so that its inaccuracy was a breach of contract. All of the members of the Court of Appeal rejected this but we do not know the reasons without looking at the judgments.

Secondly, the majority (Bridge and Shaw LJJ) held that the plaintiffs were liable in damages under s. 2(1) of the Misrepresentation Act 1967, and this time full reasons are given. The plaintiffs had failed to show that they had reasonable grounds to believe, and did believe up to the time the contract was made, that the facts represented were true. They had failed to show any 'objectively reasonable ground' for their actions. We are informed of a statement by Bridge LJ which goes further and imposes an absolute obligation not to state facts which you cannot prove you had reasonable grounds to believe.

Lord Denning MR (dissenting) considered that the burden in s. 2(1) had been discharged.

You will notice that the headnote contains references to pages and letters in the judgment. These can be very useful indeed in directing the reader to those parts of the judgments dealing with the major points of the decision. The same is true of paragraph numbers following the *Practice Direction* [2001] 1 WLR 194, *page 2*.

■ QUESTION

There were two other arguments addressed by the Court of Appeal, namely the claim in tort based on breach of a duty of care and the question of whether the exemption clause applied to allow the owners to escape liability. What did the majority of the Court of Appeal decide on these issues and what did Lord Denning decide?

NOTE: If you examine Lord Denning's judgment in this case you will discover that having explained the facts in a very clear and readable way he then deals with each of the issues under an appropriate heading. At pp. 590–95 of the report he examines first the collateral warranty argument, then the claim based on the tort of negligent misstatement and the claim under the Misrepresentation Act 1967, before discussing the exemption clause.

Look for these same issues in the judgments of Bridge LJ and Shaw LJ.

2. *Williams* v *Roffey Brothers and Nicholls (Contractors) Ltd* [1991] 1 QB 1 (CA). Read this case and attempt to answer the questions set out below before you consider the extracts and discussion of this case at *pages 135–40, 143–5, 171–3*, and *262*. You might bear in mind the broader policy considerations favouring enforcement of alteration promises and holding a person to their word. Further guidance can be found by visiting the companion website.

(a) Identify the arguments put on behalf of the plaintiff to support the enforceability of the alteration promise. What difficulty did counsel for the plaintiff face in establishing the argument that the promise was supported by consideration?

(b) Why was there no argument based on promissory estoppel? What, if anything, did each member of the Court of Appeal have to say concerning the scope of that doctrine and its application to facts such as these?

(c) What did the Court of Appeal decide in relation to consideration to support the promise and what did it decide in relation to the defendants' argument that, if there was a binding promise, the terms were that payment was to be on complete performance of the carpentry work for each flat and this had not occurred when the plaintiff left the site?

(d) On what basis did the Court of Appeal justify not applying *Stilk* v *Myrick*?

(e) On what basis was it argued that the principles in *Williams* v *Roffey* do not contravene the principle in *Stilk* v *Myrick*?

(f) Consider the nature of the consideration which the Court of Appeal held supported the defendants' promise. What did the Court of Appeal decide constituted the factual benefit? How is this consideration generated and how did the Court of Appeal avoid the potential technical difficulties associated with this?

3. *Great Peace Shipping Ltd* v *Tsavliris Salvage (International) Ltd* [2002] EWCA Civ 1407, [2003] QB 679. This case provides an example of a decision of the Court of Appeal reported since the introduction of neutral citation and paragraph numbering for judgments. It is a single judgment on behalf of the court, given by Lord Phillips MR, and the judgment addresses the question of whether a mistaken assumption on which both parties contracted was sufficiently fundamental to render the contract void at common law and, if not, whether it was nevertheless possible to rescind such a contract in equity (i.e., set it aside on terms). However, the judgment is complicated because it contains a detailed examination of the context, the applicable legal principles governing common mistake and their historical development by means of detailed examination of existing case authorities.

Read the case and then attempt to answer the questions set out below. Try to do this before checking your answers against the references given to pages in Chapter 11, where the relevant parts of the judgment are extracted and discussed. Further guidance can be found by visiting the companion website.

(a) What happened on the facts and what did each party claim? [See *pages 514–15*]

(b) What did Lord Phillips say concerning the contractual allocation of the risk of impossibility? What effect does this have in terms of the legal treatment of the impossibility? [Paragraph numbers [75]–[85], extracted *at 502*]

(c) What did Lord Phillips claim was the legal or theoretical basis for the decision of the House of Lords in *Bell* v *Lever Brothers*? On what basis did he reach this conclusion and how does this relate to previous case law? [Paragraph numbers [61]–[74] and [82]–[83], extracted *at 508–9*]

(d) Is it possible to secure a remedy at common law where it is still technically possible to perform in accordance with the contractual terms? What did Lord Phillips identify as the test to determine whether a common mistaken assumption renders performance of the contract, as originally agreed, impossible? [Paragraph number [55], extracted *at 516*]

(e) How likely is it that this test will be satisfied? [Paragraph number [86], extracted *at 516*]

(f) What did Lord Phillips say on the question of the relationship between the decision of the House of Lords in *Bell* v *Lever Brothers* and the decision of the Court of Appeal in *Solle* v *Butcher*? [Paragraph numbers [153]–[160], extracted *at 522–3*]

(g) Most significantly, what is the effect of this decision in terms of the availability of remedies for common mistake? What practical consequences might follow? [Paragraph numbers [157] and [161], extracted *at 523*, and see discussion *at pages 523–4*]

(h) What was the effect of this decision on previous case law authority, i.e., which case(s) were applied and which case was not followed? [Examine the headnote].

2

Agreement

A contract is an agreement that is legally enforceable. This chapter deals with how we determine the existence of the agreement.

SECTION 1: SUBJECTIVITY VERSUS OBJECTIVITY

A: Objectivity prevails

Smith v Hughes
(1871) LR 6 QB 597

BLACKBURN J: ... If, whatever a man's real intention may be, he so conducts himself that a reasonable man would believe that he was assenting to the terms proposed by the other party, and that other party upon that belief enters into the contract with him, the man thus conducting himself would be equally bound as if he had intended to agree to the other party's terms. ...

Centrovincial Estates plc v Merchant Investors Assurance Company Ltd
[1983] Com LR 158 (CA)

Offices were let to the defendants at a yearly rent of £68,320 subject to review from 25 December 1982. The rent review clause provided that the rent reserved should on that date be increased to the then current market rental value, such value to be agreed by the parties or in default of agreement to be assessed by an independent surveyor or valuer. There was a proviso that in no circumstances should the rent be reduced below that which was payable immediately before the review.

On 22 June 1982 solicitors wrote to the defendants, inviting them to agree the figure of £65,000 per annum as the current market rental value. On 23 June, the defendants replied agreeing that figure. On receiving that reply, the solicitors telephoned to say that the letter of 22 June had contained an error and that the plaintiffs had intended to propose £126,000. A further letter invited the defendants to treat the letter of 22 June as though it had contained the figure of £126,000, but the defendants refused to accept this and said that they wished to hold the plaintiffs to the binding agreement constituted by the letters of 22 and 23 June.

The plaintiffs commenced proceedings for, *inter alia*, a declaration that no legally binding agreement had been made. The Court of Appeal refused to grant such a declaration. Held: there was agreement at a figure of £65,000.

SLADE LJ: . . . In the absence of any proof, as yet, that the defendants either knew or ought reasonably to have known of the plaintiffs' error at the time when they purported to accept the plaintiffs' offer, why should the plaintiffs now be allowed to resile from that offer? It is a well-established principle of the English law of contract that an offer falls to be interpreted not subjectively by reference to what has actually passed through the mind of the offeror, but objectively, by reference to the interpretation which a reasonable man in the shoes of the offeree would place on the offer. It is an equally well established principle that ordinarily an offer, when unequivocally accepted according to its precise terms, will give rise to a legally binding agreement as soon as acceptance is communicated to the offeror in the manner contemplated by the offer, and cannot thereafter be revoked without the consent of the other party.

Paal Wilson & Co. A/S v Partenreederei Hannah Blumenthal, The Hannah Blumenthal
[1983] 1 AC 854 (HL)

Arbitration proceedings to settle a dispute were commenced by the buyer in 1972 but nothing happened apart from an intermittent exchange of letters between the parties from 1974 until 1980. The sellers argued that the delay amounted to an agreement to abandon the arbitration clause. Held: there was no evidence of abandonment.

LORD BRIGHTMAN: . . . To entitle the sellers to rely on abandonment, they must show that the buyers so conducted themselves as to entitle the sellers to assume, *and that the sellers did assume*, that the contract was agreed to be abandoned sub silentio. The evidence which is relevant to that inquiry will consist of or include: (1) What the buyers did or omitted to do *to the knowledge of the sellers*. Excluded from consideration will be the acts of the buyers of which the sellers were ignorant, because those acts will have signalled nothing to the sellers and cannot have founded or fortified any assumption on the part of the sellers. (2) What the sellers did or omitted to do, *whether or not to the knowledge of the buyers*. These facts evidence the state of mind of the sellers, and therefore the validity of the assertion by the sellers that they assumed that the contract was agreed to be abandoned. The state of mind of the buyers is irrelevant to a consideration of what the sellers were entitled to assume. The state of mind of the sellers is vital to what the sellers in fact assumed.

NOTE: This formula includes a subjective element, in that it is necessary to consider what it was reasonable for the offeree to believe with regard to the offer and then to examine what the offeree actually did believe.

Robert Goff LJ in *Allied Marine Transport Ltd* v *Vale do Rio doce Navegacao SA, The Leonidas D* [1985] 1 WLR 925, commented on *The Hannah Blumenthal* as follows:

> In his speech Lord Brightman was, as we understand it, asserting that if one party, O, so acts that his conduct, objectively considered, constitutes an offer, and the other party, A, believing that the conduct of O represents his actual intention, accepts O's offer, then a contract will come into existence, and on those facts it will make no difference if O did not in fact intend to make an offer, or if he misunderstood A's acceptance, so that O's state of mind is, in such circumstances, irrelevant. With that proposition we very respectfully agree . . .

The offeree must believe that the offer represents the actual intentions of the offeror.

B: Subjectivity has some relevance

If the offeree *knows or ought reasonably to have known* at the time of the purported acceptance that the offeror had made a mistake relating to the terms of the offer, the offeree cannot purport to accept that offer.

Hartog v *Colin & Shields*
[1939] 3 All ER 566

The defendants contracted to sell 30,000 Argentine hare skins to the plaintiff, but by mistake they were offered at a price per pound instead of per piece. In the pre-sale negotiations reference had always been made to the price per piece and never to the price per pound, and there was expert evidence that Argentine hare skins were generally sold at prices per piece. Held: since the plaintiff could not reasonably have supposed that the offer contained the offerors' real intention, there was no binding contract.

NOTE: Thus it is first necessary to examine how the offeror's words and conduct might reasonably have appeared to the offeree. The offeree cannot then accept if he knew, or it can be established that he ought reasonably to have known, that the offeror was making a mistake. Compare with the position where rectification is sought; here the requirement is for actual knowledge of the mistake, see *Commission for the New Towns* v *Cooper (GB) Ltd* [1995] Ch 259, *page 112*, although actual knowledge for this purpose (see note 2) extends to 'wilfully and recklessly failing to make such inquiries as an honest and reasonable man would make' (category (iii) actual knowledge).

■ QUESTIONS

1. What should the position be if the offeree has simply not addressed his mind to the question of whether the offeror in fact has this intention? (See Treitel, *The Law of Contract*, 11th edn, 2003, p. 9.)
2. Should the defendants in *Centrovincial Estates plc* v *Merchant Investors Assurance Company Ltd*, *page 18*, have known of the plaintiffs' mistake given the terms of the rent review clause?

SECTION 2: **THE CRITERIA TO DETERMINE AGREEMENT**

Traditionally the courts have required that agreement be demonstrated by an offer made by one party and by complete acceptance of that offer by the other party. However, Lord Denning, in particular, took the view that the circumstances as a whole should be examined in an attempt to discover whether there was agreement (*Butler Machine Tool Co. Ltd* v *Ex-Cell-O Corporation (England) Ltd* [1979] 1 WLR 401, *page 38*).

The majority of the Court of Appeal in the following case (Lord Denning and Ormrod LJ) also adopted this new approach.

Gibson v *Manchester City Council*
[1978] 1 WLR 520 (CA)

The facts of this case appear at *page 23.*

LORD DENNING MR: . . . To my mind it is a mistake to think that all contracts can be analysed into the form of offer and acceptance. I know in some of the text books it has been the custom to do so: but, as I understand the law, there is no need to look for a strict offer and acceptance. You should look at the correspondence as a whole and at the conduct of the parties and see therefrom whether the parties have come to an agreement on everything that was material. If by their correspondence and their conduct you can see an agreement on all material terms—which was intended thenceforward to be binding—then there is a binding contract in law even though all the formalities have not been gone through: see *Brogden* v *Metropolitan Railway Co.* (1877) 2 App Cas 666.

It seems to me that on the correspondence I have read—and, I may add, on what happened after—the parties had come to an agreement in the matter which they intended to be binding. . . .

NOTE: Although this approach was rejected by the House of Lords, Lord Diplock stated [1979] 1 WLR 294, at page 297:

> My Lords, there may be certain types of contract, though I think they are exceptional, which do not fit easily into the normal analysis of a contract as being constituted by offer and acceptance; but a contract alleged to have been made by an exchange of correspondence between the parties in which the successive communications other than the first are in reply to one another, is not one of these. I can see no reason in the instance case for departing from the conventional approach of looking at the handful of documents relied upon as constituting the contract sued upon and seeing whether upon their true construction there is to be found in them a contractual offer by the corporation to sell the house to Mr Gibson and an acceptance of that offer by Mr Gibson. I venture to think that it was by departing from this conventional approach that the majority of the Court of Appeal was led into error.

Adams and Brownsword, *Understanding Contract Law*, 4th edn, 2004, p. 53, conclude that 'in *Gibson* the consumer-welfarists were outvoted by formalists and market-individualists who refused to derogate from the general rule'. For an explanation of this terminology, see Adams and Brownsword, pp. 36–44 and Chapter 8.

In *New Zealand Shipping Co. Ltd* v *A. M. Satterthwaite & Co. Ltd, The Eurymedon* [1975] AC 154 (PC), Lord Wilberforce expressed some dissatisfaction with the traditional approach when he stated:

. . . English law, having committed itself to a rather technical and schematic doctrine of contract, in application takes a practical approach, often at the cost of forcing the facts to fit uneasily into the marked slots of offer, acceptance and consideration.

It appears that a contract may be found to exist, despite the fact that it cannot be analysed precisely into an offer and corresponding acceptance, where the terms have been fully agreed and executed by the parties.

Trentham Ltd v *Archital Luxfer*
[1993] 1 Lloyd's Rep 25 (CA)

Trentham were main contractors who were employed to design and build industrial units. This work included 'window works', i.e. the supply and installation of aluminium windows and doors. The defendants, Archital, were manufacturers, suppliers and installers of these products, and had actually carried out this work for Trentham and been paid. Trentham alleged that the defendants' work was defective and that they were therefore in breach of binding subcontracts between them. The defendants denied that any binding subcontracts had ever come into existence. Held: binding subcontracts had been concluded for the window works.

STEYN LJ: Before I turn to the facts it is important to consider briefly the approach to be adopted to the issue of contract formation in this case. It seems to me that four matters are of importance. The first is the fact that English law generally adopts an objective theory of contract formation. That means that in practice our law generally ignores the subjective expectations and the unexpressed mental reservations of the parties. Instead the governing criterion is the reasonable expectations of honest men. And in the present case that means that the yardstick is the reasonable expectations of sensible businessmen. Secondly, it is true that the coincidence of offer and acceptance will in the vast majority of cases represent the mechanism of contract formation. It is so in the case of a contract alleged to have been made by an exchange of correspondence. But it is not necessarily so in the case of a contract alleged to have come into existence during and as a result of performance. See *Brogden* v *Metropolitan Railway*, (1877) 2 AC 666; *New Zealand Shipping Co. Ltd* v *A.M. Satterthwaite & Co. Ltd* [1974] 1 Lloyd's Rep 534 at p. 539, col. 1; [1975] AC 154 at p. 167 D–E; *Gibson* v *Manchester City Council* [1979] 1 WLR 294. The third matter is the impact of the fact that the transaction is executed rather than executory. It is a consideration of the first importance on a number of levels. See *British Bank for Foreign Trade Ltd* v *Novinex* [1949] 1 KB 628, at p. 630. The fact that the transaction was performed on both sides will often make it unrealistic to argue that there was no intention to enter into legal relations. It will often make it difficult to submit that the contract is void for vagueness or uncertainty. Specifically, the fact that the transaction is executed makes it easier to imply a term resolving any uncertainty, or, alternatively, it may make it possible to treat a matter not finalised in negotiations as inessential. In this case fully executed transactions are under consideration. Clearly, similar considerations may sometimes be relevant in partly executed transactions. Fourthly, if a contract only comes into existence during and as a result of performance of the transaction it will frequently be possible to hold that the contract impliedly and retrospectively covers pre-contractual performance. See *Trollope & Colls Ltd* v *Atomic Power Constructions Ltd* [1963] 1 WLR 333. . . . The contemporary exchanges, and the carrying out of what was agreed in those exchanges, support the view that there was a course of dealing which on Trentham's side created a right to performance of the work by Archital, and on Archital's side it created a right to be paid on an agreed basis. What the parties did in respect of phase 1 is only explicable on the basis of what they had agreed in respect of phase 1. The Judge analysed the matter in terms of offer and acceptance. I agree with his conclusion. But I am, in any event, satisfied that in this fully executed transaction a contract came into existence during performance even if it cannot be precisely analysed in terms of offer and acceptance. And it does not matter that a contract came into existence after part of the work had been carried out and paid for. The conclusion must be that when the contract came into existence it impliedly governed pre-contractual performance . . .

NOTES
1. The significant factor in the decision was the fact that the arrangement was executed by the parties. Steyn LJ (with whose judgment Ralph Gibson and Neill LJJ agreed) accepted the decision of the judge at first instance which was based on offer and acceptance, but was also prepared to conclude that a contract can come into existence as a result of performance of an executed contract by relying on the decision in *Brogden* v *Metropolitan Railway Co.* (1877) 2 App Cas 666, *page 37*.
2. Compare this decision with the decision in *British Steel Corporation* v *Cleveland Bridge & Engineering Co. Ltd* [1984] 1 All ER 504, *page 78*, where despite the fact of performance, it was concluded that there was no binding contract.

■ QUESTION

Can the distinction in result between *Trentham* v *Luxfer* and *BSC* v *Cleveland Bridge* be explained on the basis of the different remedies being sought and the certainty or uncertainty of terms?

SECTION 3: OFFER DISTINGUISHED FROM INVITATION TO TREAT

If the statement maker clearly intends to be bound by acceptance of the stated terms the statement will amount to an offer, and on acceptance there will be a binding contract. However, if there is no such intention the statement will be part of the negotiating process (an invitation to treat) and any response to it will at best be no more than an offer.

Much depends upon whether the language used indicates 'a definite promise to be bound'.

Gibson v *Manchester City Council*
[1979] 1 WLR 294 (HL)

The City Council adopted a policy of selling council houses to tenants. The respondent tenant applied on a printed form for details of the price and mortgage terms. The city treasurer wrote to the respondent that the Council 'may be prepared to sell the house to you at the purchase price of £2,725 less 20% = £2,180'. The letter gave details of the mortgage likely to be made available and stated 'If you would like to make a formal application to buy . . . please complete the enclosed application form and return it to me as soon as possible.' The respondent completed the application form and returned it on 5 March. He wrote again on 18 March, requesting the Council to carry on with the purchase in accordance with his application. Before contracts were prepared and exchanged, political control of the Council changed and the Council decided to proceed with sales only where contracts had already been exchanged. The respondent sought specific performance of the contract, claiming that the offer in the city treasurer's letter had been accepted by him in his letters of 5 and 18 March. Held: there was no binding contract because no offer capable of acceptance had been made by the Council. The statements in the city treasurer's letter that the Council '*may be prepared to sell*' and inviting Mr Gibson '*to make a formal application to buy*' were not an offer to sell but merely an invitation to treat.

LORD DIPLOCK: My Lords, the words I have italicised [see facts, above] seem to me, as they seemed to Geoffrey Lane LJ, to make it quite impossible to construe this letter as a contractual offer capable of being converted into a legally enforceable open contract for the sale of land by Mr Gibson's written acceptance of it. The words 'may be prepared to sell' are fatal to this; so is the invitation, not, be it noted, to accept the offer, but 'to make formal application to buy' upon the enclosed application form. It is, to quote Geoffrey Lane LJ, a letter setting out the financial terms on which it may be the council will be prepared to consider a sale and purchase in due course.

Storer v *Manchester City Council*
[1974] 1 WLR 1403 (CA)

The Council decided to sell council houses to tenants and instructed the town clerk to devise a simple form for quick agreements which dispensed with legal formalities. The plaintiff applied to buy his council house, and on 9 March 1971 the town clerk wrote to him 'I understand you wish to purchase your council house and enclose the Agreement for Sale. If you will sign the Agreement and return it to me I will send you the Agreement signed on behalf of the [Council] in exchange'. The enclosed 'Agreement for Sale' had been filled in with details which included the purchase price, the amount of the mortgage and the monthly repayments, although the date when the tenancy was to cease and the mortgage repayments begin had been left blank. On 20 March, the plaintiff signed and returned this Agreement for Sale, but before the town clerk had signed the Agreement on the Council's behalf the Council changed political control and discontinued such sales unless contracts had already been exchanged. The plaintiff sought specific performance alleging a binding contract. Held: a binding contract had been concluded. The Council's intention was to become contractually bound when the plaintiff had signed the Agreement and returned it.

LORD DENNING: [Mr Storer] had done everything which he had to do to bind himself to the purchase of the property. The only thing left blank was the date when the tenancy ceased.

. . . The corporation put forward to the tenant a simple form of agreement. The very object was to dispense with legal formalities. One of the formalities—exchange of contracts—was quite unnecessary. The contract was concluded by offer and acceptance. The offer was contained in the letter of March 9 in which the town clerk said:

'I enclose the agreement for sale. If you will sign the agreement and return it to me I will send you the agreement signed on behalf of the corporation in exchange.'

The acceptance was made when Mr Storer did sign it, as he did, and return it, as he did on March 20. It was then that a contract was concluded. The town clerk was then bound to send back the agreement signed on behalf of the corporation. The agreement was concluded on Mr Storer's acceptance. It was not dependent on the subsequent exchange.

I appreciate that there was one space in the form which was left blank. It was No. 7 for 'the date when your tenancy ceases'. That blank did not mean there was no concluded contract. It was left blank simply for administrative convenience. . . .

The final point was this: [counsel for the corporation] said that the town clerk did not intend to be bound by the letter of March 9 1971. He intended that the corporation should not be bound except on exchange. There is nothing in this point. In contracts you do not look into the actual intent in a man's mind. You look at what he said and did. A contract is formed when there is, to all outward appearances, a contract. A man cannot get out of a contract by saying: 'I did not intend to contract' if by his words he has done so. His intention is to be found only in the outward expression which his letters convey. If they show a concluded contract, that is enough.

■ QUESTIONS

1. Lord Denning stated that Mr Storer 'had done everything which he had to do to bind himself to the purchase of the property'. Could the same be said of Mr Gibson?

2. If difference in language has such an impact, how would you advise parties to conduct their negotiations?

NOTE: In *Gibson* v *Manchester CC*, there was no firm offer of a mortgage by the Council, and it is unlikely that Mr Gibson would have intended to bind himself in the absence of a firm commitment on this matter.

In determining whether a communication is an invitation to treat or an offer, it is necessary to consider not just the literal meaning of the words used but also the context in which they are used.

ISOFT Group plc v *Misys Holdings Ltd*
[2003] EWCA Civ 229, unrep. 28 February 2003 (CA)

Misys had agreed to sell ACT, a UK information technology company, to iSOFT. By clause 11.4.2 of this agreement, if Misys acquired an entity carrying on a restricted business in the UK it had to 'offer to sell it' to iSOFT. Misys subsequently acquired such an entity and discussions took place between Misys and iSOFT concerning the operation of clause 11.4. ISOFT then alleged that Misys was in breach of the clause because it had not made the necessary 'offer to sell'. Held: a commercial reading of the clause required only that the procedure should commence with an invitation to treat rather than an offer capable of immediate acceptance. Any other interpretation would have required the court to construct a contract from scratch.

A: Advertisements

Generally advertisements are invitations to treat.

Partridge v *Crittenden*
[1968] 1 WLR 1204 (QB)

The plaintiff had inserted an advertisement in a periodical which read 'Bramblefinch cocks, Bramblefinch hens, 25s each'. The plaintiff was charged with unlawfully offering for sale a wild live bird contrary to s. 6(1) and sch. 4 of the Protection of Birds Act 1954. Held: the advertisement was an invitation to treat, not an offer for sale and therefore the plaintiff could not be guilty of the offence charged.

■ QUESTION

It is argued that if an advertisement is an offer, then the trader will have to supply the quantity ordered when the stock available to do so is limited. In *Grainger & Son* v *Gough* [1896] AC 325 Lord Herschell said (at p. 334):

> The transmission of such a price-list does not amount to an offer to supply an unlimited quantity of the wine described at the price named, so that as soon as an order is given there is a binding contract to supply that quantity. If it were so, the merchant might find himself involved in any number of contractual obligations to supply wine of a particular description which he would be quite unable to carry out, his stock of wine of that description being necessarily limited.

What would the position be if the advertisement specifically stated:

(a) that supplies were unlimited; and

(b) that supplies were limited, e.g., goods in a sale?

NOTES

1. A unilateral advertisement is an offer (see *Carlill* v *Carbolic Smoke Ball Company* [1893] 1 QB 256, *page 13*).

   If a shop advertises 'Sale—15 video recorders at the knock-down price of £60 each. First come first served', the wording may convert this advertisement into a unilateral offer requiring the performance of an act, namely being the first person at the sale to offer to purchase a video recorder at the knock-down price. There is American authority that this type of advertisement amounts to an offer (*Lefkowitz* v *Great Minneapolis Surplus Store* 86 NW 2d 689 (1957)). If such an advertisement were considered to be an invitation to treat, the shopkeeper would retain control over the formation of the contract, despite the customer's performance of the requested act.

2. A notice which detailed the ABTA scheme of protection was held by a majority of the Court of Appeal in *Bowerman* v *ABTA Ltd* [1996] CLC 451, discussed at *page 184*, to be a unilateral offer which customers accepted by booking a holiday with an ABTA member. The result was a unilateral contract between the customer and ABTA.

3. In *O'Brien* v *MGN Ltd* [2001] EWCA Civ 1279, [2002] CLC 33, the advertisement of a newspaper scratch card game with a prize of £50,000 was held to be a contractual offer which was accepted when those with eligible cards rang the telephone hotline.

B: Display of goods

Fisher v *Bell*
[1961] 1 QB 394 (QB)

A shopkeeper displayed a flick knife in his shop window with a ticket behind it stating 'Ejector knife—4s'. He was charged with offering the knife for sale contrary to s. 1(1) of the Restriction of Offensive Weapons Act 1959. Held: a display of goods in a shop window with a price ticket attached was merely an invitation to treat and not an offer for sale so that no offence had been committed.

Pharmaceutical Society of Great Britain v *Boots Cash Chemists (Southern) Ltd*
[1953] 1 QB 401 (CA)

Boots was charged with an offence under the Pharmacy and Poisons Act 1933, s. 18, which required that sales of poisons in Part I of the Poisons List take place under the supervision of a registered pharmacist. Boots operated a self-service system, and a pharmacist at the cash desk was authorised to prevent the removal of any drug from the premises. The factor determining whether an offence had been committed was the point at which the sale in this self-service shop took place. The Court of Appeal agreed with Lord Goddard CJ. Held: Boots had not committed the offence. The display of goods on a supermarket's shelves was merely an invitation to customers to make offers to buy.

Court of Queen's Bench
[1952] 2 QB 795

LORD GODDARD CJ: . . . I think that it is a well-established principle that the mere exposure of goods for sale by a shopkeeper indicates to the public that he is willing to treat but does not amount to an offer to sell. I do not think I ought to hold that that principle is completely reversed merely because there is a self-service scheme, such as this, in operation. In my opinion it comes to no more than that the customer is informed that he may himself pick up an article and bring it to the shopkeeper with a view to buying it, and if, but only if, the shopkeeper then expresses his willingness to sell, the contract for sale is completed. In fact, the offer is an offer to buy, and there is no offer to sell; the customer brings the goods to the shopkeeper to see whether he will sell or not. In 99 cases out of a 100 he will sell and, if so, he accepts the customer's offer, but he need not do so. The very fact that the supervising pharmacist is at the place where the money has to be paid is an indication to the purchaser that the shopkeeper may not be willing to complete a contract with anybody who may bring the goods to him.

Ordinary principles of common sense and of commerce must be applied in this matter, and to hold that in the case of self-service shops the exposure of an article is an offer to sell, and that a person can accept the offer by picking up the article, would be contrary to those principles and might entail serious results. On the customer picking up the article the property would forthwith pass to him and he would be able to insist upon the shopkeeper allowing him to take it away, though in some particular cases the shopkeeper might think that very undesirable. On the other hand, if a customer had picked up an article, he would never be able to change his mind and to put it back; the shopkeeper could say, 'Oh no, the property has passed and you must pay the price.'

It seems to me, therefore, that the transaction is in no way different from the normal transaction in a shop in which there is no self-service scheme. I am quite satisfied it would be wrong to say that the shopkeeper is making an offer to sell every article in the shop to any person who might come in and that that person can insist on buying any article by saying 'I accept your offer.' I agree with the illustration put forward during the case of a person who might go into a shop where books are displayed. In most book-shops customers are invited to go in and pick up books and look at them even if they do not actually buy them. There is no contract by the shopkeeper to sell until the customer has taken the book to the shopkeeper or his assistant and said 'I want to buy this book' and the shopkeeper says 'Yes.' That would not prevent the shopkeeper, seeing the book picked up, saying: 'I am sorry I cannot let you have that book; it is the only copy I have got and I have already promised it to another customer.' Therefore, in my opinion, the mere fact that a customer picks up a bottle of medicine from the shelves in this case does not amount to an acceptance of an offer to sell. It is an offer by the customer to buy and there is no sale effected until the buyer's offer to buy is accepted by the acceptance of the price. The offer, the acceptance of the price, and therefore the sale, take place under the supervision of the pharmacist.

Court of Appeal
[1953] 1 QB 401

SOMERVELL LJ: I agree with the Lord Chief Justice in everything that he said, but I will put the matter shortly in my own words. Whether the view contended for by the plaintiffs is a right view depends on what are the legal implications of this layout—the invitation to the customer. Is a contract to be regarded as being completed when the article is put into the receptacle, or is this to be regarded as a more organised way of doing what is done already in many types of shops—and a bookseller is perhaps the best example—namely, enabling customers to have free access to what is in the shop, to look at the different articles, and then, ultimately, having got the ones which they wish to buy, to come up to the assistant saying 'I want this'? The assistant in 999 times out of 1,000 says 'That is all right,' and the money passes and the transaction is completed. I agree with what the Lord Chief Justice has said, and with the reasons which he has given for his conclusion, that in the case of an ordinary shop, although goods are displayed and it is intended that customers should go and choose what they want, the contract is not completed until, the customer having indicated the articles which he needs, the shopkeeper, or someone on his behalf, accepts that offer. Then the contract is completed. I can see no reason at all, that being clearly the normal position, for drawing any different implication as a result of this layout.

The Lord Chief Justice, I think, expressed one of the most formidable difficulties in the way of the plaintiffs' contention when he pointed out that, if the plaintiffs are right, once an article has been placed in the receptacle the customer himself is bound and would have no right, without paying for the first article, to substitute an article which he saw later of a similar kind and which he perhaps preferred. I can see no reason for implying from this self-service arrangement any implication other than that which the Lord Chief Justice found in it, namely, that it is a convenient method of enabling customers to see what there is and choose, and possibly put back and substitute, articles which they wish to have, and then to go up to the cashier and offer to buy what they have so far chosen. On that conclusion the case fails, because it is admitted that there was supervision in the sense required by the Act and at the appropriate moment of time.

NOTES

1. Lord Goddard and the Court of Appeal assumed that if they held that the display was an offer, the acceptance would be the customer's act of placing the goods selected in the wire basket. However, the acceptance might be the customer's act of handing the goods to the cashier. (See Jackson (1979) 129 NLJ 775 and the American case of *Lasky* v *Economy Grocery Stores* (1946) 163 ALR 235, where it was held that the display was an offer but that acceptance did not take place until the goods were handed to the cashier.)
2. Misleading pricing constitutes a criminal offence (Consumer Protection Act 1987, ss. 20–26).

■ QUESTIONS

1. Both Lord Goddard and the Court of Appeal considered that the offer must come from the customer and acceptance must be by or on behalf of the shop-keeper, but what did they say would constitute the offer and what act would be the acceptance? Montrose (1955) 4 Am J Comp Law 235, argued that the offer occurs when the customer hands the goods to the cashier, as opposed to when they are placed in the wire basket, because until that point the customer has not evinced a definite intention to be bound.

2. What is the position if there is a non-self-service counter inside a supermarket? For example, I request that a joint of beef be cut to my specifications but before I reach the cash desk I change my mind. Has a contract of sale already been concluded?

3. In *Chapelton* v *Barry Urban District Council* [1940] 1 KB 532 (*page 216*), the Court of Appeal held that a pile of deck chairs accompanied by a notice indicating the hire charge and stating that tickets should be obtained from the attendants, amounted to an offer.

   If automatic machines represent standing offers (*Thornton* v *Shoe Lane Parking Ltd* [1971] 2 QB 163, see *page 217*), why are goods on supermarket shelves not classified as a standing offer? (See Unger (1953) 16 MLR 369.)

4. If goods are advertised/displayed on a retailer's website, does this website constitute an invitation to treat or an offer? See the discussion of the Argos website incident (September 1999) in J. Poole, *Textbook on Contract*, 7th edn, 2004: Oxford University Press, pp. 43–4, and the Kodak incident (December 2001) where £329 cameras were displayed at a price of £100.

   Regulation 12 of the Electronic-Commerce (EC Directive) Regulations 2002, SI 2002/2013, suggests that a website may be an invitation to treat since it provides that an order 'may be but need not be the contractual offer'. Due to the ambiguity of Regulation 12, it does not follow that the supplier's acknowledgement of receipt of the order will definitely constitute formal acceptance. However, if it does, the contract will be concluded when the purchaser is able to access that acknowledgement (Reg. 11(2)(a)).

   These Regulations relate to information to be supplied to customers where contracts are made via the web and do allow the service provider to specify when and where a contract will be concluded online since Regulation 9 requires the service provider to communicate in advance 'the different technical steps to follow to conclude the contract'.

C: Tenders

A request for tenders is an invitation to treat and each tender is an offer. The requestor is free to accept or reject any tender to purchase goods, even if it is the highest bid.

Spencer v *Harding*
(1870) LR 5 CP 561 (CP)

WILLES J: . . . The action is brought against persons who issued a circular offering a stock for sale by tender, to be sold at a discount in one lot. The plaintiffs sent in a tender which turned out to be the highest, but which was not accepted. They now insist that the circular amounts to a contract or promise to sell the goods to the highest bidder, that is, in this case, to the person who should tender for them at the smallest rate of discount; and reliance is placed on the cases as to rewards offered for the discovery of an offender. In those cases, however there never was any doubt that the advertisement amounted to a promise to pay the money to the person who first gave information. The difficulty suggested was that it was a contract with all the world. But that, of course, was soon overruled. It was an offer to become liable to any person who before the offer should be retracted should happen to be the person to fulfil the contract of which the advertisement was an offer or tender. That is not the sort of difficulty which presents itself here. If the circular had gone on, 'and we undertake to sell to the highest bidder,' the reward cases would have applied, and there would have been a good contract in respect of the persons. But the question is, whether there is here any offer to enter into a contract at all, or whether the circular amounts to anything more than a mere proclamation that the defendants are ready to chaffer for the sale of the goods, and to receive offers for the purchase of them. In advertisements for tenders for buildings it is not usual to say that the contract will be given to the lowest bidder, and it is not always that the contract is made with the lowest bidder. Here there is a total absence of any words to intimate that the highest bidder is to be the purchaser. It is a mere attempt to ascertain whether an offer can be obtained within such a margin as the sellers are willing to adopt.

NOTE: These are the generally applicable principles. However, there are various controls placed upon the tendering process and the award of contracts by public bodies, see the Public Works Contracts Regulations 1991, SI 1991/2680, the Public Services Contracts Regulations 1993, SI 1993/3228, the Public Supply Contracts Regulations 1995, SI 1995/201, and the Utilities Contracts Regulations 1996, SI 1996/2911 (all amended by the Public Contracts (Works, Services and Supply) and Utilities Contracts (Amendment) Regulations 2003, SI 2003/46). See also EU Directives 2004/17/EC (coordinating the procurement procedures of entities operating in the water, energy, transport and postal services sectors) and 2004/18/EC (coordinating the procedures for the award of public works contracts, public supply contracts and public service contracts). The deadline for implementation of these Directives is the end of January 2006.

In some circumstances, there may be a binding contractual obligation to consider tenders conforming to the bid conditions.

Blackpool & Fylde Aero Club Ltd v *Blackpool Borough Council*
[1990] 1 WLR 1195 (CA)

The plaintiff club and six other parties were invited by the Council to tender for a concession to operate pleasure flights from the airport. Tenders would not be considered if they were received after 12 noon on 17 March 1983. The club's tender was put in the Town Hall letter box at 11 a.m. on 17 March but the letter box was not cleared, as it should have been, at 12 noon. The club's tender was not considered on the basis that it was received too late. On discovering what had happened, the Council decided to carry out the tendering exercise again. However, when the successful tenderer threatened to sue, the Council retracted. The club sought damages for breach of warranty, arguing that the Council had warranted that if the tender was received by the deadline it would be considered. Held: an invitation to tender could give rise to a binding contractual obligation to consider tenders conforming to the conditions of tender in these circumstances, namely:

(a) The tenders had been solicited by the Council from specified parties who were known to the Council.

(b) There were absolute conditions governing submission including an absolute deadline.

BINGHAM LJ: . . . During the hearing the questions were raised: what if, in a situation such as the present, the council had opened and thereupon accepted the first tender received, even though the deadline had not expired and other invitees had not yet responded? Or if the council had considered and accepted a tender admittedly received well after the deadline? [Counsel] answered that although by so acting the council might breach its own standing orders, and might fairly be accused of discreditable conduct, it would not be in breach of any legal obligation because at that stage there would be none to breach. This is a conclusion I cannot accept. And if it were accepted there would in my view be an unacceptable discrepancy between the law of contract and the confident assumptions of commercal parties, both tenderers (as reflected in the evidence of Mr Bateson) and invitors (as reflected in the immediate reaction of the council when the mishap came to light).

A tendering procedure of this kind is, in many respects, heavily weighted in favour of the invitor. He can invite tenders from as many or as few parties as he chooses. He need not tell any of them who else, or how many others, he has invited. The invitee may often, although not here, be put to considerable labour and expense in preparing a tender, ordinarily without recompense if he is unsuccessful. The invitation to tender may itself, in a complex case, although again not here, involve time and expense to prepare, but the invitor does not commit himself to proceed with the project, whatever it is; he need not accept the highest tender; he need not accept any tender; he need not give reasons to justify his acceptance or rejection of any tender received. The risk to which the tenderer is exposed does not end with the risk that his tender may not be the highest or, as the case may be, lowest. But where, as here, tenders are solicited from selected parties all of them known to the invitor, and where a local authority's invitation prescribes a clear, orderly and familiar procedure—draft contract conditions available for inspection and plainly not open to negotiation, a prescribed common form of tender, the supply of envelopes designed to preserve the absolute anonymity of tenderers and clearly to identify the tender in question and an absolute deadline—the invitee is in my judgment protected at least to this extent: if he submits a conforming tender before the deadline he is entitled, not as a matter of mere expectation but of contractual right, to be sure that his tender will after the deadline be opened and considered in conjunction with all other conforming tenders or at least that his tender will be considered if others are. Had the club, before tendering, inquired of the council whether it could rely on any timely and conforming tender being considered along with others, I feel quite sure that the answer would have been 'of course'. The law would, I think, be defective if it did not give effect to that. . . .

I readily accept that contracts are not to be lightly implied. Having examined what the parties said and did, the court must be able to conclude with confidence both that the parties intended to create contractual relations and that the agreement was to the effect contended for. . . . [Counsel for the club] was in my view right to contend for no more than a contractual duty to consider. I think it plain that the council's invitation to tender was, to this limited extent, an offer, and the club's submission of a timely and conforming tender an acceptance.

■ QUESTION

If the remedy available for breach of such a duty to consider tenders is to be damages, how might those damages be measured? Should damages be limited to the recovery of reliance loss or would loss of chance damages be more appropriate? See the discussion of measures of damages at *pages 363–78* and *Fairclough Building* v *Port Talbot BC*, note 4 below.

NOTES

1. Bingham LJ refers to this decision as avoiding 'an unacceptable discrepancy between the law of contract and the confident assumptions of commercial parties', i.e., the club would not have bothered to tender unless its tender was to be considered, and on discovering its failure to consider the club's tender, the Council had declared the tendering process invalid until the successful tenderer had threatened legal action.

2. This decision can be analysed as an example of an implied unilateral contract, i.e., an offer to consider conforming tenders which is accepted by submitting a conforming tender.

3. For further discussion of this case see Adams and Brownsword (1991) 54 MLR 281, McKendrick [1991] LMCLQ 31 and Phang (1991) 4 JCL 46.

4. In *Fairclough Building Ltd* v *Port Talbot Borough Council* (1992) 62 Build LR 82, 33 Con LR 24, the Court of Appeal also recognised the existence of a contractual obligation to consider tenders from contractors on a Council short-list, 'unless there were reasonable grounds for not doing so'. On the facts in *Fairclough*, the Council did have reasonable grounds for removing the plaintiffs from the short-list so that there was no breach of contract and *Blackpool* was therefore distinguished.

   The Court of Appeal in *Fairclough* also suggested that had there been a breach, damages would be based on the loss of a chance to be considered.

5. In *Harmon CFEM Facades (UK) Ltd* v *Corporate Officer of the House of Commons* (1999) 67 Con LR 1, an implied contractual obligation to act fairly in the tendering process was imposed on public sector clients. See also the decision of the Privy Council in *Pratt Contractors Ltd* v *Transit New Zealand* [2003] UKPC 83, [2004] BLR 143, recognising implied terms of good faith and fair dealing in competitive tendering for work on a state highway in New Zealand. Should such an obligation be imposed on those in the private sector who request the submission of tenders?

What if the invitation to tender expressly contains an undertaking to accept the highest (or lowest) bid?

Harvela Investments Ltd v *Royal Trust Co. of Canada (CI) Ltd*
[1985] Ch 103; [1986] AC 207 (HL)

The plaintiff and the second defendant (Sir Leonard) were rival offerors for a parcel of shares belonging to the first defendants (Royal Trust). The first defendants invited both parties to submit a sealed offer or confidential telex by a stipulated date. They stated in the invitation to tender that they bound themselves to accept the highest offer they received which complied with the terms of the invitation. The plaintiff tendered a bid of $2,175,000, and the second defendant's bid was $2,100,000 or $101,000 in excess of any other offer. The first defendants accepted the second defendant's bid as being $2,276,000 and entered into a sale contract. The plaintiff brought proceedings contending that the second defendant's bid was invalid. At first instance Peter Gibson J held that the invitation to bid constituted an offer to be bound by the highest bid. This offer was unilateral in that it requested the performance of an act, submitting the highest bid, and performance of this act constituted the acceptance of that offer. The plaintiff's bid was the only valid bid so that there was a contract with the plaintiff. The Court of Appeal agreed but refused to imply a term excluding referential bids. Held: (in the House of Lords) referential bids were invalid, so that the only valid bid was the plaintiff's and the first defendants were bound to accept it. Lord Diplock confirmed the analysis of Peter Gibson J on the effect of the invitation to tender.

LORD DIPLOCK: The construction question turns upon the wording of the telex of 15 September 1981 referred to by Lord Templeman as 'the invitation' and addressed to both Harvela and Sir Leonard. It was not a mere invitation to negotiate for the sale of the shares in Harvey & Co. Ltd of which the vendors were the registered owners in the capacity of trustees. Its legal nature was that of a unilateral or 'if' contract, or rather of two unilateral contracts in identical terms to one of which the vendors and Harvela were the parties as promisor and promisee respectively, while to the other the vendors were promisor and Sir Leonard was promisee. Such unilateral contracts were made at the time when the invitation was received by the promisee to whom it was addressed by the vendors; under neither of them did the promisee, Harvela and Sir Leonard respectively, assume any legal obligation to anyone to do or refrain from doing anything.

The vendors, on the other hand, did assume a legal obligation to the promisee under each contract. That obligation was conditional upon the happening, after the unilateral contract had been made, of an event which was specified in the invitation; the obligation was to enter into a synallagmatic contract to sell the shares to the promisee, the terms of such synallagmatic contract being also set out in the invitation. The event upon the happening of which the vendors' obligation to sell the shares to the promisee arose was the doing by the promisee of an act which was of such a nature that it might be done by either promisee or neither promisee but could not be done by both. The vendors thus did not by entering into the two unilateral contracts run any risk of assuming legal obligations to enter into conflicting synallagmatic contracts to sell the shares to each promisee.

The two unilateral contracts were of short duration; for the condition subsequent to which each was subject was the receipt by the vendors' solicitors on or before 3 pm on the following day, 16 September 1981, of a sealed tender or confidential telex containing an offer by the promisee to buy the shares for a single sum of money in Canadian dollars. If such an offer was received from each of the promisees under their respective contracts, the obligation of the promisor, the vendors, was to sell the shares to the promisee whose offer was the higher; and any obligation which the promisor had assumed to the promisee under the other unilateral contract came to an end, because the event the happening of which was the condition subsequent to which the vendors' obligation to sell the shares to that promisee was subject had not happened before the unilateral contract with that promisee expired.

Since the invitation in addition to containing the terms of the unilateral contract also embodied the terms of the synallagmatic contract into which the vendors undertook to enter upon the happening of the specified event, the consequence of the happening of that event would be to convert the invitation into a synallagmatic contract between the vendors and whichever promisee had offered, by sealed tender or confidential telex, the higher sum. . . .

NOTE: This is another example of an 'implied' unilateral contract. The invitation to tender was a unilateral offer to accept the highest bid. This was accepted by everyone who bid. It was then followed by a synallagmatic (bilateral) contract with whoever was the highest bidder. If the person inviting tenders did not comply with the offer terms, then he would be in breach of the unilateral contract and would be liable in damages.

However, *Harvela* differs from *Blackpool* in that in *Harvela* the obligation forming the basis for the implied unilateral contract is an express promise rather than one implied from the circumstances.

D: Auction sales

An auctioneer's request for bids is an invitation to treat. The bid is the offer which the auctioneer can accept or reject. The Sale of Goods Act 1979, s. 57(2) provides that acceptance occurs on the fall of the hammer and any bidder may withdraw his bid before that time.

Harris v *Nickerson*
(1873) LR 8 QB 286 (QB)

The defendant auctioneer advertised that lots including certain office furniture would be sold by him at Bury St Edmunds on specified days. The plaintiff had a commission to buy this furniture and travelled from London for the sale. However, the lots were withdrawn from sale. The plaintiff brought an action against the defendant to recover for his loss of time and expenses. Held: he had no such right of action. The advertisement was only an invitation to treat and did not amount to a promise that all the articles advertised would be put up for sale.

What if the auction is advertised as being 'without reserve' (i.e., there is to be no reserve price and the property will be sold to the highest bidder)?

Warlow v *Harrison*
(1859) 1 E & E 309; 120 ER 925 (Exchequer Chamber)

The defendant, an auctioneer, advertised the sale without reserve of a horse by public auction. The plaintiff attended the sale and bid 60 guineas. The horse's owner bid 61 guineas. The plaintiff refused to make any further bid and the defendant (who, it appears, did not know that the bidder was the owner) knocked down the horse to the owner for 61 guineas. The plaintiff claimed that the horse was his since he was the highest bona fide purchaser at an unreserved sale. In his pleadings the plaintiff alleged that the defendant was the plaintiff's agent to complete this contract. Held: on the pleadings the plaintiff had no claim since there was no agency relationship between the plaintiff and the defendant. The pleadings required amendment.

MARTIN B (*obiter*): . . . The sale was announced . . . to be 'without reserve.' This, according to all the cases both at law and equity, means that neither the vendor nor any person in his behalf shall bid at the auction, and that the property shall be sold to the highest bidder, whether the sum bid be equivalent to the real value or not. We cannot distinguish the case of an auctioneer putting up property for sale upon such a condition from the case of the loser of property offering a reward. . . . Upon the same principle, it seems to us that the highest bonâ fide bidder at an auction may sue the auctioneer as upon a contract that the sale shall be without reserve. We think the auctioneer who puts the property up for sale upon such a condition pledges himself that the sale shall be without reserve; or, in other words, contracts that it shall be so; and that this contract is made with the highest bonâ fide bidder; and, in case of a breach of it, that he has a right of action against the auctioneer.

NOTES

1. There were two agreements. First, the plaintiff's bid was an offer, but since his bid was not accepted he was not entitled to the horse which was knocked down to the owner. However, the advertisement of an auction sale without reserve is a unilateral offer by the auctioneer that no reserve will be applied. Martin B indicates that only the highest bona fide bidder can accept this unilateral offer. The plaintiff clearly accepted *this* offer and the auctioneer would be liable in damages for breach of his promise that there would be no reserve. (Compare this with the analysis of invitations to tender agreeing to accept the highest bid in *Harvela Investments Ltd* v *Royal Trust Co. of Canada Ltd*, at *page 32*.)

2. See Slade (1952) 68 LQR 288, Gower (1952) 68 LQR 457 and Slade (1953) 69 LQR 21.

■ QUESTIONS

1. Might it be argued that the unilateral offer to hold an auction without reserve could be accepted by all those who bid at such an auction but that only the highest bona fide bidder would suffer loss in the event of breach and be entitled to recover damages? See the discussion in the notes relating to the decision of the Court of Appeal in *Barry* v *Davies* [2000] 1 WLR 1962, *below*.

2. The *obiter* statement in *Warlow* v *Harrison* was set in the context of the position of the highest genuine bidder at an auction without reserve where the owner is permitted to bid. However, what is the position if the auctioneer, having received one or more bids at an auction without reserve, then withdraws those goods and does not allow the hammer to fall? The Court of Appeal applied *Warlow* v *Harrison* in answering this question in the following case.

Barry v *Davies (t/a Heathcote Ball & Co.)*
[2000] 1 WLR 1962 (CA)

At an auction without reserve the plaintiff had made the only bid (of £200 each) for two engine analysers. The auctioneer considered this bid to be too low (on the basis that each machine was worth about £14,000) and withdrew the engine analysers from the sale. They were sold privately a few days later for £750 each.

The plaintiff sought damages alleging breach of contract by the auctioneer since he was the highest bidder at an auction without reserve. The plaintiff claimed damages of £27,600, being the difference between the value of both machines (£28,000) less the amount of his bid (£400). Held: the auctioneer was liable. Following *Warlow* v *Harrison*, at an auction without reserve there was a collateral contract between the auctioneer and the highest bidder based on the auctioneer's undertaking to sell to the highest bidder. By withdrawing the machines from the auction, the auctioneer was in breach of this contract and was liable to pay the highest bidder the difference between the bid amount and the market price at the date of the auction of the goods withdrawn. The only evidence of market price was the manufacturer's list price for new machines, namely £14,000 each.

SIR MURRAY STUART SMITH LJ: . . . The judge held that it would be the general and reasonable expectation of persons attending at an auction sale without reserve that the highest bidder would and should be entitled to the lot for which he bids. Such an outcome was in his view fair and logical. As a matter of law he held that there was a collateral contract between the auctioneer and the highest bidder constituted by an offer by the auctioneer to sell to the highest bidder which was accepted when the bid was made. In so doing he followed the views of the majority of the Court of Exchequer Chamber in *Warlow* v *Harrison* (1859) 1 E & E 309. . . .

[Counsel] on behalf of the defendant criticised this conclusion on a number of grounds. First, he submitted that the holding of an auction without reserve does not amount to a promise on the part of the auctioneer to sell the lots to the highest bidder. There are no express words to the effect, merely a statement of fact that the vendor has not placed a reserve on the lot. Such an intention, he submitted, is inconsistent with two principles of law, namely that the auctioneer's request for bids is not an offer which can be accepted by the highest bidder (*Payne* v *Cave* (1789) 3 Durn & E 148) and that there is no completed contract of sale until the auctioneer's hammer falls and the bidder may withdraw his bid up until that time (Sale of Goods Act 1979, s. 57(2), which reflects the common law). There should be no need to imply such a promise into a statement that the sale is without reserve, because there may be other valid reasons why the auctioneer should be entitled to withdraw the lot, for example if he suspected an illegal ring or that the vendor had no title to sell.

Secondly, [counsel] submitted that there is no consideration for the auctioneer's promise. He submitted that the bid itself cannot amount to consideration because the bidder has not promised to do anything, he can withdraw the bid until it is accepted and the sale completed by the fall of the hammer. At most the bid represents a discretionary promise, which amounts to illusory consideration, for example promising to do something 'if I feel like it'. The bid only had real benefit to the auctioneer at the moment the sale is completed by the fall of the hammer. Furthermore, the suggestion that consideration is provided because the auctioneer has the opportunity to accept the bid or to obtain a higher bid as the bidding is driven up depends upon the bid not being withdrawn. . . .

The authorities, such as they were, do not speak with one voice. The starting point is s. 57 of the Sale of Goods Act 1979, which re-enacted the Sale of Goods Act 1893 (56 & 57 Vict. c. 71), itself in this section a codification of the common law. . . .

Subsections (3) and (4) are . . . important. They provide:

(3) A sale by auction may be notified to be subject to a reserve or upset price, and a right to bid may also be reserved expressly by or on behalf of the seller. (4) Where a sale by auction is not notified to be subject to the right to bid by or on behalf of the seller, it is not lawful for the seller to bid himself or to employ any person to bid at the sale, or for the auctioneer knowingly to take any bid from the seller or any such person.

Although the Act does not expressly deal with sales by auction without reserve, the auctioneer is the agent of the vendor and, unless subsection (4) has been complied with, it is not lawful for him to make a bid. Yet withdrawing the lot from the sale because it has not reached the level which the auctioneer considers appropriate is tantamount to bidding on behalf of the seller. The highest bid cannot be rejected simply because it is not high enough. . . .

[He then discussed *Warlow* v *Harrison* as being authoritative on the question of the collateral contract and continued:] As to consideration, in my judgment there is consideration both in the form of detriment to the bidder, since his bid can be accepted unless and until it is withdrawn, and benefit to the auctioneer as the bidding is driven up. Moreover, attendance at the sale is likely to be increased if it is known that there is no reserve. . . .

For these reasons I would uphold the judge's decision on liability.

NOTES

1. It also appears from this decision that a bid at an auction without reserve can be withdrawn at any time before the hammer falls. This suggests that the unilateral (collateral) offer to apply the reserve and not to allow the owner to bid, cannot be accepted by every bidder at an auction without reserve. If the acceptance of the offer can only be made by the highest bona fide bidder, that person's identity will not be revealed, and acceptance will not occur, until the hammer falls or the goods are withdrawn from the sale. Such an analysis preserves the ability to withdraw bids at an auction without reserve.

2. The Court of Appeal rejected the argument that the measure of damages should be restricted to £1,500, which the defendant alleged was the value of the machines, having sold them for this figure. The problem was that on the facts there was no evidence of market value other than the manufacturer's list price and the court accepted that this was the only available market to purchase a substitute. Normally there will be evidence of second-hand market

value which will be applied in fixing the damages award. In his judgment Pill LJ makes it clear that the plaintiff was 'fortunate' in relation to the damages award because there was no evidence of value other than the list price.

SECTION 4: ACCEPTANCE

A: The mirror image rule

Hyde v *Wrench*
(1840) 3 Beav 334; 49 ER 132 (Rolls Court)

The defendant on 6 June offered in writing to sell his farm for £1,000; but the plaintiff offered £950, which the defendant, on 27 June, refused to accept. On 29 June, the plaintiff, by letter, agreed to give £1,000, but the defendant did not indicate assent to this. Held: there was no binding contract for the purchase of the farm.

LORD LANGDALE MR: . . . Under the circumstances stated in this bill, I think there exists no valid binding contract between the parties for the purchase of the property. The defendant offered to sell it for £1,000, and if that had been at once unconditionally accepted, there would undoubtedly have been a perfect binding contract; instead of that, the plaintiff made an offer of his own to purchase the property for £950, and he thereby rejected the offer previously made by the defendant. I think that it was not afterwards competent for him to revive the proposal of the defendant, by tendering an acceptance of it; and that, therefore, there exists no obligation of any sort between the parties . . .

Does the correspondence amount to a counter-offer?

(1) A request for further information before the offeree makes up his mind is not a counter-offer.

Stevenson, Jacques & Co. v *McLean*
(1880) 5 QBD 346 (QB)

The defendant wrote to the plaintiffs giving 40s net cash per ton as the lowest price at which he could sell iron and stating that he would hold the offer open until the following Monday. The plaintiffs telegraphed 'Please wire whether you would accept forty for delivery over two months, or, if not, the longest limit you could give'. The defendant did not reply. One of the issues before Lush J was whether this amounted to a counter-offer thereby rejecting the defendant's offer to sell at 40s net cash per ton. Held: the telegram was not a rejection of the defendant's offer but merely an inquiry as to whether the defendant would modify the terms of his offer.

LUSH J: . . . [T]he form of the telegram is one of inquiry. It is not 'I offer forty for delivery over two months,' which would have likened the case to *Hyde* v *Wrench* (1840) 3 Beav 334, where one party offered his estate for 1,000*l*., and the other answered by offering 950*l*. Lord Langdale, in that case, held that after the 950*l*. had been refused, the party offering it could not, by then agreeing to the original proposal, claim the estate, for the negotiation was at an end by the refusal of his counter proposal. Here there is no counter proposal. The words are, 'Please wire whether you would accept forty for delivery over two months, or, if not, the longest limit you would give.' There is nothing specific by way of offer or rejection, but a mere inquiry, which should have been answered and not treated as a rejection of the offer.

(2) What is the position if the offeree purports to accept in one document but attaches a covering letter asserting that he will not be in a position to comply with the terms of that acceptance? Does this make the acceptance conditional and hence ineffective as an acceptance? The Court of Appeal in *The Society of Lloyds* v *Twinn* (2000) 97 (15) LSG 40, *The Times*, 4 April 2000 recognised that there were circumstances when an offeree might wish to accept even though he was unable to perform at that time. The inclusion of an apparently inconsistent covering letter might be regarded as collateral to the concluded contract rather than rendering the acceptance conditional. The effect of the covering letter would need to be judged objectively depending on the language used and the surrounding circumstances. It was clear in this case that the agreement was regarded as concluded despite the existence of the covering letter.

There can be acceptance of a counter-offer by conduct

Brogden v *Metropolitan Railway Company*
(1877) 2 App Cas 666 (HL)

Brogden had suggested that the Company should enter into a formal contract for the supply of coal. The Company sent terms of agreement. Brogden added the name of an arbitrator to settle any differences before writing 'approved' and signing the document. The agreement was returned to the Company's manager, who put it in his desk. The manager then ordered and received coal on the basis of the arrangements in this document. When disputes arose Brogden denied that there was any binding contract. Held: By inserting the name of an arbitrator, Brogden had rejected the offer and made a counter-offer. This counter-offer had been accepted by the Company when it ordered and had taken delivery of coal upon the terms of the agreement. There had therefore been acceptance by conduct.

LORD BLACKBURN: . . . I have always believed the law to be this, that when an offer is made to another party, and in that offer there is a request express or implied that he must signify his acceptance by doing some particular thing, then as soon as he does that thing, he is bound. If a man sent an offer abroad saying: I wish to know whether you will supply me with goods at such and such a price, and, if you agree to that, you must ship the first cargo as soon as you get this letter, there can be no doubt that as soon as the cargo was shipped the contract would be complete, and if the cargo went to the bottom of the sea, it would go to the bottom of the sea at the risk of the orderer. So again, where, as in the case of *Ex parte Harris* [*In re Imperial Land Co. of Marseilles* (1871–72) 7 LR Ch App 587], a person writes a letter and says, I offer to take an allotment of shares, and he expressly or impliedly says, If you agree with me send an answer by the post, there, as soon as he has sent that answer by the post, and put it out of his control, and done an extraneous act which clenches the matter, and shews beyond all doubt that each side is bound, I agree the contract is perfectly plain and clear.

But when you come to the general proposition which [the judge at first instance] seems to have laid down, that a simple acceptance in your own mind, without any intimation to the other party, and expressed by a mere private act, such as putting a letter into a drawer, completes a contract, I must say I differ from that. . . .

But my Lords, while, as I say, this is so upon the question of law, it is still necessary to consider this case farther upon the question of fact. I agree, and I think every Judge who has considered the case does agree, certainly Lord Chief Justice Cockburn does, that though the parties may have gone no farther than an offer on the one side, saying, Here is the draft,—(for that I think is really what this case comes to,)—and the draft so offered by the one side is approved by the other, everything being agreed to except the name of the arbitrator, which the one side has filled in and the other has not yet assented to, if both parties have acted upon that draft and treated it as binding, they will be bound by it. . . .

NOTE: In *Pickfords Ltd* v *Celestica Ltd* [2003] EWCA Civ 1741, 19 November 2003, *page 53*, the Court of Appeal considered that a purported acceptance fax was in fact a counter-offer since it purported to accept the first price offer although this first price offer had been revoked by a second price offer on different terms. The 'acceptance' fax therefore represented an offer on the terms of the first price offer with the addition of a cap of £100,000 (a material new term added in the counter-offer). This counter-offer had then been accepted by conduct when the claimant carried out the removal work under the contract.

Battle of forms and the counter-offer analysis

Butler Machine Tool Co. Ltd v *Ex-Cell-O Corporation (England) Ltd*
[1979] 1 WLR 401 (CA)

On 23 May 1969, the sellers issued a quotation offering to sell a machine tool to the buyers for £75,535, delivery to be in 10 months' time. The offer was stated to be subject to certain terms and conditions which 'shall prevail over any terms and conditions in the buyer's order'. The conditions included a price variation clause providing for the goods to be charged at the price on the date of delivery. On 27 May, the buyers replied by placing an order for the machine. The order was stated to be subject to certain terms and conditions, which were materially different from those put forward by the sellers and which, in particular, made no provision for a variation in price. At the foot of the buyers' order there was a tear-off acknowledgement of receipt of the order stating that 'We accept your order on the Terms and Conditions stated thereon'. On 5 June the sellers completed and signed the acknowledgement and returned it to the buyers with a letter stating that the buyers' order was being entered in accordance with the sellers' quotation of 23 May. When the sellers came to deliver the machine they claimed that the price had increased by £2,892. The buyers refused to pay the increase in price and the sellers brought an action claiming that the price variation clause contained in their offer entitled them to the increased price. The buyers contended that the contract had been concluded on the buyers' terms and was therefore a fixed-price contract. Held: the contract had been concluded on the buyers' terms. The majority, Lawton and Bridge LJJ, held that the buyers' order was a counter-offer which the sellers had accepted by completing and returning the acknowledgement.

LAWTON LJ: The modern commercial practice of making quotations and placing orders with conditions attached, usually in small print, is indeed likely, as in this case to produce a battle of forms. The problem is how should that battle be conducted? The view taken by Thesiger J was that the battle should extend over a wide area and the court should do its best to look into the minds of the parties and make certain assumptions. In my judgment, the battle has to be conducted in accordance with set rules. It is a battle more on classical 18th century lines when convention decided who had the right to open fire first rather than in accordance with the modern concept of attrition.

   The rules relating to a battle of this kind have been known for the past 130-odd years. They were set out by Lord Langdale MR in *Hyde* v *Wrench*, 3 Beav 334, 337, . . . and, if anyone should have thought they were obsolescent, Megaw J in *Trollope & Colls Ltd* v *Atomic Power Constructions Ltd* [1963] 1 WLR 333, 337 called attention to the fact that those rules are still in force.

When those rules are applied to this case, in my judgment, the answer is obvious. The sellers started by making an offer. That was in their quotation. The small print was headed by the following words:

> 'General. All orders are accepted only upon and subject to the terms set out in our quotation and the following conditions. These terms and conditions shall prevail over any terms and conditions in the buyer's order.'

That offer was not accepted. The buyers were only prepared to have one of these very expensive machines on their own terms. Their terms had very material differences in them from the terms put forward by the sellers. They could not be reconciled in any way. In the language of article 7 of the Uniform Law on the Formation of Contracts for the International Sale of Goods (see Uniform Laws on International Sales Act 1967, Schedule 2) they did 'materially alter the terms' set out in the offer made by the plaintiffs.

As I understand *Hyde* v *Wrench*, 3 Beav 334, and the cases which have followed, the consequence of placing the order in that way, if I may adopt Megaw J's words [1963] 1 WLR 333, 337, was 'to kill the original offer.' It follows that the court has to look at what happened after the buyers made their counter-offer. By letter dated June 4, 1969, the plaintiffs acknowledged receipt of the counter-offer, and they went on in this way:

> 'Details of this order have been passed to our Halifax works for attention and a formal acknowledgment of order will follow in due course.'

That is clearly a reference to the printed tear-off slip which was at the bottom of the buyers' counter-offer. By letter dated June 5, 1969, the sales office manager at the plaintiffs' Halifax factory completed that tear-off slip and sent it back to the buyers.

It is true, [counsel for the plaintiffs] has reminded us, that the return of that printed slip was accompanied by a letter which had this sentence in it: 'This is being entered in accordance with our revised quotation of May 23 for delivery in 10/11 months.' I agree with Lord Denning MR that, in business sense, that refers to the quotation as to the price and the identity of the machine, and it does not bring into the contract the small print conditions on the back of the quotation. Those small print conditions had disappeared from the story. That was when the contract was made. At that date it was a fixed price contract without a price escalation clause.

NOTE: Lord Denning also allowed the appeal but came to his conclusion by a different route:

LORD DENNING: . . . I have much sympathy with the judge's [Thesiger J] approach to this case. In many of these cases our traditional analysis of offer, counter-offer, rejection, acceptance and so forth is out of date. This was observed by Lord Wilberforce in *New Zealand Shipping Co. Ltd* v *A.M. Satterthwaite & Co. Ltd* [1975] AC 154, 167. The better way is to look at all the documents passing between the parties—and glean from them, or from the conduct of the parties, whether they have reached agreement on all material points—even though there may be differences between the forms and conditions printed on the back of them. As Lord Cairns said in *Brogden* v *Metropolitan Railway Co.* (1877) 2 App Cas 666, 672:

> . . . there may be a *consensus* between the parties far short of a complete mode of expressing it, and that *consensus* may be discovered from letters or from other documents of an imperfect and incomplete description; . . .

Applying this guide, it will be found that in most cases when there is a 'battle of forms', there is a contract as soon as the last of the forms is sent and received without objection being taken to it. That is well observed in *Benjamin* [on Sale]. The difficulty is to decide which form, or which part of which form, is a term or condition of the contract. In some cases the battle is won by the man who fires the last shot. He is the man who puts forward the latest terms and conditions: and, if they are not objected to by the other party, he may be taken to have agreed to them. Such was *British Road Services Ltd* v *Arthur V. Crutchley & Co. Ltd* [1968] 1 Lloyd's Rep 271, 281–2, per Lord Pearson; and the illustration given by Professor Guest in *Anson's Law of Contract* when he says that 'the terms of the contract consist of the terms of the offer subject to the modifications contained in the acceptance'. In some cases the battle is won by the man who gets the blow in first. If he offers to sell at a named price on the terms and conditions stated on the back: and the buyer orders the goods purporting to accept the offer—on an order form with his own different terms and conditions on the back—then if the difference is so material that it would affect the price, the buyer ought not to be allowed to take advantage of the difference unless he draws it specifically to the attention of the seller. There are yet other cases where the battle depends on the shots fired on both sides. There is a concluded contract but the forms vary. The terms and conditions of both parties are to be construed together. If they can be reconciled so as to give a harmonious result, all well and good. If differences are irreconcilable—so that they are mutually contradictory—then the conflicting terms may have to be scrapped and replaced by a reasonable implication.

In the present case the judge thought that the sellers in their original quotation got their blow in first: especially by the provision that 'these terms and conditions shall prevail over any terms and conditions in the buyer's order'. It was so emphatic that the price variation clause continued through all the subsequent dealings and that the buyers must be taken to have agreed to it. I can understand that point of view. But I think that the documents have to be considered as a whole. And, as a matter of construction, I think the acknowledgment of June 5 1969, is the decisive document. It makes it clear that the contract was on the buyers' terms and not on the sellers' terms: and the buyers' terms did not include a price variation clause.

NOTES

1. In *Butler* v *Ex-Cell-O Corp.* there was an express acceptance of the counter-offer. In *Sauter Automation Ltd* v *Goodman (Mechanical Services) Ltd* (1986) 34 Build LR 81, the last form was accepted by conduct, namely acts of performance. See also *Nissan UK Ltd* v *Nissan Motor Manufacturing (UK) Ltd*, unrep. 26 October 1994 for a further example of acceptance of counter-offer by conduct.

2. This encourages so called 'to-ing and fro-ing with offer and counter-offer' (*per* Nourse LJ in *Nissan*), whereby businessmen send their own terms and conditions to each other in an attempt to ensure that their terms prevail.

3. Case note on *Butler* v *Ex-Cell-O Corp.*: Adams (1979) 95 LQR 481.

4. If there is already a contract between the parties, a subsequent exchange of standard forms is an attempt to vary this contract and requires specific agreement (*Lidl UK GmbH* v *Hertford Foods Ltd* [2001] EWCA Civ 938, unrep. 20 June 2001). Since no agreement had been reached, the proper inference was that neither set of standard terms was applicable. The *Butler* analysis will therefore be relevant where it is not possible to identify the existence of a prior contract containing the essential terms.

■ QUESTIONS

1. What would you advise a party to do to seek to ensure that his terms prevail? Consider the effect of Article 19, Vienna Convention (United Nations Convention on Contracts for the International Sale of Goods) (not ratified by the UK) and § 2–207 of the US Uniform Commercial Code. For an assessment of solutions to battle of forms in the international context, see Honduis and Mahe, 'The Battle of Forms: Towards a Uniform Solution' (1997) 12 JCL 268.

2. Lord Denning's approach separates the issue of formation from the question of content of the contract. Is there any empirical evidence to support Lord Denning's assessment that businessmen pay no attention to fine print and consider that they have a deal when the major terms are agreed? (See Beale and Dugdale (1975) 2 Br J Law & Soc 45, 49–51.)

3. What does Lord Denning mean when he refers to the parties reaching agreement 'on all material points'? What difficulties exist with his categorisation of terms? (See Rawlings (1979) 42 MLR 715.)

B: Acceptance must be made in response to the offer

An offer is not 'accepted' by doing the required act in ignorance of the offer. However, if the offeree responds with knowledge, his motive in so doing is irrelevant.

R v Clarke
(1927) 40 CLR 227 (High Court of Australia)

A reward was offered by the Government of Western Australia for information leading to the arrest and conviction of the persons who committed the murders of two police officers. Clarke gave this information after he had been arrested for this crime, and it was found as a fact that his only intention was to save himself from an unfounded charge so that he had not acted on the faith of, or in reliance upon, the offer. In reaching the conclusion that he could not recover, the High Court had to distinguish *Williams* v *Carwardine* (1833) 5 C & P 566, 172 ER 1101, where the plaintiff had given the information requested because she thought she was dying. It was held in that case that she could recover the reward which had been offered because she knew about the reward. Her motive in supplying the information was not material because she had acted on the offer.

HIGGINS J: . . . That case [*Williams* v *Carwardine*] seems to me not to deal with the essential elements for a contract at all: it shows merely that the *motive* of the informer in accepting the contract offered (and the performing the conditions is usually sufficient evidence of acceptance) has nothing to do with his right to recover under the contract. The reports show (as it was assumed by the Judges after the verdict of the jury in favour of the informer), that the informer *knew* of the offer when giving the information, and meant to accept the offer though she had also a *motive* in her guilty conscience.

. . . The reasoning of Woodruff J in *Fitch* v *Snedaker* [(1868) 38 NY 248] seems to me to be faultless; and the decision is spoken of in *Anson* as being undoubtedly correct in principle:—'The motive inducing consent may be immaterial, but the consent is vital. Without that there is no contract. How then can there be consent or assent to that of which the party has never heard?' Clarke had seen the offer, indeed; but it was not present to his mind—he had forgotten it, and gave no consideration to it, in his intense excitement as to his own danger. There cannot be assent without knowledge of the offer; and ignorance of the offer is the same thing whether it is due to never hearing of it or to forgetting it after hearing. But for this candid confession of Clarke's it might fairly be presumed that Clarke, having once seen the offer, acted on the faith of it, in reliance on it; but he has himself rebutted that presumption.

Gibbons v Proctor
(1891) 64 LT 594

On 29 May, the defendant instructed handbills to be printed offering a reward of £25 to the person who gave information, leading to the conviction of the perpetrator of a particular crime, to police Superintendent Penn. The plaintiff, a police officer, had already communicated the required information to a colleague, named Coppin, with instructions to forward it to Superintendent Penn. Coppin had communicated the information to his superior, Inspector Lennan, who had passed it on to Superintendent Penn. The information reached Penn on 30 May, which was after the time when the handbills had been distributed to police stations. Held: the plaintiff was entitled to the reward. Coppin and Lennan were the plaintiff's agents for the purposes of conveying the information. The terms of the offer required the information to be given to Penn. The acceptance was the supply of the information to Penn, and at that time the plaintiff knew that a reward had been offered.

NOTES
1. Hudson (1968) 84 LQR 503 argues that on grounds of policy the law should encourage rather than penalise people who do not know about a reward and who act under a sense of moral duty.
2. It is also objectionable to allow the offeror of a reward to escape liability on his promise when he has had the benefit of seeing his conditions fulfilled. (Avoidance of this situation is the very reason for holding such a promise to be an offer and not an invitation to treat.)

C: The offeror prescribes the method of acceptance

Manchester Diocesan Council for Education v *Commercial & General Investments Ltd*
[1970] 1 WLR 241 (ChD)

Condition 4 of a request for tenders stated that the person whose tender was accepted would be informed by letter sent to him at the address given in the tender. On 15 September 1964, the plaintiff wrote to the defendant company's surveyor stating that the sale to the company had been approved, but it was not until 7 January 1965 that the plaintiff's solicitors wrote to the defendant company at the address given in the tender giving formal notification of acceptance of its offer. It was alleged that the offer in the tender had lapsed so that it was necessary to decide when the contract had been concluded.

BUCKLEY J: . . . Condition 4, however, does not say that that shall be the sole permitted method of communicating an acceptance. It may be that an offeror, who by the terms of his offer insists on acceptance in a particular manner, is entitled to insist that he is not bound unless acceptance is effected or communicated in that precise way, although it seems probable that, even so, if the other party communicates his acceptance in some other way, the offeror may by conduct or otherwise waive his right to insist on the prescribed method of acceptance. Where, however, the offeror has prescribed a particular method of acceptance, but not in terms insisting that only acceptance in that mode shall be binding, I am of opinion that acceptance communicated to the offeror by any other mode which is no less advantageous to him will conclude the contract. Thus in *Tinn* v *Hoffman & Co.* (1873) 29 LT 271, where acceptance was requested by return of post, Honeyman J, said at p. 274:

> That does not mean exclusively a reply by letter by return of post, but you may reply by telegram or by verbal message or by any means not later than a letter written and sent by return of post.

If an offeror intends that he shall be bound only if his offer is accepted in some particular manner, it must be for him to make this clear. Condition 4 in the present case has not, in my judgment, this effect.

Moreover, the inclusion of condition 4 in the defendant's offer was at the instance of the plaintiff, who framed the conditions and the form of tender. It should not, I think, be regarded as a condition or stipulation imposed by the defendant as offeror upon the plaintiff as offeree, but as a term introduced into the bargain by the plaintiff and presumably considered by the plaintiff as being in some way for the protection or benefit of the plaintiff. It would consequently be a term strict compliance with which the plaintiff could waive, provided the defendant was not adversely affected. The plaintiff did not take advantage of the condition which would have resulted in a contract being formed as soon as a letter of acceptance complying with the condition was posted, but adopted another course, which could only result in a contract when the plaintiff's acceptance was actually communicated to the defendant.

For these reasons, I have reached the conclusion that in accordance with the terms of the tender it was open to the plaintiff to conclude a contract by acceptance actually communicated to the defendant in any way; and, in my judgment, the letter of September 15 constituted such an acceptance . . .

Yates Building Co. Ltd v *Pulleyn & Sons (York) Ltd*
(1975) 237 EG 183; (1975) 119 SJ 370 (CA)

The defendants granted the plaintiffs an option to buy building plots for £18,900 'exercisable by notice in writing . . . between 6 April and 6 May 1973 . . . to be sent by registered or recorded delivery post' to the defendants or their solicitors. The option was exercised by a letter of 30 April 1973 sent by ordinary post but the defendants refused to accept it as a valid acceptance. Held: as the method was not clearly stated to be mandatory, any acceptance which was communicated to the offeror by any other no less advantageous method would conclude the contract. The provision was for the benefit of the plaintiffs, and they could waive the requirement and take the risk of ordinary post.

D: Communication of the acceptance to the offeror

(a) Implied waiver of the need to communicate

Carlill v *Carbolic Smoke Ball Co.* (*Chapter 1*), is authority for the general principle that in a unilateral contract the performance of the act is the acceptance and there is no need to communicate the attempt to perform it.

However, as a general rule, silence in a bilateral contract will not constitute acceptance.

Felthouse v *Bindley*
(1862) 11 CB (NS) 869; 142 ER 1037 (CP)

The plaintiff and his nephew were negotiating for the sale of a horse. The plaintiff wrote to the nephew stating 'If I hear no more about him, I consider the horse is mine at £30 15s'. The nephew did not respond but did instruct the defendant, an auctioneer, to reserve the horse in question as it had already been sold. By mistake the defendant put the horse up for sale and it was sold. The plaintiff sued the auctioneer for the conversion of the horse (which meant that he had to show that the horse was his property at the time that it was sold). Held: the plaintiff did not have property in the horse.

WILLES J: . . . [I]t is clear that the uncle had no right to impose upon the nephew a sale of his horse for 30*l*. 15s. unless he chose to comply with the condition of writing to repudiate the offer. The nephew might, no doubt, have bound his uncle to the bargain by writing to him: the uncle might also have retracted his offer at any time before acceptance. It stood an open offer: and so things remained until the 25th of February, when the nephew was about to sell his farming stock by auction. The horse in question being catalogued with the rest of the stock, the auctioneer (the defendant) was told that it was already sold. It is clear, therefore, that the nephew in his own mind intended his uncle to have the horse at the price which he (the uncle) had named,—30*l*. 15s.: but he had not communicated such his intention to his uncle, or done anything to bind himself. Nothing, therefore, had been done to vest the property in the horse in the plaintiff down to the 25th of February, when the horse was sold by the defendant. It appears to me that, independently of the subsequent letters, there had been no bargain to pass the property in the horse to the plaintiff . . .

■ QUESTIONS

1. Why had the nephew not accepted by his act of informing the auctioneer that the horse had been sold?

2. What would the position have been if the nephew had been trying to enforce the sale contract against his uncle based upon the uncle's statement that silence would constitute acceptance?

NOTE: Section 69 of the American Restatement (2d) Contracts (1979), contains this principle but also lists a number of exceptions. Treitel, *The Law of Contract*, 11th edn, pp. 33–5, considers that there are some situations in English law where both the offeree and offeror may find themselves bound by silent acceptance.

(b) The postal rule of acceptance

If the post is the proper method to communicate acceptance, then the acceptance is deemed complete as soon as the letter of acceptance is posted.

Adams v *Lindsell*
(1818) 1 B & Ald 681; 106 ER 250 (KB)

On 2 September, the defendants wrote to the plaintiffs offering to sell them certain fleeces of wool and requiring an answer in the course of post. The defendants misdirected this letter so that the plaintiffs did not receive it until 5 September. The plaintiffs posted their acceptance on the same day but it was not received until 9 September. Meanwhile, on 8 September, the defendants, not having as they expected received an answer by 7 September, sold the wool to someone else. Held: there was a contract on 5 September when the plaintiffs posted their acceptance. In answer to the argument that the acceptance had to be communicated the court said, that if that were so, no contract could ever be completed by the post. If the defendants were not bound by their offer when accepted by the plaintiffs till the answer was received, then the plaintiffs ought not to be bound till after they had received the notification that the defendants had received their answer and assented to it. And so it might go on *ad infinitum*. The court stressed the fact that the delay in notifying the acceptance was solely the result of the defendants' mistake and 'it therefore must be taken as against them, that the plaintiffs' answer was received in course of post'.

NOTE: The following case considers the question of when the post is a proper method for communicating acceptance.

Henthorn v *Fraser*
[1892] 2 Ch 27 (CA)

The facts of this case appear at *page 55*.

LORD HERSCHELL: . . . Where the circumstances are such that it must have been within the contemplation of the parties that, according to the ordinary usages of mankind, the post might be used as a means of communicating the acceptance of an offer, the acceptance is complete as soon as it is posted.

NOTE: The offer in this case had not been made by post. The offeree had been handed an option to purchase by the offeror in Liverpool. The offeree lived in Birkenhead. Therefore it was held that acceptance by post must have been within the parties' contemplation.

Household Fire and Carriage Accident Insurance Company (Ltd) v *Grant*
(1879) 4 Ex D 216 (CA)

The defendant applied for shares in the plaintiff company. The company allotted the shares to the defendant, and addressed to him and posted a letter containing the notice of allotment, but the letter was never received by him. Held: (Thesiger and Baggally LJJ; Bramwell LJ dissenting) the defendant had become a shareholder. Acceptance was complete when the letter of allotment was posted and it was irrelevant that it never arrived.

THESIGER LJ: . . . An acceptance, which only remains in the breast of the acceptor without being actually and by legal implication communicated to the offerer, is no binding acceptance. How then are these elements of law to be harmonised in the case of contracts formed by correspondence through the post? I see no better mode than that of treating the post office as the agent of both parties, and it was so considered by Lord Romilly in *Hebb's Case* (1867) LR 4 Eq 9, when in the course of his judgment he said: '*Dunlop* v *Higgins* (1848) 1 HLC 381 decides that the posting of a letter accepting an offer constitutes a binding contract, but the reason of that is, that the post office is the common agent of both parties.' Alderson, B., also in *Stocken* v *Collin* (1841) 7 M & W 515, a case of notice of dishonour, . . . says: 'If the doctrine that the post office is only the agent for the delivery of the notice were correct no one could safely avail himself of that mode of transmission.' But if the post office be such common agent, then it seems to me to follow that, as soon as the letter of acceptance is delivered to the post office, the contract is made as complete and final and absolutely binding as if the acceptor had put his letter into the hands of a messenger sent by the offerer himself as his agent to deliver the offer and receive the acceptance. What other principle can be adopted short of holding that the contract is not complete by acceptance until and except from the time that the letter containing the acceptance is delivered to the offerer, a principle which has been distinctly negatived? . . . The acceptor, in posting the letter, has, to use the language of Lord Blackburn, in *Brogden* v *Directors of Metropolitan Ry. Co.* (1877) 2 App Cas 666, 'put it out of his control and done an extraneous act which clenches the matter, and shews beyond all doubt that each side is bound.' How then can a casualty in the post, whether resulting in delay, which in commercial transactions is often as bad as no delivery, or in non-delivery, unbind the parties or unmake the contract? To me it appears that in practice a contract complete upon the acceptance of an offer being posted, but liable to be put an end to by an accident in the post, would be more mischievous than a contract only binding upon the parties to it upon the acceptance actually reaching the offerer, and I can see no principle of law from which such an anomalous contract can be deduced.

There is no doubt that the implication of a complete, final, and absolutely binding contract being formed, as soon as the acceptance of an offer is posted, may in some cases lead to inconvenience and hardship. But such there must be at times in every view of the law. It is impossible in transactions which pass between parties at a distance, and have to be carried on through the medium of correspondence, to adjust conflicting rights between innocent parties, so as to make the consequences of mistake on the part of a mutual agent fall equally upon the shoulders of both. At the same time I am not prepared to admit that the implication in question will lead to any great or general inconvenience or hardship. An offerer, if he chooses, may always make the formation of the contract which he proposes dependent upon the actual communication to himself of the acceptance. If he trusts to the post he trusts to a means of communication which, as a rule, does not fail, and if no answer to his offer is received by him, and the matter is of importance to him, he can make inquiries of the person to whom his offer was addressed. On the other hand, if the contract is not finally concluded, except in the event of the acceptance actually reaching the offerer, the door would be opened to the perpetration of much fraud, and, putting aside this consideration, considerable delay in commercial transactions, in which despatch is, as a rule, of the greatest consequence, would be occasioned; for the acceptor would never be entirely safe in acting upon his acceptance until he had received notice that his letter of acceptance had reached its destination.

NOTE: Bramwell LJ delivered an important dissenting judgment.

BRAMWELL LJ: . . . That because a man, who may send a communication by post or otherwise, sends it by post, he should bind the person addressed, though the communication never reaches him, while he would not so bind him if he had sent it by hand, is impossible. There is no reason in it; it is simply arbitrary. I ask whether any one who thinks so is prepared to follow that opinion to its consequence; suppose the offer is to sell a particular chattel, and the letter accepting it never arrives, is the property in the chattel transferred? Suppose it is to sell an estate or grant a lease, is the bargain completed? The lease might be such as not to require a deed, could a subsequent lessee be ejected by the would-be acceptor of the offer because he had posted a letter? Suppose an article is advertised at so much, and that it would be sent on receipt of a post office order. Is it enough to post the letter? If the word 'receipt' is relied on, is it really meant that that makes a difference? If it should be said let the offerer wait, the answer is, may be he may lose his market meanwhile. Besides, his offer may be by advertisement to all mankind. Suppose a reward for information, information posted does not reach, some one else gives it and is paid, is the offerer liable to the first man?

It is said that a contrary rule would be hard on the would-be acceptor, who may have made his arrangements on the footing that the bargain was concluded. But to hold as contended would be equally hard on the offerer, who may have made his arrangements on the footing that his offer was not accepted; his non-receipt of any communication may be attributable to the person to whom it was made being absent. What is he to do but to act on the negative, that no communication has been made to him? Further, the use of the post office is no more authorised by the offerer than the sending an answer by hand, and all these hardships would befall the person posting the letter if he sent it by hand. Doubtless in that case he would be the person to suffer if the letter did not reach its destination. Why should his sending it by post relieve him of the loss and cast it on the other party. It was said, if he sends it by hand it is revocable, but not if he sends it by post, which makes the difference. But it is revocable when sent by post, not that the letter can be got back, but its arrival might be anticipated by a letter by hand or telegram, and there is no case to shew that such anticipation would not prevent the letter from binding. It would be a most alarming thing to say that it would. That a letter honestly but mistakenly written and posted must bind the writer if hours before its arrival he informed the person addressed that it was coming, but was wrong and recalled . . .

NOTES
1. Evans (1966) 15 ICLQ 553 and Winfield (1939) 55 LQR 499 contain criticisms and justifications of the postal rule. See also Gardner, 'Trashing with Trollope: A Deconstruction of the Postal Rules in Contract', (1992) 12 OJLS 170.
2. One justification for the postal rule is the fact that it prevents the offeror revoking his offer once the offeree has posted an acceptance. However, the Unidroit Principles of International Commercial Contracts advocate a 'receipt' rule for any postal acceptance (article 2.6(2)), but provide protection for the offeree who posts his acceptance since a revocation will be effective only if it reaches the offeree before the offeree has posted his acceptance (article 2.4). This is also the position in the Principles of European Contract Law (PECL) articles 2:205 and 2:202.

(i) Avoiding the postal rule

The offeror can always require actual communication of the acceptance to him which will oust the operation of the postal rule. This leads to fine distinctions between words requiring actual communication and those which do not.

Holwell Securities Ltd v Hughes

[1974] 1 WLR 155 (CA)

On 19 October 1971, the plaintiffs were granted an option by the defendant 'exercisable by notice in writing to [the defendant] at any time within six months from the date hereof'. On 14 April 1972, the plaintiffs wrote to the defendant giving notice of the exercise of the option but the letter did not arrive. The plaintiffs sought specific performance of the option agreement, arguing that it was complete on 14 April when the acceptance was posted. Held: the option had not been validly exercised because actual communication was required.

RUSSELL LJ: . . . It is the law in the first place that, prima facie, acceptance of an offer must be communicated to the offeror. Upon this principle the law has engrafted a doctrine that, if in any given case the true view is that the parties contemplated that the postal service might be used for the purpose of forwarding an acceptance of the offer, committal of the acceptance in a regular manner to the postal service will be acceptance of the offer so as to constitute a contract, even if the letter goes astray and is lost. Nor, as was once suggested, are such cases limited to cases in which the offer has been made by post. It suffices I think at this stage to refer to *Henthorn v Fraser* [1892] 2 Ch 27. In the present case, as I read a passage in the judgment below . . ., Templeman J concluded that the parties here contemplated that the postal service might be used to communicate acceptance of the offer (by exercise of the option); and I agree with that.

But that is not and cannot be the end of the matter. In any case, before one can find that the basic principle of the need for communication of acceptance to the offeror is displaced by this artificial concept of communication by the act of posting, it is necessary that the offer is in its terms consistent with such displacement and not one which by its terms points rather in the direction of actual communication. . . .

The relevant language here is, 'The said option shall be exercisable by notice in writing to the intending vendor . . .', a very common phrase in an option agreement. There is, of course, nothing in that phrase to suggest that the notification to the defendant could not be made by post. But the requirement of 'notice . . . to', in my judgment, is language which should be taken expressly to assert the ordinary situation in law that acceptance requires to be communicated or notified to the offeror, and is inconsistent with the theory that acceptance can be constituted by the act of posting, referred to by *Anson's Law of Contract* . . . as 'acceptance *without notification*'.

It is of course true that the instrument could have been differently worded. An option to purchase within a period given for value has the characteristic of an offer that cannot be withdrawn. The instrument might have said 'The offer constituted by this option may be accepted in writing within six months': in which case no doubt the posting would have sufficed to form the contract. But that language was not used, and, as indicated, in my judgment, the language used prevents that legal outcome. . . .

LAWTON LJ: . . . Does the [postal] rule apply in *all* cases where one party makes an offer which both he and the person with whom he was dealing must have expected the post to be used as a means of accepting it? In my judgment, it does not. First, it does not apply when the express terms of the offer specify that the acceptance must reach the offeror. The public nowadays are familiar with this exception to the general rule through their handling of football pool coupons. Secondly, it probably does not operate if its application would produce manifest inconvenience and absurdity. This is the opinion set out in Cheshire and Fifoot, *Law of Contract* . . . It was the opinion of Lord Bramwell as is seen by his judgment in *British & American Telegraph Co.* v *Colson* (1871) LR 6 Exch 108, and his opinion is worthy of consideration even though the decision in that case was overruled by this court in *Household Fire and Carriage Accident Insurance Co.* v *Grant* (1879) 4 Ex D 216. The illustrations of inconvenience and absurdity which Lord Bramwell gave are as apt today as they were then. Is a stockbroker who is holding shares to the orders of his client liable in damages because he did not sell in a falling market in accordance with the instructions in a letter which was posted but never received? Before the passing of the Law Reform (Miscellaneous Provisions) Act 1970 (which abolished actions for breach of promise of marriage), would a young soldier ordered overseas have been bound in contract to marry a girl to whom he had proposed by letter, asking her to let him have an answer before he left and she had replied affirmatively in good time but the letter had never reached him? In my judgment, the factors of inconvenience and absurdity are but illustrations of a wider principle, namely, that the rule does not apply if, having regard to all the circumstances, including the nature of the subject matter under consideration, the negotiating parties cannot have intended that there should be a binding agreement until the party accepting an offer or exercising an option had in fact communicated the acceptance or exercise to the other. In my judgment, when this principle is applied to the facts of this case it becomes clear that the parties cannot have intended that the posting of a letter should constitute the exercise of the option.

■ QUESTIONS

1. How would you advise an offeror to phrase his offer to ensure that any acceptance must be actually communicated? Which form of wording will have this effect and which will not? Would 'let me know your answer' suffice to oust the postal rule?

2. Lawton LJ states that the postal rule will not apply where its application 'would produce manifest inconvenience and absurdity'. What situations would this cover, and are the examples he gives appropriate?

NOTE: The Contracts (Rights of Third Parties) Act 1999, s. 2(2)(b), requires actual receipt and expressly ousts the postal rule in the context of third party assent to a term which will operate to prevent the parties cancelling or varying that contract term without that third party's consent.

(ii) May a postal acceptance be recalled or overtaken before it reaches the offeror?

Countess of Dunmore v *Alexander*
(1830) 9 S 190 (Court of Session)

The Countess wished to change a servant and wrote to Lady Agnew mentioning this fact, stating the wages to be paid and asking for a reference for a certain Elizabeth Alexander who was leaving Lady Agnew's employment. Lady Agnew replied 'If Lady Dunmore decides on taking Betty Alexander, perhaps she will have the goodness to mention whether she expects her at the new or the old term'. On 5 November the Countess wrote to Lady Agnew asking her to engage Betty Alexander and that she wished her to start at the new term. This was forwarded to Alexander. In the meantime, on 6 November the Countess wrote another letter to Lady Agnew stating that she no longer needed Alexander. The second letter was forwarded to Alexander by express and both were delivered at the same moment to Alexander. Alexander argued that there was a concluded contract. Held: there was no concluded contract.

LORD BALGRAY: The admission that the two letters were simultaneously received puts an end to the case. Had the one arrived in the morning and the other in the evening of the same day, it would have been different. Lady Dunmore conveys a request to Lady Agnew to engage Alexander, which request she recalls by a subsequent letter, that arrives in time to be forwarded to Alexander as soon as the first. This, therefore, is just the same as if a man had put an order into the Post Office, desiring his agent to buy stock for him. He afterwards changes his mind, but cannot recover his letter from the Post Office. He therefore writes a second letter countermanding the first. They both arrive together, and the result is, that no purchase can be made to bind the principal.

LORD CRAIGIE (dissenting): . . . Every letter between the principals, relative to an offer or an acceptance respectively was, as soon as it reached Lady Agnew, the same as delivered for behoof of the party on whose account it was written. I hold, therefore, that when Lady Dunmore's letter reached Lady Agnew, the contract of hiring Alexander was complete,—the offer on the part of Alexander being met by an intimated acceptance on the part of the Countess. No subsequent letter from the Countess to Lady Agnew could annul what had passed by the mere circumstance of its being delivered, at the same time with the first, into the hands of Alexander. I do not think the servant could have retracted after the first letter reached Lady Agnew; and if she was bound, it seems clear that the Countess could not be free.

NOTES

1. The case is of questionable authority in support of the proposition that it is possible to overtake a postal acceptance because the court appears to treat the letter from the Countess on 5 November as an offer and the letter of 6 November as a valid revocation of that offer.
2. Allowing a letter of acceptance to be withdrawn once posted is contrary to the postal rule and would give the offeree the best of both worlds, i.e., on posting he could decide whether to hold the offeror to the contract or recall his acceptance. However, Evans (1966) 15 ICLQ 553, argues in favour of allowing a revocation to overtake a postal acceptance and it is clear that Bramwell LJ in *Household Fire* supported this position, *page 46* above. See also Hudson (1966) 82 LQR 169, who argues that there is no disadvantage to the offeror since the offeror will act on the first communication he receives.

(iii) Are acceptances by telephone, telex, and fax subject to the postal rule?

Where an acceptance is instantaneous, actual communication is required and the postal rule does not apply.

Entores Ltd v *Miles Far East Corporation*
[1955] 2 QB 327 (CA)

An English company received a telex offer from a Dutch company and made a counter-offer which the Dutch company accepted by telex. The English company needed to establish that the contract was made within the jurisdiction. Held: since the acceptance was received in England, the contract was made within the jurisdiction.

DENNING LJ: . . . Let me first consider a case where two people make a contract by word of mouth in the presence of one another. Suppose, for instance, that I shout an offer to a man across a river or a courtyard but I do not hear his reply because it is drowned by an aircraft flying overhead. There is no contract at that moment. If he wishes to make a contract, he must wait till the aircraft is gone and then shout back his acceptance so that I can hear what he says. Not until I have his answer am I bound. . . .

Now take a case where two people make a contract by telephone. Suppose, for instance, that I make an offer to a man by telephone and, in the middle of his reply, the line goes 'dead' so that I do not hear his words of acceptance. There is no contract at that moment. The other man may not know the precise moment when the line failed. But he will know that the telephone conversation was abruptly broken off: because people usually say something to signify the end of the conversation. If he wishes to make a contract, he must therefore get through again so as to make sure that I heard. Suppose next, that the line does not go dead, but it is nevertheless so indistinct that I do not catch what he says and I ask him to repeat it. He then repeats it and I hear his acceptance. The contract is made, not on the first time when I do not hear, but only the second time when I do hear. If he does not repeat it, there is no contract. The contract is only complete when I have his answer accepting the offer.

Lastly, take the Telex. Suppose a clerk in a London office taps out on the teleprinter an offer which is immediately recorded on a teleprinter in a Manchester office, and a clerk at that end taps out an acceptance. If the line goes dead in the middle of the sentence of acceptance, the teleprinter motor will stop. There is then obviously no contract. The clerk at Manchester must get through again and send his complete sentence. But it may happen that the line does not go dead, yet the message does not get through to London. Thus the clerk at Manchester may tap out his message of accept- ance and it will not be recorded in London because the ink at the London end fails, or something of that kind. In that case, the Manchester clerk will not know of the failure but the London clerk will know of it and will immediately send back a message 'not receiving'. Then, when the fault is rectified, the Manchester clerk will repeat his message. Only then is there a contract. If he does not repeat it, there is no contract. It is not until his message is received that the contract is complete.

In all the instances I have taken so far, the man who sends the message of acceptance knows that it has not been received or he has reason to know it. So he must repeat it. But suppose that he does not know that his message did not get home. He thinks it has. This may happen if the listener on the telephone does not catch the words of acceptance, but nevertheless does not trouble to ask for them to be repeated: or if the ink on the teleprinter fails at the receiving end, but the clerk does not ask for the message to be repeated: so that the man who sends an acceptance reasonably believes that his message has been received. The offeror in such circumstances is clearly bound, because he will be estopped from saying that he did not receive the message of acceptance. It is his own fault that he did not get it. But if there should be a case where the offeror without any fault on his part does not receive the message of acceptance—yet the sender of it reasonably believes it has got home when it has not—then I think there is no contract.

My conclusion is, that the rule about instantaneous communications between the parties is different from the rule about the post. The contract is only complete when the acceptance is received by the offeror: and the contract is made at the place where the acceptance is received.

NOTES

1. Difficulties are bound to arise over exactly what is meant by the acceptance 'being received'. In *Tenax Steamship Co. Ltd* v *The Brimnes (Owners), The Brimnes* [1975] QB 929, a telex with- drawal had appeared on the charterers' telex machine between 17.30 and 18.00 (within office hours) on 2 April but it was not noted until the following day. The Court of Appeal held that the withdrawal was received when it appeared on the machine rather than when it was actually read the following day. The owners, having sent their message within office hours, had done all that they could be expected to do to transmit their message, and they would not know that it was not actually read until the following day. Megaw LJ said:

   > . . . I think that the principle which is relevant is this: if a notice arrives at the address of the person to be notified, at such a time and by such a means of communication that it would in the normal course of business come to the attention of that person on its arrival, that person cannot rely on some failure of himself or his servants to act in a normal businesslike manner in respect of taking cognisance of the communication so as to postpone the effective time of the notice until some later time when it in fact came to his attention.

   By analogy, if an acceptance was sent during office hours it would be received when it was received by the telex or fax machine. There is support for this view in the judgment of Lord Fraser in *Brinkibon Ltd* v *Stahag Stahl GmbH* (below).

2. It appears that the position will be different if the communication is sent outside office hours. Such a communication will inevitably be 'non-instantaneous'.

Brinkibon Ltd v Stahag Stahl GmbH
[1983] 2 AC 34 (HL)

A telex acceptance was sent from London to Vienna. The English company could only serve a writ for breach of contract on the Austrian company if the contract was made in England. Held: (approving *Entores*), that the contract in question had been concluded where the telex acceptance had been received, in Vienna.

LORD FRASER: . . . I have reached the opinion that, on balance, an acceptance sent by telex directly from the acceptor's office to the offeror's office should be treated as if it were an instantaneous communication between principals, like a telephone conversation. One reason is that the decision to that effect in *Entores v Miles Far East Corporation* [1955] 2 QB 327 seems to have worked without leading to serious difficulty or complaint from the business community. Secondly, once the message has been received on the offeror's telex machine, it is not unreasonable to treat it as delivered to the principal offeror, because it is his responsibility to arrange for prompt handling of messages within his own office. Thirdly, a party (the acceptor) who tries to send a message by telex can generally tell if his message has not been received on the other party's (the offeror's) machine, whereas the offeror, of course, will not know if an unsuccessful attempt has been made to send an acceptance to him. It is therefore convenient that the acceptor, being in the better position, should have the responsibility of ensuring that his message is received. For these reasons I think it is right that in the ordinary simple case, such as I take this to be, the general rule and not the postal rule should apply. But I agree with both my noble and learned friends that the general rule will not cover all the many variations that may occur with telex messages.

LORD WILBERFORCE (*obiter*): Since 1955 the use of telex communication has been greatly expanded, and there are many variants on it. The senders and recipients may not be the principals to the contemplated contract. They may be servants or agents with limited authority. The message may not reach, or be intended to reach, the designated recipient immediately: messages may be sent out of office hours, or at night, with the intention, or upon the assumption, that they will be read at a later time. There may be some error or default at the recipient's end which prevents receipt at the time contemplated and believed in by the sender. The message may have been sent and/or received through machines operated by third persons. And many other variations may occur. No universal rule can cover all such cases: they must be resolved by reference to the intentions of the parties, by sound business practice and in some cases by a judgment where the risks should lie. . . .

NOTE: Lord Brandon expressed agreement with Lord Wilberforce on this point and Lord Wilberforce's *obiter* comment was relied on by Gatehouse J in the following decision.

Mondial Shipping and Chartering BV v *Astarte Shipping Ltd*
[1995] CLC 1011

The issue in the case was whether a telex notice of intention to withdraw the vessel for non-payment of hire, sent by the shipowners to the charterers late on the evening of Friday, 2 December 1994 (at 23.41 hours), was received instantaneously or at the start of business on the next working day. This was important on the facts because payment of the hire could lawfully have been made at any time before midnight on Friday, 2 December and, if the notice took effect at 23.41 on Friday, 2 December, the charterers would not have been in default at the time the notice was served. On the other hand, the notice would have been valid if it had not taken effect until the next working day, Monday, 5 December. Held: the notice was communicated at the start of business on the next working day, namely Monday, 5 December. Accordingly it was not served before the charterers were in breach of the charterparty which occurred at midnight on the Friday night. (However, the notice was nevertheless invalid because it did not indicate the action required of the charterers.)

GATEHOUSE J: . . . It was not in dispute in the present case that a notice under cl. 27 is not effective until it is actually received by the charterer—the 'postal rule' referable to the conclusion of a contract has no application. The crucial question is what is meant by 'received'? The charterers contended that this must be the moment when it was printed out on their telex machine; that this occurred before the time when they would be in default under cl. 7, and accordingly the notice was premature and invalid for that reason, apart from its want of proper form. The owners contended that the moment of receipt was when the telex message was, or must be taken to have been, first read by a responsible member of the charterers' organisation, i.e., at or shortly after 9 am on Monday 5 December; that the charterers were by then in default of their duty of punctual payment: accordingly the notice was not then premature; it gave the charterers 48 hours from that moment to remedy their default, and the owners were accordingly entitled to withdraw the vessel when they did, at about 9.25 am on the morning of 7 December, no hire having been received within the 48-hour grace period.

There is no authority on this. The question has not arisen in any reported decision. In *The Afovos* [*Afovos Shipping Co. SA* v *R. Pagnan and F. Illi, The Afovos* [1983] 1 Lloyd's Rep 335] and other similar cases of instantaneous transmission the message was sent during ordinary business hours so the time of sending the notice by the owners and its receipt by the charterers was identical. It is therefore not significant that various judges have referred to the time when the notice was 'sent', or 'issued' . . .

What matters is not when the notice is given/sent/despatched/issued by the owners but when its content reaches the mind of the charterer. If the telex is sent in ordinary business hours, the time of receipt is the same as the time of despatch because it is not open to the charterer to contend that it did not in fact then come to his attention (see *The Brimnes* per Brandon J [1973] 1 WLR 386 at p. 406, and per the Court of Appeal [1975] QB 929).

The problem has, of course, been referred to. See the well-known passage in the speech of Lord Wilberforce in *Brinkibon Ltd* v *Stahag Stahl and Stahlwarenhandelsgesellschaft mbH* [1983] 2 AC 34 at p. 42. [Gatehouse J went on to consider this *obiter* statement, *page 51 above* . . .] Brandon J also referred, in passing, to an out-of-hours telex in *The Brimnes*. . . .

The charterers in order to found their contention that the telex message was premature, are in fact contending for a universal rule for telex communications which, they say, has the commercial advantage of certainty. But I propose to follow Lord Wilberforce's words and resolve this issue by reference to the particular circumstances. His Lordship's words, . . . were spoken with reference to where a contract is to be regarded as having been concluded: hence, as I think, his reference to the intentions of the parties and in some cases, where the risks should lie (both the cases cited were concerned with the risks which arise from a postal acceptance). A notice such as the one with which I am concerned is clearly of a quite different type and does not involve any consideration of the mutual intentions of contracting parties or of where the risks should lie. But I think the tribunal were entitled to find (para. 25 of their reasons) that a notice which arrives at 23.41 on a Friday night is not to be expected to be read before opening hours on the following Monday, and that was a conclusion of fact arrived at by the arbitrators as a matter of commercial common sense.

Why the telex was sent when it was is not explained. It may be that the owners or their agents, forgetful of the midnight rule (or, more likely, wholly ignorant of it) assumed that as the vessel had been delivered at 23.00 hours that was the moment each successive 15 days after which hire became overdue. If they had waited a further 20 minutes this problem would not have arisen.

In my judgment the tribunal were right to find that the notice under cl. 31 was not received by charterers until the opening of business on 5 December, and was not premature.

■ QUESTIONS

1. This decision clarifies the position on communication where the message is very evidently sent 'outside ordinary business hours'. However, this expression is not defined and it is possible to imagine a situation arising where a message is sent within the communicator's business hours but outside the recipient's business hours.

   Should this be judged by reference to the parties' own hours and knowledge of their respective practices?

   Would it be preferable to adopt a clear and certain definition of what will constitute receipt? The Unidroit Principles of International Commercial Contracts contain a definition of 'receipt' in the context of non-oral communications such as fax, telex, or computer, as occurring when there is delivery at the offeror's place of business or mailing address (article 1.9(3)). See also article 1:303 of the Principles of European Contract Law (PECL).

2. When are messages left on telephone answering machines communicated? See the arguments of Coote (1971) 4 *New Zealand UL Rev* 331.

3. Does the postal rule apply to acceptance messages sent by electronic mail? (Contracts made by exchange of e-mail messages are expressly excluded from the operation of the Electronic Commerce (EC Directive) Regulations 2002, Regs. 9(4) and 11(3).) This may depend on the precise method of transmitting the messages and whether, for example, the parties communicate via a common server, whether the messages are sent directly to the recipient's server or whether they are stored before dispatch. Given the many variables, it may be advisable expressly to avoid the postal rule and require actual receipt. If this solution is adopted, it may also be helpful to define what will constitute 'receipt' for this purpose. This might be when the recipient is able to access the message (by analogy with the position under Reg. 11(2)(a) of the E-Commerce Regulations 2002, *page 28*), and assuming that acceptance by e-mail is contemplated. For further discussion, see J. Poole, *Textbook on Contract*, 7th edn, 2004: Oxford University Press, pp. 43–4, 60–1.

SECTION 5: REVOCATION OF AN OFFER

An offer can be revoked at any time before it is accepted.

A second offer *may* revoke an earlier offer. Will a second quotation price from the same supplier automatically revoke the first quotation price?

Pickfords Ltd v *Celestica Ltd*
[2003] EWCA Civ 1741, 19 November 2003 (CA)

The defendant had been sent a fax (13 September 2001) containing an estimated price of £100,000 for moving office equipment based on a fixed price per vehicle load (referred to as 'the budget estimate'). After the claimant had carried out a survey, it sent a further fax (27 September 2001) containing a fixed price quotation of £98,760. On 15 October 2001 the defendant sent a fax to the claimant which was headed 'Confirmation' and stated that an order had been raised to cover the quotation and that the cost was not to exceed £100,000. The claimant carried out the work and claimed the fixed sum of £98,760 referred to in the fax of 27 September, alleging that the defendant had accepted this in the fax of 15 October. However, the defendant claimed that the contract was based on the first fax so that the price per vehicle load applied. Held: the second fax (27 September) superseded and revoked the first fax offer because there were substantial differences between the two offers. The defendant's fax of 15 October had purported to accept the first offer since the inclusion of the words 'not to exceed £100,000' made no commercial sense if the defendant was purporting to accept the second fixed price offer. Since the first offer had been revoked by the second offer, the defendant's fax of 15 October amounted to a counter-offer to accept the services offered by the claimant on the terms in the first fax, subject to the cap of £100,000 (the additional term in the fax of 15 October). The claimant had accepted this counter-offer by conduct in carrying out the work. However, even if the first offer had not been revoked, the fax of 15 October would have constituted a counter-offer because it added a new material term, i.e. the cap of £100,000.

DYSON LJ:

14 I start therefore with the question whether the first offer was revoked. The fax of 13 September 2001 was an offer to do the work of relocation at a rate of £890 excluding VAT per vehicle load, plus various extras (for example for insurance and hire of crates). The document stated that it was estimated that the work required 96 vehicle loads which was the basis of the estimated budget figure of £100,000. But it did not offer to do the work for £100,000. It was not a fixed price offer: it was an offer to do the work for a fixed price per vehicle load.

15 The proposal of 27 September 2001 contained a great deal more detail than the first offer. One essential difference between the two offers was that the second was an offer to do the work for a fixed price of £98,760. But there were many other differences between the two documents. The second offer set out in far more detail than the first precisely what services were being offered, what was expected of the client (the defendant) and provisions with regard to health and safety. It also incorporated the claimant's standard terms and conditions, which the first offer did not.

16 It is trite law that an offer may be withdrawn at any time before it is accepted. The first offer had not been accepted before the second offer was made. The only fact relied on by the claimant as evidence of the withdrawal of the first offer is the sending of the second offer. At one stage I thought that this was not enough to constitute a revocation of the first offer. An offer may be withdrawn in a number of ways. The most obvious is an express withdrawal; that did not occur here. Another is where the offeror acts in a way that is inconsistent with the continuing existence of the offer and the offeree knows of that fact. Thus if A offers to sell goods to B, and before B accepts the offer A sells to C and the fact of the sale is communicated to B, then A's offer to sell to B is withdrawn.

17 What is the position where A makes an offer to B and then makes a later offer to B? By making the later offer, does A withdraw the earlier one? That is the first question that arises in this case. No authority has been cited to us in which this question has been considered. In my judgment it must depend on the nature of the two offers and the circumstances in which they are made. Take a simple case where A asks B, a decorator, to quote for the painting of his house. Suppose, further, that B quotes A a figure of £200 per day, plus materials. Before deciding whether to instruct B to proceed, A decides to ask B to provide a fixed price quotation. B provides a fixed price quotation of £1500. In those circumstances B's later quotation does not, without more, amount to a withdrawal of the first offer. It is produced at the request of A so that A can decide which of the two quotations to accept. That is the basis upon which the second quotation is sought and provided.

18 In such a case, in my judgment, something more than the mere submission of the second quotation is required to indicate that A has withdrawn the first offer. The two offers are inconsistent with each other only in the sense that they cannot both be accepted. But the question is not whether both offers can be accepted, but whether the making of the second offer clearly indicates an intention on the part of the offeror to withdraw the first offer.

19 That simple case is, however, very different from what happened here. It is true that there are no findings of fact as to the circumstances which gave rise to the second offer. The substantial differences between the two offers in this case went far beyond a mere difference in price which could have been explained as consistent with two alternative offers both being on the table for the defendant to choose which to accept. In the absence of any findings of fact as to the circumstances which gave rise to the second offer, I would hold that the second offer did supersede and revoke the first offer.

A: Communication of the revocation

A revocation of an offer must actually be communicated to the offeree. The postal rule applies only to acceptances and not to revocations.

Henthorn v Fraser
[1892] 2 Ch 27 (CA)

A withdrawal of an offer had been posted at midday but it was not received until 5 p.m. In the meantime an acceptance had been posted at 3.50 p.m. Held: there was a binding contract at 3.50 p.m. on posting the acceptance.

LORD HERSCHELL: If the acceptance by the Plaintiff of the Defendants' offer is to be treated as complete at the time the letter containing it was posted, I can entertain no doubt that the society's attempted revocation of the offer was wholly ineffectual. I think that a person who has made an offer must be considered as continuously making it until he has brought to the knowledge of the person to whom it was made that it is withdrawn. . . .

KAY LJ: Then what was the effect of the withdrawal by the letter posted between 12 and 1 the same day, and received in the evening? Did that take effect from the time of posting? It has never been held that this doctrine applies to a letter withdrawing the offer. Take the cases alluded to by Lord Bramwell in the *Household Fire and Carriage Accident Insurance Company* v *Grant* (1879) 4 ExD 216. A notice by a tenant to quit can have no operation till it comes to the actual knowledge of the person to whom it is addressed. An offer to sell is nothing until it is actually received. No doubt there is the seeming anomaly pointed out by Lord Bramwell that the same letter might contain an acceptance, and also such a notice or offer as to other property, and that when posted it would be effectual as to the acceptance, and not as to the notice or offer. But the anomaly, if it be one, arises from the different nature of the two communications. As to the acceptance, if it was contemplated that it might be sent by post, the acceptor, in Lord Cottenham's language, has done all that he was bound to do by posting the letter, but this cannot be said as to the notice of withdrawal. That was not a contemplated proceeding. The person withdrawing was bound to bring his change of purpose to the knowledge of the said party, and as this was not done in this case till after the letter of acceptance was posted, I am of opinion that it was too late.

Byrne & Co. v Van Tienhoven & Co.
(1880) 5 CPD 344 (CP)

On 1 October the defendants in Cardiff wrote to the plaintiffs in New York offering to sell goods. The plaintiffs received this offer on 11 October, and accepted it by telegram on the same day. On 8 October the defendants posted a revocation of their offer which reached the plaintiffs on 20 October. The plaintiffs brought an action for non-delivery. Held: a revocation of an offer is not effective until it is communicated to the offeree. The offer was therefore available for acceptance until 20 October, and a binding contract was entered into on 11 October when the acceptance telegram was sent.

LINDLEY J: . . . It may be taken as now settled that where an offer is made and accepted by letters sent through the post, the contract is completed the moment the letter accepting the offer is posted: *Harris' Case* (1872) LR 7 Ch App 587; *Dunlop* v *Higgins* (1848) 1 HLC 381, even although it never reaches its destination. When, however, these authorities are looked at, it will be seen that they are based upon the principle that the writer of the offer has expressly or impliedly assented to treat an answer to him by a letter duly posted as a sufficient acceptance and notification to himself, or, in other words, he has made the post office his agent to receive the acceptance and notification of it. But this principle appears to me to be inapplicable to the case of the withdrawal of an offer. In this particular case I can find no evidence of any authority in fact given by the plaintiffs to the defendants to notify a withdrawal of their offer by merely posting a letter; and there is no legal principle or decision which compels me to hold, contrary to the fact, that the letter of the 8th of October is to be treated as communicated to the plaintiff on that day or on any day before the 20th, when the letter reached them. But before that letter had reached the plaintiffs they had accepted the offer, both by telegram and by post; and they had themselves resold the tin plates at a profit. In my opinion the withdrawal by the defendants on the 8th of October of their offer of the 1st was inoperative; and a complete contract binding on both parties was entered into on the 11th of October, when the plaintiffs accepted the offer of the 1st, which they had no reason to suppose had been withdrawn. Before leaving this part of the case it may be as well to point out the extreme injustice and inconvenience which any other conclusion would produce. If the defendants' contention were to prevail no person who had received an offer by post and had accepted it would know his position until he had waited such a time as to be quite sure that a letter withdrawing the offer had not been posted before his acceptance of it. It appears to me that both legal principles, and practical convenience require that a person who has accepted an offer not known to him to have been revoked, shall be in a position safely to act upon the footing that the offer and acceptance constitute a contract binding on both parties.

Stevenson, Jacques & Co. v McLean
(1880) 5 QBD 346

The defendant had made an offer to sell iron at 40s net cash per ton to the plaintiffs, and stated that he would hold the offer open until the following Monday. On the Monday the defendant sold the iron and informed the plaintiffs of this by a telegram sent at 1.25 p.m. Before this arrived (at 1.46 p.m.) the plaintiffs, having found a purchaser for the iron, sent an acceptance telegram to the defendant at 1.34 p.m. The plaintiffs brought an action for non-delivery. Held: although the defendant was free to revoke his offer before the close of the day on Monday, any revocation would not have effect until it reached the plaintiffs. Consequently, the defendant's offer was still open when the plaintiffs accepted it at 1.34 p.m. (on sending the acceptance telegram).

The revocation need not be communicated by the offeror himself

Dickinson v Dodds
(1876) 2 ChD 463 (CA)

On Wednesday 10 June 1874, the defendant offered to sell his house to the plaintiff, stating that 'This offer to be left over until Friday 9 a.m.'. On the Thursday afternoon the plaintiff was informed by Berry that the defendant had been offering or agreeing to sell the property to Allan. The plaintiff therefore went to the house where the defendant was staying and left a formal written acceptance there (the evidence was that the defendant did not receive this document). On the Friday at 7 a.m., Berry, who was acting as agent for the plaintiff, found the defendant at the railway station, handed him a copy of the plaintiff's acceptance and stated its contents. The defendant had sold the property to Allan on Thursday 11 June. Held: the offer might be withdrawn at any time before acceptance since there was no consideration for the promise to keep the offer open until 9 a.m. on the Friday. Had it in fact been withdrawn?

JAMES LJ: . . . [I]t is said that the only mode in which Dodds could assert that freedom was by actually and distinctly saying to Dickinson, 'Now I withdraw my offer.' It appears to me that there is neither principle nor authority for the proposition that there must be an express and actual withdrawal of the offer, or what is called a retraction. It must, to constitute a contract, appear that the two minds were at one, at the same moment of time, that is, that there was an offer continuing up to the time of the acceptance. If there was not such a continuing offer, then the acceptance comes to nothing. Of course it may well be that the one man is bound in some way or other to let the other man know that his mind with regard to the offer has been changed; but in this case, beyond all question, the Plaintiff knew that Dodds was no longer minded to sell the property to him as plainly and clearly as if Dodds had told him in so many words, 'I withdraw the offer.'

. . . It is to my mind quite clear that before there was any attempt at acceptance by the Plaintiff, he was perfectly well aware that Dodds had changed his mind, and that he had in fact agreed to sell the property to Allan. It is impossible, therefore, to say there was ever that existence of the same mind between the two parties which is essential in point of law to the making of an agreement. I am of opinion, therefore, that the Plaintiff has failed to prove that there was any binding contract between Dodds and himself.

NOTES
1. Unless the promise to keep an offer open for a stated period is supported by consideration, the offeror is free to revoke the offer at any time before acceptance (*Routledge* v *Grant* (1828) 4 Bing 653, 130 ER 920). This may be harsh where the offeree has relied on this 'firm offer' promise. See the proposals of the Law Commission Working Paper No. 60, 'Firm Offers', (1975).
2. Treitel cites *Dickinson* v *Dodds* as authority for the proposition that there is sufficient communication if the offeree knows from 'any reliable source' that the offeror no longer intends to contract with him. What problems might exist in deciding who is a 'reliable source'?
3. Although this decision appears to suggest that it is not necessary to communicate a revocation, it is based on a subjective approach to contract formation and is now incorrect on this point.
4. In *Pickfords Ltd* v *Celestica Ltd* [2003] EWCA Civ 1741, unrep. 19 November 2003, Arden LJ noted, at [32], that '[t]he revocation of an offer must be communicated to the offeree, but where the offeree is an organisation, it is sufficient if the organisation receives notice of the withdrawal', as opposed to an individual employee. The same should apply to communication of acceptances where the offeror is an organisation.

B: Revocation of a unilateral offer

Since the acceptance is the complete performance of the act in unilateral contracts, if (to use the classical example of a unilateral contract quoted by Brett J in *Great Northern Railway Company* v *Witham* (1873) LR 9 CP 16, at p. 19) I offer you £100 if you will walk to York, I could revoke my offer at any time before you reached York.

Petterson v *Pattberg*
161 NE 428 (1928); 248 NY 86 (Court of Appeals of New York)

Pattberg wrote to Petterson agreeing to discount the amount owing under Petterson's mortgage by $780 if the mortgage was paid on or before 31 May 1924. Within this time Petterson went to Pattberg's home to pay but Pattberg refused to let him in or to accept the money. Petterson sued for his loss of $780 in having to pay off the mortgage in full.

KELLOGG J: An interesting question arises when, as here, the offeree approaches the offeror with the intention of proffering performance and, before actual tender is made, the offer is withdrawn. Of such a case Williston says:

> The offeror may see the approach of the offeree and know that an acceptance is contemplated. If the offeror can say 'I revoke' before the offeree accepts, however brief the interval of time between the two acts, there is no escape from the conclusion that the offer is terminated. *Williston on Contracts*, § 60b.

. . . We think that in this particular instance the offer of the defendant was withdrawn before it became a binding promise, and therefore that no contract was ever made for the breach of which the plaintiff may claim damages.

NOTE: It is now accepted that in English law the offer may contemplate that it is not possible to revoke once the offeree has started to perform.

Errington v *Errington & Woods*
[1952] 1 KB 290 (CA)

A father purchased a house with the aid of a building society mortgage. He promised his son and daughter-in-law that if they continued in occupation and paid all the mortgage instalments he would transfer the house to them. They duly paid the instalments, but when the father died he left the house to his widow who sought possession. The issue in the judgments is whether the couple were tenants at will or had a contractual licence to occupy. Held: they were contractual licensees.

DENNING LJ: It is to be noted that the couple never bound themselves to pay the instalments to the building society; and I see no reason why any such obligation should be implied. It is clear law that the court is not to imply a term unless it is necessary; and I do not see that it is necessary here. Ample content is given to the whole arrangement by holding that the father promised that the house should belong to the couple as soon as they paid off the mortgage. The parties did not discuss what was to happen if the couple failed to pay the instalments to the building society, but I should have thought it clear that, if they did fail to pay the instalments, the father would not be bound to transfer the house to them. The father's promise was a unilateral contract—a promise of the house in return for their act of paying the instalments. It could not be revoked by him once the couple entered on performance of the act, but it would cease to bind him if they left it incomplete and unperformed, which they have not done. If that was the position during the father's lifetime, so it must be after his death. If the daughter-in-law continues to pay all the building society instalments, the couple will be entitled to have the property transferred to them as soon as the mortgage is paid off; but if she does not do so, then the building society will claim the instalments from the father's estate and the estate will have to pay them. I cannot think that in those circumstances the estate would be bound to transfer the house to them, any more than the father himself would have been.

. . . [I]t is clear that the father expressly promised the couple that the property should belong to them as soon as the mortgage was paid, and impliedly promised that so long as they paid the instalments to the building society they should be allowed to remain in possession. They were not purchasers because they never bound themselves to pay the instalments, but nevertheless they were in a position analogous to purchasers. They have acted on the promise, and neither the father nor his widow, his successor in title, can eject them in disregard of it. . . .

NOTES
1. What do you think is the basis of the decision in *Errington*? Are the words 'acted on the promise' significant? (See promissory estoppel, at *pages 147–73*.) What difficulties would exist in using promissory estoppel as the basis of this principle?
2. McGovney (1914) 27 Harv L Rev 644, 659, suggested that there are two separate offers in the unilateral offeror's statement, namely an express offer to pay on performance of the act and

an implied offer not to revoke once the offeree starts to perform. This implied offer is accepted by beginning performance, and if the offeror attempted to revoke he would be liable for breach of this promise. The problem with this analysis is that it would not prevent revocation but would only mean that damages would be payable for breach of the implied offer not to revoke. *Errington*, however, appears to be based on the view that revocation is not possible once the offeree has started to perform.

3. The other suggested explanation (*Pollock on Contract*) is based on the fact that in a unilateral contract performance of the act requested is both the acceptance and the consideration. Acceptance is stated to occur when the offeree starts to perform so that revocation is no longer possible, but the consideration is the completion of the act, and until that time no reward is payable. This is somewhat difficult to justify since at the point of starting to perform the offeree would also be bound to perform, which defeats the very nature of the unilateral contract.

4. Lord Denning may well have supported this approach (i.e. acceptance on starting to perform). See his comments in *Ward* v *Byham* [1956] 1 WLR 496, *page 127*. However, in his judgment in *Errington*, Lord Denning very clearly states that the couple were not under any obligation.

5. The crucial question is how the courts will determine when an offeree 'enters on performance of the act'. Will it cover preparation to perform, e.g., when walking shoes are purchased in preparation for the walk to York?

There is *obiter* support for the decision in *Errington* in the Court of Appeal's decision in the next case, although the approach taken appears to support McGovney's analysis.

Daulia v *Four Mill Bank Nominees Ltd*
[1978] Ch 231 (CA)

The plaintiffs wished to purchase property. They were told by the defendants that if they attended the next day at 10 a.m. with a banker's draft for the deposit and a signed and engrossed contract, the defendants would exchange contracts. The plaintiffs did this but the defendants refused to exchange because they had found another purchaser at an increased price. Held: the promise amounted to a unilateral offer, and since the plaintiffs had fulfilled the conditions they had accepted the offer.

GOFF LJ: . . . Was there a concluded unilateral contract by the . . . defendants to enter into a contract for sale on the agreed terms? The concept of a unilateral or 'if contract' is somewhat anomalous, because it is clear that, at all events until the offeree starts to perform the condition, there is no contract at all, but merely an offer which the offeror is free to revoke.

Doubts have been expressed whether the offeror becomes bound so soon as the offeree starts to perform or satisfy the condition, or only when he has fully done so.

In my judgment, however, we are not concerned in this case with any such problem, because in my view the plaintiffs had fully performed or satisfied the condition when they presented themselves at the time and place appointed with a banker's draft for the deposit, and their part of the written contract for sale duly engrossed and signed and there tendered the same, which I understand to mean proferred it for exchange. Actual exchange, which never took place, would not in my view have been part of the satisfaction of the condition but something additional which was inherently necessary to be done by the plaintiffs to enable, not to bind, the . . . defendants to perform the unilateral contract.

Accordingly, in my judgment, the answer to the . . . question must be in the affirmative.

Even if my reasoning so far be wrong the conclusion in my view is still the same for the following reasons. Whilst I think the true view of a unilateral contract must in general be that the offeror is entitled to require full performance of the condition which he has imposed and short of that he is not bound, that must be subject to one important qualification, which stems from the fact that there must be an implied obligation on the part of the offeror not to prevent the condition becoming satisfied, which obligation it seems to me must arise as soon as the offeree starts to perform. Until then the offeror can revoke the whole thing, but once the offeree has embarked on performance it is too late for the offeror to revoke his offer.

Luxor (Eastbourne) Ltd v Cooper
[1941] AC 108 (HL)

The owners (two companies) orally agreed with the agent that if he introduced someone who purchased their cinemas for at least £185,000 they would each pay him £5,000 *on the completion of the sale*. He produced purchasers who were willing to pay the price but a sale did not take place. The agent brought an action claiming the £10,000 commission, or alternatively £10,000 in damages for breach of the implied term by which the owners undertook not to do anything to prevent him earning his commission. Held: as the commission was payable only on completion, the nature of the offer contemplated that the offeror reserved the right to revoke at any time before completion. The House of Lords refused, in the circumstances of the case, to imply a term that the owners had undertaken not to prevent the sale.

LORD RUSSELL: A few preliminary observations occur to me. (1) Commission contracts are subject to no peculiar rules or principles of their own; the law which governs them is the law which governs all contracts and all questions of agency. (2) No general rule can be laid down by which the rights of the agent or the liability of the principal under commission contracts are to be determined. In each case these must depend upon the exact terms of the contract in question, and upon the true construction of those terms. And (3) contracts by which owners of property, desiring to dispose of it, put it in the hands of agents on commission terms, are not (in default of specific provisions) contracts of employment in the ordinary meaning of those words. No obligation is imposed on the agent to do anything. The contracts are merely promises binding on the principal to pay a sum of money upon the happening of a specified event, which involves the rendering of some service by the agent. There is no real analogy between such contracts, and contracts of employment by which one party binds himself to do certain work, and the other binds himself to pay remuneration for the doing of it.

I do not assent to the view, which I think was the view of the majority in the first *Trollope* case [1934] 2 KB 436, that a mere promise by a property owner to an agent to pay him a commission if he introduces a purchaser for the property at a specified price, or at a minimum price, ties the owner's hands, and compels him (as between himself and the agent) to bind himself contractually to sell to the agent's client who offers that price, with the result that if he refuses the offer he is liable to pay the agent a sum equal to or less than the amount of the commission either (a) on a quantum meruit or (b) as damages for breach of a term to be implied in the commission contract. As to the claim on a quantum meruit, I do not see how this can be justified in the face of the express provision for remuneration which the contract contains. This must necessarily exclude such a claim, unless it can (upon the facts of a particular case) be based upon a contract subsequent to the original contract, and arising from some conduct on the part of the principal.

As to the claim for damages, this rests upon the implication of some provision in the commission contract, the exact terms of which were variously stated in the course of the argument, the object always being to bind the principal not to refuse to complete the sale to the client whom the agent has introduced.

I can find no safe ground on which to base the introduction of any such implied term. Implied terms, as we all know, can only be justified under the compulsion of some necessity. No such compulsion or necessity exists in the case under consideration. The agent is promised a commission if he introduces a purchaser at a specified or minimum price. The owner is desirous of selling. The chances are largely in favour of the deal going through, if a purchaser is introduced. The agent takes the risk in the hope of a substantial remuneration for comparatively small exertion. In the case of the plaintiff his contract was made on September 23, 1935; his client's offer was made on October 2, 1935. A sum of 10,000*l.* (the equivalent of the remuneration of a year's work by a Lord Chancellor) for work done within a period of eight or nine days is no mean reward, and is one well worth a risk. There is no lack of business efficacy in such a contract, even though the principal is free to refuse to sell to the agent's client.

The position will no doubt be different if the matter has proceeded to the stage of a binding contract having been made between the principal and the agent's client. In that case it can be said with truth that a 'purchaser' has been introduced by the agent; in other words the event has happened upon the occurrence of which a right to the promised commission has become vested in the agent. From that moment no act or omission by the principal can deprive the agent of that vested right. . . .

■ QUESTIONS

1. On the facts, the House of Lords refused to imply a promise not to revoke (prevent the sale). Does this support McGovney's analysis and indicate that the implication of a promise will turn on what is contemplated by the wording of the offer?

2. Is Lord Russell suggesting that if the reward is great compared to the actual effort needed to earn it, then the offeree must take the risk of the offer being withdrawn?

C: Communication of revocation in unilateral contracts

A unilateral offer *to unascertained offerees* can be revoked through the same channel as the offer was made.

Shuey v United States
23 L ed 697 (1875); 92 US 73 (US Supreme Court)

A proclamation dated 20 April 1865 had been published offering a reward of $25,000 for the apprehension of a particular criminal. On 24 November 1865, a notice revoking the offer was published. In 1866, the plaintiff discovered the criminal and informed the authorities. He was unaware that the offer of the reward had been revoked. Held: he had not actually apprehended the criminal as required by the terms of the offer. Strong J also made the following statement on the revocation:

STRONG J: The offer of a reward for the apprehension of Surratt was revoked on the twenty-fourth day of November, 1865; and notice of the revocation was published. It is not to be doubted that the offer was revocable at any time before it was accepted, and before anything had been done in reliance upon it. There was no contract until its terms were complied with. Like any other offer of a contract, it might, therefore, be withdrawn before rights had accrued under it; and it was withdrawn through the same channel in which it was made. The same notoriety was given to the revocation that was given to the offer; and the findings of fact do not show that any information was given by the claimant, or that he did anything to entitle him to the reward offered, until five months after the offer had been withdrawn. True, it is found that then, and at all times until the arrest was actually made, he was ignorant of the withdrawal; but that is an immaterial fact. The offer of the reward not having been made to him directly, but by means of a published Proclamation, he should have known that it could be revoked in the manner in which it was made.

■ QUESTIONS

1. What do you think would be covered by the expression 'withdrawn through the same channel in which it was made'? I advertise a reward in a particular national newspaper but I issue a notice of revocation in a different national newspaper— would this be revocation through the same channel?

2. Could this authority be distinguished where the offeree has taken steps to perform (i.e. has relied upon the offer) before the publication of the revocation? See Strong J's reference to 'before anything had been done in reliance upon' the offer. Does this amount to an acceptance of Pollock's analysis, *page 59*?

3

Certainty and Agreement Mistakes

There are two separate issues to consider in this chapter: First, the agreement must be sufficiently certain in its terms for the court to enforce it. Second, certain types of mistake will 'negative consent' and so prevent a contract coming into existence.

SECTION 1: CERTAINTY

Traditionally, the courts have considered that their function is limited to interpreting the words that the parties have used, so that if an agreement is uncertain the courts will not construct a binding contract for the parties.

A: Vagueness

Scammell & Nephew Ltd v *Ouston*
[1941] AC 251 (HL)

The respondents agreed to purchase a van on hire-purchase terms over a period of two years. However, before the hire-purchase agreement itself could be entered into, and before any hire-purchase terms could be settled, the appellants refused to proceed. When the respondents brought an action claiming damages for breach of contract, the appellants argued that there was no contract because the agreement was void for uncertainty. Held: there was no enforceable contract because the clause relating to the hire-purchase terms was too vague and uncertain and required further agreement to be reached between the parties.

VISCOUNT MAUGHAM: . . . In order to constitute a valid contract the parties must so express themselves that their meaning can be determined with a reasonable degree of certainty. It is plain that unless this can be done it would be impossible to hold that the contracting parties had the same intention; in other words the consensus ad idem would be a matter of mere conjecture. This general rule, however, applies somewhat differently in different cases. In commercial documents connected with dealings in a trade with which the parties are perfectly familiar the court is very willing, if satisfied that the parties thought that they made a binding contract, to imply terms and in particular terms as to the method of carrying out the contract which it would be impossible to supply in other kinds of contract: see *Hillas & Co.* v *Arcos, Ld.* . . .

. . . [A] hire-purchase agreement may assume many forms and some of the variations in those forms are of the most important character, e.g., those which relate to termination of the agreement, warranty of fitness, duties as to repair, interest, and so forth.

Bearing these facts in mind, what do the words as to 'hire-purchase terms' mean in the present case? They may indicate that the hire-purchase agreement was to be granted by the appellants or on the other hand by some finance company acting in collaboration with the appellants; they may contemplate that the appellants were to receive by instalments a sum of 168*l.* spread over a period of two years upon delivering the new van and receiving the old car, or, on the other hand, that the appellants were to receive from a third party a lump sum of 168*l.* and that the third party, presumably a finance company, was to receive from the respondents a larger sum than 168*l.* to include interest and profit spread over a period of two years. Moreover, nothing is said (except as to the two years period) as to the terms of the hire-purchase agreement, for instance, as to the interest payable, and as to the rights of the letter whoever he may be in the event of default by the respondents in payment of the instalments at the due dates. As regards the last matters there was no evidence to suggest that there are any well known 'usual terms' in such a contract; and I think it is common knowledge that in fact many letters though by no means all of them insist on terms which the legislature regards as so unfair and unconscionable that it was recently found necessary to deal with the matter in the recent Act entitled the Hire-Purchase Act, 1938.

These, my Lords, are very serious difficulties, and when we find as we do in this curious case that the trial judge and the three Lords Justices, and even the two counsel who addressed your Lordships for the respondents, were unable to agree upon the true construction of the alleged agreement, it seems to me that it is impossible to conclude that a binding agreement has been established by the respondents. . . .

NOTE: In a hire-purchase contract the supplier hires the goods to the customer, but on payment of a specified number of 'hire instalments' the hirer will have the option to buy the goods. There are many different types of hire-purchase agreement with different terms, and it was not clear what type of hire-purchase contract was envisaged here.

Where an agreement has been acted upon the courts are reluctant to declare it unenforceable and have sought to imply terms based on 'the parties' intentions'.

Hillas & Co. Ltd v *Arcos Ltd*
(1932) 147 LT 503 (HL)

By an agreement made on 21 May 1930, the plaintiffs agreed 'to buy 22,000 standards of softwood goods of fair specification over the season 1930'. Clause 9 also stated that 'the buyers shall also have the option of entering into a contract with the sellers for the purchase of 100,000 standards for delivery during 1931. Such contract to stipulate that, whatever the conditions are, buyers shall obtain the goods on conditions and at prices which show to them a reduction of 5 per cent on the f.o.b. value of the official price list at any time ruling during 1931. Such option to be declared before 1 January 1931'. The option clause did not specify what qualities or type of goods were to be supplied. On 22 December 1930, the plaintiffs purported to exercise the option, but the defendants could not perform as they had already sold their supply to a third party. The plaintiffs sued for damages for breach of contract and the defendants argued that the agreement was void for uncertainty. Held: the agreement was binding and was not dependent on any future agreement for its validity.

LORD TOMLIN: First, the parties were both intimately acquainted with the course of business in the Russian softwood timber trade and had without difficulty carried out the sale and purchase of 22,000 standards under the first part of the document of the 21st May 1930;

Secondly, although the question here is whether clause 9 of the document of the 21st May 1930, with the letter of the 22nd Dec. 1930, constitutes a contract, the validity of the whole of the document of the 21st May 1930 is really in question so far as the matter depends upon the meaning of the phrase 'of fair specification'; and

Thirdly, it is indisputable, having regard to clause 11, which provides that 'this agreement cancels all previous agreements,' that the parties intended by the document of the 21st May 1930 to make, and believed that they had made, some concluded bargain.

. . . [I]t is said that there is in clause 9 no sufficient description of the goods to be sold . . . it is plain that something must necessarily be implied in clause 9. The words '100,000 standards' without more do not even indicate that timber is the subject-matter of the clause. The implication at the least of the words 'of softwood goods' is, in my opinion, inevitable, and if this is so I see no reason to separate the words 'of fair specification' from the words 'of softwood goods.' In my opinion there is a necessary implication of the words 'of softwood goods of fair specification' after the words '100,000 standards' in clause 9.

What then is the meaning of '100,000 standards of softwood goods of fair specification for delivery during 1931'?

If the words 'of fair specification' have no meaning which is certain or capable of being made certain, then not only can there be no contract under clause 9 but there cannot have been a contract with regard to the 22,000 standards mentioned at the beginning of the document of the 21st May 1930. This may be the proper conclusion; but before it is reached it is, I think, necessary to exclude as impossible all reasonable meanings whch would give certainty to the words. In my opinion this cannot be done.

The parties undoubtedly attributed to the words in connection with the 22,000 standards, some meaning which was precise or capable of being made precise. . . .

Reading the document of the 21st May 1930 as a whole, and having regard to the admissible evidence as to the course of the trade, I think that upon their true construction the words 'of fair specification over the season, 1930,' used in connection with the 22,000 standards, mean that the 22,000 standards are to be satisfied in goods distributed over kinds, qualities, and sizes in the fair proportions having regard to the output of the season 1930, and the classifications of that output in respect of kinds, qualities, and sizes. That is something which if the parties fail to agree can be ascertained just as much as the fair value of a property.

NOTES

1. In *Hillas* v *Arcos* the contract had been performed and the option had been exercised by the plaintiffs. In *Scammell* v *Ouston* the respondents were asking the court to enforce an executory contract (one which had not been performed in any respect). In addition, in *Hillas* v *Arcos* the court was able to imply terms based on commercial practice, whereas in *Scammell* v *Ouston* there were no such common terms.

2. Lord Wright made clear how important it was to find the certainty that businessmen intended but had not included in their agreement:

   The document of the 21st May 1930 cannot be regarded as other than inartistic, and may appear repellent to the trained sense of an equity draftsman. But it is clear that the parties both intended to make a contract and thought they had done so. Business men often record the most important agreements in crude and summary fashion; modes of expression sufficient and clear to them in the course of their business may appear to those unfamiliar with the business far from complete or precise. It is accordingly the duty of the court to construe such documents fairly and broadly, without being too astute or subtle in finding defects; but, on the contrary, the court should seek to apply the old maxim of English law, *verba ita sunt intelligenda ut res magis valeat quam pereat*. That maxim, however, does not mean that the court is to make a contract for the parties, or to go outside the words they have used, except in so far as there are appropriate implications of law, as for instance, the implication of what is just and reasonable to be ascertained by the court as matter of machinery where the contractual intention is clear, but the contract is silent on some detail. Thus in contracts for future performance over a period, the parties may neither be able nor desire to specify many matters of detail, but leave them to be adjusted in the working out of the contract. Save for the legal implication I have mentioned, such contracts might well be incomplete or uncertain; with that implication in reserve they are neither incomplete nor uncertain. As obvious illustrations I may refer to such matters as prices or times of delivery in contracts for the sale of goods, or times for loading or dis-charging in a contract of sea carriage. Furthermore, even if the construction of the words used may be difficult, that is not a reason for holding them too ambiguous or uncertain to be enforced if the fair meaning of the parties can be extracted.

3. In *Baird Textiles Holdings Ltd* v *Marks & Spencer plc* [2001] EWCA Civ 274, [2002] 1 All ER (Comm) 737 (for facts and further discussion see *page 194*) *Hillas & Co Ltd* v *Arcos Ltd* could be distinguished as the claim on these facts was based on implied contract and there was no evidence on which to determine the essential terms of the contract.

MORRITT VC:

26 . . . The distinction between those cases in which the implication of reasonableness pro-vides for certainty and those in which it does not appears most clearly from the speech of Lord Thankerton [in *Hillas* v *Arcos Ltd*]. He distinguished ((1932) 147 LT 503 at 513, [1932] All ER Rep 494 at 501) between cases where the contract provides for an objective standard which the court applies by ascertaining what is reasonable and those where, there being no such standard, the test of reasonableness is being used to make an agreement for the parties which they have not made for themselves. He was impressed by the consideration that a commercial matter was involved and the parties themselves thought that they had made a contract.

. . .

29   The issue of certainty arises, not with regard to the alleged obligation to give reasonable notice of termination, but with the allegation that—

'during the subsistence of the relationship Marks & Spencer would acquire garments from BHT in quantities and at prices which in all the circumstances were reasonable.'

Counsel for Baird accepted that this involved an obligation on Baird to supply such garments irrespective of whether it had accepted the order. It is not alleged that there was some objective criteria by which to assess what was a reasonable quantity or price. Counsel disclaimed any contention that M&S in fact allocated business from year to year in accordance with some formula of its own. The annual allocation was separately determined in each year in the light of the circumstances then prevailing.

30   I agree with the conclusion of the judge. The alleged obligation on M&S to acquire gar-ments from Baird is insufficiently certain to found any contractual obligation because there are no objective criteria by which the court could assess what would be reasonable either as to quantity or price. This is not a case in which, the parties having evidently sought to make a contract, the court seeks to uphold its validity by construing the terms to produce certainty. Rather it is a case in which the lack of certainty confirms the absence of any clear evidence of an intention to create legal relations. The allegation in para 9.28 also confirms the lack of intention to create legal relations, for if there had been the requisite certainty because of the objective criteria, then to that extent there would have been a detailed contract and a loss of flexibility. It cannot be said, let alone with confidence, that the conduct of the parties is more consistent with the existence of the contract sought to be implied than with its absence. The implication of the alleged contract is not necessary to give business reality to the commercial relationship between M&S and Baird. In agreement with the judge, I do not think that Baird has a real prospect of success on its claim in contract.

B: Severing a meaningless clause

Nicolene Ltd v *Simmonds*
[1953] 1 QB 543 (CA)

The acceptance of an offer to sell a quantity of steel bars stated that 'I assume that we are in agreement that the usual conditions of acceptance apply'. There were no 'usual conditions' operating between the parties. The defendant failed to deliver and the plaintiffs brought an action for breach of contract. Held: the clause specifying 'usual conditions' was meaningless and could be severed from the rest of the contract without impairing the sense or reasonableness of the contract as a whole.

DENNING LJ: . . . In my opinion a distinction must be drawn between a clause which is meaningless and a clause which is yet to be agreed. A clause which is meaningless can often be ignored, whilst still leaving the contract good; whereas a clause which has yet to be agreed may mean that there is no contract at all, because the parties have not agreed on all the essential terms.

I take it to be clear law that if one of the parties to a contract inserts into it an exempting condition in his own favour, which the other side agrees, and it afterwards turns out that that condition is meaningless, or what comes to the same thing, that it is so ambiguous that no ascertainable meaning can be given to it, that does not mean that the whole contract is a nullity. It only means that the exempting condition is a nullity and must be rejected. It would be strange indeed if a party could escape from every one of his obligations by inserting a meaningless exception from some of them.

C: Incompleteness

(a) Agreements to negotiate

Courtney & Fairbairn Ltd v Tolani Brothers (Hotels) Ltd
[1975] 1 WLR 297 (CA)

Tolani wished to develop a site and got in touch with Courtney, a property developer, who could obtain finance for the development. It was proposed that Courtney should introduce a financier and Tolani should employ the company which Courtney represented to construct the buildings. Courtney wrote to Tolani 'I would be very happy to know that, if my discussions and arrangements with interested parties lead to a financial arrangement acceptable to both parties you will be prepared to instruct your quantity surveyor to negotiate fair and reasonable contract sums in respect of each of the three projects as they arise. (These would incidentally be based upon agreed estimates of the net cost of work and general overheads with a margin for profit of 5 per cent) which, I am sure you will agree is, indeed reasonable'. Courtney introduced a financier and Tolani instructed his quantity surveyor to negotiate with Courtney on the price for building works, but no agreement could be reached and negotiations broke down. Courtney claimed there was an enforceable contract to employ the company as builders. Held: there was no binding contract. This was only an agreement between the parties to negotiate about the price.

LORD DENNING MR: . . . I can find no agreement on the price or on any method by which the price was to be calculated. The agreement was only an agreement to 'negotiate' fair and reasonable contract sums. The words of the letter are 'your quantity surveyor to *negotiate* fair and reasonable contract sums in respect of each of the three projects as they arise.' Then there are words which show that estimates had not yet been agreed, but were yet to be agreed. The words are: 'These [the contract sums] would, incidentally be based upon agreed estimates of the net cost of work and general overheads with a margin for profit of 5 per cent'. Those words show that there were no estimates agreed and no contract sums agreed. All was left to be agreed in the future. It was to be agreed between the parties themselves. If they had left the price to be agreed by a third person such as an arbitrator, it would have been different. But here it was to be agreed between the parties themselves.

Now the price in a building contract is of fundamental importance. It is so essential a term that there is no contract unless the price is agreed or there is an agreed method of ascertaining it, not dependent on the negotiations of the two parties themselves. In a building contract both parties must know at the outset, before the work is started, what the price is to be, or, at all events, what agreed estimates are. No builder and no employer would ever dream of entering into a building contract for over £200,000 without there being an estimate of the cost and an agreed means of ascertaining the price.

. . . There is no machinery for ascertaining the price except by negotiation. In other words, the price is still to be agreed. Seeing that there is no agreement on so fundamental [a] matter as the price, there is no contract.

But then this point was raised: even if there was not a contract actually to build, was not there a contract to negotiate? In this case Mr Tolani did instruct his quantity surveyor to negotiate, but the negotiations broke down. . . . If the law does not recognise a contract to enter into a contract (when there is a fundamental term yet to be agreed) it seems to me it cannot recognise a contract to negotiate. The reason is because it is too uncertain to have any binding force. No court could estimate the damages because no one can tell whether the negotiations would be successful or would fall through: or if successful, what the result would be. It seems to me that a contract to negotiate, like a contract to enter into a contract, is not a contract known to the law. . . .

NOTE: In *Cable & Wireless plc* v *IBM United Kingdom Ltd* [2002] EWHC 2059, [2002] 2 All ER (Comm) 1041, it was held that a clause referring disputes to alternative dispute resolution, although in effect an agreement to agree, was sufficiently certain to be enforced. Since the clause prescribed the means by which the attempt to mediate was to be made and required the parties to participate, it was sufficiently certain for a court to determine compliance. The judge recognised that any other result would 'fly in the face of public policy' since the promotion of alternative dispute resolution (A.D.R.) is a clear objective underpinning the CPR (Civil Procedure Rules); *Dunnett* v *Railtrack plc* [2002] EWCA Civ 303, [2002] 1 WLR 2434.

Walford v *Miles*
[1992] 2 AC 128 (HL)

The defendants, owners of a company, were negotiating for the sale of the company to the plaintiffs. On 17 March 1987, they had entered into an agreement whereby in return for the provision of a comfort letter from the plaintiffs' bank (indicating that loan facilities had been granted to cover the price of £2m), the defendants agreed to terminate any negotiations with third parties, not to entertain offers from any other prospective purchasers and to deal exclusively with the plaintiffs. Although the plaintiffs complied with their side of the agreement, the defendants withdrew from the negotiations and decided to sell to a third party.

The plaintiffs claimed damages for breach of this collateral agreement, which arguably was both a lock-out and a lock-in agreement. The Court of Appeal held that the collateral agreement alleged was only an agreement to negotiate and was therefore unenforceable. The plaintiffs appealed. Held (dismissing the appeal): although a lock-out agreement (not to negotiate with any other person) could be enforceable if it was made for good consideration and covered a fixed period of time, where, as here, it covered an unspecified period of time it was unenforceable. There could be no implied term to negotiate in good faith for a reasonable period of time.

LORD ACKNER: . . . I believe it is helpful to make these observations about a so-called 'lock-out' agreement. There is clearly no reason in the English contract law why A, for good consideration, should not achieve an enforceable agreement whereby B, agrees for a specified period of time, not to negotiate with anyone except A in relation to the sale of his property. There are often good commercial reasons why A should desire to obtain such an agreement from B. B's property, which A contemplates purchasing, may be such as to require the expenditure of not inconsiderable time and money before A is in a position to assess what he is prepared to offer for its purchase or whether he wishes to make any offer at all. A may well consider that he is not prepared to run the risk of expending such time and money unless there is a worthwhile prospect, should he desire to make an offer to purchase, of B, not only then still owning the property, but of being prepared to consider his offer. A may wish to guard against the risk that, while he is investigating the wisdom of offering to buy B's property, B may have already disposed of it or, alternatively, may be so advanced in negotiations with a third party as to be unwilling or for all practical purposes unable, to negotiate with A. But I stress that this is a negative agreement—B by agreeing not to negotiate for this fixed period with a third party, locks himself out of such negotiations. He has in no legal sense locked himself *into* negotiations with A. What A has achieved is an exclusive opportunity, for a fixed period, to try and come to terms with B, an opportunity for which he has, unless he makes his agreement under seal, to give good consideration . . .

The agreement alleged . . . contains the essential characteristics of a basic valid lock-out agreement, save one. It does not specify for how long it is to last. Bingham LJ [in the Court of Appeal] sought to cure this deficiency by holding that the obligation upon [the respondents] not to deal with other parties should continue to bind them 'for such time as is reasonable in all the circumstances'. He said:

> the time would end once the parties acting in good faith had found themselves unable to come to mutually acceptable terms . . . the defendants could not . . . bring the reasonable time to an end by procuring a bogus impasse, since that would involve a breach of the duty of reasonable good faith which parties such as these must, I think, be taken to owe to each other.

However, as Bingham LJ recognised, such a duty, if it existed, would indirectly impose upon [the respondents] a duty to negotiate in good faith. Such a duty, for the reasons which I have given [*see extract below*], cannot be imposed. . . .

NOTES

1. It was also held that: any lock-in agreement (to negotiate only with a particular party) was unenforceable because it was inherently uncertain (approving *Courtney & Fairbairn Ltd* v *Tolani Bros (Hotels) Ltd, page 67*).

2. The argument that it was necessary to imply a term that the defendants were obliged to negotiate in good faith, and only terminate the agreement for subjectively assessed 'proper reasons', was rejected.

   Lord Ackner said (at p. 138 of the report):

   > . . . The reason why an agreement to negotiate, like an agreement to agree, is unenforceable, is simply because it lacks the necessary certainty. The same does not apply to an agreement to use best endeavours. This uncertainty is demonstrated in the instant case by the provision which it is said has to be implied in the agreement for the determination of the negotiations. How can a court be expected to decide whether, *subjectively*, a proper reason existed for the termination of negotiations? The answer suggested depends upon whether the negotiations have been determined 'in good faith'. However, the concept of a duty to carry on negotiations in good faith is inherently repugnant to the adversarial position of the parties when involved in negotiations. Each party to the negotiations is entitled to pursue his (or her) own interest, so long as he avoids making misrepresentations. To advance that interest he must be entitled, if he thinks it appropriate, to threaten to withdraw from further negotiations or to withdraw in fact, in the hope that the opposite party may seek to reopen the negotiations by offering him improved terms. [Counsel for the plaintiffs] of course, accepts that the agreement upon which he relies does not contain a duty to complete the negotiations. But that still leaves the vital question—how is a vendor ever to know that he is entitled to withdraw from further negotiations? How is the

court to police such an 'agreement'? A duty to negotiate in good faith is as unworkable in practice as it is inherently inconsistent with the position of a negotiating party. It is here that the uncertainty lies. In my judgment, while negotiations are in existence either party is entitled to withdraw from those negotiations, at any time and for any reason. There can be thus no obligation to continue to negotiate until there is a 'proper reason' to withdraw. Accordingly a bare agreement to negotiate has no legal content.

■ QUESTION

Do you agree with Lord Ackner's assertion that parties in negotiations are in an adversarial position?

NOTES
1. See Brown [1992] JBL 353, Buckley (1993) 6 JCL 58 and Neill (1992) 108 LQR 405.
2. The House of Lords firmly rejected any suggestion of a duty to negotiate in good faith in English Law. Although a distinction was drawn between an obligation to use best endeavours and to negotiate in good faith, that distinction was not explained.
3. The decision of the Court of Appeal in *Pitt* v *PHH Asset Management Ltd* [1994] 1 WLR 327, is an example of an enforceable lock-out agreement for good consideration because the duration of the agreement was fixed at 14 days. This may indicate that the fixed period will itself need to be fairly short. As on the facts of *Pitt*, this device may prove popular with prospective purchasers of land who fear that they may be 'gazumped' and seek some protection. However, if there is a breach of an enforceable lock-out agreement, it seems that the remedy will be damages, so that the device will not secure the eventual purchase of that property.

■ QUESTIONS

1. Should an injunction be available to prevent a vendor from considering offers from third parties during the period of the lock-out agreement?
2. Do you consider that there is any real difference in terms of practical effect between a lock-in and a lock-out agreement?

(b) The price

SALE OF GOODS ACT 1979

8. Ascertainment of price

(1) The price in a contract of sale may be fixed by the contract, or may be left to be fixed in a manner agreed by the contract, or may be determined by the course of dealing between the parties.

(2) Where the price is not determined as mentioned in subsection (1) above the buyer must pay a reasonable price.

(3) What is a reasonable price is a question of fact dependent on the circumstances of each particular case.

SUPPLY OF GOODS AND SERVICES ACT 1982

15. Implied term about consideration

(1) Where, under a contract for the supply of a service, the consideration for the service is not determined by the contract, left to be determined in a manner agreed by the contract or determined by the course of dealing between the parties, there is an implied term that the party contracting with the supplier will pay a reasonable charge.

(2) What is a reasonable charge is a question of fact.

If the contract provides a mechanism for fixing the price but it has not been implemented, s. 8(2) of the Sale of Goods Act 1979 will not allow the implication of a reasonable price.

May and Butcher Ltd v *R*
[1934] 2 KB 17n (HL)

The parties entered into a contract under which the Government were to sell 'the whole of the tentage which might become available in the UK for disposal up to 31 March 1923'. The relevant terms were:

> (3) The price or prices to be paid, and the date or dates on which payment is to be made by the purchasers to the Commission for such old tentage shall be agreed upon from time to time between the Commission and the purchasers as the quantities of the said old tentage become available for disposal, and are offered to the purchasers by the Commission. . . .
>
> (10) It is understood that all disputes with reference to or arising out of this agreement will be submitted to arbitration in accordance with the provisions of the Arbitration Act, 1889.

The appellants argued that the agreement should be construed as an agreement to sell at a fair or reasonable price, or alternatively at a price to be fixed under the arbitration clause in the agreement. Held: as there was no agreement on these matters, there was no concluded contract.

> VISCOUNT DUNEDIN: To be a good contract there must be a concluded bargain, and a concluded contract is one which settles everything that is necessary to be settled and leaves nothing to be settled by agreement between the parties. Of course it may leave something which still has to be determined, but then that determination must be a determination which does not depend upon the agreement between the parties. In the system of law in which I was brought up, that was expressed by one of those brocards of which perhaps we have been too fond, but which often express very neatly what is wanted: 'Certum est quod certum reddi potest.' Therefore, you may very well agree that a certain part of the contract of sale, such as price, may be settled by some one else. As a matter of the general law of contract all the essentials have to be settled. What are the essentials may vary according to the particular contract under consideration. We are here dealing with sale, and undoubtedly price is one of the essentials of sale, and if it is left still to be agreed between the parties, then there is no contract. It may be left to the determination of a certain person, and if it was so left and that person either would not or could not act, there would be no contract because the price was to be settled in a certain way and it has become impossible to settle it in that way, and therefore there is no settlement. No doubt as to goods, the Sale of Goods Act, 1893, says that if the price is not mentioned and settled in the contract it is to be a reasonable price. The simple answer in this case is that the Sale of Goods Act provides for silence on the point and here there is no silence, because there is a provision that the two parties are to agree. . . . Here there was clearly no contract. There would have been a perfectly good settlement of price if the contract had said that it was to be settled by arbitration by a certain man, or it might have been quite good if it was said that it was to be settled by arbitration under the Arbitration Act so as to bring in a material plan by which a certain person could be put in action. The question then arises, has anything of that sort been done? I think clearly not. The general arbitration clause is one in very common form as to disputes arising out of the arrangements. In no proper meaning of the word can this be described as a dispute arising between the parties; it is a failure to agree, which is a very different thing from a dispute.

Where the price is to be fixed by agreement between the parties, it may make a difference that the agreement has been executed.

Foley v *Classique Coaches Ltd*
[1934] 2 KB 1 (CA)

The defendants entered into an agreement to purchase all their petrol requirements from the plaintiff 'at a price to be agreed by the parties in writing and from time to time'. There was also an arbitration clause should disputes arise. After the defendants had purchased their petrol from the plaintiff for three years, the defendants purported to repudiate the agreement on the ground that there was no agreement in writing as to the price. Held: the agreement was valid and binding, and if any dispute arose as to the reasonable price, the parties had provided for it to be determined by arbitration. After considering *May & Butcher* v *R* and *Hillas* v *Arcos* Scrutton LJ continued:

SCRUTTON LJ: . . . In the present case the parties obviously believed they had a contract and they acted for three years as if they had; they had an arbitration clause which relates to the subject-matter of the agreement as to the supply of petrol, and it seems to me that this arbitration clause applies to any failure to agree as to the price. By analogy to the case of a tied house there is to be implied in this contract a term that the petrol shall be supplied at a reasonable price and shall be of reasonable quality. For these reasons I think the Lord Chief Justice was right in holding that there was an effective and enforceable contract, although as to the future no definite price had been agreed with regard to the petrol.

NOTES
1. Since the parties had acted on this agreement for three years, the court was unwilling to undo it simply to serve the commercial interests of the defendants who had obtained better terms elsewhere. In addition, the petrol agreement was linked to a contract for the sale of land by the plaintiff to the defendants and, arguably, was part of the consideration for that sale.
2. In *British Bank for Foreign Trade Ltd* v *Novinex Ltd* [1949] 1 KB 623, an agreement provided that 'an agreed commission' would be payable if the plaintiffs put the defendants in direct contact with a supplier. The plaintiffs did this but were not paid any commission. The Court of Appeal held that the defendants were bound to pay a 'reasonable sum' and stressed the fact that the plaintiffs had executed their part of the agreement. Cohen LJ said (at pp. 629–630 of the report):

   . . . if there is an essential term which has yet to be agreed and there is no express or implied provision for its solution, the result in point of law is that there is no binding contract. In seeing whether there is an implied provision for its solution, however, there is a difference between an arrangement which is wholly executory on both sides, and one which has been executed on one side or the other. In the ordinary way, if there is an arrangement to supply goods at a price 'to be agreed,' or to perform services on terms 'to be agreed,' then although, while the matter is still executory, there may be no binding contract, nevertheless, if it is executed on one side, that is, if the one does his part without having come to an agreement as to the price or the terms, then the law will say that there is necessarily implied, from the conduct of the parties a contract that, in default of agreement, a reasonable sum is to be paid . . .

3. In *Mamidoil-Jetoil Greek Petroleum Co. SA* v *Okta Crude Oil Refinery (No. 1)* [2001] EWCA Civ 406, [2001] 2 Lloyd's Rep 76, the Court of Appeal held that a term for price fixing will not amount to an 'agreement to agree' where this agreement on price is not required for the conclusion of the contract. The fee was fixed for the first two years of the 10-year term of the contract (1993 and 1994) but the fee for the remaining eight years was left open. The evidence was that agreement had been reached on this fee after the initial two-year period expired, but that problems had arisen after 1999 when the parties became subject to the same group control. In addition, to this factor, the Court of Appeal stressed the history of commercial

dealings between these parties and the necessity to uphold an existing contract and held that in the event that there was a failure to fix the fee in the remaining period of the contract, a term would be implied providing for a reasonable fee to be fixed.

RIX LJ (with whose judgment Schiemann LJ and Sir Ronald Waterhouse agreed)

69 In my judgment the following principles relevant to the present case can be deduced from [the] authorities, but this is intended to be in no way an exhaustive list:

Each case must be decided on its own facts and on the construction of its own agreement. Subject to that:

Where no contract exists, the use of an expression such as 'to be agreed' in relation to an essential term is likely to prevent any contract coming into existence, on the ground of uncertainty. This may be summed up by the principle that 'you cannot agree to agree'.

Similarly, where no contract exists, the absence of agreement on essential terms of the agreement may prevent any contract coming into existence, again on the ground of uncertainty.

However, particularly in commercial dealings between parties who are familiar with the trade in question, and particularly where the parties have acted in the belief that they had a binding contract, the Courts are willing to imply terms, where that is possible, to enable the contract to be carried out.

Where a contract has once come into existence, even the expression 'to be agreed' in relation to future executory obligations is not necessarily fatal to its continued existence.

Particularly in the case of contracts for future performance over a period, where the parties may desire or need to leave matters to be adjusted in the working out of their contract, the Courts will assist the parties to do so, so as to preserve rather than destroy bargains, on the basis that what can be made certain is itself certain. Certum est quod certum reddi potest.

This is particularly the case where one party has either already had the advantage of some performance which reflects the parties' agreement on a long term relationship, or has had to make an investment premised on that agreement.

For these purposes, an express stipulation for a reasonable or fair measure or price will be a sufficient criterion for the courts to act on. But even in the absence of express language, the Courts are prepared to imply an obligation in terms of what is reasonable.

Such implications are reflected but not exhausted by the statutory provision for the implication of a reasonable price now to be found in s. 8(2) of the Sale of Goods Act, 1979 (and, in the case of services, in s. 15(1) of the Supply of Goods and Services Act, 1982).

The presence of an arbitration clause may assist the Courts to hold a contract to be sufficiently certain or to be capable of being rendered so, presumably as indicating a commercial and contractual mechanism, which can be operated with the assistance of experts in the field, by which the parties, in the absence of agreement, may resolve their dispute.

. . .

73 In my judgment, the 1993 contract should be viewed as a contract for a fixed period of at least 10 years and a term should be implied that in the absence of agreement reasonable fees should be determined for the period after 1994. I would seek to put the matter in the following way.

(i) The context is that of a long term (10 year) commercial agreement between parties who have had long familiarity with the subject matter of agreement and with each other.

(ii) The agreement in question undoubtedly arises out of a contract, the 1993 contract. This is not, therefore, one of those cases where the initial issue is whether the parties have ever reached the stage of contractual relations. If the question is whether any contract has ever been arrived at, lack of certainty in essential terms may well make it difficult or impossible to say that the parties ever intended to have legal relations, or even if they did, whether they had reached sufficient certainty to enable a Court to find a contract. If they never achieved a contract in the first place, then there is no assistance to be gained from agreement of an arbitration clause, or from statutory or any other implications. That is not to say, however, that the possibility of such implications or the presence of such an arbitration clause may not assist the Court in the overall question of whether a contract can be found. However, once a contract exists, it not only needs to be construed for its terms, but the Courts will seek to make it work, as the parties must have intended, in accordance with its terms, that it should. . . .

(v) The contract does not expressly state that the fee after the end of 1994 is 'to be agreed'. It is simply silent as to what is to happen in that period. Therefore, this case is simply not presented with the difficulties which arise, in the face of 'to be agreed' language, where it is uncertain whether there is any contract at all. It cannot be said, as was said in *May and Butcher* v *The King*, that the statutory implication of a reasonable price, or an implication that the fee should be such reasonable fee as the arbitrator may decide, is excluded by express agreement that the parties were to agree the figure.

(vi) There is no evidence that the resolution of a reasonable fee would cause any difficulty at all. On the contrary, the evidence is the other way. . . . In the absence of evidence to the contrary, I would infer that it was perfectly possible to derive from the agreements of price and price increases over the years objective criteria for working out a reasonable fee. Thus, although it is true to say that the contract itself contained no mechanism or guidance (other than the arbitration clause) as to how a reasonable fee would be derived, I do not consider that the contract should fail on that ground. Contractually derived criteria or guidance may be of assistance in finding an implied term for a reasonable price: but the authorities indicate that the Courts are well prepared to make the implication even in their absence.

4. In *Alstom Signalling Ltd (t/a Alstom Transport Information Solutions)* v *Jarvis Facilities Ltd* [2004] EWHC 1232 (TCC), 95 Con LR 55, the contract between the main contractor and subcontractor referred to an agreement to agree on pain/gain sharing. Since this was a commercial contract which had been performed, the court concluded that it was not an unenforceable agreement to agree and sought to find a fair and reasonable mechanism to determine this sharing. In the absence of agreement, the court would determine the matter under the terms of the subcontract which gave the court the power to determine any differences. Colin Reese QC stated ([61]): 'Once parties have contracted, the commercial considerations which need to be weighed are quite different from those which fall to be considered when negotiations are broken off before a transaction is agreed or before performance of a project is commenced'.

Compare *May & Butcher Ltd* v *R* [1934] 2 KB 17, *page 71*, with the next case.

Sudbrook Trading Estate Ltd v Eggleton
[1983] 1 AC 444 (HL)

A lease granted the lessees the option of purchasing the reversion 'at such price not being less than £12,000 as may be agreed by two valuers, one to be nominated by the lessor and the other by the lessee and in default of such agreement by an umpire appointed by . . . valuers'. The lessees exercised the option but the lessors refused to appoint a valuer and claimed that the option was void for uncertainty. Held: where machinery was in place which had broken down and that machinery was simply a means of ensuring that a fair price was paid, as opposed to an essential factor in determining the price, then the court could substitute its own machinery to ascertain a fair and reasonable price.

LORD FRASER OF TULLYBELTON: [The courts have] laid down the principle that where parties have agreed on a particular method of ascertaining the price, and that method has for any reason proved ineffective, the court will neither grant an order for specific performance to compel parties to operate the agreed machinery, nor substitute its own machinery to ascertain the price, because either of these clauses would be to impose upon parties an agreement that they had not made. . . .

I recognise the logic of the reasoning which has led to the courts' refusing to substitute their own machinery for the machinery which has been agreed upon by the parties. But the result to which it leads is so remote from that which parties normally intend and expect, and is so inconvenient in practice, that there must in my opinion be some defect in the reasoning. I think the defect lies in construing the provisions for the mode of ascertaining the value as an essential part of the agreement. That may have been perfectly true early in the 19th century, when the valuer's profession and the rules of valuation were less well established than they are now. But at the present day these provisions are only subsidiary to the main purpose of the agreement which is for sale and purchase of the property at a fair or reasonable value. In the ordinary case parties do not make any substantial distinction between an agreement to sell at a fair value, without specifying the mode of ascertaining the value, and an agreement to sell at a value to be ascertained by valuers appointed in the way provided in these leases. The true distinction is between those cases where the mode of ascertaining the price is an essential term of the contract, and those cases where the mode of ascertainment, though indicated in the contract, is subsidiary and non-essential. . . .

The present case falls, in my opinion, into the latter category. Accordingly when the option was exercised there was constituted a complete contract for sale, and the clause should be construed as meaning that the price was to be a fair price. On the other hand where an agreement is made to sell at a price to be fixed by a valuer who is named, or who, by reason of holding some office such as auditor of a company whose shares are to be valued, will have special knowledge relevant to the question of value, the prescribed mode may well be regarded as essential. Where, as here, the machinery consists of valuers and an umpire, none of whom is named or identified, it is in my opinion unrealistic to regard it as an essential term. If it breaks down there is no reason why the court should not substitute other machinery to carry out the main purpose of ascertaining the price in order that the agreement may be carried out.

LORD RUSSELL OF KILLOWEN (dissenting): Basically the assumption is made that the parties intended that the exercise of the option should involve payment of a 'fair price' or a 'fair value.' Of course parties to such a contract could in terms so agree, and I am not concerned to deny that in such a case a court could enforce the contract by ascertainment of a fair price or fair value, treating specific provisions in the contract for methods (which proved to be unworkable) of ascertaining that fair price or valuation as being inessential. But that is not this case. Why should it be thought that potential vendor and purchaser intended the price to be 'fair'? The former would intend the price to be high, even though 'unfairly' so. And the latter vice versa. Vendors and purchasers are normally greedy.

■ QUESTIONS

1. Is it possible to distinguish an agreement whereby the price will be fixed by the parties themselves and an agreement whereby the price will be fixed by valuers appointed by the parties?

2. Is it correct to say that the parties intended to sell and buy at a fair price? Whose approach is the more realistic, Lord Fraser's or Lord Russell's?

Sudbrook v *Eggleton* was distinguished by the Court of Appeal in the following case.

Gillatt v Sky Television Ltd
[2000] 1 All ER (Comm) 461 (CA)

By an agreement Sky had acquired shares in Tele-Aerials Satellite Ltd (TAS) and by clause 6 it had been agreed that if Sky sold or disposed of this shareholding Sky would pay M Ltd '55% of the open market value' of these shares 'as determined by an independent chartered accountant'. M had subsequently assigned this right to G.

When Sky transferred the shares to a wholly owned subsidiary, G claimed to be entitled to the payment under clause 6. However, there had been no attempt to appoint an independent accountant to determine the value of the shares and, since a reasonable time had elapsed, it was no longer possible to do so. G sought to rely on *Sudbrook* to argue that this was not an essential element of the machinery for fixing the value of the shareholding so that, since this machinery had failed, the court could substitute its own machinery. Held: the court would not interfere. The machinery specified was both integral and essential. In any event, the failure of the machinery was due to the claimant's own action in not making the necessary appointment.

MUMMERY LJ: . . . [*Sudbrook Trading Estate Ltd* v *Eggleton, Re Malpass (decd)* [1985] Ch 42 and *Didymi Corporation* v *Atlantic Lines and Navigation Co. Inc* [1988] 2 Lloyd's Rep 108] are relevant to the resolution of this appeal to the extent that (a) they identify the importance of distinguishing between essential and inessential contractual terms and the different consequences of them becoming ineffective; (b) they indicate the factors to be considered in determining whether a term is an essential one or not; (c) they emphasise the importance of upholding, if possible, the validity of the contract and the intentions of the parties; and (d) they illustrate the approach of the court in seeking to prevent contracts from becoming ineffective in consequence of a party taking advantage of either his own failure to perform his contractual obligations or of the refusal or inability of a non-party to fulfil the role which the parties contractually anticipated he would fulfil.

Those cases do not, however, determine the decision in this case. The critical question is, as the judge appreciated, to determine whether cl 6 of the TAS agreement, construed both linguistically and contextually, made the determination of the independent chartered accountant essential to Mr Gillatt's entitlement to payment for the shares in TAS. Only the terms and the surrounding circumstances of the TAS agreement can supply the answer to that question.

THE TERMS AND CIRCUMSTANCES OF THE TAS AGREEMENT

(a) As a matter of the natural and ordinary meaning of the language of cl 6.1 I would hold that the expression 'as determined by an independent chartered accountant' is an integral and essential part of the definition of the payments to which Mallard (and now Mr Gillatt) is entitled on a sale of the shares in TAS. In answer to the question 'What are you entitled to be paid for the TAS shares?' the correct contractual response is not simply '55 per cent of their open market value'; according to cl 6.1 it is that percentage of that value 'as determined by an independent chartered accountant'.

(b) It follows that I would reject the contention that the reference in cl 6.1 to the determination of the independent accountant is merely a mechanism or permissive procedure for dispute resolution . . .

(c) I do not accept the submission that the reference in cl 6.1 to 'open market value' of the shares in TAS would provide the court with adequate objective criteria in this case for the court to determine the value of the TAS shares. I recognise that the concept of open market value is objective in the sense that expert valuers called by the parties would be able to offer to the court reasoned opinions on the value of the TAS shares. The real difficulty for the experts and the court, however, would be that the TAS agreement does not contain any definition of 'open market value' or any indication of the basis on which it is to be ascertained, otherwise than by reference to the opinion of the independent accountant. . . . [T]here is more than one possible approach to such a valuation of shares in a private company: an earnings basis, an assets basis, a discounted cash flow basis, or a combination of these approaches. The fact is that in this case the parties expressly recognised that such a valuation is pre-eminently a matter of judgment for the independent accountant entrusted with the task by the parties. The TAS agreement did not prescribe for him any detail of the basis on which he was to approach the determination of open market value. It was treated as a matter of judgment entrusted to his decision which the parties agreed to accept as final and binding. It is the duty of the court to give effect to the parties' agreement on ascertainment of entitlement to the final payment and to payment for the TAS shares. It is not the function of the court to modify cl 6.1 of the TAS agreement so as to enable it to intervene and make its own valuation.

(d) There is no question in this case of the 'breakdown' of machinery for the determination of value, either as a result of the parties failing to perform their legal obligations or as a result of the nominated valuer being unable or unwilling to fulfil his role. There was no legal obligation on the parties in the TAS agreement to agree on the value of the shares or to agree on the accountant to be appointed or to agree on invoking the assistance of the president of the institute. It was open to Mr Gillatt before this action was started to seek the appointment and the determination of the independent accountant without the cooperation of Sky. But for reasons of his own, which are not disclosed in the evidence, he did not attempt to do so. It is not a case of a breakdown of contractual machinery; it is a case of a failure by the party claiming payment to take the necessary contractual steps to ascertain entitlement to payment. There is, in my view, no question of the court becoming entitled in these circumstances to substitute something different (i.e. its own opinion on open market value) in place of what was contractually agreed between the parties (i.e. the opinion of the accountant) for the determination of Mr Gillatt's entitlement, but which Mr Gillatt has simply disregarded.

(e) Commercial considerations indicate that, contrary to the submission made on behalf of Mr Gillatt, the parties probably intended that the determination of the open market value of the TAS shares should be by an independent accountant and not by the court. Assuming that such considerations are relevant to the question of construction (and both sides agreed that they are), they favour Sky's construction as being more likely to produce an outcome reflecting the probable common intention of the parties. The determination of the independent accountant is more expeditious, less expensive and more certain than litigation. It would have a final and binding effect consistent with the intended termination of the relationship between the parties. . . .

NOTES

1. This case indicates that *Sudbrook* may be limited to instances where the appointee is unwilling or unable to act or where a joint appointment is required and one party is obstructing the other's attempts to appoint in an effort to avoid the application of the agreed machinery. On the other hand, having failed to follow the agreed procedure of appointing an independent chartered accountant, Mr Gillatt could not argue that the provision meant nothing and should be replaced by a determination of the court.

2. In *Infiniteland Ltd* v *Artisan Contracting Ltd* [2004] EWHC 955 (Ch), 30 April 2004, *Sudbrook* was distinguished and *Gillatt* applied on the basis that the machinery in the clause allowing for price adjustment was essential and had not been waived. In addition, this machinery had not broken down but the problem was, as in *Gillatt*, caused by the failure of the party seeking the adjustment to operate the machinery in the clause. (The clause required Infiniteland, as purchaser, to produce a calculation of net asset value as a first step in the procedure, and it had failed to do so. In the event of any dispute on net asset value, an independent chartered accountant who was an experienced auditor of building construction companies was to certify this matter. It followed that a court could not provide this figure as it did not possess the expertise.) Park J noted that *Sudbrook* 'is not authority for the proposition that, whenever a contract provides a specific method of fixing a price but the parties do not use it, the court will always fill the gap itself'. Thus it was recognised that *Sudbrook* was a case which turned on its particular facts.

3. This case is important in indicating that where a person is not specifically named in the machinery for fixing price or value, it does not follow that the machinery is to be regarded as non-essential.

D: Paying for performance under an uncertain contract

British Steel Corporation v *Cleveland Bridge & Engineering Co. Ltd*
[1984] 1 All ER 504

The defendants entered into negotiations with the plaintiffs for the plaintiffs to manufacture steel nodes. The defendants sent the plaintiffs a letter of intent stating their intention to place an order for the steel nodes, and proposed that the contract be on the defendants' standard terms (providing for unlimited liability of the plaintiffs in respect of consequential loss from late delivery). The letter of intent requested the plaintiffs to commence work immediately pending the issue of the official contract. The plaintiffs refused to contract on the proposed terms, and although detailed negotiations took place, no agreement was reached on the question of losses following late delivery and no formal contract was concluded. In the meantime the plaintiffs had gone ahead with the manufacture of the nodes as requested. All but one of the nodes had been delivered but the last one was delayed by an industrial dispute at the plaintiffs' plant. The defendants refused to pay and sought damages on the basis that there had been a breach of a binding contract. The plaintiffs sued for the value of the nodes on a *quantum meruit* basis, contending that there was no binding contract. Held: as the parties had not reached agreement it was impossible to say what the material terms were. Consequently there was no formal contract. Since there was no contract, the work performed under the letter of intent was not referable to any contractual terms as to payment and performance. However, as the defendants had requested the plaintiffs to deliver the nodes, and had therefore received a benefit at the expense of the plaintiffs, it would be unjust for them to retain that benefit without recompensing the plaintiff for the reasonable value of the nodes.

ROBERT GOFF J: No doubt it was envisaged by CBE at the time they sent the letter that negotiations had reached an advanced stage, and that a formal contract would soon be signed; but, since the parties were still in a state of negotiation, it is impossible to say with any degree of certainty what the material terms of that contract would be. I find myself quite unable to conclude that, by starting work in these circumstances, BSC bound themselves to complete the work. In the course of argument, I put to counsel for CBE the question whether BSC were free at any time, after starting work, to cease work. His submission was that they were not free to do so, even if negotiations on the terms of the formal contract broke down completely. I find this submission to be so repugnant to common sense and the commercial realities that I am unable to accept it. . . .

I therefore reject CBE's submission that a binding executory contract came into existence in this case.

In my judgment, the true analysis of the situation is simply this. Both parties confidently expected a formal contract to eventuate. In these circumstances, to expedite performance under that anticipated contract, one requested the other to commence the contract work, and the other complied with that request. If thereafter, as anticipated, a contract was entered into, the work done as requested will be treated as having been performed under that contract; if, contrary to their expectation, no contract was entered into, then the performance of the work is not referable to any contract the terms of which can be ascertained, and the law simply imposes an obligation on the party who made the request to pay a reasonable sum for such work as has been done pursuant to that request, such an obligation sounding in quasi contract or, as we now say, in restitution.

NOTES

1. See Ball, 'Work Carried Out in Pursuance of Letters of Intent—Contract or Restitution' (1983) 99 LQR 572.

2. See also *Marston Construction Co. Ltd* v *Kigass Ltd* (1989) 15 Con LR 116 and *Yule* v *Little Bird Ltd*, unrep., 5 April 2001.

3. In *Regalian Properties plc* v *London Dockland Development Corp* [1995] 1 WLR 212, Rattee J held that there could be no recovery of pre-contractual expenses when a contract did not result between the parties. By using the expression 'subject to contract' in their negotiations the parties had accepted that any pre-contract costs were incurred at that party's own expense. There could also be no recovery on a *quantum meruit* since (distinguishing *BSC* v *Cleveland Bridge & Engineering*), the costs that Regalian (a property development company) wanted to recover were costs it had incurred for the purpose of putting itself into a position where it could obtain and perform a proposed contract to build, namely professional fees, site investigations, and detailed costings. They were not costs incurred 'by way of accelerated performance of the anticipated contract at the request of LDDC'. (See McKendrick [1995] RLR 100.)

4. In *Countrywide Communications Ltd* v *ICL Pathway Ltd* [2000] CLC 324, the plaintiff had been persuaded to carry out public relations work (regarded as a benefit) in connection with a bid to supply a particular system on the basis of an assurance that, if the bid succeeded, the plaintiff would be appointed as public relations consultant for the project. The bid succeeded but another consultant was appointed. A claim for damages for breach of contract failed because there was no binding contract to employ the plaintiff. However, the judge, Nicholas Strauss QC, accepted that in 'exceptional cases' where a contract failed to materialise a claimant would be able to recover on a *quantum meruit* for expenditure incurred in anticipation of such a contract. This was such a case so that the plaintiff was able to recover the costs associated with the work it had carried out. Nicholas Strauss QC stated:

> . . . I have found it impossible to formulate a clear general principle which satisfactorily governs the different factual situations which have arisen, let alone those which could easily arise in other cases. Perhaps, in the absence of any recognition in English law of a general duty, of good faith in contractual negotiations, this is not surprising. Much of the difficulty is caused by attempting to categorise as an unjust enrichment of the defendant, for which an action in restitution is available, what is really a loss unfairly sustained by the plaintiff. There is a lot to be said for a broad principle enabling either to be recompensed, but no such principle is clearly established in English law. Undoubtedly the court may impose an obligation to pay for benefits resulting from services performed in the course of a contract which is expected to, but does not, come into existence. This is so, even though, in all cases, the defendant is *ex hypothesi* free to withdraw from the proposed contract, whether the negotiations were expressly made 'subject to contract' or not. Undoubtedly, such an obligation will be imposed only if justice requires it or, which comes to much the same thing, if it would be unconscionable for the plaintiff not to be recompensed.
>
> Beyond that, I do not think that it is possible to go further than to say that, in deciding whether to impose an obligation and if so its extent, the court will take into account and give appropriate weight to a number of considerations which can be identified in the authorities. The first is whether the services were of a kind which would normally be given free of charge. Secondly, the terms in which the request to perform the services was made may be important in establishing the extent of the risk (if any) which the plaintiffs may fairly be said to have taken that such services would in the end be unrecompensed. What may be important here is whether the parties are simply negotiating, expressly or impliedly 'subject to contract', or whether one party has given some kind of assurance or indication that he will not withdraw, or that he will not withdraw except in certain circumstances. Thirdly, the nature of the benefit which has resulted to the defendants is important, and in particular whether such benefit is real (either 'realised' or 'realisable') or a fiction. . . . Plainly, a court will at least be more inclined to impose an obligation to pay for a real benefit, since otherwise the abortive negotiations will leave the defendant with a windfall and the plaintiff out of pocket. However, the judgment of Denning LJ in [*Brewer Street*

Investments Ltd v *Barclays Woollen Co. Ltd* [1954] 1 QB 428] suggests that the performance of services requested may of itself suffice [sic] amount to a benefit or enrichment. Fourthly, what may often be decisive are the circumstances in which the anticipated contract does not materialise and in particular whether they can be said to involve 'fault' on the part of the defendant, or (perhaps of more relevance) to be outside the scope of the risk undertaken by the plaintiff at the outset. I agree with the view of Rattee J [in *Regalian plc* v *LDDC*] that the law should be flexible in this area, and the weight to be given to each of these factors may vary from case to case.

There is in my view considerable doubt whether an obligation can be imposed in a case in which the plaintiff has not provided a benefit of any kind, even of the 'fictional' kind discussed earlier of performing services at the request of the defendant albeit without enriching him in any real sense. Thus I doubt whether an obligation can be imposed on a contracting party to repay a plaintiff for expense incurred, reasonably or even necessarily, in anticipation of a contract which does not materialise, where this is not in the course of providing services requested by the defendant. Such an obligation would not be restitutionary. . . .

SECTION 2: AGREEMENT MISTAKES

A mistake may occur which will 'negative consent' and prevent agreement. In *Great Peace Shipping Ltd* v *Tsavliris Salvage (International) Ltd* [2002] EWCA Civ 1407, [2003] QB 679, Lord Phillips MR stated that:

> **28** A mistake can be simply defined as an erroneous belief. Mistakes have relevance in the law of contract in a number of different circumstances. They may prevent the mutuality of agreement that is necessary for the formation of a contract. In order for two parties to conclude a contract binding in law each must agree with the other the terms of the contract. Whether two parties have entered into a contract in this way must be judged objectively, having regard to all the material facts. . . .

Traditionally, there are two categories of agreement mistakes relating to contractual formation: mutual mistakes (where the parties are at cross purposes) and unilateral mistake (where one party is mistaken and the other knows or ought to know this).

A: Mutual mistake

Raffles v *Wichelhaus*
(1864) 2 H & C 906; 159 ER 375 (ExD)

Agreement was reached at Liverpool that the plaintiff should sell the defendants 125 bales of Surat cotton to arrive ex *Peerless* from Bombay. However, there were two ships called *Peerless* sailing from Bombay; one sailed in October and the other sailed in December. The plaintiff brought an action against the defendants for refusing to take delivery of the goods which were shipped on the *Peerless* leaving in December. The defendants argued that there was a latent ambiguity in the contract (i.e., one which does not appear on the face of the contract) and that they should be allowed to adduce evidence of their intention. The defendants alleged that they understood the ship in the agreement to be the ship sailing in October. The Court found for the defendants. However, as no detailed judgment was given, the only indications of the reasoning underlying this decision must be sought in the questions put to counsel.

> . . . Milward, in support of the demurrer [for the plaintiff]. The contract was for the sale of a number of bales of cotton of a particular description, which the plaintiff was ready to deliver. It is immaterial by what ship the cotton was to arrive, so that it was a ship called the *Peerless*. The words 'to arrive ex *Peerless*,' only mean that if the vessel is lost on the voyage, the contract is to be at an end. [Pollock CB It would be a question for the jury whether both parties meant the same ship called the *Peerless*.] That would be so if the contract was for the sale of a ship called the *Peerless*; but it is for the sale of cotton on board a ship of that name. [Pollock CB The defendant only bought that cotton which was to arrive by a particular ship. It may as well be said, that if there is a contract for the purchase of certain goods in warehouse A, that is satisfied by the delivery of goods of the same description in warehouse B.] In that case there would be goods in both warehouses; here it does not appear that the plaintiff had any goods on board the other *Peerless*. [Martin B It is imposing on the defendant a contract different from that which he entered into. Pollock CB It is like a contract for the purchase of wine coming from a particular estate in France or Spain, where there are two estates of that name.] The defendant has no right to contradict by parol evidence a written contract good upon the face of it. He does not impute misrepresentation or fraud, but only says that he fancied the ship was a different one. Intention is of no avail, unless stated at the time of the contract. [Pollock CB One vessel sailed in October and the other in December.] The time of sailing is no part of the contract.
>
> Mellish (Cohen with him), in support of the plea [for the defendants]. There is nothing on the face of the contract to shew that any particular ship called the *Peerless* was meant; but the moment it appears that two ships called the *Peerless* were about to sail from Bombay there is a latent ambiguity, and parol evidence may be given for the purpose of shewing that the defendant meant one *Peerless*, and the plaintiff another. That being so, there was no consensus ad idem, and therefore no binding contract. He was then stopped by the Court.

NOTES
1. The decision may be limited to the fact that the defendants were allowed to adduce evidence of their intentions due to the latent ambiguity (as an exception to the parol evidence rule, see *page 207*). It is not clear whether the court accepted the argument that there was no agreement because of the mistake. *Raffles* v *Wichelhaus* was treated as a case of latent ambiguity by Lord Phillips MR in *Great Peace Shipping* v *Tsavliris Salvage*.
2. Although reference is made to the subjective approach to contract formation, the facts of the case can be used to illustrate an objective approach. Having allowed the introduction of evidence of each party's intentions, it would be for the jury to decide which party's interpretation was the more reasonable. If this could not be resolved because the agreement was totally ambiguous, then the mistake would prevent the existence of a contract.

    (This case is discussed by Grant Gilmore, *The Death of Contract*, pp. 35–44, and see Simpson, 'Contracts for Cotton to Arrive: the Case of the Two Ships *Peerless*' (1989) 11 Cardozo L Rev 287.)

■ QUESTION

It appears that the court treated the ship to be used as a term of the contract, and that performance could not be achieved by shipment on a different vessel. Is it correct to argue that this was part of the agreed means of performance?

Scriven Brothers & Co. v Hindley
[1913] 3 KB 564

The plaintiffs instructed an auctioneer to sell a number of bales of hemp and of tow. The goods were described in the auctioneer's catalogue as a number of bales in different lots with the same shipping marks. The catalogue did not indicate that some were hemp and some were tow, although it was extremely rare for different commodities to bear the same shipping marks. The defendants' manager examined only a sample, which was hemp. When the lots of tow were put up for sale the defendants successfully bid for them at a price which was extravagant for tow. The plaintiffs sued for the price of the tow and the defendants alleged a mistake as to the subject matter of the proposed contract. The jury found as facts that the auctioneer intended to sell tow and the defendants intended to bid for hemp. Held: the parties were never *ad idem* as to the subject matter of the proposed sale, so that there was no contract and the defendants did not have to pay the price. The judge (A. T. Lawrence J) appears to have been influenced by the fact that the auctioneers had contributed to the mistake by not identifying the individual lots, and therefore the plaintiffs should not benefit from their agent's mistake. The defendant buyer owed no duty to inspect lots that he did not wish to purchase.

■ QUESTION

Is this a case of unilateral mistake, in that the auctioneer ought to have known of the mistake because it was unusual for different lots to bear the same shipping marks?

Tamplin v *James*
(1880) 15 ChD 215

Property was sold as 'All that inn with the brewhouse, outbuildings and premises known as *The Ship* together with the saddler's shop and premises adjoining thereto, situated at N., Nos 454 and 455 on the tithe map'. Plans of Nos. 454 and 455 were available for inspection in the sale room. At the back of the property there were two pieces of garden occupied with the inn and saddler's shop which were not owned by the vendor and not included in the plans as part of the land for sale. The defendant knew about the occupation of the pieces of garden and purchased the property, without checking the plan, in the belief that the property purchased included the two pieces of garden. Baggallay LJ and, on appeal, the Court of Appeal held: the defendant could not resist an order of specific performance of the sale on the ground of mistake.

BAGGALLAY LJ: It is doubtless well established that a Court of Equity will refuse specific performance of an agreement when the Defendant has entered into it under a mistake, and where injustice would be done to him were performance to be enforced. The most common instances of such refusal on the ground of mistake are cases in which there has been some unintentional misrepresentation on the part of the Plaintiff (I am not now referring to cases of intentional misrepresentation which would fall rather under the category of fraud), or where from the ambiguity of the agreement different meanings have been given to it by the different parties. . . . But where there has been no misrepresentation, and where there is no ambiguity in the terms of the contract, the Defendant cannot be allowed to evade the performance of it by the simple statement that he has made a mistake. Were such to be the law the performance of a contract could rarely be enforced upon an unwilling party who was also unscrupulous. . . .

Court of Appeal
(1880) 15 ChD 215, at 221

JAMES LJ: . . . If a man will not take reasonable care to ascertain what he is buying, he must take the consequences. The defence on the ground of mistake cannot be sustained. It is not enough for a purchaser to swear, 'I thought the farm sold contained twelve fields which I knew, and I find it does not include them all,' or, 'I thought it contained 100 acres and it only contains eighty.' It would open the door to fraud if such a defence was to be allowed. Perhaps some of the cases on this subject go too far, but for the most part the cases where a Defendant has escaped on the ground of a mistake not contributed to by the Plaintiff, have been cases where a hardship amounting to injustice would have been inflicted upon him by holding him to his bargain, and it was unreasonable to hold him to it. *Webster* v *Cecil* (1861) 30 Beav 62 is a good instance of that. It is said that it is hard to hold a man to a bargain entered into under a mistake, but we must consider the hardship on the other side. Here are trustees realizing their testator's estate, and the reckless conduct of the Defendant may have prevented their selling to somebody else. If a man makes a mistake of this kind without any reasonable excuse he ought to be held to his bargain.

NOTE: The argument that the parties were at cross purposes and therefore no agreement resulted cannot be used by a party whose own interpretation is not a reasonable one. The defendant here had been reckless and could not be allowed to avoid the contract based upon his subjective intention.

B: Unilateral mistake

If there is a mistake by one party as to a *term* of the contract, and the other party knew or ought to have realised, then there will be no binding contract. See *Hartog* v *Colin & Shields* [1939] 3 All ER 566, at *page 20*, where Singleton J held that the plaintiff must have realised that a mistake was made in the offer and therefore there was no binding contract. The offeree could not be allowed to 'snap up' the offeror's mistake.

However, if it is not a mistake relating to a term of the contract but concerns a 'collateral' matter (Adams & Brownsword, *Understanding Contract Law*, 4th edn, pp. 64–5) or a matter relating to a quality of the subject matter, then it will not prevent agreement, and there is no requirement that the offeror correct the offeree's mistake where he knows it has been made.

Smith v Hughes
(1871) LR 6 QB 597 (QB)

The plaintiff offered to sell oats to the defendant and showed the defendant a sample. The defendant wrote to say that he would take the whole quantity of oats at 34s per quarter. However, he later refused to accept the oats on the ground that they were new and he thought he was buying old oats. The plaintiff only intended to offer to sell 'green' oats and had no old oats to sell. The plaintiff brought an action for non-acceptance, and the defendant alleged that the plaintiff knew he required old oats as the defendant had expressly said that he was a buyer of 'good old oats'. The appeal concerned the correctness of the judge's direction to the jury. The judge had left two questions to the jury:

(1) Had the word 'old' been used by the plaintiff or the defendant in making the contract? If so, they had to return a verdict for the defendant. However, if they thought it had not been so used, then the second question had to be considered.

(2) Was the evidence that the plaintiff believed the defendant to believe that he was contracting for old oats? If yes, then the verdict was to be for the

defendant, but if the evidence was that the plaintiff did not have such a belief, then they would find for the plaintiff. Held: the Court found that there had been a misdirection on the second question and ordered a new trial.

COCKBURN CJ: It is to be regretted that the jury were not required to give specific answers to the questions so left to them. For, it is quite possible that their verdict may have been given for the defendant on the first ground; in which case there could, I think, be no doubt as to the propriety of the judge's direction; whereas now, as it is possible that the verdict of the jury—or at all events of some of them—may have proceeded on the second ground, we are called upon to consider and decide whether the ruling of the learned judge with reference to the second question was right.

For this purpose we must assume that nothing was said on the subject of the defendant's manager desiring to buy *old* oats, nor of the oats having been said to be old; while, on the other hand, we must assume that the defendant's manager believed the oats to be old oats and that the plaintiff was conscious of the existence of such belief, but did nothing, directly or indirectly, to bring it about, simply offering his oats and exhibiting his sample, remaining perfectly passive as to what was passing in the mind of the other party. The question is whether, under such circumstances, the passive acquiescence of the seller in the self-deception of the buyer will entitle the latter to avoid the contract. I am of opinion that it will not. . . .

I take the true rule to be, that where a specific article is offered for sale, without express warranty, or without circumstances from which the law will imply a warranty—as where, for instance, an article is ordered for a specific purpose—and the buyer has full opportunity of inspecting and forming his own judgment, if he chooses to act on his own judgment, the rule caveat emptor applies. If he gets the article he contracted to buy, and that article corresponds with what it was sold as, he gets all he is entitled to, and is bound by the contract. Here the defendant agreed to buy a specific parcel of oats. The oats were what they were sold as, namely, good oats according to the sample. The buyer persuaded himself they were old oats, when they were not so; but the seller neither said nor did anything to contribute to his deception. He has himself to blame. The question is not what a man of scrupulous morality or nice honour would do under such circumstances. The case put of the purchase of an estate, in which there is a mine under the surface, but the fact is unknown to the seller, is one in which a man of tender conscience or high honour would be unwilling to take advantage of the ignorance of the seller; but there can be no doubt that the contract for the sale of the estate would be binding. . . .

Now, in this case, there was plainly no legal obligation in the plaintiff in the first instance to state whether the oats were new or old. He offered them for sale according to the sample, as he had a perfect right to do, and gave the buyer the fullest opportunity of inspecting the sample, which, practically, was equivalent to an inspection of the oats themselves. What, then, was there to create any trust or confidence between the parties, so as to make it incumbent on the plaintiff to communicate the fact that the oats were not, as the defendant assumed them to be, old oats? If, indeed, the buyer, instead of acting on his own opinion, had asked the question whether the oats were old or new, or had said anything which intimated his understanding that the seller was selling the oats as old oats, the case would have been wholly different; or even if he had said anything which shewed that he was not acting on his own inspection and judgment, but assumed as the foundation of the contract that the oats were old, the silence of the seller, as a means of misleading him, might have amounted to a fraudulent concealment, such as would have entitled the buyer to avoid the contract. Here, however, nothing of the sort occurs. The buyer in no way refers to the seller, but acts entirely on his own judgment.

It only remains to deal with an argument which was pressed upon us, that the defendant in the present case intended to buy old oats, and the plaintiff to sell new, so the two minds were not *ad idem*; and that consequently there was no contract. This argument proceeds on the fallacy of confounding what was merely a motive operating on the buyer to induce him to buy with one of the essential conditions of the contract. Both parties were agreed as to the sale and purchase of this particular parcel of oats. The defendant believed the oats to be old, and was thus induced to agree to buy them, but he omitted to make their age a condition of the contract. All that can be said is, that the two minds were not *ad idem* as to the age of the oats; they certainly were *ad idem* as to the sale and purchase of them. Suppose a person to buy a horse without a warranty, believing him to be sound; and the horse turns out unsound, could it be contended that it would be open to him to say that, as he had intended to buy a sound horse, and the seller to sell an unsound one, the contract was void, because the seller must have known from the price the buyer was willing to give, or from his general habits as a buyer of horses, that he thought the horse was sound? The cases are exactly parallel.

The result is that, in my opinion, the learned judge of the county court was wrong in leaving the second question to the jury, and that, consequently, the case must go down to a new trial.

NOTES

1. The parties had agreed the terms for the sale and purchase of the oats, and the question of the age had not been mentioned and as such was a 'collateral' matter. Consequently, unlike the mistake in *Hartog v Colin & Shields*, this was not a true agreement mistake since it did not relate to offer and acceptance and did not prevent agreement.

2. Brownsword, 'New Note on the Old Oats' (1987) 131 SJ 384, argued that this case supports the principle that a party will not easily be relieved of a bad bargain. If the buyer wanted old oats he should have ensured that he bought old oats. Any other conclusion would encourage imprudent conduct by buyers.

3. In *Clarion Ltd v National Provident Institution* [2000] 1 WLR 1888, Rimer J refused to grant relief where the mistake related to the commercial effect of an agreement, rather than a mistake as to its terms.

   The agreement in question provided for the block switching of investments. However, the defendant, issuing the pension scheme policies, did not appreciate that the effect of the agreement was that the bid prices for units in pension funds were known to Clarion when it took the decision to transfer units between the funds. Clarion was aware of the defendant's mistaken understanding relating to the use and likely effect of the agreement. The defendant sought relief alleging mistake but Rimer J refused such relief and held that this was a mistake as to the commercial effect and advantage of the agreement since the defendant did not appreciate that the terms agreed would effectively protect Clarion from the risks of forward pricing.

C: Unilateral mistake as to identity

One party (commonly termed 'the rogue') may misrepresent his or her identity in order to persuade the other contracting party to contract or allow him or her to take away goods on credit. In the majority of situations the rogue will then sell the goods to an innocent third party.

The mistaken party will normally have to seek to recover the goods and damages for conversion from the innocent third party. This is only possible if the contract is void for mistake as to identity so that the rogue did not acquire any title to pass on.

Prior to the decision of the House of Lords in *Shogun Finance Ltd v Hudson* [2003] UKHL 62, [2004] 1 AC 919, the law as to mistaken identity was generally recognised to be in an unsatisfactory state.

(a) Background to the decision of the House of Lords in *Shogun v Hudson*

The courts have been faced with the difficult task of deciding which of two innocent parties should suffer because of the fraud of a third. Since the consequences for the innocent third party are regarded as harsh, the usual approach had been to protect that party by concluding that the contract was voidable for fraudulent misrepresentation relating to identity, rather than void for mistake as to identity. If the contract is merely voidable, since the right to rescind is lost when an innocent third party purchases the goods, the goods could not then be recovered from that innocent third party (Sale of Goods Act 1979, s. 23) and the innocent third party would not be liable in damages for their conversion.

However, this policy objective was furthered by an unfortunate distinction, which was difficult to explain and justify, between mistake as to identity, and mistake as to attributes such as creditworthiness (attribute mistakes being insufficiently fundamental to render the contract void). More significantly, there could be a true mistake as to identity only where identity was regarded as crucial to the decision to contract and that would be presumed not to be the case in face to face contracts, the presumption being that there was an intention to contract with the person physically present. Even in this context, there were apparently irreconcilable decisions: *Phillips* v *Brooks Ltd* and *Lewis* v *Averay* (voidable for fraudulent misrepresentation), and *Ingram* v *Little* (treated as void by the majority of the Court of Appeal on the basis that the offer was intended for the real P.G.M. Hutchinson and therefore only he could accept it, despite the fact that this was a face to face dealing).

Many years earlier, the House of Lords in *Cundy* v *Lindsay* had concluded, in the context of a contract by written correspondence, that identity was crucially important to the decision to contract, and had therefore held the contract to be void for mistake as to identity. Both *Cundy* v *Lindsay* and the majority of the Court of Appeal in *Ingram* v *Little* focused on an offer and acceptance analysis of the question of the identity of the parties to the contract.

(b) The key cases prior to the decision in *Shogun* v *Hudson*

(i) Face to face case law
In a face-to-face situation the actual decision to sell does not normally rest on the question of the identity of the buyer, although the decision to allow the goods to be taken on credit will often be influenced by the attributes of the buyer.

Phillips v *Brooks Ltd*
[1919] 2 KB 243

A man called North had entered the plaintiff's jewellery shop and asked to see some pearls and a ring. He selected pearls at a price of £2,550 and a ring at the price of £450. He wrote out a cheque for £3,000, saying, 'You see who I am, I am Sir George Bullough', and he gave an address in St James's Square. The plaintiff knew there was such a person and, having checked the address in a directory, asked the man if he would like to take the articles with him. The man replied that he would like to take the ring with him because it was his wife's birthday the following day. The cheque was dishonoured, but in the meantime North had pledged the ring with the defendants—pawn brokers who acted without notice. The plaintiff sued the defendants for the return of the ring (or its value) and damages for its detention. Held: the plaintiff intended to contract, and did contract, with the person in the shop. The mistake related to allowing the goods to be taken away on credit.

HORRIDGE J: . . . I have carefully considered the evidence of the plaintiff, and have come to the conclusion that, although he believed the person to whom he was handing the ring was Sir George Bullough, he in fact contracted to sell and deliver it to the person who came into his shop, and who was not Sir George Bullough, but a man of the name of North, who obtained the sale and delivery by means of the false pretence that he was Sir George Bullough. . . . The following expressions seem to me to fit the facts in this case: 'The minds of the parties met and agreed upon all the terms of the sale, the thing sold, the price and time of payment, the person selling and the person buying. The fact that the seller was induced to sell by fraud of the buyer made the sale voidable, but not void. He could not have supposed that he was selling to any other person; his intention was to sell to the person present, and identified by sight and hearing; it does not defeat the sale because the buyer assumed a false name or practised any other deceit to induce the vendor to sell.' . . .

NOTES
1. Viscount Haldane in *Lake* v *Simmons* [1927] AC 487 considered that the sale in the shop had been concluded before there was any mention of Sir George Bullough so that any identity mistake could not be linked to the decision to contract. (Other reports of this case, e.g., 88 LJKB 952, suggest that North identified himself as Sir George Bullough as soon as he entered the shop.)
2. *Hardman* v *Booth* (1863) 1 H & C 803, 158 ER 1107, for facts see the speech of Lord Phillips in *Shogun* v *Hudson* [128]–[130], established an exception to the usual position in face to face dealings. The contract will be void where the intention is to contract with a company and the contract purports to be made by a person on behalf of that company who in fact has no such authority to act.

The next case proved difficult to reconcile with *Phillips* v *Brooks Ltd*.

Ingram v *Little*
[1961] 1 QB 31 (CA)

The three elderly plaintiffs, the joint owners of a car, advertised it for sale. A rogue, introducing himself as Hutchinson, offered to buy it. When he produced his cheque book to pay, the plaintiffs told him that they expected cash and were not prepared to accept payment by cheque. The rogue then said he was P.G.M. Hutchinson, a reputable businessman who lived at Stanstead House, Stanstead Road, Caterham, and that he had business interests in Caterham. The plaintiffs had never heard of this person but one of them slipped out, went to the post office and, on checking the telephone directory, ascertained that there was a P.G.M. Hutchinson living at that address. The plaintiffs, believing the rogue was this person, let him have the car in exchange for the cheque. He was not the real P.G.M. Hutchinson. The rogue's cheque was not met. Meanwhile, the rogue had sold the car to the defendant who bought in good faith. The plaintiffs sought the return of the car from the defendant, or alternatively damages for its conversion. Held: (Devlin LJ dissenting) since the plaintiffs had made an offer to the real P.G.M. Hutchinson, the rogue could not accept it.

SELLERS LJ: It [*Phillips* v *Brooks Ltd* [1919] 2 KB 243] is not an authority to establish that where an offer or acceptance is addressed to a person (although under a mistake as to his identity) who is present in person, then it must in all circumstances be treated as if actually addressed to him. I would regard the issue as a question of fact in each case depending on what was said and done and applying the elementary principles of offer and acceptance . . .

The question in each case should be solved, in my opinion, by applying the test, which Slade J applied, 'How ought the promisee to have interpreted the promise' in order to find whether a contract has been entered into. . . .

Phillips v *Brooks Ltd* [1919] 2 KB 243 is the closest authority on which the defendant relies. Once that is distinguished on its facts, without going so far as to say it is wrong, authority leans strongly in favour of the judgment appealed from.

Cundy v *Lindsay* (1878) 3 App Cas 459, on the findings of the Court of Appeal and the House of Lords, was to the same effect as the present case. The plaintiffs intended to sell to Blenkiron & Co. but Blenkarn fraudulently assumed the position of the buyer. Therefore, an offer to sell to Blenkiron & Co. was knowingly 'accepted' by Blenkarn and there was no contract.

. . . There is a difference between the case where A makes an offer to B in the belief that B is not B but is someone else, and the case where A makes an offer to B in the belief that B is X. In the first case B does in fact receive an offer, even though the offeror does not know that it is to B he is making it, since he believes B to be someone else. In the second case, A does not in truth make any offer to B at all; he thinks B is X, for whom alone the offer is meant. There was an offer intended for and available only to X. B cannot accept it if he knew or ought to have known that it was not addressed to him.

PEARCE LJ: I agree. The question here is whether there was any contract, whether offer and acceptance met. . . .

The real problem in the present case is whether the plaintiffs were in fact intending to deal with the person physically present, who had fraudulently endowed himself with the attributes of some other identity, or whether they were intending only to deal with that other identity. If the former, there was a valid but voidable contract and the property passed. If the latter, there was no contract and the property did not pass. . . .

An apparent contract made orally *inter praesentes* raises particular difficulties. The offer is apparently addressed to the physical person present. Prima facie, he, by whatever name he is called, is the person to whom the offer is made. His physical presence identified by sight and hearing preponderates over vagaries of nomenclature. 'Praesentia corporis tollit errorem nominis' said Lord Bacon (*Law Tracts* (1737), p. 102). Yet clearly, though difficult, it is not impossible to rebut the prima facie presumption that the offer can be accepted by the person to whom it is physically addressed. To take two extreme instances. If a man orally commissions a portrait from some unknown artist who had deliberately passed himself off, whether by disguise or merely by verbal cosmetics, as a famous painter, the impostor could not accept the offer. For though the offer is made to him physically, it is obviously, as he knows, addressed to the famous painter. The mistake in identity on such facts is clear and the nature of the contract makes it obvious that identity was of vital importance to the offeror. At the other end of the scale, if a shopkeeper sells goods in a normal cash transaction to a man who misrepresents himself as being some well-known figure, the transaction will normally be valid. For the shopkeeper was ready to sell goods for cash to the world at large and the particular identity of the purchaser in such a contract was not of sufficient importance to override the physical presence identified by sight and hearing. Thus the nature of the proposed contract must have a strong bearing on the question of whether the intention of the offeror (as understood by his offeree) was to make his offer to some other particular identity rather than to the physical person to whom it was orally offered.

In our case, the facts lie in the debatable area between the two extremes. At the beginning of the negotiations, always an important consideration, the name or personality of the false Hutchinson were of no importance and there was no other identity competing with his physical presence. The plaintiffs were content to sell the car for cash to any purchaser. The contractual conversation was orally addressed to the physical identity of the false Hutchinson. The identity was the man present, and his name was merely one of his attributes. Had matters continued thus, there would clearly have been a valid but voidable contract.

I accept the judge's view that there was no contract at the stage when the man pulled out his cheque book. From a practical point of view negotiations reached an impasse at that stage. For the vendor refused to discuss the question of selling on credit. . . . Payment and delivery still needed to be discussed and the parties would be expecting to discuss them. Immediately they did discuss them it became plain that they were not *ad idem* and that no contract had yet been created. But, even if there had been a concluded agreement before discussion of a cheque, it was rescinded. The man tried to make Miss Ingram take a cheque. She declined and said that the deal was off. He did not demur but set himself to reconstruct the negotiations. For the moment had come, which he must all along have anticipated, as the crux of the negotiations, the vital crisis of the swindle. He wanted to take away the car on credit against his worthless cheque, but she refused. Thereafter, the negotiations were of a different kind from what the vendor had mistakenly believed them to be hitherto. The parties were no longer concerned with a cash sale of goods where the identity of the purchaser was prima facie unimportant. They were concerned with a credit sale in which both parties knew that the identity of the purchaser was of the utmost importance. . . .

NOTES

1. The decision may be explained on policy grounds. Normally the court is concerned to protect the innocent third-party purchaser, but in *Ingram* this third party was a car dealer, and the Court of Appeal may have felt that the old ladies were more in need of protection.
2. Devlin LJ (dissenting) considered that the presumption in face to face contracts had not been rebutted and that this contract was voidable rather than void. The policy issues behind the distinction between void and voidable contracts where identity is in issue were discussed by Devlin LJ.

DEVLIN LJ *dissenting*: There can be no doubt, as all this difference of opinion shows, that the dividing line between voidness and voidability, between fundamental mistake and incidental deceit, is a very fine one. That a fine and difficult distinction has to be drawn is not necessarily any reproach to the law. But need the rights of the parties in a case like this depend on such a distinction? The great virtue of the common law is that it sets out to solve legal problems by the application to them of principles which the ordinary man is expected to recognise as sensible and just; their application in any particular case may produce what seems to him a hard result, but as principles they should be within his understanding and merit his approval. But here, contrary to its habit, the common law, instead of looking for a principle that is simple and just, rests on theoretical distinctions. Why should the question whether the defendant should or should not pay the plaintiff damages for conversion depend upon voidness or voidability, and upon inferences to be drawn from a conversation in which the defendant took no part? The true spirit of the common law is to override theoretical distinctions when they stand in the way of doing practical justice. For the doing of justice, the relevant question in this sort of case is not whether the contract was void or voidable, but which of two innocent parties shall suffer for the fraud of a third. The plain answer is that the loss should be divided between them in such proportion as is just in all the circumstances. If it be pure misfortune, the loss should be borne equally; if the fault or imprudence of either party has caused or contributed to the loss, it should be borne by that party in the whole or in the greater part. In saying this, I am suggesting nothing novel, for this sort of observation has often been made. But it is only in comparatively recent times that the idea of giving to a court power to apportion loss has found a place in our law. I have in mind particularly the Law Reform Acts of 1935, 1943 and 1945, that dealt respectively with joint tortfeasors, frustrated contracts and contributory negligence. These statutes, which I believe to have worked satisfactorily, show a modern inclination towards a decision based on a just apportionment rather than one given in black or in white according to the logic of the law. I believe it would be useful if Parliament were now to consider whether or not it is practicable by means of a similar act of law reform to provide for the victims of a fraud a better way of adjusting their mutual loss than that which has grown out of the common law.

The Law Reform Committee in its Twelfth Report (*Transfer of Title to Chattels*), Cmnd 2958, 1966, had considered the possibility of apportionment in instances of mistake as to identity but considered it impractical. However, the Committee did conclude that fine distinctions had developed which were a reproach to the law and recommended that a contract entered into as a result of a mistake as to identity should be voidable rather than void, thus protecting the innocent purchaser. This recommendation was not implemented although it was clearly supported by Lord Denning in *Lewis* v *Averay*.

Lewis v *Averay*
[1972] 1 QB 198 (CA)

The plaintiff advertised his car for sale. A rogue came to see the car, introduced himself as 'Richard Green' and made the plaintiff believe that he was the well-known film actor Richard Greene (of Robin Hood fame). The rogue said he would like to buy the car and take it away that night. He wrote out a cheque, signing it 'R. A. Green'. The plaintiff asked for proof that he was Richard Greene and the rogue showed him a pass to Pinewood Studios in the name of 'Richard A. Green' bearing a photograph of the rogue and an official stamp. The plaintiff was satisfied and let the rogue have the logbook and the car. The cheque had come from a stolen cheque book and was dishonoured. Meanwhile the rogue sold the car to Averay who bought it in good faith. The plaintiff brought an action against Averay for the return of the car, or its value and damages for conversion. Held: approving *Phillips* v *Brooks Ltd*, the presumption that the plaintiff had concluded a contract with the person physically present had not been rebutted. It was a mistake as to credit-worthiness, rather than identity, which did not render the contract void. Averay had good title to the car.

LORD DENNING MR: The real question in the case is whether on May 8, 1969, there was a contract of sale under which the property in the car passed from Mr Lewis to the rogue. If there was such a contract, then, even though it was voidable for fraud, nevertheless Mr Averay would get a good title to the car. But if there was no contract of sale by Mr Lewis to the rogue—either because there was, on the face of it, no agreement between the parties, or because any apparent agreement was a nullity and void ab initio for mistake, then no property would pass from Mr Lewis to the rogue. Mr Averay would not get a good title because the rogue had no property to pass to him.

. . . Who is entitled to the goods? The original seller? Or the ultimate buyer? The courts have given different answers. In *Phillips* v *Brooks*, the ultimate buyer was held to be entitled to the ring. In *Ingram* v *Little* the original seller was held to be entitled to the car. . . .

It seems to me that the material facts in each case are quite indistinguishable the one from the other. In each case there was, to all outward appearance, a contract: but there was a mistake by the seller as to the identity of the buyer. This mistake was fundamental. In each case it led to the handing over of the goods. Without it the seller would not have parted with them.

. . . [I]t has been suggested that a mistake as to the identity of a person is one thing: and a mistake as to his attributes is another. A mistake as to identity, it is said, avoids a contract: whereas a mistake as to attributes does not. But this is a distinction without a difference. A man's very name is one of his attributes. It is also a key to his identity. If then, he gives a false name, is it a mistake as to his identity? or a mistake as to his attributes? These fine distinctions do no good to the law.

As I listened to the argument in this case, I felt it wrong that an innocent purchaser (who knew nothing of what passed between the seller and the rogue) should have his title depend on such refinements. After all, he has acted with complete circumspection and in entire good faith: whereas it was the seller who let the rogue have the goods and thus enabled him to commit the fraud. I do not, therefore, accept the theory that a mistake as to identity renders a contract void. I think the true principle is that which underlies the decision of this court in *King's Norton Metal Co. Ltd* v *Edridge Merrett & Co. Ltd* (1897) 14 TLR 98 and of Horridge J in *Phillips* v *Brooks* [1919] 2 KB 243, which has stood for these last 50 years. It is this: When two parties have come to a contract—or rather what appears, on the face of it, to be a contract—the fact that one party is mistaken as to the identity of the other does not mean that there is no contract, or that the contract is a nullity and void from the beginning. It only means that the contract is voidable, that is, liable to be set aside at the instance of the mistaken person, so long as he does so before third parties have in good faith acquired rights under it.

Applied to the cases such as the present, this principle is in full accord with the presumption stated by Pearce LJ and also Devlin LJ in *Ingram* v *Little* [1961] 1 QB 31, 61, 66. When a dealing is had between a seller like Mr Lewis and a person who is actually there present before him, then the presumption in law is that there is a contract, even though there is a fraudulent impersonation by the buyer representing himself as a different man than he is. There is a contract made with the very person there, who is present in person. It is liable no doubt to be avoided for fraud, but it is still a good contract under which title will pass unless and until it is avoided. In support of that presumption, Devlin LJ quoted, at p. 66, not only the English case of *Phillips* v *Brooks*, but other cases in the United States where 'the courts hold that if A appeared in person before B, impersonating C, an innocent purchaser from A gets the property in the goods against B.' That seems to me to be right in principle in this country also.

In this case Mr Lewis made a contract of sale with the very man, the rogue, who came to the flat. I say that he 'made a contract' because in this regard we do not look into his intentions, or into his mind to know what he was thinking or into the mind of the rogue. We look to the outward appearances. On the face of the dealing, Mr Lewis made a contract under which he sold the car to the rogue, delivered the car and the logbook to him, and took a cheque in return. The contract is evidenced by the receipts which were signed. It was, of course, induced by fraud. The rogue made false representations as to his identity. But it was still a contract, though voidable for fraud. It was a contract under which this property passed to the rogue, and in due course passed from the rogue to Mr Averay, before the contract was avoided.

Though I very much regret that either of these good and reliable gentlemen should suffer, in my judgment it is Mr Lewis who should do so.

MEGAW LJ: For myself, with very great respect, I find it difficult to understand the basis, either in logic or in practical considerations, of the test laid down by the majority of the court in *Ingram* v *Little* [1961] 1 QB 31. That test is, I think, accurately recorded in the headnote, as follows:

— where a person physically present and negotiating to buy a chattel fraudulently assumed the identity of an existing third person, the test to determine to whom the offer was addressed was how ought the promisee to have interpreted the promise.

The promisee, be it noted, is the rogue. The question of the existence of a contract and therefore the passing of property, and therefore the right of third parties, if this test is correct, is made to depend upon the view which some rogue should have formed, presumably knowing that he is a rogue, as to the state of mind of the opposite party to the negotiation, who does not know that he is dealing with a rogue.

. . . [I]n my view this appeal can be decided on a short and simple point.

. . . The well-known textbook *Cheshire and Fifoot on the Law of Contract* 7th ed. (1969), 213 and 214, deals with the question of invalidity of a contract by virtue of unilateral mistake, and in particular unilateral mistake relating to mistaken identity. The editors describe what in their submission are certain facts that must be established in order to enable one to avoid a contract on the basis of unilateral mistake by him as to the identity of the opposite party. The first of those facts is that at the time when he made the offer he regarded the identity of the offeree as a matter of vital importance. To translate that into the facts of the present case, it must be established that at the time of offering to sell his car to the rogue, Mr Lewis regarded the identity of the rogue as a matter of vital importance. . . . [T]he mistake of Mr Lewis went no further than a mistake as to the attributes of the rogue. It was simply a mistake as to the creditworthiness of the man who was there present and who described himself as Mr Green. . . .

NOTES
1. Lord Denning stressed the need to protect the innocent third party. He saw the third party as being more innocent than the seller, who he said had allowed the rogue to have the goods in the first place and had thus enabled the rogue to commit the fraud. Unlike the position in

Ingram v *Little*, in *Lewis* v *Averay* the seller and innocent third party were on an equal footing so that there was not the same desire to protect the seller.

2. The other factor which has influenced the courts has been the need to ensure the certainty of transactions so that an innocent third party need not find himself in the position of having to return the goods when he purchased in good faith.

It would help matters still further if contracts were always voidable in cases of mistake as to identity, as suggested by Lord Denning, since the present position in itself causes uncertainty.

3. In *Lewis* v *Averay*, Lord Denning stated that there was no distinction between identity and attributes. Arguably a person's identity is made up of his attributes so that this distinction is meaningless.

(ii) Contracts made by written correspondence

There is House of Lords' authority that where a contract is made at a distance identity will be vital so that a mistaken party will intend to deal with the person named in the correspondence.

Cundy v Lindsay
(1878) 3 App Cas 459 (HL)

The plaintiffs, linen manufacturers in Belfast, received a written order for hand-kerchiefs from a rogue, Blenkarn, who gave his address as 37 Wood Street, Cheapside. The name was written to appear as 'Blenkiron & Co.' which was a highly respected firm carrying on business at 123 Wood Street, Cheapside. The plaintiffs had heard of Blenkiron & Co.'s reputation, although they did not know the number in Wood Street from which they carried on business. The plaintiffs sent the goods on credit to 'Messrs Blenkiron & Co., 37 Wood Street'. They were never paid. Blenkarn sold the goods to bona fide purchasers who included the defendants. The plaintiffs brought an action against the defendants for unlawful conversion of the handkerchiefs, which meant that they had to establish that the defendants had not obtained title to them. Held: the contract was void for mistake as to identity.

LORD CAIRNS LC: . . . Was there any contract which, with regard to the goods in question in this case, had passed the property in the goods from the Messrs. Lindsay to Alfred Blenkarn? If there was any contract passing that property, even although, as I have said, that contract might afterwards be open to a process of reduction, upon the ground of fraud, still, in the meantime, Blenkarn might have conveyed a good title for valuable consideration to the present Appellants.

. . . The principal parties concerned, the Respondents and Blenkarn, never came in contact personally—everything that was done was done by writing. What has to be judged of, and what the jury in the present case had to judge of, was merely the conclusion to be derived from that writing, as applied to the admitted facts of the case.

Now, my Lords, discharging that duty and answering that inquiry, what the jurors have found is in substance this: it is not necessary to spell out the words, because the substance of it is beyond all doubt. They have found that by the form of the signatures to the letters which were written by Blenkarn, by the mode in which his letters and his applications to the Respondents were made out, and by the way in which he left uncorrected the mode and form in which, in turn, he was addressed by the Respondents; that by all those means he led, and intended to lead, the Respondents to believe, and they did believe, that the person with whom they were communicating was not Blenkarn, the dishonest and irresponsible man, but was a well known and solvent house of Blenkiron & Co., doing business in the same street. My Lords, those things are found as matters of fact, and they are placed beyond the range of dispute and controversy in the case.

If that is so, what is the consequence? It is that Blenkarn—the dishonest man, as I call him—was acting here just in the same way as if he had forged the signature of Blenkiron & Co., the respectable firm, to the applications for goods, and as if, when, in return, the goods were forwarded and letters were sent, accompanying them, he had intercepted the goods and intercepted the letters, and had taken possession of the goods, and of the letters which were addressed to, and intended for, not himself but, the firm of Blenkiron & Co. Now, my Lords, stating the matter shortly in that way, I ask the question, how is it possible to imagine that in that state of things any contract could have arisen between the Respondents and Blenkarn, the dishonest man? Of him they knew nothing, and of him they never thought. With him they never intended to deal. Their minds never, even for an instant of time rested upon him, and as between him and them there was no *consensus* of mind which could lead to any agreement or any contract whatever. As between him and them there was merely the one side to a contract, where, in order to produce a contract, two sides would be required. With the firm of Blenkiron & Co. of course there was no contract, for as to them the matter was entirely unknown, and therefore the pretence of a contract was a failure.

The result, therefore, my Lords, is this, that your Lordships have not here to deal with one of those cases in which there is *de facto* a contract made which may afterwards be impeached and set aside, on the ground of fraud; but you have to deal with a case which ranges itself under a completely different chapter of law, the case namely in which the contract never comes into existence. My Lords, that being so, it is idle to talk of the property passing. The property remained, as it originally had been, the property of the Respondents, and the title which was attempted to be given to the Appellants was a title which could not be given to them.

NOTES

1. Since the contract was held to be void, the innocent party was the loser.
2. It appears to have been important on the facts that the plaintiffs knew of the existence of Blenkiron & Co so that they were able to show they had mistaken one existing entity for another.

■ QUESTION

Did the plaintiffs send the goods because they thought that the buyer was a highly respected firm and would pay for the goods?

(c) The opportunity presented by *Shogun Finance* v *Hudson*

The Court of Appeal in *Shogun Finance* criticised the law governing mistake as to identity. Brooke LJ referred to the law as 'still in the sorry condition' as when it had been considered by the Law Reform Committee in 1966 and Sedley LJ noted 'the illogical and sometimes barely perceptible distinctions made in earlier decisions' which he acknowledged in some cases represented 'an unarticulated judicial policy on the incidence of loss as between innocent parties'. *Cundy* v *Lindsay*, as a decision of the House of Lords, was recognised by Sedley LJ, as preventing comprehensive adjustment and he noted that Lord Denning had not referred to it in his analysis in *Lewis* v *Averay*. The legal principles were in desperate need of clarification and simplification by the House of Lords. However, whilst their Lordships have provided *some* clarification, the principles are far from simple and an arbitrary distinction between written contracts and face to face dealings has been put on a formal footing.

Shogun Finance Ltd v Hudson
[2003] UKHL 62, [2004] 1 AC 919 (HL)

The rogue had expressed an interest in purchasing a Mitsubishi Shogun car from a motor dealer. The rogue pretended to be a Mr Durlabh Patel, had given Mr Patel's address and had produced Mr Patel's stolen driving licence as proof of his identity. The dealer agreed the price for the car (£22,250) and had then faxed a draft hire purchase agreement to the claimant finance company with a copy of the driving licence. This hire purchase agreement had named Mr Patel as the customer but had been signed by the rogue, forging the signature on Mr Patel's driving licence. The finance company checked Mr Patel's credit rating and approved the finance. The dealer therefore allowed the rogue to take possession of the vehicle whereupon the rogue sold the car to Hudson, a purchaser in good faith, for £17,000. [Note that the dealer sells the car to the finance company which then 'hires' it to the purchaser.]

The finance company brought a claim against the defendant, Hudson, for damages in the tort of conversion and the defendant counterclaimed that he had acquired good title in accordance with section 27 of the Hire Purchase Act 1964. This counterclaim turned on the question of whether the rogue was a 'debtor' under the hire purchase agreement; if so, the defendant would have acquired good title.

The judge at first instance held that the defendant was not a 'debtor' and the majority of the Court of Appeal agreed on the basis that the hire purchase agreement had not been made with the rogue but with Mr Patel, the person whose identity he had taken. The real Mr Patel could not be liable on such an agreement because his signature had been forged. The majority of the Court of Appeal rejected the defendant's alternative argument that this was a face to face contract made between the rogue and the finance company via the dealer as agent, thereby raising the presumption that the finance company intended to deal with the rogue, as the person present. The basis for this rejection was that the dealer was not the agent for the finance company.

On appeal to the House of Lords, Held: dismissing the appeal (3:2; Lords Nicholls and Millett dissenting) that the written agreement was made between the finance company and the real Mr Patel. However, this was a nullity because it had been made without Mr Patel's authority. There was no valid contract between the rogue and the finance company. Accordingly the defendant was not protected by section 27 as he was not the 'debtor'.

The speeches of the majority reveal some differences in reasoning, if not in outcome, although all five Law Lords treat the basic issue as involving offer and acceptance, objectively ascertained.

Lord Hobhouse considered that the case was concerned only with the construction of the written hire purchase agreement. The written contract explicitly named Mr Patel and was described as an offer by Mr Patel to the finance company. Therefore, the finance company's acceptance related to that offer. Only the finance company and Mr Patel could be parties to the agreement. In accordance with the parol evidence rule, extrinsic oral evidence was not admissible to contradict the terms of the writing, e.g. to demonstrate that in accordance with the face to face presumption the rogue was the true 'debtor'.

Lord Walker stated that he was dismissing the appeal for the reasons given by Lord Hobhouse but, unlike Lord Hobhouse, his speech deals with the broader issues arising in the mistake as to identity cases. *Lord Phillips* (also in the majority) considered that the effect of mistake as to identity depended on whether there could be said to be an offer and acceptance. Lords Phillips and Walker drew a distinction between contracts made face to face (which might include telephone dealings, *per* Lord Walker) and contracts made through correspondence. In face to face situations there is said to be a presumption that the offer is intended to be made to the person physically present and therefore that person can accept. It followed that *Ingram* v *Little* was wrongly decided. However, this presumption could not apply to contracts made by means of written documents, including contracts made by post, email, and the present situation. In these cases the offer and acceptance issue turned on the written documents. (Lords Phillips and Walker rejected the opinion of Sedley LJ dissenting in the Court of Appeal that this was a face to face dealing conducted through the dealer as agent for the finance company.)

Lords Nicholls and Millett (dissenting): The dissenting speeches focus on the arbitrary distinction between contracts made by post and face to face dealings. Lords Nicholls and Millett objected to a distinction depending on the mode by which a transaction is completed. They therefore favoured a more general 'dealing' principle to replace the presumption (although this can be seen more clearly in the speech delivered by Lord Millett).

LORD PHILLIPS OF WORTH MATRAVERS:

119   The critical issue in this case is whether a hire-purchase agreement was ever concluded between Shogun and the rogue. If an agreement was concluded, then the rogue was the 'debtor' under section 27 of the 1964 Act and passed good title in the vehicle to Mr Hudson. If no agreement was concluded, then the rogue stole the vehicle by deception and passed no title to Mr Hudson.

'What's in a name?'

120   This area of the law has developed because of confusion about names and it may be helpful at the outset to reflect on the nature of a name. Words in a language have one or more ordinary meaning, which will be known to anyone who speaks that language. Names are not those kind of words. A name is a word, or a series of words, that is used to identify a specific individual. It can be described as a label. Whenever a name is used, extrinsic evidence, or additional information, will be required in order to identify the specific individual that the user of the name intends to identify by the name—the person to whom he intends to attach the label. Almost all individuals have two or more names which they use to identify themselves and where a name is mentioned in a particular context, or a particular milieu, those who hear it may have the additional information that they need to identify to whom the speaker is referring.

121   Where a name appears in a written document, the document itself may contain additional information which will enable the reader to identify the individual to whom the writer intended to refer when he wrote the name.

122   Where a person introduces himself by name to someone, his intention will normally be to tell that person the name that he uses to identify himself. This may also assist that other person to identify him in the future. If a person introduces himself by a false name, that may be because he does not wish to be identified in the future. If a person introduces himself by the name of somebody else, that may be because he wishes the person to whom he introduces himself to believe that he is that other person.

Formation of contract

123   A contract is normally concluded when an offer made by one party ('the offeror') is accepted by the party to whom the offer has been made ('the offeree'). Normally the contract is only concluded when the acceptance is communicated by the offeree to the offeror. A contract will not be concluded unless the parties are agreed as to its material terms. There must be 'consensus ad idem'. Whether the parties have reached agreement on the terms is not determined by evidence of the subjective intention of each party. It is, in large measure, determined by making an objective appraisal of the exchanges between the parties. If an offeree understands an offer in accordance with its natural meaning and accepts it, the offeror cannot be heard to say that he intended the words of his offer to have a different meaning. The contract stands according to the natural meaning of the words used. There is one important exception to this principle. If the offeree knows that the offeror does not intend the terms of the offer to be those that the natural meaning of the words would suggest, he cannot, by purporting to accept the offer, bind the offeror to a contract: *Hartog* v *Colin & Shields* [1939] 3 All ER 566; *Smith* v *Hughes* (1871) LR 6 QB 597. Thus the task of ascertaining whether the parties have reached agreement as to the terms of a contract can involve quite a complex amalgam of the objective and the subjective and involve the application of a principle that bears close comparison with the doctrine of estoppel. Normally, however, the task involves no more than an objective analysis of the words used by the parties. The object of the exercise is to determine what each party *intended*, or must be deemed to have *intended*.

124　The task of ascertaining whether the parties have reached agreement as to the terms of a contract largely overlaps with the task of ascertaining what it is that the parties have agreed. The approach is the same. It requires the construction of the words used by the parties in order to deduce the *intention* of the parties—see Chitty on Contracts, 28th ed (1999), vol 1, p 604, paras 12–042, 12–043 and the cases there cited. This is true, whether the contract is oral or in writing. The words used fall to be construed having regard to the relevant background facts and extrinsic evidence may be admitted to explain or interpret the words used. Equally, extrinsic evidence may be necessary to identify the subject matter of the contract to which the words refer.

125　Just as the parties must be shown to have agreed on the terms of the contract, so they must also be shown to have agreed the one with the other. If A makes an offer to B, but C purports to accept it, there will be no contract. Equally, if A makes an offer to B and B addresses his acceptance to C there will be no contract. Where there is an issue as to whether two persons have reached an agreement, the one with the other, the courts have tended to adopt the same approach to resolving that issue as they adopt when considering whether there has been agreement as to the terms of the contract. The court asks the question whether each *intended*, or must be deemed to have *intended*, to contract with the other. That approach gives rise to a problem where one person is mistaken as to the identity of the person with whom he is dealing, as the cases demonstrate. . . .

The decided cases

126　In *Boulton* v *Jones* (1857) 27 LJ Ex 117 the owner of a shop named Brocklehurst sold his stock-in-trade and assigned his business to the plaintiff. The same day the plaintiff received an order in writing, addressed to Brocklehurst, from the defendant. The defendant had had previous dealings with Brocklehurst and proposed to set off against the price a debt owed by Brocklehurst. The plaintiff supplied the goods and the defendant consumed them. When the plaintiff sent an invoice the defendant denied that he had concluded any contract with him. The court ruled that there was no contract. Pollock CB said, at pp 118–19: 'Now the rule of law is clear, that if you propose to make a contract with A, then B cannot substitute himself for A without your consent and to your disadvantage, securing to himself all the benefit of the contract.' . . .

127　This early case does not demonstrate the full application of the principles that I have set out in relation to formation of contract, although the result accords with them. The focus was, however, on the *intention* of the defendant.

128　In *Hardman* v *Booth* (1863) 1 H & C 803 a fraud was perpetrated by one Edward Gandell who, it seems, carried on business in two capacities: (1) as clerk of a well known firm, Gandell & Co, of which his father was sole proprietor. There he had neither authority to contract nor was held out as having such authority. (2) He had formed a partnership with a man called Todd, which carried on business as Gandell & Todd. He purported to conclude a contract to purchase cloth from the plaintiffs, holding himself out as a member of Gandell & Co. The first instalment of the cloth was delivered to the premises of Gandell & Co and the second instalment was collected by Edward Gandell in a cart owned by Gandell & Co. Edward Gandell took the cloth to the defendant and purported to pledge it to secure a loan to Gandell & Todd. The issue was whether in these circumstances any contract was concluded between the plaintiffs and Gandell & Todd, under which the property in the cloth passed to them. The court held that no contract had been concluded.

129　Once again the court attached critical importance to the intention of the vendors. . . .

130　Martin B, at p 807, emphasised that he had no doubt that the plaintiffs believed 'that they were dealing with Gandell & Co'. Channell B remarked, at p 808: 'I do not think there was a sale to

Gandell & Todd . . . for it is evident that the plaintiffs believed that they were dealing with Gandell & Co . . .' Wilde B's judgment was to similar effect. Thus the court proceeded on the simple premise that there could not be a contract between A and B if A did not intend to contract with B. The courts had not at this time begun to apply an objective test to the question of whether an agreement had been concluded between the parties.

[Lord Phillips then examined *Cundy* v *Lindsay* (1878) 3 App Cas 459, for facts and decision see *page 92*, and concluded:]

133 Here, once again, the focus was on the intention of the offeree. In deciding that his intention was to contract with Blenkiron & Co, the House had regard to the fact that the order was apparently signed 'Blenkiron & Co' and to the fact that the plaintiffs knew of a firm of that name and intended to deal with that firm. Thus extrinsic evidence was admitted in addition to the wording of the order in order to ascertain the intention of the plaintiffs.

[His Lordship then discussed *King's Norton Metal Co Ltd* v *Edridge, Merrett & Co Ltd* (1897) 14 TLR 98, discussed *at page 108 below* and concluded:]

135 This case demonstrates that, if a person describes himself by a false name in contractual dealings, this will not, of itself, prevent the conclusion of a contract by a person who deals with him in that name. A L Smith LJ did not refer to 'intention' in his reported judgment. The result is, however, consistent with the approach to which I have referred in relation to formation of contract. The plaintiffs intended to deal with whoever was using the name of Hallam & Co. Extrinsic evidence was needed to identify who that was but, once Wallis was identified as the user of that name, the party with whom the plaintiffs had contracted was established. They could not demonstrate that their acceptance of the offer was intended for anyone other than Wallis.

136 *Phillips* v *Brooks Ltd* [1919] 2 KB 243 is the first case that involved a face-to-face transaction.

[Lord Phillips set out the facts and noted the passage from the judgment of Horridge J, extracted *at page 87*]

138 *Phillips* v *Brooks Ltd* well illustrates the conundrum that the application of the test of *intention* raises when terms are negotiated between two persons who are face to face. It arises where the two persons, A and B, are not known to each other and where A gives a name which is not his own. If B is unaware of the existence of a third person who bears that name, there will be no problem. B will clearly intend to contract with A, treating the name given by A simply as the label by which A identifies himself. Equally A will know that B intends to contract with him. The problem arises where B is aware of a third person, C, who bears the name falsely adopted by A. In that situation it is B's intention to contract both with A and with C, for he does not distinguish between the two. No sensible answer can be given to the question: does B intend to contract with A or C? Nor can any sensible answer be given to the question: does A believe that B intends to contract with him or with C?

139 Horridge J solved the conundrum by drawing an 'inference' that the plaintiff intended to contract with the rogue, who was present, and not with the individual whose identity the rogue had assumed.

[In relation to *Ingram* v *Little* [1961] 1 QB 31, Lord Phillips noted that:]

147 All three members of the court adopted the approach of identifying the intention of Miss Ingram. The difference between them was as to the manner of application of that approach where an agreement was negotiated face to face. The majority considered that a sensible answer could be given to the question 'with whom did Miss Ingram intend to contract?' as a question of fact. Devlin LJ considered that this question could only be answered by the application of a legal presumption, which would not be rebutted where the only reason for interest in the identity of the contracting party was concern that the contracting party should be creditworthy.

[Lord Phillips then discussed the facts and decision in *Lewis* v *Averay* [1972] 1 QB 198 and the declared preference for *Phillips* v *Brooks* over *Ingram* v *Little*. He noted that:]

152 Lord Denning MR did not apply the approach of attempting to identify the intention of the plaintiff. He proceeded on the simple basis that, to all outward appearances, the plaintiff entered into an agreement with the rogue, with whom he was dealing. Both he and Phillimore LJ considered that the case was on all fours with *Phillips* v *Brooks Ltd*, which had been rightly decided.

153 The difficulty in applying a test of *intention* to the identification of the parties to a contract arises, so it seems to me, only where the parties conduct their dealings in some form of inter-personal contact, and where one purports to have the identity of a third party. There the innocent party will have in mind, when considering with whom he is contracting, both the person with whom he is in contact and the third party whom he imagines that person to be.

154 The same problem will not normally arise where the dealings are carried out exclusively in writing. The process of construction of the written instruments, making appropriate use of extrinsic evidence, will normally enable the court to reach a firm conclusion as to the person with whom a party intends to contract. This was the position in *Boulton* v *Jones* 27 LJ Ex 117, *Cundy* v *Lindsay* 3 App Cas 459 and *King's Norton Metal Co Ltd* v *Edridge, Merrett & Co Ltd* 14 TLR 98. There is a substantial body of authority that demonstrates that the identity of a party to a contract in writing falls to be determined by a process of construction of the putative contract itself.

[Lord Phillips then referred to a number of authorities on the construction of written documents and concluded:]

161 The effect of these authorities is that a person carrying on negotiations in writing can, by describing as one of the parties to the putative agreement an individual who is unequivocally identifiable from that description, preclude any finding that the party to the putative agreement is other than the person so described. The process of construction will lead inexorably to the conclusion that the person with whom the other party intended to contract was the person thus described.

162 That the identification of the parties to a written contract involves construing the contract was the basis of the decision in *Hector* v *Lyons* (1988) 58 P & CR 156. The majority of the Court of Appeal in the present case considered that this decision weighed conclusively in favour of Shogun. *Hector* v *Lyons* involved a claim for specific performance of a contract to buy a house. The plaintiff ('the father') rejoiced in the name Martin Aloysius Handel Hector. He had a son, aged less than 18, more modestly christened Martin Aloysius Hector. The father negotiated the purchase of the house face to face with the defendant, who at all times understood that she was contracting with the father. The father instructed solicitors to draw up the formal contract for exchange. For reasons not apparent he led them to understand that the purchaser was to be his son, and they described the purchaser in the contract as 'Martin Aloysius Hector', understanding that they were thereby identifying the son. The father signed the purchaser's copy of the contract with a signature that differed from his normal signature. . . .

163 The father sought to enforce the contract on the footing that he was the purchaser. The defendant argued that he was not a party to the written contract; the purchaser under that contract was the son. The trial judge found in her favour. The basis upon which he did so was that the solicitors handed over the purchaser's part of the contract as being the document of the son and the signature that it bore purported to be that of the son.

164 In the Court of Appeal counsel for the father argued that the contract had been concluded between the father and the defendant, relying on the line of cases ending with *Lewis* v *Averay* [1972] 1 QB 198. Sir Nicolas Browne-Wilkinson V-C dismissed this argument, at pp 158–159:

In the case of a face-to-face sale, where the sale is over a counter or between two individuals, the law is well established that the mere fact that the vendor V is under a misapprehension as to the identity of the person in front of him does not operate so as to render the contract void for mistake, it being a mere unilateral mistake as to a quality of the purchaser; only in cases where the identity of the purchaser is of direct and important materiality in inducing the vendor to enter into the contract is a mistake of the kind capable of avoiding the contract. With one exception those cases are entirely concerned with transactions between two individuals face to face entering into oral agreement. In my judgement the principle there enunciated has no application to a case such as the present where there is a contract and wholly in writing. There the identity of the vendor and the purchaser is established by the names of the parties included in the written contract. Once those names are there in the contract, the only question for the court is to identify who they are. In the present case the deputy judge has found as a fact that the party named in the written contract was Mr Hector junior. It follows, in my judgment, that in the absence of rectification, which has not been claimed, or Mr Cogley's alternative argument [for the father] based on agency, the only person who can enforce that contract is the party to it, namely Mr Hector junior. He has never at any stage sought to do so. It is for these purposes in my judgment irrelevant whom [the defendant] Mrs Lyons thought she was contracting with: she is entitled to say 'I entered into a contract with the person named in the contract, and nobody else.' As the deputy judge pointed out, if Mrs Lyons had sought to enforce the contract against Mr Hector senior, the position might have been different, in that Mr Hector senior might have estopped himself by his conduct from denying that he was the person named in the contract. But that is quite a different case. . . .

166 . . . While the facts of this decision are not easy to follow, it supports the proposition that the identity of the parties to a contract in writing fall to be determined by a process of construction of the contract.

The result in the present case

167 I have had the advantage of reading in draft the opinions of my noble and learned friends who have sat with me on this appeal. Lord Hobhouse of Woodborough and Lord Walker of Gestingthorpe have concluded that, as the contract was a written document, the identity of the hirer falls to be ascertained by construing that document. Adopting that approach, the hirer was, or more accurately purported to be, Mr Patel. As he had not authorised the conclusion of the contract, it was void.

168 Lord Nicholls of Birkenhead and Lord Millett have adopted a different approach. They point out the illogicality of applying a special approach to face-to-face dealings. What of dealings on the telephone, or by videolink? There also it could be said that each of the parties to the dealings is seeking to make a contract with the other party to the dealings. And this can even be said when the dealings are conducted by correspondence. If A writes to B making an offer and B writes back responding to that offer, B is intending to contract with the person who made that offer. If a contract is concluded in face-to-face dealings, notwithstanding that one party is masquerading as a third party, why should the result be different when the dealings are by letter?

169 Lord Nicholls of Birkenhead and Lord Millett propose an elegant solution to this illogicality. Where two individuals *deal with each other*, by whatever medium, and agree terms of a contract, then a contract will be concluded between them, notwithstanding that one has deceived the other into thinking that he has the identity of a third party. In such a situation the contract will be voidable but not void. While they accept that this approach cannot be reconciled with *Cundy* v *Lindsay* 3 App Cas 459, they conclude that *Cundy* v *Lindsay* was wrongly decided and should no longer be followed.

170 While I was strongly attracted to this solution, I have found myself unable to adopt it. *Cundy* v *Lindsay* exemplifies the application by English law of the same approach to identifying the parties as is applied to identifying the terms of the contract. In essence this focuses on deducing the intention of the parties from their words and conduct. Where there is some form of personal contact between individuals who are conducting negotiations, this approach gives rise to problems. In such a situation I would favour the application of a strong presumption that each intends to contract with the other, with whom he is dealing. Where, however, the dealings are exclusively conducted in writing, there is no scope or need for such a presumption. This can be illustrated by a slight adaption of the facts of the present case. Assume that the rogue had himself filled in the application form and sent it and a photocopy of Mr Patel's driving licence to Shogun. Assume further that he had been authorised to do so by Mr Patel. There can be no doubt that a contract would have been concluded between Shogun and Mr Patel. Mr Patel would have intended to contract with Shogun; Shogun would have intended to contract with Mr Patel; and this would have been demonstrated by the application form.

171   Assume now that the rogue had wrongly understood that he had been requested by Mr Patel to fill in and submit the application form on his behalf, but in fact had no authority to do so. In this situation, according to established principles of the law of agency, an apparent contract would have been concluded between Shogun and Mr Patel but, being concluded without the latter's authority, it would be a nullity. Shogun might have a claim against the rogue for breach of warranty of authority, but could not have demonstrated that a contract had been concluded with the rogue.

172   Turning to the true position—that the rogue knew he had no authority to conclude a contract in the name of Mr Patel, but fraudulently wished to induce Shogun to believe that they were entering into such a contract—I do not see by what legal principle this change in the mental attitude of the rogue could result in a binding contract being concluded with him.

173   The position is not, of course, as simple as that. Negotiations between the rogue and Shogun were not conducted exclusively by written correspondence. They were conducted with the aid of the dealer and the use of fax and telephone communications. Acceptance of the offer was conveyed by telephone via the dealer—and this might have been capable of concluding a contract, notwithstanding that clause 1 of the standard terms provided for acceptance by signature: see the discussion in Chitty on Contracts, 28th ed, vol 1, p 117, para 2–062. Sedley LJ considered that the dealings were analogous to face-to-face dealings and that the dealer was, in effect, the face of Shogun Finance Ltd. He considered that the face-to-face presumption should be applied.

174   The majority of the Court of Appeal considered that *Hector* v *Lyons* 58 P & CR 156 required them to determine the identity of the parties to the putative contract as a simple question of construction. On that basis they concluded that the putative hirer was Mr Patel and that, as the apparent contract was concluded without his authority, it was a nullity.

175   Dyson LJ considered what the result would have been had the negotiations been treated as face-to-face. He concluded [2002] QB 834, 853–4, paras 45–46 that the presumption would have been displaced by the importance that Shogun attached to the identity of the person with whom they were contracting.

176   My Lords, I started this opinion by quoting Gresson P's remark (*Fawcett* v *Star Car Sales Ltd* [1960] NZLR 406, 413) that the difficulty in a case such as this is a proper assessment of the facts rather than an assessment of the law. I have not found the assessment of the law easy, but nor is the application of the law to the facts. Shogun's representatives were aware of the presence of the prospective hirer in the dealer's showrooms in Leicester. To an extent the dealings were inter-personal through the medium of the dealer. Should one treat them as comparable to face-to-face dealings and conclude that there was a presumption that Shogun intended to contract with the man with whom they were dealing? Should one treat the written agreement as no more than peripheral to the dealings and conclude that it does not override that presumption? I have concluded that the answer to these questions is 'no'.

177   . . . Shogun put in place a system for concluding contracts that required both regulated and unregulated agreements to be entered into in writing in a form which provided essential information, including the identity of the parties to the agreement.

178   These considerations lead me to conclude that the correct approach in the present case is to treat the agreement as one concluded in writing and to approach the identification of the parties to that agreement as turning upon its construction. The particulars given in the agreement are only capable of applying to Mr Patel. It was the intention of the rogue that they should identify Mr Patel as

the hirer. The hirer was so identified by Shogun. Before deciding to enter into the agreement they checked that Mr Patel existed and that he was worthy of credit. On that basis they decided to contract with him and with no one else. Mr Patel was the hirer under the agreement. As the agreement was concluded without his authority, it was a nullity. The rogue took no title under it and was in no position to convey any title to Mr Hudson.

179   For these reasons I would dismiss this appeal.

LORD MILLETT (dissenting):

56   My Lords, A makes an offer to B. B accepts it, believing that he is dealing with C. A knows of B's mistake, and may even have deliberately caused it. What is the result of the transaction? Is there a contract at all? There is obviously no contract with C, who is not a party to the transaction and knows nothing of it. But is there a contract with A? And if so is it void or merely voidable?

57   Generations of law students have struggled with this problem. They may be forgiven for thinking that it is contrived by their tutors to test their mettle. After all, the situation seems artificial and is one which is seldom likely to arise in practice, at least in the absence of fraud. Unfortunately fraudulent impersonation is not at all uncommon today. The growth in the number of credit transactions, often entered into electronically between persons unknown to each other, has led to a surge in what has been called 'theft of identity', that is the fraudulent assumption of another's identity by a customer in order to have the wrong account debited or to misdirect inquiries into his own creditworthiness. In the classic case A, fraudulently masquerading as C, buys goods on credit from B; B, having conducted appropriate checks to satisfy himself that C is worthy of credit and believing A to be C, lets A have possession of the goods; and A thereupon sells the goods to D, an unsuspecting purchaser, before disappearing without paying for them. Who is to bear the loss? That depends on whether D, who has paid for the goods, has obtained title to them, for if not then B can reclaim them. But D will have obtained title only if A was able to transfer title to him, and this turns on whether the transaction between A and B resulted in a voidable contract for the purchase of the goods by A (which B will have been unable to avoid in time) or no contract at all.

58   The problem is sometimes mentioned in the textbooks in the section which deals with the formation of contract, where the question is whether a contract has been concluded; but it is more usually dealt with in the section which is concerned with the effect of mistake and in particular 'mistaken identity', where the question is said to turn on whether A's identity is (i) 'fundamental' (in which case the contract is completely void) or (ii) 'material' but not 'fundamental' (in which case the contract is merely voidable). In his dissenting judgment in *Ingram v Little* [1961] 1 QB 31, 64 Devlin LJ distinguished between the two questions and observed that it was easy to fall into error if one did not begin with the first question, whether there is sufficient correlation between offer and acceptance to bring a contract into existence. But if there is, I question whether the contract should be held to be void for mistake rather than merely voidable.

59   As I have said, the situation is seldom likely to arise in practice in the absence of fraud, and where the fraud is not directed to the identity of the offeror the contract is only voidable, not void, for the victim of deception ought to be able to elect to affirm the contract if he chooses to do so. It seems anomalous that a mistake which is induced by fraud should have a less vitiating effect than one which is not; and it is difficult to see why a mistake induced by fraud should make a contract altogether void if it is a mistake as to the offeror's identity (whatever that may mean) and not if it is a mistake as to some other attribute of his such as his creditworthiness which may be equally or more material.

60   As Treitel observes (The Law of Contract, 10th ed (1999), p 277) it is often difficult to say precisely what mistake has been made and, even when this is clear, it is often difficult to say whether it should be classified as a mistake of identity or of attribute. As between A and B themselves, of course, it does not normally matter whether the contract is void or merely voidable; it obviously cannot be enforced by A against B's wishes in either case. The question usually assumes importance only where an innocent third party is involved, and then it is critical. Under the law as it stands at present, his title depends on whether the fraudster obtained the goods in his own name by means of a false or forged credit reference or in the name of another by means of a genuine reference relating to that other. This is indefensible. I take the view that the law should if at all possible favour a solution which protects innocent third parties by treating the contract as voidable rather than void, whether for fraud or for mistake.

61   My Lords, I think that the time has come to follow the lead given by Lord Denning MR more than 30 years ago in *Lewis* v *Averay* [1972] 1 QB 198. He roundly rejected the theory that if a party is *mistaken* as to the identity of the person with whom he is contracting there is no contract, or that if there is a contract it is null and void so that no property can pass under it: see pp 206–7. He thought that the doctrine, derived from the writings of Pothier, should not be admitted as part of English law but should be 'dead and buried'. As he observed, it gives rise to fine distinctions which do no good to the law, and it is unjust that an innocent third party, who knows nothing of what passed between the rogue and his vendor, should have his title depend on such refinements.

62   But it is still necessary to answer the logically anterior and more difficult question: does the transaction result in the formation of a contract between A and B? There is clearly a transaction between them, for B has let A have possession of the goods and take them away, usually with the intention that he should be free to deal with them as owner. But is the transaction contractual?

63   It is trite law, as Devlin LJ explained in the passage immediately following that cited above, that before a contract can come into existence there must be offer and acceptance, and these must correspond. The offer must be addressed to the offeree, either as an individual or as a member of a class or of the public. The acceptance must come from one who is so addressed and must itself be addressed to the offeror. It is not possible in law for a person to accept an offer made to someone else; or to intercept an acceptance of someone else's offer and treat it as an acceptance of his own.

64   This is usually straightforward enough, at least in the absence of fraud. As my noble and learned friend, Lord Phillips of Worth Matravers, observes, there is normally no difference between the identity of the person to whom the offer or acceptance is directed and the person for whom it is intended. But what if, by reason of fraud, the two are not the same? What if A, posing as C, makes an offer to B which B purports to accept? B *directs* his acceptance to A, but *intends* it for C. It does not help to substitute the question: 'To whom was B's acceptance made?' This merely raises the question: 'What do you mean by "made"?'

65   The outcome is said to depend on B's intention objectively ascertained, and this is usually treated as if it were a straightforward question of fact to be determined on the evidence. In *Ingram* v *Little* [1961] 1 QB 31 Pearce LJ said, at p 61, that 'Each case must be decided on its own facts.' This is singularly unhelpful, since it involves asking: did B intend to contract with A believing him to be C? Or with C believing him to be A? The question is meaningless. As Devlin LJ pointed out in *Ingram* v *Little*, at p 65:

> If Miss Ingram had been asked whether she intended to contract with the man in the room or with P G M Hutchinson, the question could have no meaning for her, since she believed them both to be one and the same . . .

66   In this situation the courts have distinguished between transactions entered into in writing and transactions entered into orally between parties who are in the presence of each other. In the former case B's intention is ascertained by construing the description of the counterparty in the contract. This naturally identifies C, the person whose identity A has fraudulently assumed, and (provided that C actually exists) invariably leads to the conclusion that there is no counterparty and therefore no contract. In the latter case, the courts have adopted a different approach. They have introduced a rebuttable presumption that, where parties deal with each other face-to-face, each of them intends to contract with the physical person to whom he addresses the words of contract. Unless the presumption is rebutted, this must lead to the conclusion that there is a contract with the impostor.

67   I do not find this satisfactory. What evidence is sufficient to rebut the presumption? As Devlin LJ stressed, it cannot be rebutted by piling up evidence that B would never have accepted the offer if he had not thought that it had been made by C. Such evidence merely shows that the deception was

material; it does not establish the identity of B's counterparty. There might perhaps be something to be said for making the presumption conclusive. . . .

68   But the real objection to the present state of the law, in my view, is that the distinction between the face-to-face contract and other contracts is unrealistic. . . . My difficulty is that I cannot see that there is any difference in principle between the two situations when it comes to identifying B's counterparty. In both cases B's acceptance is directed to the impostor but intended for the person whose identity he has assumed. . . .

69   In *Ingram* v *Little* [1961] 1 QB 31 Devlin LJ said, at p 66, that 'the presumption that a person is intending to contract with the person to whom he is actually addressing the words of contract seems to me to be a simple and sensible one . . .' I respectfully agree. But why should it be adopted only in the case of a contract entered into between persons who deal in the physical presence of each other? If the offeree's words of acceptance are taken to be addressed to the physical person standing in his presence who made the offer, what is the position where they deal with each other by telephone? Is the disembodied voice to be equated with physical presence? Is it sufficient that the parties are in the hearing of each other? Does it make a difference if the dealing is by televisual link, so that the parties are in the hearing and sight but not the presence of each other? New means of communication make the distinction untenable.

70   But in truth the distinction was always unsound. If the offeree's words of acceptance are taken to be addressed to the physical person standing in his presence who made the offer, why is the contract entered into by correspondence different? Why is the offeree's letter of acceptance not taken to be addressed to the physical person who made the written offer which he is accepting? The offeree addresses the offeror by his assumed name in both cases. Why should this be treated as decisive in the one case and disregarded in the other? Indeed, the correlation between offer and acceptance is likely to be greater in the case of a contract entered into by correspondence, since the offeree's letter of acceptance will either be sent to the impostor at his own address or be delivered to him personally and it will almost certainly contain internal references to his offer.

71   In my opinion there are only two principled solutions to the problem. The law must give preference, either to the person for whom the offer or acceptance is intended, or to the person to whom it is directed, and must do so in all cases as a matter of law. The difficulty is in deciding which solution should be adopted, for there is much to commend each of them.

72   The first solution, which gives preference to the person for whom the offer or acceptance is intended, possibly accords more closely to the existing authorities, which treat the face-to-face transaction as an exception to the general rule, and with the decision in *Cundy* v *Lindsay* 3 App Cas 459, the only case on the subject which has come before the House. It also accords more closely with the parties' subjective intentions, for B intends to deal with C, especially if he has checked his creditworthiness, and not with A, of whom he has never heard; while A has no intention of being bound by contract at all. From his point of view the supposed contract is merely a pretence to enable him to get hold of goods without paying for them. He does not need a contract, for he is content with possession without title . . . .

73   The strongest argument in favour of this solution, I suppose, is that it could be said to be based on the parties' own assessment of what they mean by the counterparty's 'identity'. Ultimately this must refer to a physical person, but a physical person can only be identified by describing his or her attributes. For this purpose it is customary to refer to a person's name and address, which are usually though not always unique to one person. But names are merely identifying labels and can be assumed without any intention to deceive. A person is free to adopt whatever name suits his fancy, and may validly contract under an alias. Even if he has assumed a false name for the sole purpose of deceiving the counterparty, there is a contract so long, at least, as there is no real person of that name: see *King's Norton Metal Co Ltd* v *Edridge, Merrett & Co Ltd* 14 TLR 98.

74   But as Treitel observes (The Law of Contract, 10th ed, p 277) a person may be identified by reference to any one of his attributes. He may be identified as 'the person in the room', 'the person who spoke on the telephone', 'the person who appended the illegible signature', 'the writer of the letter under reply', or 'the person who made the offer'; but he may also be identified, and sometimes more relevantly, as 'the person whose creditworthiness has been checked and found to be satis-factory'. Any of these may be the means of identifying a unique person. An automated telling machine is programmed to identify a customer by a combination of a PIN number and a number encrypted on the card which is inserted into the machine. In an increasingly electronic age we are accustomed to identifying ourselves by PIN numbers and passwords; the need to eliminate fraud may in time cause us to identify ourselves by retinal imagery, which at least has the advantage of being a feature of the physical body. But even in the case of a credit card transaction there is an ambiguity. Is the customer to be identified as the person who produces the card? Or as the person whose card is produced? The whole point of a credit card fraud is that the goods should be supplied to the person who produces the card while the cost is debited to the account of the person whose card is produced.

75   Given the equivocal nature of a person's 'identity', there is something to be said for selecting those aspects of the offeror's identity which are material in causing the other party to accept the offer. In the present case, for example, Mr Patel's name, address and date of birth had no intrinsic relevance in themselves. The claimant would have entered into the transaction with anyone, what-ever his name and address or date of birth, so long as it was satisfied that he was worthy of credit. Mr Patel's personal details were merely the information which enabled it to conduct inquiries into the credit of the person it assumed to be its customer. It makes commercial sense to treat a contract made in these circumstances as purporting to be made between the finance company and the subject of its inquiries rather than with the person who merely produced the information necessary to enable it to make them.

76   Nevertheless I have come to the conclusion that it is the second solution which ought to be adopted. All the considerations which I have mentioned, and which seem to favour the first solution, when properly analysed go to the mechanics of the deception and its materiality rather than to the identity of the offeror. They ought to come into play when consideration is given to the second question, whether the contract is voidable, rather than to the first, whether there is sufficient correlation between offer and acceptance ('consensus an idem') to bring a contract into existence. Until the fraud is exposed and it is discovered that A is *not* C, the existence of a contract is not in doubt. The fraud is relevant to the question whether the contract is enforceable against B rather than its existence.

[Lord Millett then examined *King's Norton Metal Co. Ltd* v *Edridge, Merrett & Co Ltd* (1897) 14 TLR 98, discussed *at page 108*]

79   The typical fraudulent credit card transaction is also illuminating. There is clearly a transac-tion with the impostor who produces the card and who receives cash or goods (say a cinema ticket) in exchange. If the transaction is contractual in nature (as in the case of the cinema ticket) why should the transaction be thought to be with one person and the contract with another? There is only one transaction whether the party who parts with the goods debits the right account or is deceived into debiting the wrong one. Where cash is extracted from an ATM the fraud is possible because the machine is programmed to supply the cash to the person who produces the card and to debit the account of the person whose card is produced. In the same way the staff who handled the transaction in the present case on behalf of the claimant were instructed (programmed) to obtain the customer's personal details, run credit checks on the person whose details were produced, and authorise the dealer to deliver possession of the vehicle to the person who produced them. . . .

81   In my opinion, once one accepts that there are two questions involved: (i) did a contract come into existence at all? and (ii) if so was the contract vitiated by fraud or mistake? there is only one principled conclusion. Whatever the medium of communication, a contract comes into exist-ence if, on an objective appraisal of the facts, there is sufficient correlation between offer and acceptance to make it possible to say that the impostor's offer has been accepted by the person to whom it was addressed. While a person cannot intercept and accept an offer made to some one else, he should normally be treated as intending to contract with the person with whom he is dealing. Provided that the offer is made to him, then whether his acceptance of the offer is obtained by deception or mistake and whether his mistake is as to the identity of the offerer or some material attribute of his, the transaction should result in a contract, albeit one which is voidable.

82   This rule is easy to apply and accords with principle by distinguishing between the formation of a contract as a question of fact to be determined objectively and the consequences of mistake or fraud which depend on its effect on the mind of the person affected. It avoids undesirable refinements and gives a measure of protection to innocent third parties. Of course, someone has to bear the loss where there is fraud, but it is surely fairer that the party who was actually swindled and who had an opportunity to uncover the fraud should bear the loss rather than a party who entered the picture only after the swindle had been carried out and who had none. In the present case, the claimant could easily have exposed the fraud by writing to Mr Patel, whose address it had been given, and asking him to confirm his intention to proceed with the proposed transaction. If it had been one for which statute required a cooling-off period, it no doubt would have done.

83   In the Court of Appeal [2002] QB 834 both Sedley LJ (who dissented) and Brooke LJ, at p 855, para 51, expressed disquiet at 'the sorry condition' of the law. In the former's view, with which I agree, the decision in *Cundy* v *Lindsay* 3 App Cas 459 stands in the way of a coherent development of this branch of the law. We have the opportunity to restate the law, and cannot shirk the duty of putting it on a basis which is both just and principled, even if it means deciding that we should no longer follow a previous decision of the House.

84   We cannot leave the law as it is. It is neither fair nor principled, and not all the authorities from which it is derived can be reconciled; some, at least, must be overruled if it is to be extricated from the present quagmire. If the law is to be rationalised and placed on a proper footing, the formulation which I have proposed has the merit of according with the recommendations made in the Twelfth Report of the Law Reform Committee on the Transfer of Title to Chattels (Cmnd 2958) and in Anson's Law of Contract, 28th ed, p 332. It would also bring English law into line with the law both in the United States and in Germany.

[Lord Millett then examined the law in the United States and Germany and continued:]

87   Where does this leave the authorities? Most of those which are concerned with face-to-face transactions can stand with the exception of the decision of the majority of the Court of Appeal in *Ingram* v *Little* [1961] 1 QB 31, which is inconsistent with *Lewis* v *Averay* [1972] 1 QB 198 and should be overruled. I would confirm the decision in *Phillips* v *Brooks Ltd* [1919] 2 KB 243, 246–247 where Horridge J held that the shopkeeper had

> contracted to sell and deliver [the ring] to the person who came into his shop . . . who obtained the sale and delivery by means of the false pretence that he was Sir George Bullough . . . [The shopkeeper's] intention was to sell to the person present, and identified by sight and hearing . . .

In my opinion the judge's reasoning cannot be faulted. He distinguished between the two questions, and treated the identity of the purchaser as a question of fact to be determined objectively and without regard to the evidence that the shopkeeper had no intention of selling the goods to anyone other than Sir George Bullough.

[Lord Millett then reviewed more authorities, including *Hardman* v *Booth* (1863) 1 H & C 803, discussed by Lord Phillips, *page 96*]

90   The principal obstacle which has prevented the courts from rationalising this branch of the law has been *Cundy* v *Lindsay* 3 App Case 459, a decision of this House . . .

[After reviewing the facts and speeches in this case, see *page 92*, Lord Millett continued:]

93 In my view the proper conclusion on these facts is that the plaintiffs contracted with Blenkarn in the mistaken belief, induced by his fraud, that they were dealing with Blenkiron & Co, and that the resulting contract was voidable for fraud. If the plaintiffs' subjective state of mind, induced by the fraud, is put on one side, there is no justification for the question-begging assumption that the plaintiffs' letter of acceptance was directed to Blenkiron & Co and that it was the name which was right and the address which was wrong. Nor is there any justification for the suggestion that the signature was a forgery. Blenkarn, who signed the letter, did not claim that it was someone else's signature; he acknowledged and asserted that it was his own. Even those who consider that the case was rightly decided concede that the rogue could have been sued for the price of the goods: see Treitel, The Law of Contract, p 284. But that presupposes that there was sufficient correlation between offer and acceptance to bring a contract into existence, albeit one which was void (or voidable) at the instance of the party deceived. Yet this was the very proposition which the House rejected.

94 The case can usefully be contrasted with *Boulton* v *Jones* (1857) 2 H & N 564, which falls on the other side of the line and was in my opinion rightly decided.

[For facts see *page 96*]

97 The contractual claim arising from the defendant's original order failed because, objectively speaking, there was no correlation between offer and acceptance. This is the same ground as that which was later to form the basis of the decision in *Cundy* v *Lindsay* 3 App Cas 459 but the facts of the two cases are very different. In *Boulton* v *Jones* 2 H & N 564 the goods were ordered from Brocklehurst but supplied and invoiced by Boulton; the acceptance did not correspond with the offer. In *Cundy* v *Lindsay* the goods were ordered by Blenkarn posing as Blenkiron & Co and supplied and invoiced to him in that name. Outwardly the acceptance did correspond with the offer. Objectively speaking there was consensus ad idem, though this was vitiated by the fraud which produced it. . . .

103 My Lords, the identification of the parties to a written instrument is, . . . only partly a question of construction. That is the first step in the process, and it will often be enough. It would have been enough in *Boulton* v *Jones* 2 H & N 564 if the court had accepted the submission that the order was addressed to the proprietor of the shop for the time being and not to Mr Brocklehurst personally. But once it is established that the person whose name and other personal details are stated in the contract and the person who stated them and signed the contract are not the same, the question immediately arises: which of them should be treated as the counterparty? Do the name and other details included in the contract refer to the person to whom they belong or to the impostor who included them in order to identify himself? This is not simply a question of construction. It is partly a question of fact and partly a question of law. To say, as my noble and learned friend, Lord Hobhouse of Woodborough, does, that it is a question of construction which admits of only one answer, with respect simply begs the question.

104 How should the question be answered in the present case? The case is not unlike *Hector* v *Lyons* 58 P & CR 156 with the important difference that in the present case the deception was material and induced the making of the contract. If there was a contract with the rogue, it was voidable for fraud.

105 But was there such a contact [sic] at all? The contact [sic] came into being when the claimant executed its part of the agreement. The two parts corresponded in every material particular. They made it clear that the hirer was the person named on the front of the document and who had signed the document. This appeared to be a Mr Durlabh Patel, with an address in Leicester, whose personal details were given. But in fact it was not Mr Durlabh Patel at all. He knew nothing of the transaction and his driving licence had been stolen. The person who identified himself as Mr Durlabh Patel, provided Mr Durlabh Patel's personal details, and signed the document in Mr Durlabh Patel's name was not Mr Durlabh Patel but an impostor.

106 The object of the deception was to misdirect the claimant's credit inquiries. In this it succeeded. Having satisfied itself that Mr Durlabh Patel, whom it believed to be its customer, was worthy of credit, it accepted the offer which the impostor had made, signed its part of the agreement, and authorised the dealer to deliver possession of the car to his customer as hirer under the agreement.

107 But who was his customer? It was not Mr Durlabh Patel. In my opinion it was plainly the impostor. Any other conclusion would mean that the dealer parted with the vehicle to the impostor without authority and would, presumably, be liable in conversion if the vehicle proved to be irrecoverable. This is far removed from reality. The claimant and the dealer both believed that the customer who was hiring the car and Mr Durlabh Patel were one and the same; but the claimant did not make that a condition of the dealer's authority to part with the car. From first to last it believed that the impostor who attended the dealer's showroom, gave his name as Mr Durlabh Patel, and signed the agreement in that name, was indeed Mr Durlabh Patel; in that belief it entered into a hiring agreement and authorised the dealer to deliver possession of the car to the customer who had so identified himself. In my opinion, the claimant not only took a credit risk, but also took the risk that the customer who was hiring the car was not Mr Durlabh Patel and that its credit inquiries had been fraudulently misdirected. I would hold that there was a hiring, and the impostor was the hirer.

108 This conclusion involves a departure from *Cundy* v *Lindsay* 3 App Cas 459, a decision of this House which has stood for more than 120 years. But its reasoning is unsound. It is vitiated by its subjective approach to the formation of contract and the necessary correlation between offer and acceptance; which may be why textbook writers treat it as an example of unilateral mistake even though this was not the basis on which it was decided. For the same reason it cannot be regarded as authoritative on the question whether a contract otherwise properly entered into is void for mistake rather than voidable. It has had an unfortunate influence on the development of the law, leading to an unprincipled distinction between face-to-face transactions and others and the indefensible conclusion that an innocent purchaser's position depends on the nature of the mistake of a third party or the precise mechanics of the fraud which had been perpetrated on him. In my view it should now be discarded and the law put on a simpler and more principled and defensible basis.

109 In my opinion only the decision in *Cundy* v *Lindsay* stands in the way of a rational and coherent restatement of the law. My noble and learned friend, Lord Phillips of Worth Matravers, has expressed the view that the conclusion to which Lord Nicholls and I have come conflicts not only with that case but with the approach in almost all the numerous cases which he has cited. If they had preceded *Cundy* v *Lindsay*, that would be a strong reason for not adopting it. But they were merely following a decision of this House by which they were bound. Far from applying it generally, they attempted to distinguish it by carving out an unprincipled exception from it which Lord Nicholls has shown cannot be supported. While departing from *Cundy* v *Lindsay* would make obsolete the reasoning in those cases, dictated as it was by that decision, it would undermine the actual decision in very few cases. There is no long line of authority to be overruled. Indeed, only two cases need to be overruled; and neither of them can be supported even on the view that *Cundy* v *Lindsay* was rightly decided.

110 In my opinion *Cundy* v *Lindsay* 3 App Cas 459 should no longer be followed and *Ingram* v *Little* [1961] 1 QB 31 and *Hector* v *Lyons* 58 P & CR 156 should be overruled. I would allow the appeal.

NOTES

1. Despite the fundamental difference in approach between the majority and minority speeches, there is a degree of unanimity on the application of the presumption in face to face dealings that there is an intention to deal with the person physically present. It follows that *Ingram* v *Little* should not be followed.

2. The minority approach involves two steps (or questions). The first step is to determine the existence of a contract. The second step is then to assess the effect of the fraud; this relates to the enforceability of the contract as fraud negatives the rights which would normally follow from contract. Thus, on the minority view, there was a contract between the finance company and the rogue because the car was being sold to the person physically present, i.e. the mistaken party is treated as possessing an intention to sell to that person and consents to the contract. The fact that this contract was the result of a fraud could not affect the formation of

the contract itself, although it would render the contract voidable. By comparison the approach of Lords Phillips and Walker focuses only on the question of agreement and this is determined by asking whether the parties intended to deal with one another, as judged by their words and conduct. It is arguable that the majority view fails to place sufficient emphasis on the fraud.

3. Although Lord Hobhouse clearly takes the view that extrinsic evidence is not generally admissible (absent ambiguity or agency), it is far from clear that Lord Phillips felt himself to be similarly restricted by the written document. See [120]–[122]. However, the evidence of subsequent case law is that a strict interpretation will be taken on construction and extrinsic evidence, see the decision of the Court of Appeal in *Dumford Trading AG* v *OAO Atlantrybflot* [2005] EWCA Civ 24, [2005] 1 Lloyd's Rep 289, and especially comments of Rix LJ at [36].

4. The result of the majority speeches is that finance companies granting hire purchase facilities to car buyers are given protection against the consequences of fraud. If it were conceivable that they might end up in a position of losing both the car and the finance despite having carried out credit checks, it might prove to be a disincentive to lending in such circumstances, especially given the rise in cases of identity fraud. Thus, the primacy of the written document ensures that this possibility is avoided. This position contrasts with the view taken by Sedley LJ in the Court of Appeal who considered that the finance company had agreed to extend credit of over £20,000 'in a matter of minutes', i.e. it was a question of business judgment.

   There will always be policy considerations when deciding which of two innocent parties should be responsible for the fraud of a third and, whereas Lord Denning — and the minority in *Shogun* — clearly felt that the 'degrees of innocence' position favours the innocent third party purchaser, the majority position results in a distinction based on whether there is a written contract or whether the parties are dealing in a face to face situation. However, in many situations (outside the context of regulated credit agreements) it may be a matter of chance whether there is a written document or oral contract.

5. See Chandler & Devenney 'Mistake as to Identity and the Threads of Objectivity' (2004) 1 JOR 7 and Macmillan (2004) 120 LQR 369.

■ QUESTIONS

1. What would the position be if there are written documents but the contract is the result of face to face dealing?

2. What would the position be in face to face dealings where the rogue impersonates a person who is known to the mistaken party?

3. How can the decision in *King's Norton Metal Co. Ltd* v *Edridge, Merrett & Co. Ltd* (1897) 14 TLR 98, be explained?

King's Norton Metal Co. Ltd v Edridge, Merrett & Co. Ltd
(1897) 14 TLR 98 (CA)

The plaintiffs received a letter purporting to come from Hallam & Co. in Sheffield. The letter heading depicted a large factory and included a statement that the company had depots and agencies at Belfast, Lille, and Ghent. Hallam & Co. requested a quotation for brass rivet wire, which the plaintiffs sent. Hallam & Co. then sent a written order for the goods. The goods were dispatched to them but never paid for. A rogue named Wallis had in fact fraudulently used the name Hallam & Co. to obtain the goods, and had then sold the goods to the defendants who were innocent purchasers. The plaintiffs brought a damages action for conversion of the wire and alleged that they intended to deal only with Hallam & Co. and had never heard of Wallis. Held: this was not a case of mistaking one person for another because there was only one person, and the plaintiffs intended to deal with the writer of the letters whoever it was. Accordingly, a contract had come into existence between the plaintiffs and Wallis, although it was voidable for fraud.

The report refers to the judgment of A. L. Smith LJ.

> . . . The question was, With whom, upon this evidence, which was all one way, did the plaintiffs contract to sell the goods? Clearly with the writer of the letters. If it could have been shown that there was a separate entity called Hallam and Co. and another entity called Wallis then the case might have come within the decision in *Cundy* v *Lindsay* (1878) 3 App Cas 459. In his opinion there was a contract by the plaintiffs with the person who wrote the letters by which the property passed to him. There was only one entity, trading it might be under an alias, and there was a contract by which the property passed to him.

This is a contract contained in written documents rather than a face to face contract and was bound to cause difficulties for the majority approach. Lord Phillips (at [135]) concluded that 'the plaintiff intended to deal with whoever was using the name Hallam & Co. Extrinsic evidence was needed to identify who that was but, once Wallis was identified as the user of that name, the party with whom the plaintiffs had contracted was established'. Thus, the party named must actually exist if the name in the written document is to be conclusive. However, as Lord Millett stated in *Shogun Finance* v *Hudson*, the non-existence of another entity seems relevant to the fraud rather than to the formation of the contract so that the result in the case (voidable for fraud) would be correct on the minority analysis. He stated:

> **78**   It is unclear whether it would have made a difference if, unknown to the plaintiffs, there had been an entity called Hallam and Co; or if to the knowledge of both parties there were many such entities, as in the cases where a man used to book a hotel room for himself and a girlfriend under a common but fictitious name in order to give the impression (when such things mattered) that they were married. The case is different where the impostor assumes the name and address of a real person of substance when entering into a credit transaction. In such a case his purpose is to direct inquiries to that person's credit rather than his own. A better explanation of *King's Norton Metal Co Ltd* v *Edridge, Merrett & Co Ltd* is that the rogue merely assumed a false name and did not go further and assume another person's identity. But the distinction is a fine one which it may not always be possible to draw, and in any case depends on the nature and purpose of the deception and is accordingly relevant to its effect on the mind of the offeree and not to the correlation between offer and acceptance.

The fact that this may not be a formation issue at all may also be accepted by Lord Walker, who refers to the case as involving a deceit as to the standing and credit-worthiness of Wallis. In essence, this 'mistake' involved an error of judgment on the part of the plaintiffs in that they intended to send goods on credit to the company only because they thought that the company was creditworthy. Such an error should not affect the offer and acceptance question.

A: Rectification

The court may be asked to rectify a written document to reflect accurately what the parties in fact agreed. (This is an exception to the parol evidence rule, see *page 207*, since oral evidence is admissible to show the error in the written document.)

Frederick E. Rose (London) Ltd v *William H. Pim Junior & Co. Ltd*
[1953] 2 QB 450 (CA)

Buyers asked the plaintiffs to supply them with 'Moroccan horsebeans described as feveroles'. The plaintiffs did not know what feveroles were but were informed by the defendants that feveroles and horsebeans were the same thing. The plaintiffs entered into a contract with the defendants whereby the defendants were to supply them with 'horsebeans' which the plaintiffs would then sell to the buyers, both parties believing that feveroles were just horsebeans. In fact 'feveroles' were a superior type of horsebean, and the buyers had claimed damages from the plaintiffs for not supplying 'feveroles'. The plaintiffs wanted to have their written contract with the defendants rectified to read 'feveroles' (so that the defendants would have been in breach in supplying the wrong goods). Held: the Court of Appeal refused to rectify the agreement since the parties had agreed on the sale of horsebeans and the agreement correctly reflected this. The problem was that both parties mistakenly thought that horsebeans were feveroles.

DENNING LJ: . . . Rectification is concerned with contracts and documents, not with intentions. In order to get rectification it is necessary to show that the parties were in complete agreement on the terms of their contract, but by an error wrote them down wrongly; and in this regard, in order to ascertain the terms of their contract, you do not look into the inner minds of the parties—into their intentions—any more than you do in the formation of any other contract. You look at their outward acts, that is, at what they said or wrote to one another in coming to their agreement, and then compare it with the document which they have signed. If you can predicate with certainty what their contract was, and that it is, by a common mistake, wrongly expressed in the document, then you rectify the document; but nothing less will suffice. . . . There is a passage in *Crane* v *Hegeman-Harris Co. Inc.* ([1939] 1 All ER 662, 664), which suggests that a continuing common intention alone will suffice; but I am clearly of opinion that a continuing common intention is not sufficient unless it has found expression in outward agreement. There could be no certainty at all in business transactions if a party who had entered into a firm contract could afterwards turn round and claim to have it rectified on the ground that the parties intended something different. He is allowed to prove, if he can, that they *agreed something different*: see *Lovell & Christmas* v *Wall* ([1911] 104 LT 85, 88), per Lord Cozens-Hardy, MR, and per Buckley LJ (93) but not that they *intended* something different.

The present case is a good illustration of the distinction. The parties no doubt intended that the goods should satisfy the inquiry of the Egyptian buyers, namely, 'horsebeans described in Egypt as feveroles.' They assumed that they would do so, but they made no contract to that effect. Their agreement, as outwardly expressed, both orally and in writing, was for 'horsebeans'. That is all that the defendants ever committed themselves to supply, and all they should be bound to. There was, no doubt, an erroneous assumption underlying the contract—an assumption for which it might have been set aside on the ground of misrepresentation or mistake—but that is very different from an erroneous expression of the contract, such as to give rise to rectification.

NOTES

1. On the facts there was a mistake as to quality and at the time it was recognised that a contract could be set aside on terms in equity. (The Court of Appeal in *Great Peace Shipping Ltd* v *Tsavliris Salvage (International) Ltd* [2002] EWCA Civ 1407, [2003] QB 679 has since denied the existence of such an equitable jurisdiction, see *page 514*.) However, on the facts in *Rose* v *Pim*, rescission was barred since the buyers and sub-buyers had accepted the goods.

2. However, the Court of Appeal in *Joscelyne* v *Nissen* [1970] 2 QB 86, made it clear that *Rose* v *Pim* was not authority for the fact that an antecedent complete concluded contract is required for rectification. Russell LJ stated that *Rose* v *Pim* 'only shows that prior accord on a term or the meaning of a phrase to be used must have been outwardly expressed or communicated between the parties'.

Joscelyne v Nissen
[1970] 2 QB 86 (CA)

The plaintiff father and his daughter, the defendant, shared a house owned by the daughter. They agreed that the father was to transfer his car hire business to his daughter, and in return the daughter was to pay him a weekly pension and pay certain household expenses such as gas, electricity, and coal bills. The contract specified that she was to 'discharge all expenses in connection with the whole premise . . . and shall indemnify [the plaintiff] from and against any claim arising in respect of the same'. At first the defendant paid several of the household bills but then stopped paying. The plaintiff sought rectification of this contract to provide for the payment of gas, electricity, and coal bills on the basis that this reflected what had been orally agreed between the parties during negotiations. At first instance the judge had found that although there was no complete concluded antecedent agreement, the agreement should be rectified. Held: dismissing the appeal, it was not necessary to find a concluded contract antecedent to the agreement. Rectification could be ordered as long as there was a common continuing intention (demonstrated by outward expression) regarding a particular provision.

RUSSELL LJ: [Russell LJ relied on the following statement by Simonds J in *Crane* v *Hegeman-Harris Co. Inc.* [1939] 1 All ER 662, 664]

. . . I am clear that I must follow the decision of Clauson J, as he then was in *Shipley Urban District Council* v *Bradford Corpn.* [1936] 1 Ch 375, the point of which is that, in order that this court may exercise its jurisdiction to rectify a written instrument, it is not necessary to find a concluded and binding contract between the parties antecedent to the agreement which it is sought to rectify. The judge held, and I respectfully concur with his reasoning and his conclusion, that it is sufficient to find a common continuing intention in regard to a particular provision or aspect of the agreement. If one finds that, in regard to a particular point, the parties were in agreement up to the moment when they executed their formal instrument, and the formal instrument does not conform with that common agreement, then this court has jurisdiction to rectify, although it may be that there was, until the formal instrument was executed, no concluded and binding contract between the parties. That is what the judge decided, and, as I say, with his reasoning I wholly concur, and I can add nothing to his authority in the matter, except that I would say that, if it were not so, it would be a strange thing, for the result would be that two parties binding themselves by a mistake to which each had equally contributed by an instrument which did not express their real intention, would yet be bound by it. That is a state of affairs which I hold is not the law, and, until a higher court tells me it is the law, I shall continue to exercise the jurisdiction which Clauson J, as I think rightly, held might be entertained by this court.

Secondly, I want to say this upon the principle of the jurisdiction. It is a jurisdiction which is to be exercised only upon convincing proof that the concluded instrument does not represent the common intention of the parties. That is particularly the case where one finds prolonged negotiations between the parties eventually assuming the shape of a formal instrument in which they have been advised by their respective skilled legal advisers. The assumption is very strong in such a case that the instrument does represent their real intention, and it must be only upon proof which Lord Eldon, I think, in a somewhat picturesque phrase described as 'irrefragable' that the court can act. I would rather, I think, say that the court can only act if it is satisfied beyond all reasonable doubt that the instrument does not represent their common intention, and is further satisfied as to what their common intention was. For let it be clear that it is not sufficient to show that the written instrument does not represent their common intention unless positively also one can show what their common intention was. It is in the light of those principles that I must examine the facts of this somewhat complicated case.

In our judgment the law is as expounded by Simonds J in *Crane's* case with the qualification that some outward expression of accord is required. We do not wish to attempt to state in any different phrases that with which we entirely agree, except to say that it is in our view better to use only the phrase 'convincing proof' without echoing an old-fashioned word such as 'irrefragable' and without importing from the criminal law the phrase 'beyond all reasonable doubt.' Remembering always the strong burden of proof that lies on the shoulders of those seeking rectification, and that the requisite accord and continuance of accord of intention may be the more difficult to establish if a complete antecedent concluded contract be not shown, it would be a sorry state of affairs if when that burden is discharged a party to a written contract could, on discovery that the written language chosen for the document did not on its true construction reflect the accord of the parties on a particular point, take advantage of the fact.

The contention in law for the daughter would, we apprehend, involve this proposition, that if all the important terms of an agreement were set out in correspondence with clarity, but expressly 'subject to contract,' and the contract by a slip of the copyist unnoticed by either party departed from what had been 'agreed,' there could not be rectification. . . .

NOTE: Rectification will, in general, be ordered only if the contractual document fails to record the agreement of *both* parties. However, it is also available where the document does not accurately record the understanding of *one* of the parties and the other knew this and failed to draw attention to it.

Commission for the New Towns v *Cooper (GB) Ltd*
[1995] Ch 259 (CA)

In 1986, the plaintiff's predecessor had made four agreements by deed with Edison-Halo Ltd (the tenant of commercial premises). The deeds concerned (i) building works (the plaintiff was to undertake specified repair work on the premises), (ii) a 'put' option, whereby the plaintiff agreed to take an assignment of the underlease without penalty if Edison gave notice of termination on the fifth anniversary of the deed, (iii) the 'larger premises' option, whereby Edison could at any time surrender the lease if it took on the lease of larger premises from the plaintiff, (iv) a 'side land' option, whereby the plaintiff granted an option enabling Edison to acquire the lease of an adjacent site. The right granted in (ii) expressly stated that it could not be assigned.

The defendant (CoopInd) acquired the unexpired residue of the underlease by assignment in December 1988. By 1990, the defendant was considering closing down its business on the site. However, since a substantial penalty would have been payable if the defendant had simply surrendered the underlease, the defendant wished to obtain the 'put option' in the 1986 deed to enable it to surrender in 1991 without penalty. The defendant held a meeting with the plaintiff at which there was no mention of the 'put option'. Agreement was reached on terms whereby the defendant was to be treated 'in all respects as having the same rights and benefits under the original documentation' as Edison. Once this agreement was confirmed, the defendant gave notice of its intention to exercise the 'put option' requiring the plaintiff to take the assignment of the underlease. The plaintiff denied having granted a 'put option' and sought rectification of the agreement. Held: on its construction what had been agreed did not extend to granting the defendant the 'put option'. On that basis it was not strictly necessary to consider the rectification issue, but the Court of Appeal did so.

STUART-SMITH LJ (with whose reasoning Evans and Farquharson LJJ agreed): . . . The commonest circumstance in which rectification is granted is where the written contract does not accurately record the parties' joint agreement. In other words, there is a mistake common to both parties. In the case of unilateral mistake, that is to say where only one party is mistaken as to the meaning of the contract, rectification is not ordinarily appropriate. This follows from the ordinary rule that it is the objective intention of the parties which determines the construction of the contract and not the subjective intention of one of them. Also, it would generally be inequitable to compel the other party to execute a contract, which he had no intention of making, simply to accord with the mistaken interpretation of the other party: see *Olympia Sauna Shipping Co. S.A.* v *Shinwa Kaiun Kaisha Ltd* [1985] 2 Lloyd's Rep 364, 371, *per* Bingham J. But the court will intervene if there are 'additional circumstances that render unconscionable reliance on the document by the party who has intended that it should have effect according to its terms:' *Spry, Equitable Remedies*, 4th ed. (1990), p. 599. The debate in this case turns on what amounts to unconscionable conduct. The judge held that nothing less than actual knowledge of M.K.'s mistake was sufficient, and although CoopInd's representatives suspected that it was mistaken, it was not proved that it actually did.

. . . [Counsel for the plaintiff] submits, even if there was no actual knowledge and no false representation, CoopInd was guilty of such sharp and unconscionable practice that rectification should be granted. [Counsel] relies upon a dictum of Buckley LJ in *Thomas Bates & Son Ltd* v *Wyndham's (Lingerie) Ltd* [1981] 1 WLR 505 at 515, where he said:

> Undoubtedly I think in any such case the conduct of the defendant must be such as to make it inequitable that he should be allowed to object to the rectification of the document. If this necessarily implies some measure of 'sharp practice', so be it; but for my part I think that the doctrine is one which depends more on the equity of the position. The graver the character of the conduct involved, no doubt the heavier the burden of proof may be; but, in my view, the conduct must be such as to affect the conscience of the party who has suppressed the fact that he has recognised the presence of a mistake.

. . . But [counsel for the defendant] submits that it is not open to the court to adopt this approach. Nothing short of actual knowledge of the mistake, which creates an estoppel against the party with knowledge of the mistake or fraud, will suffice, though in this context fraud includes equitable fraud in the sense of undue influence of abuse of a fiduciary relationship. In support of this submission he cited the authority of this court in *Agip SpA* v *Navigazione Alta Italia SpA* [1984] 1 Lloyd's Rep 353. After reviewing *A Roberts & Co. Ltd* v *Leicestershire CC* [1961] Ch 555, *Riverlate Properties Ltd* v *Paul* [1975] Ch 133 and *Thomas Bates & Son Ltd* v *Wyndham's (Lingerie) Ltd* [1981] 1 WLR 505, which were all cases of actual knowledge of the mistake, Slade LJ, with whose judgment Oliver and Robert Goff LJJ agreed, said [1984] 1 Lloyd's Rep 353, 361–362:

> One significant feature however is common to all of the *Roberts, Riverlate* and *Bates* decisions. In all the various formulations of the relevant principle in the judgments in those cases, none of the members of the respective courts suggested that rectification can properly be granted on account of unilateral mistake unless the defendant had *actual knowledge* of the existence of the plaintiff's mistake at the time when the contract was signed. Since, in the present case, the judge has specifically found that the defendants were not aware of the

mistake of IIP at the time of signature of the charterparties, and there is no appeal against this finding, it is obvious that the plaintiffs, if they are to succeed on this appeal, must in some way succeed in persuading the court to extend the frontiers of the circumstances in which rectification may be granted on the grounds of mere unilateral mistake, beyond the frontiers established by any of the cases cited. The court, therefore, must in my opinion proceed all the more cautiously before granting rectification of these two written instruments against defendants who at the time when the negotiations first ripened into a binding contract, intended to contract on the terms which were reflected in the written charterparties and on no other terms.

Slade LJ expressed his opinion in these terms at p. 365:

While it is not necessary to go so far for the purpose of this present decision, I might perhaps add that I strongly incline to the view that in the absence of estoppel, fraud, undue influence or a fiduciary relationship between the parties, the authorities do not in any circumstances permit the rectification of a contract on the grounds of unilateral mistake, unless the defendant had actual knowledge of the existence of the relevant mistaken belief at the time when the mistaken plaintiff signed the contract. In view of the drastic nature of such an order, so far as the non-mistaken defendant is concerned, the consequences of any such conclusion may not appear unduly harsh. I do not say that even where estoppel, fraud, undue influence or a fiduciary relationship exists rectification will necessarily be an available or appropriate remedy.

It is only with great diffidence that I venture to think that this may not be an exhaustive statement of the law, although it undoubtedly covers the majority of situations. But were it necessary to do so in this case, I would hold that where A intends B to be mistaken as to the construction of the agreement, so conducts himself that he diverts B's attention from discovering the mistake by making false and misleading statements, and B in fact makes the very mistake that A intends, then notwithstanding that A does not actually know, but merely suspects that B is mistaken, and it cannot be shown that the mistake was induced by any misrepresentation, rectification may be granted. A's conduct is unconscionable and he cannot insist on performance in accordance to the strict letter of the contract; that is sufficient for rescission. But it may also not be unjust or inequitable to insist that the contract be performed according to B's understanding, where that was the meaning that A intended that B should put upon it. That is so here because, although on the assumption that CoopInd's construction is correct and the put option was included, the contract appeared to be a whole package; in truth CoopInd thought it was getting something for nothing.

NOTES

1. It would appear that this apparent extension of rectification in the case of unilateral mistakes must be confined to cases where there is an intention to deceive.

2. Counsel for the plaintiff had also disputed the judge's finding that the defendant's representatives did not have actual knowledge of the mistake. Stuart-Smith LJ found that the judge at first instance had not considered the extended definition of actual knowledge given by Peter Gibson J in *Baden* v *Société Générale pour Favoriser le Développement du Commerce et de l'Industrie en France SA (1982)* [1993] 1 WLR 509, 575–6. Peter Gibson J had included 'willfully shutting one's eyes to the obvious' (category (ii) actual knowledge) and 'willfully and recklessly failing to make such inquiries as an honest and reasonable man would make' (category (iii) actual knowledge). Stuart-Smith LJ concluded that:

   . . . In my judgment, it must have been plain that neither Mr Hill nor Mr Barton had any idea that they were dealing with the put option, far less agreeing to grant it to CoopInd. It did not suit CoopInd's plan, as the judge found, to draw attention to this or ask any questions about it. Their (CoopInd's representatives') conduct in raising the smokescreen in relation to the side land was dishonest and intended to deceive. If the question is posed as a jury question, I find it impossible to reach any other conclusion but that an honest and reasonable man would have mentioned the point expressly.

. . . I am persuaded in this case that the judge misdirected himself as to what amounts to actual knowledge and that on his own findings, to which I have referred, the case falls within categories (ii) and/or (iii) of Peter Gibson J's analysis.

3. *Commission for the New Towns* v *Cooper (GB) Ltd* was applied in two recent cases concerning claims for rectification based on unilateral mistake. In *Hurst Stores & Interiors Ltd* v *ML Europe Property Ltd* [2004] EWCA Civ 490, [2004] BLR 249, the final version of a statement of account differed from all previous versions which had passed between the parties during their negotiations and did not reflect the agreement which had been reached between the parties governing the basis of valuations of certain works. This difference had not been drawn to the attention of the project manager who had signed the document on behalf of the construction company and the Court of Appeal considered that the employer's construction manager who had prepared the final document had actual or 'shut eye' knowledge of this mistake (within category (ii) actual knowledge identified by Peter Gibson J in *Baden* v *Société Générale*). Accordingly, the judge at first instance had been correct to order rectification of the document.

By comparison, in *George Wimpey UK Ltd* v *VI Components Ltd* [2005] EWCA Civ 77, [2005] BLR 135, the claim to rectify for unilateral mistake was rejected because the purchaser of the land had failed to prove that the vendor had actual knowledge (which included category (ii) and category (iii) actual knowledge) of the purchaser's mistake relating to the formula for calculating the 'overage payment' (i.e. an extra payment that would become payable if the sale prices of flats to be built on the land exceeded a particular figure) which had been changed at the last minute. The judge at first instance had held that the vendor had shut its eyes to the fact that the purchaser was making a mistake and had failed to draw the purchaser's attention to the difference in the formula. The Court of Appeal allowed the appeal from the judge's decision on the basis that neither matter was proven on the facts. Instead, the Court of Appeal stressed the exceptional nature of the jurisdiction to rectify for unilateral mistake and the purchaser's vast experience of sales of property for residential development as compared to that of the vendor (VI Components Ltd). The implication appears to be that VI was entitled to assume that Wimpey knew what it was doing but made 'an error of judgment in entering into the contract', which has no relevance to the law of unilateral mistake (*per* Sedley LJ, [62]).

B: The plea of *non est factum*

The general principle is that a person will be bound by a written document which he has signed, whether or not he has read or understood it (see *L'Estrange* v *F. Graucob Ltd* [1934] 2 KB 394, at *page 212*).

Where it is not possible to rely on misrepresentation or mistake, the plea of *non est factum* ('this is not my deed') may be a last resort. A successful plea renders the contract void so that a third party cannot acquire a good title under it. However, as innocent third parties may have relied to their detriment upon this signature as being binding, the plea has been very narrowly construed.

Saunders v *Anglia Building Society (sub nom Gallie* v *Lee)*
[1971] AC 1004 (HL)

An elderly widow of 78 had a leasehold interest in a house. She knew her nephew wished to raise money on the house and that his business associate, Lee, was to assist him in obtaining this. The widow wanted to be sure that she could live in the house for the rest of her life. Lee asked her to sign a document, but she had broken her spectacles and could not read it. She asked what the document was and signed it when Lee told her that it was a deed of gift of the house to her nephew. In fact it was an assignment of the house to Lee for £3,000. Lee mortgaged the house for £2,000 to the building society (the innocent third party). When Lee defaulted on the mortgage instalments the building society sought possession of the house. The widow pleaded *non est factum* and asked for a declaration against the building society that the assignment was void. Held: the plea failed because the transaction she had entered into was not fundamentally different in substance from that which she had intended to enable the nephew to raise money on the security of the house. She had also been careless in signing the document.

LORD REID: The plea of *non est factum* obviously applies when the person sought to be held liable did not in fact sign the document. But at least since the sixteenth century it has also been held to apply in certain cases so as to enable a person who in fact signed a document to say that it is not his deed. Obviously any such extension must be kept within narrow limits if it is not to shake the confidence of those who habitually and rightly rely on signatures when there is no obvious reason to doubt their validity. Originally this extension appears to have been made in favour of those who were unable to read owing to blindness or illiteracy and who therefore had to trust someone to tell them what they were signing. I think it must also apply in favour of those who are permanently or temporarily unable through no fault of their own to have without explanation any real understanding of the purport of a particular document, whether that be from defective education, illness or innate incapacity.

But that does not excuse them from taking such precautions as they reasonably can. The matter generally arises where an innocent third party has relied on a signed document in ignorance of the circumstances in which it was signed, and where he will suffer loss if the maker of the document is allowed to have it declared a nullity. So there must be a heavy burden of proof on the person who seeks to invoke this remedy. He must prove all the circumstances necessary to justify its being granted to him, and that necessarily involves his proving that he took all reasonable precautions in the circumstances. I do not say that the remedy can never be available to a man of full capacity. But that could only be in very exceptional circumstances: certainly not where his reason for not scrutinising the document before signing it was that he was too busy or too lazy. In general I do not think he can be heard to say that he signed in reliance on someone he trusted. But, particularly when he was led to believe that the document which he signed was not one which affected his legal rights, there may be cases where this plea can properly be applied in favour of a man of full capacity.

The plea cannot be available to anyone who was content to sign without taking the trouble to try to find out at least the general effect of the document. Many people do frequently sign documents put before them for signature by their solicitor or other trusted advisers without making any inquiry as to their purpose or effect. But the essence of the plea *non est factum* is that the person signing believed that the document he signed had one character or one effect whereas in fact its character or effect was quite different. He could not have such a belief unless he had taken steps or been given information which gave him some grounds for his belief. The amount of information he must have and the sufficiency of the particularity of his belief must depend on the circumstances of each case. . . .

Finally, there is the question as to what extent or in what way must there be a difference between that which in fact he signed and that which he believed he was signing. In an endeavour to keep the plea within bounds there have been many attempts to lay down a dividing line. . . .

There must, I think, be a radical difference between what he signed and what he thought he was signing—or one could use the words 'fundamental' or 'serious' or 'very substantial.' But what amounts to a radical difference will depend on all the circumstances. If he thinks he is giving property to A whereas the document gives it to B, the difference may often be of vital importance, but in the circumstances of the present case I do not think that it is. I think that it must be left to the courts to determine in each case in light of all the facts whether there was or was not a sufficiently great difference. The plea *non est factum* is in a sense illogical when applied to a case where the man in fact signed the deed. But it is none the worse for that if applied in a reasonable way.

NOTE: The plea was also rejected by the Court of Appeal in the following case:

Norwich & Peterborough Building Society v Steed (No. 2)
[1993] Ch 116 (CA)

The appellant, Steed, sought to rely on the plea of *non est factum* on the basis that he had executed a power of attorney in favour of his mother but, as a result of trickery, his mother had then transferred his house to his sister and her husband who had used the house as security for a loan on which they had defaulted. He alleged that his mother thought she was signing a document concerning her own affairs and did not know that she was signing a transfer of the property. She was therefore mistaken as to the essential character of the document signed. Held: the plea could not succeed.

SCOTT LJ: . . . Submissions on these lines, . . . place Mr Steed on a species of Morton's fork. Let it be supposed that Mrs Steed was a lady of sufficient general understanding and capability to be a suitable donee of the power of appointment. Why then did she not inform herself of the purport and effect of the transfer before signing it? . . . On the other hand, let it be supposed that she lacked ordinary competence and capacity. Lord Wilberforce [in *Saunders* v *Anglia Building Society*] referred to persons 'illiterate, or blind, or lacking in understanding'. If Mrs Steed falls into this category, what was Mr Steed about when he appointed her his attorney? The donor of a power of attorney who appoints as his attorney a person incapable of understanding the import of a simple transfer can hardly be allowed, if the donee signs a transfer without any understanding of what he or she is doing, to repudiate the transfer on the ground of a lack of understanding on the part of the donee.

As to Mrs Steed's ignorance of the power of attorney, if she was ignorant of it, the ignorance was attributable to Mr Steed's incomprehensible failure to tell her either that he was about to or that he had made the appointment. It is known that he and she spoke on the telephone at about the time the power of attorney was executed. If it was really the case that he did not mention the power of attorney when speaking to her on that occasion and left her in ignorance of her responsibilities and status, his failure shows, in my opinion, such a want of care as to preclude him from relying, in support of his non est factum plea, on her ignorance of the power. As between an innocent third party purchaser such as the building society on the one hand, and Mr Steed on the other hand, his failure to take the ordinary precautionary and prudent step of informing his mother of her appointment as his attorney requires, in my judgment, that the building society be preferred. . . .

Avon Finance Co. Ltd v Bridger
[1985] 2 All ER 281 (CA)

The defendants, an elderly couple, purchased a house for their retirement for £9,275, the arrangements being conducted by their son. The son was to contribute £2,500 to the purchase price. Without telling the defendants, the son obtained a loan from the plaintiff finance company on the security of the retirement home. He obtained the defendants' signatures to the charge by telling them that the documents they were signing related to their own mortgage with the building society. The son failed to make the finance payments and the finance company sought possession against the defendants. The defendants pleaded *non est factum*. Held: such a plea could not operate because the defendants had not exercised reasonable care in entering into the transaction.

■ QUESTION

The Court of Appeal held that the contract was nevertheless voidable for undue influence (i.e., it could be set aside by the defendants). Does this mean that in future such cases are more likely to turn on the issue of undue influence? (Such an argument would not have been helpful on the facts in *Norwich & Peterborough BS* v *Steed (No. 2)*, because the alleged transaction would be the initial transfer of the property. Therefore, the appellant could only seek rectification of the register under the Land Registration Act 1925. On the facts this claim also failed.)

4

Consideration, Promissory Estoppel, and Form

In addition to any formalities requirements (section 3), a promise must either be expressed in the form of deed or be supported by consideration in order to be enforceable. This is because English contract law assumes that only bargains should be enforced (i.e., the promisor must get something in exchange for his promise).

The case law has been concerned with identifying what can constitute consideration and whether it is possible to enforce a promise in the absence of consideration.

Section 1: CONSIDERATION

A: What is consideration?

The traditional approach is to identify consideration as a detriment to the promisee and/or a benefit to the promisor. See, for example, *Currie v Misa* (1875) LR 10 Ex 153, where Lush J said (at p. 162):

A valuable consideration, in the sense of the law, may consist either in some right, interest, profit, or benefit accruing to the one party, or some forbearance, detriment, loss, or responsibility, given, suffered, or undertaken by the other . . .

The second approach is to define consideration as the price requested by the promisor, in exchange for which the promisor's promise was bought. Such a definition was adopted by Lord Dunedin in *Dunlop Pneumatic Tyre Co. Ltd v Selfridge & Co. Ltd* [1915] AC 847, where he said (at p. 855):

An act or forbearance of one party, or the promise thereof, is the price for which the promise of the other is bought, and the promise thus given for value is enforceable.

B: Consideration distinguished from a condition imposed on recipients of gifts

Thomas v Thomas
(1842) 2 QB 851; 114 ER 330 (QB)

Shortly before his death, the testator stated before witnesses that he wished his wife, Eleanor Thomas, to have their house during her lifetime and while she remained his widow, or £100 instead. However, there was no provision to this effect in his will. The executors of the will, wishing to comply with the testator's intentions, made an agreement with the plaintiff widow 'in consideration of such desire' to convey the house to her for her life 'provided nevertheless and it is further agreed' that during that time the plaintiff would pay £1 yearly towards the ground rent for the property and keep the house 'in good and tenantable repair'. The plaintiff obtained possession but the defendant executors refused to convey the house and ejected her. The issue was whether any consideration had been provided for the executors' promise. Held: although the testator's desire was only the motive for the agreement and a motive could not be consideration, the widow's promise to pay £1 towards the ground rent and to keep the house in repair was good consideration to support the promise to convey the house to her. The promise to perform these acts had some value in the eyes of the law and the court did not have to inquire as to the adequacy of the widow's promise.

PATTERSON J: . . . Motive is not the same thing with consideration. Consideration means something which is of some value in the eye of the law, moving from the plaintiff: it may be some benefit to the plaintiff, or some detriment to the defendant; but at all events it must be moving from the plaintiff. Now that which is suggested as the consideration here, a pious respect for the wishes of the testator, does not in any way move from the plaintiff; it moves from the testator; therefore, legally speaking, it forms no part of the consideration. Then it is said that, if that be so, there is no consideration at all, it is a mere voluntary gift: but when we look at the agreement we find that this is not a mere proviso that the donee shall take the gift with the burthens; but it is an express agreement to pay what seems to be a fresh apportionment of a ground rent, and which is made payable not to a superior landlord but to the executors. So that this rent is clearly not something incident to the assignment of the house; for in that case, instead of being payable to the executors, it would have been payable to the landlord. Then as to the repairs: these houses may very possibly be held under a lease containing covenants to repair; but we know nothing about it: for any thing that appears, the liability to repair is first created by this instrument. The proviso certainly struck me at first . . . that the rent and repairs were merely attached to the gift by the donors; and, had the instrument been executed by the donors only, there might have been some ground for that construction; but the fact is not so. . . .

NOTES
1. At the time of this decision it was a requirement that consideration had to move from the promisee (*Tweddle* v *Atkinson* (1861) B & S 393, *page 438*). Therefore, the testator's desire could not have amounted to consideration in any event because it did not move from the promisee, the widow.
2. As the Law Commission acknowledged in its 1996 Report on Privity of Contract, the maxim that 'consideration must move from the promisee' is ambiguous. On the one hand, it can be understood to mean 'consideration must move from the claimant' (and this is the expression used by Patterson J in *Thomas* v *Thomas*). On this interpretation the consideration would need to be provided by the person seeking to enforce the promise. However, it can be interpreted to mean only that consideration must be provided to support a promise. On this basis it is possible to reform the third party rule without altering the law on consideration, since the third party's ability to enforce a promise for his benefit could not be defeated by arguing that *he* had not provided any consideration to support that promise where the contracting party had provided that consideration. This second interpretation was the interpretation favoured by the Law Commission.

   On this basis, it was considered that the reform of the third party rule did not require a specific legislative provision on consideration since the main provision, giving third parties enforceable rights in certain circumstances, would necessarily be effective only if this interpretation of the maxim was adopted. (See Law Commission, *Privity of Contract: Contracts for*

the Benefit of Third Parties (Law Com. No. 242, Cm 3329, 1996), paras 6.1–6.8, *pages 438–40*.) Since the Contracts (Rights of Third Parties) Act 1999 it therefore seems that consideration need not be provided by a claimant but must be provided by someone if the promise is to be enforceable.

3. Since there must be a benefit to the promisor moving from the promisee, and the person whose promise it was sought to enforce on the facts in *Thomas* v *Thomas* was the defendant, the true statement should have been that the consideration must be 'some benefit to the defendant or some detriment to the plaintiff'.

4. In practice it is not easy to distinguish a party's motive from the consideration provided. It may be preferable to regard a motive as consideration provided it is of economic value rather than purely sentimental (see *pages 122–4*).

■ QUESTIONS

1. Why did the court consider that this was not a gratuitous promise to convey the house conditional on the promise to make this £1 payment and to carry out repairs?

2. Treitel, *The Law of Contract*, 11th edn, p. 72, argues that in *Carlill* v *Carbolic Smoke Ball Company* [1893] 1 QB 256, the consideration was using the smoke ball in accordance with the instructions but that the promise was conditional on the user catching influenza. Should a wider interpretation be used so that consideration consists of whatever has been requested by the promisor in exchange for his promise? (See *Chappell & Co. Ltd* v *Nestlé Co. Ltd* [1960] AC 87, *below*.)

C: Consideration must be sufficient but need not be adequate

(a) Adequacy

If what is given in exchange for the promise has value in the eyes of the law, the court will not question whether that value is adequate and will not interfere with the fairness of the bargain made by the parties.

Trivial acts have been held to amount to consideration because they have been requested by the promisor.

Chappell & Co. Ltd v *Nestlé Co. Ltd*
[1960] AC 87 (HL)

The plaintiffs owned the copyright in a piece of music, 'Rockin' Shoes'. The defendants, Nestlé, arranged for copies of this tune to be manufactured into records, and they offered these records to the public for 1s 6d plus three wrappers from their 6d chocolate bars. Section 8 of the Copyright Act 1956 permitted the making of records for retail sale provided that a royalty of 6¼ per cent on 'the ordinary retail selling price' was paid to the plaintiffs. The plaintiffs were informed that 1s 6d was the ordinary retail selling price. They sought an injunction claiming breach of copyright. Held: (Viscount Simonds and Lord Keith of Avonholm dissenting) the wrappers were part of the consideration for the sale of the records, although they were of very trivial economic value and were thrown away by Nestlé. Section 8 of the Copyright Act 1956 was intended to apply where a money sum was the entire consideration for the sale, and since this sale was outside s. 8, there was a breach of copyright.

LORD SOMERVELL: The question, then, is whether the three wrappers were part of the consideration or, as Jenkins LJ held, a condition of making the purchase, like a ticket entitling a member to buy at a co-operative store.

I think they are part of the consideration. They are so described in the offer. 'They,' the wrappers, 'will help you to get smash hit recordings.' They are so described in the record itself—'all you have to do to get such new record is to send three wrappers from Nestlé's 6d. milk chocolate bars, together with postal order for 1s. 6d.' This is not conclusive but, however described, they are, in my view, in law part of the consideration. It is said that when received the wrappers are of no value to Nestlé's. This I would have thought irrelevant. A contracting party can stipulate for what consideration he chooses. A peppercorn does not cease to be good consideration if it is established that the promisee does not like pepper and will throw away the corn. As the whole object of selling the record, if it was a sale, was to increase the sales of chocolate, it seems to me wrong not to treat the stipulated evidence of such sales as part of the consideration.

LORD REID: The respondents [submit] that acquiring and delivering the wrappers was merely a condition which gave a qualification to buy and was not part of the consideration for sale. Of course, a person may limit his offer to persons qualified in a particular way, e.g., members of a club. But where the qualification is the doing of something of value to the seller, and where the qualification only suffices for one sale and must be re-acquired before another sale, I find it hard to regard the repeated acquisitions of the qualification as anything other than parts of the consideration for the sales. The purchaser of records had to send three wrappers for each record, so he had first to acquire them. The acquisition of wrappers by him was, at least in many cases, of direct benefit to the Nestlé Co., and required expenditure by the acquirer which he might not otherwise have incurred. To my mind the acquiring and delivering of the wrappers was certainly part of the consideration in these cases, and I see no good reason for drawing a distinction between these and other cases.

NOTES

1. Lord Somervell indicated that there was a benefit to Nestlé through increased chocolate sales by requiring the wrappers (although Atiyah has argued that this was only the motive which inspired the promise). He also considered that the wrappers were part of the consideration because they were asked for. In *Carlill v Carbolic Smoke Ball Company* [1893] 1 QB 256 (*page 4*), catching influenza was a stipulated act and arguably, therefore, should form part of the consideration for the promise of the reward.

2. Viscount Simonds (dissenting) in *Chappell & Co. Ltd v Nestlé Co. Ltd* was firmly of the view that the wrappers were not part of the consideration:

   In my opinion, my Lords, the wrappers are not part of the selling price. They are admittedly themselves valueless and are thrown away and it was for that reason, no doubt, that Upjohn J was constrained to say that their value lay in the evidence they afforded of success in an advertising campaign. That is what they are. But what, after all, does that mean? Nothing more than that someone, by no means necessarily the purchaser of the record, has in the past bought not from Nestlé's but from a retail shop three bars of chocolate and that the purchaser has thus directly or indirectly acquired the wrappers. How often he acquires them for himself, how often through another, is pure speculation. The only thing that is certain is that, if he buys bars of chocolate from a retail shop or acquires the wrappers from another who has bought them, that purchase is not, or at the lowest is not necessarily, part of the same transaction as his subsequent purchase of a record from the manufacturers.

   I conclude, therefore, that the objection fails, whether it is contended that (in the words of Upjohn J) the sale 'bears no resemblance at all to the transaction to which the section . . . is pointing' or that the three wrappers form part of the selling price and are incapable of valuation. Nor is there any need to take what, with respect, I think is a somewhat artificial view of a simple transaction. What can be easier than for a manufacturer to limit his sales to those members of the public who fulfil the qualification of being this or doing that? It may be assumed that the manufacturer's motive is his own advantage. It is possible that he

achieves his object. But that does not mean that the sale is not a retail sale to which the section applies or that the ordinary retail selling price is not the price at which the record is ordinarily sold, in this case 1s. 6d.

3. The fact that the courts will not inquire into the adequacy of the consideration is further illustrated by the Unfair Terms in Consumer Contracts Regulations 1999, SI 1999/2083, regulation 6(2)(b), which specifically excludes the adequacy of the price or remuneration from the assessment of the fairness of contractual terms in the consumer context.

(b) Sufficiency ('of value in the eyes of the law')

The consideration provided must be capable of expression in economic terms.

White v Bluett
(1853) 23 LJ Ex 36 (Court of Exchequer)

Bluett had given his father a promissory note for money that his father had lent him. His father's executor sued him on the note, and he claimed in his defence that his father had promised to discharge him from the obligation if he would stop complaining about the father's distribution of his property among his children. (A promissory note is a promise to pay contained in a written document, e.g., a bank note.) Held: Bluett had not provided any consideration for such a promise by his father; the son was not under any legal duty to refrain from complaining; and therefore his forbearance could not amount to consideration.

POLLOCK CB: . . . If such a plea as this could be supported, the following would be a binding promise: A man might complain that another person used the public highway more than he ought to do, and that other might say, do not complain, and I will give you five pounds. It is ridiculous to suppose that such promises could be binding. So, if the holder of a bill of exchange were suing the acceptor, and the acceptor were to complain that the holder had treated him hardly, or that the bill ought never to have been circulated, and the holder were to say, Now, if you will not make any more complaints, I will not sue you. Such a promise would be like that now set up. In reality, there was no consideration whatever. The son had no right to complain, for the father might make what distribution of his property he liked; and the son's abstaining from doing what he had no right to do can be no consideration.

NOTE: *White* v *Bluett* can be contrasted with the following American case.

Hamer v Sidway
(1891) 27 NE 256 (Court of Appeals of New York)

An uncle promised his nephew $5,000 if the nephew would refrain from 'drinking liquor, using tobacco, swearing and playing cards or billiards for money until he should become 21 years of age'. The nephew complied but the defendant, the uncle's executor, refused to make the payment. The question was whether the nephew had provided sufficient consideration to support the promise to pay. Held: the promise was enforceable because the nephew had provided consideration by restricting his lawful freedom of action.

PARKER J: . . . The defendant contends that the contract was without consideration to support it, and therefore invalid. He asserts that the promisee, by refraining from the use of liquor and tobacco, was not harmed, but benefited; that that which he did was best for him to do, independently of his uncle's promise, — and insists that it follows that, unless the promisor was benefited, the contract was without consideration, — a contention which, if well founded, would seem to leave open for controversy in many cases whether that which the promisee did or omitted to do was in fact of such benefit to him as to leave no consideration to support the enforcement of the promisor's agreement. Such a rule could not be tolerated, and is without foundation in the law. . . . ' "Consideration" means not so much that one party is profiting as that the other abandons some legal right in the present, or limits his legal freedom of action in the future, as an inducement for the promise of the first.' Now, applying this rule to the facts before us, the promisee used tobacco, occasionally drank liquor, and he had a legal right to do so. That right he abandoned for a period of years upon the strength of the promise of the testator that for such forbearance he would give him $5,000. We need not speculate on the effort which may have been required to give up the use of those stimulants. It is sufficient that he restricted his lawful freedom of action within certain prescribed limits upon the faith of his uncle's agreement, and now, having fully performed the conditions imposed, it is of no moment whether such performance actually proved a benefit to the promisor, and the court will not inquire into it; but, were it a proper subject of inquiry, we see nothing in this record that would permit a determination that the uncle was not benefited in a legal sense. . . .

NOTES
1. It is difficult to see how this consideration could be classified as having 'economic value'. The decision may rest on policy, in that it is more socially acceptable to enforce this promise than to enforce the father's promise in *White* v *Bluett*. It may also be explained on the ground of the nephew's detrimental reliance.
2. Arguably, there is a benefit to the uncle from ensuring that his nephew refrains from these activities (see *Shadwell* v *Shadwell* (1860) 9 CBNS 159, *page 129*), although some commentators would argue that this is the uncle's motive rather than a benefit to him.
3. An important point on the facts was that the nephew had used tobacco and drunk liquor in the past. In *Arrale* v *Costain Civil Engineering Ltd* [1976] 1 Lloyd's Rep 98, Geoffrey Lane LJ stated that consideration was not provided by refraining from a course of conduct which it was never intended to pursue.

Past consideration is not a good (sufficient) consideration

Any act carried out *before* a promise is made cannot be a sufficient consideration to support the promise because it is not carried out in exchange for the promise.

Re McArdle
[1951] Ch 669 (CA)

The testator's widow had a life interest in a property which was held upon trust for the testator's five children. In 1943, improvements were carried out to the property which were paid for by the wife of one of the beneficiaries. (She had not been requested to do this.) In 1945, after this work had been completed, the five children signed a document addressed to the wife which stated, 'in consideration of your carrying out certain alterations and improvements to the property. . . . We the beneficiaries under the will of [the testator] hereby agree that the executors . . . shall repay to you from the said estate when so distributed the sum of £488 in settlement of the amount spent on the improvements'. When the testator's widow died the wife claimed this sum under the agreement. Held: since the work had been completed before the agreement of 1945, the consideration for it was past consideration and the agreement was unenforceable.

NOTE: There is a device which can be employed by the courts to avoid the literal nature of the past consideration rule and to allow such promises to be enforced. There must be a prior request to carry out the act, which carries with it a promise to pay or benefit the performer of the act in some way. In relation to this earlier promise the act is not past consideration.

Pao On v Lau Yiu Long
[1980] AC 614 (PC)

The plaintiffs owned shares in a private company, Shing On, whose principal asset was a building under construction. The defendants were the majority shareholders in the Fu Chip Investment Company which wished to acquire the building. In February 1973, the plaintiffs agreed with the Fu Chip Company to sell their shares in Shing On to Fu Chip in return for shares in Fu Chip. To avoid depressing the market for shares in Fu Chip, the defendants requested that the plaintiffs retain 60 per cent of their shares until after 30 April 1974, and it was agreed that the defendants would protect the plaintiffs against any loss from a fall in the value of those shares during that period. A subsidiary agreement was entered into by which the defendants agreed to buy and the plaintiffs agreed to sell 60 per cent of the shares on or before 30 April 1974 at $2.50 a share. The plaintiffs realised, however, that with such an agreement they would lose the benefit of any possible rise in the market price of that 60 per cent holding, and they refused to complete the sale of the shares in Shing On to Fu Chip unless the defendants agreed to replace the subsidiary agreement with an indemnity. The defendants signed an indemnity in consideration of the plaintiffs having agreed to sell their shares in Shing On. The plaintiffs later sought to rely on the indemnity and one issue before the court was whether they had provided any consideration for the indemnity. The Privy Council applied *Re Casey's Patents* [1892] 1 Ch 104. Held: the consideration was the plaintiffs' promise not to sell 60 per cent of their Fu Chip shares for one year. Although this promise had been made before the indemnity was given, it had been made at the request of the defendants and on the understanding that the plaintiffs were to be protected against the risk that the value of their shareholding might fall in this period.

LORD SCARMAN. The first question is whether upon its true construction the written guarantee of May 4, 1973, states a consideration sufficient in law to support the defendants' promise of indemnity against a fall in value of the Fu Chip shares. . . . [C]ounsel for the plaintiffs before their Lordships' Board but not below, contends that the consideration stated in the agreement is not in reality a past one. It is to be noted that the consideration was not on May 4, 1973, a matter of history only. The instrument by its reference to the main agreement with Fu Chip incorporates as part of the stated consideration the plaintiffs' three promises to Fu Chip: to complete the sale of Shing On, to accept shares as the price for the sale, and not to sell 60 per cent of the shares so accepted before April 30, 1974. Thus, on May 4, 1973, the performance of the main agreement still lay in the future. Performance of these promises was of great importance to the defendants, and it is undeniable that, as the instrument declares, the promises were made to Fu Chip at the request of the defendants. It is equally clear that the instrument also includes a promise by the plaintiffs to the defendants to fulfil their earlier promises given to Fu Chip.

The Board agrees with [counsel for the plaintiffs'] submission that the consideration expressly stated in the written guarantee is sufficient in law to support the defendants' promise of indemnity. An act done before the giving of a promise to make a payment or to confer some other benefit can sometimes be consideration for the promise. The act must have been done at the promisors' request: the parties must have understood that the act was to be remunerated either by a payment or the conferment of some other benefit: and payment, or the conferment of a benefit, must have been legally enforceable had it been promised in advance. All three features are present in this case. The promise given to Fu Chip under the main agreement not to sell the shares for a year was at the first defendant's request. The parties understood at the time of the main agreement that the restriction on selling must be compensated for by the benefit of a guarantee against a drop in price: and such a guarantee would be legally enforceable. The agreed cancellation of the subsidiary agreement left, as the parties knew, the plaintiffs unprotected in a respect in which at the time of the main agreement all were agreed they should be protected.

[Counsel for the plaintiffs'] submission is based on *Lampleigh* v *Brathwait* (1615) Hobart 105. In that case the judges said, at p. 106:

> First. . . . a meer voluntary courtesie will not have a consideration to uphold an assumpsit. But if that courtesie were moved by a suit or request of the party that gives the assumpsit, it will bind, for the promise, though it follows, yet it is not naked, but couples it self with the suit before, and the merits of the party procured by that suit, which is the difference.

The modern statement of the law is in the judgment of Bowen LJ in *In re Casey's Patents* [1892] 1 Ch 104, 115–116; Bowen LJ said:

> Even if it were true, as some scientific students of law believe, that a past service cannot support a future promise, you must look at the document and see if the promise cannot receive a proper effect in some other way. Now, the fact of a past service raises an implication that at the time it was rendered it was to be paid for, and, if it was a service which was to be paid for, when you get in the subsequent document a promise to pay, that promise may be treated either as an admission which evidences or as a positive bargain which fixes the amount of that reasonable remuneration on the faith of which the service was originally rendered. So that here for past services there is ample justification for the promise to give the third share.

. . . [Counsel] for the defendants, does not dispute the existence of the rule but challenges its application to the facts of this case. He submits that it is not a necessary inference or implication from the terms of the written guarantee that any benefit or protection was to be given to the plaintiffs for their acceptance of the restriction on selling their shares. Their Lordships agree that the mere existence or recital of a prior request is not sufficient in itself to convert what is prima facie past consideration into sufficient consideration in law to support a promise as they have indicated, it is only the first of three necessary preconditions. As for the second of those preconditions, whether the act done at the request of the promisor raises an implication of promised remuneration or other return is simply one of the construction of the words of the contract in the circumstances of its making. Once it is recognised, as the Board considers it inevitably must be, that the expressed consideration includes a reference to the plaintiffs' promise not to sell the shares before April 30, 1974 — a promise to be performed in the future, though given in the past — it is not possible to treat the defendants' promise of indemnity as independent of the plaintiffs' antecedent promise, given at the first defendant's request, not to sell. The promise of indemnity was given because at the time of the main agreement the parties intended that the first defendant should confer upon the plaintiffs the benefit of his protection against a fall in price. When the subsidiary agreement was cancelled, all were well aware that the plaintiffs were still to have the benefit of his protection as consideration for the restriction on selling. . . . Their Lordships, therefore, accept the submission that the contract itself states a valid consideration for the promise of indemnity.

NOTE: Although it may be possible to imply a promise to remunerate, in each case it must be asked whether it was reasonable in the circumstances for the parties to assume that the act would be remunerated.

There is some strength in the argument that it is more likely that such an implication of remuneration will arise in commercial cases or cases involving professional services (such as *Re Casey's Patents* and *Pao On* v *Lau Yiu Long*) than in cases involving arrangements between friends and family (*Re McArdle*) or where the services are not professional.

If you are drowning and I rescue you, although a request might be inferred from your call for help, because of the nature of the service I provide in rescuing you, it is most unlikely that the request carries with it any understanding that the rescue will be remunerated. The act of rescue cannot be consideration for any promise of reward.

Performance of existing duties

If a person either does or promises to do what they are already legally bound to do in exchange for a promise made to them, they suffer no legal detriment and confer no legal benefit so that, traditionally, this has not been accepted as constituting sufficient consideration.

Until the decision of the Court of Appeal in *Williams* v *Roffey Brothers & Nicholls (Contractors) Ltd* [1991] 1 QB 1 (see *page 135*), it was generally held to be insufficient that a factual detriment had been incurred or a factual benefit had been conferred. Lord Denning had been alone in accepting this as sufficient consideration in itself. The device employed to avoid the rule in practice was to hold that a promisee had gone beyond the scope of his existing duty and had thereby provided the necessary consideration.

(i) Performance of a duty imposed by law is not a good (sufficient) consideration

In *Collins* v *Godefroy* (1831) 1 B & Ad 950, 109 ER 1040, the Court of King's Bench held that a promise by Godefroy to pay Collins, whom he had subpoenaed, six guineas for attending as a witness was unenforceable, because if a person was subpoenaed he was under a duty imposed by law to attend and give evidence, and therefore performance of that duty could not support a promise to pay.

If a promisee has done more than he was legally obliged to do, that will constitute consideration for a promise to pay.

Ward v Byham

[1956] 1 WLR 496 (CA)

The father of an illegitimate child made the following promise to the child's mother: 'I am prepared to let you have [the child] and pay you up to £1 a week allowance for her providing you can prove that she will be well looked after and happy and also that she is allowed to decide for herself whether or not she wishes to come and live with you'. The father later stopped making these payments and the mother sought to enforce his promise. Held: the promise was supported by consideration and therefore enforceable. The majority (Morris and Parker LJJ) considered that although the mother was required by statute to maintain her child, she had gone beyond that statutory duty by complying with the father's request, and this was a sufficient consideration for the father's promise to pay.

Denning LJ considered that the factual benefit to the father was sufficient.

DENNING LJ: I approach the case, . . . on the footing that the mother, in looking after the child, is only doing what she is legally bound to do. Even so, I think that there was sufficient consideration to support the promise. I have always thought that a promise to perform an existing duty, or the performance of it, should be regarded as good consideration, because it is a benefit to the person to whom it is given. Take this very case. It is as much a benefit for the father to have the child looked after by the mother as by a neighbour. If he gets the benefit for which he stipulated, he ought to honour his promise, and he ought not to avoid it by saying that the mother was herself under a duty to maintain the child.

I regard the father's promise in this case as what is sometimes called a unilateral contract, a promise in return for an act, a promise by the father to pay £1 a week in return for the mother's looking after the child. Once the mother embarked on the task of looking after the child, there was a binding contract. So long as she looked after the child, she would be entitled to £1 a week.

■ QUESTION

How realistic is the view of the majority that the mother had suffered 'extra detriment'? It could be argued that the mother's promise to ensure that the child was happy was not capable of expression in economic terms.

Lord Denning also repeated his view of the correct principles in the next case.

Williams v Williams
[1957] 1 WLR 148 (CA)

In January 1952, a wife deserted her husband, and in March of that year the parties signed an agreement whereby the husband promised to pay the wife £1 10s a week for their joint lives so long as the wife led a chaste life. The wife promised to use this sum to support and maintain herself, 'and promised not to pledge her husband's credit and to indemnify him against any debts she incurred.' The wife later claimed arrears of this maintenance, but the husband argued that she had provided no consideration for his promise to pay since a husband was not bound to maintain a wife who had deserted him and a wife who had deserted her husband was not entitled to pledge her husband's credit. Held: the wife's promise did constitute good consideration since she could return at any time and had therefore only suspended her right to be maintained by her husband.

DENNING LJ: Now I agree that, in promising to maintain herself whilst she was in desertion, the wife was only promising to do that which she was already bound to do. Nevertheless, a promise to perform an existing duty is, I think, sufficient consideration to support a promise, so long as there is nothing in the transaction which is contrary to the public interest. Suppose that this agreement had never been made, and the wife had made no promise to maintain herself and did not do so. She might then have sought and received public assistance or have pledged her husband's credit with tradesmen: in which case the National Assistance Board might have summoned him before the magistrates, or the tradesmen might have sued him in the county court. It is true that he would have an answer to those claims because she was in desertion, but nevertheless he would be put to all the trouble, worry and expense of defending himself against them. By paying her 30s. a week and taking this promise from her that she will maintain herself and will not pledge his credit, he has an added safeguard to protect himself from all this worry, trouble and expense. That is a benefit to him which is good consideration for his promise to pay maintenance. . . .

NOTE: Denning LJ's qualification 'so long as there was nothing in the transaction which was contrary to the public interest' refers to public policy reasons why a promise should not be enforced (e.g., *Collins* v *Godefroy* (1831) 1 B & Ad 950 *page 127*). This might now be covered by the operation of the doctrine of economic duress (*page 611*).

(ii) Performance of an existing contractual duty owed to a third party is a good (sufficient) consideration
If B promises A that B will do something which he is already bound by a contract with C to do, then B can rely upon that promise (or his performance of that promise to C) as consideration to support a promise by A.

Shadwell v *Shadwell*

(1860) 9 CB NS 159; 142 ER 62 (Court of Common Bench)

After his engagement to Ellen Nicholl, the plaintiff received the following letter from his uncle:

'I am glad to hear of your intended marriage with Ellen Nicholl; and, as I promised to assist you at starting, I am happy to tell you that I will pay to you £150 yearly during my life and until your annual income derived from your profession of a Chancery barrister shall amount to 600 guineas . . .'

The plaintiff claimed arrears in these yearly sums from the uncle's executors, alleging the consideration for the promise to be his marriage to Ellen Nicholl. Held: (Erle CJ and Keating J) the promise was binding since it was supported by good consideration.

ERLE CJ (giving his own judgment and that of Keating J): Now, do these facts shew that the promise was in consideration either of a loss to be sustained by the plaintiff or a benefit to be derived from the plaintiff to the uncle, at his, the uncle's request? My answer is in the affirmative.

First, do these facts shew a loss sustained by the plaintiff at his uncle's request? When I answer this in the affirmative, I am aware that a man's marriage with the woman of his choice is in one sense a boon, and in that sense the reverse of a loss: yet, as between the plaintiff and the party promising to supply an income to support the marriage, it may well be also a loss. The plaintiff may have made a most material change in his position, and induced the object of his affection to do the same, and may have incurred pecuniary liabilities resulting in embarrassments which would be in every sense a loss if the income which had been promised should be withheld; and, if the promise was made in order to induce the parties to marry, the promise so made would be in legal effect a request to marry.

Secondly, do these facts shew a benefit derived from the plaintiff to the uncle, at his request? In answering again in the affirmative, I am at liberty to consider the relation in which the parties stood and the interest in the settlement of his nephew which the uncle declares. The marriage primarily affects the parties thereto; but in a secondary degree it may be an object of interest to a near relative, and in that sense a benefit to him. This benefit is also derived from the plaintiff at the uncle's request. If the promise of the annuity was intended as an inducement to the marriage, and the averment that the plaintiff, relying on the promise, married, is an averment that the promise was one inducement to the marriage, this is the consideration averred in the declaration; and it appears to me to be expressed in the letter, construed with the surrounding circumstances.

. . . [T]he decision turns upon the question of fact, whether the consideration for the promise is proved as pleaded. I think it is; and therefore my judgment . . . is for the plaintiff.

BYLES J (*dissenting*): . . . I am of opinion that the defendant is entitled to the judgment of the court . . .

The inquiry . . . narrows itself to this question, — Does the letter itself disclose any consideration for the promise? the consideration relied on by the plaintiff's counsel being the subsequent marriage of the plaintiff. I think the letter discloses no consideration. . . .

It is by no means clear that the words 'at starting' mean 'on marriage with Ellen Nicholl,' or with anyone else. The more natural meaning seems to me to be, 'at starting in the profession;' for, it will be observed that those words are used by testator in reciting a prior promise made when the testator had not heard of the proposed marriage with Ellen Nicholl, or, so far as appears, heard of any proposed marriage. This construction is fortified by the consideration that the annuity is not in terms made to begin from the marriage, but, as it should seem, from the date of the letter: neither is it in terms made defeasible if Ellen Nicholl should die before marriage.

But, even on the assumption that the words 'at starting' mean on marriage, I still think that no consideration appears, sufficient to sustain the promise. The promise is one which by law must be in writing; and the fourth plea shows that no consideration or request dehors the letter existed, and therefore that no such consideration or request can be alluded to by the letter.

Marriage of the plaintiff at the testator's express request would be no doubt an ample consideration. But marriage of the plaintiff without the testator's request is no consideration to the testator. It is true that marriage is or may be a detriment to the plaintiff: but detriment to the plaintiff is not enough, unless it either be a benefit to the testator, or be treated by the testator as such by having been suffered at his request. Suppose a defendant to promise a plaintiff, — 'I will give you 500*l.* if you break your leg,' — would that detriment to the plaintiff, should it happen, be any consideration? If it be said that such an accident is an involuntary mischief, would it have been a binding promise if the testator had said, — 'I will give you 100*l.* a year while you continue in your present chambers? I conceive that the promise would not be binding, for want of a previous request by the testator.

Now, the testator in the case before the court derived, so far as appears, no personal benefit from the marriage. The question, therefore, is still further narrowed to this point, — Was the marriage at the testator's request? Express request there was none. Can any request be implied? The only words from which it can be contended that it is to be implied, are the words 'I am glad to hear of your intended marriage with Ellen Nicholl.' But it appears from the fourth plea that the marriage had already been agreed on, and that the testator knew it. These words, therefore, seem to me to import no more than the satisfaction of the testator at the engagement, — an accomplished fact. No request can, as it seems to me, be inferred from them. And, further, how does it appear that the testator's implied request, if it could be implied, or his promise, if that promise alone would suffice, or both together, were intended to cause the marriage or did cause it, so that the marriage can be said to have taken place at the testator's request? or, in other words, in consequence of that request?

It seems to me not only that this does not appear, but that the contrary appears; for, the plaintiff before the letter had already bound himself to marry, by placing himself not only under a moral but under a legal objection to marry; and the testator knew it.

The well-known cases which have been cited at the bar in support of the position that a promise based on the consideration of doing that which a man is already bound to do is invalid, apply in this case. . . . The reason why the doing what a man is already bound to do is no consideration, is, not only because such a consideration is in judgment of law of no value, but because a man can hardly be allowed to say that the prior legal obligation was not his determining motive. But, whether he can be allowed to say so or not, the plaintiff does not say so here. He does, indeed, make an attempt to meet this difficulty by alleging in the replication to the fourth plea that he married relying on the testator's promise: but he shrinks from alleging, that, though he had promised to marry before the testator's promise to him, nevertheless he would have broken his engagement, and would not have married without the testator's promise. A man may rely on encouragements to the performance of his duty, who yet is prepared to do his duty without those encouragements. At the utmost the allegation that he relied on the testator's promise seems to me to import no more than that he believed the testator would be as good as his word.

It appears to me, for these reasons, that this letter is no more than a letter of kindness, creating no legal obligation.

NOTES

1. It is highly questionable whether the majority judgments support the principle that the performance by the nephew of his contractual duty owed to Ellen Nicholl (a third party) to marry her, was a good consideration for the uncle's promise. The majority judgments do not refer to the fact that the nephew was already contractually bound to his fiancée to marry her (at this time an action existed for breach of a promise to marry).

2. Erle CJ refers to the fact that the marriage could be seen as a detriment to the nephew, and stresses that the nephew might well have relied upon this promise in incurring additional expenses. Erle CJ also considered that there was a benefit to the uncle in seeing his nephew well settled. This so-called benefit is, of course, purely sentimental and is not capable of expression in economic terms.

3. Erle CJ also considered that the uncle's letter had requested the plaintiff to marry Ellen

Nicholl, whereas Byles J, dissenting, thought it did not, but had there been such a request, he was clear that the marriage would have been a good consideration for the promise.

4. Byles J considered that on its construction the marriage was a *condition* rather than the intended consideration for the uncle's promise. In any event, he considered that there was no intention to create legal relations (see *page 178*). This dissenting judgment was approved by Salmon LJ in *Jones* v *Padavatton* [1969] 1 WLR 328.

■ QUESTIONS

1. Is the true reason for enforcement the fact that the nephew had relied on his uncle's promise?

2. Byles J, dissenting, was clearly of the opinion that a detriment could be a sufficient consideration only if it was requested by the promisor. Is this a necessary requirement?

However, the principle, that performance of an existing contractual duty owed to a third party can be a good consideration, has been approved by the Privy Council in two more recent cases, namely *New Zealand Shipping Co. Ltd* v *A. M. Satterthwaite, The Eurymedon* and *Pao On* v *Lau Yiu Long* (see *below and page 125*).

New Zealand Shipping Co. Ltd v A. M. Satterthwaite, The Eurymedon
[1975] AC 154 (PC)

The shipper entered into a contract of carriage with the carrier for the carriage of a drilling machine from Liverpool to Wellington in New Zealand. This contract of carriage exempted the carrier from all liability for loss or damage unless the action was brought within one year, and this immunity was extended to the carrier's servants, agents, or independent contractors:

> It is hereby expressly agreed that no servant or agent of the carrier (including every independent contractor from time to time employed by the carrier) shall in any circumstances whatsoever be under any liability whatsoever to the shipper, consignee or owner of the goods or to any holder of this bill of lading for any loss or damage or delay of whatsoever kind arising or resulting directly or indirectly from any act neglect or default on his part while acting in the course of or in connection with his employment and, without prejudice to the generality of the foregoing provisions in this clause, every exemption, limitation, condition and liberty herein contained and every right, exemption from liability, defence and immunity of whatsoever nature applicable to the carrier or to which the carrier is entitled hereunder shall also be available and shall extend to protect every such servant or agent of the carrier acting as aforesaid and for the purpose of all the foregoing provisions of this clause the carrier is or shall be deemed to be acting as agent or trustee on behalf of and for the benefit of all persons who are or might be his servants or agents from time to time (including independent contractors as aforesaid) and all such persons shall to this extent be or be deemed to be parties to the contract in or evidenced by this bill of lading.

The carrier was a wholly-owned subsidiary company of the stevedores who were employed to unload the machine at Wellington. While unloading the machine, the stevedores were negligent and damaged it. The plaintiff cargo owner brought an action against the stevedores for the cost of repairing the drill. The stevedores pleaded the time limit in the contract of carriage between the shipper and the carrier. The Privy Council analysed the clause in the contract of carriage as a promise of exemption made to the stevedores through the carrier as their agent. In order to accept this promise, the stevedores had to provide consideration for the promise, and this was held to be the services of unloading which were of benefit to the shipper. The stevedores were already bound to perform these services under their contract with the carrier, and this could be a good consideration to support the shipper's promise.

LORD WILBERFORCE: If the choice, and the antithesis, is between a gratuitous promise, and a promise for consideration, as it must be in the absence of a tertium quid, there can be little doubt which, in commercial reality, this is. The whole contract is of a commercial character, involving service on one side, rates of payment on the other, and qualifying stipulations as to both. The relations of all parties to each other are commercial relations entered into for business reasons of ultimate profit. To describe one set of promises, in this context, as gratuitous, or nudum pactum, seems paradoxical and is prima facie implausible. It is only the precise analysis of this complex of relations into the classical offer and acceptance, with identifiable consideration, that seems to present difficulty, but this same difficulty exists in many situations of daily life, e.g., sales at auction; supermarket purchases; boarding an omnibus; purchasing a train ticket; tenders for the supply of goods; offers of rewards; acceptance by post; warranties of authority by agents; manufacturers' guarantees; gratuitous bailments; bankers' commercial credits. These are all examples which show that English law, having committed itself to a rather technical and schematic doctrine of contract, in application takes a practical approach, often at the cost of forcing the facts to fit uneasily into the marked slots of offer, acceptance and consideration. . . .

There is possibly more than one way of analysing this business transaction into the necessary components; that which their Lordships would accept is to say that the bill of lading brought into existence a bargain initially unilateral but capable of becoming mutual, between the shipper and the appellant, made through the carrier as agent. This became a full contract when the appellant performed services by discharging the goods. The performance of these services for the benefit of the shipper was the consideration for the agreement by the shipper that the appellant should have the benefit of the exemptions and limitations contained in the bill of lading. The conception of a 'unilateral' contract of this kind was recognised in *Great Northern Railway Co.* v *Witham* (1873) LR 9 CP 16 and is well established. This way of regarding the matter is very close to if not identical to that accepted by Beattie J in the Supreme Court: he analysed the transaction as one of an offer open to acceptance by action such as was found in *Carlill* v *Carbolic Smoke Ball Co.* [1893] 1 QB 256. . . .

The following points require mention. 1. In their Lordships' opinion, consideration may quite well be provided by the appellant, as suggested, even though (or if) it was already under an obligation to discharge to the carrier. (There is no direct evidence of the existence or nature of this obligation, but their Lordships are prepared to assume it.) An agreement to do an act which the promisor is under an existing obligation to a third party to do, may quite well amount to valid consideration and does so in the present case: the promisee obtains the benefit of a direct obligation which he can enforce. This proposition is illustrated and supported by *Scotson* v *Pegg* (1861) 6 H & N 295 which their Lordships consider to be good law. . . .

NOTES

1. The principle was extended to *promises* to perform an existing contractual duty owed to a third party, not just the performance of that duty, in *Pao On* v *Lau Yiu Long* (see *page 125*). The Privy Council held the consideration for the defendants' promise to be the plaintiffs' promise to the Fu Chip Company (the third party) to retain 60 per cent of their shares for one year. Lord Scarman said: 'Their Lordships do not doubt that a promise to perform, or the performance of, a pre-existing contractual obligation to a third party can be valid consideration.'

2. In *Scotson* v *Pegg* (1861) 6 H & N 295, 158 ER 121, the Court of Exchequer held that it was necessary for the promisee's action, which he was contractually bound to the third party to perform, to also be a benefit to the promisor.

   Clearly, the defendants in *Pao On* v *Lau Yiu Long*, as majority shareholders, benefited by seeing the main agreement with the company performed. The Privy Council in *The Eurymedon* also appeared to treat it as a benefit to the shipper to have the goods unloaded by the stevedores. If the stevedores failed to unload the goods, that would inevitably cause loss to the shipper, but the only party with a remedy in breach of contract would be the carrier.

It might be argued that in all these cases the promisor does get a benefit from the performance of a contractual duty owed to a third party, but it is a *factual benefit*. Should this be sufficient? (See *page 135*.)

3. The difficulty is to find additional detriment to the promisee. If there is none, does it matter? (See the discussion of *Williams* v *Roffey Brothers & Nicholls (Contractors) Ltd* [1991] 1 QB 1, at *pages 139–40*.)

(iii) Performance of a contractual duty owed to the promisor

This arises in the context of a promise to alter an existing contract between the parties.

Stilk v Myrick

The two reports of this case give different explanations of why the claim was unenforceable.

(1809) 2 Camp 317; 170 ER 1168, Campbell's Report

On a voyage from London to the Baltic, two of the seamen deserted and, because the captain could not find replacements at Cronstadt, he promised the remaining crew that he would divide the wages of the deserters between them if they sailed the ship back to London. Was this promise enforceable?

Garrow for the defendant insisted, that this agreement was contrary to public policy, and utterly void. In West India voyages, crews are often thinned greatly by death and desertion; and if a promise of advanced wages were valid, exorbitant claims would be set up on all such occasions. This ground was strongly taken by Lord Kenyon in *Harris* v *Watson* (1791) Peake 102, where that learned judge held, that no action would lie at the suit of a sailor on a promise of a captain to pay him extra wages, in consideration of his doing more than the ordinary share of duty in navigating the ship; and his Lordship said, that if such a promise could be enforced, sailors would in many cases suffer a ship to sink unless the captain would accede to any extravagant demand they might think proper to make.

LORD ELLENBOROUGH: I think *Harris* v *Watson* was rightly decided; but I doubt whether the ground of public policy, upon which Lord Kenyon is stated to have proceeded, be the true principle on which the decision is to be supported. Here, I say, the agreement is void for want of consideration. There was no consideration for the ulterior pay promised to the mariners who remained with the ship. Before they sailed from London they had undertaken to do all that they could under all the emergencies of the voyage. They had sold all their services till the voyage should be completed. If they had been at liberty to quit the vessel at Cronstadt, the case would have been quite different; or if the captain had capriciously discharged the two men who were wanting, the others might not have been compellable to take the whole duty upon themselves, and their agreeing to do so might have been a sufficient consideration for the promise of an advance of wages. But the desertion of a part of the crew is to be considered an emergency of the voyage as much as their death; and those who remain are bound by the terms of their original contract to exert themselves to the utmost to bring the ship in safety to her destined port. Therefore, without looking to the policy of this agreement, I think it is void for want of consideration . . .

NOTE: This report stresses that the desertions were covered by the agreed terms of the contract, so that by sailing the ship home shorthanded the sailors had not done any more than they were already bound to do. Consequently, the master's promise was not supported by any consideration and was unenforceable.

Espinasse's Report stresses the policy grounds, stated by Lord Kenyon in *Harris* v *Watson* (1791) Peake 102, for refusing enforcement.

(1809) 6 Esp 129; 170 ER 851

Lord Ellenborough ruled, That the plaintiff could not recover this part of his demand. His Lordship said, That he recognised the principle of the case of *Harris* v *Watson* as founded on just and proper policy. When the defendant entered on board the ship, he stipulated to do all the work his situation called upon him to do. Here the voyage was to the Baltick and back, not to Cronstadt only; if the voyage had then terminated, the sailors might have made what terms they pleased. If any part of the crew had died, would not the remainder have been forced to work the ship home? If that accident would have left them liable to do the whole work without any extraordinary remuneration, why should not desertion or casualty equally demand it?

NOTES

1. Espinasse appeared in this case as counsel for the plaintiff, but his report is not accepted as authoritative.
2. If his report were correct, it might be argued that, in the absence of circumstances of extortion, there is no reason why such a promise should not be enforced. However, Mocatta J in *North Ocean Shipping* v *Hyundai Construction Co. Ltd* [1979] QB 705, accepted *Campbell's Report* as the correct one, and it is also implicit in the judgment of the Court of Appeal in *Williams* v *Roffey Brothers & Nicholls (Contractors) Ltd* (*page 135*), since the Court did not question the need to establish consideration although there was no extortion on the facts. There also appears to be no evidence of extortion on the facts of *Stilk* v *Myrick* itself, since the initiative for the payment came from the ship's captain and not the crew.
3. Although there was a factual benefit to the captain from the sailors' promise to sail the ship home, that was not accepted as sufficient consideration.
4. The principle in *Stilk* v *Myrick* applies to variations but not to instances of rescission and replacement. The question facing the Court of Appeal in *Compagnie Noga D'Importation et D'Exportation* v *Abacha (No. 4)* [2003] EWCA Civ 1100, [2003] 2 All ER (Comm) 915, related to an agreement to settle a claim. Under the first agreement (13 August) FGN had waived all claims against SJB in return for a specified payment. However, this agreement was rescinded and replaced by an agreement of 16 August under which only certain clauses were waived. The agreement of 16 August expressly provided that it superseded the earlier agreement. FGN sought to rely on the 16 August agreement but SJB argued that it was not supported by consideration since it amounted to no more than a promise to perform an existing contractual obligation (in the agreement of 13 August) and was therefore unenforceable (*Stilk* v *Myrick*). However, the Court of Appeal held that the effect of rescission was to bring the agreement of 13 August to an end. It followed that the principle in *Stilk* did not apply since it depended on the continuation of the obligations in the old agreement (13 August) whereas they had come to an end by mutual release. The consideration for the 16 August agreement consisted of the mutual promises in that new agreement and the mutual release from the earlier agreement.

It has always been accepted that if a promisee has done more than he was contractually obliged to do, then the extra performance is consideration to support the promisor's promise.

North Ocean Shipping Co. Ltd v Hyundai Construction Co. Ltd, The Atlantic Baron
[1979] QB 705

(The full facts of this case appear at *page 613*.)

A shipbuilding company agreed to build a tanker for the owners, and opened a letter of credit to provide security for repayment of the instalments paid by the owners in the event of the shipbuilding company's default. The owners promised to pay an additional 10 per cent in the instalments when the US dollar was devalued, and asked the company to make a corresponding increase in the letter of credit, which the company did. Held: (although with some hesitation) in agreeing to increase the letter of credit, the company had undertaken an additional contractual obligation which rendered them liable to an increased detriment, and that this constituted consideration for the promise by the owners to increase the instalment payments.

MOCATTA J: [Counsel for the owners'] argument that the agreement to pay the extra 10 per cent was void for lack of consideration was based upon the well-known principle that a promise by one party to fulfil his existing contractual duty towards his other contracting party is not good consideration; he relied upon the well-known case of *Stilk* v *Myrick* (1809) 2 Camp 317; 6 Esp 129 for this submission. Accordingly there was no consideration for the owner's agreement to pay the further 10 per cent, since the Yard were already contractually bound to build the ship and it is common ground that the devaluation of the dollar had in no way lessened the Yard's legal obligation to do this. There has of course been some criticism in the books of the decision in *Stilk* v *Myrick*, which is somewhat differently reported in the two sets of reports, but Campbell's Reports have the better reputation and what I have referred to as being the law on this point is referred to as 'the present rule' in *Chitty on Contracts, General Principles*, 24th ed. (1977), p. 86: see, also, *Cheshire and Fifoot, Law of Contract*, 9th ed. (1976), p. 83. . . .

[Counsel for the ship building company] relied upon what Denning LJ said in two cases dealing with very different subject matters [*Ward* v *Byham, page 127* and *Williams* v *Williams, page 128*]. . . . I do not . . . think either of these cases successfully enables [counsel] to avoid the rule in *Stilk* v *Myrick*, 2 Camp 317.

What I have, however, found more difficult is whether the Yard did not give some consideration for the extra 10 per cent on the contract price, on which they insisted, in the form of their agreement to increase pro tanto what was for short called in argument 'the return letter of credit.' . . . I remain unconvinced . . . that by merely securing an increase in the instalments to be paid of 10 per cent the Yard automatically became obliged to increase the return letter of credit pro tanto and were therefore doing no more than undertaking in this respect to fulfil their existing contractual duty. I think that here they were undertaking an additional obligation or rendering themselves liable to an increased detriment. I therefore conclude, though not without some doubt, that there was consideration for the new agreement.

The decision of the Court of Appeal in *Williams* v *Roffey Brothers & Nicholls (Contractors) Ltd* demonstrates that, since the recognition of a doctrine of economic duress (*page 611*), as the protection against extortion, it is no longer necessary to adopt a rule requiring legal benefit or detriment, and that consideration may be found where there is a factual benefit to the promisor or avoidance of a disbenefit arising from a promise to pay more money under an existing contract.

Williams v *Roffey Brothers & Nicholls (Contractors) Ltd*
[1991] 1 QB 1 (CA)

The defendant building contractors had entered into a contract to refurbish a block of 27 flats. They subcontracted the carpentry work to the plaintiff carpenter for a price of £20,000. When the plaintiff had completed the carpentry work on the roof and only nine of the flats, and carried out only preliminary work on the others, the plaintiff found that he was in financial difficulties, despite the fact that he had already received interim payments of £16,200. The difficulties were due in part to the fact that he had underestimated the cost of doing the work, and in part because of his failure to supervise the work properly. The defendants were liable under a 'penalty clause' in the main contract if the flats were not completed on time. They were aware of the plaintiff's difficulties and that the subcontract had been under-priced. The defendants called a meeting and agreed to pay the plaintiff an extra £10,300 at the rate of £575 on completion of each flat. The plaintiff completed eight further flats and the defendants made one further payment of £1,500. The plaintiff stopped work and sued the defendants on their promise, which the defendants claimed was unenforceable because it was not supported by any con-sideration. Held: Although the plaintiff was doing no more than he was already legally obliged to do, as the defendants had obtained a benefit in making this promise, the promise was enforceable against them (in the absence of economic duress or fraud). The Court of Appeal stated that this did not overrule or contravene the principle in *Stilk* v *Myrick* (1809) 2 Camp 317, 6 Esp 129.

GLIDEWELL LJ: In his address to us [counsel for the defendants] outlined the benefits to his clients, the defendants, which arose from their agreement to pay the additional £10,300 as: (i) seeking to ensure that the plaintiff continued work and did not stop in breach of the sub-contract; (ii) avoiding the penalty for delay; and (iii) avoiding the trouble and expense of engaging other people to com-plete the carpentry work.

However, [counsel] submits that, though his clients may have derived, or hoped to derive, prac-tical benefits from their agreement to pay the 'bonus', they derived no benefit in law, since the plaintiff was promising to do no more than he was already bound to do by his subcontract, i.e. continue with the carpentry work and complete it on time. Thus there was no consideration for the agreement.

[Counsel for the defendants] relies on the principle of law which, traditionally, is based on the decision in *Stilk* v *Myrick* . . .

In *North Ocean Shipping Co. Ltd* v *Hyundai Construction Co. Ltd* [1979] QB 705, Mocatta J regarded the general principle of the decision in *Stilk* v *Myrick* as still being good law. . . .

It was suggested to us in argument that, since the development of the doctrine of promissory estoppel, it may well be possible for a person to whom a promise has been made, on which he has relied, to make an additional payment for services which he is in any event bound to render under an existing contract or by operation of law, to show that the promisor is estopped from claiming that there was no consideration for his promise. However, the application of the doctrine of promisory estoppel to facts such as those of the present case has not yet been fully developed: see e.g. the judgment of Lloyd J in *Syros Shipping Co. SA* v *Elaghill Trading Co.* [1980] 2 Lloyd's Rep 390, 392. Moreover, this point was not argued in the court below, nor was it more than adumbrated before us. Interesting though it is, no reliance can in my view be placed on this concept in the present case.

There is, however, another legal concept of relatively recent development which is relevant, namely that of economic duress. Clearly, if a subcontractor has agreed to undertake work at a fixed price, and before he has completed the work declines to continue with it unless the contractor agrees to pay an increased price, the subcontractor may be held guilty of securing the contractor's promise by taking unfair advantage of the difficulties he will cause if he does not complete the work. In such a case an agreement to pay an increased price may well be voidable because it was entered into under duress. Thus this concept may provide another answer in law to the question of policy which has troubled the courts since before *Stilk* v *Myrick* . . ., and no doubt led at the date of that decision to a rigid adherence to the doctrine of consideration.

. . . [T]he present state of the law on this subject can be expressed in the following proposition: (i) if A has entered into a contract with B to do work for, or to supply goods or services to, B in return for payment by B; and (ii) at some stage before A has completely performed his obligations under the contract B has reason to doubt whether A will, or will be able to, complete his side of the bargain; and (iii) B thereupon promises A an additional payment in return for A's promise to perform his contractual obligations on time; and (iv) as a result of giving his promise, B obtains in practice a benefit, or obviates a disbenefit; and (v) B's promise is not given as a result of economic duress or fraud on the part of A; then (vi) the benefit to B is capable of being consideration for B's promise, so that the promise will be legally binding.

As I have said, [counsel for the defendants] accepts that in the present case by promising to pay the extra £10,300 his client secured benefits. There is no finding, and no suggestion, that in this case the promise was given as a result of fraud or duress. If it be objected that the propositions above contravene the principle in *Stilk* v *Myrick*, I answer that in my view they do not; they refine, and limit the application of that principle, but they leave the principle unscathed e.g. where B secures no benefit by his promise. It is not in my view surprising that a principle enunciated in relation to the rigours of seafaring life during the Napoleonic wars should be subjected during the succeeding 180 years to a process of refinement and limitation in its application in the present day. It is therefore my opinion that on his findings of fact in the present case, the judge was entitled to hold, as he did, that the defendants' promise to pay the extra £10,300 was supported by valuable consideration, and thus constituted an enforceable agreement.

As a subsidiary argument, [counsel for the defendants] submits that on the facts of the present case the consideration, even if otherwise good, did not 'move from the promisee'. This submission is based on the principle illustrated in the decision in *Tweddle* v *Atkinson* (1861) 1 B & S 393. My understanding of the meaning of the requirement that 'consideration must move from the promisee' is that such consideration must be provided by the promisee, or arise out of his contractual relationship with the promisor. It is consideration provided by somebody else, not a party to the contract, which does not 'move from the promisee'. This was the situation in *Tweddle* v *Atkinson*, but it is, of course, not the situation in the present case. Here the benefits to the defendants arose out of their agreement of 9 April 1986 with the plaintiff, the promisee. In this respect I would adopt the following passage from *Chitty on Contracts*, 26th ed. (1989), p. 126, para. 183, and refer to the authorities there cited:

> The requirement that consideration must move from the promisee is most generally satisfied where some detriment is suffered by him e.g. where he parts with money or goods, or renders services, in exchange for the promise. But the requirement may equally well be satisfied where the promisee confers a benefit on the promisor without in fact suffering any detriment.'

That is the situation in this case.

RUSSELL LJ: . . . Speaking for myself—and I notice it is touched on in the judgment of Glidewell LJ—I would have welcomed the development of argument, if it could have been properly raised in this court, on the basis that there was here an estoppel and that the defendants, in the circumstances prevailing, were precluded from raising the defence that their undertaking to pay the extra £10,300 was not binding. For example, in *Amalgamated Investment and Property Co Ltd* v *Texas Commerce Internatonal Bank Ltd* [1982] QB 84 Robert Goff J said, at p. 105:

> it is in my judgment not of itself a bar to an estoppel that its effect may be to enable a party to enforce a cause of action which, without the estoppel, would not exist. It is sometimes said that an estoppel cannot create a cause of action, or that an estoppel can only act as a shield, not as a sword. In a sense this is true—in the sense that estoppel is not, as a contract is, a source of legal obligation. But, as Lord Denning MR pointed out in *Crabb* v *Arun District Council* [1976] Ch 179, 187, an estoppel may have the effect that a party can enforce a cause of action which, without the estoppel, he would not be able to do.

[For the speech of Lord Denning MR in the Court of Appeal ([1982] QB 84 at 122) see *page 162*]: Brandon LJ said, at pp. 131–132:

> while a party cannot in terms found a cause of action on an estoppel, he may, as a result of being able to rely on an estoppel, succeed on a cause of action on which, without being able to rely on that estoppel, he would necessarily have failed.

These citations demonstrate that while consideration remains a fundamental requirement before a contract not under seal can be enforced, the policy of the law in its search to do justice between the parties has developed considerably since the early nineteenth century when *Stilk* v *Myrick* 2 Camp 317 was decided by Lord Ellenborough CJ. In the late 20th century I do not believe that the rigid approach to the concept of consideration to be found in *Stilk* v *Myrick* is either necessary or desirable. Consideration there must still be but in my judgment the courts nowadays should be more ready to find its existence so as to reflect the intention of the parties to the contract where the bargaining powers are not unequal and where the finding of consideration reflects the true intention of the parties.

. . . The plaintiff has got into financial difficulties. The defendants, through their employee Mr Cottrell, recognised that the price that had been agreed originally with the plaintiff was less than what Mr Cottrell himself regarded as a reasonable price. There was a desire on Mr Cottrell's part to retain the services of the plaintiff so that the work could be completed without the need to employ another subcontractor. There was further a need to replace what had hitherto been a haphazard method of payment by a more formalised scheme involving the payment of a specified sum on the completion of each flat. These were all advantages accruing to the defendants which can fairly be said to have been in consideration of their undertaking to pay the additional £10,300. True it was that the plaintiff did not undertake to do any work additional to that which he had originally undertaken to do but the terms on which he was to carry out the work were varied and, in my judgment, that variation was supported by consideration which a pragmatic approach to the true relationship between the parties readily demonstrates.

For my part I wish to make it plain that I do not base my judgment on any reservation as to the correctness of the law long ago enunciated in *Stilk* v *Myrick*. A gratuitous promise, pure and simple, remains unenforceable unless given under seal. But where, as in this case, a party undertakes to make a payment because by so doing it will gain an advantage arising out of the continuing relationship with the promisee the new bargain will not fail for want of consideration.

PURCHAS LJ: The point of some difficulty which arises on this appeal is whether the judge was correct in his conclusion that the agreement reached on 9 April did not fail for lack of consideration because the principle established by the old cases of *Stilk* v *Myrick* 2 Camp 317, approving *Harris* v *Watson* Peake 102, did not apply. [Counsel] for the plaintiff, was bold enough to submit that . . . this court was bound by neither authority. I feel I must say at once that, for my part, I would not be prepared to overrule two cases of such veneration involving judgments of judges of such distinction except on the strongest possible grounds since they form a pillar stone of the law of contract which has been observed over the years and is still recognised in principle in recent authority: see the decision of *Stilk* v *Myrick* to be found in *North Ocean Shipping Co Ltd* v *Hyundai Construction Co Ltd* [1979] QB 705, 712 *per* Mocatta J. With respect, I agree with his view of the two judgments of Denning LJ in *Ward* v *Byham* [1956] 1 WLR 496 and *Williams* v *Williams* [1957] 1 WLR 148 in concluding that these judgments do not provide a sound basis for avoiding the rule in *Stilk* v *Myrick*. Although this rule has been the subject of some criticism it is still clearly recognised in current textbooks of authority: see *Chitty on Contracts*, 28th ed. (1989) and *Cheshire Fifoot and Furmston's Law of Contract*, 11th ed. (1986). . . .

In my judgment, therefore, the rule in *Stilk* v *Myrick* remains valid as a matter of principle, namely that a contract not under seal must be supported by consideration. . . . The modern cases tend to depend more on the defence of duress in a commercial context rather than lack of consideration for the second agreement. In the present case the question of duress does not arise. The initiative in coming to the agreement of 9 April came from Mr Cottrell and not from the plaintiff. It would not, therefore, lie in the defendants' mouth to assert a defence of duress. Nevertheless, the court is more ready in the presence of this defence being available in the commercial context to look for mutual advantages which would amount to sufficient consideration to support the second agreement under which the extra money is paid. Although the passage cited below from the speech of Lord Hailsham LC in *Woodhouse AC Israel Cocoa Ltd SA* v *Nigerian Produce Marketing Co Ltd* [1972] AC 741 was strictly obiter dicta I respectfully adopt it as an indication of the approach to be made in modern times. . . .

. . . Business men know their own business best even when they appear to grant an indulgence, and in the present case I do not think that there would have been insuperable difficulty in spelling out consideration from the earlier correspondence.

The question must be posed: what consideration has moved from the plaintiff to support the promise to pay the extra £10,300 added to the lump sum provision? In the particular circumstances . . . there was clearly a commercial advantage to both sides from a pragmatic point of view in reaching the agreement of 9 April. The defendants were on risk that as a result of the bargain they had struck the plaintiff would not or indeed possibly could not comply with his existing obligations without further finance. As a result of the agreement the defendants secured their position commercially. There was, however, no obligation added to the contractual duties imposed on the plaintiff under the original contract. Prima facie this would appear to be a classic *Stilk* v *Myrick* case. It was, however, open to the plaintiff to be in deliberate breach of the contract in order to 'cut his losses' commercially. In normal circumstances the suggestion that a contracting party can rely on his own breach to establish consideration is distinctly unattractive. In many cases it obviously would be and if there was any element of duress brought upon the other contracting party under the modern development of this branch of the law the proposed breaker of the contract would not benefit. With some hesitation and comforted by the passage from the speech of Lord Hailsham of St. Marylebone LC in *Woodhouse AC Israel Cocoa Ltd SA* v *Nigerian Produce Marketing Co Ltd* [1972] AC 741, 757–758 to which I have referred. I consider that the modern approach to the question of consideration would be that where there were benefits derived by each party to a contract of variation even though one party did not suffer a detriment this would not be fatal to the establishing of sufficient consideration to support the agreement. If both parties benefit from an agreement it is not necessary that each also suffers a detriment. In my judgment, on the facts as found by the judge, he was entitled to reach the conclusion that consideration existed and in those circumstances I would not disturb that finding. . . .

NOTES

1. The Court of Appeal affirmed the need for consideration to support such a promise but made it much easier to establish its existence, at least in the context of alteration promises to pay more. (There are other signs of relaxation of the strict rules relating to consideration. See, e.g., Law Commission, *Privity of Contract: Contracts for the Benefit of Third Parties* (Law Com. No. 242, Cm 3329, 1996), paras 6.13–6.17, discussed at *pages 439–40*.)

2. The 'penalty clause' was in fact an enforceable liquidated damages clause rather than a true penalty clause. The term 'penalty clause' is often used in a very general sense. (For a discussion of liquidated damages and penalty clauses, see *page 414*.)

3. In future it will be necessary, first, to ensure that the promise was not obtained under duress and, secondly, to ascertain whether there is any factual benefit to the promisor arising from the making of this promise. Coote 'Consideration and benefit in fact and in law' (1990) 3 JCL 23, argued that a promise of further payment would not be made if the performance of the contract would not benefit the promisor, since this would amount to throwing good money after bad.

4. The benefit arose from the fact that the promisor agreed to pay more money in order to secure completion on time, and it was not conferred by anything that the promisee did.

   The Court of Appeal held that the benefit could be generated by the compromise itself. This is the case, e.g., with agreements to discharge a contract, where both parties get the benefit of not having to fulfil their obligations under the contract, and it seems to have been extended to any situation where the courts are seeking to find the necessary benefit. That consideration may consist only of benefit to the promisor, without any corresponding detriment to the promisee, is further evidenced in the decision of the Court of Appeal in *Edmonds* v *Lawson* [2000] QB 501, *page 196*. The consideration consisted only of benefit, the benefit to chambers in securing suitable pupils who might be considered for future tenancies and the educational benefit to the pupil. There was no requirement that the pupil had to suffer any detriment, for example, in the form of a fee to undertake pupillage.

5. Adams and Brownsword, 'Contract, consideration and the critical path' (1990) 53 MLR 536,

considered that the decision reflects a change in approach and that, when deciding to enforce a promise, the courts are likely to be guided by considerations such as the fairness and reasonableness of the agreement and the need to reflect commercial realities rather than relying on the technical requirements of the doctrine of consideration. This shifts the burden from consideration onto the doctrine of economic duress, which is a developing doctrine and still requires further refinement (Phang (1991) 107 LQR 21).

6. The Court of Appeal in this case seemed quite willing to relieve the carpenter from the consequences of his own inaccurate tender. Once a contract has been made at a fixed price, the courts are not normally as willing to disturb it where there is no evidence of duress, mistake or misrepresentation. For example, in *Davis Contractors Ltd* v *Fareham UDC* [1956] AC 696 (*page 505*), the House of Lords held that where, due to shortages of labour and materials, the building work took longer than planned so that the price tendered did not reflect the value of the work, the contract was not frustrated and the contractors could not claim the additional sums on a *quantum meruit*.

   The result of *Williams* v *Roffey* is that if a promise to pay more is actually made, then it is enforceable; but, in the absence of such a promise, the carpenter cannot avoid performance if he finds that he has tendered too low.

7. It appears that *Williams* v *Roffey* does not apply in the context of alteration promises to accept less. Relevant case law is discussed at *pages 143–5* below, where the current standing of the decision in *Williams* v *Roffey* is also assessed.

D: Part payment of a debt

Where a creditor promises to accept a smaller sum than is due from a debtor and promises not to sue for the balance, this is a promise to alter an existing contract (the debt contract). In *Pinnel's Case* (1602) 5 CoRep 117a, the Court of Common Pleas held that in such circumstances the debtor must provide consideration for the creditor's promise to release him. Simply paying a smaller sum than that owed will not be sufficient, since the debtor has done only what he was legally obliged to do anyway under the debt contract. Traditionally, the factual benefit that might accrue to the creditor from securing some payment rather than nothing at all, was not regarded as sufficient and some separate consideration was required. However, the 'gift of a horse, hawk or robe' would be good consideration for a promise to forgo the balance if accepted by the creditor, since the court will not inquire into the adequacy of the consideration.

Payment before the due date is a good consideration, as is payment at a different place (as long as the change of venue is at the creditor's request and not the debtor's since if it were at the debtor's request there would be neither a benefit to the creditor, nor a detriment to the debtor, *Vanbergen* v *St. Edmunds Properties Ltd* [1933] 2 KB 223).

The principle in *Pinnel's Case* was confirmed by the House of Lords in the next case.

Foakes v *Beer*
(1884) 9 App Cas 605 (HL)

In August 1875, Julia Beer had obtained a High Court judgment against Dr Foakes for £2,090 19s. It was agreed in writing in December 1876, that if Dr Foakes paid £500 immediately and paid £150 on two occasions each year until the whole sum of £2,090 19s had been paid, then Julia Beer promised that she 'would not take any proceedings whatever on the said judgment'. (As a judgment debtor Dr Foakes was liable for the interest that had accrued on the judgment debt, but the agreement had not mentioned this.) Dr Foakes paid the judgment debt in accordance with the agreement but Julia Beer then brought an action claiming the interest on the debt. The House of Lords was divided on the question of whether the agreement amounted to a promise to excuse Dr Foakes from payment of the interest. Held: in any event, Dr Foakes had not provided any consideration for Julia Beer's promise not to take any proceedings on the judgment, and therefore the promise was unenforceable. He had only done what he was legally bound to do anyway.

EARL OF SELBORNE LC: . . . [T]he question remains, whether the agreement is capable of being legally enforced. Not being under seal, it cannot be legally enforced against the respondent, unless she received consideration for it from the appellant, or unless, though without consideration, it operates by way of accord and satisfaction, so as to extinguish the claim for interest. What is the consideration? On the face of the agreement none is expressed, except a present payment of £500, on account and in part of the larger debt then due and payable by law under the judgment. The appellant did not contract to pay the future instalments of £150 each, at the times therein mentioned; much less did he give any new security; in the shape of negotiable paper, or in any other form. The promise de futuro was only that of the respondent, that if the half-yearly payments of £150 each were regularly paid, she would 'take no proceedings whatever on the judgment.' No doubt if the appellant had been under no antecedent obligation to pay the whole debt, his fulfilment of the condition might have imported some consideration on his part for that promise. But he was under that antecedent obligation; and payment at those deferred dates, by the forbearance and indulgence of the creditor, of the residue of the principal debt and costs, could not (in my opinion) be a consideration for the relinquishment of interest and discharge of the judgment, unless the payment of the £500, at the time of signing the agreement, was such a consideration. As to accord and satisfaction, in point of fact there could be no complete satisfaction, so long as any future instalment remained payable; and I do not see how any mere payments on account could operate in law as a satisfaction ad interim, conditionally upon other payments being afterwards duly made, unless there was a consideration sufficient to support the agreement while still unexecuted. Nor was anything, in fact, done by the respondent in this case, on the receipt of the last payment, which could be tantamount to an acquittance, if the agreement did not previously bind her.

The question, therefore, is nakedly raised by this appeal, whether your Lordships are now prepared, not only to overrule, as contrary to law, the doctrine stated by Sir Edward Coke to have been laid down by all the judges of the Common Pleas in *Pinnel's Case* (1602) 5 CoRep 117a, . . . but to treat a prospective agreement, not under seal, for satisfaction of a debt, by a series of payments on account to a total amount less than the whole debt, as binding in law, provided those payments are regularly made; the case not being one of a composition with a common debtor, agreed to, inter se, by several creditors. . . . The doctrine itself, as laid down by Sir Edward Coke, may have been criticised, as questionable in principle, by some persons whose opinions are entitled to respect, but it has never been judicially overruled; on the contrary I think it has always, since the sixteenth century, been accepted as law. If so, I cannot think that your Lordships would do right, if you were now to reverse, as erroneous, a judgment of the Court of Appeal, proceeding upon a doctrine which has been accepted as part of the law of England for 280 years. . . .

The distinction between the effect of a deed under seal, and that of an agreement by parol, or by writing not under seal, may seem arbitrary, but it is established in our law; nor is it really unreasonable or practically inconvenient that the law should require particular solemnities to give to a gratuitous contract the force of a binding obligation. If the question be (as, in the actual state of the law, I think it is), whether consideration is, or is not, given in a case of this kind, by the debtor who pays down part of the debt presently due from him, for a promise by the creditor to relinquish, after certain further payments on account, the residue of the debt, I cannot say that I think consideration is given, in the sense in which I have always understood that word as used in our law. It might be (and indeed I think it would be) an improvement in our law, if a release or acquittance of the whole debt, on payment of any sum which the creditor might be content to receive by way of accord and satisfaction (though less than the whole), were held to be, generally, binding, though not under seal; nor should I be unwilling to see equal force given to a prospective agreement, like the present, in writing though not under seal; but I think it impossible, without refinements which practically alter the sense of the word, to treat such a release or acquittance as supported by any new consideration proceeding from the debtor.

. . . What is called 'any benefit, or even any legal possibility of benefit,' in Mr Smith's notes to *Cumber* v *Wane* (1721) 1 Stra 426, is not (as I conceive) that sort of benefit which a creditor may derive from getting payment of part of the money due to him from a debtor who might otherwise keep him at arm's length, or possibly become insolvent, but is some independent benefit, actual or contingent, of a kind which might in law be a good and valuable consideration for any other sort of agreement not under seal. . . .

Lord Blackburn, however, accepted that in practice, agreements to accept part payment in full satisfaction often have factual benefits for the creditor. His position recognises the practical realities.

LORD BLACKBURN: [Lord Blackburn referred to the decision in *Pinnel's Case* and continued:]

There are two things here resolved. First, that where a matter paid and accepted in satisfaction of a debt certain might by any possibility be more beneficial to the creditor than his debt, the Court will not inquire into the adequacy of the consideration. If the creditor, without any fraud, accepted it in satisfaction when it was not a sufficient satisfaction it was his own fault. And that payment before the day might be more beneficial, and consequently that the plea was in substance good, and this must have been decided in the case.

There is a second point stated to have been resolved, viz.: 'That payment of a lesser sum on the day cannot be any satisfaction of the whole, because it appears to the judges that by no possibility a lesser sum can be a satisfaction to the plaintiff for a greater sum.' This was certainly not necessary for the decision of the case; but though the resolution of the Court of Common Pleas was only a dictum, it seems to me clear that Lord Coke deliberately adopted the dictum, and the great weight of his authority makes it necessary to be cautious before saying that what he deliberately adopted as law was a mistake, and though I cannot find that in any subsequent case this dictum has been made the ground of the decision . . . yet there certainly are cases in which great judges have treated the dictum in *Pinnel's Case* as good law.

. . . I doubt much whether any judge sitting in a Court of the first instance would be justified in treating the question as open. But as this has very seldom, if at all, been the ground of the decision even in a Court of the first instance, and certainly never been the ground of a decision in the Court of Exchequer Chamber, still less in this House, I did think it open in your Lordships' House to reconsider this question. And, notwithstanding the very high authority of Lord Coke, I think it is not the fact that to accept prompt payment of a part only of a liquidated demand, can never be more beneficial than to insist on payment of the whole. And if it be not the fact, it cannot be apparent to the judges. . . .

What principally weighs with me in thinking that Lord Coke made a mistake of fact is my conviction that all men of business, whether merchants or tradesmen, do every day recognise and act on the ground that prompt payment of a part of their demand may be more beneficial to them than it would be to insist on their rights and enforce payment of the whole. Even where the debtor is perfectly solvent, and sure to pay at last, this often is so. Where the credit of the debtor is doubtful it must be more so. I had persuaded myself that there was no such long-continued action on this dictum as to render it improper in this House to reconsider the question. I had written my reasons for so thinking; but as they were not satisfactory to the other noble and learned Lords who heard the case, I do not now repeat them nor persist in them.

I assent to the judgment proposed, though it is not that which I had originally thought proper.

■ **QUESTIONS**

1. Was the House of Lords in fact bound to follow *Pinnel's Case*?

2. Do you consider that the creditor should be able to sue for the balance where the debtor has relied on the promise to forgo the balance, and has spent it or incurred other obligations in the belief that he was no longer bound to pay it? (See promissory estoppel, at *pages 147–73.*)

NOTES
1. *Foakes* v *Beer* was applied by the Court of Appeal in *Ferguson* v *Davies* [1997] 1 All ER 315.
2. Julia Beer clearly secured a factual benefit in ensuring payment of the judgment debt and avoiding enforcement proceedings. However, the Court of Appeal has stated that *Williams* v *Roffey* cannot apply in this context.

A factual benefit to the promisor (creditor) will not constitute consideration for an alteration promise to accept less.

Re Selectmove Ltd
[1995] 1 WLR 474 (CA)

In July 1991, a company which owed the Inland Revenue considerable sums in income tax and national insurance contributions had made a proposal at a meeting with the collector of taxes that in future it should pay the tax as it fell due and repay the arrears in instalments (commencing in February 1992). The collector stated that he would have to seek the approval of his superiors and would advise the company if the proposal was unacceptable. The company heard nothing, but the Revenue later demanded payment of the arrears in full and eventually presented a petition for winding up. The company argued that the petition should be dismissed on the ground that the proposal of July 1991 had been accepted by the Revenue, or that the Revenue was estopped from relying on this debt as being due. The judge ordered compulsory winding up on the basis that there was no such agreement and, in any event, no consideration to support it. The judge also rejected the claim based on estoppel because there was no promise which could give rise to an estoppel. On appeal the company argued, *inter alia*, that its promise to pay an existing debt was a good consideration because it amounted to a practical benefit to the Revenue. Held: there was no agreement by the Revenue to accept the company's proposal since the official in question did not have the authority to bind the Revenue. The comments relating to the arguments based on consideration and promissory estoppel were therefore *obiter.*

PETER GIBSON LJ (with whose judgment Balcombe and Stuart-Smith LJJ agreed): . . . The judge held that the case fell within the principle of *Foakes* v *Beer* (1884) 9 App Cas 605. In that case a judgment debtor and creditor agreed that in consideration of the debtor paying part of the judgment debt and costs immediately and the remainder by instalments the creditor would not take any proceedings on the judgment. The House of Lords held that the agreement was nudum pactum, being without consideration, and did not prevent the creditor, after payment of the whole debt and costs, from proceeding to enforce payment of the interest on the judgment. Although their Lordships were unanimous in the result, that case is notable for the powerful speech of Lord Blackburn, who made plain his disagreement with the course the law had taken in and since *Pinnel's Case* (1602) 5 Co Rep 117a and which the House of Lords in *Foakes* v *Beer* 9 App Cas 605 decided should not be reversed. . . . Yet it is clear that the House of Lords decided that a practical benefit of that nature is not good consideration in law.

Foakes v *Beer* has been followed and applied in numerous cases subsequently . . . [Peter Gibson LJ referred to *Vanbergen* v *St. Edmunds Properties Ltd* [1933] 2 KB 223 and *D. & C. Builders Ltd* v *Rees* [1966] 2 QB 617 as examples.] [Counsel] however submitted that an additional benefit to the revenue was conferred by the agreement in that the revenue stood to derive practical benefits therefrom: it was likely to recover more from not enforcing its debt against the company, which was known to be in financial difficulties, than from putting the company into liquidation. He pointed to the fact that the company did in fact pay its further PAYE and NIC liabilities and £7,000 of its arrears. He relied on the decision of this court in *Williams v Roffey Bros & Nicholls (Contractors) Ltd* [1991] 1 QB 1 for the proposition that a promise to perform an existing obligation can amount to good consideration provided that there are practical benefits to the promisee.

[Peter Gibson LJ referred to the propositions expressed by Glidewell LJ in that case, and continued . . .] [Counsel] submitted that although Glidewell LJ in terms confined his remarks to a case where B is to do the work for or supply goods or services to A, the same principle must apply where B's obligation is to pay A, and he referred to an article by Adams and Brownsword 'Contract, Consideration and the Critical Path' (1990) 53 MLR 536, 539–540 which suggests that *Foakes v Beer* might need reconsideration. I see the force of the argument, but the difficulty that I feel with it is that if the principle of *Williams v Roffey Bros. & Nicholls (Contractors) Ltd* is to be extended to an obligation to make payment, it would in effect leave the principle in *Foakes v Beer* without any application. When a creditor and a debtor who are at arm's length reach agreement on the payment of the debt by instalments to accommodate the debtor, the creditor will no doubt always see a practical benefit to himself in so doing. In the absence of authority there would be much to be said for the enforceability of such a contract. But that was a matter expressly considered in *Foakes v Beer* yet held not to constitute good consideration in law. *Foakes v Beer* was not even referred to in *Williams v Roffey Bros. & Nicholls (Contractors) Ltd*, and it is in my judgment impossible, consistently with the doctrine of precedent, for this court to extend the principle of *Williams'* case to any circumstances governed by the principle of *Foakes v Beer*. If that extension is to be made, it must be by the House of Lords or, perhaps even more appropriately, by Parliament after consideration by the Law Commission.

In my judgment, the judge was right to hold that if there was an agreement between the company and the revenue it was unenforceable for want of consideration.

NOTES

1. Although this result was inevitable given the doctrine of precedent, it is nevertheless difficult to justify the arbitrary distinction which now exists between alteration promises to pay more and alteration promises to accept less.

2. In *Re C (A Debtor), The Times*, 11 May 1994, a differently constituted Court of Appeal in *obiter* remarks also confirmed this restrictive approach to part payments of debts. Bingham MR stressed the fact that the relevant case law had not been referred to in *Willams v Roffey*, and he also appeared to consider that there are important differences between alteration promises to pay more and alteration promises to accept less. See also O'Sullivan, 'In Defence of *Foakes v Beer*' (1996) 55 CLJ 219, although compare Adams and Brownsword (1990) 53 MLR 536, 540, Carter, Phang, and Poole (1995) 8 JCL 248, 266–7 and (in Australia) the judgment of Santow J in *Musumeci v Winadell Pty Ltd* (1994) 34 NSWLR 723, 747.

3. Counsel for the company had argued that, even if consideration did not exist, promissory estoppel operated to prevent the Revenue from going back on its implied promise not to enforce the debt since the company had acted on this promise and it would be inequitable for the Revenue to go back on it. The Court of Appeal rejected this argument on the basis that the official in question had no authority to make such a promise and, since the company had not complied with the terms of any such 'promise', it was not inequitable for the Revenue to insist on payment.

4. *Williams v Roffey*, although initially criticised for its refusal to accept that in reality it was striking at the heart of *Stilk v Myrick*, was nevertheless welcomed as a pragmatic means of enabling alteration promises to be enforced. (See Adams and Brownsword (1990) 53 MLR 536 and Coote (1990) 3 JCL 23.) It is now the subject of more vocal academic criticism suggesting that the decision is wrong and that alteration promises should instead be enforceable by extending the doctrine of estoppel following the approach taken in the Australian decision of *Waltons Stores v Maher* (discussed at *page 165 below*). (See Carter, Phang, and Poole, 'Reactions to *Williams v Roffey*' (1995) 8 JCL 248; Chen-Wishart, 'Consideration: Practical Benefit and

the Emperor's New Clothes', in Beatson and Friedmann (eds), *Good Faith and Fault in Contract Law* (OUP, 1995); Hird and Blair, 'Minding Your Own Business—*Williams* v *Roffey* Re-visited: Consideration Reconsidered' [1996] JBL 254.) The Court of Appeal of New Zealand in *Antons Trawling Co. Ltd* v *Smith* [2003] 2 NZLR 23, *page 171*, preferred to accept that variations which have been relied upon should be binding, despite the absence of consideration, unless affected by 'duress or other policy factors'.

The consequences of *Foakes* v *Beer* will be avoided where the part payment is made by a third party and the creditor promises to accept this in full satisfaction. The creditor cannot then go back on his promise to the third party and sue the debtor for the balance.

Hirachand Punamchand v Temple
[1911] 2 KB 330 (CA)

Lieutenant Temple had borrowed money from the plaintiffs, money lenders, and had given them a promissory note. The plaintiffs had pressed Lieutenant Temple for payment on the note but, having had no success, they had informed his father. The father had sent a draft for a smaller sum than that due on the promissory note in full satisfaction of his son's debt. The plaintiffs cashed the draft but then brought an action on the note against Lieutenant Temple for the balance. Held: this action could not be maintained.

VAUGHAN WILLIAMS LJ: The learned judge [Scrutton J] dealt with the case largely on the footing that the question was whether the effect of the transaction between the plaintiffs and the father was that there had been an accord and satisfaction in respect of the debt due upon the note, and he came to the conclusion that there had been no such accord and satisfaction. Personally, I am inclined to agree that prima facie such an accord and satisfaction must be by virtue of an agreement made between a person who is under an obligation to another person, which he ought to have and has not performed, and that other person. I should hesitate to say that there can, properly speaking, be an accord and satisfaction in respect of a contractual obligation as between one of the parties to the contract, who ought to have but has not performed that obligation, and a stranger to the contract. . . . I shall assume that there was such an agreement as I have mentioned entered into between Sir Richard Temple and the plaintiffs by reason of their keeping the draft. They not only kept it, but they cashed it, and, if they changed their minds afterwards, it was too late. Under these circumstances, assuming that there was no accord and satisfaction, what form of defence, if any, could be pleaded by the defendant? In my judgment it would be that the plaintiffs had ceased really to be holders of the negotiable instrument on which they sued. They had ceased to be such holders, because, in effect, in their hands the document had ceased to be a negotiable instrument quite as much as if there had been on the acceptance of the draft by the plaintiffs an erasure of the writing of the signature to the note. There was not in fact such an erasure, but to my mind the case must be considered as standing on the same footing as if there been an erasure of the signature, and a cancellation by reason of that erasure of the promissory note, in which case, I think, the maker of the note would have had a defence, though he was not a party to the transaction in pursuance of which the note was cancelled, in the sense of being a contracting party. His defence would then have been that the document in the circumstances had ceased to be a promissory note. But, alternatively, assuming that this was not so, and that the instrument did not cease to be a negotiable instrument, then, in my judgment, from the moment when the draft sent by Sir Richard Temple was cashed by the plaintiffs a trust was created as between Sir Richard Temple and the money-lenders in favour of the former, so that any money which the latter might receive upon the promissory note, if they did receive any, would be held by them in trust for him. I wish to say here that I do not think that it makes any difference under the circumstances that the amount of the draft sent by Sir Richard Temple was not the full amount of the promissory note, but a smaller amount, because, as between Sir Richard

Temple and these plaintiffs, there was an agreement by the plaintiffs for good consideration to receive that amount in satisfaction of the note, which agreement arose from their having retained and cashed the draft. . . .

Having said thus much, I desire to add a word or two with regard to the case of *Cook* v *Lister* (1863) 13 CBNS 543 in the Common Pleas. If the judgments in that case are looked at, it will be found that Willes J said, in explaining the grounds of his judgment, that, under circumstances like those of the present case, the debt is gone, because it would be a fraud upon the stranger who pays part of a debt in discharge of the whole, that an action should be brought for the debt. I have founded my judgment upon the grounds which I have already expressed, but I do not wish to be understood as thereby negativing the proposition that a defence might be set up on the alternative basis mentioned by Willes J.

FLETCHER MOULTON LJ: I am of opinion that by that transaction between the plaintiffs and Sir Richard Temple the debt on the promissory note became extinct. I agree with the view expressed by Willes J in *Cook* v *Lister* (1863) 13 CBNS 543. The effect of such an agreement between a creditor and a third party with regard to the debt is to render it impossible for the creditor afterwards to sue the debtor for it. The way in which this is worked out in law may be that it would be an abuse of the process of the Court to allow the creditor under such circumstances to sue, or it may be, and I prefer that view, that there is an extinction of the debt; but, whichever way it is put, it comes to the same thing, namely that, after acceptance by the creditor of a sum offered by a third party in settlement of the claim against the debtor, the creditor cannot maintain an action for the balance. . . .

FARWELL LJ: In my opinion, it is clear that in the events that have happened the debt became extinguished. Assuming that an accord and satisfaction must be by agreement between the debtor and the creditor, it occurs to me from what was said by Willes J in *Cook* v *Lister* (1863) 13 CBNS 543 that the facts in this case might support such a plea. That learned judge there said, 'if a stranger pays a part of a debt in discharge of the whole, the debt is gone because it would be a fraud on the stranger to proceed. So, in the case of a composition made with a body of creditors, the assent to receive the composition discharges the debt, because otherwise fraud would be committed against the rest of the creditors'. . . . We were pressed with *Day* v *McLea* (1889) 22 QBD 610, where the debtor himself sent a cheque for an amount smaller than that of the debt to the creditor on the terms that it should be in satisfaction of the debt. In that case, there being no consideration for the discharge of the balance of the debt, it was held that the creditor could retain the money, and sue for the balance. The same reasoning does not apply where the money is sent by a stranger, in which case it can only be accepted on the terms upon which it is sent. In the former case the creditor can reply to the debtor, 'you owe me more than this, and, if you sue for a return of this, I shall set off my larger claim against it.' In the latter case, the creditor has no excuse or justification for retaining the stranger's money, unless he complies with the condition on which it was paid. I agree with Fletcher Moulton LJ that the plaintiffs cannot be heard to say that they have acted dishonestly when an honest construction can be put upon their conduct by treating their acceptance and retention of the money as being upon the terms on which it was offered. If there be any difficulty in formulating a defence at common law in such case, I have no hesitation in saying that a Court of Equity would have regarded the plaintiffs as disentitled to sue except as trustees for the father, and would have restrained them from suing under such circumstances as existed in the present case.

NOTES
1. The precise reason for this decision is unclear. The Court of Appeal appeared to consider that in cashing the draft the plaintiffs accepted the father's terms, and this had the effect of extinguishing the promissory note. It was also considered to be a fraud on the father for the plaintiffs to go back on their promise, but breach of contract will not normally constitute a fraud.
2. If the test of enforceability in section 1 of the Contracts (Rights of Third Parties) Act 1999 is satisfied (see *page 442* for details), the debtor (as third party) may rely on a contractual term in the contract between the creditor and the person making part payment which excludes the

debtor's liability for the balance. In such a situation, it would be sufficient that the consideration was provided by the person making the part payment, *page 440*, rather than the debtor.

3. In *Bracken* v *Billinghurst* [2003] EWHC 1333 (TCC), [2004] TCLR 4, it was held that by cashing a cheque issued by the defendant's company (a third party), the claimants had compromised their claims against the defendant. It was clear that this cheque was being offered as a full and final compromise of the claim and that it was accepted on that basis. Accordingly, the defendant had a complete defence to a claim for summary judgment made by the claimants.

SECTION 2: PROMISSORY ESTOPPEL

If a creditor promises to accept a smaller sum in full settlement intending the debtor to rely on that promise, and the debtor does rely on it, the debtor may have a defence of promissory estoppel when sued for the balance by the creditor. The promise will in this way be enforceable despite the absence of consideration to support it.

A: Origins of the doctrine

Central London Property Trust Ltd v *High Trees House Ltd*
[1947] KB 130

In September 1937, the plaintiffs let a block of flats in London to the defendants for a term of 99 years at a rent of £2,500 a year. In 1940, owing to the war-time conditions and bombing raids over London, only a few of the flats were actually let to tenants, and it became apparent that the defendants would not be able to pay the rent under the main lease. Following discussions, the plaintiffs agreed to reduce the rent from £2,500 to £1,250, and thereafter the defendants paid the reduced rent. By the beginning of 1945, all the flats were let, but the defendants continued to pay the reduced rent. In September 1945, the plaintiffs wrote to the defendants claiming rent at the rate of £2,500 a year, and they brought an action claiming the full rent for the last two quarters of 1945. Held: since the plaintiffs knew that their promise would be acted upon and it had been acted upon, it was enforceable despite the absence of consideration while the conditions giving rise to it continued to exist; and when they ceased to do so in 1945, the plaintiffs were entitled to claim the full rent.

DENNING J: . . . If I were to consider this matter without regard to recent developments in the law, there is no doubt that had the plaintiffs claimed it, they would have been entitled to recover ground rent at the rate of 2,500*l*. a year from the beginning of the term, since the lease under which it was payable was a lease under seal which, according to the old common law, could not be varied by an agreement by parol (whether in writing or not), but only by deed. Equity, however stepped in, and said that if there has been a variation of a deed by a simple contract (which in the case of a lease required to be in writing would have to be evidenced by writing), the courts may give effect to it. . . . That equitable doctrine, however, could hardly apply in the present case because the variation here might be said to have been made without consideration. With regard to estoppel, the representation made in relation to reducing the rent, was not a representation of an existing fact. It was a representation, in effect, as to the future, namely, that payment of the rent would not be enforced at the full rate but only at the reduced rate. Such a representation would not give rise to an estoppel, because, as was said in *Jorden* v *Money* (1854) 5 HL 185, 10 ER 868, a representation as to the future must be embodied as a contract or be nothing.

But what is the position in view of developments in the law in recent years? The law has not been standing still since *Jorden* v *Money*. There has been a series of decisions over the last fifty years which, although they are said to be cases of estoppel are not really such. They are cases in which a promise was made which was intended to create legal relations and which, to the knowledge of the person making the promise, was going to be acted on by the person to whom it was made, and which was in fact so acted on. In such cases the courts have said that the promise must be honoured. The cases to which I particularly desire to refer are: *Fenner* v *Blake* [1900] 1 QB 426, *In re Wickham*, (1917) 34 TLR 158, *Re William Porter & Co. Ltd* [1937] 2 All ER 361 and *Buttery* v *Pickard* [1946] WN 25. As I have said they are not cases of estoppel in the strict sense. They are really promises—promises intended to be binding, intended to be acted on, and in fact acted on. *Jorden* v *Money* can be distinguished, because there the promisor made it clear that she did not intend to be legally bound, whereas in the cases to which I refer the proper inference was that the promisor did intend to be bound. In each case the court held the promise to be binding on the party making it, even though under the old common law it might be difficult to find any consideration for it. The courts have not gone so far as to give a cause of action in damages for the breach of such a promise, but they have refused to allow the party making it to act inconsistently with it. It is in that sense, and that sense only, that such a promise gives rise to an estoppel. The decisions are a natural result of the fusion of law and equity: for the cases of *Hughes* v *Metropolitan Ry. Co.* (1877) 2 App Cas 439, *Birmingham and District Land Co.* v *London & North Western Ry. Co.* (1888) 40 ChD 268 and *Salisbury (Marquess)* v *Gilmore* [1942] 2 KB 38, afford a sufficient basis for saying that a party would not be allowed in equity to go back on such a promise. In my opinion, the time has now come for the validity of such a promise to be recognised. The logical consequence, no doubt is that a promise to accept a smaller sum in discharge of a larger sum, if acted upon, is binding notwithstanding the absence of consideration: and if the fusion of law and equity leads to this result, so much the better. That aspect was not considered in *Foakes* v *Beer* (1884) 9 App Cas 605. At this time of day however, when law and equity have been joined together for over seventy years, principles must be reconsidered in the light of their combined effect. It is to be noticed that in the Sixth Interim Report of the Law Revision Committee, pars. 35, 40, it is recommended that such a promise as that to which I have referred, should be enforceable in law even though no consideration for it has been given by the promisee. It seems to me that, to the extent I have mentioned, that result has now been achieved by the decisions of the courts.

I am satisfied that a promise such as that to which I have referred is binding and the only question remaining for my consideration is the scope of the promise in the present case. I am satisfied on all the evidence that the promise here was that the ground rent should be reduced to 1,250*l.* a year as a temporary expedient while the block of flats was not fully, or substantially fully let, owing to the conditions prevailing. That means that the reduction in the rent applied throughout the years down to the end of 1944, but early in 1945 it is plain that the flats were fully let. . . . I find that the conditions prevailing at the time when the reduction in rent was made, had completely passed away by the early months of 1945. I am satisfied that the promise was understood by all parties only to apply under the conditions prevailing at the time when it was made, namely, when the flats were only partially let, and that it did not extend any further than that. When the flats became fully let, early in 1945, the reduction ceased to apply.

If the case had been one of estoppel, it might be said that in any event the estoppel would cease when the conditions to which the representation applied came to an end, or it also might be said that it would only come to an end on notice. In either case it is only a way of ascertaining what is the scope of the representation. I prefer to apply the principle that a promise intended to be binding, intended to be acted on and in fact acted on, is binding so far as its terms properly apply. Here it was binding as covering the period down to the early part of 1945, and as from that time full rent is payable.

I therefore give judgment for the plaintiff company for the amount claimed.

■ QUESTIONS

1. Although the plaintiff company did not make a retrospective claim for the full rent for the war years, Denning *obiter* indicated that such a claim would fail because of promissory estoppel. Can this be reconciled with *Foakes* v *Beer*, which held that it was possible to go back on such a promise and sue for the balance?

2. Could the defendants in *High Trees* have sued the plaintiffs if the plaintiffs had not complied with their promise to accept the reduced rent? (See *page 151*.)

NOTE: Denning J purported to rely in particular on the decision and statement of principle in *Hughes* v *Metropolitan Railway Company* (1877) 2 App Cas 439, as justifying his use of a doctrine of promissory estoppel. It is interesting, however, that this case was not seen as being relevant in *Foakes* v *Beer*.

Hughes v *Metropolitan Railway Company*
(1877) 2 App Cas 439 (HL)

On 22 October 1874, the landlords gave the tenants six months' notice to repair the premises. However, on 28 November, negotiations began between the parties for the sale of the lease to the landlords. The tenants stated that they would defer commencing the repairs until they had heard whether their proposal was acceptable. After the six months had elapsed, the landlords claimed that the lease was forfeited for breach of covenant and sought to eject the tenants. The tenants sought a stay of execution. Held: the tenants were entitled in equity to be relieved against forfeiture because the negotiations had the effect of suspending the notice, and while they continued the six-month period did not run. It ran again only from the time the negotiations ended.

LORD CAIRNS: . . . It was not argued at your Lordships' Bar, and it could not be argued, that there was any right of a Court of Equity, or any practice of a Court of Equity, to give relief in cases of this kind, by way of mercy, or by way merely of saving property from forfeiture, but it is the first principle upon which all Courts of Equity proceed, that if parties who have entered into definite and distinct terms involving certain legal results—certain penalties or legal forfeiture—afterwards by their own act or with their own consent enter upon a course of negotiation which has the effect of leading one of the parties to suppose that the strict rights arising under the contract will not be enforced, or will be kept in suspense, or held in abeyance, the person who otherwise might have enforced those rights will not be allowed to enforce them where it would be inequitable having regard to the dealings which have thus taken place between the parties. . . .

NOTES
1. While the negotiations continued the landlords had impliedly promised not to enforce the notice, and the tenants had relied on this in not carrying out the repairs.
2. The principle in *Hughes* v *Metropolitan Railway Co.* appears to be intended to cover a different situation to that which arose on the facts in *High Trees*. If a landlord tells the tenant that he does not have to perform an obligation under the contract, and consequently the tenant does not do so, then the landlord cannot treat this as a breach of contract (and in *Hughes* could not forfeit the lease). In *High Trees* the landlord was not alleging that the tenant was in breach of contract by paying half the rent.
3. In *Foakes* v *Beer* (1884) 9 App Cas 605 (*page 140*), the issue was the same as in *High Trees*, namely that if one party tells the other that the other does not have to perform a contractual obligation, can that party change his mind and insist on the performance if performance is still possible? In *High Trees* the landlords were seeking to change their minds and insist on proper performance of the contract.

B: When will the doctrine operate and in what way?

(a) Clear and unequivocal promise

There must be a clear and unequivocal promise or representation that existing legal rights will not be fully enforced. This representation can be implied, as in *Hughes* v *Metropolitan Railway* (1877) 2 App Cas 439.

Woodhouse A. C. Israel Cocoa Ltd SA v *Nigerian Produce Marketing Co. Ltd*
[1972] AC 741 (HL)

A sale contract provided for payment in Nigerian pounds in Lagos. The buyers had asked if the sellers would be prepared to accept sterling in Lagos, and the sellers had replied on 30 September 1967 that 'payment can be made in sterling and in Lagos'. The pound sterling was devalued so that it was worth 15 per cent less than the Nigerian pound. The buyers argued that the seller's letter amounted either to a variation (supported by consideration) or a representation that they could make payment in sterling in Lagos on the basis of one pound sterling for one Nigerian pound, so that the sellers were estopped from going back on it. Held: to found a promissory estoppel a representation had to be clear and unequivocal (i.e., expressed so that it would be understood in the sense required). The seller's representation was not sufficiently precise either to amount to a variation of the contract terms (i.e., an alteration supported by consideration) or to found an estoppel.

LORD HAILSHAM LC: Counsel for the [buyers] was asked whether he knew of any case in which an ambiguous statement had ever formed the basis of a purely promissory estoppel, as contended for here, as distinct from estoppel of a more familiar type based on factual misrepresentation. He candidly replied that he did not. I do not find this surprising, since it would really be an astonishing thing if, in the case of a genuine misunderstanding as to the meaning of an offer, the offeree could obtain by means of the doctrine of promissory estoppel something that he must fail to obtain under the conventional law of contract. I share the feeling of incredulity expressed by Lord Denning MR in the course of his judgment in the instant case when he said [1971] 2 QB 23, 59–60:

> If the judge be right, it leads to this extraordinary consequence: A letter which is not sufficient to *vary* a contract is, nevertheless, sufficient to work an *estoppel*— which will have the same effect as a *variation*.

There seem to me to be so many and such conclusive reasons for dismissing this appeal that it may be thought a work of supererogation to add yet another. But basically I feel convinced that there was never here any real room for the doctrine or estoppel at all. If the exchange of letters was not variation, I believe it was nothing. The buyers asked for a variation in the mode of discharge of a contract of sale. If the proposal meant what they claimed, and was accepted and acted upon, I venture to think that the vendors would have been bound by their acceptance at least until they gave reasonable notice to terminate, and I imagine that a modern court would have found no difficulty in discovering consideration for such a promise. Business men know their own business best even when they appear to grant an indulgence, and in the present case I do not think that there would have been insuperable difficulty in spelling out consideration from the earlier correspondence. If, however, the two letters were insufficiently unambiguous and precise to form the basis, if accepted, for a variation in the contract I do not think their combined effect is sufficiently unambiguous or precise to form the basis of an estoppel which would produce the result of reducing the purchase price by no less than 14 per cent against a vendor who had never consciously agreed to the proposition. . . .

NOTE: In *Baird Textiles Holdings Ltd* v *Marks & Spencer plc* [2001] EWCA Civ 274, [2002] 1 All ER (Comm) 737, see *page 194* for the facts, one reason why the claim based on estopped failed was because the alleged representation was not sufficiently certain for a court to be able to give effect to it. Baird attempted to sidestep this deficiency (and the formal requirements for a binding contract) by limiting the claim to the recovery of reliance loss (discussed at *page 372*), as opposed to an expectation loss claim. The Court of Appeal considered there was no authority justifying such a radical conclusion.

MANCE LJ stated:

91   In the present case, what is submitted is that the law ought to attach legal consequences to a bare assurance or conventional understanding (falling short of contract) between two parties, without any actual contract or third party being involved or affected. The suggested justification is the limitation of the relief claimed to reliance loss. On this submission, the requirements of contract (consideration, certainty and an intention to create legal relations) are irrelevant because no contract is asserted. The requirements of estoppel (eg that is an unequivocal promise to found a promissory estoppel or conventional conduct of sufficient clarity to found an estoppel by convention and, secondly, the objective intention to affect some actual or apparent pre-existing legal relationship) are bypassed by the limitation of relief. But no authority in this jurisdiction supports the submission that estoppel can here achieve so expanded an application, simply by limiting recovery to reliance loss (assuming that reliance loss could anyway be distinguished satisfactorily from expectation loss—an apparent difficulty which I have already mentioned). Any development of English law in such a direction could and should, in my view, now take place in the highest court.

(b) A defence and not a cause of action

Combe v *Combe*
[1951] 2 KB 215 (CA)

An ex-husband promised to pay his ex-wife £100 per annum maintenance, free of income tax. However, he failed to pay, and six years later the wife brought an action claiming the arrears. She had given no consideration for her husband's promise, since she had chosen not to apply to the Divorce Court for maintenance and had not refrained from doing so at her husband's request (her income in fact being greater than her husband's). Nevertheless, Byrne J gave judgment for the wife on the basis of the doctrine in *High Trees*. He held that the husband's promise was clear, it was intended to be binding and acted upon, and it was acted upon by the wife. The Court of Appeal allowed the husband's appeal. Held: the wife had provided no consideration for the husband's promise and could not rely on promissory estoppel which did not give rise to a cause of action.

DENNING LJ: . . . Much as I am inclined to favour the principle stated in the *High Trees* case [1947] KB 130, it is important that it should not be stretched too far, lest it should be endangered. That principle does not create new causes of action where none existed before. It only prevents a party from insisting upon his strict legal rights, when it would be unjust to allow him to enforce them, having regard to the dealings which have taken place between the parties. That is the way it was put in *Hughes* v *Metropolitan Railway* (1877) 2 App Cas 439, the case in the House of Lords in which the principle was first stated, and in *Birmingham, etc., Land Company* v *London and North-Western Railway Co.* (1888) 40 ChD 268, the case in the Court of Appeal where the principle was enlarged. It is also implicit in all the modern cases in which the principle has been developed. Sometimes it is a plaintiff who is not allowed to insist on his strict legal rights. Thus, a creditor is not allowed to enforce a debt which he has deliberately agreed to waive, if the debtor has carried on business or in some other way changed his position in reliance on the waiver . . . On other occasions it is a defendant who is not allowed to insist on his strict legal rights. His conduct may be such as to debar him from relying on some condition, denying some allegation, or taking some other point in answer to the claim. . . .

The principle, as I understand it, is that, where one party has, by his words or conduct, made to the other a promise or assurance which was intended to affect the legal relations between them and to be acted on accordingly, then, once the other party has taken him at his word and acted on it, the one who gave the promise or assurance cannot afterwards be allowed to revert to the previous legal relations as if no such promise or assurance had been made by him, but he must accept their legal relations subject to the qualification which he himself has so introduced, even though it is not supported in point of law by any consideraton but only by his word.

Seeing that the principle never stands alone as giving a cause of action in itself, it can never do away with the necessity of consideration when that is an essential part of the cause of action. The doctrine of consideration is too firmly fixed to be overthrown by a side-wind. Its ill-effects have been largely mitigated of late, but it still remains a cardinal necessity of the formation of a contract, though not of its modification or discharge. I fear that it was my failure to make this clear which misled Byrne J, in the present case. He held that the wife could sue on the husband's promise as a separate and independent cause of action by itself, although as he held, there was no consideration for it. That is not correct. The wife can only enforce it if there was consideration for it. That is, therefore, the real question in the case: was there sufficient consideration to support the promise? . . .

There was, . . . clearly no promise by the wife, express or implied, to forbear from applying to the court. All that happened was that she did in fact forbear — that is, she did an act in return for a promise. Is that sufficient consideration? Unilateral promises of this kind have long been enforced, so long as the act or forbearance is done on the faith of the promise and at the request of the promissor, express or implied. . . . my difficulty is to accept the finding of Byrne J, that the promise was 'intended to be acted upon'. I cannot find any evidence of any intention by the husband that the wife should forbear from applying to the court for maintenance, or, in other words, any request by the husband, express or implied, that the wife should so forbear. He left her to apply if she wished to do so. She did not do so, and I am not surprised, because it is very unlikely that the Divorce Court would have then made any order in her favour, seeing that she had a bigger income than her husband. Her forbearance was not intended by him, nor was it done at his request. It was therefore no consideration.

ASQUITH LJ: The judge has decided that, while the husband's promise was unsupported by any valid consideration, yet the principle in *Central London Property Trust Ltd.* v *High Trees House Ltd.* [1947] KB 130 entitles the wife to succeed. It is unnecessary to express any view as to the correctness of that decision, though I certainly must not be taken to be questioning it; and I would remark, in passing, that it seems to me a complete misconception to suppose that it struck at the roots of the doctrine of consideration. But assuming, without deciding, that it is good law, I do not think, however, that it helps the plaintiff at all. What that case decides is that when a promise is given which (1) is intended to create legal relations, (2) is intended to be acted upon by the promisee, and (3) is in fact so acted upon, the promisor cannot bring an action against the promisee which involves the repudiation of his promise or is inconsistent with it. It does not, as I read it, decide that a promisee can sue on the promise. On the contrary, Denning, J, expressly stated the contrary . . .

NOTES

1. Promissory estoppel is available only where there has been an alteration to an existing contract. It cannot be used to render unnecessary consideration on the formation of a contract.
2. Birkett LJ explicitly approved counsel for the husband's argument that promissory estoppel can be 'used as a shield and not a sword'. It cannot be used to force a party to comply with a promise, and can only be used to prevent a party from ignoring his promise that he would not insist on his strict legal rights. This explains why the tenants in *High Trees* could not have sued on the landlord's promise to enforce their claim to pay reduced rent and why the plaintiff carpenter in *Williams* v *Roffey Brothers* [1991] 1 QB 1, *page 135*, did not base the claim on promissory estoppel.

In *Baird Textiles Holdings Ltd* v *Marks & Spencer plc* [2001] EWCA Civ 274, [2002] 1 All ER

(Comm) 737, Judge LJ at [52], referred to Birkett LJ's statement that estoppel is 'used as a shield and not a sword' as a 'misleading aphorism'. However, his reasoning was based on the fact that this limitation does not extend to proprietary estoppel, see *page 163*, rather than that it was inaccurate in respect of promissory estoppel in English law.

3. Compare these limitations with the scope of the doctrine as enunciated by Denning J in *High Trees* (*page 147*).

4. The future of this limitation on the doctrine of promissory estoppel in English law is the subject of debate in the light of the approach adopted by the High Court of Australia in *Walton Stores (Interstate) Ltd* v *Maher* (1988) 164 CLR 387, *page 165*, and comments made in the judgments of Glidewell and Russell LJJ in *Williams* v *Roffey Brothers* [1991] 1 QB 1, *page 135*. In *Baird Textile Holdings Ltd* v *Marks & Spencer plc* [2001] EWCA Civ 274, [2002] 1 All ER (Comm) 737, there was an unsuccessful attempt to rely on a general category of estoppel (based on *Walton Stores*). However, the judgments disclose that, faced with an appropriate case, the House of Lords might well reconsider this limitation, *page 168*.

(c) The representation or promise was intended to be binding and acted upon and was in fact acted upon

E. A. Ajayi v R. T. Briscoe (Nigeria) Ltd
[1964] 1 WLR 1326 (PC)

The defendant had hired a number of lorries from the plaintiffs on hire-purchase and was paying the purchase price in instalments. Some were withdrawn from service because of difficulties with service arrangements. The defendant wrote to the plaintiffs asking that they carry out the repairs and proposing that this would be paid for when the lorries were back in service. By a letter of 22 July 1957, the plaintiffs replied that they were agreeable to the defendant 'withholding instalments due on [the lorries] as long as they are withdrawn from active service'. The plaintiffs later claimed the full instalments due. On appeal the defendant raised the defence of promissory estoppel, arguing that the estoppel applied because he had relied upon the promise in not putting forward alternative proposals on payment for the repairs, and he had organised his business on the basis that he would not have to make the payments until the lorries were back in service. Held: the defendant had failed to establish the defence of promissory estoppel since he had not altered his position as a result of the plaintiffs' letter. The lorries had been withdrawn from service before this promise.

LORD HODSON: . . . The principle, which has been described as quasi estoppel and perhaps more aptly as promissory estoppel, is that when one party to a contract in the absence of fresh consideration agrees not to enforce his rights an equity will be raised in favour of the other party. This equity is, however, subject to the qualifications (1) that the other party has altered his position, (2) that the promisor can resile from his promise on giving reasonable notice, which need not be a formal notice, giving the promisee a reasonable opportunity of resuming his position, (3) the promise only becomes final and irrevocable if the promisee cannot resume his position . . .

The question remains whether the defendant has made good the defence. In their Lordships' opinion he has not succeeded in so doing.

The defendant did not alter his position by not putting forward counter-proposals after receipt of the letter of July 22, 1957. There is no evidence to support the contention that he did so by organising his business in a different way having regard to the fact that the lorries were out of service, and it cannot be inferred from the evidence given that such reorganisation was necessary . . .

The defendant has accordingly failed to establish any defence to the plaintiffs' claim.

■ QUESTION

Was this a clear and unequivocal promise? Does 'withhold' mean that the promisee does not have to pay those instalments at all, or only that the instalments do not have to be paid while the lorries are not in service but can be recovered later?

NOTE: The requirement that the promisee 'alter his position' was interpreted in *Ajayi* v *Briscoe* to mean altered in a detrimental way. However, Lord Denning has confirmed that detrimental reliance is not necessary.

W. J. Alan & Co. Ltd v El Nasr Export and Import Co.
[1972] 2 QB 189 (CA)

The sellers in Kenya contracted to sell coffee to the buyers at 262 (Kenyan) shillings per cwt. Two shipments were to be made and payment was to be 'by confirmed irrevocable letter of credit to be opened one month prior to shipment'. The irrevocable letter of credit was opened in sterling rather than Kenyan shillings, but the sellers operated the credit by presenting invoices in sterling for payment in sterling. The second shipment was made on 16 November 1967, and the sellers made out an invoice in sterling. However, before it could be presented for payment, sterling was devalued on 18 November. Payment under the credit was made against the invoice and the sellers then claimed an additional sum to bring the price they received up to 262 Kenyan shillings. Held: by accepting payment under the sterling letter of credit the sellers had irrevocably 'waived' their right to be paid in Kenyan currency. The majority (Megaw and Stephenson LJJ) considered that this was a variation of the sale contract (supported by consideration), whereas Lord Denning relied on the doctrine of promissory estoppel.

LORD DENNING MR: The principle of waiver is simply this: If one party, by his conduct, leads another to believe that the strict rights arising under the contract will not be insisted upon, intending that the other should act on that belief, and he does act on it, then the first party will not afterwards be allowed to insist on the strict legal rights when it would be inequitable for him to do so: see *Plasticmoda Societa per Azioni* v *Davidsons (Manchester) Ltd* [1952] 1 Lloyd's Rep 527, 539. There may be no consideration moving from him who benefits by the waiver. There may be no detriment to him by acting on it. There may be nothing in writing. Nevertheless, the one who waives his strict rights cannot afterwards insist on them. His strict rights are at any rate suspended so long as the waiver lasts. He may on occasion be able to revert to his strict legal rights for the future by giving reasonable notice in that behalf, or otherwise making it plain by his conduct that he will thereafter insist upon them: *Tool Metal Manufacturing Co. Ltd* v *Tungsten Electric Co. Ltd* [1955] 1 WLR 761. But there are cases where no withdrawal is possible. It may be too late to withdraw: or it cannot be done without injustice to the other party. In that event he is bound by his waiver. He will not be allowed to revert to his strict legal rights. He can only enforce them subject to the waiver he has made.

Instances of these principles are ready to hand in contracts for the sale of goods. A seller may, by his conduct, lead the buyer to believe that he is not insisting on the stipulated time for exercising an option: *Bruner* v *Moore* [1904] 1 Ch 305. A buyer may, by requesting delivery, lead the seller to believe that he is not insisting on the contractual time for delivery: *Charles Rickards Ltd* v *Oppenhaim* [1950] 1 KB 616, 621. A seller may, by his conduct, lead the buyer to believe that he will not insist on a confirmed letter of credit: *Plasticmoda* [1952] 1 Lloyd's Rep. 527, but will accept an unconfirmed one instead: *Panoutsos* v *Raymond Hadley Corporation of New York* [1917] 2 KB 473; *Enrico Furst & Co* v *W.E. Fischer* [1960] 2 Lloyd's Rep 340. A seller may accept a less sum for his goods than the contracted price, thus inducing him to believe that he will not enforce payment of the balance: *Central London Property Trust Ltd* v *High Trees House Ltd* [1947] KB 130 and *D. & C. Builders Ltd* v

Rees [1966] 2 QB 617, 624. In none of these cases does the party who acts on the belief suffer any detriment. It is not a detriment, but a benefit to him, to have an extension of time or to pay less, or as the case may be. Nevertheless, he has conducted his affairs on the basis that he has that benefit and it would not be equitable now to deprive him of it.

The judge rejected this doctrine because, he said, 'there is no evidence of the buyers having acted to their detriment.' I know that it has been suggested in some quarters that there must be detriment. But I can find no support for it in the authorities cited by the judge. The nearest approach to it is the statement of Viscount Simonds in the *Tool Metal* case [1955] 1 WLR 761, 764, that the other must have been led 'to alter his position,' which was adopted by Lord Hodson in *Ajayi* v *R.T. Briscoe (Nigeria) Ltd* [1964] 1 WLR 1326, 1330. But that only means that he must have been led to act differently from what he otherwise would have done. And if you study the cases in which the doctrine has been applied, you will see that all that is required is that the one should have '*acted* on the belief induced by the other party.' That is how Lord Cohen put it in the *Tool Metal* case [1955] 1 WLR 761, 799, and that is how I would put it myself . . .

MEGAW LJ: As I see it, the necessary consequence of that offer and acceptance of a sterling credit is that the original term of the contract of sale as to the money of account was varied from Kenyan currency to sterling. The payment, and the sole payment, stipulated by the contract of sale was by the letter of credit. The buyers, through the confirming bank, had opened a letter of credit which did not conform because it provided sterling as the money of account. The sellers accepted that offer by making use of the credit to receive payment for a part of the contractual goods. By that acceptance, as the sellers must be deemed to have known, not only did the confirming bank become irrevocably bound by the terms of the offer (and by no other terms), but so also did the buyers become bound. Not only did they incur legal obligations as a result of the sellers' acceptance—for example, an obligation to indemnify the bank—but also the buyers could not thereafter have turned round and said to the sellers (for example, if Kenyan currency had been devalued against sterling) that the bank would thereafter pay less for the contractual goods than the promised sterling payment of £262 per ton. If the buyers could not revert unilaterally to the original currency of account, once they had offered a variation which had been accepted by conduct, neither could the sellers so revert. The contract had been varied in that respect . . .

In my view, if there were no variation, the buyers would still be entitled to succeed on the ground of waiver. The relevant principle is, in my opinion, that which was stated by Lord Cairns LC in *Hughes* v *Metropolitan Railway Co.* (1877) 2 App Cas 439, 448 . . .

STEPHENSON LJ: By not objecting to the non-conforming letter of credit, by obtaining payment on it in sterling from the bank and by extending it the sellers clearly accepted and agreed to it and were treated as having done so not only by the bank but by the buyers, who may be presumed (although there was no evidence about it) to have paid charges and incurred liabilities such as a liability to indemnify the bank. The sellers never indicated any reservations about the change from Kenya shillings to pounds sterling or asked for any adjustment, probably for the simple reason that they considered sterling as good as Kenya shillings if not better. When after devaluation of sterling they invoiced the balance of the goods against part payment of the balance of the price and claimed the difference created by devaluation from the buyers, they were attempting to assert a liability which, whether by variation or waiver, they had allowed the buyers to alter.

. . . I would leave open the question whether the action of the other party induced by the party who 'waives' his contractual rights can be any alteration of his position, as Lord Denning MR has said, or must, as the judge thought, be an alteration to his detriment, or for the worse, in some sense. In this case the buyers did, I think, contrary to the judge's view, act to their detriment on the sellers' waiver, if that is what it was, and the contract was varied for good consideration, which may be another way of saying the same thing: so that I need not, and do not, express a concluded opinion on that controversial question . . .

■ **QUESTION**

Stephenson LJ considered that the buyers had acted to their detriment as a result of the seller's representation. This detriment was the possibility that Kenyan shillings might have been devalued and they would have been bound to pay more under the sterling letter of credit. Was this the consideration for the seller's promise so that a binding variation had been made? Does this mean that if a promisee acts to his detriment there will be a binding variation, and therefore promissory estoppel will be irrelevant?

NOTE: Although detriment is not essential, where the promisee has acted to his detriment it will be easier to establish that it is inequitable for the promisor to go back on that promise (see *page 157*).

Société Italo-Belge pour le Commerce et l'Industrie SA v *Palm and Vegetable Oils (Malaysia) Sdn Bhd, The Post Chaser*
[1982] 1 All ER 19

The sellers agreed to sell palm oil to the buyers, who in turn contracted to sell it to sub-buyers. The sellers failed to advise the buyers of the ship used until a month after it had sailed. This would have justified the buyers in refusing to accept the documents. However, the buyers did not protest, and instead requested the sellers to hand the documents relating to the consignment to the sub-buyers. Two days later, when the sub-buyers rejected the documents, the buyers also rejected them, and the sellers were forced to sell the palm oil elsewhere at a loss. The sellers claimed this loss from the buyers, and the crucial question was whether the buyers had waived their right to reject the documents. Held: the buyers had waived their right to reject the documents by requesting that the sellers hand the documents to the sub-buyers, since this was a representation that they were prepared to accept the documents. However, although the sellers had acted on this representation, by presenting the documents as requested, their position had not been prejudiced because of the very short time between the date of the representation and reliance and the date of rejection. Therefore, it was not inequitable for the buyers to enforce their legal right to reject.

ROBERT GOFF J: I approach the matter as follows. The fundamental principle is that stated by Lord Cairns LC [in *Hughes* v *Metropolitan Rlwy Co.*, see *page 149*], viz that the representor will not be allowed to enforce his rights 'where it would be inequitable having regard to the dealings which have thus taken place between the parties'. To establish such inequity, it is not necessary to show detriment; indeed, the representee may have benefited from the representation, and yet it may be inequitable, at least without reasonable notice, for the representor to enforce his legal rights. Take the facts of *Central London Property Trust Ltd* v *High Trees House Ltd* (*1946*) [1956] 1 All ER 256, [1947] KB 130, the case in which Denning J breathed new life into the doctrine of equitable estoppel. The representation was by a lessor to the effect that he would be content to accept a reduced rent. In such a case, although the lessee has benefited from the reduction in rent, it may well be inequitable for the lessor to insist on hs legal right to the unpaid rent, because the lessee has conducted his affairs on the basis that he would only have to pay rent at the lower rate; and a court might well think it right to conclude that only after reasonable notice could the lessor return to charging rent at the higher rate specified in the lease. Furthermore it would be open to the court, in any particular case, to infer from the circumstances of the case that the representee must have conducted his affairs in such a way that it would be inequitable for the representor to enforce his rights, or to do so without reasonable notice. But it does not follow that in every case in which the representee has acted, or failed to act, in reliance on the representation, it will be inequitable for the representor to enforce his rights for the nature of the action, or inaction, may be insufficient to give rise to the equity, in which event a necessary requirement stated by Lord Cairns LC for the application of the doctrine would not have been fulfilled.

(d) It must be inequitable to allow the promisor to go back on his promise

D. & C. Builders Ltd v Rees
[1966] 2 QB 617 (CA)

In July 1964, the defendant owed the plaintiff, builders, £482. In November, the defendant still had not paid. The plaintiff was in desperate financial straits, and it was alleged that the defendant's wife knew this when she offered to pay the plaintiff £300 in full settlement, indicating that if this was not accepted the plaintiff would get nothing. The plaintiff said it had no choice but to accept, and received a cheque for £300 'in completion of the account'. The plaintiff then claimed the balance. Held: there was no binding settlement. Danckwerts and Winn LJJ concentrated on rejecting the argument that consideration had been provided because the payment of a smaller amount had been made by cheque. Lord Denning examined promissory estoppel, but held that it could not operate on these facts because it was not inequitable for the plaintiff to go back on its promise which was not freely given.

LORD DENNING MR: . . . [The] doctrine of the common law [relating to part payment of debts] has come under heavy fire. It was ridiculed by Sir George Jessel in *Couldery* v *Bartram* [(1881) 19 Ch D 394, 399]. It was said to be mistaken by Lord Blackburn in *Foakes* v *Beer*. It was condemned by the Law Revision Committee (1945 Cmd 5449), paras 20 and 21. But a remedy has been found. The harshness of the common law has been relieved. Equity has stretched out a merciful hand to help the debtor. The courts have invoked the broad principle stated by Lord Cairns in *Hughes* v *Metropolitan Railway Co*.

. . . It is worth noticing that the principle may be applied, not only so as to suspend strict legal rights, but also so as to preclude the enforcement of them.

This principle has been applied to cases where a creditor agrees to accept a lesser sum in discharge of a greater. So much so that we can now say that, when a creditor and a debtor enter upon a course of negotiation, which leads the debtor to suppose that, on payment of the lesser sum, the creditor will not enforce payment of the balance, and on the faith thereof the debtor pays the lesser sum and the creditor accepts it as satisfaction: then the creditor will not be allowed to enforce payment of the balance when it would be inequitable to do so. This was well illustrated during the last war. Tenants went away to escape the bombs and left their houses unoccupied. The landlords accepted a reduced rent for the time they were empty. It was held that the landlords could not afterwards turn round and sue for the balance, see *Central London Property Trust Ltd* v *High Trees House Ltd* [1947] KB 130. This caused at the time some eyebrows to be raised in high places. But they have been lowered since. The solution was so obviously just that no one could well gainsay it.

In applying this principle, however, we must note the qualification: The creditor is only barred from his legal rights when it would be *inequitable* for him to insist upon them. Where there has been a *true accord*, under which the creditor voluntarily agrees to accept a lesser sum in satisfaction, and the debtor *acts upon* that accord by paying the lesser sum and the creditor accepts it, then it is inequitable for the creditor afterwards to insist on the balance. But he is not bound unless there has been truly an accord between them.

In the present case, on the facts as found by the judge, it seems to me that there was no true accord. The debtor's wife held the creditor to ransom . . .

In my opinion there is no reason in law or equity why the creditor should not enforce the full amount of the debt due to him. . . .

■ QUESTION

This promise would now be voidable under the doctrine of economic duress (*page 611*). It is not clear, however, what the position will be if the pressure is not as explicit as in *D. & C. Builders* v *Rees*. It appears from *Williams* v *Roffey Brothers* (*page 135*) to make a difference who initiates a compromise. Was any pressure exerted in *High Trees House*?

(e) Does promissory estoppel extinguish rights or merely suspend them?

This is a vital question, since if promissory estoppel is capable of operating to extinguish the right for all time, then it will conflict with *Foakes* v *Beer* (1884) 9 App Cas 605 (*page 140*) which held that if a promisor represented that he would not insist on his strict contractual rights, in the absence of consideration provided by the promisee, the promisor was free to change his mind.

Tool Metal Manufacturing Co. Ltd v ***Tungsten Electric Co. Ltd***
[1955] 1 WLR 761 (HL)

By a contract in 1938, Tool Metal (TMMC) granted Tungsten Electric (TECO) a licence to import, manufacture, use and sell certain hard metal alloys covered by patents owned by TMMC. If TECO's sales exceeded a set quota in any given month they were to pay 'compensation' of 30 per cent to TMMC. After the outbreak of war in 1939, TMMC agreed not to enforce their right to the 'compensation', and no compensation was paid after 31 December 1939. In 1945, TECO commenced an action against TMMC, and in March 1946 TMMC counterclaimed for the compensation in respect of the material used from June 1945 but not for the period before this. The Court of Appeal held that the counterclaim failed, because this temporary arrangement to suspend compensation could be terminated only by giving reasonable notice and this had not been done. In this action in 1950, TMMC claimed the compensation from January 1947, and the issue was whether reasonable notice had been given by TMMC to resume their strict legal rights. Held: TMMC were entitled to the compensation claimed since the delivery of the counterclaim in March 1946 constituted notice by TMMC that they intended to resume their legal rights, and the period of nine months between the date of the counterclaim and the date from which the compensation was claimed was a sufficient period of notice.

LORD TUCKER: . . . The sole question, therefore, before the courts on this issue in the present action has been throughout: Was the counterclaim in the first action a sufficient intimation to terminate the period of suspension which has been found to exist? . . . It is, of course, clear, . . . that there are some cases where the period of suspension clearly terminates on the happening of a certain event or the cessation of a previously existing state of affairs or on the lapse of a reasonable period thereafter. In such cases no intimation or notice of any kind may be necessary. But in other cases where there is nothing to fix the end of the period which may be dependent on the will of the person who has given or made the concession, equity will no doubt require some notice or intimation together with a reasonable period for readjustment before the grantor is allowed to enforce his strict rights. No authority has been cited which binds your Lordships to hold that in all such cases the notice must take any particular form or specify a date for the termination of the suspensory period.

This is not surprising having regard to the infinite variety of circumstances which may give rise to this principle which was stated in broad terms and must now be regarded as of general application. It should, I think, be applied with great caution to purely creditor and debtor relationships which involve no question of forfeiture or cancellation, and it would be unfortunate if the law were to introduce into this field technical requirements with regard to notice and the like which might tend to penalise or discourage the making of reasonable concessions.

NOTES

1. This case confirms the view that promissory estoppel is merely suspensory, and that the promisor can resume his rights under the contract after giving reasonable notice of his intention to do so.

2. Both the *High Trees* and the *Tool Metal* cases concerned individual periodic payments (of rent and monthly compensation), and in both cases it seems that it would not have been possible to claim back the instalments before notice was given or the estoppel ceased. Thus, there is an important difference between the general right, which can be revived once the conditions under which the estoppel operated cease to exist or at the end of a period of reasonable notice, and individual periodic payments, which are extinguished. It follows that there is a practical difference between the operation of promissory estoppel in the context of single-debt obligations (where promissory estoppel operates only to allow more time to pay) and debt obligations taking the form of instalment payments (where, in the period covered by the estoppel, the balance on the individual instalments is extinguished).

   Lord Denning MR in *D. & C. Builders Ltd* v *Rees* [1966] 2 QB 617 (*page 157*) stated (at p. 624): 'It is worth noticing that the principle may be applied, not only so as to suspend strict legal rights, but also so as to preclude the enforcement of them.' It is possible to reconcile this statement with the case law by arguing that Lord Denning was referring to the individual periodic payments which could be extinguished by promissory estoppel.

C: How far can the doctrine be extended?

The exact scope of promissory estoppel is unclear. In particular, questions have been raised as to whether it can be extended to give rise to a cause of action, whether it can be applied where there is no existing legal relationship between the parties, the exact scope and meaning of its suspensory effect, and the extent to which the concept of inequitable conduct will affect the estoppel.

Brikom Investments Ltd v *Carr*
[1979] 1 QB 467 (CA)

The landlords of four blocks of flats offered to sell 99-year leases to their sitting tenants. The roofs of the blocks were in need of repair, and the landlords made oral representations to the tenants that the landlords would repair the roofs at their own expense. The subsequent leases contained a covenant by the landlords to repair the roofs but also stipulated that the tenants would pay an annual contribution in respect of the maintenance expenses incurred by the landlords. The leases were signed, the landlords repaired the roofs and then claimed contributions from the tenants. The tenants refused to pay, relying on the representations of the landlords. In the action the first defendant admitted that she would have taken the lease in any event, and the second and third defendants were assignees of the original tenants to whom the representations had been made. The majority of the Court of Appeal (Roskill and Cumming-Bruce LJJ) dismissed the landlords' claim on the basis that there was a collateral contract (see *page 209*) between the landlords and the original tenants, and the tenants had given consideration for the landlords' promise by entering into the leases in reliance upon it. Lord Denning held that the tenants could rely on the defence of promissory estoppel.

LORD DENNING MR: [Counsel] for the landlords submitted that [the first defendant] could not rely on the principle in the *High Trees* case [1947] KB 130, because it was essential that she should have *acted* on the representation: and here she had not acted on it. On her own admission, he said, she would have gone on and taken the lease even if she had not been told about the roof. In all the cases, [counsel for the landlords] said, the courts had said that the party must have '*acted*' on the promise or representation in the sense that he must have altered his position on the faith of it, meaning that he must have been led to act differently from what he would otherwise have done: see *Alan & Co* v *El Nasr Export & Import Co* [1972] 2 QB 189, 213. This argument gives, I think, too limited a scope to the principle. The principle extends to all cases where one party makes a promise or representation, intending that it should be binding, intending that the other should rely on it, and on which that other does in fact rely—by acting on it, by altering his position on the faith of it, by going ahead with a transaction then under discussion, or by any other way of reliance. It is no answer for the maker to say: 'You would have gone on with the transaction anyway.' That must be mere speculation. No one can be sure what he would, or would not, have done in a hypothetical state of affairs which never took place. . . . Once it is shown that a representation was calculated to influence the judgment of a reasonable man, the presumption is that he was so influenced.

[Lord Denning then considered the position of the second and third defendants who were assignees and a sub-assignee.]

[Counsel for the landlords] submitted that the doctrine of promissory estoppel (as enunciated in the *High Trees* case) was personal to the person to whom the representation or promise was made. So the original tenants . . . could rely on the estoppel, but no one else. [Counsel] said that the assignees could not rely on it. They took their assignments in the usual conveyancing way. They take the benefit and burden of the covenants in the lease itself which run with the land at law or in equity, but not of estoppels such as this.

The judge did not accept that contention. We have had it elaborately argued before us today. It was suggested that if assignees are able to rely on an oral or written representation (not contained in the deeds) it would cause chaos and confusion amongst conveyancers. No one buying property would know where he stood.

I am not disturbed by those forebodings. I prefer to see that justice is done: and let the conveyancers look after themselves. Suppose that the landlords here (before or after doing the repairs to the roofs) had assigned their reversion to a purchaser; and then that purchaser sought to recover the contribution from the tenants—contrary to the promise made by the original landlords. Surely the assignee of the reversion would be bound by the promise made by the original landlords. It would be most unjust and unfair if he could go back on the promise. Equity would not allow him to do it.

Now if the assignee of the reversion takes subject to the *burden* of the estoppel, so also the assignee of the tenant should take subject to the *benefit* of it. . . . So when the original tenant assigns the lease over to an assignee, the benefit of the promise passes to the assignee. The burden and the benefit run down the line of assignor and assignee on each side. Especially in this case, because it is plain (as the judge found) that when the landlords made this promise they intended it to be for the benefit of all those from time to time holding the leases, realising that each in turn would tell their successors that the landlords were going to repair the roofs at their own expense. The landlords, having made a representation of that kind, knowing that it would be passed on, cannot escape from it by simply saying: 'These people are assignees.'

So it seems to me that the judge was quite right in the way he put the case. He held that in all these cases the landlords could not go back to the strict rights under the lease. They had given the tenants their promise or representation to repair the roofs at their own cost, and the tenants relied on it. That gives rise to an equity which makes it unjust and inequitable for the landlords to seek to charge the tenants for a contribution; and the benefit of this equity avails the assignees of the tenants also.

But I may say there is another way in which the case can be put which seems to me equally valid. Although this is called a 'promise' or 'representation', it seems to me that it might also qualify for what we call a 'collateral contract' or 'collateral warranty'. On the faith of it these tenants signed the leases. After the first day in the county court, [the assignees] pleaded that they took from their predecessors an assignment of the benefit of the collateral contract or warranty. That enables them to take advantage of it as against the landlords. This seems to me a roundabout way of reaching the same result as the *High Trees* principle. It is a technical way of overcoming technical difficulties. I prefer the simple way . . .

ROSKILL LJ: . . . While I agree this appeal should be dismissed, I wish, with respect, to make plain that my reasons differ from those of the judge given in his judgment. I do not rest my decision on any question of promissory estoppel; and I do not think it necessary on the facts of this case to investigate the jurisprudential basis of that doctrine in order to arrive at what I conceive to be the right decision. It is necessary to do no more than to apply that which was said by the House of Lords and especially by Lord Cairns LC in *Hughes* v *Metropolitan Railway Co.* (1877) 2 App Cas 439. . . .

[I]t would be wrong to extend the doctrine of promissory estoppel, whatever its precise limits at the present day, to the extent of abolishing in this backhanded way the doctrine of consideration . . .

It seems to me in the present case that [counsel for the tenants'] argument (in so far as it rests on promissory estoppel) involves taking that doctrine a great deal further than it has hitherto been taken. With great respect, I would not go as far as Lord Denning MR in saying it is now the law that benefits and burdens arising from a promise made in circumstances such as those presently found by the judge, to quote the phrase he used a few moments ago, 'run down both sides'. It seems to me that the problem is far more complex. Accordingly, I do not rest my conclusion that this appeal should be dismissed on any question of promissory estoppel.

. . . I entertain no doubt . . . that there was a perfectly clear agreement between the landlords and [the tenants] . . . that those who took these 99-year leases from the landlords would not be liable for their share of the cost of repairing the roofs if the time ever came to do those repairs.

. . . I do not see how the landlords can escape from the bond of the promises which were given and which seem to me to have been given for perfectly good consideration.

. . . But if I am wrong about that, I think . . . there was a plain waiver by the landlords of their right to claim the cost of these repairs from these tenants. . . . If that be right, then it seems to me that that waiver subsists notwithstanding any subsequent assignment of the lease to assignees and sub-assignees from the first assignee; because what was then assigned and reassigned was a lease, the relevant obligation in which had before assignment been waived by the landlords.

I think it necessary to go no further than what Lord Cairns LC said in *Hughes* v *Metropolitan Railway Co.* where the matter was put not as one of promissory estoppel but as a matter of contract law or equity (call it which you will) . . .

For my own part, I would respectfully prefer to regard that as an illustration of contractual variation of strict contractual rights. But it could equally well be put as an illustration of equity relieving from the consequences of strict adherence to the letter of the lease.

But, whichever is the right way of putting it, ever since *Hughes* v *Metropolitan Railway Co.*, through a long line of cases of which there are many examples in the books, one finds that where parties have made a contract which provides one thing and where, by a subsequent course of dealing, the parties have worked that contract out in such a way that one party leads the other to believe that the strict rights under that contract will not be adhered to, the courts will not allow that party who has led the other to think the strict rights will not be adhered to, suddenly to seek to enforce those strict rights against him. That seems to me to be precisely what the landlords are trying to do here. . . . I do not think that the common law or equity will allow them to take that step; and for my part, with profound respect to Lord Denning MR, I do not think it is necessary in order to reach that result to resort to the somewhat uncertain doctrine of promissory estoppel.

(a) Can estoppel found a cause of action?

(i) Estoppel by convention

Amalgamated Investment & Property Co. Ltd (in liquidation) v *Texas Commerce International Bank Ltd*

[1982] QB 84 (CA)

The defendant bank agreed to make a loan to the plaintiffs' subsidiary company (ANPP) which was based in the Bahamas. This 'Nassau' loan was to be secured by a guarantee from the plaintiffs. For exchange control purposes the money was lent to Portsoken, a subsidiary company which the bank acquired in the Bahamas, and Portsoken then lent the money to ANPP. The plaintiffs' guarantee in fact referred only to loans made by the defendant bank rather than the defendant's subsidiary. However, it was assumed by both the plaintiffs and the defendant bank that the guarantee covered this 'Nassau' loan made by the defendant's subsidiary, Portsoken. When the plaintiff company was wound up the liquidator sought a declaration that the guarantee did not cover this 'Nassau' loan. Held: since the parties had acted upon the agreed assumption that the plaintiffs were liable for the 'Nassau' loan, the plaintiffs were estopped by convention from denying that they were bound to discharge any indebtedness of ANPP to the defendant's subsidiary. (In effect the defendant bank was establishing that the guarantee was enforceable. The majority (Lord Denning and Brandon LJ) considered that the estoppel could operate so as to enable a party to succeed on a cause of action.)

LORD DENNING MR: The doctrine of estoppel is one of the most flexible and useful in the armoury of the law. But it has become overloaded with cases. It has evolved during the last 150 years in a sequence of separate developments: proprietary estoppel, estoppel by representation of fact, estoppel by acquiescence, and promissory estoppel. At the same time it has been sought to be limited by a series of maxims: estoppel is only a rule of evidence, estoppel cannot give rise to a cause of action, estoppel cannot do away with the need for consideration, and so forth. All these can now be seen to merge into one general principle shorn of limitations. When the parties to a transaction proceed on the basis of an underlying assumption—either of fact or of law—whether due to misrepresentation or mistake makes no difference—on which they have conducted the dealings between them—neither of them will be allowed to go back on that assumption when it would be unfair or unjust to allow him to do so. If one of them does seek to go back on it, the courts will give the other such remedy as the equity of the case demands.

BRANDON LJ: I turn to the second argument advanced on behalf of the plaintiffs, that the bank is here seeking to use estoppel as a sword rather than a shield, and that that is something which the law of estoppel does not permit. Another way in which the argument is put is that a party cannot found a cause of action on an estoppel.

In my view much of the language used in connection with these concepts is no more than a matter of semantics. Let me consider the present case and suppose that the bank had brought an action against the plaintiffs before they went into liquidation to recover moneys owed by ANPP to Portsoken. In the statement of claim in such an action the bank would have pleaded the contract of loan incorporating the guarantee, and averred that, on the true construction of the guarantee, the plaintiffs were bound to discharge the debt owed by ANPP to Portsoken. By their defence the plaintiffs would have pleaded that, on the true construction of the guarantee, the plaintiffs were only bound to discharge debts owed by ANPP to the bank, and not debts owed by ANPP to Portsoken. Then in their reply the bank would have pleaded that, by reason of an estoppel arising from the matters discussed above, the plaintiffs were precluded from questioning the interpretation of the guarantee which both parties had, for the purpose of the transactions between them, assumed to be true.

In this way the bank, while still in form using the estoppel as a shield, would in substance be founding a cause of action on it. This illustrates what I would regard as the true proposition of law, that, while a party cannot in terms found a cause of action on an estoppel, he may, as a result of being able to rely on an estoppel, succeed on a cause of action on which, without being able to rely on that estoppel, he would necessarily have failed. That, in my view, is, in substance, the situation of the bank in the present case.

NOTES

1. Brandon LJ, at p. 130, relying on the definition given in Spencer Bower and Turner, *Estoppel by Representation*, 3rd edn (1977), stated that estoppel by convention is founded:

   on an agreed statement of facts the truth of which has been assumed by the convention of the parties, as the basis of a transaction into which they are about to enter. When the parties have acted in their transaction upon the agreed assumption that a given state is to be accepted between them as true, then as regards that transaction each will be estopped as against the other from questioning the truth of the statement of facts so assumed.

2. In *Amalgamated Investment* Brandon LJ appears to assume that it would be the contract of guarantee which created the cause of action and not the estoppel. However, if the estoppel was being relied upon to ensure that the guarantee was enforceable, then it must be the estoppel which establishes the cause of action.

3. The passage from the judgment of Lord Denning in *Amalgamated Investment & Property* v *Texas Commerce* was quoted by Lord Bingham in *Johnson* v *Gore Wood & Co* [2001] 2 WLR 72. Lord Bingham based his decision, at least in part, on estoppel by convention. The issue in *Johnson* v *Gore Wood & Co* arose in the context of a professional negligence claim brought by a company against a firm of solicitors. Before settling the company's claim, the solicitors had been made aware that a director of the company would make a similar claim and a term of the settlement had limited some of the director's personal claims. The director later made other personal claims and the solicitors sought to have these claims struck out as an abuse of process. The House of Lords rejected this claim. Lord Bingham considered that the settlement of the company's claim was based on the common assumption that a personal claim by the director would not be an abuse of process and that it would be unfair to allow the solicitors to go back on this. However, none of the other speeches refers to estoppel by convention as the basis for the decision.

4. It is not necessarily clear that estoppel by convention gives rise to a cause of action. Although in *Baird Textiles Holdings Ltd* v *Marks & Spencer plc* [2001] EWCA Civ 274, [2002] 1 All ER (Comm) 737, Mance LJ was clearly of the opinion that both Lord Denning and Brandon LJ in *Amalgamated Investment* considered that the estoppel operated so as to enable the bank to enforce the guarantee, counsel for Baird did not dispute the claim put on behalf of M&S that *Amalgamated Investment* was authority for the proposition that estoppel by convention cannot create a cause of action, [34] and [35]. Instead, counsel for Baird, put the argument on a different basis (see the discussion at *page 168*).

   In *Johnson* v *Gore Wood & Co.* the argument based on estoppel by convention would have to be used as a cause of action in order to prevent the solicitors striking out the director's personal claim as an abuse of process.

5. The estoppel argument in *Baird Textiles* v *Marks & Spencer plc* had proceeded at first instance as an estoppel by convention. However, the Court of Appeal preferred to avoid the 'rigid classification' of types of estoppel, whilst accepting that the doctrine 'may take different shapes to fit the context of different fields' (*per* Mance LJ at [83] and [84]).

(ii) *Proprietary estoppel*

This estoppel can arise despite the absence of a clear and unequivocal representation, e.g., in the belief or expectation that the property interest will be granted, and it can give rise to a cause of action.

Crabb v Arun District Council
[1976] Ch 179 (CA)

The plaintiff owned land which had an access point (at A) onto the road owned by the defendant council, and he had a right of way along the road. The plaintiff wished to sell his land in two parts, and the defendants' representative indicated that he would be given a second point of access (at B) and a second right of way. The council subsequently fenced the boundary between its road and the plaintiff's land and erected gates at points A and B. The plaintiff sold the land with the access (A) but the defendant removed the access point (at B) so that the plaintiff's land was landlocked. The plaintiff claimed that the defendant was estopped from denying the right of access at B and right of way along the road. Held: the defendant had encouraged the plaintiff to act to his detriment in selling part A without reserving any access. This gave rise to an equity in the plaintiff which would be satisfied by granting him the relevant access point at B and right of way along the road.

LORD DENNING MR: When [counsel] for the plaintiff, said that he put his case on an estoppel, it shook me a little: because it is commonly supposed that estoppel is not itself a cause of action. But that is because there are estoppels and estoppels. Some do give rise to a cause of action. Some do not. In the species of estoppel called proprietary estoppel, it does give rise to a cause of action. We had occasion to consider it a month ago in *Moorgate Mercantile Co. Ltd* v *Twitchings* [1976] QB 225 where I said, at p. 242, that the effect of estoppel on the true owner may be that:

> . . . his own title to the property, be it land or goods, has been held to be limited or extinguished, and new rights and interests have been created therein. And this operates by reason of his conduct—what he has led the other to believe—even though he never intended it.

The new rights and interests, so created by estoppel, in or over land, will be protected by the courts and in this way give rise to a cause of action.

The basis of this proprietary estoppel—as indeed of promissory estoppel—is the interposition of equity. Equity comes in, true to form, to mitigate the rigours of strict law. The early cases did not speak of it as 'estoppel.' They spoke of it as 'raising an equity.' If I may expand what Lord Cairns LC said in *Hughes* v *Metropolitan Railway Co.* (1877) 2 App Cas 439, 448: 'it is the first principle upon which all courts of equity proceed,' that it will prevent a person from insisting on his strict legal rights— whether arising under a contract, or on his title deeds, or by statute—when it would be inequitable for him to do so having regard to the dealings which have taken place between the parties.

What then are the dealings which will preclude him from insisting on his strict legal rights? If he makes a binding contract that he will not insist on the strict legal position, a court of equity will hold him to his contract. Short of a binding contract, if he makes a promise that he will not insist upon his strict legal rights—then, even though that promise may be unenforceable in point of law for want of consideration . . .—then, if he makes the promise knowing or intending that the other will act upon it, and he does act upon it, then again a court of equity will not allow him to go back on that promise: see *Central London Property Trust Ltd* v *High Trees House Ltd* [1947] KB 130 and *Charles Rickards Ltd* v *Oppenhaim* [1950] 1 KB 616, 623. Short of an actual promise, if he, by his words or conduct, so behaves as to lead another to believe that he will not insist on his strict legal rights—knowing or intending that the other will act on that belief—and he does so act, that again will raise an equity in favour of the other; and it is for a court of equity to say in what way the equity may be satisfied. The cases show that this equity does not depend on agreement but on words or conduct. In *Ramsden* v *Dyson* (1866) LR 1 HL 129, 170 Lord Kingsdown spoke of a verbal agreement 'or what amounts to the same thing, an expectation, created or encouraged.' In *Birmingham and District Land Co.* v *London and North-Western Railway Co.* (1888) 40 ChD 268, 277, Cotton LJ said that '. . . what passed did not make a new agreement, but . . . what took place . . . raised an equity against him.' . . .

The question then is: were the circumstances here such as to raise an equity in favour of the plaintiff? True the defendants on the deeds had the title to their land, free of any access at point B. But they led the plaintiff to believe that he had or would be granted a right of access at point B. . . . The defendants actually put up the gates at point B at considerable expense. That certainly led the plaintiff to believe that they agreed that he should have the right of access through point B without more ado.

It was their conduct which led him to act as he did: and this raises an equity in his favour against them.

■ QUESTIONS

1. Do you consider that the Court of Appeal was enforcing a contract in this case based on the fact that the plaintiff had acted to his detriment? (See Atiyah (1976) 92 LQR 174 and Millett (1976) 92 LQR 342.)

2. Scarman LJ considered that the distinction between promissory estoppel and proprietary estoppel was not a helpful one. Would it be preferable to accept a general doctrine based on the fact that it is unconscionable for the promisor to go back on his promise, e.g., because he had acquiesced in the detrimental conduct or encouraged it?

(b) A new flexibility?

Waltons Stores (Interstate) Ltd v Maher
(1988) 164 CLR 387 (High Court of Australia)

Waltons had negotiated with Maher, land owners, that Maher would demolish a building and construct a new one in accordance with Waltons' specifications, and then lease the building to Waltons as retail premises. Maher did not wish to start until it was clear that there were no problems with the lease. Maher signed its part of the lease and forwarded it to Waltons' solicitors for execution 'by way of exchange', and then began to demolish the building. Waltons had second thoughts about proceeding and told its solicitors to 'go slow'. Waltons knew that 40 per cent of the work had been completed when it informed Maher that it would not proceed. Maher sought specific performance and, on appeal, sought to argue that Waltons was estopped from going back on its implied promise to complete the lease contract. Waltons argued that even if it had made a representation as to its future conduct, there was no pre-existing legal relationship between the parties and Maher could not use the estoppel to create a cause of action. Held: Waltons knew Maher was exposed to a detriment in carrying out the demolition and building work in reliance on the representation, and since it was unconscionable to adopt a course of inaction encouraging that detriment, Waltons was estopped from denying that it was bound. The majority (Mason CJ, Wilson J, and Brennan J) appeared to confirm that promissory estoppel could create a cause of action, and that this could be reconciled with the doctrine of consideration on the ground that the object of the promissory estoppel doctrine was not to enforce promises but to avoid detriment to the promisee resulting from the unconscionable departure by the promisor from the terms of his promise. In addition, it was not necessary to establish a pre-existing relationship between the parties before this estoppel could be relied upon.

MASON CJ AND WILSON J: There has been for many years a reluctance to allow promissory estoppel to become the vehicle for the positive enforcement of a representation by a party that he would do something in the future. Promissory estoppel, it has been said, is a defensive equity: *Hughes* v *Metropolitan Railway Co.* (1877) 2 App Cas 439; *Combe* v *Combe* [1951] 2 KB 215 and the traditional notion has been that estoppel could only be relied upon defensively as a shield and not as a sword . . . *High Trees* [1947] KB 130 itself was an instance of the defensive use of promissory estoppel. But this does not mean that a plaintiff cannot rely on an estoppel. Even according to traditional orthodoxy, a plaintiff may rely on an estoppel if he has an independent cause of action, where in the words of Denning LJ in *Combe* v *Combe*, the estoppel 'may be part of a cause of action, but not a cause of action in itself'.

But the respondents ask us to drive promissory estoppel one step further by enforcing directly in the absence of a pre-existing relationship of any kind a non-contractual promise on which the representee has relied to his detriment. For the purposes of discussion, we shall assume that there was such a promise in the present case. The principal objection to the enforcement of such a promise is that it would outflank the principles of the law of contract. Denning LJ in *Combe* v *Combe* after noting that 'The doctrine of consideration is too firmly fixed to be overthrown by a side-wind', said that such a promise could only be enforced if it was supported by sufficient consideration. . . .

There is force in these objections and it may not be a sufficient answer to repeat the words of Lord Denning MR in *Crabb* v *Arun District Council* [1976] 1 Ch 179: 'Equity comes in, true to form, to mitigate the rigours of strict law.' True it is that in the orthodox case of promissory estoppel, where the promisor promises that he will not exercise or enforce an existing right, the elements of reliance and detriment attract equitable intervention on the basis that it is unconscionable for the promisor to depart from his promise, if to do so will result in detriment to the promisee. And it can be argued that there is no justification for applying the doctrine of promissory estoppel in this situation, yet denying it in the case of a non-contractual promise in the absence of a pre-existing relationship. The promise, if enforced, works a change in the relationship of the parties, by altering an existing legal relationship in the first situation and by creating a new legal relationship in the second. The point has been made that it would be more logical to say that when the parties have agreed to pursue a course of action, an alteration of the relationship by non-contractual promise will not be countenanced, whereas the creation of a new relationship by a simple promise will be recognised: see D. Jackson, 'Estoppel as a Sword', *Law Quarterly Review*, vol. 81 (1965) 223, at p. 242.

[T]he doctrine [of promissory estoppel] extends to the enforcement of voluntary promises on the footing that a departure from the basic assumptions underlying the transaction between the parties must be unconscionable. As failure to fulfil a promise does not of itself amount to unconscionable conduct, mere reliance on an executory promise to do something, resulting in the promisee changing his position or suffering detriment, does not bring promissory estoppel into play. Something more would be required. *Humphreys Estate* [AG (Hong Kong) v *Humphreys Estate Ltd* [1987] 1 AC 114] suggests that this may be found, if at all, in the creation or encouragement by the party estopped in the other party of an assumption that a contract will come into existence or a promise will be performed and that the other party relied on that assumption to his detriment to the knowledge of the first party. . . . [T]he crucial question remains: was the appellant entitled to stand by in silence when it must have known that the respondents were proceeding on the assumption that they had an agreement and that completion of the exchange was a formality? The mere exercise of its legal right not to exchange contracts could not be said to amount to unconscionable conduct on the part of the appellant. But there were two other factors present in the situation which require to be taken into consideration. The first was the element of urgency that pervaded the negotiation of the terms of the proposed lease . . . The respondents' solicitor had said to the appellant's solicitor on 7 November that it would be impossible for Maher to complete the building within the agreed time unless the agreement were concluded 'within the next day or two'. The outstanding details were agreed within a day or two thereafter, and the work of preparing the site commenced almost immediately.

The second factor of importance is that the respondents executed the counterpart deed and it was forwarded to the appellant's solicitor on 11 November. The assumption on which the respondents acted thereafter was that completion of the necessary exchange was a formality. The next their solicitor heard from the appellant was a letter from its solicitors dated 19 January, informing him that the appellant did not intend to proceed with the matter. It had known, at least since 10 December, that costly work was proceeding on the site.

It seems to us, in the light of these considerations, that the appellant was under an obligation to communicate with the respondents within a reasonable time after receiving the executed counterpart deed and certainly when it learnt on 10 December that demolition was proceeding. . . .

. . . The appellant's inaction, in all the circumstances, constituted clear encouragement or inducement to the respondents to continue to act on the basis of the assumption which they had made. It was unconscionable for it, knowing that the respondents were exposing themselves to detriment by acting on the basis of a false assumption, to adopt a course of inaction which encouraged them in the course they had adopted. To express the point in the language of promissory estoppel the appellant is estopped in all the circumstances from retreating from its implied promise to complete the contract.

NOTES

1. It must be doubted whether *Waltons Stores* is strictly speaking a promissory estoppel case, since it appears to support a single general doctrine of estoppel preventing unconscionable conduct. This idea of a unifying estoppel is supported by the judgments in *Commonwealth of Australia* v *Verwayen* (1990) 170 CLR 394, which require that the doctrine should not be seen as a 'series of independent rules'.

2. Duthie, 'Equitable estoppel, unconscionability and the enforcement of promises' (1988) 104 LQR 362, argues that the denial of a future right should be treated in the same way as insistence on an existing right, so that if the legal relationship would exist were it not for the unconscionable conduct, the lack of such a relationship should not prevent reliance on the doctrine of promissory estoppel.

3. The decision has not determined the type of conduct which will be unconscionable and prevent a promisor from going back on his promise in these circumstances (although see the judgment of Mason CJ and Wilson J for guidance). It appeared that 'detrimental reliance' was required in order for a promise to found a claim based on this estoppel. Significantly, however, in *Giumelli* v *Giumelli* (1999) 163 ALR 473, the High Court of Australia was of the opinion that this is not the only basis for the estoppel.

4. The advantage of this approach is that it allows the doctrine of consideration to be reconciled with more flexible requirements for the promissory estoppel doctrine. Thus, in theory, Maher was not seeking to enforce an implied promise but to avoid the detriment that would be suffered if Waltons was permitted to continue in its unconscionable conduct of not complying with the promise.

5. In *Tanwar Enterprises Pty Ltd* v *Cauchi* (2003) 201 ALR 359, in the context of whether it was unconscionable for vendors to exercise a right of termination of contracts for the sale of land, the High Court of Australia adopted a restrictive interpretation of equitable intervention based on unconscionability, limiting it to instances of 'fraud, accident, mistake or surprise'. It was noted that 'unconscionability' was apt to mislead because it implied that intervention in contractual relationships required nothing more than 'an element of hardship or unfairness in the terms of the transaction in question, or in the manner of its performance'. The High Court's limited interpretation has, however, been subject to criticism; see, for example, Tolhurst and Carter (2004) 20 JCL 74.

6. In *Waltons Stores* the High Court of Australia gave effect to the estoppel by awarding damages in lieu of specific performance. An interesting debate surrounds the remedy required to satisfy the 'minimum equity' and, in particular, it might appear that reliance damages would be the appropriate remedy in this context (see Furmston, Norisada, and Poole, *Contract Formation and Letters of Intent*, 1997, pp. 293–6, and Robertson, 'Reliance and expectation in estoppel remedies' [1998] LS 360). However, in *Giumelli* v *Giumelli* (see Edelman (1999) 15 JCL 179), the High Court of Australia considered that *prima facie* the remedy should fulfil the promisee's expectation engendered by the promise so that the expectation measure of

damages would be appropriate. The High Court considered that it was only in instances of detrimental reliance that a reliance-based remedy would be appropriate.

7. § 90(1) of the American Restatement (2d) Contracts (1979) allows promissory estoppel to operate as a cause of action, but the courts are given a discretion to determine the appropriate remedy so that there may not be full enforcement of the promise:

> A promise which the promisor should reasonably expect to induce action or forbearance on the part of the promisee or a third person and which does induce such action or forbearance is binding if injustice can be avoided only by enforcement of the promise. The remedy granted for breach may be limited as justice requires.

8. This flexible estoppel has been advocated for use by the English courts (see discussion at *pages 144–5*). A requirement of detrimental reliance would have seriously limited the usefulness of such an estoppel and it is important that it was rejected in *Giumelli* v *Giumelli*. However, it remains to be seen whether the English courts will be prepared to adopt such an estoppel.

This argument proved unsuccessful before the Court of Appeal in *Baird Textile Holdings Ltd* v *Marks & Spencer plc* [2001] EWCA Civ 274, [2002] 1 All ER (Comm) 737, see *page 194* for the facts and the argument based on implied contract. One aspect of the pleadings was that the defendant was prevented by estoppel from determining the arrangements between the parties without giving reasonable notice and from denying the understanding that the relationship was long-term. The latter argument had been permitted to proceed to trial by the judge at first instance. However, the defendant claimed that, on the basis of established authority, such a claim had no prospect of success. The Court of Appeal agreed that the estoppel claim had no real prospect of success since English law did not currently create or recognise the right contended for on these facts. Quite apart from the fact that the obligation alleged was insufficiently certain to found an estoppel (see *page 151*), the estoppel alleged did not create a cause of action.

MORRITT VC: . . .

34 Counsel for M&S submits that the judge was wrong. He contends, . . . that this court is, as the judge was, bound by three decisions of the Court of Appeal to conclude that the estoppel claim has no real prospect of success either. The three decisions and the propositions they respectively established are: (1) a common law or promissory estoppel cannot create a cause of action (*Combe* v *Combe* [1951] 1 All ER 767, [1951] 2 KB 215); (2) an estoppel by convention cannot create a cause of action either (*Amalgamated Investment and Property Co Ltd (in liq)* v *Texas Commerce International Bank Ltd* [1981] 3 All ER 577, [1982] QB 84); and (3) accepting that a proprietary or equitable estoppel may create a cause of action it is limited to cases involving property rights, whether or not confined to land (*Western Fish Products Ltd* v *Penwith DC* [1981] 2 All ER 204 at 217).

35 Counsel for Baird did not dispute that those cases established the propositions for which M&S contended. Rather, he submitted, it is wrong to categorise particular types of estoppel and then impose limitations in each category not applicable to one or more of the other categories. He suggested that English law permits some cross-fertilisation between one category and another. He contended that English law should follow where the High Court of Australia has led in *Waltons Stores (Interstate) Ltd* v *Maher* (1988) 164 CLR 387 and *Commonwealth of Australia* v *Verwayen* (1990) 170 CLR 394 and permit estoppel to create causes of action in non-proprietary cases. In reply counsel for M&S conceded that if the Australian cases, to the effect that promissory estoppel extends to the enforcement of voluntary promises, represent the law of England then the judge was right and the cross-appeal must fail.

36 Warnings against categorisation have been given by Robert Goff J and Lord Denning MR in the *Amalgamated Investment* case [1981] 1 All ER 923 at 935, 936 and 584 [sic], [1982] QB 84 at 103, 104 and 122, by Scarman LJ in *Crabb* v *Arun DC* [1975] 3 All ER 865 at 875, [1976] Ch 179 at 192, 193 and by Lord Bingham of Cornhill in *Johnson* v *Gore Wood & Co* [2001] 1 All ER 481, [2001] 2 WLR 72. But dicta to the contrary effect are to be found in *First National Bank plc* v *Thompson* [1996] 1 All ER 140 at 144, [1996] Ch 231 at 236 per Millett LJ, *McIlkenny* v *Chief Constable of West Midlands Police Force* [1980] 2 All ER 227 at 235, [1980] 1 QB 283 at 317 per Lord Denning MR and in *Johnson* v *Gore Wood & Co* [2001] 1 All ER 481 at 507, 508, [2001] 2 WLR 72 at 99 per Lord Goff of Chieveley.

37 As in the case of the contractual claim, it is important to appreciate exactly what is being alleged and why. The material allegation in para 15 is that M&S is estopped from denying that 'the relationship with BTH could only be determined by the giving of reasonable notice'. But by itself this claim, which has undoubted echoes of *Hughes* v *Metropolitan Rly Co* (1877) 2 App Cas 439, [1874–80] All ER Rep 187 and *Central London Property Trust Ltd* v *High Trees House Ltd* (1946) [1956] 1 All ER 256, [1947] 1 KB 130, does not lead to the relief sought. For that purpose it is essential to establish an obligation by estoppel that, in the words of para 12, 'during the subsistence of the relationship Marks & Spencer would acquire garments from BTH in quantities and at prices which in all the circumstances were reasonable'. As counsel for Baird put it in their written argument, 'BTH contends that an equity generated by estoppel can be a cause of action'. They rely on a series of dicta as pointers in that direction contained in *Amalgamated Investment and Property Co Ltd* (in liq) v *Texas Commerce International Bank Ltd* [1981] 1 All ER 923, [1982] QB 84, *Taylor Fashions Ltd* v *Liverpool Victoria Trustees Co Ltd* [1981] 1 All ER 897, [1982] QB 133, *Habib Bank Ltd* v *Habib Bank AG Zurich* [1981] 2 All ER 650, [1981] 1 WLR 1265, *Pacol Ltd* v *Trade Lines Ltd, The Henrik Sif* [1982] 1 Lloyd's Rep 456, *Holiday Inns Inc* v *Broadhead, Holiday Inns Inc* v *Yorkstone Properties* (Harlington) *Ltd* (1974) 232 EG 951, *Re Basham* (decd) [1987] 1 All ER 405, [1986] 1 WLR 1498 and *Gillett* v *Holt* [2000] 2 All ER 289, [2001] Ch 210.

38 In my view English law, as presently understood, does not enable the creation or recognition by estoppel of an enforceable right of the type and in the circumstances relied on in this case. First, it would be necessary for such an obligation to be sufficiently certain to enable the court to give effect to it. That such certainty is required in the field of estoppels such as is claimed in this case as well as in contract was indicated by the House of Lords in *Woodhouse AC Israel Cocoa Ltd SA* v *Nigerian Produce Marketing Co Ltd* [1972] 2 All ER 271, [1972] AC 741 and by Ralph Gibson LJ in *Troop* v *Gibson* [1986] 1 EGLR 1 at 6. For the reasons I have already given I do not think that the alleged obligation is sufficiently certain. Second, in my view, the decisions in the three Court of Appeal decisions on which M&S rely do establish that such an enforceable obligation cannot be established by estoppel in the circumstances relied on in this case. This conclusion does not involve the categorisation of estoppels but is a simple application of the principles established by those cases to the obligation relied on in this. I do not consider that any of the dicta in the line of cases relied on by Baird could entitle this court to decline to apply those principles.

39 Counsel for M&S was, at one stage, inclined to concede that if we considered that the House of Lords, after the facts had been found at a trial, might adopt the propositions formulated by Mason CJ, Wilson and Brennan JJ in the *Waltons Stores* case, then it might be said that there was a real prospect of succeeding on the estoppel issue so that judgment under CPR 24.2 should not be given at this stage. In reply he submitted that the possibility that the House of Lords might adopt those propositions was an inadequate reason for allowing a trial. I agree. If I am right in believing that English law, as it now stands, does not permit the enforcement of an estoppel in the form alleged in this case then it is the duty of this court to apply it, notwithstanding that it may be developed by the House of Lords, who are not bound by any of the cases relied on, in the future. . . .

JUDGE LJ:

49 The interesting question therefore is whether equity can provide a remedy which cannot be provided by contract. It seems clear that the principles of the law of estoppel have not yet been fully developed, and during the course of the argument I was greatly attracted by the consideration that if summary judgment were entered against BTH under CPR 24.2 in a case such as this, the effect would be to stultify the possible development of the substantive law, or the correction of what Lord Hoffmann, in *Kleinwort Benson Ltd* v *Lincoln City Council* [1999] 2 AC 349, [1998] 4 All ER 513, described as 'ancient heresies'.

50   Two specific aspects of the current principles of the law of estoppel which may be open for reconsideration need mention. First, it is possible to envisage that the different principles encapsulated under the heading 'Estoppel' should cease to be treated as if they were individually compartmentalised. The most illuminating analysis of the disadvantages of rigidity was summarised by Robert Goff J in *Amalgamated Investment and Property Co Ltd (in liq) v Texas Commerce International Bank Ltd* [1981] 1 All ER 923, [1982] QB 84, where he said:

> 'Of all doctrines, equitable estoppel is surely one of the most flexible . . . It is no doubt helpful to establish, in broad terms, the criteria which, in certain situations, must be fulfilled before an equitable estoppel can be established; but it cannot be right to restrict equitable estoppel to certain defined categories, and indeed some of the categories proposed are not easy to defend . . . Thus in Snell . . . the learned editors isolate two categories of equitable estoppel, promissory estoppel and proprietary estoppel. It may be possible nowadays to identify the former with some degree of precision; but the latter is much more difficult to accept as a separate category . . . As a separate category, proprietary estoppel may be regarded as an amalgam of doubtful utility . . . It is not therefore surprising to discover a tendency in the more recent authorities to reject any rigid classification of equitable estoppel into exclusive and defined categories . . .' (See [1981] 1 All ER 923 at 935, 936, [1982] QB 84 at 103, 104.)

(See also per Oliver J in *Taylor Fashions Ltd v Liverpool Victoria Trustees Co Ltd* [1981] 1 All ER 897, [1982] QB 133 and further, per Lord Denning MR in the *Amalgamated Investment* case: but, see to the contrary, his earlier observations in *McIlkenny v Chief Constable of West Midlands Police Force* [1980] 2 All ER 227, [1980] 1 QB 283, and his description of the House 'called Estoppel', with its many rooms).

51   The less graphic, but equally trenchant comment by Millett LJ, as he then was, in *First National Bank plc v Thompson* [1996] 1 All ER 140 at 144, [1996] Ch 231 at 236, summarises the opposite contention:

> '. . . (the) attempt . . . to demonstrate that all estoppels other than estoppel by record are now subsumed in the single and all-embracing estoppel by representation and that they are all governed by the same requirements has never won general acceptance.'

52   The removal of formal classifications would represent the starting point from which to consider the second possible development, consigning to history the misleading aphorism that estoppel is a shield, not a sword. In reality that principle has no application to what is described as a proprietary estoppel. The cause of action founded on proprietary estoppel may, and should, so the argument runs, be extended generally in this jurisdiction, both in accordance with the recent decisions in the High Court of Australia in *Waltons Stores (Interstate) Ltd v Maher* (1988) 164 CLR 387 and *Commonwealth of Australia v Verwayen* (1990) 170 CLR 394, and perhaps also by reference in this jurisdiction to *Plimmer v Wellington Corp* (1884) 9 App Cas 699, which involved a contractual interest in a licence over land, and also on the basis that if the compartmentalisation of 'estoppel' were broken down, the remedies provided for one form of estoppel (proprietary estoppel) would then be extended to the others.

53   These, very briefly summarised, were the considerations which led me to the preliminary view that although BTH's argument in contract was unsustainable, the possible development of the law in relation to estoppel might properly justify allowing the case to proceed to trial.

54   If it did, however, both the trial judge and this court would be bound to hold that the principles relating to proprietary estoppel are limited to 'rights and interests created in and over land' and, possibly, 'to other forms of property'. (*Western Fish Products v Penwith DC* [1981] 2 All ER 204 at 218, where, in this specific context, Megaw LJ observed: 'The question of new rights and remedies is a matter for Parliament, not the judges.') Moreover, assuming for present purposes only that this authority could be distinguished, the difficulties arising from the underlying uncertainties referred to in the judgment of the Vice-Chancellor extend to the estoppel as well as the contractual issue (*Woodhouse AC Israel Cocoa Ltd SA v Nigerian Produce Marketing Co Ltd* [1972] 2 All ER 271, [1972] AC 741). In reality, BTH's possible success in this litigation would depend on establishing liability against M&S in equity when it would not otherwise be liable in contract, and would represent a dramatic, if not indeed a revolutionary, development of the legal principles governing the enforcement of private obligations.

55   On reflection, I am persuaded by the judgments of the Vice-Chancellor and Mance LJ, and for the reasons given by them, that there is no real prospect of the claim succeeding unless and until the law is developed, or corrected, by the House of Lords. In my judgment, however, such a possibility would not normally justify a case proceeding to, nor provide a compelling reason for, trial. However settled the law may appear to be, one of its strengths is that the possibility of development, or change, remains. In my view, even for the purposes of CPR 24.2, we must apply the law as it is, not as it *may* possibly one day become (my emphasis).

56   I do not believe that this approach means that the development of the law is likely to be stultified. If, for example, there were a significant conflict in the authorities, or if the law could reasonably be described as uncertain, or perhaps also, if there were a substantial body of academic or judicial opinion that the law as currently understood produced injustice and should be considered by the House of Lords, but simultaneously the essential facts were heavily in dispute, considerations such as these might provide a compelling reason for trial. Although the House of Lords in *Barrett* v *Enfield London Borough Council* [1999] 3 All ER 193, [2001] 2 AC 550 has recently emphasised that the law should be developed on the basis of established rather than assumed facts, in this case, as I have explained, many of the essential facts are not in reality in dispute. If Morison J's order were set aside, as I think it should be, without suggesting that this court should grant permission to appeal to the House of Lords, it would be open to BTH to seek permission either from this court, or, if refused, directly from the House of Lords, which could then decide whether the principles of estoppel should be re-examined, and whether this case provides an appropriate vehicle for that examination.

NOTE: The *Waltons Stores* argument was doomed to failure because of the deficiencies of the representation or promise relied upon. Although at [56], Judge LJ refers to the possibility that Baird Textiles might appeal to the House of Lords, this leave was in fact refused. Thus the reconsideration of the scope of the category or categories of estoppel by the House of Lords is still awaited.

D: Binding variations in New Zealand

The Court of Appeal of New Zealand introduced a further alternative approach and suggested that consideration would not be required to enforce alteration promises where those promises had been acted upon.

Antons Trawling Co Ltd v *Smith*
[2003] 2 NZLR 23 (Court of Appeal of New Zealand)

The plaintiff was employed as master of one of the defendants' fishing vessels. The defendants held a small fishing quota. The plaintiff claimed that he had been promised a 10 per cent share of any additional quota allocated to the defendants if the plaintiff was able to demonstrate that there were fish in sufficient commercial quantities to justify the Government setting a larger quota. The Government increased the quota for policy reasons without establishing any increase in commercial quantities and the defendants' catch increased by 80 tonnes. The defendants argued that the increased quota was not the result of any actions by the plaintiff and he had therefore supplied no consideration to support the promise of the 10 per cent share. He was required to fish under the terms of his contract and had done no more than he was contractually bound to do. Held: there was a binding variation. Where an alteration promise had been acted upon, in the absence of policy reasons to the contrary, the parties should be bound by such an alteration agreement.

BARAGWANATH J (giving the judgment of the court):

[92]   The reasoning in *Williams* v *Roffey Bros & Nicholls (Contractors) Ltd*, accepted by this Court in *Attorney-General for England and Wales* ([2002] 2 NZLR 91), has been trenchantly criticised by Professor Coote in (1990) 3 JCL 23. He argues with force that mere performance of a duty already owed to the promisee under a contract cannot constitute consideration and that the only principled way to such a result is to decide that consideration should not be necessary for the variation of contract. That is the approach of the Uniform Commercial Code, s 2–209(1) and it is vigorously supported by Reiter in 'Courts, Consideration, and Commonsense' (1977) 27 University of Toronto Law Journal 439 especially at p 507, observing that a rigid requirement of consideration in the context of modern commercial contract modifications fails to recognise:

> . . . the illogicality of equating modifying with originating promises or to see that, insofar as consideration serves to exclude gratuitous promise, it is of little assistance in the context of on-going, arms-length, commercial transactions where it is utterly fictional to describe what is being conceded as a gift, and in which there ought to be a strong presumption that good commercial 'considerations' underlie any seemingly detrimental modification. . . .

[93]   We are satisfied that *Stilk* v *Myrick* can no longer be taken to control such cases as *Roffey Bros*, *Attorney-General for England and Wales* and the present case where there is no element of duress or other policy factor suggesting that an agreement, duly performed, should not attract the legal consequences that each party must reasonably be taken to have expected. On the contrary, a result that deprived Mr Smith of the benefit of what Antons promised he should receive would be inconsistent with the essential principle underlying the law of contract, that the law will seek to give effect to freely accepted reciprocal undertakings. The importance of consideration is as a valuable signal that the parties intend to be bound by their agreement, rather than an end in itself. Where the parties who have already made such intention clear by entering legal relations have acted upon an agreement to a variation, in the absence of policy reasons to the contrary they should be bound by their agreement. Whichever option is adopted, whether that of *Roffey Bros* or that suggested by Professor Coote and other authorities, the result is in this case the same.

NOTES

1. The Court of Appeal of New Zealand seems to be suggesting that such a radical approach is the net effect of the decision in *Williams* v *Roffey, page 135*, since factual benefit amounts to invented consideration. However, it is clear that because *Roffey* and *Stilk* v *Myrick* are difficult to reconcile, the court considered the Coote approach to be preferable. The result would be that variations would be binding unless 'duress or other policy factors' are at work. However, it is unclear what would be included within 'other policy factors'. Given the importance of the issue of duress to the enforceability of promises (as is already clear from *Roffey*) it will be imperative to establish where the line will be drawn between threats and simple statements of fact, see *page 619 below*.

2. The *Antons Trawling* solution would eliminate many of the limitations on the scope of promissory estoppel under English law (such as whether promissory estoppel can create a cause of action) by removing the need to rely on this equitable doctrine. However, since *Antons Trawling* is limited in its application to variations, there would still be scope for the development of an estoppel based on unconscionability in the formation context, as in *Waltons Stores* v *Maher*, and the debate on this issue would be likely to continue.

3. This case is discussed by Professor Coote at (2004) 120 LQR 19.

■ QUESTION

The Court of Appeal of New Zealand appears to restrict the binding nature of variation promises where consideration need not be established to those promises which have been relied upon/performed. Is this tantamount to stating that reliance replaces consideration as the enforceability criterion in the context of alterations?

SECTION 3: FORMALITIES

Contrary to what is commonly presumed, contracts do not generally need to be in writing. If, however, a contract is contained in a deed, then consideration need not be shown to support the promises it contains.

(a) Deeds

Section 1(1)(b) of the Law of Property (Miscellaneous Provisions) Act 1989, abolished the requirement that a deed executed by an individual required a seal. The requirements for a valid deed are contained in s. 1(2) and (3).

LAW OF PROPERTY (MISCELLANEOUS PROVISIONS) ACT 1989

1. Deeds and their execution

(2) An instrument shall not be a deed unless—

(a) it makes it clear on its face that it is intended to be a deed by the person making it or, as the case may be, by the parties to it (whether by describing itself as a deed or expressing itself to be executed or signed as a deed or otherwise); and

(b) it is validly executed as a deed by that person or, as the case may be, one or more of those parties.

(3) An instrument is validly executed as a deed by an individual if, and only if—

(a) it is signed—

(i) by him in the presence of a witness who attests the signature; or

(ii) at his direction and in his presence and the presence of two witnesses who each attest the signature; and

(b) it is delivered as a deed by him or a person authorised to do so on his behalf.

(b) Contracts supported by consideration which must be made in writing

(i) Contracts for the sale or other disposition of an interest in land

LAW OF PROPERTY (MISCELLANEOUS PROVISIONS) ACT 1989

2. Contracts for sale etc. of land to be made by signed writing

(1) A contract for the sale or other disposition of an interest in land can only be made in writing and only by incorporating all the terms which the parties have expressly agreed in one document or, where contracts are exchanged, in each.

(2) The terms may be incorporated in a document either by being set out in it or by reference to some other document.

(3) The document incorporating the terms or, where contracts are exchanged, one of the documents incorporating them (but not necessarily the same one) must be signed by or on behalf of each party to the contract.

NOTES
1. Section 40 of the Law of Property Act 1925, which was repealed by s. 2(8), had stipulated that the contract or *some memorandum or note thereof* had to be in writing. However, it is no longer possible to have an oral contract for the sale of land which is evidenced in writing, since the contract itself must be in writing and must incorporate all the terms that the parties have expressly agreed. In addition, this document incorporating all the terms must be signed by or on behalf of each of the parties.
2. The Land Registration Act 2002 permits the creation of a framework to transfer and create interests in registered land by electronic means. The formalities requirements are set out in section 91.

LAND REGISTRATION ACT 2002

91. Electronic dispositions: formalities

(1) This section applies to a document in electronic form where—
  (a) the document purports to effect a disposition which falls within subsection (2), and
  (b) the conditions in subsection (3) are met.
(2) A disposition falls within this subsection if it is—
  (a) a disposition of a registered estate or charge,
  (b) a disposition of an interest which is the subject of a notice in the register, or
  (c) a disposition which triggers the requirement of registration, which is of a kind specified by rules.
(3) The conditions referred to above are that—
  (a) the document makes provision for the time and date when it takes effect,
  (b) the document has the electronic signature of each person by whom it purports to be authenticated,
  (c) each electronic signature is certified, and
  (d) such other conditions as rules may provide are met.
(4) A document to which this section applies is to be regarded as—
  (a) in writing, and
  (b) signed by each individual, and sealed by each corporation, whose electronic signature it has.
(5) A document to which this section applies is to be regarded for the purposes of any enactment as a deed.
(6) If a document to which this section applies is authenticated by a person as agent, it is to be regarded for the purposes of any enactment as authenticated by him under the written authority of his principal.
(7) If notice of an assignment made by means of a document to which this section applies is given in electronic form in accordance with rules, it is to be regarded for the purposes of any enactment as given in writing.
(8) The right conferred by section 75 of the Law of Property Act 1925 (c. 20) (purchaser's right to have the execution of a conveyance attested) does not apply to a document to which this section applies.
(9) If subsection (4) of section 36A of the Companies Act 1985 (c. 6) (execution of documents) applies to a document because of subsection (4) above, subsection (6) of that section (presumption of due execution) shall have effect in relation to the document with the substitution of 'authenticated' for 'signed'. . . .
(10) In this section, references to an electronic signature and to the certification of such a signature are to be read in accordance with section 7(2) and (3) of the Electronic Communications Act 2000 (c. 7).

For electronic signatures, see section 7, Electronic Communications Act 2000, *page 176.*

(ii) Bills of exchange, promissory notes and bills of sale must be in writing
See the Bills of Exchange Act 1882, s. 3(1) and s. 17(2) and the Bills of Sale Act (1878) Amendment Act 1882, s. 9 and Schedule.

(iii) Regulated consumer credit agreements
The Consumer Credit Act 1974 requires regulated consumer credit agreements to be in writing, in a specific form, and signed.

CONSUMER CREDIT ACT 1974

61. Signing of agreement

(1) A regulated agreement is not properly executed unless—

(a) a document in the prescribed form itself containing all the prescribed terms and conforming to regulations under section 60(1) is signed in the prescribed manner both by the debtor or hirer and by or on behalf of the creditor or owner, and

(b) the document embodies all the terms of the agreement, other than implied terms, and

(c) the document is, when presented or sent to the debtor or hirer for signature, in such a state that all its terms are readily legible.

Section 127(3) of the Consumer Credit Act 1974 provides that if the debtor does not sign the s. 60 document containing the prescribed terms, the creditor cannot enforce the credit agreement. In *Wilson* v *First County Trust Ltd (No. 2)* [2003] UKHL 40, [2004] 1 AC 816, the House of Lords had to consider whether this provision was incompatible with the rights guaranteed by the human rights legislation. The House of Lords held that this legislation did not have retrospective effect but that in any event this interference with the contractual rights of the creditor (alleged to be in breach of Article 1 of the First Protocol of the European Convention on Human Rights) was justified in the light of the policy of consumer protection underpinning this consumer credit legislation.

LORD NICHOLLS:

74 . . . I have no difficulty in accepting that in suitable instances it is open to Parliament, when Parliament considers the public interest so requires, to decide that failure to comply with certain formalities is an essential prerequisite to enforcement of certain types of agreements. This course is open to Parliament even though this will sometimes yield a seemingly unreasonable result in a particular case. Considered overall, this course may well be a proportionate response in practice to a perceived social problem. Parliament may consider the response should be a uniform solution across the board. A tailor-made response, fitting the facts of each case as decided in an application to the court, may not be appropriate. This may be considered an insufficient incentive and insufficient deterrent. And it may fail to protect consumers adequately. Persons most in need of protection are perhaps the least likely to participate in court proceedings. They may well let proceedings go by default . . .

However, it does not follow that all absolute bars on enforcement due to failure to meet formalities requirements will be beyond the scope of Article 1. There must be strong policy reasons favouring such an absolute bar.

There are also particular formalities required to conclude distant sale or supply contracts under the Consumer Protection (Distance Selling) Regulations 2000 (SI 2000/2334). There are also further information requirements in the context of consumer credit agreements; see, for example, The Consumer Credit (Disclosure of Information) Regulations 2004, SI 2004/1481, in force 31 May 2005.

(c) Contracts which must be evidenced in writing even where consideration has been provided

Section 4 of the Statute of Frauds 1677, as amended by the Law Reform (Enforcement of Contracts) Act 1954, requires contracts of guarantee to be evidenced in writing.

> No action shall be brought . . . whereby to charge the defendant upon any special promise to answer for the debt, default or miscarriages of another person . . . unless the agreement upon which such action shall be brought, or some memorandum or note thereof shall be in writing, and signed by the party to be charged therewith or some other person thereunto by him lawfully authorised.

In *Actionstrength Ltd* v *International Glass Engineering SpA* [2003] UKHL 17, [2003] 2 AC 541, the subcontractors argued that the employers were estopped from relying upon s. 4 of the Statute of Frauds in order to deny enforceability to the guarantee. The subcontractors alleged that this estoppel arose because they had acted to their detriment on the faith of the oral agreement. This argument would have permitted s. 4 to be avoided and was rejected by the House of Lords as inconsistent with the aim of the legislation. The formalities requirements relating to guarantees are designed to ensure that the guarantor appreciates the serious consequences attaching to a guarantee promise. However, as Lord Bingham recognised, whereas that rationale could be justified in the consumer context, it was more difficult to do so where an oral promise of guarantee was given by one experienced commercial concern in favour of another.

(d) Electronic signatures

Electronic signatures may fulfil the same function as a handwritten signature in the context of electronic communications.

ELECTRONIC COMMUNICATIONS ACT 2000

7. Electronic signatures and related certificates

    (1) In any legal proceedings—
        (a) an electronic signature incorporated into or logically associated with a particular electronic communication or particular electronic data, and
        (b) the certification by any person of such a signature, shall each be admissible in evidence in relation to any question as to the authenticity of the communication or data or as to the integrity of the communication or data.

The Electronic Signatures Regulations 2002, SI 2002/318 provide for supervision and liability of 'certification-service-providers' relating to electronic signatures and certification (i.e., electronic attestation linking signature-verification data to an individual confirming their identity).

(e) Formalities and electronic contracts

The Law Commission's Advice ('Electronic Commerce: Formal Requirements in Commercial Transactions, Advice from the Law Commission', December 2001) considered the implications of Article 9 of the E-Commerce Directive (2000/31/EC) requiring Member States to ensure that formalities requirements do not impede or invalidate the making of electronic contracts (although this does not affect for-malities requirements for contracts that create or transfer rights in real estate except for rental rights and for certain guarantees). The Law Commission concluded that the statutory formalities requirements would conflict with Article 9 'only in very rare cases', such as sections 63 and 64 of the Consumer Credit Act 1974, requiring certain documents to be 'sent by post', but acknowledged (paras 3.47 and 3.48) that where requirements existed which could not be satisfied electronically, there would need to be statutory reform. The Consumer Credit Act 1974 (Electronic Communi-cations) Order 2004, SI 2004/3236, in force 31 December 2004, provides that any references to the need for documents to be 'in writing' include electronic com-munications, and documents can be transmitted electronically if the consumer has agreed to the method of communication and the particular electronic form of communication. However, default notices will still need to be written on paper and given to the debtor or hirer in that format.

5

Intention to Create Legal Relations

Intention to create legal relations is dependent upon the parties' intentions, object-ively judged. The traditional starting point for determining this intention is the use of different presumptions for domestic and commercial agreements.

There is a presumption in the case of domestic and social agreements that there is no intention to create legal relations.

A: Husband and wife

Balfour v Balfour
[1919] 2 KB 571 (CA)

The defendant husband held a post in Ceylon. He and his wife, the plaintiff, returned to England on leave in 1915. However, when the defendant returned to Ceylon in 1916, the plaintiff remained temporarily in England on medical advice. The plaintiff alleged that before the defendant returned to Ceylon they had entered into an oral agreement by which the defendant agreed to pay her £30 a month in consideration for her agreeing not to call upon him for further maintenance. The parties later became estranged and the plaintiff sought to enforce the agreement. Held: since it was a domestic agreement between husband and wife, it was not an enforceable contract.

ATKIN LJ: . . . The defence to this action on the alleged contract is that the defendant, the husband, entered into no contract with his wife, and for the determination of that it is necessary to remember that there are agreements between parties which do not result in contracts within the meaning of that term in our law. The ordinary example is where two parties agree to take a walk together, or where there is an offer and an acceptance of hospitality. Nobody would suggest in ordinary circum-stances that those agreements result in what we know as a contract, and one of the most usual forms of agreement which does not constitute a contract appears to me to be the arrangements which are made between husband and wife. It is quite common, and it is the natural and inevitable result of the relationship of husband and wife, that the two spouses should make arrangements between themselves—agreements such as are in dispute in this action—agreements for allowances, by which the husband agrees that he will pay to his wife a certain sum of money, per week, or per month, or per year, to cover either her own expenses or the necessary expenses of the household and of the children of the marriage, and in which the wife promises either expressly or impliedly to apply the allowance for the purpose for which it is given. To my mind those agreements, or many of them, do not result in contracts at all, and they do not result in contracts even though there may be what as between other parties would constitute consideration for the agreement. . . . [T]hey are not contracts because the parties did not intend that they should be attended by legal consequences. To my mind it would be of the worst possible example to hold that agreements such as this resulted in legal obligations which could be enforced in the Courts. It would mean this, that when the husband makes his wife a promise to give her an allowance of 30s. or 2l. a week, whatever he can afford to give her, for the maintenance of the household and children, and she promises so to apply it, not only could she sue him for his failure in any week to supply the allowance, but he could sue her for non-performance of the obligation, express or implied, which she had undertaken upon her part. All I can say is that the small Courts of this country would have to be multiplied one hundredfold if these arrangements were held to result in legal obligations. They are not sued upon, not because the parties are reluctant to enforce their legal rights when the agreement is broken, but because the parties, in the inception of the arrangement, never intended that they should be sued upon. Agreements such as these are outside the realm of contracts altogether. The common law does not regulate the form of agreements between spouses. Their promises are not sealed with seals and sealing wax. The consideration that really obtains for them is that natural love and affection which counts for so little in these cold Courts. The terms may be repudiated, varied or renewed as performance proceeds or as disagreements develop, and the principles of the common law as to exoneration and discharge and accord and satisfaction are such as find no place in the domestic code. . . . it appears to me to be plainly established that the promise here was not intended by either party to be attended by legal consequences. I think the onus was upon the plaintiff, and the plaintiff has not established any contract. The parties were living together, the wife intending to return. The suggestion is that the husband bound himself to pay 30l. a month under all circumstances, and she bound herself to be satisfied with that sum under all circumstances, and, although she was in ill-health and alone in this country, that out of that sum she undertook to defray the whole of the medical expenses that might fall upon her, whatever might be the development of her illness, and in whatever expenses it might involve her. To my mind neither party contemplated such a result. . . .

NOTES
1. Although Atkin LJ states that objectively the parties did not intend that legal consequences should follow, the decision appears to rest on the argument that such agreements should not be enforceable for reasons of public policy.

   Specific reference is made to two policy factors, namely the floodgates argument and the argument that as such agreements are the result of 'natural love and affection which counts for so little in these cold courts', they are outside the jurisdiction of the courts.
2. It has been argued that, given that a criterion for the enforceability of an agreement is the presence of consideration (or a bargain), there is no additional necessity to require intention to create legal relations (see Hepple [1970] CLJ 122). The decision in *Shadwell* v *Shadwell* (1860) 9 CB NS 159, 142 ER 62 (*page 129*) supports the proposition that consideration should be sufficient. However, in *Balfour* v *Balfour*, Atkin LJ confirms that both requirements are necessary. In future it is likely that intention to be legally bound will replace consideration as the sole criterion for enforceability since consideration is not a concept recognised in continental jurisdictions. Article 2:101 of the *Principles of European Contract Law* (ed. Lando and Beale, Kluwer Law International, 2000) provides that the only factors required to establish the existence of a contract are agreement and that the parties intend to be legally bound. See also the comments of the Court of Appeal of New Zealand in *Antons Trawling Co. Ltd* v *Smith* [2003] 2 NZLR 23, discussed at *page 171*, suggesting that consideration is no more than evidence of the existence of an intention to create legal relations.

Merritt v Merritt
[1970] 1 WLR 1211 (CA)

After the husband had left his wife, he stated that he would pay her £40 a month from which she had to pay the outstanding mortgage payments on the house. He also signed a written note which provided that when the mortgage payments had all been made he would transfer the house to his wife in consideration for her paying all charges in connection with the house. The wife paid off the mortgage using this monthly payment from the husband and her own earnings. However, the husband refused to transfer the house to her. Held: the written agreement was intended to create legal relations between the parties. The presumption against such an intention did not apply when the husband and wife were not living in amity but were separated or about to separate.

LORD DENNING MR: The first point taken on his behalf by [counsel for the husband] is that the agreement was not intended to create legal relations. It was, he says, a family arrangement such as was considered by the court in *Balfour* v *Balfour* [1919] 2 KB 571 and in *Jones* v *Padavatton* [1969] 1 WLR 328. So the wife could not sue upon it.

I do not think those cases have any application here. The parties there were living together in amity. In such cases their domestic arrangements are ordinarily not intended to create legal relations. It is altogether different when the parties are not living in amity but are separated, or about to separate. They then bargain keenly. They do not rely on honourable understandings. They want everything cut and dried. It may safely be presumed that they intend to create legal relations.

[Counsel for the husband] then relied on the recent case of *Gould* v *Gould* [1970] 1 QB 275, when the parties had separated, and the husband agreed to pay the wife £12 a week 'so long as he could manage it'. The majority of the court thought that those words introduced such an element of uncertainty that the agreement was not intended to create legal relations. But for that element of uncertainty, I am sure that the majority would have held the agreement to be binding. They did not differ from the general proposition which I stated [in *Gould* v *Gould*] at p. 280 that:

> when . . . husband and wife, at arm's length, decide to separate, and the husband promises to pay a sum as maintenance to the wife during the separation, the court does, as a rule, impute to them an intention to create legal relations.

NOTES
1. The other important factor stressed by the Court of Appeal was that the terms of the agreement in this case were sufficiently certain to enable it to be enforced, and it appears from *Gould* v *Gould* [1970] 1 QB 275, that if the terms are uncertain the language will indicate that the parties do not intend to be bound even if they are separated.
2. The fact that the wife in *Merritt* v *Merritt* relied on the agreement in paying the mortgage repayments is an additional reason why the Court of Appeal held there to be an intention to create legal relations here.
3. *Merritt* v *Merritt* clearly demonstrates that agreements between husband and wife in a 'business context' which are sufficiently certain will rebut the presumption. The same is true of dealings between relatives in a business context, e.g., *Snelling* v *John G. Snelling Ltd* [1973] 1 QB 87 (*page 485*).

B: Parent and child

There is a presumption against an intention to create legal relations in agreements between parent and child. There must be clear evidence of an intention to give rise to legal consequences, reliance on the agreement, and certainty of terms, before the presumption can be rebutted.

Jones v *Padavatton*
[1969] 1 WLR 328 (CA)

In August 1962, a daughter accepted her mother's offer to go to England and study for the Bar. The agreement, which was not put in writing, was on terms that the mother was to pay the fees and provide maintenance of $200 a month. The mother had intended this to be in West Indian dollars (£42 a month), whereas the daughter thought it was to be in US dollars (£70 a month). However, when the maintenance payments arrived the daughter accepted them without objection. In 1964, the mother orally agreed to buy a house where the daughter could live, and it was agreed that the rents from letting the other rooms were to provide the maintenance in place of the £42 a month. In 1967, the mother claimed possession of the house. At the date of the hearing the daughter had still not completed her studies for the Bar. The daughter relied upon the agreement as her defence to the possession action. Held: (Danckwerts and Fenton Atkinson LJJ) the mother was entitled to possession because the agreement was a family arrangement and not intended to be legally binding. In addition, it was far too vague and uncertain to be enforceable as a contract.

FENTON ATKINSON LJ: . . . The problem is, in my view, a difficult one, because though one would tend to regard a promise by a parent to pay an allowance to a child during a course of study as no more than a family arrangement, on the facts of this case this particular daughter undoubtedly gave up a great deal on the strength of the mother's promise.

In my judgment it is the subsequent history which gives the best guide to the parties' intention at the material time. There are three matters which seem to me important: (1) The daughter thought that her mother was promising her 200 United States dollars, or £70 a month, which she regarded as the minimum necessary for her support. The mother promised 200 dollars, but she had in mind 200 British West Indian dollars, £42 a month, and that was what she in fact paid from November 1962 to December 1964. Those payments were accepted by the daughter without any sort of suggestion at any stage that the mother had legally contracted for the larger sum. (2) When the arrangements for the purchase of No. 181, Highbury Quadrant were being discussed, and the new arrangement was made for maintenance to come out of the rents, many material matters were left open: how much accommodation was the daughter to occupy; how much money was she to have out of the rents; if the rents fell below expectation, was the mother to make up the difference below £42, or £42 less the sum saved by the daughter in rent; for how long was the arrangement to continue, and so on. The whole arrangement was, in my view, far too vague and uncertain to be itself enforceable as a contract; but at no stage did the daughter bring into the discussions her alleged legal right to £42 per month until her studies were completed, and how that right was to be affected by the new arrangement. (3) It is perhaps not without relevance to look at the daughter's evidence in cross-examination. She was asked about the occasion when the mother visited the house, and she, knowing perfectly well that the mother was there, refused for some hours to open the door. She said: 'I didn't open the door because a normal mother doesn't sue her daughter in court. Anybody with normal feelings would feel upset by what was happening.' Those answers and the daughter's conduct on that occasion provide a strong indication that she had never for a moment contemplated the possibility of her mother or herself going to court to enforce legal obligations, and that she felt it quite intolerable that a purely family arrangement should become the subject of proceedings in a court of law.

At the time when the first arrangement was made, mother and daughter were, and always had been, to use the daughter's own words, 'very close'. I am satisfied that nether party at that time intended to enter into a legally binding contract, either then or later when the house was bought. The daughter was prepared to trust her mother to honour her promise of support, just as the mother no doubt trusted her daughter to study for the Bar with diligence, and to get through her examinations as early as she could.

NOTES

1. Salmon LJ came to the same conclusion, namely, that the mother was entitled to possession, but he reached it by a different route. Although he stressed the daughter's reliance in giving up her job and moving to England, and considered that the agreement as originally made was intended by both parties to have contractual force, Salmon LJ implied a term that the agreement would last for a reasonable time to enable the daughter to complete her studies. The reasonable period was five years, which had elapsed at the time of the action, and so the daughter could not rely on the agreement.

2. Although there was reliance in *Jones* v *Padavatton*, the presumption of no intention to create legal relations was not rebutted since the terms were uncertain. However, the presumption was rebutted in *Parker* v *Clark* [1960] 1 WLR 286, where there was both reliance and certainty of terms. An intention to create legal relations was found by Devlin J in an agreement between relatives to share a home. Their agreement contained very detailed terms as to the payment of household expenses, and the plaintiffs had relied upon it in selling their own home and lending the money to their daughter to buy a flat. The defendants had also made a will leaving the house to the female plaintiff, her sister, and daughter.

C: Lifts to work

Coward v *Motor Insurers' Bureau*
[1963] 1 QB 259 (CA)

There was evidence of an arrangement between Coward and Cole, whereby Cole drove Coward to work on Cole's motor cycle in return for a weekly amount of money. Both were killed in an accident owing to the negligence of Cole, and Coward's widow obtained judgment against Cole's personal representatives. This judgment was not satisfied because Coward had been a pillion passenger and Cole's insurance policy did not cover pillion passengers. The widow therefore brought an action against the Motor Insurers' Bureau, which was obliged by statute to pay unsatisfied judgments in respect of a 'liability which is required to be covered by a policy or a security' under the Road Traffic Act 1930. She argued that Coward was a person who was required to be insured because he was carried for 'hire or reward'. The Court of Appeal considered that it was necessary to decide whether there was a contract between Coward and Cole. Held: despite the evidence that Coward had paid regular weekly sums for the lifts, neither person contemplated a legally binding contract.

UPJOHN LJ: . . . [I]f the question had been posed to Coward or Cole: 'Did you intend to enter into a legal relationship?' each would probably have answered 'I never gave it a thought.'

The practice whereby workmen go to their place of business in the motor-car or on the motor-cycle of a fellow-workman upon the terms of making a contribution to the costs of transport is well known and widespread. In the absence of evidence that the parties intended to be bound contractually, we should be reluctant to conclude that the daily carriage by one of another to work upon payment of some weekly (or it may be daily) sum involved them in a legal contractual relationship. The hazards of everyday life, such as temporary indisposition, the incidence of holidays, the possibility of a change of shift or different hours of overtime, or incompatibility arising, make it most unlikely that either contemplated that the one was legally bound to carry and the other to be carried to work. It is made all the more improbable in this case by reason of the fact that alternative means of transport seem to have been available to Coward.

NOTES

1. In reality, Upjohn LJ is treating this as a policy question rather than a question of what the parties intended.

2. The majority of the House of Lords in *Albert* v *Motor Insurers' Bureau* [1972] AC 301, disapproved of the approach in *Coward* v *MIB* and considered that for the purposes of applying the Road Traffic Act it was not necessary to look for a contract.

   The House of Lords assessed whether the giving of lifts was a systematic carrying of passengers which was predominantly a business arrangement rather than a social one. On the facts, the majority found that the driver, Quirk, had engaged in a regular and systematic arrangement for which he expected to be paid. Lord Cross, however, was of the opinion that it was necessary to decide if there was a legally enforceable contract.

Albert v *Motor Insurers' Bureau*
[1972] AC 301 (HL)

LORD CROSS: . . . It is not necessary in order that a legally binding contract should arise that the parties should direct their minds to the question and decide in favour of the creation of a legally binding relationship. If I get into a taxi and ask the driver to drive me to Victoria Station it is extremely unlikely that either of us directs his mind to the question whether we are entering into a contract. We enter into a contract not because we form any intention to enter into one but because if our minds were directed to the point we should as reasonable people both agree that we were in fact entering into one. When one passes from the field of transactions of an obviously business character between strangers to arrangements between friends or acquaintances for the payment by the passenger of a contribution towards expenses the fact that the arrangement is not made purely as a matter of business and that if the anticipated payment is not made it would probably never enter into the head of the driver to sue for it disposes one to say that there is no contract, but in fact the answer to the question 'contract' or 'no contract' does not depend on the likelihood of an action being brought to enforce it in case of default.

   Suppose that when one of Quirk's fellow workers got in touch with him and asked him whether he could travel in his car to Tilbury and back next day an 'officious bystander' had asked: 'Will you be paying anything for your transport?' the prospective passenger would have answered at once: 'Of course I will pay'. If the 'officious bystander' had gone on to ask Quirk whether, if he was not paid, he would sue the man in the county court, Quirk might well have answered in the words used by the driver in *Connell's* case [1969] 2 QB 494: 'Not bloody likely.' But the fact that if default was made Quirk would not have started legal proceedings but would have resorted to extra-judicial remedies does not mean that an action could not in theory have been brought to recover payment for the carriage. If one imagines such proceedings being brought a plea on the part of the passenger that he never meant to enter into a contract would have received short shrift and so, too, would a plea that the contract was void for uncertainty because no precise sum was mentioned. If the evidence did not establish a regular charge for the Tilbury trip the judge would have fixed the appropriate sum.

NOTES

1. It may be that the majority view is preferable as a matter of policy, since if the decision in *Coward* v *MIB* is correct, then the carrier of passengers who receives payment can avoid the obligation to insure against claims by those passengers simply by stipulating that there is no legally binding contract between the parties. Viscount Dilhorne makes the point in *Albert* v *MIB* that this cannot have been Parliament's intention.

2. Lord Cross was clearly of the opinion that it was not possible to judge the existence of a contract by assessing whether it was likely to be enforced by court action in the case of default

(see the discussion of *Esso Petroleum* v *Commissioners of Customs & Excise*, at *page 188*). Indeed, Lord Cross considered, reflecting the objective evaluation of intention, that a contract could arise without the parties directing their minds to the possibility of there being a contract; whereas in *Coward* v *MIB*, Upjohn LJ's judgment concentrates on there being evidence that the parties subjectively intended to be bound contractually.

3. Stephen Hedley argued ((1985) 5 OJLS 391) that when determining the enforceability of domestic agreements, the courts appear to be adopting a policy of enforcing an agreement only at the instance of a party who has performed one side of the bargain (i.e., executed contracts). *Merritt* v *Merritt* is an example of this.

In *Coward* v *MIB* there was no contract because the Court of Appeal was concentrating on the question of whether the driver could be compelled to carry others in future, and the courts will not enforce such executory domestic arrangements. However, Lord Cross in *Albert* v *MIB* looked at the issue in terms of a service which *had been* rendered and concluded that the lift, once given, would have to be paid for.

SECTION 2: COMMERCIAL AGREEMENTS

There is a presumption of an intention to create legal relations in commercial agreements.

A mere puff is not enforceable because it is not intended to be taken literally and is not promissory in nature. One of the arguments put forward by counsel for the Smoke Ball Company in *Carlill* v *Carbolic Smoke Ball Company* [1893] 1 QB 256, was that the advertisement was no more than an advertising gimmick. However, this was rejected by the Court of Appeal because the Company had deposited £1,000 with their bank as proof of their intention to be bound (see Chapter 1).

Bowerman v Association of British Travel Agents Ltd
[1996] CLC 451 (CA)

The plaintiffs had booked a school skiing holiday through a tour operator, which was an ABTA member. Shortly before the date of the holiday, the tour operator had become insolvent and had ceased to trade. ABTA reimbursed the cost of the holiday but deducted £10 per head to represent the holiday insurance premium paid on the basis that this sum was excluded from the ABTA protection scheme. The plaintiffs sought the return of these insurance premiums claiming a direct contractual relationship with ABTA entitling them to full reimbursement of the holiday cost, on the basis of an ABTA notice displayed by tour operators, para. 5 of which provided that '(5) Where holidays or other travel arrangements have not yet commenced at the time of failure, ABTA arranges for you to be reimbursed the money you have paid in respect of your holiday arrangements'. The trial judge had accepted, and it was common ground, that the correct approach was to read the notice as the public would understand it. However, he rejected the plaintiffs' claim on the basis that there was no offer, no intention to create legal relations, and that the terms of the notice were too vague and inconsistent to constitute a legally enforceable promise. Held: (Waite and Hobhouse LJJ; Hirst LJ dissenting) there was a direct contractual relationship between ABTA and members of the public who booked their holidays with ABTA members. The ABTA notice displayed on the premises of each member tour operator constituted a contractual offer on terms obliging ABTA to reimburse the cost of insurance since it was intended to be read, and would reasonably be read, as an offer which a customer would accept by booking a holiday with an ABTA member.

HOBHOUSE LJ: . . . The relevant consideration is what if anything the document says or offers as between ABTA and the member of the public who reads it and then books with an ABTA member.

Turning to the document itself, it is accepted that the words of Bowen LJ [in *Carlill* v *Carbolic Smoke Ball Co., page 8 above*] are apt:

> It was intended to be issued to the public and to be read by the public. How would an ordinary person reading this document construe it?

The rival contentions, both of which can be persuasively argued for as is demonstrated by the difference of judicial opinion to which this case has given rise, are whether the document is simply telling the public about a scheme which ABTA has for its own members or whether it goes further than this and contains an offer which a member of the public can take up and hold ABTA to should the ABTA member with whom the member of the public is dealing fail financially.

I prefer the latter view. I recognise that the document is headed 'Notice describing ABTA's scheme of protection' and that in para. 4 and 5 the present tense is used—'ABTA seeks'—'ABTA ensures'—'ABTA arranges'—and not the future tense—'ABTA will ensure' or 'ABTA will arrange'. These points undoubtedly support the view of the judge and the defendants' argument. But the document has to be read as a whole. It is clearly intended to have an effect on the reader and to lead him to believe that he is getting something of value. The scheme is an ABTA scheme in relation to its members but it is a scheme of protection of the customers of ABTA members. It emphasises that it is 'to protect you their customers' and is 'for your benefit'. This is further underlined in para. 3 where the final sentence reads:

> If an ABTA member ceases to belong to ABTA and thereafter fails financially ABTA still protects you if you made the booking before the time when ABTA membership ceased.

ABTA is offering to protect the reader of the notice, the prospective customer. It is an inevitable inference that what ABTA is saying is that it, ABTA, will do something for the customer if the member should fail financially.

. . . In my judgment this document is intended to be read and would be reasonably be read by a member of the public as containing an offer of a promise which the customer is entitled to accept by choosing to do business with an ABTA member. A member of the public would not analyse his situation in legal terms but he would clearly understand that this notice would only apply to him if he should choose to do business with an ABTA member and he would also understand that if he did do so he would be entitled to hold ABTA to what he understood ABTA to be promising in this document. In my judgment it satisfies the criteria for a unilateral contract and contains promises which are sufficiently clear to be capable of legal enforcement. The principles established in the *Carbolic Smoke Ball* case apply. The plaintiffs are entitled to enforce the right of reimbursement given to them in para. 5.

This conclusion also covers ABTA's further argument that it had no intention to create legal relations. The document as reasonably read by a member of the public would be taken to be an offer of a legally enforceable promise. Given that this is the effect of the document which ABTA has chosen to publish, it does not advance ABTA's case to say that ABTA privately did not intend to expose itself to any legal liability to the public. It suffices that ABTA intentionally published a document which had that effect. A contracting party cannot escape liability by saying that he had his fingers crossed behind his back.

. . . Like in the *Carbolic Smoke Ball* case, we have had urged on us the potential size of the obligations which ABTA would be accepting should a number of its members fail and the difficulty of meeting all the claims which might be made on ABTA. This was a matter for the judgment of ABTA before it chose to issue the notice. It is the job of ABTA and no concern of the customer to see that its bonding and mutual and external insurance arrangements suffice. The argument has no more merit than the equivalent argument which was advanced in the *Carbolic Smoke Ball* case.

The existence of consideration to support the contractual obligation of ABTA is clear. A picture was presented to us, wholly unrealistically, of ABTA as some benevolent body which gained no benefit from and had no interest in travellers choosing to deal with ABTA members. The function of ABTA is to promote its members. It was also argued that as Mr Wallace was required by the local education authority and by the children's parents to buy only ABTA backed holidays that meant that Mr Wallace and those on whose behalf he was acting gave no consideration because, so it was argued, Mr Wallace was already under an obligation to buy an ABTA backed holiday. Mr Wallace was under no obligation to buy any holiday at all nor were the parents. No doubt there are other tour operators and travel agents, not members of ABTA, who are able to undercut ABTA prices. ABTA's members prominently market themselves as members of ABTA and anybody who chooses to do business with them is certainly giving consideration to ABTA for any contract or 'collateral' contract which may ensue. The analogy with such cases as *Shanklin Pier Ltd* v *Detel Products Ltd* [1951] 2 KB 854 [*page 461*] is fully made out.

I therefore cannot agree with the judgment of Mitchell J and consider that this appeal should be allowed. The plaintiffs were entitled to and did accept the offer contained in the document issued by ABTA and it fills one with disquiet that any organisation in the position of ABTA should after the event, when it finds that its liabilities are greater than it had anticipated, seek to contend otherwise. As counsel pointed out, if ABTA had wished to deny that it was accepting any legal obligation to the traveller or wished to say that it was not making any promises, nothing would have been simpler than for it to have said so in the document. For obvious commercial reasons ABTA did not choose this course. To have included such words would have destroyed the value of the document in the eyes of the public and nullified the very effect which ABTA intended it to, and which it did, achieve— to induce the public to book with and entrust their money to ABTA members.

I would allow the appeal.

NOTES

1. Hirst LJ (dissenting) considered that this was a non-promissory notice intended only to reassure:

> . . . In his argument [counsel for the plaintiffs] submitted that on its proper construction the language of the notice was the language of contract. He drew particular attention to the two subsidiary headings 'Scheme of protection' and 'The protection is that . . .', which he submitted were indicating a promise; he emphasised the repeated use of the personal pronoun or adjective 'you' and 'your', and submitted that it was a highly personal notice honing in on the individual customer; he contended that the reference in para. (1) to the provision by the tour operators of bonds guarantees and other securities to ABTA added legitimacy to the binding obligation which he submitted the document conveyed; he drew particular attention to the words 'ensures' and 'arranges' in para. (4) and (5) which he submitted were words of commitment; and he submitted that the final four paragraphs under the heading 'Limitations' reinforced the contractual commitment in the earlier part of the document.
>
> In support of his argument [counsel for the plaintiffs] placed strong reliance on the famous case of *Carlill* v *Carbolic Smoke Ball Co.* [1893] 1 QB 256 [*see chapter 1*]. . . .
>
> This advertisement, he submitted, was comparable with the ABTA notice in the present case, and I accept without reservation that, if the words of this notice are truly promissory in character, it would be capable of constituting a contractual offer to the public in general.
>
> The crucial point is therefore to determine whether, on its proper construction, the notice is indeed promissory in character, and on this I am unable to accept [counsel for the plaintiffs'] arguments.
>
> First, it is essential in my judgment to give full weight to the main heading, to which I attach great importance, viz.: 'Notice describing ABTA's scheme of protection against the financial failure of ABTA members'. This in my view is an accurate epitome of the terms of the notice as a whole, which is descriptive rather than contractual in character.
>
> The headings 'Scheme of protection' and 'The protection is that . . .' are no more than subheadings characterising the details of the scheme. Equally the language, in particular the verbs used in para. (3) to (5) ('protects', 'seeks to arrange' 'ensures' and 'arranges') are

grammatically descriptive, rather than promissory phrases such as, for example, 'will insure', 'will arrange', etc. By the same token the statement in para. (1) that 'all ABTA tour operators are required to provide bonds guarantee or other securities to ABTA', is also essentially descriptive.

Indeed, nowhere in the first five paragraphs of the notice do I find any specific words of promise or any firm commitment, and nothing in the last four paragraphs headed 'Limitation' points in a different direction.

By contrast, the crisp wording of the advertisement in the *Carlill* case ('£100 reward *will be paid* . . .') is essentially promissory in character, and indeed to my mind highlights the shortcomings from the appellant's point of view of the wording in the present notice.

My view as to the non-contractual nature of this document is reinforced by the vague and equivocal nature of several of the statements contained in the following numbered paragraphs:

(3) . . . other travel arrangements . . .
(4) . . . seeks to arrange . . .
(5) . . . other travel arrangements . . . your holidays arrangements . . . [and] . . . in some instances ABTA may however be able to arrange . . . or offer . . .

All these considerations to my mind strongly support the view that the ordinary member of the public would not interpret this document as constituting a contractual offer to him personally—and the use of the direct words 'you', and 'your', which carry no contractual commitment, do no more than focus the attention of the customer personally on the information contained in the notice, rather like Lord Kitchener's famous recruiting poster in the First World War.

I wish to make it clear that I do not doubt that the ordinary member of the public would interpret the notice as drawing his attention to something of value to him, but that does not seem to me to assist either way in determining whether its character is informative or contractual.

I also wish to make it clear that in reaching my conclusion I have, I believe correctly, confined my attention solely to the wording of the notice itself, and I have left out of account both the submissions from both sides as to surrounding circumstances, which were unknown to [the second plaintiff, the teacher who had booked the trip]. . . . On similar grounds, I would hold that there was no intention on ABTA's part to create a legal relationship with the individual customer.

In support of her argument on this first and main point [counsel for the defendants] relied on the case of *Kleinwort Benson* v *Malaysia Mining Corp Berhad* [1989] 1 WLR 379; (1989) 5 BCC 337 [see *page 190*] in which the Court of Appeal held that a paragraph in a letter of comfort did not have contractual status, but was no more than a representation as to the current policy adopted by the defendant company.

Although as [counsel for the plaintiffs] rightly pointed out that the facts of that case are very different from the present, seeing that the parties involved were two very large commercial enterprises, I think that the judge was right in concluding that the analogy between that case and the present one is sound, in that the essential function of the present notice is to reassure the customer by reference to the existence of the ABTA scheme of protection which it describes. . . .

For these reasons, which are closely in accord with the judge's analysis, I would dismiss this appeal.

The different approaches may be explained by the fact that, whereas the majority considered all the background circumstances and the position of the holiday consumer, Hirst LJ expressly limited himself to considering only the wording of the notice itself.

2. The approach of the majority might rightly be considered as 'consumer-welfarist' and result-orientated. See further, Adams and Brownsword, *Understanding Contract Law*, 4th edn, 2004 (see *page 21 above*). In addition, the majority were clearly influenced by the consumers' reliance.

3. This decision is also significant in providing a further practical example of the use of the unilateral collateral contract in order to bind a third party to his statements (assuming these statements to be promissory) where they induced the making of a contract. See the discussions at *pages 209–10* and *461*.

4. The majority judgments also reinforce the need expressly to exclude any intention to be legally bound if this is the desired objective. See honour clauses, *page 191 below*.

Esso Petroleum Ltd v Commissioners of Customs and Excise
[1976] 1 WLR 1 (HL)

Esso had a sales promotion scheme by which garage owners offered a 'free' World Cup coin with every four gallons of petrol. The Customs and Excise Commissioners claimed that the coins were chargeable to purchase tax because they were 'produced in quantity for general sale'. Held: (Lord Fraser dissenting) that the coins were not being sold since, if there was a contract (an issue on which there was some disagreement), the consideration for the transfer of the coin was not money but the customer's undertaking to enter into a collateral contract to purchase four gallons of petrol. The majority reasoning differed as to whether there was a contract relating to the coins. Viscount Dilhorne and Lord Russell considered the coins to be a gift (as opposed to a sale) on the basis that the coins had little intrinsic value so that there was no intention to create legal relations in such an arrangement. Lords Simon and Wilberforce came to the opposite conclusion on the basis that the arrangement was set in the context of business relations.

LORD RUSSELL: . . . The first question . . . is whether, notwithstanding the liberal references in the documents attending the promotion scheme to 'giving', 'gifts', and 'free', that which would and did take place gave rise to a contract, enforceable by a motorist who bought four gallons from a participating proprietor, that he should receive one of these medals. It is to be borne in mind in this connection that the mere fact that Esso and the garage proprietors undoubtedly had a commercial aim in promoting the scheme does not deprive the delivery of a medal of the quality of a gift as distinct from a sale: for benevolence is not a necessary feature of a gift, which may well be motivated by self interest. On the other hand it is trite law that if on analysis a transaction has in law one character, the fact that the parties either accidentally or deliberately frame the transaction in language appropriate to a transaction of a different character will not deny to it its true character.

We have here, my Lords, a promotion scheme initiated by Esso, who procured the production of the medals. Each medal was of negligible intrinsic value, though the incentive to soccer enthusiasts to collect all 30 may have been strong. Plainly it was never in Esso's mind that this negligible intrinsic value should be reflected in an increase in the pump price of petrol, and it never was: indeed the price of a gallon could not be increased by $\frac{3}{16}$ of a penny. In my opinion it would have been thought by Esso, and rightly, that there could have been no occasion, in order to ensure success of the scheme, for an outlet proprietor to subject himself to a contractual liability to deliver a coin to a motorist who had bought four gallons. The subject matter was trivial: the proprietor was directly interested in the success of the scheme and would be in the highest degree unlikely to renege on the free gift offer, and indeed there is no suggestion that a motorist who qualified and wanted a medal ever failed to get one: from the motorist's viewpoint, if this had ever happened, I cannot think that he would have considered that he had a legal grievance, though he might have said that he would not patronise that outlet again: similarly in my opinion if a garage advertised 'Free Air' and after buying petrol or oil the motorist was told that the machine was out of order that day. In my opinion, the incentive for the garage proprietor to carry out the scheme was such as to make it quite unnecessary to invest, or for Esso to intend to invest, the transaction with the additional compulsion of a contractual obligation, and in all the circumstances of the case I am unable to regard that which under the scheme was intended by Esso to take place in relation to the medals, and did take place, as something which would be intended to or regarded as creating a legal contractual relationship. In forming that opinion I regard the minimal intrinsic value of a medal as important. I would not wish it to be thought that my opinion, if correct, would, in other cases in which a sales promotion scheme involves substantial benefits, give carte blanche to participants to renege on 'free' offers. I am simply of opinion, in agreement with the Court of Appeal, though not I fear with the majority of your Lordships, that in the instant case, because of the absence of any contractual element, it should not be said that any medal was produced for general sale.

LORD SIMON: . . . I am, however, my Lords, not prepared to accept that the promotion material put out by Esso was not envisaged by them as creating legal relations between the garage proprietors who adopted it and the motorists who yielded to its blandishments. In the first place, Esso and the garage proprietors put the material out for their commercial advantage, and designed it to attract the custom of motorists. The whole transaction took place in a setting of business relations. In the second place, it seems to me in general undesirable to allow a commercial promoter to claim that what he has done is a mere puff, not intended to create legal relations (cf *Carlill* v *Carbolic Smoke Ball Co.* [1893] 1 QB 256). The coins may have been themselves of little intrinsic value; but all the evidence suggests that Esso contemplated that they would be attractive to motorists and that there would be a large commercial advantage to themselves from the scheme, an advantage to which the garage proprietors also would share. Thirdly, I think that authority supports the view that legal relations were envisaged.

. . . I venture to add that it begs the question to assert that no motorist who bought petrol in consequence of seeing the promotion material prominently displayed in the garage forecourt would be likely to bring an action in the county court if he were refused a coin. He might be a suburb Hampden who was not prepared to forgo what he conceived to be his rights or to allow a tradesman to go back on his word.

Believing as I do that Esso envisaged a bargain of some sort between the garage proprietor and the motorist, I must try to analyse the transaction. The analysis that most appeals to me is one of the ways in which Lord Denning MR considered the case [1975] 1 WLR 406, 409B–D, namely a collateral contract of the sort described by Lord Moulton in *Heilbut, Symons & Co* v *Buckleton* [1913] AC 30, 47:

> . . . there may be a contract the consideration for which is the making of some other contract. 'If you will make such and such a contract I will give you £100', is in every sense of the word a complete legal contract. It is collateral to the main contract, . . .

So here. The law happily matches the reality. The garage proprietor is saying, 'If you will buy four gallons of my petrol, I will give you one of these coins'. None of the reasons which have caused the law to consider advertising or display material as an invitation to treat rather than an offer applies here. What the garage proprietor says by his placards is in fact and in law an offer of consideration to the motorist to enter into a contract of sale of petrol. Of course, not every motorist will notice the placard, but nor will every potential offeree of many offers be necessarily conscious that they have been made. However, the motorist who does notice the placard, and in reliance thereon drives in and orders the petrol, is in law doing two things at the same time. First, he is accepting the offer of a coin if he buys four gallons of petrol. Secondly, he is himself offering to buy four gallons of petrol: this offer is accepted by the filling of his tank.

. . . Here the coins were not transferred for a money consideration. They were transferred in consideration of the motorist entering into a contract for the sale of petrol. The coins were therefore not produced for sale, and do not fall within the schedule. They are exempt from purchase tax.

NOTES
1. Lord Simon takes the same view as Lord Cross in *Albert* v *MIB*, that the determining factor cannot be whether the parties would actually sue to enforce the agreement. Atiyah has very firmly argued ((1976) 39 MLR 335) that the triviality of the transaction and the unwillingness to litigate are not the tests of an intention to create legal relations.
2. The majority decision was that there was no contract of sale because the consideration for the transfer of the coin was not money but the entering of a contract to purchase the petrol. This

is somewhat artificial since, in order to get the coin, the customer had to pay the price of the four gallons of petrol, and the price would appear to be part of the consideration.
3. Lord Fraser (dissenting) considered that it was a single contract of sale to purchase four gallons of petrol and a coin.

(a) Comfort letters

The Court of Appeal in the next case held that a comfort letter was not legally enforceable since it did not constitute a promise.

Kleinwort Benson Ltd v *Malaysia Mining Corporation Berhad*
[1989] 1 WLR 379 (CA)

A comfort letter was given to the plaintiff merchant bank by the parent company of the subsidiary company MMC Metals Ltd. The comfort letter stated, 'it is our policy to ensure that the business of Metals is at all times in a position to meet its liabilities to you under the above arrangements'. When the subsidiary company went into liquidation, the plaintiff merchant bank sought to recover from the parent company on the basis of the comfort letter. Held: the correct test to determine the status of a comfort letter was to ask whether a promise was being made, rather than the test applied by Hirst J at first instance ([1988] 1 WLR 799) of whether there was an intention to create legal relations. The words of this comfort letter amounted to a policy statement only and did not constitute a promise.

RALPH GIBSON LJ: . . . The argument [at first instance] concentrated on whether paragraph 3 was to be treated in law as a contractual promise: Hirst J. [1988] 1 WLR 799, 801G referred to the main question as being whether paragraph 3 was 'contractual in status,' and his conclusion was, as I have said, that the presumption laid down in *Edwards* v *Skyways Ltd* [1964] 1 WLR 349 applied and that the defendants had failed to displace the presumption. [Counsel for the plaintiffs] before Hirst J, had placed strong reliance on *Edwards* v *Skyways Ltd* (see [1988] 1 WLR 799, 807C), and his submission was recorded by Hirst J: 'there was a heavy onus on the defendants to prove that there was no intention to create contractual relations.' . . .

To explain why, in my view, the presumption applied by Hirst J had no application to this case it is necessary to examine in some detail the issues in *Edwards* v *Skyways Ltd* [1964] 1 WLR 349. In that case Skyways Ltd, the defendants, found it necessary to declare redundant some 15 per cent of the pilots in their employ. The secretary of Skyways Ltd, at a meeting with representatives of the Air Pilots Union, agreed:

'pilots declared redundant and leaving the company would be given an ex gratia payment equivalent to the company's contribution to the pension fund' and, in addition, 'a refund of their own contributions to the fund.'

Edwards, in reliance upon that agreement, left the company and claimed payment under it. The company purported to rescind its decision to make the ex gratia payment on the ground that it had obligations to creditors and the promised ex gratia payments were not enforceable in law. The company admitted that a promise had been made to make the payments (see p. 354) and that the promise was supported by consideration, but contended (in reliance upon *Rose and Frank Co.* v *J. R. Crompton & Brothers Ltd* [1923] 2 KB 261, 288) that the promise or agreement had no legal effect because there was no intention to enter into legal relations in respect of the promised payment. It was argued (see p. 356) that the mere use of the phrase 'ex gratia,' as part of the promise to pay, showed that the parties contemplated that the promise when accepted would have no binding force in law and, further, that there was background knowledge, concerned with the tax consequences of legally enforceable promises to pay, and present to the minds of the representatives of the parties, which gave unambiguous significance to the words 'ex gratia' as excluding legal relationships. Megaw J rejected these arguments upon the facts and upon his construction of the meaning in the context of the words 'ex gratia.' The company thus failed to show that what was otherwise admittedly a promise, supported by consideration, was to be denied legal effect because of the common intention of the parties that it should not have such effect and, accordingly, the company failed to displace the presumption. Megaw J was not dealing with the sort of question which is raised in this case, namely, whether, given that the comfort letters were intended to express the legal relationship between the parties, the language of paragraph 3 does or does not contain a contractual promise.

The central question in this case . . . is whether the words of paragraph 3, considered in their context, are to be treated as a warranty or contractual promise. Paragraph 3 contains no express words of promise. Paragraph 3 is in its terms a statement of present fact and not a promise as to future conduct. . . .

The concept of a comfort letter was, as [counsel for the defendants] acknowledged, not shown to have acquired any particular meaning at the time of the negotiations in this case with reference to the limits of any legal liability to be assumed under its terms by a parent company. . . . The court would not, merely because the parties had referred to the document as a comfort letter, refuse to give effect to the meaning of the words used. But in this case it is clear, in my judgment, that the concept of a comfort letter, to which the parties had resort when the defendants refused to assume joint and several liability or to give a guarantee, was known by both sides at least to extend to or to include a document under which the defendants would give comfort to the plaintiffs by assuming, not a legal liability to ensure repayment of the liabilities of their subsidiary, but a moral responsibility only . . . The comfort letter was drafted in terms which in paragraph 3 do not express any contractual promise and which are consistent with being no more than a representation of fact. If they are treated as no more than a representation of fact, they are in that meaning consistent with the comfort letter containing no more than the assumption of moral responsibility by the defendants in respect of the debts of Metals. There is nothing in the evidence to show that, as a matter of commercial probability or common sense, the parties must have intended paragraph 3 to be a contractual promise, which is not expressly stated, rather than a mere representation of fact, which is so stated.

NOTES

1. Clearly this agreement was a commercial agreement, and thus it appears that the presumption of an intention to create legal relations can be rebutted in relation to comfort letters where the wording used does not amount to a promise. This is likely to lead to fine distinctions dependent on the wording of the comfort letter. See Brown, 'The Letter of Comfort: Placebo or Promise?' [1990] JBL 281.

2. This case was relied upon by Hirst LJ (dissenting) in *Bowerman* v *ABTA Ltd* [1996] CLC 451, *page 184*, in reaching his conclusion that ABTA's notice was not promissory in nature but merely a statement of policy or reassurance.

(b) Honour clauses

The presumption of intention to create legal relations can also be rebutted by the use of an 'honour clause', which excludes the courts and states that the agreement is binding in honour only.

Rose and Frank Company v *J. R. Crompton and Brothers Ltd*

By an agreement the plaintiffs had been appointed sole United States agents of the defendants. The agreement contained the following clause:

This arrangement is not entered into, nor is this memorandum written, as a formal or legal agreement, and shall not be subject to legal jurisdiction in the Law Courts either of the United States or England, but it is only a definite expression and record of the purpose and intention of the three parties concerned to which they each honourably pledge themselves with the fullest confidence, based on past business with each other, that it will be carried through by each of the three parties with mutual loyalty and friendly co-operation.

The defendants terminated the agency agreement without the required notice and refused to execute orders received before termination. The plaintiffs brought an action for breach of contract and non-delivery of the goods for which orders had already been placed. Held: (in the Court of Appeal) there was no binding contract and consequently there could be no action based upon it. A majority (Atkin LJ dissenting) also held that the orders and acceptances of those orders were not legally binding contracts to deliver.

Court of Appeal
[1923] 2 KB 261

ATKIN LJ: . . . To create a contract there must be a common intention of the parties to enter into legal obligations, mutually communicated expressly or impliedly. Such an intention ordinarily will be inferred when parties enter into an agreement which in other respects conforms to the rules of law as to the formation of contracts. It may be negatived impliedly by the nature of the agreed promise or promises, as in the case of offer and acceptance of hospitality, or of some agreements made in the course of family life between members of a family as in *Balfour* v *Balfour* [1919] 2 KB 571. If the intention may be negatived impliedly it may be negatived expressly. In this document, construed as a whole, I find myself driven to the conclusion that the clause in question expresses in clear terms the mutual intention of the parties not to enter into legal obligations in respect to the matters upon which they are recording their agreement. I have never seen such a clause before, but I see nothing necessarily absurd in business men seeking to regulate their business relations by mutual promises which fall short of legal obligations, and rest on obligations of either honour or self-interest, or perhaps both. In this agreement I consider the clause a dominant clause, and not to be rejected, as the learned judge thought, on the ground of repugnancy.

The House of Lords agreed that there was no legally binding contract because of the honour clause, but considered (agreeing with Atkin LJ in the Court of Appeal) that the orders had been accepted and delivery was therefore legally required.

House of Lords
[1925] AC 445

LORD PHILLIMORE: According to the course of business between the parties which is narrated in the unenforceable agreement, goods were ordered from time to time, shipped, received, and paid for, under an established system; but the agreement being unenforceable, there was no obligation on the American company to order goods or upon the English companies to accept an order. Any actual transaction between the parties, however, gave rise to the ordinary legal rights; for the fact that it was not of obligation to do the transaction did not divest the transaction when done of its ordinary legal significance. This, my Lords, will, I think, be plain if we begin at the latter end of each transaction.

Goods were ordered, shipped, and received. Was there no legal liability to pay for them? One stage further back. Goods were ordered, shipped, and invoiced. Was there no legal liability to take delivery? I apprehend that in each of these cases the American company would be bound. If the goods were short-shipped or inferior in quality, or if the nature of them was such as to be deleterious to other cargo on board or illegal for the American company to bring into their country, the American company would have its usual legal remedies against the English companies or one of them. Business usually begins in some mutual understanding without a previous bargain. . . .

NOTE: Clearly the House of Lords was influenced by a desire to hold parties to their obligations under executed agreements, even though there was technically no contractual obligation. This seems to be the same principle which influenced the House of Lords in *Albert* v *MIB* (*page 183*).

Jones v *Vernon's Pools Ltd*
[1938] 2 All ER 626

The plaintiff alleged that he had sent in a pools coupon to the defendants, and the defendants denied having received it. The conditions on the pools coupon stated that 'the sending in of the coupon or any transaction entered into in respect of the pool should not be attended by or give rise to any legal relationship, rights, duties or consequences whatsoever, or be legally enforceable or the subject of litigation, but that all such arrangements, agreements and transactions should be binding in honour only'. Held: this condition prevented any action relating to the pools coupon.

ATKINSON J: If it means what I think that they intend it to mean, and what certainly everybody who sent a coupon and who took the trouble to read it would understand, it means that they all trusted to the defendants' honour, and to the care they took, and that they fully understood that there should be no claim possible in respect of the transactions.

One can see at once the impossibility of any other basis. I am told that there are a million coupons received every week-end. Just imagine what it would mean if half the people in the country could come forward and suddenly claim that they had posted and sent in a coupon which they never had, bring actions against the pool alleging that, and calling evidence to prove that they had sent in a coupon containing the list of winning teams, and if Vernons had to fight case after case to decide whether or not those coupons had been sent in and received. The business could not be carried on for a day on terms of that kind. It could only be carried on on the basis that everybody is trusting them, and taking the risk themselves of things going wrong. It seems to me that, even if the plaintiff established that this coupon was received, it was received on the basis of these rules, and that he has agreed in the clearest way that, if anything does go wrong, he is to have no legal claim. In other words, he has agreed that the money which *prima facie* became due to him if that coupon reached them is not to be the subject of an action at law. There is to be no legal liability to pay. He has got to trust to them, and, if something goes wrong, as I say, it is his funeral, and not theirs. I am convinced that that is the position here, and, even if the coupon were received, he has failed to establish that he would have a claim which he could come to the courts to enforce. . . .

(c) Collective agreements

In the absence of writing and an express declaration of contractual intention, the presumption of intention to create legal relations has also been rebutted in relation to collective agreements, i.e., agreements between trade unions and employers regulating rates of pay, conditions of work, dispute procedures, etc. In fact, the presumption is that there is *no* intention to be legally bound.

TRADE UNION AND LABOUR RELATIONS (CONSOLIDATION) ACT 1992

179. Enforceability of collective agreements

(1) A collective agreement shall be conclusively presumed not to have been intended by the parties to be a legally enforceable contract unless the agreement—
    (a) is in writing, and
    (b) contains a provision which (however expressed) states that the parties intend that the agreement shall be a legally enforceable contract.

(2) A collective agreement which does satisfy those conditions shall be conclusively presumed to have been intended by the parties to be a legally enforceable contract.

(d) Implied agreements in the commercial context

In the commercial context the presumption of intention to create legal relations does not apply where the allegation is that a contract should be implied from the parties' conduct, as opposed to a contract between them resulting from express agreement. The party asserting the existence of such a contract has the burden of establishing the necessity for implying it and this depends on the ability to establish the existence of an intention to be legally bound. This, in turn, appears to be linked to the issue of certainty of terms, e.g. the majority of the Court of Appeal in *Modahl* v *British Athletic Federation Ltd* [2001] EWCA Civ 1447, [2002] 1 WLR 1192 considered that a contract could be implied between the parties following from the fact that over a number of years the claimant had competed in athletic meetings under the auspices of the BAF. Such a contract was based on the rules of the British Athletic Federation, which were contractual in nature.

Baird Textiles Holdings Ltd v Marks & Spencer plc
[2001] EWCA Civ 274, [2001] 1 All ER (Comm) 737 (CA)

The claimant had been one of the principal suppliers for the defendant retailer for 30 years. In October 1999, the defendant cancelled the arrangement from the end of that season. The claimant sought damages on the basis that the arrangement could only be terminated on reasonable notice of three years. This was in part based on an allegation that there was an implied contractual obligation to that effect, there being no express contract between the parties. [See also *page 168* for discussion of the alternative argument based on estoppel.] Held: the argument based on the implied contract failed because there was no intention to create legal relations since the alleged contract was not sufficiently certain in its terms [see the discussion at *page 66*]. In addition, it was clear that the reason why there was no express contract was the deliberate decision by the defendants to maintain flexibility in the commercial relationship. Mance LJ explained the position and the burden of proof in such cases.

MANCE LJ: . . .

59 . . . For a contract to come into existence, there must be both (a) an agreement on essentials with sufficient certainty to be enforceable and (b) an intention to create legal relations.

60 Both requirements are normally judged objectively. Absence of the former may involve or be explained by the latter. But this is not always so. A sufficiently certain agreement may be reached, but there may be either expressly (ie by express agreement) or impliedly (eg in some family situations) no intention to create legal relations.

61 An intention to create legal relations is normally presumed in the case of an express or apparent agreement satisfying the first requirement: see *Chitty on Contracts* (28th edn, 1999) vol 1, para 2–146. It is otherwise when the case is that an implied contract falls to be inferred from parties' conduct: *Chitty*, para 2–147. It is then for the party asserting such a contract to show the necessity for implying it. As Morison J [the judge at first instance] said . . ., if the parties would or might have acted as they did without any such contract, there is no necessity to imply any contract. It is merely putting the same point another way to say that no intention to make any such contract will then be inferred.

62   That the test of any such implication is necessity is, in my view, clear, both on the authority of *The Aramis* [1989] I Lloyd's Rep 213, *Blackpool and Fylde Aero Club Ltd* v *Blackpool BC* [1990] 3 All ER 25, [1990] 1 WLR 1195, *Wilson & Co A/S* v *Partenreederei Hannah Blumenthal, The Hannah Blumenthal* [1983] 1 All ER 34, [1983] 1 AC 854 and *Mitsui & Co Ltd* v *Novorossiysk Shipping Co, The Gudermes* [1993] 1 Lloyd's Rep 311, cited by [Morritt VC] the Vice-Chancellor, and also a matter of consistency. It could not be right to adopt a test of necessity when implying terms into a contract and a more relaxed test when implying a contract—which must itself have terms.

63   Here it is sought by the claimant to argue in reverse. First, the issue of intention to create legal relations is addressed and it is suggested that the judge gave only one reason (based on para 9.28 of the claim) for negativing any such intention. Then, having sought to show that reason as ill-founded, it is argued that the only barrier to an enforceable contract is 'essentially one of interpretation' and of giving effect to an intention on the part of the parties to contract.

64   It is, in my judgment, more appropriate to take the requirements in the order in which I have set them out, and to recognise their potential interrelationship. If there is no sufficient agreement on essentials, that is on any view fundamental, and it may well also reflect an absence of intention to create legal relations.

65   Here, Baird has pleaded in detail facts and matters showing and concerning an exceptionally close and interactive commercial relationship with M&S. The more I have heard and read about the closeness of the parties' commercial co-operation in the past, the less able I have felt to see how its effect could be expressed in terms having any contractual certainty. The parties were in constant contact, discussing, developing, adapting or altering their arrangements. Baird submits that the answer lies in recognising that there were on each side broad obligations (a) to continue the long-standing purchaser-supplier relationship (unless and until one or other gave reasonable notice to determine it, put at three years) and, in that context, (b) for M&S to purchase and for Baird to supply a 'reasonable' or 'appropriate' share of whatever were M&S's requirements from time to time, so as (c) to ensure, at least to that extent, that the production facilities that Baird had devoted to M&S's business to date were maintained, or (at all events) run down in a less abrupt and painful way than actually occurred.

66   The terms of the suggested contract are more particularly contained in para 9 of the claim:

'. . . in exchange for BTH [Baird] agreeing (a) to supply [M&S] with garments year by year on a seasonal basis; (b) to allow [M&S] to be closely involved in the design and manufacture of the garments so supplied; (c) to establish and maintain a workforce and manufacturing capacity sufficient to meet and be highly responsive to [M&S] continuing requirements; (d) not to act in a manner which in the view of [M&S] was contrary to its interests; and (e) to deal with [M&S] in good faith and reasonably having regard to the objective of the relationship, the relationship would continue long term and would be terminable only upon the giving of reasonable notice; and that during the subsistence of the relationship [M&S] would acquire garments from BTH in quantities and at prices which in all the circumstances were reasonable and would deal with BTH in good faith and reasonably having regard to the objective of the relationship.'

. . .

68   When the suggested long-term contract is put in these terms, it becomes clear that it would, in case of any dispute, involve the court writing a 'reasonable' contract for the parties, after making a complete review of their situations, needs, abilities and expectations. It could only become relevant to seek to identify the impact of such long-term obligations in a situation where actual co-operation had broken down or one or the other party wanted to reduce its commitment to the minimum. So the court would be expected to undertake the exercise in the very situation where the parties' actual behaviour could no longer serve as a guide to the answer. I agree with the Vice-Chancellor that this is not an exercise that the court can or should undertake, or, indeed, which the parties can objectively be taken to have intended. The presence in the suggested contractual formulation of implied duties of good faith is an additional barrier in the way of the conclusion for which Baird contends, in view of English law's general refusal to recognise any duty of this nature as an implied contractual term.

69 Objectively, the only sensible analysis of the present situation is in my judgment that the parties had an extremely good long-term commercial relationship, but not one which they ever sought to express, or which the court would ever seek to express, in terms of long-term contractual obligations. The upshot is that I agree with the judge's conclusion that there was never here any agreement on essentials.

70 In addition, I consider that the fact that there was never any agreement to reach or even to set out the essential principles which might govern any legally binding long-term relationship indicates that neither party can objectively be taken to have intended to make any legally binding commitment of a long-term nature. Their conduct in this regard contrasts with their conduct in entering into short-term commitments relating to each season . . .

SECTION 3: A DIFFERENT APPROACH?

There is some evidence that the courts are placing less emphasis on a determination of the nature of the agreement as domestic or commercial. In *Edmonds* v *Lawson* [2000] QB 501 the Court of Appeal made no such determination but focused on the specific context surrounding the making of an offer of pupillage in chambers.

Edmonds v *Lawson*
[2000] QB 501 (CA)

A pupil barrister claimed that her unpaid 12 month pupillage constituted a contract of employment so that she was a 'worker' within the meaning of the National Minimum Wage Act 1998. Chambers argued that the offer of pupillage was not enforceable as a contract since there was no intention to create legal relations and Ms Edmonds had not provided any consideration. It was argued that the provisions of the Bar Council's Code of Conduct regulated the relationship and that no further contract was therefore necessary. The judge at first instance held that this was a contract of apprenticeship as it was a business arrangement and the presumption of intention to create legal relations applied. Accordingly, the claimant was a 'worker' within the Act. On appeal held: allowing the appeal, that although there was a binding contract because the context indicated that there was the necessary intention to create legal relations and the agreement was supported by consideration, this was not a contract of apprenticeship and the claimant therefore did not qualify as a 'worker' within the meaning of the National Minimum Wage Act 1998.

LORD BINGHAM CJ (giving the judgment of the court):

The first issue: was there a contract?

The claimant contended, and the judge held, that there was a contract between her and all those who were members of Mr Lawson's chambers on 1 October 1998, made by the chambers' offer of a 12-month pupillage and her acceptance of that offer. Before the judge and on appeal before us the defendants resisted that conclusion. The grounds of resistance were, first, that there was no intent to create legal relations and, secondly, that the pupillage agreement was unsupported by consideration moving from the claimant as promisee and so lacked an essential ingredient of a legally binding contract.

Whether the parties intended to enter into legally binding relations is an issue to be determined objectively and not by inquiring into their respective states of mind. The context is all-important.

From the defendants' point of view the written offer of pupillage to the claimant came at the end of a long, time-consuming and expensive process. It was also a process of great long-term consequence to them since, although barristers in practice are independent self-employed practitioners, it is of benefit to all, at every level, that chambers as a whole consist of talented and hardworking members, and the defendants, like other chambers, recruit most of their tenants from the pool of those recruited as pupils. So, quite apart from considerations of professional duty and the public interest, it is of direct practical consequence to chambers to attract and select the ablest pupils. That is why, in part at least, many chambers including the defendants' fund pupillages for a proportion of their pupils, sometimes very generously. From the pupil's point of view, obtaining a pupillage in a flourishing set of chambers practising in the pupil's chosen field is a step with potentially immense consequences, both professional and financial, in both the short and the long term. Obtaining a pupillage does not of course guarantee a tenancy, but it guarantees the pupil an opportunity to show his quality and thereby seek a tenancy. When, as the culmination of a long process of application, short-listing and interview an offer is formally made and formally accepted it would in our judgment be surprising to infer that the parties intended to bind themselves in honour only.

In arguing that there was no intent to create legal relations [counsel] for the defendants relied on the educational nature of the arrangement, suggesting that it lacked the characteristics of a commercial contract and involved no payment by the pupil. It was a voluntary and gratuitous offer by the chambers to provide education and training. He also relied on the doubt which, he said, existed as to who entered into the arrangement on the chambers' side. There was, he suggested, no need for a contract because the relationship was already regulated by the documents to which reference has been made above [Bar Council's Code of Conduct], and if chambers should resile from a undertaking to provide pupillage the pupil would have ample redress through the Bar disciplinary machinery, which would in practice preclude such dishonourable behaviour. The absence of written terms and conditions, he argued, pointed strongly against any intention to contract.

Neither singularly nor cumulatively do we find these points in any way persuasive on the question of intent. It is true that the content of the arrangement was educational, but as already pointed out the practical implications of the arrangement for both parties were potentially very significant and, subject to the point on consideration discussed below, there is no reason why a binding contract cannot be made for the provision of education and training. Whereas once the arrangement of pupillage was a one-to-one engagement between pupil and pupil master, that has ceased to be so, as evidenced by the responsibility imposed on and accepted by heads of chambers, by the procedure in practice adopted by chambers and by the management of pupillage as a chambers responsibility. The claimant was not interviewed, nor was the offer of pupillage made, by either of those who became her successive pupil masters, and when the offer was made and accepted she did not know who they would be. The regulatory materials governing pupillage . . . were impliedly incorporated by reference into the arrangement made between the parties, and to that extent the terms of the arrangement were recorded in writing; but the functions and obligations of the parties were so clearly specified in these materials that any detailed negotiation of terms and conditions to be recorded in a written agreement between the parties was rendered unnecessary. It is of course unlikely that any chambers, certainly any reputable chambers, having made an offer of pupillage which has been accepted, would resile from that arrangement without very good reason, but the existence of a disciplinary sanction does not in our view point against the existence of a contract. To our mind this arrangement had all the characteristics of a binding contract. It makes no difference that, if the pupil defaulted, the chambers would be most unlikely to sue; the same is true if an employer engages a junior employee under an employment contract which is undoubtedly binding, and the employee fails to turn up on the appointed day.

The defendants' argument on consideration is, we think, much stronger, for while chambers undertake to provide a closely prescribed curriculum of education and training the pupil no longer pays any fee and does not in our view undertake to do anything beyond that which is conducive to his or her education and training. In working on the pupil master's papers (making factual summaries, or drafting chronologies, or writing advices or preparing pleadings) the pupil will be seeking to acquire, under the tutelage of the pupil master, the skills of a professional adviser, pleader and advocate, even though the pupil master will often benefit from the pupil's work and from discussion with him. If the pupil carries out legal research or keeps a note in court, he is again learning and applying professional skills necessary for practice. If the pupil produces any work of real value, whether to the pupil master or any other member of the Bar, the beneficiary is under a professional duty to remunerate the pupil. While any pupil of ordinary common sense would, if asked, carry out mundane tasks (such as photocopying authorities or making a cup of tea) which do not in any way promote his professional development, there is in our view no obligation or duty on the pupil to do anything for the pupil master which is not conducive to his own professional development.

This conclusion, if correct, would we think be fatal to any argument that there was a contract between the pupil and the individual pupil master, for the pupil would provide no consideration for the pupil master's educational services. But the claimant does not rely on any contract said to have been made with an individual pupil master and we think a broader view has to be taken of the relationship between chambers and pupil. For reasons on which we have already touched, members of chambers have a strong incentive to attract talented pupils, and their future prospects will to some extent depend on their success in doing so. The funding of awards is not an exercise in pure altruism but reflects an obvious (and wholly unobjectionable) element of self-interest. The agreement of the claimant and other pupils to undertake pupillage at chambers such as the defendants' provides a pool of selected candidates who can be expected to compete with each other for recruitment as tenants. We do not regard this argument as undermined by the fact that some pupils who are accepted as such may be regarded as unlikely candidates for tenancy. The process must be viewed in the round, and not on a pupil by pupil basis, and chambers may well see an advantage in developing close relationships with pupils who plan to practise as employed barristers or to practise overseas. On balance we take the view that pupils such as the claimant provide consideration for the offer made by chambers such as the defendants' by agreeing to enter into the close, important and potentially very productive relationship which pupillage involves.

We agree with the judge, although for somewhat different reasons, that the claimant did make a legally binding contract with the defendants.

NOTES
1. This decision may indicate a change in the basic approach to a concentration on the context as indicative of the seriousness of the arrangement for all parties concerned. This approach also neatly avoided the potential difficulty of classification of this essentially educational relationship.
2. Presumptions are not used in the *Principles of European Contract Law*. Instead, Article 2:102 states that 'intention to be legally bound is determined from the party's statements or conduct as they are reasonably understood by the other party.' The certainty of any statements made and any action taken in reliance by the other party are factors to consider when making the necessary objective assessment of intention.

6

Terms

The next step is to consider what it is that the parties have undertaken to do, i.e., the terms of the contract.

SECTION 1: PRE-CONTRACTUAL STATEMENTS—TERMS OR MERE REPRESENTATIONS?

If a mere representation is false, it gives rise to remedies in the law of misrepresentation (see *pages 543–606*); if a term is broken, remedies are for breach of contract.

If there is a breach of contract there is an automatic right to claim damages. However, damages for misrepresentation can only be claimed on proof of fault.

The measure of damages recoverable for breach of contract aims to put the claimant into the position that he would have been in had the contract been properly performed; the tortious measure of damages for misrepresentation puts the claimant into the position that he would have been in had the misrepresentation not been made.

A claimant in a claim for breach of contract can recover for all losses which were within both parties' reasonable contemplation when they made the contract as the probable result of the breach of it. This is a far more restrictive test than the remoteness test for misrepresentation which, for fraudulent misrepresentation and negligent misrepresentation under the Misrepresentation Act 1967, s. 2(1), allows the recovery of all direct loss regardless of whether it was foreseeable (*page 584*).

The distinction between terms and representations rests upon the intentions of the parties as objectively ascertained, i.e. did the parties intend that the statement maker was making a binding promise as to the truth of the statement? The courts have determined some guidelines to assist in ascertaining this intention. Lord Moulton in *Heilbut, Symons & Co.* v *Buckleton* [1913] AC 30, warned that these guidelines are not decisive tests of intention:

[T]hey cannot be said to furnish decisive tests, because it cannot be said as a matter of law that the presence or absence of those features is conclusive of the intention of the parties. The intention of the parties can only be deduced from the totality of the evidence and no secondary principles of such a kind can be universally true.

(a) Accepting responsibility or advising on verification

Schawel v Reade
[1913] 2 IR 81 (HL)

The plaintiff required a stallion for stud purposes and went to the defendant's stables where he began examining a horse. He was told by the defendant, 'You need not look for anything; the horse is perfectly sound. If there was anything the matter with the horse I would tell you'. Therefore the plaintiff did not continue the examination. The price was agreed a few days later and the delivery of the horse took place after three weeks. The horse was found to be totally unfit for stud purposes, and the question in the case was whether the defendant's statement amounted to a term or a representation. The jury had answered 'yes' to the questions: Did the defendant represent to the plaintiff, in order that the plaintiff might purchase the horse, that the horse was fit for stud purposes, and did the plaintiff act upon that representation in purchasing the horse? Held: the jury had found that it was a warranty.

LORD MOULTON: Now, it would be impossible, in my mind, to have a clearer example of an express warranty where the word 'warrant' was not used. The essence of such warranty is that it becomes plain by the words, and the action, of the parties that it is intended that in the purchase the responsibility of the soundness shall rest upon the vendor; and how in the world could a vendor more clearly indicate that he is prepared and intends to take upon himself the responsibility of the soundness than by saying, 'You need not look at that horse, because it is perfectly sound,' and sees that the purchaser thereupon desists from his immediate independent examination?

My Lords, it seems to me, as found by the jury in their answer to the first question, we have clearly and unmistakably all the elements of an express warranty . . .

NOTES
1. The courts generally use the word 'warranty' to mean a term of the contract. A warranty is also a particular type of term (see *section 5, page 242*).
2. In *Hopkins* v *Tanqueray* (1854) 15 CB 130, 139 ER 369, the plaintiff purchased the defendant's horse at auction. The previous day the defendant had found the plaintiff examining the horse's legs and had said, 'You need not examine his legs: you have nothing to look for. I assure you that he is perfectly sound in every respect'. The Court of Common Pleas held that the defendant's statement was not a warranty, only a representation.

   How can these cases be reconciled? Arguably, the important fact was the evidence of the defendant in *Hopkins* v *Tanqueray* that horses that were sold at auction were never warranted unless this was expressly stated in the catalogue.
3. In *Harling* v *Eddy* [1951] 2 KB 739, Evershed MR distinguished these cases on the ground that in *Hopkins* v *Tanqueray* the statement was made the day before the contract, whereas in *Schawel* v *Reade* the statement was made the same day. If there is a delay between the time the statement was made and the formation of the contract, then it is less likely that it would be intended as a term.
4. If the statement indicates that the recipient of the statement should check it, then the statement maker is indicating that the statement is not intended to be a contractual term since he is explicitly refusing to take responsibility for its truth.

Ecay v Godfrey
(1947) 80 Lloyd's Rep 286

The plaintiff orally agreed to buy the defendant's motor cruiser for £750. There was evidence of a conversation between the parties in which the plaintiff had asked questions relating to the condition of the cruiser. The defendant had asked whether the plaintiff was going to have a survey completed and the plaintiff replied that he would not. The cruiser was in fact unsound, and the plaintiff claimed damages for breach of warranty. Held: it had to be shown that there was an undertaking by the defendant that the boat was a sound boat. Looking at the whole of the conversation, including the question about the survey, it amounted to no more than an innocent misrepresentation, so that the plaintiff's claim failed.

LORD GODDARD CJ: . . . I often think that a very useful test in these cases is one that Mr Justice Horridge . . . used . . . when he was trying cases in which a warranty was set out. He said:

What you have got to think of is: If the parties sat down here and wrote out their contract, would you find in that contract an undertaking by the defendant that so and so existed or so and so was the fact?

If we apply that test to the case here, having heard all the evidence, I think it is impossible to come to the conclusion that if these two parties had sat down and written out their contract, intending thereby to put down on paper exactly what they bargained about and all the terms of their bargain, Mr Godfrey would have said, 'And I promise you' (or 'And I undertake') 'that the vessel is in good condition.' It would be quite inconsistent, I think, with his statement to the plaintiff at the time, 'Aren't you going to have a survey?' or 'Are you intending to have a survey?', because if he was intending to warrant at the time that this boat was in good condition, there would be no point in having a survey. I will not go quite so far as that, because a man might say: 'Although you are willing to warrant, I am not going to be satisfied with that, because your warranty may turn out to be wrong and if I am going to part with £750 I should like to have your warranty confirmed by a survey'; but I think that the conversation with regard to the survey is material in coming to the conclusion whether there was a warranty or not.

Whatever was said here no doubt was said in the course of the negotiations leading up to the sale, but the sale did not in fact take place on that day. It did not take place until the next day, because after the meeting at the boat the plaintiff had not made up his mind and went away to think about it. Then, without any further communication with Mr Godfrey, he bought the boat. It may very likely be that the plaintiff does not understand, or did not understand—there are a great many buyers who do not understand—the difference between a representation and a warranty; but if he wanted a warranty, I think he should have got it and got it in very much more precise terms than anything that was said, or is alleged to have been said, here. . . .

(b) Importance attached test

Bannerman v *White*

(1861) 10 CB NS 844; 142 ER 685 (Court of Common Pleas)

A prospective buyer of hops asked the seller if any sulphur had been used in the growth or treatment of the hops, adding that he would not even ask the price if sulphur had been used. The seller replied that sulphur had not been used when in fact it had. Held: this statement was a term of the contract entitling the buyer to terminate for breach.

Couchman v *Hill*

[1947] KB 554 (CA)

The plaintiff bought the defendant's heifer at auction. The catalogue described the heifer as unserved and the plaintiff required an unserved heifer for service by his bull. The catalogue also stated that the auctioneers were not responsible for the correct description or any fault or defect in any lot and were not giving any warranty. Before the sale, the plaintiff asked the defendant and the auctioneer to confirm that the heifer was unserved, which they did. Seven weeks later, the heifer suffered a miscarriage and died. The plaintiff brought an action for damages for breach of warranty. Held: that the statement amounted to a warranty by the defendant which overrode the condition in the printed terms.

SCOTT LJ: . . . There was no contract in existence until the hammer fell. The offer was defined, the auctioneer's authority was defined, but it was in law open to any would-be purchaser to intimate in advance before bidding for any particular heifer offered from the rostrum that he was not willing to bid for the lot unless the defendant modified the terms of sale contained in the two documents in some way specified by him. There is no doubt that the plaintiff did make some attempt of the kind in order to protect himself from the risk of buying an animal that was not of the kind described.

The real question is,: What did the parties understand by the question addressed to and the answer received from both the defendant and the auctioneer? It is contended by the defendant that the question meant 'having regard to the onerous stipulations which I know I shall have to put up with if I bid and the lot is knocked down to me, can you give me your honourable assurance that the heifers have in fact not been served? If so, I will risk the penalties of the catalogue.' The alternative meaning is: 'I am frightened of contracting on your published terms, but I will bid if you will tell me by word of mouth that you accept full responsibility for the statement in the catalogue that the heifers have not been served, or, in other words, give me a clean warranty. That is the only condition on which I will bid.' If that was the meaning there was clearly an oral offer of a warranty which over-rode the stultifying condition in the printed terms, that offer was accepted by the plaintiff when he bid, and the contract was made on that basis when the lot was knocked down to him. . . .

■ QUESTIONS

1. Is it correct that one bidder at an auction should be able to negotiate for a warranty in advance where the auction is to be one without warranty?

    In *Hopkins* v *Tanqueray* in such circumstances it was held that a representation made the day before the auction was not a contractual term. There is an editorial note to the report of *Couchman* v *Hill* indicating that if this authority had been cited in *Couchman* the result may well have been different. On the other hand, the statement in *Couchman* v *Hill* was made on the same day as the auction, whereas that in *Hopkins* v *Tanqueray* was made the previous day.

2. Is this a case of a collateral warranty (*page 206*) since the warranty existed before the contract itself and was the consideration for entering into the main sale contract?

(c) **Special knowledge of the statement maker**

Oscar Chess Ltd v *Williams*
[1957] 1 WLR 370 (CA)

In June 1955, the defendant sold a secondhand Morris car to the plaintiffs, motor dealers, for £290. The registration book, which was examined by the plaintiffs' representative, showed that the car was first registered in 1948, and the defendant honestly believed that it was a 1948 model. The purchase price was calculated on this basis. In January 1956, the plaintiffs discovered from the manufacturers that the car was a 1939 model (so the true price was £175) and claimed damages for breach of warranty. Held (Denning and Hodson LJJ; Morris LJ dissenting): the defendant was not liable to the plaintiffs in damages for breach of warranty because, as the plaintiffs knew, the defendant had no personal knowledge of the date of the manufacture of the car and the plaintiffs were in at least as good a position to know this. The defendant had made an innocent misrepresentation, i.e., non-fraudulent. (Damages were only available at this time if the misrepresentation was fraudulent.)

DENNING LJ: . . . The crucial question is: was it a binding promise or only an innocent misrepresentation? The technical distinction between a 'condition' and a 'warranty' is quite immaterial in this case, because it is far too late for the buyer to reject the car. He can at best only claim damages. The material distinction here is between a statement which is a term of the contract and a statement which is only an innocent misrepresentation. This distinction is best expressed by the ruling of Lord Holt: Was it intended as a warranty or not? using the word warranty there in its ordinary English meaning: because it gives the exact shade of meaning that is required. It is something to which a man must be taken to bind himself.

In applying Lord Holt's test, however, some misunderstanding has arisen by the use of the word 'intended'. It is sometimes supposed that the tribunal must look into the minds of the parties to see what they themselves intended. That is a mistake. Lord Moulton made it quite clear [in *Heilbut, Symons & Co.* v *Buckleton* ([1913] AC at p. 51)] that 'The intention of the parties can only be deduced from the totality of the evidence . . .'. The question whether a warranty was intended depends on the conduct of the parties, on their words and behaviour, rather than on their thoughts. If an intelligent bystander would reasonably infer that a warranty was intended, that will suffice. And this, when the facts are not in dispute, is a question of law. . . .

It is instructive to take some recent instances to show how the courts have approached this question. When the seller states a fact which is or should be within his own knowledge and of which the buyer is ignorant, intending that the buyer should act on it and he does so, it is easy to infer a warranty; see *Couchman* v *Hill* ([1947] KB 554), where the farmer stated that the heifer was unserved, and *Harling* v *Eddy* ([1951] KB 739), where he stated that there was nothing wrong with her. So also if he makes a promise about something which is or should be within his own control: see *Birch* v *Paramount Estates Ltd* ((1956) 16 Estates Gazette 396), decided on October 2, 1956, in this court, where the seller stated that the house would be as good as the show house. But if the seller, when he states a fact, makes it clear that he has no knowledge of his own but has got his information elsewhere, and is merely passing it on, it is not so easy to imply a warranty. Such a case was *Routledge* v *McKay* ([1954] 1 WLR 615, 636), where the seller 'stated that a motor cycle combination was a 1942 model, and pointed to the corroboration of that statement to be found in the book', and it was held that there was no warranty.

Turning now to the present case, much depends on the precise words that were used. If the seller says 'I believe it is a 1948 Morris. Here is the registration book to prove it', there is clearly no warranty. It is a statement of belief, not a contractual promise. But if the seller says: 'I guarantee that it is a 1948 Morris. This is borne out by the registration book, but you need not rely solely on that. I give you my own guarantee that it is', there is clearly a warranty. The seller is making himself contractually responsible, even though the registration book is wrong.

. . . What is the proper inference from the known facts? It must have been obvious to both that the seller had himself no personal knowledge of the year when the car was made. He only became owner after a great number of changes. He must have been relying on the registration book. It is unlikely that such a person would warrant the year of manufacture. The most that he would do would be to state his belief, and then produce the registration book in verification of it. In these circumstances the intelligent bystander would, I suggest, say that the seller did not intend to bind himself so as to warrant that it was a 1948 model. If the seller was asked to pledge himself to it, he would at once have said 'I cannot do that. I have only the log-book to go by, the same as you'.

. . . It seems to me clear that the motor dealers who bought the car relied on the year stated in the log-book. If they had wished to make sure of it, they could have checked it then and there, by taking the engine number and chassis number and writing to the makers. They did not do so at the time, but only eight months later. They are experts, and, not having made that check at the time, I do not think that they should now be allowed to recover against the innocent seller who produced to them all the evidence he had, namely, the registration book. I agree that it is hard on the dealers to have paid more than the car is worth: but it would be equally hard on the seller to make him pay the difference. He would never have bought the Hillman at all unless he had got the allowance of £290 for the Morris. The best course in all these cases would be to 'shunt' the difference down the train of innocent sellers until one reached the rogue who perpetrated the fraud: but he can rarely be traced, or if he can, he rarely has the money to pay the damages. So one is left to decide between a number of innocent people who is to bear the loss. That can only be done by applying the law about representations and warranties as we know it: and that is what I have tried to do. If the rogue can be traced, he can be sued by whosoever has suffered the loss: but if he cannot be traced, the loss must lie where it falls. It should not be inflicted on innocent sellers, who sold the car many months, perhaps many years before, and have forgotten all about it and have conducted their affairs on the basis that the transaction was concluded. Such a seller would not be able to recollect after all this length of time the exact words he used, such as whether he said 'I believe it is a 1948 model', or 'I warrant it is a 1948 model'. The right course is to let the buyer set aside the transaction if he finds out the mistake quickly and comes promptly before other interests have irretrievably intervened, otherwise the loss must lie where it falls: and that is, I think, the course prescribed by law. . . .

■ QUESTION

This case involved the question of which of two innocent parties should suffer for the loss caused by a third party (the person who altered the registration book). Was the loss correctly placed on the party who was better able to bear it (the motor dealers)?

NOTES

1. See *page 242* for the meaning of 'condition'.
2. The decision of the majority seems to be the result of a desire to protect a layman who had acted in good faith on the basis of the registration book.
3. If we apply the importance attached test here, had the plaintiffs known the true age of the car they would probably still have offered to part exchange it at the 1939 valuation because they wanted the sale of the new car. This would indicate that their decision to contract did not turn on the age of manufacture of the car; only the price did. This test was not mentioned by the Court of Appeal.
4. Denning LJ in *Oscar Chess* discussed the question of whether there had been any acceptance of responsibility for the statement by the defendant. The important fact was that the registration book had been used as justifying the statement as to the age of the car. There was no independent guarantee of the truth of the statement.
5. The courts have sometimes placed exclusive reliance on *one* of these guidelines when it can be argued that they should all be considered in order to determine the parties' intentions. In *Pritchard* v *Cook* (unrep.) 4 June 1998, the Court of Appeal took account of each of the guidelines as part of its assessment of the transaction as a whole.

   The plaintiff had purchased a collectors' rally car from the defendant. The defendant's advertisement had referred to the fact that the full specification was available on request, and the plaintiff had asked to see this before purchasing the car. However, the invoice of sale made no reference to this specification. In fact the specification had been provided by Red Ltd and the defendant had simply copied the details onto his own headed notepaper. The Court of Appeal held that the specification was contractual because, looking at the transaction as a whole, it was clear that the specification was a matter of importance to both parties. The plaintiff had specifically asked to see it, and the evidence was that he would not have purchased the car without it. The defendant also regarded it as important in securing the sale because he had mentioned it in his advertisement and had copied it onto his own notepaper without issuing a disclaimer. Therefore the Court considered that the parties had made the specification the basis of the sale.

   Evans LJ specifically distinguished both *Oscar Chess* v *Williams* and *Routledge* v *McKay* [1954] 1 WLR 615. In both cases, the sellers had indicated that their statements were derived from the registration books, and the purchasers had inspected and relied directly on those books. Therefore the sellers had not taken responsibility for them. However, in *Pritchard* v *Cook*, it was clear that the defendant had adopted the specification as his own and was taking responsibility for it.

The Court of Appeal also rejected the defendant's argument that he had less technical knowledge than the plaintiff, who was a motor trader and experienced rally driver. The defendant was also in the motor business and was a collector and seller of classic cars. The Court found that both were dealing in a personal capacity for the purposes of this contract, and therefore appeared to treat them as being in a similar position with regard to knowledge of the subject matter. This is another ground on which this decision can be distinguished from *Oscar Chess*.

Compare the following case.

Dick Bentley Productions Ltd v Harold Smith (Motors) Ltd
[1965] 1 WLR 623 (CA)

The plaintiff asked the defendants, who were car dealers, to find him a 'well vetted' Bentley car. A car was found. The defendants informed the plaintiff that they were in a position to find out the history of cars and this car had been fitted with a replacement engine and gear box and had since travelled only 20,000 miles. The defendants relied on the odometer reading and had not checked the details. The plaintiff bought the car and discovered that this representation as to the mileage was untrue. The plaintiff sued the defendants seeking damages for breach of contract. Held: the statement amounted to a warranty, and therefore the plaintiff was entitled to damages.

LORD DENNING MR: . . . The first point is whether this representation, namely, that it had done 20,000 miles only since it had been fitted with a replacement engine and gearbox, was an innocent misrepresentation (which does not give rise to damages), or whether it was a warranty. It was said by Holt CJ and repeated in *Heilbut, Symons & Co.* v *Buckleton* ([1913] AC 30, 49) that: 'An affirmation at the time of the sale is a warranty, provided it appear on evidence to be so intended.' But that word 'intended' has given rise to difficulties. I endeavoured to explain in *Oscar Chess Ltd* v *Williams* ([1957] 1 WLR 370, 375) that the question whether a warranty was intended depends on the conduct of the parties, on their words and behaviour, rather than on their thoughts. If an intelligent bystander would reasonably infer that a warranty was intended, that will suffice. What conduct, then? What words and behaviour lead to the inference of a warranty?

Looking at the cases once more, as we have done so often, it seems to me that if a representation is made in the course of dealings for a contract for the very purpose of inducing the other party to act upon it, and actually inducing him to act upon it by entering into the contract, that is prima facie ground for inferring that it was intended as a warranty. It is not necessary to speak of it as being collateral. Suffice it that it was intended to be acted upon and was in fact acted on. But the maker of the representation can rebut this inference if he can show that it really was an innocent misrepresentation, in that he was in fact innocent of fault in making it, and that it would not be reasonable in the circumstances for him to be bound by it. In the *Oscar Chess* case the inference was rebutted. There a man had bought a second-hand car and received with it a log-book, which stated the year of the car, 1948. He afterwards resold the car. When he resold it he simply repeated what was in the log-book and passed it on to the buyer. He honestly believed on reasonable grounds that it was true. He was completely innocent of any fault. There was no warranty by him, but only an innocent misrepresentation. Whereas in the present case it is very different. The inference is not rebutted. Here we have a dealer, Smith, who was in a position to know, or at least to find out, the history of the car. He could get it by writing to the makers. He did not do so. Indeed, it was done later. When the history of this car was examined, his statement turned out to be quite wrong. He ought to have known better. There was no reasonable foundation for it.

■ QUESTION

Is this another example of consumer protection, since had the statement not been held to be a term of the contract, there would have been no remedy in damages? (The statement was made negligently, and before the Misrepresentation Act 1967 damages were available only for fraudulent misrepresentations.)

NOTES

1. Applying the importance attached test, the plaintiff made it clear that he wanted a car that was 'well vetted', and it is unlikely that he would have purchased the car had its actual mileage been disclosed.
2. Lord Denning suggests that the test of whether there is a warranty depends upon whether the seller is actually at fault. The dealer here was negligent in not checking the mileage, whereas in *Oscar Chess* v *Williams* there was no such requirement for the individual seller to check the registration book. Unfortunately, the wording of Lord Denning's test is too closely tied to misrepresentation, and the true test is surely that the dealer was in a better position to discover the truth.

Esso Petroleum Co. Ltd v *Mardon*
[1976] QB 801 (CA)

In 1961, the plaintiffs' employee, with 40 years' experience, calculated that the potential throughput of a petrol station was likely to reach 200,000 gallons by the third year of operation of the station. The local planning authority refused permission for the pumps to front on to the street so they had to be placed at the back of the site. In 1963, the defendant, a prospective tenant for the petrol station, was given the same estimate of throughput by the plaintiffs' employee. The defendant suggested that 100,000 or 150,000 gallons was a more likely figure, but his doubts were quelled by his trust in the greater experience of the plaintiffs' employee. The defendant entered into a three-year tenancy. In the first 15 months the throughput was only 78,000 gallons. The losses continued, and eventually the plaintiffs cut off the defendant's supply of petrol due to non-payment. They sought possession of the station and sums they were owed. The defendant claimed damages, *inter alia*, for breach of warranty as to the potential throughput of the station. Held: the statement was a contractual warranty because it was a factual statement on a crucial matter by a party professing to have special knowledge in order to induce the defendant to enter into the contract. This warranty was not a promise that the station would in fact have this throughput but a warranty that the forecast had been made with reasonable care and skill. The plaintiffs were liable in damages for the amount that the defendant had lost by being induced to enter into the contract.

LORD DENNING MR:

Collateral warranty

Ever since *Heilbut, Symons & Co.* v *Buckleton* [1913] AC 30, we have had to contend with the law as laid down by the House of Lords that an innocent misrepresentation gives no right to damages. In order to escape from that rule, the pleader used to allege—I often did it myself—that the misrepresentation was fraudulent, or alternatively a collateral warranty. At the trial we nearly always succeeded on collateral warranty. We had to reckon, of course, with the dictum of Lord Moulton, at p. 47, that 'such collateral contracts must from their very nature be rare.' But more often than not the court elevated the innocent misrepresentation into a collateral warranty: and thereby did justice—in advance of the Misrepresentation Act 1967. I remember scores of cases of that kind, especially on the sale of a business. A representation as to the profits that had been made in the past was invariably held to be a warranty. Besides that experience, there have been many cases since I have sat in this court where we have readily held a representation—which induces a person to enter into a contract—to be a warranty sounding in damages. . . . [This] was not a warranty—in this sense—that it did not *guarantee* that the throughput *would be* 200,000 gallons. But, nevertheless, it was a forecast made by a party—Esso—who had special knowledge and skill. It was the yardstick . . . by which they measured the worth of a filling station. They knew the facts. They knew the traffic in the town. They knew the throughput of comparable stations. They had much experience and expertise at their disposal. They were in a much better position than Mr Mardon to make a forecast. It seems to me that if such a person makes a forecast, intending that the other should act upon it—and he does act upon it, it can well be interpreted as a warranty that the forecast is sound and reliable in the sense that they made it with reasonable care and skill. It is just as if Esso said to Mr Mardon: 'Our forecast of throughput is 200,000 gallons. You can rely upon it as being a sound forecast of what the service station should do. The rent is calculated on that footing.' If the forecast turned out to be an unsound forecast such as no person of skill or experience should have made, there is a breach of warranty. . . .

In the present case it seems to me that there was a warranty that the forecast was sound, that is, Esso made it with reasonable care and skill. That warranty was broken.

NOTES
1. Now that damages are available for negligent misrepresentation (on a very favourable basis) under the Misrepresentation Act 1967, there will be no need to resort to the collateral warranty in order to secure a damages award in such circumstances.
2. In *Pritchard* v *Cook* (unrep.) 4 June 1998, *page 204*, Evans LJ stressed that the traditional dichotomy between representations and contractual terms is often insignificant in practice because a pre-contractual statement can be both a representation, inducing the contract, and a contractual promise as to its truth once a contract is made.
3. In *Howard Marine* v *Ogden & Sons* [1978] QB 574 (for facts see *page 582*), the defendants argued that the marine manager's statement amounted to a collateral oral warranty as to the carrying capacity of the barges which had induced them to hire the barges. The Court of Appeal held that it was not a warranty because it was not given in circumstances indicating that a contractual promise was being made. (Compare Lord Denning's test in *Dick Bentley* v *Harold Smith* with that in *Howard Marine* v *Ogden* some 13 years later. In *Howard Marine* v *Ogden* the test is whether the statement was intended to be binding rather than whether the statement maker is at fault.)

SECTION 2: WRITTEN CONTRACTS

Contracts can be written or oral, or partly written and partly oral.

A: The parol evidence rule

The parol evidence rule applies to written contracts and prevents the parties adducing extrinsic evidence to add to, vary, or contradict the writing. (For a recent application of the parol evidence rule see the speech of Lord Hobhouse in *Shogun Finance Ltd* v *Hudson* [2003] UKHL 62, [2004] 1 AC 919, page 94.) However, a party cannot rely on a written contract when he has only secured the other's consent by means of an oral assurance.

(a) Contracts partly written and partly oral

Construing a contract as partly written and partly oral will always enable the courts to avoid the parol evidence rule, which applies only to those contracts where the writing was intended to contain the whole of the agreement.

J. Evans & Son (Portsmouth) Ltd v *Andrea Merzario Ltd*
[1976] 1 WLR 1078 (CA)

The plaintiffs, importers of machines, contracted with the defendants for carriage of machines to England. The contract was on the standard conditions of the forwarding trade, giving the defendants complete freedom as to the method of transportation unless the plaintiffs gave express written instructions. The conditions exempted the defendants from liability for loss or damage of the goods. Prior to 1967, because the machines were liable to rust if carried on deck, the defendants had arranged for the transportation of the machines in crates or trailers below deck. In 1967, the defendants proposed changing over to containers and, in discussions on the matter between the plaintiffs and the defendants, the defendants gave the plaintiffs an oral assurance that these containers would be shipped below deck. The plaintiffs therefore agreed to containerised transportation of the machines. Due to an oversight by the defendants, a container was shipped on deck and fell overboard. The plaintiffs claimed damages from the defendants for loss of the machine, alleging that the carriage of the container on deck had been a breach of the carriage contract. Held: (Roskill and Geoffrey Lane LJJ) the oral assurance was an express term of the contract, and as the contract was partly oral and partly written, evidence of the oral term was admissible. The defendants were therefore liable for breach of this oral promise unless they could rely on the printed conditions (see *page 280*).

ROSKILL LJ: . . . The real question, as I venture to think, is not whether one calls this an assurance or a guarantee, but whether that which was said amounted to an enforceable contractual promise by the defendants to the plaintiffs that any goods thereafter entrusted by the plaintiffs to the defendants for carriage from Milan to the United Kingdom via Rotterdam and thence by sea to England would be shipped under deck. The matter was apparently argued before the judge on behalf of the plaintiffs on the basis that the defendants' promise (if any) was what the lawyers sometimes call a collateral oral warranty . . . But that doctrine, as it seems to me, has little or no application where one is not concerned with a contract in writing (with respect I cannot accept [counsel for the defendants'] argument that there was here a contract in writing) but with a contract which, as I think, was partly oral, partly in writing and partly by conduct. In such a case the court does not require to have recourse to lawyers' devices such as collateral oral warranty in order to seek to adduce evidence which would not otherwise be admissible. The court is entitled to look at and should look at all the evidence from start to finish in order to see what the bargain was that was struck between the parties . . . When one does that, one finds first, as I have already mentioned, that these parties had been doing business in transporting goods from Milan to England for some time before; secondly, that transportation of goods from Milan to England was always done on trailers which were always under deck; thirdly, that the defendants wanted a change in the practice—they wanted containers used instead of trailers; fourthly, that the plaintiffs were only willing to agree to that change if they were promised by the defendant that those containers would be shipped under deck, and would not have agreed to the change but for that promise. The defendants gave such a promise, which to my mind against this background plainly amounted to an enforceable contractual promise. In those circumstances it seems to me that the contract was this: 'If we continue to give you our business, you will ensure that those goods in containers are shipped under deck'; and the defendants agreed that this would be so. Thus there was a breach of that contract by the defendants when this container was shipped on deck; and it seems to me to be plain that the damage which the plaintiffs suffered resulted from that breach. . . .

NOTE: Wedderburn [1959] CLJ 58, argued that this device means that the parol evidence rule is no more than a 'self evident tautology'. It will always be correct, because if there is a written contract the rule applies and oral evidence cannot be admitted. If the contract is not completely written, then the rule does not apply and the oral evidence is admissible.

(b) Collateral contract

The court may hold that in fact there are two contracts—the written contract to which the parol evidence rule applies, and the oral collateral contract (without which the main written contract would not have been made) to which the rule does not apply.

Lord Moulton's statement in *Heilbut, Symons & Co.* v *Buckleton* [1913] AC 30, relating to collateral contracts, is restrictive and confusing because the distinction between a collateral warranty (*page 206*) and a collateral contract is not preserved:

[T]here may be a contract the consideration for which is the making of some other contract. 'If you will make such and such a contract I will give you one hundred pounds,' is in every sense of the word a complete legal contract. It is collateral to the main contract, but each has an independent existence, and they do not differ in respect of their possessing to the full the character and status of a contract. But such collateral contracts must from their very nature be rare. The effect of a collateral contract such as that which I have instanced would be to increase the consideration of the main contract by 100*l.*, and the more natural and usual way of carrying this out would be by so modifying the main contract and not by executing a concurrent and collateral contract. Such collateral contracts, the sole effect of which is to vary or add to the terms of the principal contract, are therefore viewed with suspicion by the law. They must be proved strictly. Not only the terms of such contracts but the existence of an animus contrahendi on the part of all the parties to them must be clearly shewn. Any laxity on these points would enable parties to escape from the full performance of the obligations of contracts unquestionably entered into by them and more especially would have the effect of lessening the authority of written contracts by making it possible to vary them by suggesting the existence of verbal collateral agreements relating to the same subject-matter.

Lord Denning MR adopted the device of the collateral contract in *J. Evans* v *Andrea Merzario* (for facts see *page 208*):

[T]he forwarding agents said there was no contractual promise that the goods would be carried under deck. Alternatively, if there was, they relied on the printed terms and conditions. The judge held there was no contractual promise that these containers should be carried under deck. He thought that, in order to be binding, the initial conversation ought to be contemporaneous; and that here it was too remote in point of time from the actual transport. Furthermore that, viewed objectively, it should not be considered binding. The judge quoted largely from the well known case of *Heilbut, Symons & Co.* v *Buckleton* [1913] AC 30 in which it was held that a person is not liable in damages for an innocent misrepresentation; and that the courts should be slow to hold that there was a collateral contract. I must say that much of what was said in that case is entirely out of date. We now have the Misrepresentation Act 1967 under which damages can be obtained for innocent misrepresentation of fact. This Act does not apply here because we are concerned with an assurance as to the future. But even in respect of promises as to the future, we have a different approach nowadays to collateral contracts. When a person gives a promise or an assurance to another, intending that he should act on it by entering into a contract, and he does act on it by entering into the contract, we hold that it is binding: see *Dick Bentley Productions Ltd* v *Harold Smith (Motors) Ltd* [1965] 1 WLR 623. That case was concerned with a representation of fact, but it applies also to promises as to the future. Following this approach, it seems to me plain that Mr Spano gave an oral promise or assurance that the goods in this new container traffic would be carried under deck. He made the promise in order to induce Mr Leonard to agree to the goods being carried in containers. On the faith of it, Mr Leonard accepted the quotations and gave orders for transport. In those circumstances the promise was binding. There was a breach of that promise and the forwarding agents are liable—unless they can rely on the printed conditions.

The terms of the collateral contract may even override conflicting terms in the main written contract.

City and Westminster Properties (1934) Ltd v Mudd
[1959] Ch 129

The defendant was a tenant of a lock up shop and had slept in the office at the back of the shop. In 1947, during negotiations for a new lease, the defendant was sent a draft contract containing a covenant by the lessee 'not to permit or suffer the demised premises or any part thereof to be used as a place for lodging, dwelling or sleeping'. The plaintiffs' agent told the defendant that if he signed the lease, the plaintiffs would not object to his continuing to live in the shop. The defendant therefore executed the lease. In 1956, the plaintiffs sought forfeiture of the lease on the ground of breach of this covenant. The defendant denied that he was in breach, claiming that the plaintiffs had waived the covenant or were estopped from relying on it (see the discussion of promissory estoppel, at *page 147*). Held: as the defendant had signed the lease only because of the promise by the plaintiffs' agent, he was entitled to rely on that promise as long as he was in occupation of the shop.

HARMAN J: . . . This is not a case of a representation made after contractual relations existed between the parties to the effect that one party to the contract would not rely on his rights. If the defendant's evidence is to be accepted, as I hold it is, it is a case of a promise made to him before the execution of the lease that, if he would execute it in the form put before him, the landlord would not seek to enforce against him personally the covenant about using the property as a shop only. The defendant says that it was in reliance on this promise that he executed the lease and entered on the onerous obligations contained in it. He says, moreover, that but for the promise made he would not have executed the lease, but would have moved to other premises available to him at the time. If these be the facts, there was a clear contract acted upon by the defendant to his detriment and from which the plaintiffs cannot be allowed to resile. . . . The promise was that so long as the defendant personally was tenant, so long would the landlords forbear to exercise the rights which they would have if he signed the lease. He did sign the lease on this promise and is therefore entitled to rely on it so long as he is personally in occupation of the shop.

NOTES
1. It was not a case based on the promissory estoppel doctrine, because it was a promise to induce a contract rather than a promise to induce an alteration to an existing contract. (See *Brikom Investments Ltd* v *Carr* [1979] QB 467, *page 159*.)
2. The collateral contract device gave more effective protection than the doctrine of promissory estoppel, since it is possible to go back on an estopped promise after giving reasonable notice of an intention to do so (*page 158*).

(c) Entire agreement clauses

The presence of an entire agreement clause will deprive a collateral warranty of its legal effect. An entire agreement clause states that the written document is intended and agreed to contain the entirety of the contract between the parties and each party acknowledges that it has not relied upon any promise or undertaking in entering into the agreement which is not expressly contained in the written document.

Inntrepreneur Pub Co. v *East Crown Ltd*
[2000] 2 Lloyd's Rep 611

The claimant sought to enforce a covenant in a lease for a public house whereby the defendant had agreed to purchase its supply of beer from the claimant. The defendant alleged a collateral warranty whereby the covenant had been released but the claimant alleged that as the lease contained an entire agreement clause, the defendant could not rely on this alleged collateral undertaking. Held: even if a collateral warranty could be established (and this had not been established on the facts), it would be deprived of legal effect by the entire agreement clause making it clear that the only agreed terms were those in the written agreement.

LIGHTMAN J:

Entire agreement clause
The purpose of an entire agreement clause is to preclude a party to a written agreement from threshing through the undergrowth and finding in the course of negotiations some (chance) remark or statement (often long forgotten or difficult to recall or explain) on which to found a claim such as the present to the existence of a collateral warranty. The entire agreement clause obviates the occasion for any such search and the peril to the contracting parties posed by the need which may arise in its absence to conduct such a search. For such a clause constitutes a binding agreement between the parties that the full contractual terms are to be found in the document containing the clause and not elsewhere, and that accordingly any promises or assurances made in the course of the negotiations (which in the absence of such a clause might have effect as a collateral warranty) shall have no contractual force, save insofar as they are reflected and given effect in that document. The operation of the clause is not to render evidence of the collateral warranty inadmissible in evidence as is suggested in *Chitty on Contract*, 28th ed., vol. 1, para. 12–102: it is to denude what would otherwise constitute a collateral warranty of legal effect.

Entire agreement clauses come in different forms. In the leading case of *Deepak* v *Imperial Chemical Industries plc* [1998] 2 Lloyd's Rep 139, affirmed [1999] 1 Lloyd's Rep 387 the clause read as follows:

10.16 Entirety of Agreement
This contract comprises the entire agreement between the PARTIES . . . and there are not any agreements, understandings, promises or conditions, oral or written, express or implied, concerning the subject matter which are not merged into this CONTRACT and superseded thereby . . .

Mr Justice Rix and the Court of Appeal held in that case (in particular focusing on the words 'promises or conditions') that this language was apt to exclude all liability for a collateral warranty. In *Alman & Benson* v *Associated Newspapers Group Ltd*, unreported, 20 June 1980 (cited by Mr Justice Rix at p. 168), Mr Justice Browne-Wilkinson reached the same conclusion where the clause provided that the written contract 'constituted the entire agreement and understanding between the parties with respect to all matters therein referred to' focusing on the word 'understanding'. In neither case was it necessary to decide whether the clause would have been sufficient if it had been worded merely to state that the agreement containing it comprised or constituted the entire agreement between the parties. That is the question raised in this case, where the formula of words used in the clause is abbreviated to an acknowledgement by the parties that the agreement constitutes the entire agreement between them. In my judgment that formula is sufficient, for it constitutes an agreement that the full contractual terms to which the parties agree to bind themselves are to be found in the agreement and nowhere else and that what might otherwise constitute a side agreement or collateral warranty shall be void of legal effect. That can be the only purpose of the provision. This view is entirely in accord with the judgment of Mr John Chadwick QC (as he then was) sitting as a deputy High Court Judge in *McGrath* v *Shah* (1987) 57 P & CR 452. . . .

It seems to me therefore that cl. 14.1 of the agreement provides in law a complete answer to any claim by Crown based on the alleged collateral warranty.

NOTES

1. In *Inntrepreneur Pub Co.* v *Sweeney* [2002] EWHC 1060, [2002] 2 EGLR 132, also discussed at *page 551*, Park J held that Lightman J's analysis of the effect of an entire agreement clause applied even where the pre-contractual statement relied upon as founding the collateral contract was clear and obvious (although on the facts any assurances were not sufficiently categorical to have created a collateral contract).

2. *Inntrepreneur* v *East Crown* was applied in *S.E.R.E. Holdings Ltd* v *Volkswagen Group UK Ltd* [2004] EWHC 1551 (Ch). The judge stating that the effect of Lightman J's decision in *East Crown* was to 'effectively rob any pre-contractual or collateral agreement of legal effect'. He added: 'I can see no reason why parties who have in fact reached an agreement in pre-contractual negotiations that would otherwise constitute a collateral contract should not subsequently agree in their formal contract that any such collateral agreement should have no legal effect, or in other words should be treated as if the parties had not intended to create legal relations; and for the reasons given by Lightman J this is precisely what an entire agreement clause on its face does'.

3. In *Exxonmobil Sales & Supply Corp* v *Texaco Ltd* [2003] EWHC 1964 (Comm), [2004] 1 All ER (Comm) 435, the judge considered that whereas an entire agreement clause defeated the argument for an implied term based on usage or custom, the same might not be true in the case of implied terms based upon business efficacy (see terms implied in fact, *page 234 below*). He stated: 'It seems to me arguable that where it is necessary to imply a term in order to make the express terms work, such an implied term may not be excluded by the entire agreement clause because it could be said that such a term is to be found in the document or documents forming part of the contract'.

(d) Reform

See the Law Commission Working Paper (1976) No. 70 and the Law Commission Report (No. 154 Cmnd 9700 (1986)), Marston [1986] CLJ 192.

B: The effect of signature

As a general rule, if a person signs a contractual document, he will be bound by its terms even if he has not read the document.

L'Estrange v *F. Graucob Ltd*
[1934] 2 KB 394 (Divisional Court)

The plaintiff bought an automatic cigarette vending machine from the defendants. She signed an order form which contained the following term in small print, 'any express or implied condition, statement or warranty, statutory or otherwise not stated herein is hereby excluded'. The defendants gave her a printed confirmation of this order. When the machine was delivered it did not work satisfactorily and the plaintiff sought damages for breach of the implied statutory term that the machine was fit for the purpose for which it was sold. The defendants sought to rely on the exemption clause, but the plaintiff argued that she had not read the order form and did not know what it contained. Held: as the plaintiff had signed the written contract and had not been induced to do so by any misrepresentation, she was bound by its terms. It was wholly immaterial that she had not read the document and did not know its contents.

> SCRUTTON LJ: . . . In cases in which the contract is contained in a railway ticket or other unsigned document, it is necessary to prove that an alleged party was aware, or ought to have been aware, of its terms and conditions. These cases have no application when the document has been signed. When a document containing contractual terms is signed, then, in the absence of fraud, or, I will add, misrepresentation, the party signing it is bound, and it is wholly immaterial whether he has read the document or not.

NOTES

1. Signature, for these purposes, includes electronic signature (see s. 7, Electronic Communications Act 2000, *page 176*).
2. Section 6(3) of the Unfair Contract Terms Act 1977 would now govern this exemption clause. The implied condition that goods are fit for the purpose can be excluded as against a person dealing otherwise than as consumer only if the exclusion satisfies the reasonableness requirement. Schedule 2(c) provides that a relevant factor in assessing reasonableness is 'whether the customer knew or ought reasonably to have known of the existence and extent of the term'.

   The Court of Appeal in *AEG (UK) Ltd* v *Logic Resource Ltd* [1996] CLC 265, *page 220 below*, has clarified the relationship between the question of whether a term has been incorporated and Sch. 2(c) of the 1977 Act. The Court made it quite clear that they are separate issues and that Sch. 2(c) addressed the actuality of the consent (viewed subjectively) for the purposes of assessing the reasonableness of the clause. However, reasonableness was an issue only once it had first been established that the clause had been validly incorporated so as to become a term of the contract.
3. If a party signs a written document, the written terms it contains will be incorporated and this includes any terms incorporated by reference, such as a set of standard terms even if the person signing has not read those standard terms. *BCT Software Solutions Ltd* v *Arnold Laver & Co Ltd* [2002] EWHC 1298, [2002] 2 All ER (Comm) 85, provides a recent illustration of this principle, although on the facts the standard terms could not be relied upon as they were inconsistent with the express terms agreed by the parties.
4. The decision in *Grogan* v *Robin Meredith Plant Hire* [1996] CLC 1127, *page 216*, makes it clear that terms in a document which is not a formation document, e.g., a time sheet, will not be incorporated by signature.
5. Scrutton LJ makes it quite clear that a person will not be bound by a signed document if the other party misrepresented its effect.

Curtis v *Chemical Cleaning & Dyeing Co.*
[1951] 1 KB 805 (CA)

The plaintiff took a white satin wedding dress to the defendants' shop to be cleaned. The shop assistant asked her to sign a 'receipt', which in fact contained a condition excluding the defendants' liability for any damage however arising. When the plaintiff asked why she had to sign, the assistant told her that the defendants would not accept liability for damage to the beads and sequins with which the dress was trimmed. The plaintiff signed. When the dress was returned it was stained. The defendants argued that the clause excluded their liability. Held: the defendants could not rely on the exemption clause because of the assistant's innocent misrepresentation which had misled the plaintiff as to the extent of the exemption and thereby induced her to sign the receipt.

DENNING LJ: In my opinion any behaviour, by words or conduct, is sufficient to be a misrepresentation if it is such as to mislead the other party about the existence or extent of the exemption. If it conveys a false impression, that is enough. If the false impression is created knowingly, it is a fraudulent misrepresentation; if it is created unwittingly, it is an innocent misrepresentation; but either is sufficient to disentitle the creator of it to the benefit of the exemption. . . . When one party puts forward a printed form for signature, failure by him to draw attention to the existence or extent of the exemption clause may in some circumstances convey the impression that there is no exemption at all, or at any rate not so wide an exemption as that which is in fact contained in the document. The present case is a good illustration. The customer said in evidence: 'When I was asked to sign the document I asked 'why? The assistant said I was to accept any responsibility for damage to beads and sequins. I did not read it all before I signed it'. In those circumstances, by failing to draw attention to the width of the exemption clause, the assistant created the false impression that the exemption only related to the beads and sequins, and that it did not extend to the material of which the dress was made. It was done perfectly innocently, but nevertheless a false impression was created.

NOTES
1. The decision of the Court of Appeal in *Interfoto Picture Library Ltd* v *Stiletto Visual Programmes Ltd* [1989] QB 433 indicates that onerous or unusual terms will need to be expressly disclosed if they are to be incorporated (*page 219*).
2. It is important to bear in mind that even if the document containing the terms has been signed, it may still be unenforceable as a result of the application of the Unfair Contract Terms Act 1977 or, in the context of consumer contracts, the Unfair Terms in Consumer Contracts Regulations 1999. (See *Chapter 7, section 5.*)

SECTION 3: ORAL CONTRACTS—INCORPORATION OF WRITTEN TERMS

A: Reasonable notice

Parker v *South Eastern Railway*
(1877) 2 CPD 416 (CA)

The plaintiff deposited his bag in the defendants' cloakroom, paid 2d and received a ticket. On the face of the ticket the words 'see back' were printed, and on the back a notice stated that the company would not be responsible for the value of any package in excess of £10. A notice containing the same condition was displayed in the cloakroom. The plaintiff's bag was lost or stolen and he claimed its value, which was more than £10. He argued that he had taken the ticket without reading it and thought it was only a receipt for 2d or evidence that the company had possession of his bag. He had not seen the notice in the cloakroom. Held: the trial judge had misdirected the jury since he had not asked them whether the defendants had taken reasonable steps to give the plaintiff notice of the condition.

MELLISH LJ: . . . The question then is, whether the plaintiff was bound by the conditions contained in the ticket. In an ordinary case, where an action is brought on a written agreement which is signed by the defendant, the agreement is proved by proving his signature, and, in the absence of fraud, it is wholly immaterial that he has not read the agreement and does not know its contents. The parties may, however, reduce their agreement into writing, so that the writing constitutes the sole evidence of the agreement, without signing it; but in that case there must be evidence independently of the agreement itself to prove that the defendant has assented to it. In that case, also, if it is proved that the defendant has assented to the writing constituting the agreement between the parties, it is, in the absence of fraud, immaterial that the defendant had not read the agreement and did not know its contents. Now if in the course of making a contract one party delivers to another a paper containing writing, and the party receiving the paper knows that the paper contains conditions which the party delivering it intends to constitute the contract, I have no doubt that the party receiving the paper does, by receiving and keeping it, assent to the conditions contained in it, although he does not read them, and does not know what they are. . . .

Now, I am of opinion that we cannot lay down, as a matter of law, either that the plaintiff was bound or that he was not bound by the conditions printed on the ticket, from the mere fact that he knew there was writing on the ticket, but did not know that the writing contained conditions. I think there may be cases in which a paper containing writing is delivered by one party to another in the course of a business transaction, where it would be quite reasonable that the party receiving it should assume that the writing contained in it no condition, and should put it in his pocket unread. For instance, if a person driving through a turnpike-gate received a ticket upon paying the toll, he might reasonably assume that the object of the ticket was that by producing it he might be free from paying toll at some other turnpike-gate, and might put it in his pocket unread. On the other hand, if a person who ships goods to be carried on a voyage by sea receives a bill of lading signed by the master, he would plainly be bound by it, although afterwards in an action against the shipowner for the loss of the goods, he might swear that he had never read the bill of lading, and that he did not know that it contained the terms of the contract of carriage, and that the shipowner was protected by the exceptions contained in it. Now the reason why the person receiving the bill of lading would be bound seems to me to be that in the great majority of cases persons shipping goods do know that the bill of lading contains the terms of the contract of carriage; and the shipowner, or the master delivering the bill of lading, is entitled to assume that the person shipping goods has that knowledge. It is, however, quite possible to suppose that a person who is neither a man of business nor a lawyer might on some particular occasion ship goods without the least knowledge of what a bill of lading was, but in my opinion such a person must bear the consequences of his own exceptional ignorance, it being plainly impossible that business could be carried on if every person who delivers a bill of lading had to stop to explain what a bill of lading was.

Now the question we have to consider is whether the railway company were entitled to assume that a person depositing luggage, and receiving a ticket in such a way that he could see that some writing was printed on it, would understand that the writing contained the conditions of contract, and this seems to me to depend upon whether people in general would in fact, and naturally, draw that inference. The railway company, as it seems to me, must be entitled to make some assumptions respecting the person who deposits luggage with them: I think they are entitled to assume that he can read, and that he understands the English language, and that he pays such attention to what he is about as may be reasonably expected from a person in such a transaction as that of depositing luggage in a cloak-room. The railway company must, however, take mankind as they find them, and if what they do is sufficient to inform people in general that the ticket contains conditions, I think that a particular plaintiff ought not to be in a better position than other persons on account of his exceptional ignorance or stupidity or carelessness. But if what the railway company do is not sufficient to convey to the minds of people in general that the ticket contains conditions, then they have received goods on deposit without obtaining the consent of the persons depositing them to the conditions limiting their liability. I am of opinion, therefore, that the proper direction to leave to the jury in these cases is, that if the person receiving the ticket did not see or know that there was any writing on the ticket, he is not bound by the conditions; that if he knew there was writing, and knew or believed that the writing contained conditions, then he is bound by the conditions; that if he knew there was writing on the ticket, but did not know or believe that the writing contained conditions, nevertheless he would be bound, if the delivering of the ticket to him in such a manner that he could see there was writing upon it, was, in the opinion of the jury, reasonable notice that the writing contained conditions.

NOTES

1. It is clear that there is no requirement that the contracting party be fully aware of what the terms state.
2. Mellish LJ refers to the fact that *the terms must be contained in or referred to in a contractual document*. If the document is a 'mere receipt' for money paid, it will not be a contractual document.

Chapelton v Barry Urban District Council
[1940] 1 KB 532 (CA)

The plaintiff wished to hire a deck chair to sit on the beach. The defendant council had left a pile of deck chairs with a notice giving the hire charge and stating that tickets were obtainable from the deck chair attendant. The notice itself contained no exempting conditions. The plaintiff obtained two chairs from the attendant and received two tickets. The plaintiff did not know that the tickets contained conditions because he simply glanced at them and put them into his pocket. In fact, on the reverse side of the ticket were the words: 'The council will not be liable for any accident or damage arising from the hire of the chair.' Due to the negligence of the defendant council, the canvas on the plaintiff's chair gave way when he sat on it. The council argued that the clause on the ticket exempted them from liability. Held: the ticket was a mere voucher or receipt. Only the notice was capable of containing conditions, and that made no mention of an exemption. Slesser LJ stressed that there was no reason why a person taking a chair should obtain the ticket at that time. They might sit on the chair for an hour or more before the attendant came for the money.

NOTES

1. In *Chapelton v Barry UDC*, the pile of deck chairs was held to constitute a standing offer so that a contract was formed when a deck chair was removed from the pile. The ticket might be obtained some time later and could not therefore be seen as a 'contractual document' because notice of any terms it contained would be given too late.
2. The fact that a document is called a 'receipt' is not conclusive.
3. In *Grogan v Robin Meredith Plant Hire* [1996] CLC 1127, the Court of Appeal held that a condition on a time sheet was not incorporated into the hire contract. The hire contract had already been made before the time sheet was signed. In addition, the signed time sheet did not vary the original contract because it was not a document which a reasonable man would expect to contain relevant contractual conditions. Auld LJ stated that documents such as a time sheet, an invoice, or a statement of account do not normally have contractual purpose as a document making or varying a contract. They are normally intended to record the performance of an existing contractual obligation rather than evidencing its terms.

As Mellish LJ makes clear in *Parker v South Eastern Railway*, it is sufficient that reasonable steps have been taken to bring the clause to the notice of people in general.

Thompson v London, Midland & Scottish Railway
[1930] 1 KB 41 (CA)

The plaintiff's excursion ticket contained a notice on its reverse side stating that it was issued subject to the conditions in the defendant company's timetables.

The timetables, which could be obtained for 6d, stated (on p. 552) that the ticket was issued subject to the condition that no action would lie against the company 'in respect of injury (fatal or otherwise) . . . however caused'. The plaintiff, who could not read, was injured when she got off the train when, due to the defendant's negligence, it was not safe to do so. She sought damages and the defendant company relied on the exemption clause. Held: the fact that the plaintiff could not read did not alter the fact that she was bound by the condition on the ticket. An indication of where a condition could be found in another document was sufficient notice of the existence of the clause so that it was validly incorporated.

NOTES
1. This particular clause would now be unenforceable as a result of the legislative regulation of exemption clauses by s. 2(1) of UCTA 1977 (*page 296*) and see also the Unfair Terms in Consumer Contracts Regulations 1999, reg. 5 and Sch. 2, para. 1(a) (*pages 319 and 320*).
2. In *O'Brien* v *MGN Ltd* [2001] EWCA Civ 1279, [2002] CLC 33, discussed at *page 26*, one issue was whether the 'Normal Mirror Group rules' as a whole had been incorporated into the scratch card contract since the rules had not been published in full in the newspaper on the relevant day (3 July, 1995). It was held that reasonable steps had been taken to achieve incorporation of the rules in a general sense since there was a reference to the rules on the face of the scratch card, the rules could be ascertained from back issues of the newspaper or on request from the offices of the newspaper. This case further illustrates that it is sufficient that the terms are contained in a separate document as long as there is sufficient reference to it. (The question of whether there had been sufficient incorporation of rule 5 is discussed at *page 224*.)

Before or at the time of contracting

In *Olley* v *Marlborough Court Ltd* [1949] 1 KB 532, a contract was made at a hotel reception desk. In the hotel room upstairs there was a notice excluding the hotel's responsibility for articles lost or stolen unless they were deposited for safe custody. When the plaintiff's furs and jewellery were stolen she brought an action for damages against the hotel. The Court of Appeal held that since the contract was made at the reception desk, the terms of the notice in the bedroom came too late and were not incorporated.

Thornton v Shoe Lane Parking Ltd
[1971] 2 QB 163 (CA)

The plaintiff went to park his car in the defendants' automatic car park. A notice at the entrance to the car park gave details of the charges and stated that all cars were 'parked at owner's risk'. When a car was driven up to it, a machine dispensed a ticket. The plaintiff took the ticket which gave the car's time of arrival and stated in small print that it was 'issued subject to conditions displayed on the premises'. Inside the car park there was a notice which stated, *inter alia*, that the defendants would not be liable for any injury to customers which occurred when their cars were on the premises. The plaintiff was injured in the car park, and in a negligence action the defendants relied on the exemption in the ticket. Held: the ticket came too late since the contract was concluded when the motorist drove up to the machine. The ticket exemption was the only one wide enough to exempt from liability for personal injury.

LORD DENNING MR: . . . [T]he company seek by this condition to exempt themselves from liability, not only for damage to the car, but also for injury to the customer howsoever caused. The condition talks about insurance. It is well known that the customer is usually insured against damage to the car. But he is not insured against damage to himself. If the condition is incorporated into the contract of parking, it means that Mr Thornton will be unable to recover any damages for his personal injuries which were caused by the negligence of the company.

We have been referred to the ticket cases of former times from *Parker* v *South Eastern Railway Co.* (1877) 2 CPD 416 to *McCutcheon* v *David MacBrayne Ltd* [1964] 1 WLR 125. They were concerned with railways, steamships and cloakrooms where booking clerks issued tickets to customers who took them away without reading them. In those cases the issue of the ticket was regarded as an *offer* by the company. If the customer took it and retained it without objection, his act was regarded as an acceptance of the offer: see *Watkins* v *Rymill* (1833) 10 QBD 178, 188 and *Thompson* v *London, Midland and Scottish Railway Co.* [1930] 1 KB 41, 47. These cases were based on the theory that the customer, on being handed the ticket, could refuse it and decline to enter into a contract on those terms. He could ask for his money back. That theory was, of course, a fiction. No customer in a thousand ever read the conditions. If he had stopped to do so, he would have missed the train or the boat.

None of those cases has any application to a ticket which is issued by an automatic machine. The customer pays his money and gets a ticket. He cannot refuse it. He cannot get his money back. He may protest to the machine, even swear at it. But it will remain unmoved. He is committed beyond recall. He was committed at the very moment when he put his money into the machine. The contract was concluded at that time. It can be translated into offer and acceptance in this way: the offer is made when the proprietor of the machine holds it out as being ready to receive the money. The acceptance takes place when the customer puts his money into the slot. The terms of the offer are contained in the notice placed on or near the machine stating what is offered for the money. The customer is bound by those terms as long as they are sufficiently brought to his notice before-hand, but not otherwise. He is not bound by the terms printed on the ticket if they differ from the notice, because the ticket comes too late. The contract has already been made: see *Olley* v *Marlborough Court Ltd* [1949] 1 KB 532. The ticket is no more than a voucher or receipt for the money that has been paid (as in the deckchair case, *Chapelton* v *Barry Urban District Council* [1940] 1 KB 532) on terms which have been offered and accepted before the ticket is issued.

In the present case the offer was contained in the notice at the entrance giving the charges for garaging and saying 'at owner's risk,' i.e., at the risk of the owner so far as damage to the car was concerned. The offer was accepted when Mr Thornton drove up to the entrance and, by the movement of his car, turned the light from red to green, and the ticket was thrust at him. The contract was then concluded, and it could not be altered by any words printed on the ticket itself. In particular, it could not be altered so as to exempt the company from liability for personal injury due to their negligence.

NOTES

1. Lord Denning thought it was possible to declare a clause void for unreasonableness. However, it was generally considered that there was no such doctrine at common law.

2. Lord Denning's judgment sets out the process of offer and acceptance in ticket cases (which is based on a fiction) and the process of offer and acceptances using automatic machines.

   Automatic machines have altered over the years, and it is now possible to purchase a railway ticket from such a machine. If I buy a ticket at Paddington station to travel to Cardiff, is the offer and acceptance position different depending on whether I buy my ticket from the automatic machine or the ticket office?

3. Another controversial statement made by Lord Denning was that the clause exempting from personal injury was too wide and took away important rights. He suggested that in such cases the clause would need explicitly to be drawn to the car park user's attention.

Interfoto Picture Library Ltd v ***Stiletto Visual Programmes Ltd***
[1989] QB 433 (CA)

The defendants ordered photographic transparencies from the plaintiffs. The transparencies were sent packed in a bag with a delivery note. This delivery note stated that the transparencies had to be returned by 19 March and that a holding fee of £5 per day plus VAT would be charged for each day they were retained beyond that. The defendants did not use the transparencies and completely forgot about them. They were eventually returned on 2 April. The plaintiffs sent an invoice for £3,783.50 (the holding charge per transparency per day from 19 March to 2 April). The defendants refused to pay. Held: if the condition is a particularly onerous or unusual one which would not generally be known to the other party, then the party seeking to enforce it had to show that it had fairly and reasonably been brought to the other party's attention. Condition 2 was unreasonable and extortionate, and the plaintiffs had not brought it to the attention of the defendants. Instead, the plaintiffs were entitled to an award of £3.50 per transparency per week.

DILLON LJ: . . . The question is therefore whether condition 2 was sufficiently brought to the defendants' attention to make it a term of the contract which was only concluded after the defendants had received, and must have known that they had received the transparencies *and* the delivery note.

This sort of question was posed, in relation to printed conditions, in the ticket cases, such *Parker* v *South Eastern Rly Co* (1877) 2 CPD 416, in the last century. At that stage the printed conditions were looked at as a whole and the question considered by the courts was whether the printed conditions as a whole had been sufficiently drawn to a customer's attention to make the whole set of conditions part of the contract; if so the customer was bound by the printed conditions even though he never read them.

More recently the question has been discussed whether it is enough to look at a set of printed conditions as a whole. When for instance one condition in a set is particularly onerous does something special need to be done to draw customers' attention to that particular condition? In an obiter dictum in *J. Spurling Ltd* v *Bradshaw* [1956] 1 WLR 461, 466 (cited in *Chitty on Contracts*, 25th ed. 1983) vol 1, (p. 408) Denning LJ stated:

> Some clauses which I have seen would need to be printed in red ink on the face of the document with a red hand pointing to it before the notice could be held to be sufficient.

Then in *Thornton* v *Shoe Lane Parking Ltd* [1971] 2 QB 163 both Lord Denning MR and Megaw LJ held as one of their grounds of decision, as I read their judgments, that where a condition is particularly onerous or unusual the party seeking to enforce it must show that that condition, or an unusual condition of that particular nature, was fairly brought to the notice of the other party. Lord Denning MR, at pp. 169H–170D, restated and applied what he had said in the *Spurling* case, and held that the court should not hold any man bound by such a condition unless it was drawn to his attention in the most explicit way . . .

At the time of the ticket cases in the last century it was notorious that people hardly ever troubled to read printed conditions on a ticket or delivery note or similar document. That remains the case now. In the intervening years the printed conditions have tended to become more and more complicated and more and more one-sided in favour of the party who is imposing them, but the other parties, if they notice that there are printed conditions at all, generally still tend to assume that such conditions are only concerned with ancillary matters of form and are not of importance. In the ticket cases the courts held that the common law required that reasonable steps be taken to draw the other parties' attention to the printed conditions or they would not be part of the contract. It is, in my judgment, a logical development of the common law into modern conditions that it should be held, as it was in *Thornton* v *Shoe Lane Parking Ltd* [1971] 2 QB 163, that, if one condition in a set of printed conditions is particularly onerous or unusual, the party seeking to enforce it must show that that particular condition was fairly brought to the attention of the other party.

In the present case, nothing whatever was done by the plaintiffs to draw the defendants' attention particularly to condition 2; it was merely one of four columns' width of conditions printed across the foot of the delivery note. Consequently condition 2 never, in my judgment, became part of the contract between the parties.

■ QUESTION

Was this condition invalid as a penalty? (See *page 414*.)

NOTES
1. It is difficult to see why such a rule affecting incorporation is needed in the light of the protection provided by the Unfair Contract Terms Act 1977 and the Unfair Terms in Consumer Contracts Regulations 1999.
2. The difficulty resulting from *Interfoto* v *Stiletto* is how to decide whether a clause is onerous or unreasonable.

AEG (UK) Ltd v Logic Resource Ltd
[1996] CLC 265 (CA)

This case concerned a clause in a sale contract whereby the purchaser was to return defective goods at his own expense. The majority of the Court of Appeal (Hirst and Waite LJJ) held that the clause was onerous as it imposed the costs of returning the goods on the buyer. It was also held to be unusual on the basis that the majority did not regard it as a standard or common term. Applying the test in *Interfoto*, the existence of the clause had not fairly and reasonably been brought to the defendant's attention and was therefore not incorporated.

However, Hobhouse LJ delivered a strong dissenting judgment on this issue, distinguishing *Interfoto*:

HOBHOUSE LJ (dissenting): The point on which the plaintiffs have to rely . . . is that to be found in the *Interfoto* case. The judgment of Dillon LJ in the report at [1989] 1 QB 433, sets out the historical background to their decision. It includes references to *Parker* v *South Eastern Railway Co.* and to the colourful dictum of Denning LJ in *Spurling* v *Bradshaw* [1956] 1 WLR 461 at p. 466, where he postulated that in certain circumstances a red hand might have to be used in order to draw a clause sufficiently to the notice of the other party.

The main authority upon which Dillon LJ and Bingham LJ founded was *Thornton* v *Shoe Lane Parking Ltd* [1971] 2 QB 163, and in particular the judgment of Megaw LJ in the passage which starts at p. 172 of the report . . . I will re-read two short quotations from what Dillon LJ chose to quote (p. 437F):

'But at least where the particular condition relied on involves a sort of restriction that is not shown to be usual in that class of contract, a defendant must show that his intention to attach an unusual condition *of that particular nature* was fairly brought to the notice of the other party. How much is required as being, in the words of Mellish LJ, [in *Parker* v *South Eastern Railway Co.*] 2 CPD 416, 424, "reasonably sufficient to give the plaintiff notice of the condition," depends upon the nature of the restrictive condition.'

Then, having referred to the attempt to exclude liability for personal injuries under the Occupiers Liability Act, the second quote begins at p. 438B:

'In my view, however, before it can be said that a condition of that sort, restrictive of statutory rights, has been fairly brought to the notice of a party to a contract there must be some clear indication which would lead an ordinary sensible person to realise, at or before the time of making the contract, that a term of that sort, relating to personal injury, was sought to be included.'

The emphasis in those passages which were quoted was to the 'sort' of provision. This was directly germane to the *Interfoto Picture* case where what was fairly described as an extortionate stipulation was introduced which imposed a wholly excessive and unexpected collateral financial obligation upon the hirer in a certain situation. It was a sort of clause that no one would expect to find in the standard terms which were being referred to. . . .

The clause which we are concerned with here is cl. 7. It is a clause which covers a topic which is commonly, and indeed normally, dealt with in the standard conditions of sellers of goods. It is in no way unusual nor is it suggested that it is unusual for standard conditions in some way to qualify the obligations of the sellers under a contract of sale. Nor is it suggested that it is unusual for such clauses to include warranty conditions, which have a limited effect both in time and obligation. In my judgment, the clauses which we find in cl. 7 deal with a topic which one would expect to be dealt with in the conditions of sale of a supplier of manufactured goods and they cover the type of points which would commonly be dealt with.

The problem in the present case arises from the fact that these clauses have been unreasonably drafted. As is almost inevitable in printed standard terms, they are not related to the particular circumstances of the case and, furthermore, they stipulate for a greater protection of the seller than is reasonable, or anyway is reasonable without some special justification. In my judgment, and this is where I part company from Hirst and Waite LJJ, it is necessary before excluding the incorporation of a clause in limine to consider the type of clause it is. Is it a clause of the type which you would expect to find in the printed conditions? If it is, then it is only in the most exceptional circumstances that a party will be able to say that it was not adequately brought to his notice by standard words of incorporation. If a party wishes to find out precisely how a clause of a normal sort has been worded, he should ask for the actual text of the clause. This case is not analogous to either of the two cases upon which the appellant founds. The *Interfoto* case involved an extortionate clause which did not relate directly to the expected rights and obligations of the parties. In the *Shoe Lane Parking* case, it related to personal injuries and the state of the premises and not to the subject matter of the car parking contract, which would, in the view of the Court of Appeal, have been concerned with damage to property.

Therefore, in my judgment, it is necessary to consider the type of clause, and only if it is a type of clause which it is not to be expected will be found in the printed conditions referred to then to go on to question its incorporation. These conditions do include clauses which, in my judgment, do fall foul of the *Interfoto* principle, but I do not consider that cl. 7 comes into that category. In my judgment, it is desirable as a matter of principle to keep what was said in the *Interfoto* case within its proper bounds. A wide range of clauses are commonly incorporated into contracts by general words. If it is to be the policy of English law that in every case those clauses are to be gone through with, in effect, a toothcomb to see whether they were entirely usual and entirely desirable in the particular contract, then one is completely distorting the contractual relationship between the parties and the ordinary mechanisms of making contracts. It will introduce uncertainty into the law of contract.

In the past there may have been a tendency to introduce more strict criteria but this is no longer necessary in view of the Unfair Contract Terms Act. The reasonableness of clauses is the subject matter of the Unfair Contract Terms Act and it is under the provisions of that Act that problems of unreasonable clauses should be addressed and the solution found. In the present case, it is my opinion that the Act provides the answer to the question which has been raised.

■ QUESTIONS

1. Is the approach of the majority tantamount to assessing whether this was a reasonable term to include? See Bradgate, 'Unreasonable Standard Terms' (1997) 60 MLR 582.

2. Do you agree with Hobhouse LJ that the *Interfoto* rule causes uncertainty and is no longer required in the light of UCTA 1977 and the Unfair Terms in Consumer Contracts Regulations 1999? (See *Chapter 7, section 5.*)

3. Is it sufficient that the clause in question should be onerous *or* unusual or does the clause need to be both onerous *and* unusual for the higher standard of incorporation to apply? In *HIH Casualty & General Insurance Ltd* v *New Hampshire Insurance Co* [2001] EWCA Civ 735, [2001] 2 Lloyd's Rep 161, Rix LJ (with whose judgment Mummery and Peter Gibson LJJ agreed), at [211] stated that the requirement for a higher standard of incorporation was not satisfied simply because the term was unusual; the term in question would *also* need to be 'onerous, unreasonable and extortionate'. This issue appears to be linked to the question of whether the type of clause or the particular clause needs to be onerous or unusual. If it is the type of clause which is examined for these purposes, it is not unusual for certain types of clauses to appear in contracts although the particular clause in question might be a particularly onerous version of this type of term. On the other hand, if it is accepted that it is the particular clause which is assessed, then either requirement ought to be sufficient to attract the need for the higher standard of incorporation. (See the decision of the Court of Appeal in *Ocean Chemical Transport*, below.)

In *AEG (UK) Ltd* v *Logic Resource Ltd*, the majority of the Court of Appeal considered that it was the particular clause in the context of its use which needed to be onerous or unusual, whereas Hobhouse LJ (dissenting) considered that the type of clause needed to be onerous or unusual. Since Hobhouse LJ considered that the type of clause was not unusual, the higher standard was not required. The approach adopted by Hobhouse LJ would restrict the operation of the *Interfoto* principle. However, in *Ocean Chemical Transport* it was confirmed that it is the meaning and effect of the *particular clause* that must be onerous or unusual, rather than clauses of that general type.

Ocean Chemical Transport Inc v *Exnor Craggs Ltd*
[2000] 1 All ER (Comm) 519, [2000] 1 Lloyd's Rep 446 (CA)

The case concerned the purchase of bunkers by an American company. Clause 10 of the contract provided that 'all liability whatsoever on [the seller's] part shall cease unless suit is brought within six months after delivery of the goods or the date when the goods should have been delivered'. The bunkers were supplied and 17 months later it was alleged that the seller had not paid the original supplier for the bunkers and the vessel to which they had been supplied was arrested in Egypt. The buyer paid for the release of the vessel and then sought to claim damages for breach of contract against the seller. The judge applied clause 10 and held that the claim was time-barred. One of the issues on appeal was whether the seller had taken sufficient steps to bring this clause to the attention of the buyer given that no prominence had been given to it. The judge had considered the clause in a general sense as a clause which sought to prevent claims being brought after a specified period and concluded that the clause in question was therefore neither onerous nor unusual. Counsel argued that the correct approach was to examine the particular clause and the specific circumstances of the case. On appeal held (dismissing the appeal): that on the assumption that clause 10 was capable of being construed as onerous or unusual, the *Interfoto* test applied and the seller had a duty to bring the existence of the clause to the notice of the buyer. On the facts the duty had been discharged because there had been an express acknowledgement of the existence of the terms.

> EVANS LJ (with whose judgment Henry and Waller LJJ agreed): With regard to incorporation, [counsel for the buyer] referred us to the authorities which were also referred to by the judge; in particular, to the fact that in the *Interfoto* case, different reasons for reaching the same conclusion were given by Dillon LJ on the one hand and by Bingham LJ on the other hand. The former concluded that the clause was not incorporated in the contract; the latter that, although incorporated, the clause should not be given effect to in the circumstances of the case. Where the two judgments are at one is in upholding the approach which is summarised in the passage from Chitty [*Chitty on Contracts* (28th edn, 1999) vol. I, p. 590, para. 12–015 as follows:
>
> > *Onerous or unusual terms*. Although the party receiving the document knows it contains conditions, if the particular condition relied on is one which is a particularly onerous or unusual term, or is one which involves the abrogation of a right given by statute, the party tendering the document must show that it has been brought fairly and reasonably to the other's attention. 'Some clauses which I have seen,' said Denning LJ, 'would need to be printed in red ink on the face of the document with a red hand pointing to it before the notice could be held to be sufficient.']
>
> With regard to the judgments in the *AEG* case, [counsel] showed us that the majority held that, in applying the test of incorporation as set out in *Chitty*, it was appropriate to consider what may be called, for short, the construction and effect of the particular clause. That appears specifically in the judgment of Hirst LJ ([1996] CLC 265 at 273). On the other hand, Hobhouse LJ, who dissented, held that the proper approach was to consider what kind of clause was in issue, and then to decide whether sufficient steps had been taken to bring the existence of that kind of clause to the notice of the other party and also to decide whether the particular clause was onerous or unusual by reference to the kind of clause that it was. It was wrong, he said, to apply that test to the specific terms of the clause in question. As he pointed out ([1996] CLC 265 at 277 and following) that was a case where difficulties arose because the clauses, which were not of an unusual kind, were unreasonably drafted. He thought that to concentrate upon the precise meaning of the particular clause in question meant that ([1996] CLC 265 at 277):
>
> > . . . one is completely distorting the contractual relationship between the parties and the ordinary mechanisms of making contracts. It will introduce uncertainty into the law of . contract.
>
> [Counsel] emphasised that diversity of view because in the present case the learned judge referred to the judgment of Hobhouse LJ with approval and it was that which had led him, [counsel] submitted, to consider not so much the effect of this particular clause as simply the kind of clause which it was.
>
> . . . It seems to me that the question of incorporation must always depend upon the meaning and effect of the clause in question. It may be that the type of clause is relevant. It may mean that the effect of the particular clause in the particular case is relevant. That, of course, was the division of opinion in the *AEG* case. But whichever it is, applying that test in the present case, the first stage is to ask what type of clause cl 10 is. It is a clause which has the effect of a time-bar clause which excludes liability after a certain period has passed. [Counsel] does not submit, as I understand it, that that type of clause could properly be regarded as either onerous or even unusual in a contract of this kind. But, assuming in his favour that it is necessary to apply the majority test in the *AEG* case, then the question arises whether this clause, which provides a six-month time limit, can justify either of those adjectives. Then the preliminary question, which was decided by the learned judge as his first ground of decision, was that the authorities are of doubtful application in a case such as the present where there was an express acknowledgement in the contractual documents that the terms and conditions in question were incorporated.
>
> [Counsel] submits that the *Interfoto* test, as he called it, has to be applied, even in a case where the other party has signed an acknowledgement of the terms and conditions and their incorporation. It seems to me that [counsel] could be right in what might be regarded as an extreme case,

where a signature was obtained under pressure of time or other circumstances, and where it was possible to satisfy the *Interfoto* test; that is to say, that the clause was one which was particularly onerous or unusual for incorporation in the contract in question. I would prefer to put the matter more broadly and to say that the question is whether the defendants have discharged the duty which lies upon them of bringing the existence of the clause upon which they rely (and, if [counsel] is right, of the effect of that particular clause) to the notice of the other party in the circumstances of the particular case.

As I have indicated, in some extreme circumstances, even a signature might not be enough. On the other hand, in the present case there was an express acknowledgement. It seems to me that, given the nature of this term and condition and its effect, as relied upon by the respondents, it cannot be said that the respondents failed in their duty to bring the existence of that term to the notice of the buyers, through, of course, their agents, to whom the term had been long available for their perusal. [Counsel] does not hesitate to submit that the clause in question should have had, as he puts it, the red hand approach. I would doubt very much whether that is practical in the context of a commercial contract such as this. In my view, the respondents did, in this particular case, where there was an express acknowledgement of the existence of the terms, certainly discharge their duty of bringing it sufficiently to the notice of the buyers for the clause to form part of the contract. That makes it unnecessary to make any explicit findings, as the learned judge did, as to whether this clause was properly to be regarded as onerous or unusual; but, as I have already indicated, I have taken account of the effect of this clause in reaching the conclusion which I have already stated. It seems to me that there is in fact no evidence which supports the proposition that this clause is in any way extreme or totally unexpected to be found in a contract such as this.

NOTES

1. See MacDonald [1999] CLJ 413.
2. The judgment of Evans LJ contains a broad formulation of the *Interfoto* requirement in which a duty is imposed to bring the existence of the clause to the other's attention in the circumstances of the case. This is little more than the test in *Parker* v *SE Railway* and does not indicate precisely what will be required in individual instances.
3. In *O'Brien* v *MGN Ltd* [2001] EWCA Civ 1279, [2002] CLC 33, *page 26*, the critical question was whether rule 5 of the newspaper's rules was an unusual or onerous term so that the *Interfoto* test of incorporation applied. Rule 5 provided that 'should more prizes be claimed than are available in any prize category . . ., a simple draw will take place for the prize'. The claimant alleged that the effect of this term was to 'turn winners into losers'. The majority of the Court of Appeal considered that this rule was not onerous or unusual (whereas Evans LJ considered that it did require greater prominence but was not prepared to interfere with a finding of fact by the judge at first instance).

HALE LJ . . (with whose judgment Potter LJ agreed): . . .

19 In my view the judge was right to hold that the contract was made on 3 July. The offer was contained in the paper that day. In my view it was accepted when the claimant telephoned to claim his prize. The offer and therefore the contract clearly incorporated the term 'Normal Mirror Group rules apply'. The words were there to be read and it makes no difference whether or not the claimant actually read or paid attention to them.

20 The question, therefore, is whether those words, in the circumstances, were enough to incorporate the rules, including r. 5, into the contract. In the words of Bingham LJ in *Interfoto Library* v *Stiletto* [1989] QB 433 at p. 445E, can the defendant 'be said fairly and reasonably to have brought [those rules] to the notice of the claimant?' This is a question of fact. It is clear from the passage in the same judgment quoted earlier (at para. 13) that one has to look at the particular contract made on the particular day between the particular parties. But what is fair and reasonable notice will depend upon the nature of the transaction and upon the nature of the term. As Dillon LJ summed it up in *Interfoto* at pp. 438H–439A:

'In the ticket cases the courts held that the common law required that reasonable steps be taken to draw the other parties' attention to the printed conditions or they would not be part of the contract. It is, in my judgment, a logical development of the common law into modern conditions that it should be held, as it was in *Thornton* v *Shoe Lane Parking Ltd* [1971] 2 QB 163, that if one condition in a set of printed conditions is particularly onerous or unusual, the party seeking to enforce it must show that that particular condition was fairly brought to the attention of the other party.'

Bingham LJ put the same point in this way at p. 443C:

'what would be good notice of one condition would not be good notice of another. The reason is that the more outlandish the clause the greater the notice which the other party, if he is to be bound, must in all fairness be given.'

21 In my view, although r. 5 does turn an apparent winner into a loser, it cannot by any normal use of language be called 'onerous' or 'outlandish'. It does not impose any extra burden upon the claimant, unlike the clause in *Interfoto*. It does not seek to absolve the defendant from liability for personal injuries negligently caused, unlike the clause in *Thornton* v *Shoe Lane Parking*. It merely deprives the claimant of a windfall for which he has done very little in return. He bought two newspapers, although in fact he could have acquired a card and discovered the hotline number without doing either. He made a call to a premium rate number, which will have cost him some money and gained the newspaper some, but only a matter of pennies, not pounds.

22 The more difficult question is whether the rule is 'unusual' in this context. The judge found that the claimant knew that there was a limit on the number of prizes and that there were relevant rules. Miss Platell's evidence [for the defendant] was that these games and competitions always have rules. Indeed I would accept that this is common knowledge. This is not a situation in which players of the game would assume that the newspaper bore the risk of any mistake of any kind which might lead to more people making a claim than had been intended. Some people might assume that the 'get out' rule would provide for the prize to be shared amongst the claimants. Some might assume that it would provide for the drawing of lots. In the case of a single prize some might think drawing lots more appropriate; but it seems to me impossible to say that either solution would be 'unusual'. There is simply no evidence to that effect. Such evidence as there is was to the effect that such rules are not unusual.

23 In any event, the words 'onerous or unusual' are not terms of art. They are simply one way of putting the general proposition that reasonable steps must be taken to draw the particular term in question to the notice of those who are to be bound by it and that more is required in relation to certain terms than to others depending on their effect. In the particular context of this particular game, I consider that the defendants did just enough to bring the rules to the claimant's attention. There was a clear reference to rules on the face of the card he used. There was a clear reference to rules in the paper containing the offer of a telephone prize. There was evidence that those rules could be discovered either from the newspaper offices or from back issues of the paper. The claimant had been able to discover them when the problem arose.

24 The judge had 'great sympathy for Mr O'Brien who struck me as a thoroughly decent young man who must have suffered a cruel disappointment when his hopes were raised only to be dashed'. There can be little sympathy for a newspaper which introduces such a game to attract publicity and readers, and then devotes space which could have been devoted to printing the rules to hyperbole about the prizes to be won and the people who have won them. But the fact of the matter is that there was nothing at all outlandish about the rules of this game and indeed it would have been surprising if there had been no protection on the lines of r. 5. I would dismiss this appeal.

SIR ANTHONY EVANS LJ:

25 I agree that the appeal should be dismissed, but I do so for one reason only. I feel constrained to accept [counsel for the respondents'] final submission, that this court should not interfere with the judge's finding on an issue of fact, unless the finding is clearly wrong. The issue is whether the respondents took reasonable steps to draw the particular term to the notice of those who are to be bound by it (quoting from the judgment of Hale LJ, para. 23).

26 The words 'Normal Mirror Group rules apply' clearly formed part of the contract. Unless it was established that the claimant had actual knowledge of r. 5, which it was not, it is immaterial in my judgment that he had had the opportunity to read it on previous occasions, or was aware from the earlier editions of the newspapers that some rules did exist. If those matters were relevant, it would mean that whether he was bound by it would itself be a matter of chance in the individual case.

27 There was no obvious reason why the rules could not appear in every edition which offered tickets for the game, except as Hale LJ has said the editor's wish to use the space for publishing hyperbole about the prizes to be won and the people who had won them. The reference to the rules could have been accompanied by some indication of where they had been printed or could be found, for example 'last Friday's copy' or 'published on' a particular weekday. Instead, on Monday 3 July the only publication in the Daily Mirror during the previous month had been on 10 June and 30 June. A person reading the offer on 3 July could not be expected to have ready access to back issues, even if he or she knew what date to look for. Whether the reader could discover what the rules were was left essentially as a matter of chance. The promise of significant riches, in my judgment, deserves more.

28 I would also have considered that a rule which gave the 'winner' no more than a further chance to obtain the prize was sufficiently onerous, if not unusual, to require greater prominence than was given to this one. This, in my judgment, was the strength of [Counsel's] main submission.

29 However, the judge concluded differently, and my colleagues agree with him. I cannot say that he was clearly wrong, and so reluctantly, I must agree that the appeal should be dismissed.

NOTE: This case provides a further useful illustration of the divergence of opinion that can exist on this question of whether a term is onerous or unusual.

B: Course of dealing

Incorporation by this method is not easy to establish because of the requirement that it be a *consistent* course of dealing.

McCutcheon v *David MacBrayne Ltd*
[1964] 1 WLR 125 (HL)

The respondents carried goods by sea from the western Isles of Scotland to the mainland. The appellant asked his brother-in-law, McSporran, to arrange for the appellant's car to be shipped to the mainland. The usual practice of the respondents was to ask customers to sign a risk note by which they agreed to be bound by the conditions printed on it. The conditions included a statement that the goods were shipped at the owner's risk. On this occasion the risk note had been made out but McSporran had not been asked to sign it. McSporran had shipped goods in a similar manner on previous occasions. He had sometimes signed risk notes but had never read the conditions. The ship sank due to the negligence of the respondents and the car was lost. The respondents argued that the exclusion clause on the risk note was incorporated by reason of the previous dealings. Held: there was no consistent course of dealing by which the clause could have been incorporated. Lords Pearce,

Hodson, and Guest considered that this was because the pattern of dealings was inconsistent; the past dealings had all involved written terms (incorporation via signing the risk note), whereas this contract was entirely oral. Lord Reid considered that there was no need for the present transaction to be consistent in this sense with the previous transactions. However, it was inconsistent because on some occasions McSporran had been asked to sign the risk note and on others he had not.

> LORD REID: . . . The only other ground on which it would seem possible to import these conditions is that based on a course of dealing. If two parties have made a series of similar contracts each containing certain conditions, and then they make another without expressly referring to those conditions it may be that those conditions ought to be implied. If the officious bystander had asked them whether they had intended to leave out the conditions this time, both must, as honest men, have said 'of course not'. But again the facts here will not support that ground. According to Mr McSporran, there had been no constant course of dealing; sometimes he was asked to sign and sometimes not. And, moreover, he did not know what the conditions were. This time he was offered an oral contract without any reference to conditions, and he accepted the offer in good faith. . . .
>
> > The judicial task is not to discover the actual intentions of each party: it is to decide what each was reasonably entitled to conclude from the attitude of the other. (Gloag on Contract, 2nd ed., p. 7)
>
> In this case I do not think that either party was reasonably bound or entitled to conclude from the attitude of the other, as known to him, that these conditions were intended by the other party to be part of this contract.

NOTES
1. The reasoning of Lord Reid has been accepted as correct. The approach taken by Lords Pearce, Hodson, and Guest has been criticised as taking 'consistency too far'.
2. In *Petrotrade Inc* v *Texaco Ltd* [2000] CLC 1,341 the commercial contract had been concluded by telephone before the telex was sent which specified the terms and conditions. The Court of Appeal held that these terms were incorporated on the basis of the previous dealings between the parties since over a 13-month period prior to this contract there had been five other contracts between the parties for the sale of the same or similar products.
3. However, it is very difficult to establish a consistent course of dealing where the terms in question are being relied upon as against a consumer. In *Hollier* v *Rambler Motors (AMC) Ltd* [1972] 2 QB 71 (*page 276*), the plaintiff (consumer) had had his car repaired at the defendants' garage on three or four occasions over a five-year period. On at least two of these occasions he had signed a form containing an exemption clause which he had not read. The Court of Appeal held that this was not a sufficient course of dealing for the clause to be incorporated.
   Hollier v *Rambler Motors* can be contrasted with the decision in the following case.

Henry Kendall & Sons v William Lillico & Sons Ltd
(Appeals from *Hardwick Game Farm* v *Suffolk Agricultural Poultry Producers Association*)
[1969] 2 AC 31 (HL)

The sellers had sold goods to the buyers under an oral contract. The next day the sellers had sent the buyers a 'sold note' containing a clause stating that the buyer took responsibility for latent defects in the goods. There had been three or four transactions a month between the parties over a three-year period using the same 'note', although the buyers never read the clause. Held: the clause did not cover the breach. However, *obiter*, it was found to have been validly incorporated by a consistent course of dealing (the buyers had received well over 100 sold notes containing the condition). *McCutcheon* v *David MacBrayne* was distinguished on the ground that in all the transactions in *Kendall* v *Lillico*, the same document had been sent.

NOTE: In *Hollier* v *Rambler Motors*, Salmon LJ had distinguished *Kendall* v *Lillico* with the following comment:

> That case is obviously very different from the present case. The *Hardwick Game Farm* case seems to be a typical case where a consistent course of dealing between the parties makes it imperative for the court to read into the contract the condition for which the sellers were contending. Everything that the buyer had done, or failed to do, would have convinced any ordinary seller that the buyer was agreeing to the terms in question. The fact that the buyer had not read the term is beside the point. The seller could not be expected to know that the buyer had not troubled to acquaint himself with what was written in the form that had been sent to him so often, year in and year out during the previous three years, in transactions exactly the same as the transaction then in question.

C: Common understanding of the parties

British Crane Hire Corporation v Ipswich Plant Hire Ltd
[1975] QB 303 (CA)

Both the plaintiffs and the defendants hired out heavy earth-moving equipment. The defendants hired a dragline crane by telephone from the plaintiffs. After delivery the plaintiffs sent the defendants a printed form setting out the conditions of hire, which were similar to those used by all plant-hiring firms and which stated that the defendants were liable to indemnify the plaintiffs against all expenses in connection with the use of the crane. Before this form was signed by the defendants, the crane sank in marshy ground. The plaintiffs sought to recover the cost of the crane, and the defendants claimed that the conditions had not been incorporated. Held: the defendants knew that printed conditions in similar terms to the plaintiffs' were in common use in the business, and the plaintiffs were therefore entitled to conclude that the defendants were accepting the crane on the terms in their conditions.

LORD DENNING MR: In support of the course of dealing, the plaintiffs relied on two previous transactions in which the defendants had hired cranes from the plaintiffs. One was February 20, 1969; and the other October 6, 1969. Each was on a printed form which set out the hiring of a crane, the price, the site, and so forth; and also setting out the conditions the same as those here. There were thus only two transactions many months before and they were not known to the defendants' manager who ordered this crane. In the circumstances I doubt whether those two would be sufficient to show a course of dealing.

In *Hollier* v *Rambler Motors (AMC) Ltd* [1972] 2 QB 71, 76, Salmon LJ said he knew of no case

> in which it has been decided or even argued that a term could be implied into an oral contract on the strength of a course of dealing (if it can be so called) which consisted at the most of three or four transactions over a period of five years.

That was a case of a private individual who had had his car repaired by the defendants and had signed forms with conditions on three or four occasions. The plaintiff there was not of equal bargaining power with the garage company which repaired the car. The conditions were not incorporated.

But here the parties were both in the trade and were of equal bargaining power. Each was a firm of plant hirers who hired out plant. The defendants themselves knew that firms in the plant-hiring trade always imposed conditions in regard to the hiring of plant: and that their conditions were on much the same lines. The defendants' manager, Mr Turner (who knew the crane), was asked about it. He agreed that he had seen these conditions or similar ones in regard to the hiring of plant. He said that most of them were, to one extent or another, variations of a form which he called 'the Contractors'

Plant Association form'. The defendants themselves (when they let out cranes) used the conditions of that form. The conditions on the plaintiffs' form were in rather different words, but nevertheless to much the same effect. . . .

From that evidence it is clear that both parties knew quite well that conditions were habitually imposed by the supplier of these machines: and both parties knew the substance of those conditions. In particular that if the crane sank in soft ground it was the hirer's job to recover it: and that there was an indemnity clause. In these circumstances, I think the conditions on the form should be regarded as incorporated into the contract. I would not put it so much on the course of dealing, but rather on the common understanding which is to be derived from the conduct of the parties, namely, that the hiring was to be on the terms of the plaintiffs' usual conditions. . . .

It seems to me that, in view of the relationship of the parties, when the defendants requested this crane urgently and it was supplied at once—before the usual form was received—the plaintiffs were entitled to conclude that the defendants were accepting it on the terms of the plaintiffs' own printed conditions—which would follow in a day or two. It is just as if the plaintiffs had said: 'We will supply it on our usual conditions', and the defendants said 'Of course, that is quite understood'.

■ QUESTIONS

1. Considerable stress was put on the fact that this was not a case involving business reliance on a clause against a consumer. The knowledge of business practice required to establish common understanding is far more likely to be held by a businessman than a consumer.

   This case is said to turn on the fact that the parties were 'of equal bargaining power'. However, is the crucial point that they were both in the same business, since only on that basis could such common knowledge of terms used in the business be attributed?

2. In *Grogan* v *Robin Meredith Plant Hire* [1996] CLC 1127, *page 216*, the judge at first instance had disputed the conclusion that the Contractors' Plant Association conditions were common knowledge within the industry. Was it important that the parties in *Grogan* were not in exactly the same business? (Triact was a civil engineering company laying pipes and Meredith was in the plant hire business.)

SECTION 4: IMPLIED TERMS

See Phang 'Implied Terms Revisited' [1990] JBL 394 and 'Implied Terms in English Law: Some Recent Developments' [1993] JBL 242.

A: Terms implied at common law by the courts

Liverpool City Council v *Irwin*
[1977] AC 239 (HL)

A local authority owned the tower block in which the appellants lived. The tenancy agreement contained a list of obligations imposed on the tenants and made no mention of any obligations imposed on the landlords. The appellants withheld their rent as a protest against conditions in the block. The local authority sought possession, and the appellants counterclaimed for nominal damages alleging that the local authority was in breach of its duty to repair and maintain the common parts of the building. They alleged that the lifts did not work, that the lighting on the stairs was inadequate and that the rubbish chutes were blocked. The question was whether there was any implied duty to this effect in the absence of any express provision. Held: the nature of the contract required a term to be implied that there was an obligation to take reasonable care to keep the common parts in reasonable repair and in use. However, on the facts the local authority had taken reasonable care in the circumstances and there was no breach. The House of Lords expressly rejected the suggestion of Lord Denning in the Court of Appeal that a term could be implied if it was reasonable.

LORD WILBERFORCE: . . . [T]here are varieties of implications which the courts think fit to make and they do not necessarily involve the same process. Where this is, on the face of it, a complete, bilateral contract, the courts are sometimes willing to add terms to it, as implied terms: this is very common in mercantile contracts where there is an established usage: in that case the courts are spelling out what both parties know and would, if asked, unhesitatingly agree to be part of the bargain. In other cases, where there is an apparently complete bargain, the courts are willing to add a term on the ground that without it the contract will not work—this is the case, if not of *The Moorcock* (1889) 14 PD 64 itself on its facts, at least of the doctrine of *The Moorcock* as usually applied. This is, as was pointed out by the majority in the Court of Appeal, a strict test—though the degree of strictness seems to vary with the current legal trend—and I think that they were right not to accept it as applicable here. There is a third variety of implication, that which I think Lord Denning MR favours, or at least did favour in this case, and that is the implication of reasonable terms. But though I agree with many of his instances, which in fact fall under one or other of the preceding heads, I cannot go so far as to endorse his principle; indeed, it seems to me, with respect, to extend a long, and undesirable, way beyond sound authority.

The present case, in my opinion, represents a fourth category, or I would rather say a fourth shade on a continuous spectrum. The court here is simply concerned to establish what the contract is, the parties not having themselves fully stated the terms. In this sense the court is searching for what must be implied.

What then should this contract be held to be? There must first be implied a letting, that is, a grant of the right of exclusive possession to the tenants. With this there must, I would suppose, be implied a covenant for quiet enjoyment, as a necessary incident of the letting. The difficulty begins when we consider the common parts. We start with the fact that the demise is useless unless access is obtained by the staircase; we can add that, having regard to the height of the block, and the family nature of the dwellings, the demise would be useless without a lift service; we can continue that, there being rubbish chutes built into the structures and no other means of disposing of light rubbish, there must be a right to use the chutes. The question to be answered—and it is the only question in this case—is what is to be the legal relationship between landlord and tenant as regards these matters.

There can be no doubt that there must be implied (i) an easement for the tenants and their licensees to use the stairs, (ii) a right in the nature of an easement to use the lifts, (iii) an easement to use the rubbish chutes.

But are these easements to be accompanied by any obligation upon the landlord, and what obligation? There seem to be two alternatives. The first, for which the council contends, is for an easement coupled with no legal obligation, except such as may arise under the Occupiers' Liability Act 1957 as regards the safety of those using the facilities, and possibly such other liability as might exist under the ordinary law of tort. The alternative is for easements coupled with some obligation on the part of the landlords as regards the maintenance of the subject of them, so that they are available for use.

My Lords, in order to be able to choose between these, it is necessary to define what test is to be applied, and I do not find this difficult. In my opinion such obligation should be read into the contract as the nature of the contract itself implicitly requires, no more, no less: a test, in other words, of necessity. The relationship accepted by the corporation is that of landlord and tenant: the tenant accepts obligations accordingly, in relation inter alia to the stairs, the lifts and the chutes. All these are not just facilities, or conveniences provided at discretion: they are essentials of the tenancy without which life in the dwellings, as a tenant, is not possible. To leave the landlord free of contractual obligation as regards these matters, and subject only to administrative or political pressure, is, in my opinion, inconsistent totally with the nature of this relationship. The subject matter of the lease (high rise blocks) and the relationship created by the tenancy demand of their nature some contractual obligation . . .

I do not think that this approach involves any innovation as regards the law of contract. The necessity to have regard to the inherent nature of a contract and of the relationship thereby established was stated in this House in *Lister* v *Romford Ice and Cold Storage Co. Ltd* [1957] AC 555. That was a case between master and servant and of a search for an 'implied term.' Viscount Simonds, at p. 579, makes a clear distinction between a search for an implied term such as might be necessary to give 'business efficacy' to the particular contract and a search, based on wider considerations, for such a term as the nature of the contract might call for, or as a legal incident of this kind of contract. If the search were for the former, he says, '. . . I should lose myself in the attempt to formulate it with the necessary precision.' (p. 576.) We see an echo of this in the present case, when the majority in the Court of Appeal, considering a 'business efficacy term'—i.e., a '*Moorcock*' term (*The Moorcock*, 14 PD 64)—found themselves faced with five alternative terms and therefore rejected all of them. But that is not, in my opinion, the end, or indeed the object, of the search. . . .

It remains to define the standard. My Lords, if, as I think, the test of the existence of the term is necessity the standard must surely not exceed what is necessary having regard to the circumstances. To imply an absolute obligation to repair would go beyond what is a necessary legal incident and would indeed be unreasonable. An obligation to take reasonable care to keep in reasonable repair and usability is what fits the requirements of the case. Such a definition involves—and I think rightly—recognition that the tenants themselves have their responsibilities. What it is reasonable to expect of a landlord has a clear relation to what a reasonable set of tenants should do for themselves.

. . . It has not been shown in this case that there was any breach of [the] obligation.

. . . My Lords, it will be seen that I have reached exactly the same conclusion as that of Lord Denning MR, with most of whose thinking I respectfully agree. I must only differ from the passage in which, more adventurously, he suggests that the courts have power to introduce into contracts any terms they think reasonable or to anticipate legislative recommendations of the Law Commission. A just result can be reached, if I am right, by a less dangerous route.

NOTES

1. Lord Denning in *Shell UK Ltd* v *Lostock Garage Ltd* [1976] 1 WLR 1187 (*page 234*), explained this decision:

    . . . As I read the speeches, there are two broad categories of implied terms.

    (i) The first category
    The first category comprehends all those relationships which are of common occurrence. Such as the relationship of seller and buyer, owner and hirer, master and servant, landlord and tenant, carrier by land or by sea, contractor for building works, and so forth. In all those relationships the courts have imposed obligations on one party or the other, saying they are 'implied terms'. These obligations are not founded on the intention of the parties, actual or presumed, but on more general considerations: see *Luxor (Eastbourne) Ltd* v *Cooper* [1941] AC 108 per Lord Wright; *Lister* v *Romford Ice and Cold Storage Co* [1957] AC 555, 576 per Viscount Simonds, and at p. 594 by Lord Tucker (both of whom give interesting illustrations); and *Liverpool City Council* v *Irwin* [1976] 2 WLR 562, 571 per Lord Cross of Chelsea and at p. 579 by Lord Edmund-Davies. In such relationships the problem is not solved by asking what did the parties intend? Or, would they have unhesitatingly agreed to it, if asked? It is to be solved by asking: has the law already defined the obligation or the extent of it? If so, let it be followed. If not, look to see what would be reasonable in the general run of such cases: see by Lord Cross of Chelsea at p. 570H: and then say what the obligation

shall be. The House in *Liverpool City Council* v *Irwin* went through that very process. They examined the existing law of landlord and tenant, in particular that relating to easements, to see if it contained the solution to the problem: and, having found that it did not, they imposed an obligation on the landlord to use reasonable care. In these relationships the parties can exclude or modify the obligation by express words; but unless they do so, the obligation is a legal incident of the relationship which is attached by the law itself and not by reason of any implied term. . . .

(ii) The second category

The second category comprehends those cases which are not within the first category. These are cases—not of common occurrence—in which from the particular circumstances a term is to be implied. In these cases the implication is based on an intention imputed to the parties from their actual circumstances: see *Luxor (Eastbourne) Ltd* v *Cooper* [1941] AC 108, 137 by Lord Wright. Such an imputation is only to be made when it is necessary to imply a term to give efficacy to the contract and make it a workable agreement in such manner as the parties would clearly have done if they had applied their mind to the contingency which has arisen. These are the 'officious bystander' types of case: see *Lister* v *Romford Ice & Cold Storage Co. Ltd* [1957] AC 555, 594, by Lord Tucker. In such cases a term is not to be implied on the ground that it would be reasonable: but only when it is necessary and can be formulated with a sufficient degree of precision.

Thus, there are two categories of terms implied by the courts: First, a term can be implied if it is a necessary incident of this type of contract. (Treitel, *The Law of Contract*, refers to this as 'terms implied in law'.) Such a term is implied into all contracts of a particular type as a matter of policy rather than because that is what the parties intended. Such a term must be a reasonable one to imply (see Peden (2001) 117 LQR 459). Secondly, a term can be implied on a 'one off' basis because it is necessary to give business efficacy to the particular contract. (Treitel refers to this as 'terms implied in fact'.) The implication of this type of term is based on what the parties must have intended. The test, known as the 'officious bystander test', was formulated by Scrutton LJ in *Reigate* v *Union Manufacturing Co.* [1918] 1 KB 592, at p. 605:

> A term can only be implied if it is necessary in the business sense to give efficacy to the contract; that is, if it is such a term that it can confidently be said that if at the time the contract was being negotiated some one had said to the parties, 'What will happen in such a case,' they would both have replied, 'Of course, so and so will happen; we did not trouble to say that; it is too clear.' . . .

In *Scally* v *Southern Health and Social Services Board* [1992] 1 AC 294, Lord Bridge stated that:

> . . . A clear distinction is drawn in the speeches of Viscount Simonds in *Lister* v *Romford Ice and Cold Storage Co. Ltd* [1957] AC 555 and Lord Wilberforce in *Liverpool City Council* v *Irwin* [1977] AC 239 between the search for an implied term necessary to give business efficacy to a particular contract and the search, based on wider considerations, for a term which the law will imply as a necessary incident of a definable category of contractual relationship. . . .

2. *Liverpool City Council* v *Irwin* is an example of a term implied in law into all contracts of a particular type because it is necessary. Another example is *Scally* v *Southern Health and Social Services Board*.

   In this category of implication of a term, the term must be a reasonable one to imply as well as being necessary in this type of contract. However, a term cannot be implied simply on the basis that it is reasonable. As Lord Bridge stated in *Scally* v *Southern Health and Social Services Board*, 'I fully appreciate that the criterion to justify an implication of this kind is necessity, not reasonableness'.

An example of a term *implied in law* into employment contracts is provided by the decision of the House of Lords in *Mahmud* v *Bank of Credit and Commerce International SA (in Liquidation)* (also known as *Malik* v *BCCI*).

Mahmud v *Bank of Credit and Commerce International SA (in Liquidation)*
[1998] AC 20 (HL)

BCCI's banking business had collapsed and the regulatory authorities had then discovered that the business had been carried on fraudulently over a number of years. The applicants were former employees who found that they could not obtain employment in the financial services industry. They alleged that this was because of the stigma attached to the fact that they were former employees of BCCI and they sought compensation for the financial consequences of this alleged stigma. Held: as an aspect of the implied obligation not to undermine the relationship of trust and confidence, an employer was under an implied obligation to its employees not to conduct a dishonest or corrupt business. Therefore, if it was reasonably foreseeable that a breach of this implied obligation would result in the serious possibility of damage to the employee's future employment prospects, that employee could recover damages for the financial loss resulting from that breach. (This case is also discussed at *page 394*.)

LORD STEYN: . . .

The implied term of mutual trust and confidence

The applicants do not rely on a term implied in fact. They do not therefore rely on an individualised term to be implied from the particular provisions of their employment contracts considered against their specific contextual setting. Instead they rely on a standardised term implied by law, that is, on a term which is said to be an incident of all contracts of employment: *Scally* v *Southern Health and Social Services Board* [1992] 1 A.C. 294, 307B. Such implied terms operate as default rules. The parties are free to exclude or modify them. But it is common ground that in the present case the particular terms of the contracts of employment of the two applicants could not affect an implied obligation of mutual trust and confidence.

The employer's primary case is based on a formulation of the implied term that has been applied at first instance and in the Court of Appeal. It imposes reciprocal duties on the employer and employee. Given that this case is concerned with alleged obligations of an employer I will concentrate on its effect on the position of employers. For convenience I will set out the term again. It is expressed to impose an obligation that the employer shall not:

> 'without reasonable and proper cause, conduct itself in a manner calculated and likely to destroy or seriously damage the relationship of confidence and trust between employer and employee:' see *Woods* v *W. M. Car Services (Peterborough) Ltd.* [1981] I.C.R. 666, 670 (Browne-Wilkinson J.), approved in *Lewis* v *Motorworld Garages Ltd.* [1986] I.C.R. 157 and *Imperial Group Pension Trust Ltd.* v *Imperial Tobacco Ltd.* [1991] 1 W.L.R. 589.

A useful anthology of the cases applying this term, or something like it, is given in *Sweet & Maxwell's Encyclopedia of Employment Law* (looseleaf ed.), vol. 1, para. 1.5107, pp. 1467–1470. The evolution of the term is a comparatively recent development. The obligation probably has its origin in the general duty of co-operation between contracting parties: *Hepple & O'Higgins, Employment Law*, 4th ed. (1981), pp. 134–135, paras. 291–292. The reason for this development is part of the history of the development of employment law in this century. The notion of a 'master and servant' relationship became obsolete. Lord Slynn of Hadley recently noted 'the changes which have taken place in the employer-employee relationship, with far greater duties imposed on the employer than in the past, whether by statute or by judicial decision, to care for the physical, financial and even psychological welfare of the employee:' *Spring* v *Guardian Assurance Plc.* [1995] 2 A.C. 296, 335B. A striking illustration of this change is *Scally's* case [1992] 1 A.C. 294, to which I have already referred, where the House of Lords implied a term that all employees in a certain category had to be notified by an employer of their entitlement to certain benefits. It was the change in legal culture which made possible the evolution of the implied term of trust and confidence.

There was some debate at the hearing about the possible interaction of the implied obligation of confidence and trust with other more specific terms implied by law. It is true that the implied term adds little to the employee's implied obligations to serve his employer loyally and not to act contrary to his employer's interests. The major importance of the implied duty of trust and confidence lies in its impact on the obligations of the employer: Douglas Brodie, 'Recent cases, Commentary, The Heart of the Matter: Mutual Trust and Confidence' (1996) 25 I.L.J. 121. And the implied obligation as formulated is apt to cover the great diversity of situations in which a balance has to be struck between an employer's interest in managing his business as he sees fit and the employee's interest in not being unfairly and improperly exploited.

The evolution of the implied term of trust and confidence is a fact. It has not yet been endorsed by your Lordships' House. It has proved a workable principle in practice. It has not been the subject of adverse criticism in any decided cases and it has been welcomed in academic writings. I regard the emergence of the implied obligation of mutual trust and confidence as a sound development.

Given the shape of the appeal my preceding observations may appear unnecessary. But I have felt it necessary to deal briefly with the existence of the implied term for two reasons. First, the implied obligation involves a question of pure law and your Lordships' House is not bound by any agreement of the parties on it or by the acceptance of the obligation by the judge or the Court of Appeal. Secondly, in response to a question counsel for the bank said that his acceptance of the implied obligation is subject to three limitations: (1) that the conduct complained of must be conduct involving the treatment of the employee in question; (2) that the employee must be aware of such conduct while he is an employee; (3) that such conduct must be calculated to destroy or seriously damage the trust between the employer and employee.

In order to place these suggested limitations in context it seemed necessary to explain briefly the origin, nature and scope of the implied obligation. But subject to examining the merits of the suggested limitations, I am content to accept the implied obligation of trust and confidence as established.

NOTE: In both *Mahmud* v *BCCI* and *Scally* v *Southern Health*, the implied terms are formulated and applied as narrow principles. An attempt to achieve a more general implied term failed in *Crossley* v *Faithful & Gould Holdings Ltd* [2004] EWCA Civ 293, [2004] 4 All ER 447. In *Crossley* the Court of Appeal held that, in the context of terms implied in law, it was better to focus on questions of reasonableness, fairness, and the balancing of competing policy considerations (referring to the comments of Peden (2001) 117 LQR 459), rather than the elusive concept of 'necessity'. The Court rejected the argument for an implied term that an employer should take reasonable care of an employee's economic well being (by advising him of the financial consequences of his early retirement). Such a term was considered to involve too large an extension of the law in this area and to place an unfair and unreasonable burden upon employers.

Although this case may be limited factually to the employment context, Dyson LJ's negative comment concerning the 'necessity' requirement has wider significance for terms implied in law. It is clear that the necessity test for terms implied in law is very different from the necessity test in the context of terms implied in fact and different terminology should be employed to avoid any confusion. Unfortunately, although Dyson LJ hints at this, he fails to go further and to reformulate the test other than in vague terms of reasonableness, fairness, and policy.

For terms to be *implied in fact*, both parties must have considered the term to be strictly necessary.

Shell UK Ltd v *Lostock Garage Ltd*
[1976] 1 WLR 1187 (CA)

Lostock operated a 'tied' garage (it could sell only petrol supplied by Shell). In December 1975, a petrol price 'war' began, and in Lostock's neighbourhood two garages which were not tied to Shell reduced their petrol price. As a result Shell introduced a support scheme, whereby it subsidised two Shell garages in that neighbourhood so that they could compete. Lostock's garage was excluded from the support scheme and was forced to trade at a loss. Lostock obtained petrol from another supplier. Shell brought an action seeking damages for breach of contract and an injunction against Lostock. Lostock argued, *inter alia*, that the agreement was subject to an implied obligation placed upon Shell not to discriminate abnormally against Lostock in favour of competing and neighbouring garages so as to render Lostock's petrol uneconomic, and that Shell were in breach of that term by operating the support scheme and excluding Lostock from it. Held: (Bridge LJ dissenting) the court refused to imply the term on the basis that it was not necessary to give efficacy to the agreement and that such a term could not be formulated with sufficient precision. However, they held that no injunction could be issued to restrain a breach of the tie provision while the support scheme was in place.

LORD DENNING MR: . . . Into which of the two categories does the present case come? I am tempted to say that a solus agreement between supplier and buyer is of such common occurence [sic] nowadays that it could be put into the first category: so that the law could imply a term based on general considerations. But I do not think this would be found acceptable. Nor do I think the case can be brought within the second category. If the Shell company had been asked at the beginning: 'Will you agree not to discriminate abnormally against the buyer?' I think they would have declined. It might be a reasonable term, but it is not a necessary term. Nor can it be formulated with sufficient precision. . . . In the circumstances, I do not think any term can be implied.

NOTES

1. In *Hughes* v *Greenwich London Borough Council* [1993] 3 WLR 821, the House of Lords rejected an argument for a term implied in fact on the basis that the term in question had to be 'essential' and that there had to be a 'compelling reason' for it to be included. (See Phang [1994] JBL 255.)

2. It is not clear whether a term implied in fact must be both so obvious that 'it goes without saying' *and* necessary to give business efficacy to the contract (see *The Moorcock* (1889) 14 PD 64, *page 238*) so that no term will be implied if the contract is effective without it. The Court of Appeal in *Suriya & Douglas (a firm)* v *Midland Bank plc* [1999] 1 All ER (Comm) 612 considered an argument that it was sufficient that the term was obvious even though the term contended for was not necessary to give business efficacy to the contract. In this case it was alleged that a term could be implied into a banking contract imposing a duty on the bank to inform customers of a new interest-bearing account. Schiemann LJ (with whose judgment Henry and Butler-Sloss LJJ agreed) stated that:

   The implication of the terms for which [counsel for the plaintiff] contends is not necessary to give efficacy to the contract between the bank and its customer: the bank could carry out their customers' instructions in respect of the existing accounts and keep those accounts without the need to tell its customer about new facilities being introduced which might interest him. [Counsel] did not contend to the contrary.

   He submitted however that the terms which he sought to imply were so obviously stipulations in the agreement that the parties must have intended them to form part of their contract. In short that one or more of them were terms which can be described as obvious. [Counsel] submitted that when the bank's marketing managers decided to seek new business by promoting the special account and circulating all solicitors they did not intend to pick and choose between them and had they been asked whether some solicitors were to be excluded from the possibility of taking advantage from them they would have replied 'Of course not'. He submitted that the bank's business would be quite chaotic if different bank managers were free to decide whether a particular class of customers were to have the opportunity of opening such a special account. He submitted that it must have been obvious to the manager of the plaintiff's branch that the plaintiff would prefer an arrangement which would result in it receiving interest on the surplus moneys to an arrangement in which it did not receive such interest. In short, he repeatedly invited the court to consider the events which had happened and then to reason backwards from them so as to make the implication.

That is an improper approach to the decision whether or not a term is to be implied. That decision has to be made in the light of the facts as they are, or, perhaps in some circumstances, are perceived to be, at the time of the conclusion of the contract. I think that [counsel] accepts that and so formulates the implied term as to be a term which imposes at the conclusion of the contract an obligation on the bank to inform the customer of new accounts as and when that facility is provided to other customers. I see no reason why at that time the bank should have regarded as obvious the implication of any of the terms contended for. To do so would be to add to the bank's burdens to its customer without any correlative benefit to the bank.

I accept that there might well be a benefit to the bank in adopting a *policy of telling* all customers of all changes which would be to their benefit. Indeed there is reason to suppose that the bank did indeed have, at any event, a policy of informing solicitor clients of the introduction of the special account, albeit that this policy could not be demonstrated at trial to have succeeded in the case of this plaintiff. But the mere adoption of such a policy would not give any right to the customer in respect of its non-observance. . . .

3. The tests tend to produce the same result and this has led Phang ([1998] JBL 1) to argue that there is no difference between them, the officious bystander test being no more than a general way of expressing the business efficacy test.

Both tests were applied to produce the same result, rejecting the implication of the suggested term, in *Ultraframe (UK) Ltd* v *Tailored Roofing Systems Ltd* [2004] EWCA Civ 585, [2004] 2 All ER (Comm) 692. The Court of Appeal rejected an attempt to imply a term that the claimant should not act in such a way as to deliberately prejudice or undermine the defendant's business in circumstances where the claimant had an exclusive supply agreement with the defendant. Under the terms of the contract the defendant was bound to purchase supplies of components from the claimant in return for a discount on the price, and the exclusivity could be ended by giving 12 months' notice. The defendant claimed that the claimant was in repudiatory breach by attempting to deal directly with the defendant's customers. The question was whether there was an implied term that the claimant would not do so. The Court of Appeal held that there could be no such term since it was not necessary to give business efficacy to the contract *and* the officious bystander would not have considered that the parties intended such a term. There was no provision in the contract preventing such direct selling. In addition, the alleged implied term would not have prevented the defendant from undercutting the claimant during any notice period when the defendant would inevitably have been in a stronger position as the claimant would have a reduced discount to pass on to its customers. There was nothing to suggest that the position on competition should be any different during the currency of the exclusivity and during the notice period.

Waller LJ also made reference to the difficulty in formulating such an implied term and establishing that it had been breached. A similar point was made in *Shell* v *Lostock*.

In *Equitable Life Assurance Society* v *Hyman*, the House of Lords accepted the implication of a term in fact based on a test of strict necessity.

Equitable Life Assurance Society v Hyman
[2002] 1 AC 408 (HL)

The Society had been issuing retirement 'with-profits' policies with a guaranteed annuity rate (GAR). However, the Society found this commitment to be too expensive to honour when the general annuity rate fell below this guaranteed rate. Therefore, in the mid-1990s, the Society adopted a policy of declaring a lower final bonus on such policies and cited a provision in its articles of association (constitutional document) giving the directors an absolute discretion as to the amount of any bonus and stating that the directors' decision on the award of bonuses was final and conclusive. This action of declaring a lower final bonus was held to be lawful at first instance but reversed by the Court of Appeal. On appeal Held: (affirming the decision of the Court of Appeal) it was necessary to imply a term to the effect that the directors were not to adopt a policy depriving the GAR policies of the value inherent in their original purpose. The whole purpose of such a policy had been to protect holders of such policies in the event of a fall in market rates by ensuring that they would be better off. Therefore, there was a reasonable expectation that the directors would not exercise any discretion so as to conflict with this. It was necessary to imply a term to give effect to these expectations.

LORD STEYN: . . . If properly construed the powers of the directors under article 65 are wide enough to override the terms of the guaranteed annuity rates, the GAR policyholders can have no valid complaint. On the other hand, if article 65 expressly or impliedly contains a prohibition on directors exercising their discretion to override or undermine guaranteed annuity rates, the Society's practice is invalid. Beyond that there can be no liability on the Society. It follows that there are not two separate principal issues but only one. In the circumstances of the present case one never reaches the question whether the power was exercised for an improper or collateral purpose: see *Howard Smith Ltd* v *Ampol Petroleum Ltd* [1974] AC 821. Everything hinges on the meaning of article 65.

The meaning of article 65
It is necessary to distinguish between the processes of interpretation and implication. The purpose of interpretation is to assign to the language of the text the most appropriate meaning which the words can legitimately bear. The language of article 65(1) contains no relevant express restriction on the powers of the directors. It is impossible to assign to the language of article 65(1) by construction a restriction precluding the directors from overriding GARs. To this extent I would uphold the submissions made on behalf of the Society. The critical question is whether a relevant restriction may be implied into article 65(1). It is certainly not a case in which a term can be implied by law in the sense of incidents impliedly annexed to particular forms of contracts. Such standardised implied terms operate as general default rules: see *Scally* v *Southern Health and Social Services Board* [1992] 1 AC 294. If a term is to be implied, it could only be a term implied from the language of article 65 read in its particular commercial setting. Such implied terms operate as ad hoc gap fillers. In *Luxor (Eastbourne) Ltd* v *Cooper* [1941] AC 108, 137 Lord Wright explained this distinction as follows:

> The expression 'implied term' is used in different senses. Sometimes it denotes some term which does not depend on the actual intention of the parties but on a rule of law, such as the terms, warranties or conditions which, if not expressly excluded, the law imports, as for instance under the Sale of Goods Act and the Marine Insurance Act . . . But a case like the present is different because what it is sought to imply is based on an intention imputed to the parties from their actual circumstances.

It is only an individualised term of the second kind which can arguably arise in the present case. Such a term may be imputed to parties: it is not critically dependent on proof of an actual intention of the parties. The process 'is one of construction of the agreement as a whole in its commercial setting': *Banque Bruxelles Lambert SA* v *Eagle Star Insurance Co Ltd* [1997] AC 191, 212e, per Lord Hoffmann. This principle is sparingly and cautiously used and may never be employed to imply a term in conflict with the express terms of the text. The legal test for the implication of such a term is a standard of strict necessity. This is how I must approach the question whether a term is to be implied into article 65(1) which precludes the directors from adopting a principle which has the effect of overriding or undermining the GARs.

The inquiry is entirely constructional in nature: proceeding from the express terms of article 65, viewed against its objective setting, the question is whether the implication is strictly necessary. My Lords, as counsel for the GAR policyholders observed, final bonuses are not bounty. They are a significant part of the consideration for the premiums paid. And the directors' discretions as to the amount and distribution of bonuses are conferred for the benefit of policyholders. In this context the self-evident commercial object of the inclusion of guaranteed rates in the policy is to protect the policyholder against a fall in market annuity rates by ensuring that if the fall occurs he will be better off than he would have been with market rates. The choice is given to the GAR policyholder and not to the Society. It cannot be seriously doubted that the provision for guaranteed annuity rates was a good selling point in the marketing by the Society of the GAR policies. It is also obvious that it would have been a significant attraction for purchasers of GAR policies. The Society points out that no special charge was made for the inclusion in the policy of GAR provisions. So be it. This factor does not alter the reasonable expectations of the parties. The supposition of the parties must be presumed to have been that the directors would not exercise their discretion in conflict with contractual rights. These are the circumstances in which the directors of the Society resolved upon a differential policy which was designed to deprive the relevant guarantees of any substantial value. In my judgment an implication precluding the use of the directors' discretion in this way is strictly necessary. The implication is essential to give effect to the reasonable expectations of the parties. The stringent test applicable to the implication of terms is satisfied.

In substantial agreement with Lord Woolf MR. I would hold that the directors were not entitled to adopt a principle of making the final bonuses of GAR policyholders dependent on how they exercised their rights under the policy. In adopting the principle of a differential policy in respect of GAR policyholders the directors acted in breach of article 65(1).

■ QUESTION

Would both parties have considered such a term to be essential at the time of making the contract? It is at least arguable that they would have done so. The Society had sold the GAR policies on the basis of this protective feature.

NOTES
1. An attempt to imply a broader term 'to act in good faith' based on the test of necessity was rejected in *Redwood Master Fund Ltd* v *TD Bank Europe Ltd* [2002] EWHC 2703 (Ch), *The Times*, 30 January 2003. A majority of syndicate lenders had decided to vary the terms of a syndicated loan facility. The terms of the syndication agreement provided that the consent of the majority bound all lenders. A minority challenged the variation alleging that the majority had acted contrary to good faith in deciding on a course of action that was detrimental to the minority. As there was no such express term, it was argued that such an obligation should be implied. The judge rejected this argument on the basis that such a term was not necessary to give effect to the commercial intentions of the parties and there was no obvious inference that it was intended to be implied by the parties. In the context of commercial lending, no one lender could go back on its contractual commitments merely because the particular decision affected it more seriously than other lenders.
2. In *Paragon Finance plc* v *Nash* [2001] EWCA Civ 1466, [2002] 1 WLR 685, the Court of Appeal held that a lender's entitlement to vary interest rates was subject to an implied term that interest rates were not to be set dishonestly, for an improper purpose, capriciously, or arbitrarily. It was necessary to imply such a term to give effect to the reasonable expectations of the parties and it was a term of which it could be said, 'it goes without saying'. The Court of Appeal was also prepared to extend the scope of such a term to include the fact that the claimant would not act when setting interest rates in a way that no reasonable mortgagee, acting reasonably, would do (by analogy with *Wednesbury* unreasonableness: *Associated Provincial Picture Houses Ltd* v *Wednesbury Corp* [1948] 1 KB 223). This was not the same thing as implying a term not to set unreasonable rates.

The Moorcock
(1889) 14 PD 64 (CA)

The defendants had contracted to allow the plaintiffs to load and unload at the defendants' wharf on the River Thames. It was known to both parties that at low tide any vessel at the wharf would be grounded but there was no express provision governing this in the contract. The plaintiffs' ship moored alongside the wharf, settled on the ground and was damaged because of the condition of the river bed. The defendants had taken no steps to ascertain the condition of the river bed. The plaintiffs brought an action for damages in respect of the damage done to the ship. The Court of Appeal implied a term whereby the defendants warranted that they had taken reasonable care to see that the berth was safe. Held: they were in breach of such term.

BOWEN LJ: The question which arises here is whether when a contract is made to let the use of this jetty to a ship which can only use it, as is known by both parties, by taking the ground, there is any implied warranty on the part of the owners of the jetty, and if so, what is the extent of the warranty. Now, an implied warranty, or, as it is called, a covenant in law, as distinguished from an express contract or express warranty, really is in all cases founded on the presumed intention of the parties, and upon reason. The implication which the law draws from what must obviously have been the intention of the parties, the law draws with the object of giving efficacy to the transaction and preventing such a failure of consideration as cannot have been within the contemplation of either side; and I believe if one were to take all the cases, and they are many, of implied warranties or covenants in law, it will be found that in all of them the law is raising an implication from the presumed intention of the parties with the object of giving to the transaction such efficacy as both parties must have intended that at all events it should have. In business transactions such as this, what the law desires to effect by the implication is to give such business efficacy to the transaction as must have been intended at all events by both parties who are business men; not to impose on one side all the perils of the transaction, or to emancipate one side from all the chances of failure, but to make each party promise in law as much, at all events, as it must have been in the contemplation of both parties that he should be responsible for in respect of those perils or chances.

Now what did each party in a case like this know? For if we are examining into their presumed intention we must examine into their minds as to what the transaction was. Both parties knew that this jetty was let out for hire, and knew that it could only be used under the contract by the ship taking the ground. They must have known that it was by grounding that she used the jetty; in fact, except so far as the transport to the jetty of the cargo in the ship was concerned, they must have known, both of them, that unless the ground was safe the ship would be simply buying an opportunity of danger, and that all consideration would fail unless some care had been taken to see that the ground was safe. In fact the business of the jetty could not be carried on except upon such a basis. The parties also knew that with regard to the safety of the ground outside the jetty the shipowner could know nothing at all, and the jetty owner might with reasonable care know everything. The owners of the jetty, or their servants, were there at high and low tide, and with little trouble they could satisfy themselves, in case of doubt, as to whether the berth was reasonably safe. The ship's owner, on the other hand, had not the means of verifying the state of the jetty, because the berth itself opposite the jetty might be occupied by another ship at any moment.

Now the question is how much of the peril of the safety of this berth is it necessary to assume that the shipowner and the jetty owner intended respectively to bear—in order that such a minimum of efficacy should be secured for the transaction, as both parties must have intended it to bear? . . . The berth outside the jetty was not under the actual control of the jetty owners. It is in the bed of the river, and it may be said that those who owned the jetty had no duty cast upon them by statute or common law to repair the bed of the river, and that they had no power to interfere with the bed of the river unless under the licence of the Conservators. . . .

[I]t may well be said that the law will not imply that the persons who have not the control of the place have taken reasonable care to make it good, but it does not follow that they are relieved from all responsibility. They are on the spot. They must know that the jetty cannot be used unless reasonable care is taken, if not to make it safe, at all events to see whether it is safe. No one can tell whether reasonable safety has been secured except themselves, and I think if they let out their jetty for use they at all events imply that they have taken reasonable care to see whether the berth, which is the essential part of the use of the jetty, is safe, and if it is not safe, and if they have not taken such reasonable care, it is their duty to warn persons with whom they have dealings that they have not done so. . . .

NOTES

1. It appears that the decision is based upon the term being one implied in fact, based on the presumed intentions of the parties to give business efficacy to the contract. It concerns only this transaction and was a term implied on a 'one off' basis. The fact that there are references to reasonableness relates, with one exception, to the nature of the obligation imposed, and should not obscure the fact that the term was imposed in fact.
2. There is authority to support the conclusion that a term may be implied in fact *either* on the basis of the business efficacy test in *The Moorcock* (i.e. would the contract be commercially unworkable without the term?) *or* on the basis of the officious bystander test, see *Ashmore* v *Corp of Lloyd's (No. 2)* [1992] 2 Lloyd's Rep 620. However, the courts tend to apply both and, as discussed above *page 236*, both tend to produce the same result. In *Ashmore* the implication failed on both tests; see also *Suriya & Douglas (a firm)* v *Midland Bank plc* [1999] 1 All ER (Comm) 612.

B: Terms implied by statute

(a) Terms implied into a contract for the sale of goods

SALE OF GOODS ACT 1979 (AS AMENDED BY THE SALE AND SUPPLY OF GOODS ACT 1994 AND THE SALE AND SUPPLY OF GOODS TO CONSUMERS REGULATIONS 2002, SI 2002/3045)

12. Implied terms about title, etc.

(1) In a contract of sale, . . . there is an implied term on the part of the seller that in the case of a sale he has a right to sell the goods, and in the case of an agreement to sell he will have such a right at the time when the property is to pass.

(2) In a contract of sale there is also an implied term that—

(a) the goods are free, and will remain free until the time when the property is to pass, from any charge or encumbrance not disclosed or known to the buyer before the contract is made, and

(b) the buyer will enjoy quiet possession of the goods except so far as it may be disturbed by the owner or other person entitled to the benefit of any charge or encumbrance so disclosed or known.

. . .

(5A) As regards England and Wales and Northern Ireland, the term implied by subsection (1) above is a condition and the terms implied by subsections (2) . . . above are warranties.

13. Sale by description

(1) Where there is a contract for the sale of goods by description, there is an implied term that the goods will correspond with the description.

(1A) As regards England and Wales and Northern Ireland, the term implied by subsection (1) above is a condition.

14. Implied terms about quality or fitness

(1) Except as provided by this section and section 15 below and subject to any other enactment, there is no implied term about the quality or fitness for any particular purpose of goods supplied under a contract of sale.

(2) Where the seller sells goods in the course of a business, there is an implied term that the goods supplied under the contract are of satisfactory quality.

(2A) For the purposes of this Act, goods are of satisfactory quality if they meet the standard that a reasonable person would regard as satisfactory, taking account of any description of the goods, the price (if relevant) and all the other relevant circumstances.

(2B) For the purposes of this Act, the quality of goods includes their state and condition and the following (among others) are in appropriate cases aspects of the quality of goods—

  (a) fitness for all the purposes for which goods of the kind in question are commonly supplied,

  (b) appearance and finish,

  (c) freedom from minor defects,

  (d) safety, and

  (e) durability.

(2C) The term implied by subsection (2) above does not extend to any matter making the quality of goods unsatisfactory—

  (a) which is specifically drawn to the buyer's attention before the contract is made,

  (b) where the buyer examines the goods before the contract is made, which that examination ought to reveal, or

  (c) in the case of a contract for sale by sample, which would have been apparent on a reasonable examination of the sample.

(2D) If the buyer deals as consumer . . ., the relevant circumstances mentioned in subsection (2A) above include any public statements on the specific characteristics of the goods made about them by the seller, the producer or his representative, particularly in advertising or on labelling.

(2E) A public statement is not by virtue of subsection (2D) above a relevant circumstance for the purposes of subsection (2A) above in the case of a contract of sale, if the seller shows that—

  (a) at the time the contract was made, he was not, and could not reasonably have been, aware of the statement,

  (b) before the contract was made, the statement had been withdrawn in public or, to the extent that it contained anything which was incorrect or misleading, it had been corrected in public, or

  (c) the decision to buy the goods could not have been influenced by the statement.

(2F) Subsections (2D) and (2E) above do not prevent any public statement from being a relevant circumstance for the purposes of subsection (2A) above (whether or not the buyer deals as consumer) if the statement would have been such a circumstance apart from those subsections.

(3) Where the seller sells goods in the course of a business and the buyer, expressly or by implication, makes known—

  (a) to the seller, or

  (b) where the purchase price or part of it is payable by instalments and the goods were previously sold by a credit-broker to the seller, to that credit-broker, any particular purpose for which the goods are being bought, there is an implied term that the goods supplied under the contract are reasonably fit for that purpose, whether or not that is a purpose for which such goods are commonly supplied, except where the circumstances show that the buyer does not rely, or that it is unreasonable for him to rely, on the skill or judgment of the seller or credit-broker.

. . .

(6) As regards England and Wales and Northern Ireland, the terms implied by subsections (2) and (3) above are conditions.

15. Sale by sample

(1) A contract of sale is a contract for sale by sample where there is an express or implied term to that effect in the contract.

(2) In the case of a contract for sale by sample there is an implied term—

  (a) that the bulk will correspond with the sample in quality;

(b) that the goods will be free from any defect, making their quality unsatisfactory, which would not be apparent on reasonable examination of the sample.

(3) As regards England and Wales and Northern Ireland, the term implied by subsection (2) above is a condition.

(b) Terms implied into contracts of hire-purchase

A contract of hire-purchase is defined at *page 64*. See the Supply of Goods (Implied Terms) Act 1973, ss. 8–11, as amended by the Sale and Supply of Goods Act 1994 and the Sale and Supply of Goods to Consumers Regulations 2002, reg. 13 amending s. 10.

(c) Terms implied into contracts for work and materials in relation to the materials supplied

These are contracts which primarily relate to the provision of work but under which goods are also supplied, e.g., car repairs, building contracts.

The Supply of Goods and Services Act 1982, ss. 2–5 (as amended by the Sale and Supply of Goods Act 1994 and the Sale and Supply of Goods to Consumers Regulations 2002, reg. 7 amending s. 4) relating to the materials supplied, are in similar terms to the above provisions.

(d) Terms implied into hire contracts

These are contracts where the hirer gains possession but not ownership. See Supply of Goods and Services Act 1982, ss. 7–10 as amended by the Sale and Supply of Goods Act 1994 and the Sale and Supply of Goods to Consumers Regulations 2002, reg. 10 amending s. 9.

(e) Terms implied into contracts for the supply of a service

These are contracts whereby a supplier agrees to carry out a service. In a contract for work and materials the service element will be combined with a transfer of property in goods (see (c) above for implied obligations in relation to the materials supplied).

For implied obligations relating to contracts for the supply of a service, see the Supply of Goods and Services Act 1982, ss. 13–15 (s. 13 appears at *page 330* and s. 15 at *page 70* of this casebook).

SECTION 5: TYPES OF CONTRACTUAL TERMS

See Brownsword, 'Retrieving Reasons, Retrieving Rationality? A New Look at the Right to Withdraw for Breach of Contract' (1992) 5 JCL 83.

The traditional distinction is between two types of contractual terms: conditions and warranties. A condition is an important term 'going to the root of the contract'; a warranty is a less important term not going to the substance of the contract, the breach of which can be compensated for adequately by the payment of money.

It is important to distinguish 'conditions' in the sense used here (i.e., promissory conditions which give rise to remedies for breach in the event of non-performance) from non-promissory contingent conditions. If a condition is contingent it means that the obligation will not come into force until the happening of that event.

As a general principle a breach of a promissory condition gives the innocent party the option of either terminating the performance of the contract and obtaining damages for his loss caused by the breach, or affirming the contract and recovering damages for the breach. However, if a warranty is broken, it gives rise only to a right for the innocent party to claim damages, and both parties must continue to perform their obligations under the contract.

A: Is the term a condition?

Does statute classify the term? See, for example, the Sale of Goods Act 1979, ss. 12–15. However, note s. 15A of the Sale of Goods Act 1979, introduced by s. 4 of the Sale and Supply of Goods Act 1994, which applies to breaches of ss. 13, 14, or 15 of the Sale of Goods Act 1979 where the buyer does *not* deal as consumer.

SALE OF GOODS ACT 1979 (AS AMENDED BY THE SALE AND SUPPLY OF GOODS ACT 1994)

15A.
   (1) Where in the case of a contract of sale—
      (a) the buyer would, apart from this subsection, have the right to reject goods by reason of a breach on the part of the seller of a term implied by section 13, 14 or 15 above, but
      (b) the breach is so slight that it would be unreasonable for him to reject them,
then, if the buyer does not deal as consumer, the breach is not to be treated as a breach of condition but may be treated as a breach of warranty.
   (2) This section applies unless a contrary intention appears in, or is to be implied from, the contract.
   (3) It is for the seller to show that a breach fell within subsection (1)(b) above.

■ QUESTION

Does this amount to no more than an extension of the *de minimis* principle in *Arcos Ltd* v *Ronaasen & Son* [1933] AC 470?

NOTES
1. See also the Supply of Goods (Implied Terms) Act 1973, s. 11A, and the Supply of Goods and Services Act 1982, ss. 5A and 10A for the equivalent provisions in relation to hire-purchase, work and materials, and hire contracts.
2. This will inevitably lead to uncertainty in individual cases over whether the breach of a condition will be treated as giving rise to the right to reject in relation to ss. 13–15 breaches in a non-consumer contract. The consequences normally attributed to a breach of condition will not now automatically follow.
    While flexibility may be no bad thing, this provision does not assist the clarity of the law in this area. Significantly, even if the breach is so slight that it would be unreasonable for the non-consumer buyer to reject, it does not necessarily follow that the only remedy will be damages because the section is drafted so as to give the court a discretion. Section 15A(1) provides that although the breach is not to be treated as a breach of condition (with an automatic right to reject), it '*may* be treated as a breach of warranty' (damages only).
3. Section 15A(2), however, provides for the uncertainty to be excluded by the terms of the contract, for example, by including an express provision that there is to be a right to reject.
4. Section 15A applies to *non-consumer* buyers and has the potential to limit remedies. By com-

parison, the Sale and Supply of Goods to Consumers Regulations 2002 introduced new provisions relating to the remedies available to *consumer* buyers for breaches of sections 13, 14, or 15 of the Sale of Goods Act 1979 (and equivalents) which make amendments to the Sale of Goods Act 1979 (ss. 48A–F) (and other supply of goods legislation) extending the range of possible remedies rather than restricting them. It remains possible to reject the goods for breach of condition and the provisions also provide that, for these purposes, goods will be deemed to be non-conforming (and in breach of these goods obligations) if they are non-conforming at any time within six months of delivery. The Regulations provide that 'consumer' buyers (defined in reg. 2) *have the option* to require the seller to repair or replace such non-conforming goods within a reasonable time where this is possible and not disproportionate in comparison to other available remedies. Alternatively, the buyer may require the seller to either reduce the purchase price of the goods or reject the defective goods.

Have the parties classified the term? If they have, does it operate as a condition?

Lombard North Central plc v Butterworth
[1987] QB 527 (CA)

The plaintiffs leased a computer to the defendant. Clause 2(a) of the agreement made punctual payment of each instalment of hire *of the essence* of the agreement, and under clause 5 failure to make due and punctual payment entitled the plaintiffs to terminate the agreement. The defendant was late in paying the third, fourth, and fifth instalments, and when the sixth instalment was six weeks overdue the plaintiffs terminated the agreement and sought damages for breach of contract. The Court of Appeal stressed that the parties were free to classify the relative importance of the terms of their contract. Held: clause 2(a) made prompt payment a condition of the contract, so that if any payment was not made on time there was a breach of the agreement entitling the plaintiffs to terminate the contract and recover damages for the loss of the transaction, even though the breach itself was not regarded as giving rise to serious consequences.

MUSTILL LJ: . . . The reason why I am impelled to hold that the plaintiffs' contentions are well-founded can most conveniently be set out in a series of propositions.

1. Where a breach goes to the root of the contract, the injured party may elect to put an end to the contract. Thereupon both sides are relieved from those obligations which remain unperformed.

2. If he does so elect, the injured party is entitled to compensation for (a) any breaches which occurred before the contract was terminated, and (b) the loss of his opportunity to receive performance of the promisor's outstanding obligations.

3. Certain categories of obligation, often called conditions, have the property that any breach of them is treated as going to the root of the contract. Upon the occurrence of any breach of condition, the injured party can elect to terminate and claim damages, whatever the gravity of the breach.

4. It is possible by express provision in the contract to make a term a condition, even if it would not be so in the absence of such a provision.

5. A stipulation that time is of the essence, in relation to a particular contractual term, denotes that timely performance is a condition of the contract. The consequence is that delay in performance is treated as going to the root of the contract, without regard to the magnitude of the breach.

6. It follows that where a promisor fails to give timely performance of an obligation in respect of which time is expressly stated to be of the essence, the injured party may elect to terminate

and recover damages in respect of the promisor's outstanding obligations, without regard to the magnitude of the breach . . .

NOTES

1. See Bojczuk, 'When is a condition not a condition?' [1987] JBL 353.
2. Diplock LJ in *Hong Kong Fir* v *Kawasaki* (*page 250*), and Lord Wilberforce in *Bunge Corporation* v *Tradax SA* (*page 255*) also indicated that the parties were free to make a particular term a condition. *Lombard* v *Butterworth* appears to have provided a simple formulation to achieve this. This effect can also be achieved by expressly stipulating that the remedy is to be the right to terminate (or reject the goods). See Ormrod LJ in *The Hansa Nord, page 256*.
3. See *Union Eagle Ltd* v *Golden Achievement Ltd* [1997] AC 514, *page 425*, for a further illustration of the effect of 'time is of the essence'.
4. However, in the next case, the House of Lords considered that a term described as a 'condition' could not have been intended by the parties to have this effect.

L. Schuler AG v Wickman Machine Tool Sales

[1974] AC 235 (HL)

Wickman, an English company, was given the sole selling rights for the German company's panel presses for four and a half years. Clause 7(b) of the distributorship contract provided that 'It shall be [a] condition of the agreement that (i) [Wickman] shall send its representative to visit (the six largest UK motor manufacturers) at least once in every week' to solicit orders. Wickman failed to make a number of these visits and Schuler terminated the agreement under clause 11(a) on the basis that Wickman had committed a material breach of its obligations which it had failed to remedy within 60 days of being required in writing to do so. Wickman claimed damages for wrongful repudiation. Held: (Lord Wilberforce dissenting) clause 7(b) was not a condition in the sense that a single breach, however trivial, would entitle the innocent party to terminate the contract.

LORD REID: Sometimes a breach of a term gives that option [to terminate for repudiatory breach] to the aggrieved party because it is of a fundamental character going to the root of the contract, sometimes it gives that option because the parties have chosen to stipulate that it shall have that effect. Blackburn J said in *Bettini* v *Gye* (1876) 1 QBD 183, 187: 'Parties may think some matter, apparently of very little importance, essential; and if they sufficiently express an intention to make the literal fulfilment of such a thing a condition precedent, it will be one; . . .'

In the present case it is not contended that Wickman's failures to make visits amounted in themselves to fundamental breaches. What is contended is that the terms of clause 7 'sufficiently express an intention' to make any breach, however small, of the obligation to make visits a condition so that any breach shall entitle Schuler to rescind the whole contract if they so desire.

Schuler maintains that the use of the word 'condition' is in itself enough to establish this intention. No doubt some words used by lawyers do have a rigid inflexible meaning. But we must remember that we are seeking to discover intention as disclosed by the contract as a whole. Use of the word 'condition' is an indication—even a strong indication—of such an intention but it is by no means conclusive.

The fact that a particular construction leads to a very unreasonable result must be a relevant consideration. The more unreasonable the result the more unlikely it is that the parties can have intended it, and if they do intend it the more necessary it is that they shall make that intention abundantly clear.

Clause 7(b) requires that over a long period each of the six firms shall be visited every week by one or other of two named representatives. It makes no provision for Wickman being entitled to substitute others even on the death or retirement of one of the named representatives. Even if one could imply some right to do this, it makes no provision for both representatives being ill during a particular week. And it makes no provision for the possibility that one or other of the firms may tell Wickman that they cannot receive Wickman's representative during a particular week. So if the parties gave any thought to the matter at all they must have realised the probability that in a few cases out of the 1,400 required visits a visit as stipulated would be impossible. But if Schuler's contention is right, failure to make even one visit entitle them to terminate the contract however blameless Wickman might be.

This is so unreasonable that it must make me search for some other possible meaning of the contract. If none can be found then Wickman must suffer the consequences. But only if that is the only possible interpretation. . . . If I have to construe clause 7 standing by itself then I do find difficulty in reaching any other interpretation. But if clause 7 must be read with clause 11 the difficulty disappears. The word 'condition' would make any breach of clause 7(b), however excusable, a material breach. That would then entitle Schuler to give notice under clause 11(a)(i) requiring the breach to be remedied. There would be no point in giving such a notice if Wickman were clearly not in fault but if it were given Wickman would have no difficulty in showing that the breach had been remedied. If Wickman were at fault then on receiving such a notice they would have to amend their system so that they could show that the breach had been remedied. If they did not do that within the period of the notice then Schuler would be entitled to rescind.

In my view, that is a possible and reasonable construction of the contract and I would therefore adopt it. The contract is so obscure that I can have no confidence that this is its true meaning but for the reasons which I have given I think that it is the preferable construction. It follows that Schuler was not entitled to rescind the contract as it purported to do. . . .

■ QUESTION

Could the majority of the House of Lords be accused of rewriting the parties' agreement?

NOTES

1. Lord Wilberforce (dissenting) was of the opinion that the term was clearly a condition because that was the word that the parties had used. He also stressed that if it was not a condition, then Schuler would find themselves in breach, having wrongfully repudiated.

2. The majority of the House of Lords, in interpreting what the parties intended, appears to have ignored the clear use of the word 'condition', on the basis that they considered this interpretation was so unreasonable that it could not have been intended by the parties.

3. If the word 'condition' is not conclusive of the fact that a right to terminate was intended, then much uncertainty will exist over what form of wording will be effective to achieve this objective. One particular problem resulting from uncertainty is that the innocent party has to judge whether he has the right to terminate for the breach. As noted above, it may later be decided that there was no such right because it was not a breach of a condition, so that the repudiating party will have wrongfully repudiated and find himself in breach of contract.

4. In *Rice (T/A The Garden Guardian)* v *Great Yarmouth Borough Council* [2003] TCLR 1, (2001) 3 LGLR 4, *The Times*, 26 July 2000, a clause in the contract provided for a right to terminate for the breach of 'any' obligations and the Court of Appeal held that it could not have been intended that there should be a right to terminate for any breach of any term since this 'flies in the face of commercial common sense'. The breach would have to be a repudiatory breach to justify termination. Thus whatever the parties may believe the terms to mean on a literal interpretation, the court may consider that this could not have been their intention.

What if the parties have not made a successful classification?

The courts must seek to ascertain the parties' intentions by looking at the relative importance of the term in the context of the contract as a whole, to see whether it 'goes to the root of the contract' (as the majority of the House of Lords did in *Schuler* v *Wickman Machine Tool Sales, page 245*).

In *Couchman* v *Hill* [1947] KB 554 (*page 201*) the term was considered to be a condition because the heifer being unserved was 'a substantial ingredient in the identity of the thing sold'. A similar principle can be seen in *Bannerman* v *White* (1861) 10 CB NS 844 (*page 201*) since if the term was so important to the buyer that he would not have purchased without it, it is more likely to be construed as a condition.

In *Barber* v *NWS Bank plc* [1996] 1 All ER 906, the Court of Appeal held that in a conditional sale agreement for the purchase of a car, whereby the property in the car remained vested in the finance company until the hirer had paid the balance and all sums owing, it was a condition that the finance company was the owner of the car at the date of the agreement. The Court of Appeal ruled out the possibility that such a term was innominate (see *page 250*) because it was clearly fundamental to the transaction and could only be broken in one way which would necessarily be serious. Sir Roger Parker stated (at p. 911) that 'This term is not one which admits of different breaches, some of which are trivial, for which damages are an adequate remedy, and others of which are sufficiently serious to warrant rescission. There is here one breach only'.

The need for certainty has, in the main, resulted in time stipulations in mercantile contracts being classified as conditions without it having to be established that they go to the root of the contract. Where the same term is used in a standard form, subsequent parties can rely on it and know in advance what the remedies for breach will be.

Maredelanto Compania Naviera SA v *Bergbau-Handel GmbH, The Mihalis Angelos*
[1971] 1 QB 164 (CA)

By a charterparty dated 25 May 1965, the *Mihalis Angelos* was chartered to proceed to Haiphong and load a cargo there. The charterparty described the vessel as 'expected ready to load under this charter about 1 July 1965'. On 23 June, the vessel arrived at Hong Kong to discharge a cargo from the previous voyage, and was still there on 17 July 1965 when the charterers purported to cancel the charterparty. They did so on the grounds of *force majeure* (*page 495*) because there was no cargo at Haiphong due to conditions of war. The owners accepted this action as a repudiation of the contract and claimed damages for their loss of profit. The arbitrator had found that there were no grounds to terminate for *force majeure*, so the question was whether the charterers nevertheless had the right to terminate. Held: the expected readiness to load clause was a condition which the owners had broken, since on 25 May, when the contract was made, they could not reasonably have expected that the ship would be ready to load in Haiphong on 1 July. Therefore, the charterers did have the right to terminate on 17 July.

MEGAW LJ: In my judgment, such a term in a charterparty ought to be regarded as being a condition of the contract, in the old sense of the word 'condition': that is, that when it has been broken, the other party can, if he wishes, by intimation to the party in breach, elect to be released from performance of his further obligations under the contract; and he can validly do so without having to establish that on the facts of the particular case the breach has produced serious consequences whch can be treated as 'going to the root of the contract' or as being 'fundamental,' or whatever other metaphor may be thought appropriate for a frustration case. . . .

... One of the essential elements of law is some measure of uniformity. One of the important elements of the law is predictability. At any rate in commercial law, there are obvious and substantial advantages in having, where possible, a firm and definite rule for a particular class of legal relationship: for example, as here, the legal categorisation of a particular, definable type of contractual clause in common use. It is surely much better, both for shipowners and charterers (and, incidentally, for their advisers), when a contractual obligation of this nature is under consideration, and still more when they are faced with the necessity for an urgent decision as to the effects of a suspected breach of it, to be able to say categorically: 'If a breach is proved, then the charterer can put an end to the contract,' rather than that they should be left to ponder whether or not the courts would be likely, in the particular case, when the evidence has been heard, to decide that in the particular circumstances the breach was or was not such as 'to go to the root of the contract.' Where justice does not require greater flexibility, there is everything to be said for, and nothing against, a degree of rigidity in legal principle.

NOTES

1. The need for commercial certainty (and efficiency) was stressed by the House of Lords in *Compagnie Commerciale Sucres et Denrées* v *C. Czarnikow Ltd, The Naxos* [1990] 3 All ER 641, in the context of a readiness to load clause in a mercantile contract which was construed as a condition. See also *Bunge Corporation* v *Tradax SA, page 253,* and *BS & N Ltd (BVI)* v *Micado Shipping Ltd (Malta), The Seaflower* [2001] 1 Lloyd's Rep 341.

2. The drawback with this approach is that once a term is classified as a condition it will always give rise to a right to terminate if it is broken, even if the particular breach causes little or no damage. The *Mihalis Angelos* illustrates how a party can escape from a contract which he will not be able to perform or which has become more expensive, simply on the ground that the other party has committed a breach of a condition.

3. The House of Lords has, however, stated that timely redelivery of a vessel at the end of a time charterparty is not a condition but an innominate term, despite the fact that it is essentially a time stipulation in a mercantile contract.

Torvald Klaveness A/S v *Arni Maritime Corp, The Gregos*
[1994] 1 WLR 1465 (HL)

Under the terms of the time charterparty the last date for redelivery of the vessel by the charterers to the owners was 18 March 1988. On 9 February, the charterers ordered the vessel from Matanzas in Venezuela to the port of Palua in order to load a cargo for delivery to Fos in Italy prior to redelivery to the owners by 18 March. The order of readiness to load in Palua was given on 25 February, but the Orinoco River was blocked by another vessel so that the owners considered that if a cargo was loaded the vessel would not be redelivered in time. They therefore requested fresh orders from the charterers but the charterers refused.

The owners claimed that the order was therefore a repudiatory breach and accepted it as terminating the contract. Held: The charterers had committed a repudiatory breach. The majority (Lord Mustill, with whom Lords Ackner, Slynn, and Woolf agreed) held that the obligation to redeliver on time was innominate, so that the issuing of the order for the voyage did not in itself constitute a repudiatory breach, but that the charterers' persistence in the order which had become illegitimate amounted to a renunciation of the contract, i.e. a repudiatory breach. However, Lord Templeman considered that the obligation to redeliver at the end of a time charter is of the essence of the contract, and that since the charterers had given an order which would prevent the vessel being redelivered on time, the owners could accept that repudiatory breach as terminating the contract.

LORD MUSTILL: . . . I find it hard to accept that timely redelivery is a condition of the contract. The classification of an obligation as a condition or an 'innominate' term is largely determined by its practical importance in the scheme of the contract, and this is not easily judged in relation to the obligation to redeliver, since the occasions for the cancellation of a charter on the ground of a few days' delay at the end of the chartered service are likely to be few. If the ship is laden when the final date arrives the shipowner will often have obligations to third party consignees which make it impossible for him to cut short the voyage, quite apart from the improbability that he will go to the trouble and expense of arranging for the discharge and receipt of the cargo at an alternative destination, just to save a few days' delay. These problems will not arise if the vessel is ballasting to the redelivery port, but even if the shipowner really wants the vessel back on time, rather than a few days late, he will not usually need to have recourse to a cancellation, since the charterer will have no motive to keep the charter in being, with its obligation to pay hire for an empty ship. Even acknowledging the importance given in recent years to time clauses in mercantile contracts (see, for example, *Bunge Corporation New York* v *Tradax Export SA Panama* [1981] 1 WLR 711 and *Compagnie Commerciale Sucres et Denrées* v *C Czarnikow Ltd* [1990] 1 WLR 1337) I would incline to the view that this particular obligation is 'innominate' and that a short delay in redelivery would not justify the termination of the contract.

LORD TEMPLEMAN: My Lords, in a time charter, the time for redelivery of the vessel by the charterer to the owner at the end of the charter is of the essence of the contract, absent any provision in the contract to the contrary. If the charterer in the course of the charterparty evinces an intention not to redeliver the vessel by the date or last date fixed for redelivery, the charterer will evince an intention no longer to be bound by the contract and will thus repudiate the contract. The owner may ignore the repudiation and claim damages resulting from breach of contract by any late delivery or accept the repudiation, withdraw the vessel from the control of the charterer and claim damages resulting from repudiation. . . .

There was a good deal of discussion about legitimate and illegitimate last voyages but to my mind this appeal falls to be determined by the application of elementary principles of contract. The charterer agrees to redeliver on time and must therefore give orders which ensure that the vessel will be redelivered on time. If the charterer gives an order which will not enable the vessel to be redelivered on time, the owner may treat that order as a repudiatory breach of contract. If the owner complies with the order he loses his right to repudiate but is entitled to damages for any late delivery. In the present case, the crucial date was 25 February when the charterers could have given an order which would have enabled redelivery on time but insisted on an order which did not allow the vessel to be redelivered on time. The order to load at Palua on 25 February was a repudiatory breach of contract. If the *Gregos* had been loaded, pursuant to that order, the owners would have lost their right to repudiate but would have remained entitled to damages for late delivery. The owners accepted the repudiation and withdrew the vessel. . . .

NOTES
1. This decision is indicative of the tensions in approach in this area between certainty and flexibility.
2. It may be advisable to judge the decision of the majority in the light of the background facts, namely a rising market and evidence that the owners wished to recharter at the earliest possible opportunity to take advantage of these higher rates of charter. Lord Mustill expressly commented on the dangers of concluding that this term was a condition when he stated (at p. 1475): 'My Lords, although it is well established that certain obligations under charterparties do have the character of conditions I would not for my part wish to enlarge the category unduly, given the opportunity which this provides for a party to rely on an innocuous breach as a means of escaping from an unwelcome bargain'.
3. See Girvin [1995] JBL 200.
4. In *Universal Bulk Carriers Ltd* v *Andre et Cie SA* [2001] EWCA Civ 588, [2001] 2 Lloyd's Rep 65, a time stipulation was considered not to be a condition on the basis that, in the light of the nature of the subject matter of the contract and the surrounding circumstances, it could not

have been intended that any breach of this term should give rise to an option to terminate the contract.

B: More flexibility at a price

Hong Kong Fir Shipping Co. Ltd v *Kawasaki Kisen Kaisha Ltd*
[1962] 2 QB 26 (CA)

The charterers hired a ship for 24 months, 'being in every way fitted for ordinary cargo service'. The ship was delivered on 13 February 1957, and sailed that day to pick up a cargo in the United States and take it to Osaka. Because of the age of the ship's machinery it needed to be maintained by an experienced, competent, careful, and adequate engine room staff. There were insufficient numbers of staff and the chief engineer was incompetent. As a result, there were many serious breakdowns in the machinery. On the voyage at sea for eight and a half weeks the ship was off hire for five weeks for repairs and, on reaching Osaka on 25 May, required 15 weeks of repairs to make her seaworthy. In June 1957, the charterers repudiated the charterparty (freight rates having fallen in the interim). There were no reasonable grounds for thinking that the ship would not be seaworthy in mid-September, and in fact she was seaworthy on 15 September, which left 17 months of the original charter period. The owners sought damages for wrongful repudiation. Held: although there was a breach of the charterparty because the ship was unseaworthy, seaworthiness was not a condition of the charterparty entitling the charterer to terminate. The delay caused by the breakdowns and the repairs was not so great as to frustrate the commercial purpose of the charterparty.

DIPLOCK LJ: Every synallagmatic contract contains in it the seeds of the problem: in what event will a party be relieved of his undertaking to do that which he has agreed to do but has not yet done? The contract may itself expressly define some of these events, as in the cancellation clause in a charterparty; but, human prescience being limited, it seldom does so exhaustively and often fails to do so at all. In some classes of contracts such as sale of goods, marine insurance, contracts of affreightment evidenced by bills of lading and those between parties to bills of exchange, Parliament has defined by statute some of the events not provided for expressly in individual contracts of that class; but where an event occurs the occurrence of which neither the parties nor Parliament have expressly stated will discharge one of the parties from further performance of his undertakings, it is for the court to determine whether the event has this effect or not.

The test whether an event has this effect or not has been stated in a number of metaphors all of which I think amount to the same thing: does the occurrence of the event deprive the party who has further undertakings still to perform of substantially the whole benefit which it was the intention of the parties as expressed in the contract that he should obtain as the consideration for performing those undertakings?

This test is applicable whether or not the event occurs as a result of the default of one of the parties to the contract, but the consequences of the event are different in the two cases. Where the event occurs as a result of the default of one party, the party in default cannot rely upon it as relieving himself of the performance of any further undertakings on his part, and the innocent party, although entitled to, need not treat the event as relieving him of the further performance of his own undertakings. This is only a specific application of the fundamental legal and moral rule that a man should not be allowed to take advantage of his own wrong. Where the event occurs as a result of the default of neither party, each is relieved of the further performance of his own undertakings, and their rights in respect of undertakings previously performed are now regulated by the Law Reform (Frustrated Contracts) Act, 1943.

This branch of the common law has reached its present stage by the normal process of historical growth, and the fallacy in [counsel for the charterers'] contention that a different test is applicable when the event occurs as a result of the default of one party from that applicable in cases of frustration where the event occurs as a result of the default of neither party lies, in my view, from a failure to view the cases in their historical context. The problem: in what event will a party to a contract be relieved of his undertaking to do that which he has agreed to do but has not yet done? has exercised the English courts for centuries . . .

Once it is appreciated that it is the event and not the fact that the event is a result of a breach of contract which relieves the party not in default of further performance of his obligations, two consequences follow. (1) The test whether the event relied upon has this consequence is the same whether the event is the result of the other party's breach of contract or not, as Devlin J pointed out in *Universal Cargo Carriers Corporation* v *Citati* [1957] 2 QB 401. (2) The question whether an event which is the result of the other party's breach of contract has this consequence cannot be answered by treating all contractual undertakings as falling into one of two separate categories: 'conditions' the breach of which gives rise to an event which relieves the party not in default of further performance of his obligations, and 'warranties' the breach of which does not give rise to such an event.

Lawyers tend to speak of this classificaton as if it were comprehensive, partly for the historical reasons which I have already mentioned and partly bcause Parliament itself adopted it in the Sale of Goods Act, 1893, as respects a number of implied terms in contracts for the sale of goods and has in that Act used the expressions 'condition' and 'warranty' in that meaning. But it is by no means true of contractual undertakings in general at common law.

No doubt there are many simple contractual undertakings, sometimes express but more often because of their very simplicity ('It goes without saying') to be implied, of which it can be predicated that every breach of such an undertaking must give rise to an event which will deprive the party not in default of substantially the whole benefit which it was intended that he should obtain from the contract. And such a stipulation, unless the parties have agreed that breach of it shall not entitle the non-defaulting party to treat the contract as repudiated, is a 'condition.' So too there may be other simple contractual undertakings of which it can be predicated that *no* breach can give rise to an event which will deprive the party not in default of substantially the whole benefit which it was intended that he should obtain from the contract; and such a stipulation, unless the parties have agreed that breach of it shall entitle the non-defaulting party to treat the contract as repudiated, is a 'warranty.'

There are, however, many contractual undertakings of a more complex character which cannot be categorised as being 'conditions' or 'warranties,' if the late nineteenth-century meaning adopted in the Sale of Goods Act, 1893, and used by Bowen LJ in *Bentsen* v *Taylor, Sons & Co.* [1893] 2 QB 274 be given to those terms. Of such undertakings all that can be predicated is that some breaches will and others will not give rise to an event which will deprive the party not in default of substantially the whole benefit which it was intended that he should obtain from the contract; and the legal consequences of a breach of such an undertaking, unless provided for expressly in the contract, depend upon the nature of the event to which the breach gives rise and do not follow automatically from a prior classification of the undertaking as a 'condition' or a 'warranty.' For instance, to take Bramwell B's example in *Jackson* v *Union Marine Insurance Co. Ltd* (1874) LR 10 CP 125 itself, breach of an undertaking by a shipowner to sail with all possible dispatch to a named port does not necessarily relieve the charterer of further performance of his obligation under the charterparty, but if the breach is so prolonged that the contemplated voyage is frustrated it does have this effect. . . .

As my brethren have already pointed out, the shipowners' undertaking to tender a seaworthy ship has, as a result of numerous decisions as to what can amount to 'unseaworthiness,' become one of the most complex of contractual undertakings. It embraces obligations with respect to every part of the hull and machinery, stores and equipment and the crew itself. It can be broken by the presence of trivial defects easily and rapidly remediable as well as by defects which must inevitably result in a total loss of the vessel.

Consequently the problem in this case is, in my view, neither solved nor soluble by debating whether the shipowner's express or implied undertaking to tender a seaworthy ship is a 'condition' or a 'warranty.' It is like so many other contractual terms an undertaking one breach of which may give rise to an event which relieves the charterer of further performance of his undertakings if he so elects and another breach of which may not give rise to such an event but entitle him only to monetary compensation in the form of damages. . . .

What the judge had to do in the present case, as in any other case where one party to a contract relies upon a breach by the other party as giving him a right to elect to rescind the contract, and the contract itself makes no express provision as to this, was to look at the events which had occurred as a result of the breach at the time at which the charterers purported to rescind the charterparty and to decide whether the occurrence of those events deprived the charterers of substantially the whole benefit which it was the intention of the parties as expressed in the charterparty that the charterers should obtain from the further performance of their own contractual undertakings. . . .

The question which the judge had to ask himself was, as he rightly decided, whether or not at the date when the charterers purported to rescind the contract, namely, June 6, 1957, or when the shipowners purported to accept such rescission, namely, August 8, 1957, the delay which had already occurred as a result of the incompetence of the engine-room staff, and the delay which was likely to occur in repairing the engines of the vessel and the conduct of the shipowners by that date in taking steps to remedy these two matters, were, when taken together, such as to deprive the charterers of substantially the whole benefit which it was the intention of the parties they should obtain from further use of the vessel under the charterparty. . . .

UPJOHN LJ: Why is this apparently basic and underlying condition of seaworthiness not, in fact, treated as a condition? It is for the simple reason that the seaworthiness clause is breached by the slightest failure to be fitted 'in every way' for service. Thus, to take examples from the judgments in some of the cases I have mentioned above, if a nail is missing from one of the timbers of a wooden vessel or if proper medical supplies or two anchors are not on board at the time of sailing, the owners are in breach of the seaworthiness stipulation. It is contrary to common sense to suppose that in such circumstances the parties contemplated that the charterer should at once be entitled to treat the contract as at an end for such trifling breaches. . . .

It is open to the parties to a contract to make it clear either expressly or by necessary implication that a particular stipulation is to be regarded as a condition which goes to the root of the contract, so that it is clear that the parties contemplate that any breach of it entitles the other party at once to treat the contract as at an end. That matter has to be determined as a question of the proper interpretation of the contract. . . . Where, however, upon the true construction of the contract, the parties have not made a particular stipulation a condition, it would in my judgment be unsound and misleading to conclude that, being a warranty, damages is necessarily a sufficient remedy.

In my judgment the remedies open to the innocent party for breach of a stipulation which is not a condition strictly so called, depend entirely upon the nature of the breach and its foreseeable consequences. Breaches of stipulation fall, naturally, into two classes. First there is the case where the owner by his conduct indicates that he considers himself no longer bound to perform his part of the contract; in that case, of course, the charterer may accept the repudiation and treat the contract as at an end. The second class of case is, of course, the more usual one and that is where, due to misfortune such as the perils of the sea, engine failures, incompetence of the crew and so on, the owner is unable to perform a particular stipulation precisely in accordance with the terms of the contract try he never so hard to remedy it. In that case the question to be answered is, does the breach of the stipulation go so much to the root of the contract that it makes further commercial performance of the contract impossible, or in other words is the whole contract frustrated? If yea, the innocent party may treat the contract as at an end. If nay, his claim sounds in damages only.

If I have correctly stated the principles, then as the stipulation as to the seaworthiness is not a condition in the strict sense the question to be answered is, did the initial unseaworthiness as found by the judge, and from which there has been no appeal, go so much to the root of the contract that the charterers were then and there entitled to treat the charterparty as at an end? The only unseaworthiness alleged, serious though it was, was the insufficiency and incompetence of the crew, but that surely cannot be treated as going to the root of the contract for the parties must have contemplated that in such an event the crew could be changed and augmented. . . .

NOTES

1. Diplock LJ suggested the introduction of a third category of term—the intermediate or innominate term. However, the approach of Upjohn LJ has more to commend it. Upjohn LJ argues that the crucial test is to see if the term is a condition, and if it is not, then it should not be assumed that the remedy for breach of this non-condition is always damages. Instead, the effects of the breach should be examined, and if they were nevertheless serious effects, then the contract could be terminated. This approach avoids the uncomfortable task of distinguishing an intermediate term from a warranty. (See Reynolds (1981) 97 LQR 541 and Treitel, *The Law of Contract*, 11 edn, pp. 796–7, on the question of whether there are two or three types of terms.)

2. Diplock LJ also suggested that a term would be a condition only if every breach of the particular term would deprive the innocent party of substantially the whole benefit of the contract. However, this test was rejected by the House of Lords in *Bunge Corporation* v *Tradax SA*.

Bunge Corporation v Tradax SA
[1981] 1 WLR 711

The buyers agreed to purchase 15,000 tons of soya bean meal from the sellers. The terms of the shipment contract required three shipments of 5,000 tons each from a port in the Gulf of Mexico to be nominated by the sellers. The parties agreed that one shipment would be made in June 1975 and the buyers would provide a vessel at the nominated port. Clause 7 of the standard form stated that the buyers were to 'give at least 15 consecutive days' notice' of their probable readiness to load the vessel. In order for the goods to be shipped in June, this notice had to be given by 13 June. The notice was not given until 17 June, and the sellers claimed that the late notice was a breach amounting to a repudiation of the contract. They claimed damages from the buyers on the basis that by that time the market price of the soya bean meal had fallen by over $US 60 a ton. The buyers contended that the term as to notice was an intermediate term and the effect of the breach was not sufficiently serious for the sellers to treat the contract as repudiated.

Court of Appeal
[1980] 1 Lloyd's Rep 294

Held: it was not an intermediate term.

MEGAW LJ: . . . Mr Justice Parker was of the opinion that the term could not be a condition because of what he regarded as being 'the principles established in the *Hong Kong Fir* case' (*Hong Kong Shipping Co. Ltd* v *Kawasaki Kisen Kaisha Ltd* [1961] 2 Lloyd's Rep 478, [1962] 2 QB 26) and *The Hansa Nord Cehave* v *Bremer handelsgesellschaft mbH* [1975] 2 Lloyd's Rep 445, [1976] QB 44. The Judge goes on at p. 488:

> In the latter case, Lord Justice Roskill, while recognising that some terms of a contract of sale may be conditions, expressed the view that 'a Court should not be over ready unless required by statute or authority so to do, to construe a term in a contract as a condition . . .'.

The passage in the *Hong Kong Fir* case, to which Mr Justice Parker referred, was where Lord Justice Diplock said this: the passage at pp. 493 and 69

> No doubt there are many simple contractual undertakings sometimes express but more often because of their very simplicity ('It goes without saying') to be implied, of which it can be predicated that every breach of such an undertaking must give rise to an event which will deprive the party not in default of substantially the whole benefit which it was intended that he should obtain from the contract. And such a stipulation, unless the parties have agreed

that breach of it shall not entitle the non-defaulting party to treat the contract as repudiated, is a condition.

If that statement is intended to be a definition of the requirements which must always be satisfied, in all types of contract and all types of clauses, in order that a term may qualify as a condition, I would very respectfully express the view that it is not a correct statement of the law. . . . I think it can fairly be said that in mercantile contracts stipulations as to time not only may be, but usually are, to be treated as being 'of the essence of the contract', even though this is not expressly stated in the words of the contract. It would follow that in a mercantile contract it cannot be predicated that, for time to be of the essence, any and every breach of the term as to time must necessarily cause the innocent party to be deprived of substantially the whole of the benefit which it was intended that he should have. . . .

In my opinion in the term with which we are concerned the provision as to time is of the essence of the contract. The term is a condition.

It is, I believe, a factor which is not without weight in that conclusion that, at least, it tends towards certainty in the law. Lord Hailsham of St. Marylebone, Lord Chancellor, has said '. . . in legal matters, some degree of certainty is at least as valuable a part of justice as perfection'. [See *Broome* v *Cassell* [1972] AC 1027, at p. 1054]. I adhere to what I said in that respect in *The Mihalis Angelos* [1970] 2 Lloyd's Rep 43; [1971] 1 QB 164, at pp. 55 and 205. The parties, where time is of the essence, will at least know where they stand when the contractually agreed time has passed and the contract has been broken. They will not be forced to make critical decisions by trying to anticipate how serious, in the view of arbitrators or Courts, in later years, the consequences of the breach will retrospectively be seen to have been, in the light, it may be, of hindsight.

I must, however, return to the *Hong Kong Fir* case [1961] 2 Lloyd's Rep 478, [1962] 2 QB 26. No one now doubts the correctness of that decision: that there are 'intermediate' terms, breach of which may or may not entitle the innocent party to treat hmself as discharged from the further performance of his contractual obligation. No one now doubts that a term as to seaworthiness in a charter-party, in the absence of express provision to the opposite effect, is not a condition, but is an 'intermediate' term. The question arising on that case which I think we are compelled to examine in the present case is the test by which it falls to be decided whether a term is a condition.

I have previously quoted a passage from the judgment of Lord Justice Diplock at pp. 495 and 69. In its literal sense, the words there used would mean that the test whether a term is a condition is whether *every* breach of such an undertaking *must* give rise to an event which will deprive the party not in default of *substantially the whole benefit which it was intended that he should obtain from the contract* . . . If this is a definition of the requirements which, in English law, must always be fulfilled before any contractual term (in the absence, of course, of express words) can achieve the legal status of a condition, then the term with which we are here concerned would not pass the test. The view which I have expressed that it is a condition would necessarily be wrong.

There are various reasons why I do not think that this was intended to be a literal, definitive and comprehensive statement of the requirements of a condition; and also, if it were, why, with great respect, I do not think that it represents the law as it stands today.

First, if it were intended to cover terms as to time in mercantile contracts, how could the requirements be said to be met in respect of stipulations in contracts of types in which . . . time may be of the essence . . . It could never be said, as I see it, in any real sense, that *any* breach of such a stipulation *must necessarily* cause the innocent party to be deprived of *substantially all the benefit*.

. . . I do not see how any contractual term, whether as to time or otherwise, could ever pass the test. Conditions would no longer exist in the English law of contract. For it is always possible to suggest hypothetically some minor breach or breaches of any contractual term which might, without undue use of the imagination, be wholly insufficient to produce serious effects for the innocent party, let alone the loss of substantially all the benefit.

. . . [I]t is clear law, reaffirmed by the House of Lords since *Hong Kong Fir* was decided, that where there has been a breach of a condition the innocent party is entitled to elect whether or not to treat the contract as repudiated. . . . How could this right of election be anything other than a legal fiction, a chimera, if the election can arise only in circumstances in which, as a result of the breach, an event has happened which will deprive the innocent party of substantially the whole benefit which it was intended that he should receive? This test, it is to be observed, is regarded (*Hong Kong Fir*, pp. 495 and 72) as applying also where the term is an intermediate term, except that you then look to what has actually happened in order to see if the innocent party has lost substantially all the benefit. So, again, if the test be right, the former principle of English law that the innocent party has the right to elect is no longer anything but an empty shadow, for a right to elect to continue a contract, with the result that the innocent party will be bound to continue to perform his own contractual obligations, when he will, by definition, have lost substantially all his benefit under the contract, does not appear to me to make sense. . . .

[Megaw LJ applied the test given in the judgment of Sellers LJ in *Hong Kong Fir*:]

There is no way of deciding that question except by looking at the contract in the light of the surrounding circumstances, and then making up one's mind whether the intention of the parties, as gathered from the instrument itself, will best be carried out by treating the promise as a warranty sounding only in damages, or as a condition precedent by the failure to perform which the other party is relieved of his liability.

Applying that test, for the reasons which I have sought to give I would hold that the term here in question is a condition.

House of Lords

[1981] 1 WLR 711

Held: it was a condition since it was a stipulation as to time in a mercantile contract.

LORD WILBERFORCE: . . . As to such a clause there is only one kind of breach possible, namely to be late, and the questions which have to be asked are, first, what importance have the parties expressly ascribed to this consequence, and second, in the absence of expressed agreement, what consequence ought to be attached to it having regard to the contract as a whole.

The test suggested by the appellants was a different one. One must consider, they said, the breach actually committed and then decide whether that default would deprive the party not in default of substantially the whole benefit of the contract. . . .

One may observe in the first place that the introduction of a test of this kind would be commercially most undesirable. It would expose the parties, after a breach of one, two, three, seven and other numbers of days to an argument whether this delay would have left time for the seller to provide the goods. It would make it, at the time, at least difficult, and sometimes impossible, for the supplier to know whether he could do so. It would fatally remove from a vital provision in the contract that certainty which is the most indispensable quality of mercantile contracts, and lead to a large increase in arbitrations. It would confine the seller—perhaps after arbitration and reference through the courts—to a remedy in damages which might be extremely difficult to quantify. These are all serious objections in practice. But I am clear that the submission is unacceptable in law. . . . It remains true, as Lord Roskill has pointed out in *Cehave NV* v *Bremer Handelsgesellschaft mbH (The Hansa Nord)* [1976] QB 44, that the courts should not be too ready to interpret contractual clauses as conditions. And I have myself commended, and continue to commend, the greater flexibility in the law of contracts to which *Hong Kong Fir* points the way (*Reardon Smith Line Ltd* v *Hansen-Tangen* [1976] 1 WLR 989 at 998). But I do not doubt that, in suitable cases, the courts should not be reluctant, if the intentions of the parties as shown by the contract so indicate, to hold that an obligation has the force of a condition, and that indeed they should usually do so in the case of time clauses in mercantile contracts. To such cases the 'gravity of the breach' approach of *Hong Kong Fir* case would be unsuitable. . . .

NOTE: With the innominate term approach a party cannot use a minor breach by the other party to justify terminating a contract which has proved to be a bad bargain. For example, in *Reardon Smith Line Ltd* v *Hansen Tangen* [1976] 3 All ER 570, the fact that there was an error in stating the yard where a vessel was built did not enable the charterers to avoid the contract which had turned out to be unprofitable.

Relying upon *Cehave NV v Bremer Handelsgesellschaft mbH, The Hansa Nord*, Weir argued ([1976] CLJ 33) that the *Hong Kong Fir* v *Kawasaki* approach 'rewards incompetence'.

Cehave NV v *Bremer Handelsgesellschaft mbH, The Hansa Nord*
[1976] QB 44 (CA)

The German sellers agreed to sell to Dutch buyers 12,000 tons of US citrus pulp pellets for use as animal feed. The contract provided 'shipment to be made in good condition'. Following payment of the price of £100,000 by the buyers and receipt of shipping documents, a shipment arrived at the destination port with 1,260 tons in one hold of the *Hansa Nord* and 2,053 tons in the second hold. By this time the market price of citrus pulp pellets had fallen. Much of the cargo in the first hold was found to be damaged, while the goods in the second hold were undamaged. The buyers rejected the whole cargo from both holds, and claimed the repayment of the price on the ground that shipment was not made in good condition. The goods had been sold for £30,000 to an importer, who had resold them on the same day to the buyers at the same price of £30,000. The buyers then used the entire cargo to manufacture cattle feed (the original purpose). Held: the term 'shipment in good condition' was an intermediate term which did not give a right to reject unless the breach went to the root of the contract. Since the entire cargo was used for its intended purpose as animal feed, the breach did not go to the root of the contract and the buyers, though entitled to damages, were not entitled to reject the goods.

ORMROD LJ: . . . [Counsel for the sellers] relying on s. 11(1)(b) [Sale of Goods Act 1893], argued that in a contract of sale, the court was required to categorise all relevant stipulations as conditions or warranties, that this must be done by way of construction of the contract, and that, once done, the buyer's remedy for breach was determined; if a condition, he could reject, subject to the other provisions of the Act; if a warranty, he had no right to reject in any circumstances, his only remedy being damages. Construction, at least in theory, means ascertaining the intention of the parties in accordance with the general rules. If this submission is right, it means that a buyer can always reject for breach of a condition, however trivial the consequences, subject only to the so-called de minimis rule, and never reject for breach of warranty, however serious the consequences. So, on a falling market the buyer can take advantage of a minor breach of condition and, on a rising market, waive the breach and sue for damages. It also means, as Mocatta J pointed out . . . that if breach of a stipulation could have potentially serious consequences for a buyer, the court may be obliged, whatever the results in the instant case, to construe the stipulation as a condition. Moreoever, where the contract is in a standard form as in this case, a decision in one case will, in effect, categorise the stipulation for other cases in which the same form is used. . . .

If one asks oneself the question in the form, 'Did the parties intend that the buyer should be entitled to reject the goods if they were not shipped in good condition?' the answer must be that it depends on the nature and effects of the breach. This is directly in line with Diplock LJ's approach in the *Hong Kong Fir Shipping Co.* case [1962] 2 QB 26, 69–70, not surprisingly, since there can be very little difference in principle between whether the ship is seaworthy and whether goods are in good condition. There is obviously a strong case for applying the general principle of the *Hong Kong Fir Shipping Co.* case to contracts for the sale of goods. The question remains, however and it is the kernel of [counsel for the sellers'] submission, whether it is open to the court to do so. The parties themselves, of course, can do it by express agreement . . . If it can be done expressly, it can be done by implication, unless it is in some way prohibited. [Counsel for the sellers] argues that s. 11(1)(b) compels the court to choose between condition and warranty. I do not think that the subsection was intended to have any prohibitory effect. It is essentially a definition section, defining 'condition' and 'warranty' in terms of remedies. Nor is the classification absolutely rigid, for it provides that a buyer may treat a condition as a warranty if he wishes, by accepting the goods. It does not, however, envisage the possibility that a breach of warranty might go to the root of the contract, and so, in certain circumstances, entitle the buyer to treat the contract as repudiated. But the law has developed since the Act was passed. It is now accepted as a general principle since the *Hong Kong Fir Shipping Co.* case [1962] 2 QB 26 that it is the events resulting from the breach, rather than the breach itself, which may destroy the consideration for the buyer's promise and so enable him to treat the contract as repudiated.

The problem is how to integrate this principle with s. 11(1)(b). In practice it may not arise very often. Faced with a breach which has had grave consequences for a buyer, the court may be disposed to hold that he was entitled ex post facto, to rescind, or reject the goods, without categorising the broken stipulation, applying the general principles of the law of contract. The difficulty only arises if the court had already categorised the stipulation as a warranty. The present case provides an example. If the relevant part of clause 7 is construed as a warranty in this case, and later, another dispute occurs in relation to another contract in the same form, between the same parties, for the sale of similar goods, in which the breach of clause 7 has produced much more serious consequences for the buyer, is the court bound by its decision in this case to hold that the buyer is precluded from rejecting the goods under the later contract because, as a matter of construction, it has already categorised the stipulation as a warranty? This is the converse of *The Mihalis Angelos* [1971] 1 QB 164 situation. If the answer is in the affirmative s. 11(1)(b) has, by implication, excluded one of the general common law rules of contract. It was clearly not intended to have this effect and I agree with Lord Denning MR, for the reasons that he has given in his judgment, that the Act should not, if it can be avoided, be construed in this way. Section 61(2) seems to provide an answer. If this view is correct it is bound to have important repercussions on the way in which courts in future will approach the construction of stipulations in contracts for the sale of goods. It will no longer be necessary to place so much emphasis on the potential effects of a breach on the buyer, and to feel obliged, as Mocatta J did in this case, to construe a stipulation as a condition because in other cases or in other circumstances the buyer ought to be entitled to reject. Consequently, the court will be freer to regard stipulations, as a matter of construction, as warranties, if what might be called the 'back-up' rule of the common law is available to protect buyers who ought to be able to reject in proper circumstances. I doubt whether, strictly speaking, this involves the creation of a third category of stipulations; rather, it recognises another ground for holding that a buyer is entitled to reject, namely, that, de facto, the consideration for his promise has been wholly destroyed.

The result may be summarised in this way. When a breach of contract has taken place the question arises: 'Is the party who is not in breach entitled in law to treat the contract as repudiated or, in the case of a buyer, to reject the goods? The answer depends on the answers to a series of other questions. Adopting Upjohn LJ's judgment in the *Hong Kong Fir Shipping Co.* case [1962] 2 QB 26, 64, the first question is: 'Does the contract expressly provide that in the event of the breach of the term in question the other party is entitled to terminate the contract or reject the goods?' If the answer is No, the next question is: 'Does the contract when correctly construed so provide?' The relevant term, for example, may be described as a 'condition.' The question then arises whether this word is used as a code word for the phrase 'shall be entitled to repudiate the contract or reject the goods,' or in some other sense, as in *Wickman Machine Tool Sales Ltd* v *L. Schuler AG* [1972] 1 WLR 840. The next question is whether the breach of the relevant term creates a right to repudiate or reject. This may arise either from statute or as a result of judicial decision on particular contractual terms. For example, if the requirements of s. 14(1) or (2) of the Sale of Goods Act 1893 are fulfilled, the buyer will be entitled to reject the goods, as a result of this section, read with s. 11(2). In fact, in all those sections of the Sale of Goods Act 1893 which create implied conditions the word 'condition' is, by definition a code word for 'breach of this term will entitle the buyer to reject the goods,' subject to any other relevant provision of the Act. In other cases, the courts have decided that breach of some specific terms, such as, for example, an 'expected ready to load' stipulation, will ipso facto give rise to a right in the other party to repudiate the contract: *The Mihalis Angelos* [1971] 1 QB 164, 194, *per* Lord Denning MR. In these two classes of case the consequences of the breach are irrelevant or, more accurately, are assumed to go to the root of the contract, and to justify repudiation. There remains the non-specific class where the events produced by the breach are such that it is reasonable to describe the breach as going to the root of the contract and so justifying repudiation.

If this approach is permissible in the present case I would unhesitatingly hold that the stipulation in clause 7 that the goods were to be shipped in good condition was not a condition, and that on the facts of this case the breach did not go to the root of the contract, and that, consequently, the buyers were not entitled to reject the goods.

NOTES

1. Weir's argument is that, because the Court of Appeal did not want the buyers to get the cargo for substantially less than its true value, they made the buyers pay the true value of the spoilt cargo (and the sellers' profit) even though the initial breach was by the sellers in shipping goods which were not in good condition. The buyers were punished for wrongfully rejecting the goods. Weir argued that the guilty party gets all that he bargained for, unless there is a breach of a condition so that he gets no part of what he bargained for. (Ormrod LJ's judgment must now be read in the light of s. 15A of the Sale of Goods Act 1979, inserted by the Sale and Supply of Goods Act 1994, *page 243*.)

2. The next case is one of the rare examples where the effects of the breach of an intermediate term were sufficiently serious to justify termination.

Federal Commerce & Navigation Co. Ltd v *Molena Alpha Inc.*
[1979] AC 757 (HL)

Clause 9 of a charter provided that the charterers were to sign bills of lading stating that the freight had been correctly paid. After a dispute arose concerning deductions made by the charterers, the shipowners withdrew this authority, contrary to the terms of the charter. The master was instructed not to sign bills of lading with the indorsement 'freight pre paid' or which did not contain an indorsement giving the owners a lien over the cargo for freight. This meant that the charterers would be put in an impossible position commercially. The charterers treated the owner's actions as a repudiation of the charter. Held: although the term broken was not a condition, the breach went to the root of the contract by depriving the charterers of virtually the whole benefit of the contract because the issue of such bills was essential to the charterers' trade.

Aerial Advertising Co. v *Batchelors Peas Ltd (Manchester)*
[1938] 2 All ER 788

The plaintiffs and the defendants entered into a contract whereby the plaintiffs were to advertise the defendants' goods by flying over various towns trailing a banner reading 'Eat Batchelors' Peas'. The pilot was to telephone the defendants each day to get their approval for what he proposed to do that day. He failed to do this on 11 November 1937, and flew over the main square in Salford during the two minutes' silence on Armistice Day, towing his banner, much to the indignation of the thousands of people there. The defendants received many letters announcing that their goods would be boycotted, and there was a marked drop in demand for their goods. The defendants sought damages and a declaration that they would no longer be bound by the contract. Atkinson J released them on the ground that it was commercially wholly unreasonable to continue with the contract. However, this was based on the seriousness of the consequences of the breach.

NOTE: This last case pre-dates *Hong Kong Fir* v *Kawasaki*.

SECTION 6: ENTIRE OBLIGATIONS

A contractual obligation may be construed as 'entire'. This means that it must be completely and precisely performed before the other party is obliged to perform his contractual obligations.

Cutter v *Powell*
(1795) 6 Term Rep 320; 101 ER 573 (Court of King's Bench)

Cutter was employed as second mate for a sea voyage from Jamaica to Liverpool. It was agreed that 10 days after the ship's arrival in Liverpool, Cutter was to receive 'thirty guineas, provided he proceeds, continues and does his duty as second mate in the said ship from hence to the port of Liverpool'. The ship sailed on 2 August 1793, but Cutter died on 20 September, before the ship arrived in Liverpool on 9 October. Cutter's widow sought wages for the work he had completed before his death on a *quantum meruit* basis (i.e., reasonable value of work done). The usual wages of a second mate were £4 a month and this voyage usually took eight weeks. Held: Cutter's obligation in respect of the voyage was entire and the defendant's promise depended upon the condition precedent being performed. Emphasis was placed on the fact that a second mate would normally expect to earn £8 on such a voyage, whereas Cutter had been promised £30 if he fulfilled these conditions.

ASHHURST J: . . . This is a written contract, and it speaks for itself. And as it is entire, and as the defendant's promise depends on a condition precedent to be performed by the other party, the condition must be performed before the other party is entitled to receive any thing under it. It has been argued however that the plaintiff may now recover on a quantum meruit: but she has no right to desert the agreement; for wherever there is an express contract the parties must be guided by it; and one party cannot relinquish or abide by it as it may suit his advantage. Here the intestate was by the terms of his contract to perform a given duty before he could call upon the defendant to pay him any thing; it was a condition precedent, without performing which the defendant is not liable. And that seems to me to conclude the question: the intestate did not perform the contract on his part; he was not indeed to blame for not doing it; but still as this was a condition precedent, and as he did not perform it, his representative is not entitled to recover.

NOTES
1. In the light of the fact that the promised sum was considerably in excess of the market rate for the job, it is hardly surprising that the court interpreted this express stipulation as meaning that Cutter was to receive 30 guineas if he performed and nothing if he did not. The contract placed the risk of non-completion on Cutter.
2. The courts lean against construing obligations as entire, so that such obligations are the exception rather than the rule. If an obligation is severable or divisible, then the defaulting party can recover at the stipulated rate for each instalment provided, subject to a set-off or counterclaim for damages for breach (for example, the Apportionment Act 1870 provides that 'salaries' and 'other periodical payments in the nature of income' are severable).
3. A contract can have both entire and severable obligations.
4. Statute provides that the obligation to deliver the correct quantity in a sale of goods contract, which is not an instalment contract and where the buyer is a consumer, is entire (Sale of Goods Act 1979, s. 30 as amended by the Sale and Supply of Goods Act 1994), so that if a seller delivers too much or too little the buyer is entitled to refuse to accept the goods and pay for them (subject to the *de minimis* rule, i.e., minor discrepancies). However, if goods supplied are defective in quality, that is not a breach of an entire obligation.

5. Building contracts which provide for a lump sum payment on completion will be construed as entire, because it is not possible to apportion the price over the work completed.

It is possible to recover on a *quantum meruit* for work done if the injured party had the option to accept or reject the partial performance and voluntarily accepted it.

Sumpter v Hedges
[1898] 1 QB 673 (CA)

The plaintiff builder contracted with the defendant to build two houses and stables on the defendant's land for a lump sum of £565. The plaintiff did work amounting to £333 in value, but then informed the defendant that he had no money and could not go on with the work. The defendant finished the building himself, using building materials belonging to the plaintiff which the plaintiff had left on the defendant's land. Held: the obligation to do the building work was entire. The defendant had not voluntarily adopted the partial performance, so that there was no new implied contract to pay for the partial performance on a *quantum meruit* basis.

COLLINS LJ: . . . There are cases in which, though the plantiff has abandoned the performance of a contract, it is possible for him to raise the inference of a new contract to pay for the work done on a quantum meruit from the defendant's having taken the benefit of that work, but, in order that that may be done, the circumstances must be such as to give an option to the defendant to take or not to take the benefit of the work done. It is only where the circumstances are such as to give that option that there is any evidence on which to ground the inference of a new contract. Where, as in the case of work done on land, the circumstances are such as to give the defendant no option whether he will take the benefit of the work or not, then one must look to other facts than the mere taking the benefit of the work in order to ground the inference of a new contract. In this case I see no other facts on which such an inference can be founded. The mere fact that a defendant is in possession of what he cannot help keeping, or even has done work upon it, affords no ground for such an inference. He is not bound to keep unfinished a building which in an incomplete state would be a nuisance on his land. I am therefore of opinion that the plaintiff was not entitled to recover for the work which he had done. . . .

NOTE: The injured party must have the option whether to accept the partial performance. In cases of unfinished buildings on the injured party's land, there is no practical choice. However, the defendant did not have to accept the materials left on his land but decided to do so. Bruce J, at first instance, held that the defendant had to pay for these materials.

If the party in breach has 'substantially performed' his obligations as to quality under the contract, then he can claim the price less damages in respect of the defective performance.

Hoenig v Isaacs
[1952] 2 All ER 176 (CA)

The defendant employed the plaintiff to decorate and furnish the defendant's flat for the sum of £750 'net cash as the work proceeds and the balance on completion'. The defendant refused to pay the balance of £350 on the ground that certain of the work done and articles supplied were defective. The defendant contended that the plaintiff could not recover the balance since this was an entire obligation which the plaintiff had not performed. The official referee found that a wardrobe door needed replacing and a bookcase required alterations and assessed the cost of remedying the defects at £55. Held: in the case of an entire contract, the defendant cannot repudiate liability on the ground that the work, though substantially performed, is in some respects not in accordance with the contract. The defendant was therefore liable for the balance, less a deduction for the cost of putting right the defects.

SOMERVELL LJ: . . . Each case turns on the construction of the contract. [*Cutter* v *Powell*] clearly decided that his continuing as mate during the whole voyage was a condition precedent to payment. It did not decide that if he had completed the main purpose of the contract, namely, serving as mate for the whole voyage, the defendant could have repudiated his liability by establishing that in the course of the voyage the sailor had, possibly through inadvertence, failed on some occasion in his duty as mate whereby some damage had been caused. . . .

The principle that fulfilment of every term is not necessarily a condition precedent in a contract for a lump sum is usually traced back to a short judgment of Lord Mansfield CJ in *Boone* v *Eyre* (1779) 1 Hy Bl 273n—the sale of the plantation with its slaves. Lord Mansfield said:

. . . where mutual covenants go to the whole of the consideration on both sides, they are mutual conditions, the one precedent to the other. But where they go only to a part, where a breach may be paid for in damages, there the defendant has a remedy on his covenant, and shall not plead it as a condition precedent.

The learned official referee regarded *H. Dakin & Co. Ltd* v *Lee* [1916] 1 KB 566 as laying down that the price must be paid subject to set-off or counterclaim if there was a substantial compliance with the contract. I think on the face of this case where the work was finished in the ordinary sense, though in part defective, this is right. It expresses in a convenient epithet what is put from another angle in the Sale of Goods Act, 1893. The buyer cannot reject if he proves only the breach of a term collateral to the main purpose. . . .

DENNING LJ: In determining this issue the first question is whether, on the true construction of the contract, entire performance was a condition precedent to payment. It was a lump sum contract, but that does not mean that entire performance was a condition precedent to payment. When a contract provides for a specific sum to be paid on completion of specified work, the courts lean against a construction of the contract which would deprive the contractor of any payment at all simply because there are some defects or omissions. The promise to complete the work is, therefore, construed as a term of the contract, but not as a condition. It is not every breach of that term which absolves the employer from his promise to pay the price, but only a breach which goes to the root of the contract, such as an abandonment of the work when it is only half done. Unless the breach does go to the root of the matter, the employer cannot resist payment of the price. He must pay it and bring a cross-claim for the defects and omissions, or, alternatively, set them up in diminution of the price. It is, of course, always open to the parties by express words to make entire performance a condition precedent. A familiar instance is when the contract provides for progress payments to be made as the work proceeds, but for retention money to be held until completion. Then entire performance is usually a condition precedent to payment of the retention money, but not, of course, to the progress payments. The contractor is entitled to payment pro rata as the work proceeds, less a deduction for retention money. But he is not entitled to the retention money until the work is entirely finished, without defects or omissions. In the present case the contract provided for 'net cash, as the work proceeds; and balance on completion.' If the balance could be regarded as retention money, then it might well be that the contractor ought to have done all the work correctly, without defects or omissions, in order to be entitled to the balance. But I do not think the balance should be regarded as retention money. Retention money is usually only ten per cent, or fifteen per cent, whereas this balance was more than fifty per cent. I think this contract should be regarded as an ordinary lump sum contract. It was substantially performed. The contractor is entitled, therefore, to the contract price, less a deduction for the defects.

ROMER LJ: . . . In certain cases it is right that the rigid rule for which the defendant contends should be applied, for example, if a man tells a contractor to build a ten foot wall for him in his garden and agrees to pay £x for it, it would not be right that he should be held liable for any part of the contract price if the contractor builds the wall to two feet and then renounces further performance of the contract, or builds the wall of a totally different material from that which was ordered, or builds it at the wrong end of the garden. The work contracted for has not been done and the corresponding obligation to pay consequently never arises. But when a man fully performs his contract in the sense that he supplies all that he agreed to supply but what he supplies is subject to defects of so minor a character that he can be said to have substantially performed his promise, it is, in my judgment, far more equitable to apply the *H. Dakin & Co. Ltd* v *Lee* [1916] 1 KB 566 principle than to deprive him wholly of his contractual rights and relegate him to such remedy (if any) as he may have on a quantum meruit. . . .

NOTES

1. *Hoenig* v *Isaacs* concerned defective performance, whereas *Cutter* v *Powell* concerned the order of performance. In *Cutter* v *Powell*, although the obligation to serve as second mate for the entire voyage was entire, Cutter could have recovered the 30 guineas less a deduction for breach if he had completed the voyage but in serving in that capacity he had been guilty of any breach of duty.

   Although the obligation to deliver the correct quantity in a sale of goods contract where the buyer is a consumer is entire, the obligation that the goods should be fit for the purpose and of satisfactory quality is not entire. If the correct quantity of goods is delivered but they are defective, then the consumer buyer can terminate the contract (subject to the option to require repair or replacement, reg. 5 of the Sale and Supply of Goods to Consumers Regulations 2002, inserting s. 48A–F Sale of Goods Act 1979) because of the breach of the s. 14 condition, so that he does not have to pay, but that has nothing to do with the entire obligation rule.

   In *Hoenig* v *Isaacs*, the obligation to decorate and furnish the flat was entire but the quality obligation was not entire. It may therefore be the case that the substantial performance doctrine is being applied to the quality obligation and not to the entire obligation itself.

2. In *Williams* v *Roffey Brothers & Nicholls (Contractors) Ltd* [1991] 1 QB 1 (*page 135*), it was argued by the defendants that the alteration provided that the plaintiff would be paid on completion of each of the flats. The Court of Appeal, relying on *Hoenig* v *Isaacs*, held that the plaintiff had 'substantially completed' and was entitled to the payment for the eight flats, less a deduction for defects and incomplete work.

■ QUESTION

Was there any incomplete work in *Hoenig* v *Isaacs*? It appears that the Court of Appeal in *Williams* v *Roffey* failed to appreciate that the obligation actually to finish the work is entire.

Bolton v Mahadeva
[1972] 1 WLR 1009 (CA)

The plaintiff agreed with the defendant that he would install central heating in the defendant's house for a lump sum of £560. When the work was completed, the defendant complained that it was defective and refused to pay. The judge found that the flue was defective so that it gave off fumes making the rooms uncomfortable, and the system was inefficient in that the amount of heat varied from one room to another. The cost of rectifying these defects was £174. Held: the plaintiff was not entitled to recover as there had been no substantial performance.

CAIRNS LJ: The main question in the case is whether the defects in workmanship found by the judge to be such as to cost £174 to repair—that is, between one third and one quarter of the contract price—were of such a character and amount that the plaintiff could not be said to have substantially performed his contract. That is, in my view, clearly the legal principle which has to be applied to cases of this kind. . . .

In considering whether there was substantial performance I am of opinion that it is relevant to take into account both the nature of the defects and the proportion between the cost of rectifying them and the contract price. It would be wrong to say that the contractor is only entitled to payment if the defects are so trifling as to be covered by the de minimis rule.

The main matters that were complained of in this case were that when the heating system was put on, fumes were given out which made some of the living rooms (to put it at the lowest) extremely uncomfortable and inconvenient to use; secondly, that by reason of there being insufficient radiators and insufficient insulation, the heating obtained by the central heating system was far below what it should have been. . . .

Now, certainly it appears to me that the nature and amount of the defects in this case were far different from those which the court had to consider in *H. Dakin & Co. Ltd* v *Lee* [1916] 1 KB 566 and *Hoenig* v *Isaacs* [1952] 2 All ER 176. For my part, I find it impossible to say that the judge was right in reaching the conclusion that in those circumstances the contract had been substantially performed. The contract was a contract to install a central heating system. If a central heating system when installed is such that it does not heat the house adequately and is such, further, that fumes are given out, so as to make living rooms uncomfortable, and if the putting right of those defects is not something which can be done by some slight amendment of the system, then I think that the contract is not substantially performed.

NOTES

1. This type of breach clearly goes to the root of the contract, and it appears that on that basis the performance could not be 'substantial'. It is very similar to the nature of the effects of the breach approach adopted in *Hong Kong Fir* v *Kawasaki*, *page 250*. If the actual defects are serious, the contract is repudiated; if they are trivial, it is not.

2. This decision shows that it can be difficult to distinguish between fulfilling performance (finishing the work) which is an entire obligation, and the quality obligation (which is not). This difficulty may explain the treatment of this issue by the Court of Appeal in *Williams* v *Roffey*, *page 262*.

3. The Law Commission's Report No. 121, *Pecuniary Restitution for Breach of Contract* (1983) (Burrows (1984) 47 MLR 76), recommended that a party who partly performs an entire contract should be permitted to recover in respect of benefits he has conferred on the other as a result of that part performance. These recommendations have not been implemented.

7

Exemption Clauses and Unfair Contract Terms

As a general definition, an exemption clause is a term in a contract or notice which either seeks to exclude liability or remedies for breach of contract and/or negligence (referred to as 'exclusion clauses' in this casebook), or which seeks to limit that liability to a specified sum (referred to as 'limitation clauses').

SECTION 1: THE NATURE OF EXEMPTION CLAUSES

Do exemption clauses operate purely as a defence once the breach of contract or negligence has been established, or are they to be construed with all the other terms of the contract so as to define the initial obligations of the parties?

The general approach of the courts has been to treat an exclusion clause as a defence, i.e., as removing liability for breach of an existing obligation. The definitional approach involves construing all of the terms together so that the party is not taken to have accepted this liability at all. Lord Diplock adopted this approach in *Photo Production Ltd* v *Securicor Transport Ltd* [1980] AC 827, at pp. 850 and 851 (for the full facts and discussion of this case, see *page 283*):

My Lords, an exclusion clause is one which excludes or modifies an obligation, whether primary, general secondary or anticipatory secondary that would otherwise arise under the contract by implication of law. Parties are free to agree to whatever exclusion or modification of all types of obligations as they please within the limits that the agreement must retain the legal characteristics of a contract . . . [I]n the absence of the exclusion clause which Lord Wilberforce has cited, a primary obligation of Securicor under the contract, which would be implied by law, would be an absolute obligation to procure that the visits by the night patrol to the factory were conducted by natural persons who would exercise reasonable skill and care for the safety of the factory. That primary obligation is modified by the exclusion clause. Securicor's obligation to do this is not to be absolute, but is limited to exercising due diligence in its capacity as employer of the natural persons by whom the visits are conducted, to procure that those persons shall exercise reasonable skill and care for the safety of the factory.

SECTION 2: THE GENERAL APPROACH TO EXEMPTION CLAUSES

There are some distinct advantages in the use of exemption clauses to allocate risk, e.g., the avoidance of duplicate insurance and lower pricing. However, at common law, the courts were very concerned to protect a party against an exemption clause imposed without negotiation by a party who had superior bargaining power. The courts could achieve this by finding that the clause had not been incorporated as a term of the contract, e.g. *Thornton* v *Shoe Lane Parking Ltd* [1971] 2 QB 163, *page 217,* although this option was not available in the majority of cases where the weaker party had signed a standard form contract without reading it (*L'Estrange* v *Graucob Ltd* [1934] 2 KB 394, see *page 212*). More frequently, they resorted to construing the clause so that it did not provide protection for the stronger party in the circumstances which had occurred. To achieve this, the courts often construed the clause artificially (*Hollier* v *Rambler Motors (AMC) Ltd* [1972] 2 QB 71, see *page 276*).

Since the Unfair Contract Terms Act 1977 (and the Unfair Terms in Consumer Contracts Regulations 1999), there is no longer a need for the courts to adopt such restrictive approaches to incorporation and construction. Lord Diplock stated in *Photo Production Ltd* v *Securicor Transport Ltd* (at p. 851).

My Lords, the reports are full of cases in which what would appear to be very strained constructions have been placed upon exclusion clauses, mainly in what today would be called consumer contracts and contracts of adhesion. As Lord Wilberforce has pointed out, any need for this kind of judicial distortion of the English language has been banished by Parliament's having made these kinds of contracts subject to the Unfair Contract Terms Act 1977. In commercial contracts negotiated between businessmen capable of looking after their own interests and of deciding how risks inherent in the performance of various kinds of contract can be most economically borne (generally by insurance), it is, in my view, wrong to place a strained construction upon words in an exclusion clause which are clear and fairly susceptible of one meaning only even after due allowance has been made for the presumption in favour of the implied primary and secondary obligations.

SECTION 3: REQUIREMENTS THAT MUST BE SATISFIED BEFORE AN EXEMPTION CLAUSE CAN BE RELIED UPON

A party seeking to rely on an exemption clause must show:

(a) that it has been incorporated as a term of the contract (see the discussion of incorporation of terms at *pages 212–29*);

(b) that, on its natural and ordinary meaning, it covers the event(s) which has/have occurred (see *section 4, below*);

(c) that it is not rendered unenforceable by the Unfair Contract Terms Act 1977 (UCTA 1977) or the Unfair Terms in Consumer Contracts Regulations 1999 (see *section 5, below*).

SECTION 4: CONSTRUCTION—ON ITS NATURAL AND ORDINARY MEANING THE CLAUSE COVERED WHAT HAPPENED

Before UCTA 1977, the courts adopted a restrictive and often artificial approach to construction in order to protect the weaker party. Lord Denning admitted this in the Court of Appeal in *George Mitchell (Chesterhall) Ltd* v *Finney Lock Seeds Ltd* [1983] QB 284 (at p. 297):

The heyday of freedom of contract

None of you nowadays will remember the trouble we had—when I was called to the Bar—with exemption clauses. They were printed in small print on the back of tickets and order forms and invoices. They were contained in catalogues or timetables. They were held to be binding on any person who took them without objection. No one ever did object. He never read them or knew what was in them. No matter how unreasonable they were, he was bound. All this was done in the name of 'freedom of contract.' But the freedom was all on the side of the big concern which had the use of the printing press. No freedom for the little man who took the ticket or order form or invoice. The big concern said, 'Take it or leave it.' The little man had no option but to take it. The big concern could and did exempt itself from liability in its own interest without regard to the little man. It got away with it time after time. When the courts said to the big concern, 'You must put it in clear words,' the big concern had no hesitation in doing so. It knew well that the little man would never read the exemption clauses or understand them.

It was a bleak winter for our law of contract. It is illustrated by two cases, *Thompson* v *London, Midland and Scottish Railway Co.* [1930] 1 KB 41 (in which there was exemption from liability, not on the ticket, but only in small print at the back of the timetable, and the company were held not liable) and *L'Estrange* v *F. Graucob Ltd* [1934] 2 KB 394 (in which there was complete exemption in small print at the bottom of the order form, and the company were held not liable).

The secret weapon

Faced with this abuse of power—by the strong against the weak—by the use of the small print of the conditions—the judges did what they could to put a curb upon it. They still had before them the idol, 'freedom of contract.' They still knelt down and worshipped it, but they concealed under their cloaks a secret weapon. They used it to stab the idol in the back. This weapon was called 'the true construction of the contract.' They used it with great skill and ingenuity. They used it so as to depart from the natural meaning of the words of the exemption clause and to put upon them a strained and unnatural construction. In case after case, they said that the words were not strong enough to give the big concern exemption from liability; or that in the circumstances the big concern was not entitled to rely on the exemption clause . . .

When examining many of the cases that follow, it is important to bear in mind that the courts are unlikely to adopt such a restrictive approach to the question of construction after UCTA 1977 and the Unfair Terms in Consumer Contracts Regulations 1999.

A: *Contra proferentem*

Any ambiguity in an exemption clause will be resolved against the party seeking to rely upon it.

Houghton v *Trafalgar Insurance Co. Ltd*

[1954] 1 QB 247 (CA)

A car insurance policy excluded liability for damage 'caused or arising whilst the car is conveying any load in excess of that for which it was constructed'. At the time of an accident there were six people in a car with seating accommodation for five and the insurers denied liability claiming that this was a load in excess of that for which the car was constructed. Held: the word 'load' only covered cases where there was a specified weight which must not be exceeded, as in the case of lorries or vans.

ROMER LJ: . . . I think that it would be most regrettable if a provision of this kind were held to have the force for which the defendants contend. It would be a serious thing for a motorist involved in a collision if he were told that the particular circumstances of the accident excluded him from the benefit of the policy. I think that any clause or provision that purports to have that effect ought to be clear and unambiguous so that the motorist knows exactly where he stands. This provision is neither clear nor unambiguous. If applied to a private motor-car I have not the least idea what it means . . .

NOTES

1. As Romer LJ appears to be suggesting, policy reasons may also have caused the Court of Appeal to reject the insurers' suggested interpretation, since it would have had a devastating effect on the ability of innocent third parties to recover on car insurance policies in those circumstances.
2. In *Andrews Brothers (Bournemouth) Ltd* v *Singer & Co. Ltd* [1934] 1 KB 17, the exemption covered all implied obligations, but the Court of Appeal held that the defendants could not rely on this as exempting them from liability for breach of the express obligation that the car be 'new'.
3. Regulation 7(2) of the Unfair Terms in Consumer Contracts Regulations 1999 incorporates *contra proferentem* in legislative form and reg. 7(1) imposes a duty to avoid ambiguity.

UNFAIR TERMS IN CONSUMER CONTRACTS REGULATIONS 1999

7. Written contracts

(1) A seller or supplier shall ensure that any written term of a contract is expressed in plain, intelligible language.

(2) If there is doubt about the meaning of a written term, the interpretation which is most favourable to the consumer shall prevail but this rule shall not apply in proceedings brought under regulation 12.

B: Liability for negligence

It is often difficult to grasp the concept that in an action in negligence, the defendant may seek to rely on an exemption clause in a contract to which he is a party in order to protect himself (as to the position where a third party seeks to do this see *Chapter 10*).

The approach of the courts has been to limit the scope of the exemption clause and construe it so that it covers only contractual liability unless the clause expressly extends to negligence.

In *Canada Steamship Lines Ltd* v *R* [1952] AC 192, at p. 208 Lord Morton of Henryton laid down a construction test to ascertain whether the clause covers negligence liability:

Their Lordships think that the duty of a court in approaching the consideration of such clauses may be summarised as follows:—

(1) If the clause contains language which expressly exempts the person in whose favour it is made (hereafter called 'the proferens') from the consequence of the negligence of his own servants, effect must be given to that provision. . . .

(2) If there is no express reference to negligence, the court must consider whether the words used are wide enough, in their ordinary meaning, to cover negligence on the part of the servants of the proferens. If a doubt arises at this point, it must be resolved against the proferens . . .

(3) If the words used are wide enough for the above purpose, the court must then consider whether 'the head of damage may be based on some ground other than that of negligence,' to quote again Lord Greene, in the *Alderslade* case [1945] KB 189. The 'other ground' must not be so fanciful or remote that the proferens cannot be supposed to have desired protection against it; but subject to this qualification, which is no doubt to be implied from Lord Greene's words, the existence of a possible head of damage other than that of negligence is fatal to the proferens even if the words used are prima facie wide enough to cover negligence on the part of his servants. . . .

NOTE: The first possibility is that the clause expressly refers to negligence or a synonym of negligence. Most clauses will use more general words. The following case concerned a clause that covered negligence liability, as the words 'neglect or default' were synonymous with negligence.

Monarch Airlines Ltd v *London Luton Airport Ltd*
[1997] CLC 698 (QBD—Admiralty)

Loose paving blocks had damaged one of the plaintiff airline's aircraft as it was preparing to take off from the airport. When the plaintiff sued to recover damages for negligence and/or breach of duty under s. 2 of the Occupiers' Liability Act 1957, the defendant sought to rely on clause 10 of its standard conditions which excluded the liability of the airport, its servants, and agents for any damage to aircraft 'arising or resulting directly or indirectly from any act, omission, neglect or default . . . unless done with intent to cause damage or recklessly and with knowledge that damage would probably result'. The plaintiff submitted that this clause did not cover the liability that had occurred since, applying the test in *Canada Steamship* v *R*, clause 10 did not cover negligence liability. However, Clarke J held: the clause excluded liability for negligence and any breach of statutory duty unless the negligence or breach was caused either with intent to cause damage or recklessly and with knowledge that damage would probably result. The words 'neglect or default' were synonymous with negligence.

CLARKE J: [Clarke J referred to the following statement by Lloyd J in *The Golden Leader* [1980] 2 Lloyd's Rep 573, at 574:]

> Like all rules of construction Lord Morton's test is a guide designed to ascertain the true intention of the parties. It should not be applied rigidly or mechanically so as to defeat their intentions. In the present case the owners have, by clause 2, accepted liability in three cases, and three cases only, namely improper or negligent stowage, personal want of due diligence to make the vessel seaworthy, and personal act or default of the owners or their manager. By accepting liability in respect of those three matters only, and I emphasise the word 'only', they have beyond doubt excluded liability in respect of all other causes: see *Westfal-Larsen and Co. A/S* v *Colonial Sugar Refining Co. Ltd* [1960] 2 Lloyd's Rep 206, expressly approved by McNair J in *The Brabant* . . . [1967] 1 QB 588. . . . The clause adverts specifically to negligence. It accepts liability for negligence in some respects, but in those respects only. It follows that it excludes negligence in all other respects. There is no ambiguity. To hold the owners liable for negligence in any respect other than those mentioned would be to defeat the plain intention of the clause.

I respectfully agree with the approach adopted by Lloyd J in that passage. All depends upon the particular clause, but, like him, it appears to me that where the clause is in the form of 'not liable unless' or 'only liable if' it may well not be appropriate to consider each of the questions raised by Lord Morton. In any event, in my judgment the clause with which I am concerned can properly be analysed in much the same way as Lloyd J analysed the clause in *The Golden Leader*. Under cl. 10 there is to be no liability arising from any act, omission, neglect or default unless done with intent to cause damage or recklessly and with knowledge that damage would probably result. Thus there is only to be liability in any of those cases if there is an intention to cause damage or if there is relevant recklessness. . . .

[Counsel for the defendant] submits that if it is necessary to consider each of Lord Morton's tests, the question under test one is whether, as Steyn LJ put it in *EE Caledonia* (at p. 651H) the clause contains words which are 'synonymous with negligence, or words which in the case law have acquired a status equivalent to a reference to negligence'. That is in my opinion the correct approach. In this connection [counsel] submits that the case law shows that the words 'neglect or default' have been treated as synonymous with negligence. He relies upon the decision of the Divisional Court in *Shaw* v *Great Western Railway Co.* [1894] 1 QB 373.

. . . It is true that the court was considering the words in a particular context, but I accept [counsel's] submission that it treated them as synonymous with negligence, as in my judgment they are. It follows that the clause passes Lord Morton's first test.

It seems to me that the words 'any, act, omission, neglect or default' were clearly intended to include negligent acts and that the whole purpose of the clause was to exclude the consequences of all deliberate and negligent acts unless they were done with the intention or recklessness described in the clause. I do not think that there is anything in the decision of the Court of Appeal in the *EF Caledonia* case to lead to any other conclusion, if only because the clause with which the court was concerned there was not a 'not liable unless' or 'only liable if' clause. . . .

If the clause does not pass Lord Morton's first test, it passes the second because the words are wide enough in their ordinary meaning to cover negligence on the part of the servants of the defendant. In that event the question is whether they pass Lord Morton's third test. . . . The modern approach to the third test is summarised by May LJ in *The Raphael* [1982] 2 Ll Rep 42. In that case the parties had discussed in detail possible heads of liability other than negligence. May LJ said (at p. 50):

> With respect to both sides in this appeal, I think that this is an over-legalistic approach to this problem. When two commercial concerns contract with one another, they do not, neither should they be deemed to, concern themselves with the legal subtleties of private nuisance or the like. They in fact approach the problem, and so also should the Courts, with a much broader brush. They consider, or must be deemed to have in mind, their respective responsibilities one to another more from a factual standpoint than a legalistic one. In seeking to apply Lord Morton's third test, we should not ask now whether there is or might be a technical alternative head of legal liability which the relevant exemption clause might cover and, if there is, immediately construe the clause as inapplicable to negligence. We should look at the facts and realities of the situation as they did or must be deemed to have presented themselves to the contracting parties at the time the contract was made, and ask what potential liabilities the one to the other did the parties apply their minds, or must they be deemed to have done so.

Before turning to the facts of the instant case, I observe in passing that in the *EE Caledonia* case the court held that there were other grounds of liability which might form the basis of liability and it was conceded that those grounds were not fanciful or remote.

In the instant case [counsel for the plaintiff] submits that the draftsman may well have had in mind grounds of liability other than negligence, namely private nuisance and breach of statutory duty. I am however unable to accept that submission. If I ask myself the question posed by May LJ, namely what, having regard to the facts and realities of the situation, are the potential liabilities to which each party must be deemed to have applied its mind when the contract was made or the notice given, I do not think that the answer would include private nuisance. It is a tort which involves interference with an interest in or the enjoyment of land. [Counsel] submits that the plaintiff had such an interest because it was the lessee of a hangar or hangars on the airport, but it seems to me that the chances the [sic] either the draftsman or the parties had any such liability in mind is very remote indeed.

The position is, however, somewhat different in the case of non-negligent breach of statutory duty. . . . [Counsel] submits that one of the potential liabilities which the parties must be taken to have had in mind would be a breach of such duties. I accept that submission, but it does not lead to the conclusion that the defendant is not entitled to rely upon cl. 10. I have already expressed my view that, even if the clause does not satisfy Lord Morton's first test, it was clearly intended to protect the airport from negligence unless the relevant act or omission was done with intent to cause damage or recklessly and with knowledge that damage would probably result.

NOTES
1. The second possibility requires that the words be wide enough to cover negligence. In *Lamport & Holt Lines Ltd* v *Coubro & Scrutton (M & I) Ltd, The Raphael* [1982] 2 Lloyd's Rep 42, the words 'any act or omission' were held to be words that were wide enough to cover negligence.
2. Assuming that the words are wide enough to cover negligence, the next step is to ask whether there is any other liability which exists on these facts, e.g., breach of an absolute contractual obligation. If so, then the clause will be confined to this alternative liability and will not apply to cover the liability in negligence.

White v *John Warwick & Co. Ltd*
[1953] 1 WLR 1285 (CA)

The plaintiff contracted with the defendants for the hire of a tradesman's tricycle. The tricycle supplied under the agreement had a defective saddle. The plaintiff was thrown off the tricycle when the saddle tipped up, and was injured. Clause 11 of their agreement provided that the defendants would not be liable 'for any personal injuries to the riders of the machines hired'. The plaintiff sought damages, alleging (i) that the defendants were strictly liable in supplying a tricycle which was not reasonably fit for the purpose for which it was required, and (ii) they were negligent in that they had failed to take care to ensure that the tricycle supplied was in a proper state of repair and in working condition. Counsel for the plaintiff argued that although clause 11 might apply to the breach of contract claim, it did not, and could not, apply to the negligence. The Court of Appeal agreed. Held: the clause applied only to exempt the defendants from liability under the contract.

DENNING LJ: . . . In this type of case two principles are well settled. The first is that if a person desires to exempt himself from a liability which the common law imposes on him, he can only do so by a contract freely and deliberately entered into by the injured party in words that are clear beyond the possibility of misunderstanding. The second is: if there are two possible heads of liability on the part of defendant, one for negligence, and the other a strict liability, an exemption clause will be construed, so far as possible, as exempting the defendant only from his strict liability and not as relieving him from his liability for negligence.

In the present case, there are two possible heads of liability on the defendants, one for negligence, the other for breach of contract. The liability for breach of contract is more strict than the liability for negligence. The defendants may be liable in contract for supplying a defective machine even though they were not negligent. (See *Hyman* v *Nye* (1881) 6 QBD 685). In these circumstances, the exemption clause must, I think, be construed as exempting the defendants only from their liability in contract, and not from their liability for negligence.

[Counsel for the defendants] admitted that, if the negligence was a completely independent tort, the exemption clause would not avail; but he said that the negligence here alleged was a breach of contract, not an independent tort. The facts which give rise to the tort are, he said, the same as those which give rise to the breach of contract, and the plaintiff should not be allowed to recover merely by framing his action in tort instead of contract. That was the view which appealed to Parker J, but I cannot agree with it.

In my opinion, the claim for negligence in this case is founded in tort and not on contract. That can be seen by considering what would be the position if, instead of the newsvendor himself, it was his servant who had been riding the cycle and had been injured. If the servant could show that the defendants had negligently sent out a defective machine for immediate use, he would have had a cause of action in negligence on the principle stated in *Donoghue* v *Stevenson* [1932] AC 562, and, as against the servant, the exemption clause would be no defence. That shows that the defendants owed a duty of care to the servant. A fortiori they owed a like duty to the newsvendor himself. In either case a breach of that duty is a tort, which can be established without relying on any contract at all. It is true that the newsvendor could also rely on a contract, if he had wished, but he is not bound to do so; and if he can avoid the exemption clause by framing his claim in tort he is, in my judgment, entitled to do so.

NOTES

1. The net effect was that the clause could not operate in a negligence action. Since UCTA 1977, even if the clause is wide enough to cover negligence, it will still need to satisfy s. 2 (see *page 296*). Section 2 of UCTA 1977 provides wide protection, and it may no longer be necessary to adopt such a restrictive approach to construction and negligence liability in order to protect the weak.

2. It appears from the comments of Denning LJ that in order to avoid the exemption clause the claim in negligence must be founded upon breach of a duty of care in tort, even though there may also be liability for contractual negligence (breach of a qualified contractual obligation). It is necessary to look at the position of, in this case, a third party who rode the tricycle, and ask whether he would have been owed a duty of care in the circumstances. If he is owed the duty of care, then a duty is also owed to the contractual party, and it is not necessary to rely on the contract to establish it. By comparison, Gower (1954) 17 MLR 155, at p. 157, argued that the parties cannot have intended to contract out of negligence liability pleaded in tort but not contractual negligence.

3. There is evidence that a more relaxed approach may be taken to Lord Morton's third test, at least in the context of 'not liable unless' clauses. See *Monarch Airlines Ltd* v *London Luton Airport Ltd*, *page 268* above.

4. In *Ailsa Craig Fishing Co. Ltd* v *Malvern Fishing Co. Ltd* [1983] 1 WLR 964, at p. 970, Lord Fraser indicated that the test in *Canada Steamship Lines Ltd* v *R* [1952] AC 192, would not be applied as strictly to limitation clauses as it was to exemption and indemnity clauses (see *page 278*). Whether it is correct to make this distinction is another matter.

EE Caledonia Ltd v *Orbit Valve plc*
[1994] 1 WLR 1515 (CA)

The plaintiffs operated an oil drilling platform and entered into a contract with the defendants whereby the defendants provided a service engineer to work on the platform. There was an indemnity clause (art. 10(b)) in the contract whereby each party was to indemnify the other in respect of 'any claim, demand, cause of action, loss, expense or liability' arising from the death of an employee of the indemnifying party in the performance of the contract. The defendants' employee died due to the negligence of the plaintiffs, who were also in breach of health and safety regulations. The plaintiffs settled the claim brought by the employee's estate and sought to rely on the indemnity clause to recover from the defendants. They argued that it covered negligence, but that in any event the indemnity applied because they could also have been held liable for breach of statutory duty. Held: the plaintiffs were not entitled to claim the indemnity. Each party had assumed a risk in respect of their own employees, subject to the proviso that each had agreed to bear the risk in respect of their own negligence. As the indemnity clause allocated the risk between the parties, it was also held that it did not apply to an action based on breach of statutory duty.

STEYN LJ:

The first question: does article 10(b) cover negligence?

The question before us is not to divine what the parties in fact intended. Our task is to determine what the words of article 10(b) mean. The plaintiffs argue that the language of article 10(b) covers negligence. The judge accepted the defendants' submission to a contrary effect. Our task is to decide which is the best interpretation.

. . . In article 10(b) there is no reference to negligence nor words to a like effect. It is plain that neither the other parts of article 10 nor the rest of the agreement assist the plaintiffs' interpretation. That brings me back to article 10(b). Given that the words of article 10(b), although not indicative of an intent to cover negligence are nevertheless wide enough to cover the negligence of the parties, Lord Morton's second proposition is satisfied. Lord Morton's third proposition must therefore be considered. The question is whether liability may be based on some other ground than negligence. The answer is plainly 'Yes'. But that leaves the question whether such other heads of liability were fanciful or remote. The judge dealt with this matter [1994] 1 WLR 221, 228:

> In article 10(b) there is no express reference to negligence; therefore there is no express provision that the right to an indemnity should cover a liability arising out of negligence of the party seeking the indemnity. However, the words used are wide enough potentially to cover a liability arising from negligence. The words are 'any claim . . . or liability'. Clearly such liability could, and will often be, a liability which has arisen from the negligence of the party liable or of those for whom he is responsible. But the liability need not arise from such negligence. It could arise as a result of a breach of a statutory duty which has occurred without any negligence of the party liable or his servants. This could be the situation with regard to both the company and the contractor; both are subject to statutory duties which could give rise to civil liabilities for death or personal injury. The examples are not fanciful; in an environment such as an offshore platform in an oilfield where a strict statutory regime operates, the possibility of a strict liability arising is a real one and is directly within the contemplation of this contract. Accordingly it is clear that art. 10(b), like (a) and (c), is capable of applying to situations where there has been no actual negligence of the relevant party or his own servants. This could have been the situation in the present case. The breaches of the regulations could in fact have been solely those of the employees of independent contractors working on the platform. In fact the disaster was also a result of the actual negligence of one of the plaintiffs' own servants.

. . . It follows that Lord Morton's third proposition is applicable. Reading article 10(b) against this well established aid to construction, it seems to me that article 10(b) should be construed as not covering the consequences of the negligence of the parties and their servants.

. . . [I]n my judgment, even in the case of a bilateral clause, such as the one before us, it is prima facie implausible that the parties would wish to release one another from the consequences of the other's negligence and agree to indemnify the other in respect of such consequences. . . .

The second question: does article 10(b) cover breach of a statutory duty even if there is negligence?

[Counsel for the plaintiffs] argued at first instance, and on this appeal, that since article 10(b) is wide enough to cover the plaintiffs' breaches of statutory duties it followed that the indemnity is applicable. He said that all that mattered was that the plaintiffs were liable for breaches of statutory duties. He said it was irrelevant that they were also liable in negligence.

The judge did not accept this argument. He said that the second question was closely related to the first. He then observed, at pp. 231–232:

> The question is one of construction but is not one which derives much assistance from a detailed analysis of the language of article 10(b). That clause makes no reference to statutory duties or to negligence. The question which I have to consider arises from the rules of

construction which I have to apply to that clause and the principles upon which those rules of construction are based.

I consider that the plaintiffs' arguments cannot be accepted. Where there are concurrent causes, each cause is a cause of the consequent event. If the event would have occurred in the absence of a particular fault, that fault is not a cause of the event. Accordingly, it is not correct to say in the present case that the plaintiffs were liable in respect of the death of Mr Quinn because of the breaches of statutory duty; they were liable because of the breaches of statutory duty *and* the negligence of their servant. It was the concurrent effect of both those causes that gave rise to the death of Mr Quinn and without either of those causes the death would not have occurred and the plaintiffs would not have been liable. Therefore the correct question remains whether the plaintiffs have a right to an indemnity from the defendants in respect of a liability of which *a* cause was the negligence of one of their servants. It is still necessary to ask whether, as a matter of the construction of the clause, it does cover such a liability.

For the purposes of considering the first question I have already quoted from judgments which state the principle to be applied. The principle is that in the absence of clear words parties to a contract are not to be taken to have intended that an exemption or indemnity clause should apply to the consequences of a party's negligence. Applying that principle and adopting a correct understanding of causation, the parties to a contract such as that with which I am concerned should not be taken to have intended that a party whose servant has been negligent should be entitled to an exemption or an indemnity although there has also been, as a concurrent cause of the relevant loss, a breach of a strict statutory duty. The principle still applies. . . .

I agree with the judge that on the supposition that article 10(b) does not apply to negligence, there is still a question of interpretation to be addressed, namely whether, despite their negligence, the plaintiffs are nevertheless entitled to an indemnity by the defendants. I further agree that the judge answered that question correctly. I would, however, express my reasons for that conclusion somewhat differently.

. . . On the assumed facts there were two concurrent causes, each of which was in the eye of the law effective to cause the event which led to Mr Quinn's death. The plaintiffs' negligence was an effective cause of Mr Quinn's death and the plaintiffs' breaches of statutory duty were also an effective cause of Mr Quinn's death.

That brings me directly to the issue of construction. It seems to me right to approach the interpretation of article 10(b) not in a technical way but in the way in which the commercial parties to the agreement would probably have approached it. The observations of Lord Diplock in *Photo Production Ltd* v *Securicor Transport Ltd* [1980] AC 827, 851F–G encourage me to think that such an approach to the construction of article 10(b) is realistic. And the supposition is that article 10(b) does not apply to negligence. Given this premise it seems realistic to view article 10(b), operating as it does by way of reciprocal exceptions and indemnities, as an agreed distribution or allocation of risks. The rationale was that each party would bear the risk in respect of his own property and employees. To the extent that they released each other from liability, they thereby contractually assumed the risk. But article 10(b) should be construed as containing a reservation of each party's right to sue the other in negligence and a correlative agreement that the indemnities would not avail either if so sued in negligence. Properly construed, article 10(b) provides that each party shall bear and assume the risk of his own negligence. If the approach I have adopted is correct, as I believe it is, the consequence is that article 10(b) should be construed as providing that the indemnities are not applicable if the event in question has been caused not only by a party's breach of statutory duty but also by his negligence. The short point is that the plaintiffs have contractually assumed the risk of their own negligence and cannot seek to avoid the consequences of that assumption of risk by seeking to rely on a breach of statutory duty.

I would add that this interpretation also better matches the reasonable expectations of the parties than the somewhat technical approach of the plaintiffs. Given that article 10(b) must be construed as not covering negligence, the judge's interpretation is in my view the more reasonable interpretation.

After all, it is inherently improbable even in a bilateral clause such as article 10(b) that a party would be willing to assume a risk of loss caused by the negligence of the other, notably when there is probably an imbalance and inequality in the risks of negligence by the one employee of the defendants and the many employees of the plaintiffs.

NOTES
1. This decision adds further strength to the proposition that clauses will be construed to prevent a party transferring responsibility for his own negligence.
2. One factor influencing this decision may have been that s. 4 of UCTA 1977 would not have been relevant as a final line of defence, since s. 4 does not apply to commercial indemnity clauses.
3. Steyn LJ's comment that the plaintiff's argument was 'somewhat technical' may indicate a willingness to be less mechanical in the application of the *Canada Steamship* principles. On a literal interpretation, since there was some other liability on the facts, the indemnity should cover the other liability, and not the negligence. Hoffmann J had regarded the liabilities as concurrent to avoid this consequence, but such a conclusion would fit uneasily with *White v John Warwick*. The Court of Appeal's approach is to avoid such technical difficulties by simply regarding the clause as allocating risk in a general way.
4. Further evidence of a more relaxed approach to Lord Morton's guidelines can be found in the speeches of the House of Lords in *HIH Casualty & General Insurance Ltd* v *Chase Manhattan Bank* [2003] UKHL 6, [2003] 1 All ER (Comm) 349. Lord Bingham stated at [11] that Lord Morton 'was giving helpful guidance on the proper approach to interpretation and not laying down a code. The passage does not provide a litmus test which, applied to the terms of the contract, yields a certain and predictable result. The courts' task of ascertaining what the particular parties intended in their particular commercial context, remains.' Similarly, Lord Scott stated at [116] that Lord Morton was expressing 'broad guidelines not prescribing rigid rules'. He added that the guidelines were not to be applied so as to produce a result which was inconsistent with the commercial purpose of the contract in question.

Where the only basis of liability is negligence, the courts are more willing to construe the clause to cover that negligence.

Alderslade v *Hendon Laundry Ltd*
[1945] 1 KB 189 (CA)

The plaintiff left 10 large Irish linen handkerchiefs with the defendants to be washed. The laundry lost the handkerchiefs, but in an action by the plaintiff for damages for £2 1s 5d (the cost of replacement handkerchiefs), the defendants sought to rely on condition 3 of the conditions on which the handkerchiefs had been accepted. This provided that 'The maximum amount allowed for lost or damaged articles is 20 times the charge made for laundering' (calculated as 11s 5½d here). Held: the only liability that could arise from the loss of the handkerchiefs by the defendants was by establishing that the defendants were negligent. They owed only *a duty to take reasonable care* of the handkerchiefs, so that there could be no strict liability for such loss. As a result, the condition could be applied to limit that negligence liability and the damages payable to the plaintiff.

LORD GREENE MR: It was argued before us for the defendants that the clause did apply and was effective to limit liability for lost articles; and reliance was placed on a well-known line of authority dealing with clauses of this description. The effect of those authorities can I think be stated as follows: where the head of damage in respect of which limitation of liability is sought to be imposed by such a clause is one which rests on negligence and nothing else, the clause must be construed as extending to that head of damage, because it would otherwise lack subject-matter. Where, on the other hand, the head of damage may be based on some other ground than that of negligence, the general principle is that the clause must be confined in its application to loss occurring through that other cause, to the exclusion of loss arising through negligence. The reason is that if a contracting party wishes in such a case to limit his liability in respect of negligence, he must do so in clear terms in the absence of which the clause is construed as relating to a liability not based on negligence. A common illustration of the principle is to be found in the case of common carriers. A common carrier is frequently described, though perhaps not quite accurately, as an insurer, and his liability in respect of articles entrusted to him is not necessarily based on negligence. Accordingly if a common carrier wishes to limit his liability for lost articles and does not make it quite clear that he is desiring to limit it in respect of his liability for negligence, then the clause will be construed as extending only to his liability on grounds other than negligence. If, on the other hand, a carrier not being a common carrier, makes use of such a clause, then unless it is construed so as to cover the case of negligence there would be no content for it at all seeing that his only obligation is to take reasonable care. That, broadly speaking, is the principle which falls to be applied in this case.

It was argued by counsel for the plaintiff that the clause must be construed in the present case so as to exclude loss by negligence. . . . It was said that the loss of a customer's property might take place for one of two reasons, namely, negligence and mere breach of contract, and that in the absence of clear words referring to negligence, loss through negligence cannot be taken to be covered by the clause. In my opinion that argument fails. It is necessary to analyse the legal relationship between the customer and the defendants. What I may call the hard core of the contract, the real thing to which the contract is directed, is the obligation of the defendants to launder. That is the primary obligation. It is the contractual obligation which must be performed according to its terms, and no question of taking due care enters into it. The defendants undertake, not to exercise due care in laundering the customer's goods, but to launder them, and if they fail to launder them it is no use their saying, 'We did our best, we exercised due care and took reasonable precautions, and we are very sorry if as a result the linen is not properly laundered.' That is the essence of the contract, and in addition there are certain ancillary obligations into which the defendants enter if they accept goods from a customer to be laundered. The first relates to the safe custody of the goods while they are in the possession of the defendants. The customer's goods may have to wait for a time in the laundry premises to be washed, and while they are so waiting there is an obligation to take care of them, but it is in my opinion not the obligation of an insurer but the obligation to take reasonable care for the protection of the goods. If while they are waiting to be washed in the laundry a thief, through no fault of the defendants, steals them, the defendants are not liable. The only way in which the defendants could be made liable for the loss of articles awaiting their turn to be washed would, I think, quite clearly be if it could be shown that they had been guilty of negligence in performing their duty to take care of the goods. That is one ancillary obligation which is inherent in a contract of this kind. Another relates to the delivery of the goods. The laundry company in most cases, and indeed in this case, make a practice of delivering the goods to the customer, and in the ordinary way the customer expects to receive that service. But what is the precise obligation of the laundry in respect of the return of the goods after the laundering has been completed? In my opinion it stands on the same footing as the other ancillary obligation that I have mentioned, namely, the obligation to take reasonable care in looking after and safeguarding the goods. It cannot I think be suggested that the obligation of the laundry company in the matter of returning the goods after they have been laundered is the obligation of an insurer. To say that they have undertaken by contract an absolute obligation to see that they are returned seems to me to go against common sense. Supposing the defendants are returning the goods by van to their customer and while the van is on its way a negligent driver of a lorry drives into it and overturns it with the result that it is set on fire and the goods destroyed. No action would lie by the customer for damages for the loss of those goods any more than it would lie against any ordinary transport undertaking which was not a common carrier. To hold otherwise would mean that in respect of that clearly ancillary service the defendants were undertaking an absolute obligation that the goods would, whatever happened, be returned to the customer. It seems to me that the only obligation on the defendants in the matter of returning the goods is to take reasonable care.

In the present case all that we know about the goods is that they are lost. There seems to me to be no case of lost goods in respect of which it would be necessary to limit liability, unless it be a case where the goods are lost by negligence. Goods sent to the laundry will not be lost in the act of washing them. On the other hand, they may be lost while they are in the custody of the defendants before washing or after washing has been completed. They may be lost in the process of returning them to the customer after they have been washed, but in each of those two cases, if my view is right, the obligation of the defendants is an obligation to take reasonable care and nothing else. Therefore, the claim of a customer that the defendants are liable to him in respect of articles that have been lost must, I think, depend on the issue of due care on their part. If that be right, to construe this clause, so far as it relates to loss, in such a way as to exclude loss occasioned by lack of proper care, would be to leave the clause so far as loss is concerned—I say nothing about damage—without any content at all. The result is in my opinion is that the clause must be construed as applying to the case of loss through negligence. . . .

NOTES
1. Since the laundry company would be supplying a service in the course of a business, it would impliedly undertake 'to carry out the service with reasonable care and skill' (Supply of Goods and Services Act 1982, s. 13). Therefore it seems that Lord Greene's identification of a strict obligation to launder properly would need to be amended in the light of this provision. However, s. 16 of the 1982 Act leaves open the possibility that a court may imply terms which are stricter than the qualified standard in s. 13.
2. Lord Greene indicated that it was an *automatic* conclusion that where negligence is the only liability that can arise, the exemption clause *must* be construed as applying to it. However, this was not accepted by the Court of Appeal in the next case.

Hollier v *Rambler Motors (AMC) Ltd*
[1972] 2 QB 71 (CA)

The plaintiff's car was being repaired at the defendants' garage when it was damaged by a fire caused by the defendants' negligence. The plaintiff claimed damages for breach of the implied term that the defendant would take reasonable care of his car. The defendants sought to rely on a clause in their standard form for repair that 'The Company is not responsible for damage caused by fire to customers' cars on the premises'. Held: the clause had not been incorporated because there was not a consistent course of dealing (see *page 227*). It was also held that in any event, the language of this clause did not exclude liability for the defendants' negligence but was merely a 'warning' that the defendants would not be liable for fire damage which was not attributable to their own negligence.

SALMON LJ: . . . It is well settled that a clause excluding liability for negligence should make its meaning plain on its face to any ordinarily literate and sensible person. The easiest way of doing that, of course, is to state expressly that the garage, tradesman or merchant, as the case may be, will not be responsible for any damage caused by his own negligence. No doubt merchants, tradesmen, garage proprietors and the like are a little shy of writing in an exclusion clause quite so bluntly as that. Clearly it would not tend to attract customers, and might even put many off. I am not saying that an exclusion clause cannot be effective to exclude negligence unless it does so expressly, but in order for the clause to be effective the language should be so plain that it clearly bears that meaning. I do not think that defendants should be allowed to shelter behind language which might lull the customer into a false sense of security by letting him think—unless perhaps he happens to be a lawyer—that he would have redress against the man with whom he was dealing for any damage which he, the customer, might suffer by the negligence of that person.

The principles are stated by Scrutton LJ with his usual clarity in *Rutter* v *Palmer* [1922] 2 KB 87, 92:

For the present purposes a rougher test will serve. In construing an exemption clause certain general rules may be applied: First the defendant is not exempted from liability for the negligence of his servants unless adequate words are used; secondly, the liability of the defendant apart from the exempting words must be ascertained; then the particular clause in question must be considered; and if the only liability of the party pleading the exemption is a liability for negligence, the clause will more readily operate to exempt him.

Scrutton LJ was far too great a lawyer, and had far too much robust common sense, if I may be permitted to say so, to put it higher than that 'if the only liability of the party pleading the exemption is a liability for negligence, the clause will more readily operate to exempt him.' He does not say that 'if the only liability of the party pleading the exemption is a liability for negligence, the clause will necessarily exempt him.' After all, there are many cases in the books dealing with exemption clauses, and in every case it comes down to a question of construing the alleged exemption clause which is then before the court. It seems to me that in *Rutter* v *Palmer*, although the word 'negligence' was never used in the exemption clause, the exemption clause would have conveyed to any ordinary, literate and sensible person that the garage in that case was inserting a clause in the contract which excluded their liability for the negligence of their drivers. The clause being considered in that case—and it was without any doubt incorporated in the contract—was: 'Customers' cars are driven by your staff at customers' sole risk.' Any ordinary man knows that when a car is damaged it is not infrequently damaged because the driver has driven it negligently. He also knows, I suppose, that if he sends it to a garage and a driver in the employ of the garage takes the car on the road for some purpose in connection with the work which the customer has entrusted the garage to do, the garage could not conceivably be liable for the car being damaged in an accident unless the driver was at fault. It follows that no sensible man could have thought that the words in that case had any meaning except that the garage would not be liable for the negligence of their own drivers. That is a typical case where, on the construction of the clause in question, the meaning for which the defendant was there contending was the obvious meaning of the clause.

The next case to which I wish to refer is the well-known case of *Alderslade* v *Hendon Laundry Ltd* [1945] 1 KB 189. . . . Again, this was a case where negligence was not expressly excluded. The question was: what do the words mean? I have no doubt that they would mean to the ordinary housewife who was sending her washing to the laundry that, if the goods were lost or damaged in the course of being washed through the negligence of the laundry, the laundry would not be liable for more than 20 times the charge made for the laundering. I say that for this reason. It is, I think, obvious that when a laundry loses or damages goods it is almost invariably because there has been some neglect or default on the part of the laundry. I think that the ordinary sensible housewife, or indeed anyone else who sends washing to the laundry, who saw that clause must have appreciated that almost always goods are lost or damaged because of the laundry's negligence, and therefore this clause could apply only to limit the liability of the laundry, when they were in fault or negligent.

But [counsel for the defendants] has drawn our attention to the way in which the matter was put by Lord Greene MR in delivering the leading judgment in this court, and he contends that Lord Greene MR was in fact making a considerable extension to the law as laid down by Scrutton LJ in the case to which I have referred. . . .

I do not think that Lord Greene MR was intending to extend the law in the sense for which [counsel for the defendants] contends. If it were so extended, it would make the law entirely artificial by ignoring that rules of construction are merely our guides and not our masters; in the end you are driven back to construing the clause in question to see what it means. Applying the principles laid down by Scrutton LJ, they lead to the result at which the court arrived in *Alderslade* v *Hendon Laundry Ltd* [1945] 1 KB 189. In my judgment these principles lead to a very different result in the present case. The words are: 'The company is not responsible for damage caused by fire to customers' cars on the premises.' What would that mean to any ordinarily literate and sensible car owner? I do not suppose that any such, unless he is a trained lawyer, has an intimate or indeed any knowledge of the liability of bailees in law. If you asked the ordinary man or woman: 'Supposing you send your car to the garage to be repaired, and there is a fire, would you suppose that the garage would be liable?' I should be surprised if many of them did not answer, quite wrongly: 'Of course they are liable if there is a fire.' Others might be more cautious and say: 'Well, I had better ask my solicitor,' or, 'I do not know. I suppose they may well be liable.' That is the crucial difference, to my mind, between the present case and *Alderslade* v *Hendon Laundry Ltd* and *Rutter* v *Palmer* [1922] 2 KB 87. In those two cases, any ordinary man or woman reading the conditions would have known that all that was being excluded was the negligence of the laundry, in the one case, and the garage, in the other. But here I think the ordinary man or woman would be equally surprised and horrified to learn that if the garage was so negligent that a fire was caused which damaged their car, they would be without remedy because of the words in the condition. I can quite understand that the ordinary man or woman would consider that, because of these words, the mere fact that there was a fire would not make the garage liable. Fires can occur from a large variety of causes, only one of which is negligence on the part of the occupier of the premises, and that is by no means the most frequent cause. The ordinary man would I think say to himself: 'Well, what they are telling me is that if there is a fire due to any cause other than their own negligence they are not responsible for it.' To my mind, if the defendants were seeking to exclude their responsibility for a fire caused by their own negligence, they ought to have done so in far plainer language than the language here used. . . .

NOTE: This decision was severely criticised (see Barendt (1972) 35 MLR 644).

■ QUESTION

Do you consider that this case would be decided the same way today?

If the clause is held to cover negligence UCTA 1977, s. 2(2) would apply so that the clause would have to satisfy the reasonableness requirement. Would it satisfy this requirement? (See *page 304* on reasonableness.) In addition, the Unfair Terms in Consumer Contracts Regulations 1999 would apply. Would this term be 'unfair'? (See *pages 318–27*.)

C: Limitation clauses

Ailsa Craig Fishing Co. Ltd v *Malvern Fishing Co. Ltd*
[1983] 1 WLR 964 (HL)

Securicor had agreed to provide a security service in Aberdeen harbour for the fishing boats of the members of an association which were berthed there. Ailsa Craig's vessel fouled another boat in the harbour and sank. Clause 2(f) purported to limit Securicor's liability to £1,000. Ailsa Craig claimed damages against Securicor, alleging that the loss was caused by breach of contract and/or negligence. The trial judge awarded damages of £55,000. Securicor appealed against this award, alleging that condition 2(f) applied. Held: the limitation clause operated to limit liability to £1,000. Limitation clauses were not to be construed by the exacting standards applicable to exclusion clauses, and since this clause was clear and unambiguous, it was wide enough to cover liability in negligence.

LORD WILBERFORCE: Whether a clause limiting liability is effective or not is a question of construction of that clause in the context of the contract as a whole. If it is to exclude liability for negligence, it must be most clearly and unambiguously expressed, and in such a contract as this, must be construed contra proferentem. I do not think that there is any doubt so far. But I venture to add one further qualification, or at least clarification: one must not strive to create ambiguities by strained construction, as I think that the appellants have striven to do. The relevant words must be given, if possible, their natural, plain meaning. Clauses of limitation are not regarded by the courts with the same hostility as clauses of exclusion: this is because they must be related to other contractual terms, in particular to the risks to which the defending party may be exposed, the remuneration which he receives, and possibly also the opportunity of the other party to insure.

LORD FRASER: . . . In my opinion these principles [per Lord Morton of Henryton in *Canada Steamship Lines Ltd* v *R* [1952] AC 192] are not applicable in their full rigour when considering the effect of clauses merely limiting liability. Such clauses will of course be read contra proferentem and must be clearly expressed, but there is no reason why they should be judged by the specially exacting standards which are applied to exclusion and indemnity clauses. The reason for imposing such standards on these clauses is the inherent improbability that the other party to a contract including such a clause intended to release the proferens from a liability that would otherwise fall upon him. But there is no such high degree of improbability that he would agree to a limitation of the liability of the proferens, especially when . . . the potential losses that might be caused by the negligence of the proferens or its servants are so great in proportion to the sums that can reasonably be charged for the services contracted for. It is enough in the present case that the clause must be clear and unambiguous.

NOTE: It appears that a limitation clause can provide protection against liability in negligence in circumstances where an exclusion clause might not, since the negligence construction test is whether the clause is clear and unambiguous.

This distinction in treatment for construction purposes has been endorsed by Lord Bridge in *George Mitchell* v *Finney Lock Seeds* [1983] 2 AC 803, at p. 814 (see *page 286*), in *EE Caledonia Ltd* v *Orbit Valve plc* [1994] 1 WLR 1515, *per* Steyn LJ at p. 1521 and in *BHP Petroleum* v *British Steel* [2000] 2 All ER (Comm) 133, at p. 143 (per Evans LJ).

■ QUESTION

Is this special approach to the construction of limitation clauses justifiable? UCTA 1977 applies equally to limitation and exclusion clauses, and it may just be that many limitation clauses are more likely to satisfy the reasonableness requirement in s. 11 of UCTA 1977. The High Court of Australia in *Darlington Futures Ltd* v *Delco Australia Pty Ltd* (1986) 161 CLR 500, (1986) 61 ALJR 76, considered this distinction in construction to be unsupportable, since if the limitation clause sets the figure for recovery at a very low level, its effects would be much the same as those applicable to total exclusion clauses.

D: Inconsistent terms

If an exemption clause is inconsistent with another express term of the contract or an oral undertaking given at or before the time of contracting, then the exemption clause will be overridden by that term or undertaking.

Mendelssohn v *Normand Ltd*
[1970] 1 QB 177 (CA)

The plaintiff, wishing to park his car, was told by the car park attendant that the rules required the car to be left unlocked. The plaintiff explained that he had a suitcase in the car containing valuables, and the attendant agreed to lock the car as soon as he had moved it. The plaintiff was then given a ticket exempting the garage from responsibility for loss or damage to vehicles or their contents, however caused. On his return the plaintiff found the car unlocked and later discovered that his suitcase was missing. Were the defendants liable for the loss of the suitcase?

Held: the defendants were liable, since the attendant's promise (to lock up the car, which implied that he would see that the contents were safe) took priority over the printed condition because the printed condition was repugnant to that express promise.

LORD DENNING MR: . . . Such a statement is binding on the company. It takes priority over any printed condition. There are many cases in the books when a man has made, by word of mouth, a promise or a representation of fact, on which the other party acts by entering into the contract. In all such cases the man is not allowed to repudiate his representation by reference to a printed condition, see *Couchman* v *Hill* [1947] KB 554; *Curtis* v *Chemical Cleaning & Dyeing Co.* [1951] 1 KB 805; and *Harling* v *Eddy* [1951] 2 KB 739; nor is he allowed to go back on his promise by reliance on a written clause, see *City and Westminster Properties (1934) Ltd* v *Mudd* [1959] Ch 129, 145 by Harman J. The reason is because the oral promise or representation has a decisive influence on the transaction—it is the very thing which induces the other to contract—and it would be most unjust to allow the maker to go back on it. The printed condition is rejected because it is repugnant to the express oral promise or representation. As Devlin J said in *Firestone Tyre and Rubber Co. Ltd* v *Vokins & Co. Ltd* [1951] 1 Lloyd's Rep 32, 39: 'It is illusory to say: "We promise to do a thing, but we are not liable if we do not do it".' To avoid this illusion, the law gives the oral promise priority over the printed clause.

NOTE: Another example is provided by the Court of Appeal's decision in *J. Evans & Son (Portsmouth)* v *Andrea Merzario Ltd* [1976] 1 WLR 1078, *page 208*. The printed conditions gave the defendants complete freedom to decide the method of transportation of goods and exempted the defendants for loss of or damage to the goods. However, the plaintiffs had been given an oral assurance that the containers would be stored below deck. It was held that the defendants were not entitled to rely upon the printed conditions to exempt them from liability for this breach because this would render the oral promise illusory. (See also *Couchman* v *Hill* [1947] KB 554, at *page 201*.)

E: Fundamental breach

In the 1950s and early 1960s, as part of their restrictive approach to construction, the courts took particular exception to the use of an exemption clause to protect against liability where the breach in question was 'fundamental' (particularly serious), and held in a series of cases that exemption clauses could not operate to exclude liability for such breaches. While this device was designed to protect the weak from the strong, it operated in all cases, including situations where the clause in question was freely negotiated between two parties of equal bargaining power.

In *Suisse Atlantique Société d'Armement Maritime SA* v *NV Rotterdamsche Kolen Centrale* the House of Lords held *obiter* that there was no such rule of law applicable to fundamental breaches.

Suisse Atlantique Société d'Armement Maritime SA v *NV Rotterdamsche Kolen Centrale*
[1967] 1 AC 361 (HL)

The respondents agreed to charter a ship from the appellants 'for a total of two years' consecutive voyages'. The charter provided for fixed periods within which the respondents had to load and discharge on each voyage (laytime). If they exceeded this, they had to pay 'demurrage' at $1,000 per day. There were considerable delays, and between October 1957 and the end of the charter the ship made eight round voyages, whereas the appellants alleged that a further six voyages could have been performed if the respondents had kept within laytime. The appellants brought an action to claim the freight that they would have earned on these extra voyages, claiming that the demurrage clause was a limitation clause and the delays were so extensive that they amounted to a fundamental breach entitling them to repudiate the contract. Held: there was no fundamental breach by detaining the ship beyond the laytime and, in any event, the demurrage clause was a liquidated damages clause (*page 414*) and not a limitation clause. It was not possible for the appellants to recover any more than the liquidated damages amount. The House of Lords also considered (as has been subsequently confirmed in *Photo Production Ltd* v *Securicor Transport Ltd, page 283*) that it was a question of construction whether an exemption clause covered a fundamental breach, or any breach, of contract.

LORD REID: The new contention submitted by the appellants is that the breaches of contract which caused these delays amounted to fundamental breach or breach going to the root of the contract so that at some time during the currency of the agreement the appellants would have been entitled to treat the breaches as a repudiation, to terminate or rescind the contract and to claim damages at common law. It is, I think, clear that if they did have that right they must be held to have elected not to treat the breaches as repudiatory. But they argue that nevertheless the fact that there was a fundamental breach prevents the respondents from relying on the demurrage clause as limiting their responsibility.

So the first question must be whether these delays can be regarded as involving fundamental breach. . . . General use of the term 'fundamental breach' is of recent origin and I can find nothing to indicate that it means either more or less than the well known type of breach which entitles the innocent party to treat it as repudiatory and to rescind the contract. The appellants allege that the respondents caused these delays deliberately (i.e., with the wilful intention of limiting the number of contractual voyages). They do not allege fraud or bad faith. This allegation would appear to cover a case where the charterers decided that it would pay them better to delay loading and discharge and pay the resulting demurrage at the relatively low agreed rate, rather than load and discharge more speedily and then have to buy more coal and pay the relatively high agreed freight on the additional voyages which would then be possible. If facts of that kind could be proved I think that it would be open to the arbitrators to find that the respondents had committed a fundamental or repudiatory breach. One way of looking at the matter would be to ask whether the party in breach has by his breach produced a situation fundamentally different from anything which the parties could as reasonable men have contemplated when the contract was made. Then one would have to ask not only what had already happened but also what was likely to happen in future. And there the fact that the breach was deliberate might be of great importance.

If fundamental breach is established the next question is what effect, if any, that has on the applicability of other terms of the contract. This question has often arisen with regard to clauses excluding liability, in whole or in part, of the party in breach. I do not think that there is generally much difficulty where the innocent party has elected to treat the breach as a repudiation, bring the contract to an end and sue for damages. Then the whole contract has ceased to exist including the exclusion clause, and I do not see how that clause can then be used to exclude an action for loss which will be suffered by the innocent party after it has ceased to exist, such as loss of the profit which would have accrued if the contract had run its full term. But that is not the situation in the present case, where in my view the appellants elected that the contract should continue in force.

Where the contract has been affirmed by the innocent party, at first sight the position is simple. You must either affirm the whole contract or rescind the whole contract: you cannot approbate and reprobate by affirming part of it and disaffirming the rest—that would be making a new contract. So the clause excluding liability must continue to apply. But that is too simple and there is authority for two quite different ways of holding that, in spite of affirmation of the contract as a whole by the innocent party, the guilty party may not be entitled to rely on a clause in it. One way depends on construction of the clause. The other way depends on the existence of a rule of substantive law.

As a matter of construction it may appear that the terms of the exclusion clause are not wide enough to cover the kind of breach which has been committed. Such clauses must be construed strictly and if ambiguous the narrower meaning will be taken. Or it may appear that the terms of the clause are so wide that they cannot be applied literally: that may be because this would lead to an absurdity or because it would defeat the main object of the contract or perhaps for other reasons. And where some limit must be read into the clause it is generally reasonable to draw the line at fundamental breaches. There is no reason why a contract should not make a provision for events which the parties do not have in contemplation or even which are unforeseeable, if sufficiently clear words are used. But if some limitation has to be read in it seems reasonable to suppose that neither party had in contemplation a breach which goes to the root of the contract. Then the true analysis seems to me to be that the whole contract, including the clause excluding liability, does survive after election to affirm it, but that does not avail the party in breach. The exclusion clause does not change its meaning: as a matter of construction it never did apply and does not after election apply to this type of breach, and therefore is no answer to an action brought in respect of this type of breach.

But applying a strict construction to these clauses is not sufficient to exclude them in all cases of fundamental breach. It cannot be said as a matter of law that the resources of the English language are so limited that it is impossible to devise an exclusion clause which will apply to at least some cases of fundamental breach without being so widely drawn that it can be cut down on any ground by applying ordinary principles of construction. So, if there is to be a universal rule that, no matter how the exclusion clause is expressed, it will not apply to protect a party in fundamental breach, any such rule must be a substantive rule of law nullifying any agreement to the contrary and to that extent restricting the general principle of English law that parties are free to contract as they may see fit.

There is recent authority for the existence of such a rule of law but I cannot find support for it in the older authorities. . . . In my view no such rule of law ought to be adopted. I do not take that view merely because any such rule is new or because it goes beyond what can be done by developing or adapting existing principles. Courts have often introduced new rules when, in their view, they were required by public policy. . . . But my main reason is that this rule would not be a satisfactory solution of the problem which undoubtedly exists.

Exemption clauses differ greatly in many respects. Probably the most objectionable are found in the complex standard conditions which are now so common. In the ordinary way the customer has no time to read them, and if he did read them he would probably not understand them. And if he did understand and object to any of them, he would generally be told he could take it or leave it. And if he then went to another supplier the result would be the same. Freedom to contract must surely imply some choice or room for bargaining.

At the other extreme is the case where parties are bargaining on terms of equality and a stringent exemption clause is accepted for a quid pro quo or other good reason. But this rule appears to treat all cases alike. There is no indication in the recent cases that the courts are to consider whether the exemption is fair in all the circumstances or is harsh and unconscionable or whether it was freely agreed by the customer. And it does not seem to me to be satisfactory that the decision must always go one way if, e.g., defects in a car or other goods are just sufficient to make the breach of contract a fundamental breach, but must always go the other way if the defects fall just short of that. This is a complex problem which intimately affects millions of people and it appears to me that its solution should be left to Parliament. If your Lordships reject this new rule there will certainly be a need for urgent legislative action but that is not beyond reasonable expectation.

NOTES

1. While there are clear statements in the speeches that there is no such rule of law applicable to fundamental breaches, and it is a question of construction of the clause as to whether it covers the breach, there was also a need to address the arguments put before the House, so that the fundamental breach rule, which had just been rejected, also seems to be applied. In particular, the speeches of Lord Reid and Lord Upjohn seem to imply that where a contract is

terminated, any exemption clause in that contract can no longer apply. In *Suisse Atlantique* the contract was affirmed.

2. The inconclusive nature of the judgments allowed the Court of Appeal in *Harbutts' 'Plasticine' Ltd* v *Wayne Tank & Pump Co. Ltd* [1970] 1 QB 447, to continue to deny the operation of an exemption clause where there was a fundamental breach and the contract had been terminated.

The House of Lords was finally able to confirm the construction approach in the next case.

Photo Production Ltd v Securicor Transport Ltd
[1980] AC 827 (HL)

The plaintiffs, factory owners, entered into a contract with the defendants whereby the defendants would patrol the factory at a cost of £8 15s per week. The contract was on the defendants' standard form, which included the following clause:

> Under no circumstances shall the company [Securicor] be responsible for any injurious act or default by any employee of the company unless such act or default could have been foreseen and avoided by the exercise of due diligence on the part of the company as his employer; nor, in any event, shall the company be held responsible for (a) any loss suffered by the customer through burglary, theft, fire or any other cause, except insofar as such loss is solely attributable to the negligence of the company's employees acting within the course of their employment. . . .

One of the defendants' employees was patrolling the factory when he deliberately started a fire by discarding a lighted match. The flames spread and the factory was destroyed, causing a loss of £615,000. The plaintiffs claimed damages from the defendants. The Court of Appeal applied the 'fundamental breach rule' and held that the contract had been brought to an end so that the defendants were not able to rely on this clause as excluding their liability. The House of Lords allowed the defendants' appeal. Held:

(a) It was not good law to say that on termination of a contract for a fundamental breach the contract terms (including any exemption clauses) came to an end.

(b) The question whether and to what extent an exemption clause was to be applied to any breach of contract was a question of construction of the contract.

(c) Normally, when the parties were bargaining on equal terms they should be free to apportion the risks as they saw fit.

(d) On their true construction, the words of the exclusion clause covered deliberate acts, and therefore the defendants were relieved from responsibility for breach of their implied duty to operate with due regard to the safety of the premises.

> LORD WILBERFORCE: It is first necessary to decide upon the correct approach to a case such as this where it is sought to invoke an exception or limitation clause in the contract. The approach of Lord Denning MR in the Court of Appeal was to consider first whether the breach was 'fundamental.' If so, he said, the court itself deprives the party of the benefit of an exemption or limitation clause ([1978] 1 WLR 856, 863). Shaw and Waller LJJ substantially followed him in this argument.
>
> Lord Denning MR in this was following the earlier decision of the Court of Appeal, and in particular his own judgment in *Harbutt's 'Plasticine' Ltd* v *Wayne Tank & Pump Co. Ltd* . . .

My Lords, whatever the intrinsic merit of this doctrine, as to which I shall have something to say later, it is clear to me that so far from following this House's decision in the *Suisse Atlantique* it is directly opposed to it and that the whole purpose and tenor of the *Suisse Atlantique* was to repudiate it. The lengthy, and perhaps I may say sometimes indigestible speeches of their Lordships, are correctly summarised in the headnote—holding No. 3 [1967] 1 AC 361, 362—'That the question whether an exceptions clause was applicable where there was a fundamental breach of contract was one of the true construction of the contract.' That there was any rule of law by which exceptions clauses are eliminated, or deprived of effect, regardless of their terms, was clearly not the view of Viscount Dilhorne, Lord Hodson, or of myself. The passages invoked for the contrary view of a rule of law consist only of short extracts from two of the speeches—on any view a minority. But the case for the doctrine does not even go so far as that. Lord Reid, in my respectful opinion, and I recognise that I may not be the best judge of this matter, in his speech read as a whole, cannot be claimed as a supporter of a rule of law. . . . I am convinced that, with the possible exception of Lord Upjohn whose critical passage, when read in full, is somewhat ambiguous, their Lordships, fairly read, can only be taken to have rejected those suggestions for a rule of law which had appeared in the Court of Appeal and to have firmly stated that the question is one of construction, not merely of course of the exclusion clause alone, but of the whole contract.

Much has been written about the *Suisse Atlantique* case. Each speech has been subjected to various degrees of analysis and criticism, much of it constructive. Speaking for myself I am conscious of imperfections of terminology, though sometimes in good company. But I do not think that I should be conducing to the clarity of the law by adding to what was already too ample a discussion a further analysis which in turn would have to be interpreted. I have no second thoughts as to the main proposition that the question whether, and to what extent, an exclusion clause is to be applied to a fundamental breach, or a breach of a fundamental term, or indeed to any breach of contract, is a matter of constructon of the contract. Many difficult questions arise and will continue to arise in the infinitely varied situations in which contracts come to be breached—by repudiatory breaches, accepted or not, by anticipatory breaches, by breaches of conditions or of various terms and whether by negligent, or deliberate action or otherwise. But there are ample resources in the normal rules of contract law for dealing with these without the superimposition of a judicially invented rule of law. I am content to leave the matter there with some supplementary observations.

1.   The doctrine of 'fundamental breach' in spite of its imperfections and doubtful parentage has served a useful purpose. There was a large number of problems, productive of injustice, in which it was worse than unsatisfactory to leave exception clauses to operate. Lord Reid referred to these in the *Suisse Atlantique* case [1967] 1 AC 361, 406, pointing out at the same time that the doctrine of fundamental breach was a dubious specific. But since then Parliament has taken a hand: it has passed the Unfair Contract Terms Act 1977. This Act applies to consumer contracts and those based on standard terms and enables exception clauses to be applied with regard to what is just and reasonable. It is significant that Parliament refrained from legislating over the whole field of contract. After this Act, in commercial matters generally, when the parties are not of unequal bargaining power, and when risks are normally borne by insurance, not only is the case for judicial intervention undemonstrated, but there is everything to be said, and this seems to have been Parliament's intention, for leaving the parties free to apportion the risks as they think fit and for respecting their decisions.

At the stage of negotiation as to the consequences of a breach, there is everything to be said for allowing the parties to estimate their respective claims according to the contractual provisions they have themselves made, rather than for facing them with a legal complex so uncertain as the doctrine of fundamental breach must be. What, for example, would have been the position of the respondents' factory if instead of being destroyed it had been damaged, slightly or moderately or severely? At what point does the doctrine (with what logical justification I have not understood) decide, ex post facto, that the breach was (factually) fundamental before going on to ask whether legally it is to be regarded as fundamental? How is the date of 'termination' to be fixed? Is it the date of the incident causing the damage, or the date of the innocent party's election, or some other date? All these difficulties arise from the doctrine and are left unsolved by it.

At the judicial stage there is still more to be said for leaving cases to be decided straightforwardly on what the parties have bargained for rather than upon analysis, which becomes progressively more refined, of decisions in other cases leading to inevitable appeals. The learned judge was able to decide this case on normal principles of contractual law with minimal citation of authority. I am sure that most commercial judges have wished to be able to do the same . . . In my opinion they can and should.

2.   The case of *Harbutt* [1970] 1 QB 447 must clearly be overruled. It would be enough to put that upon its radical inconsistency with the *Suisse Atlantique* case [1967] 1 AC 361. But even if the matter were res integra I would find the decision to be based upon unsatisfactory reasoning as to the 'termination' of the contract and the effect of 'termination' on the plaintiffs' claim for damage. I have, indeed, been unable to understand how the doctrine can be reconciled with the well accepted principle of law, stated by the highest modern authority, that when in the context of a breach of contract one speaks of 'termination,' what is meant is no more than that the innocent party or, in some cases, both parties, are excused from further performance. Damages, in such cases, are then claimed under the contract, so what reason in principle can there be for disregarding what the contract itself says about damages—whether it 'liquidates' them, or limits them, or excludes them? These difficulties arise in part from uncertain or inconsistent terminology. A vast number of expressions are used to describe situations where a breach has been committed by one party of such a character as to entitle the other party to refuse further performance: discharge, rescission, termination, the contract is at an end, or dead, or displaced; clauses cannot survive, or simply go. I have come to think that some of these difficulties can be avoided; in particular the use of 'rescission,' even if distinguished from rescission ab initio, as an equivalent for discharge, though justifiable in some contexts (see *Johnson* v *Agnew* [1980] AC 367) may lead to confusion in others. To plead for complete uniformity may be to cry for the moon. But what can and ought to be avoided is to make use of these confusions in order to produce a concealed and unreasoned legal innovation: to pass, for example, from saying that a party, victim of a breach of contract, is entitled to refuse further performance, to saying that he may treat the contract as at an end, or as rescinded, and to draw from this the proposition, which is not analytical but one of policy, that all or (arbitrarily) some of the clauses of the contract lose, automatically, their force, regardless of intention.

In this situation the present case has to be decided. As a preliminary, the nature of the contract has to be understood. Securicor undertook to provide a service of periodical visits for a very modest charge which works out at 26p per visit. It did not agree to provide equipment. It would have no knowledge of the value of the plaintiffs' factory: that, and the efficacy of their fire precautions, would be known to the respondents. In these circumstances nobody could consider it unreasonable, that as between these two equal parties the risk assumed by Securicor should be a modest one, and that the respondents should carry the substantial risk of damage or destruction.

The duty of Securicor was, as stated, to provide a service. There must be implied an obligation to use due care in selecting their patrolmen, to take care of the keys and, I would think, to operate the service with due and proper regard to the safety and security of the premises. The breach of duty committed by Securicor lay in a failure to discharge this latter obligation. Alternatively it could be put upon a vicarious responsibility for the wrongful act of Musgrove—viz., starting a fire on the premises: Securicor would be responsible for this upon the principle stated in *Morris* v *C.W. Martin & Sons Ltd* [1966] 1 QB 716, 739. This being the breach, does condition 1 apply? It is drafted in strong terms, 'Under no circumstances' . . . 'any injurious act or default by any employee.' These words have to be approached with the aid of the cardinal rules of construction that they must be read contra proferentem and that in order to escape from the consequences of one's own wrongdoing, or that of one's servant, clear words are necessary. I think that these words are clear. The respondents in fact relied upon them for an argument that since they exempted from negligence they must be taken as not exempting from the consequence of deliberate acts. But this is a perversion of the rule that if a clause can cover something other than negligence, it will not be applied to negligence. Whether, in addition to negligence, it covers other, e.g., deliberate, acts, remains a matter of construction requiring, of course, clear words. I am of opinion that it does, and being free to construe and apply the clause, I must hold that liability is excluded. . . .

NOTES

1. This confirms that there is now a general construction test and it is no longer necessary to distinguish a fundamental breach. It appears that the only relevance of a fundamental breach is that clearer words will be required for the clause to cover it.

2. Lord Wilberforce rejects any substantive rule applicable to fundamental breach on the ground that it leads to uncertainty, since it is difficult to determine whether a breach is serious enough to be fundamental and it is difficult to determine the point at which the contract is terminated.

3. The House of Lords also recognised the misconception in *Harbutts' 'Plasticine' Ltd* v *Wayne Tank & Pump Co. Ltd* [1970] 1 QB 447 that the effect of termination for fundamental breach was to bring the contract to an end so that the contractual terms no longer applied. On the contrary, although future performance is no longer required, the contract is *not* treated as being void *ab initio*. The terms are still relevant, for example, for the purposes of assessing the measure of damages, and any exemption clause is still relevant for the purposes of assessing if liability has been excluded or limited. (Section 9(1) of UCTA 1977 confirms that termination does not destroy exemption clauses in the contract.)

4. The House of Lords seems to have been greatly influenced by the fact that the parties were 'of equal bargaining power', and so must be taken to have allocated the risk and, consequently, the burden of securing insurance cover. The other relevant factor was that the House viewed the cost of the service provided by Securicor as being very modest.

■ QUESTION

Is it true to say that the parties were of equal bargaining power when the plaintiffs contracted on the defendants' standard terms? See Nicol and Rawlings, 'Substantive Fundamental Breach Burnt Out' (1980) 43 MLR 567.

George Mitchell (Chesterhall) Ltd v *Finney Lock Seeds Ltd*
[1983] 2 AC 803 (HL)

The plaintiffs purchased 30lbs of Finney's Late Dutch special cabbage seed at a price of £201.60 from the defendant seed merchants with whom they had contracted for many years. The conditions of sale on the back of the invoice limited liability to replacement of the goods or a refund of the purchase price. The seed supplied was not late cabbage seed but autumn cabbage seed of inferior variety. The plaintiffs had planted the seed in 63 acres, but it did not grow into true cabbage plants and had to be ploughed in. The plaintiffs' loss was over £61,000. They claimed damages. Parker J held that since what was delivered was wholly different in kind from what had been ordered and agreed to be supplied, the clause could not operate. The majority of the Court of Appeal (Oliver and Kerr LJJ: [1983] 1 QB 284) agreed, although they also found that the clause was unenforceable by virtue of the Sale of Goods Act 1979, s. 55, since it was not 'fair and reasonable' to allow reliance on it. The House of Lords agreed with Lord Denning MR, in the minority in the Court of Appeal, that the task of the judge was to give the clause its natural meaning, and on their true construction the conditions did cover the loss which had occurred. However, the House agreed with the Court of Appeal that it would not be 'fair and reasonable' to allow reliance on them. (On the question of the reasonableness of the clause, see *page 306*.)

LORD BRIDGE: My Lords, it seems to me, with all due deference, that the judgments of the learned trial judge and of Oliver LJ on the common law issue come dangerously near to re-introducing by the back door the doctrine of 'fundamental breach' which this House in *Securicor 1* [1980] AC 827, had so forcibly evicted by the front. The learned judge discusses what I may call the 'peas and beans' or 'chalk and cheese' cases, sc. those in which it has been held that exemption clauses do not apply where there has been a contract to sell one thing, e.g. a motor car, and the seller has supplied quite another thing, e.g. a bicycle. . . .

In my opinion, this is not a 'peas and beans' case at all. The relevant condition applies to 'seeds.' Clause 1 refers to seeds 'sold' and 'seeds agreed to be sold.' Clause 2 refers to 'seeds supplied.' As I have pointed out, Oliver LJ concentrates his attention on the phrase 'seeds agreed to be sold.' I can see no justification, with respect, for allowing this phrase alone to dictate the interpretation of the relevant condition, still less for treating clause 2 as 'merely a supplement' to clause 1. Clause 2 is perfectly clear and unambiguous. The reference to 'seeds agreed to be sold' as well as to 'seeds sold' in clause 1 reflects the same dichotomy as the definition of 'sale' in the Sale of Goods Act 1979 as including a bargain and sale as well as a sale and delivery. The defective seeds in this case were seeds sold and delivered, just as clearly as they were seeds supplied, by the appellants to the respondents. The relevant condition, read as a whole, unambiguously limits the appellants' liability to replacement of the seeds or refund of the price. It is only possible to read an ambiguity into it by the process of strained construction which was deprecated by Lord Diplock [1980] AC 827, 851C in *Securicor 1* and by Lord Wilberforce in *Securicor 2* [1983] 1 WLR 964, 966G.

In holding that the relevant condition was ineffective to limit the appellants' liability for a breach of contract caused by their negligence, Kerr LJ applied the principles stated by Lord Morton of Henryton giving the judgment of the Privy Council in *Canada Steamship Lines Ltd* v *The King* [1952] AC 192, 208. The learned Lord Justice stated correctly that this case was also referred to by Lord Fraser of Tullybelton in *Securicor 2* [1983] 1 WLR 964, 970. He omitted, however, to notice that, as appears from the passage from Lord Fraser's speech which I have already cited, the whole point of Lord Fraser's reference was to express his opinion that the very strict principles laid down in the *Canada Steamship Lines* case as applicable to exclusion and indemnity clauses cannot be applied in their full rigour to limitation clauses. Lord Wilberforce's speech contains a passage to the like effect, and Lord Elwyn-Jones, Lord Salmon and Lord Lowry agreed with both speeches. Having once reached a conclusion in the instant case that the relevant condition unambiguously limited the appellants' liability, I know of no principle of construction which can properly be applied to confine the effect of the limitation to breaches of contract arising without negligence on the part of the appellants. In agreement with Lord Denning MR, I would decide the common law issue in the appellants' favour.

NOTES
1. See Adams, 'Fundamental Breach—Positively Last Appearance' (1983) 46 MLR 771.
2. It is clear that any argument based upon the 'peas and beans' cases is unlikely to succeed in future as a method of preventing reliance on an exemption clause, since, given that there are to be no strained constructions, a court may not construe what has been delivered as being wholly different from what was ordered. The House of Lords construed this contract as a contract to deliver seed, and seed had been delivered.

SECTION 5: THE CLAUSE IS NOT RENDERED UNENFORCEABLE BY THE UNFAIR CONTRACT TERMS ACT 1977 OR THE UNFAIR TERMS IN CONSUMER CONTRACTS REGULATIONS 1999

A: Scope of UCTA 1977

See Adams and Brownsword, 'The Unfair Contract Terms Act: A Decade of Discretion' (1988) 104 LQR 94, Macdonald [1994] JBL 441, 441–56 and 'Unifying Unfair Terms Legislation' (2004) 67 MLR 69.

UCTA 1977 places statutory restrictions on the extent to which liability can be *'excluded or restricted'* by means of exemption clauses.

(a) Section 13(1)

Section 13(1) extends this somewhat limited definition. (See Macdonald (1992) 12 *Legal Studies* 277.)

UNFAIR CONTRACT TERMS ACT 1977

13. Varieties of exemption clause

(1) To the extent that this Part of this Act prevents the exclusion or restriction of any liability it also prevents—

    (a) making the liability or its enforcement subject to restrictive or onerous conditions;

    (b) excluding or restricting any right or remedy in respect of the liability, or subjecting a person to any prejudice in consequence of his pursuing any such right or remedy;

    (c) excluding or restricting rules of evidence or procedure;

and (to that extent) sections 2 and 5 to 7 also prevent excluding or restricting liability by reference to terms and notices which exclude or restrict the relevant obligation or duty.

Stewart Gill Ltd v *Horatio Myer & Co. Ltd*
[1992] 1 QB 600 (CA)

The plaintiffs were to supply the defendants with an overhead conveyor system. Payment was in stages, with the final 10 per cent payable in the form of 5 per cent on completion and 5 per cent 30 days thereafter. The plaintiffs' general conditions of sale provided that the defendants could not withhold payment of any amount due on grounds of set off or counterclaim in respect of incorrect or defective goods. The defendants withheld the final 10 per cent and argued that the plaintiffs had committed various breaches of contract and that these losses could be set off against the amount claimed. Held: the clause was unenforceable. Section 13(1)(b) extended the meaning of ss. 3 and 7 to cover this clause since it excluded a right that would otherwise be available. Therefore, the clause had to be shown to be reasonable. A term preventing an overpayment being set off against a claim for the price was prima facie unreasonable, and since the offending parts could not be severed, the whole clause was unenforceable.

LORD DONALDSON MR: . . . Section 3 of the 1977 Act applies where, as here, one party to a contract deals with the other on that other's written standard terms of business. However, it is limited to terms excluding or restricting liability or entitling the party concerned to render no contractual performance or a performance which is substantially different from that which was reasonably expected of him. Clause 12.4 is not such a clause, but the section is relevant to a consideration of section 13, although it is not there referred to in express terms.

Section 7 applies where, as here, the contract transfers the ownership of goods otherwise than under a contract for the sale or hire-purchase of goods. Unlike section 3, it is referred to in section 13 but, like section 3, it is concerned with exclusion or restriction of liability.

[Lord Donaldson then referred to section 13:]

It is a trite fact (as contrasted with being trite law) that there are more ways than one of killing a cat. Section 13 addresses this problem. On behalf of the plaintiffs it was submitted that it only did so to the extent of rendering ineffective any unreasonable term which by for example introducing restrictive or onerous conditions, indirectly achieved the exclusion or restriction of liability which, if achieved directly, would fall within the scope of other sections. The plaintiffs rightly say that clause

12.4 does not have this effect. On behalf of the defendants it was submitted that it had a wider scope.

The answer is, of course, to be found in the wording of the section, but it does not exactly leap out of the print and hit one between the eyes. Analysing the section and disregarding words which are irrelevant, it seems to deal with the matter as follows: 'To the extent that this Part of this Act prevents the exclusion or restriction of any liability it also prevents . . .' This seems to me to do no more than give expression to the 'cat' approach. Both sections 3 and 7 would render ineffective any clause in the plaintiffs' written standard terms of business which excluded or restricted liability in respects which are here material and section 13 extends this in some way. In order to find out in what way, one must read on:

> it also prevents—(a) making the liability or its enforcement subject to restrictive or onerous conditions; (b) excluding or restricting any right or remedy in respect of the liability . . . (c) excluding or restricting rules of . . . procedure . . .

Now clause 12.4 can perhaps be said to make the enforcement of the plaintiffs' liability subject to a condition that the defendants shall not have sought to set off their own claims against their liability to pay the price and this might well be said to be onerous. However, I do not think it necessary to pursue this, because it is quite clear that clause 12.4 excludes the defendants' 'right' to set off their claims against the plaintiffs' claim for the price and further excludes the remedy which they would otherwise have of being able to enforce their claims against the plaintiffs by means of a set-off: see paragraph (b). It also excludes or restricts the procedural rules as to set off: see paragraph (c). Thus far, therefore, the defendants can bring themselves within the section.

We then get to the words:

> and (to that extent) sections 2 and 5 to 7 also prevent excluding or restricting liability by reference to terms and notices which exclude or restrict the relevant obligation or duty.

Although I find this obscure, I do not think that these words restrict the ambit of the preceding words. I think that they constitute an extension and that what is intended to be covered is an exclusion or restriction of liability not by contract but by reference to notices or terms of business which are not incorporated in a contract. If this is correct, it is irrelevant to the present case.

NOTE: Compare with *Schenkers Ltd* v *Overland Shoes Ltd* [1998] 1 Lloyd's Rep 498, *page 313*.

Section 13(1) provides that clauses are subject to ss. 2, 5, 6, or 7 of UCTA 1977 if they are worded as clauses which exclude or restrict the obligation or duty.

Smith v *Eric S. Bush*
[1990] 1 AC 831 (HL)

A prospective purchaser applied for a building society mortgage and the building society instructed the defendants to value the property. The applicant signed a form containing a disclaimer which stated that neither the building society nor its surveyor warranted that the report and valuation would be accurate, and the report and valuation were supplied without any acceptance of responsibility. The report also contained a similar disclaimer. The valuation stated that no essential repairs were required. It was negligently prepared and the purchaser claimed damages in tort from the defendants. The defendants argued that the disclaimer was effective to protect them and was not subject to UCTA 1977, s. 2(2) (*page 296*) because it was not a clause which excluded liability. Held: a duty of care was owed by the valuers to the prospective purchaser. The disclaimer was subject to UCTA 1977, s. 2, in that the last part of s. 13(1) stated that s. 2 applied to clauses which purported to prevent the duty ever arising.

LORD TEMPLEMAN: . . . In *Harris* v *Wyre Forest DC* [1988] QB 835 the Court of Appeal . . . accepted an argument that the 1977 Act did not apply because the council by their express disclaimer refused to obtain a valuation save on terms that the valuer would not be under any obligation to Mr and Mrs Harris to take reasonable care or exercise reasonable skill. The council did not exclude liability for negligence but excluded negligence so that the valuer and the council never came under a duty of care to Mr and Mrs Harris and could not be guilty of negligence. This construction would not give effect to the manifest intention of the Act but would emasculate the Act. The construction would provide no control over standard form exclusion clauses which individual members of the public are obliged to accept. A party to a contract or a tortfeasor could opt out of the Act of 1977 by declining in the words of Nourse LJ, at p. 845, to recognise 'their own answerability to the plaintiff'. Caulfield J said, at p. 850, that the Act 'can only be relevant where there is on the facts a potential liability'. But no one intends to commit a tort and therefore any notice which excludes liability is a notice which excludes a potential liability. Kerr LJ, at p. 853, sought to confine the Act to 'situations where the existence of a duty of care is not open to doubt' or where there is 'an inescapable duty of care'. I can find nothing in the Act of 1977 or in the general law to identify or support this distinction. In the result the Court of Appeal held that the Act does not apply to 'negligent misstatements where a disclaimer has prevented a duty of care from coming into existence'; per Nourse LJ, at p. 848. My Lords, this confuses the valuer's report with the work which the valuer carries out in order to make his report. The valuer owed a duty to exercise reasonable skill and care in his inspection and valuation. If he had been careful in his work, he would not have made a 'negligent misstatement' in his report.

Section 11(3) of the Act of 1977 provides that in considering whether it is fair and reasonable to allow reliance on a notice which excludes liability in tort, account must be taken of:

'all the circumstances obtaining when the liability arose or (but for the notice) would have arisen'.

Section 13(1) of the Act prevents the exclusion of any right or remedy and (to that extent) section 2 also prevents the exclusion of liability:

'by reference to . . . notices which exclude . . . the relevant obligation or duty'.

Nourse LJ dismissed section 11(3) as 'peripheral' and made no comment on section 13(1). In my opinion both these provisions support the view that the Act of 1977 requires that all exclusion notices which would in common law provide a defence to an action for negligence must satisfy the requirement of reasonableness.

The answer to the second question involved in these appeals is that the disclaimer of liability made by the council on its own behalf in the *Harris* case and by the Abbey National on behalf of the appellant surveyors in the *Smith* case constitute notices which fall within the Unfair Contract Terms Act 1977 and must satisfy the requirement of reasonableness.

NOTES

1. It is far from clear *which* clauses excluding or restricting a duty are covered by UCTA 1977. See MacDonald (1992) 12 *Legal Studies* 277, the 'but for' test and the 'expectations test'.
2. On the question of the application of s. 2(2) and the reasonableness of the clause, see *page 310*.

(b) Clauses transferring liability from the tortfeasor to a third party are not subject to UCTA

Thompson v ***T. Lohan (Plant Hire) Ltd & J. W. Hurdiss Ltd***
[1987] 1 WLR 649 (CA)

The defendants, a plant hire company, hired an excavator and driver to Hurdiss for use by Hurdiss at its quarry. The hire was on the terms and conditions of the Contractors' Plant Association, clause 8 of which provided:

When a driver or operator is supplied by the owner with the plant, the owner shall supply a person competent in operating the plant and such person shall be under the direction and control of the hirer. Such drivers or operators shall for all purposes in connection with their employment in the working of the plant be regarded as the servants or agents of the hirer . . . who alone shall be responsible for all claims arising in connection with the operation of the plant by the said drivers or operators. The hirer shall not allow any other person to operate such plant without the owner's previous consent to be confirmed in writing.

Clause 13 provided that the hirer was to 'fully and completely indemnify the owner in respect of all claims by any person whatsoever for injury to person or property caused by or in connection with or arising out of the use of the plant'. The plaintiff's husband was killed in an accident caused by the negligence of the driver in operating the excavator at the quarry. The plaintiff succeeded in her claim for damages in tort from the defendants, and the defendants sought to rely on clauses 8 and 13 to recover the damages from Hurdiss. Hurdiss argued, *inter alia*, that the conditions were contrary to s. 2(1) of UCTA 1977 (*page 296*) and could not be relied upon. Held: clause 8 transferred liability for the driver's negligence to the third party, Hurdiss, who therefore had to indemnify the defendants under clause 13. Section 2 of UCTA was intended to prevent the *exclusion* of liability in negligence to the victim of the negligence (the plaintiff) and was not concerned with arrangements, such as those made in clause 8, for sharing or transferring the burden of compensating the victim.

The Court of Appeal in *Thompson* v *Lohan* had been referred to the following case.

Phillips Products Ltd v Hyland

[1987] 1 WLR 659 (CA)

The plaintiffs hired an excavator and a driver from the defendants to carry out building work at the plaintiffs' factory. The contract of hire incorporated clause 8 of the Contractors' Plant Association conditions (*see above*). The driver negligently drove the excavator into a wall and caused considerable damage to the plaintiffs' property. The plaintiffs claimed damages from the defendants who sought to rely on clause 8. The plaintiffs alleged that clause 8 was subject to s. 2(2) of UCTA since it purported to 'exclude or restrict' liability in negligence. Held: in deciding whether a clause had excluded or restricted liability, the court had to look at the substance and effect of the term rather than its form. In the circumstances, the effect of clause 8 was to negative the common law duty in tort which otherwise would have been owed by the defendants. Therefore, clause 8 had the *effect* of excluding liability and fell within s. 2(2) of UCTA.

SLADE LJ (delivering the judgment of the Court): . . . The argument for Hamstead is that they do not, by reference to clause 8, '*exclude or restrict*' their liability for negligence. Clause 8, it is stressed, is not an 'excluding' or 'restricting' clause. It may have an *effect* on the liability for negligence which would otherwise have existed if there were, as there was in the present case, negligence. (For 'may' we would substitute 'must' assuming that Hamstead's submission as to the validity of clause 8 is correct.) Nevertheless, the clause does not, it is said, amount to an attempt by either party to the contract to '*exclude or restrict*' liability: it is simply an attempt on their part to divide and allocate the obligations or responsibilities arising in relation to the contract by *transferring* liability for the acts of the operator from the plant owners to the hirers. A transfer, it is suggested, is not an exclusion; hence the hirers fail at the section 2(2) hurdle.

. . . We are unable to accept that in the ordinary sensible meaning of words in the context of section 2 and the Act as a whole, the provisions of clause 8 do not fall within the scope of section 2(2). A transfer of liability from A to B necessarily and inevitably involves the exclusion of liability so far as A is concerned. . . . On the particular facts of this case the effect of clause 8, if valid, is to negative a common law liability in tort which would otherwise admittedly fall on the plant owner. The effect of clause 8 making 'the hirer alone responsible for all claims' necessarily connotes that by the clause the plant owner's responsibility is excluded. In applying section 2(2), it is not relevant to consider whether the form of a clause is such that it can aptly be given the label of an 'exclusion' or 'restriction' clause. There is no mystique about 'exclusion' or 'restriction' clauses. To decide whether a person 'excludes' liability by reference to a contract term, you look at the effect of the term. You look at its substance. The effect here is beyond doubt. Hamstead do most certainly purport to exclude their liability for negligence by *reference* to clause 8. Furthermore, clause 8 purports to 'exclude or restrict the relevant obligation or duty' within the provisions of section 13(1) of the Act. . . .

NOTES

1. In *Thompson* v *Lohan Ltd*, *Phillips Products* v *Hyland* was distinguished by Fox LJ who said (at pp. 656–7):

   In the *Phillips* case there was a tortfeasor, Hamstead, who were vicariously liable to Phillips for the damage done by their servant, Hyland. Thus Hamstead were liable to Phillips for negligence, but were seeking to exclude that liability by relying on clause 8. If that reliance had been successful, the result in the *Phillips* case would be that the victim would be left with no remedy by virtue of the operation of clause 8. Prima facie the victim was entitled to damages for negligence against Hamstead, because Hamstead were vicariously liable in negligence for the acts of their own servant. So one starts from that point. There was a plain liability of Hamstead to Phillips. That was, as Slade LJ said, a case of a plant owner excluding his liability for negligence in the relevant sense by reference to the contract term, clause 8. . . .

   If one then turns to the present case, the sharp distinction between it and the *Phillips* case is this, that whereas in the *Phillips* case there was a liability in negligence of Hamstead to Phillips (and that was sought to be excluded), in the present case there is no exclusion or restriction of the liability sought to be achieved by reliance upon the provisions of clause 8. The plaintiff has her judgment against Lohan and can enforce it. The plaintiff is not prejudiced in any way by the operation sought to be established of clause 8. All that has happened is that Lohan and the third party have agreed between themselves who is to bear the consequences of Mr Hill's negligent acts. I can see nothing in section 2(1) of the Act of 1977 to prevent that. In my opinion, section 2(1) is concerned with protecting the victim of negligence, and of course those who claim under him. It is not concerned with arrangements made by the wrongdoer with other persons as to the sharing or bearing of the burden of compensating the victim. In such a case it seems to me there is no exclusion or restriction of the liability at all. The liability has been established by Hodgson J. It is not in dispute and is now unalterable. The circumstance that the defendants have between themselves chosen to bear the liability in a particular way does not affect that liability; it does not exclude it, and it does not restrict it. The liability to the plaintiff is the only relevant liability in the case, as it seems to me, and that liability is still in existence and will continue until discharge by payment to the plaintiff. Nothing is excluded in relation to the liability, and the liability is not restricted in any way whatever. The liability of Lohan to the plaintiff remains intact. The liability of Hamstead to Phillips was sought to be excluded.

   The loss in *Phillips Products* v *Hyland* was incurred by the hirer so that the clause could easily be seen as excluding liability, whereas in *Thompson* it was the loss of a third party. They are consistent in that in both it is the position of the victim which is all important.

2. Despite the indication that it is the substance of the clause which matters rather than its form, it is not clear how this distinction will be made. In *Johnstone* v *Bloomsbury Health*

Authority [1992] 1 QB 333, there was an express term of the junior doctor's contract requiring the doctor to be available on call for up to an average of 48 hours a week in addition to the contracted 40 hours working week. The junior doctor claimed that this term was unenforceable under UCTA 1977, s. 2(1) as a clause excluding liability for personal injury arising from negligence, since it was potentially injurious to the doctor's health. All three members of the Court of Appeal considered that UCTA 1977 would apply to the express term. Unfortunately, only Stuart-Smith LJ gave brief reasons. He referred to s. 13(1) and continued:

> When considering the operation of section 2 of the Act the court is concerned with the substance and not the form of the contractual provision. . . .
>
> If, contrary to my opinion, the defendants are entitled to succeed on the submissions they advanced in support of the appeal in relation to the statement of claim, it is arguable that they can only do so because the effect of paragraph 4(b) of the contract must be construed as an express assumption of risk by the plaintiff (a plea of volenti non fit injuria) or because it operates to restrict or limit the ambit and scope of the duty of care owed by the defendants. If that is the correct analysis, then the substance and effect, though not the form, of the term is such that it can properly be argued to fall within . . . the Act.

(c) Evasion by means of secondary contract

UNFAIR CONTRACT TERMS ACT 1977

10. Evasion by means of secondary contract

A person is not bound by any contract term prejudicing or taking away rights of his which arise under, or in connection with the performance of, another contract, so far as those rights extend to the enforcement of another's liability which this Part of this Act prevents that other from excluding or restricting.

Tudor Grange Holdings Ltd v *Citibank NA*
[1992] Ch 53

Tudor Grange brought an action against Citibank. Citibank sought to have it struck out on the ground that Tudor Grange had agreed a deed of release which prevented the action. This deed of release released the bank from 'all claims, demands and causes of action whether or not presently known or suspected'. Tudor Grange claimed that this deed of release was unenforceable under s. 10 of UCTA 1977. They argued that the release took away their rights under the banking contract with Citibank, including their right to complain of breaches of the duty of care owed in the banking contract, which the bank was precluded by UCTA from excluding or restricting unless the release was shown to be reasonable. Held: section 10 did not apply to a contract to settle disputes which had arisen concerning the performance of an earlier contract. It could also not apply where the parties to both contracts were the same, so that the release was binding on Tudor Grange.

BROWNE-WILKINSON V-C: . . . This argument that s. 10 of the Act may apply to compromises or settlement of existing disputes has been foreseen by a number of textbook writers as an unfortunate possibility. They are unanimous in their hope that the courts will be robust in resisting it. If [counsel for the plaintiffs'] construction is correct, the impact will be very considerable. The Act of 1977 is normally regarded as being aimed at exemption clauses in the strict sense, that is to say, clauses in a contract which aim to cut down prospective liability arising in the course of the performance of the contract in which the exemption clause is contained. If [counsel for the plaintiffs'] argument is correct, the Act will apply to all compromises or waivers of existing claims arising from past actions.

Any subsequent agreement to compromise contractual disputes falling within sections 2 or 3 of the Act will itself be capable of being put in question on the grounds that the compromise or waiver is not reasonable. Even an action settled at the door of the court on the advice of solicitors and counsel could be reopened on the grounds that the settlement was not reasonable within the meaning of the Act. If I am forced to that conclusion by the words of section 10 properly construed, so be it. But, in my judgment, it is improbable that Parliament intended that result: it would be an end to finality in seeking to resolve disputes.

The starting point in construing section 10 is, in my judgment, to determine the mischief aimed at by the Act itself. For this purpose, it is legitimate to look at the second report on exemption clauses of the Law Commission on *Exemption Clauses* (1975) (Law Com No. 69): (see *Smith* v *Eric S Bush* [1990] AC 831, 857E, per Lord Griffiths). This report was the genesis of the Act of 1977. The report is wholly concerned with remedying injustices which are caused by exemption clauses in the strict sense. So far as I can see, the report makes no reference of any kind to any mischief relating to agreements to settle disputes.

Next, the marginal note to section 10 reads: 'Evasion by means of secondary contract.' Although the marginal note to a section cannot control the language used in the section, it is permissible to have regard to it in considering what is the general purpose of the section and the mischief at which it is aimed: see *Stephens* v *Cuckfield Rural District Council* [1960] 2 All ER 716, [1960] 2 QB 372. This sidenote clearly indicates that it is aimed at devices intended to *evade* the provisions of Pt 1 of the Act of 1977 by the use of another contract. In my judgment, a contract to settle disputes which have arisen concerning the performance of an earlier contract cannot be described as an evasion of the provisions in the Act regulating exemption clauses in the earlier contract. Nor is the compromise contract 'secondary' to the earlier contract.

The textbooks, to my mind correctly, identify at least one case which section 10 is designed to cover. Under contract 1, the supplier (S) contracts to supply a customer (C) with a product. Contract 1 contains no exemption clause. However, C enters into a servicing contract, contract 2, with another party (X). Under contract 2, C is precluded from exercising certain of his rights against S under contract 1. In such a case section 10 operates to preclude X from enforcing contract 2 against C so as to prevent C enforcing his rights against S under contract 1. The extent of the operation of section 10 in such circumstances may be doubtful: see Treitel on *The Law of Contract*, 7th edn, 1987), p. 206. But there is no doubt that such a case falls squarely within the terms of section 10.

In the case that I have just postulated, the references in section 10 to 'another's liability' and 'that other' are references to someone other than X, i.e. to the original supplier, S. On [counsel for the plaintiffs'] construction the words 'another' and 'that other' are taken as referring to someone other than C, the customer whose rights are restricted, so as to make the section apply to a case such as the present where there is no third party, X. Although as a matter of language the words of the section are capable of referring to anyone other than C, in my judgment, read in context and having regard to the purpose both of the Act and of the section itself, the reference to 'another' plainly means someone other than X, that is to say someone other than the party to the secondary contract. In my judgment, section 10 does not apply where the parties to both contracts are the same.

This view is reinforced by a further factor. If the Act were intended to apply to terms in subsequent compromise agreements between the same parties as the original contract, section 10 would be quite unnecessary. Under sections 2 and 3 there is no express requirement that the contract term excluding or restricting S's liability to C has to be contained in the same contract as that giving rise to S's liability to C. If S and C enter into two contracts, it makes no difference if the exemption clause is contained in a different contract from that under which the goods are supplied. Sections 2 and 3 by themselves will impose the test of reasonableness. Why then should Parliament have thought that in section 10 there was some possibility of evasion in such circumstances?

In my judgment, the Act of 1977 is dealing solely with exemption clauses in the strict sense (i.e. clauses in a contract modifying prospective liability) and does not affect retrospective compromises of existing claims. Section 10 is dealing only with attempts to evade the Act's provisions by the introduction of such an exemption clause into a contract with a third party. . . . Accordingly, for those reasons, section 10 cannot apply to the release. . . .

NOTE: Section 10 is therefore limited to attempts to avoid the operation of UCTA's provisions by the use of an exemption clause in a secondary contract with a third party.

(d) Business liability

The main provisions of the Act (ss. 2–7) apply only to 'business liability'.

UNFAIR CONTRACT TERMS ACT 1977

1. Scope of Part I

(3) In the case of both contract and tort, sections 2 to 7 apply (except where the contrary is stated in section 6(4)) only to business liability, that is liability for breach of obligations or duties arising—

    (a) from things done or to be done by a person in the course of a business (whether his own business or another's); or

    (b) from the occupation of premises used for business purposes of the occupier; and references to liability are to be read accordingly.

NOTE: 'Business' is defined by s. 14 as including 'a profession and the activities of any government department or local or public authority'. (See, e.g., the local authority in *St Albans City and District Council* v *International Computers Ltd* [1996] 4 All ER 481, 490, which was dealing 'in the course of a business'.) Section 6(4) extends the liabilities in s. 6 beyond business liability.

B: Basic scheme of UCTA 1977

UCTA 1977 deals with exemption clauses in one of two ways: either the clause will be rendered totally unenforceable in the circumstances; or the clause will be unenforceable unless it is established that it is reasonable. (It is important to note, therefore, that not every clause is subject to the reasonableness requirement.)

The first step is to find the section applicable to the liability sought to be excluded. This will then tell us whether the clause is totally unenforceable or subject to the reasonableness requirement.

(a) Negligence liability

UNFAIR CONTRACT TERMS ACT 1977

1. Scope of Part I

(1) For the purposes of this Part of this Act, 'negligence' means the breach—

    (a) of any obligation, arising from the express or implied terms of a contract, to take reasonable care or exercise reasonable skill in the performance of the contract;

    (b) of any common law duty to take reasonable care or exercise reasonable skill (but not any stricter duty);

    (c) of the common duty of care imposed by the Occupiers' Liability Act 1957 or the Occupiers' Liability Act (Northern Ireland) 1957.

This means that for the purposes of the Act, certain breaches of contract are treated as negligence (i.e., breaches of qualified contractual obligations to take reasonable care or exercise reasonable skill).

UNFAIR CONTRACT TERMS ACT 1977

2. Negligence liability

(1) A person cannot by reference to any contract term or to a notice given to persons generally or to particular persons exclude or restrict his liability for death or personal injury resulting from negligence.

(2) In the case of other loss or damage, a person cannot so exclude or restrict his liability for negligence except in so far as the term or notice satisfies the requirement of reasonableness.

NOTE: Clauses which purport to exclude or restrict negligence liability for death or personal injury are rendered totally unenforceable.

'Other loss or damage' means loss or damage other than death or personal injury, and would include property damage and economic loss. Clauses falling within s. 2(2) are enforceable only if shown to be reasonable.

(b) Contractual liability

This is dealt with in two places in the Act. There are special rules in ss. 6 and 7 covering certain implied obligations (e.g., as to title, description, fitness for purpose, satisfactory quality, and correspondence with sample) in sale of goods and hire-purchase contracts, and contracts for work and materials, and hire contracts (for details of these contracts and terms, see *page 240*). There is also a general provision covering contractual liability if qualifying conditions are met (s. 3).

(i) Contracts covered by ss. 6 and 7

UNFAIR CONTRACT TERMS ACT 1977

6. Sale and hire-purchase

(2) As against a person dealing as consumer, liability for breach of the obligations arising from—

  (a) section 13, 14 or 15 of the 1893 Act [now 1979 Act] (seller's implied undertakings as to conformity of goods with description or sample, or as to their quality or fitness for a particular purpose);

  (b) section 9, 10 or 11 of the 1973 Act (the corresponding things in relation to hire-purchase),

cannot be excluded or restricted by reference to any contract term.

(3) As against a person dealing otherwise than as consumer, the liability specified in subsection (2) above can be excluded or restricted by reference to a contract term, but only in so far as the term satisfies the requirement of reasonableness.

NOTES
1. Exclusion or restriction of the implied terms in s. 6 was previously governed by the Supply of Goods (Implied Terms) Act 1973.
2. Section 6(1) provides that the implied obligations as to title cannot be excluded or restricted. Section 7(3A) of UCTA provides that liability for breach of s. 2 of the Supply of Goods and Services Act 1982 (relating to the transfer of goods in a work and materials contract) cannot be excluded or restricted. However, liability for breach of s. 7 of the 1982 Act (implied obligation concerning the right to transfer possession of goods in a hire contract) can be excluded or restricted if the clause is shown to satisfy the reasonableness test (UCTA 1977, s. 7(4)).
3. Section 6(2) and (3) and s. 7(2) and (3) are to similar effect and draw an important distinction between a party 'dealing as consumer' (who is given absolute protection against the exclusion of the implied obligations as to description, fitness for purpose, satisfactory quality, and

correspondence with sample) and a non-consumer (against whom this liability can be excluded provided the clause is a reasonable one).
4. Section 12(1) provides a definition of 'dealing as a consumer'.

UNFAIR CONTRACT TERMS ACT 1977

12. 'Dealing as consumer'

(1) A party to a contract 'deals as consumer' in relation to another party if—

    (a) he neither makes the contract in the course of a business nor holds himself out as doing so; and

    (b) the other party does make the contract in the course of a business; and

    (c) in the case of a contract governed by the law of sale of goods or hire-purchase, or by section 7 of this Act, the goods passing under or in pursuance of the contract are of a type ordinarily supplied for private use or consumption.

(1A) But if the first party mentioned in subsection (1) is an individual paragraph (c) of that subsection must be ignored.

(2) But the buyer is not in any circumstances to be regarded as dealing as consumer—

    (a) if he is an individual and the goods are second hand goods sold at public auction at which individuals have the opportunity of attending the sale in person;

    (b) if he is not an individual and the goods are sold by auction or by competitive tender.

NOTES

1. S. 12(1A) and new s. 12(2) were inserted by reg. 14 of the Sale and Supply of Goods to Consumers Regulations 2002, SI 2002/3045.
2. Section 12(3) provides that 'it is for those claiming that a party does not deal as consumer to show that he does not'.

When will the making of a contract be 'in the course of a business'?

R. & B. Customs Brokers Co. Ltd v United Dominions Trust Ltd
[1988] 1 WLR 321 (CA)

A company which had only two directors and shareholders (Mr and Mrs Bell) and which operated as a freight forwarding agent, bought a car on conditional sale terms from the defendant. Clause 2(a) of the agreement purported to exclude any implied conditions as to the condition or quality of the car, or its fitness for any particular purpose in relation to business transactions. The car was for the personal and business use of the Bells. A serious leak was discovered in the vehicle so that it was rendered unfit for use on the roads (a breach of the implied term in the Sale of Goods Act 1979, s. 14(3)). The plaintiff company brought an action against the defendants to recover the amount they had paid under the conditional sale agreement. The Court of Appeal examined whether the contract was made 'in the course of a business' by relying on the meaning of 'trade or business' in the Trade Descriptions Act 1968. Held: either the contract must be an integral part of the business (which here would mean integral to the freight forwarding business), or, if it is merely incidental to the business, it must be carried out with sufficient regularity to render it a contract in the course of a business. Since this car was only the second or third vehicle acquired by the plaintiffs on credit terms, there was not a sufficient degree of regularity to establish that this contract was anything more than a consumer transaction. The plaintiff company had dealt as a consumer and clause 2(a) did not apply.

DILLON LJ: . . . Did the company neither make the contract with the defendants in the course of a business nor hold itself out as doing so?

In the present case there was no holding out beyond the mere facts that the contract and the finance application were made in the company's corporate name, and in the finance application the section headed 'Business Details' was filled in to the extent of giving the nature of the company's business as that of shipping brokers, giving the number of years trading and the number of employees, and giving the names and addresses of the directors. What is important is whether the contract was made in the course of a business.

. . . Section 12 does not require that the business in the course of which the one party, referred to in condition (a), makes the contract must be of the same nature as the business in the course of which the other party, referred to in condition (b), makes the contract, e.g., that they should both be motor dealers.

. . . [W]e have been referred to decisions under the Trade Descriptions Act 1968, and in particular to the decision of the House of Lords in *Davies* v *Sumner* [1984] 1 WLR 1301.

Under the Trade Descriptions Act 1968 any person who in the course of a trade or business applies a false trade description to goods is, subject to the provisions of the Act, guilty of an offence. It is a penal Act, whereas the 1977 Act is not, and it is accordingly submitted that decisions on the construction of the 1968 Act cannot assist on the construction of s. 12 of the Act of 1977. Also the legislative purposes of the two Acts are not the same. The primary purpose of the Trade Descriptions Act 1968 is consumer protection, and the course of business referred to is the course of business of the alleged wrongdoer. But the provisions as to dealing as a consumer in the Act of 1977 are concerned with differentiating between two classes of innocent contracting party—those who deal as consumers and those who do not—for whom differing degrees of protection against unfair contract terms are afforded by the Act of 1977. Despite these distinctions, however, it would, in my judgment, be unreal and unsatisfactory to conclude that the fairly ordinary words 'in the course of business' bear a significantly different meaning in, on the one hand, the Trade Descriptions Act 1968 and, on the other hand, section 12 of the Act of 1977. In particular I would be very reluctant to conclude that these words bear a significantly wider meaning in section 12 than in the Trade Descriptions Act 1968.

I turn therefore to *Davies* v *Sumner* [1984] 1 WLR 1301. That case was not concerned with a company, but with an individual who had used a car for the purposes of his business as a self-employed courier. When he sold the car by trading it in in part exchange for a new one, he had applied a false trade description to it by falsely representing the mileage the car had travelled to have been far less than it actually was. Lord Keith of Kinkel who delivered the only speech in the House of Lords, commented at p. 1304F, that it was clear that the transaction—sc of trading in the car on the purchase of a new one—was reasonably incidental to the carrying on of the business, but he went on to say at 1305:

> Any disposal of a chattel held for the purposes of a business may, in a certain sense, be said to have been in the course of that business, irrespective of whether the chattel was acquired with a view to resale or for consumption or as a capital asset. But in my opinion section 1(1) of the Act is not intended to cast such a wide net as this. The expression 'in the course of a trade or business' in the context of an Act having consumer protection as its primary purpose conveys the concept of some degree of regularity, and it is to be observed that the long title to the Act refers to 'misdescriptions of goods, services, accommodation and facilities provided in the course of trade'. Lord Parker CJ in the *Havering* case [*Havering London Borough* v *Stevenson* [1970] 1 WLR 1375] clearly considered that the expression was not used in the broadest sense. The reason why the transaction there in issue was caught was that in his view it was 'an integral part of the business carried on as a car hire firm'. That would not cover the sporadic selling off of pieces of equipment which were no longer required for the purposes of a business. The vital feature of the *Havering* case appears to have been, in Lord Parker's view, that the defendant's business *as part of its normal practice* bought and disposed of cars. The need for some degree of regularity does not, however, involve that a one-off adventure in the nature of trade, carried through with a view to profit, would not fall within section 1(1) because such a transaction would itself constitute a trade.

Lord Keith then held that the requisite degree of regularity had not been established on the facts of *Davies* v *Sumner* because a normal practice of buying and disposing of cars had not yet been established at the time of the alleged offence. He pointed out for good measure that the disposal of the car was not a disposal of stock in trade of the business, but he clearly was not holding that only a disposal of stock in trade could be a disposal in the course of a trade or business.

Lord Keith emphasised the need for some degree of regularity, and he found pointers to this in the primary purpose and long title of the Trade Descriptions Act 1968. I find pointers to a similar need for regularity under the Act of 1977, where matters merely incidental to the carrying on of a business are concerned, both in the words which I would emphasise, 'in the course of' in the phrase 'in the course of a business' and in the concept, or legislative purpose, which must underlie the dichotomy under the Act of 1977 between those who deal as consumers and those who deal otherwise than as consumers.

This reasoning leads to the conclusion that, in the Act of 1977 also, the words 'in the course of business' are not used in what Lord Keith called 'the broadest sense'. I also find helpful the phrase used by Lord Parker CJ and quoted by Lord Keith, 'an integral part of the business carried on'. The reconcilation between that phrase and the need for some degree of regularity is, as I see it, as follows: there are some transactions which are clearly integral parts of the business concerned, and these should be held to have been carried out in the course of those businesses; this would cover, apart from much else, the instance of a one-off adventure in the nature of trade where the transaction itself would constitute a trade or business. There are other transactions, however, such as the purchase of the car in the present case, which are at highest only incidental to the carrying on of the relevant business; here a degree of regularity is required before it can be said that they are an integral part of the business carried on, and so entered into in the course of that business.

Applying the test thus indicated to the facts of the present case, I have no doubt that the requisite degree of regularity is not made out on the facts. Mr Bell's evidence that the car was the second or third vehicle acquired on credit terms was in my judgment and in the context of this case not enough. Accordingly, I agree with the judge that, in entering into the conditional sale agreement with the defendants, the company was 'dealing as consumer'. The defendants' condition 2(a) is thus inapplicable and the defendants are not absolved from liability under section 14(3).

There is a different approach which I would wish to leave open for a future case since it was not argued before us. If the company had never been incorporated and Mr Bell had bought the car personally for personal (or domestic) and business use, it would, I apprehend, have been difficult to argue that he had not been dealing as a consumer in buying the car. On facts such as those of the present case it would seem anomalous and in some measure disquieting if a different result were reached if the car was bought by a company for the personal and business use of its two directors. It occurs to me that in such circumstances it could well be appropriate to pierce the corporate veil and look at the realities of the situation as in *DHN Food Distributors Ltd* v *Tower Hamlets London Borough Council* [1976] 1 WLR 852; see especially the comments of Lord Denning MR at p. 860, and Goff LJ at p. 861.

■ QUESTION

A company can therefore 'deal as a consumer' within UCTA 1977. Can a company seek protection under the Unfair Terms in Consumer Contracts Regulations 1999? See reg. 3 definition of consumer *page 319*.

NOTES
1. Dillon LJ rejected the argument that the plaintiffs were holding themselves out as contracting in the course of a business within s. 12(1) merely by representing that they were a company. More than this is required.
2. In circumstances such as these, the company was in the same need of protection when buying the car as an individual consumer since it was not in the business of buying cars and did not regularly purchase cars on credit so as to be in a position of knowledge. However, it is possible to consider circumstances where a company might not be in need of the same protection, e.g., a large public company.

3. It seems that 'regularly' in this context means frequently, and it is not necessary to establish a set pattern for purchases, e.g., every six months.

4. In *Stevenson* v *Rogers* [1999] QB 1028, the Court of Appeal considered the meaning of 'in the course of a business' in the context of s. 14 of the Sale of Goods Act 1979 and concluded that a sale would be in the course of a business unless it was a purely private transaction outside the scope of any business carried on by the seller. This is very different to the test in *R & B Customs Brokers* since under the test in *Stevenson* v *Rogers* a sale would be made in the course of a business where it is incidental to the seller's business. There has been some support for applying this interpretation to UCTA 1977 (see MacDonald (1999) 3 Web JCL 1) but the current test is that laid down in *R & B Customs Brokers*.

5. In *Feldaroll Foundry plc* v *Hermes Leasing (London) Ltd* [2004] EWCA Civ 747, (2004) 101 (24) LSG 32, the Court of Appeal was asked to prefer the definition in *Stevenson* v *Rogers* but applied the *R & B Customs Brokers* test when assessing whether a company could rely on the protection provided by s. 6(2) UCTA to those dealing as a consumer when it purchased a Lamborghini car for the use of the company's managing director. The *R & B* test applied because the meaning of 'in the course of a business' arose in the context of the application of UCTA. In particular, the fact that Feldaroll was a public company did not mean that *R & B* did not apply. The result was that the claimant company was dealing as a consumer and could reject the defective car despite the existence of a term excluding implied conditions of satisfactory quality and fitness for purpose.

6. This situation has been addressed in the Law Commission's Report, *Unfair Terms in Contracts*, Law Com No. 292, Cm 6464 (2005). Clause 26 of the Draft Bill defines a 'consumer contract' as a contract between '(a) an individual ("the consumer") who enters into it wholly or mainly for purposes unrelated to a business of his, and (b) the person ("the business") who enters into it wholly or mainly for purposes related to his business'. Thus, only natural persons will be consumers under the new scheme (as is currently the position under UTCCR 1999) and such a consumer must act for purposes outside the course of his business. The inclusion of the words 'wholly or mainly' addresses the classification problems where a contract is partly private and partly for business purposes. The Law Commission proposes that it should be for the courts to classify a contract as 'consumer' in accordance with what they regard as the predominant purpose of the contract. The new scheme proposes special treatment for 'small businesses' (Part 5 of the Report, clause 11 and clauses 27–29 of the draft Bill) enabling them to challenge standard terms that are not 'core' terms and which have not been individually negotiated. A term excluding liability for satisfactory quality as against a company where that term has not been negotiated would seem to be subject to the 'fair and reasonable' test if used against a small business (clause 11) or if the company is dealing on the other's written standard terms of business (draft clause 9), but not otherwise.

(ii) Section 3 (general contractual liability)

Any clause which attempts to exclude or restrict liability for *absolute obligations* arising under a contract, other than those covered by ss. 6 and 7 may be covered by this section if it applies.

UNFAIR CONTRACT TERMS ACT 1977

3. Liability arising in contract

(1) This section applies as between contracting parties where one of them deals as consumer or on the other's written standard terms of business.

(2) As against that party, the other cannot by reference to any contract term—

    (a) when himself in breach of contract, exclude or restrict any liability of his in respect of the breach; or

    (b) claim to be entitled—

        (i) to render a contractual performance substantially different from that which was reasonably expected of him, or

> (ii) in respect of the whole or any part of his contractual obligation, to render no performance at all,
>
> except in so far as (in any of the cases mentioned above in this subsection) the contract term satisfies the requirement of reasonableness.

NOTES

1. Section 3(1) states the conditions under which s. 3(2) will operate. It does not cover general contractual liability between two businesses unless one of the parties is dealing 'on the other's written standard terms of business', which is not defined by the Act. In *St Albans City and District Council* v *International Computers Ltd* [1995] FSR 686, Scott Baker J at first instance considered that it would be necessary for the other party to have drafted the *relevant exempting terms*, but that as long as there had not been any negotiation on those crucial terms, there could have been negotiation over other terms, e.g., price, quality. In the Court of Appeal ([1996] 4 All ER 481) Nourse LJ explained the position (at pp. 490–1) as follows:

   > The first question is whether, as between the plaintiffs and the defendant, the plaintiffs dealt as consumer or on the, defendant's written standard terms of business within s. 3(1). In the light of s. 12(1)(a) and the definition of 'business' in s. 14, it is accepted on behalf of the plaintiffs that they did not deal as consumer. So the question is reduced to this. Did the plaintiffs 'deal' on the defendant's written standard terms of business?
   >
   > [Counsel for the defendant] submitted that the question must be answered in the negative, on the ground that you cannot be said to deal on another's standard terms of business if, as was here the case, you negotiate with him over those terms before you enter into the contract. In my view that is an impossible construction for two reasons: first, because as a matter of plain English 'deals' means 'makes a deal', irrespective of any negotiations that may have preceded it; secondly, because s. 12(1)(a) equates the expression 'deals as consumer' with 'makes the contract'. Thus it is clear that in order that one of the contracting parties may deal on the other's written standard terms of business within s. 3(1) it is only necessary for him to enter into the contract on those terms.
   >
   > [Counsel for the defendant] sought to derive support for his submission from observations of Judge Thayne Forbes QC in *Salvage Association* v *CAP Financial Services Ltd* [1995] FSR 654 at 671–672. In my view, those observations do not assist the defendant. In that case the judge had to consider, in relation to two contracts, whether certain terms satisfied the description 'written standard terms of business' and also whether there had been a 'dealing' on those terms. In relation to the first contract he said (at 671):
   >
   > > I am satisfied that the terms in question were ones which had been written and produced in advance by CAP as a suitable set of contract terms for use in many of its future contracts of which the first contract with [the Salvage Association] happened to be one. It is true that Mr Jones felt free to and did negotiate and agree certain important matters and details relating to the first contract at the meeting of February 27, 1987. However, although he had read and briefly considered CAP's conditions of business, he did not attempt any negotiation with regard to those conditions, nor did he or Mr Ellis consider that it was appropriate or necessary to do so. The CAP standard conditions were terms that he and Mr Ellis willingly accepted as incorporated into the first contract in their predetermined form. In those circumstances, it seems to me that those terms still satisfy the description 'written standard terms of business' and, so far as concerns the first contract, the actions of Mr Jones and Mr Ellis constituted 'dealing' on the part of [the Salvage Association] with CAP on its written standard terms of business within the meaning of section 3 of the [Unfair Contract Terms Act 1977].
   >
   > It is true that the judge found that the Salvage Association did not negotiate with CAP over the latter's standard terms and that he held that, in entering into the contract, the Salvage Association dealt with CAP on those terms within s. 3. I do not, however, read his observations as indicating a view that the 'dealing' depended on the absence of negotiations. I think that even if there had been negotiations over the standard conditions his view would have been the same.

Scott Baker J dealt with this question as one of fact, finding that the defendant's general conditions remained effectively untouched in the negotiations and that the plaintiffs accordingly dealt on the defendant's written standard terms for the purposes of s. 3(1) (see [1995] FSR 686 at 706). I respectfully agree with him. . . .

More recently the courts have interpreted 'written standard terms of business' very generously in order to ensure the application of s. 3. In *Pegler* v *Wang (UK) Ltd (No. 1)* [2000] BLR 218 the only standard form clauses were the exclusion and limitation clauses inserted by the defendant. Nevertheless, since these clauses were regarded as non-negotiable and highly material, the judge considered that the claimant had clearly contracted on the defendant's 'written standard terms of business'. The crucial issue therefore seems to be the non-negotiability of the relevant terms. In *Watford Electronics Ltd* v *Sanderson CFL Ltd* [2000] 2 All ER (Comm) 984, the judge followed the approach of Nourse LJ in the *St Albans* case by indicating that a non-material variation would not necessarily prove fatal to the application of s. 3. Any amended term would have to be judged against the totality of the standard conditions and if it is was a narrow and insubstantial alteration, the contract would still be made 'on the other's written standard terms of business'. (Although *Watford* v *Sanderson* was overturned on appeal in relation to reasonableness, there was no appeal on the application of s. 3.)

2. Section 3(2)(b)(i) is designed to cover the possibility that the clause may allow the contractual performance to be altered in some way, e.g., a clause in a package holiday contract allowing the company to change the ship, the cruise details, and itineraries from those which had been booked (see *Anglo-Continental Holidays* v *Typaldos (London) Ltd* [1967] 2 Lloyd's Rep 61). Although the 'consumer' has agreed to this term which is incorporated in the contract, it is objectionable because it conflicts with what was 'reasonably expected' of the party relying on the term. However, this raises the question of how these reasonable expectations are to be established.

It is clear that for s. 3(2)(b) to apply the contract term had to be one which substantially alters the contractual performance reasonably expected of the party relying on the term. This was not the case on the facts in *Paragon Finance plc* v *Nash* (also known as *Paragon Finance plc* v *Staunton*) [2001] EWCA Civ 1466, [2002] 1 WLR 685, since the term altered the performance of the party who was objecting to the term. The interpretation of s. 3(2)(b) arose for consideration in the context of claims for possession by the claimant mortgagee following the defendants' default in the payment of mortgage instalments. The loan agreements contained variable interest clauses and in their defence the defendants sought to argue that the loan agreement was an extortionate credit bargain under the Consumer Credit Act 1974 since the applicable interest rates had been increased to a level which was considerably in excess of Bank of England or prevailing market rates. At first instance the judge had struck out the defence as having no real prospect of success. On appeal, the Court of Appeal Held: although there was an implied term relating to the exercise of the mortgagee's discretion to vary interest rates (discussed at *page 238*), there had been no breach of this term. The Court of Appeal also rejected the argument that the mortgagee's discretion to fix interest rates fell within s. 3 UCTA 1977 (and was therefore subject to the reasonableness requirement) since it amounted to altering the 'contractual performance' within s. 3(2)(b). There was no obligation on the mortgagee to perform a service and so no 'contractual performance'. When the mortgagee fixed the interest rate it was not altering the performance of *its* obligations but altering the performance required by the defendants under the contract.

DYSON LJ (with whose judgment Astill and Thorpe LJJ agreed):

Section 3(2)(b)(i) of the Unfair Contract Terms Act 1977

71 Section 3 of the Act provides, so far as material:

'(1) This section applies as between contracting parties where one of them deals as consumer or on the other's written standard terms of business.

'(2) As against that party, the other cannot by reference to any contract term . . . (b) claim to be entitled—(i) to render a contractual performance substantially different from that which was reasonably expected of him, or (ii) in respect of the whole or any part of his contractual obligation, to render no performance at all, except in so far as (in any of the cases mentioned above in this subsection) the contract term satisfies the requirement of reasonableness.'

72 It is submitted on behalf of the defendants that they were reasonably entitled to expect that, in performing their side of the bargain, the claimant would not apply rates which were substantially out of line with rates applied by comparable lenders to borrowers in comparable situations to the defendants. It is contended that the setting of interest rates is 'contractual performance' within the meaning of section 3(2)(b) of the 1977 Act, and that the claimant set interest rates that defeated that expectation.

73 The first question is whether the fixing of rates of interest under a discretion given by the contract was 'contractual performance' within the meaning of section 3(2)(b). [Counsel for the defendants] submits that it is. He relies on two authorities. The first is *Timeload Ltd* v *British Telecommunications plc* [1995] EMLR 459. In that case, the plaintiff set up a free telephone inquiry service and entered into a contract with BT whereby BT provided the plaintiff with the use of a certain telephone number. There was a clause in the contract which authorised BT to terminate apparently without reason. BT gave one month's notice of termination, and the plaintiff sought an injunction to restrain BT from terminating. It was held by the Court of Appeal that it was at least arguable that a clause purporting to authorise BT to terminate without reason purported to permit partial or different performance from that which the plaintiff was entitled to expect, and that section 3(2) of the 1977 Act applied. But the licence agreement imposed clear performance obligations on BT. Thus, clause I.I. obliged BT to provide the various services there set out. In these circumstances, it is not difficult to see why the court thought that it was at least arguable that a clause authorising termination of the obligation to provide those services for no good reason purported to permit a contractual performance different from that which the customer might reasonably expect.

74 The second authority is *Zockoll Group Ltd* v *Mercury Communications Ltd (No. 2)* [1999] EMLR 385. This was another telecommunications case. The plaintiff planned to set up a network of franchisees to provide goods and services to the public in response to telephone inquiries. It entered into a contract with Mercury under which it obtained a number of telephone numbers. Mercury wished to withdraw one number from the plaintiff and asserted that it was entitled to do so at its sole discretion. The plaintiff brought proceedings and relied on section 3(2)(b)(i) of the 1977 Act. The court held that the withdrawal of the disputed number did not render the contractual performance substantially different from what was expected. [Counsel] points out that it is implicit in the decision of the court that it was accepted that the withdrawal of the disputed number was *capable of being* contractual performance substantially different from that which it was reasonable to expect.

75 In my judgment, neither of these authorities assists [counsel's] submission. In both cases, the defendant telecommunications provider was contractually bound to provide a service. The question was whether the withdrawal of the service in the particular circumstances of the case was such as to render the contract performance (i e the provision of that service) substantially different from that which it was reasonable for the other contracting party to expect. The present cases are quite different. Here, there is no relevant obligation on the claimant, and therefore nothing that can qualify as 'contractual performance' for the purposes of section 3(2)(b)(i). Even if that is wrong, by fixing the rate of interest at a particular level the claimant is not altering the performance of any obligation assumed by it under the contract. Rather, it is altering the performance required of the defendants.

76 There appears to be no authority in which the application of section 3(2)(b)(i) to a situation similar to that which exists in this case has been considered. The editors of *Chitty on Contracts*, 28th ed (1999) offer this view, at para 14–071:

'Nevertheless it seems unlikely that a contract term entitling one party to terminate the contract in the event of a material breach by the other (eg failure to pay by the due date) would fall within paragraph (b), or, if it did so, would be adjudged not to satisfy the requirement of reasonableness. Nor, it is submitted, would that provision extend to a contract term which entitled one party, not to alter the performance expected of himself, but to alter the performance required of the other party (e g a term by which a seller of goods is entitled to increase the price payable by the buyer to the price ruling at the date of delivery, or a term by which a person advancing a loan is entitled to vary the interest payable by the borrower on the loan).'

77 In my judgment, this passage accurately states the law. The contract term must be one which has an effect (indeed a substantial effect) on the contractual performance reasonably expected of the party who relies on the term. The key word is 'performance'. A good example of what would come within the scope of the statute is given in *Chitty*, para 14–070. The editors postulate a person dealing as a consumer with a holiday tour operator who agrees to provide a holiday at a certain hotel at a certain resort, but who claims to be entitled, by reference to a term of the contract to that effect, to be able to accommodate the consumer at a different hotel, or to change the resort, or to cancel the holiday in whole or in part. In that example, the operator has an obligation to provide a holiday. The provision of the holiday is the 'contractual performance'. But that does not apply here.

3. Clauses covered by s. 3(2)(b) are clauses which define the obligation in a more limited way, so that a breach is less likely. (This is necessary because the last part of s. 13 does not apply to s. 3, see *page 288*.)
4. If section 3 applies, the clause in question must satisfy the reasonableness requirement in s. 11 in order to be enforceable.

(c) The reasonableness requirement

NOTE: Apply this test only if the applicable section requires this, e.g., s. 2(2), s. 3, s. 6(3).

UNFAIR CONTRACT TERMS ACT 1977

11. The 'reasonableness' test

(1) In relation to a contract term, the requirement of reasonableness for the purposes of this Part of this Act . . . is that the term shall have been a fair and reasonable one to be included having regard to the circumstances which were, or ought reasonably to have been, known to or in the contemplation of the parties when the contract was made.

(2) In determining for the purposes of section 6 or 7 above whether a contract term satisfies the requirement of reasonableness, regard shall be had in particular to the matters specified in Schedule 2 to this Act; but this subsection does not prevent the court or arbitrator from holding, in accordance with any rule of law, that a term which purports to exclude or restrict any relevant liability is not a term of the contract.

(3) In relation to a notice (not being a notice having contractual effect), the requirement of reasonablenes under this Act is that it should be fair and reasonable to allow reliance on it, having regard to all the circumstances obtaining when the liability arose or (but for the notice) would have arisen.

(4) Where by reference to a contract term or notice a person seeks to restrict liability to a specified sum of money, and the question arises (under this or any other Act) whether the term or notice satisfies the requirement of reasonableness, regard shall be had in particular (but without prejudice to subsection (2) above in the case of contract terms) to—

    (a) the resources which he could expect to be available to him for the purpose of meeting the liability should it arise; and

    (b) how far it was open to him to cover himself by insurance.

(5) It is for those claiming that a contract term or notice satisfies the requirement of reasonableness to show that it does.

NOTES

1. The reasonableness of the clause is to be judged at the time the contract was made. (Some of the case law on reasonableness was actually decided on the basis of the test used in the Supply of Goods (Implied Terms) Act 1973 (Sale of Goods Act 1979, s. 55), i.e., whether it is fair and reasonable to allow reliance on the term. In these cases, reasonableness was judged after the breach had occurred.) The Sale of Goods Act 1979, s. 55 (set out in Sch. 1, para. 11) applied to contracts made between the date when the 1973 Act came into force and the date when UCTA 1977 came into force.

2. What factors are relevant in determining reasonableness? Section 11(4) states two factors which are particularly relevant to the reasonableness of clauses limiting the compensation available. The availability and cost of insurance is one of these factors, but it has been used more generally by the courts (e.g., *Photo Production Ltd* v *Securicor Transport Ltd* [1980] AC 827).

3. Section 11(2) makes reference to guidelines in Sch. 2 which are stated to be relevant to reasonableness in ss. 6 and 7. Due to their factual relevancy, however, they have been used more widely. See Stuart Smith LJ in *Stewart Gill Ltd* v *Horatio Myer & Co. Ltd* [1992] 1 QB 600, 608.

UNFAIR CONTRACT TERMS ACT 1977

SCHEDULE 2 'GUIDELINES' FOR APPLICATION OF REASONABLENESS TEST

The matters to which regard is to be had in particular for the purposes of sections 6(3), 7(3) and (4), 20 and 21 are any of the following which appear to be relevant—

(a) the strength of the bargaining positions of the parties relative to each other, taking into account (among other things) alternative means by which the customer's requirements could have been met;

(b) whether the customer received an inducement to agree to the term, or in accepting it had an opportunity of entering into a similar contract with other persons, but without having to accept a similar term;

(c) whether the customer knew or ought reasonably to have known of the existence and extent of the term (having regard, among other things, to any custom of the trade and any previous course of dealing between the parties);

(d) where the term excludes or restricts any relevant liability if some condition is not complied with, whether it was reasonable at the time of the contract to expect that compliance with that condition would be practicable;

(e) whether the goods were manufactured, processed or adapted to the special order of the customer.

NOTES

1. The most fundamental factor in practice has been the question of the parties' bargaining positions. It is clearly more reasonable to use such a clause where the parties' bargaining position is equal.

2. As regards condition (c), the Court of Appeal in *AEG (UK) Ltd* v *Logic Resource Ltd* [1996] CLC 265, *page 220*, made it clear that the fact that a clause had been incorporated as a term did not mean that the clause would satisfy the reasonableness test. Schedule 2(c) requires an examination of the reality of the consent to the term. Hobhouse LJ made the following statement regarding the application of Sch. 2 and concluded that, on these facts, the plaintiffs had not established that the clause in question satisfied the reasonableness requirement since they had not shown that the defendant knew or ought reasonably to have known of the term. Accordingly, the clause could not be relied upon:

It is . . . desirable to draw specific attention to the fact that Sch. 2, para. (a) and (c), and the reference in s. 3 to standard terms to which an opposite party is required to adhere, raises a consideration of the reality of the consent of the contracting party. As I have said in the first part of my judgment, it is a necessary incident of a law of contract that in various commercial and other situations parties must objectively be taken to have agreed to clauses even though they have not actually applied to those clauses, and indeed may never have taken steps to inform themselves of their content.

What the Unfair Contract Terms Act is concerned with, and in particular Sch. 2, para. (a) and (c), is, among other aspects of reasonableness, the actuality or the reality of the consent of the party that it is sought to bind by the particular clause. Paragraph (c), 'whether the customer knew or ought reasonably to have known of the existence and extent of the term (having regard to, among other things, any custom of the trade and any previous course of dealing between the parties)', presupposes that the clause has already been incorporated in the contract; otherwise the point does not arise. It is necessary in order to assess reasonableness to consider to what extent the party has actually consented to the clause.

The judge dismissed this point in a single sentence:

> Guideline 'c' does not apply because, for the reasons stated above, the defendants were fixed with notice of the plaintiffs' conditions. It is only guideline 'a' which stands to be considered.

That is, in my judgment, a badly mistaken approach. It is essential in any question of reasonableness that the reality of the consent of the party sought to be bound by the relevant clause is considered. This also raises considerations of inequality of bargaining power which, in the present case, militate strongly in favour of the case of the defendants.

Therefore, it follows, in my judgment, that the plaintiffs did not discharge the burden of proof. Furthermore, having regard to the circumstances of this case and the effect of the provisions upon which the plaintiffs seek to rely, it is clear that on any view cl. 7 must be held to be unreasonable.

The Court of Appeal in *Britvic Soft Drinks* v *Messer UK Ltd* [2002] EWCA Civ 548, [2002] 2 Lloyd's Rep 368, *page 317*, also emphasised the fact that there is a distinction between instances of actual knowledge and consent to the term (possibly as a result of negotiation of the term), and the constructive consent (ought reasonably to have known of the existence and extent of the term) referred to in Sched. 2(c).

3. It is now clear that the presentation of the clause can be significant when assessing its reasonableness. In *Stag Line Ltd* v *Tyne Ship Repair Group Ltd, The Zinnia* [1984] 2 Lloyd's Rep 211, the most important factor affecting reasonableness was the fact that the parties were of equal bargaining power, but *obiter* Staughton J stated (at p. 222):

> I would have been tempted to hold that all the conditions are unfair and unreasonable for two reasons: first, they are in such small print that one can barely read them; secondly, the draughtsmanship is so convoluted and prolix that one almost needs an LL.B. to understand them. However, neither of those arguments was advanced before me, so I say no more about them.

(See now reg. 7 of the Unfair Terms in Consumer Contracts Regulations 1999, *page 267*.)

How should the courts approach this reasonableness requirement and what factors have been relevant?

George Mitchell (Chesterhall) Ltd v Finney Lock Seeds Ltd
[1983] 2 AC 803 (HL)

The facts of this case appear at *page 286*. Held: although on its true construction the clause applied to what had happened, it was not fair and reasonable to allow reliance on the clause (within s. 55 of the Sale of Goods Act 1979). A number of factors were stressed:

(a) It had been the defendants' practice to settle claims in excess of the limitation if they considered them to be justified. It therefore appeared that the defendants did not always consider the clause to be fair and reasonable.

(b) The defendants could have insured against crop failure without materially increasing the price of the seed.

(c) The supply of incorrect seed was due to negligence, and this was important in relation to the 'reasonableness' of the clause.

LORD BRIDGE: My Lords, at long last I turn to the application of the statutory language to the circumstances of the case. Of the particular matters to which attention is directed by paragraphs (a) to (e) of section 55(5), only those in (a) to (c) are relevant. As to paragraph (c), the respondents admittedly knew of the relevant condition (they had dealt with the appellants for many years) and, if they had read it, particularly clause 2, they would, I think, as laymen rather than lawyers, have had no difficulty in understanding what it said. This and the magnitude of the damages claimed in proportion to the price of the seeds sold are factors which weigh in the scales in the appellants' favour.

The question of relative bargaining strength under paragraph (a) and of the opportunity to buy seeds without a limitation of the seedsman's liability under paragraph (b) were inter-related. The evidence was that a similar limitation of liability was universally embodied in the terms of trade between seedsmen and farmers and had been so for very many years. The limitation had never been negotiated between representative bodies but, on the other hand, had not been the subject of any protest by the National Farmers' Union. These factors, if considered in isolation, might have been equivocal. The decisive factor, however, appears from the evidence of four witnesses called for the appellants, two independent seedsmen, the chairman of the appellant company, and a director of a sister company (both being wholly-owned subsidiaries of the same parent). They said that it had always been their practice, unsuccessfully attempted in the instant case, to negotiate settlements of farmers' claims for damages in excess of the price of the seeds, if they thought that the claims were 'genuine' and 'justified.' This evidence indicated a clear recognition by seedsmen in general, and the appellants in particular, that reliance on the limitation of liability imposed by the relevant condition would not be fair or reasonable.

Two further factors, if more were needed, weight the scales in favour of the respondents. The supply of autumn, instead of winter, cabbage seeds was due to the negligence of the appellants' sister company. Irrespective of its quality, the autumn variety supplied could not, according to the appellants' own evidence be grown commercially in East Lothian. Finally, as the trial judge found, seedsmen could insure against the risk of crop failure caused by supplying the wrong variety of seeds without materially increasing the price of seeds.

My Lords, even if I felt doubts about the statutory issue, I should not, for the reasons explained earlier, think it right to interfere with the unanimous original decision of that issue by the Court of Appeal. As it is, I feel no such doubts. If I were making the original decision, I should conclude without hesitation that it would not be fair or reasonable to allow the appellants to rely on the contractual limitation of their liability.

NOTE: Lord Bridge gave guidance on how the question of reasonableness should be approached:

This is the first time your Lordships' House has had to consider a modern statutory provision giving the court power to override contractual terms excluding or restricting liability, which depends on the court's view of what is 'fair and reasonable.' The particular provision of the modified section 55 of the Act of 1979 which applies in the instant case is of limited and diminishing importance. But the several provisions of the Unfair Contract Terms Act 1977 which depend on 'the requirement of reasonableness,' defined in section 11 by reference to what is 'fair and reasonable,' albeit in a different context, are likely to come before the courts with increasing frequency. It may, therefore, be appropriate to consider how an original decision as to what is 'fair and reasonable' made in the application of any of these provisions should be approached by an appellate court. It would not be accurate to describe such a decision as an exercise of discretion. But a decision under any of the provisions referred to will have this in common with the exercise of a discretion, that, in having regard to the various matters to which the modified section 55(5) of the Act of 1979, or section 11 of the Act of 1977 direct attention, the court must entertain a whole range of considerations, put them in the scales on one side or the other, and decide at the end of the day on which side the balance comes down. There will sometimes be room for a legitimate difference of judicial opinion as to what the answer shoud be, where it will be impossible to say that one view is demonstrably wrong and the other demonstrably right. It must follow, in my view, that, when asked to review such a decision on appeal, the appellate court should treat the original decision with the utmost respect and refrain from interference with it unless satisfied that it proceeded upon some erroneous principle or was plainly and obviously wrong.

For a recent example where an appellate court overturned a first instance finding on reasonableness, see *Watford Electronics Ltd* v *Sanderson CFL Ltd* [2001] EWCA Civ 317, [2001] 1 All ER (Comm) 696, *page 315.*

It will therefore be very difficult to give advice on whether a clause is likely to pass the reasonableness requirement in s. 11.

R. W. Green Ltd v Cade Brothers Farms
[1978] 1 Lloyd's Rep 602

The sellers, seed potato merchants, sold the buyers, who were farmers, 20 tons of uncertified King Edward potatoes at a price of £28 per ton. The sale was made on the standard terms of the National Association of Seed Potato Merchants, clause 5 of which provided that:

> . . . Time being the essence of this Contract . . . notification of rejection, claim or complaint must be made to the Seller giving a statement of the grounds for such rejection claim or complaint within three days after the arrival of the seed at its destination . . . It is specifically provided and agreed that compensation and damages payable under any claim or claims arising out of this Contract under whatsoever pretext shall not under any circumstances amount in aggregate to more than the Contract price of the potatoes forming the subject of the claim or claims.

In fact, it was later discovered that the potatoes were infected with a potato virus which could be detected only by examining the growing crop and which was not discoverable by inspecting the seeds. The sellers brought an action to recover monies owed for seed supplied, and the buyers counter-claimed to set off against this their loss of profit on the crop (£6,000). The sellers argued that they were protected from such a claim by their conditions of sale and that the buyers could recover only the price of the potatoes (£634). Held: it was not fair and reasonable (within s. 55 of the Sale of Goods Act 1979) to allow reliance on that part of the clause imposing a three-day time limit for complaints, since it was not possible to discover the defect within that time. However, the part of the clause limiting liability to the cost of the potato seeds was reasonable because the parties were of equal bargaining power, the clause had been in use for many years and had evolved as a result of trade practice and discussion between the Seed Potato Merchants Association and the National Farmers' Union. In addition, the buyers could have purchased certified seed at a higher price and would have been guaranteed against the virus.

> GRIFFITHS J: . . . This contract, like any commercial contract, must be considered and construed against the background of the trade in which it operates. The plaintiffs' conditions are based upon a standard form of conditions produced by the National Association of Seed Potato Merchants. They are used by a large majority of seed potato merchants and they have been in use in their present

form for over 20 years. They have evolved over a much longer period as the result both of trade practice and discussions between the Association and the National Farmers' Union. They are therefore not conditions imposed by the strong upon the weak; but are rather a set of trading terms upon which both sides are apparently content to do business.

It is also important to have in mind the distinction between certified and uncertified seed. The Ministry of Agriculture provides a service whereby its inspectors will inspect a potato crop during the growing season, and if it appears healthy will issue a certificate to that effect. There are various grades of certificate indicating the percentage of virus infected plants in the growing crop, ranging from an H certificate based on a tolerance of 2 per cent, to an FS certificate, based on a tolerance of 0.001 per cent. If a farmer buys certified seed, he pays a little more for it to cover the costs of the inspection and certification. The certificate cannot be an absolute guarantee that the seed will not be infected, but it is on the whole a fairly reliable system, and I have no doubt provides a very real safeguard against buying an infected batch of seed. The farmer who buys uncertified seed does not have this safeguard which is provided by the independent examination of the Ministry, and must as a general rule be taking a greater risk of buying infected seed, but of course he gets it at a cheaper price. . . .

On my findings no complaint was made about the potatoes until 13 days after delivery. The plaintiffs therefore say that the claim is out of time and barred by the condition that it must be made within three days of delivery. The plaintiffs' directors, in their evidence, explained that such a term was necessary in the trade because potatoes are a very perishable commodity and may deteriorate badly after delivery, particularly if they are not properly stored. So it was thought reasonable to give the farmer three days to inspect and make his complaint. This appears to me to be a very reasonable requirement in the case of damage that is discoverable by reasonable inspection. But the presence of virus Y in the potatoes was not discoverable by inspection, and the complaint that was made did not relate to this defect, which neither the farmer nor the potato merchant suspected.

At the time this contract was made no one would expect it to have been practicable for the farmer to complain of virus Y in the potatoes within three days of delivery, for the simple reason that he would not know of its presence. It would therefore, in my judgment, not be fair or reasonable that this claim should be defeated because no complaint was made within three days of delivery. I therefore declare that that part of cl. 5 is unenforceable in this action and provides no defence to the plaintiffs.

Is the claim to be limited to the contract price of the potatoes?

Should I exercise my discretion under s. 55, as amended, of the Sale of Goods Act and declare it to be unenforceable, because it would not be fair or reasonable to let the plaintiffs rely upon it?

I have considered the matters to which I am particularly directed to have regard by s. 55(5), in so far as they are relevant in this case. The parties were of equal bargaining strength; the buyer received no inducement to accept the term. True, it appears that he could not easily have bought potatoes without this term in the contract, but he had had the protection of the National Farmers' Union to look after his interests as the contract evolved and he knew that he was trading on these conditions.

No moral blame attaches to either party; neither of them knew, nor could be expected to know, that the potatoes were infected. There was of course a risk; it was a risk that the farmer could largely have avoided by buying certified seed, but he chose not to do so. To my mind the contract in clear language places the risk in so far as damage may exceed the contract price, on the farmer. The contract has been in use for many years with the approval of the negotiating bodies acting on behalf of both seed potato merchants and farmers, and I can see no grounds upon which it would be right for the Court to say in the circumstances of this case that such a term is not fair or reasonable.

NOTES
1. A number of the Sch. 2 guidelines were applicable in this case:
    (a) The parties were of equal bargaining power, since, although they contracted on the sellers' standard terms, these terms had been negotiated by the relevant trade bodies. It was also possible to purchase certified seed and the buyers had chosen not to do so.

(b) It was not possible to contract for the purchase of uncertified seeds and avoid this clause but this was offset by the factors in (a) above.

(c) The parties had dealt on these terms for five or six years and the buyers ought to have been aware of them.

(d) The first part of the clause requiring defects to be notified within three days of delivery is a condition affecting liability, and the test in Sch. 2 condition (d) is whether compliance with this was reasonably practicable. Griffiths J held that it was not.

2. In *Stewart Gill Ltd* v *Horatio Myer & Co. Ltd* [1992] 1 QB 600 (*page 288*), the Court of Appeal refused to sever unreasonable words in a clause when assessing reasonableness. The clause in *R. W. Green* v *Cade Bros Farms* does, however, appear to be separable into two distinct issues.

Smith v Eric S. Bush
[1990] 1 AC 831 (HL)

The facts of this case appear at *page 289*.

Since s. 2(2) applied to the disclaimer of the surveyors' liability, the House of Lords had to decide whether it was reasonable in these circumstances. Held: it was not fair and reasonable for mortgagees (such as the building society) and valuers to impose the risk of loss due to their incompetence or carelessness on purchasers, given the high cost of houses and the high interest rates payable by purchasers.

LORD GRIFFITHS: . . . Finally, the question is whether the exclusion of liability contained in the disclaimer satisfies the requirement of reasonableness provided by s. 2(2) of the Act of 1977. The meaning of reasonableness and the burden of proof are both dealt with in s. 11(3) . . . It is clear, then, that the burden is on the surveyor to establish that in all the circumstances it is fair and reasonable that he should be allowed to rely upon his disclaimer of liability.

I believe that it is impossible to draw up an exhaustive list of the factors that must be taken into account when a judge is faced with this very difficult decision. Nevertheless, the following matters should, in my view, always be considered.

1. Were the parties of equal bargaining power? If the court is dealing with a one-off situation between parties of equal bargaining power the requirement of reasonableness would be more easily discharged than in a case such as the present where the disclaimer is imposed on the purchaser who has no effective power to object.

2. In the case of advice would it have been reasonably practicable to obtain the advice from an alternative source taking into account considerations of costs and time. In the present case it is urged on behalf of the surveyor that it would have been easy for the purchaser to have obtained his own report on the condition of the house, to which the purchaser replies that he would then be required to pay twice for the same advice and that people buying at the bottom end of the market, many of whom will be young first-time buyers, are likely to be under considerable financial pressure without the money to go paying twice for the same service.

3. How difficult is the task being undertaken for which liability is being excluded. When a very difficult or dangerous undertaking is involved there may be a high risk of failure which would certainly be a pointer towards the reasonableness of excluding liability as a condition of doing the work. A valuation, on the other hand, should present no difficulty if the work is undertaken with reasonable skill and care. It is only defects which are observable by a careful visual examination that have to be taken into account and I cannot see that it places any unreasonable burden on the valuer to require him to accept responsibility for the fairly elementary degree of skill and care involved in observing, following-up and reporting on such defects. Surely it is work at the lower end of the surveyor's field of professional expertise.

4. What are the practical consequences of the decision on the question of reasonableness. This must involve the sums of money potentially at stake and the ability of the parties to bear the loss involved, which, in its turn, raises the question of insurance. There was once a time when it was

considered improper even to mention the possible existence of insurance cover in a lawsuit. But those days are long past. Everyone knows that all prudent, professional men carry insurance, and the availability and cost of insurance must be a relevant factor when considering which of two parties should be required to bear the risk of a loss. We are dealing in this case with a loss which will be limited to the value of a modest house and against which it can be expected that the surveyor will be insured. Bearing the loss will be unlikely to cause significant hardship if it has to be borne by the surveyor but it is, on the other hand, quite possible that it will be a financial catastrophe for the purchaser who may be left with a valueless house and no money to buy another. If the law in these circumstances denies the surveyor the right to exclude his liability, it may result in a few more claims but I do not think so poorly of the surveyor's profession as to believe that the floodgates will be opened. There may be some increase in surveyors' insurance premiums which will be passed on to the public, but I cannot think that it will be anything approaching the figures involved in the difference between the Abbey National's offer of a valuation without liability and a valuation with liability discussed in the speech of my noble and learned friend, Lord Templeman. The result of denying a surveyor, in the circumstances of this case, the right to exclude liability will result in distributing the risk of his negligence among all house purchasers through an increase in his fees to cover insurance, rather than allowing the whole of the risk to fall upon the one unfortunate purchaser.

. . . The evaluation of the foregoing matters leads me to the clear conclusion that it would not be fair and reasonable for the surveyor to be permitted to exclude liability in the circumstances of this case. I would therefore dismiss this appeal.

It must, however, be remembered that this is a decision in respect of a dwelling house of modest value in which it is widely recognised by surveyors that purchasers are in fact relying on their care and skill. It will obviously be of general application in broadly similar circumstances. But I expressly reserve my position in respect of valuations of quite different types of property for mortgage purposes, such as industrial property, large blocks of flats or very expensive houses. In such cases it may well be that the general expectation of the behaviour of the purchaser is quite different. With very large sums of money at stake prudence would seem to demand that the purchaser obtain his own structural survey to guide him in his purchase and, in such circumstances with very much larger sums of money at stake, it may be reasonable for the surveyors valuing on behalf of those who are providing the finance either to exclude or limit their liability to the purchaser.

NOTES

1. This is a rare assessment of reasonableness in the consumer context.
2. It is interesting that, given the fact that an alternative was available, the House of Lords was prepared to go further and consider its practical value. Most purchasers did not instruct an independent survey to be conducted but relied on that supplied through the building society because they simply could not afford to pay twice.
3. Lord Griffiths also considered the practical consequences of the decision, given that this decision had far-reaching implications. The provision of insurance was relevant to this. Either the burden would fall on the poor unfortunate victim of the negligence, or the valuers could insure against this risk, which would lead to a small increase in the price of valuations which would affect all purchasers equally.
4. If the property is not a modest dwelling house, then it appears that the burden shifts, so that it will be more reasonable for a valuer to exclude his liability in these circumstances and more reasonable to expect the purchaser to obtain an independent survey.

■ QUESTION

Why do you think there are so few reported cases concerning UCTA regulation of clauses in *consumer* contracts?

St Albans City and District Council v *International Computers Ltd*
[1995] FSR 686; [1996] 4 All ER 481 (CA)

The plaintiff, a local authority, had contracted with the defendants for the provision and installation of software to enable the local authority to create a database of eligible poll tax payers. The software contained an error so that the figure submitted to central government was overstated and the local authority therefore suffered loss. The local authority brought an action for damages and the defendants sought to rely on a limitation clause in the contract limiting their liability to £100,000. Scott Baker J, at first instance, held that the limitation clause was not reasonable and could not be relied upon.

Section 7(3) was applicable because this was a contract for goods (the software) and services and the software was not of merchantable quality or fit for the purpose. Section 3 applied to a breach of contract by the defendants' manager.

The following factors were identified as leading to the conclusion that the limitation was unreasonable:

(a) The defendant company was very substantial and, as a wholly-owned subsidiary of a multinational, had ample resources to meet any liability.

(b) The defendant company had product liability insurance cover of £50 million and could not justify the limit of liability to £100,000 which was small compared to the potential risk and the actual loss.

(c) The defendant company was in a very strong bargaining position relative to the plaintiff since it was one of a limited number of companies capable of fulfilling the local authority's requirements. The alternative companies also dealt on similar standard conditions.

(d) The practical consequence of a contrary finding of reasonableness would be that the loss would be borne by the local authority's population, either through increased taxation or reduced services, whereas the defendants were covered by insurance and should carry the risk since they were the party which stood to make the profit on the contract.

(On appeal the Court of Appeal was mainly concerned with the measure of the damages award and, in part, allowed the appeal on that issue.)

NOTES
1. These factors outweighed the factors on the other side of the balance, namely, that this contract was made between two 'businesses' who should be free to contract on whatever terms they chose, that the local authority was aware of the limitation when it contracted, and that limitations of this kind were commonplace in the industry.
2. This decision is significant in that it involves a finding of unreasonableness of a limitation clause in a contract between two 'businesses', when it had previously been considered that such clauses were likely to be held to be reasonable. However, the judge adopts a protectionist attitude towards the local authority which, although technically a non-consumer under UCTA 1977, is in a distinct position and is arguably in greater need of protection than a large public limited company.
3. On the first instance decision of Scott Baker J, see Macdonald (1995) 58 MLR 585.
4. When assessing reasonableness in the Court of Appeal, Nourse LJ (with whose judgment Hirst LJ and Sir Iain Glidewell agreed) referred to the approach to be taken on appeal which had been discussed by Lord Bridge in *George Mitchell* v *Finney Lock Seeds*, *page 307*, and concluded that he was not satisfied that there were any grounds to upset the decision of Scott

Baker J that the clause was unreasonable; and to reinforce the point, Nourse LJ added that he would have come to the same conclusion.

The recent approach to reasonableness in consumer contracts

In *Monarch Airlines Ltd* v *London Luton Airport Ltd, page 268*, Clarke J also had to consider whether cl. 10 was unenforceable as a result of the application of UCTA 1977. On the facts, s. 2(2) applied, and hence the defendant had to establish that the clause satisfied the reasonableness requirement in s. 11. The judge held that the clause was reasonable at the time the contract was made:

[Counsel] submits that the clause is not reasonable here for these . . . reasons. The defendant constructed and had sole control over the condition of the runway, whereas the plaintiff was simply a permitted user of it. The defendant would have no incentive to ensure that its runways were safe for the use of commercial passenger aircraft. It would also mean that the plaintiff would have to obtain additional cover in respect of a risk over which it could have no control with the consequence that it would either have to pass the extra cost to its customers or bear the extra cost itself.

The first of those is I think a relevant consideration, but I do not accept the second. . . . Also, there is no evidence that at any time before April 1992 the defendant regarded its responsibilities as occupier of the airport as any less onerous in practice because of the clause. As to the third point, I have already expressed my view that insurance cover was available. Whoever insured against the risk, the cost of doing so would be likely to be reflected somewhere in the ultimate cost to the consumer.

Having tried to take all the circumstances of the case into account I have reached the conclusion that, if cl. 10 is considered as at say March or April 1992, it was a fair and reasonable term to include in the terms and conditions. As already stated, it was generally accepted in the market, including the insurance market. Indeed, so far as I am aware, there has been no suggestion in the market (whether it be from the airlines, the airports or the insurers) that the clause be amended in any way. It was accepted by the plaintiff without demur. It has a clear meaning and the insurance arrangements of both parties could be made on the basis that the contract was governed by standard terms which had already been held to be reasonable in principle. It follows that, judged as at the beginning of the year in April, the terms did not fall foul of the Unfair Contract Terms Act. . . .

NOTE: This case provides a further illustration of the fact that in the context of commercial contracts it should be much easier to establish that the clause is reasonable, especially if the clause in question is contained in a standard form which is generally accepted in the industry. This accords with the approach adopted in *Photo Production* v *Securicor, page 283*, of non-interventionism and leaving it to the parties to allocate the risks and responsibility for insurance cover. In *Granville Oil & Chemicals Ltd* v *Davies Turner & Co. Ltd* [2003] EWCA Civ 570, [2003] 1 All ER (Comm) 819, Tuckey LJ (with whose judgment Potter LJ and Hart J agreed) made the following comment on the s. 11 discretion in commercial contracts:

[31] . . . The 1977 Act obviously plays a very important role in protecting vulnerable consumers from the effects of draconian contract terms. But I am less enthusiastic about its intrusion into contracts between commercial parties of equal bargaining strength, who should generally be considered capable of being able to make contracts of their choosing and expect to be bound by their terms.

Schenkers Ltd v Overland Shoes Ltd

[1998] 1 Lloyd's Rep 498 (CA)

The plaintiffs, freight forwarders, had contracted with the defendants, shoe importers, on the BIFA (British International Freight Association) standard trading conditions. Clause 23(A) of these conditions was a 'no set-off clause' in the following terms:

> The Customer shall pay to the Company in cash . . . all sums immediately when due, without reduction or deferment on account of any claim, counterclaim or set-off.

The defendants sought to set off a sum for VAT, which they claimed that the plaintiffs should have reclaimed for the benefit of the defendants. The plaintiffs sought to rely on cl. 23(A). The defendants claimed that it was unreasonable to exclude the right of set-off, that the clause had not been relied upon in practice in their long course of previous dealings and that they were in a position of unequal bargaining power. Held: the plaintiffs had proved that the clause was reasonable within s. 3 of UCTA 1977.

PILL LJ: . . . In my judgment the plaintiffs have satisfied the burden upon them of establishing that cl. 23(A) in the circumstances satisfies the requirement of reasonableness. The clause was in common use and well known in the trade following comprehensive discussions between reputable and representative bodies mindful of the considerations involved. It reflects a general view as to what is reasonable in the trade concerned. It was sufficiently well known that any failure by the defendant's officers, in the course of long and substantial dealings, to put their minds to the clause cannot be relied on to establish that it was unfair or unreasonable to include it in the contracts. I regard the level of disbursements as a factor which assists the plaintiffs to establish that it was fair and reasonable to include the term but not in itself a conclusive one. In a situation in which there was no significant inequality of bargaining position, the customs of the trade were an important factor. The parties were well aware of the circumstances in which business was conducted, the heads of expenditure to be incurred and the risks involved.

In present circumstances, I see little merit in the defendants' argument that the clause had not in practice been relied upon. The give and take practised by the parties in the course of substantial dealings upon the running account was admirable and conducive to a good business relationship but did not in my judgment prevent the plaintiffs, when the dispute arose, relying upon the term agreed. In *George Mitchell*, there was evidence that neither party expected the limitation of liability clause to [be] applied literally and a recognition that reliance on the clause was unreasonable. While there was evidence in the present case that there was no ready or frequent resort to the clause, there was no such recognition. I cannot find conduct which permits the defendants to claim that reliance on the clause would be unfair or unreasonable.

NOTES
1. It was accepted in *Stewart Gill Ltd* v *Horatio Myer & Co. Ltd, page 288*, that UCTA regulation applies to such 'no set-off' clauses as a result of s. 13. This was accepted without question in *Schenkers* v *Overland Shoes* so that the only issue was whether the clause satisfied the reasonableness test prescribed by s. 3.
2. Significantly, having regard to the scale of the defendants' operation and the fact that the freight forwarding market in Far East trade was very competitive, the Court of Appeal rejected the defendants' argument that it was in a position of unequal bargaining power.
3. It is highly relevant that the Court of Appeal chose to distinguish *George Mitchell* regarding the lack of previous reliance on the clause. This, and the trend of recent case law, may indicate that the approach of the courts to reasonableness in the context of commercial contracts may be nearer to the *Photo Production* approach than that in *George Mitchell*. See further the assessment by Adams & Brownsword, 'The Unfair Contract Terms Act: A Decade of Discretion' (1988) 104 LQR 94.

Further evidence of the non-interventionist approach to exemption clauses in commercial contracts is provided by the decision of the Court of Appeal in the following case.

Watford Electronics Ltd v *Sanderson CFL Ltd*

[2001] EWCA Civ 317, [2001] 1 All ER (Comm) 696 (CA)

A contract for the supply of a bespoke integrated software system included a clause purporting to exclude any liability for indirect or consequential losses and a clause limiting liability in a general sense to the price paid under the contract (£104,600). The system was faulty and the claimant sought damages for breach of contract amounting to £5.5m for loss of profits, the increased costs of working and reimbursement of the cost of a replacement software system. At first instance the judge held that the exemption clauses were unreasonable in their entirety. On appeal held: the clauses were reasonable having been negotiated by two experienced business people who represented substantial companies of equal bargaining power. The judge had reached his conclusion on an incorrect basis since he had failed to separate the clauses and to consider loss and reasonableness in relation to each clause.

CHADWICK LJ (with whom Peter Gibson LJ and Buckley J agreed):

Was the term a fair and reasonable one to be included?

49 . . . I am satisfied that this is a case in which, if this court takes a different view from that of the judge on the question whether the inclusion of the limit of liability clause in Sanderson's standard terms and conditions was fair and reasonable having regard to the circumstances which were, or ought reasonably to have been, known to or in the contemplation of the parties when the contract was made, it is entitled to give effect to its own view. That is because I am satisfied that the judge reached his conclusion on the wrong basis.

50 I have explained why I take the view that, on a true analysis of the limit of liability clause, it comprises two distinct contract terms in relation to which it is necessary to consider whether the requirement of reasonableness is satisfied. One (to which I shall refer for convenience as 'the term excluding indirect loss') is that contained in the first sentence of the clause. The other ('the term limiting direct loss') is contained in the second sentence. It is, I think, appropriate to consider, separately in relation to each term, whether the requirement of reasonableness is satisfied; although, of course, in considering whether that requirement is satisfied in relation to each term, the existence of the other term in the contract is relevant.

51 I turn, therefore, to consider whether the requirement of reasonableness is satisfied in relation to the term excluding indirect loss. It is important to keep in mind (i) that, as a matter of construction, the term does not seek to exclude loss resulting from pre-contractual statements in relation to which a claim lies (if at all) in tort or under the 1967 Act and (ii) that the term is qualified by the addenda so that it does not exclude indirect or consequential loss resulting from breach of warranty unless Sanderson has used its best endeavours to ensure that the equipment and the software does comply with the warranty.

52 I accept that the court is required to have regard, in the present case, to the 'guideline' matters set out in Sch 2 to the 1977 Act. There are factors, identified by the guidelines, which point to a conclusion that the term excluding indirect loss was a fair and reasonable one to include in this contract. The parties were of equal bargaining strength; the inclusion of the term was, plainly, likely to affect Sanderson's decision as to the price at which was prepared to sell its product; Watford must be taken to have appreciated that; Watford knew of the term, and must be taken to have understood what effect it was intended to have; the product was, to some extent, modified to meet the special needs of the customer. Other factors point in the opposite direction. The judge found that, although there were other mail order packages on the market, Mailbrain was the only one which appeared to fulfil Watford's needs . . .; and, further, that Watford could not reasonably have expected to have been able to have acquired a similar software package, if available, on better terms as to performance and as to the supplier's potential liability for non-performance.

53 I do not, for my part, accept that the term excluding indirect loss is a term to which s. 11(4) of the 1977 Act applies. It is not, I think, properly to be regarded as a term by which a person (Sanderson) seeks to restrict liability to a specified sum of money; rather the term seeks to exclude liability for indirect or consequential loss altogether, in those circumstances in which it is intended to have effect. Nevertheless, it seems to me right to have regard, as part of the circumstances which were, or ought reasonably to have been, known to or in the contemplation of the parties when the contract was made, both to the resources which could be expected to be available to each party for the purpose of meeting indirect or consequential loss resulting from the failure of the equipment or software to perform in accordance with specification, and to the possibility that such loss could be covered by insurance.

54 It seems to me that the starting point in an enquiry whether, in the present case, the term excluding indirect loss was a fair and reasonable one to include in the contract which these parties made is to recognise (i) that there is a significant risk that a non-standard software product, 'custom-ised' to meet the particular marketing, accounting or record-keeping needs of a substantial and relatively complex business (such as that carried on by Watford), may not perform to the customer's satisfaction, (ii) that, if it does not do so, there is a significant risk that the customer may not make the profits or savings which it had hoped to make (and may incur consequential losses arising from the product's failure to perform), (iii) that those risks were, or ought reasonably to have been, known to or in the contemplation of both Sanderson and Watford at the time when the contract was made, (iv) that Sanderson was in the better position to assess the risk that the product would fail to perform but (v) that Watford was in the better position to assess the amount of the potential loss if the product failed to perform, (vi) that the risk of loss was likely to be capable of being covered by insurance, but at a cost, and (vii) that both Sanderson and Watford would have known, or ought reasonably to have known, at the time when the contract was made, that the identity of the party who was to bear the risk of loss (or to bear the cost of insurance) was a factor which would be taken into account in determining the price at which the supplier was willing to supply the product and the price at which the customer was willing to purchase. With those considerations in mind, is reason-able to expect that the contract will make provision for the risk of indirect or consequential loss to fall on one party or the other. In circumstances in which parties of equal bargaining power negotiate a price for the supply of product under an agreement which provides for the person on whom the risk of loss will fall, it seems to me that the court should be very cautious before reaching the conclusion that the agreement which they have reached is not a fair and reasonable one.

55 Where experienced businessmen representing substantial companies of equal bargaining power negotiate an agreement, they may be taken to have had regard to the matters known to them. They should, in my view, be taken to be the best judge of the commercial fairness of the agreement which they have made; including the fairness of each of the terms in that agreement. They should be taken to be the best judge on the question whether the terms of the agreement are reasonable. The court should not assume that either is likely to commit his company to an agree-ment which he thinks is unfair, or which he thinks includes unreasonable terms. Unless satisfied that one party has, in effect, taken unfair advantage of the other—or that a term is so unreasonable that it cannot properly have been understood or considered—the court should not interfere. . . .

NOTES

1. Peel (2001) 117 LQR 545.
2. Although the Court of Appeal emphasised that commercial men 'should be taken to be the best judge of the commercial fairness of each of the terms of the agreement', it does not follow that an exemption clause in such a contract can never be unreasonable. For example, in *Overseas Medical Supplies Ltd* v *Orient Transport Services Ltd* [1999] CLC 1243, the defendant was protected by a limitation clause if it lost the equipment it was transporting. However, it was also a term of the contract that the defendant was to insure this equipment and the defendant had failed to do this. It was held that although the limitation of liability was reasonable in relation to loss of the goods, it was unreasonable in respect of the loss arising through the failure to insure.

3. It would appear that in the context of the supply of computer software, an exclusion of consequential loss will be reasonable if the contract permits some recovery for direct loss, such as a money back guarantee. *SAM Business Systems Ltd* v *Hedley & Co* [2002] EWHC 2733, [2003] 1 All ER (Comm) 465, was another example of a contract to supply computer software. The software was defective and the supplier sought to rely on an exclusion clause, excluding any liability for incidental or consequential loss, and a limitation clause, limiting liability for direct loss to the amount of the licence fee paid for the software (i.e., a money-back guarantee). Judge Bowsher QC held that the exclusion clause was rendered reasonable by the existence of the money-back guarantee.

4. In *Motours Ltd* v *Euroball (West Kent) Ltd* [2003] EWHC 614 (QB), [2003] All ER (D) 165, the judge avoided the non-interventionist approach advocated for commercial contracts and concluded that a clause in standard conditions of a telephone service supplier excluding liability for consequential losses was unreasonable. He concluded that the parties were not of equal bargaining power and there had been no discussion or negotiations about the terms of the contract.

5. In *Watford Electronics* v *Sanderson*, the Court of Appeal stressed the fact that the clauses had been negotiated by experienced businessmen. On the other hand, in *SAM Business Systems* v *Hedley*, the judge accepted that the exclusion of consequential losses was a common clause in relation to the supply of computer software and must have been accepted because there had been no attempt to try to negotiate its terms. This would imply that the existence or absence of negotiation could be used to establish reasonableness in accordance with a broader objective. The underlying explanation of the finding of reasonableness of these terms in computer software contracts is disclosed in the 'soft drinks' cases, namely the nature of the risk and the scope of the potential liability.

   In *Britvic Soft Drinks* v *Messer UK Ltd* [2002] EWCA Civ 548, [2002] 2 Lloyd's Rep 368, the Court of Appeal considered that the fact that the parties may not have discussed or negotiated the clause in a standard form was relevant when applying the Sched. 2(c) guideline, i.e., the extent to which the party knew of the existence and extent of the clause and therefore had impliedly consented to its use. This does not fit easily with the approach in *SAM Business Systems* on the question of non-negotiation and the scope of the potential liability may be the dominant factor in that case.

6. The 'soft drinks' cases can usefully be contrasted with the approach to exemption clauses in the context of computer software where the commercial risk is much greater. These cases concerned the supply of carbon dioxide to manufacturers of soft drinks where that supply was found to be contaminated with traces of benzene. In *Britvic Soft Drinks* v *Messer UK Ltd* [2002] EWCA Civ 548, [2002] 2 Lloyd's Rep 368 and *Bacardi-Martini Beverages Ltd* v *Thomas Hardy Packaging* [2002] EWCA Civ 549, [2002] 2 Lloyd's Rep 379, the exclusion clause relied upon purported to exclude implied warranties and conditions as to quality, description, and fitness for purpose. The Court of Appeal in each case held that the clause was unreasonable.

   In *Britvic Soft Drinks* v *Messer UK Ltd*, Mance LJ criticised the approach of the judge at first instance in relation to the assessment of reasonableness and distinguished *Watford Electronics* v *Sanderson*:

> **21** The Judge accepted that the parties were to be regarded as having been of equal bargaining power—see par. (a) in Sch 2 to the Act. There were other suppliers (Hydrogas and BOC) to which THP and Brothers could have gone. The Judge also treated it as axiomatic for the purposes of par. (c) that 'on the footing that the terms are applicable at all' the buyers 'must be regarded as cognizant of their existence and effect'. I am not satisfied that par. (c) can be quite so easily disposed of. Contractual incorporation may in some circumstances occur without a party either knowing, or being realistically in a position where he or it can be blamed for not knowing, of the extent of certain terms. Take someone contracting for the carriage of a parcel by rail or air on the carriers' standard conditions. No-one really expects him to obtain or read the terms. Nor do I think that par. (c) is to be necessary even to be read as equating the positions of someone who

actually knows and someone who 'ought reasonably to have known' of the existence and extent of a term. It seems to me legitimate to consider and take into account the actual extent and quality of the knowledge of a party, however much he or it may, under ordinary contractual principles, have become contractually bound by the particular term(s).

22 Thus, in the case of *Watford Electronics Ltd* v *Sanderson CFL Ltd* [2001] EWCA Civ 317, [2001] 1 All ER (Comm) 696, cited to the Judge and to us, the Judge found as a relevant factor under par. (c) that the buyer of the relevant software was—

. . . aware of the existence of the term, only first learned of its existence towards the end of the pre-contract discussions, attempted unsuccessfully to have it substantially amended, only succeeded in achieving a make-weight amendment and learnt from Sanderson [the supplier] that a term excluding liability was standard software industry practice.

23 The Court of Appeal in *Watford*, in upholding the validity of an exclusion of liability for any 'claims for indirect or consequential losses whether arising from negligence or otherwise', regarded that as a most material factor, as appears from the judgment given by Lord Justice Chadwick (with which Mr Justice Buckley agreed) at pars. 54(vii) and 56 and that of Lord Justice Peter Gibson at par. 62(4). In the present case, the commercial and contractual background were significantly different. The manufacture of carbon dioxide so as to exclude benzene does not compare with the provision of software (an exercise notoriously liable to give rise to problems). No-one would have contemplated that the manufacturing process would allow benzene in, or (despite cl 11.2) that the buyers (THP and Brothers) would test for benzene, or indeed for compliance with BS 4105, which Messer anyway warranted. The parties did not discuss or negotiate with regard to the specific provisions of the contract, cll 11.1 and 11.2 in particular. Clauses 11.1 and 11.2 were simply incorporated as part of Messer's standard provisions. Although this is not a consideration specifically identified in Schedule 2 [to the 1977 Act], it seems to me that it can be relevant under par. (c) and anyway as a general consideration under s. 11(2) (cf also by analogy s. 3(1)).

Thus, the fact that the contamination of the carbon dioxide would not have been contemplated was a reason favouring acceptance of liability rather than a reason favouring the reasonableness of exclusion of that liability.

It was also considered important in *Bacardi-Martini* v *Thomas Hardy* that the contamination was due to a manufacturing error and it was considered that the supplier ought not to be able to transfer responsibility for that risk to the buyer. The same might be said of defective computer software but it appears to be accepted that such defects are considerably more likely and therefore it is appropriate and reasonable at least to limit liability.

■ QUESTION

How do you think these cases would be decided if the draft Unfair Contract Terms Bill was applicable? What would the crucial factors be? See *section 6* discussion of Law Commission Report and draft Bill.

C: The Unfair Terms in Consumer Contracts Regulations 1999

These Regulations (SI 1999 No. 2083 as amended by SI 2001 No. 1186) revoke the 1994 Regulations (SI 1994 No. 3159) of the same name which were intended to implement the EC Directive on Unfair Terms in Consumer Contracts (93/13/EC). (See MacDonald [1994] JBL 441 on the Directive and Beale, 'Legislative Control of Fairness: The Directive on Unfair Terms in Consumer Contracts' in *Good Faith and Fault in Contract Law*, Beatson and Friedmann (eds) (OUP, 1995).) The 1999 Regulations came into force on 1 October 1999.

The Directive was intended to harmonise laws on unfair terms in contracts between a seller or supplier and a consumer. There is some overlap in terms of scope between UCTA 1977 and the Directive, but the UK Government in its consultation documents of October 1993 and September 1994 indicated that it did not propose a single piece of legislation combining UCTA and the Directive but would instead implement the Directive separately, so that there are currently two pieces of legislation with the potential to regulate exemption clauses. This has inevitably led to complexity and uncertainty and is the subject of a proposal for reform from the Law Commission, discussed in *section 6*.

However, whereas UCTA 1977 can cover contracts between two businesses (and see *R & B Customs Brokers* v *UDT, page 297*, where a company was held to be dealing as a consumer), the Regulations cover consumer contracts which have not been individually negotiated, and 'consumer' is defined to mean 'any natural person who, in contracts covered by these Regulations, is acting for purposes which are outside his trade, business or profession'. A company cannot therefore rely on the protection contained in the Regulations. UCTA 1977 may extend to business contracts and negotiated contracts. On the other hand, the Regulations are broader in their general coverage since they apply to any non-negotiated term in the relevant contract, other than terms covered by reg. 4(2) and reg. 6(2), and therefore are not limited in their coverage to exclusion or limitation clauses.

UNFAIR TERMS IN CONSUMER CONTRACTS REGULATIONS 1999

4. Terms to which these Regulations apply

(1) These Regulations apply in relation to unfair terms in contracts concluded between a seller or a supplier and a consumer.

(2) These Regulations do not apply to contractual terms which reflect—

(a) mandatory statutory or regulatory provisions (including such provisions under the law of any Member State or in Community legislation having effect in the United Kingdom without further enactment);

(b) the provisions or principles of international conventions to which the Member States or the Community are party.

5. Unfair terms

(1) A contractual term which has not been individually negotiated shall be regarded as unfair if, contrary to the requirement of good faith, it causes a significant imbalance in the parties' rights and obligations arising under the contract, to the detriment of the consumer.

(2) A term shall always be regarded as not having been individually negotiated where it has been drafted in advance and the consumer has therefore not been able to influence the substance of the term.

(3) Notwithstanding that a specific term or certain aspects of it in a contract has been individually negotiated, these Regulations shall apply to the rest of a contract if an overall assessment of it indicates that it is a pre-formulated standard contract.

(4) It shall be for any seller or supplier who claims that a term was individually negotiated to show that it was.

(5) Schedule 2 to these Regulations contains an indicative and non-exhaustive list of the terms which may be regarded as unfair.

6. Assessment of unfair terms

(1) Without prejudice to regulation 12, the unfairness of a contractual term shall be assessed, taking into account the nature of the goods or services for which the contract was concluded and

by referring, at the time of conclusion of the contract, to all the circumstances attending the conclusion of the contract and to all the other terms of the contract or of another contract on which it is dependent.

(2) In so far as it is in plain intelligible language, the assessment of fairness of a term shall not relate—

(a) to the definition of the main subject matter of the contract, or

(b) to the adequacy of the price or remuneration, as against the goods or services supplied in exchange.

NOTES

1. In *London Borough of Newham* v *Khatun* [2004] EWCA Civ 55, [2004] 3 WLR 417, the Court of Appeal held that UTCCR 1999 applied to contracts relating to land and, in particular, to local authorities carrying out their statutory duties to house homeless persons by making offers of leased accommodation available in the private sector. Accordingly, for these purposes the local authority was regarded as a seller or supplier within reg. 3 and the homeless persons were consumers.

2. These Regulations introduce the concept of 'good faith' into English contract law. However, there is no definition of what is meant by 'good faith' and the only assistance in determining whether a term is unfair is provided by reg. 6(1) and reg. 5(5). In particular, reg. 6(1) stresses the importance of the circumstances surrounding the making of the contract and its other terms. Regulation 5(5) refers to the indicative and non-exhaustive list of the terms which may be regarded as unfair contained in sch. 2 (the so-called 'grey list'). It is important to bear in mind that the list is not conclusive and unfairness must still be established on the facts.

SCHEDULE 2 INDICATIVE AND NON-EXHAUSTIVE LIST OF TERMS WHICH MAY BE REGARDED AS UNFAIR

1. Terms which have the object or effect of—

(a) excluding or limiting the legal liability of a seller or supplier in the event of the death of a consumer or personal injury to the latter resulting from an act or omission of that seller or supplier;

(b) inappropriately excluding or limiting the legal rights of the consumer vis-à-vis the seller or supplier or another party in the event of total or partial non-performance or inadequate performance by the seller or supplier of any of the contractual obligations, including the option of offsetting a debt owed to the seller or supplier against any claim which the consumer may have against him;

(c) making an agreement binding on the consumer whereas provision of services by the seller or supplier is subject to a condition whose realisation depends on his own will alone;

(d) permitting the seller or supplier to retain sums paid by the consumer where the latter decides not to conclude or perform the contract, without providing for the consumer to receive compensation of an equivalent amount from the seller or supplier where the latter is the party cancelling the contract;

(e) requiring any consumer who fails to fulfil his obligation to pay a disproportionately high sum in compensation;

(f) authorising the seller or supplier to dissolve the contract on a discretionary basis where the same facility is not granted to the consumer, or permitting the seller or supplier to retain the sums paid for services not yet supplied by him where it is the seller or supplier himself who dissolves the contract;

(g) enabling the seller or supplier to terminate a contract of indeterminate duration without reasonable notice except where there are serious grounds for doing so; . . .

3. If a term is regarded as 'unfair' then it will not be binding on the consumer.

4. The main purpose of the 1999 Regulations was to further implement Article 7 of the Directive, which requires member States to ensure that there is a right of pre-emptive challenge to unfair terms including the ability of bodies having a legitimate interest under national law as protecting consumers to pursue representative actions. Regulation 8 of the 1994 Regulations (now reg. 10 of the 1999 Regulations) imposed a statutory duty on the Director General of Fair Trading to consider complaints of unfairness relating to terms in general use and, if required, to bring proceedings for an injunction to ensure that the use of any unfair term was discontinued. The 1999 Regulations extended this power to various qualifying bodies, notably utility regulators and weights and measures authorities (see regs 10–15 and sch. 1). The OFT publishes regular bulletins detailing policy and any action taken. For more information consult http://www.oft.gov.uk.

5. Part 8 of the Enterprise Act 2002 permitted secondary legislation to be enacted to enable certain designated bodies to obtain an order stopping infringements of consumer protection legislation, including the Unfair Terms in Consumer Contracts Regulations 1999, where the infringement is shown to harm the collective interests of consumers in the UK. The legislation also allows for corrective statements to be ordered. The Enterprise Act (Part 8 Community Infringements Specified UK Laws) Order 2003, SI 2003/1374 and the Enterprise Act (Part 8 Domestic Infringements) Order 2003 SI 2003/1593 have since been enacted. Infringements of UCTA 1977 are also covered by this legislation, together with infringements of the distance selling and electronic commerce regulations.

Case law examining the Regulations

In response to an application for an injunction at the instance of the Director General of Fair Trading, the House of Lords examined and applied the Regulations (1994 version).

Director General of Fair Trading v *First National Bank plc*
[2001] UK HL 52, [2002] 1 AC 481 (HL)

A term in a consumer loan agreement provided for interest to be paid at the contractual rate on sums owing both before and after any judgment. Thus if judgment on the debt was obtained, interest at the contractual rate remained payable until the judgment was discharged despite the fact that all the instalments due under the judgment had been paid. This meant that a debtor might budget on the basis of the judgment instalments and then, having paid these instalments, discover that he owed a further sum in interest. The Director General of Fair Trading considered that this term was 'unfair' and sought an injunction to prevent its continued use. The bank claimed that (i) the Regulations had no application to the term in question because it was a 'core term' defining the main subject matter of the contract or concerning the adequacy of the price or remuneration (old reg. 3(2), now reg. 6(2) of the 1999 Regulations, *page 320*); (ii) in any event, the term was not unfair. The judge at first instance had considered that the term was not a 'core term' and that it was not unfair. Although the Court of Appeal agreed that it was not a 'core term', it overturned that decision because it considered the term to be unfair in view of the element of unfair surprise for the debtor. On appeal Held: (1) the term did not fall within reg. 3(2)(b) as it was an incidental term setting out the consequences of a borrower's default. The term did not concern the adequacy of the interest earned by the bank as remuneration for the loan and so did not express the substance of the parties' bargain. Accordingly the Regulations applied to the term; (2) the term was not unfair within the test prescribed in the Regulations and contained nothing detrimental to the consumer.

LORD BINGHAM (with whose reasons the other members of the House of Lords agreed):

8 . . . [T]he Director's challenge, although addressed only to the bank's use of and reliance on the term, if upheld, may well invalidate any similar term in any other regulated agreement made by any other lender with any borrower. The questions at issue are accordingly of general public importance.

(1) The applicability of the Regulations

9 Regulation 3(2) of the Regulations provides:

'In so far as it is in plain, intelligible language, no assessment shall be made of the fairness of any term which—(a) defines the main subject matter of the contract, or (b) concerns the adequacy of the price or remuneration, as against the goods or services sold or supplied.'. . .

10 In reliance on regulation 3(2)(b) [counsel] on behalf of the bank, submitted that no assessment might be made of the fairness of the term because it concerns the adequacy of the bank's remuneration as against the services supplied, namely the loan of money. A bank's remuneration under a credit agreement is the receipt of interest. The term, by entitling the bank to post-judgment interest, concerns the quantum and thus the adequacy of that remuneration. . . .

12 In agreement with the judge and the Court of Appeal, I do not accept the bank's submission on this issue. The Regulations, as Professor Sir Guenter Treitel QC has aptly observed (Treitel The Law of Contract, 10th ed (1999), p 248), 'are not intended to operate as a mechanism of quality or price control' and regulation 3(2) is of 'crucial importance in recognising the parties' freedom of contract with respect to the essential features of their bargain': p 249. But there is an important 'distinction between the term or terms which express the substance of the bargain and "incidental" (if important) terms which surround them': Chitty on Contracts, 28th ed (1999), vol 1, ch 15 'Unfair Terms in Consumer Contracts', p 747, para 15–025. The object of the Regulations and the Directive is to protect consumers against the inclusion of unfair and prejudicial terms in standard-form contracts into which they enter, and that object would plainly be frustrated if regulation 3(2)(b) were so broadly interpreted as to cover any terms other than those falling squarely within it. In my opinion the term, as part of a provision prescribing the consequences of default, plainly does not fall within it. It does not concern the adequacy of the interest earned by the bank as its remuneration but is designed to ensure that the bank's entitlement to interest does not come to an end on the entry of judgment. . . . [The term is] an ancillary provision and not one concerned with the adequacy of the bank's remuneration as against the services supplied. It is therefore necessary to address the second question.

(2) Unfairness

13 Regulation 4 of the Regulations is entitled 'Unfair terms' and provides:

(1) In these Regulations, subject to paragraphs (2) and (3) below, 'unfair term' means any term which contrary to the requirement of good faith causes a significant imbalance in the parties' rights and obligations under the contract to the detriment of the consumer.
(2) An assessment of the unfair nature of a term shall be made taking into account the nature of the goods or services for which the contract was concluded and referring, as at the time of the conclusion of the contract, to all circumstances attending the conclusion of the contract and to all the other terms of the contract or of another contract on which it is dependent.
(3) In determining whether a term satisfies the requirement of good faith, regard shall be had in particular to the matters specified in Schedule 2 to these Regulations.
(4) Schedule 3 to these Regulations contains an indicative and non-exhaustive list of the terms which may be regarded as unfair.

Schedule 2 to the Regulations provides

'In making an assessment of good faith, regard shall be had in particular to—(a) the strength of the bargaining positions of the parties; (b) whether the consumer had an inducement to agree to the term; (c) whether the goods or services were sold or supplied to the special order of the consumer, and (d) the extent to which the seller or supplier has dealt fairly and equitably with the consumer.'

Each of (a), (b) and (c) also appear in Schedule 2 to the Unfair Contract Terms Act 1977 among the guidelines for application of the reasonableness test laid down by that statute, suggesting that some similarity of approach in applying the two tests may be appropriate. In a case such as the present, where the fairness of a term is challenged in the absence of any individual consumer, little attention need be paid to (b) and (c). It may however be assumed that any borrower is in a much weaker bargaining position than a large bank contracting on its own standard form. (d) applies a general test of fair and equitable dealing between supplier and consumer. Schedule 3 contains a list of indicative and illustrative terms which may because of their object or effect be regarded as unfair. Examples are terms which have the object or effect of '(e) requiring any consumer who fails to fulfil his obligation to pay a disproportionately high sum in compensation', '(i) irrevocably binding the consumer to terms with which he had no real opportunity of becoming acquainted before the conclusion of the contract', or '(k) enabling the seller or supplier to alter unilaterally without a valid reason any characteristics of the product or service to be provided'. It is not suggested that the term falls within any specific entry in the list. It is common ground that fairness must be judged as at the date the contract is made, although account may properly be taken of the likely effect of any term which is then agreed and said to be unfair.

. . .

17   The test laid down by regulation 4(1), deriving as it does from article 3(1) of the Directive, has understandably attracted much discussion in academic and professional circles and helpful submissions were made to the House on it. It is plain from the recitals to the Directive that one of its objectives was partially to harmonise the law in this important field among all member states of the European Union. The member states have no common concept of fairness or good faith, and the Directive does not purport to state the law of any single member state. It lays down a test to be applied, whatever their pre-existing law, by all member states. If the meaning of the test were doubtful, or vulnerable to the possibility of differing interpretations in differing member states, it might be desirable or necessary to seek a ruling from the European Court of Justice on its interpretation. But the language used in expressing the test, so far as applicable in this case, is in my opinion clear and not reasonably capable of differing interpretations. A term falling within the scope of the Regulations is unfair if it causes a significant imbalance in the parties' rights and obligations under the contract to the detriment of the consumer in a manner or to an extent which is contrary to the requirement of good faith. The requirement of significant imbalance is met if a term is so weighted in favour of the supplier as to tilt the parties' rights and obligations under the contract significantly in his favour. This may be by the granting to the supplier of a beneficial option or discretion or power, or by the imposing on the consumer of a disadvantageous burden or risk or duty. The illustrative terms set out in Schedule 3 to the Regulations provide very good examples of terms which may be regarded as unfair; whether a given term is or is not to be so regarded depends on whether it causes a significant imbalance in the parties' rights and obligations under the contract. This involves looking at the contract as a whole. But the imbalance must be to the detriment of the consumer; a significant imbalance to the detriment of the supplier, assumed to be the stronger party, is not a mischief which the Regulations seek to address. The requirement of good faith in this context is one of fair and open dealing. Openness requires that the terms should be expressed fully, clearly and legibly, containing no concealed pitfalls or traps. Appropriate prominence should be given to terms which might operate disadvantageously to the customer. Fair dealing requires that a supplier should not, whether deliberately or unconsciously, take advantage of the consumer's necessity, indigence, lack of experience, unfamiliarity with the subject matter of the contract, weak bargaining position or any other factor listed in or analogous to those listed in Schedule 2 to the Regulations. Good faith in this context is not an artificial or technical concept; nor, since Lord Mansfield was its champion, is it a concept wholly unfamiliar to British lawyers. It looks to good standards of commercial morality and practice. Regulation 4(1) lays down a composite test, covering both the making and the substance of the contract, and must be applied bearing clearly in mind the objective which the Regulations are designed to promote.

. . .

20   In judging the fairness of the term it is necessary to consider the position of typical parties when the contract is made. The borrower wants to borrow a sum of money, often quite a modest sum, often for purposes of improving his home. He discloses an income sufficient to finance repayment by instalments over the contract term. If he cannot do that, the bank will be unwilling to lend. The essential bargain is that the bank will make funds available to the borrower which the borrower will repay, over a period, with interest. Neither party could suppose that the bank would willingly forgo any part of its principal or interest. If the bank thought that outcome at all likely, it would not lend. If there were any room for doubt about the borrower's obligation to repay the principal in full with interest, that obligation is very clearly and unambiguously expressed in the conditions of contract. There is nothing unbalanced or detrimental to the consumer in that obligation; the absence of such a term would unbalance the contract to the detriment of the lender. . . .

LORD STEYN: . . .

36 . . . There are three independent requirements. But the element of detriment to the consumer may not add much. But it serves to make clear that the Directive is aimed at significant imbalance against the consumer, rather than the seller or supplier. The twin requirements of good faith and significant imbalance will in practice be determinative. Schedule 2 to the Regulations, which explains the concept of good faith, provides that regard must be had, amongst other things, to the extent to which the seller or supplier has dealt fairly and equitably with the consumer. It is an objective criterion. Good faith imports, as Lord Bingham of Cornhill has observed in his opinion, the notion of open and fair dealing: see also *Interfoto Picture Library Ltd* v *Stiletto Visual Programmes Ltd* [1989] QB 433. And helpfully the commentary to *Lando & Beale, Principles of European Contract Law, Parts I and II* (combined and revised 2000), p 113 prepared by the Commission of European Contract Law, explains that the purpose of the provision of good faith and fair dealing is 'to enforce community standards of decency, fairness and reasonableness in commercial transactions'; a fortiori that is true of consumer transactions. Schedule 3 to the Regulations (which corresponds to the annex to the Directive) is best regarded as a check list of terms which must be regarded as potentially vulnerable. The examples given in Schedule 3 convincingly demonstrate that the argument of the bank that good faith is predominantly concerned with procedural defects in negotiating procedures cannot be sustained. Any purely procedural or even predominantly procedural interpretation of the requirement of good faith must be rejected.

37 That brings me to the element of significant imbalance. It has been pointed out by Hugh Collins that the test 'of a significant imbalance of the obligations obviously directs attention to the substantive unfairness of the contract': 'Good Faith in European Contract Law' (1994) 14 Oxford Journal of Legal Studies 229, 249. It is however, also right to say that there is a large area of overlap between the concepts of good faith and significant imbalance.

38 It is now necessary to turn to the application of these requirements to the facts of the present case. The point is a relatively narrow one. I agree that the starting point is that a lender ought to be able to recover interest at the contractual rate until the date of payment, and this applies both before and after judgment. On the other hand, counsel for the Director advanced a contrary argument. Adopting the test of asking what the position of a consumer is in the contract under consideration with or without clause 8, he said that the consumer is in a significantly worse position than he would have been if there had been no such provision. Certainly, the consumer is worse off. The difficulty facing counsel, however, is that this disadvantage to the consumer appears to be the consequence not of clause 8 but of the County Courts (Interest on Judgment Debts) Order 1991. Under this Order no statutory interest is payable on a county court judgment given in proceedings to recover money due under a regulated agreement: see article 2. Counsel said that for policy reasons it was decided that in such a case no interest may be recovered after judgment. He said that it is not open to the House to criticise directly or indirectly this legal context. In these circumstances he submitted that it is not legitimate for a court to conclude that fairness requires that a lender must be able to insist on a stipulation designed to avoid the statutory regime under the 1991 Order. Initially I was inclined to uphold this policy argument. On reflection, however, I have been persuaded that this argument cannot prevail in circumstances where the legislature has neither expressly nor by necessary implication barred a stipulation that interest may continue to accrue after judgment until payment in full.

39 For these reasons as well as the reasons given by Lord Bingham I agree that clause 8 is not unfair . . .

NOTES
1. MacDonald (2002) 65 MLR 763.
2. In *Bairstow Eves London Central Ltd* v *Smith* [2004] EWHC 263 (QB), [2004] 2 EGLR 25, it was held that reg. 6(2) ('core terms') is to be interpreted restrictively, thereby allowing more terms to be assessed for unfairness. The case concerned a term in an estate agency contract providing for commission at the rate of 1.5 per cent if paid in full within 10 days of completion or agreed alternative payment date. Otherwise commission was payable at 3 per cent on the sale price with interest at 3 per cent above base. The judge had concluded that this was not a 'core term' (i.e. did not concern the adequacy of the price or remuneration) and that the 3 per cent term was unfair and so not binding on the vendors. The estate agents appealed on the applicability of the Regulations and the judge held that the issue here was whether the core rate was 3 per cent with an option to pay 1.5 per cent (in which case reg. 6(2) was applicable) or whether the core rate was 1.5 per cent with a 'default' provision of 3 per cent. He concluded that the 1.5 per cent was contemplated as the price, with a default position of 3 per cent if the vendors failed to pay within 10 days. Accordingly reg. 6(2) did not apply and the Regulations as a whole were applicable. The issue of unfairness was not appealed.

Relying on the guidance in *Director General of Fair Trading* v *First National Bank*, Gross J concluded:

> **25** . . . Guided by this authority, the landscape becomes clear. The object of the Regulations is *not* price control nor are the Regulations intended to interfere with the parties' freedom of contract as to the essential features of their bargain. But, that said, regulation 6(2) must be given a restrictive interpretation; otherwise a coach and horses could be driven through the Regulations. So, while it is not for the Court to re-write the parties' bargain as to the fairness or adequacy of the price itself, regulation 6(2) may be unlikely to shield terms as to price escalation or default provisions from scrutiny under the fairness requirement contained in regulation 5(1). I say 'may be unlikely' because, of course, much depends on the individual contract under consideration. When, however, regulation 6(2) is inapplicable so that regulation 5(1) is engaged, it does not follow that a term will be adjudged unfair; whether or not a term is unfair involves a separate inquiry but one which cannot be undertaken at all insofar as regulation 6(2) is applicable and bars the way.

3. 'Significant imbalance' imports considerations of the substantive fairness of the term judged in the context of the contract terms as a whole.
4. Professor Beale in 'Legislative Control of Fairness: The Directive on Unfair Terms in Consumer Contracts' in Beatson and Friedmann, *Good Faith and Fault in Contract Law* (OUP, 1995, at page 245), had referred to good faith as having a dual operation, namely the procedural aspects of good faith (preventing unfair surprise) and the substantive aspect concerning any imbalance in the content of the clause to the detriment of the consumer. Their Lordships clearly accept that 'significant imbalance' is substantive but appear to consider that 'good faith' refers to both procedural and substantive unfairness. Lord Bingham identified 'good faith' as a requirement of 'fair and open dealing'. Whereas openness clearly refers to procedural matters, fairness can encompass both substantive and procedural matters and Lord Bingham's examples refer to issues of unconscionability such as taking advantage of a weakness in bargaining position. Lord Steyn comments (at [37]) that 'there is a large area of overlap between the concepts of good faith and significant imbalance', which also suggests that he sees good faith as involving substantive fairness.
5. The House of Lords was prepared to accept that the position for consumers was unsatisfactory. However, any unfairness did not result from the term in question but the inability of the county court to take account of contractual interest when giving judgment on a debt.

6. It is important to appreciate that this decision relates to the 1994 Regulations so that although the majority of provisions are in identical terms to those under the 1999 Regulations, the number of the applicable regulation may be different. The exception is the reference in Lord Bingham's speech to Schedule 2 of the 1994 Regulations, which resembled Schedule 2 of UCTA 1977. There is no equivalent provision in the 1999 Regulations (although reg. 6(1) provides a general statement on assessing unfairness).

7. The European Commission has reviewed the implementation and operation of the Directive (see DTI Consultation Paper, 'European Commission Review of Directive 93/13/EEC on Unfair Terms in Consumer Contracts', July 2000 and the European Commission Report on Unfair Terms, Com (2000) 248).

Bankers Insurance Co Ltd v *South*
[2003] EWHC 380 (QB), [2004] Lloyd's Rep IR 1

The defendant, South, had purchased holiday insurance for a trip to Cyprus. The policy contained an exclusion of liability for accidents 'involving your ownership or possession of any . . . motorised waterborne craft'. While South was driving a jet ski he was involved in a collision and the other person (the second defendant) was seriously injured. The second defendant commenced proceedings against South who did not notify his insurer (Bankers Insurance) until six months later (some three and a half years after the accident). The insurer sought a declaration that because of the exclusion it was not liable to indemnify South. Alternatively, the insurer claimed that South was in breach of conditions (d) and (e) of his policy which provided that payment under the policy was contingent upon the insured reporting full details of any incidents 'as soon as reasonably possible' and 'immediately upon receipt' was to forward any writ or other communication in connection with the claim. Held: the exclusion clause clearly covered the jet ski accident (its terms were in 'plain and intelligible' language) and since it related to the definition of the subject matter of the contract (within reg. 6(2) UTCCR 1999), the Regulations did not apply and the term could not be assessed for fairness. *Obiter*, Buckley J also examined the notification conditions which were conditions precedent to liability. There was agreement that the Regulations did apply to these conditions and so the question of unfairness would have arisen. He concluded that whereas non-compliance with these conditions could have prejudiced the position of the insurer (e.g. in respect of its right of subrogation and the chance of recovering from another party), there might well be circumstances in which the conditions might have caused a significant imbalance in the party's obligations to the detriment of the insured, e.g. if the insurer was able to deny liability on the basis of a purely technical breach of such a condition. The best solution was to undertake a balancing exercise between the seriousness of the actual breach of the conditions and the prejudice caused to the insurers. On these facts there was tangible prejudice to the insurers since they had lost three and a half years in which they might have investigated the claim.

NOTE: A further consideration of unfairness under the Regulations was undertaken by Judge Thornton QC in *Westminster Building Co. Ltd* v *Beckingham* [2004] EWHC 138 (TCC), 94 Con LR 107. The consumer who had commissioned builders to renovate his property was held bound by an adjudication clause in the contract.

1. The terms in this case were not individually negotiated but were couched in plain and intelligible language.

2. The terms of the contract were decided upon by Mr Beckingham's agent, who are chartered surveyors, and Mr Beckingham had, or had available to him, competent and objective advice as to the existence and effect of the adjudication clause before he proffered and entered into the contract. Westminster did no more than accept the contract terms offered and had no reasonable need to draw to Mr Beckingham's attention the potential pitfalls to be found in the adjudication clause and in its operation during the course of the work. The clause did not, therefore contravene the requirement of good faith (see especially the speech of Lord Bingham in the Director General of Fair Trading case at page 494).

3. The clause did not, if considered at the time of making the contract, constitute a significant imbalance as to Mr Beckingham's rights . . .

4. The clause does not significantly exclude or hinder the consumer's right to take legal action or other legal remedy or restrict the evidence available to him.

SECTION 6: REFORM—LAW COMMISSION REPORT, UNFAIR TERMS IN CONTRACTS

In August 2002, the Law Commission published a Consultation Paper, No. 166, on 'Unfair Terms in Contracts'. In broad terms, this Consultation Paper recommended that the existing legislative provisions applicable to consumer contracts (in both UCTA and UTCCR) should be replaced by a unified regime, designed to be clearer and more accessible. The Consultation Paper contained specific proposals concerning current difficulties in interpreting some provisions and proposed that there should be detailed guidance on the application of the 'fair and reasonable' test, together with a presumptive list of unfair terms (i.e., terms presumed to be unfair unless shown to be otherwise). The current position is that under the Regulations it is the consumer who has the burden of establishing that the term is unfair should he wish to avoid its application.

The Law Commission also asked for responses to proposals to widen controls over terms in commercial contracts (between two businesses), possibly along similar lines to the control contained in the Regulations.

[See Macdonald, 'Unifying Unfair Terms Legislation' (2004) 67 MLR 69]

In February 2005 the Law Commission published its Report, *Unfair Terms in Contracts*, Law Com No. 292, Cm 6464, containing a draft Bill. As anticipated, the draft Bill contains a draft for unified legislation with the aim of simplifying and clarifying concepts in the regulation of unfair terms. [What follows is a summary of the main recommendations in this Report and draft legislation to enable readers to evaluate the case law which is the concern of this book (for example, see the evaluation at *page 300* concerning the definition of 'consumer contracts'). Further evaluation and possible impact on case law is provided on the website.]

The Report's recommendations and the draft Bill provide a single regime for 'consumer contracts' covering unfair terms (and not just exemption clauses). This consumer regime will extend to negotiated terms as well as standard or non-negotiated terms and will alter the burden of proof that currently exists under the Regulations so that the business will have the burden of showing that a term is fair and reasonable where the term is detrimental to the consumer (unless there is a pre-emptive challenge by the OFT or other body when that body will have the burden of establishing that the term is unfair). This general provision (draft clause 4(1)) will not apply to a term which defines the main subject matter of a consumer contract as long as the term is transparent and substantially the same as the definition the consumer reasonably expected (an interesting legislative inclusion of reasonable expectations although one that will inevitably give rise to case law). Of particular significance, is the clarity provided by express recognition that terms which currently are unenforceable under UCTA s. 2(1) (death or personal injury resulting from negligence) and s. 6(2) (exclusion or limitation of liability for breaches of basic obligations in the sales legislation, e.g. satisfactory quality) will remain unenforceable. Although it should have been possible to establish that such terms were unfair under the Regulations, they were not automatically unfair.

In the business context, the Report and draft legislation distinguishes between 'small businesses' and other businesses. 'Small businesses' are considered to warrant protection which should not be extended to other business to business contracts. Under the legislation small businesses will be able to challenge any standard term which has not been altered through negotiation, as long as it is not concerned with the main subject matter of the contract or the price. If the term is detrimental to the small business and the small business wishes to challenge it, it has the burden of establishing that the term is not 'fair and reasonable' (i.e. the reverse of the burden of proof for consumers). While it is commendable to wish to protect such businesses, there are difficulties in deciding where to draw the line and the draft Bill contains complex definitions of small business in an attempt to avoid the difficulties encountered in other areas of law in ensuring that 'small businesses' are in fact 'small'. In any event, some important categories of contracts are excluded from this protection and, as small businesses are not covered by the pre-emptive challenges, they will need to possess sufficient resources to pursue court action challenging terms as unfair.

The approach to other business to business contracts is non-interventionist (see the discussion above at *pages 313–18* on the approach to the reasonableness requirement under UCTA 1977 in commercial contracts). This differs from the more radical suggestion on business to business contracts proposed in the Consultation Paper. The s. 6(3) protection against exemptions of the implied obligations under sales law if the term is not shown to be reasonable is not contained in the draft Bill in its current form. Instead, such a term in a business to business contract will only have to be shown to be fair and reasonable if one business deals on the other's written standard terms of business (draft clause 9). It is envisaged that the current case law on the meaning of 'written standard terms of business' will continue to assist (Report, paras 4.45–4.57).

The test of 'fair and reasonable' is contained in clause 14 of the Draft Bill (now extended to apply to notices as well as contractual terms) and refers to the need to take into account 'the extent to which the term is transparent' (defined in clause 14(3) in presentational terms) and 'the substance and effect of the term, and all the circumstances existing at the time it was agreed' (substantive and procedural fairness and reasonableness). In examining this second aspect of the test the court is to have regard to the facts listed in clause 14(4). This list will replace the guidelines in Schedule 2 of UCTA and extends the relevant factors. Clause 14(6) refers to the Schedule 2 indicative list of consumer contract terms and small business contract terms which may be regarded as not being fair and reasonable. This list is based on Schedule 2 of UTCCR but is expressed in clearer terms and includes examples. The problem would seem to be the relationship between the Schedule 2 list and the various factors identified in clause 14(4).

Finally, there is an equivalent to s. 13 UCTA to explain the extended meaning of terms which exclude or restrict liability. The provision covering negligence liability is in similar terms to section 2 of UCTA (clause 1 of the draft Bill) although certain issues are clarified in the clause 2 exceptions.

This draft legislation will inevitably be a great improvement on the current law, although the difficulties of the exercise in relation to some issues which the Law Commission recognises, mean that it is unlikely to be a complete panacea. The 'good news' is that if the draft Bill is enacted in its current form, much of the existing case law will remain relevant for purposes of interpretation, e.g. the case law discussing 'written standard terms of business' in s. 3 UCTA 1977.

8

Discharge for Breach of Contract

The contractual terms determine the performance obligations of the parties. Since a failure to comply in full with a performance obligation, without lawful excuse, is a breach of contract, it is vital to know the standard of performance required.

SECTION 1: ABSOLUTE AND QUALIFIED CONTRACTUAL OBLIGATIONS

If a contractual obligation is strict, non-compliance will be a breach of contract irrespective of fault, e.g., the obligations imposed on sellers in sale of goods contracts by the Sale of Goods Act 1979, ss. 13–15, are strict.

Contractual obligations which are qualified impose a duty to take reasonable care. For example, in *Liverpool City Council* v *Irwin* [1977] AC 239, the House of Lords held that the local authority owed a duty to take reasonable care to ensure that the common parts of a block of flats were in reasonable repair and in use. Since the local authority had taken reasonable care there was no breach. Similarly, a surgeon owes a duty to exercise reasonable care and skill in the performance of an operation but cannot guarantee the result (*Thake* v *Maurice* [1986] 1 All ER 497). A further example of a qualified obligation is s. 13 of the Supply of Goods and Services Act 1982.

SUPPLY OF GOODS AND SERVICES ACT 1982

13. Implied term about care and skill

In a contract for the supply of a service where the supplier is acting in the course of a business, there is an implied term that the supplier will carry out the service with reasonable care and skill.

NOTE: On standards of performance, see Treitel, *The Law of Contract*, 11th edn, pp. 838–41.

SECTION 2: CONSEQUENCES OF BREACH

Subject to an enforceable exemption clause, a breach of contract entitles the injured party to damages to compensate for the loss suffered as a result of the breach.

Photo Production Ltd v *Securicor Transport Ltd*
[1980] AC 827 (HL)

The facts of this case appear at *page 283*. Lord Diplock explained the effects of a breach of a contractual obligation.

LORD DIPLOCK: . . . [B]reaches of primary obligations give rise to substituted or secondary obligations on the part of the party in default, and, in some cases, may entitle the other party to be relieved from further performance of his own primary obligations. . . .

Every failure to perform a primary obligation is a breach of contract. The secondary obligation on the part of the contract breaker to which it gives rise by implication of the common law is to pay monetary compensation to the other party for the loss sustained by him in consequence of the breach; but, with two exceptions, the primary obligations of both parties so far as they have not yet been fully performed remain unchanged. This secondary obligation to pay compensation (damages) for non-performance of primary obligations I will call the 'general secondary obligation.' It applies in the cases of the two exceptions as well.

The exceptions are: (1) Where the event resulting from the failure by one party to perform a primary obligation has the effect of depriving the other party of substantially the whole benefit which it was the intention of the parties that he should obtain from the contract, the party not in default may elect to put an end to all primary obligations of both parties remaining unperformed. (If the expression 'fundamental breach' is to be retained, it should, in the interests of clarity, be confined to this exception.) (2) Where the contracting parties have agreed, whether by express words or by implication of law, that *any* failure by one party to perform a particular primary obligation ('condition' in the nomenclature of the Sale of Goods Act 1893), irrespective of the gravity of the event that has in fact resulted from the breach, shall entitle the other party to elect to put an end to all primary obligations of both parties remaining unperformed. (In the interests of clarity, the nomenclature of the Sale of Goods Act 1893, 'breach of condition' should be reserved for this exception.)

Where such an election is made (a) there is substituted by implication of law for the primary obligations of the party in default which remain unperformed a secondary obligation to pay monetary compensation to the other party for the loss sustained by him in consequence of their non-performance in the future and (b) the unperformed primary obligations of that other party are discharged. This secondary obligation is additional to the general secondary obligation; I will call it 'the anticipatory secondary obligation.'

NOTES
1. The primary obligations are the performance obligations in the contract. Breaches of these obligations give rise to secondary obligations to pay damages.
2. A breach of contract will not necessarily result in the termination of the contract, so that the primary obligations of both parties may continue. However, if there has been a repudiatory breach of contract, then the injured party has an option to terminate or affirm the contract. In order for the contract to be terminated, the injured party must have accepted the repudiatory breach as terminating the contract. See *Decro-Wall International SA* v *Practitioners in Marketing Ltd* [1971] 1 WLR 361: where Sachs LJ stated (at p. 375):

   The general law as to the effect of repudiation has long been settled. The locus classicus for reference purposes is the statement in plain and simple terms in the speech of Viscount Simon LC in *Heyman* v *Darwins Ltd* [1942] AC 356, 361: 'But repudiation by one party standing alone does not terminate the contract. It takes two to end it, by repudiation, on the one side, and acceptance of the repudiation, on the other'. Whether the other party accepts is a matter for his option: if he does not, the contract remains alive. . . .

   See *Vitol SA* v *Norelf Ltd, The Santa Clara* [1996] AC 800, *page 350*, on the question of what constitutes 'acceptance' of a repudiatory breach.

   By termination, we mean that performance of future obligations under the contract is no longer required. It does not mean that the contract is treated as if it never existed. (Care should therefore be taken with the expression 'rescission for breach of contract'.)

In *Johnson* v *Agnew* [1980] AC 367, Lord Wilberforce stated (at pp. 392–3):

> . . . [I]t is important to dissipate a fertile source of confusion and to make clear that although the vendor is sometimes referred to in the above situation as 'rescinding' the contract, this so-called 'rescission' is quite different from rescission ab initio, such as may arise for example in cases of mistake, fraud or lack of consent. In those cases, the contract is treated in law as never having come into existence. . . . In the case of an accepted repudiatory breach the contract has come into existence but has been put an end to or discharged. Whatever contrary indications may be disinterred from old authorities, it is now quite clear, under the general law of contract, that acceptance of a repudiatory breach does not bring about 'rescission ab initio.' I need only quote one passage to establish these propositions.

In *Heyman* v *Darwins Ltd* [1942] AC 356 Lord Porter said, at p. 399:

> To say that the contract is rescinded or has come to an end or has ceased to exist may in individual cases convey the truth with sufficient accuracy, but the fuller expression that the injured party is thereby absolved from future performance of his obligations under the contract is a more exact description of the position. Strictly speaking, to say that on acceptance of the renunciation of a contract the contract is rescinded is incorrect. In such a case the injured party may accept the renunciation as a breach going to the root of the whole of the consideration. By that acceptance he is discharged from further performance and may bring an action for damages, but the contract itself is not rescinded.

3. Lord Diplock refers to two situations where the primary obligations which have not yet been performed are discharged. They correspond with breaches of conditions (*page 243*) and breaches of non-conditions which deprive the injured party of substantially the whole benefit of the contract (see *Hong Kong Fir Shipping* v *Kawasaki Kishen Kaisha* [1962] 2 QB 26, at *page 250*), i.e. repudiatory breaches which have been accepted as terminating the contract.

    In this situation there is a secondary obligation to pay damages for the breach (referred to as the 'general secondary obligation'), and the primary obligations which remain unperformed are replaced by a secondary obligation to pay damages for the loss resulting from non-performance of these primary obligations due in the future (referred to as 'the anticipatory secondary obligation').

SECTION 3: ANTICIPATORY BREACH

An anticipatory breach occurs where, before the time for performance, one party informs the other that they will not perform their contractual obligations. This type of breach will normally be repudiatory, since the contract is renounced or the party incapacitates himself from performing the obligations under the contract.

Renunciation of the contract in advance of the time for performance occurs where one party evinces an unconditional intention not to perform his contractual obligations or not to be bound by the contract.

What will constitute renunciation?

Woodar Investment Development Ltd v Wimpey Construction UK Ltd
[1980] 1 WLR 277 (HL)

The full facts of this case appear at *page 468*. Wimpey sought to terminate the contract to purchase land on the ground that the Secretary of State for the Environment had commenced a compulsory acquisition procedure in respect of the land. The contract expressly reserved the right to terminate in these circumstances. Woodar, the vendors, claimed that Wimpey had repudiated the contract. Held: (Lord Salmon and Lord Russell of Killowen dissenting) in order to constitute a renunciation of the contract there had to be an intention to abandon the contract and instead of abandoning the contract Wimpey were relying on its terms as justifying their right to terminate.

LORD WILBERFORCE: . . . [I]t would be a regrettable development of the law of contract to hold that a party who bona fide relies upon an express stipulation in a contract in order to rescind or terminate a contract should, by that fact alone, be treated as having repudiated his contractual obligations if he turns out to be mistaken as to his rights. Repudiation is a drastic conclusion which should only be held to arise in clear cases of a refusal, in a matter going to the root of the contract, to perform contractual obligations. To uphold the respondents' contentions in this case would represent an undesirable extension of the doctrine.

As with all repudiatory breaches, where an anticipatory breach occurs the injured party has the option of affirming or terminating the contract.

A: Affirmation

If the injured party chooses to affirm, the contract continues in force and the injured party awaits performance on the performance date. However, this does not mean that no damages will be recoverable by the injured party, since if the guilty party does not perform on the performance date, the injured party can seek damages for this *actual* breach of contract (subject to there being no subsequent frustration or breach by the injured party, see below *pages 341–2*).

What will constitute affirmation?

Yukong Line Ltd of Korea v Rendsburg Investments Corporation of Liberia
[1996] 2 Lloyd's Rep 604 (Commercial Court)

In June 1995 the plaintiffs chartered a vessel to the defendants, Rendsburg, for three years. However, on 23 January 1996, the charterers sent a message stating that they were 'unable to perform any further'. The following day the plaintiffs sent the following telex message in response:

really upset to receive notice of non-performance from charterers. Charterers' cancellation is totally unacceptable and charterers are strongly requested to honour their contractual obligations according to the charterparty . . . In case of non-performance all damages, loss and any other costs incurred directly or indirectly to be for charterers' responsibility and liability.

Look forward to receiving honourable confirmation from charterers . . .

Having received no response to this message, on 1 February the plaintiffs advised the charterers that they were accepting the repudiation as terminating the contract.

As a preliminary question of law, Moore-Bick J had to determine whether the plaintiffs' telex of 24 January amounted to an affirmation of the contract. Held: it did not affirm the repudiatory breach. The judge stressed the need for very clear evidence of the intention to continue with the contract.

MOORE-BICK J: From . . . [the] authorities, one can deduce the following principles which are applicable to the present case and which were not in dispute:

(1)   A renunciation of the contract by one party, prior to the time for performance is not itself a breach but it gives the other party, the injured party, the right to treat it as a breach in anticipation and thus to treat the contract as discharged immediately. In other words, if a person says he will not perform, the law allows the other to take him at his word and act accordingly.

(2)   In such a case the injured party is not ordinarily bound to treat the contract as discharged: the law gives him a choice. He may treat the contract as discharged or he may disregard the repudiation and treat the contract as continuing in full effect, notwithstanding what has occurred. He can, in other words, elect to affirm it.

(3)   If the injured party elects to affirm the contract, both parties' rights and obligations under it remain completely unaffected; the renunciation is 'writ in water', to use the well-known expression of Lord Justice Asquith in *Howard* v *Pickford Tool Co. Ltd* [1951] 1 KB 417 at p. 421.

(4)   The choice placed before the injured party is between inconsistent rights, and once the choice has been made and communicated to the other party to the contract, it is irrevocable. Unlike estoppel, election does not depend upon any change in position by the party to whom it is communicated.

(5)   Although the injured party is bound by his election once it has been made, the fact that he has affirmed the contract does not of course preclude him from treating it as discharged on a subsequent occasion if the other party again repudiates it.

(6)   The injured party will not be treated as having elected to affirm the contract in the face of the renunciation unless it can be shown that he knew of the facts giving rise to his right to treat the contract as discharged and of his right to choose between affirming the contract and treating it as discharged.

(7)   A binding election requires the injured party to communicate his choice to the other party in clear and unequivocal terms. In particular, he will not be held bound by a qualified or conditional decision.

(8)   Election can be express or implied and will be implied where the injured party acts in a way which is consistent only with a decision to keep the contract alive or where he exercises rights which would only be available to him if the contract had been affirmed.

As I say, none of these principles was in dispute.

Two observations in the authorities cited to me strike me as being of particular significance in the context of this case in which the argument has turned mainly on the proper construction to be placed upon the owners' response to the charterers' original message that they could not per-form. In *Johnson and Another* v *Agnew* [[1980] AC 367] Lord Wilberforce said, at p. 398E of the report:

Election, though the subject of much learning and refinement, is in the end a doctrine based on simple considerations of common sense and equity.

And in *Peyman* v *Lanjani and Others* [[1985] Ch 457], Lord Justice Slade, having held that actual knowledge of the right to choose is essential to support an election, pointed out, at p. 501B of the report, that the doctrine of estoppel will often operate to prevent any injustice in a case where the repudiating party has relied on an apparent election by the injured party.

These comments seem to me to provide strong support for the view that the Court should not adopt an unduly technical approach to deciding whether the injured party has affirmed the contract and should not be willing to hold that the contract has been affirmed without very clear evidence that the injured party has indeed chosen to go on with the contract notwithstanding the other party's repudiation. In my view, the Court should generally be slow to accept that the injured party has committed himself irrevocably to continuing with the contract in the knowledge that if, without finally committing himself, the injured party has made an unequivocal statement of some kind on which the party in repudiation has relied, the doctrine of estoppel is likely to prevent any injustice being done.

Considerations of this kind are perhaps most likely to arise when the injured party's initial response to the renunciation of the contract has been to call on the other to change his mind, accept his obligations and perform the contract. That is often the most natural response and one which, in my view, the Court should do nothing to discourage. It would be highly unsatisfactory, if, by responding in that way, the injured party were to put himself at risk of being held to have irrevocably affirmed the contract whatever the other's reaction might be, and in my judgment he does not do so. The law does not require an injured party to snatch at a repudiation and he does not automatically lose his right to treat the contract as discharged merely by calling on the other to reconsider his position and recognise his obligations.

[The judge then considered whether the telex of 24 January constituted an affirmation by the plaintiffs:]

. . . [Counsel for the defendants] reminded me of the passage in the speech of Lord Ackner in *The Simona* [[1988] 2 Lloyd's Rep 199] where he said at p. 203, col. 2; p. 799 of the reports [i.e. Appeal Cases]:

> When one party wrongly refuses to perform obligations, this will not automatically bring the contract to an end. The innocent party has an option. He may either accept the wrongful repudiation as determining the contract and sue for damages, or he may ignore or reject the attempt to determine the contract and affirm its continued existence. Cockburn CJ in *Frost* v *Knight* [(1872) LR 7 Ex 111] put the matter thus:
>
> . . .
>
> The promisee, if he pleases, may, treat the notice of intention as inoperative, and await the time when the contract is to be executed, and then hold the other party responsible for all the consequences of non-performance.

He submitted that in their message the owners quite clearly rejected any cancellation of the charter and made it clear that as far as they were concerned the contract was going ahead. They demanded that the charterers should perform their obligations and threatened to hold them liable in damages if in the event they failed to do so. This, [counsel] submitted, was a plain case of the owners 'rejecting the attempt to determine the contract' in the words of Lord Ackner, and 'choosing to treat the charterers' notice as inoperative', to use the words of Cockburn, CJ. Accordingly, he said, they affirmed the charter.

[Counsel for the plaintiffs] submitted that the telex cannot properly be read in that way at all. What it amounted to, he said, was an expression of outrage and a demand that the charterers withdraw their repudiation and perform their obligations. The threat to hold them responsible in damages if they did not do so was, he said, wholly consistent with the retaining of the option to treat the contract as discharged, and the final sentence containing the request for 'an honourable confirmation' made it clear that their willingness to proceed with the contract depended on their receiving confirmation from the charterers that they would honour their obligations.

This telex, of course, has to be read as a whole. It would be quite wrong to take it apart and seek to attach a particular meaning to one section while ignoring what precedes and follows it. And it must also be remembered that it is not a formal document but one drafted by businessmen whose native language was not English.

In my view, this message, read as a whole, can only be read as a cry of protest at what the owners regarded as a dishonourable attempt by the charterers to abandon their obligations. Far from rejecting the idea that the charter might be discharged, as [counsel for the defendants] suggests, what the owners are here saying is that they regard the charterers' conduct in seeking to abandon it as totally unacceptable behaviour. Likewise, I cannot read the final sentence as simply inviting the charterers to confirm that if in due course their failure [sic] to perform the contract they would be liable in damages. The threat to report the charterers' attitude as well as their actions shows clearly that it is their present conduct which concerned the owners. The only meaning one can sensibly give to the final sentence of the telex is that the owners were asking the charterers to withdraw their repudiation and confirm their willingness to perform the contract. However one reads this telex, it is impossible, in my view, to find in it an unequivocal statement on the part of the owners that they will proceed with the contract and await performance in due course regardless of the position adopted by the charterers. That being so, the argument that the owners affirmed the contract by sending this message must fail.

. . . It follows that, in my judgment, the owners had not previously elected to affirm the contract when on Feb. 1 they accepted the charterers' repudiation as discharging it and that they were entitled to take that step. When doing so, they referred expressly to the charterers' failure to confirm that they would fulfil the contract. That, in my view, was an understandable reference back to their telex of Jan. 24 in which they had asked for an honourable confirmation of the charterers' intention to perform. . . .

NOTES

1. It is apparent from this judgment that there must be an unequivocal affirmation of the contract which firmly commits the injured party to continuing with the contract. This appears to be because the consequences of affirmation are viewed as being strict, i.e. the injured party cannot later change his mind and accept the repudiatory breach as terminating the contract. Thus, the implication is that the election to affirm is irrevocable. However, this may not be the case if the breach is continuing (see discussion below).

2. This decision on affirmation can usefully be compared with the approach taken by the House of Lords in *Vitol SA* v *Norelf Ltd, The Santa Clara, page 350*, to what can constitute acceptance of a repudiatory breach.

3. Moore-Bick J considers that this restrictive approach to affirmation is tempered by the fact that the doctrine of estoppel will prevent injustice to a defendant who has relied on unequivocal statements by the claimant that appeared to constitute affirmation of the repudiatory breach (see *Fercometal* v *Mediterranean Shipping, page 341*). However, it will be necessary to clearly distinguish those actions that are not sufficiently unequivocal to constitute affirmations but are sufficiently unequivocal to found an estoppel.

Is the election to affirm irrevocable or can the injured party having first affirmed then accept the repudiation and bring the contract to an end before the date of an actual breach?

In *Yukong Line* v *Rendsburg* [1996] 2 Lloyd's Rep 604, *page 333*, the question of whether the election to affirm was irrevocable did not arise for decision, since once the judge had concluded that there was no affirmation on 24 January he did not then need to consider whether the plaintiffs could terminate on 1 February. It was, however, a matter considered by Colman J and Thomas J in separate actions in *Stocznia Gdanska SA* v *Latvian Shipping Co.* [1997] 2 Lloyd's Rep 228 (Colman J), [2001] 1 Lloyd's Rep 537 (Thomas J) and by the Court of Appeal on appeal from the decision of Thomas J.

Stocznia Gdanska SA v Latvian Shipping Co. (No. 3)
[2002] EWCA Civ 889, [2002] 2 All ER (Comm) 768 (CA)

The plaintiffs, a shipbuilding company ('the yard'), had entered into six contracts to build six refrigerated vessels. The contract terms provided that the price was payable by instalments, with 5 per cent becoming payable after receipt of the plaintiffs' bank guarantee and the second instalment of 20 per cent of the purchase price becoming payable five banking days after the plaintiffs had given the purchasers telex notice of the laying of the keel. The defendant purchasers repudiated the contracts after the first instalment had been paid by stating that they were financially unable to perform. The plaintiffs carried on with performance and claimed the second instalment for each vessel, having given notice of keel laying for all six vessels. In fact keels had been laid only for vessels 1 and 2 and the plaintiffs had renumbered those vessels in order to serve notice of keel laying for vessels 3, 4, 5, and 6.

Since the defendants did not pay any of the second instalments of 20 per cent on keel laying, the plaintiffs issued notices under cl. 5.05 of the contract. This clause gave the plaintiffs the right to rescind for non-payment of these instalments and provided for financial compensation.

The plaintiffs claimed, *inter alia*, the defendants were in anticipatory repudiatory breach and that they had accepted this breach as terminating the contracts so that they were entitled to recover damages at common law. The defendants argued that the plaintiffs had affirmed by tendering the keel laying notices following the breach and that this election was irrevocable. Colman J agreed that this conduct amounted to an unequivocal affirmation so that the contracts continued and, since this affirmation was irrevocable, the plaintiffs had to permit the defendants to pay the second instalments if they were able. However, another claim for leave to amend the pleadings was heard by Thomas J ([2001] 1 Lloyd's Rep 537), who concluded that the tendering of the keel laying notices did not amount to affirmation but stated in *obiter* comments that the election to affirm was not irrevocable in relation to continuing or renewed anticipatory breach in the period between affirmation and the date set for contractual performance.

THOMAS J: Once the innocent party has affirmed, he must going on performing. He must then be able to point to behaviour that amounts to a repudiation after the affirmation either by way of some fresh conduct amounting to repudiation or by way of the continuing refusal to perform amounting to a repudiation. I cannot see any reason why the innocent party must wait until there is an actual repudiatory breach . . . To require an innocent party, who has by pressing for performance of the contract affirmed it, to wait until there is an actual breach by the party in breach before he can bring the contract to an end might well, as in this case, have required that innocent party to engage in performance that is entirely pointless and wasteful as the party in breach would, when he became under an obligation to accept performance, refuse to do so . . .

The question therefore is whether the breach was a continuing one and amounted to repudiatory conduct. In my view it was. As I have set out, the yard pressed for performance on 19 April 1994 and 4 May 1994; there was no response. It does not seem to me that the failure to respond can make a difference; if, for example, Latreefers had replied and said that they were not going to perform, then there would clearly have been a new repudiatory act. Can it make a difference that they were silent in the face of a demand for performance, if the inference from silence was their continuing refusal to perform? As that is the inference I draw, I do not think it can make a difference, as by not responding in the circumstances of this case they were making clear that they were not going to perform. The matter can be tested by asking whether in such circumstances, the yard were meant to proceed to start to build the vessels and wait until such time as there was some act of Latreefers that amounted to a fresh actual breach. Had they done so, I am sure that it would be said rightly that they had failed to mitigate in circumstances where it was obvious that Latreefers were not going to take the vessels.

The Court of Appeal Held: There was a middle ground between acceptance of the repudiation as terminating the contract and affirmation. This was the period prior to any election when the innocent party was making up his mind what action to take. During this period the contract was kept in being but the right to treat it as repudiated was reserved. (This was a completely different position to affirming but excusing the innocent party from performance of his own obligations until the guilty party indicates a willingness to perform; a position that had been firmly rejected in *The Simona* [1989] AC 788, 801. In that situation an election had occurred.)

RIX LJ (with whose judgment Tuckey and Aldous LJJ agreed):

87 In my judgment, there is of course a middle ground between acceptance of repudiation and affirmation of the contract, and that is the period when the innocent party is making up his mind what to do. If he does nothing for too long, there may come a time when the law will treat him as having affirmed. If he maintains the contract in being for the moment, while reserving his right to treat it as repudiated if his contract partner persists in his repudiation, then he has not yet elected. As long as the contract remains alive, the innocent party runs the risk that a merely anticipatory repudiatory breach, a thing 'writ in water' until acceptance, can be overtaken by another event which prejudices the innocent party's rights under the contract—such as frustration or even his own breach. He also runs the risk, if that is the right word, that the party in repudiation will resume performance of the contract and thus end any continuing right in the innocent party to elect to accept the former repudiation as terminating the contract.

In the circumstances the tendering of the keel laying notices did not constitute affirmation as the validity of these notices had always been disputed. As a result, the contracts remained in force until the exercise of the contractual mechanism to terminate under cl. 5.05.

The Court of Appeal agreed with Thomas J that affirmation for anticipatory breach would not prevent the innocent party terminating for continuing anticipatory breach in the period prior to the contractual date for performance.

RIX LJ:

Acceptance of anticipatory breach as a repudiation following an affirmation

93 Was the yard entitled to say that Latreefers was still in repudiation of contracts 3–6 following the (assumed) affirmation of those contracts at the time of serving the keel-laying notices? That is the question which arises on the hypothesis of affirmation.

94 [Counsel for the defendants] makes two submissions in this context. First, he says that nothing that happened after the affirmation amounted to a further repudiation of the contracts. Nothing can be inferred from mere silence, especially where the notices were invalid and therefore did not call for a response. Secondly, he says that an affirmation of one kind of conduct in the past is also an affirmation for the future of conduct of the same kind. There must be a qualitative difference in the conduct after affirmation to entitle the affirming party to claim a valid right to terminate. Therefore, the doctrine of *Safehaven Investments Inc v Springbok Ltd* (1995) 71 P&CR 59 . . . needs on any view to be qualified to this extent. Again, he relies on the analysis of Colman J:

'The one course that the yard could not take following its service of the keel-laying notices was to revert to the right which it did have in the face of the prior anticipatory breach to bring the contract to an end. The reason for this is very clear. The facility which the law provides to the innocent party in the face of an anticipatory repudiatory breach is to elect to terminate the contract or to keep it alive for the benefit of both parties: see *Fercometal S.A.R.L.* v *Mediterranean Shipping Co. S.A.* ([1988] 2 All ER 742 at 747–8, [1989] AC 788 at 799–802 per Lord Ackner). If, with full knowledge of the facts, the innocent party affirms the contract by words, conduct or in some cases inactivity, he cannot subsequently treat the contract as terminated on the grounds of the same anticipatory breach in relation to which he has made his election to affirm. The irrevocability of an election to affirm once made has long been recognised: see, for example, *Bentsen* v *Taylor & Sons Co.*, [1893] 2 Q.B. 274, and had been repeatedly stated: see, for example, *The Kanchenjunga*, [1990] 1 Lloyd's Rep. 391, per Lord Goff of Chieveley at pp. 398–399. In the area of anticipatory breach the guilty party needs to know with certainty whether the contract which he has repudiated has been terminated or kept alive, for, if it is still alive, he will yet have the opportunity of performance. For this reason the innocent party who has affirmed the contract cannot revert to his right to treat the contract as terminated on the grounds of the same pre-existing anticipatory breach. As it is often said, he cannot reprobate having already approbated.' (See [1997] 2 Lloyd's Rep 228 at 235.)

95 [He referred to the analysis of Thomas J on this matter and continued:] [Counsel for the yard] submits that the judge was right for the reasons he gave. There was a continuing repudiation and the judge was entitled to evaluate the nature of Latreefers' post-affirmation conduct against the background of its pre-affirmation conduct. In such circumstances, Latreefers' silence was not mere silence but what has sometimes been called a pregnant silence, a silence that speaks of maintained recalcitrance. Moreover the silence continued in circumstances where there was a duty to speak, a duty on Latreefers to make clear that it was no longer continuing with its previous repudiatory attitude to the effect that it was unwilling to proceed unless the contracts were renegotiated on a 'take it or leave it' basis.

96 In my judgment the judge was right to adopt and apply [the] ratio in the *Safehaven Investments* case and right to conclude on the facts that there was a continuing repudiation after affirmation. I would also accept [counsel for the yard's] submissions about Latreefers' silence to the extent that they may go beyond the judge's analysis. The silence was not mere silence, it was overlaid with all that had gone before. It was a speaking silence. The difficulty with silence is that it is normally equivocal. Where, however, it is part of a course of consistent conduct it may be a silence which not only speaks but does so unequivocally. Where silence speaks, there may be a duty on the silent party in turn to speak to rectify the significance of his silence. The circumstances of this case demonstrate the importance of these principles. This was not a case where a party seeks to derive assent out of mere silence. These parties were in contractual relations, and the question was whether the yard should continue to perform in circumstances where Latreefers had made it clear that it did not want performance on the terms of the existing contracts. The yard needed to know where it stood. Whether the notices were valid or not, if Latreefers wished the yard to proceed with building the vessels in circumstances where it had previously made clear that it did not, then it had an obligation to clarify its new intentions. If its position, paradoxical as it might be, was that if only the yard would get itself where it could serve valid keel-laying notices, Latreefers would pay, even though it had refused to pay in response to the valid keel-laying notices on vessels 1 and 2, then it should have made that position clear. In the commercial context no other response makes any sense at all, and the law should not adopt a position where it cannot respond adequately to such a situation. I am satisfied that legal principle is well able to derive the right answer from the facts of this case, and that the answer is that given by the judge.

97 That means that it is unnecessary to rule on a further submission based on an article written by Professor Sir Gunther Treitel QC 'Affirmation after repudiatory breach' (1998) 114 LQR 22 in response to the facts of this very case, to the effect that affirmation should not necessarily be regarded as irrevocable. In the House of Lords ([1998] 1 All ER 883 at 902, [1998] 1 WLR 574 at 594) Lord Goff thought it right that Colman J's judgment should be set aside 'in toto' so that full consideration could be given at trial to the yard's argument on continuing repudiation. Lord Goff continued:

'That this argument is of a substantial nature is fortified by Sir Gunther Treitel's note on the present case ((1998) 114 LQR 22); I wish to add that the point in question did not arise for consideration in *Motor Oil Hellas (Corinth) Refineries SA* v *Shipping Corp of India, The Kanchenjunga* [1990] 1 Lloyd's Rep 391, a case relied upon by Colman J in his judgment.'

98 Lord Goff had in mind a sentence in his own speech in *The Kanchenjunga* that 'Once an election is made, however, it is final' (see [1990] 1 Lloyd's Rep 391 at 398). Professor Treitel argues powerfully that such an election, if indeed the concept of election is the correct concept at all in this context, should not be final or binding, in the sense of irrevocable, in the face of a continuing anticipatory repudiation.

99 It seems to me that an affirmation of a repudiatory actual breach may differ from an affirmation of a merely anticipatory repudiatory breach in that the former breach is complete at the time it occurs whereas the latter breach looks to the future. An affirmation of an actual breach may therefore be said to leave nothing outstanding for the future, in that the worst has already occurred, whereas an affirmation of an anticipatory breach still leaves the future open. Prima facie an election or waiver looks to the past, even if it is possible, in a very clear case, to waive one's rights for the future too. Two views might therefore be taken as to the effect of an affirmation of an anticipatory breach. One is that it is a waiver for the future as well: that was what Colman J decided and [counsel for the defendants] submitted. The other is that the affirmation prima facie relates only to the past, leaving open the question of a continuing or renewed anticipatory breach. It seems to me that the latter view is to be preferred, and is inherent in the decision in the *Safehaven Investments* case and in the decision already taken in relation to this case. That would still leave open of course the question of how one tells whether an anticipatory breach is a continuing one, and the correct way of viewing silence. Professor Treitel highlights ((1998) 114 LQR 22 at 26) the undesirability of subverting considerations of substance or policy to the accidents of negotiation. I wonder whether each case does not in truth have to be decided on its own facts. However, substance and principle suggest that silence should not in this context be too readily regarded as equivocal; and that against the background of an earlier anticipatory repudiation it should not take much further to prove continuing repudiatory conduct.

100 It also occurs to me that even in the case of an actual repudiatory breach, where the breach is of a continuing nature, such as a failure to pay or to deliver, an affirmation at one stage is not necessarily an irrevocable affirmation for all time in the future. If it were otherwise, the law could not have developed the doctrine of *Charles Rickards Ltd* v *Oppenheim* [1950] 1 All ER 420, [1950] 1 KB 616.

101 I express these thoughts in response to the interesting arguments deployed in this case, but it is not necessary to decide the issue and I refrain from doing so.

NOTES
1. Affirmation following an anticipatory repudiatory breach does not prevent the injured party from later accepting the *actual* repudiatory breach as terminating the contract (i.e. the failure to perform on the date set for contractual performance). (See Carter (1998) 12 JCL 247, 250: 'If the promisor fails to perform, and that failure gives rise to a right to terminate, there is a fresh right of termination not affected by the prior affirmation'.)
2. The observations in *Stocznia* have resolved the question of whether an election to affirm is irrevocable in the period between the affirmation and the date for contractual performance. At least in those instances where there has been no change of position by the guilty party in reliance on the affirmation so that they would be prejudiced by the change of heart, the innocent party is entitled to go back on his affirmation where there has been a continuing or renewed anticipatory breach by the guilty party. This is the position advocated by Treitel in 'Affirmation after Repudiatory Breach' (1998) 114 LQR 22 and has the support of Thomas J and Rix LJ, giving the judgment of the Court of Appeal.

   The result is that there is a distinction between anticipatory breaches that cannot be remedied prior to the date set for performance, e.g., because the subject matter has been destroyed or sold to a third party, and anticipatory breaches that can be remedied, such as a statement that the party is unable to pay. Clearly, if the anticipatory breach can be remedied but the guilty expressly states that he will not do so, there will be a renewed repudiation and the innocent party should be able to terminate. However, the difficulties of analysis will arise where there is silence on the part of the guilty party. Both Thomas J and Rix LJ considered that the inference from such silence was of a continuing refusal to perform. Rix LJ went further and considered that where there was a clear duty to rectify the inferences from silence in the context of a continuing obligation to perform, such silence might be 'a speaking silence'. The adoption of this position reflects the commercial need for the yard to know whether it should continue with construction of the vessels, expenditure that might be 'entirely pointless and wasteful' (*per* Thomas J).

3. It is important to bear in mind that if the injured party elects to affirm, the contract remains in force and any damages award will not be available until (at the earliest) the contractual date for performance. These damages will then be assessed on the basis of loss resulting from the actual breach at the date when the contract ought to have been performed rather than the date of the anticipatory repudiatory breach.

Since the effect of affirmation is that the contract continues in force, this presents some risks to the injured party. The same risks exist in the 'middle ground' position prior to making the election (see Rix LJ in *Stocznia Gdanska SA* v *Latvian Shipping Co. (No. 3)* [2002] EWCA Civ 889, [2002] 2 All ER (Comm) 768, [87], *page 338 above*).

(a) Subsequent breach by the injured party

If the injured party subsequently breaches the contract in the intervening period, the injured party is liable to pay damages for his breach and cannot argue that the guilty party's anticipatory breach excused further performance of the contractual obligations.

Fercometal SARL v Mediterranean Shipping Co. SA, The Simona
[1989] AC 788 (HL)

Under a charterparty for the carriage of steel coils from Durban to Bilbao, the charterers were entitled to cancel if the vessel was not ready to load on or before 9 July. On 2 July the charterers committed an anticipatory repudiatory breach by chartering another vessel to carry the cargo when the owners had requested an extension to 13 July. The owners did not accept this repudiation and notified the charterers that the vessel would start loading on 8 July. This notice was invalid because the vessel was not in fact ready to load. Consequently, the owners were committing a breach of contract. The charterers sought to cancel the charterparty relying on the express cancellation provision. Held: if the injured party elects to affirm the contract following an anticipatory repudiatory breach, then that party is not absolved from tendering further performance of his obligations under the contract. The charterers therefore retained the right to cancel the charterparty. The House of Lords did state, however, that if the charterers had indicated that the owner was no longer required to perform, and the owner had relied upon that as excusing the performance, then the charterers would be estopped from relying on the breach and could not have cancelled the charterparty.

LORD ACKNER: . . . When A wrongfully repudiates his contractual obligations in anticipation of the time for their performance, he presents the innocent party B with two choices. He may either affirm the contract by treating it as still in force or he may treat it as finally and conclusively discharged. There is no third choice, as a sort of via media, to affirm the contract and yet be absolved from tendering further performance unless and until A gives reasonable notice that he is once again able and willing to perform. Such a choice would negate the contract being kept alive for the benefit of *both* parties and would deny the party who unsuccessfully sought to rescind, the right to take advantage of any supervening circumstance which would justify him in declining to complete.

[Counsel for the owners] submitted that the charterers' conduct had induced or caused the owners to abstain from having the ship ready prior to the cancellation date. Of course, it is always open to A, who has refused to accept B's repudiation of the contract, and thereby kept the contract alive, to contend that in relation to a particular right or obligation under the contract, B is estopped from contending that he, B, is entitled to exercise that right or that he, A, has remained bound by that obligation. If B represents to A that he no longer intends to exercise that right or requires that obligation to be fulfilled by A and A acts upon that representation, then clearly B cannot be heard thereafter to say that he is entitled to exercise that right or that A is in breach of contract by not fulfilling that obligation. If, in relation to this option to cancel, the owners had been able to establish that the charterers had represented that they no longer required the vessel to arrive on time because they had already fixed the *Leo Tornado* and in reliance upon that representation, the owners had given notice of readiness only after the cancellation date, then the charterers would have been estopped from contending they were entitled to cancel the charterparty. There is, however, no finding of any such representation, let alone that the owners were induced thereby not to make the vessel ready to load by 9 July. On the contrary, the owners on 5 July on two occasions asserted that the vessel would start loading on 8 July and on 8 July purported to tender notice of readiness. . . . The non-readiness of the vessel by the cancelling date was in no way induced by the charterers' conduct. It was the result of the owners' decision to load other cargo first.

In short in affirming the continued existence of the contract, the owners could only avoid the operation of the cancellation clause by tendering the vessel ready to load on time (which they failed to do), or by establishing (which they could not) that their failure was the result of the charterers' conduct in representing that they had given up their option, which representation the owners had acted on by not presenting the vessel on time . . .

(b) Frustration between affirmation and date for performance

If the contract is frustrated between the date of affirmation and the date fixed for performance, then the injured party will lose his right to remedies for the breach.

Avery v *Bowden*
(1855) 5 E & B 714; 119 ER 647 (QB), affirmed Exchequer Chamber (1856) 6 E & B 953

A ship was required to load cargo at Odessa within 45 days. The ship's master was told before the expiry of these laydays that no cargo would be available. He elected to affirm the contract and remained in port hoping that a cargo would be provided. Before the expiry of the 45-day period the contract was frustrated by the outbreak of war, which made it illegal to load a cargo at an enemy port. Held: the shipowners could not recover damages for the anticipatory repudiatory breach in failing to provide a cargo since the master had affirmed. If the master had sailed away on receiving that information, then not only could another cargo have been loaded at a friendly port, but the shipowner would have had a right to claim damages for the loss caused by the breach.

(c) Claiming the contract price as an alternative to damages

It has been held that the injured party can continue his performance of the contract and claim the contract price (as an action for a liquidated sum) rather than suing for damages for the breach. This is controversial, since the performance clearly is not required and the expenditure in performing is wasted.

White & Carter (Councils) Ltd v *McGregor*
[1962] AC 413 (HL)

The plaintiffs, advertising contractors, had contracted with the defendant garage proprietor to display advertisements for the garage on litter bins for a three-year period. On the same day the defendant requested that the agreement be cancelled, but the plaintiffs refused. The plaintiffs displayed the advertisements for 156 weeks and then claimed the contract price of £196 4s. Held: (Lords Morton and Keith dissenting) the plaintiffs were entitled to carry out the contract and claim the full contract price. They were not bound to accept the repudiation and sue for the lost profit on the contract as their damages. The minority were of the opinion that there could be no recovery of unwanted wasted expenditure and that the plaintiffs should have mitigated (*page 408*).

LORD REID: . . . If one party to a contract repudiates it in the sense of making it clear to the other party that he refuses or will refuse to carry out his part of the contract, the other party, the innocent party, has an option. He may accept that repudiation and sue for damages for breach of contract, whether or not the time for performance has come; or he may if he chooses disregard or refuse to accept it and then the contract remains in full effect. . . .

I need not refer to the numerous authorities. They are not disputed by the respondent but he points out that in all of them the party who refused to accept the repudiation had no active duties under the contract. The innocent party's option is generally said to be to *wait* until the date of performance and then to claim damages estimated as at that date. There is no case in which it is said that he may, in face of the repudiation, go on and incur useless expense in performing the contract and then claim the contract price. The option, it is argued, is merely as to the date as at which damages are to be assessed.

Developing this argument, the respondent points out that in most cases the innocent party cannot complete the contract himself without the other party doing, allowing or accepting something, and that it is purely fortuitous that the appellants can do so in this case. In most cases by refusing co-operation the party in breach can compel the innocent party to restrict his claim to damages. Then it was said that, even where the innocent party can complete the contract without such co-operation, it is against the public interest that he should be allowed to do so. An example was developed in argument. A company might engage an expert to go abroad and prepare an elaborate report and then repudiate the contract before anything was done. To allow such an expert then to waste thousands of pounds in preparing the report cannot be right if a much smaller sum of damages would give him full compensation for his loss. It would merely enable the expert to extort a settlement giving him far more than reasonable compensation.

. . . It might be, but it never has been, the law that a person is only entitled to enforce his contractual rights in a reasonable way, and that a court will not support an attempt to enforce them in an unreasonable way. One reason why that is not the law is, no doubt, because it was thought that it would create too much uncertainty to require the court to decide whether it is reasonable or equitable to allow a party to enforce his full rights under a contract.

. . . It may well be that, if it can be shown that a person has no legitimate interest, financial or otherwise, in performing the contract rather than claiming damages, he ought not to be allowed to saddle the other party with an additional burden with no benefit to himself. If a party has no interest to enforce a stipulation, he cannot in general enforce it: so it might be said that, if a party has no interest to insist on a particular remedy, he ought not to be allowed to insist on it. And, just as a party is not allowed to enforce a penalty, so he ought not to be allowed to penalise the other party by taking one course when another is equally advantageous to him. If I may revert to the example which I gave of a company engaging an expert to prepare an elaborate report and then repudiating before anything was done, it might be that the company could show that the expert had no substantial or legitimate interest in carrying out the work rather than accepting damages: I would think that the de minimis principle would apply in determining whether his interest was substantial, and that he might have a legitimate interest other than an immediate financial interest. But if the expert had no such interest then that might be regarded as a proper case for the exercise of the general equitable jurisdiction of the court. But that is not this case. Here the respondent did not set out to prove that the appellants had no legitimate interest in completing the contract and claiming the contract price rather than claiming damages; there is nothing in the findings of fact to support such a case, and it seems improbable that any such case could have been proved. It is, in my judgment, impossible to say that the appellants should be deprived of their right to claim the contract price merely because the benefit to them, as against claiming damages and re-letting their advertising space, might be small in comparison with the loss to the respondent: that is the most that could be said in favour of the respondent. Parliament has on many occasions relieved parties from certain kinds of improvident or oppressive contracts, but the common law can only do that in very limited circumstances.

LORD HODSON: In *Howard* v *Pickford Tool Co. Ltd* [1951] 1 KB 417 Asquith LJ said: 'An unaccepted repudiation is a thing writ in water and of no value to anybody: it confers no legal rights of any sort or kind.'

It follows that, if, as here, there was no acceptance, the contract remains alive for the benefit of both parties and the party who has repudiated can change his mind but it does not follow that the party at the receiving end of the proffered repudiation is bound to accept it before the time for performance and is left to his remedy in damages for breach.

[Counsel] for the respondent, did not seek to dispute the general proposition of law to which I have referred but sought to argue that if at the date of performance by the innocent party the guilty party maintains his refusal to accept performance and the innocent party does not accept the repudiation, although the contract still survives, it does not survive so far as the right of the innocent party to perform it is concerned but survives only for the purpose of enforcing remedies open to him by way of damages or specific implement.

This produces an impossible result; if the innocent party is deprived of some of his rights it involves putting an end to the contract except in cases, unlike this, where, in the exercise of the court's discretion, the remedy of specific implement is available.

The true position is that the contract survives and does so not only where specific implement is available. When the assistance of the court is not required the innocent party can choose whether he will accept repudiation and sue for damages for anticipatory breach or await the date of performance by the guilty party. Then, if there is failure in performance, his rights are preserved.

It may be unfortunate that the appellants have saddled themselves with an unwanted contract causing an apparent waste of time and money. No doubt this aspect impressed the Court of Session but there is no equity which can assist the respondent. It is trite that equity will not rewrite an improvident contract where there is no disability on either side. There is no duty laid upon a party to a subsisting contract to vary it at the behest of the other party so as to deprive himself of the benefit given to him by the contract. To hold otherwise would be to introduce a novel equitable doctrine that a party was not to be held to his contract unless the court in a given instance thought it reasonable so to do. In this case it would make an action for debt a claim for a discretionary remedy. . . .

LORD MORTON OF HENRYTON *dissenting*: My Lords, I think that this is a case of great importance, although the claim is for a comparatively small sum. If the appellants are right, strange consequences follow in any case in which, under a repudiated contract, services are to be performed by the party who has not repudiated it, so long as he is able to perform these services without the co-operation of the repudiating party. Many examples of such contracts could be given. One, given in the course of the argument and already mentioned by my noble and learned friend, Lord Reid, is the engagement of an expert to go abroad and write a report on some subject for a substantial fee plus his expenses. If the appellants succeed in the present case, it must follow that the expert is entitled to incur the expense of going abroad, to write his unwanted report, and then to recover the fee and expenses, even if the other party has plainly repudiated the contract before any expense has been incurred.

It is well established that repudiation by one party does not put an end to a contract. The other party can say 'I hold you to your contract, which still remains in force.' What then is his remedy if the repudiating party persists in his repudiation and refuses to carry out his part of the contract? The contract has been broken. The innocent party is entitled to be compensated by damages for any loss which he has suffered by reason of the breach, and in a limited class of cases the court will decree specific implement. The law of Scotland provides no other remedy for a breach of contract, and there is no reported case which decides that the innocent party may act as the appellants have acted. The present case is one in which specific implement could not be decreed, since the only obligation of the respondent under the contract was to pay a sum of money for services to be rendered by the appellants. Yet the appellants are claiming a kind of inverted specific implement of the contract. They first insist on performing their part of the contract, against the will of the other party, and then claim that he must perform his part and pay the contract price for un-wanted services. In my opinion, my Lords, the appellants' only remedy was damages, and they were bound to take steps to minimise their loss, according to a well-established rule of law. Far from doing this, having incurred no expense at the date of the repudiation, they made no attempt to procure another advertiser, but deliberately went on to incur expense and perform unwanted services with the intention of creating a money debt which did not exist at the date of the repudiation.

. . . The course of action followed by the appellants seems to me unreasonable and oppressive, but it is not on that ground that I would reject their claim. I would reject it for the reasons which I have already given.

NOTES

1. In effect the majority was stating that the right to affirm includes the right to earn the contract price by performing the contract, as long as this can be achieved without the other party's cooperation. However, the actual result has been criticised, partly on the ground that it achieves the same effect as an order for specific performance where specific performance would not have been available.

2. The majority considered that there was no duty to mitigate because they felt that on affirm-ation there was no breach. However, if on the contractual date for performance there is no performance, there will inevitably be a breach, which on these facts the plaintiffs affirmed. Arguably, therefore, the plaintiffs should have mitigated as from this date.

   It is true that the claim here was an action for an agreed sum, so that damages rules such as that relating to mitigation do not apply. This decision illustrates the unsatisfactory nature of the consequences that follow from this distinction. It is submitted that the duty to mitigate should apply to both types of claim.

3. *White & Carter* v *McGregor* has been limited in subsequent decisions by reference to two apparent limitations placed upon it by Lord Reid. The first is that the claimants must have been able to perform without the cooperation of the defendant and the second, that the claimants must have a legitimate interest in continuing to perform rather than claiming damages.

   In *Clea Shipping Corp* v *Bulk Oil International Ltd, The Alaskan Trader* (*page 348*), Lloyd J explained these limitations:

   > Lord Reid agreed with Lord Hodson and Lord Tucker that on the facts the plaintiffs' claim in debt must succeed. But his speech contains two important observations on the law. First, he pointed out that it is only in rare cases that the innocent party will be able to complete performance of his side of the contract, without the assent or cooperation of the party in breach. Obviously, if the innocent party cannot complete performance, he is restricted to his claim for damages. A buyer who refuses to accept delivery of the goods, and thereby prevents property passing, cannot, in the ordinary case, be made liable for the price. The peculiarity of *White & Carter* v *McGregor* [1961] 3 All ER 1178 at 182, [1962] AC 413 at 429, as Lord Reid pointed out, was that the plaintiffs could completely fulfil their part of the contract without any cooperation from the defendant.
   >
   > The second observation which Lord Reid made as to the law was that a party might well be unable to enforce his contractual remedy if 'he had no legitimate interest, financial or otherwise, in performing the contract rather than claiming damages'. Lord Reid did not go far in explaining what he meant by legitimate interest except to say that the de minimis principle would apply. Obviously it would not be sufficient to establish that the innocent party was acting unreasonably. . . .
   >
   > It is clear that, on the facts, no attempt had been made by the defendant to establish absence of legitimate interest. Accordingly, counsel for the owners was right when he

submitted that the two observations which I have mentioned were both, strictly speaking, obiter.

In the following case, Megarry J considered that cooperation in this context meant passive as well as active cooperation.

Hounslow London Borough Council v Twickenham Garden Developments Ltd
[1971] Ch 233

Contractors were working on a site belonging to the local authority. The local authority 'repudiated' their contract but the contractors refused to accept this and elected to proceed with the work on site. The question was whether they had the right to insist on continuing to perform the contract. Held: they did not have that right.

MEGARRY J: . . . The case before me is patently one in which the contractor cannot perform the contract without any co-operation by the borough. The whole machinery of the contract is geared to acts by the architect and quantity surveyor, and it is a contract that is to be performed on the borough's land. True, the contractor already has de facto possession or control of the land; there is no question of the borough being required to do the act of admitting the contractor into possession, and so in that respect the contractor can perform the contract without any 'co-operation' by the borough. But I do not think that the point can be brushed aside so simply. Quite apart from questions of active co-operation, cases where one party is lawfully in possession of property of the other seem to me to raise issues not before the House of Lords in *White and Carter (Councils) Ltd v McGregor* [1962] AC 413. Suppose that A, who owns a large and valuable painting, contracts with B, a picture restorer, to restore it over a period of three months. Before the work is begun, A receives a handsome offer from C to purchase the picture, subject to immediate delivery of the picture in its unrestored state, C having grave suspicions of B's competence. If the work of restoration is to be done in A's house, he can effectually exclude B by refusing to admit him to the house: without A's 'co-operation' to this extent B cannot perform his contract. But what if the picture stands in A's locked barn, the key of which he has lent to B so that he may come and go freely, or if the picture has been removed to B's premises? In these cases can B insist on performing his contract, even though this makes it impossible for A to accept C's offer? In the case of the barn, A's co-operation may perhaps be said to be requisite to the extent of not barring B's path to the barn or putting another lock on the door: but if the picture is on B's premises, no active co-operation by A is needed. Nevertheless, the picture is A's property, and I find it difficult to believe that Lord Reid intended to restrict the concept of 'co-operation' to active co-operation. In *White and Carter (Councils) Ltd v McGregor* no co-operation by the proprietor, either active or passive, was required: the contract could be performed by the agents wholly without reference to the proprietor or his property. The case was far removed from that of a property owner being forced to stand impotently aside while a perhaps ill-advised contract is executed on property of his which he has delivered into the possession of the other party, and is powerless to retrieve.

Accordingly, I do not think that *White and Carter (Councils) Ltd v McGregor* has any application to the case before me. I say this, first, because a considerable degree of active co-operation under the contract by the borough is requisite, and second, because the work is being done to property of the borough. I doubt very much whether the *White* case can have been intended to apply where the contract is to be performed by doing acts to property owned by the party seeking to determine it. I should add that it seems to me that the ratio of the *White* case involves acceptance of Lord Reid's limitations, even though Lord Tucker and Lord Hodson said nothing of them: for without Lord Reid there was no majority for the decision of the House. Under the doctrine of precedent, I do not think that it can be said that a majority of a bare majority is itself the majority.

■ QUESTIONS

1. This interpretation has considerably diminished the scope of *White & Carter (Councils) Ltd* v *McGregor*, since the performance of many contracts will require at least passive cooperation from the other party. There appears to be a difference between a contractor working on the site of the owner and working on the site of a third party. Should this make a difference?

2. Did the plaintiffs in *White & Carter* v *McGregor* have a legitimate interest in performing the contract?

NOTES

1. Where the anticipatory breach is of a contract for the sale or supply of unascertained or future goods and the buyer indicates that he does not want the goods, the seller will not be able to perform so as to be entitled to claim the price since the buyer will not accept the goods. (See J. Poole, *Textbook on Contract*, 7th edn, 2004: Oxford University Press, p. 266, for a full explanation.)

2. Lord Reid's comment on the need to establish a legitimate interest in continuing to perform rather than claim damages was not accepted by the other members of the House of Lords, but Megarry J appears to treat it as part of the *ratio* of the case.

3. The restriction in *White & Carter* that a claimant was limited to a remedy in damages where he could not perform without the cooperation of the contract-breaker applies only where the performance which had been prevented by the breach was a pre-condition to the payment obligation, i.e. the performance obligation was entire (as in *White & Carter*): *Ministry of Sound (Ireland) Ltd* v *World Online Ltd* [2003] EWHC 2178 (Ch), [2003] 2 All ER (Comm) 823. In *Ministry of Sound* the innocent party could perform only if CDs were supplied by the guilty party. However, since there was no link between the required performance and the right to receive the contractual payment, and since the contract had not been terminated for the repudiatory breach, in principle (although not on the facts) the contract term as to payment could be enforced via a claim in debt. As there was no link between performance and payment, it did not matter whether performance was impossible without cooperation.

4. In *Attica Sea Carriers Corporation* v *Ferrostaal Poseidon Bulk Reederei GmbH, The Puerto Buitrago* [1976] 1 Lloyd's Rep 250, the Court of Appeal was faced with the question of whether the shipowners could ignore a repudiation by the charterers in redelivering a vessel in breach of a repair obligation and sue for the charter hire until the repairs were completed (the evidence being that the repairs would cost $2 million which would be greatly in excess of the value of the vessel). Orr LJ (with whose conclusion Browne LJ agreed) referred to the judgment of Lord Reid in *White & Carter Ltd* v *McGregor*, and continued:

> The present case differs from that case in that here it cannot be said that the owners could fulfil the contract without any cooperation from the charterers and also because in this case the charterers have set out to prove that the owners have no legitimate interest in claiming the charter hire rather than claiming damages, and the passages above quoted strongly suggest to me that if either or both of these factors had been present in *White & Carter* v *McGregor* Lord Reid might well have agreed with Lord Morton and Lord Keith as to the outcome of the appeal, with the result that there would have been a majority in favour of dismissing it.

Lord Denning MR stated:

> . . . [*White & Carter Ltd* v *McGregor*] has been criticized in a leading textbook (Cheshire & Fifoot, pp. 600 and 601). It is said to give a 'grotesque' result. Even though it was a Scots case, it would appear that the House of Lords, as at present constituted, would expect us to follow it in any case that is precisely on all fours with it. But I would not follow it otherwise. It has no application whatever in a case where the plaintiff ought, in all reason, to accept the repudiation and sue for damages—provided that damages would provide an adequate remedy for any loss suffered by him. The reason is because, by suing for the money, the plaintiff is seeking to enforce specific performance of the contract—and he should not be

allowed to do so when damages would be an adequate remedy. Take a servant, who has a contract for six months certain, but is dismissed after one month. He cannot sue for his wages for each of the six months by alleging that he was ready and willing to serve. His only remedy is damages. Take a finance company which lets a machine or motor-car on hire purchase, but the hirer refuses to accept it. The finance company cannot sue each month for the instalments. Its only remedy is in damages: see *National Cash Register Co.* v *Stanley* [1921] 3 KB 292; *Karsales (Harrow)* v *Wallis* [1956] 1 WLR 936 (2nd point). So here, when the charterers tendered redelivery at the end of the period of the charter—in breach of the contract to repair—the shipowners ought in all reason to have accepted it. They cannot sue for specific performance—either of the promise to pay the charter hire, or of the promise to do the repairs—because damages are an adequate remedy for the breach. What is the alternative which the shipowners present to the charterers? Either the charterers must pay the charter hire for years to come, whilst the vessel lies idle and useless for want of repair. *Or* the charterers must do repairs which would cost twice as much as the ship would be worth when repaired—after which the shipowners might sell it as scrap, making the repairs a useless waste of money. In short, on either alternative, the shipowners seek to compel specific performance of one or other of the provisions of the charter—with most unjust and unreasonable consequences—when damages would be an adequate remedy. I do not think the law allows them to do this. I think they should accept redelivery and sue for damages. . . .

Clea Shipping Corp. v Bulk Oil International Ltd, The Alaskan Trader
[1984] 1 All ER 129

After 12 months of a two-year charter, the vessel suffered a serious engine break-down necessitating several months of repair. The charterers indicated that they would not require the vessel but the owners went ahead with repairs costing £800,000 which were completed in April 1981. They informed the charterers that the vessel was available and maintained a full crew ready to sail between April and December 1981. The charterers sought repayment of the hire they had paid between April and December, alleging that the owners should have accepted the charterers' conduct as repudiating the contract and claimed damages. The owners argued that they were free to elect to affirm and keep the vessel at the disposal of the charterers. Held: although in general, there was an unfettered right to elect, in exceptional cases the court would exercise its general equitable jurisdiction to refuse to allow the injured party to affirm if there was no legitimate interest in performing the contract rather than claiming damages. The arbitrator had found that the plaintiffs had acted wholly unreasonably and Lloyd J upheld this finding. Therefore, although the charterers were liable in damages, they could recover the hire.

LLOYD J: . . . Whether one takes Lord Reid's language, which was adopted by Orr and Browne LJJ in *The Puerto Buitrago*, or Lord Denning MR's language in that case ('in all reason'), or Kerr J's language in *The Odenfeld* ('wholly unreasonable . . . quite unrealistic, unreasonable and untenable'), there comes a point at which the court will cease, on general equitable principles, to allow the innocent party to enforce his contract according to its strict legal terms. How one defines that point is obviously a matter of some difficulty, for it involves drawing a line between conduct which is merely unreasonable (see per Lord Reid in *White & Carter* v *McGregor* [1961] 3 All ER 1178 at 1182, [1962] AC 413 at 429–430) and conduct which is wholly unreasonable (see per Kerr J in *The Odenfeld* [1978] 2 Lloyd's Rep 357 at 374). But however difficult it may be to define the point, that there is such a point seems to me to have been accepted both by the Court of Appeal in *The Puerto Buitrago* and by Kerr J in *The Odenfeld*.

I appreciate that the House of Lords has recently re-emphasised the importance of certainty in commercial contracts, when holding that there is no equitable jurisdiction to relieve against the consequences of the withdrawal clause in a time charter: see *Scandinavian Trading Tanker Co. AB* v *Flota Petrolera Ecuatoriana, The Scaptrade* [1983] 2 All ER 763, [1983] 3 WLR 203. I appreciate, too, that the importance of certainty was one of the main reasons urged by Lord Hodson in *White & Carter* v *McGregor* in upholding the innocent party's unfettered right to elect. But, for reasons already mentioned, it seems to me that this court is bound to hold that there is *some* fetter, if only in extreme cases; and, for want of a better way of describing that fetter, it is safest for this court to use the language of Lord Reid, which, as I have already said, was adopted by a majority of the Court of Appeal in *The Puerto Buitrago*.

NOTE: In *Ocean Marine Navigation Ltd* v *Koch Carbon Inc., The Dynamic* [2003] EWHC 1936 (Comm), [2003] 2 Lloyd's Rep 693, the owner of a vessel claimed to be entitled to rely on the right to hire, available in accordance with the terms of the charterparty, rather than being limited to damages for the charterers' repudiatory breach in not redelivering the vessel on time. The judge, Simon J, considered Lord Reid's limitation in *White & Carter (Councils) Ltd* v *McGregor* [1962] AC 413: 'It may well be that, if it can be shown that a person has no legitimate interest financial or otherwise, in performing the contract rather than claiming damages, he ought not to be allowed to saddle the other party with an additional burden with no benefit to himself' and went on to examine the authorities where the interpretation of this limitation has been discussed, such as *The Puerto Buitrago* [1976] 1 Lloyd's Rep 250, *The Odenfeld* [1978] 2 Lloyd's Rep 357 and *The Alaskan Trader* [1983] 2 Lloyd's Rep 645. He cited the statement by Kerr J in *The Odenfeld* [1978] 2 Lloyd's Rep 357 at p. 373 that 'any fetter on the innocent party's right of election whether or not to accept a repudiation will only be applied in extreme cases, viz. where damages would be an adequate remedy and where an election to keep the contract alive would be wholly unreasonable'. The word 'wholly' in 'wholly unreasonable' added nothing to the test itself and only made it clear that 'the rule is general and the exception only applies in extreme cases'. Simon J considered the binding principles to be:

> **23.** These cases establish the following exception to the general rule that the innocent party has an option whether or not to accept a repudiation: (i)The burden is on the *contract-breaker* to show that the innocent party has no legitimate interest in performing the contract rather than claiming damages. (ii) This burden is not discharged merely by showing that the benefit to the other party is small in comparison to the loss to the contract-breaker. (iii) The exception to the general rule applies only in extreme cases: where damages would be an adequate remedy and where an election to keep the contract alive would be unreasonable.

This approach means that the innocent party's right to elect to affirm is not as restricted as might have been thought and it requires an 'extreme case' for the ability to affirm to be lost. Nevertheless, having affirmed, the ability to continue performance and claim the contract price, is limited by the need to be able to do this without the cooperation of the contract-breaker. Thus, Lord Reid's two limitations relate to two different issues.

B: Termination

The innocent party 'accepts' the repudiatory breach as terminating the contract. Can the innocent party 'accept' the repudiation merely by failing to perform his own future obligations under the contract?

Vitol SA v Norelf Ltd, The Santa Clara
[1996] AC 800 (HL)

Under the terms of the contract for the sale of a cargo, the ship carrying the cargo was to arrive, berth and leave Houston between 1–7 March 1991. After loading the cargo, the contract required specific actions to be taken by the parties. While the cargo was being loaded, the plaintiff buyers sent a telex (on 8 March) purporting to reject the cargo for breach of condition on the basis that the loading would not be completed within the contractual period. The vessel completed loading and sailed on 9 March, but thereafter neither party took any steps to perform the contract. The market price of the cargo fell and the sellers resold it for a much reduced price. The arbitrator held that the buyers' telex constituted an anticipatory repudiatory breach which had been accepted by the sellers as terminating the contract since, to the knowledge of the buyers, they had not taken any steps thereafter to perform the contract. The buyers appealed on this point, arguing that mere inactivity could not constitute acceptance of the repudiation.

Whereas Phillips J, at first instance, upheld the arbitrator's decision and held that the sellers' failure to perform their own contractual obligations constituted 'acceptance' of the buyers' repudiation, the Court of Appeal allowed the buyers' appeal and held that a mere failure to perform contractual obligations could not as a matter of law constitute such acceptance. The sellers appealed. Held: although it was possible as a matter of law for an innocent party to accept a repudiatory breach as terminating the contract simply by failing to perform his own contractual obligations, whether it did so was a question of fact depending on the particular contractual relationship and the particular circumstances of the case. The House of Lords accepted that the factual question of whether there had been an acceptance sufficient to communicate the fact of election to terminate was a matter within the exclusive jurisdiction of the arbitrator (who had found that, by not tendering the bill of lading, the sellers had accepted the buyers' repudiatory breach in the telex as terminating the contract).

LORD STEYN (with whose reasoning the other members of the House of Lords agreed): My Lords, the question of law before the House does not call for yet another general re-examination of the principles governing an anticipatory breach of a contract and the acceptance of the breach by an aggrieved party. For present purposes I would accept as established law the following propositions. (1) Where a party has repudiated a contract the aggrieved party has an election to accept the repudiation or to affirm the contract: *Fercometal SARL v Mediterranean Shipping Co. SA* [1989] AC 788. (2) An act of acceptance of a repudiation requires no particular form: a communication does not have to be couched in the language of acceptance. It is sufficient that the communication or conduct clearly and unequivocally conveys to the repudiating party that that aggrieved party is treating the contract as at an end. (3) It is rightly conceded by counsel for the buyers that the aggrieved party need not personally, or by an agent, notify the repudiating party of his election to treat the contract as at an end. It is sufficient that the fact of the election comes to the repudiating party's attention, e.g. notification by an unauthorised broker or other intermediary may be sufficient: *Wood Factory Pty Ltd v Kiritos Pty Ltd* [1985] 2 NSWLR 105, 146 per McHugh JA, *Majik Markets Pty Ltd v S & M Motor Repairs Pty Ltd (No. 1)* (1987) 10 NSWLR 49, 54 per Young J, and Carter and Harland: *Contract Law in Australia*, 3rd ed. (1996), pp. 689–691, para 1970.

The arbitrator did not put forward any heterodox general theory of the law of repudiation. On the contrary he expressly stated that unless the repudiation was accepted by the sellers and the acceptance was communicated to the buyers the election was of no effect. It is plain that the arbitrator directed himself correctly in accordance with the governing general principle. The criticism of the arbitrator's reasoning centres on his conclusion that 'the failure of [the sellers] to take any further step to perform the contract which was apparent to [the buyers] constituted sufficient communication of acceptance'. By that statement the arbitrator was simply recording a finding that the buyers knew that the sellers were treating the contract as at an end. That interpretation is reinforced by the paragraph in his award read as a whole. The only question is whether the relevant holding of the arbitrator was wrong in law.

It is now possible to turn directly to the first issue posed, namely whether non-performance of an obligation is ever as a matter of law capable of constituting an act of acceptance. On this aspect I found the judgment of Phillips J entirely convincing. One cannot generalise on the point. It all depends on the particular contractual relationship and the particular circumstances of the case. But, like Phillips J, I am satisfied that a failure to perform may sometimes signify to a repudiating party an election by the aggrieved party to treat the contract as at an end. Postulate the case where an employer at the end of a day tells a contractor that he, the employer, is repudiating the contract and that the contractor need not return the next day. The contractor does not return the next day or at all. It seems to me that the contractor's failure to return may, in the absence of any other explanation, convey a decision to treat the contract as at an end. Another example may be an overseas sale providing for shipment on a named ship in a given month. The seller is obliged to obtain an export licence. The buyer repudiates the contract before loading starts. To the knowledge of the buyer the seller does not apply for an export licence with the result that the transaction cannot proceed. In such circumstances it may well be that an ordinary businessman, circumstanced as the parties were, would conclude that the seller was treating the contract as at an end. Taking the present case as illustrative, it is important to bear in mind that the tender of a bill of lading is the pre-condition to payment of the price. Why should an arbitrator not be able to infer that when, in the days and weeks following loading and the sailing of the vessel, the seller failed to tender a bill of lading to the buyer, he clearly conveyed to a trader that he was treating the contract as at an end? In my view therefore the passage from the judgment of Kerr LJ in the *Golodetz* case [*State Trading Corp. of India Ltd v M. Golodetz Ltd (now Transcontinental Affiliates Ltd)*] [1989] 2 Lloyd's Rep 277 at 286, if it was intended to enunciate a general and absolute rule, goes too far. It will be recalled, however, that Kerr LJ spoke of a *continuing* failure to perform. One can readily accept that a continuing failure to perform, i.e. a breach commencing before the repudiation and continuing thereafter, would necessarily be equivocal. In my view too much has been made of the observation of Kerr LJ. Turning to the observation of Nourse LJ [1996] QB 108, 116–117 that a failure to perform a contractual obligation is necessarily and always equivocal I respectfully disagree. Sometimes in the practical world of businessmen an omission to act may be as pregnant with meaning as a positive declaration. While the analogy of offer and acceptance is imperfect it is not without significance that while the general principle is that there can be no acceptance of an offer by silence, our law does in exceptional cases recognise acceptance of an offer by silence. Thus in *Rust* v *Abbey Life Assurance Co. Ltd* [1979] 2 Lloyd's Rep 334 the Court of Appeal held that a failure by a proposed insured to reject a proffered insurance policy for seven months justified on its own an inference of acceptance. See also Treitel *The Law of Contract*, 9th ed. (1995), pp. 30–32. Similarly, in the different field of repudiation, a failure to perform may sometimes be given a colour by special circumstances and may only be explicable to a reasonable person in the position of the repudiating party as an election to accept the repudiation.

My Lords, I would answer the question posed by this case in the same way as Phillips J did. In truth the arbitrator inferred an election, and communication of it, from the tenor of the rejection telex and the failure *inter alia* to tender the bill of lading. That was an issue of fact within the exclusive jurisdiction of the arbitrator.

For these reasons I would allow the appeal of the sellers.

NOTE: In a case note ([1996] CLJ 430), Hedley effectively summarised the position as being that, although acceptance of a repudiation must be communicated, that will be achieved where the 'repudiator has been left in no doubt' that the repudiation has been accepted.

If the injured party accepts the anticipatory repudiatory breach as terminating the contract, then the injured party can claim damages from that time and does not have to wait for the time fixed for performance.

Hochster v De La Tour
(1853) 2 E & B 678; 118 ER 922 (QB)

On 12 April 1852, the defendant agreed to employ the plaintiff as a courier for three months as from 1 June 1852. On 11 May, the defendant wrote to the plaintiff stating that he had changed his mind and that the plaintiff's services were no longer required. On 22 May the plaintiff commenced an action for breach of contract, and the defendant argued that there could be no breach of contract before 1 June. Held: the plaintiff was entitled to commence an action for damages on 22 May and did not have to wait until 1 June.

LORD CAMPBELL CJ: . . . [I]t cannot be laid down as a universal rule that, where by agreement an act is to be done on a future day, no action can be brought for a breach of the agreement till the day for doing the act has arrived. If a man promises to marry a woman on a future day, and before that day marries another woman, he is instantly liable to an action for breach of promise of marriage. If a man contracts to execute a lease on and from a future day for a certain term, and, before that day, executes a lease to another for the same term, he may be immediately sued for breaking the contract. So, if a man contracts to sell and deliver specific goods on a future day, and before the day he sells and delivers them to another, he is immediately liable to an action at the suit of the person with whom he first contracted to sell and deliver them. One reason alleged in support of such an action is, that the defendant has, before the day, rendered it impossible for him to perform the contract at the day: but this does not necessarily follow; for, prior to the day fixed for doing the act, the first wife may have died, a surrender of the lease executed might be obtained, and the defendant might have repurchased the goods so as to be in a situation to sell and deliver them to the plaintiff.
. . . If the plaintiff has no remedy for breach of the contract unless he treats the contract as in force, and acts upon it down to the 1 June 1852, it follows that, till then, he must enter into no employment which will interfere with his promise 'to start with the defendant on such travels on the day and year,' and that he must then be properly equipped in all respects as a courier for a three months' tour on the continent of Europe. But it is surely much more rational, and more for the benefit of both parties, that, after the renunciation of the agreement by the defendant, the plaintiff should be at liberty to consider himself absolved from any future performance of it, retaining his right to sue for any damage he has suffered from the breach of it. Thus, instead of remaining idle and laying out money in preparations which must be useless, he is at liberty to seek service under another employer, which would go in mitigation of the damages to which he would otherwise be entitled for a breach of the contract. It seems strange that the defendant, after renouncing the contract, and absolutely declaring that he will never act under it, should be permitted to object that faith is given to his assertion, and that an opportunity is not left to him of changing his mind. If the plaintiff is barred of any remedy by entering into an engagement inconsistent with starting as a courier with the defendant on the 1 June, he is prejudiced by putting faith in the defendant's assertion: and it would be more consonant with principle, if the defendant were precluded from saying that he had not broken the contract when he declared that he entirely renounced it. Suppose that the defendant, at the time of his renunciation, had embarked on a voyage for Australia, so as to render it physically impossible for him to employ the plaintiff as a courier on the continent of Europe in the months of June, July and August 1852: according to decided cases, the action might have been brought before the 1 June; but the renunciation may have been founded on other facts, to be given in evidence, which would equally have rendered the defendant's performance of the contract impossible. The man who wrongfully renounces a contract into which he has deliberately entered cannot justly complain if he is immediately sued for a compensation in damages by the man whom he has injured: and it seems reasonable to allow an option to the injured party, either to sue immediately, or to wait till the time when the

act was to be done, still holding it as prospectively binding for the exercise of this option, which may be advantageous to the innocent party, and cannot be prejudicial to the wrongdoer. . . . If it should be held that, upon a contract to do an act on a future day, a renunciation of the contract by one party dispenses with a condition to be performed in the meantime by the other, there seems no reason for requiring that other to wait till the day arrives before seeking his remedy by action: and the only ground on which the condition can be dispensed with seems to be, that the renunciation may be treated as a breach of the contract.

NOTE: The injured party must mitigate (see *page 408*) from the date of accepting the breach as terminating the contract. On the facts, the plaintiff had found another engagement to start later in June.

9

Remedies for Breach of Contract

SECTION 1: DAMAGES FOR BREACH OF CONTRACT

The aim of contractual damages is to compensate the injured party for the loss suffered as a result of the other party's breach of contract.

Contractual damages are not punitive and, where the innocent party has suffered no loss, it is not generally considered possible to recover damages which transfer the benefit gained by the guilty party as a result of the breach of contract, even if that breach was deliberate. The innocent party can recover only for his actual loss.

Surrey County Council v *Bredero Homes Ltd*
[1993] 1 WLR 1361 (CA)

The council had sold land to the defendant developer on the basis of a contract which required the developer to develop the land in accordance with the already granted planning permission for 72 houses. After the sale, however, the defendant obtained a new planning permission allowing an additional five houses to be built on the site. The defendant then deliberately breached the contract term requiring it to abide by the original planning permission and constructed the extra houses. The council sought damages for the breach based on the sum from the defendant's profits which they argued the defendant would have had to pay to the council in order to obtain a relaxation of the covenant in the contract. Held: the council was entitled to recover only nominal damages since it had not suffered any loss as a result of the breach, and in financial terms was already in the position it would have been had the covenant been performed.

NOTES
1. See Burrows [1993] LMCLQ 453.
2. It has been argued that the law should be prepared to award restitutionary damages to reverse enrichment gained by a breach of contract (see *pages 435–7*). See Birks (1993) 109 LQR 518. The argument is that this would counter deliberate breaches of contract in these circumstances since there would then be no advantage to the party in breach. Steyn LJ rejected this, partly on the basis that the motive of the party committing the breach is not a factor in assessing damages for breach of contract and also because of reasons of policy:

   . . . The introduction of restitutionary remedies to deprive cynical contract breakers of the fruits of their breaches of contract will lead to greater uncertainty in the assessment of damages in commercial and consumer disputes. It is of paramount importance that the way in which disputes are likely to be resolved by the courts must be readily predictable. Given the premise that the aggrieved party has suffered no loss, is such a dramatic extension of restitutionary remedies justified in order to confer a windfall in each case on the aggrieved party? I think not. In any event such a widespread availability of restitutionary remedies will have a tendency to discourage economic activity in relevant situations. In a range of cases such liability would fall on underwriters who have insured relevant liability risks. Inevitably underwriters would have to be compensated for the new species of potential claims. Insurance premiums would have to go up. That, too, is a consequence which militates against the proposed extension. The recognition of the proposed extension will in my view not serve the public interest. It is sound policy to guard against extending the protection of the law of obligations too widely. For these substantive and policy reasons I regard it as undesirable that the range of restitutionary remedies should be extended in the way in which we have been invited to do so.

See Goodhart, 'Restitutionary Damages for Breach of Contract' [1995] RLR 3.

3. The Law Commission Consultation Paper No. 132, 'Aggravated, Exemplary and Restitutionary Damages', 1993, suggested that gain-based damages should be available if the gain was attributable to an interference with a proprietary or analogous right, or to deliberate wrongdoing which could have been restrained by injunction. If this were accepted much would depend on the meaning of 'proprietary interest'. However, Steyn LJ expressly stated that he considered the link with the availability of a remedy of injunction was unsatisfactory since this was a 'wholly different and discretionary' remedy.

4. In its 1997 Report, 'Aggravated, Exemplary and Restitutionary Damages', No. 247, the Law Commission (paras 3.38–3.47) recommended that there should be no legislation on the question of restitutionary damages for breach of contract as it would be dangerous to attempt to 'freeze' the position in legislative form. Instead, it recommended that the availability of such damages should be left to common law development following support for such a position from those responding to the Consultation Paper.

The House of Lords in *Attorney-General* v *Blake* has held that in very exceptional circumstances it may be possible to obtain an order that the party in breach has to account for a profit made as a result of that breach of contract. This decision has, in principle, the potential to revolutionise the basis on which damages are awarded in contract by introducing a punitive element. Its exact scope is unclear but, because the principle was devised against a very specific and limited factual background, it seems to have been envisaged that the principle would be tightly circumscribed.

Attorney-General v Blake
[2001] 1 AC 268 (HL)

The defendant was a former member of the intelligence services but had become an agent for the Soviet Union. He had been tried and imprisoned for treason but had escaped from prison and fled to Moscow, where he had written his autobiography. The autobiography had been published in England in breach of a term of the defendant's former employment contract that he would not divulge official information. The Attorney-General wished to prevent payment of the book royalties to the defendant. A number of arguments were put at various stages of the action including an argument that the defendant owed a fiduciary duty to the Crown not to use information gained in his former position (rejected at first instance) and a claim in public law to prevent the receipt of any benefit resulting from criminal conduct (rejected by the House of Lords). The Court of Appeal had accepted that the defendant was in breach of contract but held that since the Crown could not establish that it had suffered loss as a result of this breach, it was limited to the recovery of nominal damages. The Court of Appeal did, however, indicate its support for the availability of restitutionary damages for breach of contract in some circumstances, which Lord Woolf MR (giving the judgment of the Court of Appeal) identified as instances of 'skimped performance', i.e. charging the full price but not providing the full performance contracted for, and instances where the profit is obtained by doing the very thing which the person in question contracted not to do. A claim for restitutionary relief was argued on appeal to the House of Lords. Held: (Lord Hobhouse dissenting) in an exceptional case where the normal remedies for breach of contract provided inadequate compensation, the court could grant the discretionary remedy of requiring the defendant to account to the plaintiff for the benefits received from the breach of contract even where the breach of contract did not involve the use of, or interference with, a property interest of the claimant. Such a remedy would give effect to the plaintiff's interest in performance and on these facts it was just that such an account of profits be ordered.

LORD NICHOLLS (with whom Lords Goff, Browne-Wilkinson and Steyn agreed): . . . The basic remedy [for breach of contract] is an award of damages. In the much quoted words of Baron Parke, the rule of the common law is that where a party sustains a loss by reason of a breach of contract, he is, so far as money can do it, to be placed in the same position as if the contract had been performed: *Robinson* v *Harman* (1848) 1 Exch 850, 855. Leaving aside the anomalous exception of punitive damages, damages are compensatory. That is axiomatic. It is equally well established that an award of damages, assessed by reference to financial loss, is not always 'adequate' as a remedy for a breach of contract. The law recognises that a party to a contract may have an interest in performance which is not readily measurable in terms of money. On breach the innocent party suffers a loss. He fails to obtain the benefit promised by the other party to the contract. To him the loss may be as important as financially measurable loss, or more so. An award of damages, assessed by reference to financial loss, will not recompense him properly. For him a financially assessed measure of damages is inadequate.

The classic example of this type of case, as every law student knows, is a contract for the sale of land. The buyer of a house may be attracted by features which have little or no impact on the value of the house. An award of damages, based on strictly financial criteria, would fail to recompense a disappointed buyer for this head of loss. The primary response of the law to this type of case is to ensure, if possible, that the contract is performed in accordance with its terms. The court may make orders compelling the party who has committed a breach of contract, or is threatening to do so, to carry out his contractual obligations. To this end the court has wide powers to grant injunctive relief. The court will, for instance, readily make orders for the specific performance of contracts for the sale of land, and sometimes it will do so in respect of contracts for the sale of goods. In *Beswick* v *Beswick* [1968] AC 58 the court made an order for the specific performance of a contract to make payments of money to a third party. The law recognised that the innocent party to the breach of contract had a legitimate interest in having the contract performed even though he himself would suffer no financial loss from its breach. Likewise, the court will compel the observance of negative obligations by granting injunctions. This may include a mandatory order to undo an existing breach, as where the court orders the defendant to pull down building works carried out in breach of covenant.

All this is trite law. In practice, these specific remedies go a long way towards providing suitable protection for innocent parties who will suffer loss from breaches of contract which are not adequately remediable by an award of damages. But these remedies are not always available. For instance, confidential information may be published in breach of a non-disclosure agreement before the innocent party has time to apply to the court for urgent relief. Then the breach is irreversible. Further, these specific remedies are discretionary. Contractual obligations vary infinitely. So do the circumstances in which breaches occur, and the circumstances in which remedies are sought. The court may, for instance, decline to grant specific relief on the ground that this would be oppressive.

An instance of this nature occurred in *Wrotham Park Estate Co. Ltd* v *Parkside Homes Ltd* [1974] 1 WLR 798. For social and economic reasons the court refused to make a mandatory order for the demolition of houses built on land burdened with a restrictive covenant. Instead, Brightman J made an award of damages under the jurisdiction which originated with Lord Cairns's Act. The existence of the new houses did not diminish the value of the benefited land by one farthing. The judge considered that if the plaintiffs were given a nominal sum, or no sum, justice would manifestly not have been done. He assessed the damages at five per cent of the developer's anticipated profit, this being the amount of money which could reasonably have been demanded for a relaxation of the covenant.

In reaching his conclusion the judge applied by analogy the cases . . . concerning the assessment of damages when a defendant has invaded another's property rights but without diminishing the value of the property. I consider he was right to do so. Property rights are superior to contractual rights in that, unlike contractual rights, property rights may survive against an indefinite class of persons. However, it is not easy to see why, as between the parties to a contract, a violation of a party's contractual rights should attract a lesser degree of remedy than a violation of his property rights. As Lionel D. Smith has pointed out in his article 'Disgorgement of the profits of Breach of Contract: Property, Contract and "Efficient Breach" ' (1995) 24 Can BLJ 121, it is not clear why it should be any more permissible to expropriate personal rights than it is permissible to expropriate property rights.

[He then considered *Surrey C.C.* v *Bredero Homes Ltd* and continued:]

[*Surrey* v *Bredero*] is a difficult decision. It has attracted criticism from academic commentators and also in judgments of Sir Thomas Bingham MR and Millett LJ in *Jaggard* v *Sawyer* [1995] 1 WLR 269. I need not pursue the detailed criticisms. In the *Bredero* case Dillon LJ himself noted, at p. 1364, that had the covenant been worded differently, there could have been provision for payment of an increased price if a further planning permission were forthcoming. That would have been enforceable. But, according to the *Bredero* decision, a covenant not to erect any further houses without permission, intended to achieve the same result, may be breached with impunity. That would be a sorry reflection on the law. Suffice to say, in so far as the *Bredero* decision is inconsistent with the approach adopted in the *Wrotham Park* case, the latter approach is to be preferred.

The *Wrotham Park* case, therefore, still shines, rather as a solitary beacon, showing that in contract as well as tort damages are not always narrowly confined to recoupment of financial loss. In a suitable case damages for breach of contract may be measured by the benefit gained by the wrongdoer from the breach. The defendant must make a reasonable payment in respect of the benefit he has gained. In the present case the Crown seeks to go further. The claim is for all the profits of Blake's book which the publisher has not yet paid him. This raises the question whether an account of profits can ever be given as a remedy for breach of contract. The researches of counsel have been unable to discover any case where the court has made such an order on a claim for breach of contract. In *Tito* v *Waddell (No. 2)* [1977] Ch 106, 332, a decision which has proved controversial, Sir Robert Megarry VC said that, as a matter of fundamental principle, the question of damages was 'not one of making the defendant disgorge' his gains, in that case what he had saved by committing the wrong, but 'one of compensating the plaintiff.' In *Occidental Worldwide Investment Corporation* v *Skibs A/S Avanti* [1976] 1 Lloyd's Rep 293, 337, Kerr J summarily rejected a claim for an account of profits when ship owners withdrew ships on a rising market.

There is a light sprinkling of cases where courts have made orders having the same effect as an order for an account of profits, but the courts seem always to have attached a different label. A person who, in breach of contract, sells land twice over must surrender his profits on the second sale to the original buyer. Since courts regularly make orders for the specific performance of contracts for the sale of land, a seller of land is, to an extent, regarded as holding the land on trust for the buyer: *Lake* v *Bayliss* [1974] 1 WLR 1073. In *Reid-Newfoundland Co.* v *Anglo-American Telegraph Co. Ltd* [1912] AC 555 a railway company agreed not to transmit any commercial messages over a particular telegraph wire except for the benefit and account of the telegraph company. The Privy Council held that the railway company was liable to account as a trustee for the profits it wrongfully made from its use of the wire for commercial purposes. In *British Motor Trade Association* v *Gilbert* [1951] 2 All ER 641 the plaintiff suffered no financial loss but the award of damages for breach of contract effectively stripped the wrongdoer of the profit he had made from his wrongful venture into the black market for new cars.

These cases illustrate that circumstances do arise when the just response to a breach of contract is that the wrongdoer should not be permitted to retain any profit from the breach. In these cases the courts have reached the desired result by straining existing concepts. Professor Peter Birks has deplored the 'failure of jurisprudence when the law is forced into this kind of abusive instrumentalism:' see 'Profits of Breach of Contract' (1993) 109 LQR 518, 520). Some years ago Professor Dawson suggested there is no inherent reason why the technique of equity courts in land contracts should not be more widely employed, not by granting remedies as the by-product of a phantom 'trust' created by the contract, but as an alternative form of money judgment remedy. That well known ailment of lawyers, a hardening of the categories, ought not to be an obstacle: see 'Restitution or Damages' (1959) 20 Ohio SLJ 175.

My conclusion is that there seems to be no reason, *in principle*, why the court must in all circumstances rule out an account of profits as a remedy for breach of contract. I prefer to avoid the unhappy expression 'restitutionary damages'. Remedies are the law's response to a wrong (or, more precisely, to a cause of action). When, exceptionally, a just response to a breach of contract so requires, the court should be able to grant the discretionary remedy of requiring a defendant to account to the plaintiff for the benefits he has received from his breach of contract. In the same way as a plaintiff's interest in performance of a contract may render it just and equitable for the court to make an order for specific performance or grant an injunction, so the plaintiff's interest in performance may make it just and equitable that the defendant should retain no benefit from his breach of contract.

The state of the authorities encourages me to reach this conclusion rather than the reverse. The law recognises that damages are not always a sufficient remedy for breach of contract. This is the foundation of the court's jurisdiction to grant the remedies of specific performance and injunction. Even when awarding damages, the law does not adhere slavishly to the concept of compensation for financially measurable loss. When the circumstances require, damages are measured by reference to the benefit obtained by the wrongdoer. This applies to interference with property rights. Recently, the like approach has been adopted to breach of contract. Further, in certain circumstances an account of profits is ordered in preference to an award of damages. Sometimes the injured party is given the choice: either compensatory damages or an account of the wrongdoer's profits. Breach of confidence is an instance of this. If confidential information is wrongfully divulged in breach of a non-disclosure agreement, it would be nothing short of sophistry to say that an account of profits may be ordered in respect of the equitable wrong but not in respect of the breach of contract which governs the relationship between the parties. With the established authorities going thus far, I consider it would be only a modest step for the law to recognise openly that, exceptionally, an account of profits may be the most appropriate remedy for breach of contract. It is not as though this step would contradict some recognised principle applied consistently throughout the law to the grant or withholding of the remedy of an account of profits. No such principle is discernible.

The main argument against the availability of an account of profits as a remedy for breach of contract is that the circumstances where this remedy may be granted will be uncertain. This will have an unsettling effect on commercial contracts where certainty is important. I do not think these fears are well founded. I see no reason why, *in practice*, the availability of the remedy of an account of profits need disturb settled expectations in the commercial or consumer world. An account of profits will be appropriate only in exceptional circumstances. Normally the remedies of damages, specific performance and injunction, coupled with the characterisation of some contractual obligations as fiduciary, will provide an adequate response to a breach of contract. It will be only in exceptional cases, where those remedies are inadequate, that any question of accounting for profits will arise. No fixed rules can be prescribed. The court will have regard to all the circumstances, including the subject matter of the contract, the purpose of the contractual provision which has been breached, the circumstances in which the breach occurred, the consequences of the breach and the circumstances in which relief is being sought. A useful general guide, although not exhaustive, is whether the plaintiff had a legitimate interest in preventing the defendant's profit-making activity and, hence, in depriving him of his profit.

It would be difficult, and unwise, to attempt to be more specific. In the Court of Appeal [1998] Ch 439 Lord Woolf MR suggested there are at least two situations in which justice requires the award of restitutionary damages where compensatory damages would be inadequate: see p. 458. Lord Woolf

MR was not there addressing the question of when an account of profits, in the conventional sense, should be available. But I should add that, so far as an account of profits is concerned, the suggested categorisation would not assist. The first suggested category was the case of 'skimped' performance, where the defendant fails to provide the full extent of services he has contracted to provide. He should be liable to pay back the amount of expenditure he saved by the breach. This is a much discussed problem. But a part refund of the price agreed for services would not fall within the scope of an account of profits as ordinarily understood. Nor does an account of profits seem to be needed in this context. The resolution of the problem of cases of skimped performance, where the plaintiff does not get what was agreed, may best be found elsewhere. If a shopkeeper supplies inferior and cheaper goods than those ordered and paid for, he has to refund the difference in price. That would be the outcome of a claim for damages for breach of contract. That would be so, irrespective of whether the goods in fact served the intended purpose. There must be scope for a similar approach, without any straining of principle, in cases where the defendant provided inferior and cheaper services than those contracted for.

The second suggested category was where the defendant has obtained his profit by doing the very thing he contracted not to do. This category is defined too widely to assist. The category is apt to embrace all express negative obligations. But something more is required than mere breach of such an obligation before an account of profits will be the appropriate remedy.

Lord Woolf MR [1998] Ch 439, 457, 458, also suggested three facts which should not be a sufficient ground for departing from the normal basis on which damages are awarded: the fact that the breach was cynical and deliberate; the fact that the breach enabled the defendant to enter into a more profitable contract elsewhere; and the fact that by entering into a new and more profitable contract the defendant put it out of his power to perform his contract with the plaintiff. I agree that none of these facts would be, by itself, a good reason for ordering an account of profits.

The present case

The present case is exceptional. The context is employment as a member of the security and intelligence services. Secret information is the lifeblood of these services. In the 1950s Blake deliberately committed repeated breaches of his undertaking not to divulge official information gained as a result of his employment. He caused untold and immeasurable damage to the public interest he had committed himself to serve. In 1990 he published his autobiography, a further breach of his express undertaking. By this time the information disclosed was no longer confidential. In the ordinary course of commercial dealings the disclosure of non-confidential information might be regarded as venial. In the present case disclosure was also a criminal offence under the Official Secrets Acts, even though the information was no longer confidential. . . .

When he joined the Secret Intelligence Service Blake expressly agreed in writing that he would not disclose official information, during or after his service, in book form or otherwise. He was employed on that basis. That was the basis on which he acquired official information. The Crown had and has a legitimate interest in preventing Blake profiting from the disclosure of official information, whether classified or not, while a member of the service and thereafter. Neither he, nor any other member of the service, should have a financial incentive to break his undertaking. It is of paramount importance that members of the service should have complete confidence in all their dealings with each other, and that those recruited as informers should have the like confidence. Undermining the willingness of prospective informers to co-operate with the services, or undermining the morale and trust between members of the services when engaged on secret and dangerous operations, would jeopardise the effectiveness of the service. An absolute rule against disclosure, visible to all, makes good sense.

In considering what would be a just response to a breach of Blake's undertaking the court has to take these considerations into account. The undertaking, if not a fiduciary obligation, was closely akin to a fiduciary obligation, where an account of profits is a standard remedy in the event of breach. Had the information which Blake has now disclosed still been confidential, an account of profits would have been ordered, almost as a matter of course. In the special circumstances of the intelligence services, the same conclusion should follow even though the information is no longer confidential. That would be a just response to the breach. . . .

NOTES

1. This decision will inevitably lead to yet more academic debate on this fundamental issue. See, e.g., Hedley (2000) 4 Web JCL 1 and Campbell (2002) 65 MLR 256. In particular, the debate will focus on the circumstances when this principle will be applicable. The comments of Lord Nicholls on this matter are far too general to be of much assistance although it seems that, as a general guide, it will be necessary for a claimant to establish that he has 'a legitimate interest in preventing the defendant's profit-making activity and, hence, in depriving him of his profit'. It is submitted that this is far too wide and gives the green light to the formulation of claims despite the alternative emphasis on the exceptional nature of this remedy. It may also be significant that, as Lord Steyn noted, the defendant's position in *Blake* was closely analogous to that of a fiduciary and this may well prove to be the factor used by the courts to limit the scope of this remedy to the 'exceptional case' envisaged.

2. It is important to note that the House of Lords does not accept the categories for any restitutionary remedy of disgorgement which had been identified by Lord Woolf in the Court of Appeal.

3. Only Lord Hobhouse dissented on the issue of liability to account for profits. He emphasised the essential distinction between restitution (property based) and contract (based on the compensation principle). He regarded the essence of restitutionary remedies as 'the procuring by the courts of the *performance* by the defendant of his obligations. The plaintiff recovers what he is actually entitled to, not some monetary substitute for it. If what the plaintiff is entitled to is wealth expressed in monetary terms, the order will be for the payment of money but this does not alter the character of the remedy or of the right being recognised. He gets the money because it was his property or he was in some other way entitled to it. It is still the enforced performance of an obligation'. Lord Hobhouse did not see how this could be relevant on the facts since the Crown no longer had any right to enforce against the defendant. The remedy being awarded by the majority was 'a remedy based on proprietary principles when the necessary proprietary principles are absent'.

4. Lord Hobhouse (dissenting) also expressed some concern that the principle formulated by the majority should not be extended without a full appreciation of the consequences in the context of commercial contracts.

> LORD HOBHOUSE (dissenting): . . . I must also sound a further note of warning that if some more extensive principle of awarding non-compensatory damages for breach of contract is to be introduced into our commercial law the consequences will be very far reaching and disruptive. I do not believe that such is the intention of your Lordships but if others are tempted to try to extend the decision of the present exceptional case to commercial situations so as to introduce restitutionary rights beyond those presently recognised by the law of restitution, such a step will require very careful consideration before it is acceded to.

In the event of a breach of a commercial contract, the innocent party would be expected to mitigate and would only recover damages to compensate for losses on this basis. The remedy of an account of profits would bypass mitigation and would almost certainly involve causation questions and complex and difficult calculations in arriving at the appropriate profit figure.

5. There is evidence that an account of profits is increasingly being claimed as a potential remedy in the commercial context. In *Esso Petroleum Co Ltd* v *Niad Ltd*, unrep. 22 November 2001 (noted by Beatson (2002) 118 LQR 377), Morritt VC applied the principle in *Blake* in concluding that an account of profits was an available remedy on the facts, involving a breach of a commercial contract.

Esso Petroleum Co Ltd v *Niad Ltd*
Unrep. 22 November 2001

The defendant was the owner of a petrol service station and had a solus agreement (for the exclusive supply of petrol) with the claimant oil company. In 1996 the claimant had introduced a marketing scheme, 'Pricewatch', which the defendant had agreed to implement. This involved the owners of petrol stations reporting prices charged by local competitors which the claimant took into account in setting the price to be charged by its petrol stations. In return for implementing the scheme and agreeing to charge the price specified, the defendant received a discount on the price it paid the claimant for petrol. The evidence was that, in breach of contract, the defendant had failed to implement the scheme, despite repeated assurances that he would do so, and had kept the discount received from the claimant. The claimant therefore wished to determine whether in principle it was entitled to an account of profits or restitution of the amount charged by the defendant in excess of the price recommended by the claimant. Held: in principle alternative remedies of an account of profits or restitution of the amount by which the charges for petrol exceeded the claimant's recommended prices, were available. On the basis of the decision in *Blake*, an account of profits would only be granted in exceptional circumstances where the usual remedies for breach of contract were inadequate and the claimant had a legitimate interest in preventing the defendant from profiting from the breach. This was such an exceptional case since damages were inadequate. The claimant was unable to recover damages for this breach because it could not establish the lost sales attributable to the individual defendant's failure to implement the scheme. However, the defendant's obligation to implement the price reductions had been fundamental to the 'Pricewatch' scheme and, since the breach threatened to undermine this scheme, the claimant had the necessary legitimate interest in preventing the defendant from profiting from the breach to allow an account of profits to be ordered.

NOTES

1. Although the remedy of account of profits was available in principle, Morritt VC recognised that in practice that it might not be easily obtained since the claimant would have to establish the necessary causal link between the defendant's breach and lost sales. He concluded (at [56]) that, as a result, the claimant would not be able to recover as much as in relation to a restitutionary claim. The restitutionary claim was clearly regarded as the more appropriate remedy [at 64] since this would permit the recovery on the basis of unjust enrichment of the full amount by which the charges for petrol exceeded the claimant's recommended prices. In the light of the fact that the case of *Esso Petroleum* v *Niad* hardly has an 'exceptional' set of case facts in the commercial context and in view of the alternative restitutionary remedy, it is difficult to see how the argument in favour of allowing such a use of the *Blake* principle can be defended.

2. The decision of the Court of Appeal in *Experience Hendrix LLC* v *PPX Enterprises Inc* [2003] EWCA Civ 323, [2003] 1 All ER (Comm) 830, has provided some assistance in setting the limits for the use of the *Blake* principle in the commercial context and explaining its relationship with the principle in *Wrotham Park Estate Co Ltd* v *Parkside Homes Ltd* [1974] 1 WLR 798 (discussed by Lord Nicholls in *Blake*, extract at *page 356*). This case concerned breaches of a 1973 settlement agreement relating to masters of titles and licences of the music of Jimi Hendrix. Injunctions had been issued to prevent breaches by PPX of the settlement agreement but Buckley J had dismissed a claim for damages and an account of profits relating to past breaches. The claimant had therefore appealed on this question to the Court of Appeal. There was no evidence to establish the financial loss suffered by the appellant as a result of the breaches so it sought the amount it could reasonably have demanded to relax the prohibitions in the settlement agreement or the profit attributable to the exploitation of the material (i.e., the *Wrotham Park* principle; the loss was the sum that could have been extracted as the price of consent to the development). Mance LJ (with whose judgment Peter Gibson LJ and Hooper J agreed) noted the exceptional features of *Blake*:

(i) The context of Blake's employment in the security and intelligence service whose operation was dependent on secret information;

(ii) The deliberate and repeated breaches and the fact that Blake's notoriety meant that he could command considerable sums for his publication;

(iii) The contractual undertaking he had given was closely akin to a fiduciary obligation where an account of profits is a common remedy.

However, the Court of Appeal concluded that *Hendrix* was not an exceptional case within the principle in *Blake*. Mance LJ noted that features (i) and (iii) were missing on these facts (and, of course, they were also missing in *Esso* v *Niad*), although the fact that an injunction had been issued in relation to future breaches established that the appellant had a legitimate interest in preventing this profit-making activity. *Niad* was distinguished on the basis that in that case the defendant's breaches were fundamental to the scheme and questioned its viability. Mance LJ added (at [44]), as a practical point, that 'Here, the breaches, though deliberate, took place in a commercial context. PPX, though knowingly and deliberately breaching its contract, acted as it did in the course of a business, to which it no doubt gave some expenditure of time and effort and probably the use of connections and some skill . . . An account of profits would involve a detailed assessment of such matters, which, as is very clear from *Blake*, should not lightly be ordered.' Accordingly, he concluded that PPX should pay the sum that might reasonably be demanded by the Hendrix estate to release the prohibition (*Wrotham Park*). Such an assessment would allow such commercial considerations and the broader context to be taken into account and, it is submitted, will often be a more appropriate remedy in this context than an account of profits.

Peter Gibson LJ agreed that this was not an appropriate case for ordering an account of profits, adding (at [53]) 'No doubt deliberate breaches of contract occur frequently in the commercial world; yet something more is needed to make the circumstances exceptional enough to justify ordering an account of profits, particularly when another remedy is available.' It is to be hoped that this may impose some restraint on claims for accounts of profits in relation to commercial contracts.

3. In *Lane* v *O'Brien Homes Ltd* [2004] EWHC 303 (QB), unrep. 5 February 2004 (noted Campbell (2004) 67 MLR 817), Clarke J awarded substantial damages on the basis of the *Wrotham Park* principle. Lane had sold a site to O'Brien on which O'Brien was to build houses. The sale was subject to an oral collateral contract limiting the number of houses to be built to three. O'Brien built four houses in breach of this oral collateral contract and damages of £150,000 had been awarded representing the value of the 'loss of chance of the bargaining position' that Lane possessed when negotiating any release from the undertaking to build only three houses. Clarke J, hearing the appeal, considered that *Wrotham Park Estate Company* v *Parkside Homes* was the proper basis for the award, rather than any reference to damages for loss of chance. This principle required the court to consider hypothetical negotiations for the release from the restriction to build three houses at the time of the grant of planning permission to build four houses on the land and award damages to represent the amount reasonably required to secure relaxation of the 'covenant' (or undertaking in this case). (There was no restrictive covenant in this case, only an oral collateral undertaking to build no more than three houses.) Clarke J considered that the case law did not provide that such damages were limited to a small percentage of the purchaser's potential profit arising from the breach of the undertaking (although only 5 per cent had been awarded in *Wrotham Park*). He did not think that the judge had acted erroneously in awarding damages of £150,000. Thus it is clear that the potential profit is the starting point for any assessment of such damages and the actual award in *Lane* represents a sizeable proportion of the profit made on the sale of the fourth house, around £280,000. Counsel had argued that the decision in *Blake* suggested that the law was moving to a position of accepting awards of the entire profit rather than a share of it. However, the judge considered that 'the factual context of that case . . . is so far from the present case that I do not find it helpful in my task'.

Counsel did not pursue an argument that Lane should be limited to nominal damages since no loss had been suffered and Clarke J noted that such a result would not have appealed to the court. This decision indicates that in the lower courts there has been a movement away from *Surrey CC* v *Bredero* to widespread acceptance of the *Wrotham Park* principle, i.e. damages as the price of release from the contractual obligation.

■ QUESTION

Is a *Wrotham Park* award compensatory, or does it make restitution for wrongful enrichment?

A: Expectation loss

Contractual damages are usually awarded to compensate for the injured party's loss of expectation, i.e., what the injured party would have received had the contract been properly performed. In *Robinson* v *Harman* (1848) 1 Exch 850, Parke B said (at p. 855): 'The rule of the common law is, that where a party sustains a loss by reason of a breach of contract, he is, so far as money can do it, to be placed in the same situation, with respect to damages, as if the contract had been performed.'

(a) Measurement: difference in value

One measure is the difference in value between what the injured party expected to receive and what he actually did receive, e.g., in relation to defective goods, the measure will be the difference in value between the goods as promised and the goods actually received.

SALE OF GOODS ACT 1979

50. Damages for non-acceptance

(3) Where there is an available market for the goods in question the measure of damages is prima facie to be ascertained by the difference between the contract price and the market or current price at the time or times when the goods ought to have been accepted or (if no time was fixed for acceptance) at the time of the refusal to accept.

51. Damages for non-delivery

(3) Where there is an available market for the goods in question the measure of damages is prima facie to be ascertained by the difference between the contract price and the market or current price of the goods at the time or times when they ought to have been delivered or (if no time was fixed) at the time of the refusal to deliver.

■ QUESTION

Can the damages awarded to the seller, in the event of the buyer's failure to accept, include the loss of profit on this sale which does not actually take place (a 'lost volume' sale)?

If there is an unlimited supply of the goods in question, one sale will have been lost and the loss of profit on that sale can be recovered.

Thompson (W. L.) Ltd v *Robinson (Gunmakers) Ltd*
[1955] Ch 177

The defendant company refused to accept delivery of a 'Vanguard' motor car which they had contracted to buy from the plaintiffs, who were motor dealers. The

'Vanguard' car was readily available. Although the dealers took the car back, the plaintiffs contended that they were still entitled to the lost profit on the repudiated sale, namely £61. The defendants, relying on s. 50(3), Sale of Goods Act contended that the plaintiffs' loss was only nominal. Held: there was no available market for the goods within s. 50(3), and therefore the loss of the bargain meant a loss of profit.

UPJOHN J: . . . [I]t would seem to me on the facts which I have to consider to be quite plain that the plaintiffs' loss in this case is the loss of their bargain. They have sold one 'Vanguard' less than they otherwise would. The plaintiffs, as the defendants must have known, are in business as dealers in motor-cars and make their profit in buying and selling motor-cars, and what they have lost is their profit on the sale of this 'Vanguard.' There is no authority exactly in point in this country, although it seems to me that the principle to be applied is a clear one. It is to be found in *In re Vic Mill Ltd* [1913] 1 Ch 465. In that case the supplier was to supply certain machines which he had to make, and they were to be made to the particular specification of the purchaser although they were of a type generally in common use. It was not the present case of a sale by a motor-dealer of a standardised product. The purchaser repudiated his order, and with a view to mitigating damages the supplier, on getting another order for somewhat similar machinery, very sensibly made such alterations as were necessary to the machinery that he had made for the original purchaser and sold the machinery so altered to the second purchaser. His costs of doing that were comparatively trivial. It was said by the supplier that the measure of his damages was the loss of his bargain; by the purchaser that the measure of damages was merely the cost of the conversion of the machinery for the second purchaser and his slight loss on the re-sale . . .

Buckley LJ put the matter succinctly in this way:

> As regards No. 1, where the goods were manufactured, the respondents are, I think, entitled to both profits, because they were not bound to give the appellants the benefit of another order that the respondents had received. The respondents were left with these goods on their hands. They altered them and sold them to another buyer, but they could have made, and would otherwise, I suppose, have made, other goods for that buyer, and not employed these goods for that purpose. If they had done so, they would have made both profits.

It seems to me that in principle that covers this case. True, the motor-car in question was not sold to another purchaser, but the plaintiffs did what was reasonable, they got out of their bargain with George Thompson Ld., but they sold one less 'Vanguard,' and lost their profit on that transaction . . .

The main case, however, put by the defendants is this: they submit that subsection (3) of section 50 applies, because they say that there is an available market for the goods in question, and in that available market we know that the price of the 'Vanguard' is fixed. It is fixed by the manufacturers. Therefore, they say, the measure of damages must necessarily be little more than nominal. Had the plaintiffs kept the car and sold it to another at a later stage, no doubt they would have been entitled to the costs of storage in the meantime, possibly interest on their money laid out, and so on, but as they had in fact mitigated their damages by getting out of the contract, damages are nil.

. . . [A]n 'available market' merely means that the situation in the particular trade in the particular area was such that the particular goods could freely be sold, and that there was a demand sufficient to absorb readily all the goods that were thrust on it, so that if a purchaser defaulted, the goods in question could readily be disposed of. Indeed, such was the situation in the motor trade until very recently. It was, of course, notorious that dealers all over the country had long waiting lists for new motor-cars. People put their names down and had to wait five or six years, and whenever a car was spared by the manufacturer from export it was snatched at, and if any purchaser fell out there were many waiting to take his place, and it was conceded that if those circumstances were still applicable to the 'Vanguard' motor-car the claim for damages must necessarily have been purely nominal. But on the assumed facts circumstances had changed in relation to 'Vanguard' motor-cars, and in March of this year there was not a demand in the East Riding which could readily absorb all the 'Vanguard' motor-cars available for sale. If a purchaser defaults, that sale is lost, and there is no means of readily disposing of the 'Vanguard' contracted to be sold so that there is not even on the extended definition an available market.

NOTES
1. If demand exceeds supply then loss of profit is not recoverable (*Charter* v *Sullivan* [1957] 2 QB 117).
2. In *Lazenby Garages Ltd* v *Wright* [1976] 1 WLR 459, the Court of Appeal held that there was no 'available market' for secondhand cars within s. 50(3) since a secondhand car was 'unique'. Therefore, the measure was that in s. 50(2), and the fact that the plaintiffs would sell one car less out of their total of secondhand car sales could not have been contemplated by the defendant. Lord Denning MR stated (at p. 462):

> ... The cases show that if there are a number of new cars, all exactly of the same kind, available for sale, and the dealers can prove that they sold one car less than they otherwise would have done, they would be entitled to damages amounting to their loss of profit on the one car: see the judgment of Upjohn J in *W. L. Thompson* v *Robinson (Gunmakers) Ltd* [1955] Ch 177 ...
>
> But it is entirely different in the case of a secondhand car. Each secondhand car is different from the next, even though it is the same make. The sales manager of the garage admitted in evidence that some secondhand cars, of the same make, even of the same year, may sell better than others of the same year. Some may sell quickly, others may be sluggish. You simply cannot tell why. But they are all different.
>
> In the circumstances the cases about new cars do not apply. We have simply to apply to section 50 of the Sale of Goods Act 1893. There is no 'available market' for secondhand cars. So it is not sub-section (3) but sub-section (2). The measure of damages is the estimated loss directly and naturally resulting in the ordinary course of events from the buyer's breach of contract. That throws us back to the test of what could reasonably be expected to be in the contemplation of the parties as a natural consequence of the breach. The buyer in this case could not have contemplated that the dealer would sell one car less. At most he would contemplate that, if they resold this very car at a lower price, they would suffer by reason of that lower price and should recover the difference. But if they resold this very car at a higher price, they would suffer no loss.
>
> Seeing that these plaintiffs resold this very car for £100 more than the sale to Mr Wright, they clearly suffered no damage at all.

3. Although the normal measure of damages where a supply contract is repudiated will be the loss of profit (net profit) on that contract, in some circumstances (where it is not possible to replace the contract with other work) gross profit can be recovered (less expenses of performance). In *Western Webb Offset Printers Ltd* v *Independent Media Ltd* [1996] CLC 77, the defendant, publishers of a local newspaper, had a printing contract with the plaintiff printers. The defendant repudiated this contract before the end of the contract period. The plaintiff accepted the repudiation as terminating the contract and sought damages of its gross profit on the contract (£176,903, namely the price it would have been paid for the remaining printing under the contract after deducting the direct expenses of carrying out the work, e.g., paper and ink). The plaintiff argued that as a result of the recession it was unable to replace the defendant's contract with other work so that this sum was a loss of turnover otherwise available to cover its fixed overheads. The Court of Appeal awarded damages of £176,903 since the purpose of damages was to compensate the plaintiff for loss caused by the breach. Normally this would be achieved by awarding net profit following a cancellation of a supply contract but where due to the recession it was not possible to find an alternative contract to defray overheads, the plaintiff's loss included loss of gross profit intended to cover these expenses.

(b) Measurement: cost of cure

When, if ever, can the cost of cure be recovered?

Ruxley Electronics & Construction Ltd v *Forsyth*
[1996] 1 AC 344 (HL)

The defendant contracted with the two plaintiff companies for the construction of an enclosed swimming pool in his garden. The contract terms required that the maximum depth of the pool should be 7'6". In fact it was later discovered to be only 6'9" as a maximum, and only 6' at the diving point. When the plaintiffs claimed the unpaid balance of the purchase price, the defendant counterclaimed for breach of contract. The trial judge found as a fact that the pool as constructed was perfectly safe to dive into and that there was no difference in value between the swimming pool contracted for and that supplied. He refused to award the claimed cost of cure damages of £21,560 so that the specified depth could be achieved, on the basis that it would be unreasonable to award such damages which were 'wholly disproportionate to the disadvantage' of having a pool of this depth, and he was not satisfied that the defendant intended to carry out the reconstruction work. Instead the judge awarded £2,500 for loss of amenity. The majority of the Court of Appeal (Staughton and Mann LJJ; Dillon LJ dissenting), allowing the appeal, awarded cost of cure damages on the basis that it was the only way to fulfil the defendant's contractual objective. Reasonableness was not a factor in its own right but was only relevant to mitigation and, given that there was no cheaper way of compensating for the loss, it was not unreasonable to award such cost of cure damages. Although the defendant had given an undertaking to rebuild on the appeal, it was held that this was irrelevant. On appeal Held: (restoring the award of the trial judge) that cost of cure damages could be recovered only if it was reasonable to do so, and it would be reasonable only if the cost was not out of all proportion to the benefit to be obtained. The intention to rebuild was relevant to the reasonableness of awarding cost of cure because otherwise there would not be a loss needing to be compensated. The House of Lords confirmed the award of £2,500 for loss of amenity.

LORD JAUNCEY: . . . Damages are designed to compensate for an established loss and not to provide a gratuitous benefit to the aggrieved party, from which it follows that the reasonableness of an award of damages is to be linked directly to the loss sustained. If it is unreasonable in a particular case to award the cost of reinstatement it must be because the loss sustained does not extend to the need to reinstate. A failure to achieve the precise contractual objective does not necessarily result in the loss which is occasioned by a total failure. This was recognised by the High Court of Australia in the passage in *Bellgrove* v *Eldridge* [(1954) 90 CLR 613, 617–18], where it was stated that the cost of reinstatement work subject to the qualification of reasonableness was the extent of the loss, thereby treating reasonableness as a factor to be considered in determining what was that loss rather than, as the respondents argued, merely a factor in determining which of two alternative remedies were appropriate for a loss once established. Further support for this view is to be found in the following passage in the judgment of Sir Robert Megarry V-C in *Tito* v *Waddell (No. 2)* [1977] Ch 106, 332:

> Per contra, if the plaintiff has suffered little or no monetary loss in the reduction of value of his land, and he has no intention of applying any damages towards carrying out the work contracted for, or its equivalent, I cannot see why he should recover the cost of doing work which will never be done. It would be a mere pretence to say that this cost was a loss and so should be recoverable as damages.

The Vice-Chancellor was as I understand it there saying that it would be unreasonable to treat as a loss the cost of carrying out work which would never in fact be done.

I take the example suggested during argument by my noble and learned friend Lord Bridge of

Harwich. A man contracts for the building of a house and specifies that one of the lower courses of brick should be blue. The builder uses yellow brick instead. In all other respects the house conforms to the contractual specification. To replace the yellow bricks with blue would involve extensive demolition and reconstruction at a very large cost. It would clearly be unreasonable to award to the owner the cost of reconstructing because his loss was not the necessary cost of reconstruction of his house, which was entirely adequate for its design purpose, but merely the lack of aesthetic pleasure which he might have derived from the sight of blue bricks. Thus in the present appeal the respondent has acquired a perfectly serviceable swimming pool, albeit one lacking the specified depth. His loss is thus not the lack of a useable pool with consequent need to construct a new one. Indeed were he to receive the cost of building a new one and retain the existing one he would have recovered not compensation for loss but a very substantial gratuitous benefit, something which damages are not intended to provide.

What constitutes the aggrieved party's loss is in every case a question of fact and degree. Where the contract breaker has entirely failed to achieve the contractual objective it may not be difficult to conclude that the loss is the necessary cost of achieving that objective. Thus if a building is constructed so defectively that it is of no use for its designed purpose the owner may have little difficulty in establishing that his loss is the necessary cost of reconstructing. Furthermore in taking reasonableness into account in determining the extent of loss it is reasonableness in relation to the particular contract and not at large. Accordingly if I contracted for the erection of a folly in my garden which shortly thereafter suffered a total collapse it would be irrelevant to the determination of my loss to argue that the erection of such a folly which contributed nothing to the value of my house was a crazy thing to do. As Oliver J said in *Radford* v *De Froberville* [1977] 1 WLR 1262, 1270:

> If he contracts for the supply of that which he thinks serves his interests—be they commercial, aesthetic or merely eccentric—then if that which is contracted for is not supplied by the other contracting party I do not see why, in principle, he should not be compensated by being provided with the cost of supplying it through someone else or in a different way, subject to the proviso, of course, that he is seeking compensation for a genuine loss and not merely using a technical breach to secure an uncovenanted profit.

However where the contractual objective has been achieved to a substantial extent the position may be very different.

It was submitted that where the objective of a building contract involved satisfaction of a personal preference the only measure of damages available for a breach involving failure to achieve such satisfaction was the cost of reinstatement. In my view this is not the case. Personal preference may well be a factor in reasonableness and hence in determining what loss has been suffered but it cannot per se be determinative of what that loss is.

My Lords, the trial judge found that it would be unreasonable to incur the cost of demolishing the existing pool and building a new and deeper one. In so doing he implicitly recognised that the respondent's loss did not extend to the cost of reinstatement. He was, in my view, entirely justified in reaching that conclusion. It therefore follows that the appeal must be allowed.

. . . The appellant argued that the cost of reinstatement should only be allowed as damages where there was shown to be an intention on the part of the aggrieved party to carry out the work. Having already decided that the appeal should be allowed I no longer find it necessary to reach a conclusion on this matter. However I should emphasise that in the normal case the court has no concern with the use to which a plaintiff puts an award of damages for a loss which has been established. Thus irreparable damage to an article as a result of a breach of contract will entitle the owner to recover the value of the article irrespective of whether he intends to replace it with a similar one or to spend the money on something else. Intention, or lack of it, to reinstate can have relevance only to reasonableness and hence to the extent of the loss which has been sustained. Once that loss has been established intention as to the subsequent use of the damages ceases to be relevant. . . .

LORD MUSTILL: . . . In my opinion there would indeed be something wrong if, on the hypothesis that cost of reinstatement and the depreciation in value were the only available measures of recovery, the rejection of the former necessarily entailed the adoption of the latter; and the court might be driven to opt for the cost of reinstatement, absurd as the consequence might often be, simply to escape from the conclusion that the promisor can please himself whether or not to comply with the wishes of the promisee which, as embodied in the contract, formed part of the consideration for the price. Having taken on the job the contractor is morally as well as legally obliged to give the employer what he stipulated to obtain, and this obligation ought not to be devalued. In my opinion, however, the hypothesis is not correct. There are not two alternative measures of damage, at opposite poles, but only one: namely, the loss truly suffered by the promisee. In some cases the loss cannot be fairly measured except by reference to the full cost of repairing the deficiency in performance. In others, and in particular those where the contract is designed to fulfil a purely commercial purpose, the loss will very often consist only of the monetary detriment brought about by the breach of contract. But these remedies are not exhaustive, for the law must cater for those occasions where the value of the promise to the promisee exceeds the financial enhancement of his position which full performance will secure. This excess, often referred to in the literature as the 'consumer surplus' (see for example the valuable discussion by Harris, Ogus and Phillips (1979) 95 LQR 581) is usually incapable of precise valuation in terms of money, exactly because it represents a personal, subjective and non-monetary gain. Nevertheless, where it exists the law should recognise it and compensate the promisee if the misperformance takes it away. The lurid bathroom tiles, or the grotesque folly instanced in argument by my noble and learned friend Lord Keith of Kinkel, may be so discordant with general taste that in purely economic terms the builder may be said to do the employer a favour by failing to install them. But this is too narrow and materialistic a view of the transaction. Neither the contractor nor the court has the right to substitute for the employer's individual expectation of performance a criterion derived from what ordinary people would regard as sensible. As my Lords have shown, the test of reasonableness plays a central part in determining the basis of recovery, and will indeed be decisive in a case such as the present when the cost of reinstatement would be wholly disproportionate to the non-monetary loss suffered by the employer. But it would be equally unreasonable to deny all recovery for such a loss. The amount may be small, and since it cannot be quantified directly there may be room for difference of opinion about what it should be. But in several fields the judges are well accustomed to putting figures to intangibles, and I see no reason why the imprecision of the exercise should be a barrier, if that is what fairness demands.

My Lords, once this is recognised the puzzling and paradoxical feature of this case, that it seems to involve a contest of absurdities, simply falls away. There is no need to remedy the injustice of awarding too little by unjustly awarding far too much. The judgment of the trial judge acknowledges that the employer has suffered a true loss and expresses it in terms of money. Since there is no longer any issue about the amount of the award, as distinct from the principle, I would simply restore his judgment by allowing the appeal.

LORD LLOYD: [Lord Lloyd cited the judgment of Cardozo J in *Jacob & Youngs Inc.* v *Kent* (1921) 230 NY 239 and continued:]

Cardozo J's judgment is important, because it establishes two principles which I believe to be correct and which are directly relevant to the present case: first, the cost of reinstatement is not the appropriate measure of damages if the expenditure would be out of all proportion to the benefit to be obtained, and secondly, the appropriate measure of damages in such a case is the difference in value, even though it would result in a nominal award.

The first of these principles is contrary to Staughton LJ's view that the plaintiff is entitled to reinstatement, however expensive, if there is no cheaper way of providing what the contract requires. The second principle is contrary to the whole thrust of [counsel for the defendant's] argument that the judge had no alternative but to award the cost of reinstatement, once it became apparent that the difference in value produced a nil result.

[He then cited *Bellgrove* v *Eldridge* (1954) 90 CLR 613, *East Ham BC* v *Bernard Sunley & Sons Ltd* [1966] AC 406 and *G W Atkins Ltd* v *Scott* (1991) 7 Const LJ 215.] . . . It seems to me that in the light of these authorities . . . [counsel for the plaintiff] was right when he submitted, and Dillon LJ was right when he held, that mitigation is not the only area in which the concept of reasonableness has an impact on the law of damages.

If the court takes the view that it would be unreasonable for the plaintiff to insist on reinstatement, as where, for example, the expense of the work involved would be out of all proportion to the benefit to be obtained, then the plaintiff will be confined to the difference in value. If the judge had assessed the difference in value in the present case at, say, £5,000, I have little doubt that the Court of Appeal would have taken that figure rather than £21,560. The difficulty arises because the judge has, in the light of the expert evidence, assessed the difference in value as nil. But that cannot make reasonable what he has found to be unreasonable.

So I cannot accept that reasonableness is confined to the doctrine of mitigation. It has a wider impact . . .

How then does [counsel for the defendant] seek to support the majority judgment? It can only be, I think, by attacking the judge's finding of fact that the cost of rebuilding the pool would have been out of all proportion to the benefit to be obtained. [Counsel] argues that this was not an ordinary commercial contract but a contract for a personal preference. . . .

I am far from saying that personal preferences are irrelevant when choosing the appropriate measure of damages ('predilections' was the word used by Ackner LJ in *G W Atkins Ltd* v *Scott* 7 Const LJ 215, 221, adopting the language of Oliver J in *Radford* v *De Froberville* [1977] 1 WLR 1262). But such cases should not be elevated into a separate category with special rules. If, to take an example mentioned in the course of argument, a landowner wishes to build a folly in his grounds, it is no answer to a claim for defective workmanship that many people might regard the presence of a well-built folly as reducing the value of the estate. The eccentric landowner is entitled to his whim, provided the cost of reinstatement is not unreasonable. But the difficulty of that line of argument in the present case is that the judge, as is clear from his judgment, took Mr Forsyth's personal preferences and predilections into account. Nevertheless, he found as a fact that the cost of reinstatement was unreasonable in the circumstances. The Court of Appeal ought not to have disturbed that finding. . . .

Intention

I fully accept that the courts are not normally concerned with what a plaintiff does with his damages. But it does not follow that intention is not relevant to reasonableness, at least in those cases where the plaintiff does not intend to reinstate. Suppose in the present case Mr Forsyth had died, and the action had been continued by his executors. Is it to be supposed that they would be able to recover the cost of reinstatement, even though they intended to put the property on the market without delay?

There is, as Staughton LJ observed, a good deal of authority to the effect that intention may be relevant to a claim for damages based on cost of reinstatement. The clearest decisions on the point are those of Sir Robert Megarry V-C in *Tito* v *Waddell (No. 2)* [1977] Ch 106 and Oliver J in *Radford* v *De Froberville* [1977] 1 WLR 1262. One of the many questions in the former case was whether the plaintiffs could recover the cost of replanting the plots of land in question, or whether the recovery of damages was limited to the difference in the market value of the land by reason of the work not having been done. Sir Robert Megarry V-C said ([1977] Ch 106, 332): [see extract quoted in the speech of Lord Jauncey, *page 366 above*].

In the present case the judge found as a fact that Mr Forsyth's stated intention of rebuilding the pool would not persist for long after the litigation had been concluded. In these circumstances it would be 'mere pretence' to say that the cost of rebuilding the pool is the loss which he has in fact suffered. This is the critical distinction between the present case and the example given by Staughton LJ of a man who has had his watch stolen. In the latter case, the plaintiff is entitled to recover the value of the watch because that is the true measure of his loss. He can do what he wants with the damages. But if, as the judge found, Mr Forsyth had no intention of rebuilding the pool, he has lost nothing except the difference in value, if any . . .

Does Mr Forsyth's undertaking to spend any damages which he may receive on rebuilding the pool make any difference? Clearly not. He cannot be allowed to create a loss, which does not exist, in order to punish the defendants for their breach of contract. The basic rule of damages, to which exemplary damages are the only exception, is that they are compensatory not punitive.

NOTES

1. See Poole, 'Damages for Breach of Contract—Compensation and "Personal Preferences" ' (1996) 59 MLR 272.
2. Cost of cure damages are an example of compensation that takes account of the innocent party's subjective contractual preferences or subjective valuation of the contractual perform- ance, i.e., that the innocent party's loss may be more than the objective difference in value measure and that the only way to compensate that party is to provide him with the means to fulfil that subjective requirement. (See Harris, Ogus and Phillips, 'The Consumer Surplus' (1979) 95 LQR 581.) In *Attorney-General* v *Blake* [2001] 1 AC 268, Lord Nicholls stated that 'the law recognises that a party to a contract may have an interest in performance which is not readily measured in terms of money'. See also Lord Goff (dissenting) in *Alfred McAlpine Con- struction* v *Panatown Ltd* [2001] 1 AC 518 at 551 (extract at *page 477*).
3. The arguments in favour of awarding cost of cure damages on facts such as these are, first, that not to do so sends the wrong signals to the construction industry by indicating that they will not have to pay substantial damages if they do not fulfil the subjective preferences of the other party specified in the contract where there is no difference in value; second, it can be argued that otherwise the innocent party does not actually receive what he specifically requested under the contract. This assumes that there are to be no limits set by the courts on the ability to compensate for loss of subjective preferences when some limit is clearly called for in order to avoid windfall damages and unjust enrichment to the innocent party as a result of a damages award. The crucial factor in *Ruxley* appears to have been the relative triviality of the breach. Although Mr Forsyth's wishes were relevant, they could not dictate an award of cost of cure damages when reconstruction was not a reasonable course of action in the circumstances. However, the House of Lords did make it clear that there can be no objection in principle to fulfilling unusual tastes where these are contracted for.
4. The conclusion of Staughton and Mann LJJ in the Court of Appeal that there was no require- ment to establish an intention to carry out the repair had also received support from Steyn and Dillon LJJ in *Darlington BC* v *Wiltshier Northern Ltd* [1995] 1 WLR 68, *page 473*, but it has now been revived by the House of Lords as being relevant to reasonableness and estab- lishing the loss sustained. (See the speech of Lord Lloyd *above*.) Thus, there is a distinction between intention for the purposes of identifying a loss, and the situation where there is a clear loss when it is no concern of the courts to assess what the claimant will do with his damages award. See Lord Clyde in *Alfred McAlpine* v *Panatown* [2001] 1 AC 518, extract at *page 475*.
5. It has been argued that the damages in a case like *Ruxley* should be restitutionary damages to prevent unjust enrichment of the contractor by making him liable for the amount he has saved by not performing the obligation in question. However, this was not argued in *Ruxley* and it was rejected in *Surrey* v *Bredero* [1993] 1 WLR 1361. For an outline of other suggested alternatives on damages see Poole (1996) 59 MLR 272, 284–5. Interestingly, in *Attorney- General* v *Blake* [1998] Ch 439 Lord Woolf MR in the Court of Appeal identified cases of 'skimped performance' where compensatory damages would be inadequate, as one of the situations in which restitutionary damages for breach of contract ought to be available. However, this was rejected by the House of Lords in *Attorney-General* v *Blake* [2001] 1 AC 268 in relation to an account of profits. Lord Nicholls considered that 'skimped performance' might be addressed in other ways. It is therefore unlikely that restitutionary damages will be seen as a future solution.
6. For further discussion of the award for loss of amenity see *pages 380–1 below*.
7. See also Loke, 'Cost of Cure or Difference in Market Value? Toward a Sound Choice in the Basis for Quantifying Expectation Damages' (1996) 10 JCL 189, Phang [1996] JBL 362 and O'Sullivan, 'Loss and Gain at Greater Depth: The Implications of the *Ruxley* Decision', in Rose (ed), *Failure of Contracts: Contractual, restitutionary and proprietary consequences* (Hart Publish- ing: Oxford, 1997).

■ **QUESTION**

The example of the folly in the judgment of Lord Jauncey is a useful one in explaining why and where the line on recovery is likely to be drawn. What would the position be if the breach was that the folly had been constructed six inches to the right of the preferred spot? Would counsel for Mr Forsyth have argued that Mr Forsyth was entitled to substantial damages if the pool had been constructed to a depth of 7 feet 5 inches?

Watts v *Morrow*
[1991] 1 WLR 1421 (CA)

The plaintiffs purchased a country house for £177,500 in reliance on the defendant's survey, in which he stated that overall the dwelling house was sound, stable, and in good condition, although there were minor defects. When the plaintiffs took possession, they discovered that there were substantial defects not mentioned in the report which required urgent repair, including renewal of the roof, windows and floor boards. The true value of the house at the date of purchase was therefore only £162,500 (a difference in value of £15,000). The plaintiffs carried out the repairs at a cost of nearly £34,000 and brought an action to recover those costs. At first instance the cost of repairs was awarded. Held: although it was reasonable for the plaintiffs to retain the property and carry out the repairs, the proper measure of damages was the difference in value, since this was the amount required to put the plaintiffs in the position that they would have been in had the survey been carried out properly and the true value of the house paid. If they recovered the cost of repairs they would be recovering damages for breach of warranty as to the condition of the house when no such warranty had been given.

RALPH GIBSON LJ: It was rightly acknowledged for [the plaintiffs] that proof that the plaintiff, properly advised, would not have bought the property does not by itself cause the diminution in value rule to be inapplicable. It was contended, however, that it becomes inapplicable if it is also proved that it is reasonable for the plaintiff to retain the property and to do the repairs. I cannot accept that submission for the following reasons.

(1)   The fact that it is reasonable for the plaintiff to retain the property and to do the repairs seems to me to be irrelevant to determination of the question whether recovery of the cost of repairs is justified in order to put the plaintiff in the position in which he would have been if the contract, i.e. the promise to make a careful report, had been performed. The position is no different from that in *Philips* v *Ward* [1956] 1 WLR 471: the plaintiff would either have refused to buy or he would have negotiated a reduced price. Recovery of the cost of repairs after having gone into possession: that is to say in effect the acquisition of the house at the price paid less the cost of repairs at the later date of doing those repairs, is not a position into which the plaintiff could have been put as a result of proper performance of the contract. Nor is that cost recoverable as damages for breach of any promise by the defendant because, as stated above, there was no promise that the plaintiff would not incur any such cost.

(2)   In the context of the contract proved in this case, I have difficulty in seeing when or by reference to what principle it would not be reasonable for the purchaser of a house to retain it and to do the repairs. He is free to do as he pleases. He can owe no duty to the surveyor to take any cheaper course. The measure of damages should depend, and in my view does depend, upon proof of the sum needed to put the plaintiff in the position in which he would have been if the contract was properly performed, and a reasonable decision by him to remain in the house and to repair it, upon discovery of the defects, cannot alter that primary sum, which remains the amount by which he was caused to pay more than the value of the house in its condition.

NOTE: The surveyor owed a duty to exercise reasonable care and skill in carrying out the survey. He had not warranted that no repairs would be needed. To award the cost of repair would involve treating the surveyor's obligation as strict when it was only qualified. In *Farley* v *Skinner (No. 2)* [2001] UKHL 49, [2002] 2 AC 732, *page 382*, whereas the House of Lords disapproved of the distinction between strict and qualified obligations for the purposes of determining the availability of damages for distress and disappointment, it remains a relevant distinction in terms of recovery of the basic measure of damages.

B: Reliance loss

The injured party may wish to claim for reliance loss ('wasted expenditure'), i.e., the expenses incurred in preparing to perform or performing the contract which have now been wasted as a result of the breach. When can reliance interest damages be claimed?

(a) Where expectation or profit is too speculative

An injured party will be forced to claim for his reliance interest damages where the expectation or profit under the contract is too speculative to establish.

McRae v *Commonwealth Disposals Commission*
(1951) 84 CLR 377 (High Court of Australia)

The Commission invited tenders 'for the purchase of an oil tanker lying on Jourmaund Reef. The vessel is said to contain oil'. The plaintiff's tender of £285 was accepted. The plaintiff spent money in fitting out a salvage expedition but there was no tanker at the location. Held: the Commission was in breach of contract since it had promised that there was an oil tanker at the location given (see *page 495*). The amount that the plaintiff was entitled to recover was £285 (the purchase price) and damages of £3,000 (being the cost of the salvage expedition which was wasted in reliance on the promise that the oil tanker was at the stated location). This salvage expedition was within the reasonable contemplation of the parties. However, since the Commission had not promised to deliver any oil or a tanker of any specified size, the claim for the loss of profit on the tanker and the oil was too speculative.

DIXON J and FULLAGER J (McTiernan J concurring): . . . [I]t is quite impossible to place any value on what the Commission purported to sell. The plaintiffs indeed, on one basis of claim which is asserted in their statement of claim, assessed their damages on the basis of an 'average-sized tanker, 8,000–10,000 ton oil tanker, valued at £1,000,000, allowing for the said tanker lying on Jourmaund Reef, valued at £250,000', and, for good measure, they added their 'estimated value of cargo of oil' at the figure of £50,000. But this, as a basis of damages, seems manifestly absurd. The Commission simply did not contract to deliver a tanker of any particular size or of any particular value or in any particular condition, nor did it contract to deliver any oil.

It was strongly argued for the plaintiffs that mere difficulty in estimating damages did not relieve a tribunal from the responsibility of assessing them as best it could. This is undoubtedly true. In the well-known case of *Chaplin* v *Hicks* [1911] 2 KB 786 Vaughan Williams LJ said:—'The fact that damages cannot be assessed with certainty does not relieve the wrongdoer of the necessity of paying damages for his breach of contract'. That passage, and others from the same case, are quoted by Street CJ in *Howe* v *Teefy* (1927) 27 SR (NSW) 301, but the learned Chief Justice himself states the position more fully. He says:—'The question in every case is: has there been any assessable loss resulting from the breach of contract complained of? There may be cases where it would be impossible to say that any assessable loss had resulted from a breach of contract, but, short of that, if a plaintiff has been deprived of something which has a monetary value, a jury is not relieved from the duty of assessing the loss merely because the calculation is a difficult one or because the circumstances do not admit of the damages being assessed with certainty' . . . It does not seem possible to say that 'any assessable loss has resulted from' non-delivery as such. In *Chaplin* v *Hicks* [1911] 2 KB 786, if the contract had been performed, the plaintiff would have had a real chance of winning the prize, and it seems proper enough to say that that chance was worth something. It is only in another and quite different sense that it could be said here that, if the contract had been performed, the plaintiffs would have had a chance of making a profit. The broken promise itself in *Chaplin* v *Hicks* [1911] 2 KB 786 was, in effect, 'to give the plaintiff a chance': here the element of chance lay in the nature of the thing contracted for itself. Here we seem to have something which cannot be assessed. If there were nothing more in this case than a promise to deliver a stranded tanker and a failure to deliver a stranded tanker, the plaintiffs would, of course, be entitled to recover the price paid by them, but beyond that, in our opinion, only nominal damages.

NOTE: There is a distinction between a loss which is merely speculative and a 'real' loss of a chance, as in *Chaplin* v *Hicks*, where the court should seek to quantify the loss. See also *Allied Maples Group Ltd* v *Simmons & Simmons (a firm)* [1995] 1 WLR 1602, where the plaintiff's loss resulting from the defendant's negligence depended on the hypothetical action of a third party. The Court of Appeal held that the plaintiff could succeed if he proved on the balance of probabilities that there was a substantial chance of the action being taken and not merely a speculative chance. This substantial chance could then be evaluated by the court and would lie 'somewhere between something that just qualifies as real or substantial on the one hand and near certainty on the other'. In *Bank of Credit and Commerce International SA (In Liquidation)* v *Ali (No. 3)* [2002] EWCA Civ 82, [2002] 3 All ER 750, the Court of Appeal applied the same principle and held, in relation to the loss of the chance of employment, that a claimant must show on the balance of probabilities that he had lost 'a substantial chance rather than a speculative one'.

Anglia Television Ltd v *Reed*
[1972] 1 QB 60 (CA)

The defendant, an American actor, contracted with the plaintiffs to play the leading male role in a television play from 9 September to 11 October. On 3 September, the defendant repudiated. The plaintiffs could not get a substitute and abandoned the production. The plaintiffs sued the defendant for damages of £2,750, their total wasted expenditure on the production. The defendant argued that they could only recover the expenditure incurred after they made the contract (£854). The Court of Appeal awarded £2,750. Held: since the plaintiffs had elected to claim their wasted expenditure instead of loss of profits, they could also recover pre-contract expenditure as long as it was reasonably in the contemplation of the parties as likely to be wasted if the contract was broken. (For a discussion of remoteness, see *page 401*.)

LORD DENNING MR: . . . Anglia Television do not claim their profit. They cannot say what their profit would have been on this contract if Mr Reed had come here and performed it. So, instead of claim for loss of profits, they claim for the wasted expenditure. They had incurred the director's fees, the designer's fees, the stage manager's and assistant manager's fees, and so on. It comes in all to £2,750. Anglia Television say that all that money was wasted because Mr Reed did not perform his contract.

Mr Reed's advisers take a point of law. They submit that Anglia Television cannot recover for expenditure incurred *before* the contract was concluded with Mr Reed. They can only recover the expenditure *after* the contract was concluded. They say that the expenditure *after* the contract was only £854.65, and that is all that Anglia Television can recover.

The master rejected that contention: he held that Anglia Television could recover the whole £2,750; and now Mr Reed appeals to this court.

. . . It seems to me that a plaintiff in such a case as this has an election: he can either claim for loss of profits; or for his wasted expenditure. But he must elect between them. He cannot claim both. If he has not suffered any loss of profits—or if he cannot prove what his profits would have been—he can claim in the alternative the expenditure which has been thrown away, that is, wasted, by reason of the breach. That is shown by *Cullinane* v *British 'Rema' Manufacturing Co. Ltd* [1954] 1 QB 292, 303, 308.

If the plaintiff claims the wasted expenditure, he is not limited to the expenditure incurred *after* the contract was concluded. He can claim also the expenditure incurred *before* the contract, provided that it was such as would reasonably be in the contemplation of the parties as likely to be wasted if the contract was broken. Applying that principle here, it is plain that, when Mr Reed entered into this contract, he must have known perfectly well that much expenditure had already been incurred on director's fees and the like. He must have contemplated—or, at any rate, it is reasonably to be imputed to him—that if he broke his contract, all that expenditure would be wasted, whether or not it was incurred before or after the contract. He must pay damages for all the expenditure so wasted and thrown away. This view is supported by the recent decision of Brightman J in *Lloyd* v *Stanbury* [1971] 1 WLR 535. There was a contract for the sale of land. In anticipation of the contract—and before it was concluded—the purchaser went to much expense in moving a caravan to the site and in getting his furniture there. The seller afterwards entered into a contract to sell the land to the purchaser, but afterwards broke his contract. The land had not increased in value, so the purchaser could not claim for any loss of profit. But Brightman J held, at p. 547, that he could recover the cost of moving the caravan and furniture, because it was 'within the contemplation of the parties when the contract was signed.' That decision is in accord with the correct principle, namely, that wasted expenditure can be recovered when it is wasted by reason of the defendant's breach of contract. It is true that, if the defendant had never entered into the contract, he would not be liable, and the expenditure would have been incurred by the plaintiff without redress: but, the defendant having made his contract and broken it, it does not lie in his mouth to say he is not liable, when it was because of his breach that the expenditure has been wasted.

NOTES
1. Expectation loss (i.e., the loss of profits on the television film) was too speculative to be claimed.
2. Although Lord Denning states that an election must be made between recovering expectation and reliance loss, the position is that the injured party cannot recover gross profit as expectation loss as well as the costs of performing the contract, since the gross profit figure includes those costs and it is not possible to recover twice for the same loss. There is no reason, however, why a claim could not be combined for net profit and wasted expenditure since there would then be no double recovery.

In *CCC Films (London) Ltd* v *Impact Quadrant Films Ltd* [1985] 1 QB 16, Hutchison J said (at p. 32):

. . . the plaintiff has an unfettered choice: it is not only in those cases where he establishes by evidence that he cannot prove loss of profit or that such loss of profits as he can prove is small that he is permitted to frame his claim as one for wasted expenditure. I consider that when Lord Denning MR says, 'If he has not suffered any loss of profits—or if he cannot prove what his profits would have been—he can claim in the alternative the expenditure which has been thrown away . . .' and when Sir Raymond Evershed MR says in *Cullinane* v *British 'Rema' Manufacturing Co. Ltd* [1954] 1 QB 292, 303 'if it were shown that the profit-earning capacity was in fact very small, the plaintiff would probably elect so to base his claim', each is describing factors which would be likely to motivate the plaintiff to elect to claim on the lost expenditure basis rather than laying down what must be proved before such a claim can be entertained. In other words, I consider that those cases are authority for the proposition that a plaintiff may always frame his claim in the alternative way if he chooses. I reach this conclusion all the more readily when I reflect that to hold that there had to be evidence of the impossibility of making profits might in many cases saddle the plaintiff with just the sort of difficulties of proof that this alternative measure is designed to avoid.

3. However, the judgment of the High Court of Australia in *Commonwealth of Australia* v *Amann Aviation Pty Ltd* (1991) 66 ALJR 123 (noted Treitel (1992) 108 LQR 226), suggests that there is no right of election between expectation and reliance interest damages. Toohey and McHugh JJ considered that reliance damages could only be recovered in cases where there was either no profit, or where it was not possible to establish a profit with any certainty.

(b) 'Bad bargains'

It is not possible to recover reliance loss to compensate the claimant for having made a 'bad bargain', since this would put an injured party in a better position than if the contract were performed.

C & P Haulage v Middleton
[1983] 1 WLR 1461 (CA)

The defendant granted the plaintiff a contractual licence to occupy premises for the purposes of the plaintiff's work. The plaintiff spent money making the premises suitable by building an enclosing wall and putting in electricity, even though it was expressly provided that fixtures put in by him were not to be removed when the licence expired. The plaintiff was unlawfully ejected by the defendant but the local authority allowed him to use his own garage for business purposes which meant that he saved £60–£100 a week rent. The plaintiff claimed the cost of the improvements to the premises. Held: the court had to endeavour to put the plaintiff in the position that he would have been in had the contract been performed and since the plaintiff had suffered no loss his damages were nominal.

ACKNER LJ: . . . [The defendant] is not claiming for the loss of his bargain, which would involve being put in the position that he would have been in if the contract had been performed. He is not asking to be put in that position. He is asking to be put in the position he would have been in if the contract had never been made at all. If the contract had never been made at all, then he would not have incurred these expenses, and that is the essential approach he adopts in mounting this claim; because if the right approach is that he should be put in the position in which he would have been had the contract been performed, then it follows that he suffered no damage. He lost his entitlement to a further ten weeks of occupation after October 5, and during that period he involved himself in no loss of profit because he found other accommodation, and in no increased expense—in fact the contrary—because he returned immediately to his own garage, thereby saving whatever would have been the agreed figure which he would have to have paid the plaintiffs. . . .

The case which I have found of assistance—and I am grateful to counsel for their research—is a case in the British Columbia Supreme Court: *Bowlay Logging Ltd.* v *Domtar Ltd.* [1978] 4 W.W.R. 105. Berger J., in a very careful and detailed judgment, goes through various English and American authorities and refers to the leading textbook writers, and I will only quote a small part of his judgment. At the bottom of p. 115 he refers to the work of Professor L.L. Fuller and William R. Perdue, Jr., in 'The Reliance Interest in Contract Damages: 1' (1936), 46 Yale Law Jour, 52 and their statement, at p. 79:

'We will not in a suit for reimbursement for losses incurred in reliance on a contract knowingly put the plaintiff in a better position than he would have occupied had the contract been fully performed.'

Berger J., at p. 116, then refers to L. *Albert & Son* v *Armstrong Rubber Co.* (1949) 178 F. 2d 182 in which Learned Hand C.J., speaking for the Circuit Court of Appeals, Second Circuit:

'held that on a claim for compensation for expenses in part performance the defendant was entitled to deduct whatever he could prove the plaintiff would have lost if the contract had been fully performed.'

What Berger J. had to consider was this, p. 105:

'The parties entered into a contract whereby the plaintiff would cut timber under the defendant's timber sale, and the defendant would be responsible for hauling the timber away from the site of the timber sale. The plaintiff claimed the defendant was in breach of the contract as the defendant had not supplied sufficient trucks to make the plaintiff's operation, which was losing money, viable, and claimed not for loss of profits but for compensation for expenditures. The defendant argued that the plaintiff's operation lost money not because of a lack of trucks but because of the plaintiff's inefficiency, and, further, that even if the defendant had breached the contract the plaintiff should not be awarded damages because its operation would have lost money in any case.'

This submission was clearly accepted because the plaintiff was awarded only nominal damages, and Berger J. said, at p. 117:

'The law of contract compensates a plaintiff for damages resulting from the defendant's breach; it does not compensate a plaintiff for damages resulting from his making a bad bargain. Where it can be seen that the plaintiff would have incurred a loss on the contract as a whole, the expenses he has incurred are losses flowing from entering into the contract, not losses flowing from the defendant's breach. In these circumstances, the true consequence of the defendant's breach is that the plaintiff is released from his obligation to complete the contract—or in other words, he is saved from incurring further losses. If the law of contract were to move from compensating for the consequences of breach to compensating for the consequences of entering into contracts, the law would run contrary to the normal expectations of the world of commerce. The burden of risk would be shifted from the plaintiff to the defendant. The defendant would become the insurer of the plaintiff's enterprise. Moreover, the amount of the damages would increase not in relation to the gravity or consequences of the breach but in relation to the inefficiency with which the plaintiff carried out the contract. The greater his expenses owing to inefficiency, the greater the damages. The fundamental principle upon which damages are measured under the law of contract is restitutio in integrum. The principle contended for here by the plaintiff would entail the award of damages not to compensate the plaintiff but to punish the defendant.' . . .

In my judgment, the approach of Berger J. is the correct one. It is not the function of the courts where there is a breach of contract knowingly, as this would be the case, to put a plaintiff in a better financial position than if the contract had been properly performed. In this case the defendant who is the plaintiff in the counterclaim, if he was right in his claim, would indeed be in a better position because, as I have already indicated, had the contract been lawfully determined as it could have been in the middle of December, there would have been no question of his recovering these expenses. . . .

■ QUESTION

Who bears the burden of proving whether the claimant has made a bad bargain, i.e., whether the expenditure would have been recouped?

CCC Films (London) Ltd v *Impact Quadrant Films Ltd*
[1985] 1 QB 16

The plaintiffs had been given a licence by the defendants to exploit, distribute, and exhibit films, but due to the defendants' breach of contract the plaintiffs did not receive the tapes of the films and so could not exploit the licence. Held: where the plaintiff was claiming for reliance expenditure (here the US$12,000 spent on the licence) and had been prevented by the defendant's breach of contract from recouping his expenditure, the onus was on the defendant to show that the expenditure would not have been recouped even if the plaintiff had been able to exploit the licence. On the facts the defendants had not discharged this burden.

HUTCHISON J: . . . (Hutchison J quoted from the judgment of Learned Hand CJ in *L. Albert & Son* v *Armstrong Rubber Co.* (1949) 178 F 2d 182, 189.)

In cases where the venture would have proved profitable to the promisee there is no reason why he should not recover his expenses. On the other hand, on those occasions in which the performance would not have covered the promisee's outlay, such a result imposes the risk of the promisee's contract upon the promisor. We cannot agree that the promisor's default in performance should under this guise make him an insurer of the promisee's venture; yet it does not follow that the breach should not throw upon him the duty of showing that the value of the performance would in fact have been less than the promisee's outlay. It is often very hard to learn what the value of the performance would have been; and it is a common expedient, and a just one, in such situations to put the peril of the answer upon that party who by his wrong has made the issue relevant to the rights of the other. On principle, therefore, the proper solution would seem to be that the promisee may recover this outlay in preparation for the performance, subject to the privilege of the promisor to reduce it by as much as he can show that the promisee would have lost, if the contract had been performed.

[Hutchison J continued:] . . . It seems to me that at least in those cases where the plaintiff's decision to base his claim on abortive expenditure was dictated by the practical impossibility of proving loss of profit rather than by unfettered choice, any other rule would largely, if not entirely, defeat the object of allowing this alternative method of formulating the claim. This is because, notwithstanding the distinction to which I have drawn attention between proving a loss of net profit and proving in general terms the probability of sufficient returns to cover expenditure, in the majority of contested cases impossibility of proof of the first would probably involve like impossibility in the case of the second. It appears to me to be eminently fair that in such cases where the plaintiff has by the defendant's breach been prevented from exploiting the chattel or the right contracted for and, therefore, putting to the test the question of whether he would have recouped his expenditure, the general rule as to the onus of proof of damage should be modified in this manner.

It follows that, the onus being on the defendants to prove that the expenditure incurred by the plaintiffs is irrecoverable because they would not have recouped their expenditure (and that onus admittedly not having been discharged), the plaintiffs are entitled to recover such expenditure as was wasted as a result of such breach or breaches of contract as they have proved.

NOTES
1. Although this case is traditionally cited as authority for the fact that the burden of establishing that it is not a good bargain rests with the guilty party, the Court of Appeal in *Dataliner Ltd* v *Vehicle Builders & Repairers Association* (1995) *Independent*, 30 August, has explained the statement of Hutchison J in *CCC Films* as being that the burden of proof actually depends on the effect of the breach. In general the burden will lie on the innocent party to establish on the balance of probabilities that he made a good bargain (i.e., that but for the defendant's breach he would have recouped this expenditure). For example, in *Dataliner*, where the plaintiff had wasted expenses in attending a trade show which the defendants, as conference organisers, had failed properly to promote, the judge found that the plaintiff's expectation that it would at least recover its expenditure was reasonable and justified. However, if, as in *CCC Films*, the defendant's breach makes it impossible for the claimant to prove that the expenditure would have been recouped, then the burden shifts to the defendant to establish that the claimant would not have recovered his expenditure in any event.
2. This is clearly a preferable position on the burden of proof because, in general, the guilty party will have difficulty discharging this burden where the relevant information is more readily available to the innocent party. However, where it is the guilty party's breach that

prevents the claimant being able to establish that he would have recovered his expenses, the burden should lie with the defendant.

3. The decision in *Commonwealth of Australia* v *Amann Aviation Pty Ltd* (1991) 66 ALJR 123, is a good illustration of the difficulties in establishing whether the expenditure would have been recouped. On the facts it would seem that, even if the contract had not been wrongfully terminated, the company would have recouped its expenditure only if the contract had been renewed for a further term.

C: Damages for disappointment and distress

See Phang 'The Crumbling Edifice? The Award of Contractual Damages for Mental Distress' [2003] JBL 341.

In *Addis* v *Gramophone Company Ltd* [1909] AC 488, the House of Lords held that any damages award for wrongful dismissal must not compensate for injured feelings. (See the attempt to circumvent this in *Johnson* v *Unisys Ltd* [2001] UKHL 13, [2001] 2 WLR 1076, *page 397*.) The House of Lords in *Johnson* v *Gore Wood & Co (A Firm)* [2002] 2 AC 1, approved the general principle in *Addis* that damages for breach of contract should not generally include damages for disappointment and distress (non-pecuniary loss).

There are two exceptional cases where such damages for distress can be recovered in contract.

The authoritative statement of the law is the statement of Bingham LJ in *Watts* v *Morrow* [1991] 1 WLR 1421, 1445:

BINGHAM LJ: . . .

A contract-breaker is not in general liable for any distress, frustration, anxiety, displeasure, vexation, tension or aggravation which his breach of contract may cause to the innocent party. This rule is not, I think, founded on the assumption that such reactions are not foreseeable, which they surely are or may be, but on considerations of policy.

But the rule is not absolute. Where the very object of a contract is to provide pleasure, relaxation, peace of mind or freedom from molestation, damages will be awarded if the fruit of the contract is not provided or if the contrary result is procured instead. If the law did not cater for this exceptional category of case it would be defective. A contract to survey the condition of a house for a prospective purchaser does not, however, fall within this exceptional category.

In cases not falling within this exceptional category, damages are in my view recoverable for physical inconvenience and discomfort caused by the breach and mental suffering directly related to that inconvenience and discomfort. If those effects are foreseeably suffered during a period when defects are repaired I am prepared to accept that they sound in damages even though the cost of the repairs is not recoverable as such. But I also agree that awards should be restrained, and that the awards in this case far exceeded a reasonable award for the injury shown to have been suffered.

This statement was cited with approval by Lord Cooke in *Johnson* v *Gore Wood & Co* [2002] 2 AC 1, at p. 49, and by Lord Steyn in *Farley* v *Skinner (No. 2)* [2001] UKHL 49, [2002] 2 AC 732, at [14]. It was also cited by Lord Bingham himself in *Johnson* v *Gore Wood & Co* at p. 37.

(a) Contracts whose object is to provide peace of mind or freedom from distress

Bliss v South East Thames Regional Health Authority
[1987] ICR 700 (CA)

The plaintiff was employed by the defendant health authority as a consultant orthopaedic surgeon. Following a dispute with a colleague, the Regional Health Authority required him to undergo a psychiatric examination, but the plaintiff refused to comply and was suspended. The plaintiff's solicitors alleged that the defendant had repudiated the plaintiff's employment contract. The plaintiff then brought an action against the defendant health authority for damages for breach of contract, and the judge's award included £2,000 damages for mental distress. Held on appeal: in contract it was not possible to recover damages for distress in cases of wrongful dismissal. The Court of Appeal overruled *Cox* v *Philips Industries Ltd* [1976] 3 All ER 161, which had suggested that such damages were more widely available.

DILLON LJ: It remains to consider . . . the validity of the judge's award of £2,000 with interest by way of general damages for frustration and mental distress. In making such an award, the judge considered that he was justified by the decision of Lawson J in *Cox* v *Philips Industries Ltd* [1976] ICR 138. With every respect to them, however, the views of Lawson J in that case and of the judge in the present case are on this point, in my judgment, wrong.

The general rule laid down by the House of Lords in *Addis* v *Gramophone Co. Ltd* [1909] AC 488 is that where damages fall to be assessed for breach of contract rather than in tort it is not permissible to award general damages for frustration, mental distress, injured feelings or annoyance occasioned by the breach. Modern thinking tends to be that the amount of damages recoverable for a wrong should be the same whether the cause of action is laid in contract or in tort. But in the *Addis* case Lord Loreburn regarded the rule that damages for injured feelings cannot be recovered in contract for wrongful dismissal as too inveterate to be altered, and Lord James of Hereford supported his concurrence in the speech of Lord Loreburn by reference to his own experience at the Bar.

There are exceptions now recognised where the contract which has been broken was itself a contract to provide peace of mind or freedom from distress: see *Jarvis* v *Swans Tours Ltd* [1973] QB 233 and *Heywood* v *Wellers* [1976] QB 446. Those decisions, do not however cover this present case.

In *Cox* v *Philips Industries Ltd* [1976] ICR 138 Lawson J took the view that damages for distress, vexation and frustration, including consequent ill-health, could be recovered for breach of a contract of employment if it could be said to have been in the contemplation of the parties that the breach would cause such distress etc. For my part, I do not think that that general approach is open to this court unless and until the House of Lords has reconsidered its decision in the *Addis* case.

Holiday contracts fall within the category of contracts 'to provide peace of mind' where such damages are recoverable.

Jarvis v Swans Tours Ltd
[1973] QB 233 (CA)

As his annual fortnight's holiday, the plaintiff booked a Christmas skiing holiday with the defendants for £63.45. The defendants' brochure described the holiday as a 'House party' and stated that the hotel had its own 'Alphutte Bar' which would be open several evenings a week. It was also stated that a welcome party, afternoon tea and cakes, a fondue party, and yodeller evening were included in the price. In fact there were only 13 people at the hotel in the first week, and in the second week the plaintiff was the only resident so that there was no house party at all. The skiing did not correspond to the claims in the brochure, the cakes consisted of potato crisps and dry nut cakes, and the yodeller was a man who came in in his working clothes and quickly sang a few songs. The bar was open on one evening. The plaintiff claimed damages for these breaches of contract. Held: the plaintiff was entitled to be compensated for his disappointment and distress at the loss of his holiday and the loss of the facilities which had been promised in the brochure.

LORD DENNING MR: . . . In a proper case damages for mental distress can be recovered in contract, just as damages for shock can be recovered in tort. One such case is a contract for a holiday, or any other contract to provide entertainment and enjoyment. If the contracting party breaks his contract, damages can be given for the disappointment, the distress, the upset and frustration caused by the breach. I know, that it is difficult to assess in terms of money, but it is no more difficult than the assessment which the courts have to make every day in personal injury cases for loss of amenities. Take the present case. Mr Jarvis has only a fortnight's holiday in the year. He books it far ahead, and looks forward to it all that time. He ought to be compensated for the loss of it.

A good illustration was given by Edmund Davies LJ in the course of the argument. He put the case of a man who has taken a ticket for Glyndbourne. It is the only night on which he can get there. He hires a car to take him. The car does not turn up. His damages are not limited to the mere cost of the ticket. He is entitled to general damages for the disappointment he has suffered and the loss of the entertainment which he should have had. Here, Mr Jarvis's fortnight's winter holiday has been a grave disappointment. It is true that he was conveyed to Switzerland and back and had meals and bed in the hotel. But that is not what he went for. He went to enjoy himself with all the facilities which the defendants said he would have. He is entitled to damages for the lack of those facilities and for his loss of enjoyment . . .

I think the judge was in error in taking the sum paid for the holiday £63.45 and halving it. The right measure of damages is to compensate him for the loss of entertainment and enjoyment which he was promised, and which he did not get.

Looking at the matter quite broadly, I think the damages in this case should be the sum of £125.

NOTES

1. An example of a contract the purpose of which is freedom from distress is provided by *Heywood* v *Wellers* [1976] QB 446. The plaintiff employed the defendant solicitors to secure a method of preventing a former male friend from pestering her. The solicitors sought a non-molestation injunction but were negligent in making the application so that the injunction was ineffective, and the plaintiff was molested on three or four further occasions, causing her mental distress and upset. The Court of Appeal awarded damages which included a sum to compensate her for the anxiety and distress she had suffered in consequence of the continued molestation, since this was a direct and foreseeable consequence of the solicitors' failure to obtain the relief which it was *the very purpose* of the contract to secure.

2. In these examples it appears that damages for distress were available in order to compensate the claimant for loss of expectation under those contracts, thereby taking account of 'subjective' losses. *The very purpose* of the contracts had been lost.

3. The scope of this exception had always been limited by the need to show this purpose was 'the very object' of the contract. (See Macdonald (1994) 7 JCL 134, and the 'objects' exception.) This limitation necessarily resulted in the exclusion of commercial contracts from the scope of the exception.

4. In *Ruxley Electronics* v *Forsyth* [1996] 1 AC 344, *page 366*, the House of Lords confirmed the trial judge's award of £2,500 for loss of pleasurable amenity. For tactical reasons there was no substantial argument before the House of Lords regarding this figure or the basis for the award. The only judgment to deal with the matter in any depth is that of Lord Lloyd:

Loss of amenity

I turn last to the head of damages under which the judge awarded £2,500. . . . In the Court of Appeal Mr Forsyth sought to increase the award under this head. According to Staughton LJ this led to an interesting argument. But the Court of Appeal did not find it necessary to deal with the point.

Before your Lordships, [counsel for the defendant] abandoned the point altogether, for what [counsel for the plaintiff] described as forensic reasons. It undermined the main theme of his argument that since difference in value gave Mr Forsyth nothing by way of damages, he must be entitled to the cost of reinstatement. So [counsel for the defendant] was contending that the judge's award of £2,500 was without precedent in the field of damages, and was fundamentally inconsistent with the decision of this House in *Addis* v *Gramophone Co. Ltd* [1909] AC 488. For obvious reasons, [counsel for the plaintiff] did not press the contrary argument. So your Lordships are placed in something of a difficulty. The House does not have the benefit of the views of the Court of Appeal on the point, and the submissions before your Lordships have been artificially restricted.

Addis v *Gramophone Co. Ltd* established the general rule that in claims for breach of contract, the plaintiff cannot recover damages for his injured feelings. But the rule, like most rules, is subject to exceptions. One of the well-established exceptions is when the object of the contract is to afford pleasure, as, for example, where the plaintiff has booked a holiday with a tour operator. If the tour operator is in breach of contract by failing to provide what the contract called for, the plaintiff may recover damages for his disappointment: see *Jarvis* v *Swans Tours Ltd* [1973] QB 233 and *Jackson* v *Horizon Holidays Ltd* [1975] 1 WLR 1468.

This was, as I understand it, the principle which Judge Diamond applied in the present case. He took the view that the contract was one 'for the provision of a pleasurable amenity'. In the event, Mr Forsyth's pleasure was not so great as it would have been if the swimming pool had been 7 feet 6 inches deep. This was a view which the judge was entitled to take. If it involves a further inroad on the rule in *Addis* v *Gramophone Co. Ltd* [1909] AC 488, then so be it. But I prefer to regard it as a logical application or adaptation of the existing exception to a new situation. I should, however, add this note of warning. Mr Forsyth was, I think, lucky to have obtained so large an award for his disappointed expectations. But as there was no criticism from any quarter as to the quantum of the award as distinct from the underlying principle, it would not be right for your Lordships to interfere with the judge's figure.

That leaves one last question for consideration. I have expressed agreement with the judge's approach to damages based on loss of amenity on the facts of the present case. But in most cases such an approach would not be available. What is then to be the position where, in the case of a new house, the building does not conform in some minor respect to the contract, as, for example, where there is a difference in level between two rooms, necessitating a step. Suppose there is no measurable difference in value of the complete house, and the cost of reinstatement would be prohibitive. Is there any reason why the court should not award by way of damages for breach of contract some modest sum, not based on difference in value, but solely to compensate the buyer for his disappointed expectations? Is the law of damages so inflexible, as I asked earlier, that it cannot find some middle ground in such a case? I do not give a final answer to that question in the present case. But it may be that it would have afforded an alternative ground for justifying the judge's award of damages. And if the judge had wanted a precedent, he could have found it in Sir David Cairns' judgment in *G W Atkins Ltd* v *Scott* 7 Const LJ 215, where, it will be remembered, the Court of Appeal upheld the judge's award of £250 for defective tiling. Sir David Cairns said, at p. 221:

> There are many circumstances where a judge has nothing but his common sense to guide him in fixing the quantum of damages, for instance, for pain and suffering, for loss of pleasurable activities or for inconvenience of one kind or another.

The House of Lords has awarded distress damages for so-called 'loss of amenity' on the basis that the *major or important object* of the contract was to provide pleasure, relaxation, or peace of mind.

Farley v *Skinner (No. 2)*
[2001] UKHL 49, [2002] 2 AC 732 (HL)

The plaintiff was considering the purchase of a house situated 15 miles from Gatwick Airport. He employed the defendant surveyor and specifically requested that the defendant should investigate whether the property would be affected by aircraft noise, since he did not wish to live on a flight path. The surveyor's report stated that it was unlikely that the property would suffer greatly from such noise. The plaintiff purchased the property and spent money on modernisation. However, when he moved in, he discovered that the property was badly affected by aircraft noise as it was close to a navigation beacon where aircraft were 'stacked' at busy times awaiting clearance to land. He decided not to sell but wanted to recover damages for the breach of contract. The judge at first instance found that there was no difference between the purchase price and the market value of the property (i.e. no difference in value) but awarded £10,000 as damages for distress consequent upon physical discomfort (see *page 392*) since the noise was 'a confounded nuisance'. The majority of the Court of Appeal allowed the defendant's appeal against this award on the basis that there was no physical inconvenience and the case did not fall within the exceptional category since 'the very object' of the contract was to undertake the survey with reasonable care and skill rather than the provision of pleasure, relaxation, or peace of mind. The obligation to investigate the aircraft noise was a minor aspect of the overall contract purpose. On appeal Held: allowing the appeal and restoring the award of the trial judge, although distress damages for breach of contract were not generally available, they could be awarded for distress and disappointment at the loss of a pleasurable amenity where the provision of that amenity was 'a major or important part of the contract rather than its sole object'. The obligation to investigate the aircraft noise was *a major or important* part of this contract as the plaintiff had specifically asked for confirmation on this matter. Alternatively, and *obiter*, their Lordships considered that the plaintiff might have recovered damages for distress consequent on physical inconvenience. (This aspect of the decision is discussed at *page 392*.)

LORD STEYN (with whose reasons Lord Browne-Wilkinson and Lord Scott agreed):

[Lord Steyn referred to the two exceptions identified by Bingham LJ in *Watts* v *Morrow* [1991] 1 WLR 1421, 1445, *page 378*, and continued:]

. . . The scope of these exceptions is in issue in the present case. It is, however, correct, as counsel for the surveyor submitted, that the entitlement to damages for mental distress caused by a breach of contract is not established by mere foreseeability: the right to recovery is dependent on the case falling fairly within the principles governing the special exceptions. So far there is no real disagreement between the parties.

VI. The very object of the contract: the framework

17 I reverse the order in which the Court of Appeal considered the two issues. I do so because the issue whether the present case falls within the exceptional category governing cases where the very object of the contact is to give pleasure, and so forth, focuses directly on the terms actually agreed between the parties. It is concerned with the reasonable expectations of the parties under the specific terms of the contract. Logically, it must be considered first.

18   It is necessary to examine the case on a correct characterisation of the plaintiff's claim. Stuart-Smith LJ [in the Court of Appeal] [2000] Lloyd's Rep PN 516, 521 thought that the obligation undertaken by the surveyor was 'one relatively minor aspect of the overall instructions'. What Stuart-Smith and Mummery LJJ would have decided if they had approached it on the basis that the obligation was a major or important part of the contract between the plaintiff and the surveyor is not clear. But the Court of Appeal's characterisation of the case was not correct. The plaintiff made it crystal clear to the surveyor that the impact of aircraft noise was a matter of importance to him. Unless he obtained reassuring information from the surveyor he would not have bought the property. That is the tenor of the evidence. It is also what the judge found. The case must be approached on the basis that the surveyor's obligation to investigate aircraft noise was a major or important part of the contract between him and the plaintiff. It is also important to note that, unlike in *Addis* v *Gramophone Co Ltd* [1909] AC 488, the plaintiff's claim is not for injured feelings caused by the breach of contract. Rather it is a claim for damages flowing from the surveyor's failure to investigate and report, thereby depriving the buyer of the chance of making an informed choice whether or not to buy resulting in mental distress and disappointment.

19   The broader legal context of *Watts* v *Morrow* [1991] 1 WLR 1421 must be borne in mind. The exceptional category of cases where the very object of a contract is to provide pleasure, relaxation, peace of mind or freedom from molestation is not the product of Victorian contract theory but the result of evolutionary developments in case law from the 1970s. Several decided cases informed the description given by Bingham LJ of this category. The first was the decision of the sheriff court in *Diesen* v *Samson* 1971 SLT (Sh Ct) 49. A photographer failed to turn up at a wedding, thereby leaving the couple without a photographic record of an important and happy day. The bride was awarded damages for her distress and disappointment. In the celebrated case of *Jarvis* v *Swans Tours Ltd* [1973] QB 233, the plaintiff recovered damages for mental distress flowing from a disastrous holiday resulting from a travel agent's negligent representations: compare also *Jackson* v *Horizon Holidays Ltd* [1975] 1 WLR 1468. In *Heywood* v *Wellers* [1976] QB 446, the plaintiff instructed solicitors to bring proceedings to restrain a man from molesting her. The solicitors negligently failed to take appropriate action with the result that the molestation continued. The Court of Appeal allowed the plaintiff damages for mental distress and upset. While apparently not cited in *Watts* v *Morrow* [1991] 1 WLR 1421, *Jackson* v *Chrysler Acceptances Ltd* [1978] RTR 474 was decided before *Watts* v *Morrow*. In Jackson's case the claim was for damages in respect of a motor car which did not meet the implied condition of merchantability in section 14 of the Sale of Goods Act 1893 (56 & 57 Vict c 71). The buyer communicated to the seller that one of his reasons for buying the car was a forthcoming touring holiday in France. Problems with the car spoilt the holiday. The disappointment of a spoilt holiday was a substantial element in the award sanctioned by the Court of Appeal.

20   At their Lordships' request counsel for the plaintiff produced a memorandum based on various publications which showed the impact of the developments already described on litigation in the county courts. Taking into account the submissions of counsel for the surveyor and making due allowance for a tendency of the court sometimes not to distinguish between the cases presently under consideration and cases of physical inconvenience and discomfort, I am satisfied that in the real life of our lower courts non-pecuniary damages are regularly awarded on the basis that the defendant's breach of contract deprived the plaintiff of the very object of the contract, viz pleasure, relaxation, and peace of mind. The cases arise in diverse contractual contexts, e g the supply of a wedding dress or double glazing, hire purchase transactions, landlord and tenant, building contracts, and engagements of estate agents and solicitors. The awards in such cases seem modest. For my part what happens on the ground casts no doubt on the utility of the developments since the 1970s in regard to the award of non-pecuniary damages in the exceptional categories. But the problem persists of the precise scope of the exceptional category of case involving awards of non-pecuniary damages for breach of contract where the very object of the contract was to ensure a party's pleasure, relaxation or peace of mind.

21   An important development for this branch of the law was *Ruxley Electronics and Construction Ltd* v *Forsyth* [1996] AC 344 . . .

[Lord Steyn discussed the award of £2,500 for the disappointment in not receiving the swimming pool depth that had been specified, see discussion *page 381*, and continued:]

. . . I am satisfied that the principles enunciated in Ruxley's case in support of the award of 2,500 for a breach of respect of the provision of a pleasurable amenity have been authoritatively established.

VII. The very object of the contract: the arguments against the plaintiff's claim

22   Counsel for the surveyor advanced three separate arguments each of which he said was sufficient to defeat the plaintiff's claim. First, he submitted that even if a major or important part of the contract was to give pleasure, relaxation and peace of mind, that was not enough. It is an indispensable requirement that the object of the entire contract must be of this type. Secondly, he submitted that the exceptional category does not extend to a breach of a contractual duty of care, even if imposed to secure pleasure, relaxation and peace of mind. It only covers cases where the promiser guarantees achievement of such an object. Thirdly, he submitted that by not moving out of Riverside House the plaintiff forfeited any right to recover non-pecuniary damages.

23   The first argument fastened onto a narrow reading of the words 'the very object of [the] contract' as employed by Bingham LJ in *Watts* v *Morrow* [1991] 1 WLR 1421, 1445. Cases where a major or important part of the contract was to secure pleasure, relaxation and peace of mind were not under consideration in *Watts* v *Morrow*. It is difficult to see what the principled justification for such a limitation might be. After all, in 1978, the Court of Appeal allowed such a claim in *Jackson* v *Chrysler Acceptances Ltd* [1978] RTR 474 in circumstances where a spoiled holiday was only one object of the contract. Counsel was, however, assisted by the decision of the Court of Appeal in *Knott* v *Bolton* (1995) 11 Const LJ 375 which in the present case the Court of Appeal treated as binding on it. In *Knott* v *Bolton* an architect was asked to design a wide staircase for a gallery and impressive entrance hall. He failed to do so. The plaintiff spent money in improving the staircase to some extent and he recovered the cost of the changes. The plaintiff also claimed damages for disappointment and distress at the lack of an impressive staircase. In agreement with the trial judge the Court of Appeal disallowed this part of his claim. Reliance was placed on the dicta of Bingham LJ in *Watts* v *Morrow* [1991] 1 WLR 1421, 1445.

24   Interpreting the dicta of Bingham LJ in *Watts* v *Morrow* narrowly the Court of Appeal in *Knott* v *Bolton* ruled that the central object of the contract was to design a house, not to provide pleasure to the occupiers of the house. It is important, however, to note that *Knott* v *Bolton* was decided a few months before the decision of the House in *Ruxley Electronics and Construction Ltd* v *Forsyth* [1996] AC 344. In any event, the technicality of the reasoning in *Knott* v *Bolton*, and therefore in the Court of Appeal judgments in the present case, is apparent. It is obvious, and conceded, that if an architect is employed only to design a staircase, or a surveyor is employed only to investigate aircraft noise, the breach of such a distinct obligation may result in an award of non-pecuniary damages. Logically the same must be the case if the architect or surveyor, apart from entering into a general retainer, concludes a separate contract, separately remunerated, in respect of the design of a staircase or the investigation of aircraft noise. If this is so the distinction drawn in *Knott* v *Bolton* and in the present case is a matter of form and not substance. David Capper, 'Damages for Distress and Disappointment The Limits of Watts v Morrow' (2000) 116 LQR 553, 556 has persuasively argued:

> 'A ruling that intangible interests only qualify for legal protection where they are the "very object of the contract" is tantamount to a ruling that contracts where these interests are merely important, but not the central object of the contract, are in part unenforceable. It is very difficult to see what policy objection there can be to parties to a contract agreeing that these interests are to be protected via contracts where the central object is something else. If the defendant is unwilling to accept this responsibility he or she can say so and either no contract will be made or one will be made but including a disclaimer.'

There is no reason in principle or policy why the scope of recovery in the exceptional category should depend on the object of the contract as ascertained from all its constituent parts. It is sufficient if a major or important object of the contract is to give pleasure, relaxation or peace of mind. In my view *Knott* v *Bolton* 11 Const LJ 375 was wrongly decided and should be overruled.

To the extent that the majority in the Court of Appeal relied on *Knott* v *Bolton* their decision was wrong.

25 That brings me to the second issue, namely whether the plaintiff's claim is barred by reason of the fact that the surveyor undertook an obligation to exercise reasonable care and did not guarantee the achievement of a result. This was the basis upon which Hale LJ after the first hearing in the Court of Appeal thought that the claim should be disallowed. This reasoning was adopted by the second Court of Appeal and formed an essential part of the reasoning of the majority. This was the basis on which they distinguished *Ruxley Electronics and Construction Ltd* v *Forsyth* [1996] AC 344. Against the broad sweep of differently framed contractual undertakings, and the central purpose of contract law in promoting the observance of contractual promises. I am satisfied that this distinction ought not to prevail. It is certainly not rooted in precedent. I would not accept the suggestion that it has the pedigree of an observation of Ralph Gibson LJ in *Watts* v *Morrow* [1991] 1 WLR 1421, 1442b–d: his emphasis appears to have been on the fact that the contract did not serve to provide peace of mind, and so forth. As far as I am aware the distinction was first articulated in the present case. In any event, I would reject it. I fully accept, of course, that contractual guarantees of performance and promises to exercise reasonable care are fundamentally different. The former may sometimes give greater protection than the latter. Proving breach of an obligation of reasonable care may be more difficult than proving breach of a guarantee. On the other hand, a party may in practice be willing to settle for the relative reassurance offered by the obligation of reasonable care undertaken by a professional man. But why should this difference between an absolute and relative contractual promise require a distinction in respect of the recovery of non-pecuniary damages? Take the example of a travel agent who is consulted by a couple who are looking for a golfing holiday in France. Why should it make a difference in respect of the recoverability of non-pecuniary damages for a spoiled holiday whether the travel agent gives a guarantee that there is a golf course very near the hotel, represents that to be the case, or negligently advises that all hotels of the particular chain of hotels are situated next to golf courses? If the nearest golf course is in fact 50 miles away a breach may be established. It may spoil the holiday of the couple. It is difficult to see why in principle only those plaintiffs who negotiate guarantees may recover non-pecuniary damages for a breach of contract. It is a singularly unattractive result that a professional man, who undertakes a specific obligation to exercise reasonable care to investigate a matter judged and communicated to be important by his customer, can in Lord Mustill's words in *Ruxley Electronics and Construction Ltd* v *Forsyth* [1996] AC 344, 360 'please himself whether or not to comply with the wishes of the promise which, as embodied in the contract, formed part of the consideration for the price'. If that were the law it would be seriously deficient. I am satisfied that it is not the law. In my view the distinction drawn by Hale LJ and by the majority in the Court of Appeal between contractual guarantees and obligations of reasonable care is unsound.

26 The final argument was that by failing to move out the plaintiff forfeited a right to claim non-pecuniary damages. This argument was not advanced in the Court of Appeal. It will be recalled that the judge found as a fact that the plaintiff had acted reasonably in making 'the best of a bad job'. The plaintiff's decision also avoided a larger claim against the surveyor. It was never explained on what legal principle the plaintiff's decision not to move out divested him of a claim for non-pecuniary damages. Reference was made to a passage in the judgment of Bingham LJ in *Watts* v *Morrow* [1991] 1 WLR 1421, 1445c. Examination showed, however, that the observation, speculative as it was, did not relate to the claim for non-pecuniary damages: see the criticism of Professor M P Furmston, 'Damages Diminution in Value or Cost of Repair? Damages for Distress' (1993) 6 JCL 64, 65. The third argument must also be rejected.

27 While the dicta of Bingham LJ are of continuing usefulness as a starting point, it will be necessary to read them subject to the three points on which I have rejected the submissions made on behalf of the surveyor.

VIII. Quantum

28 In the surveyor's written case it was submitted that the award of 10,000 was excessive. It was certainly high. Given that the plaintiff is stuck indefinitely with a position which he sought to avoid by the terms of his contract with the surveyor I am not prepared to interfere with the judge's evaluation on the special facts of the case. On the other hand, I have to say that the size of the award appears to be at the very top end of what could possibly be regarded as appropriate damages. Like Bingham LJ in *Watts* v *Morrow* [1991] 1 WLR 1421, 1445h I consider that awards in this area should be restrained and modest. It is important that logical and beneficial developments in this corner of the law should not contribute to the creation of a society bent on litigation.

LORD SCOTT: . . .

74 The reason why such an apparently straightforward issue has caused such division of opinion is because it has been represented as raising the question whether and when contractual damages for mental distress are available. It is highly desirable that your Lordships should resolve the present angst on this subject and avoid the need in the future for relatively simple claims, such as Mr Farley's, to have to travel to the appellate courts for a ruling.

75 In my opinion, the issue can and should be resolved by applying the well known principles laid down in *Hadley* v *Baxendale* (1854) 9 Exch 341 (as restated in *Victoria Laundry (Windsor) Ltd* v *Newman Industries Ltd* [1949] 2 KB 528) in the light of the recent guidance provided by Bingham LJ in *Watts* v *Morrow* [1991] 1 WLR 1421 and by this House in *Ruxley Electronics and Construction Ltd* v *Forsyth* [1996] AC 344.

76 The basic principle of damages for breach of contract is that the injured party is entitled, so far as money can do it, to be put in the position he would have been in if the contractual obligation had been properly performed. He is entitled, that is to say, to the benefit of his bargain: see *Robinson* v *Harman* (1848) 1 Exch 850, 855.

[Lord Scott then referred to *Ruxley Electronics* v *Forsyth* and continued:]

79 Ruxley's case establishes, in my opinion, that if a party's contractual performance has failed to provide to the other contracting party something to which that other was, under the contract, entitled, and which, if provided, would have been of value to that party, then, if there is no other way of compensating the injured party, the injured party should be compensated in damages to the extent of that value. Quantification of that value will in many cases be difficult and may often seem arbitrary. In Ruxley's case the value placed on the amenity value of which the pool owner had been deprived was 2,500. By that award, the pool owner was placed, so far as money could do it, in the position he would have been in if the diving area of the pool had been constructed to the specified depth.

80 In Ruxley's case the breach of contract by the builders had not caused any consequential loss to the pool owner. He had simply been deprived of the benefit of a pool built to the depth specified in the contract. It was not a case where the recovery of damages for consequential loss consisting of vexation, anxiety or other species of mental distress had to be considered.

81 In *Watts* v *Morrow* [1991] 1 WLR 1421, however, that matter did have to be considered. As in the present case, the litigation in *Watts* v *Morrow* resulted from a surveyor's report. The report had negligently failed to disclose a number of defects in the property. The clients, who had purchased the property in reliance on the report, remedied the defects and sued for damages. The judge awarded them the costs of the repairs and also general damages of 4,000 each for 'distress and inconvenience' (p 1424). As to the cost of repairs, the Court of Appeal substituted an award of damages based on the difference between the value of the property as the surveyor's report had represented it to be and the value as it actually was. Nothing for present purposes, turns on that. As to the damages for 'distress and inconvenience' the Court of Appeal upheld the award in principle but held that the damages should be limited to a modest sum for the physical discomfort endured and reduced the award to 750 for each plaintiff . . .

[Lord Scott cited the statement of Bingham LJ in *Watts* v *Morrow*, extract at *page 378* and continued:]

82   In the passage I have cited, Bingham LJ was dealing with claims for consequential damage consisting of the intangible mental states and sensory experiences to which he refers. Save for the matters referred to in the first paragraph, all of which reflect or are brought about by the injured party's disappointment at the contract breaker's failure to carry out his contractual obligations, and recovery for which, if there is nothing more, is ruled out on policy grounds. Bingham LJ's approach is, in my view, wholly consistent with established principles for the recovery of contractual damages.

[He then cited two qualifications to the principle relating to recovery of distress damages for physical inconvenience, discussed *page 392,* and continued:]

86   In summary, the principle expressed in *Ruxley Electronics and Construction Ltd* v *Forsyth* [1996] AC 344 should be used to provide damages for deprivation of a contractual benefit where it is apparent that the injured party has been deprived of something of value but the ordinary means of measuring the recoverable damages are inapplicable. The principle expressed in *Watts* v *Morrow* [1991] 1 WLR 1421 should be used to determine whether and when contractual damages for inconvenience or discomfort can be recovered.

87   These principles, in my opinion, provide the answer, not only to the issue raised in the present case, but also to the issues raised in the authorities which were cited to your Lordships.

88   In *Hobbs* v *London and South Western Railway Co.* LR 10 QB 111 the claim was for consequential damage caused by the railway company's breach of contract. Instead of taking the plaintiff, his wife and two children to Hampton Court, their train dumped them at Esher and they had to walk five miles or so home in the rain. The plaintiff's wife caught a cold as a result of the experience. The plaintiff was awarded damages for the inconvenience and discomfort of his and his family's walk home but his wife's cold was held to be too remote a consequence. The plaintiff's recovery of damages attributable, in part, to the discomfort suffered by his wife and children was in accordance with principle. The contractual benefit to which he was entitled was the carriage of himself and his family to Hampton Court. It was reasonable in my opinion, to value that benefit, of which he had been deprived by the breach of contract, by reference to the discomfort to the family of the walk home. This was, in my view, a *Ruxley Electronics* case.

89   *Jarvis* v *Swans Tours Ltd* [1973] QB 233 was a case in which the plaintiff had contracted for a holiday with certain enjoyable qualities. He had been given a holiday which lacked those qualities. His holiday had caused him discomfort and distress. The trial judge awarded him 31.72, one-half of the price of the holiday. This must, I think have been the value attributed by the judge to the contractual benefit of which the plaintiff had been deprived. But on the plaintiff's appeal against so low an award, the Court of Appeal allowed him 125.

90   Somewhat different reasons were given by the three members of the court. Lord Denning MR said, at pp 237–238:

'In a proper case damages for mental distress can be recovered in contract . . . One such case is a contract for a holiday, or any other contract to provide entertainment and enjoyment. If the contracting party breaks his contract, damages can be given for the disappointment, the distress, the upset and frustration caused by the breach.'

The reference in this passage to the 'contract for a holiday, or any other contract to provide entertainment and enjoyment' is consistent with an intention to compensate the plaintiff for the contractual benefit of which he had been deprived. The reference, however, to 'the disappointment, the distress' etc reads like a reference to consequential damage.

91   Edmund Davies LJ based his decision on the defendant's failure to provide a holiday of the contractual quality'. He held that the amount of damages was not limited by the price for the holiday. He said, at p 239: 'The court is entitled, and indeed bound, to contrast the overall quality of the holiday so enticingly promised with that which the defendants in fact provided'. He regarded the plaintiff's vexation and disappointment as relevant matters to take into account in 'determining what would be proper compensation for the defendants' marked failure to fulfil their undertaking'. This was a *Ruxley Electronics and Construction Ltd* v *Forsyth* [1996] AC 344 approach. Stephenson LJ, at p 240, based his decision on the 'reasonable contemplation of the parties . . . as a likely result of [the holiday contract] being so broken'. He said, at pp 240–241, that where there are contracts 'in which the parties contemplate inconvenience on breach which may be described as mental: frustration, annoyance, disappointment . . .' damages for breach should take that inconvenience into account. This was a *Watts* v *Morrow* [1991] 1 WLR 1421 approach . . .

93 *Knott* v *Bolton* 11 Const LJ 375 is, in my opinion, inconsistent with Ruxley's case and should now be regarded as having been wrongly decided. The plaintiffs had been deprived of the wide staircase and gallery and baronial entrance hall to which they were contractually entitled and had to put up with lesser facilities. A value should, in my opinion, have been placed on the benefit of which they had been deprived . . .

105 It is time for me to turn to the present case and apply the principles expressed in *Ruxley Electronics and Construction Ltd* v *Forsyth* [1996] AC 344 and *Watts* v *Morrow* [1991] 1 WLR 1421. In my judgment. Mr Farley is entitled to be compensated for the 'real discomfort' that the judge found he suffered. He is so entitled on either of two alternative bases.

106 First, he was deprived of the contractual benefit to which he was entitled. He was entitled to information about the aircraft noise from Gatwick-bound aircraft that Mr Skinner, through neg-ligence, had failed to supply him with. If Mr Farley had, in the event, decided not to purchase Riverside House, the value to him of the contractual benefit of which he had been deprived would have been nil. But he did buy the property. And he took his decision to do so without the advantage of being able to take into account the information to which he was contractually entitled. If he had had that information he would not have bought. So the information clearly would have had a value to him. Prima facie, in my opinion, he is entitled to be compensated accordingly.

107 In these circumstances, it seems to me, it is open to the court to adopt a *Ruxley Electronics and Construction Ltd* v *Forsyth* [1996] AC 344 approach and place a value on the contractual benefit of which Mr Farley has been deprived. In deciding on the amount, the discomfort experienced by Mr Farley can, in my view, properly be taken into account. If he had had the aircraft noise information he would not have bought Riverside House and would not have had that discomfort.

[Lord Scott then discussed the alternative basis for an award of distress damages, see *page 392*, and continued:]

109 I would add that if there had been an appreciable reduction in the market value of the property caused by the aircraft noise. Mr Farley could not have recovered both that difference in value and damages for discomfort. To allow both would allow double recovery for the same item.

110 Whether the approach to damages is on *Ruxley Electronics and Construction Ltd* v *Forsyth* [1996] AC 344 lines, for deprivation of a contractual benefit, or on *Watts* v *Morrow* [1991] 1 WLR 1421 lines, for consequential damage within the applicable remoteness rules, the appropriate amount should, in my opinion, be modest. The degree of discomfort experienced by Mr Farley, although 'real', was not very great. I think 10,000 may have been on the high side. But in principle, in my opinion, the judge was right to award damages and I am not, in the circumstances, disposed to disagree with his figure.

111 For the reasons I have given and for the reasons contained in the opinion of my noble and learned friend, Lord Steyn, I would allow the appeal and restore the judge's order.

NOTES

1. McKendrick and Graham [2002] LMCLQ 161, Capper (2002) 118 LQR 193.
2. Although Lord Scott stated that he was agreeing with the reasons given in the speech of Lord Steyn, his approach, although not the outcome, may be very different since it does not appear to be linked explicitly to the provision of pleasure or relaxation. (Of course, this may be no bad thing since performance can have a subjective value without it necessarily involv-ing an object of pleasure, see Poole (1996) 59 MLR 272, at 280–85.) Although within the

scope of recovery for loss of amenity in *Ruxley*, Lord Scott appears to be stating that distress damages will be available in accordance with the principle in that case where the non-performance has resulted in the loss of contractual performance having a value to the claimant. The damages award will represent that value. On the other hand, based on this interpretation, such a principle has the potential to extend considerably the ability to recover damages for distress, at least in instances where such recovery can be said to fall within the remoteness principle.

3. The Court of Appeal had followed the approach in *Watts* v *Morrow* in refusing to award damages for distress on the basis that, since the surveyor had not guaranteed a particular result and owed only a duty of reasonable care and skill, it was not possible to award damages for distress. This was also stated to be a factor distinguishing this case from *Ruxley Electronics* where there was an absolute obligation to construct a swimming pool of the required depth. The House of Lords has rejected such a distinction, at least in the context of awarding damages for distress. It cannot make a difference to the award of such damages that the obligation is expressed in absolute or qualified terms. It does, however, make a difference to the ability to award cost of cure damages rather than difference in value, see *page 372*.

4. The significant factor in this case was that the plaintiff had specifically requested some reassurance on the question of aircraft noise and, given that the judge had found there to be no difference in value, awarding damages for distress ensured that the plaintiff had a remedy for breach of the defendant's undertaking on this matter. However, as Lord Scott noted, it is important to remember that in many instances there will be a difference in value and damages will be awarded on this basis.

Hamilton-Jones *v David & Snape (a firm)*
[2003] EWHC 3147 (Ch), [2004] 1 WLR 924

The claimant instructed the defendant solicitors to take action to ensure that her husband, from whom she was separated, was unable to remove the children from the country. Court orders were obtained for residence and to prevent this removal and although the defendant notified the UK Passport Agency of these orders in 1994 and asked them not to issue a passport to the husband or in the names of the children, the defendant failed to renew the notification after 12 months, despite being warned by the Passport Agency that the notice would require renewal after 12 months. In 1996 the husband was able to obtain a passport and removed two of the children from the jurisdiction. The claimant brought an action for breach of contract which included a claim for damages for distress. Neuberger J adopted the traditional approach on the question of recovery of damages for mental distress, i.e. that the general rule is that such damages are not recoverable (*Addis* v *Gramophone Co. Ltd* [1909] AC 488) unless the case fell within one of the established exceptions stated by Bingham LJ in *Watts* v *Morrow* and approved by Lords Bingham and Cooke in *Johnson* v *Gore Wood & Co.* [2002] 2 AC 1. Whilst Bingham LJ in *Watts* v *Morrow* had originally expounded the exception as requiring that '*the very object* of a contract is to provide pleasure, relaxation, peace of mind or freedom from molestation', Lord Steyn, and the majority, in *Farley* v *Skinner (No. 2)* had relaxed this requirement so that it required only that '*a major or important object* of the contract is to give pleasure, relaxation or peace of mind'. Held: the claimant was awarded £20,000 as damages for the distress since a major object of the contract was to ensure that for her peace of mind the claimant should retain custody of her children.

Neuberger J stated: '**61**. . . .[O]n any view, it appears to me that both the claimant and the defendants would have had in mind that a significant reason for the claimant instructing the defendants was with a view to ensuring, so far as possible, that the claimant retained custody of her children for her own pleasure and peace of mind' and 'it appears to me unrealistic to suggest that a significant part of the purpose of the claimants instructing the defendants, and the defendants accepting the claimants' instructions, was not to protect the claimant's peace of mind in respect of the very event which happened, namely the removal of the twins from this country'.

Thus, given the purpose behind the instruction, peace of mind was at least 'an important' object of the contract and part of the reason for contracting, albeit that it was not the sole purpose since the primary purpose under the relevant legislation was to protect the child. The solicitors had been engaged to minimise the inevitable distress associated with these circumstances or the risk of that distress and had failed to do so.

NOTES

1. This case is similar to *Heywood* v *Wellers* [1976] QB 446 and *McLeish* v *Amoo-Gottfried & Co.* (1993) 10 PN 102 in that peace of mind and the avoidance of distress were integral to the performance contracted for. This contracted for performance will, it seems, need to be quite specific. These cases can be compared with *Channon* v *Lindley Johnstone* [2002] EWCA Civ 353, [2002] Lloyd's Rep PN 342, where the claimant alleged distress suffered in consequence of having to pay more in ancillary relief to his ex-wife due to the negligence of his solicitors. The claim failed because there was no particular undertaking by the solicitors as to his property or to achieve a particular result. It follows that even in the context of a contract made with a consumer, something akin to the type of specific request in *Farley* v *Skinner* may be required in order to permit recovery of damages for distress in the context of contracts for the provision of a service. Such a position would fit with the policy considerations in relation to recovery of distress damages in the context of the exceptions.

2. Neuberger J cannot be said to have extended the principle in *Farley* v *Skinner* although he clearly felt the need to seek to justify the decision by reference to the perceived relaxing of the House of Lords' authority of *Addis* v *Gramophone*.

   > **63** The issue is perhaps particularly difficult because, as has been pointed out in more than one case, the question of whether or not damages are recoverable for mental distress in favour of a claimant in professional negligence proceedings is, at least to a significant extent, a matter of policy. In reaching the conclusion that the claimant in the present case is entitled to damages for mental distress, I must admit to drawing some encouragement from recent observations in the House of Lords which tend to suggest a relatively more liberal approach to the exceptions to the general rule laid down in *Addis* v *Gramophone Co Ltd* [1909] AC 488. Thus, in *Johnson* v *Gore Wood & Co* [2002] 2 AC I, 50F Lord Cooke doubted 'the permanence of *Addis* v *Gramophone Co Ltd* in English law', and Lord Hoffmann, in *Johnson* v *Unisys Ltd* [2003] 1 AC 518, 541, para 44, suggested that he would have felt able 'to circumvent or overcome the obstacle of *Addis*'. Furthermore, as is pointed out in *Halsbury's Laws of England*, 4th ed reissue, vol 12(1) (1998), para 961, the tendency over the past few years has been to extend, rather than restrict, the exceptions to the general principle in *Addis*, 'particularly . . . in claims by private consumers of goods and services': see also *McGregor on Damages*, 17th ed (2003), para 3–030.

3. The judge did not follow the approach advocated by Lord Scott in *Farley* v *Skinner* and it would seem unlikely that a first instance decision will do so.

Damages for distress will not be available in relation to a breach of a commercial contract since, as Lord Cooke stated in *Johnson* v *Gore Wood & Co (A Firm)* [2002] 2 AC 1, at p. 49: 'Contract-breaking is treated as an incident of commercial life which players in the game are expected to meet with mental fortitude.'

Hayes v *James and Charles Dodd*
[1990] 2 All ER 815 (CA)

The plaintiffs wished to purchase larger premises for their motor repair business. The premises they wished to purchase had only a narrow access through a tunnel at the front, but the plaintiffs' solicitor negligently informed them that there was a right of way over land at the rear so that there would be access to the garage. The plaintiffs purchased the property but the owner of the land at the rear blocked the access. This had a devastating effect on the plaintiffs' business and after 12 months the business was closed down. At first instance the damages award included £1,500 damages for each plaintiff for anguish and vexation. The Court of Appeal overturned this award. Held: such damages were not available if, as here, they arose out of a breach of a purely commercial contract.

STAUGHTON LJ: Like the judge, I consider that the English courts should be wary of adopting what he called 'the United States practice of huge awards'. Damages awarded for negligence or want of skill, whether against professional men or anyone else, must provide fair compensation, but no more than that. And I would not view with enthusiasm the prospect that every shipowner in the Commercial Court, having successfully claimed for unpaid freight or demurrage, would be able to add a claim for mental distress suffered while he was waiting for his money.

In a sense, the wrong done to the plaintiffs in this action, for which they seek compensation under this head, lay in the defendants' failure to admit liability at an early stage. On 6 July 1983 the defendants acknowledged that there was no right of way, but denied negligence. Had they on that very day admitted liability and tendered a sum on account of damages, or offered interim reparation in some other form, the anxiety of the plaintiffs, and their financial problems, could have been very largely relieved. But liability was not admitted until January 1987. I believe that in one or more American states damages are awarded for wrongfully defending an action. But there is no such remedy in this country so far as I am aware.

In *Perry* v *Sidney Phillips & Son (a firm)* [1982] 3 All ER 705, [1982] 1 WLR 1297 damages were awarded for the distress, worry, inconvenience and trouble which the plaintiff had suffered while living in the house he bought, owing to the defects which his surveyor had overlooked. Lord Denning MR considered that these consequences were reasonably foreseeable (see [1982] 3 All ER 705 at 709, [1982] 1 WLR 1297 at 1302). Kerr LJ stated a narrower test ([1982] 3 All ER 705 at 712, [1982] 1 WLR 1297 at 1307):

> So far as the question of damages for vexation and inconvenience is concerned, it should be noted that the deputy judge awarded these not for the tension or frustration of a person who is involved in a legal dispute in which the other party refuses to meet its liabilities. If he had done so, it would have been wrong, because such aggravation is experienced by almost all litigants. He awarded these damages because of the physical consequences of the breach, which were all foreseeable at the time. The fact that in such cases damages under this head may be recoverable, if they have been suffered but not otherwise, is supported by the decision of this court in *Hutchinson* v *Harris* (1978) 10 Build LR 19.
>
> I would emphasise the reference to physical consequences of the breach.

I am not convinced that it is enough to ask whether mental distress was reasonably foreseeable as a consequence, or even whether it should reasonably have been contemplated as not unlikely to result from a breach of contract. It seems to me that damages for mental distress in contract are, as a matter of policy, limited to certain classes of case. I would broadly follow the classification provided by Dillon LJ in *Bliss* v *South East Thames Regional Health Authority* [1987] ICR 700 at 718:

> . . . where the contract which has been broken was itself a contract to provide peace of mind or freedom from distress . . .

It may be that the class is somewhat wider than that. But it should not, in my judgment, include any case where the object of the contract was not comfort or pleasure, or the relief of discomfort, but simply carrying on a commercial activity with a view to profit. So I would disallow the item of damages for anguish and vexation.

NOTES

1. Staughton and Purchas LJJ stressed the fact that such damages could be recovered only for distress caused by the breach rather than the litigation process. On the facts the distress was primarily caused by the fact that the plaintiffs had financial difficulties and the solicitors did not admit liability until 1987.

2. In *Alexander* v *Rolls Royce Motor Cars* [1996] RTR 95, the Court of Appeal rejected the argument that a contract to repair a car was akin to a contract to provide freedom from worry and anxiety, so that damages for distress or loss of enjoyment in the use of the car were not available if the car was not repaired in breach of contract.

3. See Enonchong (1996) 16 OJLS 617.

4. The availability of damages for distress in relation to contracts which can be classified as commercial has changed little as a result of *Farley* v *Skinner*. Distress damages will not be available in the absence of a specific undertaking on a matter of importance which brings the contract within the peace of mind or pleasure exception. This limited relaxation would also be the position for consumer contracts if the majority approach is adopted, as initial indications suggest will be the case. Of course, this statement of the position presupposes the continued existence of the general rule in *Addis* v *Gramophone* (but see discussion at *page 398*).

(b) Distress directly consequent on physical inconvenience caused by the defendant's breach of contract

---

Perry v *Sidney Phillips & Son*
[1982] 1 WLR 1297 (CA)

The plaintiff purchased a house in reliance on a survey report prepared by the defendants. This stated that the house was in good order. After moving in the plaintiff discovered that the roof leaked and was in poor condition, and that the septic tank was inefficient and caused a nuisance by its smell. The Court of Appeal awarded damages for discomfort caused by the repairs since this was foreseeable.

This is the second exception discussed in the third paragraph of Bingham LJ's statement of principle in *Watts* v *Morrow* [1991] 1 WLR 1421, 1445, extract at *page 378*. It was the basis for the award of damages for distress in *Watts* v *Morrow*, i.e., damages for the distress caused by the physical inconvenience of living in the house whilst repairs were carried out.

Farley v *Skinner (No. 2)*
[2001] UKHL 49, [2002] 2 AC 732

For facts see *page 382*.

The House of Lords accepted that, as an alternative basis for its decision, it would have been possible for Mr Farley to have recovered damages for distress under this exception, although Lord Scott added some qualifications to the principle as stated by Bingham LJ.

LORD SCOTT: . . .

84   First, there will, in many cases, be an additional remoteness hurdle for the injured party to clear. Consequential damage, including damage consisting of inconvenience or discomfort, must, in order to be recoverable, be such as, at the time of the contract, was reasonably foreseeable as liable to result from the breach: see McGregor on Damages, 16th ed, pp 159–160, para 250.

85   Second, the adjective 'physical', in the phrase 'physical inconvenience and discomfort', requires, I think, some explanation or definition. The distinction between the 'physical' and the 'non-physical' is not always clear and may depend on the context. Is being awoken at night by aircraft noise 'physical'? If it is, is being unable to sleep because of worry and anxiety 'physical'? What about a reduction in light caused by the erection of a building under a planning permission that an errant surveyor ought to have warned his purchaser-client about but had failed to do so? In my opinion, the critical distinction to be drawn is not a distinction between the different types of inconvenience or discomfort of which complaint may be made but a distinction based on the cause of the inconvenience or discomfort. If the cause is no more than disappointment that the contractual obligation has been broken, damages are not recoverable even if the disappointment has led to a complete mental breakdown. But, if the cause of the inconvenience or discomfort is a sensory (sight, touch, hearing, smell etc) experience, damages can, subject to the remoteness rules, be recovered. . . .

108   [As an alternative basis for the decision] Mr Farley can, in my opinion, claim compensation for the discomfort as consequential loss. Had it not been for the breach of contract, he would not have suffered the discomfort. It was caused by the breach of contract in a causa sine qua non sense. Was the discomfort a consequence that should reasonably have been contemplated by the parties at the time of contract as liable to result from the breach? In my opinion, it was. It was obviously within the reasonable contemplation of the parties that, deprived of the information about aircraft noise that he ought to have had, Mr Farley would make a decision to purchase that he would not otherwise have made. Having purchased, he would, having become aware of the noise, either sell in which case at least the expenses of the resale would have been recoverable as damages or he would keep the property and put up with the noise. In the latter event, it was within the reasonable contemplation of the parties that he would experience discomfort from the noise of the aircraft. And the discomfort was 'physical' in the sense that Bingham LJ in *Watts* v *Morrow* [1991] 1 WLR 1421, 1445 had in mind. In my opinion, the application of *Watts* v *Morrow* principles entitles Mr Farley to damages for discomfort caused by the aircraft noise.

NOTES

1. Lord Scott's emphasis on the cause of the inconvenience or discomfort reflects the true nature of this exception as *distress directly consequent on physical inconvenience*. If the distress results in physical consequences there is no recovery of damages for distress within this exception, e.g. sleeplessness due to anxiety about the breach. This distress is the direct result of (caused by) the breach. On the other hand, if the breach causes a physical consequence, such as repairs, and this causes inconvenience and distress, the resultant distress is consequent on the physical inconvenience and is recoverable within the scope of the exception if it falls within the remoteness principle. This distress is caused by the physical inconvenience rather than directly by the breach. Some confusion appears to have resulted from the failure to make this distinction clear.

2. In the second part of this extract [108], Lord Scott explains that damages for distress are, in his opinion, recoverable if the distress is caused by the physical inconvenience or, on the basis of the consumer surplus, if the breach prevents the (consumer) claimant from obtaining the peace of mind he contracted for. This second exception may be put another way, i.e. the claimant can recover for the distress consequent on the consequences when he does not get the peace of mind he contracted for. Lord Scott's formulation may therefore involve only a broad exception. He makes clear that a choice of the basis (or exception) must be made in order to avoid double recovery.

D: Damages for loss of reputation

Addis v *Gramophone Co. Ltd* [1909] AC 488 has traditionally been regarded as House of Lords authority for the fact that in general there can be no damages for loss sustained due to the fact that the wrongful dismissal makes it more difficult to obtain fresh employment (see Lord Loreburn LC at p. 491).

However, in the next case the House of Lords accepted that in some very limited circumstances damages for loss of reputation might be awarded to former employees as damages for breach of their employment contracts although this would be damages to compensate for financial loss caused by this breach.

Mahmud v Bank of Credit & Commerce International SA (in liquidation) (Also known as Malik v BCCI)
[1998] AC 20 (HL)

The plaintiffs were former employees of the bank (BCCI) who submitted proof of a debt in the bank's liquidation claiming compensation for alleged stigma. They argued that on the bank's liquidation, it had been made more difficult for them to obtain alternative employment because of their previous employment with BCCI. The Court of Appeal had agreed with the liquidator and the judge at first instance that such a claim for damages could not succeed. Held on appeal: If an employer acted in breach of the employment contract by conducting the business in a dishonest and corrupt manner and if it was reasonably foreseeable that such a breach would prejudice the future employment prospects of the employees (see *page 400*), then damages for loss of reputation could be recovered by employees who established that they had in fact been handicapped in the labour market as a result of this conduct by the bank.

LORD STEYN:

. . .

The availability of the remedy of damages
In considering the availability of the remedy of damages it is important to bear in mind that the applicants claim damages for financial loss. That is the issue. It will be recalled that the Court of Appeal decided the case against the applicants on the basis that there is a positive rule debarring the recovery of damages in contract for injury to an existing reputation, and that in truth the two applicants were claiming damages for injury to their previously existing reputations. . . .

The true ratio decidendi of the House of Lords' decision in *Addis* v *Gramophone Co. Ltd* [[1909] AC 488] has long been debated. Some have understood it as authority for the proposition that an employee may not recover damages even for pecuniary loss caused by a breach of contract of the employer which damages the employment prospects of an employee. If *Addis's* case establishes such a rule it is an inroad on traditional principles of contract law. And any such restrictive rule has been criticised by distinguished writers: *Treitel, The Law of Contract*, 9th ed. (1995), p. 893, *Burrows, Remedies for Torts and Breach of Contract*, 2nd ed. (1994), pp. 221–225. Moreover, it has been pointed out that *Addis's* case was decided in 1909 before the development of modern employment law, and long before the evolution of the implied mutual obligation of trust and confidence. Nevertheless, it is necessary to take a closer look at *Addis's* case so far as it affects the issues in this case. A company had dismissed an overseas manager in a harsh and oppressive manner. The House of Lords held that the employee was entitled to recover his direct pecuniary loss, such as loss of salary and commission. But the jury had been allowed to take into account the manner in which the employee had been dismissed and to reflect this in their award. The House of Lords, with Lord Collins dissenting, held that this was wrong. The headnote to the case states that in a case of wrongful dismissal the award of damages may not include compensation for the manner of his dismissal, for his injured feelings, or for the loss he may suffer from the fact that the dismissal of itself makes it more difficult to obtain fresh employment. . . .

I would accept . . . that Lord Loreburn LC and the other Law Lords in the majority apparently thought they were applying a special rule applicable to awards of damages for wrongful dismissal. It is, however, far from clear how far the ratio of *Addis's* case extends. It certainly enunciated the principle that an employee cannot recover exemplary or aggravated damages for wrongful dismissal. That is still sound law. The actual decision is only concerned with wrongful dismissal. It is therefore arguable that as a matter of precedent the ratio is so restricted. But it seems to me unrealistic not to acknowledge that *Addis's* case is authority for a wider principle. There is a common proposition in the speeches of the majority. That proposition is that damages for breach of contract may only be awarded for breach of contract, and not for loss caused by the manner of the breach. No Law Lord said that an employee may not recover financial loss for damage to his employment prospects caused by a breach of contract. And no Law Lord said that in breach of contract cases compensation for loss of reputation can never be awarded, or that it can only be awarded in cases falling in certain defined categories. *Addis's* case simply decided that the loss of reputation in that particular case could not be compensated because it was not caused by a breach of contract: Nelson Enonchong, 'Contract Damages for Injury to Reputation' (1996) 59 MLR 592, 593. So analysed *Addis's* case does not bar the claims put forward in the present case. . . .

O'Laoire v *Jackel International Ltd (No. 2)* [1991] ICR 718, involved a claim by a dismissed employee for loss 'due to the manner and nature of his dismissal.' It was held that such a claim is excluded by *Addis's* case. But that does not affect the present case which is based not on the manner of a wrongful dismissal but on a breach of contract which is separate from and independent of the termination of the contract of employment.

In my judgment therefore the authorities relied on by Morritt LJ [in the Court of Appeal] do not on analysis support his conclusion. Moreover, the fact that in appropriate cases damages may in principle be awarded for loss or reputation caused by breach of contract is illustrated by a number of cases which Morritt LJ discussed: *Aerial Advertising Co.* v *Batchelors Peas Ltd (Manchester)* [1938] 2 All ER 788; *Foaminol Laboratories Ltd* v *British Artid Plastics Ltd* [1941] 2 All ER 393 and *Anglo-Continental Holidays Ltd* v *Typaldos Lines (London) Ltd* [1967] 2 Lloyd's Rep 61. But, unlike Morritt LJ, I regard these cases not as exceptions but as the application of ordinary principles of contract law. Moreover, it is clear that a supplier who delivers contaminated meat to a trader can be sued for loss of commercial reputation involving loss of trade: see *Cointax* v *Myham & Son* [1913] 2 KB 220 and *G.K.N. Centrax Gears Ltd* v *Matbro Ltd* [1976] 2 Lloyd's Rep 555. Rhetorically, one may ask, why may a bank manager not sue for loss of professional reputation, if it causes financial loss flowing from a breach of the contract of employment? The speeches of the majority of the House of Lords in *Spring* v *Guardian Assurance Plc* [1995] 2 AC 296 are also instructive. In that case the majority held that a former employee could recover damages for financial loss which he suffered as a result of his employer's negligent preparation of a reference. The reference affected his reputation. The majority considered that, if the reference had been given while the plaintiff was still employed, his claim could have been brought in contract. On that hypothesis he could have sued in contract for damage to his reputation. The dicta in *Spring* v *Guardian Assurance Plc* show that there is no rule preventing the recovery of damages for injury to reputation where that injury is caused by a breach of contract. The principled position is as follows. Provided that a relevant breach of contract can be established, and the requirements of causation, remoteness and mitigation can be satisfied, there is no good reason why in the field of employment law recovery of financial loss in respect of damage to reputation caused by breach of contract is necessarily excluded. I am reinforced in this view by the consideration that such losses are in principle recoverable in respect of unfair dismissal: see section 123(1) of the Employment Rights Act 1996 and *Norton Tool Co. Ltd* v *Tewson* [1973] 1 WLR 45, 50–51. It is true that the relevant statute does not govern the appeals under consideration. But in the search for the correct common law principle one is not compelled to ignore the analogical force of the statutory dispensation: see Professor Jack Beatson, 'Has the Common Law a Future,' inaugural lecture delivered on 29 April 1996, (1997) Cambridge University Press pamphlet, pp. 23–43. Not only does legal principle not support the restrictive principle, which prevailed in the Court of Appeal, but there are no sound policy reasons for it.

The effect of my conclusions

Earlier, I drew attention to the fact that the implied mutual obligation of trust and confidence applies only where there is 'no reasonable and proper cause' for the employer's conduct, and then only if the conduct is calculated to destroy or *seriously* damage the relationship of trust and confidence. That circumscribes the potential reach and scope of the implied obligation. Moreover, even if the employee can establish a breach of this obligation, it does not follow that he will be able to recover damages for injury to his employment prospects. The Law Commission has pointed out that loss of reputation is inherently difficult to prove: Consultation Paper No. 132 on Aggravated, Exemplary and Restitutionary Damages, p. 22, para 2.15. It is, therefore, improbable that many employees would be able to prove 'stigma compensation.' The limiting principles of causation, remoteness and mitigation present formidable practical obstacles to such claims succeeding. But difficulties of proof cannot alter the legal principles which permit, in appropriate cases, such claims for financial loss caused by breach of contract being put forward for consideration.

NOTES

1. It is important to bear in mind that this is a very limited decision dependent on there being a breach of the implied term that the employer will not conduct its business in a manner likely to undermine the trust and confidence required of the employment relationship. Lord Nicholls made these limitations clear when he stated, at p. 42:

   . . . [O]ne of the assumed facts in the present case is that the employer was conducting a dishonest and corrupt business. I would like to think this will rarely happen in practice . . . [T]here are many circumstances in which an employee's reputation may suffer from his having been associated with an unsuccessful business, or an unsuccessful department within a business. In the ordinary way this will not found a claim of the nature made in the present case, even if the business or department was run with gross incompetence. A key feature in the present case is the assumed fact that the business was dishonest or corrupt. Finally, although the implied term that the business will not be conducted dishonestly is a term which avails all employees, proof of consequential handicap in the labour market may well be much more difficult for some classes of employees than others. An employer seeking to employ a messenger, for instance, might be wholly unconcerned by an applicant's former employment in a dishonest business, whereas he might take a different view if he were seeking a senior executive.

2. In practice, it will be extremely difficult to establish the necessary causal link between the breach and the financial loss. In *Bank of Credit and Commerce International SA (in liquidation)* v *Ali (No. 3)* [2002] EWCA Civ 82, [2002] 3 All ER 750, the Court of Appeal accepted the principle in *Mahmud* but held that the employees in question had failed to prove that the stigma had caused them any financial loss.

3. It is also worth bearing in mind that the claim in *Mahmud* was for financial loss and the House of Lords was not dealing with a claim for damages for humiliation or distress.

4. As the speeches in *Mahmud* make clear, there are some recognised instances where damages for loss of reputation can be recovered. These relate to loss of publicity contemplated by the contract where an actor is wrongfully dismissed (*Marbe* v *George Edwardes (Daly's Theatre) Ltd* [1928] 1 KB 269), breach of a contract where the main purpose was to provide advertising or publicity (see *Aerial Advertising Co.* v *Batchelors Peas Ltd (Manchester)* [1938] 2 All ER 788, *page 258 above*) and damages for loss of credit reputation on the wrongful dishonouring of a cheque (*Kpohraror* v *Woolwich Building Society* [1996] 4 All ER 119).

5. In addition, as has been confirmed in *Johnson* v *Unisys Ltd* [2003] UKHL 13, [2003] 1 AC 518, *Mahmud* applies to a breach of this duty only during the period that the employees are employed. *Addis* v *Gramophone Co.* remains the authority concerning damages for the *manner*

of the dismissal. No damages will be obtainable as a result of difficulties in obtaining employment due to the manner of the dismissal.

Johnson v *Unisys Ltd*
[2001] UKHL 13, [2003] 1 AC 518 (HL)

The claimant had been summarily dismissed from his employment and had obtained the statutory maximum for unfair dismissal from an industrial tribunal (now called an employment tribunal). He claimed that as a result of the manner of his dismissal he had suffered psychiatric illness and considerable distress and had been unable to obtain employment. The claim was made for £400,000 in lost earnings relying on the principle in *Mahmud*, i.e., that the manner of his dismissal amounted to a breach of the implied term that his employers would not conduct themselves in such a way as to damage their relationship of trust and confidence. Held: (by majority) that the implied term of trust and confidence was an obligation in a continuing relationship rather than one applicable on its termination. In any event (Lord Steyn dissenting), Parliament had provided a statutory scheme laying down the remedy in such circumstances and the claimant could not be permitted to invoke the common law in an attempt to avoid the maximum compensation permitted under that scheme by devising a remedy of damages for the unfair manner of his dismissal.

NOTES
1. The House of Lords made it clear that the authority of *Addis* v *Gramophone* did not represent an obstacle to recovery of damages for distress or damage to reputation where the claim was based on breach of the implied term of trust and confidence. This was why *Addis* had not prevented recovery of damages for financial loss flowing from damage to reputation resulting from breach of this term in the way in which the business had been conducted (*Mahmud* v *BCCI*). However, the difficulty was that this term was inapplicable in the context of termination and the unfair dismissal scheme covered the situation. Nevertheless, the House of Lords in *Eastwood* v *Magnox Electric plc* [2004] UKHL 35, [2004] 3 WLR 322, distinguished *Johnson* v *Unisys* and held that an employee may have a claim for financial loss if a breach, which caused loss, had occurred prior to the disciplinary procedure to dismiss the employee and was independent of his subsequent unfair dismissal. In this situation the unfair dismissal claim under the statutory scheme would not preclude the award of common law damages under the principle in *Mahmud* (although there was to be no double recovery). On the facts, financial loss had been suffered by the claimant due to his psychiatric illness caused by the actions of his employer pre-dismissal. Thus the relevant question will be whether the breach complained of formed part of the dismissal procedure. (The House of Lords also confirmed that an award under the statutory unfair dismissal legislation could not include an award for injured feelings: *Dunnachie* v *Kingston upon Hull City Council* [2004] UKHL 36, [2004] 3 WLR 310 interpreting s. 123(1) of the Employment Rights Act 1996 so that a discretion to award compensation which was just and equitable in amount did not extend to a discretion as to the heads of loss for which compensation could be awarded.)
2. Outside the scope of the *Mahmud* situation, *Addis* will continue to represent the applicable authority so that damages for distress will not be available in connection with the manner of a dismissal. This was confirmed by the Court of Appeal in *Boardman* v *Copeland London Borough Council* [2001] EWCA Civ 888, unrep., 13 June 2001 and *Eastwood* v *Magnox Electric plc*.
3. In *Johnson* v *Gore Wood & Co* [2002] 2 AC 1, in the context of the existing exceptions, Lord Bingham stated, at p. 38, that he was not persuaded that the general applicability of *Addis* should be further restricted, suggesting that in terms of the general principle on non-availability of damages for distress *Addis* was predominant. However, Lord Cooke, in the

context of *Mahmud* and recovery of stigma damages, stated (at p. 50) that he took 'leave to doubt the permanence of *Addis* in English law' on the basis that the underlying philosophy had moved on. He noted that at the time of the decision in *Addis* the employment relationship was seen 'as no more than an ordinary commercial one' whereas this was 'a world away from the concept now'.

4. Lord Steyn in *Johnson* v *Unisys* also questioned the correctness of *Addis* in this context:

LORD STEYN:

I Addis v Gramophone Co Ltd

3 My Lords, the headnote of the decision of the House of Lords in *Addis* v *Gramophone Co Ltd* [1909] AC 488 purports to state the ratio decidendi of that case as follows: where a servant is wrongfully dismissed from his employment the damages for the dismissal cannot include compensation for the manner of his dismissal, for his injured feelings, or for the loss he may sustain from the fact that the dismissal of itself makes it more difficult for him to obtain fresh employment. This statement of the law was based on an observation in the speech of Lord Loreburn LC. A majority of the Law Lords expressed agreement with this speech. On the other hand, only Lord Loreburn LC specifically referred to the unavailability of special damages for loss of employment prospects. The other Law Lords concentrated on the non-pecuniary aspects of the case. The headnote is arguably wrong in so far as it states that the House decided that a wrongfully dismissed employee can never sue for special damages for loss of employment prospects arising from the harsh and humiliating manner of the dismissal: see *MacGregor* [sic] *on Damages*, 16th ed (1997), para 1242. Nevertheless, the statement of the law encapsulated in the controversial headnote has exercised an influence over this corner of the law for more than 90 years. It has had a restrictive impact on the damages which an employee may recover for financial loss actually suffered as a result of the manner of wrongful dismissal.

4 It is instructive to consider how this decision was viewed in 1909. Sir Frederic Pollock, the editor of the Law Quarterly Review, was not impressed. In a case note he contrasted 'an artificial rule or mere authority' to 'the rationale of the matter': (1910) 26 LQR 1–2. Citing cases contrary to what was perceived to be the *Addis* rule, and 'said to be exceptions', he plainly thought that as a matter of legal principle the decision was questionable. He said, at p 2:

'In the case of wrongful dismissal, a harsh and humiliating way of doing it, by the imputation which such a dismissal conveys, may make it very difficult for the servant to obtain a new situation. That was how the court looked at it in *Maw* v *Jones* [25 QBD 107]; not as a mere personal slight or affront. So in *Addis* v *Gramophone Co Ltd*. The plaintiff was dismissed summarily from an important post in India, and the whole management taken out of his hands in a way which could not but import obloquy among the commercial community of India, and as a result permanent loss. It was no mere rudeness or want of consideration. But the majority of the House of Lords thought the damages in question were really for defamation, and could be recovered only in a separate action.'

The supposed rule in *Addis* has been controversial for a long time. When the first edition of Treitel's classic book on contract was published some 40 years ago the author described the exclusion of any claim by an employee for financial loss to reputation as hard to justify: *The Law of Contract* (1962), pp 606–7. In the 10th edition (1999) of the same work Sir Guenter Treitel QC remained of the same view and was able to cite further decisions in which damages were awarded for financial loss of employment prospects or for injury to reputation resulting from a breach of contract: see pp 921–924.

5 During the course of the last century a fundamental alteration in the relationship between employer and employee has come about. And in the economic sphere that relationship has also drastically altered. This is the context in which the question of public importance now before the House is whether *Addis's* case precludes the recovery by an employee of special damages for financial loss in respect of damage to his employment prospects resulting from the manner of a wrongful dismissal. It was on this basis that the Appeal Committee granted leave to appeal rather than the particular features of the claim under consideration . . .

VI The effect of Addis v Gramophone Co Ltd

15 It is necessary to examine what was decided in *Addis's* case [1909] AC 488. The speeches in *Addis's* case are not easy to understand. Two of their Lordships spoke in terms of exemplary damages: see Lord James of Hereford, at p 492, and Lord Collins, dissenting, at pp 497 and 500–501. That could not have been an issue. In English law such damages have never and cannot be awarded for breach of any contract. That part of the discussion in the speeches in *Addis's* case can safely be put to one side. The context of the dispute has often been described. For my part it is sufficient to adopt the description of the case by Sir Frederic Pollock, 26 LQR 2, that the plaintiff:

> was dismissed summarily from an important post in India, and the whole management taken out of his hands in a way which could not but import obloquy among the commercial community of India, and as a result permanent loss.

The critical observation on the law of Lord Loreburn LC, at p 491, was undeniably to the effect stated in the headnote. On the other hand, *MacGregor* [sic] *on Damages*, para 1242 has argued that the other Law Lords in the majority confined themselves to the non-pecuniary aspects of the case. Accordingly, it is said, the headnote may not reflect the ratio decidendi of the case. Lord James of Hereford in his substantive reasons discussed the availability of general damages for injury to feelings. But he did say, at p 492, that he agreed with 'the entirety of the judgment delivered by my noble and learned friend on the Woolsack'. In my view he endorsed the relevant part of the speech of Lord Loreburn LC. On the other hand, Lord Atkinson (at p 493), Lord Gorrell (at p 502) and Lord Shaw of Dunfermline (at p 505) at most expressed general concurrence. In *Broome* v *Cassell & Co Ltd* [1972] AC 1027, 1087B Lord Reid observed: 'Concurrence with the speech of a colleague does not mean acceptance of every word which he has said. If it did there would be far fewer concurrences than there are.' When one turns to the substantive reasons given by Lord Atkinson, Lord Gorrell and Lord Shaw of Dunfermline, one finds that they dealt exclusively with the non-pecuniary aspects of the case. Only one of the Law Lords who sat in the case can realistically be regarded as having evinced a clear endorsement of Lord Loreburn LC's observation so far as it ruled out special damages for loss of employment prospects flowing from the manner of a wrongful dismissal.

16 Given the apparently harsh and humiliating manner of the dismissal, it is surprising that the other Law Lords did not consider this aspect. Indeed Lord Atkinson expressly said it was not 'necessary' to deal with it. The explanation may be the view taken of the pleadings: see Lord Atkinson's complaint [1909] AC 488, 493 about the 'unscientific form' of the pleadings and 'the loose manner in which the proceedings at the trial were conducted'. Despite assumptions to the contrary (including in particular my assumption in *Mahmud's* case [1998] AC 20, 50D–51D) it is nevertheless tolerably clear that the ratio decidendi of *Addis's* case does not preclude the recovery of special damages flowing from the manner of a wrongful dismissal.

VII The correctness of the observation of Lord Loreburn LC

17 It is still necessary to consider whether the observation of Lord Loreburn LC, although not reflecting the ratio decidendi of *Addis's* case [1909] AC 488, was nevertheless correct. This is so for two reasons. First my interpretation of *Addis's* case may not be correct. Secondly, the proposition of Lord Loreburn LC may be correct in all its constituent parts. As Sir Frederic Pollock explained in his case note in the Law Quarterly Review, Lord Loreburn LC enunciated a special and restrictive rule precluding the recovery of special damages in respect of financial loss flowing from the manner of wrongful dismissal. It was viewed as contrary to legal principle in 1909. In modern times it has been widely criticised as being in conflict with general principles of contract law. In *Mahmud's* case [1998] AC 20 Lord Nicholls of Birkenhead and I dealt with this point and it is unnecessary to cover the same ground again. But perhaps I may add that I am not aware of any modern academic writer, addressing the subject, who has tried to defend the relevant restrictive rule of Lord Loreburn LC. One is entitled to pose the question: why was the contract of employment singled out for a special rule to the disadvantage of employees?

18 *Addis's* case was decided in the heyday of a judicial philosophy of market individualism in respect of what was then called the law of master and servant. The idea that in the eyes of the law the position of a servant was a subordinate one seemed natural and inevitable. And in *Addis's* case it may have been the background to the adoption of a special restrictive rule denying in all cases to employees the right to recover financial loss which naturally flowed from the manner of their wrongful dismissal. Since 1909 there has been a fundamental change in legal culture. . . .

In *Spring* v *Guardian Assurance plc* [1995] 2 AC 296, 335, Lord Slynn of Hadley noted:

'the changes which have taken place in the employer-employee relationship, with far greater duties imposed on the employer than in the past, whether by statute or by judicial decision, to care for the physical, financial and even psychological welfare of the employee.'

One of the most important of those developments is the evolution since the mid-seventies of the obligation of trust and confidence in contracts of employment and its unanimous and unequivocal endorsement in *Mahmud's* case. . . .

19 Since 1909 our knowledge of the incidence of stress-related psychiatric and psychological problems of employees, albeit still imperfect, has greatly increased. What could in the early part of the last century dismissively be treated as mere 'injured feelings' is now sometimes accepted as a recognisable psychiatric illness. . . .

Inevitably, the incidence of psychiatric injury due to excessive stress has increased. The need for protection of employees through their contractual rights, express and implied by law, is markedly greater than in the past.

20 It is no longer right to equate a contract of employment with commercial contracts. One possible way of describing a contract of employment in modern terms is as a relational contract. If (contrary to my view) the headnote of *Addis's* case [1909] AC 488 correctly states the ratio decidendi of *Addis's* case I would now be willing to depart from it. That is not a particularly bold step. Indeed, in *Mahmud's* case [1998] AC 20 the House took that step.

21 . . . To this extent therefore the observation of Lord Loreburn LC in *Addis*, which rules out in all cases a claim for financial loss resulting from the manner of a wrongful dismissal, is qualified by the unanimous decision of the House in *Mahmud's* case.

Although, unlike the other members of the House, Lord Steyn would have been prepared to extend the application of the principle in *Mahmud* to instances of dismissal, he considered that the employees' claim would inevitably fail because they would be unable to establish that their loss was caused by the *manner* of the dismissal rather then the fact of dismissal. He referred (at [29]) to this as 'an even more formidable difficulty for the employee'. Therefore, any further extensions to the principles of recovery are unlikely to advance the practical ability to recover in such circumstances.

Lord Steyn continued his criticism in *Eastwood* v *Magnox Electric plc* [2004] UKHL 35, [2004] 3 WLR 322, whilst accepting that the difficulty was the existence of the Parliamentary scheme for unfair dismissal claims.

11 . . . The trust and confidence implied term means, in short, that an employer must treat his employees fairly. In his conduct of his business, and in his treatment of his employees, an employer must act responsibly and in good faith. In principle, this obligation should apply as much when an employer exercises his right to dismiss as it does to his exercise of other powers of his which affect a subsisting employment relationship. It makes little sense, for instance, that the implied obligation to act fairly should apply when an employer is considering whether to suspend an employee but not when the employer is proposing to take the more drastic step of dismissing him. Considerations of this nature suggest that the natural, continuing development of this aspect of the common law should be that the implied obligation to act fairly applies to dismissal decisions. This would mean that if an employee were treated today in the same shameful way as Mr Addis he would have a remedy at common law for breach of contract.

12 This development of the common law, however desirable it may be, faces one overriding difficulty. Further development of the common law along these lines cannot co-exist satisfactorily with the statutory code regarding unfair dismissal. A common law obligation having the effect that an employer will not dismiss an employee in an unfair way would be much more than a major development of the common law of this country. Crucially, it would cover the same ground as the statutory right not to be dismissed unfairly, and it would do so in a manner inconsistent with the statutory provisions. . . .

14 I recognise that, by establishing a statutory code for unfair dismissal, Parliament did not evince an intention to circumscribe an employee's rights in respect of wrongful dismissal. But Parliament has occupied the field relating to unfair dismissal. It is not for the courts now to expand a common law principle into the same field and produce an inconsistent outcome. To do so would, incidentally, have the ironic consequence that an implied term fashioned by the courts to enable employees to obtain redress under the statutory code would end up supplanting part of that code.

15 As was to be expected, the decision in *Johnson* v *Unisys Ltd* [2003] 1 AC 518 has given rise to demarcation and other problems. These were bound to arise. Dismissal is normally the culmination of a process. Events leading up to a dismissal decision take place during the subsistence of an employment relationship. If an implied term to act fairly, or a term to that effect, applies to events leading up to dismissal but not to dismissal itself unsatisfactory results become inevitable.

E: Remoteness of damage

Hadley v *Baxendale*

(1854) 9 Exch 341, 156 ER 145 (Exchequer)

The plaintiffs, owners of a flour mill, contracted with the defendant carriers for the carriage of a crank shaft to Greenwich for use as a pattern for a new crank shaft. The carriage was delayed due to the negligence of the defendants so that the new shaft was received late. The plaintiffs claimed their loss of profits in operating the mill during the delay. The defendants argued that this loss was too remote for them to be liable for it. Held: the loss of profits was not recoverable.

ALDERSON B: Now we think the proper rule in such a case as the present is this:—Where two parties have made a contract which one of them has broken, the damages which the other party ought to receive in respect of such breach of contract should be such as may fairly and reasonably be considered either arising naturally, i.e., according to the usual course of things, from such breach of contract itself, or such as may reasonably be supposed to have been in the contemplation of both parties, at the time they made the contract, as the probable result of the breach of it. Now, if the special circumstances under which the contract was actually made were communicated by the plaintiffs to the defendants, and thus known to both parties, the damages resulting from the breach of such a contract, which they would reasonably contemplate, would be the amount of injury which would ordinarily follow from a breach of contract under these special circumstances so known and communicated. But, on the other hand, if these special circumstances were wholly unknown to the party breaking the contract, he, at the most, could only be supposed to have had in his contemplation the amount of injury which would arise generally, and in the great multitude of cases not affected by any special circumstances, from such a breach of contract. For, had the special circumstances been known, the parties might have specially provided for the breach of contract by special terms as to the damages in that case; and of this advantage it would be very unjust to deprive them . . . Now, in the present case, if we are to apply the principles above laid down, we find that the only circumstances here communicated by the plaintiffs to the defendants at the time the contract was made, were, that the article to be carried was the broken shaft of a mill, and that the plaintiffs were the millers of that mill. But how do these circumstances shew reasonably that the profits of the mill must be stopped by an unreasonable delay in the delivery of the broken shaft by the carrier to the third person? Suppose the plaintiffs had another shaft in their possession put up or putting up at the time, and that they only wished to send back the broken shaft to the engineer who made it; it is clear that this would be quite consistent with the above circumstances, and yet the unreasonable delay in the delivery would have no effect upon the intermediate profits of the mill. Or, again, suppose that, at the time of the delivery to the carrier, the machinery of the mill had been in other respects defective, then, also, the same results would follow. Here it is true that the shaft was actually sent back to serve as a model for a new one, and that the want of a new one was the only cause of the stoppage of the mill, and that the loss of profits really arose from not sending down the new shaft in proper time, and that this arose from the delay in delivering the broken one to serve as a model. But it is obvious that, in the great multitude of cases of millers sending off broken shafts to third persons by a carrier under ordinary circumstances, such consequences would not, in all probability, have occurred; and these special circumstances were here never communicated by the plaintiffs to the defendants. It follows, therefore, that the loss of profits here cannot reasonably be considered such a consequence of the breach of contract as could have been fairly and reasonably contemplated by both the parties when they made this contract. For such loss would neither have flowed naturally from the breach of this contract in the great multitude of such cases occurring under ordinary circumstances, nor were the special circumstances, which, perhaps, would have made it a reason-able and natural consequence of such breach of contract, communicated to or known by the defendants. . . .

■ **QUESTION**

Is the size of the mill important to the imputed knowledge of the carrier? For example, if the mill is small would the carrier be taken to know that there was no spare shaft?

NOTES

1. There are said to be two distinct limbs to this remoteness rule:

    (a) Losses 'arising naturally' are inevitably within the parties' reasonable contemplation. The stoppage of the mill did not arise naturally from the carrier's delay because there might have been a spare shaft so that the mill could have kept working.

    (b) 'Abnormal losses' will be within the parties' reasonable contemplation only if the special circumstances giving rise to the loss were known to both parties at the time of the contract. The carriers had been told only that they were transporting a broken crank shaft to be used as a pattern for a new one. If they had been told that the mill would have to stop or that there was no spare shaft, then the loss of profits could have been recovered.

2. However, Evans LJ in *Kpohraror* v *Woolwich Building Society* [1996] 4 All ER 119, 127–8, stated that 'I would prefer to hold the starting point for any application of *Hadley* v *Baxendale* is the extent of shared knowledge of both parties when the contract was made . . . When that is established it may often be the case that the first and second parts of the rule overlap, or at least that it is unnecessary to draw a clear line of demarcation between them'. In *Jackson* v *Royal Bank of Scotland* [2005] UKHL 3, [2005] 1 WLR 377, Lord Hope recognised that there is a single principle underlying both limbs of 'what was in the contemplation of the parties at the time they made the contract'. However, the limbs are useful in terms of the application of that principle. On the facts Lord Hope (with whose reasons the other members of the House of Lords agreed) considered that the loss fell within the first limb since it was a loss arising naturally from the breach. The breach was the disclosure of confidential information so that the buyer of goods being imported by the claimant customer was able to discover the extent of the mark up and cancelled a long term supply contract.

3. In *Balfour Beatty Construction (Scotland) Ltd* v *Scottish Power plc* (1994) 71 BLR 20, the House of Lords had to consider whether knowledge of a construction process, namely the need for continuous pour of concrete, could be imputed to the electricity supplier, so that when the

electricity supply failed the consequential demolition and rebuilding costs could be recovered as 'a loss arising naturally'. The House of Lords held that there was no general rule that contracting parties were presumed to have knowledge of each other's business practices, but the simpler the activity the easier it would be to infer knowledge of the practice. However, where, as here, it was a complicated construction technique, the supplier was not deemed to know about it.

4. In *Jackson* v *Royal Bank of Scotland* [2005] UKHL 3, [2005] 1 WLR 377, the House of Lords confirmed what should have been a clear matter of principle, namely that what was in the contemplations of the parties was to be judged at the time of the contract and that the Court of Appeal had been wrong to limit the period of damages for loss of future business by reference to what was in the bank's contemplation at the time of the breach. The correct point of reference was the date of the contract.

Victoria Laundry (Windsor) Ltd v *Newman Industries Ltd*
[1949] 2 KB 528 (CA)

The plaintiffs were launderers and dyers who wished to extend their business. They contracted with the defendants, an engineering firm, for the purchase of a boiler which was to be delivered on 5 June. The boiler was damaged before delivery so that it was not delivered until 8 November. The defendants were aware of the nature of the plaintiffs' business and had been informed by letter that the plaintiffs intended to put the boiler to immediate use in their business. In an action for breach of contract the plaintiffs claimed:

(a) the profit that they would have earned using the boiler between 5 June and 8 November from the expansion of their business; and

(b) the profit on a number of highly lucrative dyeing contracts which they 'could and would have accepted' with the Ministry of Supply.

Held: although the loss of normal business profits was a *reasonably foreseeable* consequence of the delayed delivery, the defendants had no knowledge of the highly lucrative dyeing contracts so that this loss was too remote.

ASQUITH LJ (delivering the judgment of the Court): . . . What propositions applicable to the present case emerge from the authorities as a whole . . . We think they include the following:—

(1) It is well settled that the governing purpose of damages is to put the party whose rights have been violated in the same position, so far as money can do so, as if his rights had been observed: (*Sally Wertheim* v *Chicoutimi Pulp Company* [1911] AC 301). This purpose, if relentlessly pursued, would provide him with a complete indemnity for all loss de facto resulting from a particular breach, however improbable, however unpredictable. This, in contract at least, is recognised as too harsh a rule. Hence,

(2) In cases of breach of contract the aggrieved party is only entitled to recover such part of the loss actually resulting as was at the time of the contract reasonably forseeable as liable to result from the breach.

(3) What was at that time reasonably so foreseeable depends on the knowledge then possessed by the parties or, at all events, by the party who later commits the breach.

(4) For this purpose, knowledge 'possessed' is of two kinds; one imputed, the other actual. Everyone, as a reasonable person, is taken to know the 'ordinary course of things' and consequently what loss is liable to result from a breach of contract in that ordinary course. This is the subject matter of the 'first rule' in *Hadley* v *Baxendale* (1854) 9 Exch 341. But to this knowledge, which a contract-breaker is assumed to possess whether he actually possesses it or not, there may have to be added in a particular case knowledge which he actually possesses, of special circumstances outside the 'ordinary course of things,' of such a kind that a

breach in those special circumstances would be liable to cause more loss. Such a case attracts the operation of the 'second rule' so as to make additional loss also recoverable.

(5) In order to make the contract-breaker liable under either rule it is not necessary that he should actually have asked himself what loss is liable to result from a breach. As has often been pointed out, parties at the time of contracting contemplate not the breach of the contract, but its performance. It suffices that, if he had considered the question, he would as a reasonable man have concluded that the loss in question was liable to result.

(6) Nor, finally, to make a particular loss recoverable, need it be proved that upon a given state of knowledge the defendant could, as a reasonable man, foresee that a breach must necessarily result in that loss. It is enough if he could foresee it was likely so to result. It is indeed enough if the loss (or some factor without which it would not have occurred) is a 'serious possibility' or a 'real danger.' For short, we have used the word 'liable' to result. Possibly the colloquialism 'on the cards' indicates the shade of meaning with some approach to accuracy . . .

NOTES

1. The Court of Appeal applied a test of reasonable foreseeability which suggested that the test for remoteness in contract was the same as that for recovery in tort. However, this approach was criticised by the House of Lords in *The Heron II, below.*

2. Asquith LJ pointed out that the headnote to *Hadley* v *Baxendale* is misleading since it suggests that the carrier knew that the mill had stopped. If that were so then the loss should have been recoverable under the second limb of the rule.

3. It is argued that the second limb encourages the sharing of risks, and if a party is aware of the scope of likely liability, that party can take out insurance to cover it.

4. In *Seven Seas Properties Ltd* v *Al-Essa (No. 2)* [1993] 3 All ER 577, it was held that where the defendants' default had caused the plaintiffs to lose their profit on a sub-sale of property, the defendants would be liable for this loss only if, at the time of the main contract, they were aware of the intention to enter into the sub-sale. On the facts this information had been deliberately withheld, and therefore this loss was not within the parties' reasonable contemplations. (In the case of sale of goods where there is an available market for the goods in question, it is assumed that the injured party can purchase a substitute on the date of non-delivery and consequently is able to fulfil the sub-sale. This case, however, involved a sale of land.)

5. It is not clear what is required to enable recovery to occur under this second limb. Must the other party have actual knowledge of the facts, or must he actually accept the risk in question? In *Kemp* v *Intasun Holidays Ltd* [1987] FTLR 234, the casual mention by the plaintiff's wife of her husband's asthma to the travel agent at the time of booking, was not sufficient to make his attack reasonably contemplatable.

Koufos v *C. Czarnikow Ltd, The Heron II*
[1969] 1 AC 350 (HL)

Charterers chartered a vessel from the owners for the carriage of sugar from Constanza to Basrah. The shipowners knew that the charterers were sugar merchants and that there was a sugar market at Basrah but did not actually know that the charterers intended to sell the sugar promptly on arrival at Basrah. In breach of the charterparty, the vessel deviated from the voyage, so that instead of arriving at Basrah on 22 November, it did not arrive until 2 December. The market price of sugar at Basrah had fallen in this period from £32 10s per ton to £31 2s 9d per ton. Held: the charterers were entitled to recover the difference in price caused by the delay. Knowledge was imputed to them that it was *not unlikely* (to use the words of Lord Reid) that the sugar would be sold on arrival and that market prices fluctuate. Lord Reid rejected the reasonable foreseeability test used in *Victoria Laundry* v

Newman Industries (see *page 403*), since the test in contract was different to that in tort.

> LORD REID: So the question for decision is whether a plaintiff can recover as damages for breach of contract a loss of a kind which the defendant, when he made the contract, ought to have realised was not unlikely to result from a breach of contract causing delay in delivery. I use the words 'not unlikely' as denoting a degree of probability considerably less than an even chance but nevertheless not very unusual and easily foreseeable.

[Lord Reid then referred to *Hadley* v *Baxendale*. He continued:]

> Alderson B clearly did not and could not mean that it was not reasonably foreseeable that delay might stop the resumption of work in the mill. He merely said that in the great multitude—which I take to mean the great majority—of cases this would not happen. He was not distinguishing between results which were foreseeable or unforeseeable, but between results which were likely because they would happen in the great majority of cases, and results which were unlikely because they would only happen in a small minority of cases. He continued:
>
> > It follows, therefore, that the loss of profits here cannot reasonably be considered such a consequence of the breach of contract as could have been fairly and reasonably contemplated by both the parties when they made this contract.
>
> He clearly meant that a result which will happen in the great majority of cases should fairly and reasonably be regarded as having been in the contemplation of the parties, but that a result which, though foreseeable as a substantial possibility, would only happen in a small minority of cases should not be regarded as having been in their contemplation. . . .
>
> I am satisfied that the court did not intend that every type of damage which was reasonably foreseeable by the parties when the contract was made should either be considered as arising naturally, i.e., in the usual course of things, or be supposed to have been in the contemplation of the parties. Indeed the decision makes it clear that a type of damage which was plainly foreseeable as a real possibility but which would only occur in a small minority of cases cannot be regarded as arising in the usual course of things or be supposed to have been in the contemplation of the parties: the parties are not supposed to contemplate as grounds for the recovery of damage any type of loss or damage which on the knowledge available to the defendant would appear to him as only likely to occur in a small minority of cases.
>
> In cases like *Hadley* v *Baxendale* (1854) 9 Exch 341 or the present case it is not enough that in fact the plaintiff's loss was directly caused by the defendant's breach of contract. It clearly was so caused in both. The crucial question is whether, on the information available to the defendant when the contract was made, he should, or the reasonable man in his position would, have realised that such loss was sufficiently likely to result from the breach of contract to make it proper to hold that the loss flowed naturally from the breach or that loss of that kind should have been within his contemplation.
>
> The modern rule of tort is quite different and it imposes a much wider liability. The defendant will be liable for any type of damage which is reasonably foreseeable as liable to happen even in the most unusual case, unless the risk is so small that a reasonable man would in the whole circumstances feel justified in neglecting it. And there is good reason for the difference. In contract, if one party wishes to protect himself against a risk which to the other party would appear unusual, he can direct the other party's attention to it before the contract is made, and I need not stop to consider in what circumstances the other party will then be held to have accepted responsibility in that event. But in tort there is no opportunity for the injured party to protect himself in that way, and the tortfeasor cannot reasonably complain if he has to pay for some very unusual but nevertheless foreseeable damage which results from his wrongdoing. I have no doubt that today a tortfeasor would be held liable for a type of damage as unlikely as was the stoppage of Hadley's Mill for lack of a crankshaft: to anyone with the knowledge the carrier had that may have seemed unlikely but the chance of it happening would have been seen to be far from negligible. But it does not at all follow that *Hadley* v *Baxendale* (1854) 9 Exch 341 would today be differently decided.

[Lord Reid, then referred to *Victoria Laundry* v *Newman Industries* [1949] 2 KB 528 and Asquith LJ's formulation . . .]

To bring in reasonable foreseeability appears to me to be confusing measure of damages in contract with measure of damages in tort. A great many extremely unlikely results are reasonably foreseeable: it is true that Lord Asquith may have meant foreseeable as a likely result, and if that is all he meant I would not object further than to say that I think that the phrase is liable to be misunderstood. For the same reason I would take exception to the phrase 'liable to result'. Liable is a very vague word but I think that one would usually say that when a person foresees a very improbable result he foresees that it is liable to happen.

. . . It has never been held to be sufficient in contract that the loss was foreseeable as 'a serious possibility' or 'a real danger' or as being 'on the cards.' It is on the cards that one can win £100,000 or more for a stake of a few pence—several people have done that. And anyone who backs a hundred to one chance regards a win as a serious possibility—many people have won on such a chance. And the *Wagon Mound (No. 2)* [1961] AC 388 could not have been decided as it was unless the extremely unlikely fire should have been foreseen by the ship's officer as a real danger. It appears to me that in the ordinary use of language there is wide gulf between saying that some event is not unlikely or quite likely to happen and saying merely that it is a serious possibility, a real danger, or on the cards. Suppose one takes a well-shuffled pack of cards, it is quite likely or not unlikely that the top card will prove to be a diamond: the odds are only 3 to 1 against. But most people would not say that it is quite likely to be the nine of diamonds for the odds are then 51 to 1 against. On the other hand I think that most people would say that there is a serious possibility or a real danger of its being turned up first and of course it is on the cards. If the tests of 'real danger' or 'serious possibility' are in future to be authoritative then the *Victoria Laundry* case [1949] 2 KB 528 would indeed be a landmark because it would mean that *Hadley* v *Baxendale* (1854) 9 Exch 341 would be differently decided today. I certainly could not understand any court deciding that, on the information available to the carrier in that case, the stoppage of the mill was neither a serious possibility nor a real danger. If those tests are to prevail in future then let us cease to pay lip service to the rule in *Hadley* v *Baxendale* (1854) 9 Exch 341. But in my judgement to adopt these tests would extend liability for breach of contract beyond what is reasonable or desirable. From the limited knowledge which I have of commercial affairs I would not expect such an extension to be welcomed by the business community and from the legal point of view I can find little or nothing to recommend it.

■ QUESTIONS

1. Do you agree with Lord Reid that if the test is reasonable foreseeability, then the carrier in *Hadley* v *Baxendale* would have been liable?

2. Is there a distinction between 'natural losses' and 'foreseeable losses'?

3. Lord Reid justified a stricter test of remoteness in contract because the parties will know each other and are therefore in a better position to assess the risk of loss due to the breach. If we accept Lord Reid's distinction, what should the position be if a claim on the facts could lie in both contract and tort? Can the injured party choose to formulate the claim in tort so that recovery of losses will be wider?

H. Parsons (Livestock) Ltd v Uttley Ingham & Co. Ltd
[1978] 1 QB 791 (CA)

The plaintiffs, pig farmers, ordered a bulk food storage hopper for storing pig nuts from the defendants. When the defendants installed the hopper they failed to ensure that the ventilator on the top was open. The pig nuts went mouldy, and when the pigs ate them they became ill with an intestinal disease called 'e coli'. Two hundred and fifty-four pigs died. Held: (Scarman and Orr LJJ) that the death of the pigs was not too remote a loss since the parties might reasonably have contemplated some illness to the pigs resulting from this breach and they did not have to foresee the actual illness that occurred. Lord Denning also held that the death of the pigs was within the remoteness rule. He thought that the same distinction should be drawn in contract as applied in tort between physical damage and economic loss (loss of profit), and that the tort test of remoteness should apply to physical damage.

LORD DENNING MR: . . .

The law as to remoteness

Remoteness of damage is beyond doubt a question of law. In *C. Czarnikow Ltd v Koufos* [1969] AC 350 the House of Lords said that, in remoteness of damage, there is a difference between contract and tort. In the case of a *breach of contract*, the court has to consider whether the consequences were of such a kind that a reasonable man, at the time of making the contract, would *contemplate* them as being of a very substantial degree of probability. (In the House of Lords various expressions were used to describe this degree of probability, such as, not merely 'on the cards' because that may be too low: but as being 'not unlikely to occur' (see pp. 383 and 388); or 'likely to result or at least not unlikely to result' (see p. 406); or 'liable to result' (see p. 410); or that there was a 'real danger' or 'serious possibility' of them occurring (see p. 415).)

In the case of a *tort*, the court has to consider whether the consequences were of such a kind that a reasonable man, at the time of the tort committed, would *foresee* them as being of a much lower degree of probability. (In the House of Lords various expressions were used to describe this, such as, it is sufficient if the consequences are 'liable to happen in the most unusual case' (see p. 385); or in a 'very improbable' case (see p. 389); or that 'they may happen as a result of the breach, however unlikely it may be, unless it can be brushed aside as far-fetched' (see p. 422).)

I find it difficult to apply those principles universally to all cases of contract or to all cases of tort: and to draw a distinction between what a man 'contemplates' and what he 'foresees'. I soon begin to get out of my depth. I cannot swim in this sea of semantic exercises—to say nothing of the different degrees of probability—especially when the cause of action can be laid either in contract or in tort. I am swept under by the conflicting currents. I go back with relief to the distinction drawn in legal theory by Professors Hart and Honoré in their book *Causation in the Law* (1959). at pp. 281–287. They distinguish between those cases in contract in which a man has suffered no damage to person or property, but only *economic loss*, such as, loss of profit or loss of opportunities for gain in some future transaction: and those in which he claims damages for an *injury actually done* to his person or *damage actually done* to his property (including his livestock) or for ensuing expense (damnum emergens) to which he has actually been put. In the law of *tort*, there is emerging a distinction between economic loss and physical damage: see *Spartan Steel & Alloys Ltd v Martin & Co. (Contractors) Ltd* [1973] QB 27, 36–37.

It seems to me that in the law of *contract*, too, a similar distinction is emerging. It is between loss of profit consequent on a breach of contract and physical damage consequent on it.

Loss of profit cases

I would suggest as a solution that in the former class of case—loss of profit cases—the defaulting party is only liable for the consequences if they are such as, at the time of the contract, he ought reasonably to have *contemplated* as a *serious* possibility or real danger. You must assume that, at the time of the contract, he had the very kind of breach in mind—such a breach as afterwards happened, as for instance, delay in transit—and then you must ask: ought he reasonably to have *contemplated* that there was a *serious* possibility that such a breach would involve the plaintiff in loss of profit? If yes, the contractor is liable for the loss unless he has taken care to exempt himself from it by a condition in the contract—as, of course, he is able to do if it was the sort of thing which he could reasonably contemplate. The law on this class of case is now covered by the three leading cases of *Hadley v Baxendale*, 9 Exch 341; *Victoria Laundry (Windsor) Ltd v Newman Industries Ltd*

[1949] 2 KB 528; and *C. Czarnikow Ltd* v *Koufos* [1969] 1 AC 350. These were all 'loss of profit' cases: and the test of 'reasonable contemplation' and 'serious possibility' should, I suggest, be kept to that type of loss or, at any rate, to economic loss.

Physical damage cases

In the second class of case—the physical injury or expense case—the defaulting party is liable for any loss or expense which he ought reasonably to have *foreseen* at the time of the breach as a possible consequence, even if it was only a *slight* possibility. You must assume that he was aware of his breach, and then you must ask: ought he reasonably to have foreseen, at the time of the breach, that something of this kind might happen in consequence of it? This is the test which has been applied in cases of tort ever since *The Wagon Mound* cases [1961] AC 388 and [1967] 1 AC 617. But there is a long line of cases which support a like test in cases of contract. . . .

Coming to the present case, we were told that in some cases the makers of these hoppers supply them, direct to the pig farmer under contract with him, but in other cases they supply them through an intermediate dealer—who buys from the manufacturer and resells to the pig farmer on the self-same terms—in which the manufacturer delivers direct to the pig farmer. In the one case the pig farmer can sue the manufacturer in contract. In the other in tort. The test of remoteness should be the same. It should be the test in tort.

Conclusion

The present case falls within the class of case where the breach of contract causes physical damage. The test of remoteness in such cases is similar to that in tort. The contractor is liable for all such loss or expense as could reasonably have been foreseen at the time of the breach, as a possible con-sequence of it. Applied to this case, it means that the makers of the hopper are liable for the death of the pigs. They ought reasonably to have foreseen that, if the mouldy pignuts were fed to the pigs, there was a possibility that they might become ill. Not a serious possibility. Nor a real danger. But still a slight possibility. On that basis the makers were liable for the illness suffered by the pigs. They suffered from diarrhoea at the beginning. This triggered off the deadly E. coli. That was a far worse illness than could then be foreseen. But that does not lessen this liability. The type or kind of damage was foreseeable even though the extent of it was not: see *Hughes* v *Lord Advocate* [1963] AC 837. . . .

NOTES

1. Scarman and Orr LJJ expressly refused to adopt this distinction on the basis that the case law did not support it.

2. The decision of the majority means that if the type of loss is within the parties' reasonable contemplations, the extent of it need not be. See also *Brown* v *KMR Services Ltd* [1995] 4 All ER 598, where this principle was applied.

3. In *Victoria Laundry* v *Newman Industries* (*page 403*), the type of loss appears to be loss of profits but the profits on the dyeing contracts were not recoverable. Is it possible to explain this difference in treatment?

F: Mitigation

The injured party is prevented from recovering for losses which he failed to miti-gate. Viscount Haldane LC in *British Westinghouse Electric & Manufacturing Co. Ltd* v *Underground Electric Railways Company of London Ltd* [1912] AC 673, said (at p. 689):

. . . I think that there are certain broad principles which are quite well settled. The first is that, as far as possible, he who has proved a breach of a bargain to supply what he contracted to get is to be placed, as far as money can do it, in as good a situation as if the contract had been performed.

The fundamental basis is thus compensation for pecuniary loss naturally flowing from the breach; but this first principle is qualified by a second, which imposes on a plaintiff the duty of taking all reasonable steps to mitigate the loss consequent on the breach, and debars him from claiming any part of the damage which is due to his neglect to take such steps. In the words of James LJ in *Dunkirk Colliery Co.* v *Lever* (1878) 9 ChD 20, 'The person who has broken the contract is not to be exposed to additional cost by reason of the plaintiffs not doing what they ought to have done as reasonable men, and the plaintiffs not being under any obligation to do anything otherwise than in the ordinary course of business.'

As James LJ indicates, this second principle does not impose on the plaintiff an obligation to take any step which a reasonable and prudent man would not ordinarily take in the course of his business. But when in the course of his business he has taken action arising out of the transaction, which action has diminished his loss, the effect in actual diminution of the loss he has suffered may be taken into account even though there was no duty on him to act.

NOTE: Although the expression 'duty to mitigate' is used, it is not strictly accurate, since there is no liability if the injured party fails to mitigate. The effect of failure to mitigate is to reduce the damages that might otherwise have been payable.

(a) Reasonable steps

Payzu Ltd v *Saunders*
[1919] 2 KB 581 (CA)

The defendant contracted to sell crêpe de Chine to the plaintiffs, delivery as required within a nine-month period and payment within one month of delivery. When the plaintiffs failed to pay punctually for the first instalment the defendant refused to deliver any more under the contract. (This amounted to a repudiatory breach by the defendant.) However, the defendant did offer to deliver the goods at the contract price if the plaintiffs would agree to pay cash when ordering. The plaintiffs refused this offer and sought damages for breach of contract. The market price of crêpe de Chine had risen and damages of the difference between the market price and contract price were sought. Held: the plaintiffs should have mitigated their loss by accepting the defendant's offer. Damages were confined to the loss that the plaintiffs would have suffered if they had paid cash and acquired the goods at the contract price, i.e., the loss of a month's credit which had originally applied under the contract. The Court of Appeal also held that the question of whether the steps were reasonable was a question of fact in each case.

BANKES LJ: . . . It is plain that the question what is reasonable for a person to do in mitigation of his damages cannot be a question of law but must be one of fact in the circumstances of each particular case. There may be cases where as matter of fact it would be unreasonable to expect a plaintiff to consider any offer made in view of the treatment he has received from the defendant. If he had been rendering personal services and had been dismissed after being accused in presence of others of being a thief, and if after that his employer had offered to take him back into his service, most persons would think he was justified in refusing the offer, and that it would be unreasonable to ask him in this way to mitigate the damages in an action of wrongful dismissal. But that is not to state a principle of law, but a conclusion of fact to be arrived at on a consideration of all the circumstances of the case. . . . [Counsel for the appellants] complained that the respondent had treated his clients so badly that it would be unreasonable to expect them to listen to any proposition she might make. I do not agree. In my view each party was ready to accuse the other of conduct unworthy of a high commercial reputation, and there was nothing to justify the appellants in refusing to consider the respondent's offer.

■ QUESTION

Who received the benefit of the rise in market price?

NOTES
1. Bridge, 'Mitigation of damages in contract and the meaning of avoidable loss' (1989) 105 LQR 398.
2. It also appears that an injured party is not required to take action which will damage its reputation or public relations (*London & South of England Building Society* v *Stone* [1983] 1 WLR 1242).
3. In *Farley* v *Skinner* [2001] UKHL 49, [2002] 2 AC 732, *page 382*, the House of Lords considered that it was reasonable for a house purchaser not to sell and to remain in the property after discovering a breach of contract affecting his enjoyment of that property.
4. *Payzu* v *Saunders* was applied by Harman J in the next case.

Pilkington v Wood
[1953] Ch 770

The plaintiff instructed the defendant solicitor to act for him in the purchase of a house. The defendant negligently advised that the title of the vendor was good when in fact the vendor held as trustee of the property. The defendant argued that the plaintiff should have mitigated his loss by bringing legal proceedings against the vendor for having conveyed a defective title. Held: there was no duty to embark on 'a complicated and difficult piece of litigation' in order to protect the defendant from the consequences of his own carelessness.

(b) What if the reasonable steps increase the loss?

Banco de Portugal v Waterlow & Sons Ltd
[1932] AC 452 (HL)

The plaintiff bank had engaged the defendant printers to print bank notes. In breach of contract the defendants also delivered a large number of these notes to a criminal who put them into circulation in Portugal. When the bank discovered this they withdrew the complete issue of the particular note and undertook to exchange all such notes presented to them for other notes. The defendants argued that they were liable only for the cost of printing new notes and that the remaining loss was caused by the bank's action in exchanging those notes for others. Held: (Lord Warrington of Clyffe and Lord Russell of Killowen dissenting) since the bank's actions had been reasonable, the value of the currency given in exchange was also recoverable.

LORD MACMILLAN: . . . Where the sufferer from a breach of contract finds himself in consequence of that breach placed in a position of embarrassment the measures which he may be driven to adopt in order to extricate himself ought not to be weighed in nice scales at the instance of the party whose breach of contract has occasioned the difficulty. It is often easy after an emergency has passed to criticize the steps which have been taken to meet it, but such criticism does not come well from those who have themselves created the emergency. The law is satisfied if the party placed in a difficult situation by reason of the breach of a duty owed to him has acted reasonably in the adoption of remedial measures, and he will not be held disentitled to recover the cost of such measures merely because the party in breach can suggest that other measures less burdensome to him might have been taken. . . . In my opinion the action of the Bank in honouring all notes of the type in question, genuine and spurious alike, between December 7 and December 26, 1925, was reasonable and justifiable in the circumstances, and Messrs Waterlow ought to be held responsible for whatever loss was occasioned to the Bank by the adoption of that policy. . . .

G: Causation and contributory negligence

(a) Causation

The injured party must establish a causal link between his loss and the defendant's breach of contract. In *Galoo Ltd* v *Bright Grahame Murray* [1994] 1 WLR 1360, the Court of Appeal held that in a breach of contract claim a plaintiff was entitled to claim damages where the breach was the effective or dominant cause of his loss. It was not sufficient that the breach merely provided the plaintiff with the opportunity to sustain loss. This is judged 'by the application of the court's common sense' (*per* Glidewell LJ). The 'but for' test governing causation in tort was not sufficient in contract.

On the facts the breach of contract by the companies' auditors related to the fact that the audited accounts of the plaintiff companies contained substantial inaccuracies, but it was held that this merely provided the companies concerned with the opportunity to incur further trading losses and did not actually cause those losses.

In *County Ltd* v *Girozentrale Securities* [1996] 3 All ER 834, it was argued that a number of causes had combined to bring about the loss suffered by a bank in connection with the underwriting of an issue of shares. The Court of Appeal held that in such a situation a court was not required to choose which was the more effective cause. It was sufficient in a contractual claim that the cause in question (in this case a breach of contract by the brokers engaged to approach potential investors) was *an* effective cause of the loss.

However, an intervening cause may break the chain of causation.

Beoco Ltd v *Alfa Laval Co. Ltd*
[1994] 3 WLR 1179 (CA)

The first defendant installed a heat exchanger at the plaintiff company's premises. Some time later a leak was discovered and the plaintiff employed the second defendant to repair it. Without inspecting the repair, which would have revealed that it was defective, the plaintiff put the heat exchanger back into use. Two months later the heat exchanger exploded damaging the plaintiff's plant and causing loss of production.

In a claim against the first defendant for breach of warranty, the plaintiff sought the loss of profits which would have been suffered because of the defect in the heat exchanger necessitating further repair or replacement. This was a purely hypothetical loss because of the intervening explosion (which was attributed to the plaintiff's failure to inspect the repair). Held: the principles were the same as those applicable in tort (see, e.g., *Jobling* v *Associated Dairies Ltd* [1982] AC 794) so that the plaintiff could not recover for the hypothetical loss of profits when the intervening event (due to the plaintiff's negligence) had caused greater damage.

(b) Contributory negligence

If the injured party's negligent actions are not sufficient to break the chain of causation but contribute to the loss, can the damages in contract be apportioned to take account of this contributory negligence? Is the Law Reform (Contributory Negligence) Act 1945 wide enough to cover contractual actions?

LAW REFORM (CONTRIBUTORY NEGLIGENCE) ACT 1945

1. Apportionment of liability in case of contributory negligence

(1) Where any person suffers damage as the result partly of his own fault and partly of the fault of any other person or persons, a claim in respect of that damage shall not be defeated by reason of the fault of the person suffering the damage, but the damages recoverable in respect thereof shall be reduced to such extent as the court thinks just and equitable having regard to the claimant's share in the responsibility of the damage: . . .

4. Interpretation

'fault' . . . means negligence, breach of statutory duty or other act or omission which gives rise to liability in tort or would, apart from this Act, give rise to the defence of contributory negligence.

Forsikringsaktieselskapet Vesta v *Butcher*
[1989] AC 852 (CA)

The plaintiffs were seeking to vary a contract of reinsurance through the defendant brokers. The brokers failed to act. This was a breach of their duty of care owed to the plaintiffs in tort, and a breach of an implied term in their contract with the plaintiffs that they would exercise reasonable care and skill. The defendant brokers alleged that the plaintiffs had many opportunities to put the omission right and were therefore contributorily negligent. The plaintiffs alleged that by formulating their claim in contract they could avoid apportionment of damages under the 1945 Act. Held: where the defendant's liability in contract is the same as the liability in the tort of negligence (independent of the existence of any contract), the Act applied to enable the court to apportion damages even though the claim was made in contract. In the Court of Appeal O'Connor LJ explained the issues.

O'CONNOR LJ: . . . The important issue of law is whether on the facts of this case there is power to apportion under the Law Reform (Contributory Negligence) Act 1945 and thus reduce the damages recoverable by Vesta.

I start by pointing out that Vesta pleaded its claim against the brokers in contract and tort. This is but a recognition of what I regard as a clearly established principle that where under the general law a person owes a duty to another to exercise reasonable care and skill in some activity, a breach of that duty gives rise to a claim in tort notwithstanding the fact that the activity is the subject matter of a contract between them. In such a case the breach of duty will also be a breach of contract. The classic example of this situation is the relationship between doctor and patient.

Since the decision of the House of Lords in *Hedley Byrne & Co Ltd* v *Heller & Partners Ltd* [1964] AC 465 the relationship between the brokers and Vesta is another example. [Counsel] for Vesta accepts that this is so but he submits that if a plaintiff makes his claim in contract contributory negligence cannot be relied on by the defendant whereas it is available if the claim is made in tort. If this contention is sound then the law has been sadly adrift for a very long time for it would mean that in employers' liability cases an injured employee could debar the employer from relying on any contributory negligence by framing his action in contract.

. . . The judge [Hobhouse J] dealt with this submission and said [1986] 2 All ER 488, 508:

The question whether the 1945 Act applies to claims brought in contract can arise in a number of classes of case. Three categories can conveniently be identified. (1) Where the defendant's liability arises from some contractual provision which does not depend on negligence on the part of the defendant. (2) Where the defendant's liability arises from a contractual obligation which is expressed in terms of taking care (or its equivalent) but does not correspond to a common law duty to take care which would exist in the given case independently of contract. (3) Where the defendant's liability in contract is the same as his liability in the tort of negligence independently of the existence of any contract.

The present case fell fairly and squarely within the judge's category (3). He said, at p. 509:

> The category (3) question has arisen in very many different types of case and the answer is treated as so obvious that it passes without any comment. It is commonplace that actions are brought by persons who have suffered personal injuries as the result of the negligence of the person sued and that there is a contractual as well as tortious relationship. In such cases apportionment of blame is invariably adopted by the court notwithstanding that the plaintiff could sue in contract as well as in tort. The example normally cited in the present context is the decision of the Court of Appeal in *Sayers* v *Harlow Urban District Council* [1958] 2 All ER 342, [1958] 1 WLR 623, which concerned a contractual visitor to premises (a lady who had paid to use a public lavatory). The Court of Appeal said it did not matter whether the cause of action was put in tort or in contract and proceeded to apportion blame awarding her three-quarters of her damages. This was a decision on a category (3) case. The power to make an apportionment was part of the ratio decidendi and is binding on me. There are innumerable similar decisions to the same effect which could be cited, very many by appellate courts. . . .

In my judgment *Sayers* v *Harlow Urban District Council* is a category (3) case and the decision of the Court of Appeal that there is power to apportion was not only right but is binding on us just as the judge held it was binding on him. . . .

I am satisfied that the judge came to the right conclusion on this topic and in respect of it I would dismiss Vesta's appeal.

NOTES

1. This case fell within Hobhouse J's category (3) so that the Act applied. (See also *Platform Home Loans Ltd* v *Oyston Shipways Ltd* [2000] 2 AC 190.) Hobhouse J indicated that the Act did not apply to category (1) cases, i.e., breaches of strict contractual obligations. The decision of the Court of Appeal was affirmed by the House of Lords on other grounds.

2. The Law Commission Working Paper No. 114, *Contributory Negligence as a Defence in Contract* (1990) (see especially pp. 69–73), recommended that, unless the contract expressly declared to the contrary, the courts should be able to apportion damages in all three contractual cases where the plaintiff's conduct contributed to his loss. However, in its Report, Law Commission No. 219, 1993, the Law Commission recommended apportionment of damages where there is a breach of a qualified contractual obligation (contractual negligence), but not if the breach is of a strict contractual obligation. The Report recommended a separate legislative provision for the contractual position and included a draft Bill. Under the proposed legislation it would, however, be possible to exclude apportionment for contributory negligence, either expressly or by implication (e.g., using a liquidated damages clause to fix the damages in advance, see further *pages 414–17*).

Barclays Bank plc v *Fairclough Building Ltd*
[1995] QB 214 (CA)

The defendant contractor was in breach of a contract to clean roofs containing asbestos, in that it had failed to execute the work in an expeditious, efficient, and workmanlike manner and had failed to comply with statutory requirements relating to asbestos. The defendant argued that the plaintiff had failed to supervise the work and therefore damages should be reduced for this contributory negligence under the 1945 Act. Held: contributory negligence was not a defence to a claim for damages based on a breach of a strict contractual obligation, even where the defendant might have also had a parallel liability in tort.

SIMON BROWN LJ: . . . [W]hen, as in a category (1) case, the contractual liability is by no means immaterial, when rather it is a strict liability arising independently of any negligence on the defendants' part, then there seem to me compelling reasons why the contract, even assuming it is silent as to apportionment, should be construed as excluding the operation of the Act of 1945. The very imposition of a strict liability on the defendant is to my mind inconsistent with an apportionment of the loss. And not least because of the absurdities that the contrary approach carries in its wake. Assume a defendant, clearly liable under a strict contractual duty. Is his position to be improved by demonstrating that besides breaching that duty he was in addition negligent? Take this very case. Is this contract really to be construed so that the defendant is advantaged by an assertion of its own liability in nuisance or trespass as well as in contract? Are we to have trials at which the defendant calls an expert to implicate him in tortious liability, whilst the plaintiffs' expert seeks paradoxically to exonerate him? The answer to all these questions is surely 'No'. Whatever arguments exist for apportionment in other categories of case—and these are persuasively deployed in the 1993 Law Commission Report, (Law Com No. 219)—to my mind there are none in the present type of case and I for my part would construe the contract accordingly.

NOTE: This decision indicates the importance of correctly identifying the nature of the obligation broken (see *page 330*) and is in line with the Law Commission's position in its 1993 Report.

H: Agreed damages clauses

The contract may provide that specified damages shall be payable in respect of particular types of breach, thus avoiding difficulties of quantification and avoiding disruptions to a continuing legal relationship.

However, a distinction has been drawn between 'liquidated damages clauses', which are enforceable, and 'penalty clauses', which are not enforceable beyond the amount of the injured party's actual loss. Liquidated damages represent 'a genuine pre-estimate of the loss' which will be suffered as a result of the breach. A penalty clause is not an attempt to compensate for actual loss suffered but is designed as a threat to compel performance.

(a) Is an agreed damages clause a liquidated damages clause or a penalty?

Dunlop Pneumatic Tyre Co. Ltd v **New Garage & Motor Co. Ltd**
[1915] AC 79 (HL)

The appellants supplied motor tyres, covers and tubes to the respondent dealers under an agreement whereby the respondents received certain trade discounts and agreed not to tamper with the marks on the goods, not to sell or offer the goods to any private customer or to any cooperative society at less than the appellants' list prices, not to supply to persons to whom the appellants would not supply and 'to pay the sum of £5 by way of liquidated damages for every tyre, cover or tube sold or offered in breach of the agreement'. The respondents sold a tyre cover to a cooperative society at below the current list price and the appellants sought damages. The respondents pleaded that the clause was a penalty. Held: it was a liquidated damages clause, so the appellants could recover this amount as damages.

LORD DUNEDIN: . . . I shall content myself with stating succinctly the various propositions which I think are deducible from the decisions which rank as authoritative:—

1. Though the parties to a contract who use the words 'penalty' or 'liquidated damages' may prima facie be supposed to mean what they say, yet the expression used is not conclusive. The Court must find out whether the payment stipulated is in truth a penalty or liquidated damages. This doctrine may be said to be found passim in nearly every case.

2. The essence of a penalty is a payment of money stipulated as in terrorem of the offending party; the essence of liquidated damages is a genuine covenanted pre-estimate of damage (*Clydebank Engineering and Shipbuilding Co.* v *Don Jose Ramos Yzquierdo y Castaneda* [1905] AC 6).

3. The question whether a sum stipulated is penalty or liquidated damages is a question of construction to be decided upon the terms and inherent circumstances of each particular contract, judged of as at the time of the making of the contract, not as at the time of the breach . . .

4. To assist this task of construction various tests have been suggested, which if applicable to the case under consideration may prove helpful, or even conclusive. Such are:

   (a) It will be held to be penalty if the sum stipulated for is extravagant and unconscionable in amount in comparison with the greatest loss that could conceivably be proved to have followed from the breach.

   (b) It will be held to be a penalty if the breach consists only in not paying a sum of money, and the sum stipulated is a sum greater than the sum which ought to have been paid (*Kemble* v *Farren* (1829) 6 Bing 141). This though one of the most ancient instances is truly a corollary to the last test. . . .

   (c) There is a presumption (but no more) that it is penalty when 'a single lump sum is made payable by way of compensation, on the occurrence of one or more or all of several events, some of which may occasion serious and others but trifling damage'.

   On the other hand:

   (d) It is no obstacle to the sum stipulated being a genuine pre-estimate of damage, that the consequences of the breach are such as to make precise pre-estimation almost an impossibility. On the contrary, that is just the situation when it is probable that pre-estimated damage was the true bargain between the parties . . .

Turning now to the facts of the case, it is evident that the damage apprehended by the appellants owing to the breaking of the agreement was an indirect and not a direct damage. So long as they got their price from the respondents for each article sold, it could not matter to them directly what the respondents did with it. Indirectly it did. Accordingly, the agreeement is headed 'Price Maintenance Agreement,' and the way in which the appellants would be damaged if prices were cut is clearly explained in evidence by Mr Baisley, and no successful attempt is made to controvert that evidence. But though damage as a whole from such a practice would be certain, yet damage from any one sale would be impossible to forecast. It is just, therefore, one of those cases where it seems quite reasonable for parties to contract that they should estimate that damage at a certain figure, and provided that figure is not extravagant there would seem no reason to suspect that it is not truly a bargain to assess damages, but rather a penalty to be held in terrorem.

NOTES
1. The terminology used is not conclusive.
2. Recent case law has adopted the following statement of Colman J in *Lordsvale Finance plc* v *Bank of Zambia* [1996] AC 752, at 762, interpreting *Dunlop Pneumatic Tyre*: 'whether a provision is to be treated as a penalty is a matter of construction to be resolved by asking whether at the time the contract was entered into the predominant contractual function of the provision was to deter a party from breaking the contract or to compensate the innocent party for breach. That the contractual function is deterrent rather than compensatory can be deduced by comparing the amount that would be payable on breach with the loss that might be sustained if breach occurred'. (Cited with approval by the Court of Appeal in *United International Pictures* v *Cine Bes Filmcilik ve Yapimcilik AS* [2003] EWCA Civ 1669, [2004] ICLC 401,

and by Burnton J in *Murray v Leisureplay plc* [2004] EWHC 1927 (QB), unrep. 5 August 2004.) On this basis the core question is the purpose underlying the clause so that Colman J considered that there was no reason why a clause should be struck down as a penalty if it was 'commercially justifiable' and 'its dominant purpose was not to deter the other party from breach'.

3. In *Philips Hong Kong Ltd v AG of Hong Kong* (1993) 61 BLR 41, the Privy Council stressed the need for certainty in commercial contracts such as complex construction contracts, and the need for commercial parties to be able to rely upon damages clauses which they have agreed. Lord Woolf (giving the judgment) held that the general approach should therefore be against a finding that a clause was penal. In so doing he recognised the difficulty of drafting a clause that would never operate in a penal way.

It had been argued that the clause would necessarily be penal if, in the case of certain hypothetical breaches, the agreed sum would be greater than the actual loss. However, Lord Woolf stated (at pp. 58–9) that:

> Except possibly in the case of situations where one of the parties to the contract is able to dominate the other as to the choice of the terms of a contract, it will normally be insufficient to establish that a provision is objectionably penal to identify situations where the application of the provision could result in a larger sum being recovered by the injured party than his actual loss. Even in such situations so long as the sum payable in the event of non-compliance with the contract is not extravagant, having regard to the range of losses that it could reasonably be anticipated it would have to cover at the time the contract was made, it can still be a genuine pre-estimate of the loss that would be suffered and so a perfectly valid liquidated damage provision. The use in argument of unlikely illustrations should therefore not assist a party to defeat a provision as to liquidated damages . . . In seeking to establish that the sum described in the Philips contract as liquidated damages was in fact a penalty, Philips has to surmount the strong inference to the contrary resulting from its agreement to make the payments as liquidated damages and the fact that it is not suggesting in these proceedings that the sum claimed is excessive in relation to the actual loss suffered by the Government. The fact that the issue has to be determined objectively, judged at the date the contract was made, does not mean what actually happens subsequently is irrelevant. On the contrary it can provide valuable evidence as to what could reasonably be expected to be the loss at the time the contract was made. Likewise the fact that two parties who should be well capable of protecting their respective commercial interests agreed the allegedly penal provision suggests that the formula for calculating liquidated damages is unlikely to be oppressive. . . .

In the light of this pragmatic approach, it would appear that Lord Dunedin's guidelines should not be interpreted too literally in the context of commercial contracts where the parties are of equal bargaining power. However, in *Jeancharm Ltd v Barnet Football Club Ltd* [2003] EWCA Civ 58, 92 Con LR 26, the Court of Appeal made it clear that the principle in *Philips* cannot rescue a clause which, on its face, is clearly not a genuine pre-estimate of the likely loss. The clause in question provided for interest at 5 per cent per week (260 per cent per annum) if the club was late in paying its supplier for football kits. The club alleged that this clause was unenforceable as a penalty. However, the supplier argued that *Philips* required the court to assess the entire contract, including the risks on each side, and the interest clause was balanced by a clause whereby the supplier had to pay the club 20p per garment per day for late delivery. The Court of Appeal rejected this argument. *Philips* had not altered the basic principle that the clause had to be a genuine pre-estimate of the loss. Since this interest clause provided for an extravagant interest payment compared to the greatest loss that could be perceived following late delivery, it was clearly a penalty clause. For *Philips* to apply, the clause on its face should appear to be a genuine pre-estimate of the loss following from the anticipated breach or breaches, as opposed to purely hypothetical breaches that might be imagined.

4. In *Cenargo Ltd v Izar Construcciones Navales SA* [2002] EWCA Civ 524, [2002] CLC 1151, *obiter* the Court of Appeal adopted the approach in *Phillips* and considered that an agreed damages clause in a commercial contract should not be tested against trifling breaches causing trifling

loss (on the basis that this would make a freely bargained for clause an unenforceable penalty). Therefore, the clause should be construed as applying only to major breaches, for which it would be a genuine pre-estimate of the loss, and not to trifling breaches which could be easily remedied by a small award of unliquidated damages. This clearly conflicts with Lord Dunedin's guideline 4(c) and appears to be a matter of expediency to preserve something of an agreed damages clause in a commercial contract.

5. If the clause is a liquidated damages clause, then the injured party recovers that amount irrespective of the actual loss sustained.

Cellulose Acetate Silk Company Ltd v *Widnes Foundry (1925) Ltd*
[1933] AC 20 (HL)

In a contract for the delivery and erection of plant, if the work was not completed within a certain time the contractors were to pay to the purchasers by way of 'penalty' a sum of £20 for every week they were in default. The contractors were 30 weeks late in completing the work. The contractors sought the purchase price but the defendant purchasers counterclaimed for their actual loss caused by the delay (£5,850). Held: it was a liquidated damages amount (even though it was set at *less* than the estimated loss). The plaintiffs were therefore only liable to pay £600 (i.e., £20 × 30).

6. The House of Lords in *Suisse Atlantique* [1967] 1 AC 361, *page 280*, distinguished liquidated damages and limitation clauses. Whereas a liquidated damages clause fixes the amount payable irrespective of the loss, a limitation clause merely places an upper limit on the damages available so that any amount of actual loss up to the limitation figure can be claimed.

In the following case the Court of Appeal held that if a clause is a penalty it is not struck out but remains a term of the contract. However, it will not be enforced beyond the amount of the injured party's actual loss.

Jobson v *Johnson*
[1989] 1 WLR 1026 (CA)

The defendant contracted to purchase 62,566 shares in Southend United Football Club for a total price of £351,688, payable by an initial payment of £40,000 and the rest in six half-yearly instalments. If the defendant defaulted on the payment of the second or any subsequent instalment, he was required to transfer the shares back to the vendors for £40,000. The defendant defaulted when he had paid £140,000, and the vendor sought specific performance of the agreement for the retransfer of the shares. The defendant claimed that the contractual provision was a penalty and unenforceable. Held: the transfer of shares for £40,000 was not a genuine pre-estimate of the vendor's loss and was payable on the retransfer irrespective of how much the defendant had paid. Since it was a penalty, the retransfer clause could not be enforced beyond the amount of the vendor's loss.

NICHOLLS LJ: . . . [A] penalty clause in a contract is, in practice, a dead letter. An obligation to make a money payment stipulated in terrorem will not be enforced beyond the sum which represents the actual loss of the party seeking payment, namely, principal, interest and, if appropriate, costs, in those cases where (to use modern terminology) the primary obligation is to pay money, or where the primary obligation is to perform some other obligation, beyond the sum recoverable as damages for breach of that obligation. (For convenience I shall hereafter refer to that sum as 'the actual loss of the innocent party'.) Hence normally there is no advantage in suing on the penalty clause. In *Wall* v

Rederiaktiebolaget Luggude [1915] 3 KB 66, 73, Bailhache J concluded his examination of the history of this matter in the context of a penalty clause in a charterparty with these words:

> This being the state of the law as I understand it, one easily sees why in charterparty cases no one sues on the penalty clause now. You cannot under it recover more than the proved damages, and if the proved damages exceed the penal sum you are restricted to the lower amount. As the penalty clause may be disregarded it always is disregarded and has become a dead letter, or from another point of view a 'brutum fulmen' . . .

This accords with authoritative dicta in *Campbell Discount Co. Ltd* v *Bridge* [1962] AC 600 . . . Likewise Lord Radcliffe, at p. 625:

> In my opinion, a clause of this kind, when founded upon a consequence of a contractual breach, comes within the range of the court's jurisdiction to relieve against penalties, and the owners should be confined to the right of claiming from Bridge any damage that they can show themselves to have actually suffered from his falling down upon the contract. . . .

. . . Although in practice a penalty clause in a contract as described above is effectively a dead letter, it is important in the present case to note that, contrary to the submissions of [counsel for the defendant], the strict legal position is not that such a clause is simply struck out of the contract, as though with a blue pencil, so that the contract takes effect as if it had never been included therein. Strictly, the legal position is that the clause remains in the contract and can be sued upon, but it will not be enforced by the court beyond the sum which represents, in the events which have happened, the actual loss of the party seeking payment. . . .

NOTES
1. See *pages 424* for further discussion of this case.
2. Therefore, if the actual loss is lower than the penalty amount, the lower actual loss is recoverable because the penalty is invalid.
3. What is the position if a clause is a penalty and the actual loss is greater than this amount? Can the higher actual loss be recovered? There appears to be some support for concluding that it can from the decision in *Wall* v *Rederiaktiebolaget Luggude* [1915] 3 KB 66. Although the question was left open in *Cellulose Acetate Silk Co. Ltd* v *Widnes Foundry (1925) Ltd*, it would appear that the Court of Appeal in *Jobson* is suggesting that actual loss damages prevail. (See Hudson (1974) 90 LQR 31 and (1975) 91 LQR 25, and Barton (1976) 92 LQR 20.)
4. The Unfair Terms in Consumer Contracts Regulations 1999, sch. 2(1)(e) provides that in a consumer contract a term may be unfair and unenforceable if it requires 'any consumer who fails to fulfil his obligation to pay a disproportionately high sum in compensation'. This will also strike down penalty clauses. However, it will require an assessment of what is meant by a 'disproportionately high sum' in the general context of unfairness and good faith. Such an assessment will clearly turn on the facts of each case. The examples thus far given in the Office of Fair Trading *Bulletins* (*page 321*) indicate that the Director-General has intervened where no figure is given but it is a matter left within the discretion of the seller or supplier.

(b) Penalties payable on events other than breach of contract

The penalty rule applies only where the sum specified is payable on breach. The penalty will be enforceable where it operates on an event other than breach even if it is a threat to compel performance and thus penal in nature. This leads to unsatisfactory fine distinctions.

Alder v Moore

[1961] 2 QB 57 (CA)

The Association Football Players and Trainers Union took out a policy of insurance on behalf of its members. It provided that if a member of the union suffered permanent total disability which prevented him from playing as a professional footballer he would be paid £500. The defendant received an eye injury in the course of a match and was certified totally disabled. He was paid £500 under the policy and signed a declaration required by the terms of the policy agreeing to 'take no part as a playing member in any form of professional football in the future and that in the event of an infringement of this condition I will be subject to a penalty of the amount stated above' (£500). Within four months of receiving this payment the defendant began to play professional football on a part-time basis. The insurers claimed the return of the £500 and the defendant argued that it was a penalty and unenforceable. Held: (Devlin LJ dissenting) this declaration amounted to a promise to repay the £500 if the defendant played again rather than a promise not to play with a £500 penalty for breach of that promise. The penalty rule did not apply here to relieve the defendant and he had to repay the £500.

Export Credits Guarantee Department v *Universal Oil Products Co.*
[1983] 1 WLR 399 (HL)

The defendants were involved in the construction of oil refineries for the New-foundland companies. The construction was financed by a bank consortium in return for the issue of promissory notes by the Newfoundland companies. The plaintiffs guaranteed these notes to the bank consortium, and by clause 7(1) of their agreement with the defendants, the defendants were to repay the plaintiffs any sums paid by the plaintiffs under the guarantee if the defendants defaulted in the performance of their obligations under the construction contracts. The Newfound-land companies dishonoured notes and the plaintiffs indemnified the bank con-sortium for £39,571,000 but claimed this from the defendants on the basis that clause 7(1) operated because the defendants had defaulted. The defendants argued that the clause was a penalty and unenforceable. Held: it was not a penalty since it was not a sum payable on breach of any contract between the plaintiffs and the defendants. It related to the defendants' breach of contractual obligations owed to a third party (the Newfoundland companies).

NOTE: In any event, it is difficult to see what the defendants had to gain by arguing that it was a penalty, since if it was then the plaintiffs could have claimed their actual loss.

The following case concerned the status of minimum payment clauses in hire-purchase contracts (i.e., minimum sums payable if the contract is terminated).

Bridge v *Campbell Discount Co. Ltd*
[1962] AC 600 (HL)

Bridge hired a car under a hire-purchase agreement with a finance company. Clause 6 provided for termination by the hirer on giving notice. Clause 9 provided that in that event the hirer 'shall forthwith . . . pay to the owners . . . by way of agreed compensation for depreciation of the vehicle such further sums as may be neces-sary to make the rentals paid and payable equal to two-thirds of the hire-purchase price'. Bridge terminated the agreement when he had paid the initial payment and the first monthly instalment on the ground that he could not keep up the pay-ments. Held: clause 9 was a penalty since the depreciation would increase as the clause amount decreased.

LORD RADCLIFFE: . . . Since the obligation under clause 9(b) may mature at any time from the beginning to the end of the hiring, a week after the beginning or a week before the end, it seems to me impossible to take a single formula for measuring the damage as any true pre-estimate. It produces the result, absurd in its own terms, that the estimated amount of depreciation becomes progressively less the longer the vehicle is used under the hire. This is because the sum agreed upon diminishes as the total of the cash payments increases. It is a sliding scale of compensation, but a scale that slides in the wrong direction, if the measure of anticipated depreciation is to be supposed to be the basis for the compensation agreed upon. The fact that this anomalous result is deliberately produced by the formula employed suggests, I think, that the real purpose of this clause is not to provide compensation for depreciation at all but to afford the owners a substantial guarantee against the loss of their hiring contract. . . .

NOTES
1. Bridge was in breach of his contractual obligations and therefore had not terminated under the option in clause 6. Since Bridge was in breach of contract, clause 9 was unenforceable and the finance company could recover only their actual loss.
2. Paradoxically, the hirer who breaks the hire-purchase contract by failing to pay can rely on the penalty rule and avoid the minimum payment, but if the hirer is not in breach and exercises an option to terminate, the penalty is enforceable and the minimum payment must be made. Lord Denning in *Bridge* v *Campbell Discount Co. Ltd* said (at pp. 628–9):

> The truth is that this minimum-payment is not so much compensation for depreciation but rather compensation for loss of the future instalments which the hire-purchase company expected to receive, but which they had no right to receive. It is a penal sum which they exact because the hiring is terminated before two-thirds has been paid. In cases when the hiring is terminated; as it was here, within a few weeks, it is beyond doubt oppressive and unjust.
>
> . . . [I]f Bridge, after a few weeks, finds himself unable to keep up the instalments and, being a conscientious man, gives notice of termination and returns the car, without falling into arrear, he is liable to pay the penal sum of £206 3s. 4d. without relief of any kind. But if he is an unconscientious man who falls into arrear without saying a word, so that the company retake the car for his default, he will be relieved from payment of the penalty.
>
> Let no one mistake the injustice of this. It means that equity commits itself to this absurd paradox: it will grant relief to a man who breaks his contract but will penalise the man who keeps it. . . .

3. If there is a breach, the minimum payment clause will not apply because of the penalty rule. However, a failure to pay instalments is not a repudiatory breach and the owner can recover only for his loss occurring prior to termination (i.e., instalment arrears plus interest). Recovering for future losses would be similar in effect to enforcing the invalid penalty clause (*Financings Ltd* v *Baldock* [1963] 2 QB 104).
4. Although a minimum payment clause may be invalid, it appears that if the failure to pay is drafted as a breach of a condition, then the injured party can terminate for a repudiatory breach and recover the future instalments as actual loss resulting from the breach.

Lombard North Central plc v *Butterworth*
[1987] QB 527 (CA)

The full facts of this case appear at *page 244*. Clause 2 of the agreement provided that punctual payment of each instalment was of the essence of the agreement. Clause 5 contained a right to terminate in the event of default in payment, and clause 6 entitled the owner to all future instalments which would have fallen due, as well as arrears. Held: clause 6 was an unenforceable penalty but, since clause 2 made punctual payment a condition of the contract, there had been a repudiatory breach entitling the owners to terminate independently of clause 5. They could recover their actual loss, and therefore recovered what would have been recovered had clause 6 operated.

MUSTILL LJ: . . .

7. A term of the contract prescribing what damages are to be recoverable when a contract is terminated for a breach of condition is open to being struck down as a penalty, if it is not a genuine covenanted pre-estimate of the damage, in the same way as a clause which prescribes the measure for any other type of breach. No doubt the position is the same where the clause is ranked as a condition by virtue of an express provision in the contract.

8. A clause expressly assigning a particular obligation to the category of condition is not a clause which purports to fix the damages for breaches of the obligation, and is not subject to the law governing penalty clauses.

9. Thus, although in the present case clause 6 is to be struck down as a penalty, clause 2(a)(i) remains enforceable. The plaintiffs were entitled to terminate the contract independently of clause 5, and to recover damages for loss of the future instalments. . . .

I believe that the real controversy in the present case centres upon the eighth proposition. I will repeat it: a clause expressly assigning a particular obligation to the category of conditions is not a clause which purports to fix the damages for breach of the obligation, and is not subject to the law governing penalty clauses. I acknowledge, of course, that by promoting a term into the category where all breaches are ranked as breaches of condition, the parties indirectly bring about a situation where, for breaches which are relatively small, the injured party is enabled to recover damages as on the loss of the bargain, whereas without the stipulation his measure of recovery would be different. But I am unable to accept that this permits the court to strike down as a penalty the clause which brings about this promotion. To do so would be to reverse the current of more than 100 years' doctrine, which permits the parties to treat as a condition something which would not otherwise be so. I am not prepared to take this step.

NOTES
1. This continues the extract at *pages 244–5*.
2. It seems a remarkably easy method of avoiding the effects of the penalty rule simply by including a clause making punctual payment of the essence of the contract.
3. The minimum payments clause in a consumer contract may not be binding on the consumer under the Unfair Terms in Consumer Contracts Regulations 1999 (see reg. 5(5) and sch. 2(1)(e), *pages 319–20*). See also ss. 99 and 100, Consumer Credit Act 1974.

(c) Deposits and forfeiture clauses

A deposit is an advance payment, and if the payer defaults the other party is entitled to forfeit the deposit, i.e., keep it (*Howe* v *Smith* (1884) 27 ChD 89), whether or not he has suffered any loss as a result of the default. The deposit may also be seen as an incentive to perform, i.e., 'an earnest to bind the bargain'.

The only possible relief available to the defaulting payer is:

(a) if the deposit figure is unreasonable, so that the forfeiture clause is an unenforceable penalty; and/or

(b) if the court is (otherwise) prepared to grant relief against forfeiture. There is some debate concerning the jurisdiction to grant relief against forfeiture. In *Stockloser* v *Johnson* [1954] 1 QB 476, both Denning and Somervell LJJ thought that the deposit might be recoverable in equity if the forfeiture was penal and it was unconscionable for the injured party to retain the money. However, there was a strong dissent from Romer LJ, who stated that unless there was evidence of fraud or sharp practice by the payee, equity would not order repayment of the deposit. This is the view which has subsequently been followed (e.g., Sachs J in *Galbraith* v *Mitchenhall Estates Ltd* [1965] 2 QB 473).

Workers Trust and Merchant Bank Ltd v *Dojap Investments Ltd*
[1993] AC 573 (PC)

The bank, acting as second mortgagee, agreed to sell land for Jamaican $11,500,000. The purchaser paid a deposit of 25 per cent ($2,875,000) in accordance with clause 4 of the contract. The contract provided for forfeiture of the deposit in the event of default by the purchaser. The contract also required the remainder of the price to be paid within 14 days of the auction sale and stated that time was of the essence of the contract. The purchaser defaulted, and although the balance plus interest was tendered a week later than required under the contract, the bank returned it and purported to forfeit the deposit. The purchaser sought relief against forfeiture of the deposit. Held: the deposit had to be repaid once the bank had subtracted from it its actual loss suffered as a result of the breach.

LORD BROWNE-WILKINSON: . . . In general, a contractual provision which requires one party in the event of his breach of the contract to pay or forfeit a sum of money to the other party is unlawful as being a penalty, unless such provision can be justified as being a payment of liquidated damages being a genuine pre-estimate of the loss which the innocent party will incur by reason of the breach. One exception to this general rule is the provision for the payment of a deposit by the purchaser on a contract for the sale of land. Ancient law has established that the forfeiture of such a deposit (customarily 10 per cent. of the contract price) does not fall within the general rule and can be validly forfeited even though the amount of the deposit bears no reference to the anticipated loss to the vendor flowing from the breach of contract.

This exception is anomalous and at least one textbook writer has been surprised that the courts of equity ever countenanced it: see Farrand, *Contract and Conveyancing*, 4th ed. (1983), p. 204. The special treatment afforded to such a deposit derives from the ancient custom of providing an earnest for the performance of a contract in the form of giving either some physical token of earnest (such as a ring) or earnest money. The history of the law of deposits can be traced to the Roman law of arra, and possibly further back still: see *Howe* v *Smith* (1884) 27 Ch D 89, 101–102, per Fry LJ. Ever since the decision in *Howe* v *Smith* the nature of such a deposit has been settled in English law. Even in the absence of express contractual provision, it is an earnest for the performance of the contract: in the event of completion of the contract the deposit is applicable towards payment of the purchase price; in the event of the purchaser's failure to complete in accordance with the terms of the contract, the deposit is forfeit, equity having no power to relieve against such forfeiture.

However, the special treatment afforded to deposits is plainly capable of being abused if the parties to a contract, by attaching the label 'deposit' to any penalty, could escape the general rule which renders penalties unenforceable. There are two authorities which indicate that this cannot be done. In *Stockloser* v *Johnson* [1954] 1 QB 476, Denning LJ in considering the power of the court to relieve against forfeiture said, obiter, at p. 491:

> Again, suppose that a vendor of property, in lieu of the usual 10 per cent. deposit, stipulates for an initial payment of 50 per cent. of the price as a deposit and part payment, and later, when the purchaser fails to complete, the vendor re-sells the property at a profit and in addition claims to forfeit the 50 per cent. deposit. Surely the court will relieve against the forfeiture. The vendor cannot forestall this equity by describing an extravagant sum as a deposit, any more than he can recover a penalty by calling it liquidated damages.

In *Linggi Plantations Ltd* v *Jagatheesan* [1972] 1 MLJ 89 Lord Hailsham of St. Marylebone LC delivered the judgment of the Board which upheld the claim to forfeit a normal 10 per cent. deposit even though the vendor had in fact suffered no loss. He referred on a number of occasions to a requirement that the amount of a deposit should be 'reasonable' and said, at 94:

It is also no doubt possible that in a particular contract the parties may use language normally appropriate to deposits properly so called and even to forfeiture which turn out on investigation to be purely colourable and that in such a case the real nature of the transaction might turn out to be the imposition of a penalty, by purporting to render forfeit something which is in truth part payment. This no doubt explains why in some cases the irrecoverable nature of a deposit is qualified by the insertion of the adjective 'reasonable' before the noun. But the truth is that a reasonable deposit has always been regarded as a guarantee of performance as well as a payment on account, and its forfeiture has never been regarded as a penalty in English law or common English usage.

In the view of their Lordships these passages accurately reflect the law. It is not possible for the parties to attach the incidents of a deposit to the payment of a sum of money unless such sum is reasonable as earnest money. The question therefore is whether or not the deposit of 25 per cent. in this case was reasonable as being in line with the traditional concept of earnest money or was in truth a penalty intended to act in terrorem.

[The Chief Justice] tested the question of 'reasonableness' by reference to the evidence before him that it was of common occurrence for banks in Jamaica selling property at auction to demand deposits of between 15 per cent. and 50 per cent. He held that, since this was a common practice, it was reasonable. Like the Court of Appeal, their Lordships are unable to accept this reasoning. In order to be reasonable a true deposit must be objectively operating as 'earnest money' and not as a penalty. To allow the test of reasonableness to depend upon the practice of one class of vendor, which exercises considerable financial muscle, would be to allow them to evade the law against penalties by adopting practices of their own.

However, although their Lordships are satisfied that the practice of a limited class of vendors cannot determine the reasonableness of a deposit, it is more difficult to define what the test should be. Since a true deposit may take effect as a penalty, albeit one permitted by law, it is hard to draw a line between a reasonable, permissible amount of penalty and an unreasonable, impermissible penalty. In their Lordships' view the correct approach is to start from the position that, without logic but by long continued usage both in the United Kingdom and formerly in Jamaica, the customary deposit has been 10 per cent. A vendor who seeks to obtain a larger amount by way of forfeitable deposit must show special circumstances which justify such a deposit.

. . . In the view of their Lordships, since the 25 per cent. deposit was not a true deposit by way of earnest, the provision for its forfeiture was a plain penalty. There is clear authority that in a case of a sum paid by one party to another under the contract as security for the performance of that contract, a provision for its forfeiture in the event of non-performance is a penalty from which the court will give relief by ordering repayment of the sum so paid, less any damage actually proved to have been suffered as a result of non-completion: *Commissioner of Public Works* v *Hills* [1906] AC 368. Accordingly, there is jurisdiction in the court to order repayment of the 25 per cent. deposit. . . .

Finally, it appears that the bank may have suffered some damage as a result of the purchaser's failure to complete. If so, the bank is entitled to deduct the amount of such damages from the 'deposit' of 25 per cent. Such damage has not been quantified in the judgment below but appears to be small in amount. It would not be right to keep the purchaser out of all its money to await the outcome of the necessary inquiry as to damages. The bank ought accordingly to make immediate repayment of a substantial amount of the deposit, leaving a fund out of which the bank's damages, if any, can be satisfied.

NOTES
1. See Beale, 'Unreasonable Deposits' (1993) 109 LQR 524.
2. The Law Commission Working Paper No. 61, 'Penalty Clauses and Forfeiture of Monies Paid' (1975), paras 65 and 66, recommended that forfeiture clauses should be subject to the same rule as penalty clauses. The test applied by the Privy Council is different, in that the essential question determining whether a deposit is a penalty is one of 'unreasonableness' rather than whether the sum is a genuine pre-estimate of the loss.
3. If a contract requires a deposit amount which is later considered to be unreasonable, the courts will not insert a reasonable figure in its place and allow forfeiture.

4. It may be significant that it is far from clear whether the Privy Council was in fact dealing with the case on the basis of the penalty rule or on the basis of granting relief against forfeiture. Lord Browne-Wilkinson stated that it was not necessary for him to decide between the alternative positions on relief against forfeiture in *Stockloser* v *Johnson* and that the deposit was a penalty which the court would order to be repaid. If the case was being dealt with on the basis of granting equitable relief against forfeiture, the court would have far more of a discretion in terms of how the deposit should be dealt with. It is therefore suggested that this case in fact turns on the application of the penalty rule.

In *Jobson* v *Johnson* [1989] 1 WLR 1026 (*page 417*), the re-transfer agreement was not only a penalty but also a form of security for payment of the price. The defendant had alternatively counterclaimed for relief against forfeiture. This counterclaim was struck out at trial on procedural grounds, but the Court of Appeal did discuss the relationship between the penalty rule and relief against forfeiture of a deposit. Essentially, relief against a penalty is as of right and cuts down recovery to the extent of the injured party's actual loss, whereas relief against forfeiture is discretionary, granted subject to conditions, and overrides the forfeiture clause. It is helpful, therefore, if the forfeiture clause is a penalty since automatic penalty relief will follow.

Nicholls LJ in *Jobson* v *Johnson* said (at pp. 1038, 1042–3):

In considering this appeal it is right to have in mind that the legal principles applicable today regarding penalty clauses in contracts and those applicable regarding relief from forfeiture stem from a common origin. A penalty clause in a contract, as that expression is normally used today, is a provision which, on breach of the contract, requires the party in default to make a payment to the innocent party of a sum of money which, however it may be labelled, is not a genuine pre-estimate of the damage likely to be sustained by the innocent party, but is a payment stipulated in terrorem of the party in default. For centuries equity has given relief against such provisions by not permitting the innocent party to recover under the penal provision more than his actual loss. . . .

Likewise with forfeiture. Take the simple case of a provision for forfeiture of a lease on non-payment of rent. That provision was regarded by equity as a security for the rent. So that, where conscience so required, equity relieved against the forfeiture on payment of the rent with interest. . . . In the case of a penalty clause in a contract equity relieves by cutting down the extent to which the contractual obligation is enforceable: the 'scaling-down' exercise, as I have described it. In the case of forfeiture clauses equitable relief takes the form of relieving wholly against the contractual forfeiture provision, subject to compliance with conditions imposed by the court. Be that as it may, I see no reason why the court's ability to grant discretionary relief automatically granted in respect of a penalty clause if, exceptionally, a contractural provision has characteristics which enable a defendant to pray in aid both heads of relief. . . .

Paragraph 6(b) . . . is something of a hybrid. It possesses the essential characteristics of a penalty clause in a contract. It also possesses features which resemble those of a forfeiture provision. Paragraph 6(b) provided that if the purchaser failed to pay all the agreed instalments, he would retransfer to the vendors a slice (44.9 per cent.) of the issued share capital of the company equal to the slice the vendors had sold to him. In substance paragraph 6(b) is equivalent to a right to re-take the property being sold in default of payment of the full price. Paragraph 6(b) was inserted as an attempt to give the vendors some 'security' over the property being sold if the purchaser failed to pay in full. . . .

NOTES
1. See Harpum, 'Equitable relief—penalties and forfeitures' [1989] CLJ 370.
2. The Unfair Terms in Consumer Contracts Regulations 1999, sch. 2(1)(d), indicates that a term may be unfair in a consumer contract where it permits 'the seller or supplier to retain sums paid by the consumer where the latter decides not to conclude or perform the contract,

without providing for the consumer to receive compensation of any equivalent amount from the seller or supplier where the latter is the party cancelling the contract'.

Union Eagle Ltd v *Golden Achievement Ltd*
[1997] AC 514 (PC)

The plaintiff had agreed to buy a flat and had paid a deposit of 10 per cent of the purchase price. The purchase agreement specified the date, time, and place of completion and stated that time was of the essence of the contract, so that the vendor had the right to terminate the contract and forfeit the deposit if the purchaser failed to comply with any term of the agreement. The purchaser failed to complete by the stipulated time and was 10 minutes late tendering the purchase price. The vendor therefore terminated the contract and forfeited the deposit. The plaintiff sought specific performance of the agreement. The Privy Council dismissed the action seeking specific performance (upholding the decisions of the judge and of the Court of Appeal of Hong Kong). The purchaser had committed a repudiatory breach, which entitled the vendor to reject late performance and terminate the contract.

The Privy Council also rejected the plaintiff's argument seeking relief against forfeiture in the form of an extension of the time for completion. The Privy Council stressed that what was important was not the fact that performance was only slightly late but that the purchaser had failed to comply with an essential time condition.

LORD HOFFMANN (delivering the judgment of the Privy Council): The boundaries of the equitable jurisdiction to relieve against contractual penalties and forfeitures are in some places imprecise. But their Lordships do not think that it is necessary in this case to draw them more exactly because they agree with [the judge at first instance] that the facts lie well beyond the reach of the doctrine. The notion that the court's jurisdiction to grant relief is 'unlimited and unfettered' (per Lord Simon of Glaisdale in *Shiloh Spinners Ltd* v *Harding* [1973] AC 691, 726) was rejected as a 'beguiling heresy' by the House of Lords in *Scandinavian Trading Tanker Co. A.B.* v *Flota Petrolera Ecuatoriana (The Scaptrade)* [1983] 2 AC 694, 700. It is worth pausing to notice why it continues to beguile and why it is a heresy. It has the obvious merit of allowing the court to impose what it considers to be a fair solution in the individual case. The principle that equity will restrain the enforcement of legal rights when it would be unconscionable to insist upon them has an attractive breadth. But the reasons why the courts have rejected such generalisations, are founded not merely upon authority (see per Lord Radcliffe in *Campbell Discount Co. Ltd* v *Bridge* [1962] AC 600, 626) but also upon practical considerations of business. These are, in summary, that in many forms of transaction it is of great importance that if something happens for which the contract has made express provision, the parties should know with certainty that the terms of the contract will be enforced. The existence of an undefined discretion to refuse to enforce the contract on the ground that this would be 'unconscionable' is sufficient to create uncertainty. Even if it is most unlikely that a discretion to grant relief will be exercised, its mere existence enables litigation to be employed as a negotiating tactic. The realities of commercial life are that this may cause injustice which cannot be fully compensated by the ultimate decision in the case.

. . . When a vendor exercises his right to rescind, he terminates the contract. The purchaser's loss of the right to specific performance may be said to amount to a forfeiture of the equitable interest which the contract gave him in the land. But this forfeiture is different in its nature from, for example, the vendor's right to retain a deposit or part payments of the purchase price. So far as these retentions exceed a genuine pre-estimate of damage or a reasonable deposit they will constitute a penalty which can be said to be essentially to provide security for payment of the full price. No objectionable uncertainty is created by the existence of a restitutionary form of relief against forfeiture, which gives the court a discretion to order repayment of all or part of the retained money. But the right to rescind the contract, though it involves termination of the purchaser's equitable interest, stands upon a rather different footing. Its purpose is, upon breach of an essential term, to restore to the vendor his freedom to deal with his land as he pleases. In a rising market, such a right may be valuable but volatile. Their Lordships think that in such circumstances a vendor should be able to know with reasonable certainty whether he may resell the land or not.

It is for this reason that, for the past 80 years, the courts in England although ready to grant restitutionary relief against penalties, have been unwilling to grant relief by way of specific performance against breach of an essential condition as to time. In *Steedman* v *Drinkle* [1916] 1 AC 275, 279 Viscount Haldane said:

> Courts of Equity, which look at the substance as distinguished from the letter of agreements, no doubt exercise an extensive jurisdiction which enables them to decree specific performance in cases where justice requires it, even though literal terms of stipulations as to time have not been observed. But they never exercise this jurisdiction where the parties have expressly intimated in their agreement that it is not to apply by providing that time is to be of the essence of their bargain.

. . . The present case seems to their Lordships to be one to which the full force of the general rule applies. The fact is that the purchaser was late. Any suggestion that relief can be obtained on the ground that he was only slightly late is bound to lead to arguments over how late is too late, which can be resolved only by litigation. For five years the vendor has not known whether he is entitled to resell the flat or not. It has been sterilised by a caution pending a final decision in this case. In his dissenting judgment, Godfrey JA said that the case 'cries out for the intervention of equity.' Their Lordships think that, on the contrary, it shows the need for a firm restatement of the principle that in cases of rescission of an ordinary contract of sale of land for failure to comply with an essential condition as to time, equity will not intervene.

NOTES
1. The purchaser had claimed relief against forfeiture in the form of an extension of time to complete on the basis that it would be unconscionable for the vendor to exercise its contractual rights. However, this was extremely unlikely to succeed given the clear wording of the contract and, as Lord Hoffmann stressed, the need for commercial certainty. Interestingly, there was no attempt to claim relief against forfeiture of the deposit paid. Although it might be argued that it is desirable that the vendor should know the contractual position and be able to resell the property (perhaps at a profit), it is far from clear that he should also be able to keep the deposit. However, there is no relief against forfeiture of deposits unless the deposit is unreasonable.
2. The purchaser had also argued that the deposit was a penalty since it was not a genuine pre-estimate of the loss that the vendor would incur on breach. However, on the basis of *Workers Trust & Merchant Bank* v *Dojap Investments Ltd*, *page 422 above*, such an argument was bound to fail. It was a reasonable deposit to which the penalty rule does not apply and therefore it was irrelevant whether or not it was a genuine pre-estimate of the loss.

SECTION 2: **ACTION FOR AN AGREED SUM**

If one party has performed his primary contractual obligations and the other party's breach consists of a failure to pay the contractual price or other agreed sum, the performing party can claim this agreed (liquidated) sum rather than damages.

In relation to an action for the price in a contract for the sale of goods, the Sale of Goods Act 1979, s. 49, provides:

(1) Where, under a contract of sale, the property in the goods has passed to the buyer and he wrongfully neglects or refuses to pay for the goods according to the terms of the contract, the seller may maintain an action against him for the price of the goods.

Since it is a liquidated claim, the remoteness rules and duty to mitigate do not apply (see *White & Carter (Councils) Ltd* v *McGregor* [1962] AC 413 (*page 342*), which was an action for an agreed sum where the plaintiffs were able to continue with performance and claim the agreed sum without having to mitigate). In addition, because it is a liquidated claim it has the procedural advantage that summary judgment can be applied for (i.e., early judgment).

SECTION 3: SPECIFIC PERFORMANCE AND INJUNCTIONS

Specific performance is an order of the court requiring the party in breach to perform his primary obligations under the contract. In relation to the sale of goods the remedy has been put into statutory form. Section 52 of the Sale of Goods Act 1979 gives the court a discretion to order specific performance 'in any action for breach of contract to deliver specific or ascertained goods' (i.e., goods identified and agreed upon at the time of contracting or subsequently). See also s. 48E(2) of the Sale of Goods Act 1979, inserted by the Sale and Supply of Goods to Consumers Regulations 2002, SI 2002/3045, granting the discretion to order specific performance of the repair or replacement option in consumer contracts.

An injunction is an order restraining a breach of a negative stipulation in a contract, e.g., breach of a restraint of trade stipulation (*page 674*).

It is important to remember that, unlike damages, these are discretionary remedies.

Numerous restrictions are placed on the ability of the injured party to obtain an order for specific performance. These restrictions also apply to the grant of an injunction against the breach of a negative stipulation in the contract which would have the same effect as an order to perform the obligation.

(a) If damages are an adequate remedy specific performance is not available

In *Beswick* v *Beswick* [1968] AC 58 (*page 464*), the loss to the estate caused by the nephew's failure to pay the widow the annuity was nominal since it was the widow who suffered the loss. The House of Lords ordered specific performance of the contract on the ground that damages to the estate would not provide an adequate remedy.

In relation to sale of goods, damages will be an adequate remedy if it is possible for the injured party to purchase substitute goods (*Société des Industries Metallurgiques SA* v *The Bronx Engineering Co. Ltd* [1975] 1 Lloyd's Rep 465). If the goods are unique, then damages might not be adequate.

Sky Petroleum Ltd v VIP Petroleum Ltd
[1974] 1 All ER 954

The plaintiff company had agreed to buy all the petrol and diesel fuel needed for its filling stations from the defendant at fixed prices for a period of 10 years. Three and a half years later the defendant purported to terminate the contract, alleging the plaintiff was in breach. The plaintiff sought an interlocutory (or interim) injunction to restrain the defendant from withholding fuel supplies (an unascertained commodity) from the plaintiff. There was evidence that at that time, November 1973, the plaintiff would have little prospect of finding an alternative source of supply. Goulding J recognised that, if he granted the injunction, its effect would be to compel performance of the contract. He held that specific performance would be available because damages would not be an adequate remedy. The defendant was for all practical purposes the sole means of keeping the plaintiff's business going. Since specific performance would have been available, he granted an interlocutory injunction.

(b) Supervision

Specific performance may not be granted where the contract extends over a period of time because of the difficulty of constant supervision (*Ryan* v *Mutual Tontine Westminster Chambers Association* [1893] 1 Ch 116). However, Megarry J in *C. H. Giles & Co. Ltd* v *Morris* [1972] 1 All ER 960, expressed dissatisfaction with any absolute restriction based on difficulties in supervision.

The House of Lords in *Co-operative Insurance Society Ltd* v *Argyll Stores (Holdings) Ltd* clarified the restrictions on the availability of the remedy of specific performance. In particular the House of Lords has clarified what is meant by supervision and made clear that in some circumstances specific performance may still be refused even if damages would be inadequate.

Co-operative Insurance Society Ltd v Argyll Stores (Holdings) Ltd
[1997] 2 WLR 898 (HL)

The plaintiffs, developers of a shopping centre, had granted a 35-year lease of one of the major units in the centre to the defendants, a leading supermarket chain. The presence of a major supermarket was important to the success of the shopping centre since it would attract customers and therefore make it easier to let other, smaller units. The plaintiffs therefore included a covenant in the lease, which was designed to protect them against the possibility that the defendants would move out of the centre. By cl. 4(19) the defendant covenanted to keep the premises open for retail trade during the usual hours of business in the locality. The lease had commenced in August 1979, but in May 1995 the defendants closed the supermarket and moved out of the centre. The plaintiffs sought specific performance of the covenant compelling the defendants to continue to operate the supermarket. It was clear that damages would not be adequate since it would be difficult to quantify the plaintiff's loss over the rest of the term of the lease. The judge had refused to order specific performance, but a majority of the Court of Appeal had overturned this decision and ordered specific performance. The House of Lords allowed the appeal on the basis that specific performance should not be ordered in such circumstances. In particular, it would be difficult to formulate an order with sufficient precision to avoid wasteful litigation concerning compliance with it and, since the effect of such an order might be to order someone to carry on an uneconomic business, the loss might be out of all proportion to the loss being suffered by the plaintiffs as a result of the breach of covenant.

LORD HOFFMANN (with whose judgment the other members of the House of Lords agreed): [Lord Hoffmann first referred to the 'settled practice' whereby the courts would not grant mandatory injunctions requiring the carrying on of a business and continued:]

Specific performance is traditionally regarded in English law as an exceptional remedy, as opposed to the common law damages to which a successful plaintiff is entitled as of right. There may have been some element of later rationalisation of an untidier history, but by the 19th century it was orthodox doctrine that the power to decree specific performance was part of the discretionary jurisdiction of the Court of Chancery to do justice in cases in which the remedies available at common law were inadequate. This is the basis of the general principle that specific performance will not be ordered when damages are an adequate remedy. By contrast, in countries with legal systems based on civil law, such as France, Germany and Scotland, the plaintiff is prima facie entitled to specific performance. The cases in which he is confined to a claim for damages are regarded as the exceptions. In practice, however, there is less difference between common law and civilian systems than these general statements might lead one to suppose. The principles upon which English judges exercise the discretion to grant specific performance are reasonably well settled and depend upon a number of considerations, mostly of a practical nature, which are of very general application. I have made no investigation of civilian systems, but a priori I would expect that judges take much the same matters into account in deciding whether specific performance would be inappropriate in a particular case.

The practice of not ordering a defendant to carry on a business is not entirely dependent upon damages being an adequate remedy. In *Dowty Boulton Paul Ltd* v *Wolverhampton Corporation* [1971] 1 WLR 204, Sir John Pennycuick VC refused to order the corporation to maintain an airfield as a going concern because: 'It is very well established that the court will not order specific performance of an obligation to carry on a business:' see p. 211. He added: 'It is unnecessary in the circumstances to discuss whether damages would be an adequate remedy to the company:' see p. 212. Thus the reasons which underlie the established practice may justify a refusal of specific performance even when damages are not an adequate remedy.

The most frequent reason given in the cases for declining to order someone to carry on a business is that it would require constant supervision by the court. In *J.C Williamson Ltd* v *Lukey and Mulholland* (1931) 45 CLR 282, 297–298, Dixon J said flatly: 'Specific performance is inapplicable when the continued supervision of the court is necessary in order to ensure the fulfilment of the contract.'

There has, I think, been some misunderstanding about what is meant by continued superintendence. It may at first sight suggest that the judge (or some other officer of the court) would literally have to supervise the execution of the order. In *C.H. Giles & Co. Ltd* v *Morris* [1972] 1 WLR 307, 318 Megarry J said that 'difficulties of constant superintendence' were a 'narrow consideration' because:

> there is normally no question of the court having to send its officers to supervise the performance of the order . . . Performance . . . is normally secured by the realisation of the person enjoined that he is liable to be punished for contempt if evidence of his disobedience to the order is put before the court; . . .

This is, of course, true but does not really meet the point. The judges who have said that the need for constant supervision was an objection to such orders were no doubt well aware that supervision would in practice take the form of rulings by the court, on applications made by the parties, as to whether there had been a breach of the order. It is the possibility of the court having to give an indefinite series of such rulings in order to ensure the execution of the order which has been regarded as undesirable.

Why should this be so? A principal reason is that, as Megarry J pointed out in the passage to which

I have referred, the only means available to the court to enforce its order is the quasi-criminal procedure of punishment for contempt. This is a powerful weapon; so powerful, in fact, as often to be unsuitable as an instrument for adjudicating upon the disputes which may arise over whether a business is being run in accordance with the terms of the court's order. The heavy-handed nature of the enforcement mechanism is a consideration which may go to the exercise of the court's discretion in other cases as well, but its use to compel the running of a business is perhaps the paradigm case of its disadvantages and it is in this context that I shall discuss them.

The prospect of committal or even a fine, with the damage to commercial reputation which will be caused by a finding of contempt of court, is likely to have at least two undesirable consequences. First, the defendant, who ex hypothesi did not think that it was in his economic interest to run the business at all, now has to make decisions under a sword of Damocles which may descend if the way the business is run does not conform to the terms of the order. This is, as one might say, no way to run a business. In this case the Court of Appeal made light of the point because it assumed that, once the defendant had been ordered to run the business, self-interest and compliance with the order would thereafter go hand in hand. But, as I shall explain, this is not necessarily true.

Secondly, the seriousness of a finding of contempt for the defendant means that any application to enforce the order is likely to be a heavy and expensive piece of litigation. The possibility of repeated applications over a period of time means that, in comparison with a once-and-for-all inquiry as to damages, the enforcement of the remedy is likely to be expensive in terms of cost to the parties and the resources of the judicial system.

This is a convenient point at which to distinguish between orders which require a defendant to carry on an activity, such as running a business over or more or less extended period of time, and orders which require him to achieve a result. The possibility of repeated applications for rulings on compliance with the order which arises in the former case does not exist to anything like the same extent in the latter. Even if the achievement of the result is a complicated matter which will take some time, the court, if called upon to rule, only has to examine the finished work and say whether it complies with the order. This point was made in the context of relief against forfeiture in *Shiloh Spinners Ltd* v *Harding* [1973] AC 691. If it is a condition of relief that the tenant should have complied with a repairing covenant, difficulty of supervision need not be an objection. As Lord Wilberforce said, at p. 724:

> what the court has to do is to satisfy itself, ex post facto, that the covenanted work has been done, and it has ample machinery, through certificates, or by inquiry, to do precisely this.

This distinction between orders to carry on activities and to achieve results explains why the courts have in appropriate circumstances ordered specific performance of building contracts and repairing covenants: see *Wolverhampton Corporation* v *Emmons* [1901] 1 KB 515 (building contract) and *Jeune* v *Queens Cross Properties Ltd* [1974] Ch 97 (repairing covenant). It by no means follows, however, that even obligations to achieve a result will always be enforced by specific performance. There may be other objections, to some of which I now turn.

One such objection, which applies to orders to achieve a result and a fortiori to orders to carry on an activity, is imprecision in the terms of the order. If the terms of the court's order, reflecting the terms of the obligation, cannot be precisely drawn, the possibility of wasteful litigation over compliance is increased. So is the oppression caused by the defendant having to do things under threat of proceedings for contempt. The less precise the order, the fewer the signposts to the forensic minefield which he has to traverse. The fact that the terms of a contractual obligation are sufficiently definite to escape being void for uncertainty, or to found a claim for damages, or to permit compliance to be made a condition of relief against forfeiture, does not necessarily mean that they will be sufficiently precise to be capable of being specifically performed. So in *Wolverhampton Corporation* v *Emmons*, Romer LJ said, at p. 525, that the first condition for specific enforcement of a building contract was that

> the particulars of the work are so far definitely ascertained that the court can sufficiently see what is the exact nature of the work of which it is asked to order the performance.

Similarly in *Morris* v *Redland Bricks Ltd* [1970] AC 652, 666, Lord Upjohn stated the following general principle for the grant of mandatory injunctions to carry out building works:

the court must be careful to see that the defendant knows exactly in fact what he has to do and this means not as a matter of law but as a matter of fact, so that in carrying out an order he can give his contractors the proper instructions.

Precision is of course a question of degree and the courts have shown themselves willing to cope with a certain degree of imprecision in cases of orders requiring the achievement of a result in which the plaintiffs' merits appeared strong; like all the reasons which I have been discussing, it is, taken alone, merely a discretionary matter to be taken into account: see *Spry, Equitable Remedies*, 4th ed. (1990), p. 112. It is, however, a very important one. . . .

There is a further objection to an order requiring the defendant to carry on a business, which was emphasised by Millett LJ in the Court of Appeal. This is that it may cause injustice by allowing the plaintiff to enrich himself at the defendant's expense. The loss which the defendant may suffer through having to comply with the order (for example, by running a business at a loss for an indefinite period) may be far greater than the plaintiff would suffer from the contract being broken. As Professor RJ Sharpe explains in 'Specific Relief for Contract Breach,' ch. 5 of *Studies in Contract Law* (1980), edited by Reiter and Swan, p. 129:

> In such circumstances, a specific decree in favour of the plaintiff will put him in a bargaining position vis-à-vis the defendant whereby the measure of what he will receive will be the value to the defendant of being released from performance. If the plaintiff bargains effectively, the amount he will set will exceed the value to him of performance and will approach the cost to the defendant to complete.

. . . It is true that the defendant has, by his own breach of contract, put himself in such an unfortunate position. But the purpose of the law of contract is not to punish wrongdoing but to satisfy the expectations of the party entitled to performance. A remedy which enables him to secure, in money terms, more than the performance due to him is unjust. From a wider perspective, it cannot be in the public interest for the courts to require someone to carry on business at a loss if there is any plausible alternative by which the other party can be given compensation. It is not only a waste of resources but yokes the parties together in a continuing hostile relationship. The order for specific performance prolongs the battle. If the defendant is ordered to run a business, its conduct becomes the subject of a flow of complaints, solicitors' letters and affidavits. This is wasteful for both parties and the legal system. An award of damages, on the other hand, brings the litigation to an end. The defendant pays damages, the forensic link between them is severed, they go their separate ways and the wounds of conflict can heal.

The cumulative effect of these various reasons, none of which would necessarily be sufficient on its own, seems to me to show that the settled practice is based upon sound sense. Of course the grant or refusal of specific performance remains a matter for the judge's discretion. There are no binding rules, but this does not mean that there cannot be settled principles, founded upon practical considerations of the kind which I have discussed, which do not have to be re-examined in every case, but which the courts will apply in all but exceptional circumstances. . . .

NOTES

1. Until the decision of the Court of Appeal it had been assumed that breach of such a covenant would give rise to a damages claim. The decision of the Court of Appeal had far-reaching implications for retailers who might well have been forced to operate uneconomic stores. It would also have repercussions for property developers, since tenants would understandably have been reluctant to agree to covenants of this nature and have been in a good bargaining position to negotiate reduced rents on leases.

2. Although the Court of Appeal had been influenced by what it regarded as the bad behaviour of the defendants, Lord Hoffmann made the following comment:

> . . . The principles of equity have always had a strong ethical content and nothing which I say is intended to diminish the influence of moral values in their application. I can envisage cases of gross breach of personal faith, or attempts to use the threat of non-performance as blackmail, in which the needs of justice will override all the considerations which support the settled practice. But although any breach of covenant is regrettable, the

exercise of the discretion as to whether or not to grant specific performance starts from the fact that the covenant has been broken. Both landlord and tenant in this case are large sophisticated commercial organisations and I have no doubt that both were perfectly aware that the remedy for breach of the covenant was likely to be limited to an award of damages. The interests of both were purely financial: there was no element of personal breach of faith, as in the Victorian cases of railway companies which refused to honour obligations to build stations for landowners whose property they had taken: compare *Greene* v *West Cheshire Railway Co.* (1871) LR 13 Eq 44. No doubt there was an effect on the businesses of other traders in the Centre, but Argyll had made no promises to them and it is not suggested that C.I.S. warranted to other tenants that Argyll would remain. Their departure, with or without the consent of C.I.S., was a commercial risk which the tenants were able to deploy in negotiations for the next rent review. On the scale of broken promises, I can think of worse cases, but the language of the Court of Appeal left them with few adjectives to spare.

3. The Court of Appeal's order had been suspended pending assignment of the lease to another tenant. Such a tenant had been found by the time of the final appeal to the House of Lords. Therefore, in practical terms the order would never have been enforced. Nevertheless, this factor could not determine the outcome of the exercise of the discretion to award specific performance.

4. In *Rainbow Estates Ltd* v *Tokenhold Ltd* [1998] 2 All ER 860, it was held that the courts had the power in appropriate circumstances to order specific performance of a tenant's covenant to repair. This would be an order to achieve a result (as opposed to an order to carry on an activity). Accordingly, there would not be the same difficulties regarding the need for constant supervision as long as what needed to be done in order to comply with the order of specific performance was sufficiently defined by the court.

(c) Contracts for personal services

Generally a court will not order specific performance of a contract requiring personal services, e.g., where there is a negative stipulation in the contract whereby one party must render exclusive services to the other, and will not grant an injunction to restrain the breach since this would have the same effect as specific performance and compel one person to work for another.

Page One Records Ltd v *Britton*
[1968] 1 WLR 157

The plaintiffs were the managers and publishers of the pop group, 'The Troggs'. The contract between them provided that the group would not 'engage any other person firm or corporation to act as [their] managers or agents or act themselves in such capacity'. The plaintiffs sought an interlocutory (interim) injunction to restrain the group from engaging Harvey Block Associates Ltd as their manager in breach of contract, and from publishing music performed by them. The plaintiffs also sought an injunction against Harvey Block Associates Ltd restraining any inducement to the defendants to break their contract with the plaintiffs. Held: enforcement of these negative covenants would be tantamount to ordering specific performance of the contract of personal services by the plaintiffs. It would be wrong to put pressure on the defendants to continue to employ in the fiduciary capacity of a manager and agent, someone in whom they had lost confidence.

STAMP J: . . . [T]his present case, in my judgment, fails, on the facts at present before me, on a more general principle, the converse of which was conveniently stated in the judgment of Branson J in

Warner Brothers Pictures Inc v *Nelson* [1937] 1 KB 209. Branson J stated the converse of the proposition and the proposition, correctly stated, is, I think, this, that where a contract of personal service contains negative covenants the enforcement of which will amount either to a decree of specific performance of the positive covenants of the contract or to the giving of a decree under which the defendant must either remain idle or perform those positive covenants, the court will not enforce those negative covenants.

In the *Warner Brothers* case Branson J felt able to find that the injunction sought would not force the defendant to perform his contract or remain idle.

I quote from the report:

> It was also urged that the difference between what the defendant can earn as a film artiste and what she might expect to earn by any other form of activity is so great that she will in effect be driven to perform her contract. That is not the criterion adopted in any of the decided cases. The defendant is stated to be a person of intelligence, capacity and means, and no evidence was adduced to show that, if enjoined from doing the specified acts otherwise than for the plaintiffs, she will not be able to employ herself both usefully and remuneratively in other spheres of activity, though not as remuneratively as in her special line. She will not be driven, although she may be tempted, to perform the contract, and the fact that she may be so tempted is no objection to the grant of an injunction.

So it was said in this case that if an injunction is granted the Troggs could, without employing any other manager or agent, continue as a group on their own or seek other employment of a different nature. So far as the former suggestion is concerned, in the first place I doubt whether consistently with the terms of the agreements which I have read, the Troggs could act as their own managers; and, in the second place, I think I can, and should, take judicial notice of the fact that these groups, if they are to have any great success, must have managers. Indeed, it is the plaintiffs' own case that the Troggs are simple persons, of no business experience, and could not survive without the services of a manager. As a practical matter on the evidence before me, I entertain no doubt that they would be compelled, if the injunction was granted, on the terms that the plaintiffs seek, to continue to employ the first plaintiff as their manager and agent and it is, I think, on this point that this case diverges from *Lumley* v *Wagner* (1852) 1 De GM & G 604 and the cases which have followed it, including the *Warner Brothers* case [1937] 1 KB 209: for it would be a bad thing to put pressure upon these four young men to continue to employ as a manager and agent in a fiduciary capacity one who, unlike the plaintiff in those cases (who had merely to pay the defendant money) has duties of a personal and fiduciary nature to perform and in whom the Troggs, for reasons good, bad or indifferent, have lost confidence and who may, for all I know, fail in its duty to them.

On the facts before me on this interlocutory motion, I should, if I granted the injunction, be enforcing a contract for personal services in which personal services are to be performed by the first plaintiff. In *Lumley* v *Wagner* Lord St Leonards, in his judgment, disclaimed doing indirectly what he could not do directly; and in the present case, by granting an injunction I would, in my judgment, be doing precisely that. I must, therefore, refuse the injunction which the first plaintiff seeks.

NOTES

1. Particular stress was placed on the fact that this relationship was one requiring mutual trust and confidence.
2. Stamp J referred to the decision in the following case.

Warner Brothers Pictures Incorporated v Nelson
[1937] 1 KB 209

The actress, Bette Davis, had agreed to render her exclusive services as an actress to Warner Brothers for 52 weeks (with Warner Brothers having an option to renew) and undertook not to render such services to any other person. In breach of contract, she agreed with a third party to perform in the UK as a film artist. The plaintiffs sought an injunction, which in its terms was confined to forbidding the defendant, without the consent of the plaintiffs, from rendering any services in any motion picture or stage production for anyone other than the plaintiffs. (It did not require enforcement of a positive performance obligation which would not have been granted.) Branson J granted the injunction on the basis that the effect of the contract was not such as to force the defendant to perform this contract or be idle and starve. Although Bette Davis might earn more as a film actress, and therefore might be tempted to perform the contract with Warner Brothers, she could earn money in other ways and would not be *driven* to perform.

NOTES

1. This decision appears to have been influenced by a wish to prevent parties 'departing from their contracts at their pleasure', leaving the injured party to damages, which was not an adequate remedy.
2. 'The Troggs' in *Page One Records Ltd* v *Britton* did not have the experience or ability to operate as a pop group without a manager and would have been driven to continue to employ the plaintiffs.

Warren v *Mendy*
[1989] 1 WLR 853 (CA)

In January 1988, the plaintiff entered into a contract with the professional boxer, Nigel Benn, to act as Benn's manager for three years. Benn agreed to be managed and directed exclusively by the plaintiff and not to enter into any agreement with any other manager without the plaintiff's consent. By June 1988, Benn was dissatisfied with the plaintiff's management and entered into an agreement with the defendant whereby the defendant was to act as Benn's agent. The plaintiff brought an action against the defendant, claiming damages for inducing Benn to break his contract with the plaintiff and an *ex parte* (now 'without notice') injunction against the defendant to restrain him from acting as Benn's agent. However, the injunction was later discharged on the ground that restraining the defendant from acting as Benn's agent would have the effect of compelling the boxer to perform the positive obligation imposed on him to be managed and directed exclusively by the plaintiff. The plaintiff appealed. Held: the injunction was rightly discharged because it would compel Benn to use only the exclusive services of the plaintiff. It was also held that a court is less likely to grant an injunction where the contract of service contains obligations of mutual trust and confidence between the manager and the performer and the performer has genuinely lost confidence in the manager, as here.

NOURSE LJ (giving the judgment of the Court): . . . [C]onsideration of the authorities has led us to believe that the following general principles are applicable to the grant or refusal of an injunction to enforce performance of the servant's negative obligations in a contract for personal services inseparable from the exercise of some special skill or talent. (We use the expressions 'master' and 'servant' for ease of reference and not out of any regard for the reality of the relationship in many of these cases.) In such a case the court ought not to enforce the performance of the negative obligations if their enforcement will effectively compel the servant to perform his positive obligations under the contract. Compulsion is a question to be decided on the facts of each case, with a realistic regard for the probable reaction of an injunction on the psychological and material, and sometimes the physical, need of the servant to maintain the skill or talent. The longer the term for which an injunction is sought, the more readily will compulsion be inferred. Compulsion may be inferred where the injunction is sought not against the servant but against a third party, if either the third party is the only other available master or if it is likely that the master will seek relief against anyone who attempts to replace him. An injunction will less readily be granted where there are obligations of mutual trust and confidence, more especially where the servant's trust in the master may have been betrayed or his confidence in him has genuinely gone.

In stating the principles as we have, we are not to be taken as intending to pay anything less than a full and proper regard to the sanctity of contract. No judge would wish to detract from his duty to enforce the performance of contracts to the very limit which established principles allow him to go. Nowhere is that duty better indicated than in the words of Lord St Leonards LC in *Lumley* v *Wagner* (1852) 1 De GM & G 604, 619. To that end the judge will scrutinise most carefully, even sceptically, any claim by the servant that he is under the human necessity of maintaining the skill or talent and thus will be compelled to perform the contract, or that his trust in the master has been betrayed or that his confidence in him has genuinely gone. But, if, having done that, the judge is satisfied that the grant of an injunction will effectively compel performance of the contract, he ought to refuse it. To do otherwise would be to disregard the authoritative observations which were made in this court in *Whitwood Chemical Co.* v *Hardman* [1891] 2 Ch 416. . . .

■ **QUESTION**

This decision and *Page One Records* v *Britton* both involved a management contract and enforcement by the employee, whereas in *Warner Brothers* v *Nelson* the issue had been enforcement by the employer. Does this make a difference?

NOTE: The Court of Appeal stressed that Benn needed the services of a manager to arrange his fights, and he had to fight in order to maintain his talent. Therefore, the injunction would compel him to perform his contract with the plaintiff if that was the only way of exercising his talents. In *Warner Brothers* v *Nelson*, it had been assumed that Bette Davis was not solely dependent upon acting and could obtain alternative work.

SECTION 4: RESTITUTION

Restitution allows the injured party to recover money paid or the value of benefits conferred on the party in breach where it would be unjust to allow the guilty party to retain that benefit.

If the benefit consisted of a payment of money, it can be recovered where there has been a total failure of consideration (i.e., the injured party received no part of the contractual performance) but not if the failure of consideration is only partial, since the courts would have to calculate whether the contractual performance was equivalent to the sum paid. Bovill CJ in *Whincup* v *Hughes* (1871) LR 6 CP 78 explained this difficulty of apportionment (at p. 81):

This is an action brought to recover a part of the premium paid upon the execution of an apprentice-ship deed, on the ground of failure of consideration. The general rule of law is, that where a contract has been in part performed no part of the money paid under such contract can be recovered back. There may be some cases of partial performance which form exceptions to this rule, as, for instance, if there were a contract to deliver ten sacks of wheat and six only were delivered, the price of the remaining four might be recovered back. But there the consideration is clearly severable. The general rule being what I have stated, is there anything in the present case to take it out of such rule? The master instructed the apprentice under the deed for the period of a year, and then died. It is clear law that the contract being one of a personal nature, the death of the master, in the absence of any stipulation to the contrary, puts an end to it for the future. The further performance of it has been prevented by the act of God, and there is thus no breach of contract upon which any action will lie against the executor. That being so, can any action be maintained otherwise than upon the contract? The contract having been in part performed, it would seem that the general rule must apply unless the consideration be in its nature apportionable. I am at a loss to see on what principle such apportionment could be made. It could not properly be made with reference to the proportion which the period during which the apprentice was instructed bears to the whole term. In the early part of the term the teaching would be most onerous, and the services of the apprentice of little value; as time went on his services would probably be worth more, and he would require less teaching. . . .

In *Stocznia Gdanska SA* v *Latvian Shipping Co.* [1998] 1 WLR 574 (noted Jaffey [1998] RLR 157; for facts see *page 336 above*), the defendants argued that because they had not received anything under the contract, there had been a total failure of consideration. However, the House of Lords held that for there to be a total failure of consideration the test was not whether the purchasers had received anything under the contract but whether the shipbuilders had performed any part of their contractual duties. It was therefore a matter of determining what the shipbuilders had promised to do under the contract; and since the contract imposed an obligation for design and construction in addition to delivery, there was no total failure of consideration. Lord Goff stated (at pp. 587–8):

Before addressing the rival submissions of the parties, I pause to observe that these were both founded on the premise that the issue was simply one of total failure of consideration. I am, of course, well aware of the continuing debate among scholars and law reformers as to the circumstances in which, and the basis on which, a party in breach of contract can recover a benefit conferred by him on the innocent party under the contract before it was terminated by reason of his breach, as to which see, for example, the admirable discussion by Professor Jack Beatson in *The Use and Abuse of Unjust Enrichment* (1991), chapter 3. However, I am content to approach this aspect of the case on the premise, common to both parties, that the issue is one of total failure of consideration since, as I understand it, this is consistent with the approach of the majority in *Hyundai Heavy Industries Co. Ltd* v *Papadopoulos* [1980] 1 WLR 1129, which is directly in point on this aspect of the case.

I find myself to be in agreement with [counsel for the yard's] submission on this point. I start from the position that failure of consideration does not depend upon the question whether the promisee has or has not *received* anything under the contract like, for example, the property in the ships being built under contracts 1 and 2 in the present case. Indeed. if that were so, in cases in which the promisor undertakes to do work or render services which confer no direct benefit on the promisee, for example where he undertakes to paint the promisee's daughter's house, no consideration would ever be furnished for the promisee's payment. In truth, the test is not whether the promisee has received a specific benefit, but rather whether the promisor has performed any part of the contractual duties in respect of which the payment is due. The present case cannot, therefore, be approached by asking the simple question whether the property in the vessel or any part of it has passed to the buyers. That test would be apposite if the contract in question was a contract for the sale of goods (or indeed a contract for the sale of land) simpliciter under which the consideration for the price would be the passing of the property in the goods (or land). However before that test can be regarded as appropriate, the anterior question has to be asked: is the contract in question simply a contract for the sale of a ship? or is it rather a contract under which the design and construction of the vessel formed part of the yard's contractual duties, as well as the duty to transfer the finished object to the buyers? If it is the latter, the design and construction of the vessel form part of the consideration for which the price is to be paid, and the fact that the contract has been brought to an end before the property in the vessel or any part of it has passed to the buyers does not prevent the yard from asserting that there has been no total failure of consideration in respect of an instalment of the price which has been paid before the contract was terminated, or that an instalment which has then accrued due could not, if paid, be recoverable on that ground.

I am satisfied that the present case falls into the latter category. This was what the contracts provided in their terms. Moreover, consistently with those terms, payment of instalments of the price was geared to progress in the construction of the vessel. That this should be so is scarcely surprising in the case of a shipbuilding contract, under which the yard enters into major financial commitments at an early stage, in the placing of orders for machinery and materials, and in reserving and then occupying a berth for the construction of the vessel. Indeed if [counsel for the buyer's] argument is right, it would follow that no consideration would have been furnished by the yard when instalments of the price fell due before the moment of delivery, notwithstanding all the heavy and irreversible financial commitments then undertaken by the yard.

If the benefit consists of services, and there is no contractual provision for remuneration, the injured party can claim their reasonable value on a *quantum meruit* (*Planche* v *Colburn* (1831) 8 Bing 14, 131 ER 305). See also *British Steel Corporation* v *Cleveland Bridge & Engineering Co. Ltd* [1984] 1 All ER 504, *page 78*, where the services were requested by the benefited party. Compare *Regalian Properties plc* v *London Dockland Development Corp* [1995] 1 WLR 212, *page 79*.

10

Privity of Contract and Third Party Rights

The doctrine of privity of contract provides that only the parties to a contract can enjoy the benefits of that contract or suffer the burdens of it.

Consideration must move from the promisee. Traditionally, this was interpreted to mean that a person could not sue on a contract if the consideration was provided by another, even where the contract was made for his benefit.

Tweddle v *Atkinson*
(1861) 1 B & S 393; 121 ER 762 (QB)

John Tweddle and William Guy each agreed to pay a sum of money to the plaintiff (Tweddle's son) in consideration of his marrying Guy's daughter. Guy failed to pay and the plaintiff sought to enforce his promise against Guy's executor. Held: the son could not enforce the promise despite the fact that the contract was for his benefit since he had given no consideration for it.

> CROMPTON J: . . . [T]he consideration must move from the party entitled to sue upon the contract. It would be a monstrous proposition to say that a person was a party to the contract for the purpose of suing upon it for his own advantage, and not a party to it for the purpose of being sued. It is said that the father in the present case was agent for the son in making the contract, but that argument ought also to make the son liable upon it. . . .
>
> WIGHTMAN J: . . . [I]t is now established that no stranger to the consideration can take advantage of a contract, although made for his benefit.

NOTES
1. The judgments concentrate on the fact that the consideration for Guy's promise was not provided by the plaintiff but by John Tweddle. However, the plaintiff was also not a party to the contract.
2. Crompton J justified not allowing the plaintiff to enforce a contract expressly made for his benefit on the ground that it would be unfair if a person could enforce a contract under which he could not be sued. (This problem has been addressed as part of the debate concerning reform of the third party beneficiary rule. See, e.g., Iacobucci J in *London Drugs Ltd* v *Kuehne and Nagel, page 451.*)

Dunlop Pneumatic Tyre Co. Ltd v *Selfridge & Co. Ltd*
[1915] AC 847 (HL)

Dew & Co. agreed with the plaintiffs, Dunlop, to buy a specific quantity of the plaintiffs' tyres in consideration for obtaining discounts on the list price. Dew &

Co. also agreed not to sell these tyres to trade buyers for less than list price unless a similar undertaking was given by those trade buyers that they would observe the plaintiffs' list price. The defendants ordered Dunlop tyres from Dew & Co. and agreed with Dew & Co., in return for receiving a discount from Dew & Co., that they would not sell or offer these tyres to any private customers at less than list price. The defendants did sell tyres at below list price and the plaintiffs sued them for breach of their undertaking. Held: there was no consideration moving from the plaintiffs to the defendants, and therefore the contract was not enforceable by the plaintiffs. Viscount Haldane LC also recognised the doctrine of privity (i.e., that no stranger to the contract can enforce it).

VISCOUNT HALDANE LC: My Lords, in the law of England certain principles are fundamental. One is that only a person who is a party to a contract can sue on it. Our law knows nothing of a jus quaesitum tertio arising by way of contract. Such a right may be conferred by way of property, as, for example, under a trust, but it cannot be conferred on a stranger to a contract as a right to enforce the contract in personam. A second principle is that if a person with whom a contract not under seal has been made is to be able to enforce it consideration must have been given by him to the promisor or to some other person at the promisor's request. . . . A third proposition is that a principal not named in the contract may sue upon it if the promisee really contracted as his agent. But again, in order to entitle him so to sue, he must have given consideration either personally or through the promisee, acting as his agent in giving it.

My Lords, in the case before us, I am of opinion that the consideration, the allowance of what was in reality part of the discount to which Messrs Dew, the promisees, were entitled as between themselves and the appellants, was to be given by Messrs Dew on their own account, and was not in substance, any more than in form, an allowance made by the appellants. . . .

LORD DUNEDIN: . . . My Lords, I confess that this case is to my mind apt to nip any budding affection which one might have had for the doctrine of consideration. For the effect of that doctrine in the present case is to make it possible for a person to snap his fingers at a bargain deliberately made, a bargain not in itself unfair, and which the person seeking to enforce it has a legitimate interest to enforce. . . .

Now the agreement sued on is an agreement which on the face of it is an agreement between Dew and Selfridge. But speaking for myself, I should have no difficulty in the circumstances of this case in holding it proved that the agreement was truly made by Dew as agent for Dunlop, or in other words that Dunlop was the undisclosed principal, and as such can sue on the agreement. None the less, in order to enforce it he must show consideration, moving from Dunlop to Selfridge.

In the circumstances, how can he do so? The agreement in question is not an agreement for sale. It is only collateral to an agreement for sale; but that agreement for sale is an agreement entirely between Dew and Selfridge. The tyres, the property in which upon the bargain is transferred to Selfridge, were the property of Dew, not of Dunlop, for Dew under his agreement with Dunlop held these tyres as proprietor, and not as agent. What then did Dunlop do, or forbear to do, in a question with Selfridge? The answer must be, nothing. He did not do anything, for Dew, having the right of property in the tyres, could give a good title to any one he liked, subject, it might be, to an action of damages at the instance of Dunlop for breach of contract, which action, however, could never create a vitium reale in the property of the tyres. He did not forbear in anything, for he had no action against Dew which he gave up, because Dew had fulfilled his contract with Dunlop in obtaining, on the occasion of the sale, a contract from Selfridge in the terms prescribed.

To my mind, this ends the case. That there are methods of framing a contract which will cause persons in the position of Selfridge to become bound, I do not doubt. But that has not been done in this instance; and as Dunlop's advisers must have known of the law of consideration, it is their affair that they have not so drawn the contract.

NOTE: Viscount Haldane treated the privity doctrine and the rule that consideration must move from the promisee as two separate principles. Although these principles may produce the same result in a *Tweddle* v *Atkinson* situation where the promise is made to one person, they may not do so where the promise is made to more than one person but the consideration is provided by only one of these promisees. In its 1991 Consultation Paper, the Law Commission considered that the two principles were separate since the issue of the promises which are enforceable (consideration) is distinct from the issue of who may enforce a promise (privity). In its 1996 Report, *Privity of Contract: Contracts for the Benefit of Third Parties*, Law Com No. 242, Cm 3329, Part VI (6.1–6.8), the Law Commission accepted that because 'consideration must move from the promisee' can be interpreted to mean 'consideration must move from the plaintiff' its proposals for reform of the privity rule in the context of third-party beneficiaries would be ineffectual if the third party could be prevented from enforcing the contract on the basis that he had not provided consideration. However, the Law Commission considered that this was covered by the central provision of the proposed reform allowing third-party enforcement which necessarily also reformed the consideration rule where this was interpreted to mean consideration moving from the plaintiff. In other words, although consideration had to be provided, it need not be provided by the third party.

Although the Contracts (Rights of Third Parties) Act 1999 gives third parties the right to enforce contractual terms in certain circumstances, there is no provision addressing the issue of consideration. Therefore, although consideration is required, it will no longer need to be provided by a third party. Does this mean that a third party is being placed in a more advantageous position than a promisee who must supply consideration for the promise?

SECTION 2: REFORM OF THE PRIVITY DOCTRINE AND THE CONTRACTS (RIGHTS OF THIRD PARTIES) ACT 1999

It has been argued that where a third party is the intended beneficiary, he should be able to enforce the contract. To deny this would defeat the parties' intentions which are normally paramount in contract law. (See Flannigan 'The End of an Era (Error)' (1987) 103 LQR 564 and Law Commission Report, Law Com No. 242, Cm 3329 (1996), Part III, Arguments for Reform.)

In *Darlington BC* v *Wiltshier Northern Ltd* [1995] 1 WLR 68 (*page 473*), Steyn LJ commented (at pp. 76–8):

> The case for recognising a contract for the benefit of a third party is simple and straightforward. The autonomy of the will of the parties should be respected. The law of contract should give effect to the reasonable expectations of contracting parties. Principle certainly requires that a burden should not be imposed on a third party without his consent. But there is no doctrinal, logical or policy reason why the law should deny effectiveness to a contract for the benefit of a third party where that is the expressed intention of the parties. Moreover, often the parties, and particularly third parties, organise their affairs on the faith of the contract. They rely on the contract. It is therefore unjust to deny effectiveness to such a contract. I will not struggle further with the point since nobody seriously asserts the contrary; but see a valuable article by Jack Beatson, a law commissioner, now Rouseball Professor of English Law at Cambridge, 'Reforming the Law of Contracts for the Benefit of Third Parties: a Second Bite at the Cherry' (1992) 45 CLP 1.
>
> The genesis of the privity rule is suspect. It is attributed to *Tweddle* v *Atkinson* (1861) B & S 393. It is more realistic to say that the rule originated in the misunderstanding of *Tweddle* v *Atkinson*: see *Atiyah, The Rise and Fall of Freedom of Contract* (1979) p. 414 and *Simpson, A History of the Law of Contract: the Rise of the Action of Assumpsit* (1975) p. 475. While the privity rule was barely tolerable in Victorian England, it has been recognised for half a century that it has no place in our more complex commercial world. Indeed, as early as *Dunlop Pneumatic Tyre Co. Ltd* v *Selfridge & Co. Ltd*

[1915] AC 847, 855, when the House of Lords restated the privity rule, Lord Dunedin observed in a dissenting speech that the rule made—

it possible for a person to snap his fingers at a bargain deliberately made, a bargain not in itself unfair, and which the person seeking to enforce it has a legitimate interest to enforce.

Among the majority, Viscount Haldane LC asserted as a self-evident truth at p. 853, that 'only a person who is a party to a contract can sue on it'. Today the doctrinal objection to the recognition of a stipulatio alteri continues to hold sway. While the rigidity of the doctrine of consideration has been greatly reduced in modern times, the doctrine of privity of contract persists in all its artificial technicality.

In 1937 the Law Revision Committee in its Sixth Report ['Statute of Frauds and the Doctrine of Consideration'] (Cmd 5449, paras 41–8) proposed the recognition of a right of a third party to enforce the contract which by its express terms purports to confer a benefit directly on him. In 1967 *Beswick* v *Beswick* [1968] AC 58, 72, Lord Reid observed that if there was a long period of delay in passing legislation on the point the House of Lords might have to deal with the matter. Twelve years later Lord Scarman, who as a former chairman of the Law Commission usually favoured legislative rather than judicial reform where radical change was involved, reminded the House that it might be necessary to review all the cases which 'stand guard over this unjust rule': *Woodar Investment Development Ltd* v *Wimpey Construction UK Ltd* [1980] 1 WLR 277, 300G. See also Lord Keith of Kinkel, at pp. 297H–298A. In 1981 Dillon J described the rule as 'a blot on our law and most unjust': *Forster* v *Silvermere Golf and Equestrian Centre Ltd* (1981) 125 Sol Jo 397. In 1983 Lord Diplock described the rule as 'an anachronistic shortcoming that has for many years been regarded as a reproach to English private law': *Swain* v *Law Society* [1983] 1 AC 598, 611D.

But as important as judicial condemnations of the privity rule is the fact that distinguished academic lawyers have found no redeeming virtues in it: see e.g. Markesinis (1987) 103 LQR 354, Reynolds (1989) 105 LQR 1, Beatson (1992) 45 CLP 1 and Adams and Brownsword (1993) 56 MLR 722. And we do well to remember that the civil law legal systems of other members of the European Union recognise such contracts. That our legal system lacks such flexibility is a disadvantage in the single market. Indeed it is a historical curiosity that the legal system of a mercantile country such as England, which in other areas of the law of contract (such as, for example, the objective theory of the interpretation of contracts) takes great account of the interests of third parties, has not been able to rid itself of this unjust rule deriving from a technical conception of a contract as a purely bilateral vinculum juris.

In 1991 the Law Commission revisited this corner of the law. In cautious language appropriate to a consultation paper the Law Commission has expressed the provisional recommendation that 'there should be a (statutory) reform of the law to allow third parties to enforce contractual provisions made in their favour': 'Privity of Contract: Contracts for the Benefit of Third Parties', Consultation Paper No. 121, p. 132. The principal value of the consultation paper lies in its clear analysis of the practical need for the recognition of a contract for the benefit of third parties, and the explanation of the unedifying spectacle of judges trying to invent exceptions to the rule to prevent demonstrable unfairness. No doubt there will be a report by the Law Commission in the not too distant future recommending the abolition of the privity of contract rule by statute. What will then happen in regard to the proposal for legislation? The answer is really quite simple: probably nothing will happen.

But on this occasion I can understand the inaction of Parliament. There is a respectable argument that it is the type of reform which is best achieved by the courts working out sensible solutions on a case by case basis, e.g., in regard to the exact point of time when the third party is vested with enforceable contractual rights: see Consultation Paper, No. 121, para. 5.8. But that requires the door to be opened by the House of Lords reviewing the major cases which are thought to have entrenched the rule of privity of contract. Unfortunately, there will be few opportunities for the House of Lords to do so. After all, by and large, courts of law in our system are the hostages of the arguments deployed by counsel. And [counsel] for the council, the third party, made it clear to us that he will not directly challenge the privity rule if this matter should go to the House of Lords. He said that he is content to try to bring his case within exceptions to the privity rule or what Lord Diplock in *Swain* v *The Law Society* [1983] 1 AC 598, 611D, described as 'juristic subterfuges . . . to mitigate the effect of the lacuna resulting from the non-recognition of a jus quaesitum tertio . . .'

NOTES

1. Following this judgment, in 1996 the Law Commission published its Report, Cm 3329, proposing a detailed legislative scheme for reform of the third-party rule in preference to judicial reform. The Report recommended that third parties should have the right to enforce contractual provisions if they could satisfy the test of enforceability. For an account of the recommendations in this Report, see Burrows [1996] LMCLQ 467.

2. It seems that Steyn LJ was unduly pessimistic about the prospects of legislation as in December 1998 the Government introduced the Contracts (Rights of Third Parties) Bill in the House of Lords. This Bill was generally in the same terms as the draft Bill recommended in the Law Commission Report, although there were changes in terms of presentation and expression. The Contracts (Rights of Third Parties) Act 1999 received Royal Assent on 11 November 1999 and took effect in relation to contracts entered into after 11 May 2000 or, if the Act was expressly stated to be applicable in the contract itself, after 11 November 1999. For a discussion of the Act, see MacMillan (2000) 63 MLR 721 and Andrews [2001] CLJ 353.

3. The Contracts (Rights of Third Parties) Act 1999 provides that a third party may enforce a contractual term if either the contract expressly gives him the right to enforce it, or the term purports to confer a benefit on him and there is nothing in the contract to indicate that the parties did not intend that the third party should be able to enforce the term (s. 1(1) and (2)). In addition, 'the third party must be expressly identified in the contract by name, as a member of a class or as answering a particular description but need not be in existence when the contract is entered into' (s. 1(3)). It is important to bear in mind that this test is not as generous as it may appear and, without revised drafting of clauses in the light of these provisions, the legislation is unlikely to give third parties sweeping rights of enforcement. In addition, there are a number of important exceptions where third parties will not have enforcement rights (see s. 6 of the Act).

4. Section 4 of the Act makes it clear that the promisee retains the right to enforce the contract, and there is a provision to protect the promisor from double liability in the event of an action by both the third party and the promisee (s. 5).

5. Section 7(1) provides that the right of enforcement given by s. 1 does 'not affect any right or remedy of a third party that exists or is available' apart from this legislation. This means that it will still be necessary to consider the various devices that have been employed by the courts in an effort to avoid the application of the privity rule to third-party beneficiaries. It is also necessary to consider to what extent, if at all, these devices are rendered redundant by the Act.

Nisshin Shipping is the first case to examine the Contracts (Rights of Third Parties) Act 1999.

Nisshin Shipping Co. Ltd v Cleaves & Co. Ltd
[2003] EWHC 2602 (Comm), [2004] 1 Lloyd's Rep 38

The shipbrokers (Cleaves) had negotiated nine time charters on behalf of the applicant owners (Nisshin). Each contract provided for the payment of commission to the brokers; the wording in four of these contracts provided for a commission of 2 per cent as payable to the brokers on hire earned and paid under the charter. (As there were two brokers, it followed that the clause provided for commission of 1 per cent for Cleaves.) There was also an arbitration clause in each contract. Cleaves sought payment of this commission but the owners challenged the entitlement alleging that the brokers were in repudiatory breach of the agency relationship. Cleaves purported to refer the commission issue to arbitration although they were not a party to any of the nine arbitration agreements. The arbitrators' decision that they had jurisdiction was challenged by Nisshin on the grounds that Cleaves could not rely on the 1999 Act as giving them the right to rely on the arbitration clauses.

It was accepted by Cleaves that the clauses did not expressly provide that they could enforce the commission clauses directly against the owners and the central question therefore was whether they fell within s1(1)(b) of the Contracts (Rights of Third Parties) Act 1999, i.e. (i) whether the clause purported to confer a benefit on the brokers and (ii) whether, on the true construction of the clause, the parties did not intend the term to be enforceable by the third party brokers. Held: Cleaves was entitled to rely on the 1999 Act since (i) the commission clauses did purport to confer a benefit on the brokers within s. 1(1)(b). (ii) s. 1(2) did not require that for s. 1(1)(b) to apply it had to be positively shown that the parties intended that the benefit term should be enforceable by the third party, rather it merely stated that s. 1(1) (b) could not apply if on the proper construction it appeared that the parties did not intend the third party to have a right to enforcement. Thus it was for Nisshin to allege that the parties had no such intention so that s. 1(1)(b) should be disapplied. Where, as here, the contract was neutral on this question and the contract did not express an intention to deny enforceability to the third party, s. 1(1)(b) would apply. (iii) The charters created a trust of the promise to pay commission to the brokers which was enforceable by the charterers as trustees (i.e. an express trust), but it did not follow from the existence of this trust that Cleaves was denied a direct right of enforcement under the 1999 Act. (In other words, the common law exceptions continue to apply but do not detract from the s. 1 direct right unless s. 1(2) applies, i.e. there is evidence of a contrary intention to allow direct enforceability. Of course, as Colman J recognised, direct enforceability will be far simpler.) (iv) The brokers were therefore entitled to enforce the commission clauses in their own right under s. 1 of the Act.

COLMAN J:

Do Cleaves fall within s. 1 of the 1999 Act?

10. It is accepted on behalf of Cleaves that in none of the charters did the commission clauses expressly provide that Cleaves could enforce such clauses directly against the owners. However the real issues are (i) whether those clauses purported to confer a benefit on Cleaves within sub-s. (1)(b) of s. 1 and (ii) whether sub-s. 1(b) is disapplied by sub-s. (2) because 'on a proper construction of the contract it appears that the parties did not intend the term to be enforceable by the third party'.

[Colman J then considered an argument relating to whether the clauses conferred a benefit on Cleaves in its own right. He held that they did confer a benefit relating to 1 per cent commission]

15. It is then further argued by [counsel], on behalf of Nisshin, that on the proper construction of the charter-parties the parties to them did not intend the commission clause to be enforceable by Cleaves and accordingly s. 1(1)(b) of the 1999 Act is disapplied by s. 1(2).

16. In support of this argument Nisshin relies on three distinct points.

[The first argument related to the arbitration clause]

22. Secondly, it is argued by [counsel] on behalf of Nisshin that there is no positive indication in the charter-parties that the parties did intend the brokers to have enforceable rights. There is no suggestion in those contracts that the owners and charterers were mutually in agreement that the brokers should be entitled to claim against the owners as if they were parties to the contract.

23. It is to be noted that s. 1(2) of the 1999 Act does not provide that sub-s. 1(b) is disapplied unless on a proper construction of the contract it appears that the parties intended that the benefit term should be enforceable by the third party. Rather it provides that sub-s. 1(b) is disapplied if, on a proper construction, it appears that the parties did not intend third party enforcement. In other words, if the contract is neutral on this question, sub-s. (2) does not disapply sub-s. 1(b). Whether the contract does express a mutual intention that the third party should not be entitled to enforce the benefit conferred on him or is merely neutral is a matter of construction having regard to all relevant circumstances. The purpose and background of the Law Commission's recommendations in relation to sub-s. (2) are explained in a paper by Professor Andrew Burrows who, as a member of the Law Commission, made a major contribution to the drafting of the bill as enacted. He wrote at [2000] L.M.C.L.Q. 540 at p. 544:

> The second test therefore uses a rebuttable presumption of intention. In doing so, it copies the New Zealand Contracts (Privity) Act, 1982, s. 4, which has used the same approach. It is this rebuttable presumption that provides the essential balance between sufficient certainty for contracting parties and the flexibility required for the reform to deal fairly with a huge range of different situations. The presumption is based on the idea that, if you ask yourself, 'When is it that parties are likely to have intended to confer rights on a third party to enforce a term, albeit that they have not expressly conferred that right', the answer will be: 'Where the term purports to confer a benefit on an expressly identified third party'. That then sets up the presumption. But the presumption can be rebutted if, as a matter of ordinary contractual interpretation, there is something else indicating that the parties did not intend such a right to be given.

24. In the present case, apart from [counsel's] third point, the charter-parties are indeed neutral in the sense that they do not express any intention contrary to the entitlement of the brokers to enforce the commission term.

25. Thirdly, [counsel] submits that the parties' mutual intention on the proper construction of the contracts was to create a trust of a promise in favour of the brokers—a trust enforceable against the owners at the suit of the charterers as trustees. That being the proper construction of the contracts by reference to the state of the law at the time when the 1999 Act came into force, the very same contract wording did not, subsequently to that, evidence a different mutual intention. Accordingly, the mutual intention evidenced by the contracts was that the enforcement of the promise to pay commission would be at the suit of the charterers who must be joined by the brokers as co-claimants.

[The judge examined case law on creation of a trust of brokers' commission, including *Les Affréteurs Réunis SA* v *Leopold Walford (London) Ltd* [1919] AC 801, *page 462*, and concluded:]

28. Accordingly, the position in 1853 and 1919 was that when a charter-party was entered into and incorporated a term that the owners would pay commission to the brokers, the only means of enforcement of that promise was an action by the charterers and the brokers as co-plaintiff because, the charterer having contracted for commission on behalf of the broker, once the contract had been signed, the charterer became trustee of the broker's right to recover that commission, the broker being unable to enforce the promise direct and without the charterer's intervention because he was not a party to the contract and therefore had no cause of action available to him against the owner. With regard to this trustee relationship it could then be said that when the charter-party was entered into neither owners nor charterers contemplated that the brokers could sue the owners direct.

29. What is the position arising from the contract itself following the coming into force of the 1999 Act? As a matter of analysis of the underlying relationship between the parties, it must be precisely the same. Thus, the charterer is no less the trustee of the owners' promise to pay the commission, having regard to the fact that the charterer contracts for payment of the commission on behalf of a non-contracting party. Indeed, the only thing that has changed is the coming into force of the 1999 Act and the introduction of the statutory facility of a direct right of action for a non-contracting party on whom a contract purports to confer a benefit.

30. Accordingly, the argument advanced by the owners can only succeed if it is to be inferred from the existence of the underlying trustee relationship that it was the mutual intention of owners and charterers that the broker beneficiary should not be entitled to avail himself of the facility of direct action by the 1999 Act.

31. This proposition is, in my judgment, entirely unsustainable. The fact that prior to the 1999 Act it would be the mutual intention that the only available facility for enforcement would be deployed by the broker does not lead to the conclusion that, once an additional statutory facility for enforcement had been introduced, the broker would not be entitled to use it, but would instead be confined to the use of the pre-existing procedure. Indeed, quite apart from the complete lack of any logical basis for such an inference, the very cumbersome and inconvenient nature of the procedure based on the trustee relationship (described by Lord Wright as a 'cumbrous fiction') would point naturally to the preferred use by the broker of the right to sue directly provided by the 1999 Act. Not only would that original procedure be inconvenient, but it might involve risk that the broker would be prevented from recovering his commission, for example, in a case where the charterer had been dissolved in its place of incorporation or where, in the absence of cooperation by the charterer, proceedings had to be served on it outside the jurisdiction and service could not be effected. There are therefore very strong grounds pointing against any mutual intention to confine the brokers to the old procedure and to deny them the right to rely on the 1999 Act.

32. I therefore reject the third ground relied upon by Nisshin. In so doing I reach the same conclusion as the arbitrators.

33. It follows that Cleaves are entitled to enforce the commission clauses in their own right by reason of s. 1 of the 1999 Act.

SECTION 3: AGENCY

In *Dunlop Pneumatic Tyre Co. Ltd* v *Selfridge & Co. Ltd* (*page 438*) it was argued that Dew & Co. acted as Dunlop's agent for the purposes of extracting this undertaking from Selfridge. An agency relationship occurs where one party, the agent, is authorised by another, the principal, to negotiate and enter into contracts on behalf of the principal. In this example Dunlop would be the principal, so that technically the contract would be between Dunlop and Selfridge, thereby enabling Dunlop to enforce the contract.

However, the agent must have the authority to act as agent for the principal and consideration must be supplied by the principal himself. On these facts Dunlop had to have provided consideration for Selfridge's promise and the House of Lords held that none had been provided.

The agency argument often arose in the case law in the context of whether a third party could enforce a provision (such as an exemption clause) in a contract to which he is not a party when he is sued in tort by one of the contractual parties.

Scruttons Ltd v *Midland Silicones Ltd*
[1962] AC 446 (HL)

The shippers contracted with US Lines, the carrier, for the carriage of a drum containing chemicals from America to London. This contract of carriage contained an exemption clause limiting the liability of the carrier in the event of loss, damage or delay to $500 (£179) per package. Scruttons were stevedores, employed by a contract with the carrier, who negligently dropped and damaged the drum when delivering it to the consignees (Midland Silicones). Midland Silicones sued

Scruttons in tort claiming the value of the drum's contents which had been lost, namely £593. Scruttons sought to rely on the clause in the bill of lading between the shippers and US Lines which limited their liability to £179. Held: (Lord Denning dissenting) the stevedores could not rely on the clause in a contract to which they were not parties because:

(a) there was nothing in that clause which expressly or impliedly indicated that the clause was to extend to the stevedores; and

(b) the carrier did not contract as agent for the stevedores for the benefit of the clause.

LORD REID: . . . I think it is necessary to have in mind certain established principles of the English law of contract. Although I may regret it, I find it impossible to deny the existence of the general rule that a stranger to a contract cannot in a question with either of the contracting parties take advantage of provisions of the contract, even where it is clear from the contract that some provision in it was intended to benefit him. That rule appears to have been crystallised a century ago in *Tweddle* v *Atkinson* (1861) 1 B & S 393 and finally established in this House in *Dunlop Pneumatic Tyre Co. Ltd* v *Selfridge & Co. Ltd* [1915] AC 847. There are, it is true, certain well-established exceptions to that rule—though I am not sure that they are really exceptions and do not arise from other principles. But none of these in any way touches the present case.

. . . The appellants in this case seek to get round this rule . . . they say that through the agency of the carrier they were brought into contractual relation with the shipper and that they can now found on that against the consignees, the respondents. And thirdly, they say that there should be inferred from the facts an implied contract, independent of the bill of lading, between them and the respondents. . . .

I can see a possibility of success of the agency argument if (first) the bill of lading makes it clear that the stevedore is intended to be protected by the provisions in it which limit liability, (secondly) the bill of lading makes it clear that the carrier, in addition to contracting for these provisions on his own behalf, is also contracting as agent for the stevedore that these provisions should apply to the stevedore, (thirdly) the carrier has authority from the stevedore to do that, or perhaps later ratification by the stevedore would suffice, and (fourthly) that any difficulties about consideration moving from the stevedore were overcome. . . .

But again there is nothing of that kind in the present case. I agree with your Lordships that 'carrier' in the bill of lading does not include stevedore, and if that is so I can find nothing in the bill of lading which states or even implies that the parties to it intended the limitation of liability to extend to stevedores. Even if it could be said that reasonable men in the shoes of these parties would have agreed that the stevedores should have this benefit, that would not be enough to make this an implied term of the contract. And even if one could spell out of the bill of lading an intention to benefit the stevedore, there is certainly nothing to indicate that the carrier was contracting as agent for the stevedore in addition to contracting on his own behalf. So it appears to me that the agency argument must fail.

NOTE: The House of Lords rejected the agency argument on these facts but appeared to leave the way open for a suitably drafted clause to succeed. This may be because they were recognising the reality that such clauses are commercially efficient by allocating the risks and the burden of insurance in contracts. This is clearly recognised by Lord Goff in *The Mahkutai* [1996] AC 650, p. 661.

___

New Zealand Shipping Co. Ltd v *A. M. Satterthwaite & Co. Ltd, The Eurymedon*
[1975] AC 154 (PC)

The facts of this case appear at *page 131*. Held: (Viscount Dilhorne and Lord Simon of Glaisdale dissenting) the clause in question did protect the third-party stevedore.

LORD WILBERFORCE: The question in the appeal is whether the stevedore can take the benefit of the time limitation provision. The starting point, in discussion of this question, is provided by the House of Lords decision in *Midland Silicones Ltd* v *Scruttons Ltd* [1962] AC 446. There is no need to question or even to qualify that case in so far as it affirms the general proposition that a contract between two parties cannot be sued on by a third person even though the contract is expressed to be for his benefit. . . . But *Midland Silicones* left open the case where one of the parties contracts as agent for the third person: in particular Lord Reid's speech spelt out, in four propositions, the prerequisites for the validity of such an agency contract. [Lord Wilberforce referred to the four requirements stipulated by Lord Reid in *Scruttons Ltd* v *Midland Silicones Ltd*.]

The question in this appeal is whether the contract satisfies these propositions. Clause 1 of the bill of lading, whatever the defects in its drafting, is clear in its relevant terms. The carrier, on his own account, stipulates for certain exemptions and immunities: among these is that conferred by article III, rule 6, of the Hague Rules which discharges the carrier from all liability for loss or damage unless suit is brought within one year after delivery. In addition to these stipulations on his own account, the carrier as agent for, inter alios, independent contractors stipulates for the same exemptions.

Much was made of the fact that the carrier also contracts as agent for numerous other persons; the relevance of this argument is not apparent. It cannot be disputed that among such independent contractors, for whom, as agent, the carrier contracted, is the appellant company which habitually acts as stevedore in New Zealand by arrangement with the carrier and which is, moreover, the parent company of the carrier. The carrier was, indisputably, authorised by the appellant to contract as its agent for the purposes of clause 1. All of this is quite straightforward and was accepted by all the judges in New Zealand. The only question was, and is, the fourth question presented by Lord Reid, namely that of consideration.

(See the extract from this judgment at *page 132* where Lord Wilberforce analysed this transaction as a unilateral offer of exemption made by the shipper to the stevedores through the carrier as agent. This unilateral offer was accepted when the stevedores performed services for the benefit of the shipper, i.e., unloading the goods. Since this is a unilateral contract, the act of acceptance is also the consideration.) Lord Wilberforce continued:

. . . A clause very similar to the present was given effect by a United States District Court in *Carle & Montanari Inc.* v *American Export Isbrandtsen Lines Inc.* [1968] 1 Lloyd's Rep 260. The carrier in that case contracted, in an exemption clause, as agent, for, inter alios, all stevedores and other independent contractors, and although it is no doubt true that the law in the United States is more liberal than ours as regards third party contracts, their Lordships see no reason why the law of the Commonwealth should be more restrictive and technical as regards agency contracts. Commercial considerations should have the same force on both sides of the Pacific.

In the opinion of their Lordships, to give the appellant the benefit of the exemptions and limitations contained in the bill of lading is to give effect to the clear intentions of a commercial document, and can be given within existing principles. They see no reason to strain the law or the facts in order to defeat these intentions. It should not be overlooked that the effect of denying validity to the clause would be to encourage actions against servants, agents and independent contractors in order to get round exemptions (which are almost invariable and often compulsory) accepted by shippers against carriers, the existence, and presumed efficacy, of which is reflected in the rates of freight. They see no attraction in this consequence.

NOTES
1. The type of clause used here is often referred to as a 'Himalaya clause'.
2. Viscount Dilhorne and Lord Simon (dissenting) considered that the contract with the stevedores would have to be bilateral and that such a contract was not supported by consideration since the stevedores had not promised the shipper/consignee that they would unload the goods.
3. Since acceptance of the unilateral offer takes place only when the stevedore begins to unload

the goods, this agency construction cannot be used by a stevedore who damages the goods *before* starting to unload them. In *Raymond Burke Motors Ltd* v *The Mersey Docks & Harbour Co.* [1986] 1 Lloyd's Rep 155, the goods were at the terminal awaiting the arrival of the ship when they were damaged. At this time no services had been performed which were referable to the carriage contract. Inevitably this will result in fine distinctions.

It should also be noted that the courts appear to be treating an act of starting to unload as sufficient to constitute acceptance for these purposes (see *page 59* and criticisms of this).

4. It is not possible to accept an offer that you do not know about since the response must be in exchange for the promise (*R* v *Clarke* (1927) 40 CLR 227, *page 41*). Will the stevedores (third party) know of the terms of the bill of lading (contract of carriage) when they start to unload?

This appears not to have been a problem in *The Eurymedon* because the stevedore company and the carrier company were companies in the same group, and therefore the stevedores probably did know of the carriage terms.

5. One further theoretical difficulty with the unilateral contract analysis is that, since there is a contract established between the shipper and the stevedore, there is no obvious reason to seek to rely on agency. Coote, 'Pity the Poor Stevedore!' [1981] CLJ 13, suggested that it might be necessary because the terms of the bill of lading indicated an immediate bargain rather than an offer of a future contract, and the contract between the shipper and the stevedore is formed when the services are performed by the stevedore which will be after the bill of lading contract is made.

■ QUESTION

If this contract had been covered by the Contracts (Rights of Third Parties) Act 1999, would the stevedores have had a *direct* right of enforcement of the clause thereby eliminating the technicalities of the *Eurymedon* device? See *page 442*.

However, in general, the courts have shown themselves unwilling to make 'fine distinctions' in order to limit the applicability of the doctrine in *The Eurymedon*. Lord Wilberforce in *Port Jackson Stevedoring Pty Ltd* v *Salmond & Spraggon (Australia) Pty Ltd, The New York Star* [1981] 1 WLR 138 had stated that the Privy Council 'would not encourage a search for fine distinctions which would diminish the general applicability, in the light of established commercial practice, of the principle . . .'. Accordingly, the Privy Council rejected an argument that it had not been shown that the carrier had authority to act on the stevedores' behalf for the benefit of the exemption clause. On the facts, the stevedores and carriers were companies in the same group so that authority to act could be assumed.

Similarly, in *Owners of the Ship 'Borvigilant'* v *Owners of the 'Romina G'* [2003] EWCA Civ 935, [2003] 2 Lloyd's Rep 520, in relation to the requirement to establish authority to act as agent, the Court of Appeal held that it was not necessary for the relevant document, a Tug Requisition Form, to expressly state that NIOC was contracting as agent for other tug owners if it was clear by implication from the rest of the contract terms, considered against the surrounding circumstances or factual matrix, that it was intended that the other tug owners should have the benefit of the contract. The Court of Appeal held that NIOC was contracting on behalf of Borkan because '[i]t is the only conclusion which makes commercial sense' in the light of other terms. Clarke LJ considered Lord Reid's first two requirements to be closely related: 'Thus if, as here, the contract expressly provides that it is made for the benefit of another person, that seems to me to be a strong pointer to the conclusion that the contract was made on behalf of that person, especially if, . . . such a person would not be entitled to the benefit of the contract unless the contract was made on his behalf'. It was also noted that this approach accorded with the comment by Lord Goff in *The Mahkutai* [1996] AC 650, at 661:

In more recent years the pendulum has swung back again, as recognition has been given to the undesirability, especially in a commercial context, of allowing plaintiffs to circumvent contractual exception clauses by suing in particular the servant or agent of the contracting party who caused the relevant damage, thereby undermining the purpose of the exception, and so redistributing the contractual allocation of risk which is reflected in the freight rate and in the parties' respective insurance arrangements.

However, difficulties existed in the context of building contracts due to the difficulty of showing that the main contractor had been authorised to act as agent for the subcontractor at the time when the main contract was made.

Southern Water Authority v Carey

[1985] 2 All ER 1077

The predecessor of the plaintiff water authority had entered into a contract with the main contractors for the construction of sewage works. This contract provided that 12 months after completion the main contractors, their subcontractors, servants or agents were not to be liable for defects in the works or loss attributable to such defects. It also provided that the main contractors were to be deemed to have contracted on their own behalf and on behalf of their subcontractors, servants and agents. The main contractor employed the defendant subcontractors. The plaintiff brought an action against those subcontractors alleging negligence and the subcontractors sought to rely on the clause in the main contract. Held: they were not entitled to the benefit of a clause in a contract to which they were not parties. They could not claim that the main contractor acted as their agent in contracting with the plaintiffs, since at the time the main contract was made the subcontractors had not given the main contractor this authority. However, the defendants were not liable in tort because the clause in the main contract negatived the duty of care that they would normally have owed as subcontractors.

JUDGE DAVID SMOUT QC: I must be cautious before extending into a wider field those decisions in so far as they apply the principle of unilateral contract to the specialised practice of carriers and stevedores in mercantile law. To my mind the principle of the unilateral contract does not, taken by itself, fit easily onto the accepted facts in the instant case and it strikes me as uncomfortably artificial.

It is, however, the agency element in *Satterthwaite's* case that is much to the point, [He then referred to Lord Reid's four requirements mentioned in *Scruttons* v *Midland Silicones* (page 446) and continued:]

Let us then consider the four propositions in the context of the instant case. First, does the main contract make it clear that the sub-contractors are intended to be protected by the provisions in it which limit liability? To my mind the answer must be Yes. Second, does it make it clear that the main contractor in addition to contracting for these provisions on his own behalf is also contracting as agent for the subcontractors that the provisions should also apply to the sub-contractors? Again, I answer Yes: cl 30(vi) so states. The fourth proposition as to consideration poses no difficulty, for this is a contract under seal. It is the third proposition that is debatable in the instance case: had the main contractor authority from the sub-contractor, at the time of making the contract, and, if not, was there any later ratification that would suffice? Unlike *Satterthwaite's* case, there is no evidence here on which I could conclude that the main contractors had prior authority. What as to ratification? Counsel for the plaintiffs contends that there can be no ratification unless the principal was capable of being ascertained at the time when the act was done, i.e. when the deed was signed. Herein lies the defendants' difficulty . . . The fact that the fourth defendants were in the contemplation of the second defendants at the material time, as the documents show, and that it may be that the third defendants were also in contemplation, does not in my view suffice. . . . I turn now away from contract to the argument as it has been put in tort. . . .

No one would doubt that in an ordinary building case as between the subcontractors and the building owner who has suffered damage there is a sufficient relationship of proximity that in the reasonable contemplation of the sub-contractor carelessness on his part may be likely to cause damage to the building owner. Thus a prima facie duty of care lies on the sub-contractor. So also in this case. But one has to go on to consider whether there are any considerations which ought to negative or to reduce or limit the scope of that duty. And merely to ask the question in the context of this case seems to me to foretell the answer. Did not the plaintiffs' predecessor as building owner, as it were, itself stipulate that the sub-contractors should have a measure of protection following on the issue of appropriate taking-over certificates? We must look to see the nature of such limitation clause to consider whether or not it is relevant in defining the scope of the duty in tort. The contractual setting may not necessarily be overriding, but it is relevant in the consideration of the scope of the duty in tort for it indicates the extent of the liability which the plaintiffs' predecessor wished to impose. To put it more crudely, and I hope I do no injustice to counsel for the third defendants to say that that is how he emphasised the matter, the contractual setting defines the area of risk which the plaintiffs' predecessor chose to accept and for which it may or may not have sought commercial insurance. . . .

While the terms of cl 30(vi) may, if literally interpreted, exceed the bounds of common sense the intent is clear, namely that the sub-contractor whose works have been so completed as to be the subject of a valid taking-over certificate should be protected in respect of those works from any liability in tort to the plaintiffs. As the plaintiffs' predecessor did so choose to limit the scope of the sub-contractors' liability, I see no reason why such limitation should not be honoured. . . .

NOTES
1. Lord Reid in *Scruttons* v *Midland Silicones* (*page 446*) had indicated that either the agent had to be authorised to act or the contract might be subsequently ratified. Ratification was not possible here since the subcontractors were selected after the main contract was signed, whereas agency requires that the principal be capable of being ascertained at the time of the contract. This represented an important limitation on the usefulness of *The Eurymedon*, since it was interpreted to mean that the subcontract had to exist at the time of the main contract. (See now s. 1(3) of the Contracts (Rights of Third Parties) Act 1999.)
2. The practical effect of the decision on the duty of care in tort is that although the sub-contractors were not a party to the main contract, they were able to rely on its terms to protect them.

■ QUESTIONS

1. Under the provisions of the Contracts (Rights of Third Parties) Act 1999, do you think that the stevedores in *The Eurymedon* and the subcontractors in *Southern Water Authority* v *Carey* ought to be able to enforce the contractual provisions directly? In other words, would they satisfy the test of enforceability (see s. 1(1)–(3), *page 442 above*)? If so, it will eliminate the technicality and artificiality of *The Eurymedon* analysis.

2. Would the provisions of the Act enable employees in the same position as the employees in the next case to directly enforce the contractual limitation? Does the clause 'purport to confer a benefit' on the employees, and are they 'expressly identified in the contract by name, as members of a class or as answering a particular description'?

London Drugs Ltd v *Kuehne and Nagel International Ltd*
(1993) 97 DLR (4th) 261, Supreme Court of Canada

The plaintiffs delivered a transformer to Kuehne and Nagel (the corporation) for storage upon the terms of their contract, which limited 'the warehouseman's liability' to $40. The transformer was damaged during lifting as a result of the negligence of two of the corporation's employees, and the plaintiffs brought an action against them in tort claiming their full loss of $34,000. The question was whether the employees, who were not parties to the contract containing the limitation clause, could rely upon it. The Court of Appeal had reached a conclusion favourable to the employees by using two different approaches: (i) *The Eurymedon* analysis, although on the facts it was necessary to imply a term that the protection extended to employees since it did not do so expressly, and (ii) the 'tort analysis', whereby the 'contractual matrix' including the limitation clause qualified the employees' duty of care and ensuing liability to $40. Held: on appeal the majority considered that the employees could rely on the limitation clause. Since they were acting in the course of their employment and performing the very services contracted for by the plaintiffs, they were implicit third party beneficiaries of the clause.

IACOBUCCI J (L'Heureux-Dube, Sopinka and Cory JJ concurring): . . . For my part, I prefer to deal head-on with the doctrine of privity and to relax its ambit in the circumstances of this case. Some may argue that the same result can (and should) be reached by using a number of approaches which are seemingly less drastic and/or allegedly more theoretically sound . . . Except for a rigid adherence to the doctrine of privity of contract, I do not see any compelling reason based on principle, authority or policy demonstrating that this court, or any other, must embark upon a complex and somewhat uncertain 'tort analysis' in order to allow third parties such as the respondents to obtain the benefit of a contractual limitation of liability clause, once it has been established that they breached a recognised duty of care. In my view, apart from privity of contract, it is contrary to neither principle nor authority to allow such a party, in appropriate circumstances, to obtain the benefit *directly* from the contract i.e., in the same manner as would the contracting party, by resorting to what may be referred to as a 'contract analysis'. . . .

None of the traditional exceptions to privity is applicable in the case at bar. As noted by the appellant, there is no evidence to support a finding of agency or trust, and these matters were not fully argued before the courts below. While the respondents rely to a certain extent on the approach taken by Lambert J.A. in the Court of Appeal, I must say that I have much difficulty in supporting a conclusion that the approach described in *The Eurymedon*, . . . and *ITO-International Terminal Operators* [(1986) 28 DLR (4th) 641] is applicable to the facts of this case. Rather than artificially extending recognised exceptions beyond their accepted limits, I prefer approaching this matter on the basis that privity of contract would otherwise apply so as to preclude the respondents from obtaining the benefit of the limitation of liability clause. The questions I now need to address are whether this doctrine should be relaxed in the circumstances of this case and, if so, on what basis.

Should the doctrine of privity be relaxed?
Without doubt, major reforms to the rule denying third parties the right to enforce contractual provisions made for their benefit must come from the legislature. Although I have strong reservations about the rigid retention of a doctrine that has undergone systematic and substantial attack, privity of contract is an established principle in the law of contracts and should not be discarded lightly. Simply to abolish the doctrine of privity or to ignore it, without more, would represent a major change to the common law involving complex and uncertain ramifications. . . .

[T]he doctrine of privity has come under serious attack for its refusal to recognise the right of a third party beneficiary to enforce contractual provisions made for his or her benefit. Law reformers, commentators and judges have pointed out the gaps that sometimes exist between contract theory on the one hand, and commercial reality and justice on the other. We have also seen that many jurisdictions around the world, including Quebec and the United States, have chosen from an early point (as early as the doctrine became 'settled' in the English common law) to recognise third party beneficiary rights in certain circumstances. As noted by the appellant, the common law recognises certain exceptions to the doctrine, such as agency and trust, which enable courts, in appropriate circumstances, to arrive at results which conform with the true intentions of the contracting parties and commercial reality. However, as many have observed, the availability of these exceptions does not always correspond with their need. Accordingly, this court should not be precluded from developing the common law so as to recognise a further exception to privity of contract merely on the ground that some exceptions already exist.

While these comments may not, in themselves, justify doing away with the doctrine of privity, they none the less give a certain context to the principles that this court is now dealing with. This context clearly supports in my view some type of reform or relaxation to the law relating to third party beneficiaries. Again, I reiterate that any substantial amendment to the doctrine of privity is a matter properly left with the legislature. But this does not mean that courts should shut their eyes to criticisms when faced with an opportunity, as in the case at bar, to make a very specific incremental change to the common law.

There are few principled reasons for upholding the doctrine of privity in the circumstances of this case . . . most of the traditional reasons or justifications behind the doctrine are of little application in cases such as this one, when a third party beneficiary is relying on a contractual provision as a defence in an action brought by one of the contracting parties. There are no concerns about double recovery or floodgates of litigation brought by third party beneficiaries. The fact that a contract is a very personal affair, affecting only the parties to it, is simply a restatement of the doctrine of privity rather than a reason for its maintenance. Nor is there any concern about 'reciprocity', that is, there is no concern that it would be unjust to allow a party to sue on a contract when he or she cannot be sued on it.

Moreover, recognizing a right for a third party beneficiary to rely on a limitation of liability clause should have relatively little impact on the rights of contracting parties to rescind or vary their contracts, in comparison with the recognition of a third party right to sue on a contract. In the end, the most that can be said against the extension of exceptions to the doctrine of privity in this case is that the respondent employees are mere donees and have provided no consideration for the contractual limitation of liability.

The doctrine of privity fails to appreciate the special considerations which arise from the relationships of employer-employee and employer-customer. There is clearly an identity of interest between the employer and his or her employees as far as the performance of the employer's contractual obligations is concerned. When a person contracts with an employer for certain services, there can be little doubt in most cases that employees will have the prime responsibilities related to the performance of the obligations which arise under the contract. This was the case in the present appeal, clearly to the knowledge of the appellant . . . I am in no way suggesting that employees are a party to their employer's contracts in the traditional sense so that they can bring an action on the contract or be sued for breach of contract. However, when an employer and a customer enter into a contract for services and include a clause limiting the liability of the employer for damages arising from what will normally be conduct contemplated by the contracting parties to be performed by the employer's employees, and in fact so performed, there is simply no valid reason for denying the benefit of the clause to employees who perform the contractual obligations. The nature and scope of the limitation of liability clause in such a case coincides essentially with the nature and scope of the contractual obligations performed by the third party beneficiaries (employees).

Upholding a strict application of the doctrine of privity in the circumstances of this case would also have the effect of allowing the appellant to circumvent or escape the limitation of liability clause to which it had expressly consented. . . .

. . . Holding the employees liable in these circumstances could lead to serious injustice especially when one considers that the financial position of the affected employees could vary considerably such that, for example, more well-off employees would be sued and left to look for contribution from the less well-off employees. Such a result creates also uncertainty and requires excessive expenditures on insurance in that it defeats the allocations of risk specifically made by the contracting parties and the reasonable expectations of everyone involved, including the employees. When parties enter into commercial agreements and decide that one of them *and* its employees will benefit from limited liability, or when these parties choose language such as 'warehouseman' which implies that employees will also benefit from a protection, the doctrine of privity should not stand in the way of commercial reality and justice.

How should the doctrine of privity be relaxed?
Regardless of the desirability of making a particular change to the law, I have already noted that complex changes with uncertain ramifications should be left to the legislature. Our power and duty as a court to adapt and develop the common law must only be exercised generally in an incremental fashion . . .

In the end, the narrow question before this court is: in what circumstances should employees be entitled to benefit from a limitation of liability clause found in a contract between their employer and the plaintiff (customer)? Keeping in mind the comments made earlier and the circumstances of this appeal, I am of the view that employees may obtain such a benefit if the following requirements are satisfied:

(1)   the limitation of liability clause must, either expressly or impliedly, extend its benefit to the employees (or employee) seeking to rely on it; and
(2)   the employees (or employee) seeking the benefit of the limitation of liability clause must have been acting in the course of their employment *and* must have been performing the very services provided for in the contract between their employer and the plaintiff (customer) when the loss occurred. . . .

It is clear that the parties did not choose express language in order to extend the benefit of the clause to employees. For example, there is no mention of words such as 'servants' or 'employees' in s. 11(b) of the contract. As such, it cannot be said that the respondents are express third party beneficiaries with respect to the limitation of liability clause. However, this does not preclude a finding that they are *implied* third party beneficiaries . . .

When all the circumstances of this case are taken into account, including the nature of the relationship between employees and their employer, the identity of interest with respect to contractual obligations, the fact that the appellant knew that employees would be involved in performing the contractual obligations, and the absence of a clear indication in the contract to the contrary, the term 'warehouseman' in s. 11(b) of the contract must be interpreted as meaning 'warehousemen'. As such, the respondents are not complete strangers to the limitation of liability clause. Rather, they are unexpressed or implicit third party beneficiaries with respect to this clause. Accordingly, the first requirement of this new exception to the doctrine of privity is also met.

. . . While neither trust nor agency is applicable, the respondents are entitled to benefit directly from the limitation of liability clause in the contract between their employer and the appellant. This is so because they are third party beneficiaries with respect to that clause and because they were acting in the course of their employment and performing the very services contracted for by the appellant when the damages occurred. I acknowledge that this, in effect, relaxes the doctrine of privity and creates a limited *jus tertii*. However, when viewed in its proper context, it merely represents an incremental change to the law, necessary to see that the common law develops in a manner that is consistent with modern notions of commercial reality and justice.

NOTES
1. See Adams and Brownsword (1993) 56 MLR 722 for a detailed analysis of the reasoning.
2. This decision involved a totally different approach, since the Supreme Court of Canada expressly recognised a new exception allowing third party employees to rely on an exemption clause (albeit a specific and limited exception). The Court refused to extend the 'artificial' *Eurymedon* exception to enable it to apply on these facts.
3. Iacobucci J referred to this approach as 'incremental change' and justified the exception by the need to make commercial sense and avoid absurd results. Waddams (1993) 109 LQR 349, pp. 350–1, supported this 'incremental' approach to reform of the privity rule, i.e. by the

continuing development of exceptions rather than a general reform allowing third parties to enforce benefits which Waddams believed would lead to 'unacceptable results'. See, however, Huscroft (1994) 7 JCL 181, who argued that this 'incremental' response was inadequate and criticised Waddams's view that it is 'now open to any court to establish a new exception wherever justice and commercial convenience require one'.

■ QUESTION

The Law Commission Report (1996), Part V, rejected judicial reform of the third party beneficiary rule in favour of a detailed legislative scheme. Why was this?

The Supreme Court of Canada continued this 'incremental' approach to reform in *Fraser River & Dredge Ltd* v *Can-Dive Services Ltd* [2000] 1 Lloyd's Rep 199 in the context of waiver of subrogation against an additional insured third party.

Fraser River & Dredge Ltd v *Can-Dive Services Ltd*
[2000] 1 Lloyd's Rep 199 (Supreme Court of Canada)

C had chartered a barge from F to carry out work on a gas pipeline. Under the terms of the charter C was fully responsible for towing the barge to the site and for its condition. The barge sank at the site and F recovered under its insurance policy that included 'Additional Insureds' and 'Waiver of Subrogation' clauses whereby any charterer was to be regarded as an additional insured and the insurers agreed to waive any rights of subrogation against 'charterers and/or operators'. Held: these facts satisfied the criteria in *London Drugs* for relaxing the privity doctrine. C was a charterer and therefore included within the coverage of the policy. As such C was entitled to rely on the waiver of subrogation provision.

IACOBUCCI J: . . .
Is Can-Dive as a third-party beneficiary under the insurance policy pursuant to the waiver of subrogation clause, entitled to rely on that clause to defend against the insurer's subrogated action on the basis of the principled exception to the privity of contract doctrine established by the Court's decision in London Drugs?

(1) *London Drugs and a principled exception to the doctrine of privity of contract*
As stated above, Can-Dive's position is that of a third-party beneficiary who normally would be precluded from enforcing or relying on the terms of the policy in effect between Fraser River and its insurers. Accordingly, it is necessary to consider the legal status of the waiver of subrogation clause in light of the Court's decision in *London Drugs*, sup. In that case, the Court introduced what was intended as a principled exception to the common law doctrine of privity of contract.

[He discussed *London Drugs* and continued:]

(2) *Application of the principled exception to the circumstances of this appeal*
As a preliminary matter, I note that it was not our intention in *London Drugs*, sup., to limit application of the principled approach to situations involving only an employer–employee relationship. That the discussion focussed on the nature of this relationship simply reflects the prudent jurisprudential principle that a case should not be decided beyond the scope of its immediate facts.

In terms of extending the principled approach to establishing a new exception to the doctrine of privity of contract relevant to the circumstances of the appeal, regard must be had to the emphasis in *London Drugs* that a new exception first and foremost must be dependent upon the intention of the contracting parties. Accordingly, extrapolating from the specific requirements as set out in *London Drugs*, the determination in general terms is made on the basis of two critical and cumulative factors: (a) did the parties to the contract intend to extend the benefit in question to the third party seeking to rely on the contractual provision; and (b) are the activities performed by the third party seeking to rely on the contractual provision the very activities contemplated as coming within the scope of the contract in general, or the provision in particular, again as determined by reference to the intentions of the parties?

Intentions of the parties

. . .

In my opinion, the case in favour of relaxing the doctrine of privity is even stronger in the circumstances of this appeal than was the case in *London Drugs*, sup., wherein the parties did not expressly extend the benefit of a limitation of liability clause covering a 'warehouseman' to employees. Instead, it was necessary to support an implicit extension of the benefit on the basis of the relationship between the employers and its employees, that is to say, the identity of interest between the employer and its employees in terms of performing the contractual obligations. In contrast, given the express reference to 'charterer(s)' in the waiver of subrogation clause in the policy, there is no need to look for any additional factors to justify characterizing Can-Dive as a third-party beneficiary rather than a mere stranger to the contract.

Having concluded that the parties intended to extend the benefit of the waiver of subrogation clause to third parties such as Can-Dive, it is necessary to address Fraser River's argument that its agreement with the insurers to pursue legal action against Can-Dive nonetheless effectively deleted the third-party benefit from the contract. A significant concern with relaxing the doctrine of privity is the potential restrictions on freedom of contract which could result if the interests of a third-party beneficiary must be taken into account by the parties to the initial agreement before any adjustment to the contract could occur. It is important to note, however, that the agreement in question was concluded subsequent to the point at which what might be termed Can-Dive's inchoate right under the contract crystallized into an actual benefit in the form of a defence against an action in negligence by Fraser River's insurers. Having contracted in favour of Can-Dive as within the class of potential third-party beneficiaries, Fraser River and the insurers cannot revoke unilaterally Can-Dive's rights once they have developed into an actual benefit. At the point at which Can-Dive's rights crystallized, it became for all intents and purposes a party to the initial contract for the limited purposes of relying on the waiver of subrogation clause. Any subsequent alteration of the waiver provision is subject to further negotiation and agreement among all of the parties involved, including Can-Dive.

I am mindful, however, that the principle of freedom of contract must not be dismissed lightly. Accordingly, nothing in these reasons concerning the ability of the initial parties to amend contractual provisions subsequently should be taken as applying other than to the limited situation of a third-party seeking to rely on a benefit conferred by the contract to defend against an action initiated by one of the parties, and only then in circumstances where the inchoate contractual right has crystallized prior to any purported amendment. Within this narrow exception, however, the doctrine of privity presents no obstacle to contractual rights conferred on third-party beneficiaries.

Third-party beneficiary is performing the activities contemplated in the contract

. . . At issue is whether the purported third-party beneficiary is involved in the very activity contemplated by the contract containing the provision upon which he or she seeks to rely. In this case, the relevant activities arose in the context of the relationship of Can-Dive to Fraser River as a charterer, the very activity anticipated in the policy pursuant to the waiver of subrogation clause. Accordingly, I conclude that the second requirement for relaxing the doctrine of privity has been met.

Policy reasons in favour of an exception in these circumstances

. . .

Fraser River has also argued that to relax the doctrine of privity of contract in the circumstances of this appeal would be to introduce a significant change to the law that is better left to the legislature. As was noted in *London Drugs*, privity of contract is an established doctrine of contract law, and should not be lightly discarded through the process of judicial decree. Wholesale abolition of the doctrine would result in complex repercussions that exceed the ability of the Courts to anticipate and address. It is by now a well-established principle that the Courts will not undertake judicial reform of this magnitude, recognizing instead that the legislature is better placed to appreciate and accommodate the economic and policy issues involved in introducing sweeping legal reforms.

That being said, the corollary principle is equally compelling, which is that in appropriate circumstances, the Courts must not abdicate their judicial duty to decide on incremental changes to the common law necessary to address emerging needs and values in society: *Watkins* v *Olafson* [1989] 2 SCR 750, at pp. 760–761, and *R* v *Salituro* [1991] 3 SCR 654, at pp. 665–670. In this case, I do not accept Fraser River's submission that permitting third-party beneficiaries to rely on a waiver of subrogation clause represents other than an incremental development. To the contrary, the factors present in *London Drugs*, in support of the incremental nature of the exception are present as well in the circumstances of this appeal. As in *London Drugs*, a third-party beneficiary is seeking to rely on a contractual provision in order to defend against an action initiated by one of the contracting parties. Fraser River's concerns regarding the potential for double recovery are unfounded, as relaxing the doctrine to the extent contemplated by these reasons does not permit Can-Dive to rely on any provision in the policy to establish a separate claim. In addition, the exception is dependent upon the express intentions of the parties, evident in the language of the waiver of subrogation clause, to extend the benefit of the provision to certain named classes of third-party beneficiaries.

Conclusion and disposition

I conclude that the circumstances of this appeal nonetheless meet the requirements established in *London Drugs*, for a third-party beneficiary to rely on the terms of a contract to defend against a claim initiated by one of the parties to the contract. As a third-party beneficiary to the policy, Can-Dive is entitled to rely on the waiver of subrogation clause whereby the insurers expressly waived any right of subrogation against Can-Dive as a 'charterer' of a vessel included within the policy's coverage.

NOTES

1. As Iacobucci J emphasises, the merits of this situation called for intervention to ensure that the charterers could rely on the waiver of subrogation clause because they were expressly mentioned as having that benefit. This can be compared with *London Drugs* where some implication had to be made from the term 'warehouseman'. It would appear that a third party in the position of the charterer in *Fraser River* would fall within s. 1(1)(b) of the Contracts (Rights of Third Parties) Act 1999 (subject to s. 1(2)) as the term expressly purports to confer a benefit on the charterer who is expressly identified in the contract as a member of a class. Compare this with *London Drugs*.
2. The argument that the waiver of subrogation clause had been varied by the agreement with the insurers to commence proceedings against the charterer was rejected by the court on the basis that the third party had not consented to such a variation. Compare Iacobucci J's comments on variation with s. 2 of the Contracts (Rights of Third Parties) Act 1999.
3. See Nicholson [2000] LMCLQ 322.

In Commonwealth jurisdictions there is evidence of a more relaxed approach to the privity doctrine, both in terms of statutory reform of the third party rule and in terms of case law (see the Canadian case law discussed above). The decision of the High Court of Australia in *Trident General Insurance Co. Ltd* v *McNiece Brothers Pty Ltd* is a useful illustration of this approach, and the judgments are helpful in discussing the difficulties faced when reforming the third party rule.

Trident General Insurance Co. Ltd v *McNiece Brothers Proprietary Ltd*
(1988) 165 CLR 107; (1988) 80 ALJR 574 (High Court of Australia)

In 1977, Blue Circle took out a policy of insurance with Trident covering the public liability of Blue Circle, all its subsidiaries, associated and related companies, and all its contractors and subcontractors and/or suppliers. In 1978, McNiece Bros. were employed as subcontractors on one of Blue Circle's construction contracts, and due to their alleged negligence an employee of a labour subcontractor was injured. McNiece sought an indemnity from Trident under the policy. Trident denied liability, arguing that McNiece Bros. were not Blue Circle's contractors at the date of the policy. A majority of a seven member High Court of Australia (5:2) thought that McNiece Bros. were entitled to this indemnity against their liability to pay damages. However, only three of the majority (Mason CJ, Wilson J, and Toohey J) based their decision on privity, and the decision may well be restricted to the special case of insurance contracts.

MASON CJ AND WILSON J: [This judgment identifies some of the difficulties presented by allowing third parties to enforce contractual benefits.] In order to justify the privity and consideration rules, three practical policy considerations are sometimes invoked. First, they preclude the risk of double recovery from the promisor by the third party as well as the promisee. If the third party is permitted to sue the risk of double recovery arises from the possibility that the one party may seek specific performance after another has recovered damages. The risk is insignificant; joinder of all parties in the first action will make the resulting decision binding on all.

The second point is that the privity requirement imposes an effective barrier to liability on the part of a contracting party to a vast range of potential plaintiffs. This may be significant in the case of government contracts intended to benefit a class of persons. But it is difficult to justify the existence of a rule by reference to one of its indirect results, if in other respects its operation is unsatisfactory.

The third matter is more important. The recognition of an unqualified entitlement in a third party to sue on the contract would severely circumscribe the freedom of action of the parties, particularly the promisee. He may rescind or modify the contract with the assent of the promisor, arrive at a compromise or assign his contractual rights. He may even modify the contract so that he diverts to himself the benefit initially intended for the third party. Professor Corbin suggested that any entitlement in the third party to enforce the provision in his favour would necessarily exist at the expense of the rights, privileges and liberties that the contracting parties enjoy under the common law rules: 'Third Party Beneficiary Contracts in England', *University of Chicago Law Review*, vol 35 (1968) 544, at p. 549. But this does not entirely follow. The entitlement of the third party to enforce the provision in his favour can be subordinated to the right of the contracting parties to rescind or modify the contract, in which event the third party would lose his rights except in so far as he relied on the promise to his detriment. . . . To subordinate the third party's entitlement in this way would accord with legal principle and with the protection of the interests of the parties to the contract. There is to our minds no compelling reason why the interests of the third party should be preferred. . . .

Should it be a sufficient foundation for the existence of a third party entitlement to sue on the contract that there is a contractual intention to benefit a third party? Or, should an intention that the third party should be able to sue on the contract be required? Under s. 48 of the Insurance Contracts Act 1984 (Cth) and in the United States an intention to benefit a third party alone is necessary and that seems to be the position in Western Australia. But in Queensland (Property Law Act 1974, ss. 55(1), 55(6)(c)(ii)) and in New Zealand (Contracts (Privity) Act 1982, ss. 4, 8) an intention that the third party should be able to sue is required. This requirement again seems to have its origin in the recommendations of the English Law Revision Committee. As the contracting parties are unlikely to turn their attention to the enforcement by the third party, the ascertainment of this intention may well be fraught with similar problems to those that have surrounded the trust concept.

The variety of these responses to the problems arising from contracts to benefit a third party indicate the range of the policy choices to be made and that there is room for debate about them. A simple departure from the traditional rules would lead to third party enforceability of such a contract, subject to the preservation of a contracting party's right to rescind or vary, in the absence of reliance by the third party to his detriment, and to the availability in an action by the third party of defences against a contracting party. The adoption of this course would represent less of a departure from the traditional exposition of the law than other legislative choices which have been made. . . .

In the ultimate analysis the limited question we have to decide is whether the old rules apply to a policy of insurance. The injustice which would flow from such a result arises not only from its failure to give effect to the expressed intention of the person who takes out the insurance but also from the common intention of the parties and the circumstance that others, aware of the existence of the policy, will order their affairs accordingly. We doubt that the doctrine of estoppel provides an adequate protection of the legitimate expectations of such persons and, even if it does, the rights of persons under a policy of insurance should not be made to depend on the vagaries of such an intricate doctrine. In the nature of things the likelihood of some degree of reliance on the part of the third party in the case of a benefit to be provided for him under an insurance policy is so tangible that the common law rule should be shaped with that likelihood in mind.

This argument has even greater force when it is applied to an insurance against liabilities which is expressed to cover the insured and its sub-contractors. It stands to reason that many sub-contractors will assume that such an insurance is an effective indemnity in their favour and that they will refrain from making their own arrangements for insurance on that footing. That, it seems, is what happened in the present case. But why should the respondent's rights depend entirely on its ability to make out a case of estoppel?

In the circumstances, notwithstanding the caution with which the Court ordinarily will review earlier authorities and the operation of long-established principle, we conclude that the principled development of the law requires that it be recognized that McNiece was entitled to succeed in the action.

NOTES

1. McNiece Bros was able to obtain the benefit of a contract to which it was not a party without having to resort to agency or trust arguments. Compare with *Southern Water Authority* v *Carey*, *page 449*.
2. The case facts pre-dated an Australian statute allowing third parties to sue on insurance contracts. This factor clearly influenced the judgments.
3. Brennan J and Dawson J considered that the privity rule could not be modified judicially. Gaudron J held Trident liable in restitution on the basis of unjust enrichment. Deane J would have preferred a trust argument (which had not been pleaded).
4. Section 2 of the Contracts (Rights of Third Parties) Act 1999 addresses the question of whether the contracting parties can vary or cancel the contract where a third party has a right to enforce a term under s. 1.

■ QUESTION

To what extent are the reform issues identified in this judgment adequately addressed by the Contracts (Rights of Third Parties) Act 1999?

SECTION 4: **JOINT PROMISEES**

Where a promise is made to joint promisees but only one of them provides the consideration, can both enforce the contract?

Coulls v *Bagot's Executor & Trustee Co. Ltd*
(1967) 119 CLR 460; [1967] ALR 385 (High Court of Australia)

By an agreement headed 'Agreement between Arthur Coulls and O'Neil Construction Company', Coulls granted the company quarrying rights over his land in return for royalties. The agreement also provided that Coulls could instruct the company to pay these royalties to him and his wife as joint tenants. (This meant that the survivor would be solely entitled.) This agreement was signed by the company and by both Coulls and his wife. After the death of Coulls, a dispute arose between his executors and his widow as to who was entitled to these royalty payments. Held: (McTiernan, Taylor, and Owen JJ) the company was bound to pay the royalties to the husband's estate on his death because the wife was not a party to the agreement and when he died the mandate to pay the money to the wife was revoked.

Barwick CJ and Windeyer J dissented on the ground that the husband and wife were joint promisees. The problem was that the wife had not provided any consideration for the company's promise to make the payments in this way. Barwick CJ held that there would need to be a joint action with the husband's executor for her to be able to enforce the promise.

BARWICK CJ: Before turning to discuss its enforceability it is convenient to determine with whom the promise was made. As I have already said, there is nothing in the writing to indicate expressly to whom the promise of the company was given. But, bearing in mind the matters to which I have already referred, the grant of a licence to quarry for a cash consideration, the participation of the company's representative in the discussion as to the payees and the signature of all three parties in what was regarded as a single arrangement, I have come to the conclusion that not only was the promise to pay a promise to pay the deceased and the respondent during their joint lifetime and thereafter the survivor of them but that it was a promise given to both of them to make those payments.

It must be accepted that, according to our law, a person not a party to a contract may not himself sue upon it so as directly to enforce its obligations. For my part, I find no difficulty or embarrassment [sic] in this conclusion. Indeed, I would find it odd that a person to whom no promise was made could himself in his own right enforce a promise made to another. But that does not mean that it is not possible for that person to obtain the benefit of a promise made with another for his benefit by steps other than enforcement by himself in his own right: see the recent case of *Beswick* v *Beswick* [1966] Ch 538; [1968] AC 58. I would myself, with great respect, agree with the conclusion that where A promises B for a consideration supplied by B to pay C then B may obtain specific performance of A's promise, at least where the nature of the consideration given would have allowed the debtor to have obtained specific performance. I can see no reason whatever why A in those circumstances should not be bound to perform his promise. That C provided no part of the consideration seems to me irrelevant. Questions of consideration and of privity are not always kept distinct. Indeed, on some occasions when lack of privity is the real reason for not allowing a plaintiff to succeed on a promise not made with him, an unnecessary and irrelevant reason is given that the plaintiff was a stranger to the consideration; that is to say, that he was not merely not a party to the agreement but was not a party to the bargain. In *Dunlop Pneumatic Tyre Co. Ltd* v *Selfridge & Co. Ltd* [1915] AC 847 privity was not lacking because it was assumed, but the promise made by the defendant to the plaintiff was as between them gratuitous. But in this case whether the promise was made by the company to the deceased alone or to the deceased and the respondent, it was not as between promisor and promisee a gratuitous promise.

But as I construe this writing, we have here not a promise by A with B for consideration supplied by B to pay C. It was, in my opinion, a promise by A made to B and C for consideration to pay B and C. In such a case it cannot lie in the mouth of A, in my opinion, to question whether the consideration which he received for his promise moved from both B and C or, as between themselves, only from one of them. His promise is not a gratuitous promise as between himself and the promisees as on the view I take of the agreement it was a promise in respect of which there was privity between A on the one hand and B and C on the other. Such a promise, in my opinion, is clearly enforceable in the joint lifetime of B and C: But it is only enforceable if both B and C are parties to the action to enforce it. B, though he only supplied the consideration, could not sue alone. If C were unwilling to join in the action as plaintiff, B no doubt, after suitable tender of costs, could join C as a defendant. And A's promise could be enforced. But the judgment would be for payment to B and C. If B would not join in an action to enforce A's promise, I see no reason why C should not sue joining B as a defendant. Again, in my opinion, A's promise would be enforced and a judgment in favour of B and C would result. In neither of these cases could A successfully deny either privity or consideration. I find nothing in *Dunlop Pneumatic Tyre Co. Ltd* v *Selfridge & Co. Ltd* [1915] AC 847 to suggest that he could.

Upon the death of one of the joint promisees the promise remains on foot and remains enforceable but it is still the same promise given to B and C though, because of the death of one and the right of survivorship, the promise is now to pay the survivor. C, it seems to me, being the survivor, may enforce the promise by an action to which both B's estate and C are parties. However, C could not, in any event, in my opinion, be the sole plaintiff against A because A's promise was not made with C alone. Consequently, B's personal representative would need to be either a co-plaintiff or joined as a defendant, though in this case the judgment would be for C alone, the promise with B and C being to pay the survivor of them. . . .

Windeyer J considered that as long as consideration had been provided by one joint promisee they could both enforce the promise, and the wife alone could do so on the death of her husband because of the survivorship terms.

WINDEYER J: My reasons for saying that the promise by the construction company was made to Coulls and Mrs Coulls as joint promisees are as follows. Mrs Coulls was present when the agreement was drawn up: she wrote the document from dictation: she, Coulls and O'Neil all took part in a discussion of how an arrangement for payment to the deceased and herself jointly and then to the survivor solely should be expressed. . . . [T]aken with the fact of Mrs Coulls being one of the signatories to the document, and with the fact that the promise was to pay the deceased and her jointly during their lives, . . . she and he were joint promisees. On that basis she was not a stranger to the contract, but a party to it with him.

Still, it was said, no consideration moved from her. But that, I consider, mistakes the nature of a contract made with two or more persons jointly. The promise is made to them collectively. It must, of course, be supported by consideration, but that does not mean by considerations furnished by them separately. It means a consideration given on behalf of them all, and therefore moving from all of them. In such a case the promise of the promisor is not gratuitous; and, as between him and the joint promisees, it matters not how they were able to provide the price of his promise to them. That is the position as I see it. It accords with the very old decision in *Rookwood's Case* (1589) Cro Eliz 164, 78 ER 421 and with general principle.

On this view, that Coulls and Mrs Coulls were joint promisees, an action against the construction company would, during their joint lives, have had to be brought in the names of both. If one had refused to be joined as a plaintiff, he or she could, after an offer of indemnity against costs, have been made a defendant. After the death of either of two joint promisees an action on a contract can be brought by the survivor alone: see *Halsbury's Laws of England*, 3rd ed., vol. 8, p. 67. Therefore Mrs Coulls, on the basis that she is a surviving joint promisee, could now bring an action on the contract; and in respect of moneys becoming due and payable under it since the death of her husband recover them for herself alone.

NOTES
1. Four members of the court (Barwick CJ, Taylor, Windeyer, and Owen JJ) considered that *if* both the husband and wife were parties to the contract as joint promisees, the wife could enforce the promise to make payments to her even though she had provided no consideration. McTiernan J did not express an opinion on this issue. See Coote (1978) 37 CLJ 301.
2. The Law Commission's Report (1996) Cm 3329 considered that a joint promisee could not be treated as a third party for the purposes of its proposed reform since he was privy to the contract. However, the Law Commission did not resolve the precise rights of a joint promisee, preferring to leave appropriate reform to the courts. Clearly if, under these recommendations and the provisions of the Contracts (Rights of Third Parties) Act 1999, a third party's right of enforcement could not be defeated on the ground that the third party had not provided consideration, a joint promisee should not be in a more disadvantageous position.

SECTION 5: THE COLLATERAL CONTRACT

If a court can find the existence of a separate (collateral) contract (*page 209*) between the promisor and the third party, it can avoid the difficulties of privity.

Shanklin Pier Ltd v *Detel Products Ltd*
[1951] 2 KB 854

Contractors were employed by the plaintiffs, owners of a pier, to paint the pier. The contract permitted the plaintiffs to specify the paint the contractors were to use. The defendant company told the plaintiffs that the paint they manufactured, known as DMU, would be suitable for the work and that two coats would have a life of at least seven years. On the faith of these statements the plaintiffs instructed the contractors to use two coats of DMU, and the contractors purchased the paint from the defendants. In fact the paint lasted only three months. The plaintiffs brought an action in breach of contract against the defendants. The problem was that the plaintiffs were not party to the purchase contract between the contractors and the defendants. Held: the plaintiffs could succeed because there was a collateral contract between the defendants and the plaintiffs that the paint would last at least seven years. The consideration for this contract was the plaintiffs' action in instructing the contractors to buy DMU from the defendants.

NOTES
1. This device has proved to be of particular use in combating the privity difficulties arising from hire-purchase agreements.

   In hire-purchase agreements the dealer may make statements, for example, relating to a car, but the actual contract of hire-purchase is made between the finance company and the customer. There is no contract between the dealer and the customer. If the dealer makes a warranty to induce the contract with the finance company, a collateral contract will allow the customer to enforce that warranty against the dealer (*Andrews* v *Hopkinson* [1957] 1 QB 229).
2. In *Wells (Merstham) Ltd* v *Buckland Sand & Silica Ltd* [1964] 1 All ER 41, the plaintiffs, chrysanthemum growers, asked the defendants, who were sand merchants, whether their sand would be suitable for growing chrysanthemums. The defendants confirmed that it was suitable. The plaintiffs then bought this sand from a third party. Edmund Davies J held that the defendants were liable in contract (following *Shanklin Pier* v *Detel*) when the sand did not conform to the warranty, since they had given a 'collateral undertaking' and the plaintiffs had acquired the sand in reliance on it.

   At the time of the undertaking the plaintiffs did not contemplate making any specific main contract but Edmund Davies J considered it sufficient that it was within the plaintiffs' and defendants' contemplation that a contract based upon the promise would be entered into shortly.
3. A further example of the application of this principle is provided by the decision of the majority of the Court of Appeal in *Bowerman* v *ABTA Ltd* [1996] CLC 451, *page 184*.
4. It must be doubtful whether parties in the same position as the plaintiffs in *Shanklin Pier* v *Detel* would be able to satisfy the test of enforceability in the Contracts (Rights of Third Parties) Act 1999, thereby enabling them directly to enforce a contract to which they were not parties (such as the sale contract for the paint). This is because such a sale contract is unlikely expressly to identify them as being intended beneficiaries. In any event, as s. 7(1) of the Act makes clear, it will still be possible to argue that there is a collateral contract in such circumstances.

5. As a result of reg. 15 of the Sale and Supply of Goods to Consumers Regulations 2002, SI 2002/3045, 'a consumer guarantee' given with goods which are sold or supplied to a consumer, is enforceable 'as a contractual obligation' in circumstances which might not satisfy the requirements to establish a collateral contract. By reg. 2, 'a consumer guarantee' is defined as 'any undertaking to a consumer [same definition as under the UTCC Regulations 1999, *page 319*] by a person acting in the course of his business, given without extra charge, [therefore excludes manufacturers' extended warranties] to reimburse the price paid or to replace, repair or handle consumer goods in any way if they do not meet the specifications set out in the guarantee statement or in the relevant advertising.' An enforcement authority may apply for an injunction to require compliance with such a guarantee (reg. 15(6)).

SECTION 6: TRUSTS OF CONTRACTUAL OBLIGATIONS

A trust is an equitable obligation placed on a trustee to hold property on behalf of another, the beneficiary. Is it possible to avoid the privity doctrine by showing that the contractual party holds the benefit of the promise on trust for the third party?

At one time this device was frequently used to evade privity where a third party was intended to have the benefit of a contract. There was no requirement that the third-party beneficiary had to provide any consideration for the promise.

Les Affréteurs Réunis SA v Leopold Walford (London) Ltd
[1919] AC 801 (HL)

In a charterparty contract the shipowners promised the charterer that they would pay the broker 3 per cent commission. They later refused to pay this to the broker. The broker's action was treated as if the charterers had been added as plaintiffs. Held: the broker was entitled to the commission since the charterers, as trustees for the broker, could enforce the clause against the shipowners.

NOTE: However, there must now be a clear expression of intent to create a trust; a trust will not be implied. This is undoubtedly more realistic, since the difficulty with using a trust is that it is irrevocable and the parties cannot vary the terms of their agreement in the future. It must be doubtful if contracting parties would intend this, and if they do, they must make that intention clear.

Re Schebsman
[1944] Ch 83 (CA)

Mr Schebsman was employed by a Swiss company and its English subsidiary. His employment ended and he entered into an agreement with the two companies whereby the English company agreed to pay him £5,500 as compensation for loss of his employment, in six annual instalments. If Schebsman died the payments were to be made to his widow and daughter. During the period of the agreement Schebsman was adjudicated bankrupt and then died. His trustee in bankruptcy claimed that the amounts to be paid under the agreement were part of Schebsman's estate and available to pay his creditors. Held: the manifest intention of the agreement was that the widow should benefit, and therefore the company was bound to make the payments to her. However, it was also held that the contract did not create a trust in favour of the widow and daughter.

LORD GREENE MR: The first question which arises is whether or not the debtor was a trustee for his wife and daughter of the benefit of the undertaking given by the English company in their favour. An examination of the decided cases does, it is true, show that the courts have on occasions adopted what may be called a liberal view on questions of this character, but in the present case I cannot find in the contract anything to justify the conclusion that a trust was intended. It is not legitimate to import into the contract the idea of a trust when the parties have given no indication that such was their intention. To interpret this contract as creating a trust would, in my judgment, be to disregard the dividing line between the case of a trust and the simple case of a contract made between two persons for the benefit of a third. That dividing line exists, although it may not always be easy to determine where it is to be drawn. In the present case I find no difficulty. . . .

DU PARCQ LJ: . . . It is true that, by the use possibly of unguarded language, a person may create a trust . . . without knowing it, but unless an intention to create a trust is clearly to be collected from the language used and the circumstances of the case, I think that the court ought not to be astute to discover indications of such an intention. I have little doubt that in the present case both parties (and certainly the debtor) intended to keep alive their common law right to vary consensually the terms of the obligation undertaken by the company, and if circumstances had changed in the debtor's life-time injustice might have been done by holding that a trust had been created and that those terms were accordingly unalterable. . . .

NOTE: In *Rolls-Royce Power Engineering plc* v *Ricardo Consulting Engineers Ltd* [2003] EWHC 2871 (TCC), [2004] 2 All ER (Comm) 129, it was held that B (a contracting party) could not recover damages as trustee for C (a third party) unless, at the time of the contract, A (the other contracting party) knew or had reason to know that B was contracting as trustee. On the facts there was no such knowledge of the interest of the parent company in the contract since it was only subsequently that the subsidiary company's business was transferred to the parent.

SECTION 7: ACTION BY THE CONTRACTING PARTY AS A MEANS OF AVOIDING PRIVITY

Section 4 of the Contracts (Rights of Third Parties) Act 1999 makes it clear that the promisee can maintain a claim to enforce a contractual term even where a third party has enforcement rights under s. 1. In addition, where the third party is outside the scope of s. 1 and is not able to utilise a common law device, such as agency, to avoid the privity rule, his only hope of securing relief may be by means of a claim brought by the promisee.

What remedies can the contracting party secure?

A: Specific performance

Specific performance is a court order compelling the promisor to carry out his promise. However, it is a discretionary remedy and is available only if damages would be an inadequate remedy.

Beswick v *Beswick*
[1968] AC 58 (HL)

Peter Beswick agreed in writing with his nephew, the defendant, that he would transfer his coal round business to the nephew. It was further agreed that the nephew would employ him as a consultant at £6 10s a week for the rest of his life and on his death would pay his widow an annuity of £5 a week for life. The nephew took over the business but, when Peter Beswick died, the nephew paid only one sum of £5 to his widow and refused to pay any more. The widow brought an action to compel the nephew to continue making the payments. She did so in two capacities:

(a) as administratrix of her late husband's estate; and

(b) in her personal capacity.

Held: she was entitled to an order of specific performance of the promise in her capacity as administratrix. There was no problem of privity or consideration since it was as if Peter Beswick himself had been suing. However, she could not enforce the promise in her personal capacity because she was not a party to the contract.

If damages were awarded they would be nominal (but see Lord Pearce, *below*) since Peter Beswick's estate had not suffered any loss. To avoid this injustice to the widow, the House of Lords exercised its discretion and ordered specific performance.

LORD REID: For clarity I think it best to begin by considering a simple case where, in consideration of a sale by A to B, B agrees to pay the price of £1,000 to a third party X. . . . what is the nature of B's obligation and who is entitled to enforce it? . . .

Lord Denning's view, expressed in this case not for the first time, is that X could enforce this obligation. But the view more commonly held in recent times has been that such a contract confers no right on X and that X could not sue for the £1,000. Leading counsel for the respondent based his case on other grounds, and as I agree that the respondent succeeds on other grounds, this would not be an appropriate case in which to solve this question. It is true that a strong Law Revision Committee recommended so long ago as 1937 (Cmd. 5449):

That where a contract by its express terms purports to confer a benefit directly on a third party it shall be enforceable by the third party in his own name . . . (p. 31).

And, if one had to contemplate a further long period of Parliamentary procrastination, this House might find it necessary to deal with this matter. But if legislation is probable at any early date I would not deal with it in a case where that is not essential. So for the purposes of this case I shall proceed on the footing that the commonly accepted view is right.

What then is A's position? I assume that A has not made himself a trustee for X, because it was not argued in this appeal that any trust had been created. So, if X has no right, A can at any time grant a discharge to B or make some new contract with B. If there were a trust the position would be different. X would have an equitable right and A would be entitled and, indeed, bound to recover the money and account for it to X. And A would have no right to grant a discharge to B. If there is no trust and A wishes to enforce the obligation, how does he set about it? He cannot sue B for the £1,000 because under the contract the money is not payable to him, and, if the contract were performed according to its terms, he would never have any right to get the money. So he must seek to make B pay X.

The argument for the appellant is that A's only remedy is to sue B for damages for B's breach of contract in failing to pay the £1,000 to X. Then the appellant says that A can only recover nominal damages of 40s. because the fact that X has not received the money will generally cause no loss to

A: he admits that there may be cases where A would suffer damage if X did not receive the money but says that the present is not such a case.

Applying what I have said to the circumstances of the present case, the respondent in her personal capacity has no right to sue, but she has a right as administratrix of her husband's estate to require the appellant to perform his obligation under the agreement. He has refused to do so and he maintains that the respondent's only right is to sue him for damages for breach of his contract. If that were so, I shall assume that he is right in maintaining that the administratrix could then only recover nominal damages because his breach of contract has caused no loss to the estate of her deceased husband.

If that were the only remedy available the result would be grossly unjust. It would mean that the appellant keeps the business which he bought and for which he has only paid a small part of the price which he agreed to pay. He would avoid paying the rest of the price, the annuity to the respondent, by paying a mere 40s. damages. . . .

The respondent's second argument is that she is entitled in her capacity of administratrix of her deceased husband's estate to enforce the provision of the agreement for the benefit of herself in her personal capacity, and that a proper way of enforcing that provision is to order specific performance. That would produce a just result, and, unless there is some technical objection, I am of opinion that specific performance ought to be ordered. For the reasons given by your Lordships I would reject the arguments submitted for the appellant that specific performance is not a possible remedy in this case.

LORD PEARCE: . . . My Lords, if the annuity had been payable to a third party in the lifetime of Beswick senior and there had been default, he could have sued in respect of the breach. His administratrix is now entitled to stand in his shoes and to sue in respect of the breach which has occured [sic] since his death.

It is argued that the estate can only recover nominal damages and that no other remedy is open, either to the estate or to the personal plaintiff. Such a result would be wholly repugnant to justice and commonsense. And if the argument were right it would show a very serious defect in the law.

In the first place, I do not accept the view that damages must be nominal. Lush LJ in *Lloyd's* v *Harper* (1880) 16 ChD 290 said:

> Then the next question which, no doubt, is a very important and substantial one, is, that Lloyd's, having sustained no damage themselves, could not recover for the losses sustained by third parties by reason of the default of Robert Henry Harper as an underwriter. That, to my mind, is a startling and alarming doctrine, and a novelty, because I consider it to be an established rule of law that where a contract is made with A for the benefit of B, A can sue on the contract for the benefit of B, and recover all that B could have recovered if the contract had been made with B himself.

I agree with the comment of Windeyer J in the case of *Coulls* v *Bagot's Executor and Trustee Co. Ltd* (1967) 119 CLR 460 in the High Court of Australia that the words of Lush LJ cannot be accepted without qualification and regardless of context and also with his statement:

> I can see no reason why in such cases the damages which A would suffer upon B's breach of his contract to pay C $500 would be merely nominal: I think that in accordance with the ordinary rules for the assessment of damages for breach of contract they could be substantial. They would not necessarily be $500; they could I think be less or more.

In the present case I think that the damages, if assessed, must be substantial. It is not necessary, however, to consider the amount of damages more closely since this is a case in which, as the Court of Appeal rightly decided, the more appropriate remedy is that of specific performance.

The administratrix is entitled, if she so prefers, to enforce the agreement rather than accept its repudiation, and specific performance is more convenient than an action for arrears of payment followed by separate actions as each sum falls due. Moreover, damages for breach would be a less appropriate remedy since the parties to the agreement were intending an annuity for a widow; and a lump sum of damages does not accord with this. And if (contrary to my view) the argument that a derisory sum of damages is all that can be obtained be [sic] right, the remedy of damages in this case is manifestly useless.

The present case presents all the features which led the equity courts to apply their remedy of specific performance. The contract was for the sale of a business. The defendant could on his part clearly have obtained specific performance of it if Beswick senior or his administratrix had defaulted. Mutuality is a ground in favour of specific performance.

Moreover, the defendant on his side has received the whole benefit of the contract and it is a matter of conscience for the court to see that he now performs his part of it, Kay J said in *Hart v Hart* (1881) 18 ChD 670:

> ... when an agreement for valuable consideration ... has been partially performed, the court ought to do its utmost to carry out that agreement by a decree for specific performance.

What, then, is the obstacle to granting specific performance?

It is argued that since the widow personally had no rights which she personally could enforce the court will not make an order which will have the effect of enforcing those rights. I can find no principle to this effect. The condition as to payment of an annuity to the widow personally was valid. The estate (though not the widow personally) can enforce it. Why should the estate be barred from exercising its full contractual rights merely because in doing so it secures justice for the widow who, by a mechanical defect of our law, is unable to assert her own rights? Such a principle would be repugnant to justice and fulfil no other object than that of aiding the wrongdoer. I can find no ground on which such a principle should exist.

NOTES

1. Lord Reid referred in his judgment to 'Lord Denning's view'. Lord Denning in *Smith and Snipes Hall Farm Ltd* v *River Douglas Catchment Board* [1949] 2 KB 500, had expressed the view that a promise deliberately made was enforceable by the person intended to be benefited by the promise, even though that person was not a party to the contract.
2. Would Mrs Beswick be able directly to enforce the nephew's promise under the provisions of the Contracts (Rights of Third Parties) Act 1999, see *page 442 above*?
3. Specific performance will not be granted if a contract has already been performed fully but in a defective manner.
4. Lord Pearce was of the opinion that substantial rather than nominal damages should be recoverable by the contracting party in this situation.

B: Promisee's action for damages

Can the promisee recover substantial damages for the loss suffered by the third party?

Jackson v *Horizon Holidays Ltd*
[1975] 1 WLR 1468 (CA)

The plaintiff booked a holiday with the defendants, for himself, his wife, and his two small children at a price of £1,200. The plaintiff made it quite clear that he wished the holiday to be of the highest standard and specifically requested that the meals be four course with a choice of three or four dishes per course. The brochure issued by the defendants described the hotel as having excellent facilities. However, there were various breaches of these contractual terms. The plaintiff sought damages for the loss of the holiday and disappointment and distress for himself, his wife, and children. The defendants did not contest liability but appealed against the judge's award of £1,100 damages. Held: since the plaintiff had contracted for the benefit of himself and his family, as well as recovering for his own loss he could also recover for that suffered by his family as a result of the breach of contract. Therefore, the damages award was not excessive.

LORD DENNING MR: . . . We have had an interesting discussion as to the legal position when one person makes a contract for the benefit of a party. In this case it was a husband making a contract for the benefit of himself, his wife and children. Other cases readily come to mind. A host makes a contract with a restaurant for a dinner for himself and his friends. The vicar makes a contract for a coach trip for the choir. In all these cases there is only one person who makes the contract. It is the husband, the host or the vicar, as the case may be. Sometimes he pays the whole price himself. Occasionally he may get a contribution from the others. But in any case it is he who makes the contract. It would be a fiction to say that the contract was made by all the family, or all the guests, or all the choir, and that he was only an agent for them. Take this very case. It would be absurd to say that the twins of three years old were parties to the contract or that the father was making the contract on their behalf as if they were principals. It would equally be a mistake to say that in any of these instances there was a trust. The transaction bears no resemblance to a trust. There was no trust fund and no trust property. No, the real truth is that in each instance, the father, the host or the vicar, was making a contract himself for the benefit of the whole party. In short, a contract by one for the benefit of third persons.

What is the position when such a contract is broken? At present the law says that the only one who can sue is the one who made the contract. None of the rest of the party can sue, even though the contract was made for their benefit. But when that one does sue, what damages can he recover? Is he limited to his own loss? Or can he recover for the others? Suppose the holiday firm puts the family into a hotel which is only half built and the visitors have to sleep on the floor? Or suppose the restaurant is fully booked and the guests have to go away, hungry and angry, having spent so much on fares to get there? Or suppose the coach leaves the choir stranded half-way and they have to hire cars to get home? None of them individually can sue. Only the father, the host or the vicar can sue. He can, of course, recover his own damages. But can he not recover for the others? I think he can. The case comes within the principle stated by Lush LJ in Lloyd's v Harper (1880) 16 ChD 290, 321:

> I consider it to be an established rule of law that where a contract is made with A for the benefit of B, A can sue on the contract for the benefit of B, and recover all that B could have recovered if the contract had been made with B himself.

It has been suggested that Lush LJ was thinking of a contract in which A was trustee for B. But I do not think so. He was a common lawyer speaking of the common law. His words were quoted with considerable approval by Lord Pearce in Beswick v Beswick [1968] AC 58, 88. I have myself often quoted them. I think they should be accepted as correct, at any rate so long as the law forbids the third persons themselves from suing for damages. It is the only way in which a just result can be achieved. Take the instance I have put. The guests ought to recover from the restaurant their wasted fares. The choir ought to recover the cost of hiring the taxis home. There is no one to recover for them except the one who made the contract for their benefit. He should be able to recover the expense to which they have been put, and pay it over to them. Once recovered, it will be money had and received to their use. (They might even, if desired, be joined as plaintiffs.) If he can recover for the expense, he should also be able to recover for the discomfort, vexation and upset which the whole party have suffered by reason of the breach of contract, recompensing them accordingly out of what he recovers.

Applying the principles to this case, I think that the figure of £1,100 was about right. It would, I think, have been excessive if it had been awarded only for the damage suffered by Mr Jackson himself. But when extended to his wife and children, I do not think it is excessive. People look forward to a holiday. They expect the promises to be fulfilled. When it fails, they are greatly disappointed and upset. It is difficult to assess in terms of money; but it is the task of the judges to do the best they can. I see no reason to interfere with the total award of £1,100. . . .

NOTES
1. Orr LJ agreed with Lord Denning's judgment and James LJ delivered a brief judgment indicating that this was a contract for a family holiday and *the plaintiff* had not received this.

2. The Package Travel, Package Holidays and Package Tours Regulations 1992, SI 1992/3288, specifically provide that 'the consumers' who are parties to the package holiday contract include 'the principal Contractor' and 'the other beneficiaries' so that members of the party have direct contractual rights (reg. 2(2)).

3. Section 5 of the Contracts (Rights of Third Parties) Act 1999 is designed to protect the promisor from double recovery, so that where a promisee has already recovered from a promisor in respect of a third party's loss and the third party brings an action based on rights acquired under s. 1, the court has to reduce the award to the third party 'to such extent as it thinks appropriate to take account of the sum recovered by the promisee'. The section makes no express provision imposing liability on the promisee to account to the third party.

Woodar Investment Development Ltd v Wimpey Construction UK Ltd
[1980] 1 WLR 277 (HL)

Wimpey contracted to buy land for £850,000 and agreed to pay £150,000 on completion to a third party, Transworld Trade Ltd. The contract allowed the purchaser to repudiate the contract if before completion a statutory authority 'shall have commenced' to acquire the property by compulsory purchase. At the date of the contract both parties knew that a draft compulsory purchase order had been made. Wimpey purported to terminate relying on this provision, and Woodar sought damages alleging that this amounted to a wrongful repudiation. Their damages claim included the loss suffered by the third party. Held: there was not a wrongful repudiation where a party was relying on a contract term to repudiate (*page 333*). The majority considered it necessary to examine the damages question in the light of *Jackson* v *Horizon Holidays*. (These remarks are necessarily *obiter*.)

LORD WILBERFORCE: The second issue in this appeal is one of damages. Both courts below have allowed Woodar to recover substantial damages in respect of condition I under which £150,000 was payable by Wimpey to Transworld Trade Ltd on completion. On the view which I take of the repudiation issue, this question does not require decision, but in view of the unsatisfactory state in which the law would be if the Court of Appeal's decision were to stand I must add three observations:

1. The majority of the Court of Appeal followed, in the case of Goff LJ with expressed reluctance, its previous decision in *Jackson* v *Horizon Holidays Ltd* [1975] 1 WLR 1468. I am not prepared to dissent from the actual decision in that case. It may be supported either as a broad decision on the measure of damages (per James LJ) or possibly as an example of a type of contract—examples of which are persons contracting for family holidays, ordering meals in restaurants for a party, hiring a taxi for a group—calling for special treatment. As I suggested in *New Zealand Shipping Co. Ltd* v *A.M. Satterthwaite & Co. Ltd* [1975] AC 154, 167, there are many situations of daily life which do not fit neatly into conceptual analysis, but which require some flexibility in the law of contract. *Jackson's* case may well be one.

I cannot however agree with the basis on which Lord Denning MR put his decision in that case. The extract on which he relied from the judgment of Lush LJ in *Lloyd's* v *Harper* (1880) 16 ChD 290, 321 was part of a passage in which the Lord Justice was stating as an 'established rule of law' that an agent (sc. an insurance broker) may sue on a contract made by him on behalf of the principal (sc. the assured) if the contract gives him such a right, and is no authority for the proposition required in *Jackson's* case, still less for the proposition, required here that, if Woodar made a contract for a sum of money to be paid to Transworld, Woodar can, without showing that it has itself suffered loss or that Woodar was agent or trustee for Transworld, sue for damages for non-payment of that sum. That would certainly not be an established rule of law, nor was it quoted as such authority by Lord Pearce in *Beswick* v *Beswick* [1968] AC 58.

2. Assuming that *Jackson's* case was correctly decided (as above), it does not carry the present

case, where the factual situation is quite different. I respectfully think therefore that the Court of Appeal need not, and should not have followed it.

3.   Whether in a situation such as the present—viz. where it is not shown that Woodar was agent or trustee for Transworld, or that Woodar itself sustained any loss, Woodar can recover any damages at all, or any but nominal damages, against Wimpey, and on what principle, is, in my opinion, a question of great doubt and difficulty—no doubt open in this House—but one on which I prefer to reserve my opinion.

LORD KEITH: . . . That case [*Jackson* v *Horizon Holidays*] is capable of being regarded as rightly decided upon a reasonable view of the measure of damages due to the plaintiff as the original contracting party, and not as laying down any rule of law regarding the recovery of damages for the benefit of third parties. There may be a certain class of cases where third parties stand to gain indirectly by virtue of a contract, and where their deprivation of that gain can properly be regarded as no more than a consequence of the loss suffered by one of the contracting parties. In that situation there may be no question of the third parties having any claim to damages in their own right, but yet it may be proper to take into account in assessing the damages recoverable by the contracting party an element in respect of expense incurred by him in replacing by other means benefits of which the third parties have been deprived or in mitigating the consequences of that deprivation. The decision in *Jackson* v *Horizon Holidays Ltd* is not, however, in my opinion, capable of being supported upon the basis of the true ratio decidendi in *Lloyd's* v *Harper*, 16 ChD 290, which rested entirely on the principles of agency.

I would also associate myself with the observations of my noble and learned friend, Lord Scarman, as to the desirability of this House having an opportunity of reviewing, in some appropriate future case, the general attitude of English law towards the topic of jus quaesitum tertio.

LORD SCARMAN: . . . [B]ecause of its importance, I propose to say a few words on the question of damages.

The plaintiff company agreed to sell the land to the defendants for £850,000. They also required the defendants to pay £150,000 to a third party. The covenant for this payment was in the following terms:

1.   Upon completion of the purchase of the whole or any part of the land the purchaser shall pay to Transworld Trade Ltd of 25 Jermyn Street, London, SW1 a sum of £150,000.

No relationship of trust or agency was proved to exist between the plaintiff company and Transworld Trade Ltd. No doubt, it suited Mr Cornwell to split up the moneys payable under the contract between the two companies: but it is not known, let alone established by evidence (though an intelligent guess is possible) why he did so, or why the plaintiffs desired this money to be paid to Transworld Trade. It is simply a case of B agreeing with A to pay a sum of money to C.

B, in breach of his contract with A, has failed to pay C. C, it is said, has no remedy, because the English law of contract recognises no 'jus quaesitum tertio': *Tweddle* v *Atkinson* (1861) 1 B & S 393. No doubt, it was for this reason that Transworld Trade is not a party to the suit. A, it is acknowledged, could in certain circumstances obtain specific performance of the promise to pay C: *Beswick* v *Beswick* [1968] AC 58. But, since the contract in the present case is admitted (for reasons which do not fall to be considered by the House) to be no longer in existence, specific performance is not available. A's remedy lies only in an award of damages to himself. It is submitted that, in the absence of any evidence that A has suffered loss by reason of B's failure to pay C, A is only entitled to nominal damages.

I wish to add nothing to what your Lordships have already said about the authorities which the Court of Appeal cited as leading to the conclusion that the plaintiff company is entitled to substantial damages for the defendants' failure to pay Transworld Trade. I agree that they do not support the conclusion. But I regret that this House has not yet found the opportunity to reconsider the two rules which effactually prevent A or C recovering that which B, for value, has agreed to provide.

First, the 'jus quaesitum tertio.' I respectfully agree with Lord Reid that the denial by English law of a 'jus quaesitum tertio' calls for reconsideration. In *Beswick* v *Beswick* [1968] AC 58, 72 Lord Reid, after referring to the Law Revision Committee's recommendation in 1937 (Cmnd. 5449) p. 31 that the third party should be able to enforce a contractual promise taken by another for his benefit, observed:

> And, if one had to contemplate a further long period of Parliamentary procrastination, this House might find it necessary to deal with this matter.

The committee reported in 1937: *Beswick* v *Beswick* was decided in 1967. It is now 1979: but nothing has been done. If the opportunity arises, I hope the House will reconsider *Tweddle* v *Atkinson* and the other cases which stand guard over this unjust rule.

Likewise, I believe it open to the House to declare that, in the absence of evidence to show that he has suffered no loss, A, who has contracted for a payment to be made to C, may rely on the fact that he required the payment to be made as prima facie evidence that the promise for which he contracted was a benefit to him and that the measure of his loss in the event of non-payment is the benefit which he intended for C but which has not been received. Whatever the reason, he must have desired the payment to be made to C and he must have been relying on B to make it. If B fails to make the payment, A must find the money from other funds if he is to confer the benefit which he sought by his contract to confer upon C. Without expressing a final opinion on a question which is clearly difficult, I think the point is one which does require consideration by your Lordships' House.

Certainly the crude proposition for which the defendants contend, namely that the state of English law is such that neither C for whom the benefit was intended nor A who contracted for it can recover it, if the contract is terminated by B's refusal to perform, calls for review: and now, not forty years on.

NOTES

1. The facts in *Woodar* v *Wimpey* did not fall within the categories of contracts made by one person for the benefit of a group of people. There was also no evidence that Woodar had suffered any loss as a result of the non-payment to Transworld Trade Ltd, whereas in *Jackson* v *Horizon Holidays*, Mr Jackson had also suffered loss.

   Lord Scarman appeared to indicate that there might be ways of including the loss of the payment to the third party within the loss suffered by Woodar. This would presumably be the case if Woodar would otherwise have to satisfy that debt.

2. While the result in *Jackson* v *Horizon Holidays* has been confirmed, the principle has been restricted to limited circumstances, namely contracts calling for 'special treatment'.

3. The House of Lords expressed its dissatisfaction with the privity doctrine and wished it to be reconsidered at the first available opportunity.

Linden Gardens Trust Ltd v *Lenesta Sludge Disposals Ltd*
[1994] 1 AC 85 (HL)

In this case (the 'St Martin's Property' Appeal), there had been a transfer of property and an assignment of the benefit of a building contract regarding that property. Held: The House of Lords found that the assignment of the benefit of the building contract was invalid since it was in breach of a valid prohibition on assignment. As owner of the property it was the assignee who suffered damage as a result of breach of the building contract, but technically contractual rights remained with the assignor who no longer owned the property and therefore suffered no loss. Nevertheless, it was held that the assignor could recover substantial damages on the basis that it had been contemplated all along that the property development would be sold or leased, and therefore the building contract had been entered into on the basis that the assignor (first plaintiff) could enforce the contractual rights for the benefit of those suffering from defective performance (the second plaintiff, assignee); and the terms of the contract (prohibiting assignment) meant that the acquirer of the property would not be able to acquire rights to hold the defendant (McAlpines) liable for breach.

Counsel for the defendant (McAlpines) had argued that only nominal damages could be recovered by the first plaintiff (who held contractual rights but had suffered no loss), and he relied on case law concerning breaches of contracts for the carriage of goods such as *The Albazero* [1977] AC 774.

LORD BROWNE-WILKINSON: . . . Notwithstanding the apparent logic of [this] submission, I have considerable doubts whether it is correct. A contract for the supply of goods or of work, labour and materials (a supply contract) is not the same as a contract for the carriage of goods. A breach of a supply contract involves a failure to provide the very goods or services which the defendant had contracted to supply and for which the plaintiff has paid or agreed to pay. If the breach is discovered before payment of the contract price, the price is abated by the cost of making good the defects . . . [Counsel] accepted that this right to abatement of the price does not depend on ownership by the plaintiff of the goods and it would be odd if the plaintiff's rights arising from breach varied according to whether the breach was discovered before or after the payment of the price. . . .

In contracts for the sale of goods, the purchaser is entitled to damages for delivery of defective goods assessed by reference to the difference between the contract price and the market price of the defective goods, irrespective of whether he has managed to sell on the goods to a third party without loss: *Slater* v *Hoyle & Smith Ltd* [1920] 2 KB 11; see also as to non-delivery *Williams Bros* v *E T Agius Ltd* [1914] AC 510. In those cases the judgments contained no consideration of the person in whom the property in the goods was vested although it appears that some of the subcontracts had been made prior to the breach of contract.

If the law were to be established that damages for breach of a supply contract were not quantifiable by reference to the beneficial ownership of goods or enjoyment of the services contracted for but by reference to the difference in value between that which was contracted for and that which is in fact supplied, it might also provide a satisfactory answer to the problems raised where a man contracts and pays for a supply to others, e.g. a man contracts with a restaurant for a meal for himself and his guests or with a travel company for a holiday for his family. It is apparently established that, if a defective meal or holiday is supplied, the contracting party can recover damages not only for his own bad meal or unhappy holiday but also for that of his guests or family: see *Jackson* v *Horizon Holidays Ltd* [1975] 1 WLR 1468 as explained in *Woodar Investment Development Ltd* v *Wimpey Construction UK Ltd* [1980] 1 WLR 277, 283–284, 293–294, 297, 300–301.

There is therefore much to be said for drawing a distinction between cases where the ownership of goods or property is relevant to prove that the plaintiff has suffered loss through the breach of a contract other than a contract to supply those goods or property and the measure of damages in a supply contract where the contractual obligation itself requires the provision of those goods or services. I am reluctant to express a concluded view on this point since it may have profound effects on commercial contracts which effects were not fully explored in argument. In my view the point merits exposure to academic consideration before it is decided by this House. Nor do I find it necessary to decide the point since, on any view, the facts of this case bring it within the class of exceptions to the general rule to which Lord Diplock referred in *The Albazero*. . . .

In addition, the decision in *The Albazero* itself established a further exception. This House was concerned with the status of a long-established principle based on the decision in *Dunlop* v *Lambert* (1839) 6 Cl & F 600 that a consignor of goods who had parted with the property in the goods before the date of breach could even so recover substantial damages for the failure to deliver the goods. Lord Diplock identified, at p. 847, the rationale of that rule as being:

> The only way in which I find it possible to rationalise the rule in *Dunlop* v *Lambert* so that it may fit into the pattern of the English law is to treat it as an application of the principle, accepted also in relation to policies of insurance on goods, that in a commercial contract concerning goods where it is in the contemplation of the parties that the proprietary interests in the goods may be transferred from one owner to another after the contract has been entered into and before the breach which causes loss or damage to the goods, an original party to the contract, if such be the intention of them both, is to be treated in law as having entered into the contract for the benefit of all persons who have or may acquire an interest in the goods before they are lost or damaged, and is entitled to recover by way of damages for

breach of contract the actual loss sustained by those for whose benefit the contract is entered into.

. . .

In my judgment the present case falls within the rationale of the exceptions to the general rule that a plaintiff can only recover damages for his own loss. The contract was for a large development of property which, to the knowledge of both Corporation and McAlpine, was going to be occupied, and possibly purchased, by third parties and not by Corporation itself. Therefore it could be foreseen that damage caused by a breach would cause loss to a later owner and not merely to the original contracting party, Corporation. As in contracts for the carriage of goods by land, there would be no automatic vesting in the occupier or owners of the property for the time being who sustained the loss of any right of suit against McAlpine. On the contrary, McAlpine had specifically contracted that the rights of action under the building contract could *not* without McAlpine's consent be transferred to third parties who became owners or occupiers and might suffer loss. In such a case, it seems to me proper, as in the case of the carriage of goods by land, to treat the parties as having entered into the contract on the footing that Corporation would be entitled to enforce contractual rights for the benefit of those who suffered from defective performance but who, under the terms of the contract, could not acquire any right to hold McAlpine liable for breach. It is truly a case in which the rule provides 'a remedy where no other would be available to a person sustaining loss which under a rational legal system ought to be compensated by the person who has caused it'.

. . . I would therefore hold that Corporation is entitled to substantial damages for any breach by McAlpine of the building contract.

NOTES
1. See Duncan Wallace (1994) 110 LQR 42, Berg [1994] JBL 129 and Palmer and Tolhurst (1997) 12 JCL 1 and 97.
2. There were two possible grounds for entitling the assignor (first plaintiff) to recover substantial damages, namely the broad ground (which Lord Browne-Wilkinson considered required further academic consideration) and the narrow ground (on which he actually decided the case). Lord Griffiths preferred the broad ground. Lord Keith concurred with Lord Browne-Wilkinson but also stated that he had sympathy with the broad ground. Lord Bridge concurred and stated that he was 'much attracted' by the broad ground.

   Lord Griffiths stated the broad ground in the context of the *McAlpine* appeal, namely that, in the context of a contract for the supply of work and materials, the promisee did not need to show a proprietary interest in the subject matter of the contract in order to be able to recover damages for its breach:

LORD GRIFFITHS: . . . I cannot accept that in a contract of this nature, namely for work, labour and the supply of materials, the recovery of more than nominal damages for breach of contract is dependent upon the plaintiff having a proprietary interest in the subject matter of the contract at the date of breach. In everyday life contracts for work and labour are constantly being placed by those who have no proprietary interest in the subject matter of the contract. To take a common example, the matrimonial home is owned by the wife and the couple's remaining assets are owned by the husband and he is the sole earner. The house requires a new roof and the husband places a contract with a builder to carry out the work. The husband is not acting as agent for his wife, he makes the contract as principal because only he can pay for it. The builder fails to replace the roof properly and the husband has to call in and pay another builder to complete the work. Is it to be said that the husband has suffered no damage because he does not own the property? Such a result would in my view be absurd and the answer is that the husband has suffered loss because he did not receive the bargain for which he had contracted with the first builder and the measure of damages is the cost of securing the performance of that bargain by completing the roof repairs properly by the second builder. To put this simple example closer to the facts of this appeal—at the time the husband employs the builder he owns the house but just after the builder starts work the couple are advised to divide their assets so the husband transfers the house to his wife. This is no concern of the builder whose bargain is with the husband. If the roof turns out to be defective the husband can recover from the builder the cost of putting it right and thus obtain the benefit of the bargain that the builder had promised to deliver. It was suggested in argument that the answer to the example I have given is that the husband could assign the benefit of the contract to the wife. But what if, as in this case, the builder has a clause in the contract forbidding assignment without his consent and refuses to give consent as McAlpine has done. It is then said that neither husband nor wife can recover damages; this seems to me to be so unjust a result that the law cannot tolerate it.

The principle authority relied upon by McAlpine in support of the proposition that the contracting party suffers no loss if they did not have a proprietary interest in the property at the time of the breach was *The Albazero* [1977] AC 774. The situation in that case was however wholly different from the present. The *Albazero* was not concerned with money being paid to enable the bargain, i.e. the contract of carriage, to be fulfilled. The damages sought in *The Albazero* were claimed for the loss of the cargo, and as at the date of the breach the property in the cargo was vested in another with a right to sue it is readily understandable that the law should deny to the original party to the contract a right to recover damages for a loss of the cargo which had caused him no financial loss. In cases such as the present the person who places the contract has suffered financial loss because he has to spend money to give him the benefit of the bargain which the defendant had promised but failed to deliver. I therefore cannot accept that it is a condition of recovery in such cases that the plaintiff has a proprietary right in the subject matter of the contract at the date of breach.

3. For academic discussion, see Palmer and Tolhurst (1998) 13 JCL 143.

■ QUESTION

Would the new property owner be able to enforce the building contract directly under the provisions of the Contracts (Rights of Third Parties) Act 1999? See the test of enforceability, s. 1, *page 442*.

The 'St Martin's Property' exception was applied in the following case:

Darlington Borough Council v *Wiltshier Northern Ltd*
[1995] 1 WLR 68 (CA)

The building contractor, Wiltshier, had entered into a contract with Morgan Grenfell (Local Authority Services) (MG) to construct a recreation centre for the benefit of the council who owned the land on which it was to be built. It was necessary to employ MG because of restrictions on local authority expenditure, but MG validly assigned its contractual rights to the council. The council sought to bring a breach of contract action against the contractor alleging that there were serious defects which would cost £2m to remedy. The council faced a problem in that a person cannot assign greater rights than he actually has. It was successfully argued at first instance that MG only had a right to recover nominal damages, since it had no property interest in the recreation centre, so that the council was also restricted to nominal damages. Held: on appeal, applying the 'St Martin's Property' exception, the assignor (MG) had the right to recover substantial damages since it was clear to the contractor from the outset that the centre was being constructed for the benefit of the council and that the contractual rights were to be assigned to the council. Since these contractual rights had been validly assigned to the council, it followed that the council could recover substantial damages.

STEYN LJ: . . . The council, as the assignees of Morgan Grenfell, is seeking to recover substantial damages for breach of the building contract against Wiltshier, namely the cost of the remedial works to the Darlington Centre. The council accepts that, as assignees, they can recover no more in damages than Morgan Grenfell could have recovered. In other words, the question is what the assignor (Morgan Grenfell) could have recovered against the builder (Wiltshier) had the assignment not taken place: *Dawson* v *Great Northern and City Railway Co.* [1905] 1 KB 260. The council invokes in the first place the narrower principle relied on by Lord Browne-Wilkinson in *Linden Gardens Trust Ltd* v *Lenesta Sludge Disposals Ltd* [1994] 1 AC 85 and, in particular, that part of his speech, at pp. 112E–115G, which dealt with the *McAlpine* appeal. In the alternative the council invokes the wider principle enunciated by Lord Griffiths in his speech, at pp. 96D–98F, which dealt mainly with the *McAlpine* appeal.

. . . [Counsel for Wiltshier] submits that Morgan Grenfell, the party in contractual relationship with Wiltshier, suffered no loss and could transfer no claim for substantial damages; and the council, which suffered the loss, is precluded by the privity rule from claiming the damages which it suffered. He submits that established doctrine deprives the council of a remedy and allows the contract-breaker to go scot-free. Recognising that this is hardly an attractive result, he reminds us of our duty to apply the law as it stands.

That brings me to the speech of Lord Browne-Wilkinson in the *Linden Gardens* case [1994] AC 85. In his speech Lord Browne-Wilkinson rested his decision on the exception to the rule that a plaintiff can only recover damages for his own loss which was enunciated in *The Albazero* [1977] AC 774 in the context of carriage of goods by sea, bills of lading and bailment. [Steyn LJ quoted the passage cited in Lord Browne-Wilkinson's judgment in *Linden Gardens* from the judgment of Lord Diplock in *The Albazero, pages 471–2 above*, and continued:] Clearly, this passage did not exactly fit the material facts in the *Linden Gardens* case. But Lord Browne-Wilkinson extracted the rationale of the decision and by analogy applied it to the purely contractual situation in *Linden Gardens*. He particularly justified this extension of the exception in *The Albazero* by invoking Lord Diplock's words in *The Albazero*:

> there may still be occasional cases in which the rule would provide a remedy where no other would be available to a person sustaining loss which under a rational legal system ought to be compensated by the person who has caused it.

Lord Browne-Wilkinson's conclusion was supported by all members of the House of Lords although, it is right to say, Lord Griffiths wished to go further. Relying on the exception recognised in the *Linden Gardens* case, as well as on the need to avoid a demonstrable unfairness which no rational legal system should tolerate, I would rule that the present case is within the rationale of Lord Browne-Wilkinson's speech. I do not say that the relevant passages in his speech precisely fit the material facts of the present case. But it involves only a very conservative and limited extension to apply it by analogy to the present case. For these reasons I would hold that the present case is covered by an exception to the general rule that a plaintiff can only recover damages for his own loss.

The exception contained in Lord Griffiths's speech
The rationale of Lord Griffiths's wider principle is essentially that, if a party engages a builder to perform specified work and the builder fails to render the contractual service, the employer suffers a loss. He suffers a loss of bargain or of expectation interest. And that loss can be recovered on the basis of what it would cost to put right the defects. While other members of the House of Lords expressed sympathy with this view, they did not decide the point. The point has now been argued in some depth before us. We have also had the benefit of some academic comment on the point: John Cartwright 'Remedies in Respect of Defective Buildings after Linden Gardens' (1993) 9 Con LJ 281 and I N Duncan Wallace 'Assignment of Rights to Sue: Half a Loaf' (1994) 110 LQR 42. Subject to one qualification, it will be clear from what I said earlier that I am in respectful agreement with the wider principle. It seems to me that Lord Griffiths has based his principle on classic contractual theory.

The qualification is, however, important. Lord Griffiths observed at p. 97:

> The court will of course wish to be satisfied that the repairs have been or are likely to be carried out but if they are carried out the cost of doing them must fall upon the defendant who broke his contract.

There was apparently no argument on this point in the House of Lords. For my part I would hold that in the field of building contracts, like sale of goods, it is no concern of the law what the plaintiff proposes to do with his damages. It is also no precondition to the recovery of substantial damages that the plaintiff does propose to undertake the necessary repairs. In this field English law adopts an objective approach to the ascertainment of damages for breach of contract. On this point I am in agreement with the observations of Kerr LJ in *Dean v Ainley* [1987] 1 WLR 1729, 1737H–1738A and Staughton LJ in *Ruxley Electronics and Construction Ltd v Forsyth* [1994] 1 WLR 650, 656A–657D. Subject to this qualification, I am in respectful agreement with Lord Griffiths's wider principle. And I gratefully adopt it as part of my reasoning.

NOTES

1. Dillon and Waite LJJ considered that on these facts—which included a provision obliging MG to transfer all 'rights' it had against the contractor—if, before the assignment, MG had itself brought an action for breach, it could have succeeded in recovering damages for the losses of the council and would have held such damages as constructive trustee for the council.

2. There is some support in the judgment of Steyn LJ for the 'broad ground' discussed by Lord Griffiths in *Linden Gardens*. Dillon LJ found that it was not necessary to consider it and that he preferred not to do so.

3. While the Contracts (Rights of Third Parties) Act 1999 preserves the promisee's right to enforce the contract despite the fact that the third party may also have that right, it does not deal with the question of reform of the remedies available to a promisee. The Law Commission Report, Law Com No. 242, Cm 3329 (1996) recommended that this be left to the courts (para. 5.17). See Cartwright (1996) 10 JCL 244.

4. Steyn LJ's observations on the relevance of establishing what a plaintiff intends to do with his damages are discussed in the context of the decision in *Ruxley Electronics and Construction Ltd v Forsyth* [1996] 1 AC 344, *page 370.*

Alfred McAlpine Construction Ltd v Panatown Ltd
[2001] 1 AC 518 (HL)

A contract between Panatown and McAlpine provided that McAlpine was to construct an office building in Cambridge. However, the actual owner of the site on which the building was constructed was UIPL, but UIPL was not a party to the construction contract. A separate 'duty of care deed' was entered into between McAlpine and UIPL giving UIPL a direct remedy against the contractor for breaches of qualified contractual terms.

Panatown alleged that the construction work was defective and sought damages. McAlpine argued that Panatown had suffered no financial loss because it did not own the site and, in any event, the existence of the 'duty of care deed' giving UIPL a direct right of action (which UIPL had chosen not to enforce) prevented recovery of substantial damages by Panatown. The Court of Appeal ([1998] CLC 636) had applied the narrow ground in *St Martin's Property* to allow recovery of substantial damages which would be held on constructive trust for the building owner and had considered that this exception was 'contract based'. The Court of Appeal had also considered that the existence of the 'duty of care deed' was not intended to deprive Panatown of this remedy. On appeal held: by a majority (Lords Goff and Millett dissenting) that under the *St Martin's Property* exception an employer could only recover substantial damages for a third party building owner in the event of the contractor's breach of contract where that third party had no direct remedy against the contractor. Since there was a direct right to claim substantial damages under the duty of care deed, Panatown had no right to recover such damages for loss suffered by UIPL. Panatown was entitled to nominal damages only, as it had suffered no loss.

[Lord Clyde referred to the passage in Lord Diplock's speech in *The Albazero, The* [1977] AC 774 at 847 (*see pages 471–2*) and continued:]

It is particularly this passage in Lord Diplock's speech which has given rise to a question discussed in the present appeal whether *The Albazero* exception is a rule of law or is based upon the intention of the parties. The issue was identified by my noble and learned friend, Lord Goff of Chieveley, in his speech in *White* v *Jones* [1995] 2 AC 207, 267. The problem arises from two phrases in the speech of Lord Diplock the mutual relationship between which may not be immediately obvious. The two phrases, in the reverse order than that in which they appear, are 'is to be treated in law as having entered into the contract' and 'if such be the intention of the parties'. In my view it is preferable to regard it as a solution imposed by the law and not as arising from the supposed intention of the parties, who may in reality not have applied their minds to the point. On the other hand if they deliberately provided for a remedy for a third party it can readily be concluded that they have intended to exclude the operation of the solution which would otherwise have been imposed by law. The terms and provisions of the contract will then require to be studied to see if the parties have excluded the operation of the exception.

That appears to have been the conclusion adopted in *Linden Gardens Trust Ltd* v *Lenesta Sludge Disposals Ltd; St. Martins Property Corporation Ltd* v *Sir Robert McAlpine Ltd* [1994] 1 AC 85 (the *St. Martins* case), where my noble and learned friend, Lord Browne-Wilkinson, observed, at p. 115:

> In such a case, it seems to me proper, as in the case of the carriage of goods by land, to treat the parties as having entered into the contract on the footing that Corporation would be entitled to enforce contractual rights for the benefit of those who suffered from defective performance but who, under the terms of the contract, could not acquire any right to hold McAlpine liable for breach.

In that case the point was made that the contractor and the employer were both aware that the property was going to be occupied and possibly purchased by third parties so that it could be foreseen that a breach of the contract might cause loss to others than the employer. But such foresight may be an unnecessary factor in the applicability of the exception. So also an intention of the parties to benefit a third person may be unnecessary. Foreseeability may be relevant to the question of damages under the rule in *Hadley* v *Baxendale* (1854) 9 Exch 341, but in the context of liability it is a concept which is more at home in the law of tort than in the law of contract. If the exception is founded primarily upon a principle of law, and not upon the particular knowledge of the parties to the contract, then it is not easy to see why the necessity for the contemplation of the parties that there will be potential losses by third parties is essential. It appears that in the *St. Martins* case [1994] 1 AC 85 the damages claimed were in respect of the cost of remedial work which had been carried out. I see no reason why consequential losses should not also be recoverable under this exception where such loss occurs and the third party should have a right to recover for himself all the damages won by the original party on his behalf.

The Albazero exception will plainly not apply where the parties contemplate that the carrier will enter into separate contracts of carriage with the later owners of the goods, identical to the contract with the consignor. Even more clearly, as Lord Diplock explained [1977] AC 774, 848, will the exception be excluded if other contracts of carriage are made in terms different from those in the original contract. In *The Albazero* the separate contracts which were mentioned were contracts of carriage. That is understandable in the context of carriage by sea involving a charterparty and bills of lading, but the counterpart in a building contract to a right of suit under a bill of lading should be the provision of a direct entitlement in a third party to sue the contractor in the event of a failure in the contractor's performance. In the context of a building contract one does not require to look for a second building contract to exclude the exception. It would be sufficient to find the provision of a right to sue. Thus as my noble and learned friend, Lord Browne-Wilkinson, observed in the *St. Martins* case [1994] 1 AC 85, 115:

> If, pursuant to the terms of the original building contract, the contractors have undertaken liability to the ultimate purchasers to remedy defects appearing after they acquired the

property, it is manifest the case will not fall within the rationale of *Dunlop* v *Lambert* 6 Cl & F 600. If the ultimate purchaser is given a direct cause of action against the contractor (as is the consignee or endorsee under a bill of lading) the case falls outside the rationale of the rule.

In the *St. Martins* case the employer started off as the owner of the property and subsequently conveyed it to another company. In the present case the employer never was the owner. But that has not featured as a critical consideration in the present appeal and I do not see that that factor affects the application of the exception. In the *St. Martins* case there was a contractual bar on the assignment of rights of action without the consent of the contractor. In the present case the extra qualification was added that the consent should not be unreasonably withheld. But again I do not see that difference as of significance. It does not follow that the presence of a provision enabling assignment without the consent of the contractor excludes the exception. As was held in *Darlington Borough Council* v *Wiltshier Northern Ltd* [1995] 1 WLR 68 where there is a right to have an assignment of any cause of action accruing to the employer against the contractor, the exception may still apply so as to enable the assignee to recover substantial damages. It may be that the exception could be excluded through some contractual arrangement between the employer and the third party who sustained the actual loss, but the law would probably be slow to find such an intention established where it would leave the black hole. At least an express provision for assignment of the employer's rights will not suffice.

I have no difficulty in holding in the present case that the exception cannot apply. As part of the contractual arrangements entered into between Panatown and McAlpine there was a clear contemplation that separate contracts would be entered into by McAlpine, the contracts of the deed of duty of care and the collateral warranties. The duty of care deed and the collateral warranties were of course not in themselves building contracts. But they did form an integral part of the package of arrangements which the employer and the contractor agreed upon and in that respect should be viewed as reflecting the intentions of all the parties engaged in the arrangements that the third party should have a direct cause of action to the exclusion of any substantial claim by the employer, and accordingly that the exception should not apply. There was some dispute upon the difference in substance between the remedies available under the contract and those available under the duty of care deed. Even if it is accepted that in the circumstances of the present case where the eventual issue may relate particularly to matters of reasonable skill and care, the remedies do not absolutely coincide, the express provision of the direct remedy for the third party is fatal to the application of *The Albazero* exception. On a more general approach the difference between a strict contractual basis of claim and a basis of reasonable care makes the express remedy more clearly a substitution for the operation of the exception. Panatown cannot then in the light of these deeds be treated as having contracted with McAlpine for the benefit of the owner or later owners of the land and the exception is plainly excluded.

NOTES

1. This is a very significant decision as the judgments embark on an analysis of the essential nature of contractual performance and the identification of loss. See Coote, 'The performance interest, *Panatown* and the problem of loss' (2001) 117 LQR 81. It is likely that this debate will continue for some time (see Chapter 9, *pages 355* and *366*, for further relevant case law).
2. The dissenting members of the House of Lords (Lords Goff and Millett) relied on the broad ground and considered that on this basis Panatown had suffered a loss as a result of the defective performance of the obligations for which it had contracted. The duty of care deed was irrelevant to this because it dealt not with loss suffered by the employer but the ability of the third party to enforce the construction contract.

LORD GOFF (dissenting): . . . I wish to state that I find persuasive the reasoning and conclusion expressed by Lord Griffiths in his opinion in the *St. Martins* case [1994] 1 AC 85 that the employer under a building contract may in principle recover substantial damages from the building contractor, because he has not received the performance which he was entitled to receive from the contractor under the contract, notwithstanding that the property in the building site was vested in a third party.

The example given by Lord Griffiths of a husband contracting for repairs to the matrimonial home which is owned by his wife is most telling. It is not difficult to imagine other examples, not only within the family, but also, for example, where work is done for charitable purposes—as where a wealthy man who lives in a village decides to carry out at his own expense major repairs to, or renovation or even reconstruction of, the village hall, and himself enters into a contract with a local builder to carry out the work to the existing building which belongs to another, for example to trustees, or to the parish council. Nobody in such circumstances would imagine that there could be any legal obstacle in the way of the charitable donor enforcing the contract against the builder by recovering damages from him if he failed to perform his obligations under the building contract, for example because his work failed to comply with the contract specification.

At this stage I find it necessary to return to the opinion of Lord Griffiths in the *St. Martins* case. In the passage from his opinion [1994] 1 AC 85, 96–97 . . . he gave the example of a husband placing a contract with a builder for the replacement of the roof of the matrimonial home which belonged to his wife. The work proved to be defective. Lord Griffiths expressed the opinion that, in such a case, it would be absurd to say that the husband has suffered no damage because he does not own the property. I wish now to draw attention to the fact that, in his statement of the facts of his example, Lord Griffiths included the fact that the husband had to call in and pay another builder to complete the work. It might perhaps be thought that Lord Griffiths regarded that fact as critical to the husband's cause of action against the builder, on the basis that the husband only has such a cause of action in respect of defective work on another person's property if he himself has actually sustained financial loss, in this example by having paid the second builder. In my opinion, however, such a conclusion is not justified on a fair reading of Lord Griffiths's opinion. This is because he stated the answer to be that

> the husband has suffered loss because he did not receive the bargain for which he had contracted with the first builder and the measure of damages is the cost of securing the performance of that bargain by completing the roof repairs properly by the second builder.

It is plain, therefore, that the payment to the second builder was not regarded by Lord Griffiths as essential to the husband's cause of action.

The point can perhaps be made more clearly by taking a different example, of the wealthy philanthropist who contracts for work to be done to the village hall. The work is defective; and the trustees who own the hall suggest that he should recover damages from the builder and hand the damages over to them, and they will then instruct another builder, well known to them, who, they are confident, will do the work well. The philanthropist agrees, and starts an action against the first builder. Is it really to be suggested that his action will fail, because he does not own the hall, and because he has not incurred the expense of himself employing another builder to do the remedial work? Echoing the words of Lord Griffiths, I regard such a conclusion as absurd. The philanthropist's cause of action does not depend on his having actually incurred financial expense; as Lord Griffiths said of the husband in his example, he 'has suffered loss because he did not receive the bargain for which he had contracted with the first builder'.

There has been a substantial amount of academic discussion about the difference of opinion in the Appellate Committee in the *St. Martins* case and in particular about the merits of Lord Griffiths's opinion in that case. The Appellate Committee in the present case was supplied with copies of a number of relevant articles, which I have studied with interest and respect. I have not detected any substantial criticism of Lord Griffiths's broader ground, whereas there has been some criticism of the narrower ground adopted by the majority of the Appellate Committee in the *St. Martins* case [1994] 1 AC 85—see in particular the articles by Professor Treitel 'Damages in Respect of a Third Party's Loss' (1998) 114 LQR 527 and by Mr Duncan Wallace QC (the editor of *Hudson on Building Contracts*) 'Assignment of Right to Sue: Half a Loaf' (1994) 110 LQR 42 and 'Third Party Damage: No Legal Black Hole?' (1999) 115 LQR 394 (in which the writer supports Lord Griffiths's broader ground). I have found nothing in the academic material with which we were supplied which should deter those who are attracted to the broader ground from giving effect to it in an appropriate case. . . .

It follows, in my opinion, that the principal argument advanced on behalf of McAlpine is inconsistent with authority and established principle. This conclusion may involve a fuller recognition of the importance of the protection of a contracting party's interest in the performance of his contract than has occurred in the past. But not only is it justified by authority, but the principle on which it is based is supported by a number of distinguished writers, notably Professor Brian Coote and Mr Duncan Wallace QC.

In truth, no question of a *jus quaesitum tertio* arises in this case at all. Lord Griffiths's broader ground is not concerned with privity of contract as such. It is concerned with the damages recoverable by one party to a contract (the employer) against another (the contractor) for breach of a contract for labour and materials, viz, a building contract. It does not seek to establish an exception to the old privity rule, though it may provide a principled basis for the recovery of damages (by a contracting party, not by a third party) in some cases, such as *Jackson v Horizon Holidays Ltd* [1975] 1 WLR 1468, in which the privity rule has been seen as a barrier to recovery (not by a contracting party but by a third party).

Furthermore, as Professor Hugh Beale stated some years ago in 'Privity of Contract: Judicial and Legislative Reforms' (1995) 9 JCL 103, 108:

> Even if the basic doctrine of privity were to be reformed along the lines suggested by the Law Commission, I think it is vital that the promisee should have adequate remedies to take care of those cases in which the third party does not acquire rights.

I would however go further. I do not regard Lord Griffiths's broader ground as a departure from existing authority, but as a reaffirmation of existing legal principle. Indeed, I know of no authority which stands in its way. On the contrary, there have been statements in the cases which provide support for his view. Thus in *Darlington Borough Council v Wiltshier Northern Ltd* [1995] 1 WLR 68, 80, Steyn LJ described Lord Griffiths's broader ground as based on classic contractual theory, a statement with which I respectfully agree. Moreover, Lord Griffiths's reasoning was foreshadowed in the opinions of members of the Appellate Committee in *Woodar Investment Development Ltd v Wimpey Construction UK Ltd* [1980] 1 WLR 277; see especially the opinion of Lord Keith of Kinkel, at pp. 297–298, and in addition the more tentative statements of Lord Salmon, at p. 291, and Lord Scarman, at pp. 300–301. Furthermore, as I have just indicated, full recognition of the importance of the performance interest will open the way to principled solution of other well-known problems in the law of contract, notably those relating to package holidays which are booked by one person for the benefit not only of himself but of others, normally members of his family (as to which see *Jackson v Horizon Holidays Ltd* [1975] 1 WLR 1468), and other cases of a similar kind referred to by Lord Wilberforce in his opinion in the *Woodar Investment* case [1980] 1 WLR 277, 283—cases of an everyday kind which are calling out for a sensible solution on a principled basis. Even if it is not thought, as I think, that the solution which I prefer is in accordance with existing principle, nevertheless it is surely within the scope of the type of development of the common law which, especially in the law of obligations, is habitually undertaken by appellate judges as part of their ordinary judicial function. That such developments in the law may be better left to the judges, rather than be the subject of legislation, is now recognised by the Law Commission itself, because legislation within a developing part of the common law can lead to ossification and a rigid segregation of legal principle which disfigures the law and impedes future development of legal principle on a coherent basis. It comes as no surprise therefore that, in its Report on Privity of Contract: Contracts for the Benefit of Third Parties (1996) (Law Com. No. 242) para. 5.15, the Law Commission declined to make specific recommendations in relation to *the promisee's* remedies in a contract for the benefit of a third party (here referring to *The Albazero, The* [1977] AC 774 and *Linden Gardens Trust Ltd v Lenesta Sludge Disposals Ltd* (the *St. Martins* case) [1994] 1 AC 85 as cases in which 'the courts have gone a considerable way towards developing rules which in many appropriate cases do allow the promisee to recover damages on behalf of the third party'), and stated that the Commission 'certainly . . . would not wish to forestall further judicial development of this area of the law of damages'. This certainly does not sound like a warning to judicial trespassers to keep out of forbidden territory; see also para. 11.22, concerned with the problem of double liability—which I shall have to consider at a later stage.

The present case provides, in my opinion, a classic example of a case which falls properly within the judicial province. I, for my part, have therefore no doubt that it is desirable, indeed essential, that the problem in the present case should be the subject of judicial solution by providing proper recognition of the plaintiff's interest in the performance of the contractual obligations which are owed to him. I cannot see why the proposed statutory reform of the old doctrine of privity of contract should inhibit the ordinary judicial function, and so prevent your Lordships' House from doing justice between the parties in the present case. . . .

Lord Browne-Wilkinson, who was in the majority, attempted to link the two approaches by stating that because of the duty of care deed, UIPL had a remedy against the contractor and it was for this reason that Panatown had not suffered any damage to its performance interest under the construction contract.

Lord Clyde (in the majority) argued against the application of the 'broad ground' (at least where the promisee (employer) had not spent any money in carrying out relevant repairs) for the following reasons:

LORD CLYDE:

I turn accordingly to what was referred to in the argument as the broader ground. But the label requires more careful definition. The approach under *The Albazero* exception has been one of recognising an entitlement to sue by the innocent party to a contract which has been breached, where the innocent party is treated as suing on behalf of or for the benefit of some other person or persons, not parties to the contract, who have sustained loss as a result of the breach. In such a case the innocent party to the contract is bound to account to the person suffering the loss for the damages which the former has recovered for the benefit of the latter. But the so-called broader ground involves a significantly different approach. What it proposes is that the innocent party to the contract should recover damages for himself as a compensation for what is seen to be his own loss. In this context no question of accounting to anyone else arises. This approach however seems to me to have been developed into two formulations.

The first formulation, and the seeds of the second, are found in the speech of Lord Griffiths in the *St. Martins* case [1994] 1 AC 85, 96. At the outset his Lordship expressed the opinion that Corporation, faced with a breach by McAlpine of their contractual duty to perform the contract with sound materials and with all reasonable skill and care, would be entitled to recover from McAlpine the cost of remedying the defect in the work as the normal measure of damages. He then dealt with two possible objections. First, it should not matter that the work was not being done on property owned by Corporation. Where a husband instructs repairs to the roof of the matrimonial home it cannot be said that he has not suffered damage because he did not own the property. He suffers the damage measured by the cost of a proper completion of the repair:

> In cases such as the present the person who places the contract has suffered financial loss because he has to spend money to give him the benefit of the bargain which the defendant had promised but failed to deliver. (See p. 97.)

The second objection, that Corporation had in fact been reimbursed for the cost of the repairs was answered by the consideration that the person who actually pays for the repairs is of no concern to the party who broke the contract. But Lord Griffiths added, at p. 97:

> The court will of course wish to be satisfied that the repairs have been or are likely to be carried out but if they are carried out the cost of doing them must fall upon the defendant who broke his contract.

In the first formulation this approach can be seen as identifying a loss upon the innocent party who requires to instruct the remedial work. That loss is, or may be measured by, the cost of the repair. The essential for this formulation appears to be that the repair work is to be, or at least is likely to be, carried out. This consideration does not appear to be simply relevant to the reasonableness of allowing the damages to be measured by the cost of repair. It is an essential condition for the application of the approach, so as to establish a loss on the part of the plaintiff. Thus far the approach appears to be consistent with principle, and in particular with the principle of privity. It can cover the case where A contracts with B to pay a sum of money to C and B fails to do so. The loss to A is in the necessity to find other funds to pay to C and provided that he is going to pay C, or indeed has done so, he should be able to recover the sum by way of damages for breach of contract from B. If it was evident that A had no intention to pay C, having perhaps changed his mind, then he would not be able to recover the amount from B because he would have sustained no loss, and his damages would at best be nominal.

But there can also be found in Lord Griffiths's speech the idea that the loss is not just constituted by the failure in performance but indeed consists in that failure. This is the 'second formulation'. In relation to the suggestion that the husband who instructs repair work to the roof of his wife's house and has to pay for another builder to make good the faulty repair work has sustained no damage Lord Griffiths observed, at p. 97:

> Such a result would in my view be absurd and the answer is that the husband has suffered loss because he did not receive the bargain for which he had contracted with the first builder and the measure of damages is the cost of securing the performance of that bargain by completing the roof repairs properly by the second builder.

That is to say that the fact that the innocent party did not receive the bargain for which he contracted is itself a loss. As Steyn LJ put it in *Darlington Borough Council* v *Wiltshier Northern Ltd* [1995] 1 WLR 68, 80: 'He suffers a loss of bargain or of expectation interest.' In this more radical formulation it does not matter whether the repairs are or are not carried out, and indeed in the *Darlington* case that qualification is seen as unnecessary. In that respect the disposal of the damages is treated as res inter alios acta. Nevertheless on this approach the intention to repair may cast light on the reasonableness of the measure of damages adopted. In order to follow through this aspect of the second formulation in Lord Griffiths's speech it would be necessary to understand his references to the carrying out of the repairs to be relevant only to that consideration.

I find some difficulty in adopting the second formulation as a sound way forward. First, if the loss is the disappointment at there not being provided what was contracted for, it seems to me difficult to measure that loss by consideration of the cost of repair. A more apt assessment of the compensation for the loss of what was expected should rather be the difference in value between what was contracted for and what was supplied. Secondly, the loss constituted by the supposed disappointment may well not include all the loss which the breach of contract has caused. It may not be able to embrace consequential losses, or losses falling within the second head of *Hadley* v *Baxendale* 9 Exch. 341. The inability of the wife to let one of the rooms in the house caused by the inadequacy of the repair, does not seem readily to be something for which the husband could claim as his loss. Thirdly, there is no obligation on the successful plaintiff to account to anyone who may have sustained actual loss as a result of the faulty performance. Some further mechanism would then be required for the court to achieve the proper disposal of the monies awarded to avoid a double jeopardy. Alternatively, in order to achieve an effective solution, it would seem to be necessary to add an obligation to account on the part of the person recovering the damages. But once that step is taken the approach begins to approximate to *The Albazero* exception. Fourthly, the 'loss' constituted by a breach of contract has usually been recognised as calling for an award of nominal damages, not substantial damages.

The loss of an expectation which is here referred to seems to me to be coming very close to a way of describing a breach of contract. A breach of contract may cause a loss, but is not in itself a loss in any meaningful sense. When one refers to a loss in the context of a breach of contract, one is in my view referring to the incidence of some personal or patrimonial damage. A loss of expectation might be a loss in the proper sense if damages were awarded for the distress or inconvenience caused by the disappointment. Professor Coote ('Contract Damages, *Ruxley* and the Performance Interest' [1997] CLJ 537) draws a distinction between benefits in law, that is bargained-for contractual rights, and benefits in fact, that is the enjoyment of the fruits of performance. Certainly the former may constitute an asset with a commercial value. But while frustration may destroy the rights altogether so that the contract is no longer enforceable, a failure in the obligation to perform does not destroy the asset. On the contrary it remains as the necessary legal basis for a remedy. A failure in performance of a contractual obligation does not entail a loss of the bargained-for contractual rights. Those rights remain so as to enable performance of the contract to be enforced, as by an order for specific performance. If one party to a contract repudiates it and that repudiation is accepted, then, to quote

Lord Porter in *Heyman* v *Darwins Ltd* [1942] AC 356, 399, 'By that acceptance he is discharged from further performance and may bring an action for damages, but the contract itself is not rescinded'. The primary obligations under the contract may come to an end, but secondary obligations then arise, among them being the obligation to compensate the innocent party. The original rights may not then be enforced. But a consequential right arises in the innocent party to obtain a remedy from the party who repudiated the contract for his failure in performance. . . .

It seems to me that a more realistic and practical solution is to permit the contracting party to recover damages for the loss which he and a third party has suffered, being duly accountable to them in respect of their actual loss, than to construct a theoretical loss in law on the part of the contracting party, for which he may be under no duty to account to anyone since it is to be seen as his own loss. The solution is required where the law will not tolerate a loss caused by a breach of contract to go uncompensated through an absence of privity between the party suffering the loss and the party causing it. In such a case, to avoid the legal black hole, the law will deem the innocent party to be claiming on behalf of himself and any others who have suffered loss. It does not matter that he is not the owner of the property affected, nor that he has not himself suffered any economic loss. He sues for all the loss which has been sustained and is accountable to the others to the extent of their particular losses. While it may be that there is no necessary right in the third party to compel the innocent employer to sue the contractor, in the many cases of the domestic or familial situation that consideration should not be a realistic problem. In the commercial field, in relation to the interests of such persons as remoter future proprietors who are not related to the original employer, it may be that a solution by way of collateral warranty would still be required. If there is an anxiety lest the exception would permit an employer to receive excessive damages, that should be set at rest by the recognition of the basic requirement for reasonableness which underlies the quantification of an award of damages. . . .

3. In *Rolls-Royce Power Engineering plc* v *Ricardo Consulting Engineers Ltd* [2003] EWHC 2871 (TCC), [2004] 2 All ER (Comm) 129, Judge Seymour QC made the following observation concerning Lord Griffiths' broad ground:

[128] Lord Griffiths' approach has not so far been adopted as a matter of decision in any case in England and Wales which counsel had been able to discover. It seems on its face to divorce the assessment of damages for breach of contract in a case in which it is adopted from proof of any particular loss sustained by the claimant, substituting some more or less notional quantification of damages for loss of bargain. As it is a notional loss of the actual claimant, if the person who has actually sustained the loss has some independent ground of claim, for example in tort, it would seem that the wrongdoer could find himself having to pay compensation for one wrong twice over. Settlement of the claim of the other contracting party would not obviously be a defence to the claim of the person who in fact sustained loss. Again, leaving aside that difficulty, it does not seem at all easy just as a practical matter to apply Lord Griffiths' approach in any case other than one in which the alleged damage is damage to, or failure to repair, property and there is no suggestion of any consequential loss. If may be that the cost of repairing damage to a house or a car or some other type of corporeal property is likely to be similar no matter who sustains it. It may be that the diminution in the value of an item of corporeal property is likely to be similar no matter who owns it. However, the nature and extent of any consequential loss—for example, loss of income from inability for a period to turn property to account—may well depend critically upon the particular circumstances of the owner and what he or she does with the property. A simple example is that an owner of a flat may live in it as his main residence, or he may keep it empty for occasional use by himself, or he may let it and derive an income from it. Inability to use the flat because it has been damaged in some way may cause no loss beyond the cost of repair in the second case—the owner can live in his main residence—and the measure of the loss in the other two cases may well be different, either the cost of renting alternative accommodation or loss of rental income. In a case such as the present, in which there has been no damage to corporeal property as a result of the defendant's alleged breach of contract, it is impossible to

see how any assessment of damages could be made other than by reference to what actually happened to the other contracting party.

[**129**] In the *Lenesta Sludge* case itself, Lord Keith of Kinkel and Lord Bridge of Harwich expressly did not decide the appeals on the basis of the suggested principle of Lord Griffiths, whilst indicating some sympathy with his comments. Lord Ackner expressly agreed only with Lord Browne-Wilkinson and did not comment at all upon what Lord Griffiths said. In the *Darlington BC* case Dillon LJ, with whom Waite LJ agreed, expressly did not consider the principle suggested by Lord Griffiths, but the third member of the Court of Appeal, Steyn LJ, expressly adopted it as a ground for his decision concurring with the majority in the result. In the *Panatown* case [2000] 4 All ER 97 at 109–112, 143–148, [2001] 1 AC 518 at 532–535, 568–574 Lord Clyde and Lord Jauncey of Tullichettle considered Lord Griffiths' suggested approach and identified difficulties with it. Lord Goff of Chieveley ([2000] 4 All ER 97 at 122, [2001] 1 AC 518 at 546) expressed his agreement with it. Lord Browne-Wilkinson ([2000] 4 All ER 97 at 151, [2001] 1 AC 518 at 577) assumed that it was sound. Lord Millett ([2000] 4 All ER 97 at 164, [2001] 1 AC 518 at 591) approved it, but limited its application to 'building contracts and other contracts for the supply of work and materials where the claim is in respect of defective or incomplete work or delay in completing it'.

[**130**] In the result there is a lack of unanimity of judicial utterance as to the appropriateness of the approach of Lord Griffiths to any class of case, and a respectable body of opinion that in some or all classes of case it is contrary to principle and/or difficult of practical application. In these treacherous waters I prefer to navigate by already published charts and to seek to apply the law as it has already clearly developed, rather than to speculate as to how it may develop in future.

4. It is clearly accepted that there is an obligation on the employer to account to the building owner for damages received under the application of 'the narrow ground' since the recovery is for the third party's loss. Recovery on the basis of the 'broad ground' is fundamentally different because the loss is treated as being the employer's.

5. Although the 'narrow ground' in *St Martin's Property* was held to be excluded by the existence of a right of direct action for the third party, in the absence of such a direct route for redress the exception will remain applicable and this is important in the light of s. 5 of the Contracts (Rights of Third Parties) Act 1999. Significantly, however, the House of Lords regarded the exception as being imposed by law rather than being based on contractual intention and contemplations. Although this requires further theoretical justification, it does represent a practical acceptance of the realities of the situation and will avoid technical difficulties surrounding determining that intention. In future the exception ought to apply where the third party suffers loss as building owner and the employer's loss is purely nominal, either because he no longer owns the property in question or because he never owned it. It will only be in instances where there is direct redress that this operation of law will be necessarily excluded.

6. In *Rolls-Royce Power Engineering plc* v *Ricardo Consulting Engineers Ltd* [2003] EWHC 2871 (TCC), [2004] 2 All ER (Comm) 129, the judge applied the previous 'contractual' basis for the 'narrow ground' exception. Judge Seymour QC stated:

[**124**] In the existing state of the law it seems to me that a fundamental condition to be met if the rule in *Dunlop* v *Lambert* is to be applied in any case is that it should at the time the relevant contract was made have been in the actual contemplation of the parties that an identified third party or a third party who was a member of an identified class would or might suffer damage in the event of a breach of the contract. In no case to which my attention was drawn was that condition not satisfied. Moreover, if the general rule, as everyone seems to accept, is that a party to a contract may not recover in respect of a breach of it substantial damages if he himself has not suffered such loss, any exception is an exception to that rule, not a wholesale replacement of it, and there must be special circumstances which take a particular case out of the ambit of the general rule. If the special circumstances which take a case out of the general are knowledge that an identified third party or a third party who is a member of an identified class will or might suffer

damage if there is a breach of contract, that is something which ought to be capable of being readily demonstrated, it involves no obvious injustice, as the possibility of loss will have been known at the time the contract was made, and seems to do justice because it gives effect to the contemplation of the contracting parties and provides a means of compensating the third party for whose benefit, at least in part, the relevant contractual obligation was undertaken. If knowledge at the date of the contract of the interest of the third party as such or as a member of an identified class were unnecessary, the result would be that a claim for substantial damages could be advanced on behalf of anyone whomsoever who contended that they had suffered loss as a result of a breach of contract, however remote their apparent connection to the performance of the contract. Such a possibility would destroy the general rule.

[**125**] In the present case, on my findings of fact, RRPE was not a party identified either by name or by membership of an identified class as one who would or might suffer loss as a result of a breach of the definitive design contract on the part of Ricardo. The fact that it was known to be the parent company of Allen is, in my judgment, insufficient, for in that capacity it would sustain no loss in the event of a breach of the contract in respect of which Allen could recover substantial damages, and Allen would have been able to do that in the event of a claim for damages arising at any stage, had not the Allen Diesels Business been transferred to RRPE and RRPE thereafter undertaken manufacture and sale of the engines itself.

As the judge recognised, this approach is out of line with the 'rule of law' approach adopted by the House of Lords in *Panatown*. However, he did not consider that Lord Clyde in *Panatown* could have meant that there were no conditions for the narrow ground to apply.

Although this is a first instance decision, it suggests some uncertainty concerning the basis for the narrow ground exception and the matter will need clarification.

C: Staying the action

It appears that if A makes an express promise to B that A will not sue C, then, although C cannot use A's promise to B as a defence when sued by A (because of privity), B may ask the court to exercise its discretion (Supreme Court Act 1981, s. 49(3)) to stay A's action against C. It may also be possible to do this where B was under a legal obligation to reimburse C for any damages he would have to pay A.

Gore v *Van der Lann*
[1967] 2 QB 31 (CA)

Liverpool Corporation issued free bus passes to old age pensioners. The plaintiff applied for a pass and signed an application form which provided that neither the Corporation nor its servants were to be liable for any injury or loss. The pass itself contained a similar clause. While the plaintiff was boarding a bus at a bus stop the bus moved away and she was injured. The plaintiff brought an action against the Corporation's conductor, alleging that her injury was caused by his negligence. Liverpool Corporation asked the court to stay the proceedings on the ground that the plaintiff was bound by the terms of the pass. The plaintiff argued that the agreement for the pass constituted 'a contract for the conveyance of a passenger in a public service vehicle' and such contracts were void under the Road Traffic Act 1960, s. 151. Held: the contract was rendered void by s. 151 of the Road Traffic Act 1960 so that the Corporation had no ground for seeking to prevent the plaintiff's action. In addition (Willmer and Salmon LJJ; Harman LJ expressing no opinion) the Corporation were not under any contractual obligation to indemnify the conductor against sums he had to pay to the plaintiff, and the plaintiff had not promised the Corporation that she would not institute proceedings against the employee, so the Corporation had no interest entitling them to stay the action.

WILLMER LJ: . . . It is true that the conditions accepted by the plaintiff when she accepted the offer of a free pass included a provision that the employees of the corporation were not to be liable to her for any injury or loss. But I cannot construe this provision as a promise by the plaintiff not to institute proceedings against an employee. If the corporation desired such a promise from a holder of a free pass, they could have said so in clear and unambiguous terms. In my judgment the conditions are to be construed strictly against the corporation who put them forward. It is not enough to say that a promise not to sue the employee is to be implied. At the best for the corporation, the condition relied on is ambiguous, and any ambiguity must be resolved in favour of the plaintiff.

In these circumstances the corporation has not satisfied me that it has any justification for interfering with the plaintiff's prima facie right at common law to bring proceedings against the conductor whom she accuses of negligence. . . .

NOTES

1. It appears from this judgment that the intervening party (Liverpool Corporation) would *either* have to show an express promise by the plaintiff not to sue the Corporation's servants, *or* that the Corporation were legally obliged to reimburse the conductor for any damages he had to pay to the plaintiff.
2. See also *The Elbe Maru* [1978] 1 Lloyd's Rep 206.

Snelling v John G. Snelling Ltd

[1973] 1 QB 87

Three brothers were directors of a family company. They agreed in writing that if any one of them voluntarily resigned his directorship he would immediately forfeit all moneys due to him from the company. Later, Brian Snelling, the plaintiff, resigned and the company cancelled his loan account. He then commenced proceedings against the company claiming the money which he alleged the company owed him. The plaintiff's brothers, Peter and Barrie Snelling, on their application, were joined as defendants in the action. They sought to rely on their agreement with the plaintiff (to which the company was not a party) and counterclaimed for a declaration that the plaintiff had forfeited the money. Held: although the company could not rely on the agreement because it was not a party to it, the brothers were entitled to a declaration that the plaintiff was bound by the terms of the agreement so that it would have been a proper case for a stay of proceedings. As all the parties were before the court and the claim had failed, the action was dismissed.

NOTE: The judge, Ormrod J, only emphasised the need to show a promise not to sue, and there was no discussion about whether the brothers were obliged to indemnify the company if it was sued by the plaintiff. The promise itself was stated to be a necessary implication of the agreement made, whereas in *Gore* v *Van der Lann* the Court of Appeal refused to imply a promise by the plaintiff not to sue the Corporation or its servants.

SECTION 8: PRIVITY AND BURDENS

The privity doctrine provides that a third party cannot be made subject to a burden by a contract to which he is not a party.

A: Exemption clauses

Can a third party be bound by an exemption clause in a contract to which he is not a party?

Morris v *C. W. Martin & Sons Ltd*
[1966] 1 QB 716 (CA)

The plaintiff sent a mink stole to a furrier for cleaning. She agreed that it should be passed to the defendants for cleaning. The furrier contracted with the defendants for the cleaning on current trade conditions which provided that 'goods belonging to customers were held at the customer's risk' and that the defendants were not to be responsible for loss or damage during processing. M, the defendants' employee, was given the cleaning task and stole the fur while it was in his custody. The plaintiff sued the defendants for damages. Held: (Diplock and Salmon LJJ) the defendants were bailees for reward, and therefore they owed a duty to the plaintiff to take care of the fur. However, the exemption clauses in the defendants' contract of cleaning with the furrier did not extend on their wording to cover liability to the plaintiff. (They were therefore able to avoid the more difficult privity question.) Lord Denning found that the clauses on their wording did not extend to cover the plaintiff but considered that the plaintiff had impliedly consented to the furrier contracting for the cleaning on usual terms so that in principle the defendants might rely on the exemptions in the bailment contract.

LORD DENNING MR: . . . [C]an the plaintiff sue the cleaners direct for the misappropriation by their servant? And if she does, can she ignore the exempting conditions?

. . . [I]f the sub-bailment is for reward, the sub-bailee owes to the owner all the duties of a bailee for reward: and the owner can sue the sub-bailee direct for loss of or damage to the goods; and the sub-bailee (unless he is protected by any exempting conditions) is liable unless he can prove that the loss or damage occurred without his fault or that of his servants. So the plaintiff can sue the defendants direct for the loss of the goods by the misappropriation by their servant, and the cleaners are liable unless they are protected by the exempting conditions.

Now comes the question: Can the defendants rely, as against the plaintiff, on the exempting conditions although there was no contract directly between them and her? There is much to be said on each side. On the one hand, it is hard on the plaintiff if her just claim is defeated by exempting conditions of which she knew nothing and to which she was not a party. On the other hand, it is hard on the defendants if they are held liable to a greater responsibility than they agreed to undertake. As long ago as 1601 Lord Coke advised a bailee to stipulate specially that he would not be responsible for theft, see *Southcote's case* (1601) 4 Co Rep 83b, a case of theft by a servant. It would be strange if his stipulation was of no avail to him. The answer to the problem lies, I think, in this: the owner is bound by the conditions if he expressly or impliedly consented to the bailee making a sub-bailment containing those conditions, but not otherwise. Suppose the owner of goods lets them out on hire, and the hirer sends them for repair, and the repairer holds them for a lien. The owner is bound by the lien because he impliedly consented to the repairs being done, since they were reasonably incidental to the use of the car: see *Tappenden* v *Artus* [1964] 2 QB 185. So also if the owner of a ship accepts goods for carriage on a bill of lading containing exempting conditions (i.e. a 'bailment upon terms') the owner of the goods (although not a party to the contract) is bound by those conditions if he impliedly consented to them as being in 'the known and contemplated form,' . . .

In this case the plaintiff agreed that Beder should send the fur to the defendants, and by so doing I think she impliedly consented to his making a contract for cleaning on the terms usually current in the trade. But when I come to study the conditions I do not think that they are sufficient to protect the cleaners. We always construe such conditions strictly. Clause 9 applies only to 'goods belonging to customers', that is, goods belonging to Beder, and not to goods belonging to his customers such as the plaintiff. The conditions themselves draw a distinction between 'customer' and 'his own customer,' see clause 16. Clause 14 only applies to 'the loss of or damage to the goods during processing'. The loss here was not during processing. It was before or after processing.

Seeing that the conditions do not protect the defendants, I am of opinion that they are liable for the loss due to the theft by their servant.

NOTES
1. Salmon LJ stated that he was 'strongly attracted by this view'. Lord Denning's approach was adopted in *Singer Co. (UK) Ltd* v *Tees & Hartlepool Port Authority* [1988] 2 Lloyd's Rep 164.
2. Bailment involves the delivery of goods under a contract by a bailor to the bailee for some purpose and, after that purpose has been fulfilled, their return to the bailor.
3. In the following case the Privy Council applied and clarified Lord Denning's principle in *Morris* v *Martin*.

K.H. Enterprise v Pioneer Container, The Pioneer Container
[1994] 2 AC 324 (PC)

The K.H. Enterprise, a ship owned by the defendant carriers, was in collision with another ship on a journey from Taiwan to Hong Kong and was lost. Action was taken in the courts of Hong Kong by those interested in the cargo against the defendants, and this led to the arrest of another ship owned by them, namely, *The Pioneer Container*. The defendants objected to the arrest and wanted a stay of action on the ground that the cargo was carried by them under contracts which exclusively stated that disputes were to be determined in Taiwan. The plaintiff cargo owners had contracted with other carriers (Hanjin and Scandutch) for the carriage of their goods, but the contract had entitled their carriers to subcontract the carriage on any terms, and carriage had been subcontracted to the defendants. Held: the plaintiffs were bound by the exclusive jurisdiction clause in the contract between their carriers and the defendants because they had consented to their cargo being sub-bailed on terms including the jurisdiction clause and the defendants had known that the cargo belonged to the plaintiffs and not to Hanjin and Scandutch, the carriers.

LORD GOFF: . . . In order to decide whether, like Steyn J [in *Singer Co. (UK) Ltd* v *Tees and Hartlepool Port Authority*] to accept the principle so stated by Lord Denning MR [in *Morris* v *Martin*], it is necessary to consider the relevance of the concept of 'consent' in this context. It must be assumed that, on the facts of the case, no direct contractual relationship has been created between the owner and the sub-bailee, the only contract created by the sub-bailment being that between the bailee and the sub-bailee. Even so, if the effect of the sub-bailment is that the sub-bailee voluntarily receives into his custody the goods of the owner and so assumes towards the owner the responsibility of a bailee, then to the extent that the terms of the sub-bailment are consented to by the owner, it can properly be said that the owner has authorised the bailee so to regulate the duties of the sub-bailee in respect of the goods entrusted to him, not only towards the bailee but also towards the owner. (Their Lordships add in parenthesis that for this purpose it is not, in their opinion, necessary to have recourse to the doctrine of estoppel: cf *Hispanica de Petroleos SA* v *Vencedora Oceanica Navigacion SA (No. 2)* [1987] 2 Lloyd's Rep 321, 336, 340 per Nicholls and Dillon LJJ. Even where there is express or implied consent to the relevant terms by the owner of the goods, there can be no estoppel without some holding out on his part. Estoppel may however be relevant if recourse is to be had to the doctrine of ostensible authority.)

Such a conclusion, finding its origin in the law of bailment rather than the law of contract, does not depend for its efficacy either on the doctrine of privity of contract or on the doctrine of consideration

. . . [I]f the owner seeks to hold a sub-bailee responsible to him as bailee, he has to accept all the terms of the sub-bailment, warts and all; for either he will have consented to the sub-bailment on those terms or, if not, he will (by holding the sub-bailee liable to him as bailee) be held to have ratified all the terms of the sub-bailment. A negative answer to the question is however supported by other writers, notably by *Palmer's Bailment* pp. 31 et seq., where Professor Palmer cites a number of examples of bailment without the consent of the owner, and by Professor Tay in her article 'The essence of bailment' (1966) 5 Syd LR 239. On this approach, a person who voluntarily takes another person's goods into his custody holds them as bailee of that person (the owner); and he can only invoke, for example, terms of a sub-bailment under which he received the goods from an intermediate bailee as qualifying or otherwise affecting his responsibility to the owner if the owner consented to them. It is the latter approach which, as their Lordships have explained, has been adopted by English Law and, with English law, the law of Hong Kong.

Their Lordships wish to add that this conclusion, which flows from the decisions in *Morris* v *C W Martin & Sons Ltd* [1996] 1 QB 716 and the *Gilchrist Watt* case [*Gilchrist Watt and Sanderson Pty Ltd* v *York Products Pty Ltd*] [1970] 1 WLR 1262, produces a result which in their opinion is both principled and just. They incline to the opinion that a sub-bailee can only be said for these purposes to have voluntarily taken into his possession the goods of another if he has sufficient notice that a person other than the bailee is interested in the goods so that it can properly be said that (in addition to his duties to the bailee) he has, by taking the goods into his custody, assumed towards that other person the responsibility for the goods which is characteristic of a bailee. This they believe to be the underlying principle. Moreover, their Lordships do not consider this principle to impose obligations on the sub-bailee which are onerous or unfair, once it is recognised that he can invoke against the owner terms of the sub-bailment which the owner has actually (expressly or impliedly) or even ostensibly authorised. . . .

NOTES
1. Devonshire [1996] JBL 329 and Phang (1995) 58 MLR 422.
2. Lord Goff in *The Mahkutai* [1996] 3 All ER 502, distinguished *The Pioneer Container. The Pioneer Container* was concerned with the enforceability of a term in a sub-bailment against the bailor which turned on the scope of authority of the carriers to subcontract so as to bind the bailor, the plaintiff cargo owners. On the facts, the plaintiffs were bound by the terms of the sub-bailment because they had authorised the carrier to subcontract 'on any terms'. However, *The Mahkutai* dealt with the different issue of agreement and whether a subcontractor (the ship-owner) could have the benefit of a term in the main bill of lading contract as against the goods owners or consignees.
3. The Court of Appeal in *Sandeman Coprimar SA* v *Transitos y Transportes Integrales SL* [2003] EWCA Civ 113, [2003] QB 1270, applied the principle in *The Pioneer Container* since the importer had implicitly authorised the conclusion of a chain of contracts on certain terms and had therefore authorised sub-bailment on terms. An important development was that Lord Phillips MR (giving the judgment of the court) held that this was the position on the basis of bailment or alternatively there were collateral contracts between the importer and sub-bailees. He stated ([63]):

The principles of the law of bailment have always overlapped with those of the law of contract, for bailment and contract often go hand in hand. Where a bailee has the consent, and thus the authority, of the bailor to enter into a sub-bailment on particular terms and does so, and where those terms purport to govern the relationship not merely between the sub-bailee and the bailee, but between the sub-bailee and the bailor, it seems to us that all the elements of a collateral contract binding the sub-bailee and the bailor will be present, for there will be privity, via the agency of the bailee, and no difficulty in identifying consideration, at least if the terms are capable of resulting in benefit to each of the parties. It is easier to identify a contract in such circumstances than in the circumstances which led the Privy Council to identify one in *New Zealand Shipping Co Ltd* v *A M Satterthwaite & Co Ltd* [1975] AC 154.

4. The Law Commission Report Cm 3329 (1996) made recommendations in relation to benefits and the question of burdens imposed on third parties was outside its scope. Similarly, the Contracts (Rights of Third Parties) Act 1999 relates only to benefits.

B: Restrictions on the use of chattels

If there is a restriction on a chattel in a contract between A and B, and C purchases the chattel with notice of the restriction, is C bound by the restriction?

Lord Strathcona Steamship Company Ltd v Dominion Coal Company Ltd
[1926] AC 108 (PC)

The owners of a steamship chartered her to the plaintiffs for 10 successive seasons. The ship went into the plaintiffs' service in 1916 but at the end of that season was requisitioned by the British Government until 1919. The owners had sold the ship in 1917 and it had been resold in 1919. When the defendants purchased it in 1920, they had notice of the terms of the charterparty and covenanted with the sellers to perform and accept all responsibilities under it. However, they then refused to perform the charterparty for the 1920 season. The plaintiffs sought a declaration that the defendants were bound to carry out the charterparty and an injunction to restrain them from using the vessel in any way inconsistent with the charterparty. The defendants argued that they were not privy to the contract containing the restriction so that it was not binding on them. Held: (applying an *obiter dictum* of Knight Bruce LJ in *De Mattos* v *Gibson* (1858) 4 De G & J 276) since the defendants had purchased with notice of the terms of the charterparty relating to the use of the ship, the charterers could obtain an injunction to restrain them from employing the ship in any way inconsistent with the charterparty.

LORD SHAW: The position of the case is that the appellants are possessed of a ship with regard to which a long running charterparty is current, the existence of which was fully disclosed, together, indeed, with an obligation which the appellants appear to have accepted to respect and carry out that charterparty. The proposal of the appellants and the argument submitted by them is to the effect that they are not bound to respect and carry forward this charterparty either in law or in equity, but that, upon the contrary, they can, in defiance of its terms, of which they had knowledge, use the vessel at their will in any other way. It is accordingly, when the true facts are shown, a very simple case raising the question of whether an obligation affecting the user of the subject of sale, namely, a ship, can be ignored by the purchaser so as to enable that purchaser, who has bought a ship notified to be not a free ship but under charter, to wipe out the condition of purchase and use the ship as a free ship. It was not bought or paid for as a free ship, but it is maintained that the buyer can thus extinguish the charterer's rights in the vessel, of which he had notice, and that the charterer has no means, legal or equitable, of preventing this in law.

In the opinion of the Board the case is ruled by *De Mattos* v *Gibson* (1858) 4 De G & J 276 . . . Their Lordships think that the judgment of Knight Bruce LJ plainly applies to the present case:

> Reason and justice seem to prescribe that, at least as a general rule, where a man, by gift or purchase, acquires property from another, with knowledge of a previous contract, lawfully and for valuable consideration made by him with a third person, to use and employ the property for a particular purpose in a specified manner, the acquirer shall not to the material damage of the third person, in opposition to the contract and inconsistently with it, use and employ the property in a manner not allowable to the giver or seller.

. . . The general character of the principle on which a Court of equity acts was explained in *Tulk* v *Moxhay* (1848) 2 Ph 774, 41 ER 1143. . . . [*Tulk* v *Moxhay*] analyses the true situation of a purchaser who having bought upon the terms of the restriction upon free contract existing, thereafter when vested in the lands, attempts to divest himself of the condition under which he had bought: 'it is said that the covenant being one which does not run with the land, this Court cannot enforce it; but the question is, not whether the covenant runs with the land, but whether a party shall be permitted to use the land in a manner inconsistent with the contract entered into by his vendor, and with notice of which he purchased. Of course, the price would be affected by the covenant, and nothing could be more inequitable than that the original purchaser should be able to sell the property the next day for a greater price, in consideration of the assignee being allowed to escape from the liability which he had himself undertaken.'

In the opinion of the Board these views, much expressive of the justice and good faith of the situation, are still part of English equity jurisprudence, and an injunction can still be granted thereunder to compel, as in a court of conscience, one who obtains a conveyance or grant sub conditione from violating the condition of his purchase to the prejudice of the original contractor. Honesty forbids this; and a Court of equity will grant an injunction against it.

. . . [T]he person seeking to enforce such a restriction must, of course, have, and continue to have, an interest in the subject matter of the contract. For instance, in the case of land he must continue to hold the land in whose favour the restrictive covenant was meant to apply. That was clearly the state of matters in the case of *Tulk* v *Moxhay* applicable to the possession of real estate in Leicester Square. It was also clearly the case in *De Mattos* v *Gibson*, in which the person seeking to enforce the injunction had an interest in the user of the ship. In short, in regard to the user of land or of any chattel, an interest must remain in the subject matter of the covenant before a right can be conceded to an injunction against the violation by another of the covenant in question. . . . [T]he present is, as has been seen, a case as to the user of a ship, with regard to the subject matter of which, namely, the vessel, the respondent has, and will have during the continuance of the period covered by the charterparty, a plain interest so long as she is fit to go to sea. Again, to adopt the language of Knight Bruce LJ in the *De Mattos* v *Gibson* case:

> Why should it (the Court) not prevent the commission or continuance of a breach of such a contract, when, its subject being valuable, as for instance, a trading ship or some costly machine, the original owner and possessor, or a person claiming under him, with notice and standing in his right, having the physical control of the chattel, is diverting it from the agreed object, that object being of importance to the other? A system of laws in which such a power does not exist must surely be very defective. I repeat that, in my opinion, the power does exist here.

NOTES

1. A person who takes with notice of the restriction, and who probably pays a lower price in consequence, should not then be able to disregard that restriction.

2. The difficulty with this decision is its reliance on *Tulk* v *Moxhay* as establishing the principle, since the charterers lacked the independent proprietary interest which would be necessary to enforce a restrictive covenant under *Tulk* v *Moxhay*.

   It is not the case, despite what Lord Shaw suggested, that the charterparty itself could give that right, because a contract of hire gives only a personal right. In addition, as the interest is conferred by the very contract which it is sought to enforce, it could hardly be described as independent. The decision has therefore been heavily criticised as contrary to principle. (See Tettenborn 'Contracts, privity of contract and the purchaser of personal property' [1982] CLJ 58.)

3. In *Port Line Ltd* v *Ben Line Steamers Ltd* [1958] 2 QB 146, Diplock J refused to follow *Strathcona* because he considered that it was wrongly decided:

   > It seems, therefore, that it is in this case for the first time after more than 30 years that an English court has to grapple with the problem of what principle was really laid down in the *Strathcona* case, and whether that case was rightly decided. The difficulty I have found in

ascertaining its ratio decidendi, the impossibility which I find of reconciling the actual decision with well-established principles of law, the unsolved and, to me, insoluble problems which that decision raises combine to satisfy me that it was wrongly decided. I do not propose to follow it, I naturally express this opinion with great diffidence, but having reached a clear conclusion it is my duty to express it.

If I am wrong in my view that the case was wrongly decided, I am certainly averse from extending it one iota beyond that which, as I understand it, it purported to decide. In particular, I do not think that it purported to decide (1) that anything short of actual knowledge by the subsequent purchaser at the time of the purchase of the charterer's rights, the violation of which it is sought to restrain, is sufficient to give rise to the equity; (2) that the charterer has any remedy against the subsequent purchaser with notice except a right to restrain the use of the vessel by such purchaser in a manner inconsistent with the terms of the charter; (3) that the charterer has any positive right against the subsequent purchaser to have the vessel used in accordance with the terms of his charter. The third proposition follows from the second; ubi jus, ibi remedium. For failure by the subsequent purchaser to use the vessel in accordance with the terms of the charter entered into by his seller there is no remedy by specific performance as was held in the *Strathcona* case itself. There is equally no remedy in damages, a consideration which distinguishes the *Strathcona* case from such cases as *Lumley* v *Wagner* (1852) 1 De GM & G 604 and *Lumley* v *Gye* (1853) 2 E & B 216. The charterer's only right is coterminous with his remedy, namely, not to have the ship used by the purchaser in violation of his charter.

Thus, Diplock J considered that even if *Strathcona* was correctly decided, it would apply only if the purchaser took with *actual notice* of the terms of the restriction.

4. In the next case Browne-Wilkinson J followed *Strathcona*.

Swiss Bank Corporation v Lloyds Bank Ltd
[1979] Ch 548

The plaintiff agreed to lend money to IFT to enable IFT to acquire shares in FIBI. One of the terms of the loan agreement was that IFT should comply with the Bank of England's conditions attached to exchange control consents, including the conditions that the loan had to be used to acquire the FIBI securities and that interest and repayment of the loan should be made out of the proceeds of sale of those securities. Without exchange control consent, IFT purported to grant a charge over those securities to Lloyds Bank who, at the time, did not have actual notice of the terms of the exchange control consents. The securities were later sold without the knowledge of the plaintiff, and the plaintiff claimed damages and repayment of the loan out of the proceeds of sale. Held: if a person took a charge on property with *actual knowledge* of a contractual obligation in favour of another person, that person could be restrained by injunction from exercising his rights so as to interfere with the performance of that contractual obligation. Lloyds Bank had only constructive knowledge which was not sufficient.

BROWNE-WILKINSON J: . . . [I]n my judgment the authorities establish the following propositions. (1) The principle stated by Knight Bruce LJ in *De Mattos* v *Gibson*, 4 De G & J 276, is good law and represents the counterpart in equity of the tort of knowing interference with contractual rights. (2) A person proposing to deal with property in such a way as to cause a breach of a contract affecting that property will be restrained by injunction from so doing if when he acquired that property he had actual knowledge of that contract. (3) A plaintiff is entitled to such an injunction even if he has no proprietary interest in the property: his right to have his contract performed is a sufficient interest. (4) There is no case in which such an injunction has been granted against a defendant who acquired the property with only constructive, as opposed to actual, notice of the contract. In my judgment contructive notice is not sufficient, since actual knowledge of the contract is a requisite element in the tort.

NOTE: The equitable counterpart of the tort of knowing interference with contractual rights is the principle in *Lumley* v *Gye* (1853) 2 E & B 216. The plaintiff, a theatre owner, entered into a contract with Wagner whereby she was to sing at his theatre for a season and was not to sing elsewhere during that period without his written consent. The defendant, the owner of a rival theatre, persuaded Wagner to break this contract with the plaintiff by promising to pay her more. The plaintiff brought an action for damages against the defendant, alleging that the defendant had induced Wagner to break her contract with him. Held: the plaintiff was entitled to damages since the defendant had committed the tort of intentionally procuring a breach of contract.

Strathcona may well be based on this principle rather than *Tulk* v *Moxhay* because the tort of knowing interference with another's contractual rights requires the person who interferes to have actual knowledge of the contract, whereas constructive notice is all that is required in *Tulk* v *Moxhay*. This would also remove the difficulties of establishing an independent proprietary interest as required by *Tulk* v *Moxhay*. However, the *Strathcona* principle is not as wide as *Lumley* v *Gye* since it is limited to protection in the form of an injunction.

Law Debenture Trust Corp plc v Ural Caspian Oil Co. Ltd
[1993] 1 WLR 138; [1994] 3 WLR 1221 (CA)

The share capital of four companies which had carried on business in Russia before the 1917 Revolution was purchased in 1986 by L Ltd ('Overseas') under a contract containing a 'negative pledge', whereby L Ltd covenanted with the companies that it would pay any compensation received from the Soviet authorities to the plaintiff as trustee for the existing shareholders and would not transfer ownership of the companies except on terms that the transferee entered into a similar undertaking.

Subsequently L Ltd transferred its shareholding to H Ltd, but no such undertaking was entered into by H Ltd. H Ltd later transferred its shareholding to C Ltd. The Russian companies were paid £13.2m in compensation which C Ltd refused to pay to the plaintiff.

The plaintiff sought to argue that H and C were liable in tort for causing or procuring the breach of L Ltd's covenant with knowledge of the agreement between the Russian companies and L Ltd (i.e. the principle in *Lumley* v *Gye*). The plaintiff also sought to amend the statement of claim to argue that since H and C took the shares with knowledge of the covenant, they were under an obligation to perform the covenant and a positive injunction should issue (i.e. the principle in *De Mattos* v *Gibson*).

Hoffmann J accepted the equitable principle in *De Mattos* but considered that it was not a principle of general application and that it could not apply on these facts when what was being sought was a compelling remedy.

Hoffmann J ([1993] 1 WLR 138):

The plaintiff's difficulty, as it seems to me, is not whether the principle applies but the extent of the remedy which it provides. One thing is beyond doubt: it does not provide a panacea for outflanking the doctrine of privity of contract. In the *Strathcona* case [1926] AC 108, 119, Lord Shaw said:

It has sometimes been considered that *Tulk* v *Moxhay* (1848) 2 Ph 774, 777 and *De Mattos* v *Gibson* (1858) 4 De G & J 276 carried forward to and laid upon the shoulders of an alienee with notice the obligations of the alienor, and, therefore, that the former is liable to the covenantee in specific performance as by the law of contract, and under a species of implied privity. This is not so; the remedy is a remedy in equity by way of injunction against acts inconsistent with the covenant, with notice of which the land was acquired.

Thus the *De Mattos* principle permits no more than the grant of a negative injunction, to restrain the third party from doing acts which would be inconsistent with performance of the contract by the original contracting party. The terms of the injunction must be such that refraining altogether from action would constitute compliance. A time charter, as Diplock J pointed out in *Port Line Ltd* v *Ben Line Steamers Ltd* [1958] 2 QB 146 is a contract under which the owner is under a positive obligation to provide the vessel. It is clear that Lord Shaw in *Strathcona* did not intend to order the purchaser to fulfil this obligation. The injunction only prohibited him from doing an inconsistent act, namely chartering the vessel to someone else. In practice, the Board thought that this would provide the owner with an economic incentive to perform the charter: as Lord Shaw said, at p. 125: 'It is incredible that the owners will lay up the vessel rather than permit its use under the contract.' But such dog-in-the-manger behaviour would not have been a breach of the injunction.

In the *Swiss Bank* case [1979] Ch 548 Browne-Wilkinson J analysed the other cases in which it appeared that the *De Mattos* principle had been applied, and showed that in each case the remedy was a purely negative restraint . . .

On the question of the tort of inducing the breach of contract, Hoffmann J accepted that in taking the shares H Ltd was knowingly assisting in the breach of contract by L Ltd, but that C could not have participated in a breach of contract on the transfer to C by H since there was no contract between H and the plaintiff. However, he was prepared to extend the principle to interference with a remedy which would otherwise have been available on the basis that, because H knew of the breach of covenant, H could have been ordered to transfer the shares back to L in order to prevent the contractual obligation between L and the plaintiff being defeated. The transfer to C had deprived the plaintiff of this remedy and therefore there was a claim in tort against C.

The Court of Appeal ([1994] 3 WLR 1221) allowed C's appeal. In order to fall within the principle in *Lumley* v *Gye* there needed to be a right in the plaintiff which was violated by an actionable wrong on the transfer between H and C. Held: there was no actionable wrong.

SIR THOMAS BINGHAM MR: . . . It is not in dispute that Hilldon could, on timely application, have been ordered to retransfer the shares to Overseas and restrained from transferring them on to Caspian or anyone else. It is said that Hilldon could only be restrained from acting unlawfully and that it would not be liable to such restraint if such onward transfer were lawful. Therefore onward transfer is to be regarded as unlawful, as violating Law Debenture's right that it should not take place. As a party to this onward transfer Caspian are party to the unlawfulness and so liable.

To my mind this chain of reasoning harbours a fallacy. It is of course true that the courts restrain the commission of unlawful acts such as threatened breaches of contract or torts or breaches of trust and grant mandatory orders for the doing of things which it would be unlawful not to do. But all injunctive orders are not of this kind. The court will restrain a defendant and potential judgment debtor from making himself judgment-proof by dissipating his assets and may order him to give disclosure of assets in support of the injunction. But the defendant violates no legal right of the plaintiff if he makes himself judgment-proof by dissipating his assets before he is enjoined from doing so and he does not act unlawfully in failing to give disclosure before he is ordered to do so. . . .

Caspian can be liable to Law Debenture if and only if Hilldon's transfer of the shares to it was tortious. But at the time this transfer was made Hilldon was the full legal and beneficial owner of the shares. It had no contractual relationship of any kind with Law Debenture. It was liable to Law Debenture for its tortious conduct in procuring Overseas' breach of its contract with Law Debenture, but that was all. It was open to Law Debenture to seek an interlocutory injunction restraining Hilldon from making onward transfer and a final injunction ordering retransfer, but application had not been made and injunctions had not been granted. Until some injunction was granted, Hilldon was in my judgment entitled to do what it would with its own. I cannot regard the onward transfer as an actionable wrong, and it would in my view defeat the ingenuity of any pleader to frame a plausible statement of claim based on that transfer alone.

[Counsel] for Caspian criticised the judgment of Hoffmann LJ on the ground that, although the judge listed an actionable wrong as one of the ingredients of the cause of action he failed to identify any relevant actionable wrong on the part of Hilldon and Caspian. That seems to be a fair criticism. In concentrating on the right, it seems to me that the judge did take his eye off the wrong.

NOTES
1. This case rests on the assumption that the *De Mattos* and *Lumley* v *Gye* principles are not the same and that they may be pleaded as alternatives.
2. See Cane (1995) 111 LQR 400.

11

Common Mistake and Frustration

In the absence of contractual allocation of the risk in question (*William Sindall plc* v *Cambridgeshire County Council* [1994] 1 WLR 1016, *page 497*), if the parties entered into a contract under the same mistaken assumption, that contract may be void for 'common mistake' if the mistake is so fundamental that it 'nullifies' consent. This is often referred to as 'initial impossibility' because the impossibility already exists when the contract is made.

The impossibility may be 'subsequent', i.e., after the formation of the contract, events occur, without the fault of either party, which render further performance of the contract either impossible, illegal, or radically different from what was originally envisaged. In this situation the contract may be automatically discharged on the grounds of frustration and the parties will be excused further performance of their contractual obligations. Statute also provides for adjustment of obligations arising before frustration. Again, however, the frustration doctrine will apply only in the absence of an express provision in the contract allocating the risk. If the contract contains a *force majeure* clause covering the event that has occurred, that *force majeure* clause will govern and not the frustration doctrine.

The existence of express contractual provisions enables the parties to allocate the risks in the way they wish so that the use of such provisions reduces the potential scope of application of the doctrines of common mistake and frustration.

Although determining the existence of either initial or subsequent impossibility may turn on fine distinctions of timing (*page 530*), the legal consequences are quite different.

SECTION 1: CONTRACTUAL ALLOCATION OF RISK

(a) Assuming the risk

If one party has assumed the risk of the event in question or has assumed the risk of the existence of the subject matter, in the event that the risk materialises or the subject matter is found not to have existed, that party will be responsible and cannot rely on the legal doctrines of mistake (initial impossibility) or frustration (subsequent impossibility).

McRae v Commonwealth Disposals Commission
(1951) 84 CLR 377 (High Court of Australia)

The Commission invited tenders for an oil tanker lying on Jourmaund Reef and said to contain oil. The plaintiffs' tender was accepted and a sales advice note described what was sold as 'one oil tanker including contents . . .'. In fact there was no such tanker at that location. The plaintiffs sought damages for breach of contract. The Commission alleged that because the subject matter of the contract did not exist, the alleged contract was void. Held: the plaintiffs were entitled to damages for breach of contract because the Commission was in breach of its 'promise' that there was an oil tanker at the location.

DIXON AND FULLAGAR JJ: The position so far, then, may be summed up as follows. It was not decided in *Couturier* v *Hastie* (1856) 5 HL Cas 673 that the contract in that case was void. The question whether it was void or not did not arise. If it had arisen, as in an action by the purchaser for damages, it would have turned on the ulterior question whether the contract was subject to an implied condition precedent. Whatever might then have been held on the facts of *Couturier* v *Hastie*, it is impossible in this case to imply any such term. The terms of the contract and the surrounding circumstances clearly exclude any such implication. The buyers relied upon, and acted upon, the assertion of the seller that there was a tanker in existence. It is not a case in which the parties can be seen to have proceeded on the basis of a common assumption of fact so as to justify the conclusion that the correctness of the assumption was intended by both parties to be a condition precedent to the creation of contractual obligations. The officers of the Commission made an assumption, but the plaintiffs did not make an assumption in the same sense. They knew nothing except what the Commission had told them. If they had been asked, they would certainly not have said: 'Of course, if there is no tanker, there is no contract'. They would have said: 'We shall have to go and take possession of the tanker. We simply accept the Commission's assurance that there is a tanker and the Commission's promise to give us that tanker.' The only proper construction of the contract is that it included a promise by the Commission that there was a tanker in the position specified. The Commission contracted that there was a tanker there. If, on the other hand, the case of *Couturier* v *Hastie* and this case ought to be treated as cases raising a question of 'mistake', then the Commission cannot in this case rely on any mistake as avoiding the contract, because any mistake was induced by the serious fault of their own servants, who asserted the existence of a tanker recklessly and without any reasonable ground. There *was* a contract, and the Commission contracted that a tanker existed in the position specified. Since there was no such tanker, there has been a breach of contract, and the plaintiffs are entitled to damages for that breach.

The contract was made in Melbourne, and it would seem that its proper law is Victorian law. Section 11 of the Victorian Goods Act 1928 corresponds to s. 6 of the English Sale of Goods Act 1893. This has been generally supposed to represent the legislature's view of the effect of *Couturier* v *Hastie*. Whether it correctly represents the effect of the decision in that case or not, it seems clear that the section has no application to the facts of the present case. Here the goods never existed, and the seller ought to have known that they did not exist.

NOTES

1. *Couturier* v *Hastie* (1856) 5 HL Cas 673, a mistake case, is discussed below *page 510*.

2. In *Associated Japanese Bank (International) Ltd* v *Credit du Nord SA* [1989] 1 WLR 255, *page 503*, Steyn J considered that a party seeking to rely on common mistake must have reasonable grounds for his belief. He cited *McRae* in support of this principle, i.e., that the Commission had no reasonable ground for asserting that there was a tanker in the position specified and was therefore at fault in inducing any mistake. The events giving rise to a claim based on mistake or frustration must not be attributable to the fault of one of the parties or that party will be taken to have accepted responsibility for them. (In the context of frustration, the situation where the event occurs as a result of the fault of one of the parties is discussed at *page 498 below*.)

3. From a practical perspective, if the High Court had dealt with this case on the basis that it was a common mistake, the contract would have been void, and although the plaintiffs could have recovered the purchase price of the wreck, they could not have recovered the cost of the salvage expedition (see *page 372*).

William Sindall plc v Cambridgeshire County Council
[1994] 1 WLR 1016 (CA)

Builders agreed to purchase land from the county council on terms whereby the land was stated to be sold subject to easements, liabilities, and public rights affecting it, but without prejudice to the vendor's duty to disclose all latent easements and incumbrances which it knew to affect the property. The council had stated that so far as it was aware there were none, and the sale contract was concluded in March 1989 at a price of £5m. By the time that the builders had obtained planning permission for a residential development 18 months later, the land was worth less than half of that purchase price because of a fall in land values. In October 1990, the builders discovered that, unknown to either party, a foul sewer was buried under the land. The builders claimed that, since they had to leave a six-foot wide maintenance strip, this affected their plans for a residential development on the land, and they sought to rescind the contract for misrepresentation and common mistake, and to recover the purchase price. The judge at first instance held that they were entitled to rescind (exercising his discretion not to award damages in lieu of rescission under s. 2(2) of the Misrepresentation Act 1967) so that the purchase price plus interest was recoverable. Held: on appeal, it was not possible for the builders to rescind because (i) the contract terms allocated the risk of incumbrances not known to the vendor to the purchaser so that the law of mistake could not apply, and (ii) there could be no claim based on misrepresentation since the council's representation was that it had no actual knowledge of the existence of the sewer and that it had made reasonable investigations. It was held that the council had made reasonable investigations and therefore it could not be liable for a subsequently discovered defect in title. (See *pages 594–8* for discussion of misrepresentation.)

HOFFMANN LJ: The judge found that in the absence of any actionable misrepresentation, Sindall was entitled to rescind the contract for a common mistake as to the existence of a sewer. This is at first sight a startling result. As Steyn J said in *Associated Japanese Bank (International) Ltd v Crédit du Nord SA* [1989] 1 WLR 255, 268:

> Logically, before one can turn to the rules as to mistake, whether at common law or in equity, one must first determine whether the contract itself, by express or implied condition precedent or otherwise, provides who bears the risk of the relevant mistake. It is at this hurdle that many pleas of mistake will either fail or prove to have been unnecessary. Only if the contract is silent on the point is there scope for invoking mistake.

When the judge speaks of the contract allocating risk 'by express or implied condition precedent or otherwise' I think he includes rules of general law applicable to the contract and which, for example, provide that, in the absence of express warranty, the law is caveat emptor. This would, in my view, allocate the risk of an unknown defect in goods to the buyer, even though it is not mentioned in the contract. Similarly, the rule in *Hill v Harris* [1965] 2 QB 601 that a lessor or vendor does not impliedly warrant that the premises are fit for any particular purpose means that the contract allocates the risk of the premises being unfit for such a purpose. I should say that neither in *Grist v Bailey* [1967] Ch 532 nor in *Laurence v Lexcourt Holdings Ltd* [1978] 1 WLR 1128 did the judges who decided those cases at first instance advert to the question of contractual allocation of risk. I am not sure that the decisions would have been the same if they had.

In this case the contract says in express terms that it is subject to all easements other than those of which the vendor knows or has the means of knowledge. This allocates the risk of such incumbrances to the buyer and leaves no room for rescission on the grounds of mistake.

EVANS LJ: . . . [O]n any view of the matter . . . the first question is whether the contract on its true construction covers the new situation which has arisen by reason of a change of circumstances (frustration) or the emergence of a factual situation different from that which was assumed (mutual mistake). If the scope of the contrast is wide enough to cover the new, or newly discovered, situation, then there is no room either for discharge by frustration or for rescission in equity on the grounds of mistake. Put another way, if the agreed terms provide for this situation, then the parties have 'allocated the risk' as between themselves, as [counsel for the council] submits that they did in the present case.

[Evans LJ construed the terms so that they allocated the risk and continued:]

Subject, therefore, to the claims for rescission based on actionable misrepresentation, the contract for sale as a matter of construction requires the builders to accept the property notwithstanding the presence of the pipeline and the city council's easement. . . .

NOTES
1. Although the judgments refer to the possibility of rescission for mutual mistake, it is important to appreciate that the term 'mutual' is often used in the case law to refer to a common mistake but should not be confused with true mutual (or cross-purpose) mistake, discussed at *page 80*. In addition, at the time of this decision there was thought to be an equitable jurisdiction to rescind in equity (often on terms) for common mistake, although the mistake was not sufficiently fundamental at common law to render the contract void. The existence of such a an equitable jurisdiction has now been denied by the Court of Appeal in *Great Peace Shipping Ltd* v *Tsavliris (International) Ltd* [2002] EWCA Civ 1407, [2003] QB 679. This aspect of the decision is discussed at *page 514*.
2. *Kalsep Ltd* v *X-Flow BV, The Times*, 3 May 2001, provides an example of a clause in a contract which operated to exclude the doctrine of mistake.

(b) Event occurs as a result of the fault of one of the parties
This is most likely to occur in the context of subsequent impossibility. The essence of frustration is that the extraneous event, which renders the contract impossible to perform, is not attributable to any act or fault of one of the parties. If it is, the impossibility is said to be 'self-induced' and the frustration doctrine cannot apply.

Maritime National Fish Ltd v *Ocean Trawlers Ltd*
[1935] AC 524 (PC)

The defendants chartered a steam trawler, the 'St Cuthbert', from the plaintiffs solely for fishing use. It could only operate as a trawler with an otter trawl, and both parties knew that a licence was required. The defendants applied to the Minister for licences for five trawlers which they were operating (including the 'St Cuthbert'). The Minister indicated that only three would be granted and asked the defendants to name the three trawlers to which the licences would be applied. The three named by the defendants did not include the 'St Cuthbert' and licences were granted for only the three named trawlers. The plaintiffs claimed the charter hire and the defendants pleaded the charter was frustrated because it was impossible to perform. Held: it was not frustrated because the defendants' own election had prevented this trawler from having a licence to fish. Therefore the defendants were liable for the hire.

LORD WRIGHT (delivering the judgment of the court): . . . The essence of 'frustration' is that it should not be due to the act or election of the party. There does not appear to be any authority which has been decided directly on this point. There is, however, a reference to the question in the speech of Lord Sumner in *Bank Line, Ltd* v *Arthur Capel & Co.* [1919] AC 435. What he says is:

> . . . I think it is now well settled that the principle of frustration of an adventure assumes that the frustration arises without blame or fault on either side. Reliance cannot be placed on a self-induced frustration; indeed, such conduct might give the other party the option to treat the contract as repudiated. . . .

If it be assumed that the performance of the contract was dependent on a licence being granted, it was [the appellants'] election which prevented performance, and on that assumption it was the appellants' own default which frustrated the adventure: the appellants cannot rely on their own default to excuse them from liability under the contract.

NOTES

1. In *Ocean Tramp Tankers Corporation* v *V/O Sovfracht, The Eugenia* [1964] 2 QB 226, 'The Eugenia' was chartered for a voyage to India via the Black Sea. There was a clause in the charterparty which provided that the vessel was not to be taken into a war zone without the owner's consent. The vessel entered the Suez Canal in breach of this war clause and became trapped when the Canal was blocked. The charterers claimed that the charterparty was frustrated. Lord Denning MR stated that: 'One thing that is obvious is that the charterers cannot rely on the fact that the *Eugenia* was trapped in the canal; for that was their own fault. They were in breach of the war clause in entering it. They cannot rely on a self-induced frustration, see *Maritime National Fish Ltd* v *Ocean Trawlers Ltd* [1935] AC 524.'

2. If one party wishes to argue that a particular event was caused by the other's fault, he or she must prove it on the balance of probabilities (*Joseph Constantine Steamship Line Ltd* v *Imperial Smelting Corporation Ltd* [1942] AC 154). The other will then be in breach of contract.

3. The mere existence of a choice may be sufficient to establish that what follows was self-induced.

J. Lauritzen AS v Wijsmuller BV, The Super Servant Two
[1990] 1 Lloyd's Rep 1 (CA)

The defendants agreed to carry the plaintiffs' drilling rig and deliver it between 20 June and 20 August 1981, using either 'Super Servant One' or 'Super Servant Two' (the 'Dan King' contract). The defendants had intended to use 'Super Servant Two' for this contract and had entered into other contracts with third parties which they could only perform using 'Super Servant One'. On 29 January 1981, the 'Super Servant Two' sank, and in February 1981 the defendants informed the plaintiffs that they would not perform. When the plaintiffs alleged breach of contract the defendants argued that they were not liable because the contract had been frustrated by the sinking of 'Super Servant Two'. Held: according to the contract terms the defendants could have satisfied their obligation by using 'Super Servant One' after 'Super Servant Two' had sunk but had elected not to do so. The frustration doctrine could only assist a party who had contracted to perform a contract with a vessel which through no fault of his own no longer existed. It therefore could not apply here since there was an alternative and the sinking of 'Super Servant Two' did not automatically bring the contract to an end.

BINGHAM LJ: . . . The argument in this case raises important issues on the English law of frustration. . . .

Certain propositions, established by the highest authority, are not open to question:

1. The doctrine of frustration was evolved to mitigate the rigour of the common law's insistence on literal performance of absolute promises (*Hirji Mulji* v *Cheong Yue Steamship Co. Ltd* (sub

nom. *Dharsi Nanji* v *Cheong Yue Steamship Co. Ltd*), (1926) 24 Ll L Rep 209 at p. 213, col. 2; [1926] AC 497 at p. 510: *Denny, Mott & Dickson Ltd* v *James B. Fraser & Co. Ltd* [1944] AC 265 at p. 275; *Joseph Constantine Steamship Line Ltd* v *Imperial Smelting Corporation Ltd* (1941) 70 Ll L Rep 1 at p. 12, col. 2; [1942] AC 154 at p. 171). The object of the doctrine was to give effect to the demands of justice, to achieve a just and reasonable result, to do what is reasonable and fair, as an expedient to escape from injustice where such would result from enforcement of a contract in its literal terms after a significant change in circumstances (*Hirji Mulji*, sup., at p. 213, col. 2; p. 510; *Joseph Constantine Steamship Line Ltd* (sup.), at p. 18, col, 2; p. 23, col. 1; pp. 183, 193; *National Carriers Ltd* v *Panalpina (Northern) Ltd* [1981] AC 675 at p. 701).

2. Since the effect of frustration is to kill the contract and discharge the parties from further liability under it, the doctrine is not to be lightly invoked, must be kept within very narrow limits and ought not to be extended (*Bank Line Ltd* v *Arthur Capel & Co.* [1919] AC 435 at p. 459; *Davis Contractors Ltd* sup., at pp. 715, 727; *Pioneer Shipping Ltd* v *B.T.P. Tioxide Ltd (The Nema)*, [1981] 2 Lloyd's Rep 239 at p. 253, col. 2; [1982] AC 724 at 752).

3. Frustration brings the contract to an end forthwith, without more and automatically (*Hirji Mulji*, sup. at pp. 211, 212; pp. 505, 509; *Maritime National Fish Ltd* v *Ocean Trawlers Ltd* (1935) 51 Lloyd's L Rep 299 at p. 302; [1935] AC 524 at p. 527; *Joseph Constantine Steamship Line Ltd* sup., at pp. 9, 11, 12, 20, 25; pp. 163, 170, 171, 187, 200; *Denny Mott & Dickson Ltd* sup. at p. 274).

4. The essence of frustration is that it should not be due to the act or election of the party seeking to rely on it (*Hirji Mulji*, sup., at p. 213; p. 510; *Maritime National Fish Ltd* sup., at p. 303; p. 530; *Joseph Constantine Steamship Ltd* sup., at p. 12; p. 170; *Denny Mott & Dickson Ltd* sup., at p. 274; *Davis Contractors Ltd* sup., at p. 728. A frustrating event must be some outside event or extraneous change of situation *(Paal Wilson & Co. A/S* v *Partenreederi Hannah Blumenthal (The Hannah Blumenthal)*, [1983] 1 Lloyd's Rep 103 at p. 112; [1983] 1 AC 854 at p. 909).

5. A frustrating event must take place without blame or fault on the side of the party seeking to rely on it *(Bank Line Ltd* sup., at 452; *Joseph Constantine Steamship Ltd* sup., at p. 12; p. 171; *Davis Contractors Ltd* sup., at p. 729; *The Hannah Blumenthal* [1982] 1 Lloyd's Rep 582 at p. 592; [1983] 1 Lloyd's Rep 103 at p. 112; [1983] 1 AC 854 at pp. 882, 909).

. . .

Had the *Dan King* contract provided for carriage by *Super Servant Two* with no alternative, and that vessel had been lost before the time for performance, then assuming no negligence by Wijsmuller (as for purposes of this question we must), I feel sure the contract would have been frustrated. The doctrine must avail a party who contracts to perform a contract of carriage with a vessel which, through no fault of his, no longer exists. But that is not this case. The *Dan King* contract did provide an alternative. When that contract was made one of the contracts eventually performed by *Super Servant One* during the period of contractual carriage of *Dan King* had been made, the other had not, at any rate finally. Wijsmuller have not alleged that when the *Dan King* contract was made either vessel was earmarked for its performance. That, no doubt, is why an option was contracted for. Had it been foreseen when the *Dan King* contract was made that *Super Servant Two* would be unavailable for performance, whether because she had been deliberately sold or accidentally sunk, Lauritzen at least would have thought it no matter since the carriage could be performed with the other . . . the present case does not fall within the very limited class of cases in which the law will relieve one party from an absolute promise he has chosen to make.

. . . I cannot, furthermore, reconcile Wijsmuller's argument with the reasoning or the decision in *Maritime National Fish Ltd* sup. In that case the Privy Council declined to speculate why the charterers selected three of the five vessels to be licensed but, as I understand the case, regarded the interposition of human choice after the allegedly frustrating event as fatal to the plea of frustration. If Wijsmuller are entitled to succeed here, I cannot see why the charterers lost there. The cases on frustrating delay do not, I think, help Wijsmuller since it is actual and prospective delay (whether or not recognised as frustrating by a party at the time) which frustrates the contract, not a party's election or decision to treat the delay as frustrating. I have no doubt that force majeure clauses are, where their terms permit, to be construed and applied as in the commodity cases on which Wijsmuller relied, but it is in my view inconsistent with the doctrine of frustration as previously understood on high authority that its application should depend on any decision, however reasonable and commercial, of the party seeking to rely on it.

NOTES

1. Bingham LJ considered that the existence of a choice was fatal no matter how reasonable and commercial the decision to elect had been.

   Treitel's view, that if the party acted reasonably in making the election he or she could use such means as remained available to perform some of the contracts and claim that the others were frustrated by the supervening event, was rejected by the Court of Appeal. Dillon LJ stated:

   > It is the view of Professor Treitel, expressed both in his own book on the Law of Contract—see the 7th ed. at pp. 6/4–5 and 700–701— and in the current editions of well-known textbooks of which he is editor or an editor, that where a party has entered into a number of contracts with other parties and an uncontemplated supervening event has the result that he is deprived of the means of satisfying all those contracts, he can, provided he acts 'reasonably' in making his election, elect to use such means as remains available to him to perform some of the contracts, and claim that the others, which he does not perform, have been frustrated by the supervening event. The reasoning depends on the proposition that if it is known to those concerned that the party will have entered into commitments with others and if he acts 'reasonably' in his allocation of his remaining means to his commitments, the chain of causation between the uncontemplated supervening event and the non-performance of those of his contracts which will not have been performed will not have been broken by the election to apply his remaining means in a 'reasonable' way. . . . Such an approach is however inconsistent to my mind with the view expressed by Lord Wright in that passage in *Maritime National Fish* which I have already cited, where he said:
   >
   > > It is immaterial to speculate why they preferred to put forward for licences the three trawlers which they actually selected.
   >
   > It is also, as my Lord has pointed out, inconsistent with the long accepted view that frustration brings the contract to an end forthwith, without more ado automatically. Plainly the sinking of *Super Servant Two* did not do that, since even after that sinking the defendants could have used *Super Servant One* to perform the contract.

   See Treitel's assessment in *The Law of Contract*, 11th edn, pp. 907–8 and in *Frustration and Force Majeure* (Sweet & Maxwell, 2nd ed, 2004), Chapter 14.

2. It appears that the court considered that the risk of the defendant being over-committed had been placed on the defendant. If the defendant had wished to alter this, an appropriately drafted *force majeure* clause could have been incorporated.

   It is evident that the courts prefer the risk to be placed on one of the parties to the contract, thereby avoiding the application of the frustration doctrine.

3. See Swanton (1990) 2 JCL 206 and McKendrick [1990] LMCLQ 153.

Great Peace Shipping Ltd v *Tsavliris Salvage (International) Ltd*
[2002] EWCA Civ 1407, [2003] QB 679 (CA)

[For facts and further discussion of this case *see pages 508 and 514.*]

Lord Phillips MR (giving the judgment of the Court of Appeal) considered that the question of assumption of risk and whether the impossibility is attributable to the fault of one of the parties are similar in effect:

75 Just as the doctrine of frustration only applies if the contract contains no provision that covers the situation, the same should be true of common mistake. If, on true construction of the contract, a party warrants that the subject matter of the contract exists, or that it will be possible to perform the contract, there will be no scope to hold the contract void on the ground of common mistake.

76 If one applies the passage from the judgment of Lord Alverstone CJ in *Blakeley* v *Muller & Co* 19 TLR 186, . . . to a case of common mistake, it suggests that the following elements must be present if common mistake is to avoid a contract: (i) there must be a common assumption as to the existence of a state of affairs; (ii) there must be no warranty by either party that that state of affairs exists; (iii) the non-existence of the state of affairs must not be attributable to the fault of either party; (iv) the non-existence of the state of affairs must render performance of the contract impossible; (v) the state of affairs may be the existence, or a vital attribute, of the consideration to be provided or circumstances which must subsist if performance of the contractual adventure is to be possible.

77 The second and third of these elements are well exemplified by the decision of the High Court of Australia in *McRae* v *Commonwealth Disposals Commission* (1951) 84 CLR 377.

[Lord Phillips then discussed the facts and leading judgment of Dixon and Fullagar JJ, extract *at page 496*, and continued:]

[The English doctrine of mistake] fills a gap in the contract where it transpires that it is impossible of performance without the fault of either party and the parties have not, expressly or by implication, dealt with their rights and obligations in that eventuality. In *Associated Japanese Bank (International) Ltd* v *Crédit du Nord SA* [1989] 1 WLR 255, 268 Steyn J observed:

'Logically, before one can turn to the rules as to mistake, whether at common law or in equity, one must first determine whether the contract itself, by express or implied condition precedent or otherwise, provides who bears the risk of the relevant mistake. It is at this hurdle that many pleas of mistake will either fail or prove to have been unnecessary. Only if the contract is silent on the point, is there scope for invoking mistake.'

81 In *William Sindall plc* v *Cambridgeshire County Council* [1994] 1 WLR 1016, 1035 Hoffmann LJ commented that such allocation of risk can come about by rules of general law applicable to contract, such as 'caveat emptor' in the law of sale of goods or the rule that a lessor or vendor of land does not impliedly warrant that the premises are fit for any particular purpose, so that this risk is allocated by the contract to the lessee or purchaser. . . .

84 Once the court determines that unforeseen circumstances have, indeed, resulted in the contract being impossible of performance, it is next necessary to determine whether, on true construction of the contract, one or other party has undertaken responsibility for the subsistence of the assumed state of affairs. This is another way of asking whether one or other party has undertaken the risk that it may not prove possible to perform the contract, and the answer to this question may well be the same as the answer to the question of whether the impossibility of performance is attributable to the fault of one or other of the parties.

85 Circumstances where a contract is void as a result of common mistake are likely to be less common than instances of frustration. Supervening events which defeat the contractual adventure will frequently not be the responsibility of either party. Where, however, the parties agree that something shall be done which is impossible at the time of making the agreement, it is much more likely that, on true construction of the agreement, one or other will have undertaken responsibility for the mistaken state of affairs. This may well explain why cases where contracts have been found to be void in consequence of common mistake are few and far between.

NOTE: Lord Phillips made a very important practical point, namely that by its very nature initial impossibility is likely to be less common than supervening impossibility. It also follows from the nature of impossibility existing at the time of contracting, that it is more likely that the contract will in fact have allocated that risk to one of the contractual parties.

In *An Introduction to the Law of Contract* (5th edn, Clarendon, 1995), Atiyah stated, at p. 226, that 'as a rule pre-existing facts could have been discovered by the parties'. This may imply a degree of fault on the part of parties who have entered into a contract on the basis of a common mistake. It may well explain the fact that the doctrine of mistake is of limited scope and that the courts will not easily grant relief in such cases.

SECTION 2: THEORETICAL BASIS FOR THE DOCTRINES OF COMMON MISTAKE AND FRUSTRATION

(a) The implied term theory

In the context of common mistake there was alleged to be an implied condition precedent that the goods forming the subject matter of the contract should exist at the time that the contract was entered into. This was the interpretation adopted by Denning LJ in *Solle* v *Butcher* [1950] 1 KB 671 and can be seen in the analysis of common mistake in *McRae* v *Commonwealth Disposals Commission, page 495*. It was also the basis accepted by Steyn J in *Associated Japanese Bank (International) Ltd* v *Crédit du Nord*.

Associated Japanese Bank (International) Ltd v *Crédit du Nord*
[1989] 1 WLR 255

On a sale and lease back transaction, the plaintiff bank purchased four specified machines from Bennett and then leased them back to him.

Bennett received over £1 million under the transaction. As a condition of the transaction, Bennett's obligations under the lease back transaction were guaranteed by the defendant bank. Both banks believed that the four machines existed and were in Bennett's possession. After Bennett failed to keep up the payments under the lease it was discovered that the machines had never existed. When Bennett was declared bankrupt the plaintiff sought to enforce the guarantee against the defendant. The defendant argued that the guarantee was void for common mistake as to the existence of the machines. Held: on its true construction, the guarantee was subject to a condition precedent that there was a lease in respect of four existing machines. As these machines did not exist the plaintiff bank's claim failed.

STEYN J: . . . [I]t remains to be considered whether there was an *implied* condition precedent that the lease related to four existing machines. In the present contract such a condition may only be held to be implied if one of two applicable tests is satisfied. The first is that such an implication is necessary to give business efficacy to the relevant contract, i.e. the guarantee. In other words, the criterion is whether the implication is necessary to render the contract (the guarantee) workable. That is usually described as the *Moorcock* test, being a reference to *The Moorcock* (1889) 14 P.D. 64. It may well be that this stringent test is not satisfied because the guarantee is workable in the sense that all that is required is that the guarantors who assumed accessory obligations must pay what is due under the lease. But there is another type of implication, which seems more appropriate in the present context. It is possible to imply a term if the court is satisfied that reasonable men, faced with the suggested term which was ex hypothesi not expressed in the contract, would without hesitation say: yes, of course, that is 'so obvious that it goes without saying:' see *Shirlaw* v *Southern Foundries (1926) Ltd.* [1939] 2 K.B. 206, 227, *per* MacKinnon L.J. Although broader in scope than the *Moorcock* test, it is nevertheless a stringent test, and it will only be permissible to hold that an implication has been established on this basis in comparatively rare cases, notably when one is dealing with a commercial instrument such as a guarantee for reward. Nevertheless, against the contextual background of the fact that both parties were informed that the machines existed, and the express terms of the guarantee, I have come to the firm conclusion that the guarantee contained an implied condition precedent that the lease related to existing machines. . . .

For both parties the guarantee of obligations under a lease with non-existent machines was essentially different from a guarantee of a lease with four machines which both parties at the time of the contract believed to exist. The guarantee is an accessory contract. The non-existence of the subject matter of the principal contract is therefore of fundamental importance. Indeed the analogy of the classic res extincta cases, so much discussed in the authorities, is fairly close. In my judgment the stringent test of common law mistake is satisfied: the guarantee is void ab initio.

It was originally considered that the doctrine of frustration was based on the implication of a term.

Taylor v Caldwell
(1863) 3 B & S 826; 122 ER 309 (QB)

On 27 May 1862, the plaintiffs entered into a contract with the defendants by which the defendants agreed to let the plaintiffs have the use of Surrey Gardens and Music Hall on 17 June, 15 July, and 5 and 19 August for the purpose of giving a series of four grand concerts and fetes. On 11 June (before the first of these dates on which a concert was to be given), the Hall was destroyed by fire, without the fault of either party. The concerts could not be given as intended. The plaintiffs argued that the defendants were in breach of contract in failing to supply the Hall and they sought damages for their wasted advertising expenditure. Held: the continuation of the contract was subject to an implied condition that the parties would be excused if the subject matter was destroyed. Therefore, the contract was discharged by frustration and both parties were released.

BLACKBURN J (delivering the judgment of the court): . . . [W]here, from the nature of the contract, it appears that the parties must from the beginning have known that it could not be fulfilled unless when the time for the fulfilment of the contract arrived some particular specified thing continued to exist, so that, when entering into the contract, they must have contemplated such continuing existence as the foundation of what was to be done; there, in the absence of any express or implied warranty that the thing shall exist, the contract is not to be construed as a positive contract, but as subject to an implied condition that the parties shall be excused in case, before breach, performance becomes impossible from the perishing of the thing without default of the contractor.

There seems little doubt that this implication tends to further the great object of making the legal construction such as to fulfil the intention of those who entered into the contract. For in the course of affairs men in making such contracts in general would, if it were brought to their minds, say that there should be such a condition. . . .

. . . [The] excuse is by law implied, because from the nature of the contract it is apparent that the parties contracted on the basis of the continued existence of the particular person or chattel. In the present case, looking at the whole contract, we find that the parties contracted on the basis of the continued existence of the Music Hall at the time when the concerts were to be given; that being essential to their performance.

. . . We think, therefore, that the Music Hall having ceased to exist, without fault of either party, both parties are excused, the plaintiffs from taking the gardens and paying the money, the defendants from performing their promise to give the use of the Hall and Gardens and other things. . . .

However, the implied term theory was rejected by the House of Lords in the context of frustration in *Davis Contractors* v *Fareham U.D.C.* The decision of the Court of

Appeal in *Great Peace Shipping Ltd* v *Tsavliris Salvage (International) Ltd* [2002] EWCA Civ 1407, [2003] QB 679 has now confirmed that the development of these doctrines was linked so that the implied term theory is also inappropriate as the theoretical basis for common mistake.

(b) The construction theory

Davis Contractors Ltd v *Fareham Urban District Council*
[1956] AC 696 (HL)

On July 9 1946, the contractors entered into a building contract to build 78 houses for a local authority for £92,425 within a period of eight months. Without the fault of either party, adequate supplies of labour were not available and the work took 22 months to complete. The contractors argued that the contract was frustrated and they could therefore claim on a *quantum meruit* basis (which would be more than the contract price) for the houses they completed. Held: the contract had not been frustrated. The shortage of labour had rendered the contract more onerous than expected but had not altered the fundamental nature of the contractual performance.

LORD RFID: Frustration has often been said to depend on adding a term to the contract by implication: for example, Lord Loreburn in *F. A. Tamplin Steamship Co. Ltd* v *Anglo-Mexican Petroleum Products Co. Ltd* [1916] 2 AC 397, after quoting language of Lord Blackburn, said:

> That seems to me another way of saying that from the nature of the contract it cannot be supposed the parties, as reasonable men, intended it to be binding on them under such altered conditions. Were the altered conditions such that, had they thought of them, they would have taken their chance of them, or such that as sensible men they would have said 'if that happens, of course, it is all over between us'? What, in fact, was the true meaning of the contract? Since the parties have not provided for the contingency, ought a court to say it is obvious they would have treated the thing as at an end?

I find great difficulty in accepting this as the correct approach because it seems to me hard to account for certain decisions of this House in this way. . . .

I may be allowed to note an example of the artificiality of the theory of an implied term given by Lord Sands in *James Scott and Sons Ltd* v *Del Sel* (1922) SC 592:

> A tiger has escaped from a travelling menagerie. The milkgirl fails to deliver the milk. Possibly the milkman may be exonerated from any breach of contract but, even so, it would seem hardly reasonable to base that exoneration on the ground that 'tiger days excepted' must be held as if written into the milk contract.

I think that there is much force in Lord Wright's criticism in *Denny, Mott & Dickson Ltd* v *James B. Fraser & Co. Ltd* [1944] AC 265:

> The parties did not anticipate fully and completely, if at all, or provide for what actually happened. It is not possible, to my mind, to say that, if they had thought of it, they would have said: 'Well, if that happens, all is over between us.' On the contrary, they would almost certainly on the one side or the other have sought to introduce reservations or qualifications or compensations.

It appears to me that frustration depends, at least in most cases, not on adding any implied term, but on the true construction of the terms which are in the contract read in light of the nature of the contract and of the relevant surrounding circumstances when the contract was made. . . .

LORD RADCLIFFE: . . . This approach [implied term] is in line with the tendency of English courts to refer all the consequences of a contract to the will of those who made it. But there is something of a logical difficulty in seeing how the parties could even impliedly have provided for something which ex hypothesi they neither expected nor foresaw; and the ascription of frustration to an implied term of the contract has been criticised as obscuring the true action of the court which consists in applying an objective rule of the law of contract to the contractual obligations that the parties have imposed upon themselves. So long as each theory produces the same result as the other, as normally it does, it matters little which theory is avowed (see *British Movietonews Ltd* v *London and District Cinemas Ltd* [1952] AC 166, per Viscount Simon). But it may still be of some importance to recall that, if the matter is to be approached by way of implied term, the solution of any particular case is not to be found by inquiring what the parties themselves would have agreed on had they been, as they were not, forewarned. It is not merely that no one can answer that hypothetical question; it is also that the decision must be given 'irrespective of the individuals concerned, their temperaments and failings, their interest and circumstances' (*Hirji Mulji* v *Cheong Yue Steamship Co. Ltd* [1926] AC 497). The legal effect of frustration 'does not depend on their intention or their opinions, or even knowledge, as to the event.' On the contrary, it seems that when the event occurs 'the meaning of the contract must be taken to be, not what the parties did intend (for they had neither thought nor intention regarding it), but that which the parties, as fair, and reasonable men, would presumably have agreed upon if, having such possibility in view, they had made express provision as to their several rights and liabilities in the event of its occurrence' (*Dahl* v *Nelson* (1881) 6 App Cas 38 per Lord Watson).

By this time it might seem that the parties themselves have become so far disembodied spirits that their actual persons should be allowed to rest in peace. In their place there rises the figure of the fair and reasonable man. And the spokesman of the fair and reasonable man, who represents after all no more than the anthropomorphic conception of justice, is and must be the court itself. So perhaps it would be simpler to say at the outset that frustration occurs whenever the law recognises that without default of either party a contractual obligation has become incapable of being performed because the circumstances in which performance is called for would render it a thing radically different from that which was undertaken by the contract. Non haec in foedera veni. It was not this that I promised to do.

There is, however, no uncertainty as to the materials upon which the court must proceed. 'The data for decision are, on the one hand, the terms and construction of the contract, read in the light of the then existing circumstances, and on the other hand the events which have occurred' (*Denny, Mott & Dickson Ltd* v *James B. Fraser & Co. Ltd* [1944] AC 265, per Lord Wright). In the nature of things there is often no room for any elaborate inquiry. The court must act upon a general impression of what its rule requires. It is for that reason that special importance is necessarily attached to the occurrence of any unexpected event that, as it were, changes the face of things. But, even so, it is not hardship or inconvenience or material loss itself which calls the principle of frustration into play. There must be as well such a change in the significance of the obligation that the thing undertaken would, if performed, be a different thing from that contracted for.

I am bound to say that, if this is the law, the appellants' case seems to me a long way from a case of frustration. . . .

NOTES
1. Lord Radcliffe's approach has since been accepted by Lord Hailsham in *National Carriers Ltd* v *Panalpina (Northern) Ltd* [1981] AC 675 (*page 528*).
2. Much of the difficulty in reconciling the case law in this area stems from the fact that some of it is professed to be based on the implied theory in *Taylor* v *Caldwell* (e.g., *Krell* v *Henry* [1903] 2 KB 740, see *page 528*).
3. In *Davis* v *Fareham UDC*, the contractors were seeking to profit from the frustration by using it to escape the contractual price they had agreed and the terms they had agreed, and instead to claim a larger sum on a *quantum meruit*. Not surprisingly, the court rejected this (although see *page 140*).

Ocean Tramp Tankers Corporation v *V/O Sovfracht, The Eugenia*
[1964] 2 QB 226 (CA)

For facts see *page 499*.

LORD DENNING MR:

[The charterers] seek to rely on the fact that the canal itself was blocked. They assert that even if the *Eugenia* had never gone into the canal, but had stayed outside (in which case she would not have been in breach of the war clause), nevertheless she would still have had to go round by the Cape. And that, they say, brings about a frustration, for it makes the venture fundamentally different from what they contracted for. . . . I think the position is now reasonably clear. It is simply this: if it should happen, in the course of carrying out a contract, that a fundamentally different situation arises for which the parties made no provision—so much so that it would not be just in the new situation to hold them bound to its terms—then the contract is at an end.

It was originally said that the doctrine of frustration was based on an implied term. In short, that the parties, if they had foreseen the new situation, would have said to one another: 'If that happens, of course, it is all over between us.' But the theory of an implied term has now been discarded by everyone, or nearly everyone, for the simple reason that it does not represent the truth. The parties would not have said: 'It is all over between us.' They would have differed about what was to happen. Each would have sought to insert reservations or qualifications of one kind or another. Take this very case. The parties realised that the canal might become impassable. They tried to agree on a clause to provide for the contingency. But they failed to agree. So there is no room for an implied term.

It has frequently been said that the doctrine of frustration only applies when the new situation is 'unforeseen' or 'unexpected' or 'uncontemplated,' as if that were an essential feature. But it is not so. The only thing that is essential is that the parties should have made no provision for it in their contract. The only relevance of it being 'unforeseen' is this: If the parties did not foresee anything of the kind happening, you can readily infer they have made no provision for it: whereas, if they did foresee it, you would expect them to make provision for it. But cases have occurred where the parties have foreseen the danger ahead, and yet made no provision for it in the contract. Such was the case in the Spanish Civil War when a ship was let on charter to the republican government. The purpose was to evacuate refugees. The parties foresaw that she might be seized by the nationalists. But they made no provision for it in their contract. Yet, when she was seized, the contract was frustrated, see *W. J. Tatem Ltd* v *Gamboa* [1939] 1 KB 132. So here the parties foresaw that the canal might become impassable: it was the very thing they feared. But they made no provision for it. So there is room for the doctrine to apply if it be a proper case for it.

We are thus left with the simple test that a situation must arise which renders performance of the contract 'a thing radically different from that which was undertaken by the contract,' see *Davis Contractors Ltd* v *Fareham Urban District Council* [1956] AC 696 by Lord Radcliffe. To see if the doctrine applies, you have first to construe the contract and see whether the parties have themselves provided for the situation that has arisen. If they have provided for it, the contract must govern. There is no frustration. If they have not provided for it, then you have to compare the new situation with the situation for which they did provide. Then you must see how different it is. The fact that it has become more onerous or more expensive for one party than he thought is not sufficient to bring about a frustration. It must be more than merely more onerous or more expensive. It must be positively unjust to hold the parties bound. It is often difficult to draw the line. But it must be done. And it is for the courts to do it as a matter of law: see *Tsakiroglou & Co. Ltd* v *Noblee Thorl GmbH* [1962] AC 93 by Lord Simonds and by Lord Reid.

Applying these principles to this case, I have come to the conclusion that the blockage of the canal did not bring about a 'fundamentally different situation' such as to frustrate the venture. My reasons are these: (1) The venture was the *whole* trip from delivery at Genoa, out to the Black Sea, there load cargo, thence to India, unload cargo, and redelivery. The time for this vessel from Odessa to Vizagapatam via the Suez Canal would be 26 days, and via the Cape, 56 days. But that is not the right comparison. You have to take the whole venture from delivery at Genoa to redelivery at Madras. We were told that the time for the whole venture via the Suez Canal would be 108 days and via the Cape 138 days. The difference over the whole voyage is not so radical as to produce a frustration. (2) The cargo was iron and steel goods which would not be adversely affected by the longer voyage, and there was no special reason for early arrival. The vessel and crew were at all times fit and sufficient to proceed via the Cape. (3) The cargo was loaded on board at the time of the blockage of the canal. If the contract was frustrated, it would mean, I suppose, that the ship could throw up the charter and unload the cargo wherever she was, without any breach of contract. (4) The voyage round the Cape made no great difference except that it took a good deal longer and was more expensive for the charterers than a voyage through the canal.

NOTES
1. The fact that the ship had become trapped was attributable to the actions of the charterers, and they could not rely on this as being the frustrating event. Instead they had attempted to argue that the frustrating event was the closure of the canal. However, it was held that the closure did not render performance of the contract radically different (applying *Tsakiroglou* v *Noblee Thorl* [1962] AC 93, *page 527*).
2. Lord Denning is advocating that the frustration doctrine will still apply where the event is foreseen as long as no provision is included to deal with it. There is a similar *obiter* statement by Goddard J in *W.J. Tatem Ltd* v *Gamboa* [1939] 1 KB 132.

■ QUESTION

Is this asking the court to reallocate the risks that parties have freely, and with knowledge, entered upon?

Great Peace Shipping Ltd v Tsavliris Salvage (International) Ltd
[2002] EWCA Civ 1407, [2003] QB 679 (CA)

LORD PHILLIPS MR:

[Lord Phillips referred to the fact that Lord Atkin in *Bell* v *Lever Bros* had adopted the implication of a term as the alternative basis for his test to determine the existence of a fundamental common mistake, and continued:]

61 . . . It seems to us that this was a more solid jurisprudential basis for the test of common mistake that Lord Atkin was proposing. At the time of *Bell* v *Lever Bros Ltd* [1932] AC 161 the law of frustration and common mistake had advanced hand in hand on the foundation of a common principle. Thereafter frustration proved a more fertile ground for the development of this principle than common mistake, and consideration of the development of the law of frustration assists with the analysis of the law of common mistake.

[He then traced the development of frustration case law, especially the recognition that a contract would be frustrated if performance as originally envisaged would be radically different, and continued:]

70 . . . In *National Carriers Ltd* v *Panalpina (Northern) Ltd* [1981] AC 675 the House of Lords considered five different explanations for the doctrine of frustration. Lord Hailsham of St Marylebone LC and Lord Roskill favoured the exposition of the doctrine given by Lord Radcliffe in *Davis Contractors Ltd* v *Fareham Urban District Council* [1956] AC 696, 728 and Lord Simon of Glaisdale advanced the following refinement of that test [1981] AC 675, 700:

'Frustration of a contract takes place when there supervenes an event (without default of either party and for which the contract makes no sufficient provision) which so significantly changes the nature (not merely the expense or onerousness) of the outstanding contractual rights and/or obligations from what the parties could reasonably have contemplated at the time of its execution that it would be unjust to hold them to the literal sense of its stipulations in the new circumstances; in such case the law declares both parties to be discharged from further performance.' . . .

73 What do these developments in the law of frustration have to tell us about the law of common mistake? First that the theory of the implied term is as unrealistic when considering common mistake as when considering frustration. Where a fundamental assumption upon which an agreement is founded proves to be mistaken, it is not realistic to ask whether the parties impliedly agreed that in those circumstances the contract would not be binding. The avoidance of a contract on the ground of common mistake results from a rule of law under which, if it transpires that one or both of the parties have agreed to do something which it is impossible to perform, no obligation arises out of that agreement.

74 In considering whether performance of the contract is impossible, it is necessary to identify what it is that the parties agreed would be performed. This involves looking not only at the express terms, but at any implications that may arise out of the surrounding circumstances. In some cases it will be possible to identify details of the 'contractual adventure' which go beyond the terms that are expressly spelt out, in others it will not. . . .

82 Thus, while we do not consider that the doctrine of common mistake can be satisfactorily explained by an implied term, an allegation that a contract is void for common mistake will often raise important issues of construction. Where it is possible to perform the letter of the contract, but it is alleged that there was a common mistake in relation to a fundamental assumption which renders performance of the essence of the obligation impossible, it will be necessary, by construing the contract in the light of all the material circumstances, to decide whether this is indeed the case. In performing this exercise, the test advanced by Diplock LJ, applicable alike to both frustration and to fundamental breach, in *Hongkong Fir Shipping Co Ltd* v *Kawasaki Kisen Kaisha Ltd* [1962] 2 QB 26, 65–66 can be of assistance:

> Every synallagmatic contract contains in it the seeds of the problem: in what event will a party be relieved of his undertaking to do that which he has agreed to do but has not yet done? The contract may itself expressly define some of these events, as in the cancellation clause in a charterparty; but, human prescience being limited, it seldom does so exhaustively and often fails to do so at all. In some classes of contracts such as sale of goods, marine insurance, contracts of affreightment evidenced by bills of lading and those between parties to bills of exchange, Parliament has defined by statute some of the events not provided for expressly in individual contracts of that class; but where an event occurs the occurrence of which neither the parties nor Parliament have expressly stated will discharge one of the parties from further performance of his undertakings, it is for the court to determine whether the event has this effect or not. The test whether an event has this effect or not has been stated in a number of metaphors all of which I think amount to the same thing: does the occurrence of the event deprive the party who has further undertakings still to perform of substantially the whole benefit which it was the intention of the parties as expressed in the contract that he should obtain as the consideration for performing those undertakings?

83 This test may not, however, be adequate in the context of mistake, for there are cases where contracts have been held void for mistake, notwithstanding that the effect of the mistake was that the consideration proved to have substantially greater value than the parties had contemplated.

NOTE: This judgment is helpful in identifying the theoretical basis for the impossibility doctrines, i.e., the basis for judging the existence of impossibility on the facts. The relevance of the test formulated by Diplock LJ in *Hong Kong Fir Shipping* for the purposes of determining whether breach of an intermediate term amounts to a repudiatory breach (discussed at *page 250*) has long been accepted in relation to identification of a frustratory event, especially in cases of temporary unavailability. Lord Phillips recognises that it may be relevant but is unlikely to be as helpful in identifying a sufficiently fundamental common mistake.

SECTION 3: COMMON MISTAKE

The crucial characteristic of common mistake is that both parties make a mistake and it is the same mistake. In order for the contract to be void for common mistake, thereby excusing the parties from all performance, that mistake must be 'fundamental'. A mistake will be sufficiently fundamental if it involves a mistaken assumption of fact which would render performance in accordance with the contract terms essentially different from the performance originally contemplated by the parties. However, this test was described as 'narrow' by the Court of Appeal in *Great Peace Shipping Ltd* v *Tsavliris Salvage (International) Ltd* [2002] EWCA Civ 1407, [2003] QB 679 and will not be easily satisfied in the context of mistakes other than those relating to the existence of the subject matter of the contract.

A: *Res extincta*

Both parties are mistaken as to the existence of the subject matter of the contract.

Couturier v *Hastie*
(1856) 5 HL Cas 673; 10 ER 1065 (HL)

In May 1848, the parties entered into a contract for the sale of corn which was believed to be in transit from Salonica to the UK. Shipment had occurred in February 1848 and, unknown to both parties, before the contract was made in May, the corn had deteriorated to such an extent that the master of the ship had sold it at Tunis. When he discovered this fact the English buyer repudiated the contract but the seller argued that the buyer was still liable for the price. Held: the contract contemplated that there was an existing commodity to be sold and bought. Since this was not the case at the time of the sale to the buyer, he was not liable to pay the price.

NOTES
1. *Couturier* v *Hastie* is often quoted as authority for the fact that a mistake by both parties as to the existence of the subject matter of the contract renders the contract void. This interpretation was placed on *Couturier* v *Hastie* by the legislative draftsman in the Sale of Goods Act 1893. Section 6 of the 1979 Act provides:

   > Where there is a contract for the sale of specific goods, and the goods without the knowledge of the seller have perished at the time when the contract is made, the contract is void.

   However, the only issue the House of Lords had to decide was whether the buyer was liable to pay the price. The House of Lords held that he was not so bound, but this could have been because there was a contract that the goods existed and there was a total failure of consideration destroying the basis of the contract. The word 'mistake' is not even mentioned in the case, and the Lord Chancellor expressly stated that the whole question turned upon the construction of the contract.
2. Since s. 6 of the Sale of Goods Act 1979 seems to accept that the goods did once exist, it does not apply where the subject matter never existed.
   The problem with this interpretation is that it both limits the application of s. 6 (to goods which have at one time existed) and it restricts the principle in *McRae* v *Commonwealth*

Disposals Commission, page 495, to situations where one party accepts the risk that the goods do not exist at all.

3. Atiyah has argued ((1957) 73 LQR 340) that s. 6 is only a rule of construction which can be ousted by a contrary intention. However, it is not likely that this was intended, since, although other sections of the Act state that their application is subject to contrary agreement, s. 6 does not.

B: Mistakes as to quality

A mistake as to quality made by both parties does not render performance as originally agreed impossible.

Bell v *Lever Brothers Ltd*
[1932] AC 161 (HL)

Bell and Snelling entered into a contract with the plaintiff company under which they agreed to serve for five years as chairman and vice-chairman of the plaintiff's subsidiary company. While acting in these capacities and in breach of duty, they entered into secret speculations in cocoa for their own benefit. Subsequently their services were no longer required. The plaintiff company negotiated with them both to give up their appointments in return for monetary compensation. Being unaware of the breaches of duty and that these breaches would have justified terminating the agreements without compensation, the plaintiff company agreed to compensation of £30,000 and £20,000 respectively. The money was paid to the defendants, but on discovering the breaches of duty the plaintiff company sought to recover it. (The jury found that when they had agreed to the compensation the defendants had forgotten about their breaches of duty. Therefore it was a question of common mistake as both parties had made the same mistake.) Held: the majority (3:2) rejected the argument that the compensation agreement was void for the common mistake, since this was a mistake as to a quality of the service contracts. (The speeches refer to mutual mistake as meaning common mistake.) Lord Atkin referred to *res extincta* and then continued:

LORD ATKIN: . . . Mistake as to quality of the thing contracted for raises more difficult questions. In such a case a mistake will not affect assent unless it is the mistake of both parties, and is as to the existence of some quality which makes the thing without the quality essentially different from the thing as it was believed to be. Of course it may appear that the parties contracted that the article should possess the quality which one or other or both mistakenly believed it to possess. But in such a case there is a contract and the inquiry is a different one, being whether the contract as to quality amounts to a condition or a warranty, a different branch of the law.

   . . .

   We are now in a position to apply to the facts of this case the law as to mistake so far as it has been stated. . . . Is an agreement to terminate a broken contract different in kind from an agreement to terminate an unbroken contract, assuming that the breach has given the one party the right to declare the contract at an end? I feel the weight of the plaintiffs' contention that a contract immediately determinable is a different thing from a contract for an unexpired term, and that the difference in kind can be illustrated by the immense price of release from the longer contract as compared with the shorter. And I agree that an agreement to take an assignment of a lease for five years is not the same thing as to take an assignment of a lease for three years, still less a term for a few months. But, on the whole, I have come to the conclusion that it would be wrong to decide that an agreement to terminate a definite specified contract is void if it turns out that the agreement had already been broken and could have been terminated otherwise. The contract released is the identical contract in both cases, and the party paying for release gets exactly what he bargains for. It seems immaterial that he could have got the same result in another way, or that if he had known the true facts he would not have entered into the bargain. A buys B's horse; he thinks the horse is sound and he pays the price of a sound horse; he would certainly not have bought the horse if he had known as the fact is that the horse is unsound. If B has made no representation as to soundness and has not contracted that the horse is sound, A is bound and cannot recover back the price. A buys a picture from B; both A and B believe it to be the work of an old master, and a high price is paid. It turns out to be a modern copy. A has no remedy in the absence of representation or warranty. A agrees to take on lease or to buy from B an unfurnished dwelling-house. The house is in fact uninhabitable. A would never have entered into the bargain if he had known the fact. A has no remedy, and the position is the same whether B knew the facts or not, so long as he made no representation or gave no warranty. A buys a roadside garage business from B abutting on a public thoroughfare: unknown to A, but known to B, it has already been decided to construct a byepass road which will divert substantially the whole of the traffic from passing A's garage. Again A has no remedy. All these cases involve hardship on A and benefit B, as most people would say, unjustly. They can be supported on the ground that it is of paramount importance that contracts should be observed, and that if parties honestly comply with the essentials of the formation of contracts—i.e., agree in the same terms on the same subject-matter—they are bound, and must rely on the stipulations of the contract for protection from the effect of facts unknown to them.

. . . [I]f the contract expressly or impliedly contains a term that a particular assumption is a condition of the contract, the contract is avoided if the assumption is not true. But we have not advanced far on the inquiry how to ascertain whether the contract does contain such a condition. Various words are to be found to define the state of things which make a condition. 'In the contemplation of both parties fundamental to the continued validity of the contract,' 'a foundation essential to its existence,' 'a fundamental reason for making it,' are phrases found in the important judgment of Scrutton LJ in the present case. The first two phrases appear to me to be unexceptionable. They cover the case of a contract to serve in a particular place, the existence of which is fundamental to the service, or to procure the services of a professional vocalist, whose continued health is essential to performance. But 'a fundamental reason for making a contract' may, with respect, be misleading. The reason of one party only is presumedly not intended, but in the cases I have suggested above, of the sale of a horse or of a picture, it might be said that the fundamental reason for making the contract was the belief of both parties that the horse was sound or the picture an old master, yet in neither case would the condition as I think exist. Nothing is more dangerous than to allow oneself liberty to construct for the parties contracts which they have not in terms made by importing implications which would appear to make the contract more businesslike or more just. The implications to be made are to be no more than are 'necessary' for giving business efficacy to the transaction, and it appears to me that, both as to existing facts and future facts, a condition would not be implied unless the new state of facts makes the contract something different in kind from the contract in the original state of facts. . . . We therefore get a common standard for mutual mistake, and implied conditions whether as to existing or as to future facts. Does the state of the new facts destroy the identity of the subject-matter as it was in the original state of facts? To apply the principle to the infinite combinations of facts that arise in actual experience will continue to be difficult, but if this case results in establishing order into what has been a somewhat confused and difficult branch of the law it will have served a useful purpose.

NOTES

1. The principle underlying this decision is that a mistake as to quality should not enable a completed contract to be undone since the parties have agreed in the same terms on the same subject matter. The net effect of *Bell* v *Lever Bros* is that it promotes certainty but at the expense of fairness and flexibility.

2. In *Associated Japanese (International) Ltd* v *Crédit du Nord SA* [1989] 1 WLR 255, Steyn J considered that the *ratio* of *Bell* v *Lever Bros* was that in order for the contract to be void, the mistake as to quality had 'to make the thing without the quality essentially different from the

thing as it was believed to be' (*per* Lord Atkin). However, Lord Atkin's examples of mistakes which will not be sufficiently fundamental to render the contract void indicate that this principle is very restrictive indeed.

Lord Thankerton stated that the mistake must 'relate to something which both [parties] must necessarily have accepted in their minds as an essential element of the subject matter'. The evidence was that only the plaintiff company regarded the validity of the service contracts as essential.

Treitel, *The Law of Contract*, 11th edn, pp. 293–4, argues that a fundamental mistake occurs if the particular quality is so important to the parties that they actually use it to identify the subject matter. In *Bell* v *Lever Brothers Ltd*, the parties would merely have stated that they were contracting about service contracts.

3. The minority in *Bell* v *Lever Bros* (Viscount Hailsham and Lord Warrington of Clyffe) considered that this mistake was sufficiently fundamental to the bargain. This may be because of the value involved in the mistake.

Sherwood v Walker
66 Mich 568 (1887); 33 NW 919 (Supreme Court of Michigan)

The plaintiffs agreed to buy a cow from the defendants for $80. Both parties believed the cow to be barren, but the defendants then discovered that the cow was in calf at the time the contract had been entered into (as a breeding cow the value soared to between $750–1,000). The defendants refused to deliver the cow, arguing that a common mistake had been made which went to 'the very nature of the thing'. The majority of the Supreme Court agreed that this mistake went to the whole substance of the agreement, stressing the difference in the price of the cow. It was so fundamental a mistake that it went beyond a mere mistake as to quality and affected the very character of the animal for all time.

Nicholson & Venn v Smith-Marriott
(1947) 177 LT 189

A set of linen napkins and table cloths bearing a royal coat of arms was described as 'all with the crest and arms of Charles I and . . . the authentic property of that monarch'. The plaintiffs, antique dealers, paid £787 for the linen on the faith of this description in the catalogue. In fact it was Georgian and worth only £105. Held: this was a sale by description within s. 13 of the Sale of Goods Act (now 1979), and since the linen did not correspond with the description there had been a breach of contract.

HALLETT J (*obiter*): Clearly, in this case, as it seems to me, what the defendants were intending to sell and the plaintiffs intending to buy was not two fine table cloths and twelve fine table napkins as such, but something which I will describe as a Carolean relic. Using the language of Lord Atkin, I am disposed to the view that a Georgian relic, if there be such a thing—which I have no reason to suppose there is—is an 'essentially different' thing from a Carolean relic. I think that the absence of the crest and arms of Charles I—the absence of anything attesting or appearing to attest a connection between this table linen and that monarch, who at one time, after all, appeared in the English Prayer Book, if I am not mistaken, as a martyr, which none of the four Georgian kings did—did make the goods obtained different things in substance from those which the plaintiffs sought to buy and believed that they had bought. I should be disposed therefore, though recognising the great difficulties of the point and without any undue confidence in the correctness of my judgment, to hold if necessary that here there was a mutual mistake of the kind or category calculated to vitiate the assent of the parties and therefore to enable the plaintiffs to treat themselves as not bound by the contract.

NOTES
1. Applying Treitel's suggested solution (*page 513*), if the parties had been asked what they were contracting about and had replied that it was 'Charles I napkins', then the contract would be void; but if they had merely replied 'antique table linen', it would be valid.
2. In *Solle* v *Butcher* [1950] 1 KB 671, Denning LJ disagreed with the view that the contract in *Nicholson & Venn* v *Smith-Marriott* was void. This has thrown serious doubts on its application as an example of a sufficiently fundamental mistake.
3. As in *Nicholson & Venn* v *Smith-Marriott*, it may be possible to argue that a particular quality is a term of the contract. Section 13(1) of the Sale of Goods Act 1979 provides:

> Where there is a contract for the sale of goods by description, there is an implied term that the goods will correspond with the description.

However, in *Harlingdon & Leinster Enterprises Ltd* v *Christopher Hull Fine Art Ltd* [1990] 1 All ER 737, the Court of Appeal held in order for the sale of goods to be a sale 'by description' within s. 13(1), the description had to be influential in the sale. The court had to be able to impute a common intention to the parties that the description should be a term of the contract, and this depended on whether it was within the contemplation of the parties that the buyer would rely on the description.

There may be a misrepresentation as to quality. In *Leaf* v *International Galleries* [1950] 2 KB 86 (*page 556*), both parties entered into the contract mistakenly thinking that the painting was by Constable. On the facts there was a misrepresentation by the seller, but the only available remedy of rescission had been lost because of lapse of time. Evershed MR explained why such a mistake as to quality did not render the contract void:

> The plaintiff's case rested fundamentally upon this statement which he made: 'I contracted to buy a Constable. I have not had, and never had, a Constable.' Though that is, as a matter of language, perfectly intelligible, it nevertheless needs a little expansion if it is to be quite accurate. What he contracted to buy and what he bought was a specific chattel, namely, an oil painting of Salisbury Cathedral; but he bought it on the faith of a representation, innocently made, that it had been painted by John Constable. It turns out, as the evidence now stands and as the county court judge has found, that it was not so painted. Nevertheless it remains true to say that the plaintiff still has the article which he contracted to buy. The difference is no doubt considerable, but it is, as Denning LJ has observed, a difference in quality and in value rather than in the substance of the thing itself.

Great Peace Shipping Ltd v *Tsavliris Salvage (International) Ltd*
[2002] EWCA Civ 1407, [2003] QB 679 (CA)

A ship, *Cape Providence*, had suffered serious structural damage in the South Indian Ocean. As there were concerns that the vessel might sink and thereby endanger the safety of the crew before a tug arrived, the appellants, a salvage company, sought a merchant vessel in the vicinity to assist with the evacuation of the crew. The *Great Peace* was identified as the nearest vessel. It was believed to be about 35 miles away from the *Cape Providence* and able to rendezvous within a few hours. The appellants and the respondents therefore entered into a contract whereby the *Great Peace* was hired for a minimum of five days to deviate towards the *Cape Providence* and then escort and stand by the *Cape Providence* for the purposes of saving life. The contract contained a cancellation clause giving the appellants the right to cancel on payment of five days' hire. In fact the vessels were 410 miles apart (so that it would take about 39 hours for the *Great Peace* to arrive) and, after securing the services of an alternative vessel, the appellants cancelled the contract with the respondents. The respondents sought the five days' hire (US$82,500) under the terms of the contract but the appellants alleged that the contract was either void at law or voidable in equity since both parties had proceeded on the basis of the fundamental mistake of fact, namely that the two vessels were in 'close proximity' at the time of contracting. Toulson J, at first instance, had given judgment for the respondents and, in particular, had denied any equitable jurisdiction to grant relief in these circumstances. On appeal Held: the critical issue in determining the existence of a fundamental common mistake as to quality was whether the common mistaken assumption of fact underpinning the contract meant that the performance of the contract in accordance with its terms would be essentially different from the performance contemplated by the parties. In this context that was interpreted to mean whether the distance between the two vessels was such that the service which the *Great Peace* was in a position to provide was essentially different from what the parties had agreed. The fact that the appellants did not cancel the contract until they had secured the services of another vessel and the fact that the *Great Peace* would have arrived in time to provide several days escort service indicated that performance of the contractual adventure had not been impossible. The contract was therefore not void for common mistake. In addition, there was no equitable jurisdiction to grant rescission for a common mistake which was not sufficiently fundamental at common law (*Bell* v *Lever Bros* applied). Accordingly, the appellants were liable to pay the charge under the cancellation clause.

LORD PHILLIPS MR (giving the judgment of the court) . . .

31   In the present case the parties were agreed as to the express terms of the contract. The defendants agreed that the *Great Peace* would deviate towards the *Cape Providence* and, on reaching her, escort her so as to be on hand to save the lives of her crew, should she founder. The contractual services would terminate when the salvage tug came up with the casualty. The mistake relied upon by the defendants is as to an assumption that they claim underlay the terms expressly agreed. This was that the *Great Peace* was within a few hours sailing of the *Cape Providence*. They contend that this mistake was fundamental in that it would take the *Great Peace* about 39 hours to reach a position where she could render the services which were the object of the contractual adventure.

32   Thus what we are here concerned with is an allegation of a common mistaken assumption of fact which renders the service that will be provided if the contract is performed in accordance with its terms something different from the performance that the parties contemplated. This is the type of mistake which fell to be considered in *Bell* v *Lever Bros Ltd* [1932] AC 161.
We shall describe it as 'common mistake', although it is often alternatively described as 'mutual mistake'.

33   [Counsel] for the defendants puts his case in two alternative ways. First he submits that performance of the contract in the circumstances as they turned out to be would have been fundamentally different from the performance contemplated by the parties, so much so that the effect of the mistake was to deprive the agreement of the consideration underlying it. Under common law, so he submits, the effect of such a mistake is to render the contract void. [Counsel] draws a close analogy with the test to be applied when deciding whether a contract has been frustrated or whether there has been a fundamental breach. The foundation for this submission is *Bell* v *Lever Bros Ltd*.

34   If the facts of this case do not meet that test, [Counsel] submits that they none the less give rise to a right of rescission in equity. He submits that such a right arises whenever the parties contract under a common mistake as to a matter that can properly be described as 'fundamental' or 'material' to the agreement in question. Here he draws an analogy with the test for rescission where one party, by innocent misrepresentation, induces the other to enter into a contract—indeed that is one situation where the parties contract under a common mistake. The foundation for this submission is *Solle* v *Butcher* [1950] 1 KB 671. . . .

50   It is generally accepted that the principles of the law of common mistake expounded by Lord

Atkin in *Bell* v *Lever Bros Ltd* [1932] AC 161 were based on the common law. The issue raised by [Counsel's] submissions is whether there subsists a separate doctrine of common mistake founded in equity which enables the court to intervene in circumstances where the mistake does not render the contract void under the common law principles. The first step is to identify the nature of the common law doctrine of mistake that was identified, or established, by *Bell* v *Lever Bros Ltd*.

51 Lord Atkin and Lord Thankerton were breaking no new ground in holding void a contract where, unknown to the parties, the subject matter of the contract no longer existed at the time that the contract was concluded. The Sale of Goods Act 1893 (56 & 57 Vict c 71) was a statute which set out to codify the common law. Section 6, to which Lord Atkin referred, provided: 'When there is a contract for the sale of specific goods, and the goods without the knowledge of the seller have perished at the time when the contract is made, the contract is void.'

52 Judge Chalmers, the draftsman of the Act, commented in the first edition of his book on the Act, *The Sale of Goods Act 1893* (1894), p 17: 'The rule may be based either on the ground of mutual mistake, or on the ground of impossibility of performance.'

53 He put at the forefront of the authorities that he cited in support *Couturier* v *Hastie* (1856) 5 HL Cas 673. That case involved the sale of a cargo of corn which, unknown to the parties, no longer existed at the time that the contract was concluded. Other decisions where agreements were held not to be binding were *Strickland* v *Turner* (1852) 7 Exch 208—the sale of an annuity upon the life of a person who, unknown to the parties, had died—and *Pritchard* v *Merchant's and Tradesman's Mutual Life Assurance Society* (1858) 3 CBNS 622—an insurance policy renewed in ignorance of the fact that the assured had died. . . .

55 Where that which is expressly identified as the subject of a contract does not exist, the contract will necessarily be one which cannot be performed. Such a situation can readily be identified. The position is very different where there is 'a mistake as to the existence of some quality of the subject matter which makes the thing without the quality essentially different from the thing as it was believed to be'. In such a situation it may be possible to perform the letter of the contract. . . .

[Lord Phillips then considered the basis for the decision in *Bell* to have been the implied term (see *page 508*). This mirrored the development of the theoretical basis of frustration at that time. He traced the subsequent development of the doctrine of frustration and continued:]

73 What do these developments in the law of frustration have to tell us about the law of common mistake? First that the theory of the implied term is as unrealistic when considering common mistake as when considering frustration. Where a fundamental assumption upon which an agreement is founded proves to be mistaken, it is not realistic to ask whether the parties impliedly agreed that in those circumstances the contract would not be binding. The avoidance of a contract on the ground of common mistake results from a rule of law under which, if it transpires that one or both of the parties have agreed to do something which it is impossible to perform, no obligation arises out of that agreement.

74 In considering whether performance of the contract is impossible, it is necessary to identify what it is that the parties agreed would be performed. This involves looking not only at the express terms, but at any implications that may arise out of the surrounding circumstances. In some cases it will be possible to identify details of the 'contractual adventure' which go beyond the terms that are expressly spelt out, in others it will not. . . .

86 Lord Atkin himself [in *Bell* v *Lever Bros*] gave no examples of cases where a contract was rendered void because of a mistake as to quality which made 'the thing without the quality essentially different from the thing as it was believed to be'. He gave a number of examples of mistakes which did not satisfy this test, which served to demonstrate just how narrow he considered the test to be. Indeed this is further demonstrated by the result reached on the facts of *Bell* v *Lever Bros Ltd* [1932] AC 161 itself.

87   Two cases where common mistake has been held to avoid the contract under common law call for special consideration. A case which is by no means easy to reconcile with *Bell* v *Lever Bros Ltd* is *Scott* v *Coulson* [1903] 2 Ch 249. A contract for the sale of a life policy was entered into in circumstances in which both parties believed that the assured was alive. The price was paid and the policy assigned. The contract price was little more than the surrender value of the policy. In fact, the assured had died before the contract was concluded and the policy thus carried with it entitlement to the full sum assured. The vendors succeeded, in proceedings in the Chancery Division [1903] 1 Ch 453, in having the transaction set aside. In the Court of Appeal, Vaughan Williams LJ described the position [1903] 2 Ch 249, 252:

'If we are to take it that it was common ground that, at the date of the contract for the sale of this policy, both the parties to the contract supposed the assured to be alive, it is true that both parties entered into this contract upon the basis of a common affirmative belief that the assured was alive; but as it turned out that this was a common mistake, the contract was one which cannot be enforced. This is so at law; and the plaintiffs do not require to have recourse to equity to rescind the contract, if the basis which both parties recognised as the basis is not true.'

88   This case is often erroneously treated as being on all fours with *Strickland* v *Turner* 7 Exch 208: see for example in *Bell* v *Lever Bros Ltd* [1931] 1 KB 557 Wright J, at p 565, Greer LJ, at p 595, and Lord Warrington [1932] AC 161, 206–207. The two cases were, however, very different. An annuity on the life of someone deceased is self-evidently a nullity. The policy in *Scott* v *Coulson* [1903] 2 Ch 249 was very far from a nullity. The only way that the case can be explained is by postulating that a life policy before decease is fundamentally different from a life policy after decease, so that the contractual consideration no longer existed, but had been replaced by something quite different—ergo the contract could not be performed. Such was the explanation given by Lord Thankerton in *Bell* v *Lever Bros Ltd* [1932] AC 161, 236.

89   The other case is the decision of Steyn J in *Associated Japanese Bank (International) Ltd* v *Crédit du Nord SA* [1989] 1 WLR 255. The plaintiff bank entered into an agreement with a rogue under which he purported to sell and lease back four specific machines. The defendant bank agreed with the plaintiff bank to guarantee the rogue's payments under the lease-back agreement. The machines did not, in fact, exist. The rogue defaulted on his payments and the plaintiffs called on the guarantee. The defendants alleged (1) that on true construction of the agreement it was subject to an express condition precedent that the four machines existed; if this was not correct (2) that the agreement was void at law for common mistake; if this was not correct the agreement was voidable in equity on the ground of mistake and had been avoided.

90   The first head of defence succeeded. Steyn J went on, however, to consider the alternative defences founded on mistake. After reviewing the authorities on common mistake, he reached the following formulation of the law, at p 268:

'The first imperative must be that the law ought to uphold rather than destroy apparent contracts. Secondly, the common law rules as to a mistake regarding the quality of the subject matter, like the common law rules regarding commercial frustration, are designed to cope with the impact of unexpected and wholly exceptional circumstances on apparent contracts. Thirdly, such a mistake in order to attract legal consequences must substantially be shared by both parties, and must relate to facts as they existed at the time the contract was made. Fourthly, and this is the point established by *Bell* v *Lever Bros Ltd* [1932] AC 161, the mistake must render the subject matter of the contract essentially and radically different from the subject matter which the parties believed to exist. While the civilian distinction between the substance and attributes of the subject matter of a contract has played a role in the development of our law (and was cited in speeches in *Bell* v *Lever Bros Ltd*), the principle enunciated in *Bell* v *Lever Bros Ltd* is markedly narrower in scope than the civilian doctrine. It is therefore no longer useful to invoke the civilian distinction. The principles enunciated by Lord Atkin and Lord Thankerton represent the ratio decidendi of *Bell* v *Lever Bros Ltd*. Fifthly, there is a requirement which was not specifically discussed in *Bell* v *Lever Bros Ltd*. What happens if the party, who is seeking to rely on the mistake, had no reasonable grounds for his belief? An extreme example is that of the man who makes a contract with minimal knowledge of the facts to which the mistake relates but is content that it is a good speculative risk. In my judgment a party cannot be allowed to rely on a common mistake where the mistake consists of a belief which is entertained by him without any reasonable grounds for such belief: cf *McRae* v *Commonwealth Disposals Commission* 84 CLR 377, 408. That is not because principles such as estoppel or negligence require it, but simply because policy and good sense dictate that the positive rules regarding common mistake should be so qualified.'

91 The detailed analysis that we have carried out leads us to concur in this summary, subject to the proviso that the result in *McRae's* case can, we believe, be explained on the basis of construction, as demonstrated above. In agreeing with the analysis of Steyn J, we recognise that it is at odds with comments that Lord Denning MR made on more than one occasion about *Bell* v *Lever Bros Ltd* [1932] AC 161 to the effect that 'a common mistake, even on a most fundamental matter, does not make a contract void at law'. As to this Steyn J said [1989] 1 WLR 255, 267:

'With the profoundest respect to the former Master of the Rolls I am constrained to say that in my view his interpretation of *Bell* v *Lever Bros Ltd* [1932] AC 161 does not do justice to the speeches of the majority.'

92 We share both the respect and the conclusion. We shall shortly consider in some detail the effect of Lord Denning MR's treatment of the decision in *Bell* v *Lever Bros Ltd*. . . .

94 Our conclusions have marched in parallel with those of Toulson J. We admire the clarity with which he has set out his conclusions, which emphasise the importance of a careful analysis of the contract and of the rights and obligations created by it as an essential precursor to consideration of the effect of an alleged mistake. We agree with him that, on the facts of the present case, the issue in relation to common mistake turns on the question of whether the mistake as to the distance apart of the two vessels had the effect that the services that the *Great Peace* was in a position to provide were something essentially different from that to which the parties had agreed. . . .

Mistake in equity

95 In *Solle* v *Butcher* [1950] 1 KB 671 Denning LJ held that a court has an equitable power to set aside a contract that is binding in law on the ground of common mistake. Subsequently, as Lord Denning MR, in *Magee* v *Pennine Insurance Co Ltd* [1969] 2 QB 507, 514 he said of *Bell* v *Lever Bros Ltd* [1932] AC 161:

'I do not propose today to go through the speeches in that case. They have given enough trouble to commentators already. I would say simply this: a common mistake, even on a most fundamental matter, does not make a contract void at law: but it makes it voidable in equity. I analysed the cases in *Solle* v *Butcher* [1950] 1 KB 671, and I would repeat what I said there, at p 693: "A contract is also liable in equity to be set aside if the parties were under a common misapprehension either as to facts or as to their relative and respective rights, provided that the misapprehension was fundamental and that the party seeking to set it aside was not himself at fault." '

96 Neither of the other two members of the court in *Magee* v *Pennine Insurance Co Ltd* cast doubt on *Bell* v *Lever Bros Ltd*. Each purported to follow it, although reaching different conclusions on the facts. It is axiomatic that there is no room for rescission in equity of a contract which is void. Either Lord Denning MR was purporting to usurp the common law principle in *Bell* v *Lever Bros Ltd* and replace it with a more flexible principle of equity, or the equitable remedy of rescission that he identified is one that operates in a situation where the mistake is not of such a nature as to avoid the contract. Decisions have, hitherto, proceeded on the basis that the latter is the true position. Thus, in *Associated Japanese Bank (International) Ltd* v *Crédit du Nord SA* [1989] 1 WLR 255, 266 Steyn J remarked that it was clear that mistake in equity was not circumscribed by common law definitions. He went on to say, at pp 267–268:

'No one could fairly suggest that in this difficult area of the law there is only one correct approach or solution. But a narrow doctrine of common law mistake (as enunciated in *Bell* v *Lever Bros Ltd* [1932] AC 161), supplemented by the more flexible doctrine of mistake in equity (as developed in *Solle* v *Butcher* [1950] 1 KB 671 and later cases), seems to me to be an entirely sensible and satisfactory state of the law: see *Sheikh Bros Ltd* v *Ochsner* [1957] AC 136. And there ought to be no reason to struggle to avoid its application by artificial interpretations of *Bell* v *Lever Bros Ltd*.'

97   Toulson J has taken a different view. He has concluded that it is not possible to differentiate between the test of mistake identified in *Bell* v *Lever Bros Ltd* and that advanced by Lord Denning MR as giving rise to the equitable jurisdiction to rescind. He has examined the foundations upon which Lord Denning MR founded his decision in *Solle* v *Butcher* and found them defective. These are conclusions that we must review. If we agree with them the question will then arise of whether it was open to him, or is open to this court, to rule that the doctrine of common mistake leaves no room for the intervention of equity.

98   The following issues fall to be considered in relation to the effect of common mistake in equity. (1) Prior to *Bell* v *Lever Bros Ltd* was there established a doctrine under which equity permitted rescission of a contract on grounds of common mistake in circumstances where the contract was valid at common law? (2) Could such a doctrine stand with *Bell* v *Lever Bros Ltd*? (3) Is this court none the less bound to find that such a doctrine exists having regard to *Solle* v *Butcher* and subsequent decisions?

Common mistake in equity prior to Bell v Lever Bros Ltd

99   The doctrine of common mistake at common law which we have identified cannot be said to have been firmly established prior to *Bell* v *Lever Bros Ltd*: see the comments of the High Court of Australia in *McRae* v *Commonwealth Disposals Commission* 84 CLR 377 and of the authors of *Meagher, Gummow & Lehane, Equity: Doctrines and Remedies*, 3rd ed (1992), p. 372. Little wonder if litigants, confronted with what appeared to them to be agreements binding in law, should invoke the equitable jurisdiction of the court of Chancery in an attempt to be released from their obligations, when they considered justice so demanded. Nor is it surprising if the Chancery court granted the relief sought on the basis upon which it was claimed. It is not realistic to infer that when such relief was granted the court implicitly determined that the contract was binding in law.

100   The precise circumstances in which the court of Chancery would permit rescission of a contract were not clearly established in the latter half of the 19th century. . . .

While a number of 18th and 19th century cases prior to the decision in *Cooper* v *Phibbs* LR 2 HL 149 lend some support to the thesis that equity had taken that step, 'No coherent equitable doctrine of mistake can be spelt from them': see the discussion in *Goff & Jones, The Law of Restitution*, 5th ed (1998), pp 288–289 and *Meagher, Gummow & Lehane, Equity: Doctrines and Remedies*, pp 375–376. *Cooper* v *Phibbs* was however the decision primarily relied upon by Denning LJ in *Solle* v *Butcher* [1950] 1 KB 671 . . .

101   At the heart of the case was a dispute as to title to a fishery in Ireland. The fishery, together with a cottage, was the subject of an agreement for a three-year lease entered into by Phibbs, the respondent, with Cooper, the appellant. Phibbs was acting as agent for five sisters, who believed that they had inherited the fishery from their father. He, in the belief that he was the owner of the fishery in fee simple, had expended much money in improving it. Cooper contended that, after entering into the lease, he had discovered that the fishery had at all material times been trust property and that, in consequence of a series of events of very great complexity, he was entitled to an equitable life interest. It was ultimately not disputed, however, that the head lease of the cottage was vested in the sisters.

102   Cooper petitioned the Court of Chancery in Ireland seeking an order that the agreement be delivered up to be cancelled and that Phibbs be restrained from suing upon it. Cooper at all times made it plain that he was prepared to submit to any terms which the court might impose. The Lord Chancellor of Ireland, Sir Maziere Brady, dismissed the petition, without prejudice to the question as to ownership of the fishery, holding that no ground for the grant of relief had been made out. Cooper appealed, contending that the agreement ought to be set aside as made under mistake of fact and that he should be declared to have title to the fishery.

103   The House of Lords resolved the issue of title in favour of Cooper. Lord Cranworth dealt with the legal consequences of this in a short passage LR 2 HL 149, 164:

'The consequence was, that the present appellant, when, after the death of his uncle, he entered into the agreement to take a lease of this property, entered into an agreement to take a lease of what was, in truth, his own property—for, in truth, this fishery was bound by the covenant, and belonged to him, just as much as did the lands of Ballysadare; therefore, he says, I entered into the agreement under a common mistake, and I am entitled to be relieved from the consequence of it. In support of that proposition he relied upon a case which was decided in the time of Lord Hardwicke, not by Lord Hardwicke himself, but by the then Master of the Rolls, *Bingham* v *Bingham* (1748) 1 Ves Sen 126, where that relief was expressly administered. I believe that the doctrine there acted upon was perfectly correct doctrine; but even if it had not been, that will not at all show that this appellant is not entitled to this relief, because in this case the appellant was led into the mistake by the misinformation given to him by his uncle, who is now represented by the respondents. It is stated by him in his cause petition, which is verified, and to which there is no contradiction, and in all probability it seems to be the truth, that his uncle told him, not intending to misrepresent anything, but being in fact in error, that he was entitled to this fishery as his own fee simple property; and the appellant, his nephew, after his death acting on the belief of the truth of what his uncle had so told him, entered into the agreement in question. It appears to me, therefore, that it is impossible to say that he is not entitled to the relief which he asks, namely, to have the agreement delivered up and the rent repaid. That being so, he would be entitled to relief, but he is only entitled to this relief on certain terms, to which I will presently advert.' . . .

113   In the House of Lords [in *Bell* v *Lever Bros*] [1932] AC 161 the report shows that the appellants relied on both common law authorities and *Cooper* v *Phibbs* LR 2 HL 149 in support of the submission that a common mistake had to be as to the existence of the subject matter of the contract if it was to render it void. The respondents do not appear to have suggested that equity might provide relief where common law would not. They relied upon frustration cases in support of the proposition that a mistake would render a contract void if it was based on a mistaken assumption that was contractual and was as to the essence of the contract. . . .

118   . . . The House of Lords in *Bell* v *Lever Bros Ltd* [1932] AC 161 considered that the intervention of equity, as demonstrated in *Cooper* v *Phibbs* LR 2 HL 149, took place in circumstances where the common law would have ruled the contract void for mistake. We do not find it conceivable that the House of Lords overlooked an equitable right in Lever Bros to rescind the agreement, notwithstanding that the agreement was not void for mistake at common law. The jurisprudence established no such right. Lord Atkin's test for common mistake that avoided a contract, while narrow, broadly reflected the circumstances where equity had intervened to excuse performance of a contract assumed to be binding in law.

The effect of Solle v Butcher

119   The material facts of *Solle* v *Butcher* [1950] 1 KB 671 can shortly be summarised as follows. The defendant agreed to let a flat to the plaintiff for £250 a year. The flat had previously been let at a rent of £140. Substantial work had been done on the flat and both parties believed that this so altered the nature of the premises as to free them from relevant rent control. In this they were mistaken. The defendant would have been able to charge the plaintiff an increased rent of £250 to reflect the work done on the flat had he complied with the requisite formalities but, under the influence of the mistake, he failed to do so. In the result he could not lawfully charge a rent higher than £140. The plaintiff obtained a declaration in the county court that the rent was restricted to £140 and an order for repayment of rent overpaid. The judge rejected the contention that the contract had been concluded under a common mistake of fact, holding that the mistake was one of law.

120   The Court of Appeal, by a majority, reversed this decision. Bucknill LJ held, at p 685, that the parties had concluded the agreement under a common mistake of fact, namely that the alterations had turned the premises into 'in effect, a different flat'. He held that this common mistake was on a

matter of fundamental importance and that the defendant was entitled to rescind the agreement under the principle in *Cooper* v *Phibbs* LR2 HL149. He remarked that he had read the judgment of Denning LJ and agreed with the terms proposed by him on which the lease should be set aside.
. . .

122   Denning LJ first identified the effect of common mistake under principles of common law. . . .

123   Applying those principles he held that it was clear that there was a contract. The parties had agreed in the same terms on the same subject matter. True it was that there was a fundamental mistake as to the rent which could be charged, but that did not render the lease a nullity. Turning to equity, he observed that the court could set aside a contract when it was unconscientious for the other party to take advantage of it. As to what was considered unconscientious, equity had shown a progressive development. A material misrepresentation would suffice, even if not fraudulent or fundamental. He continued, at p 693:

> 'A contract is also liable in equity to be set aside if the parties were under a common misapprehension either as to facts or as to their relative and respective rights, provided that the misapprehension was fundamental and that the party seeking to set it aside was not himself at fault.'

124   . . . He added [1950] 1 KB 671, 695: '*Cooper* v *Phibbs* affords ample authority for saying that, by reason of the common misapprehension, this lease can be set aside on such terms as the court thinks fit.'

125   Denning LJ held, at p 695, that the lease should be set aside because there had been 'a common misapprehension, which was fundamental'. The terms on which the lease was set aside were such as, in effect, to give the tenant the option of substituting the lease for one at the full rent which the law permitted.

126   Toulson J described this decision by Denning LJ as one which 'sought to outflank *Bell* v *Lever Bros Ltd* [1932] AC 161'. We think that this was fair comment. It was not realistic to treat the House of Lords in *Bell* v *Lever Bros Ltd* as oblivious to principles of equity, nor to suggest that 'if it had been considered on equitable grounds the result might have been different'. For the reasons that we have given, we do not consider that *Cooper* v *Phibbs* LR2 HL149 demonstrated or established an equitable jurisdiction to grant rescission for common mistake in circumstances that fell short of those in which the common law held a contract void. In so far as this was in doubt, the House of Lords in *Bell* v *Lever Bros Ltd* delimited the ambit of operation of *Cooper* v *Phibbs* by holding, rightly or wrongly, that on the facts of that case the agreement in question was void at law and by holding that, on the facts in *Bell* v *Lever Bros Ltd*, the mistake had not had the effect of rendering the contract void.

127   It was not correct to state that *Cooper* v *Phibbs*, as interpreted by Denning LJ, was 'in no way impaired by *Bell* v *Lever Bros Ltd*', nor to make the inconsistent statement that the principle of *Cooper* v *Phibbs*, as interpreted by Denning LJ, had been 'fully restored' by *Norwich Union Fire Insurance Society Ltd* v *Wm H Price Ltd* [1934] AC 455. That was a decision of the Privy Council, on appeal from the Supreme Court of New South Wales. Insurers had paid the insured value on a cargo of lemons under a mistake, shared by the assured, that they had been destroyed by a peril insured against. In fact they had been sold in transit because they were ripening. The Privy Council allowed the insurers' appeal against the refusal of the Supreme Court to allow them to recover the insurance moneys on the ground that they had been paid under a mistake of fact. In their advice they observed, at pp 462–463:

> 'The mistake was as vital as that in *Cooper* v *Phibbs* LR2 HL149, 170 in respect of which Lord Westbury used these words: "If parties contract under a mutual mistake and misapprehension as to their relative and respective rights, the result is, that that agreement is liable to be set aside as having proceeded upon a common mistake." At common law such a contract (or simulacrum of a contract) is more correctly described as void, there being in truth no intention to contract. Their Lordships find nothing tending to contradict or overrule these established principles in *Bell* v *Lever Bros Ltd* [1932] AC 161.'

128   This passage reinforces the approach of the House of Lords in *Bell* v *Lever Bros Ltd* of equating the test of common mistake in *Cooper* v *Phibbs* with one that renders a contract void at common law.

129   Nor was it accurate to state that *Cooper* v *Phibbs* afforded ample authority for saying that the lease could be set aside 'on such terms as the court thinks fit'. As we have demonstrated, the terms imposed by the House of Lords in *Cooper* v *Phibbs* were no more than necessary to give effect to the rights and interests of those involved.

130   In *Bell* v *Lever Bros Ltd* the House of Lords equated the circumstances which rendered a contract void for common mistake with those which discharged the obligations of the parties under the doctrine of frustration. Denning LJ rightly concluded that the facts of *Solle* v *Butcher* [1950] 1 KB 671 did not amount to such circumstances. The equitable jurisdiction that he then asserted was a significant extension of any jurisdiction exercised up to that point and one that was not readily reconcilable with the result in *Bell* v *Lever Bros Ltd*.

131   If the result in *Solle* v *Butcher* [1950] 1 KB 671 extended beyond any previous decision the scope of the equitable jurisdiction to rescind a contract for common mistake, the terms of Denning LJ's judgment left unclear the precise parameters of the jurisdiction. The mistake had to be 'fundamental', but how far did this extend beyond Lord Atkin's test [1932] AC 161, 218 of a mistake 'as to the existence of some quality which makes the thing without the quality essentially different from the thing as it was believed to be'? The difficulty in answering this question was one of the factors that led Toulson J to conclude that there was no equitable jurisdiction to rescind on the ground of common mistake a contract that was valid in law. Was it open to him after half a century and is it open to this court to find that the equitable jurisdiction that Denning LJ identified in *Solle* v *Butcher* was a chimera?

. . .

Summary

153   A number of cases, albeit a small number, in the course of the last 50 years have purported to follow *Solle* v *Butcher* [1950] 1 KB 671, yet none of them defines the test of mistake that gives rise to the equitable jurisdiction to rescind in a manner that distinguishes this from the test of a mistake that renders a contract void in law, as identified in *Bell* v *Lever Bros Ltd* [1932] AC 161. This is, perhaps, not surprising, for Denning LJ, the author of the test in *Solle* v *Butcher*, set *Bell* v *Lever Bros Ltd* at nought. It is possible to reconcile *Solle* v *Butcher* and *Magee* v *Pennine Insurance Co Ltd* [1969] 2 QB 507 with *Bell* v *Lever Bros Ltd* only by postulating that there are two categories of mistake, one that renders a contract void at law and one that renders it voidable in equity. Although later cases have proceeded on this basis, it is not possible to identify that proposition in the judgment of any of the three Lords Justices, Denning, Bucknill and Fenton Atkinson, who participated in the majority decisions in the former two cases. Nor, over 50 years, has it proved possible to define satisfactorily two different qualities of mistake, one operating in law and one in equity.

154   In *Solle* v *Butcher* Denning LJ identified the requirement of a common misapprehension that was 'fundamental', and that adjective has been used to describe the mistake in those cases which have followed *Solle* v *Butcher*. We do not find it possible to distinguish, by a process of definition, a mistake which is 'fundamental' from Lord Atkin's mistake as to quality which 'makes the thing [contracted for] essentially different from the thing [that] it was believed to be': [1932] AC 161, 218.

155   A common factor in *Solle* v *Butcher* and the cases which have followed it can be identified. The effect of the mistake has been to make the contract a particularly bad bargain for one of the parties. Is there a principle of equity which justifies the court in rescinding a contract where a common mistake has produced this result?

'Equity is . . . a body of rules or principles which form an appendage to the general rules of law, or a gloss upon them. In origin at least, it represents the attempt of the English legal system to meet a problem which confronts all legal systems reaching a certain stage of development. In order to ensure the smooth running of society it is necessary to formulate general rules which work well enough in the majority of cases. Sooner or later, however, cases arise in which, in some unforeseen set of facts, the general rules produce substantial unfairness.' (*Snell's Equity*, 30th ed (2000), para 1–03.)

156 Thus the premise of equity's intrusion into the effects of the common law is that the common law rule in question is seen in the particular case to work injustice, and for some reason the common law cannot cure itself. But it is difficult to see how that can apply here. Cases of fraud and misrepresentation, and undue influence, are all catered for under other existing and uncontentious equitable rules. We are *only* concerned with the question whether relief might be given for common mistake in circumstances wider than those stipulated in *Bell* v *Lever Bros Ltd* [1932] AC 161. But that, surely, is a question as to where the common law should draw the line; not whether, given the common law rule, it needs to be mitigated by application of some other doctrine. The common law has drawn the line in *Bell* v *Lever Bros Ltd*. The effect of *Solle* v *Butcher* [1950] 1 KB 671 is not to supplement or mitigate the common law: it is to say that *Bell* v *Lever Bros Ltd* was wrongly decided.

157 Our conclusion is that it is impossible to reconcile *Solle* v *Butcher* with *Bell* v *Lever Bros Ltd*. The jurisdiction asserted in the former case has not developed. It has been a fertile source of academic debate, but in practice it has given rise to a handful of cases that have merely emphasised the confusion of this area of our jurisprudence. In paras 110 to 121 of his judgment, Toulson J has demonstrated the extent of that confusion. If coherence is to be restored to this area of our law, it can only be by declaring that there is no jurisdiction to grant rescission of a contract on the ground of common mistake where that contract is valid and enforceable on ordinary principles of contract law. That is the conclusion of Toulson J.

160 . . . In this case we have heard full argument, which has provided what we believe has been the first opportunity in this court for a full and mature consideration of the relation between *Bell* v *Lever Bros Ltd* [1932] AC 161 and *Solle* v *Butcher*. In the light of that consideration we can see no way that *Solle* v *Butcher* can stand with *Bell* v *Lever Bros Ltd*. In these circumstances we can see no option but so to hold.

161 We can understand why the decision in *Bell* v *Lever Bros Ltd* did not find favour with Lord Denning MR. An equitable jurisdiction to grant rescission on terms where a common fundamental mistake has induced a contract gives greater flexibility than a doctrine of common law which holds the contract void in such circumstances. Just as the Law Reform (Frustrated Contracts) Act 1943 was needed to temper the effect of the common law doctrine of frustration, so there is scope for legislation to give greater flexibility to our law of mistake than the common law allows.

NOTES

1. The decision of the Court of Appeal has resolved one of the areas of academic debate, namely the question of why the House of Lords in *Bell* v *Lever Bros*, having first determined that the contract was valid at common law, did not then consider the application of an equitable jurisdiction to set aside the contract on terms. There is no such equitable jurisdiction in such circumstances and *Solle* v *Butcher* and other Court of Appeal and first instance decisions applying such a jurisdiction are plainly incorrect. It also resolves what had become something of a judicial dilemma in trying to distinguish a mistake that was not sufficiently fundamental to render the contract void at common law from a mistake that was sufficiently fundamental for the contract to be set aside on terms in equity.

2. Whilst the ability to set aside the contract on terms for common mistake as to quality cannot be reconciled with *Bell* v *Lever Bros*, it did have the advantage of allowing some remedial flexibility. This point is noted by Lord Phillips at [161]. It will be difficult in instances other than common mistake as to the existence of the subject matter to obtain relief, absent other possible forms of relief such as misrepresentation, since the test in *Bell* v *Lever Bros* to determine whether a contract is void is notoriously narrow. In any event, if the contract is void it will be an 'all or nothing' remedy. There are two points that can be made relating to this: (i) instances of initial impossibility are limited and, as noted at *page 502*, it is likely that the risk of the event will have been allocated by the contract. It might be suggested, therefore, that there are likely to be few claims based only on common mistake (although a review of recent contract case law does not lend much support to such a conclusion). (ii) As Lord Phillips suggests, legislation may be necessary to provide for some adjustment to the parties' positions (bearing in mind that initial impossibility should be discovered reasonably quickly and

any adjustment to the parties' positions may not be significant) and/or the courts are likely to seek other avenues to achieve the desired remedial relief.

3. *Great Peace* confirms that in determining whether a contract is void for common mistake as to quality at common law the test is that expounded by Lord Atkin in *Bell* v *Lever Bros* of essential difference and that this is a matter of contractual construction. In addition, the context for this assessment may include the 'contractual adventure', i.e., the purpose underpinning the contract. However, this assessment is inevitably one of fact and it will be difficult to advise in individual cases whether performance will be 'essentially different'.

4. See Chandler, Devenney, and Poole, 'Common Mistake: Theoretical Justification and Remedial Inflexibility' [2004] JBL 34.

Subsequent interpretation of *Great Peace*

(a) *Brennan* v *Bolt Burdon* [2004] EWCA Civ 1017, [2004] 3 WLR 1321. The question was whether a compromise agreement was void for common mistake of law. The claimant's claim for damages for personal injury was issued on 7 June 2001, four months before the limitation period expired, and served on the defendants on 6 October. However, a judge held that it was served outside the limitation period on 8 October. Accordingly, the claimant agreed to compromise the claim. However, the case in which the decision on service had been made was subsequently overruled and the claimant successfully appealed the judge's decision that the claim form had been served out of time. The defendants applied to stay the proceedings alleging that there was a binding contractual compromise. The claimant alleged that this was void for mistake.

The Court of Appeal accepted that a mistake of law is capable of rendering a contract void (*Kleinwort Benson Ltd* v *Lincoln City Council* [1999] 2 AC 359 applied in this context) but that there would not be a mistake as to law if the law was merely in doubt and on these facts the parties could have discovered that the relevant decision was being appealed. When entering into compromise agreements each party accepted the risk that their view of the law might turn out to be mistaken. Sedley LJ considered that 'a shift in the law cannot be allowed to undo a compromise of litigation entered into in the knowledge of both how the law now stood and of the fact—for it is always a fact—that it might not remain so'.

It was a question of construction as to whether a mistake rendered the contract void and, in any event, it was doubtful that a mistake of law would be capable of passing the applicable test in *Great Peace*, namely whether the mistake rendered the agreed performance (or contractual adventure) impossible. This was not a case of impossibility of performance since the compromise was at all times performable.

Sedley LJ expressed some difficulty with this test in the context of mistakes of law and considered that 'a different test may be necessary'. He considered that: 'The equivalent question needs to be whether, had the parties appreciated that the law was what it is now known to be, there would still have been an intelligible basis for their agreement'.

(b) It appears that while accepting Lord Atkin's test in *Bell* v *Lever Brothers* of 'essential difference', the Court of Appeal has in fact reformulated it in terms similar to the test for identification of a frustratory event or a breach of an innominate term, namely whether performance as originally agreed is impossible. If this were limited to performance in accordance with the contract terms it would effectively deny the possibility that the contract might ever be void for common mistake as to quality.

However, the test does extend to a consideration of whether the contractual adventure is still possible.

In *Champion Investments Ltd* v *Ahmed* [2004] EWHC 1956 (QB) Blair QC concluded that the mistake in the parties' understanding as to the applicable rate of interest was (i) not essentially different from the position as the parties believed it to be, and (ii) did not render performance of the contract impossible. This suggests that the applicable test may still require clarification.

SECTION 4: FRUSTRATION

A contract may be automatically discharged by frustration where a frustrating event occurs without the fault of the contracting parties *after* the formation of the contract.

A: Frustrating events

(a) Impossibility

(i) *Destruction of the subject matter*
See *Taylor* v *Caldwell* (1863) 3 B & S 826, 122 ER 309 (*page 504*). This was a contract for the hire of both the Hall and Gardens. Only the Hall was destroyed but the court held the contract to be frustrated. (Compare with *Herne Bay Steam Boat Company* v *Hutton* [1903] 2 KB 683, *page 530.*)

In sale of goods contracts there are special rules governing the destruction of the subject matter.

SALE OF GOODS ACT 1979

20. Risk prima facie passes with property

(1) Unless otherwise agreed, the goods remain at the seller's risk until the property in them is transferred to the buyer, but when the property in them is transferred to the buyer the goods are at the buyer's risk whether delivery has been made or not.

7. Goods perishing before sale but after agreements to sell

Where there is an agreement to sell specific goods and subsequently the goods, without any fault on the part of the seller or buyer, perish before the risk passes to the buyer, the agreement is avoided.

NOTES
1. If the goods are destroyed after the risk has passed, the contract is not frustrated. If the goods are destroyed before the risk has passed, the contract is frustrated where the goods are specific (i.e., identified and agreed on at the time the contract is made), or if under the contract they are to come from a particular source and the entire source is destroyed.
2. If, on the other hand, the goods were not specific, sellers are obliged to deliver goods of the contractual description and cannot argue that the goods they intended to use have been destroyed. In this situation the contract cannot be frustrated.

(ii) *Temporary unavailability of the subject matter*
The question in each case is whether the contractual performance when resumed would amount to performance of a fundamentally different contract.

Jackson v *Union Marine Insurance Company Ltd*
(1874) LR 10 CP 125 (Exchequer Chamber)

A ship was chartered in November 1871. It was required to proceed 'with all possible dispatch (dangers and accidents of navigation excepted) from Liverpool to Newport, and there load a cargo for carriage to San Francisco'. The ship sailed from Liverpool on 2 January 1872, but ran aground on the way to Newport on 3 January. The ship was not repaired until the end of August. On 15 February, the charterers repudiated the charter and chartered another ship. The shipowner brought an action on his insurance policy. The question in the case was whether the shipowner could have maintained an action against the charterers for not loading. Only if no such action could have been maintained would this be a loss of freight by insured perils entitling the owners to recover under the policy. The jury found as facts that the delay due to the repairs was so long as to make it unreasonable for the charterers to supply a cargo in August for the voyage to San Francisco. Held: the contract was frustrated and the charterers were not bound to load. There was therefore a loss of the chartered freight by perils of the sea within the insurance policy.

BRAMWELL B: . . . (The jury have found that) the voyage the parties contemplated had become impossible; that a voyage undertaken after the ship was sufficiently repaired would have been a different voyage, not, indeed, different as to the ports of loading and discharge, but different as a different adventure,—a voyage for which at the time of the charter the plaintiff had not in intention engaged the ship, nor the charterers the cargo; a voyage as different as though it had been described as intended to be a spring voyage, while the one after the repair would be an autumn voyage.

NOTE: In *Bank Line Ltd* v *Arthur Capel & Co.* [1919] AC 435, a 12-month charter was to run from April 1915 to April 1916. The ship was requisitioned before delivery and not returned until September 1915. The House of Lords (Viscount Haldane dissenting) held the charterparty to have been frustrated because a September to September charter would be a substantially different charter from that which had been agreed.

(iii) Impossibility of agreed method of performing

Nickoll & Knight v *Ashton, Edridge & Co.*
[1901] 2 KB 126 (CA)

By a contract made in October 1899, the defendants sold the plaintiffs a cargo of cotton seed to be shipped by a steamship called 'Orlando' from Alexandria during January 1900. In December 1899 the 'Orlando' went aground and could not reach Alexandria in January. The plaintiffs brought an action against the defendants for failure to ship the cargo. The majority of the Court of Appeal (Vaughan Williams LJ dissenting) followed the implied term approach in *Taylor* v *Caldwell*, *page 504*. Held: the contract must be construed as subject to an implied condition that, if at the time of performance the 'Orlando' was not fit to ship the cargo, the contract would be at an end. The use of the 'Orlando' was regarded by the majority as the contractually agreed means of performance and the only means of performing.

NOTE: It is not sufficient that the parties contemplated a particular method of performance which has now become impossible. It must actually have been expressly agreed that this was the exclusive method of performing so that any other method would result in the performance being radically different from that which was envisaged.

Tsakiroglou & Co. Ltd v *Noblee Thorl GmbH*
[1962] AC 93 (HL)

On 4 October 1956, a written contract was made whereby the sellers agreed to sell Sudanese groundnuts to the buyers for shipment from Port Sudan to Hamburg during November and December 1956. Both parties expected that shipment would be made via the Suez Canal but there was no express stipulation to this effect. On 2 November, the Canal was closed to navigation but the goods could have been shipped to Hamburg via the Cape of Good Hope. This route was twice as long and the freightage was far more costly. The sellers failed to ship the goods. Held: the contract was not frustrated by the closure of the Canal. The House of Lords refused to imply a term that shipment should be made via the Suez Canal. The sellers should have shipped the goods by the alternative route which was not substantially different from that envisaged by the contract.

LORD REID: . . . The question now is whether by reason of the closing of the Suez route the contract had been ended by frustration.

The appellants' first argument was that it was an implied term of the contract that shipment should be via Suez. It is found in the case that both parties contemplated that shipment would be by that route but I find nothing in the contract or in the case to indicate that they intended to make this a term of the contract or that any such term should be implied: they left the matter to the ordinary rules of law. . . .

I turn then to consider the position after the Canal was closed, and to compare the rights and obligations of the parties thereafter, if the contract still bound them, with what their rights and obligations would have been if the Canal had remained open. As regards the sellers, the appellants, the only difference to which I find reference in the case—and indeed the only difference suggested in argument—was that they would have had to pay £15 per ton freight instead of £7 10s. They had no concern with the nature of the voyage. In other circumstances that might have affected the buyers, and it is necessary to consider the position of both parties because frustration operates without being invoked by either party and, if the market price of groundnuts had fallen instead of rising, it might have been the buyers who alleged frustration. There might be cases where damage to the goods was a likely result of the longer voyage which twice crossed the Equator, or perhaps the buyer could be prejudiced by the fact that the normal duration of the voyage via Suez was about three weeks whereas the normal duration via the Cape was about seven weeks. But there is no suggestion in the case that the longer voyage could damage the groundnuts or that the delay could have caused loss to these buyers of which they could complain. Counsel for the appellants rightly did not argue that this increase in the freight payable by the appellants was sufficient to frustrate the contract and I need not therefore consider what the result might be if the increase had reached an astronomical figure. The route by the Cape was certainly practicable. There could be, on the findings in the case, no objection to it by the buyers and the only objection to it from the point of view of the sellers was that it cost them more and it was not excluded by the contract. Where, then, is there any basis for frustration?

It appears to me that the only possible way of reaching a conclusion that this contract was frustrated would be to concentrate on the altered nature of the voyage. As I understood the argument it was based on the assumption that the voyage was the manner of performing the sellers' obligations and that therefore its nature was material. I do not think so. What the sellers had to do was simply to find a ship proceeding by what was a practicable and now a reasonable route—if perhaps not yet a usual route—to pay the freight and obtain a proper bill of lading, and to furnish the necessary documents to the buyers. That was their manner of performing their obligations, and for the reasons which I have given I think that such changes in these matters as were made necessary fell far short of justifying a finding of frustration. . . .

NOTE: It follows that it cannot be argued that a contract is frustrated if only one party contemplated its performance in a particular way (*Blackburn Bobbin Company Ltd* v *T. W. Allen & Sons Ltd* [1918] 2 KB 467).

(b) Supervening illegality

See *Fibrosa Spolka Akcyjna* v *Fairbairn Lawson Combe Barbour Ltd* [1943] AC 32, at *page 532*.

The following case concerned temporary illegality.

National Carriers Ltd v Panalpina (Northern) Ltd
[1981] AC 675 (HL)

A warehouse was leased to the defendants for 10 years from 1 January 1974. The lease contained a covenant that the premises should only be used as a warehouse. The only vehicular access to the warehouse was by a street which the local authority closed on 16 May 1979 in order to demolish a dangerous building. The street was likely to be closed for 20 months and the defendants were not able to use the warehouse in that period. The plaintiffs brought an action for unpaid rent but the defendants claimed that the lease was frustrated so that they were discharged. Held: on the facts, having regard to the period of the lease which would remain after the interruption ceased compared to the 10-year term of the lease, the defendants could not rely on frustration as a defence.

(c) Frustration of the common purpose of the parties

Since this depends upon establishing that *both* parties had the same purpose in entering into the contract and that purpose can no longer be achieved, it will rarely succeed as a frustrating event.

It will not be sufficient that the purpose has become more difficult to achieve (see *Davis Contractors* v *Fareham UDC* (*page 505*), and *Tsakiroglou & Co. Ltd* v *Noblee Thorl* (*page 527*)).

Krell v Henry
[1903] 2 KB 740 (CA)

On 20 June 1902, the defendant agreed to hire a flat in Pall Mall from the plaintiff for £75. The hire was for 26 and 27 June (days only), which were the days on which the coronation procession of Edward VII was due to take place and pass along Pall Mall. The £25 deposit was paid and the balance was due on 24 June. The contract contained no express reference to the coronation procession or to any other purpose for which the flat was taken. It was announced on 24 June that the procession would not take place on those days because the coronation had been postponed due to the King's illness. The defendant refused to pay the balance of the agreed rent. Darling J (at first instance) relying on *Taylor* v *Caldwell*, held that there was an implied condition in the contract that the procession should take place. Held: (on appeal) from the circumstances it was clear that the procession actually taking place on these days along the advertised route was regarded by both contracting parties as being of the foundation of the contract, and hence the contract was frustrated.

VAUGHAN WILLIAMS LJ: . . . I do not think that the principle of the civil law [frustration] as introduced into the English law is limited to cases in which the event causing the impossibility of performance is the destruction or non-existence of some thing which is the subject-matter of the contract or of some condition or state of things expressly specified as a condition of it. I think that you first have to ascertain, not necessarily from the terms of the contract, but, if required, from necessary inferences, drawn from surrounding circumstances recognised by both contracting parties, what is the substance of the contract, and then to ask the question whether that substantial contract needs for its foundation the assumption of the existence of a particular state of things. If it does, this will limit the operation of the general words, and in such case, if the contract becomes impossible of performance by reason of the non-existence of the state of things assumed by both contracting parties as the foundation of the contract, there will be no breach of the contract thus limited. Now what are the facts of the present case? The contract is contained in two letters of June 20 which passed between the defendant and the plaintiff's agent, Mr Cecil Bisgood. These letters do not mention the coronation, but speak merely of the taking of Mr Krell's chambers, or, rather, of the use of them, in the daytime of June 26 and 27, for the sum of 75*l.*, 25*l.* then paid, balance 50*l.* to be paid on the 24th. But the affidavits, which by agreement between the parties are to be taken as stating the facts of the case, shew that the plaintiff exhibited on his premises, third floor, 56A, Pall Mall, an announcement to the effect that windows to view the Royal coronation procession were to be let, and that the defendant was induced by that announcement to apply to the housekeeper on the premises, who said that the owner was willing to let the suite of rooms for the purpose of seeing the Royal procession for both days, but not nights, of June 26 and 27. In my judgment the use of the rooms was let and taken for the purpose of seeing the Royal procession. It was not a demise of the rooms, or even an agreement to let and take the rooms. It is a licence to use rooms for a particular purpose and none other. And in my judgment the taking place of those processions on the days proclaimed along the proclaimed route, which passed 56A, Pall Mall, was regarded by both contracting parties as the foundation of the contract; and I think that it cannot reasonably be supposed to have been in the contemplation of the contracting parties, when the contract was made, that the coronation would not be held on the proclaimed days, or the processions not take place on those days along the proclaimed route. . . . It was suggested in the course of the argument that if the occurrence, on the proclaimed days, of the coronation and the procession in this case were the foundation of the contract, and if the general words are thereby limited or qualified, so that in the event of the non-occurrence of the coronation and procession along the proclaimed route they would discharge both parties from further performance of the contract, it would follow that if a cabman was engaged to take some one to Epsom on Derby Day at a suitable enhanced price for such a journey, say 10*l.*, both parties to the contract would be discharged in the contingency of the race at Epsom for some reason becoming impossible; but I do not think this follows, for I do not think that in the cab case the happening of the race would be the foundation of the contract. No doubt the purpose of the engager would be to go to see the Derby, and the price would be proportionately high; but the cab had no special qualifications for the purpose which led to the selection of the cab for this particular occasion. Any other cab would have done as well. Moreover, I think that, under the cab contract, the hirer, even if the race went off, could have said, 'Drive me to Epsom; I will pay you the agreed sum; you have nothing to do with the purpose for which I hired the cab,' and that if the cabman refused he would have been guilty of a breach of contract, there being nothing to qualify his promise to drive the hirer to Epsom on a particular day. Whereas in the case of the coronation, there is not merely the purpose of the hirer to see the coronation procession, but it is the coronation procession and the relative position of the rooms which is the basis of the contract as much for the lessor as the hirer; and I think that if the King, before the coronation day and after the contract, had died, the hirer could not have insisted on having the rooms on the days named. It could not in the cab case be reasonably said that seeing the Derby race was the foundation of the contract, as it was of the licence in this case. Whereas in the present case, where the rooms were offered and taken, by reason of their peculiar suitability from the position of the rooms for a view of the coronation procession, surely the view of the coronation procession was the foundation of the contract, which is a very different thing from the purpose of the man who engaged the cab—namely, to see the race— being held to be the foundation of the contract. Each case must be judged by its own circumstances. In each case one must ask oneself, first, what, having regard to all the circumstances, was the foundation of the contract? Secondly, was the performance of the contract prevented? Thirdly, was the event which prevented the performance of the contract of such a character that it cannot reasonably be said to have been in the contemplation of the parties at the date of the contract? If all these questions are answered in the affirmative (as I think they should be in this case), I think both parties are discharged from further performance of the contract. In the present case the condition which fails and prevents the achievement of that which was, in the contemplation of both parties, the foundation of the contract, is not expressly mentioned either as a condition of the contract or the purpose of it; but I think for the reasons which I have given that the principle of *Taylor* v *Caldwell* (1863) 3 B & S 826 ought to be applied.

■ **QUESTION**

If a coach firm advertises a coach trip with entrance tickets to see the Derby on Derby Day, and the race is cancelled, would the coach firm be able to escape liability for breach of contract by pleading frustration?

NOTES
1. In *Krell* v *Henry*, the defendant had responded to an advertisement in a window of the plaintiff's flat to the effect that windows to view the coronation procession were to be let. In addition, since the flat was only at the defendant's disposal in the daytime, it was easier to establish that the plaintiff's purpose was to let rooms to view the procession.
2. The decision to cancel the procession took place after the hiring contract was made, but in *Griffith* v *Brymer* (1903) 19 TLR 434, a contract to hire a room to view the procession made at 11 a.m. on 24 June was held to be void for common mistake where, unknown to both parties, the decision to cancel the procession had been taken at 10 a.m. that day. If the contract had been made at 9.30 a.m. in *Griffith* v *Brymer*, the case would have turned on frustration.
3. The result in *Krell* v *Henry* would seem perfectly acceptable since the plaintiff should not have been enriched at the defendant's expense, and assuming that the procession would be rearranged, the defendant would not have had to pay twice to view it. It was not a case where the defendant was seeking to avoid an inconvenient contract.

Herne Bay Steam Boat Co. v *Hutton*
[1903] 2 KB 683 (CA)

The defendant hired a steamship from the plaintiffs which was to be at the disposal of the defendant to take passengers from Herne Bay for the purpose of viewing the naval review at Spithead on 28 and 29 June 1902, and to cruise round the fleet. The price was £250 and the defendant paid a £50 deposit. On 25 June, the review was cancelled due to the King's illness, although the fleet remained anchored at Spithead. The plaintiffs informed the defendant that the ship was ready and asked for the balance of the price. Held: the contract was not frustrated since the naval review was not the sole basis of the contract. Consequently, there was no total failure of the consideration because the cruise round the fleet could still have taken place.

VAUGHAN WILLIAMS LJ: . . . [The defendant], in hiring this vessel, had two objects in view: first, of taking people to see the naval review, and, secondly, of taking them round the fleet. Those, no doubt, were the purposes of Mr Hutton, but it does not seem to me that because, as it is said, those purposes became impossible, it would be a very legitimate inference that the happening of the naval review was contemplated by both parties as the basis and foundation of this contract, so as to bring the case within the doctrine of *Taylor* v *Caldwell* (1863) 3 B & S 826. On the contrary, when the contract is properly regarded, I think the purpose of Mr Hutton, whether of seeing the naval review or of going round the fleet with a party of paying guests, does not lay the foundation of the contract within the authorities.

Having expressed that view, I do not know that there is any advantage to be gained by going on in any way to define what are the circumstances which might or might not constitute the happening of a particular contingency as the foundation of a contract. I will content myself with saying this, that I see nothing that makes this contract differ from a case where, for instance, a person has engaged a brake to take himself and a party to Epsom to see the races there, but for some reason or other, such as the spread of an infectious disease, the races are postponed. In such a case it could not be said that he could be relieved of his bargain. So in the present case it is sufficient to say that the happening of the naval review was not the foundation of the contract.

ROMER LJ: . . . In my opinion, . . . it is a contract for the hiring of a ship by the defendant for a certain voyage, though having, no doubt, a special object, namely, to see the naval review and the fleet; but it appears to me that the object was a matter with which the defendant, as hirer of the ship, was alone concerned, and not the plaintiffs, the owners of the ship.

The case cannot, in my opinion, be distinguished in principle from many common cases in which, on the hiring of a ship, you find the objects of the hiring stated. Very often you find the details of the voyage stated with particularity, and also the nature and details of the cargo to be carried. If the voyage is intended to be one of pleasure, the object in view may also be stated, which is a matter that concerns the passengers. But this statement of the objects of the hirer of the ship would not, in my opinion, justify him in saying that the owner of the ship had those objects just as much in view as the hirer himself. The owner would say, 'I have an interest in the ship as a passenger or cargo carrying machine, and I enter into the contract simply in that capacity; it is for the hirer to concern himself about the objects.' . . .

The view I have expressed with regard to the general effect of the contract before us is borne out by the following considerations. The ship (as a ship) had nothing particular to do with the review or the fleet except as a convenient carrier of passengers to see it: any other ship suitable for carrying passengers would have done equally as well. Just as in the case of the hire of a cab or other vehicle, although the object of the hirer might be stated, that statement would not make the object any the less a matter for the hirer alone, and would not directly affect the person who was letting out the vehicle for hire. In the present case I may point out that it cannot be said that by reason of the failure to hold the naval review there was a total failure of consideration. That cannot be so. Nor is there anything like a total destruction of the subject-matter of the contract. Nor can we, in my opinion, imply in this contract any condition in favour of the defendant which would enable him to escape liability. A condition ought only to be implied in order to carry out the presumed intention of the parties, and I cannot ascertain any such presumed intention here. It follows that, in my opinion, so far as the plaintiffs are concerned, the objects of the passengers on this voyage with regard to sight-seeing do not form the subject-matter or essence of this contract. . . .

STIRLING LJ: It is said that, by reason of the reference in the contract to the 'naval review,' the existence of the review formed the basis of the contract, and that as the review failed to take place the parties became discharged from the further performance of the contract, in accordance with the doctrine of *Taylor* v *Caldwell* (1863) 3 B & S 826. I am unable to arrive at that conclusion. It seems to me that the reference in the contract to the naval review is easily explained; it was inserted in order to define more exactly the nature of the voyage, and I am unable to treat it as being such a reference as to constitute the naval review the foundation of the contract so as to entitle either party to the benefit of the doctrine in *Taylor* v *Caldwell*. I come to this conclusion the more readily because the object of the voyage is not limited to the naval review, but also extends to a cruise round the fleet. The fleet was there, and passengers might have been found willing to go round it. It is true that in the event which happened the object of the voyage became limited, but, in my opinion, that was the risk of the defendant whose venture the taking the passengers was.

NOTES

1. Arguably, in *Herne Bay Steamboat Co.* v *Hutton*, the purpose was simply to have the steamship at the defendant's disposal, whereas in *Krell* v *Henry*, it was clearly to view the procession. However, in *Krell* v *Henry* there was no express term in the contract relating to viewing the procession, whereas in *Herne Bay Steamboat Co.* v *Hutton* the contract stated that the hire was for the purpose of viewing the naval review and cruising round the fleet.

2. In *Herne Bay Steamboat Co.* v *Hutton*, although seeing the review and the fleet was the defend-

ant's purpose, it was not that of the plaintiffs. In other words, it could be similar to the position where a taxi cab is hired to go to Epsom on Derby Day. Seeing the Derby is not the taxi owner's purpose even though it is clearly the hirer's.

This type of fine distinction is unsatisfactory in an area of the law where certainty is vital.

3. Brownsword's argument ((1985) 129 SJ 860) has much to recommend it. He argues that in *Herne Bay Steamboat Co.* v *Hutton* there was an 'imprudent commercial bargain', in that the defendant had lost the commercial benefit of cashing in on the naval review. The courts will not allow frustration to be used to avoid the consequences of what turn out to be bad bargains. On the other hand, the defendant in *Krell* v *Henry* was a consumer, and the court was being asked to prevent the unjust enrichment of the plaintiff at the defendant's request.

B: The effects of frustration

Frustration discharges contractual performance from the date of frustration so that the parties are excused from future performance.

(a) At common law

(i) *Recovering money paid in advance of frustration*

Fibrosa Spolka Akcyjna v *Fairbairn Lawson Combe Barbour Ltd*
[1943] AC 32 (HL)

In July 1939, the English company agreed to sell machinery to a Polish company and to deliver it three to four months later to Gdynia in Poland. The purchase price was £4,800, of which £1,600 was to be paid when the order was placed. In fact only £1,000 of this advance sum was paid. War broke out between Germany and Britain on 3 September 1939, and Gdynia was occupied by the German army on 23 September. Held: the contract was frustrated because performance would have amounted to trading with the enemy. The House of Lords also held that since there was a total failure of consideration (i.e., the buyer got no part of what he bargained for), the buyer could recover the £1,000 advance payment and did not have to pay the outstanding balance on the advance payment of £600.

NOTES

1. *Fibrosa* v *Fairbairn* relaxed the previous common law rule that because the obligation to make the advance payment had arisen *before* the frustrating event, it had to be fulfilled (see *Chandler* v *Webster* [1904] 1 KB 493). Instead the advance payment could be recovered, but only where there was a total failure of consideration. If some of the goods had been delivered before the frustrating event occurred, then the advance payment could not have been recovered.

2. On the facts of this case, the English sellers had already incurred expenses in making machines but were not able to keep any part of the advance payment to cover this.

(ii) *Benefit provided prior to the frustrating event*

Appleby v *Myers*
(1867) LR 2 CP 651 (Exchequer Chamber)

The plaintiff contracted to install and maintain certain machinery in the defendant's factory for two years, payment to be made on completion. After some of the work of installation had been completed, the factory and the machinery were accidentally destroyed by fire. Held: the contract was frustrated so that the defendant was discharged from his obligation to pay, but the plaintiff was not entitled to recover any sum for the work that had been completed. Blackburn J referred to the normal assumption that the contract will be severable and not 'entire' (*page 259*) and continued:

> BLACKBURN J: . . . But, though this is the prima facie contract between those who enter into contracts for doing work and supplying materials, there is nothing to render it either illegal or absurd in the workman to agree to complete the whole, and be paid when the whole is complete, and not till then: and we think that the plaintiffs in the present case had entered into such a contract. Had the accidental fire left the defendant's premises untouched, and only injured a part of the work which the plaintiffs had already done, we apprehend that it is clear the plaintiffs under such a contract as the present must have done that part over again, in order to fulfil their contract to complete the whole and 'put it to work for the sums above named respectively.' As it is, they are, according to the principle laid down in *Taylor* v *Caldwell* (1863) 3 B & S 826, excused from completing the work; but they are not therefore entitled to any compensation for what they have done, but which has, without any fault of the defendant, perished. The case is in principle like that of a shipowner who has been excused from the performance of his contract to carry goods to their destination, because his ship has been disabled by one of the excepted perils, but who is not therefore entitled to any payment on account of the part-performance of the voyage, unless there is something to justify the conclusion that there has been a fresh contract to pay freight pro rata.

(b) The Law Reform (Frustrated Contracts) Act 1943

See McKendrick 'The Consequences of Frustration –The Law Reform (Frustrated Contracts) Act 1943' in *Force Majeure and Frustration of Contract*, 2nd edn (LLP Professional Publishing, 1995) and Stewart and Carter, 'Frustrated Contracts and Statutory Adjustment: The Case for a Reappraisal' [1992] CLJ 66.

(i) *Recovering money paid in advance of frustration*

LAW REFORM (FRUSTRATED CONTRACTS) ACT 1943

1. Adjustment of rights and liabilities of parties to frustrated contracts

. . . (2) All sums paid or payable to any party in pursuance of the contract before the time when the parties were so discharged (in this Act referred to as 'the time of discharge') shall, in the case of sums so paid, be recoverable from him as money received by him for the use of the party by whom the sums were paid, and, in the case of sums so payable, cease to be so payable:

Provided that, if the party to whom the sums were so paid or payable incurred expenses before the time of discharge in, or for the purpose of, the performance of the contract, the court may, if it considers it just to do so having regard to all the circumstances of the case, allow him to retain or, as the case may be, recover the whole or any part of the sums so paid or payable, not being an amount in excess of the expenses so incurred.

. . . (4) In estimating, for the purposes of the foregoing provisions of this section, the amount of any expenses incurred by any party to the contract, the court may, without prejudice to the generality of the said provisions, include such sum as appears to be reasonable in respect of overhead expenses and in respect of any work or services performed personally by the said party.

NOTES
1. Money paid before the frustrating event is recoverable, and money payable before the frustrating event ceases to be payable (irrespective of whether there has been a total failure of consideration).
2. The payee *may* be permitted by the court to set off any expenses he incurred before the frustrating event in performing the contract against the advance payment.
3. The amount of expenses that can be recovered is limited in any event to the amount of the

advance payment. This means that if there was no advance payment, s. 1(2) cannot be used to recover expenses. Similarly, if the expenses are more than the advance payment amount, it is only possible as a maximum to recover the advance payment amount.

Gamerco SA v *I.C.M./Fair Warning (Agency) Ltd*
[1995] 1 WLR 1226

The plaintiffs, Spanish pop group promoters, had agreed in a contract with the defendants that they would promote a rock concert by the group 'Guns N' Roses' at a stadium in Madrid on 4 July 1992. However, on 1 July the permit issued for the stadium was withdrawn because of safety concerns about the cement used in its construction, and the parties became aware of these events on 2 July. No other suitable venue could be found and the concert had to be cancelled. The plaintiffs had already paid $412,000 on account and were under an obligation to pay, but had not yet paid, a further $362,500. Both parties had incurred expenses in preparation for the concert. The judge, Garland J, accepted that the defendants' expenses amounted to $50,000, and the undisputed evidence was that the plaintiffs had also incurred expenses of $450,000 prior to the cancellation. The plaintiffs claimed that the contract was frustrated and sought to recover their advance payment under s. 1(2) of the Law Reform (Frustrated Contracts) Act 1943. The defendants counter-claimed for damages for breach of contract by the plaintiffs in failing to hold the concert. Held: the plaintiffs were not in breach because the contract was frustrated when the permit for the stadium was revoked. Therefore the plaintiffs were entitled to recover the advance payment of $412,000 and did not need to make the further payment of $362,500 already due (s. 1(2)). The court had a 'broad discretion' to allow the defendants to set off their expenses under the proviso to s. 1(2). In all the circumstances, and having particular regard to the expenses incurred by the plaintiffs, no deduction for the defendants' expenses was made under the proviso.

GARLAND J: . . . The issue which I have to decide is whether and, if so, to what extent the defendants can set off against the US$412,500 expenses incurred before the time of discharge in or for the purpose of the performance of the contract. It is perhaps surprising that over a period of 50 years there is no reported case of the operation of section 1(2), although it was considered obiter by Robert Goff J in *B.P. Exploration Co. (Libya) Ltd* v *Hunt (No. 2)* [1979] 1 WLR 783, 800. The section has, of course, received the attention of textbook writers, most recently that of Professor Treitel in *Frustration and Force Majeure* (1994). . . .

The approach to the proviso

The following have to be established: (1) that the defendants incurred expenses paid or payable (2) before the discharge of the contract on 2 July (3) in performance of the contract (which is not applicable) or (4) for the purposes of the performance of the contract, and (5) that it is just in all the circumstances to allow them to retain the whole or any part of the sums so paid or payable.

The onus of establishing these matters must lie on the defendant. It is, in the broad sense, his case to be made out and I am assisted by the Victorian case of *Lobb* v *Vasey Housing Auxiliary (War Widows Guild)* [1963] VR 239 under the corresponding Victorian Act of 1959, which is in very similar terms to the Act of 1943.

I have already dealt with (1), (2) and (4) so far as the evidence allows. I turn to (5). I take the following matters into consideration. (a) My assumption that the relevant expenses of US$50,000 was undisputed. (b) It was undisputed that the plaintiffs incurred expenses in excess of 52m. pesetas (approximately £285,000 or US$450,000). (c) Neither party conferred any benefit on the other or on a third party, so that subsections (3) and (6) did not apply. (d) The plaintiffs' expenditure was wholly wasted, as was the defendants'. (e) The plaintiffs were concerned with one contract only. The defendants were concerned with the last of 20 similar engagements, neither party being left with any residual benefit or advantage. (f) As already stated, I entirely ignore any insurance recoveries in accordance with subsection (5).

Various views have been advanced as to how the court should exercise its discretion and these can be categorised as follows.

(1)　*Total retention*. This view was advanced by the Law Revision Committee in 1939 (Cmd. 6009) on the questionable ground 'that it is reasonable to assume that in stipulating for prepayment the payee intended to protect himself from loss under the contract.' As the editor of *Chitty on Contracts*, 27th ed. (1994), vol. 1, p. 1141, para. 23–060, note 51, (Mr. E G McKendrick) comments: 'He probably intends to protect himself against the possibility of the other party's insolvency or default in payment.' To this, one can add: 'and secure his own cash flow.'

In *B.P. Exploration Co. (Libya) Ltd* v *Hunt (No. 2)* [1979] 1 WLR 783 Robert Goff J considered the principle of recovery under subsections (2) and (3). He said, at pp. 799–800:

> The Act is *not* designed to do certain things: (i) It is not designed to apportion the loss between the parties. There is no general power under either section 1(2) or section 1(3) to make any allowance for expenses incurred by the plaintiff (except, under the proviso to section 1(2), to enable him to enforce pro tanto payment of a sum payable but unpaid before frustration); and expenses incurred by the defendant are only relevant in so far as they go to reduce the net benefit obtained by him and thereby limit any award to the plaintiff (ii) It is not concerned to put the parties in the position in which they would have been if the contract had been performed. (iii) It is not concerned to restore the parties to the position they were in before the contract was made. A remedy designed to prevent unjust enrichment may not achieve that result; for expenditure may be incurred by either party under the contract which confers no benefit on the other, and in respect of which no remedy is available under the Act

He then turned to section 1(2) and said:

> There is no discretion in the court in respect of a claim under section 1(2), except in respect of the allowance for expenses; subject to such an allowance ... the plaintiff is entitled to repayment of the money he has paid. The allowance for expenses is probably best rationalised as a statutory recognition of the defence of change of position. True, the expenses need not have been incurred by reason of the plaintiff's payments; but they must have been incurred in, or for the purpose of, the performance of the contract under which the plaintiff's payment has been made, and for that reason it is just that they should be brought into account.

I do not derive any specific assistance from the *B.P Exploration Co.* case. There was no question of any change of position as a result of the plaintiffs' advance payment.

(2)　*Equal division*. This was discussed by Professor Treitel in *Frustration and Force Majeure*, pp. 555–556, paras 15–059 and 15–060. There is some attraction in splitting the loss, but what if the losses are very unequal? Professor Treitel considers statutory provisions in Canada and Australia but makes the point that unequal division is unnecessarily rigid and was rejected by the Law Revision Committee in the 1939 report to which reference has already been made. The parties may, he suggests have had an unequal means of providing against the loss by insurers, but he appears to overlook subsection (5). It may well be that one party's expenses are entirely thrown away while the other is left with some realisable or otherwise usable benefit or advantage. Their losses may, as in the present case, be very unequal. Professor Treitel therefore favours the third view.

(3)　*Broad discretion*. It is self-evident that any rigid rule is liable to produce injustice. The words, 'if it considers it just to do so having regard to all the circumstances of the case,' clearly confer a very broad discretion. Obviously the court must not take into account anything which is not 'a circumstance of the case' or fail to take into account anything that is and then exercise its discretion rationally. I see no indication in the Act, the authorities or the relevant literature that the court is obliged to incline towards either total retention or equal division. Its task is to do justice in a situation which the parties had neither contemplated nor provided for, and to mitigate the possible harshness of allowing all loss to lie where it has fallen.

I have not found my task easy. As I have made clear, I would have welcomed assistance on the true measure of the defendants' loss and the proper treatment of overhead and non-specific expenditure. Because the defendants have plainly suffered some loss, I have made a robust assumption. In all the circumstances, and having particular regard to the plaintiffs' loss, I consider that justice is done by making no deduction under the proviso.

■ QUESTION

Is this decision explicable on the basis that Garland J is compensating for the inadequacies of s. 1(3), namely the fact that a s. 1(3) claim by the plaintiffs was not possible because they had conferred no benefit on the defendants at the date of the frustration, so that allowing the defendants to recover their expenses would have amounted to throwing all the loss on the plaintiffs? (See *below* for discussion of s. 1(3).)

NOTES

1. Carter and Tolhurst (1996) 10 JCL 264 disagreed with the approach adopted by Garland J and argued that, given the wording of the proviso ('the whole or any part') and the restitutionary basis of the 1943 Act, 'there was no discretion to award a nil sum'. They appeared to prefer a 'total retention' approach.

2. The decision to revoke the permit was taken on 1 July, but Garland J treats 2 July as the point at which the contract was discharged by frustration. Although on these facts it can be argued that frustration would not occur until it was clear that an alternative venue could not be found, it must be the position that where it is the decision itself that causes the contract to be frustrated, frustration will normally occur when the decision is made rather than when the parties are notified of it. See *Griffith* v *Brymer* (1903) 19 TLR 434, *page 530*. Although it is not clear from the judgment in *Gamerco* v *I.C.M.*, it appears that it was the decision to revoke the permit that was crucial and not merely the fact that the stadium was unsafe, thereby making performance at the agreed venue impossible, since presumably this construction problem pre-dated the contract.

(ii) Benefit provided prior to the frustrating event

LAW REFORM (FRUSTRATED CONTRACTS) ACT 1943

1. Adjustment of rights and liabilities of parties to frustrated contracts

(3) Where any party to the contract has, by reason of anything done by any other party thereto in, or for the purpose of, the performance of the contract, obtained a valuable benefit (other than a payment of money to which the last foregoing subsection applies) before the time of discharge, there shall be recoverable from him by the said other party such sum (if any), not exceeding the value of the said benefit to the party obtaining it, as the court considers just, having regard to all the circumstances of the case and, in particular,—

(a) the amount of any expenses incurred before the time of discharge by the benefited party in, or for the purpose of, the performance of the contract, including any sums paid or payable by him to any other party in pursuance of the contract and retained or recoverable by that party under the last foregoing subsection, and

(b) the effect, in relation to the said benefit, of the circumstances giving rise to the frustration of the contract.

NOTES

1. Section 1(3) applies where one party has conferred a non-monetary 'valuable benefit' on the other party before the frustrating event. The court may award him a 'just sum' to recompense him, and this sum must not exceed the value of the benefit to the party receiving it.

2. The subsection also appears to state that when calculating this 'just sum', the court must in

particular consider the expenses incurred by the benefited party (i.e., the fact that an advance payment was made to the provider of the benefit which the provider of the benefit was permitted to retain as his expenses under s. 1(2)). The provider of the benefit cannot recover twice for the same expenses under both s. 1(2) and (3).

3. By s. 1(3)(b), the court must also consider 'the effect of the frustrating event on the benefit received'.

BP Exploration Co. (Libya) Ltd v Hunt (No. 2)
[1979] 1 WLR 783

In December 1957, the Libyan Government granted the defendant a concession to explore for, and extract, oil in a specified area in the Libyan desert. In June 1960, the defendant made an agreement with the plaintiff oil company whereby the defendant assigned a half share in the oil concession to the plaintiff and the plaintiff undertook to explore, develop, and operate the whole concession at its expense and to make payments in cash and oil to the defendant. The agreement provided that if and when oil was discovered in commercial quantities, the operating expenses were to be shared and the plaintiff was to be entitled to three-eighths of the defendant's half share of the oil produced for a particular period. The plaintiff spent considerable sums of money in exploration and development of the concession and found oil in commercially worthwhile quantities. However, following a revolution in Libya, the Libyan Government first expropriated the plaintiff's half share in the concession on 7 December 1971, and then the defendant's half share on 11 June 1973. The plaintiff brought an action against the defendant alleging that the agreement was frustrated on 7 December 1971, and claimed a 'just sum' under s. 1(3) of the 1943 Act in respect of the benefit obtained by the defendant as a result of the plaintiff's performance of the contract prior to frustration. Held: the contract was frustrated and the Act applied.

ROBERT GOFF J: . . . The principle, which is common to both s. 1 (2) and (3), and indeed is the fundamental principle underlying the Act itself, is prevention of the unjust enrichment of either party to the contract at the other's expense. It was submitted by [counsel], on behalf of BP, that the principle common to both subsections was one of restitution for net benefits received, the net benefit being the benefit less an appropriate deduction for expenses incurred by the defendant. This is broadly correct so far as s. 1 (2) is concerned; but under s. 1 (3) the net benefit of the defendant simply provides an upper limit to the award—it does not measure the amount of the award to be made to the plaintiff. This is because in s. 1 (3) a distinction is drawn between the plaintiff's performance under the contract, and the benefit which the defendant has obtained by reason of that performance, . . . and the net benefit obtained by the defendant from the plaintiff's performance may be more than a just sum payable in respect of such performance, in which event a sum equal to the defendant's net benefit would not be an appropriate sum to award to the plaintiff. I therefore consider it better to state the principle underlying the Act as being the principle of unjust enrichment, which underlies the right of recovery in very many cases in English law, and indeed is the basic principle of the English law of restitution, of which the Act forms part.

[Robert Goff J then considered the process of calculating a s. 1(3) award. He continued:]

(a) *General* . . . First, it has to be shown that the defendant has, by reason of something done by the plaintiff in, or for the purpose of, the performance of the contract, obtained a valuable benefit (other than a payment of money) before the time of discharge. That benefit has to be identified, and valued, and such value forms the upper limit of the award. Secondly, the court may award to the plaintiff such sum, not greater than the value of such benefit, as it considers just having regard to all the circumstances of the case, including in particular the matters specified in s. 1(3)(a) and (b). In the case of an award under s. 1(3) there are, therefore, two distinct stages—the identification and valuation of the benefit, and the award of the just sum. The amount to be awarded is the just sum, unless the defendant's benefit is less, in which event the award will be limited to the amount of that benefit. The distinction between the identification and valuation of the defendant's benefit, and the assessment of the just sum, is the most controversial part of the Act. It represents the solution adopted by the legislature of the problem of restitution in cases where the benefit does not consist of a payment of money; but the solution so adopted has been criticised by some commentators as productive of injustice, and it certainly gives rise to considerable problems, to which I shall refer in due course.

(b) *Identification of the defendant's benefit.* In the course of the argument before me, there was much dispute whether, in the case of services, the benefit should be identified as the services themselves, or as the end product of the services. One example canvassed (because it bore some relationship to the facts of the present case) was the example of prospecting for minerals. If minerals are discovered, should the benefit be regarded (as counsel for Mr Hunt contended) simply as the services of prospecting, or (as counsel for BP contended) as the minerals themselves being the end product of the successful exercise? Now, I am satisfied that it was the intention of the legislature, to be derived from s. 1(3) as a matter of construction, that the benefit should in an appropriate case be identified as the end product of the services. This appears, in my judgment, not only from the fact that s. 1(3) distinguishes between the plaintiff's performance and the defendant's benefit, but also from s. 1(3)(b) which clearly relates to the product of the plaintiff's performance. Let me take the example of a building contract. Suppose that a contract for work on a building is frustrated by a fire which destroys the building and which, therefore, also destroys a substantial amount of work already done by the plaintiff. Although it might be thought just to award the plaintiff a sum assessed on a quantum meruit basis, probably a rateable part of the contract price, in respect of the work he has done, the effect of s. 1(3)(b) will be to reduce the award to nil, because of the effect, in relation to the defendant's benefit, of the circumstances giving rise to the frustration of the contract. It is quite plain that, in s. 1(3)(b), the word 'benefit' is intended to refer, in the example I have given, to the actual improvement to the building, because that is what will be affected by the frustrating event; the subsection therefore contemplates that, in such a case, the benefit is the end product of the plaintiff's services, not the services themselves. This will not be so in every case, since in some cases the services will have no end product; for example, where the services consist of doing such work as surveying, or transporting goods. In each case it is necessary to ask the question: what benefit has the defendant obtained by reason of the plaintiff's contractual performance? But it must not be forgotten that in s. 1(3) the relevance of the value of the benefit is to fix a ceiling to the award. If, for example, in a building contract, the building is only partially completed, the value of the partially completed building (i.e. the product of the services) will fix a ceiling for the award; the stage of the work may be such that the uncompleted building may be worth less than the value of the work and materials that have gone into it, particularly as completion by another builder may cost more than completion by the original builder would have cost. In other cases, however, the actual benefit to the defendant may be considerably more than the appropriate or just sum to be awarded to the plaintiff, in which event the value of the benefit will not in fact determine the quantum of the award. I should add, however, that, in a case of prospecting, it would usually be wrong to identify the discovered mineral as the benefit. In such a case there is always (whether the prospecting is successful or not) the benefit of the prospecting itself, ie of knowing whether or not the land contains any deposit of the relevant minerals; if the prospecting is successful, the benefit may include also the enhanced value of the land by reason of the discovery; if the prospector's contractual task goes beyond discovery and includes development and production, the benefit will include the further enhance-ment of the land by reason of the installation of the facilities, and also the benefit of in part transforming a valuable mineral deposit into a marketable commodity.

I add by way of footnote that all these difficulties would have been avoided if the legislature had thought it right to treat the services themselves as the benefit. In the opinion of many commenta-tors, it would be more just to do so; after all, the services in question have been requested by the defendant, who normally takes the risk that they may prove worthless, from whatever cause. In the example I have given of the building destroyed by fire, there is much to be said for the view that the builder should be paid for the work he has done, unless he has (for example by agreeing to insure the works) taken on himself the risk of destruction by fire. But my task is to construe the Act as it stands. On the true construction of the Act, it is in my judgment clear that the defendant's benefit must, in an appropriate case, be identified as the end product of the plaintiff's services, despite the difficulties which this construction creates, difficulties which are met again when one comes to value the benefit.

. . .

(d) *Valuing the benefit*. Since the benefit may be identified with the product of the plaintiff's performance, great problems arise in the valuation of the benefit. First, how does one solve the problem which arises from the fact that a small service may confer an enormous benefit, and conversely, a very substantial service may confer only a very small benefit? The answer presumably is that at the stage of valuation of the benefit (as opposed to assessment of the just sum) the task of the court is simply to assess the value of the benefit to the defendant. For example, if a prospector after some very simple prospecting discovers a large and unexpected deposit of a valuable mineral, the benefit to the defendant (namely, the enhancement in the value of the land) may be enormous; it must be valued as such, always bearing in mind that the assessment of a just sum may very well lead to a much smaller amount being awarded to the plaintiff. But conversely, the plaintiff may have undertaken building work for a substantial sum which is, objectively speaking, of little or no value— for example, he may commence the redecoration, to the defendant's execrable taste, of rooms which are in good decorative order. If the contract is frustrated before the work is complete, and the work is unaffected by the frustrating event, it can be argued that the defendant has obtained no benefit, because the defendant's property has been reduced in value by the plaintiff's work; but the partial work must be treated as a benefit to the defendant, since he requested it, and valued as such. Secondly, at what point in time is the benefit to be valued? If there is a lapse of time between the date of the receipt of the benefit, and the date of frustration, there may in the meanwhile be a substantial variation in the value of the benefit. If the benefit had simply been identified as the services rendered, this problem would not arise; the court would simply award a reasonable remuneration for the services rendered at the time when they were rendered, the defendant taking the risk of any subsequent depreciation and the benefit of any subsequent appreciation in value. But that is not what the Act provides: s. 1(3)(b) makes it plain that the plaintiff is to take the risk of depreciation or destruction by the frustrating event. If the effect of the frustrating event upon the value of the benefit is to be measured, it must surely be measured upon the benefit as at the date of frustration. For example, let it be supposed that a builder does work which doubles in value by the date of frustration, and is then so severely damaged by fire that the contract is frustrated; the valuation of the residue must surely be made on the basis of the value as at the date of frustration.

But there is a further problem which I should refer to, before leaving this topic. Section 1(3)(a) requires the court to have regard to the amount of any expenditure incurred before the time of discharge by the benefited party in, or for the purpose of, the performance of the contract. The question arises—should this matter be taken into account at the stage of valuation of the benefit, or of assessment of the just sum? Take a simple example. Suppose that the defendant's benefit is valued at £150, and that a just sum is assessed at £100, but that there remain to be taken into account defendant's expenses of £75: is the award to be £75 or £25? The clue to this problem lies, in my judgment, in the fact that the allowance for expenses is a statutory recognition of the defence of change of position. Only to the extent that the position of the defendant has so changed that it would be unjust to award restitution, should the court make an allowance for expenses. Suppose that the plaintiff does work for the defendant which produces no valuable end product, or a benefit no greater in value than the just sum to be awarded in respect of the work: there is then no reason why the whole of the relevant expenses should not be set off against the just sum. But suppose that the defendant has reaped a large benefit from the plaintiff's work, far greater in value than the just sum to be awarded for the work. In such circumstances it would be quite wrong to set off the whole of the defendant's expenses against the just sum. The question whether the defendant has suffered a change of position has to be judged in the light of all the circumstances of the case. Accordingly, on the Act as it stands, under s. 1(3) the proper course is to deduct the expenses from the value of the benefit, with the effect that only in so far as they reduce the value of the benefit below the amount of the just sum which would otherwise be awarded will they have any practical bearing on the award . . .

(e) *Assessment of the just sum*. The principle underlying the Act is prevention of the unjust enrichment of the defendant at the plaintiff's expense. Where, as in cases under s. 1(2), the benefit conferred on the defendant consists of payment of a sum of money, the plaintiff's expense and the defendant's enrichment are generally equal; and, subject to other relevant factors, the award of restitution will consist simply of an order for repayment of a like sum of money. But where the benefit does not consist of money, then the defendant's enrichment will rarely be equal to the plaintiff's expense. In such cases, where (as in the case of a benefit conferred under a contract thereafter frustrated) the benefit has been requested by the defendant, the basic measure of recovery in restitution is the reasonable value of the plaintiff's performance—in a case of services, a quantum meruit or reasonable remuneration, and in a case of goods, a quantum valebat or reasonable price. Such cases are to be contrasted with cases where such a benefit has not been requested by the defendant. In the latter class of case, recovery is rare in restitution; but if the sole basis of recovery was that the defendant had been incontrovertibly benefited, it might be legitimate to limit recovery to the defendant's actual benefit—a limit which has (perhaps inappropriately) been imported by the legislature into s. 1(3) of the Act. However, under s. 1(3) as it stands, if the defendant's actual benefit is less than the just or reasonable sum which would otherwise be awarded to the plaintiff, the award must be reduced to a sum equal to the amount of the defendant's benefit.

■ QUESTIONS

1. What is the effect of the Act on the decision in *Appleby* v *Myers*?

2. Why was no s. 1(3) claim made by the plaintiffs in *Gamerco* v *I.C.M.*, *page 534*, in respect of their expenditure in preparing to perform?

3. At what point in time should the benefit be identified? The difficulty caused by identifying the benefit as the end product of the services results from s. 1(3)(b), which requires the court to consider the effect of the frustration on the benefit received. If a fire destroys that end product, then according to Goff J, there is no benefit to value and there can be no s. 1(3) award. Thus Goff J considers both s. 1(3)(a) and (b) when valuing the benefit to the party receiving it. However, the Act itself requires s. 1(3)(b) to be considered when assessing the 'just sum' and not when valuing the benefit. The benefit should be valued on the basis of circumstances existing *immediately before* the frustrating event, but the specified factors are to be taken into account when the court fixes the figure of the 'just sum' to award.

NOTES

1. See Treitel, *Law of Contract*, 11th edn, pp. 913–16.
2. It is very difficult to predict what the court will decide the reasonable value of the claimant's performance to be.
3. Haycroft and Waksman [1984] JBL 207 criticised Robert Goff J's identification of the benefit as the end product of the services, which Goff J insisted was inevitable given the wording of the Act. They preferred the benefit to be identified as the value of the services themselves.
4. The complexity in the section is caused by the need to assess two figures—the value of the benefit to the defendant and the just sum to award the claimant. Robert Goff J considered that the purpose underlying the Act was to prevent unjust enrichment of one party at the expense of the other. His view is that if the frustration destroys the benefit, there is no benefit and no unjust enrichment to be remedied.

    However, Haycroft and Waksman believe the real purpose of the Act is to provide a mechanism for apportioning the loss caused by frustration between two innocent parties. See also support for this view in relation to s. 1(3) in McKendrick, 'Frustration, Restitution, and Loss

Apportionment' in *Essays on the Law of Restitution*, ed. Burrows, Clarendon Press (1991). But compare Stewart and Carter [1992] CLJ 66, 109–10.

SECTION 5: THE RELATIONSHIP BETWEEN COMMON MISTAKE AND FRUSTRATION

Although common mistake relates to the formation of a contract and renders it void *ab initio*, and frustration relates to its discharge, the same issue is raised, namely the allocation of the risk between two parties of an extraneous event.

Amalgamated Investment & Property Co. Ltd v *John Walker & Sons Ltd*
[1977] 1 WLR 164 (CA)

In July 1973, the plaintiffs agreed to purchase some commercial property belonging to the defendants which had been advertised as suitable for redevelopment at a price of £1,710,000. The defendants were aware that the plaintiffs wished to redevelop the property. In the pre-contractual inquiries the plaintiffs specifically asked the defendants whether the property was designated as a building of special architectural or historic interest. On 14 August, the defendants replied that it was not but, unknown to both parties, the Department of the Environment had included the property in a list of buildings proposed to be designated as being of special architectural or historical interest. The parties signed the contract of sale on 25 September, and the next day the Department of the Environment informed the defendant that the property was to be listed. The listing in fact took place on 27 September and resulted in the property being worth £1,500,000 less than the contract price. The plaintiffs sought to have the contract set aside on the basis of mistake, or alternatively argued that the listing had frustrated the contract. Held: this was not a case to which common mistake could apply since that mistake had to exist at the date of the contract. The property was not listed at the date of the contract (25 September). Rejecting the frustration argument, the Court of Appeal held, applying *Davis Contractors* v *Fareham UDC (page 505)*, that performance of the contract following the listing was not radically different from the performance contemplated by the parties, it was merely economically disadvantageous. The risk of a property becoming listed was an inherent risk which was to be borne by the purchaser. The plaintiffs had even asked about this possibility.

SIR JOHN PENNYCUICK: 1. *Mistake.* At the date of the contract, namely September 25, 1973, the property had not in fact been listed. The parties were therefore under no mistake in believing that the property was not subject to any existing fetter in this respect. [Counsel for the plaintiffs] accepts that, but contends that there was a common mistake, that mistake arising from the belief of the parties that the property was ripe for development, i.e. (as he puts it) suitable for and capable of development, whereas in truth it was not ripe for development because the listing of the property was then pending and would prevent development. It is certainly true that knowledge that the listing of the property was under consideration in the office concerned would vitally affect the minds of the parties negotiating the purchase of the property. . . . The mere possibility that the property would be listed would certainly affect the mind of anybody contemplating a purchase of the property and considering what price he was prepared to pay. I think, however, that the mere possibility or probability, be it small or great, of some future event occurring is too uncertain to be taken into account in considering whether the belief of the parties as to ripeness for development should be treated as mistaken. The purchaser of property takes subject to the risk of future events, and it is for him to evaluate these risks in considering whether to buy and at what price. The possibility of listing is inherent in any building today and represents to my mind precisely such a risk. Of course, in this connection, as in many others, future events involve present intention in the minds of someone or other—here the officials of the department concerned—but I do not think it is legitimate to treat future events as present facts on this ground. I agree that this court is bound by the decision in *Solle* v *Butcher* [1950] 1 KB 671, and I will not pursue the very interesting discussion whether that decision is or is not consistent with the decision of the House of Lords in *Bell* v *Lever Brothers Ltd* [1932] AC 161.

2. *Frustration.* The contract dated September 25, 1973, is a contract for the sale and purchase of a specified property at a specified price. Certainly the purpose of the plaintiffs was to develop the property, and the plaintiffs would not have paid a fraction of the price which they contracted to pay if they had known that the property would not be available for development. Again certainly, the defendants knew the plaintiffs' purpose and knew that the price would have been much less if the plaintiffs had known that the property would not be available for development, even if the plaintiffs had been willing to purchase at all. But, on the other hand, it was not a term or condition of the contract that the property should continue to be available for development at the date of completion; nor, I think, can such a condition be implied into the contract. The subject matter of the contract is simply a specified piece of land described in the contract and nothing more. Can it then be said that listing before completion frustrated the contract?

We were referred to *Davis Contractors Ltd* v *Fareham Urban District Council* [1956] AC 696, in the House of Lords, in particular to the speech of Lord Radcliffe [see extract from judgment at *pages 505–6*]. . . . The listing struck down the value of the property as might a fire or a compulsory purchase order or a number of other events. It seems to me, however, that the listing did not in any respect prevent the contract from being carried to completion according to its terms; that is to say, by payment of the balance of the purchase price and by conveyance of the property. The property is none the less the same property by reason that listing imposed a fetter on its use. It seems to me impossible to bring the circumstances of the present case within the test enunciated by Lord Radcliffe. One cannot say that the circumstances in which performance, i.e. completion, will be called for would render that performance a thing radically different from that which was undertaken by the contract. On the contrary, completion, according to the terms of the contract, would be exactly what the purchaser promised to do, and of course the vendors.

■ **QUESTION**

Why did the listing not take place when the decision to list was made? In *Griffith* v *Brymer* (1903) 19 TLR 434 (*page 530*), the relevant time was taken to be the point when the decision to cancel the procession was made.

NOTES

1. Although the Court of Appeal in *Amalgamated Investment* v *John Walker* considered itself bound by the previous Court of Appeal decision in *Solle* v *Butcher*, the Court of Appeal in *Great Peace Shipping* rejected the equitable jurisdiction to grant rescission for common mistake, accepting that the decision in *Solle* v *Butcher* was inconsistent with the decision of the House of Lords in *Bell* v *Lever Bros*.

2. The date of the listing determined the applicable legal treatment. If it had been a common mistake as to quality, at the time of this decision the contract could have been set aside in equity on terms (*Solle* v *Butcher* [1950] 1 KB 671). This might have permitted greater flexibility than a finding that the contract was frustrated, followed by statutory adjustment of the parties' positions under the Frustrated Contracts Act 1943. As a result of the decision in *Great Peace Shipping Ltd* v *Tsavliris Salvage (International) Ltd* [2002] EWCA Civ 1407, [2003] QB 679, *page 514*, in which *Solle* v *Butcher* was not followed, there is no such flexibility in terms of the legal effect of such a mistake. At common law such a mistake would render the contract void. Therefore, greater remedial flexibility is permitted under the rules applicable to frustration.

12

Misrepresentation

A statement made during contractual negotiations may be a mere puff, a mere representation or a contractual term. The essence of a representation is that the maker asserts the truth of certain facts and this operates to induce the contract. A term, on the other hand, is essentially a *promise* so that there is an obligation to fulfil it. (See *page 199* for a discussion of the distinction between representations and terms.)

Since a representor does not make a promise, the most appropriate remedy in misrepresentation is for the party induced to be put into the position he would have been in had he not been induced to contract. An actionable misrepresentation therefore renders the contract voidable, i.e., liable to be set aside (rescinded). Damages may also be available with the aim of restoring the parties to their original positions.

(This area of contract law tends to overlap with tort. Factual situations which give rise to a claim in misrepresentation may also give rise to a claim in tort for negligent misstatement.)

SECTION 1: ACTIONABLE MISREPRESENTATION

An actionable misrepresentation is an unambiguous false statement of fact which induces the other party to enter into the contract.

A: Unambiguous false statement of fact

(a) Unambiguous

McInerny v *Lloyds Bank Ltd*
[1974] 1 Lloyd's Rep 246 (CA)

The plaintiff wished to sell some companies to Mackay and wanted payment to be guaranteed by the defendant bank. Mackay asked the bank to give the guarantee and instructed the bank's reply to be sent to the plaintiff. The bank replied that it was not permissible under banking regulations to give the guarantee and that the only available method was to establish an irrevocable credit. The plaintiff subsequently signed a contract with Mackay, who honoured only the first two payments of the purchase price. The plaintiff claimed damages for negligent misrepresentation in respect of the bank's reply which, he argued, amounted to an assurance to make the payments. Held: the bank was not responsible for the interpretation that the plaintiff put on the reply because, on a reasonable construction, the bank had given none of the assurances requested.

(b) Statement

The courts have often interpreted 'statement' to include conduct.

Gordon v Selico Co. Ltd
(1986) 278 EG 53 (CA)

The estate agents of a flat, on behalf of the owners, instructed an independent contractor to do work to the flat 'to bring it up to a very good standard for the purpose of selling'. The contractor deliberately covered up patches of dry rot without attempting to eradicate it. The plaintiffs saw the flat with a view to purchasing it, and contracts were later exchanged incorporating a standard form clause providing 'the purchaser shall buy with full notice of the actual state and condition of the property and shall take it as it stands'. Held: the Court of Appeal agreed with Goulding J at first instance that this concealment amounted to a misrepresentation to the plaintiffs that the flat did not suffer from dry rot.

GOULDING J: . . . The law must be careful not to run ahead of popular morality by stigmatising as fraudulent every trivial act designed to make buildings or goods more readily saleable, even if a highly scrupulous person might consider it dishonest. But it is to my mind quite a different matter for an intending vendor to hide so sinister and menacing a defect as active dry rot. The case is fairly comparable, in my view, with the concealment of cracks indicating the settlement of foundations, considered in *Ridge* v *Crawley* (1958) 172 Estates Gazette 637 and, in the Court of Appeal (1959) 173 Estates Gazette 959. There the plaintiff relied on a combination of words and conduct, but I believe it to be the law that conduct alone can constitute a fraudulent misrepresentation. (See *Horsfall* v *Thomas* (1862) 1 H&C 90 and *Smith* v *Hughes* (1871) LR 6 QB 597.) In my judgment the concealment of dry rot by Mr Azzam was a knowingly false representation that Flat C did not suffer from dry rot, which was intended to deceive purchasers, and did deceive the plaintiffs to their detriment. I am satisfied that the plaintiffs would not have entered into a contract or accepted the lease had they known there was dry rot inside Flat C. . . .

■ QUESTION

I wish to sell my house. I put up wood panelling in the dining room, partly because the room needs decorating and partly to hide serious cracks in a wall. You buy my house and subsequently discover that the wall is defective. Would you have a remedy in misrepresentation in these circumstances?

NOTES

1. It had been argued that the plaintiffs had inspected the flat and that this meant that they were precluded by *Horsfall* v *Thomas* (1862) 1 H & C 90 from complaining of misrepresentation. However, in *Horsfall* v *Thomas*, the defect in the gun was discoverable on inspection but no inspection had taken place, so that the plaintiff could not argue that he had relied upon the misrepresentation. Here the defect was deliberately concealed and was not discovered on routine inspection. It was intended to deceive and did deceive, so there was no question of the plaintiff not having relied upon the misrepresentation.

2. *Caveat emptor* (let the buyer beware) does not apply in cases of fraudulent misrepresentation. *Taylor* v *Hamer* [2002] EWCA Civ 1130, [2003] 1 EGLR 103, [2003] 3 EG 127, concerned the removal of flagstones after inspection and prior to the exchange of contracts. The defendant

had sought to rely on clause 8(1) of the contract ('The buyer is deemed to have inspected the property whether or not the buyer has in fact done so') and condition 3.2.1 of the National Conditions of Sale, 23rd edn. ('The buyer accepts the property in the physical state it is in at the date of the contract . . .'). The judge at first instance had considered that clause 8 assumed inspection immediately prior to exchange of contracts, with the result that there could be no claim for breach of contract. He awarded damages for deceit based on the vendor's untruthful reply to an enquiry prior to exchange asking whether flagstones had been removed. The result was that the claimant was awarded damages of the cost of replacing the flagstones but not their relaying. However, the majority of the Court of Appeal (Sedley LJ and Wall J; Arden LJ dissenting) held that the removal of the flagstones did amount to a breach of contract because this was a contract for the sale of the property including the flagstones in situ. Accordingly, the claimant was entitled to damages for breach of contract to include the cost of replacing and relaying the flagstones. The majority relied on *Gordon* v *Selico* in holding that that the principle of caveat emptor did not apply.

WALL J: . . .

70   If a vendor surreptitiously makes a material alteration to a property, and then both seeks to conceal it from, and lies about it to, the purchaser in answer to pre-contract enquiries, he cannot, in my judgment, rely upon a clause such as 8(1) to protect him from the consequences of his dishonesty. Applied specifically to the contract under discussion, he cannot use clause 8(1) to say that the purchaser should have uncovered the fraud, discovered the true state of the property on inspection, and appreciated that the flagstones *in situ* were not part of the property passing under the contract.

71   In my judgment, the principle of *caveat emptor* does not apply in these circumstances. In *Gordon* v *Selico Co Ltd* [1986] 1 EGLR 71, this court held that a vendor who had fraudulently concealed dry rot could not rely upon what was then clause 4(2)(a) of the Law Society's Conditions of Sale, under which a purchaser of property was deemed to purchase 'with full notice of its actual state and condition'. At p77, Slade LJ, giving the judgment of this court in a powerful constitution (Slade and Woolf LJJ and Sir Denys Buckley), undertook an analysis of *Horsfall* v *Thomas* (1862) 1 H&C 90 and *Smith* v *Hughes* (1871) LR 6 QB 597, and stated, at p77G:

> Both these two cases, however, are distinguishable from the present on their facts. In the former, not only was the defect in the gun patent and discoverable on inspection but the purchaser took no steps to inspect it, so that he did in fact not rely on any misrepresentation as to its condition which might have been made. In the latter case, the vendor did nothing to disguise the character of the oats sold. In the present case, on the learned judge's relevant findings of fact, with which we see no reason to disagree, not only was a fraudulent misrepresentation made, which was intended to mislead prospective purchasers of a lease of the property; the misrepresentation did mislead the purchasers and they acted to their detriment. In these circumstances, it is in our judgment no answer in law to the claim in deceit for the defendants to say that the plaintiffs or their surveyor *could have* discovered the dry rot on a closer inspection of Flat C or were content to purchase without any warranty as to the condition of the property; they and their surveyor were in fact misled by the cover-up operation, as they were intended to be. The general principle *caveat emptor* has no application where a purchaser has been induced to enter the contract of purchase by fraud.

72   *Gordon* was, of course, an action based upon fraudulent misrepresentation and deceit. I none the less find it helpful in the construction of the contract in this case, and the passage I have cited seems to me an additional basis for the proposition that clause 8(1) of the contract does not assist the respondent.

73   It also seems to me that similar considerations apply to clause 3.2.1 of the standard conditions of sale. If, unbeknown to the purchaser, the vendor makes a material alteration to the physical state of part of the property, conceals the alteration and then, in enquiries before contract, denies making it, can he really take advantage of that conduct to insist that what passes under the contract is the property in the condition to which he has reduced it? . . .

3. In *Spice Girls Ltd* v *Aprilla World Service BV* [2002] EWCA Civ 15, [2002] EMLR 27, it was held that when the pop group, the Spice Girls, took part in a photo shoot and promotions for the defendant, a motor scooter manufacturer, prior to the signing of a sponsorship agreement for their tour, this amounted to a misrepresentation by conduct. The misrepresentation was that the group did not know and had no reasonable grounds to believe that any member of the group had an intention to leave before the sponsorship agreement ended. This was false because, as the judge found on the evidence, Geri Halliwell had already declared such an intention to leave the group.

Is there a duty of disclosure? Does silence amount to misrepresentation?

Keates v The Earl of Cadogan

(1851) 10 CB 591; 138 ER 234 (Common Pleas)

The defendant let a house to the plaintiff knowing that the plaintiff wanted it for immediate occupation but did not tell the plaintiff that the house was in fact uninhabitable. Held: in the absence of fraud, the defendant was under no implied duty to disclose the state of the house.

JERVIS CJ: . . . It is not pretended that there was any warranty, express or implied, that the house was fit for immediate occupation: but it is said, that, because the defendant knew that the plaintiff wanted it for immediate occupation, and knew that it was in an unfit and dangerous state, and did not disclose that fact to the plaintiff, an action of deceit will lie. The declaration does not allege that the defendant made any misrepresentation, or that he had reason to suppose that the plaintiff would not do what any man in his senses would do, viz. make proper investigation, and satisfy himself as to the condition of the house before he entered upon the occupation of it. There is nothing amounting to deceit: it was a mere ordinary transaction of letting and hiring. . . .

NOTES
1. This case is based on the principle of *caveat emptor*. Contracting parties should not be expected to share every piece of information with one another where they deal at 'arm's length', unless the non-disclosure is fraudulent (see *Gordon* v *Selico*, *Taylor* v *Hamer*, *above*).
2. The main difficulty with accepting a duty of disclosure is to define that duty and when it will arise. See, for example, *Sykes* v *Taylor-Rose* [2004] EWCA Civ 299, [2004] 2 P & CR 30, where the vendor of a house did not disclose that a child murder had been committed in the house some years earlier. This was not a misrepresentation since the preliminary inquiries required the vendor to disclose 'any other information that you think that the buyer may have a right to know'. It was held that this was to be judged subjectively rather than needing to be objectively justified, and the vendor honestly believed the buyer had no right to be told.

(c) Exceptions to non-disclosure

(i) Misleading statements: half-truths

Dimmock v Hallett

(1866) LR 2 Ch App 21 (CA)

Land for sale was described as 'let to Hickson at £130 p.a.' and another farm was described as 'let to Wigglesworth at £160 p.a.'. Both tenants were yearly Lady Day tenants. No reference was made to the fact that they had both given notice to quit which would expire on Lady Day, although there were statements that some of the other tenants had given notice to quit. Held: it was a fair inference that these tenants had not given notice to quit so that the statement that the farms were let was misleading and amounted to a misrepresentation.

(ii) Change of circumstances

What is the position regarding statements which are true when made but which become false before the contract is made?

With v O'Flanagan

[1936] Ch 575 (CA)

In January 1934, negotiations were entered into for the sale of a medical practice which the vendor represented as having an income of £2,000 per annum. However, by the time the contract was signed in May, the practice had declined due to the vendor's illness, but this was not disclosed. The purchasers sought rescission. Held: the representation was made to induce purchasers to enter into the contract and had to be treated as continuing until the contract was signed. Once it became false, to the knowledge of the representor, there was a misrepresentation if he failed to correct it.

> ROMER LJ: . . . If A with a view to inducing B to enter into a contract makes a representation as to a material fact, then if at a later date and before the contract is actually entered into, owing to a change of circumstances, the representation then made would to the knowledge of A be untrue and B subsequently enters into the contract in ignorance of that change of circumstances and relying upon that representation, A cannot hold B to the bargain. There is ample authority for that statement and, indeed, I doubt myself whether any authority is necessary, it being, it seems to me, so obviously consistent with the plainest principles of equity.

NOTES

1. The misrepresentation occurs when the change of circumstances is not disclosed.
2. It is unlikely that such a misrepresentation would be held to be fraudulent, since it is notoriously difficult to prove fraud (although for an example, see *Banks v Cox (No. 2)*, unrep. 21 December 2000, *page 571*). As Lord Wright MR stated in *With v O'Flanagan* (at p. 584):

   . . . nowadays the Court is more reluctant to use the word 'fraud' and would not generally use the word 'fraud' in that connection because the failure to disclose, though wrong and a breach of duty, may be due to inadvertence or a failure to realise that the duty rests upon the party who has made the representation not to leave the other party under an error when the representation has become falsified by a change of circumstances. . . .

   In *Thomas Witter Ltd v TBP Industries Ltd* [1996] 2 All ER 573 (noted Beale (1995) 111 LQR 385), *page 564*, Jacob J held that a company selling a business had not been fraudulent in failing to disclose a change in accounting method affecting the profit estimates since there was no evidence of dishonesty on the part of the officers concerned. (See the definition of fraudulent misrepresentation at *page 563*.)

   However, in *Banks v Cox (No. 2)*, unrep. 21 December 2000 (discussed at *page 571* in relation to the damages award), after the date of the relevant accounts, the vendors of the nursing home business had been informed that there were to be cuts in the social services budget which would impact on the business. They also knew that there had already been a deterioration in occupancy and turnover but failed to disclose these material changes to the accounts dated five months prior to the sale contract. This failure to disclose amounted to a fraudulent misrepresentation.
3. A further example of change of circumstances and failure to disclose is provided by the decision in *Spice Girls Ltd v Aprilla World Service BV* [2002] EWCA Civ 15, [2002] EMLR 27.

4. This principle does not apply to statements of intention. If the contracting party changes his declared intention before the conclusion of the contract, there is no obligation to communicate that change of intention.

Wales v *Wadham*
[1977] 1 WLR 199

In February 1973, during divorce negotiations, the husband promised to pay the wife £13,000 to finally settle the wife's claim for financial provision. The wife remarried shortly after the divorce decree was made absolute in September 1973 so that, but for the agreement, the ex-husband would have been under no obligation to make financial provision for her. The ex-husband claimed that the agreement should be rescinded for fraudulent misrepresentation, in that the ex-wife had stated on numerous occasions that she would not remarry. Held: the wife had made an honest representation of her intention, which was not a statement of fact or an intention which she did not actually hold at the time. As a result she was under no duty to inform her husband that she had changed her mind.

TUDOR EVANS J: . . . It is submitted that even if the wife's statement that she would never remarry was honestly held, she was under a duty to tell the husband of her changed circumstances, but that she failed to do so. Counsel has referred me to *With* v *O'Flanagan* [1936] Ch 575, in the Court of Appeal . . . Lord Wright MR, at p. 582, quoted, with approval, observations of Fry J in *Davies* v *London & Provincial Marine Insurance Co.* (1878) 8 ChD 469, 475, where he said:

> So, again, if a statement has been made which is true at the time, but which during the course of negotiations becomes untrue, then the person who knows that it has become untrue is under an obligation to disclose to the other the changed circumstances.

The representations in both of these cases related to existing fact and not to a statement of intention in relation to future conduct. A statement of intention is not a representation of existing fact, unless the person making it does not honestly hold the intention he is expressing, in which case there is a misrepresentation of fact in relation to the state of that person's mind. That does not arise on the facts as I have found them. On the facts of this case, the wife made an honest statement of her intention which was not a representation of fact, and I can find no basis for holding that she was under a duty in the law of contract to tell the husband of her change of mind.

NOTE: See *page 551* on the distinction between a statement of fact and a statement of intention.

(d) Of fact

(i) *Statements of belief or opinion*
If the maker of the statement is in no better a position to know the truth of the statement than the recipient of it, and the recipient is aware of this, then the maker's statement is likely to be construed as a statement of opinion and, if false, will not amount to an actionable misrepresentation.

Bisset v *Wilkinson*
[1927] AC 177 (PC)

The owner of a farm told a prospective purchaser that he believed it would support 2,000 sheep. Held: on the evidence the statement was merely a statement of opinion which the vendor honestly held. The evidence was that the owner was not in any better position than the purchaser to know the farm's true capacity since the land had not been used as a sheep farm before. The purchaser was aware that the vendor could do no more than state his belief.

LORD MERRIVALE: . . . [I]t is . . . essential to ascertain whether that which is relied upon is a representation of a specific fact, or a statement of opinion, since an erroneous opinion stated by the party affirming the contract, though it may have been relied upon and have induced the contract on the part of the party who seeks rescission, gives no title to relief unless fraud is established. The application of this rule, however, is not always easy, as is illustrated in a good many reported cases, as well as in this. A representation of fact may be inherent in a statement of opinion and, at any rate, the existence of the opinion in the person stating it is a question of fact.

In ascertaining what meaning was conveyed to the minds of the now respondents by the appellant's statement as to the two thousand sheep, the most material fact to be remembered is that, as both parties were aware, the appellant had not and, so far as appears, no other person had at any time carried on sheep-farming upon the unit of land in question. That land as a distinct holding had never constituted a sheep-farm. . . . In these circumstances . . . the defendants were not justified in regarding anything said by the plaintiff as to the carrying capacity as being anything more than an expression of his opinion on the subject. . . .

NOTES

1. In *Economides* v *Commercial Union Assurance Co. plc* [1997] 3 WLR 1066, when the plaintiff's parents had moved into his flat, he had increased his contents insurance cover to £16,000. Subsequently, there was a burglary and jewellery and silverware belonging to his parents were stolen. The value of the contents stolen was £31,000 and the evidence was that the plaintiff should have insured the contents of the flat for £40,000. The insurance company contended that he had misrepresented the value of the contents. However, it was held that there was no misrepresentation since this was a statement of belief and the plaintiff honestly believed it to be correct. The property in question did not belong to the plaintiff so that he was not in a position to know the true value, and he was under no duty to carry out specific inquiries to establish an objectively reasonable basis for his statement of belief.
2. If, however, the statement maker is in a better position to know the facts, then his statement contains an implied assertion that he knows of facts which justify his opinion.

Smith v Land and House Property Corporation
(1884) 28 ChD 7 (CA)

The plaintiffs advertised a hotel for sale, stating in the particulars that it was let to 'Mr Frederick Fleck (a most desirable tenant)'. In fact Fleck was in arrears with his rent at the time and distress had been threatened (i.e., the taking of goods by the landlord to cover the non-payment of rent). The defendant agreed to purchase the hotel but then refused to complete. The plaintiffs sued for specific performance. Held: this description was not a mere expression of opinion but contained an implied assertion that the vendors knew of no facts leading to the conclusion that Fleck was not a most desirable tenant.

BOWEN LJ: . . . It is material to observe that it is often fallaciously assumed that a statement of opinion cannot involve the statement of a fact. In a case where the facts are equally well known to both parties, what one of them says to the other is frequently nothing but an expression of opinion. The statement of such opinion is in a sense a statement of a fact, about the condition of the man's own mind, but only of an irrelevant fact, for it is of no consequence what the opinion is. But if the facts are not equally known to both sides, then a statement of opinion by the one who knows the facts best involves very often a statement of a material fact, for he impliedly states that he knows facts which justify his opinion. Now a landlord knows the relations between himself and his tenant, other persons either do not know them at all or do not know them equally well, and if the landlord says that he considers that the relations between himself and his tenant are satisfactory, he really avers that the facts peculiarly within his knowledge are such as to render that opinion reasonable. Now are the statements here statements which involve such a representation of material facts? They are statements on a subject as to which *prima facie* the vendors know everything and the purchasers nothing. The vendors state that the property is let to a most desirable tenant, what does that mean? I agree that it is not a guarantee that the tenant will go on paying his rent, but it is to my mind a guarantee of a different sort, and amounts at least to an assertion that nothing has occurred in the relations between the landlords and the tenant which can be considered to make the tenant an unsatisfactory one. That is an assertion of a specific fact. Was it a true assertion? . . . I think that it was not. . . . Now could it . . . be said that nothing had occurred to make Fleck an undesirable tenant? In my opinion a tenant who had paid his last quarter's rent by driblets under pressure must be regarded as an undesirable tenant.

NOTES

1. In *BG plc* v *Nelson Group Services (Maintenance) Ltd* [2002] EWCA Civ 547, unrep. 24 April 2002, Kennedy LJ (with whose judgments the other members of the Court of Appeal agreed) expressed this principle in the following statement: 'When an opinion is expressed, the person who expresses it either does or does not know facts which justify that opinion. The existence of those facts, and his state of knowledge in relation to them, are themselves facts capable of being misrepresented by implication by the expression of opinion' [35].

2. This principle was further extended in *Esso Petroleum Co. Ltd* v *Mardon* [1976] QB 801 (CA) (for full facts see *page 206*). The Court of Appeal stated that where a forecast is made by a person with greater skill and expertise in relation to the subject matter, that person is impliedly stating that reasonable care and skill has been used in preparing the forecast. Lord Denning MR said (at p. 818):

   > . . . it was a forecast made by a party—Esso—who had special knowledge and skill. It was the yardstick . . . by which they measured the worth of a filling station. They knew the facts. They knew the traffic in the town. They knew the through-put of comparable stations. They had much experience and expertise at their disposal. They were in a much better position than Mr Mardon to make a forecast. It seems to me that if such a person makes a forecast, intending that the other should act upon it—and he does act upon it, it can well be interpreted as a warranty that the forecast is sound and reliable in the sense that they made it with reasonable care and skill. It is just as if Esso said to Mr Mardon: 'Our forecast of throughput is 200,000 gallons. You can rely upon it as being a sound forecast of what the service station should do. The rent is calculated on that footing.' If the forecast turned out to be an unsound forecast such as no person of skill or experience should have made, there is a breach of warranty . . . It is very different from the New Zealand case where the land had never been used as a sheep farm and both parties were equally able to form an opinion as to its carrying capacity: see particularly *Bisset* v *Wilkinson* [1927] AC 177, 183–184.

   Although this comment relates to establishing a collateral warranty (term), a statement by an expert will be a statement of fact since the expert is impliedly stating that there are facts to support his forecast.

3. According to Adams and Brownsword, *Understanding Contract Law*, the overall effect of *Esso* v *Mardon* is that people with 'special informational advantages' are held to their representations. It is interesting to compare this with the general discussion of the duty of disclosure and *Keates* v *Cadogan*. It appears that a person with special information cannot be compelled, as a general rule, to disclose that information, but if he does disclose it he will be responsible for that disclosure.

4. If the maker of the statement has no special skill or knowledge relating to the statement, his statements of opinion will not amount to misrepresentations even if his belief is unreasonable (*Hummingbird Motors Ltd* v *Hobbs* [1986] RTR 276).

(ii) Statements as to future conduct and intention

Edgington v Fitzmaurice
(1885) 29 ChD 459 (CA)

The directors of a company issued a prospectus inviting subscriptions for debentures, and stating that money raised would be used to complete alterations in the buildings of the company, to purchase horses and vans, and to develop the trade of the company. The real object of the loan was to enable the directors to pay off pressing liabilities. The plaintiff advanced money on some of the debentures under the mistaken belief that the prospectus offered a charge upon the property of the company, and stated in his evidence that he would not have advanced his money but for such belief, but that he also relied upon the statements contained in the prospectus. Held: the misstatement of object amounted to a misstatement of fact and was a material misrepresentation.

BOWEN LJ: . . . There must be a misstatement of an existing fact: but the state of a man's mind is as much a fact as the state of his digestion. It is true that it is very difficult to prove what the state of a man's mind at a particular time is, but if it can be ascertained it is as much a fact as anything else. A misrepresentation as to the state of a man's mind is, therefore, a misstatement of fact. . . .

NOTES
1. The difficulty resulting from *Edgington* v *Fitzmaurice* is an evidential one, namely to prove what the maker's true intention was at the time of making the statement.
2. In *Inntrepreneur Pub Co (CPC) Ltd* v *Sweeney* [2002] EWHC 1060 (Ch), [2003] ECC 17, [2002] 2 EGLR 132, the tenant of a public house alleged that he had been induced to take a new lease from the defendant landlord as a result of a statement predicting that the tenant would be released from an associated beer tie by the end of March 1998. This statement was no more than a statement of intention and it was honestly held since it was the defendant's policy at that time to release all pubs from the tie (the defendant having given undertakings to this effect to the Secretary of State for Trade and Industry). As a result, the statement could not constitute an actionable misrepresentation. In addition, although the statement might constitute a statement of fact on the basis that it was an opinion or prediction which impliedly stated that the defendant had good grounds for making it (*Smith* v *Land & House, Esso* v *Mardon*), it was not a *false* statement of fact precisely because there were *good grounds* to justify the statement at the time it was made.

(iii) Statements of law can give rise to a claim based on actionable misrepresentation

In *Pankhania* v *Hackney London Borough Council* [2002] EWHC 2441 (Ch), [2002] NPC 123, the claimant had bid for commercial property, part of which was occupied by NCP, National Car Parks Ltd, and used as a car park. The claimant alleged that he had been induced to purchase the properties as a result of misrepresentations in the auction brochure to the effect that NCP was a contractual licensee whose occupation could be terminated by giving three months' notice, when in fact NCP was a business tenant and protected under the Landlord and Tenant Act 1954. The claimant sought damages for misrepresentation to cover the payment made to NCP to secure its departure from the car park. The defendants claimed that any misrepresentations were misrepresentations as to law and there was a longstanding rule that statements of law were not actionable. The judge held that, since the decision of the House of Lords in *Kleinwort Benson Ltd* v *Lincoln City Council* [1999] 2 AC 349 to the effect that it was not the case that there was no remedy available for a mistake of law, a misrepresentation of law could be an actionable misrepresentation. He awarded damages under s. 2(1) of the Misrepresentation Act 1967, *page 582*, on the basis that the defendant could not show that it reasonably believed its statements relating to NCP to be true. (See *Pankhania v Hackney LBC (Damages)* [2004] EWHC 323 (Ch), [2004] 1 EGLR 135 for the damages award.)

B: Induces the contract

(a) Materiality

In *Pan Atlantic Co. Ltd* v *Pine Top Insurance Co. Ltd* [1995] 1 AC 501, the House of Lords was unanimous in considering that in a claim based on misrepresentation it was necessary to establish both that the statement was material and that it actually induced the contract. Their Lordships differed on the test of materiality. Lord Mustill (with whose reasoning Lords Goff and Slynn agreed; Lord Templeman and Lord Lloyd dissenting on this issue) stated that the test for materiality is whether the representation relates to a matter which would have influenced the reasonable man. This is an objective test, whereas a test of actual inducement is subjective. (It had previously been generally considered that materiality was relevant only in non-disclosure cases, and that the only test in a misrepresentation case was whether the misrepresentation induced the contract. For example, in *Museprime Properties Ltd* v *Adhill Properties Ltd* (1990) 36 EG 114, it had been held that if the statement had actually induced the contract there was no need to establish that it would have influenced a reasonable man to contract, or to contract on those terms.)

Pan Atlantic was confirmed by the Court of Appeal in *St Paul Fire and Marine Insurance Co. (UK) Ltd* v *McConnell Dowell Constructors Ltd* [1996] 1 All ER 96. Evans LJ (at p. 112) appears to accept that in some cases where materiality is easily established, inducement can be inferred (subject to evidence to the contrary).

(b) Inducement

Redgrave v Hurd
(1881) 20 ChD 1 (CA)

The plaintiff, a solicitor who was shortly to retire, placed an advertisement offering to take a partner in the practice who would not object to purchasing the plaintiff's suburban residence. The defendant replied to the advertisement and was told by the plaintiff that the practice brought in about £300 a year. The plaintiff had shown the defendant summaries for three years, showing a business of just less than £200 a year and stated that the rest of the income was made up of business not included in the summaries which was detailed in a bundle of papers shown to the defendant. The defendant did not examine these papers, which in fact showed that there was next to no additional business so that income from the business was only £200 a year. The defendant signed an agreement to purchase the house for £1,600 and paid a deposit of £100. Subsequently, the defendant discovered the true facts about the business and refused to complete. The plaintiff brought an action for specific performance, and the defendant counterclaimed for rescission of the contract and damages alleging misrepresentation as to the business. Held: if a material misrepresentation is made to a party, then he must be taken to have relied on it in entering into the contract, unless it can be shown that the representee knew of the facts showing the representation to be untrue or that he either expressly stated or showed by his conduct that he did not rely on the representation. The defendant was therefore entitled to have the contract rescinded and his deposit returned. (However, he was not entitled to damages because at the time of this case damages were available only where the misrepresentation was fraudulent, and fraud had not been pleaded by the defendant in his counterclaim.)

JESSEL MR: . . . If a man is induced to enter into a contract by a false representation it is not a sufficient answer to him to say, 'If you had used due diligence you would have found out that the statement was untrue. You had the means afforded you of discovering its falsity, and did not choose to avail yourself of them.' I take it to be a settled doctrine of equity, not only as regards specific performance but also as regards rescission, that this is not an answer.

. . . Nothing can be plainer, I take it, on the authorities in equity than that the effect of false representation is not got rid of on the ground that the person to whom it was made has been guilty of negligence. One of the most familiar instances in modern times is where men issue a prospectus in which they make false statements of the contracts made before the formation of a company, and then say that the contracts themselves may be inspected at the offices of the solicitors. It has always been held that those who accepted those false statements as true were not deprived of their remedy merely because they neglected to go and look at the contracts. Another instance with which we are familiar is where a vendor makes a false statement as to the contents of a lease, as, for instance, that it contains no covenant preventing the carrying on of the trade which the purchaser is known by the vendor to be desirous of carrying on upon the property. Although the lease itself might be produced at the sale, or might have been open to the inspection of the purchaser long previously to the sale, it has been repeatedly held that the vendor cannot be allowed to say, 'You were not entitled to give credit to my statement.' It is not sufficient, therefore, to say that the purchaser had the opportunity of investigating the real state of the case, but did not avail himself of that opportunity. . . .

NOTES
1. Although the normal inference is that the buyer will check all information, this was displaced in *Redgrave* v *Hurd* by the desire to make the representor responsible for his statements and prevent him shifting that responsibility to the buyer.
2. It might be argued that the buyer is negligent in failing to make inquiries where the opportunity is available to him, and his damages should consequently be reduced for contributory negligence. The argument in favour of apportionment is, however, incompatible with the tone of the judgment of Jessel MR in *Redgrave* v *Hurd* that the buyer has no obligation to investigate. (Although see the discussion of contributory negligence, *pages 589–91*.)
3. It is clear from *Horsfall* v *Thomas* (1862) 1 H & C 90, that a representation cannot induce a contract unless the representee knew of it. In that case, the defect might have been discovered by the buyer if he had inspected the gun but he did not, and the representation could not therefore have induced the contract.

Attwood v Small
(1838) 6 Cl & F 232; [1835–42] All ER Rep 258 (HL)

The vendor made statements about the earning capacity of mines he was selling. The prospective buyers arranged for their co-directors and experienced agents to examine the property and accounts. They reported (incorrectly) that the vendor's statements were true. The buyers purchased the mine but later claimed to rescind, alleging fraudulent misrepresentation by the vendor. Held: first, that there was no fraud and, secondly, the buyers had not relied on the vendor's statements because they had tested their accuracy and relied on the results of their own investigations.

NOTES

1. *Attwood* v *Small* is often cited as authority for the fact that if the representee carries out his own investigations, then he does not rely on the representation. However, it was stated *obiter* in *S. Pearson & Son Ltd* v *Dublin Corporation* [1907] AC 351, that even if a representee carries out his own investigations, the representor will be liable for misrepresentation if the misrepresentation is made fraudulently.

2. In addition, for *Attwood* v *Small* to preclude action based on a representation, the plaintiff must have relied *only* on the results of his investigations and not at all on the representation itself, since a representation need not be the only reason inducing a contract as long as it is one of the reasons (*Edgington* v *Fitzmaurice* (1885) 29 ChD 459, *page 551*). This point is aptly illustrated by *Morris* v *Jones* [2002] EWCA Civ 1790, unrep. 6 December 2002. The claimant had been negotiating to purchase a leasehold interest in a basement flat and the defendant had represented that it had been 'tanked'. However, the claimant had received three survey reports identifying problems of dampness in the basement. The defendant therefore alleged that the misrepresentation had not induced the making of the contract. The Court of Appeal held, relying on *Edgington* v *Fitzmaurice*, that the claimant could still rely on the misrepresentation as a factor inducing the making of the contract. (The judge had found that the representation was fraudulent and this point was not contested on appeal, which may explain why the fraud point in *S. Pearson & Son Ltd* v *Dublin Corporation* was not argued.)

3. In *County NatWest Bank Ltd* v *Barton* [2002] 4 All ER 494 (Note), [1999] Lloyd's Rep Bank 408, the Court of Appeal held that, in the context of a fraudulent misrepresentation, if the false statement was likely to play a part in the decision of a reasonable person to contract, inducement would be presumed (unless the representor satisfied the court to the contrary).

SECTION 2: THE REMEDY OF RESCISSION

As misrepresentation renders the contract voidable at the option of the misrepresentee, the main remedy will be rescission, which *in principle* is available for fraudulent, negligent, and innocent misrepresentation, and which involves the return from each party of anything which has passed under the contract.

A: Limits to the right to rescind

Rescission is an equitable remedy and is subject to a number of bars preventing its exercise.

(a) Affirmation

Long v Lloyd
[1958] 1 WLR 753 (CA)

The defendant advertised a lorry for sale in a newspaper and described it as being in 'exceptional condition'. The plaintiff saw the vehicle at the defendant's premises and the defendant stated that it was capable of a speed of 40 miles per hour. On 22 October, the plaintiff, accompanied by the defendant, took the lorry for a trial run and the defendant represented that the lorry's fuel consumption was 11 miles to the gallon. The plaintiff then bought the lorry for £750. Two days later, on 24 October, the plaintiff attempted a journey in the lorry but the dynamo ceased to function and the plaintiff was advised to fit a reconstructed dynamo. He also noticed that an oil seal was defective, there was a crack in one of the wheels and the vehicle had consumed eight gallons of fuel when it had travelled only 40 miles. When the defendant was advised of these defects he offered to pay half the cost of the reconstructed dynamo and the plaintiff accepted this offer. The repair having taken place, on 25 October the plaintiff's brother took the vehicle on a journey, and on 26 October the plaintiff learnt that the lorry had broken down on this journey. The plaintiff brought an action for rescission of the contract on the ground of non-fraudulent misrepresentation. (Note there was no right to damages for such a misrepresentation at this time.) Held: certainly by the time that the plaintiff sent the lorry on a journey on 25 October he had affirmed the misrepresentations and accepted the lorry in full knowledge of the condition and performance of the vehicle. (Thus the plaintiff was left with no remedy at all.)

PEARCE LJ: . . . [A] strict application to the facts of the present case of Denning LJ's view to the effect that the right (if any) to rescind after completion on the ground of innocent misrepresentation is barred by acceptance of the goods must necessarily prove fatal to the plaintiff's case. Apart from special circumstances, the place of delivery is the proper place for examination and for acceptance. It was open to the plaintiff to have the lorry examined by an expert before driving it away, but he chose not to do so. It is true, however, that the truth of certain of the representations, for example, that the lorry would do 11 miles to the gallon—could not be ascertained except by user and, there-fore—the plaintiff should have a reasonable time to test it. Until he had had such an opportunity it might well be said that he had not accepted the lorry, always assuming, of course that he did nothing inconsistent with the ownership of the seller. An examination of the facts, however, shows that on any view he must have accepted the lorry before he purported to reject it.

Thus, to recapitulate the facts, after the trial run the plaintiff drove the lorry home from Hampton Court to Sevenoaks, a not inconsiderable distance. After that experience he took it into use in his business by driving it on the following day to Rochester and back to Sevenoaks with a load. By the time he returned from Rochester he knew that the dynamo was not charging, that there was an oil seal leaking, that he had used 8 gallons of fuel for a journey of 40 miles, and that a wheel was cracked. He must also, as we think, have known by this time that the vehicle was not capable of 40 miles per hour. As to oil consumption, we should have thought that, if it was so excessive that the sump was practically dry after 300 miles, the plaintiff could have reasonably been expected to discover that the rate of consumption was unduly high by the time he had made the journey from Hampton Court to Sevenoaks and thence to Rochester and back.

On his return from Rochester the plaintiff telephoned to the defendant and complained about the dynamo, the excessive fuel consumption, the leaking oil seal and the cracked wheel. The defendant then offered to pay half the cost of the reconstructed dynamo which the plaintiff had been advised to fit, and the plaintiff accepted the defendant's offer. We find this difficult to reconcile with the continuance of any right of rescission which the plaintiff might have had down to that time.

But the matter does not rest there. On the following day the plaintiff, knowing all that he did about the condition and performance of the lorry, dispatched it, driven by his brother, on a business trip to Middlesbrough. That step, at all events, appears to us to have amounted, in all the circumstances of the case, to a final acceptance of the lorry by the plaintiff for better or for worse, and to have con-clusively extinguished any right of rescission remaining to the plaintiff after completion of the sale.

NOTE: Pearce LJ also suggested that rescission might well have been lost much earlier. He appears to have relied upon Denning LJ's comments in *Leaf* v *International Galleries*, seeking to equate this area of law with the rules in the Sale of Goods Act 1979 on the right to reject for breach of condition (*see below*). At this time there was also no available remedy in damages for such a misrepresentation, although damages were clearly available for breach of contract even where the right to reject had been lost.

(b) Lapse of time

Leaf v *International Galleries*
[1950] 2 KB 86 (CA)

In 1944, the defendants sold the plaintiff a picture which they represented to have been painted by Constable. In 1949, the plaintiff tried to sell it and discovered it was not by Constable. He sought rescission and repayment of the purchase price. Held: this remedy had been lost because it had not been exercised within a reasonable time.

DENNING LJ: . . . The question is whether the plaintiff is entitled to rescind the contract on the ground that the picture in question was not painted by Constable. I emphasise that it is a claim to rescind only: there is no claim in this action for damages for breach of condition or breach of warranty. The claim is simply one for rescission. At a very late stage before the county court judge counsel did ask for leave to amend by claiming damages for breach of warranty, but it was not allowed. No claim for damages is before us at all. The only question is whether the plaintiff is entitled to rescind.

The way in which the case is put by [counsel], on behalf of the plaintiff, is this: he says that this was an innocent misrepresentation and that in equity he is, or should be, entitled to claim rescission even of an executed contract of sale on that account. He points out that the judge has found that it is quite possible to restore the parties to their original position. It can be done by simply handing back the picture to the defendants.

In my opinion, this case is to be decided according to the well known principles applicable to the sale of goods. This was a contract for the sale of goods. There was a mistake about the quality of the subject-matter, because both parties believed the picture to be a Constable; and that mistake was in one sense essential or fundamental. But such a mistake does not avoid the contract: there was no mistake at all about the subject-matter of the sale. It was a specific picture, 'Salisbury Cathedral.' The parties were agreed in the same terms on the same subject-matter, and that is sufficient to make a contract: see *Solle* v *Butcher* [1950] 1 KB 671.

There was a term in the contract as to the quality of the subject-matter: namely, as to the person by whom the picture was painted—that it was by Constable. That term of the contract was, according to our terminology, either a condition or a warranty. If it was a condition, the buyer could reject the picture for breach of the condition at any time before he accepted it, or is deemed to have accepted it; whereas, if it was only a warranty, he could not reject it at all but was confined to a claim for damages.

I think it right to assume in the buyer's favour that this term was a condition, and that, if he had come in proper time he could have rejected the picture; but the right to reject for breach of condition has always been limited by the rule that, once the buyer has accepted, or is deemed to have accepted, the goods in performance of the contract, then he cannot thereafter reject, but is relegated to his claim for damages: see s. 11, sub-s. 1 (c), of the Sale of Goods Act, 1893, and *Wallis, Son & Wells* v *Pratt & Haynes* [1911] AC 394.

The circumstances in which a buyer is deemed to have accepted goods in performance of the contract are set out in s. 35 of the Act, which says that the buyer is deemed to have accepted the goods, amongst other things, 'when, after the lapse of a reasonable time, he retains the goods without intimating to the seller that he has rejected them.' In this case the buyer took the picture into his house and, apparently, hung it there, and five years passed before he intimated any rejection at all. That, I need hardly say, is much more than a reasonable time. It is far too late for him at the end of five years to reject this picture for breach of any condition. His remedy after that length of time is for damages only, a claim which he has not brought before the court.

Is it to be said that the buyer is in any better position by relying on the representation, not as a condition, but as an innocent misrepresentation? I agree that on a contract for the sale of goods an innocent material misrepresentation may, in a proper case, be a ground for rescission even after the contract has been executed. . . .

Although rescission may in some cases be a proper remedy, it is to be remembered that an innocent misrepresentation is much less potent than a breach of condition; and a claim to rescission for innocent misrepresentation must at any rate be barred when a right to reject for breach of condition is barred. A condition is a term of the contract of a most material character, and if a claim to reject on that account is barred, it seems to me a fortiori that a claim to rescission on the ground of innocent misrepresentation is also barred.

So, assuming that a contract for the sale of goods may be rescinded in a proper case for innocent misrepresentation, the claim is barred in this case for the self-same reason as a right to reject is barred. The buyer has accepted the picture. He had ample opportunity for examination in the first few days after he had bought it. Then was the time to see if the condition or representation was fulfilled. Yet he has kept it all this time. Five years have elapsed without any notice of rejection. In my judgment he cannot now claim to rescind. His only claim, if any, as the county court judge said, was one for damages, which he has not made in this action. . . .

NOTES
1. The damages claim to which Denning LJ was referring was that for breach of contract. Nowadays there is a right to *claim* damages in misrepresentation, but only if the misrepresentation was at least negligent.
2. Since *Leaf* v *International Galleries* was a case of non-fraudulent misrepresentation, time ran from the date of the contract. One of the advantages in alleging fraudulent misrepresentation is that time runs from the date when the fraud was, or could with reasonable diligence have been, discovered.

(c) Restitution is impossible

Clarke v *Dickson*
(1858) EB & E 148; 120 ER 463 (Queen's Bench)

In 1853, the plaintiff purchased shares in a mining company as a result of representations made by the defendants who were directors of this company. The company was later wound up. The plaintiff then discovered that the representations made to him had been fraudulent. He wanted to give up the shares and recover the purchase price. Held: he could not.

ERLE J: . . . The plaintiff claims to repudiate the contract under which shares were allotted to him; to give up the shares, and recover back the price. There are several grounds of objection, all falling under the same principle: the plaintiff cannot avoid the contract under which he took the shares, because he cannot restore them in the same state as when he took them. In 1853 the plaintiff accepted the shares; and from that time he was, in point of law, in possession of the mine, and worked it by his agent the purser. After three years working of the mine, and trying to make a profit, he cannot restore the shares as they were before this was done. But, further, he not only had the chance of profit, but dividends were declared, and received by him. They were not received in money, it is true; but the receipt of money's worth has the same effect in law. Then he has also changed the nature of the article: the shares he received were shares in a company on the cost book principle; the plaintiff offers to restore them after he has converted them into shares in a joint stock corporation. Lastly, the offer to restore these shares is not made till after the Company is in the course of being wound up, when all chance of profit is over, and the shares can only be a source of loss. . . .

In *Thomas Witter* v *TBP Industries Ltd* [1996] 2 All ER 573 (for facts see *page 564*), Jacob J held that rescission was not available:

> [Counsel for the plaintiff] tied his claim to rescission to the claim in fraud. I never was quite sure why, since rescission is available also for innocent misrepresentation. Even if I had found fraud, however, I would not have granted rescission. This remedy is not available where it is not possible to restore the parties to their position before the contract. Although Melton Medes kept the Witter business separate, it is unrealistic to regard it as the same as the business conveyed. There have been numerous changes to staff and personnel (including the departure of Mr Francis who had exceptional sales skills). Those personnel who have stayed have been in different pension schemes, there are mortgagees of the business and so on. Time has moved on and third parties would, I think, be affected. [Counsel's] actual submission was that it was not shown that third parties would be affected. So he was suggesting that the onus was on the defendants to avoid rescission by showing innocent third parties would be affected. I cannot think that is right. The Thomas Witter business has been in the hands of Melton Medes for four years. It is they who would know who or what might be affected by a transfer back to Tarmac.

This suggests that rescission of a contract to purchase a business can be lost by the vendor contesting the right to rescind so that the misrepresentee has to seek a remedy of rescission via court action. It is generally assumed that rescission is a self-help remedy, i.e. the innocent party's election to rescind is determinative rather than court action. However, the problem in practice is that the guilty party may not accept rescission and a court has to determine the innocent party's ability to rescind. In *Thomas Witter* Jacob J assessed the availability of rescission at the date of the hearing when, if rescission is achieved by the party's action, he should have considered the position at the date of that action to rescind. However, it is unrealistic for a court to evaluate the ability to achieve *restitutio in integrum* at that date since time and events will not have stood still in the interim. (See O'Sullivan 'Rescission as a Self Help Remedy: A Critical Analysis' [2000] CLJ 509). It would seem that the self-help analysis of the nature of rescission has also led to the English courts rejecting a discretion to award partial rescission.

Partial rescission is not permitted

It appears that a misrepresentee cannot rescind part of the contract but must rescind the whole. In *TSB Bank plc* v *Camfield* [1995] 1 WLR 430, the Court of Appeal rejected a claim for partial rescission and held that a charge had to be set aside in its entirety. This can be contrasted with the approach of the High Court of Australia in *Vadasz* v *Pioneer Concrete (SA) Pty* (1995) 184 CLR 102, where it was held that the court could set aside part of a contract of guarantee whilst leaving the remainder. The Privy Council in *Far Eastern Shipping Co Ltd* v *Scales Trading Ltd* [2001] 1 All ER (Comm) 319 did not decide between these competing authorities.

However, in *De Molestina* v *Ponton* [2002] 1 All ER (Comm) 587, Colman J emphatically rejected partial rescission on the basis that it conflicted with the essential nature of the remedy of rescission as restoring the parties to their original positions and the requirement of *restitutio in integrum*.

COLMAN J: . . .

(6) Rescission: the relevant principles

6.1 There can be no doubt that, according to the present state of development of English law, this court is bound by the general principle that a misrepresentee is permitted to rescind the whole of a contract but not part of it. This has been recognised as well established since the eighteenth century: see *Myddleton* v *Lord Kenyon* (1794) 2 Ves 391 at 408, 409, 30 ER 689 at 697, 698, per Lord Eldon of Loughborough LC:

> 'The deed may be set aside *in toto* . . . I cannot make a new bargain for the parties . . . The consequence is not, that a new agreement is to be made, to be introduced by this Court: but they must be reinstated in their former situation.'

The House of Lords has affirmed this position in *United Shoe Machinery Co of Canada* v *Brunet* [1909] AC 330 where Lord Atkinson observed that the defrauded party could not avoid one part of a contract and affirm another part 'unless indeed the parts are so severable from each other as to form two separate contracts'. More recently the Court of Appeal has reaffirmed this principle in *TSB Bank plc* v *Camfield* [1995] 1 All ER 951, [1995] 1 WLR 430. In that case the wife of the borrower had been induced by him to consent to stand surety and to their granting a legal mortgage over the matrimonial home as security for personal borrowing by her husband. He had innocently misrepresented to her that the security was limited to £15,000 when in truth it was unlimited. The trial judge had given judgment against the husband for the full amount due (£47,315) but against the wife for £15,000, in effect rescinding her contract of suretyship pro tanto the extent of the misrepresentation. The Court of Appeal allowed her appeal. Nourse LJ expressly rejected the argument that in a case of rescission the court could impose terms the effect of which would be that rescission was subject to the wife making the payment which she would have been obliged to make under the contract she believed herself to be entering into. In adopting the approach to a similar problem taken by Ferris J in *Allied Irish Bank plc* v *Byrne* [1995] 1 FCR 430 at 462, Nourse LJ founded his conclusion on Lord Browne-Wilkinson's speech in *Barclays Bank plc* v *O'Brien* [1993] 4 All ER 417 at 432, [1994] 1 AC 180 at 199:

> 'It seems to me that setting aside must refer to setting aside in its entirety. Indeed the concept of a partial setting aside is, to my mind, an elusive one, although I can see that if a different equitable remedy were appropriate a charge might be left on foot, but the chargee could be restrained from enforcing it beyond a particular extent. This is what Purchas L.J. seems to have had in mind. [Counsel for the bank] relied upon the flexibility of equity in relation to restitution. He cited *Chitty on Contracts*, 26th edition, para. 468 and (*O'Sullivan* v *Management Agency and Music Ltd* [1985] 3 All ER 351 at 366, [1985] QB 428 at 458). But for my part I cannot escape the fact that what Mrs. Byrne claims, and what she is in my judgment entitled to, is to set aside the transaction *which, to my mind, is an all or nothing process*. This is consistent with the fact that a party who complains of having entered into a transaction on the basis of a misrepresentation is saying that if he had been aware of the truth, he would not have entered into the transaction. If this claim is upheld, the court seeks to put that party into the position in which he would have been if the representation had not been made.' (My emphasis.)

Roch LJ observed:

> 'Normally, if the representee is entitled to rescind the legal charge, that will have been effected by the representee's pleading that the transaction has been or should be set aside; that is to say, the transaction would have been set aside before the matter reaches the court. The court is not being asked to grant equitable relief; nor is it, in my view, granting equitable relief to which terms may be attached.' (See the *TSB Bank* case [1995] 1 All ER 951 at 960, [1995] 1 WLR 430 at 438–439.)

In the earlier case of *Thorpe* v *Fasey* [1949] 2 All ER 393, [1949] Ch 649 Wynn-Parry J referred to the judgment of the Divisional Court in *Sheffield Nickel & Silver Plating Co Ltd* v *Unwin* (1877) 2 QBD 214 at 223 per Lush J:

'A contract voidable for fraud cannot be avoided when the other party cannot be restored to his status quo: *Clarke* v *Dickson* ((1858) E B & E 148, 120 ER 463). For a contract cannot be rescinded in part and stand good for the residue. If it cannot be rescinded in toto, it cannot be rescinded at all; but the party complaining of the non-performance, or the fraud, must resort to an action for damages.'

Wynn-Parry J commented:

'There, again, the language used indicates that the court there intended to pray in aid a well established general principle that a contract cannot be rescinded in part and stand good for the residue. If it cannot be rescinded *in toto* it cannot be rescinded at all, and one reason for not directing rescission is that the parties, or one of them, cannot be restored to their *status quo*.' (See [1949] 2 All ER 393 at 399, [1949] Ch 649 at 664.)

6.2   These authorities do, in my judgment, make it very clear that the principle that there cannot be partial rescission is part of the wider requirement that there cannot be rescission unless there can be restitutio in integrum. Further, that requirement is the conceptual consequence of the basic nature of the remedy of rescission which is to discharge all the parties from the bargain into which the misrepresentor has induced them to enter. It is not and never has had the function of providing compensation for the misrepresentation or some hybrid solution to reflect what would be fair between the parties having regard to the nature of the representation and the extent to which one party has been misled by another. Consistently with that, the court has no power to create a new bargain for the parties. What has been induced is the original bargain and it is the purpose of the remedy to return the parties to their position before that particular bargain was made. There is therefore no room for any form of equitable engineering directed to reconstructing the fabric of the original contract.

6.3   Consideration of those authorities which have been concerned with restitutio in integrum shows that rescission will not be withheld where substantial restitution is possible, but this remedy is not fettered by some overriding equitable test as to whether the consequences would work unfairly to the misrepresentor. Thus there are numerous cases where rescission has involved the return of property by the representee which has substantially diminished in value through no fault of the representee (eg *Armstrong* v *Jackson* [1917] 2 KB 822, [1916–17] All ER Rep 1117). That said, there is undoubtedly a degree of flexibility in the approach to restitution. It has to be possible to achieve *substantial* restitution, albeit *precise* restitution of what passed under the contract may no longer be possible. What the courts are doing in those cases where they deploy that flexibility which involves, for example, the taking of an account or an order for the payment of compensation or an indemnity, is to make adjustments ancillary to and in aid of restitution to take account of changes to property or benefits derived from the contract by one side or another during the period between the making of the contract and the proceedings for rescission. This is clearly reflected in the speech of Lord Wright in *Spence* v *Crawford* [1939] 3 All ER 271 at 288–289:

'The remedy is equitable. Its application is discretionary, and, where the remedy is applied, it must be moulded in accordance with the exigencies of the particular case. The general principal is authoritatively stated in a few words by Lord Blackburn in *Erlanger* v *New Sombrero Phosphate Co* ((1878) 3 App Cas 1218, [1874–80] All ER Rep 271), where, after referring to the common law remedy of damages, he went on to say ((1878) 3 App Cas 1218 at 1278–1279, [1874–80] All ER Rep 271 at 286): "But a court of equity could not give damages, and, unless it can rescind the contract, can give no relief. And on the other hand, it can take accounts of profits, and make allowance for deterioration. And I think the practice has always been for a court of equity to give this relief whenever, by the exercise of its powers, it can do what is practically just, though it cannot restore the parties precisely to the state they were in before the contract." In that case, Lord Blackburn is careful not to seek to tie the hands of the court by attempting to form any rigid rules. The court must fix its eyes on the goal of doing "what is practically just." How that goal may be reached must depend on the circumstances of the case, but the court will be more drastic in exercising its discretionary powers in a case of fraud than in a case of innocent misrepresentation. This is clearly recognised by Lindley, M.R., in the *Lagunas* case (*Lagunas Nitrate Co* v *Lagunas Syndicate*

[1899] 2 Ch 392). There is no doubt good reason for the distinction. A case of innocent misrepresentation may be regarded rather as one of misfortune than as one of moral obliquity. There is no deceit or intention to defraud. The court will be less ready to pull a transaction to pieces where the defendant is innocent, whereas in the case of fraud the court will exercise its jurisdiction to the full in order, if possible, to prevent the defendant from enjoying the benefit of his fraud at the expense of the innocent plaintiff. Restoration, however, is essential to the idea of restitution. To take the simplest case, if a plaintiff who has been defrauded seeks to have the contract annulled and his money or property restored to him, it would be inequitable if he did not also restore what he had got under the contract from the defendant. Though the defendant has been fraudulent, he must not be robbed, nor must the plaintiff be unjustly enriched, as he would be if he both got back what he had parted with and kept what he had received in return. The purpose of the relief is not punishment, but compensation. The rule is stated as requiring the restoration of both parties to the *status quo ante*, but it is generally the defendant who complains that restitution is impossible. The plaintiff who seeks to set aside the contract will generally be reasonable in the standard of restitution which he requires. However, the court can go a long way in ordering restitution if the substantial identity of the subject-matter of the contract remains. Thus, in the *Lagunas* case, though the mine had been largely worked under the contract, the court held that, at least if the case had been one of fraud, it could have ordered an account of profits or compensation to make good the change in the position. In *Adam* v *Newbigging* ((1888) 13 App Cas 308, [1886–90] All ER Rep 975), where the transaction related to the sale of a share in a partnership, which had become insolvent since the contract, the court ordered the rescission and mutual restitution, though the misrepresentation was not fraudulent, and gave ancillary directions so as to work out the equities. These are merely instances. Certainly in a case of fraud the court will do its best to unravel the complexities of any particular case, which may in some cases involve adjustments on both sides.' . . .

6.5   The claimants have relied on the submission that English law, or at least the common law, is in a state of development which makes it so uncertain that the issue of rescission cannot suitably be determined on an application for summary judgment dismissing the claim. In support of this argument [counsel] relies on the decision of the High Court of Australia in *Vadasz* v *Pioneer Concrete (SA) Pty Ltd* (1995) 184 CLR 102. That case dealt with the question whether, if the representee guarantor was induced to enter into a written guarantee of the past and future indebtedness of his company by a representation that it was confined to future indebtedness, he was entitled to avoid the guarantee to the extent of past, but not future, indebtedness. It was therefore similar on its material facts to *TSB Bank plc* v *Camfield* [1995] 1 All ER 951, [1995] 1 WLR 430. The High Court of Australia adopted a very different approach to that of the Court of Appeal. It held on the basis of the speech of Lord Blackburn in *Erlanger* v *New Sombrero Phosphate Co* (1878) 3 App Cas 1218, [1874–80] All ER Rep 271 and the observations of Lord Wright in *Spence* v *Crawford* [1939] 3 All ER 271, which I have already cited, that the guarantor's liability was limited to future indebtedness. The court concluded that it was appropriate to look at what was practically just for *both* parties, not only the guarantor, and stated: 'To enforce the guarantee to the extent of future indebtedness is to do no more than hold the appellant to what he was prepared to undertake independently of any misrepresentation.' (See *Vadasz'* case (1995) 184 CLR 102 at 115.) It observed that a similar approach had been taken in a number of cases, including in the footnote *Barclays Bank* v *O'Brien* [1992] 4 All ER 983, [1993] QB 109 in the Court of Appeal and noting that the appeal had been dismissed by the House of Lords ([1993] 4 All ER 417, [1994] 1 AC 180), but apparently entirely overlooking the fact that such an approach was diametrically inconsistent with the passage from the speech of Lord Browne-Wilkinson which I have already cited as one of the bases for the conclusion of the Court of Appeal in the *TSB Bank* case.

6.6   In *Far Eastern Shipping Co Public Ltd* v *Scales Trading Ltd* [2001] 1 All ER (Comm) 319, a decision of the Judicial Committee of the Privy Council on an appeal from the Court of Appeal of New Zealand in respect of the enforceability of a guarantee induced by non-disclosure, one of the arguments advanced by the guaranteed supplier was that as held by the New Zealand Court of Appeal, on the basis of *Vadasz'* case, rescission of the guarantee should be permitted only if the guarantor paid the principal debt so far accrued before rescission. The Privy Council found it unnecessary to decide whether *Vadasz'* case was to be preferred to the *TSB Bank* case and decided to allow the appeal on the grounds that there was no factual basis for the conclusion that if full disclosure had been made, the representee would still have been prepared to guarantee part of the debt. Although Lord Scott of Foscote described the issue whether *Vadasz'* case should be preferred to the *TSB Bank* case as 'an important one', there is nothing in the judgment to suggest that the Privy Council held any concluded or even provisional view on the matter.

6.7 I conclude that on this issue the present state of English law is not in any doubt at all and nothing in *Vadasz'* case renders it doubtful, whatever may be the position in Australia. By reference to the state of English law as so far developed at House of Lords level that case was wrongly decided. Unless and until the House of Lords overrules the analysis by Lord Browne-Wilkinson in the *Barclays Bank* case and its particular application in the *TSB Bank* case, the principles binding on this court are well settled. The scope of the equitable discretion in a rescission claim is confined to adjustments to achieve substantial restitution to accommodate events that have occurred after the contract has come into force and does not extend to the general reconstruction of the bargain to achieve an objectively overall fair result.

6.8 I therefore reject [counsel's] submission that, on grounds of uncertainty in the law, these applications cannot suitably be determined before a full trial.

6.9 The crucial issue in the present applications is, however, one of mixed fact and law and it is how one identifies the criteria for determining whether a number of separate contracts are part of a single overall transaction for the purposes of the rule against rescission of part of a transaction. On this point there is little or no help in the authorities, but applications of general principles strongly suggests the necessary criteria. If a representee is induced to enter into separate contracts A and B by the same misrepresentation, it may be that performance of contract B depends on the prior performance of contract A. In that case one cannot rescind contract A without also rescinding contract B. To permit the survival of contract B would be inconsistent with the principles of restitutio in integrum. But there may be cases where, although both contracts were induced by the same misrepresentation either can be performed without performance of the other. In that case the representee may rescind unless the contract not sought to be rescinded would never have been entered into by the parties without also entering into the other. Thus, for example, in a case where the transaction is divided into different contracts simultaneously negotiated, it may be that the consideration for the whole bargain is written into one contract, leaving only nominal consideration in the other contract. In that event it would not be open to the representee to leave open the contract that gave him the main consideration while rescinding the other contract under which his primary performance obligation lay. Again, to do otherwise would not effect restitutio in integrum. Or there may be cases where it is clear from the terms of the contracts and the matrix evidence that the subject matter of the contracts is so interrelated that, although it would be theoretically possible to perform each separately, one would never have been entered into without that contract sought to be rescinded. However, in the absence of structural interdependence between separate contracts, the most usual determinant of inseparability is likely to be the distribution of consideration for the whole bargain between the separate contracts.

NOTES

1. See Poole and Keyser 'Justifying Partial Rescission in English Law' (2005) 121 LQR 280 for contrary argument.
2. Colman J notes that '[t]here is . . . no room for any form of equitable engineering directed to reconstructing the fabric of the original contract' in order to achieve a fair result between the parties. This is entirely different to the flexibility available in equity to recognise changes in the value of the benefit received where substantial restitution is possible on the facts (see Lord Blackburn in *Erlanger* v *New Sombrero Phosphate Co* (1878) 3 App Cas 1218). In such circumstances, the court may exercise a discretion to allow for the payment of compensation to account for deterioration or the taking of an account to reflect changes in the value of the subject matter in the relevant period.

3. It is important to determine whether there is a single transaction or a number of separate and distinct contracts. If the contracts are separate, it may be possible to rescind only one of them unless they are interrelated in that performance of each contract is linked. This was the issue on the facts in *De Molestina* v *Ponton* and the judge seems to have considered that, in principle, the three share distribution agreements were interdependent in the sense that no one 'SDA' would have been entered into without the other two but that these agreements could be rescinded without interfering with performance of certain other agreements that had been made. However, he concluded that this question could not be conclusively determined prior to a full trial.

(d) Where a bona fide third-party purchaser has acquired the goods before rescission

See the discussion of mistake as to identity, at *page 85*.

(c) Where the court exercises its discretion under s. 2(2) to award damages instead of rescission

See *page 591*.

SECTION 3: TYPES OF MISREPRESENTATION AND DAMAGES

The nature of the damages available for the misrepresentation turns on the type of misrepresentation, but it is no longer the case that damages can only be claimed for fraudulent misrepresentations. Rescission alone may have the effect of restoring the parties to their original positions, but may not do so where, for example, the representee has incurred consequential expenses. In such cases, damages may be available *in addition* to rescission for fraudulent and negligent misrepresentations. Where rescission is not available the only remedy will be damages for misrepresentation, although damages cannot be claimed for innocent misrepresentation.

A: Fraudulent misrepresentation: the tort of deceit

Derry v *Peek*
(1889) 14 App Cas 337 (HL)

An Act incorporating a tram company provided that the carriages might be moved by steam power with the consent of the Board of Trade. The directors of the company issued a prospectus containing a statement that the Act gave the company the right to use steam power. The plaintiff bought shares relying on this statement, but the Board of Trade refused to approve the use of steam power by the company and it was later wound up. The plaintiff brought an action against the directors in deceit based upon the false statement. Held: the directors were not liable since the statement in the prospectus had been made by them in the honest belief that it was true.

LORD HERSCHELL: . . . I think the authorities establish the following propositions: First, in order to sustain an action of deceit, there must be proof of fraud, and nothing short of that will suffice. Secondly, fraud is proved when it is shewn that a false representation has been made (1) knowingly, or (2) without belief in its truth, or (3) recklessly, careless whether it be true or false. Although I have treated the second and third as distinct cases, I think the third is but an instance of the second, for one who makes a statement under such circumstances can have no real belief in the truth of what he states. To prevent a false statement being fraudulent, there must, I think, always be an honest belief in its truth. And this probably covers the whole ground, for one who knowingly alleges that which is false, has obviously no such honest belief. Thirdly, if fraud be proved, the motive of the person guilty of it is immaterial. It matters not that there was no intention to cheat or injure the person to whom the statement was made.

Thomas Witter Ltd v *TBP Industries Ltd*
[1996] 2 All ER 573

The defendants owned a carpet manufacturing business which the plaintiff wished to purchase. During the negotiations the defendants provided the plaintiff with audited accounts and management accounts for 1988 and estimated profit figures for 1989. They also allowed the plaintiff to see the October 1989 management accounts, which included a special one-off expense of £120,000 in respect of problems with carpets supplied to one customer. However, the defendants did not indicate that these accounts were prepared on a different basis to the audited accounts and contained deferred pattern book expenditure. The parties concluded the contract for the sale of the business.

Within six months, the plaintiff claimed that it had been induced by representations made in the accounts, namely (i) the statement that they included the special one-off expense of £120,000 (thereby implying that general profits would otherwise be higher) when the actual amount of this expense would be no more than £50,000, and (ii) by not disclosing the change in accounting basis, i.e. that the accounts included deferred pattern book expenditure. The allegation was that these representations had been made recklessly (and so were fraudulent). Alternatively it was alleged that they were negligent. Held: these misrepresentations were not made fraudulently. Recklessness for the purposes of fraudulent misrepresentation required the statements to have been made dishonestly. Although there was no evidence of dishonesty, since there was a belief that these statements were true, the misrepresentations were made negligently.

JACOB J:

The legal test for fraudulent misrepresentation
First then deceit. [Counsel for the plaintiff] relied upon part of the classic speech of Lord Herschell in *Derry* v *Peek* (1889) 14 App Cas 337 at 375–376, [1886–90] All ER Rep 1 at 22–23:

> The ground upon which an alleged belief was founded is a most important test of its reality. I can conceive many cases where the fact that an alleged belief was destitute of all reasonable foundation would suffice of itself to convince the Court that it was not really entertained, and that the representation was a fraudulent one. So, too . . . if I thought that a person making a false statement had shut his eyes to the facts, or purposely abstained from inquiring into them, I should hold that honest belief was absent, and that he was just as fraudulent as if he had knowingly stated that which was false.

He further submitted that where a person has made a representation of fact and, before the contract is concluded, comes to learn of its falseness, that person comes under a duty to correct the representation and, if he fails to do so, then is taken to be fraudulent. [Counsel] relied upon the speech of Lord Blackburn in *Brownlie* v *Campbell* (1880) 5 App Cas 925 at 950:

I quite agree in this, that whenever a man in order to induce a contract says that which is in his knowledge untrue with the intention to mislead the other side, and induce them to enter into the contract, that is downright fraud; in plain English, and Scotch also, it is a downright lie told to induce the other party to act upon it, and it should of course be treated as such. I further agree in this: that when a statement or representation has been made in the *bona fide* belief that it is true, and the party who has made it afterwards comes to find out that it is untrue, and discovers what he should have said, he can no longer honestly keep up that silence on the subject after that has come to his knowledge, thereby allowing the other party to go on, and still more, inducing him to go on, upon a statement which was honestly made at the time when it was made, but which he has not now retracted when he has become aware that it can be no longer honestly persevered in. That would be fraud too, I should say, as at present advised.

This argument related to the changed basis of profit forecast point. It was argued that Mr Simpson, having given to Mr Puri profit forecasts on one basis of pattern book expenditure, knew his later forecast was on a different basis and should be taken as fraudulent for not disclosing that fact.

In my judgment [counsel for the plaintiff's] argument is wrong in law. He takes the reference to 'recklessness' out of context—divorcing it from the heart of the tort of deceit, namely dishonesty. One only has to read earlier in the speech of Lord Herschell to see that this is so:

> . . . there has always been present, and regarded as an essential element, that the deception was wilful either because the untrue statement was known to be untrue, or because belief in it was asserted without such belief existing . . . I cannot assent to the doctrine that a false statement made through carelessness, and which ought to have been known to be untrue, of itself renders the person who makes it liable to an action for deceit.' (See (1889) 14 App Cas 337 at 369, 373, [1886–90] All ER Rep 1 at 19, 21.)

Findings of fact in relation to fraudulent misrepresentation

So what I have to decide is whether Mr Simpson or Mr Lloyd deliberately set out to mislead Mr Puri, not by a deliberate untruth (for that is not alleged) but by its equivalent, such recklessness as to amount to a disregard for the truth. I have no difficulty in acquitting these witnesses of any such intent. I must explain why.

So far as pattern book expenditure deferrals in the October management accounts are concerned, I accept Mr Simpson's evidence that he did not know of these right up until the time of the contract. Nor did Mr Lloyd. By the time of the contract both thought that until November pattern book expenditure was written off as it was incurred. No one had ever suggested that the management accounts sometimes had ad hoc deferrals for 'smoothing' purposes.

In relation to the Allied problem . . . it is clear that by the time of the contract the representation had been defined as set out in the disclosure letter, namely £120,000 charged to the September and October accounts.

What does matter is whether Mr Simpson was so reckless in the estimate that he should be regarded as fraudulent. He says he was given the figure of £120,000 by Mr Hogarth as a 'fag packet' calculation at a Witter board meeting on 21 November. Mr Hogarth has no recollection whatever of the cost of the Allied problem being discussed. There appears never to have been a detailed estimate of the figure being worked out. Now I accept Mr Simpson's evidence that he got a rough estimate from Mr Hogarth. It was obviously important. So I think he was negligent not to get a proper estimate, or to tell Mr Puri that he had not got a proper estimate. But it was not dishonest of him to give that rough estimate to Mr Puri. He believed it, but knowing there was no proper check, his belief was not reasonable.

NOTES
1. This case clarifies the distinction between recklessness and negligence. In order to be reckless the statement maker would need to be in a position where he does not know whether a statement is true or false but takes the risk and asserts that it is true. There is no such dishonesty involved in a statement which is negligent since the statement maker honestly

believes that his statement is true, even if he ought to have known it was false and was careless in not checking first.

2. Since an action based on fraudulent misrepresentation is in the tort of deceit, the measure of damages is tortious.

(a) Measure of damages for fraudulent misrepresentation

(i) All direct loss flowing from the transaction

The proper measure of damages for deceit was held by the Court of Appeal in *Doyle v Olby (Ironmongers) Ltd* [1969] 2 QB 158, to be 'all the damage directly flowing from the tortious act of fraudulent inducement which was not rendered too remote by the plaintiff's own conduct, whether or not the defendant could have foreseen the loss'.

Doyle v *Olby* was approved and applied in the following case:

Smith New Court Securities Ltd v Scrimgeour Vickers (Asset Management) Ltd
[1997] AC 254 (HL)

In July 1989, the plaintiff company had purchased a parcel of shares in FIS Inc. at the price of 82.25 pence per share as a result of representations by the vendors of the shares that there were two other bidders involved. In fact this was not the case. However, before this was discovered it was announced in the September that FIS Inc. had been the victim of a major fraud by a third party. This resulted in a considerable fall in the share price and the plaintiff was eventually able to sell the shares for only 30–40 pence per share. The plaintiff sought damages for fraudulent misrepresentation. The trial judge assessed the damages as being the difference between the price paid and the real value of the shares at the date of the sale taking into account the then undiscovered fraud, i.e. the difference between 82.25p and 44p. This resulted in a damages award of £10.7 million. On appeal the Court of Appeal reversed this award and held that the correct measure was the difference between the price paid and the market value at the date of the sale, i.e. the difference between 82.25p and 78p. The damages award was therefore reduced to £1,196,000. On appeal to the House of Lords it was argued that the plaintiff had caused the loss by retaining the shares rather than selling them on immediately. Held: the victim of fraud was entitled to compensation for all actual loss, including consequential loss, which flowed directly from the transaction irrespective of whether it was foreseeable loss. Although the normal method of calculating such loss would be the difference between the price paid and the real value of the shares as at the date of the share purchase, on these facts that would not compensate the plaintiff for loss suffered. The fraudulent misrepresentation had led the plaintiff to pay too high a price for the shares and, given that the shares had been purchased with a view to retaining them and selling later, the plaintiff was locked into the transaction. Therefore the damages award was the difference between 82.25p and 44p.

LORD BROWNE-WILKINSON: . . . *Doyle* v *Olby (Ironmongers) Ltd* establishes four points. First, that the measure of damages where a contract has been induced by fraudulent misrepresentation is reparation for all the actual damage directly flowing from (i.e. caused by) entering into the transaction. Second, that in assessing such damages it is not an inflexible rule that the plaintiff must bring into account the value as at the transaction date of the asset acquired: although the point is not adverted to in the judgments, the basis on which the damages were computed shows that there can be circumstances in which it is proper to require a defendant only to bring into account the actual proceeds of the asset provided that he has acted reasonably in retaining it. Third, damages for deceit are not limited to those which were reasonably foreseeable. Fourth, the damages recoverable can include consequential loss suffered by reason of having acquired the asset.

In my judgment *Doyle* v *Olby (Ironmongers) Ltd* was rightly decided on all these points. It is true, as to the second point, that there were not apparently cited to the Court of Appeal the 19th century cases which established the 'inflexible rule' that the asset acquired has to be valued as at the transaction date . . . But in my judgment the decision on this second point is correct. The old 'inflexible rule' is both wrong in principle and capable of producing manifest injustice. The defendant's fraud may have an effect continuing after the transaction is completed, e.g. if a sale of gold shares was induced by a misrepresentation that a new find had been made which was to be announced later it would plainly be wrong to assume that the plaintiff should have sold the shares before the announcement should have been made. Again, the acquisition of the asset may, as in *Doyle* v *Olby (Ironmongers) Ltd* itself, lock the purchaser into continuing to hold the asset until he can effect a resale. To say that in such a case the plaintiff has obtained the value of the asset as at the transaction date and must therefore bring it into account flies in the face of common sense: how can he be said to have received such a value if, despite his efforts, he has been unable to sell.

Doyle v *Olby (Ironmongers) Ltd* has subsequently been approved and followed by the Court of Appeal in *East* v *Maurer* [1991] 1 WLR 461 and *Downs* v *Chappell* [1997] 1 WLR 426. In both cases the plaintiffs had purchased a business as a going concern in reliance on the defendant's fraudulent misrepresentation. In each case after discovery of the fraud they sold the business at a loss and recovered by way of damages the difference between the original purchase price and the price eventually realised on a resale, i.e. the old date of transaction rule was not applied. In *Banque Bruxelles Lambert SA* v *Eagle Star Insurance Co. Ltd* [1997] AC 191 your Lordships treated the measure of damages for fraud as being in a special category regulated by the principles of *Doyle* v *Olby (Ironmongers) Ltd*.

. . . In many cases, even in deceit, it will be appropriate to value the asset acquired as at the transaction date if that truly reflects the value of what the plaintiff has obtained. Thus, if the asset acquired is a readily marketable asset and there is no special feature (such as a continuing misrepresentation or the purchaser being locked into a business that he has acquired) the transaction date rule may well produce a fair result. The plaintiff has acquired the asset and what he does with it thereafter is entirely up to him, freed from any continuing adverse impact of the defendant's wrongful act. The transaction date rule has one manifest advantage, namely that it avoids any question of causation. One of the difficulties of either valuing the asset at a later date or treating the actual receipt on realisation as being the value obtained is that difficult questions of causation are bound to arise. In the period between the transaction date and the date of valuation or resale other factors will have influenced the value or resale price of the asset. It was the desire to avoid these difficulties of causation which led to the adoption of the transaction date rule. But in cases where property has been acquired in reliance on a fraudulent misrepresentation there are likely to be many cases where the general rule has to be departed from in order to give adequate compensation for the wrong done to the plaintiff, in particular where the fraud continues to influence the conduct of the plaintiff after the transaction is complete or where the result of the transaction induced by fraud is to lock the plaintiff into continuing to hold the asset acquired.

Finally, it must be emphasised that the principle in *Doyle* v *Olby (Ironmongers) Ltd* [1969] 2 QB 158, strict though it is, still requires the plaintiff to mitigate his loss once he is aware of the fraud. So long as he is not aware of the fraud, no question of a duty to mitigate can arise. But once the fraud has been discovered, if the plaintiff is not locked into the asset and the fraud has ceased to operate on his mind, a failure to take reasonable steps to sell the property may constitute a failure to mitigate his loss requiring him to bring the value of the property into account as at the date when he discovered the fraud or shortly thereafter.

In sum, in my judgment the following principles apply in assessing the damages payable where the plaintiff has been induced by a fraudulent misrepresentation to buy property: (1) the defendant is bound to make reparation for all the damage directly flowing from the transaction; (2) although such damage need not have been foreseeable, it must have been directly caused by the transaction; (3) in assessing such damage, the plaintiff is entitled to recover by way of damages the full price paid by him, but he must give credit for any benefits which he has received as a result of the transaction; (4) as a general rule, the benefits received by him include the market value of the property acquired as at the date of acquisition; but such general rule is not to be inflexibly applied where to do so would prevent him obtaining full compensation for the wrong suffered; (5) although the circumstances in which the general rule should not apply cannot be comprehensively stated, it will normally not apply where either (a) the misrepresentation has continued to operate after the date of the acquisition of the asset so as to induce the plaintiff to retain the asset or (b) the circumstances of the case are such that the plaintiff is, by reason of the fraud, locked into the property. (6) In addition, the plaintiff is entitled to recover consequential losses caused by the transaction; (7) the plaintiff must take all reasonable steps to mitigate his loss once he has discovered the fraud. . . .

How then do those principles apply in the present case? First, there is no doubt that the total loss incurred by Smith was caused by the Roberts fraud, unless it can be said that Smith's own decision to retain the shares until after the revelation of the Guerin fraud was a causative factor. The Guerin fraud had been committed before Smith acquired the shares on 21 July 1989. Unknown to everybody, on that date the shares were already pregnant with disaster. Accordingly when, pursuant to the Roberts fraud, Smith acquired the Ferranti shares they were induced to purchase a flawed asset. This is not a case of the difficult kind that can arise where the depreciation in the asset acquired between the date of acquisition and the date of realisation may be due to factors affecting the market which have occurred after the date of the defendant's fraud. In the present case the loss was incurred by reason of the purchasing of the shares which were pregnant with the loss and that purchase was caused by the Roberts fraud.

Can it then be said that the loss flowed not from Smith's acquisition but from Smith's decision to retain the shares? In my judgment it cannot. The judge found that the shares were acquired as a market-making risk and at a price which Smith would only have paid for an acquisition as a market-making risk. As such, Smith could not dispose of them on 21 July 1989 otherwise than at a loss. Smith were in a special sense locked into the shares having bought them for a purpose and at a price which precluded them from sensibly disposing of them. It was not alleged or found that Smith acted unreasonably in retaining the shares for as long as they did or in realising them in the manner in which they did.

In the circumstances, it would not in my judgment compensate Smith for the actual loss they have suffered (i.e. the difference between the contract price and the resale price eventually realised) if Smith were required to give credit for the shares having a value of 78p on 21 July 1989. Having acquired the shares at 82¼p for stock Smith could not commercially have sold on that date at 78p. It is not realistic to treat Smith as having received shares worth 78p each when in fact, in real life, they could not commercially have sold or realised the shares at that price on that date. In my judgment, this is one of those cases where to give full reparation to Smith, the benefit which Smith ought to bring into account to be set against its loss for the total purchase price paid should be the actual resale price achieved by Smith when eventually the shares were sold.

NOTES

1. Lord Mustill suggested that 'in the future when faced with situations such as the present, courts would do well to be guided by the seven propositions set out by . . . Lord Browne-Wilkinson'.

2. Lord Steyn explained the policy rationale underlying the principles determining remedies for fraudulent misrepresentation (deceit):

> Such a policy of imposing more stringent remedies on an intentional wrongdoer serves two purposes. First it serves a deterrent purpose in discouraging fraud. . . .
>
> And in the battle against fraud civil remedies can play a useful and beneficial role. Secondly, as between the fraudster and the innocent party, moral considerations militate in favour of requiring the fraudster to bear the risk of misfortunes directly caused by his fraud. I make no apology for referring to moral considerations. The law and morality are

inextricably interwoven. To a large extent the law is simply formulated and declared morality. And, as *Oliver Wendell Holmes, The Common Law* (1968) p 106 observed, the very notion of deceit with its overtones of wickedness is drawn from the moral world.

3. Although the remoteness rules in an action for deceit and in that for negligent misrepresentation under s. 2(1) of the Misrepresentation Act 1967 allow recovery of all direct losses (see, e.g., *Naughton v O'Callaghan* [1990] 3 All ER 191, *page 588*, where Waller J allowed recovery under s. 2(1) of the difference between the price paid and the value of the horse at the time the misrepresentation was discovered, on the basis that retaining the horse in order to train it was precisely the action to be expected in the circumstances), Lord Steyn made one distinction clear by stating that 'in an action for deceit the plaintiff is entitled to recover all his loss directly flowing from the fraudulently induced *transaction*. In the case of a negligent misrepresentation the rule is narrower: the recoverable loss does not extend beyond the consequences flowing from the negligent *misrepresentation* (see *Banque Bruxelles Lambert SA v Eagle Star Insurance Co. Ltd* [1995] 2 All ER 769, [1995] QB 375)'. This may prove significant where there are a number of misrepresentations inducing the making of the contract.

4. In *Pankhania v Hackney LBC (Damages)* [2004] EWHC 323 (Ch), [2004] 1 EGLR 135 (for facts see *page 551*), Geoffrey Vos QC appeared to accept that in principle the *Smith New Court* principle could be applied to a s. 2(1) claim for damages because of the fiction of fraud (see *page 584*). However, on the facts there was no continuing misrepresentation or lock-in, and the property could have been sold at any time subject to the NCP tenancy of the car park. Thus, the *Smith New Court* measure was inapplicable on the facts. The judge therefore applied 'the normal measure' of damages (i.e. the difference between the sum paid and the actual value of the property—a figure of £500,000). He accepted that mitigation applied to claims for fraudulent misrepresentation and to damages claims under s. 2(1), but considered that the claimant had not acted unreasonably in seeking to obtain possession so that the damages would not be reduced to take account of what had happened to the property in the meantime.

In his comments on passages from the speech of Lord Browne-Wilkinson in *Smith New Court*, the judge fails to make the distinction discussed above between damages flowing from having entered into the contract and damages flowing from the specific misrepresentation (which led to the contract).

(ii) Can loss of profits be recovered if fraudulent misrepresentation induced the purchase of a business? If so, how will those lost profits be calculated?

East v *Maurer*
[1991] 1 WLR 461 (CA)

In 1979, the plaintiffs bought one of the two hair salon businesses belonging to the defendant in Bournemouth for £20,000, and were induced to do so in part by a representation by the defendant that he did not intend to work in the other salon except in emergencies. In fact he continued to work full-time at the other salon, and this had such an effect on the plaintiffs' business that it was never profitable. They eventually sold it in 1989 for £7,500 and brought an action alleging fraudulent misrepresentation. The trial judge assessed damages so as to include an award of £15,000 for loss of profits, which was based on the profit that the defendant would have made in the salon if he had not sold it, less a deduction of 25 per cent for the fact that the plaintiffs were not as experienced. The defendant appealed against this assessment of loss of profits. Held: relying on *Doyle v Olby*, that loss of profits, which is normally claimed in contract as part of the expectation, could be recovered in an action for deceit on the basis that it was actual damage directly flowing from the misrepresentation. However, this loss of profits had to be calculated using tortious principles so as to compensate the plaintiffs for the profit they might have made had the misrepresentation not been made (the profit they might have expected to make in another hairdressing business bought for a similar sum), rather than on the contractual basis of the profits that this business might have made if the representation had been true and the defendant had not worked in the other salon. Consequently, the award for loss of profits was reduced to £10,000.

BELDAM LJ: [Counsel] for the defendants, submits that there is a difference in the manner in which damages are assessed for breach of contract and for the tort of deceit. He says that the authorities show that no damages at all are recoverable for loss of profits in an action of deceit. Although there is no express decision which states that to be the case, in no case which has dealt with the proper measure of damage in an action of deceit has there been an award for loss of profits, although one would have expected to see one. . . . Finally, he submits that even if damages for loss of profit are recoverable the judge assessed the figure at too high a level, and on an incorrect basis.

That the measure of damages for the tort of deceit and for breach of contract are different no longer needs support from authority. Damages for deceit are not awarded on the basis that the plaintiff is to be put in as good a position as if the statement had been true; they are to be assessed on a basis which would compensate the plaintiff for all the loss he has suffered, so far as money can do it.

This was confirmed in *Doyle* v *Olby (Ironmongers) Ltd* [1969] 2 QB 158, to which both the judge and this court were referred and was a case in which the facts were similar to those of the present case.

. . . [I]t seems to me clear that there is no basis upon which one could say that loss of profits incurred whilst waiting for an opportunity to realise to its best advantage a business which has been purchased are irrecoverable. It is conceded that losses made in the course of running the business of a company are recoverable. If in fact the plaintiffs lost the profit which they could reasonably have expected from running a business in the area of a kind similar to the business in this case, I can see no reason why those do not fall within the words of Lord Atkin in *Clark* v *Urquhart* [1930] AC 28, 'actual damage directly flowing from the fraudulent inducement.'

So I consider that on the facts found by the judge in the present case, the plaintiffs did establish that they had suffered a loss due to the defendants' misrepresentation which arose from their inability to earn the profits in the business which they hoped to buy in the Bournemouth area. . . .

However, I am not satisfied that in arriving at the figure of £15,000 the judge approached the quantification of those damages on the correct basis. It seems to me that he was inclined to base his award on an assessment of the profits which the business actually bought by the plaintiffs might have made if the statement made by the first defendant had amounted to a warranty that customers would continue to patronise the salon in Exeter Road; further that he left out of account a number of significant factors. What he did was to found his award on an evaluation which he made of the profits of the business at Exeter Road made by the first defendant in the year preceding the purchase of the business by the plaintiffs. Basing himself on figures which had been given to him by an accountant, and making an allowance for inflation he arrived at a figure for the profits which might have been made if the first defendant had continued to run the business at Exeter Road during the 3¼ years. He then made an allowance only for the fact that the second plaintiff's experience in hair styling and hairdressing was not as extensive or as cosmopolitan as that of the first defendant. Thus he based his award on an assessment of what the profits would have been, less a deduction of 25 per cent. for the second plaintiff's lack of experience.

It seems to me that he should have begun by considering the kind of profit which the second plaintiff might have made if the representation which induced her to buy the business at Exeter Road had not been made, and that involved considering the kind of profits which *she* might have expected to make in another hairdressing business bought for a similar sum . . .

The judge, . . . had two clear starting points. First, that any person investing £20,000 in a business would expect a greater return than if the sum was left safely in the bank or in a building society earning interest, and a reasonable figure for that at the rates then prevailing would have been at least £6,000. Secondly, that the salary of a hairdresser's assistant in the usual kind of establishment was at this time £40 per week and that the assistant could expect tips in addition. That would produce a figure of over £7,000, but the proprietor of a salon would clearly expect to earn more, having risked his money in the business. It seems to me that those are valid points from which to start to consider what would be a reasonable sum to award for loss of profits of a business of this kind. As was pointed out by Winn LJ in *Doyle* v *Olby (Ironmongers) Ltd* [1969] 2 QB 158, 169, this is not a question which can be considered on a mathematical basis. It has to be considered essentially in the round, making what he described as a 'jury assessment'.

Taking all the factors into account, I think that the judge's figure was too high; for my part I would have awarded a figure of £10,000 for that head of damage, and to this extent I would allow the appeal.

NOTES
1. This is an example of a statement of intention amounting to a statement of fact, because it was found as a fact that the defendant did not actually have this intention when he made the statement. See *Edgington* v *Fitzmaurice* (*page 551*).
2. See Marks (1992) 108 LQR 386.
3. Although in *East* v *Maurer* the Court of Appeal was prepared to assess profits based upon a hypothetical identical salon without evidence that any such salon existed, in *Davis* v *Churchward* (unrep., 6 May 1993, noted Chandler (1994) 110 LQR 35) the Court of Appeal looked at actual similar public houses which could have been purchased for the same amount and held that because the weekly turnover on these public houses would have been the same as the actual weekly turnover on the public house purchased (£1,500), there could be no recovery for lost profits. In particular, unlike Beldam LJ in *East* v *Maurer*, Nourse LJ refused to take account of the profit that would have been made had the purchase money instead been invested in a building society, on the basis that this was hypothetical since it had been found as a fact that another public house would have been purchased.

    Nevertheless, this is an example of a contract induced by a fraudulent misrepresentation of weekly turnover, and it must be asked whether it is likely that the plaintiff would indeed have purchased a similar public house knowing that the actual turnover of that public house was only £1,500.
4. In *Banks* v *Cox* (*Costs*) [2002] EWHC 2166 (Ch), unrep. 25 October 2002, Mr and Mrs Banks had purchased a nursing home for £250,000 as a result of a fraudulent misrepresentation (see *page 547*), taking a fifty-year lease at a rental of £50,000 per annum. The judge considered that they were locked into the business and would have to continue with it; the change in the policy of social services meant that they were not in a position to cover their indebtedness. He therefore awarded damages of £250,000 (the return of the price paid on the basis that no benefit had been received to set off against this figure). In addition, he awarded £500,000 as compensation for the fact that the purchasers were locked into the lease and had commitments to their bank relating to this loss-making business. The judge also awarded loss of profits from the date of the contract to the date of judgment of £400,000. This figure was calculated on the basis of the profit that Mr and Mrs Banks would have made if they had purchased a comparable nursing home, discounted to take account of market conditions and what he referred to as 'the comparative lack of experience of the claimants'. The amount of the damages award was largely academic since the defendants were also in financial difficulty.
5. On the basis of *East* v *Maurer*, it will not be possible to recover damages for loss of profit where a profit is in fact being made, albeit not at the level anticipated in reliance on the misrepresentation. To award damages for loss of profit in such circumstances would amount to treating the representation as if it were a contractual promise.

Downs v Chappell
[1997] 1 WLR 426 (CA)

In 1988, the plaintiffs were interested in purchasing a bookshop business owned by Chappell, the first defendant. The sale particulars represented that in 1987 the business had a turnover of approximately £109,000 and a gross profit of £33,500. The plaintiffs asked the first defendant for independent verification, and at the first defendant's request the second defendant, accountants, wrote to the plaintiffs broadly confirming these figures. The plaintiffs therefore purchased the business for £120,000 considering that, on the basis of these figures, and with a mortgage of £60,000, they could still generate an adequate income. However, they later discovered that the figures had been overstated and that the business would not generate sufficient income to cover their costs. They therefore sought to sell it. Up until March 1990 the business was making a profit, although it did not accord with the profit level that had been represented. In March 1990 the plaintiffs refused two offers of £76,000 for the business in the belief that they could get more if they held out. However, they eventually sold the business for less than £60,000 and claimed damages in the tort of deceit against the first defendant and damages in negligence against the second defendant. They also claimed an annual alleged loss of £5,000 profit by comparing the actual profitability of the business with that represented. Held: since the plaintiffs had been induced by fraudulent and negligent misrepresentations relating to profitability to purchase a business, the damages recoverable were their income and capital losses to the date when they discovered the misrepresentations and had the opportunity to avoid further losses. However, they could not recover for income losses because they were still trading at a profit up to March 1990. In addition, as far as the capital loss was concerned, they could not recover the difference between the £120,000 price paid and the price at which they eventually sold the business. The capital loss was £44,000 (£120,000 less £76,000).

HOBHOUSE LJ (with whose judgment Butler-Sloss LJ and Roch LJ agreed): . . . It is not in dispute that it was possible for the plaintiffs to sell out in the first quarter of 1990. If necessary they would have had to abandon the business. Indeed, one or more of those expressing an interest in buying the shop and the flat in the early part of 1990 were not doing so for the purpose of running a bookshop. Since the business was unlikely to be capable of covering the cost of servicing its capital, it is not suggested that its goodwill had then a significant market value. It follows that any losses which the plaintiffs suffered after the spring of 1990 were not caused by the defendants' torts but by the plaintiffs' decision not to sell out at that date for a figure of about £75,000. The only basis upon which the plaintiffs might have been able to recover any later loss would have been that they had been reasonably but unsuccessfully attempting to mitigate their loss further and had unhappily increased their loss: see *McGregor on Damages* 15th ed. (1988), pp. 197–199, paras. 323–324. On the facts of this case the plaintiffs are unable to make such a claim and have not sought to do so. They have argued that they did not act unreasonably in rejecting the offers of £76,000 in March 1990. Even accepting that they acted reasonably, the fact remains that it was their choice, freely made, and they cannot hold the defendants responsible if the choice has turned out to have been commercially unwise. They were no longer acting under the influence of the defendants' representations. The causative effect of the defendants' faults was exhausted; the plaintiffs' right to claim damages from them in respect of those faults had likewise crystallised. It is a matter of causation.

The correct finding of fact is that the plaintiffs suffered a loss of £44,000 as a result of entering into the contract with Mr Chappell.

NOTES

1. This demonstrates the dangers of such voluntary action in trying to avoid the consequences of a purchase induced by misrepresentation. The causal link with the defendants' misrepresentations had ended. It would therefore appear sensible to accept the first reasonable offer to purchase after discovering the misrepresentation or, in preference, seek to rescind (assuming this to be possible). In both *Downs* v *Chappell* and *Smith* v *Scrimgeour Vickers* there appears to have been no attempt to rescind. (In *Smith* v *Scrimgeour Vickers* an argument to rescind after the sale of the shares was not pursued at the trial and, it is submitted, would not have succeeded because it would not have been possible to return the shares.)

2. The trial judge had held that although there were false statements made by the defendants, the plaintiffs had not established on the balance of probabilities that they would not have purchased the business had the true figures been quoted. However, not surprisingly the Court of Appeal rejected this and held that an actionable misrepresentation required only that the plaintiffs establish that the figures induced the transaction.

3. Hobhouse LJ stated that damages for fraudulent misrepresentation should not be greater than the loss which would have been suffered 'had the represented, or supposed, state of affair actually existed'. In other words, the defendant should not be liable for loss that would have been suffered by the purchaser of the business even if the representation had been true, e.g., a general fall in market price. It was therefore necessary to compare the loss suffered with the hypothetical position had the representation in fact been true. However, *Downs* v *Chappell* was overruled on this point by the House of Lords in *Smith* v *Scrimgeour Vickers* [1997] AC 254. No such check is necessary.

4. In *Standard Chartered Bank* v *Pakistan National Shipping Corp. (Assessment of Damages)* [1999] 1 Lloyd's Rep 747, Toulson J held that the test of whether the plaintiff had acted reasonably in mitigation of loss in a claim based on fraud was the same as in any tort or breach of contract action. The judge considered that if the loss could reasonably have been avoided it could not be regarded as having been caused by the misrepresentation. See also the comment of Potter LJ, on appeal to the Court of Appeal, [2001] EWCA Civ 55, [2001] 1 All ER (Comm) 822, [41], that in the tort of deceit the concepts of causation and mitigation are 'two sides of the same coin'.

5. In *Banks* v *Cox (Costs)* [2002] EWHC 2166, unrep. 25 October 2002, the claimants were unable to mitigate because they were locked in as a result of the fraudulent misrepresentation and their indebtedness to their bank resulted from the purchase. They had been advised that although they had paid £250,000 for the business, they would need to put it on the market for £120,000 in order to have any possibility of achieving a sale. However, that would not have been possible due to the level of their indebtedness to their bank.

(iii) What is the position where the contract entered into as a result of a fraudulent misrepresentation is profitable for the misrepresentee? Can the misrepresentee recover damages in deceit on the basis that he would otherwise have entered into a more profitable contract on better terms?

Clef Acquitaine SARL v *Laporte Materials (Barrow) Ltd*
[2001] QB 488 (CA)

The plaintiff company had agreed to purchase quotas of goods from the defendant and to distribute them in France. The defendant had fraudulently stated that the price list applicable represented the lowest prices at which the defendant's salesmen could sell the goods to trade customers. In fact other price lists were used for trade customers and the evidence was that certain trade customers had obtained big discounts on these prices. The plaintiff managed to resell the goods purchased at a profit but sought damages in the tort of deceit representing the difference between the price paid for the goods and the price that probably could have been negotiated but for the misrepresentation. The judge awarded such damages and the defendant appealed arguing that damages for deceit were limited to instances of loss-making transactions. Held (upholding the judge's assessment of damages): there was no absolute rule that the transaction had to be loss making before damages for deceit could be recovered. If the plaintiff could prove that a more favourable transaction would have been entered into with the defendant but for the deceit, its loss of opportunity could be recovered on that basis.

SIMON BROWN LJ:

Damages for deceit

[Counsel] for the defendants challenges the whole basis of this second head of claim. He argues that it is an attempt to obtain by another route damages for loss of a bargain which are not recoverable for the tort of deceit. Damages for deceit are only to compensate the person deceived for loss suffered. Here the plaintiffs failed to prove any such loss. . . . They can prove no more than that they would have made a still greater profit had they entered into yet more favourable agreements, and that, submits [counsel] is insufficient to sustain the claim. . . .

[T]he judge [at first instance] concluded on the balance of probabilities that, but for Mr Dent's deceit, the plaintiffs could and would have entered into the same distribution agreements but on more favourable terms as to price, and that their loss was therefore the difference between the lower prices which in those circumstances they would have paid and the prices actually paid. . . . Having been referred to a number of authorities, most notably *Smith New Court Securities Ltd* v *Scrimgeour Vickers (Asset Management) Ltd* [1997] AC 254; *East* v *Maurer* [1991] 1 WLR 461 and *Downs* v *Chappell* [1997] 1 WLR 426, the judge said:

> . . . The result may be the same as a loss of bargain claim, but, as [counsel for the plaintiff] argued, that does not mean that it is a loss of bargain claim. It is the best way of judging the loss, if any, which was caused directly to the plaintiffs by being induced by the deceit to enter the agreements which they did . . . It establishes the loss, if any, which the plaintiffs have suffered with a view to putting them in the position they would have been in if no representations had been made . . .

[Counsel for the defendant] criticises the judge's reasoning throughout that section of the judgment. It is, he submits, contrary to principle to seek to reconstruct the deal which would have been reached but for the deceit.

. . . This whole case, the defendants argue, is an attempt to create for the plaintiffs a contractual claim to which they were never entitled. These to my mind are powerful arguments and I do not pretend to have found the point an easy one.

In the *Smith New Court* case [1997] AC 254, 267 Lord Browne-Wilkinson, summarising the principles applicable in assessing damages payable where the plaintiff has been induced by a fraudulent misrepresentation to buy property, stated the first three as follows:

> (1) the defendant is bound to make reparation for all the damage directly flowing from the transaction; (2) although such damage need not have been foreseeable, it must have been directly caused by the transaction; (3) in assessing such damage, the plaintiff is entitled to recover by way of damages the full price paid by him, but he must give credit for any benefits which he has received as a result of the transaction . . .

The difficulty in the present case, as it seems to me, is in deciding whether 'all the damage (actual loss) directly flowing from the transaction' (Lord Browne-Wilkinson's first principle . . .) can encompass, in a case like the present where the actual transaction entered into has been profitable rather than loss-making, the loss occasioned through the party deceived having entered into that particular transaction rather than a different transaction which would have been yet more profitable. In submitting that it cannot, [counsel] not surprisingly places considerable reliance on Lord Steyn's statement [in *Smith New Court*] [1997] AC 254, 283 that:

> it is not necessary . . . after . . . ascertain[ing] the loss directly flowing from the victim having

entered into the transaction, to embark on a hypothetical reconstruction of what the parties would have agreed had the deceit not occurred.

Indeed this very statement, he submits, usefully contrasts 'the loss directly flowing from . . . the transaction' with any idea of comparing one profitable transaction with another in order to find a 'loss' in this way. To do that, he submits, is also to offend against Lord Steyn's first three propositions: it is to protect the plaintiffs in respect of their positive interest rather than compensate them in respect of their negative interest, in this bargain; to create for them a contractual measure of damages. It comes to this: unless and until the plaintiffs can show (which they cannot) that these distributorship agreements caused them loss, they have no claim in tort. It is not sufficient for their purpose to show only *that* other distributorship agreements would have given them greater profit.

It is helpful at this point to consider *East* v *Maurer* [1991] 1 WLR 461, the authority principally relied upon by the judge below in carrying out the exercise he did. . . .

Mustill LJ, at p. 468:

> the best course in a case of this kind is to begin by comparing the position of the plaintiff as it would have been if the act complained of had not taken place with the position of the plaintiff as it actually became. This establishes the actual loss which the plaintiff has suffered and often helps to avoid the pitfalls of double counting, omissions and impermissible awards of both a capital and an income element in respect of the same loss . . . In the present case the act complained of is the making of the fraudulent representation, coupled with the reliance placed upon it by the plaintiffs in concluding the bargain. If this had not happened the plaintiffs would, on the judge's findings, have . . . bought a new business in Bournemouth, albeit not the one in Exeter Road . . . It is objected that the loss of profits is not properly recoverable because it is appropriate not to a claim in fraud but to a claim based on a contractual warranty of profits, for in such a case the loss of profits does not stem from the making of the contract but from the fact that the profit made was not what was anticipated. I should have thought this argument sound if the judge had included an item for loss of the Exeter Road profits; but he has not done so. The loss of profits awarded relates to the hypothetical profitable business in which the plaintiffs would have engaged but for buying the Exeter Road business, and the profits of the latter are treated by the judge solely as some evidence of what the profits of the other business might have been. . . .

[Counsel for the defendant] submits that *East* v *Maurer* [1991] 1 WLR 461 was a very different case from the present and that the point established there and approved in the *Smith New Court* case [1997] AC 254 cannot avail the plaintiffs here. It is one thing to say that, in quantifying the undoubted losses resulting from the plaintiffs' tortiously induced purchase of the salon in Exeter Road, they could properly include as consequential loss the profits they might reasonably have expected to make in another business which they would, but for the defendant's fraud, have purchased; quite another to say that, even had Exeter Road proved profitable, they could have claimed in tort on the basis that, but for the fraud, it would have been more profitable still.

The novelty of the present case lies in the plaintiffs having suffered no loss from the transaction save only from having entered into that transaction rather than a still more profitable one. That distinguishes this case from all the others we were shown. Is it, however, a distinction fatal to the plaintiffs' success? [Counsel for the plaintiff] submits not. His starting point is Lord Steyn's sixth proposition in the *Smith New Court* case [1997] AC 254, 282 with regard to 'the overriding compensatory principle':

> The legal measure is to compare the position of the plaintiff as it was before the fraudulent statement was made to him with his position as it became as a result of his reliance on the fraudulent statement.

The plaintiffs' argument is quite straightforward. Before Mr Dent's fraudulent statement, the plaintiffs were anxious to become Sovereign's exclusive distributors in France and were negotiating agreements, and in particular prices and a price increase formula, to that end. In reliance on the fraudulent statement they became locked into these long-term agreements and a commitment to pay prices and price increases larger than would otherwise have been the case. The judge below did no more and no less than compensate them for having thereby worsened their position. This accorded with the overriding principle.

In my judgment this argument is correct. The judge did not, be it noted, make the mistake of awarding damages by reference to the contractual measure. . . .

As for Lord Steyn's statement [1997] AC 254, 283 that it is unnecessary 'to embark on a hypothetical reconstruction of what the parties would have agreed had the deceit not occurred,' this has to be understood in the context of Hobhouse LJ's 'qualification' in *Downs* v *Chappell* [1997] 1 WLR 426, 444, which Lord Steyn was criticising. What Hobhouse LJ had done, by way of a 'check' on the conventional measure, was 'to compare the loss consequent upon entering into the transaction with what would have been the position had the represented, or supposed, state of affairs actually existed.' To reject that exercise (a different exercise, be it noted, from that undertaken by the judge in the present case) was not to reject the possibility that the ascertainment of loss in the first place might itself require a 'hypothetical reconstruction of what the parties would have agreed had the deceit not occurred.' If, as was held in *East* v *Maurer* [1991] 1 WLR 461 (a holding expressly approved by Lord Steyn [1997] AC 254, 282), consequential loss can be established and awarded by reference to 'the hypothetical profitable business in which the plaintiff would have engaged but for [the] deceit,' why should that loss, to be recoverable, have to be parasitic on some other, more direct, loss, and why should the alternative 'hypothetical profitable business' have to be a business (or, as here, contract) notionally acquired from some third party?

True it is that in *Downs* v *Chappell* [1997] 1 WLR 426, 433 Hobhouse LJ, in a part of the judgment not criticised in the *Smith New Court* case [1997] AC 254, said:

> It was wrong both factually and legally for the judge to create the hypothesis that the second defendants could and would have given the plaintiffs accurate figures so as to give them an accurate basis upon which to decide whether to make a contract with Mr Chappell.

But that was in the context of establishing liability, not quantifying damage. True it is too that later in his judgment, having referred to *East* v *Maurer* [1991] 1 WLR 461, Hobhouse LJ said [1997] 1 WLR 426, 441:

> In general, it is irrelevant to inquire what the representee would have done if some different representation had been made to him or what other transactions he might have entered into if he had not entered onto the transaction in question. Such matters are irrelevant speculations . . .

That, however, was expressed to be 'in general' and, as I conclude, there will be particular cases, of which this is one, where to give effect to the overriding compensatory rule it will be both possible on the facts, and appropriate in law, to hypothesise. Not every hypothesis involves irrelevant speculation.

I have, in short, reached the conclusion that there is no absolute rule requiring the person deceived to prove that the actual transaction into which he was induced to enter was itself loss-making . . .

It will sometimes be possible, as it was here, to prove instead that a different and more favourable transaction (either with the defendant or with some third party) would have been entered into but for the fraud, and to measure and recover the plaintiffs' loss on that basis . . .

NOTE: There is a clear emphasis in the judgments on the need to achieve justice and some redress for the plaintiff, which had been 'overcharged'. However, the effect of this decision is to include this loss (assuming that it can be proved) as a direct loss flowing from the fraudulent misrepresentation under what Simon Brown LJ refers to as 'the overriding compensatory rule'. The tension arises because at first sight it appears to be a loss of bargain (or contractual) claim, just as the loss of profits claim appeared to be contractual in *East* v *Maurer* and similar difficulties arise in trying to assess damages based on hypotheticals. There is a fine line between putting a person in the position he would have been in had the misrepresentation not been made and putting him into the position that he would have been in had a true statement been made. This dilemma is referred to in the judgment of Ward LJ:

I confess to have been worrying whether there is any meaningful difference between, on the one hand, being put in the position one would have been in had one not been told a lie and, on the other hand, being put in the position one would have been in had one been told the truth. I think the answer is to follow Lord Steyn's approach to its logical conclusion because if one is truly to compare the position of the plaintiff as it was before the fraudulent statement was made to him with his position as it became as a result of his reliance on the fraudulent statement, then just before the fraudulent statement was made the plaintiff was battling in what he believed to be honest negotiations to ascertain the defendant's bottom line and he was denied finding it because of the lies that were told to him. My other concern, reflecting [counsel's] argument, was why, if one cannot get damages for the loss of one's bargain, should one be allowed to get damages for the loss of the bargain one might have made. On reflection, I think the answer to this argument is that the loss of the bargain contemplated in breach of warranty cases is the bargain to be made with third parties when selling on the goods whereas the bargain one might have made if told the truth is the different bargain which might have been struck with the defendant. I am now satisfied that so long as the hypothetical questions are asked and answered as the means of establishing value in the absence of a market or of any other precise means of establishing that value, then the hypothetical approach, which is essentially what [the judge] was adopting, is well justi-fied by the authorities. On this basis I would uphold [the judge's] assessment of damages.

■ QUESTION

Is the explanation offered by Ward LJ, of why it is possible to recover damages for the loss of a bargain that might have been made, i.e., loss of opportunity, but not for loss of a bargain *per se*, a convincing one?

(iv) There is no defence of contributory negligence where the defendant's misrepresentation is fraudulent

---

Standard Chartered Bank v Pakistan National Shipping Corporation (No. 2)
[2002] UKHL 43, [2003] 1 AC 959 (HL)

The seller, an English company, had contracted to ship a cargo to a Vietnamese buyer with payment to be made by a letter of credit issued by a Vietnamese bank (the issuing bank) and confirmed by Standard Chartered Bank (SCB). This letter of credit required shipment to be made before 25 October and required the docu-ments to be presented before 10 November 1993. The cargo was not shipped on time and on 8 November the shipowners and the managing director of the sellers had agreed that documents with a false shipping date would be issued. SCB accepted these documents on 15 November and authorised payment, although it knew that the documents were presented after the expiry of the credit. SCB then sought reimbursement from the issuing bank, falsely stating that the documents had been presented before the expiry date of the credit. The issuing bank refused payment because of other discrepancies in the documents. SCB claimed damages for deceit against the shipowners and managing director of the sellers based on the falsely dated documents. However, they claimed that SCB had suffered loss partly as a result of its own deceit on the issuing bank. They alleged that this constituted 'fault' within section 4 of the Law Reform (Contributory Negligence) Act 1945 so that damages were to be apportioned to take account of SCB's 'contributory neg-ligence'. Held: the defendants could not rely on the claimant's contributory neg-ligence as a defence to a claim based on fraudulent misrepresentation. There had been no such defence available at common law and, since the 1945 Act had not been intended to alter the position on absolute defences at common law, there was no such defence under that Act.

LORD HOFFMANN (with whose speech the other members of the House agreed):

10   My Lords, I shall consider first the defence of contributory negligence. The relevant provisions of the 1945 Act are sections 1(1) and the definition of 'fault' in section 4:

> '1 (1) Where any person suffers damage as the result partly of his own fault and partly of the fault of any other person or persons, a claim in respect of that damage shall not be defeated by reason of the fault of the person suffering the damage, but the damages recoverable in respect thereof shall be reduced to such extent as the court thinks just and equitable having regard to the claimant's share in the responsibility for the damage . . .'
>
> '4 . . . 'fault' means negligence, breach of statutory duty or other act or omission which gives rise to a liability in tort or would, apart from this Act, give rise to a defence of contributory negligence.'

11   In my opinion, the definition of 'fault' is divided into two limbs, one of which is applicable to defendants and the other to plaintiffs. In the case of a defendant, fault means 'negligence, breach of statutory duty or other act or omission' which gives rise to a liability in tort. In the case of a plaintiff, it means 'negligence, breach of statutory duty or other act or omission' which gives rise (at common law) to a defence of contributory negligence. The authorities in support of this construction are discussed by Lord Hope of Craighead in *Reeves* v *Comr of Police of the Metropolis* [2000] 1 AC 360, 382. It was also the view of Professor Glanville Williams in *Joint Torts and Contributory Negligence* (1951), p 318.

12   It follows that conduct by a plaintiff cannot be 'fault' within the meaning of the Act unless it gives rise to a defence of contributory negligence at common law. This appears to me in accordance with the purpose of the Act, which was to relieve plaintiffs whose actions would previously have failed and not to reduce the damages which previously would have been awarded against defendants. Section 1(1) makes this clear when it says that 'a claim in respect of that damage shall not be defeated by reason of the fault of the person suffering the damage, but [instead] the damages recoverable in respect thereof shall be reduced . . .'

13   The question is therefore whether at common law SCB's conduct would be a defence to its claim for deceit. Sir Anthony Evans thought that it would. He said that although the conduct of SCB in making a false statement about when the documents had been presented was intentional or reckless, the House of Lords had decided in *Reeves*'s case [2000] 1 AC 360 that an intentional act could give rise to a defence of 'contributory negligence' at common law and therefore count as 'fault' for the purpose of the Act. I am not sure that it was necessary to rely upon *Reeves* for this purpose, because the Act requires fault in relation to the damage which has been suffered. That damage was SCB's loss of the money it paid Oakprime. In *Reeves*, the plaintiff's husband had intended to cause the damage he suffered. He intended to kill himself. But SCB did not intend to lose its money. It would be more accurate to say that it was careless in making payment against documents which, as it knew or ought to have known, did not comply with the terms of the credit, on the assumption that it could successfully conceal these matters from Incombank. In respect of the loss suffered, SCB was in my opinion negligent.

14   Be that as it may, the real question is whether the conduct of SCB would at common law be a defence to a claim in deceit. Sir Anthony Evans said that the only rule supported by the authorities was that if someone makes a false representation which was intended to be relied upon and the other party relies upon it, it is no answer to a claim for rescission or damages that the claimant could with reasonable diligence have discovered that the representation was untrue. *Redgrave* v *Hurd* (1881) 20 Ch D 1 is a well known illustration. That was not the case here. SCB should not have paid even if they could not have discovered that the representation about the bill of lading was untrue. But in my opinion there are other cases which can be explained only on the basis of a wider rule. In *Edgington* v *Fitzmaurice* (1885) 29 ChD 459 the plaintiff invested £1,500 in debentures issued by a company formed to run a provision market in Regent Street. Five months later the company was wound up and he lost nearly all his money. He sued the directors who had issued the prospectus, alleging that they had fraudulently or recklessly represented that the debenture issue was to raise money for the expansion of the company's business ('develop the arrangements . . . for the direct supply of cheap fish from the coast') when in fact it was to pay off pressing liabilities. The judge found the allegation proved and that the representation played a part in inducing the plaintiff to take the debentures. But another reason for his taking the debentures was that he thought, without any reasonable grounds, that the debentures were secured upon the company's land. Cotton LJ said, at p 481, that this did not matter:

'It is true that if he had not supposed he would have a charge he would not have taken the debentures; but if he also relied on the misstatement in the prospectus, his loss none the less resulted from that misstatement. It is not necessary to show that the misstatement was the sole cause of his acting as he did. If he acted on that misstatement, though he was also influenced by an erroneous supposition, the defendants will still be liable.'

Bowen and Fry LJJ gave judgments to the same effect.

15 This case seems to me to show that if a fraudulent representation is relied upon, in the sense that the claimant would not have parted with his money if he had known it was false, it does not matter that he also held some other negligent or irrational belief about another matter and, but for that belief, would not have parted with his money either. The law simply ignores the other reasons why he paid. As Lord Cross of Chelsea said in *Barton* v *Armstrong* [1976] AC 104, 118–119:

'If . . . Barton relied on the [fraudulent] misrepresentation Armstrong could not have defeated his claim to relief by showing that there were other more weighty causes which contributed to his decision to execute the deed, for in this field the court does not allow an examination into the relative importance of contributory causes. 'Once make out that there has been anything like deception, and no contract resting in any degree on that foundation can stand': per Lord Cranworth LJ in *Reynell* v *Sprye* (1852) 1 De G M & G 660, 708.'

16 In *Edgington* v *Fitzmaurice* 29 ChD 459 the defence was not that the plaintiff could have discovered that the representation was false. It was that he was also induced by mistaken beliefs of his own, but for which he would not have subscribed for the debentures. That is very like the present case. It is said here that although SCB would not have paid if they had known the bill of lading to be falsely dated, they would also not have paid if they had not mistakenly and negligently thought that they could obtain reimbursement. In my opinion, the law takes no account of these other reasons for payment. This rule seems to me based upon sound policy. It would not seem just that a fraudulent defendant's liability should be reduced on the grounds that, for whatever reason, the victim should not have made the payment which the defendant successfully induced him to make.

17 As Sir Anthony Evans correctly pointed out, the rule in *Redgrave* v *Hurd* 20 ChD 1 applies to both innocent and fraudulent misrepresentations. The wider rule in *Edgington* v *Fitzmaurice* probably applies only to fraudulent misrepresentations. In *Gran Gelato Ltd* v *Richcliff (Group) Ltd* [1992] Ch 560 Sir Donald Nicholls V-C said that, in principle, a defence of contributory negligence should be available in a claim for damages under section 2(1) of the Misrepresentation Act 1967. But, since the alleged contributory negligence was that the plaintiff could with reasonable care have discovered that the representation was untrue, the rule in *Redgrave* v *Hurd* prevented the conduct of the plaintiff from being treated as partly responsible for the loss. This left open the possibility that, in a case of innocent representation, some other kind of negligent causative conduct might be taken into account.

18 In the case of fraudulent misrepresentation, however, I agree with Mummery J in *Alliance and Leicester Building Society* v *Edgestop Ltd* [1993] 1 WLR 1462 that there is no common law defence of contributory negligence. (See also Carnwath J in *Corporación Nacional del Cobre de Chile* v *Sogemin Metals Ltd* [1997] 1 WLR 1396 and Blackburn J in *Nationwide Building Society* v *Thimbleby & Co* [1999] Lloyd's Rep PN 359.) It follows that, in agreement with the majority in the Court of Appeal, I think that no apportionment under the 1945 Act is possible.

B: Negligent misrepresentation

Negligent misrepresentation involves a statement made honestly but without reasonable grounds for the belief.

(a) At common law

Hedley Byrne & Co. Ltd v Heller & Partners Ltd
[1964] AC 465 (HL)

Hedley Byrne, who were advertising agents, asked their bank to inquire as to the financial standing of Easipower Ltd. Heller & Partners, who were Easipower's bankers, replied 'without responsibility' that Easipower was 'considered good for its ordinary business engagements'. Relying on this reference, Hedley Byrne booked advertising time for Easipower on terms under which they were personally responsible for payment. Easipower went into liquidation and Hedley Byrne lost £17,000 on these contracts. They bought an action against Heller & Partners for damages for negligence. Held: such a statement could give rise to an action for damages for financial loss in tort (there being no contractual relationship between the parties concerned). This was because a duty of care would be owed where there was a special relationship between the parties. However, on these facts that duty had been expressly excluded by the disclaimer of responsibility.

LORD MORRIS OF BORTH-Y-GEST: . . . [I]rrespective of any contractual or fiduciary relationship and irrespective of any direct dealing, a duty may be owed by one person to another. It is said, however, that where careless (but not fraudulent) misstatements are in question there can be no liability in the maker of them unless there is either some contractual or fiduciary relationship with a person adversely affected by the making of them or unless, through the making of them, something is created or circulated or some situation is created which is dangerous to life, limb or property. In logic I can see no essential reason for distinguishing injury which is caused by a reliance upon words from injury which is caused by a reliance upon the safety of the staging to a ship or by a reliance upon the safety for use of the contents of a bottle of hair wash or a bottle of some consumable liquid. It seems to me, therefore, that if A claims that he has suffered injury or loss as a result of acting upon some misstatement made by B who is not in any contractual or fiduciary relationship with him, the inquiry that is first raised is whether B owed any duty to A: if he did the further inquiry is raised as to the nature of the duty. There may be circumstances under which the only duty owed by B to A is the duty of being honest: there may be circumstances under which B owes to A the duty not only of being honest but also a duty of taking reasonable care. The issue in the present case is whether the bank owed any duty to Hedleys and if so what the duty was . . .

My Lords, I consider that it follows and that it should now be regarded as settled that if someone possessed of a special skill undertakes, quite irrespective of contract, to apply that skill for the assistance of another person who relies upon such skill, a duty of care will arise. The fact that the service is to be given by means of or by the instrumentality of words can make no difference. Furthermore, if in a sphere in which a person is so placed that others could reasonably rely upon his judgment or his skill or upon his ability to make careful inquiry, a person takes it upon himself to give information or advice to, or allows his information or advice to be passed on to, another person who, as he knows or should know, will place reliance upon it, then a duty of care will arise.

NOTE: Liability under *Hedley Byrne* v *Heller* turns on whether there was a special relationship between the claimant and the defendant and an 'assumption of responsibility' for a statement (*Henderson* v *Merrett Syndicates Ltd* [1995] 2 AC 145). To establish the special relationship, the defendant must arguably either have or profess to have some special skill in relation to the subject matter or, at the very least, must have taken it upon himself to make representations and, secondly, it must have been reasonable for the claimant to rely upon the defendant's statement. As a third requirement, the defendant must either know that the claimant will rely on the statement or it must be reasonably foreseeable that he will rely on it. Finally, it appears from the decision of the House of Lords in *Caparo Industries plc* v *Dickman* [1990] 2 AC 605, that the defendant must have some knowledge of the type of transaction for which the information is required.

Hedley Byrne v *Heller* can apply to pre-contractual statements where a contract finally resulted between the parties.

Esso Petroleum Co. Ltd v Mardon
[1976] QB 801 (CA)

The facts of this case appear at *page 206.*

LORD DENNING MR:

Negligent misrepresentation

. . . [T]he question arises whether Esso are liable for negligent misstatement under the doctrine of *Hedley Byrne & Co. Ltd* v *Heller & Partners Ltd* [1964] AC 465. It has been suggested that *Hedley Byrne* cannot be used so as to impose liability for negligent pre-contractual statements: and that, in a pre-contract situation the remedy (at any rate before the Act of 1967) was only in warranty or nothing. . . .

In arguing this point, [counsel for Esso] took his stand in this way. He submitted that when the negotiations between two parties resulted in a contract between them, their rights and duties were governed by the law of contract and not by the law of tort. There was, therefore, no place in their relationship for *Hedley Byrne* [1964] AC 465, which was solely on liability in tort. He relied particularly on *Clark* v *Kirby-Smith* [1964] Ch 506 where Plowman J held that the liability of a solicitor for negligence was a liability in contract and not in tort, following the observations of Sir Wilfrid Greene MR in *Groom* v *Crocker* [1939] 1 KB 194, 206. [Counsel for Esso] might also have cited *Bagot* v *Stevens Scanlan & Co. Ltd* [1966] 1 QB 197, about an architect; and other cases too. But I venture to suggest that those cases are in conflict with other decisions of high authority which were not cited in them. These decisions show that, in the case of a professional man, the duty to use reasonable care arises not only in contract, but is also imposed by the law apart from contract, and is therefore actionable in tort. . . . A professional man may give advice under a contract for reward; or without a contract, in pursuance of a voluntary assumption of responsibility, gratuitously without reward. In either case he is under one and the same duty to use reasonable care: see *Cassidy* v *Ministry of Health* [1951] 2 KB 343, 359–360. In the one case it is by reason of a term implied by law. In the other, it is by reason of a duty imposed by law. For a breach of that duty he is liable in damages: and those damages should be, and are, the same, whether he is sued in contract or in tort.

It follows that I cannot accept [counsel for Esso's] proposition. It seems to me that *Hedley Byrne & Co. Ltd* v *Heller & Partners Ltd* [1964] AC 465, properly understood, covers this particular proposition: if a man, who has or professes to have special knowledge or skill, makes a representation by virtue thereof to another—be it advice, information or opinion—with the intention of inducing him to enter into a contract with him, he is under a duty to use reasonable care to see that the representation is correct, and that the advice, information or opinion is reliable. If he negligently gives unsound advice or misleading information or expresses an erroneous opinion, and thereby induces the other side to enter into a contract with him, he is liable in damages. . . .

Applying this principle, it is plain that Esso professed to have—and did in fact have—special knowledge or skill in estimating the throughput of a filling station. They made the representation—they forecast a throughput of 200,000 gallons—intending to induce Mr Mardon to enter into a tenancy on the faith of it. They made it negligently. It was a 'fatal error.' And thereby induced Mr Mardon to enter into a contract of tenancy that was disastrous to him. For this misrepresentation they are liable in damages.

NOTES
1. In a claim based on negligent misrepresentation the claimant has the burden of proving the existence of the special relationship.
2. It will be the only available claim where, as in *Hedley Byrne* v *Heller* itself, the misrepresentor is

not a party to the contract, or where no contract results following the negotiations in which the statement was made.

3. Damages are tortious, in that the aim is to put the claimant into the position that he would have been in had the misrepresentation not been made. Lord Denning in *Esso* v *Mardon* explained it as follows (at pp. 820–1):

> ### The measure of damages
>
> Mr Mardon is not to be compensated here for 'loss of a bargain.' He was given no bargain that the throughput *would* amount to 200,000 gallons a year. He is only to be compensated for having been induced to enter into a contract which turned out to be disastrous for him. Whether it be called breach of warranty or negligent misrepresentation, its effect was *not* to warrant the throughput, but only to induce him to enter the contract. So the damages in either case are to be measured by the loss he suffered. Just as in *Doyle* v *Olby (Ironmongers) Ltd* [1969] 2 QB 158. 167 he can say: '. . . I would not have entered into this contract at all but for your representation. Owing to it, I have lost all the capital I put into it. I also incurred a large overdraft. I have spent four years of my life in wasted endeavour without reward: and it will take me some time to re-establish myself.'
>
> For all such loss he is entitled to recover damages. It is to be measured in a similar way as the loss due to a personal injury. You should look into the future so as to forecast what would have been likely to happen if he had never entered into this contract: and contrast it with his position as it is now as a result of entering into it. The future is necessarily problematical and can only be a rough-and-ready estimate. But it must be done in assessing the loss.

Recovery is not as wide as in the case of fraudulent misrepresentation, since the claimant can only recover for loss which was reasonably foreseeable at the time of the statement.

(b) Under statute

SECTION 2(1) MISREPRESENTATION ACT 1967

MISREPRESENTATION ACT 1967

2. Damages for misrepresentation

(1) Where a person has entered into a contract after a misrepresentation has been made to him by another party thereto and as a result thereof he has suffered loss, then, if the person making the misrepresentation would be liable to damages in respect thereof had the misrepresentation been made fraudulently, that person shall be so liable notwithstanding that the misrepresentation was not made fraudulently, unless he proves that he had reasonable ground to believe and did believe up to the time the contract was made that the facts represented were true.

(i) The burden of proof

The normal burden of proof is reversed so that the representor has to disprove negligence.

Howard Marine and Dredging Co. Ltd v *A. Ogden & Sons (Excavations) Ltd*
[1978] QB 574 (CA)

During negotiations between the defendants, civil engineering contractors, and the plaintiffs, owners of two sea barges, for the hire of barges the plaintiffs' marine manager stated that the capacity of each barge was '850 cubic metres' and that this was equivalent to about 1,600 tonnes deadweight carrying capacity. He based this figure on his recollection of an entry in *Lloyd's Register* which gave the capacity of the barges as 1,800 tonnes. The register was in fact incorrect and the correct figure was 1,055 tonnes. This correct figure could have been ascertained from the ship's documents which were in the plaintiffs' possession. The defendants agreed to take the barges. Six months after taking delivery the defendants discovered the correct capacity and refused to pay the full hire. The plaintiffs claimed the outstanding hire charges and the defendants counterclaimed, *inter alia*, for damages under s. 2(1) of the Misrepresentation Act 1967 on the basis of the misrepresentation as to the barges' capacity. Held: (Bridge and Shaw LJJ) the plaintiffs had failed to prove that their marine manager had had reasonable grounds to believe and did believe up to the time the contract was made that the facts he represented were true, since the correct figure was contained in the ships' documents and they had failed to show any 'objectively reasonable ground' for relying instead on the figure in *Lloyd's Register*.

BRIDGE LJ: The first question then is whether Howards would be liable in damages in respect of Mr O'Loughlin's misrepresentation if it had been made fraudulently, that is to say, if he had known that it was untrue. An affirmative answer to that question is inescapable. The Judge found in terms that what Mr O'Loughlin said about the capacity of the barges was said with the object of getting the hire contract for Howards, in other words, with the intention that it should be acted on. This was clearly right. Equally clearly the misrepresentation was in fact acted on by Ogdens. It follows, therefore, on the plain language of the statute that, although there was no allegation of fraud, Howards must be liable unless they proved that Mr O'Loughlin had reasonable ground to believe what he said about the barges' capacity.

. . . If the representee proves a misrepresentation which, if fraudulent, would have sounded in damages, the onus passes immediately to the representor to prove that he had reasonable ground to believe the facts represented. In other words the liability of the representor does not depend upon his being under a duty of care the extent of which may vary according to the circumstances in which the representation is made. In the course of negotiations leading to a contract the statute imposes an absolute obligation not to state facts which the representor cannot prove he had reasonable ground to believe.

. . . [I]t is to be assumed that Mr O'Loughlin was perfectly honest throughout. But the question remains whether his evidence, however benevolently viewed, is sufficient to show that he had an objectively reasonable ground to disregard the figure in the ship's documents and to prefer the Lloyd's Register figure. I think it is not. Accordingly I conclude that Howards failed to prove that Mr O'Loughlin had reasonable ground to believe the truth of his misrepresentation to Mr Redpath.

Lord Denning MR (dissenting) thought that the burden of disproving negligence had been discharged.

LORD DENNING MR, *dissenting*: This enactment imposes a new and serious liability on anyone who makes a representation of fact in the course of negotiations for a contract. If that representation turns out to be mistaken—then however innocent he may be—he is just as liable as if he made it fraudulently. But how different from times past! For years he was not liable in damages at all for innocent misrepresentation: see *Heilbut, Symons & Co.* v *Buckleton* [1913] AC 30. Quite recently he was made liable if he was proved to have made it negligently: see *Esso Petroleum Co. Ltd* v *Mardon* [1976] QB 801. But now with this Act he is made liable —unless he proves—and the burden is on him to prove—that he had reasonable ground to believe and did in fact believe that it was true.

Section 2(1) certainly applies to the representation made by Mr O'Loughlin on July 11, 1974, when he told Ogdens that each barge could carry 1,600 tonnes. The judge found that it was a misrepresentation: that he said it with the object of getting the hire contract for Howards. They got it: and, as a result, Ogdens suffered loss. But the judge found that Mr O'Loughlin was not negligent: and so Howards were not liable for it.

The judge's finding was criticised before us: because he asked himself the question: was Mr O'Loughlin negligent? Whereas he should have asked himself: did Mr O'Loughlin have reasonable ground to believe that the representation was true? I think that criticism is not fair to the judge. By the word 'negligent' he was only using shorthand for the longer phrase contained in s. 2(1) which he had before him. And the judge, I am sure, had the burden of proof in mind: for he had come to the conclusion that Mr O'Loughlin was not negligent. The judge said in effect: 'I am satisfied that Mr O'Loughlin was not negligent': and being so satisfied, the burden need not be further considered.

It seems to me that when one examines the details, the judge's view was entirely justified. He found that Mr O'Loughlin's state of mind was this: Mr O'Loughlin had examined Lloyd's Register and had seen there that the deadweight capacity of each barge was 1,800 tonnes. That figure stuck in his mind. The judge found that 'the 1,600 tonnes was arrived at by knocking off what he considered a reasonable margin for fuel, and so on, from the 1,800 tonnes summer deadweight figure in Lloyd's Register, which was in the back of his mind.' The judge said that Mr O'Loughlin had seen at some time the German shipping documents and had seen the deadweight figure of 1,055–135 tonnes: but it did not register. All that was in his mind was the 1,800 tonnes in Lloyd's Register which was regarded in shipping circles as the Bible. That afforded reasonable ground for him to believe that the barges could each carry 1,600 tonnes pay load: and that is what Mr O'Loughlin believed.

So on this point, too, I do not think we should fault the judge. It is not right to pick his judgment to pieces—by subjecting it—or the shorthand note—to literal analysis. Viewing it fairly, the judge (who had s. 2(1) in front of him) must have been of opinion that the burden of proof was discharged.

NOTES

1. The decision of the majority is that in order to escape liability under s. 2(1) the representor must positively prove reasonable grounds for his belief in addition to disproving negligence. Bridge LJ went as far as stating that s. 2(1) imposed an absolute obligation on the representor not to state facts which he could not prove he had reasonable grounds to believe.

   Inevitably, this means that liability to pay damages for negligent misrepresentation will more easily be established under s. 2(1) than at common law.

2. In *Spice Girls Ltd* v *Aprilla World Services BV* [2002] EWCA Civ 15, [2002] EMLR 27 (for facts see *page 546*), Aprilla recovered damages under s. 2(1) because the onus was on the Spice Girls to show that they had reasonable grounds to believe and did believe, at the date of the agreement, that the representation was true. Since it had been established that they knew that one member intended to leave, they were unable to discharge this burden.

3. The members of the Court of Appeal in *Howard Marine* v *Ogden* also had different opinions on whether there was liability for negligent misstatement at common law. Only Shaw LJ considered that this liability was established.

4. Section 2(1) only applies where the misrepresentation induces the representee to enter into a contract with the representor, and this is the most important limitation on its application.

5. The effect of the exemption clause is discussed at *page 604*.

(ii) The measure of damages under s. 2(1)

Much emphasis has been placed on the fact that the section itself does not make clear how damages are to be assessed. The drafting of the section rests upon the 'fiction of fraud', in that *liability* in damages is said to exist where it would exist had the misrepresentation been fraudulent even though it is not fraudulent. This has been interpreted to mean that the damages are determined in accordance with the principles applicable to fraudulent misrepresentation.

***

Royscot Trust Ltd v Rogerson
[1991] 2 QB 297 (CA)

A customer agreed to buy a car for £7,600 from a dealer. The deposit was £1,200 with the balance of £6,400 on hire-purchase terms. In order to satisfy a 20 per cent deposit requirement, the dealer represented to the finance company that the purchase price was £8,000 and that a deposit of £1,600 had been paid (leaving the same balance of £6,400). The hire-purchase contract was made on this basis. When £2,775 of instalments had been paid, the customer dishonestly sold the car for £7,200 to an innocent purchaser. The company recovered damages of £1,600 against the dealer, i.e., the extra amount that the company had been induced to pay as a result of the misrepresentation (if the deposit actually paid—£1,200—had been correctly stated the true price of the car would have been £6,000 and the company would have paid the dealer £4,800, not £6,400). The finance company claimed that the damages against the dealer should be £3,625 (which was the difference between the amount paid to the dealer and the amount received from the customer). Therefore, the first issue was whether damages under s. 2(1) were tortious, so as to put the representee into the position that he would have been in had he never entered into the contract. The dealer contended that he should pay no damages because the customer's sale of the car during the continuance of the hire-purchase agreement was not a reasonably foreseeable loss. Held: the measure of damages under s. 2(1) was tortious, in that the measure had to be the same as for fraudulent misrepresentation because of the fiction of fraud. It followed that the finance company could recover for all losses directly flowing from the misrepresentation, even if that loss was unforeseeable (although on the facts it was foreseeable). The finance company was therefore entitled to recover the £3,625, being the tortious measure of damages.

BALCOMBE LJ: . . . The finance company's cause of action against the dealer is based on s. 2(1) of the Misrepresentation Act 1967. . . .

As a result of some dicta by Lord Denning MR in two cases in the Court of Appeal —*Gosling* v *Anderson* [1972] EGD 709 and *Jarvis* v *Swans Tours Ltd* [1973] QB 233, 237—and the decision at first instance in *Watts* v *Spence* [1976] Ch 165, there was some doubt whether the measure of damages for an innocent misrepresentation giving rise to a cause of action under the Act of 1967 was the tortious measure, so as to put the representee in the position in which he would have been if he had never entered into the contract, or the contractual measure, so as to put the representee in the position in which he would have been if the misrepresentation had been true, and thus in some cases give rise to a claim for damages for loss of bargain. Lord Denning MR's remarks in *Gosling* v *Anderson* were concerned with an amendment to a pleading, while his remarks in *Jarvis* v *Swans Tours Ltd* were clearly obiter. *Watts* v *Spence* was disapproved by this court in *Sharneyford Supplies Ltd* v *Edge* [1987] Ch 305, 323. However, there is now a number of decisions which make it clear that the tortious measure of damages is the true one. Most of these decisions are at first instance and will be found in *Chitty on Contract*, 26th ed. (1989), vol 1, p. 293, para 439, note 63 and in *McGregor on Damages*, 15th ed. (1988) pp 1107–1108, para 1745. One at least, *Chesneau* v *Interhome Ltd* (1983) 134 NLJ 341 . . . is a decision of this court. The claim was one under s. 2(1) of the 1967 Act and the appeal concerned the assessment of damages. In the course of his judgment Eveleigh LJ said:

> [Damages] should be assessed in a case like the present one on the same principles as damages are assessed in tort. The subsection itself says: '. . . if the person making the misrepresentation would be liable to damages in respect thereof had the misrepresentation been made fraudulently, that person shall be so liable . . .' By 'so liable' I take it to mean liable as he would be if the misrepresentation had been made fraudulently.

In view of the wording of the subsection it is difficult to see how the measure of damages under it could be other than the tortious measure and, despite the initial aberrations referred to above, that is now generally accepted. Indeed counsel before us did not seek to argue the contrary.

The first main issue before us was: accepting that the tortious measure is the right measure, is it the measure where the tort is that of fraudulent misrepresentation, or is it the measure where the tort is negligence at common law? The difference is that in cases of fraud a plaintiff is entitled to any loss which flowed from the defendant's fraud, even if the loss could not have been foreseen: see

Doyle v *Olby (Ironmongers) Ltd* [1969] 2 QB 158. In my judgement the wording of the subsection is clear: the person making the innocent misrepresentation shall be 'so liable', i.e. liable to damages as if the representation had been made fraudulently. This was the conclusion to which Walton J came in *F & B Entertainments Ltd* v *Leisure Enterprises Ltd* (1976) 240 EG 455, 461. See also the decision of Sir Douglas Franks QC sitting as a High Court judge in *McNally* v *Welltrade International Ltd* [1978] IRLR 497. In each of these cases the judge held that the basis for the assessment of damages under s. 2(1) of the Act of 1967 is that established in *Doyle* v *Olby (Ironmongers) Ltd*. This is also the effect of the judgment of Eveleigh LJ in *Chesneau* v *Interhome Ltd* already cited: 'By "so liable" I take it to mean liable as he would be if the misrepresentation had been made fraudulently.'

This was also the original view of the academic writers. In an article, 'The Misrepresentation Act 1967' (1967) 30 MLR 369 by P. S. Atiyah and G. H. Treitel, the authors say, at pp. 373–4:

> The measure of damages in the statutory action will apparently be that in an action of deceit . . . But more probably the damages recoverable in the new action are the same as those recoverable in an action of deceit . . .

Professor Treitel has since changed his view. In *Treitel, The Law of Contract*, 7th ed. (1987), p. 278, he says:

> Where the action is brought under section 2(1) of the Misrepresentation Act, one possible view is that the deceit rule will be applied by virtue of the fiction of fraud. But the preferable view is that the severity of the deceit rule can only be justified in cases of actual fraud and that remoteness under section 2(1) should depend, as in actions based on negligence, on the test of foreseeability.

The only authority cited in support of the 'preferable' view is *Shepheard* v *Broome* [1904] AC 342, a case under s. 38 of the Companies Act 1867, which provided that in certain circumstances a company director, although not in fact fraudulent, should be 'deemed to be fraudulent'. As Lord Lindley said, at p. 346: 'To be compelled by Act of Parliament to treat an honest man as if he were fraudulent is at all times painful', but he went on to say:

> 'but the repugnance which is naturally felt against being compelled to do so will not justify your Lordships in refusing to hold the appellant responsible for acts for which an Act of Parliament clearly declares he is to be held liable . . .'

The House of Lords so held.

It seems to me that that case, far from supporting Professor Treitel's view, is authority for the proposition that we must follow the literal wording of s. 2(1), even though that has the effect of treating, so far as the measure of damages is concerned, an innocent person as if he were fraudulent. *Chitty on Contracts*, 26th ed. (1989), vol. 1, p. 293, para 439, says:

> it is doubtful whether the rule that the plaintiff may recover even unforeseeable losses suffered as the result of fraud would be applied; it is an exceptional rule which is probably justified only in cases of actual fraud.

No authority is cited in support of that proposition save a reference to the passage in Professor Treitel's book cited above.

Professor Furmston in *Cheshire Fifoot, and Furmston's Law of Contract*, 11th ed. (1986) p. 286, says: 'It has been suggested—and the reference is to the passage in Atiyah and Treitel's article cited above—that damages under s. 2(1) should be calculated on the same principles as govern the tort of deceit. This suggestion is based on a theory that s. 2(1) is based on a "fiction of fraud". We have already suggested that this theory is misconceived. On the other hand the action created by s. 2(1) does look much more like an action in tort than one in contract and it is suggested that the rules for negligence are the natural ones to apply.'

The suggestion that the 'fiction of fraud' theory is misconceived occurs at p. 271, in a passage which includes:

> Though it would be quixotic to defend the drafting of the section, it is suggested that there is no such 'fiction of fraud' since the section does not say that a negligent misrepresentor shall be treated for all purposes as if he were fraudulent. No doubt the wording seeks to incorpor-

ate by reference some of the rules relating to fraud but, for instance, nothing in the wording of the subsection requires the measure of damages for deceit to be applied to the statutory action.

With all respect to the various learned authors whose works I have cited above, it seems to me that to suggest that a different measure of damage applies to an action for innocent misrepresentation under the section than that which applies to an action for fraudulent misrepresentation (deceit) at common law is to ignore the plain words of the subsection and is inconsistent with the cases to which I have referred. In my judgment, therefore, the finance company is entitled to recover from the dealer all the losses which it suffered as a result of its entering into the agreements with the dealer and the customer, even if those losses were unforeseeable, provided that they were not otherwise too remote.

NOTES
1. See Wadsley (1992) 55 MLR 698 and Hooley (1991) 107 LQR 547.
2. The application of the fiction of fraud has drawn a clear distinction between fraudulent and negligent misrepresentation under s. 2(1), and negligent misstatement at common law.
   It is difficult to see why there should be a more generous measure of damages under s. 2(1) than that available for negligent misstatement in tort when both claims could arise on the same facts. Not only does the burden of proof favour the representee under s. 2(1) but the representee can also recover for a much wider category of loss.
   Royscot Trust v *Rogerson* is likely to result in infrequent reliance on *Hedley Byrne* v *Heller* where s. 2(1) is available (namely where there is a contract between the representor and representee). It may also mean that there is little point in a representee seeking to establish fraudulent misrepresentation when the same measure of damages can be obtained under s. 2(1) with the advantage of the reversal of the burden of proof. (But see Lord Steyn's comment in *Smith New Court*, quoted in *note 3, page 569*, noting a distinction between losses flowing from the transaction and from the specific misrepresentation.)
3. It is difficult to justify a decision which will result in an honest but negligent representor being held liable as if he were fraudulent. In principle some distinction should persist.
4. In *Smith New Court Securities Ltd* v *Scrimgeour Vickers (Asset Management) Ltd* [1997] AC 254, *page 527*, Lord Steyn (at p. 283) raised the question of whether 'the rather loose wording of the statute compels the court to treat a person who was morally innocent as if he was guilty of fraud when it comes to the measure of damages'. However, since the issue did not arise directly on the facts of that case, Lord Steyn did not express any concluded view on this matter. Lord Browne-Wilkinson also stated that he was not expressing any view on the correctness of the decision in *Royscot Trust*.
5. In *Spice Girls Ltd* v *Aprilla World Service BV (Damages)* [2001] EMLR 8, Arden J held that she was bound to follow *Royscot Trust* and calculate damages under s. 2(1) on the basis of compensating Aprilla for all direct losses (i.e. the fraud measure), which included consequential loss. See also the acceptance of this position in *Pankhania* v *Hackney LBC (Damages)* [2004] EWHC 323 (Ch), [2004] 1 EGLR 135, discussed at *page 569*.
6. Remarkably in *Avon Insurance plc* v *Swire Fraser Ltd* [2000] 1 All ER (Comm) 573, Rix J considered that due to the application of the fraud principles of damages to negligent misrepresentations under s. 2(1), a court should not be too willing to find there to be an actionable misrepresentation where that court had some room for the exercise of judgment. He stated:

   If, on the other hand, the rule in the *Royscot Trust Ltd* case were one day to be found to be a misunderstanding of the 1967 Act, and the way were to become open to treat an innocent misrepresentation under s. 2(1) as though it was a case of negligence in *Hedley Byrne*, so that in the typical case of the provision of negligent information it would be possible to tailor the damages to the risk undertaken by the negligent representor, as in the *Banque Bruxelles* case, then there would be nothing to be said against adopting a more closely focused approach to the proof of misrepresentation.

This may be a sign of the deep misgivings over *Royscot Trust* but seems a wholly inappropriate solution.

Following *Royscot Trust* the crucial question will now be: Does the loss flow directly from the misrepresentation, i.e., did the misrepresentation *cause* this loss?

Naughton v *O'Callaghan*
[1990] 3 All ER 191

The plaintiffs bought a thoroughbred yearling colt for 26,000 guineas and trained the colt for two seasons. The colt was unplaced in all of its six races and its value fell to £1,500. The plaintiffs then discovered that the pedigree had not been correctly described, and sought to recover the purchase price and training fees. If the colt had originally been correctly described it would have fetched 23,500 guineas. There was a breach of contract but the contractual measure of damages was only the difference in value at the date of the contract. The plaintiffs therefore formulated their claim in misrepresentation and sought the difference between the price paid and the fall in value at the time the misrepresentation was discovered, on the basis that the fall in value was a direct loss. Waller J awarded the difference between 26,000 guineas and £1,500, accepting that the aim of damages under s. 2(1) was tortious and based on the fiction of fraud so that all direct loss flowing from the misrepresentation was recoverable. Training and racing was exactly the conduct to be expected and was reasonable conduct in the circumstances.

WALLER J: [Quoting Winn LJ in *Doyle* v *Olby* [1969] 2 QB 158:]

It appears to me that in a case where there has been a breach of warranty of authority, and still more clearly where there has been a tortious wrong consisting of a fraudulent inducement, the proper starting point for any court called on to consider what damages are recoverable by the defrauded person is to compare his position before the representation was made to him with his position after it, brought about by that representation, always bearing in mind that no element in the consequential position can be regarded as attributable loss and damage if it be too remote a consequence: it will be too remote not necessarily because it was not contemplated by the representor but in any case where the person deceived has not himself behaved with reasonable prudence, reasonable common sense or can in any true sense be said to have been the author of his own misfortune. The damage that he seeks to recover must have flowed directly from the fraud perpetrated on him.

Winn LJ then assessed the damages in that case by reference to precisely what the plaintiff had done after acquiring the business including selling the business at some later time and giving credit for that sale price. (I should perhaps make clear that *Doyle* v *Olby (Ironmongers) Ltd* was concerned with fraud, but in relation to a claim for damages under the Misrepresentation Act 1967 the approach is the same. . . .)

What, as it seems to me, makes this case different from the norm is, first, that what the plaintiffs in fact purchased in reliance on the representation in the catalogue was a different animal altogether; second, if they had known of the misrepresentation within a day or so they could, and as I have found would, have sold Fondu for its then value; third, their decision to keep Fondu and race it was precisely what the sellers would have expected: Fondu was not a commodity like, for example, rupee paper, which it would be expected that the defendants would go out and sell; fourth, the fall in Fondu's value if it did not win races was not due to a general fall in the market in racehorses, but was special to Fondu and to be expected if Fondu did not win. It might well not have happened if Fondu had been the different animal as it had been originally described.

Accordingly, in my judgment it would be unjust if the plaintiffs were not entitled to recover the difference between 26,000 guineas and £1,500, and on that aspect of the case accordingly I award that sum.

Waller J also awarded the training fees and costs of upkeep of the horse up to the date when the misrepresentation was discovered.

WALLER J: . . . It seems to me that in relation to this particular horse, applying Winn LJ's test in *Doyle v Olby (Ironmongers) Ltd* [1969] 2 All ER 119 at 123–124, [1969] 2 QB 158 at 168, the cost of training and keeping Fondu should be recoverable. But is it right to apply blinkers and consider the purchase of this particular animal and the expenditure on him? The defendant says that expenditure would have been incurred anyway on some yearling purchased at those September sales. To which the plaintiffs retort that that may be so, but if they bought the horse described by the defendant it *might* have paid for its keep and reaped for them rich rewards.

I have concluded that the plaintiffs are entitled to ask the court to look simply at the contract they made in reliance on the representation which induced them to enter into that bargain. They are entitled to say that there must be no speculation one way or the other about what would have happened if they had not purchased this horse and if no misrepresentation had been made to them. They are entitled to say (putting it in broad terms) we bought one horse and we spent money training it and entering it for races. We discovered two years after the purchase that it was not the horse we thought we had bought; it is not the horse on which we would have spent any money training or keeping, and therefore that is money only spent in reliance on the representation made.

NOTE: This case illustrates that many misrepresentation cases will turn on proving the direct loss, i.e., that the loss was caused by the misrepresentation. The representee's acts must be reasonable in the circumstances or the chain of causation may be broken.

In *Hussey v Eels* [1990] 2 QB 227, the Court of Appeal held that a profit on the sale of a bungalow which the plaintiffs had been induced to buy as a result of the defendants' misrepresentation did not have to be taken into account in assessing the damages since it was not *caused* by the misrepresentation but by the independent act of the plaintiffs in securing planning permission. Mustill LJ said (at p. 241):

> . . . Did the negligence which caused the damage also cause the profit—if profit there was? I do not think so. It is true that in one sense there was a casual link between the inducement of the purchase by misrepresentation and the sale 2½ years later, for the sale represented a choice of one of the options with which the plaintiffs had been presented by the defendants' wrongful act. But only in that sense. To my mind the reality of the situation is that the plaintiffs bought the house to live in, and did live in it for a substantial period. It was only after two years that the possibility of selling the land and moving elsewhere was explored, and six months later still that this possibility came to fruition. It seems to me that when the plaintiffs unlocked the development value of their land they did so for their own benefit, and not as part of a continuous transaction of which the purchase of land and bungalow was the inception.

(iii) Contributory negligence

Can the damages awarded to the representee under s. 2(1) be reduced for contributory negligence?

Gran Gelato Ltd v Richcliff (Group) Ltd
[1992] Ch 560

Gran Gelato had been granted a 10-year underlease by Richcliff in 1984. The headlease contained a redevelopment break clause which was exercisable by 12 months' notice expiring on or after June 1989. Gran Gelato and their solicitors had no notice of this restriction, and in reply to an inquiry Richcliff's solicitors had stated that 'to the lessor's knowledge' there were no such rights affecting the headlease which would inhibit the tenant's enjoyment of the property. In November 1988, the head lessor exercised the break clause and Gran Gelato brought an action claiming damages for negligent misstatement at common law and damages under s. 2(1) of the Misrepresentation Act 1967 for negligent misrepresentation. In answer to Richcliff's claim that Gran Gelato were contributorily negligent in proceeding without first seeing the headlease, Gran Gelato argued that s. 1 of the Law Reform (Contributory Negligence) Act 1945 did not apply to a damages claim under the Misrepresentation Act 1967. Held: since there were concurrent claims for damages for negligence at common law and under the 1967 Act, apportionment for contributory negligence under the 1945 Act applied to both claims. On the facts, however, it was not just and equitable to make a reduction in the damages.

SIR DONALD NICHOLLS VC: . . . Richcliff has advanced a defence of contributory negligence. Clearly, this is available as a defence to the claim against Richcliff for damages for breach of the common law duty of care; but is it available to the claim against Richcliff under s. 2(1) of the Misrepresentation Act 1967? In other words, does s. 1 of the Law Reform (Contributory Negligence) Act 1945 apply to a claim by a plaintiff for damages under the Misrepresentation Act 1967? So far as is material, s. 1(1) provides:

> Where any person suffers damage as the result partly of his own fault and partly of the fault of any other person or persons, a claim in respect of that damage shall not be defeated by reason of the fault of the person suffering the damage, but the damages recoverable in respect thereof shall be reduced to such extent as the court thinks just and equitable having regard to the claimant's share in the responsibility for the damage . . .'

Fault is defined in s. 4 as—

> negligence, breach of statutory duty or other act or omission which gives rise to a liability in tort or would, apart from this Act, give rise to the defence of contributory negligence.

[He referred to s. 2(1) of the Misrepresentation Act 1967 and continued:] Thus, in short, liability under the Misrepresentation Act 1967 is essentially founded on negligence, in the sense that the defendant, the representor, did not have reasonable grounds to believe that the facts represented were true. (Of course, if he did not believe the facts represented were true he will be liable for fraud.) This being so, it would be very odd if the defence of contributory negligence were not available to a claim under that Act. It would be very odd if contributory negligence were available as a defence to a claim for damages based on a breach of a duty to take care in and about the making of a particular representation, but not available to a claim for damages under the Act in respect of the same representation.

In my view, the answer to this point is provided by the decision of the Court of Appeal in *Forsikringsaktieselskapet Vesta* v *Butcher* [1989] AC 852. There the court held that the Act of 1945 applies to a case where there is a claim for damages for negligence at common law even if, in addition, there is a claim in contract to the same effect. O'Connor LJ, at p. 866, adopted the view expressed by Prichard J in *Rowe* v *Turner Hopkins & Partners* [1980] 2 NZLR 550, 556, regarding the equivalent section of the New Zealand legislation:

> I therefore conclude, in the absence of any clear authority to the contrary, that the first limb of the definition of s. 2 determines the meaning of the word 'fault' as it relates to the plaintiff's cause of action: that accordingly, the Contributory Negligence Act cannot apply unless the cause of action is founded on some act or omission on the part of the defendant which gives rise to liability in tort: that if the defendant's conduct meets that criterion, the Act can apply— whether or not the same conduct is also actionable in contract.

Neill LJ, at p. 875, agreed with this approach, and I do not read Sir Roger Ormrod's judgment as differing on this point.

In the present case the conduct of which Gran Gelato complains founds a cause of action both in negligence at common law and under the Act of 1967. As already noted, under the Act of 1967 liability is essentially founded on negligence. By parity of reasoning with the conclusion in *Forsikringsaktieselskapet Vesta* v *Butcher* [1989] AC 852 regarding concurrent claims in negligence in tort and contract, the Act of 1945 applies in the present case where there are concurrent claims against Richcliff in negligence in tort and under the Act of 1967. . . .

NOTE: It is submitted that this should also be the case where only a s. 2(1) claim is made, otherwise it would be possible to avoid apportionment by framing the claim only under the Misrepresentation Act 1967. Given that the 1945 Act applies to 'fault' on the part of the innocent party, it is wide enough to cover s. 2(1).

However, in *Alliance & Leicester Building Society* v *Edgestop Ltd* [1994] 2 All ER 38, Mummery J held that contributory negligence could not apply to apportion damages in an action in the tort of deceit. (See also *Corporacion Nacional del Cobre del Chile* v *Sogemin Metals Ltd* [1997] 1 WLR 1396.) In so doing he reaffirmed the principle enunciated by Jessel MR in *Redgrave* v *Hurd* and distinguished *Gran Gelato Ltd* v *Richcliff (Group) Ltd*. The House of Lords in *Standard Chartered Bank* v *Pakistan National Shipping Corporation (No. 2)* [2002] UKHL 43, [2003] 1 AC 959, discussed at *page 577*, has also confirmed that there is no defence of contributory negligence where the misrepresentation is fraudulent.

In this respect it appears that if the fiction of fraud were applied to assessing damages in an action under s. 2(1) of the Misrepresentation Act 1967 (*Royscot Trust* v *Rogerson, page 584*) then contributory negligence should not apply since it would not be applicable in an action for fraudulent misrepresentation. This would be highly unsatisfactory given that negligent misstatement in tort is clearly covered by the 1945 Act. Some clarification and reform in this area is urgently required. (See Chandler & Higgins [1994] LMCLQ 326 and Oakley [1994] CLJ 218.)

SECTION 2(2) MISREPRESENTATION ACT 1967—DAMAGES IN LIEU OF RESCISSION

MISREPRESENTATION ACT 1967

2. Damages for misrepresentation

(2) Where a person has entered into a contract after a misrepresentation has been made to him otherwise than fraudulently, and he would be entitled, by reason of the misrepresentation, to rescind the contract, then, if it is claimed, in any proceedings arising out of the contract, that the contract ought to be or has been rescinded, the court or arbitrator may declare the contract subsisting and award damages in lieu of rescission, if of opinion that it would be equitable to do so, having regard to the nature of the misrepresentation and the loss that would be caused by it if the contract were upheld, as well as to the loss that rescission would cause to the other party.

NOTES
1. In the context of negligent, or wholly innocent misrepresentations (i.e., honest and based on reasonable grounds), it is for the court in its discretion to decide to award damages instead of rescission if it feels that in the circumstances it would be fair to do so. In particular, if the misrepresentation was wholly innocent, then rescission may be an overreaction where damages would adequately compensate the misrepresentee, especially if the misrepresentation is on a trivial matter.
2. It had traditionally been considered that if the right to the remedy of rescission had been lost (see bars to rescission, *page 554*), then the court had no discretion to award damages in lieu of it under s. 2(2). In such cases there would be no remedy at all for innocent misrepresentation, and it may be doubtful that this is what Parliament intended. In *Thomas Witter Ltd* v *TBP Industries Ltd* [1996] 2 All ER 573, *page 564*, Jacob J *obiter* (because on the facts negligence was established) considered the issue and stated that:

   The defendants here argued that they had a defence of innocence both in relation to pattern book expenditure and in relation to the Allied problem, and so escaped s. 2(1). I reject that on the facts. . . . But even if the 'innocence defence' applies, then s. 2(2) comes into play. [Counsel for the defendants] argued that it could not do so because rescission is no longer available. He argued that the discretion under s. 2(2) to award damages crucially depends upon the rescission remedy remaining extant at the time the court comes to consider the question. Whether that argument is right has been a moot point since the Act was passed. The leading article of the time, Atiyah and Treitel 'Misrepresentation Act 1967' [1967] MLR 369, noticed the point at once. I found the argument unattractive: rescission might or might not be available at the time of trial depending on a host of factors which have nothing to do with behaviour of either party. I was not surprised to find that the authors of *Chitty on Contracts* (27th edn, 1994) para 6–058, p. 372 found the suggested construction 'strange' even though Mustill J had apparently accepted it *obiter* in *Atlantic Lines and Navigation Co. Inc.* v *Hallam Ltd, The Lucy* [1983] 1 Lloyd's Rep 188 and one of the plaintiffs conceded it in *Alman* v *Associated Newspapers Ltd* (20 June 1980, unrep.).

The argument assumes that the Act is referring to the remedy of 'rescission', though this is not clear. If it were only the remedy referred to then it is difficult to understand the reference to 'has been rescinded' in the section. It seemed to me that the reference might well be to a claim by the representee that he was entitled to rescission, in which case it would be enough for the court to find that the agreement was 'rescissionable' at least by the date when the representee first claimed rescission or at any time. There was enough ambiguity here to look to see what was said in Parliament at the time of the passing of the Act, pursuant to the limited new-found freedom given by *Pepper (Inspector of Taxes)* v *Hart* [1993] 1 All ER 42, [1993] AC 593. [Counsel for the defendants] found what the Solicitor General of the time said in the House of Commons. Even though it was against his . . . case, in the usual fine tradition of the Bar, he drew it to my attention. The Solicitor General said (741 HC Official Report (5th series) cols 1388–1389, 20 February 1967):

> . . . the hon. Gentleman put to me the case of the sale of a house. He asked me to suppose that there had been the sale of a house, some defect was discovered afterwards, it might be that a third party had come into the matter, and it might be entirely unjust or inequitable to insist on rescission in such a case. I suggest that in such a case, as the Lord Chancellor said, the conveyance is unlikely to be rescinded because of the impossibility of restitution. My answer is that a case of that sort would be covered by Clause 2(2) which says [here the material words of the present section were read]. That is the option which is given to the court, and in the sort of case which has been put to me . . . it would follow that the court or arbitrator would almost certainly award damages in lieu of rescission. Therefore that matter is really fully covered.

So the Solicitor General told the House of Commons that it was his view that damages could be awarded under s. 2(2) when there was an impossibility of restitution. Accordingly, I hold that the power to award damages under s. 2(2) does not depend upon an extant right to rescission—it only depends upon a right having existed in the past. Whether it depends upon such a right existing at any time, or depends upon such a right subsisting at the time when the representee first claims rescission, I do not have to decide. It was here first claimed by letter of 25 April 1990 which is only some four months from the contract date. In principle, however, I would have thought that it is enough that at any time a right to rescind subsisted. It is damages in lieu of that right (even if barred by later events or lapse of time) which can be awarded.

(See Beale's comments (1995) 111 LQR 60 and (1995) 111 LQR 385, 387–8. There is a danger of unjust enrichment without the ability to award damages in instances where rescission has been lost.)

However, in more recent cases the traditional interpretation has been followed on the basis that the wording of the section ('the injured party would otherwise be entitled to rescind') requires that the remedy of rescission should exist at the date of the hearing if damages are to be awarded in lieu of that remedy (*Floods of Queenferry* v *Shand Construction Ltd* [2000] BLR 81 at 93 (Humphrey Lloyd QC) and *Government of Zanzibar* v *British Aerospace (Lancaster House) Ltd* [2000] 1 WLR 2333 (Raymond Jack QC)).

Judge Raymond Jack QC in *Government of Zanzibar* v *British Aerospace (Lancaster House) Ltd* assessed the position as follows:

> To my mind the wording of s. 2(2) shows clearly enough that the effect of the subsection is to give the court an alternative to rescission where a right to rescission has been established but the court considers that damages would be a more equitable solution. I refer in particular to 'and he would be entitled,' 'if it is claimed . . . that the contract ought to be or has been rescinded,' 'the court . . . may declare the contract subsisting and award damages in lieu of rescission' and 'as well as to the loss that rescission would cause to the other party.' The last part of the section contemplates a balancing exercise between the situation if damages are awarded and that if rescission were granted: this supposes that rescission is an option open to the court. So I would disagree with the editors of *Chitty on Contracts*, 28th ed. (1999), vol. 1, pp. 383–384, para. 6–097 where it is stated that the words are far from clear.
>
> The scheme of the section is thus in my view that s. 2(1) gives a right to damages for non-fraudulent misrepresentation subject to the defence that the representor had reasonable grounds to believe his representation true, whereas s. 2(2) gives the court power to award damages where this would be more equitable than making an order for rescission or upholding a previous rescission by act of party. Because it is no defence to a claim for rescission that the representor had reasonable grounds to believe the representation true, that is not a defence where the court is considering damages under s. 2(2). In this way, where rescission remains an option, a claimant may do better under s. 2(2) because that defence is not available against him. That is no doubt why Zanzibar seeks to rely on it in addition to s. 2(1). It is also stated in *Chitty*, pp. 383–4, para. 6–097 that, if the power to award damages under s. 2(2) is restricted to situations in which rescission remains possible, then it would be strange because there would be no power to award damages in situations where the right has been lost, for example, because a car which has been misrepresented has been resold. The answer to that point is the claim to damages under s. 2(1), though here as a matter of policy it has been enacted that there should be the reasonable-grounds-of-belief defence. . . .
>
> I conclude that both the report of the Law Reform Committee (Tenth Report, 'Innocent Misrepresentation' (1962) Cmnd 1782) and the manner in which cl. 2(2) of the Bill was introduced in the House of Lords make clear that s. 2(2) gives the court a discretionary power to hold the contract to be subsisting and to award damages where it would otherwise be obliged to grant rescission or to hold that the contract had been rescinded by the representee. The court does not have that power, and does not need to have that power, where rescission is no longer available. In short, the power to award damages is an alternative to an order for rescission or the upholding of a prior rescission by the representee if that has occurred.

This appears to be yet another example of the literal approach to interpretation adopted in *Royscot Trust* and is a further indictment on the drafting of the Misrepresentation Act 1967.

In *Pankhania* v *Hackney London Borough Council* [2002] EWHC 2441 (Ch), [2002] NPC 123, *page 551*, the judge stated *obiter* [at 74] that 'the introduction of s. 2(2) was to mitigate the effect on the vendor of rescission, which would otherwise be available to the purchaser, and in certain circumstances was an over-harsh remedy, rather than to provide a remedy where there was none.' In other words, the intention was to provide an alternative remedy in a particular situation where there was an existing remedy but not to create a remedy where none existed before. This reasoning appears compelling.

Although the majority of recent first instance decisions require the continued availability of rescission in order to be able to exercise the discretion under s. 2(2), there is still some residual uncertainty on this question and a decision of a higher court would be helpful, or even consideration of this question by the Law Commission as part of a more general reconsideration of remedies for misrepresentation.

3. In *Thomas Witter* v *TBP Industries*, Jacob J sought (*obiter*) to identify the differences between damages under s. 2(1) and s. 2(2):

> ... what is the difference between s. 2(2) and s. 2(1)? In particular, since s. 2(1) has a defence of 'innocence' is that in practical terms useless because damages can be had under s. 2(2)? There is, of course, overlap between the two subsections on any construction and s. 2(3) explicitly recognises this. But if my construction covered all the cases covered by s. 2(1) then the latter would be pointless and my construction would probably be wrong. However, I do not think there is complete overlap. First, under s. 2(1) damages can be awarded in addition to rescission. So if there is 'innocence' the representor cannot have both remedies and never could, whatever the date of the decision. Secondly, the question of an award of damages under s. 2(2) is discretionary and the court must take into account the matters referred to in the concluding words of the subsection. Thirdly, the measure of damages under the two subsections may be different—s. 2(3) certainly contemplates that this may be so and moreover contemplates that s. 2(1) damages may be more than s. 2(2) damages and not the other way round. . . .

4. Although there is some assistance in the Act identifying the factors relevant to the decision to award damages in lieu of rescission, the section does not identify the measure of damages under s. 2(2).

Some further assistance on both of these questions is provided by the helpful *obiter* discussions of the Court of Appeal in the next case.

William Sindall plc v Cambridgeshire County Council
[1994] 1 WLR 1016 (CA)

For facts see *page 497*. Held: there was no misrepresentation so that rescission was not available and therefore no question of damages in lieu of rescission arose.

HOFFMANN LJ: My conclusion that there are no grounds for rescission . . . means that it is unnecessary to consider whether the judge correctly exercised his discretion under s. 2(2) of the Misrepresentation Act 1967 not to award damages in lieu of rescission. But in case this case goes further, I should say that in my judgment the judge approached this question on a false basis, arising from his mistake about the seriousness of the defect. . . .

The discretion conferred by s. 2(2) is a broad one, to do what is equitable. But there are three matters to which the court must in particular have regard.

The first is the nature of the misrepresentation. It is clear from the Law Reform Committee's Report that the court was meant to consider the importance of the representation in relation to the subject matter of the transaction. I have already said that in my view, in the context of a £5m sale of land, a misrepresentation which would have cost £18,000 to put right and was unlikely seriously to have interfered with the development or resale of the property was a matter of relatively minor importance.

The second matter to which the court must have regard is 'the loss that would be caused by it [the misrepresentation] if the contract were upheld'. The section speaks in terms of loss suffered rather than damages recoverable but clearly contemplates that if the contract is upheld, such loss will be compensated by an award of damages. Section 2(2) therefore gives a power to award damages in circumstances in which no damages would previously have been recoverable. Furthermore, such damages will be compensation for loss caused by the misrepresentation, whether it was negligent or not. This is made clear by s. 2(3), which provides:

> Damages may be awarded under subsection (2) of this section whether or not he is liable to damages under subsection (1) thereof, but where he is so liable any award under subsection (2) shall be taken into account in assessing his liability under the said subsection (1).

Damages under s. 2(2) are therefore damages for the misrepresentation as such. What would be the measure of such damages? This court is not directly concerned with quantum, which would be determined at an inquiry. But since the court, in the exercise of its discretion, needs to know whether damages under s. 2(2) would be an adequate remedy and to be able to compare such damages with the loss which rescission would cause to Cambridgeshire, it is necessary to decide in principle how the damages would be calculated. . . .

Under s. 2(1), the measure of damages is the same as for fraudulent misrepresentation i.e. all loss caused by the plaintiff having been induced to enter into the contract: *Cemp Properties (UK) Ltd* v *Dentsply Research and Development Corp* [1991] 2 EGLR 197. This means that the misrepresentor is invariably deprived of the benefit of the bargain (e.g. any difference between the price paid and the value of the thing sold) and may have to pay additional damages for consequential loss suffered by the representee on account of having entered into the contract. In my judgment, however, it is clear that this will not necessarily be the measure of damages under s. 2(2).

First, s. 2(1) provides for damages to be awarded to a person who 'has entered into a contract after a misrepresentation has been made to him by another party and as a result thereof—sc. of having entered into the contract—he has suffered loss'. In contrast s. 2(2) speaks of 'the loss which would be caused by it—sc. the misrepresentation—if the contract were upheld'. In my view, s. 2(1) is concerned with the damage flowing from having entered into the contract, while s. 2(2) is concerned with damage caused by the property not being what it was represented to be.

Secondly, s. 2(3) contemplates that damages under s. 2(2) may be less than damages under s. 2(1) and should be taken into account when assessing damages under the latter subsection. This only makes sense if the measure of damages may be different.

Thirdly, the Law Reform Committee Report makes it clear that s. 2(2) was enacted because it was thought that it might be a hardship to the representor to be deprived of the whole benefit of the bargain on account of a minor misrepresentation. It could not possibly have intended the damages in lieu to be assessed on a principle which would invariably have the same effect.

The Law Reform Committee drew attention to the anomaly which already existed by which a minor misrepresentation gave rise to a right of rescission whereas a warranty in the same terms would have grounded no more than a claim for modest damages. It said that this anomaly would be exaggerated if its recommendation for abolition of the bar on rescission after completion were to be implemented. I think that s. 2(2) was intended to give the court a power to eliminate this anomaly by upholding the contract and compensating the plaintiff for the loss he has suffered on account of the property not having been what it was represented to be. In other words, damages under s. 2(2) should never exceed the sum which would have been awarded if the representation had been a warranty. It is not necessary for present purposes to discuss the circumstances in which they may be less.

If one looks at the matter when Sindall purported to rescind, the loss which would be caused if the contract were upheld was relatively small: the £18,000 it would have cost to divert the sewer, the loss of a plot and interest charges on any consequent delay at the rate of £2,000 a day. If one looks at the matter at the date of trial, the loss would have been nil because the sewer had been diverted.

The third matter to be taken into account under s. 2(2) is the loss which would be caused to Cambridgeshire by rescission. This is the loss of the bargain at the top of the market (cf *The Lucy* [1983] 1 Lloyd's Rep 188) having to return about £8m in purchase price and interest in exchange for land worth less than £2m.

Having regard to these matters, and in particular the gross disparity between the loss which would be caused to Sindall by the misrepresentation and the loss which would be caused to Cambridgeshire by rescission, I would have exercised my discretion to award damages in lieu of rescission.

EVANS LJ: . . . Section 2(3) makes it clear that the statutory power to award damages under s. 2(2) is distinct from the plaintiff's right to recover damages under s. 2(1). Quoting from s. 2(2) itself, such damages are awarded 'in lieu of rescission' and the court has to have regard to three factors in particular, namely, the nature of the misrepresentation, the loss that would be caused by it (sc the misrepresentation) if the contract was upheld, and the loss that rescission would cause to the other party (sc the non-fraudulent author of the misrepresentation). It has not been suggested that these three are the only factors which the court may take into account. The discretion is expressed in broad terms 'if of opinion that it would be equitable to do so'. The three factors, however, in all but an exceptional case, are likely to be the ones to which most weight would be given, even if the subsection were silent in this respect.

No real difficulty arises in the present case as regards the nature of the misrepresentation, if any was made, nor as regards the loss which would be caused to the council, if rescission were upheld. There was no blameworthiness, on the judge's findings, so far as the council's officers in 1988–89 were concerned. . . . The consequences of the misrepresentation were not negligible, but they were small in relation to the purchase and the project as a whole. The loss caused to the council by rescission would be very great. They would repay in excess of £5m, together with interest, and would have restored to them land worth only a fraction of that amount. In other words, they would suffer the decline in market values which has occurred since 1988. And, even if the easement had been discovered immediately and the contract had been rescinded then, the council would have suffered significant loss, simply by reason of the need to repeat the tendering process and find another buyer.

There is, however, much room for debate as to the 'loss that would be caused if the contract were upheld'. The subsection assumes, as I read it, that this loss will be compensated by the damages awarded, if the contract is upheld. But if the measure is the same as those awarded in respect of a fraudulent misrepresentation (*Doyle* v *Olby (Ironmongers) Ltd* [1969] 2 QB 158), or under s. 2(1) (*Cemp Properties (UK) Ltd* v *Dentsply Research and Development Corp* [1991] 2 EGLR 197; cf *Royscot Trust Ltd* v *Rogerson* [1991] 2 QB 297), in cases where the contract continues in force, then two consequences seem to follow. First, damages under s. 2(2) are co-extensive with those under s. 2(1), whereas s. 2(3) suggests that they are or may be different. Secondly, an innocent and non-negligent defendant will be liable under s. 2(2) for damages which he is specifically excused under s. 2(1). Furthermore, if the plaintiff recovers full compensation under s. 2(2), if the contract is upheld, then he will not suffer any net loss, assuming that the damages are paid.

The cost of remedying the defect in the land was almost insignificant, and any delay and inconvenience suffered by Sindall can be compensated by a relatively small additional sum. The real issue is whether account should be taken of the decline in market values which affects Sindall if the contract stands, just as it would affect Cambridgeshire if rescission was upheld.

[Counsel for Sindall's] argument is that Sindall are entitled to recover the whole of the loss which they have suffered as a result of entering into the transaction, inducing the fall in market values from 1988 until at least the time of purported rescission in December 1990. . . .

In my judgment, it is not correct that the measure of damages under s. 2(2) for the loss that would be caused by the misrepresentation if the contract were upheld is the same measure as under s. 2(1). The latter is established by the common law, and it is the amount required to compensate the party to whom the misrepresentation was made for all the losses which he has sustained by reason of his acting upon it at the time when he did. But the damages contemplated by s. 2(2) are damages in lieu of rescission. The starting point for the application of the subsection is the situation where a plaintiff has established a right to rescind the contract on grounds of innocent misrepresentation; its object is to ameliorate for the innocent misrepresentor the harsh consequences of rescission for a wholly innocent (meaning, non-negligent as well as non-fraudulent) misrepresentor, in a case where it is fairer to uphold the contract and award damages against him. Such an award of damages was not permitted in law or equity before 1967. The court, therefore, exercises a statutory jurisdiction and it does so having regard to the circumstances at the date of the hearing, when otherwise rescission would be ordered. . . . When there has been a decline in market values since the date of the contract, then one party or the other will suffer that loss, depending on whether rescission is ordered or not. But that loss is not caused by the misrepresentation, except in the sense that the decline has occurred since the representation was made, and it does not measure the loss caused by the misrepresentation either when the representation was acted upon or when the court decides whether to order rescission or not. The 'loss caused by it', in my judgment, can be measured by the cost of remedying the defect, or alternatively by the reduced market value attributable to the defect, together with additional compensation, if appropriate . . .

When the court is required to form its own view of what is equitable between the parties at the date of the hearing, it is dangerous to lay down any hard-and-fast rule to the effect that no account can be taken of changed market values . . . Moreover, if it is right to take account of the current market value in assessing the loss which would be sustained by the council, if rescission was ordered, then it would be 'inequitable' not to have regard to this factor in the case of the builders also. But the effect of doing so is merely to re-state the issue which the court has to decide: in the circumstances of the case, should the loss of market remain where it presently lies?

Viewed in this way, it would be substantially unjust, in my judgment, to deprive Cambridgeshire of the bargain which it made in 1988, albeit that the bargain was induced by a misrepresentation innocently made, but which was of little importance in relation to the contract as a whole. That misrepresentation apart, Sindall made what has proved to be so far an unfortunate bargain for them (although they remain owners of an important potential development site in what is a notoriously cyclical market). To permit them to transfer the financial consequences to Cambridgeshire, in the circumstances of this case, could properly be described as a windfall for them.

For the above reasons, and taking into account the nature of the alleged representation and the history of the matter generally, including Sindall's deliberate failure to make any serious attempt to find a solution to the difficulty which arose when the sewer was discovered, the equitable balance, in my judgment, lies in favour of upholding the contract and awarding damages in lieu of rescission in this case. If there were a live issue under s. 2(2), I would award damages in lieu of rescission and order the amount of such damages to be assessed.

There remains the question of whether these damages should include the decline in the market value of the land since the contract was made. As indicated above, in my judgment they should not. This conclusion may be inconsistent with the view expressed in *McGregor on Damages* 15th ed. (1988), para. 1752, and in defence to the distinguished author I should explain my reasons briefly. He suggests that the measure to be adopted is:

> the same as the normal measure of damages in tort where the plaintiff has been induced to contract by fraudulent or negligent misrepresentation . . . The overall result, therefore, is that the damages will be held to be the difference between the value transferred and the value received   no recovery being possible for consequential losses.'

If the 'value transferred' (meaning the price paid by the plaintiff, to whom the representation was made) was the market value of the property, then there is no difference between this formula and what *McGregor* calls the contract measure, that is to say, the difference between the actual value received and the value which the property would have had, if the representation was true: see paragraph 1718. By adopting the tort measure, therefore, as he does in paragraph 1752, the author impliedly rejects the contract measure, whereas in my judgment that becomes the correct measure in circumstances where the plaintiff is entitled to an order for rescission, but rescission is refused under s. 2(2) of the Act. This is because the difference in value between what the plaintiff was misled into believing that he was acquiring, and the value of what he in fact received seems to me to be the measure of the loss caused to him by the misrepresentation in a case where he cannot rescind the contract and therefore retains the property which he received.

As *McGregor on Damages* points out, the tortious measure benefits a plaintiff who made a bad bargain, that is to say, who agreed to pay more than the market value of the property in the state in which he believed it to be, more so than the contract measure would do. Conversely, it disbenefits one who paid less than the market value, because it disentitles him from recovering the whole of the difference which the contract measure would otherwise produce. Likewise, the right to rescind benefits a plaintiff who has paid, or agreed to pay more than, with hindsight, he should have done. The period of hindsight may be short or long; where it is long, and the value has fallen in line with the market and therefore for reasons unconnected with the misrepresentation, there is no justification, in my view, for holding that the author of the misrepresentation is liable to compensate the plaintiff for that loss, in a case where rescission is refused.

It is unnecessary to explore the wider questions whether a tortious measure should ever include damages for a fall in market values, and whether this measure, as described by Lord Denning MR in *Doyle v Olby (Ironmongers) Ltd* [1969] 2 QB 158, 166, is necessarily exclusive of, or inconsistent with, the contractual measure to the extent which has been suggested. The recovery of such damages in the present case, even if the tortious measure under s. 2(2) applies, appears to be barred by the following three obstacles: (1) such damage was caused, not by the misrepresentation, but by the subsequent fall in market values, an extraneous cause; (2) the authorities suggest that the plaintiff's loss has to be assessed at the date when the property was transferred: *McGregor on Damages* 15th ed., para. 1727, citing *Waddell* v *Blockey* (1879) 4 QBD 678; and (3) if a subsequent rise, or fall, in market values is relevant at the date of trial, then a chance element enters into the calculation, whether the contract is rescinded or not. I should add, however, that the reported authorities are sparse, as *McGregor* emphasises, and as I read them they do not purport to decide the question whether a decline in value until the time of discovery of the true facts is necessarily excluded.

It is sufficient for present purposes to say that an award of damages in lieu of rescission under s. 2(2) should in my view be calculated as I have described above.

NOTES

1. See Beale (1995) 111 LQR 60.
2. Hoffmann LJ discusses the three factors identified in the subsection as relevant to the exercise of the court's discretion to award damages in lieu of rescission, namely the nature of the misrepresentation, the loss caused by the misrepresentation if the contract is upheld (i.e. damages to award to the representee instead of rescission), and the loss which would be caused to the non-fraudulent representor by rescission. The discussion of the measure of damages under s. 2(2) is relevant to the second of these factors. Significantly, unlike s. 2(1) damages, which are concerned with damages resulting from the misrepresentation leading to the making of the contract, s. 2(2) damages are to be assessed on the basis of losses caused by the misrepresentation if the contract is upheld, i.e. losses due to the subject matter of the contract not being what it was represented to be (difference in value). It follows that whereas consequential loss can be recovered under s. 2(1), such loss cannot be recovered under s. 2(2). (See Jacob J (*obiter*) in *Thomas Witter* v *TBP Industries Ltd* [1996] 2 All ER 573.) However, the measure of loss in this context cannot be contractual, which is the result of the difference in value measure. It may be that this measure would have to be limited to contracts which turn out to be bad bargains, as was the case in *Sindall*.
3. The difficulty on the facts with the measure of damages concerned whether the builders could recover for the fall in the value of the land. However, as the Court of Appeal pointed out, that loss is not actually caused by the misrepresentation but by the general fall in land values. Evans LJ argues that the loss caused by the misrepresentation is 'measured by the cost of remedying the defect, or alternatively by the reduced market value attributable to the defect', judged at the date of the contract.
4. In *UCB Corporate Services Ltd* v *Thomason* [2005] EWCA Civ 225, [2005] 1 All ER (Comm) 601, a husband and wife had given two guarantees to the bank. There had been a compromise with the husband's creditors to avoid bankruptcy and the bank agreed, on the basis that there had been full disclosure of the couple's assets, to release the liability under the guarantees (a waiver agreement). The bank later sought to enforce the guarantees or to rescind the waiver agreement for misrepresentation, on the basis that there had not been full disclosure. The Court of Appeal considered the discretion to award damages in lieu under s. 2(2) and held that the judge at first instance had been correct in that, given the financial position of the couple, the loss caused by the misrepresentation was the lost chance of recovering more money had it known the truth and therefore not agreed to the waiver at the relevant time, rather than the amount of the guaranteed debt (i.e. the difference in value). The implication was that the bank could have tried to realise the security at that time if it had not been induced to agree to the waiver. The Court also rejected the argument that the judge had been wrong in not making a specific point of the nature of the misrepresentations, although it was clear that he had been fully aware of the facts.
5. In *Thomas Witter* v *TBP Industries*, Jacob J concluded that 'The constant and justified academic criticism of the [Misrepresentation] Act indicates a subject well worth the attention of the Law Commission'.

SECTION 4: EXCLUDING LIABILITY FOR NON-FRAUDULENT MISREPRESENTATION

MISREPRESENTATION ACT 1967 (AS AMENDED)

3. Liability arising in contract

If a contract contains a term which would exclude or restrict—

    (a) any liability to which a party to a contract may be subject by reason of any misrepresentation made by him before the contract was made; or

    (b) any remedy available to another party to the contract by reason of such a misrepresentation,

that term shall be of no effect except in so far as it satisfies the requirement of reasonableness as stated in section 11(1) of the Unfair Contract Terms Act 1977; and it is for those claiming that the term satisfies that requirement to show that it does.

NOTE: Under the original s. 3 (before it was amended by s. 8 of the Unfair Contract Terms Act 1977), reasonableness was judged at the time of the judgment; it is now judged, according to the Unfair Contract Terms Act 1977, s. 11, at the time that the contract was made.

    Much of the case law, such as there is, is based on the unamended version of s. 3, and therefore it is important to be aware of this difference.

(i) Excluding liability for fraud

A party cannot exclude liability for his own fraud: *S. Pearson & Sons Ltd* v *Dublin Corporation* [1907] AC 351.

    In *HIH Casualty and General Insurance Co Ltd* v *Chase Manhattan Bank* [2003] UKHL 6, [2003] 1 All ER (Comm) 349, [2003] 2 Lloyd's Rep 61, the House of Lords confirmed that a party cannot exclude liability for his own fraud and held that in order to exclude liability for the fraud of agents a contractor would need to use clear and unambiguous words. This was the position despite the fact that the inclusion of such explicit language might deter the other party from contracting on this basis.

(ii) The crucial question is: when does s. 3 apply?

If a misrepresentation is made by an agent on behalf of a party, then any term excluding or limiting that agent's authority operates to protect the principal and is outside the scope of s. 3.

Overbrooke Estates Ltd v *Glencombe Properties Ltd*
[1974] 1 WLR 1355

The conditions of sale at an auction stated that: 'The vendors do not make or give and neither the Auctioneers nor any person in the employment of the Auctioneers has any authority to make or give any representation or warranty in relation to [the property]'. On 5 November, in response to an inquiry from the defendants, the auctioneers, who were agents for the plaintiffs, informed the defendants that no local authority had schemes or plans for the property or were interested in it for compulsory purchase. At the auction on 8 November the defendants successfully bid for the property and paid a deposit, and the auctioneers signed a memorandum of contract. The defendants later learnt that the property might well be included in a slum clearance programme, so they stopped payment on the deposit cheque and informed the plaintiffs that they would not now be proceeding. The plaintiffs claimed specific performance relying on the clause excluding any warranty or representation, and the defendants alleged in their defence that the clause relied on had to be fair and reasonable within s. 3. Held: this was not a clause which excluded or restricted liability for misrepresentation. It amounted only to a public limitation on the ostensible authority of this agent. The plaintiffs knew about this limitation before they bid, since it was contained in the conditions of sale that they received in advance. As a result, s. 3 did not apply.

NOTES

1. This limitation on the ostensible authority of the agent was defining the contractual duty itself rather than excluding or restricting liability for its breach. Section 3 of the Misrepresentation Act, it appears, has not therefore been extended by the Unfair Contract Terms Act 1977, s. 13 (*page 288*), to cover provisions which exclude or restrict the duty or obligation itself.
2. Ostensible authority occurs where an agent's usual authority to bind the principal has been restricted but the third party has no notice of this restriction and deals with the agent on the basis that there is no restriction. The principal will be bound to the third party. (Here the third party had notice of the restriction so that the principal could not be liable.)
3. The Unfair Terms in Consumer Contracts Regulations 1999, sch. 2(1)(n), provides that clauses 'limiting the seller's or supplier's obligation to respect commitments undertaken by his agents or making his commitments subject to compliance with a particular formality in consumer contracts' may be regarded as unfair. Much will depend on whether a 'commitment' is regarded as a representation or only as a contractual promise. If the former, clauses such as that in *Overbrooke Estates* may be unfair in a consumer contract.

(iii) Entire agreement clauses purporting to cover misrepresentations

A contract may contain an 'entire agreement clause', i.e., a statement that the written document comprises all the contract terms and that no representations have been made. The decision of Jacob J in *Thomas Witter* v *TBP Industries Ltd* [1996] 2 All ER 573, has proved controversial in its assessment of a previously typical entire agreement clause. The clause in question provided that the agreement was the entire agreement and that 'the purchaser acknowledges that it has not been induced to enter into this Agreement by any representation or warranty' other than the warranties in sch. 6. Jacob J rejected the claim by the defendants that this excluded them from liability for misrepresentation, whether pre-contractual or incorporated into the contract. First, it was not sufficiently clear that the purchaser was agreeing only to a remedy for breach of warranty and excluding liability for misrepresentations. He stated that a party seeking such protection cannot be 'mealy-mouthed in his clause' and this clause was not sufficiently explicit since it might be interpreted as merely setting out those representations that the purchaser thinks he is relying on at the time. Secondly, where a statement had become a warranty, an exclusion clause excluding liability for misrepresentation was ineffective because the remedy for misrepresentation in such a case is preserved by s. 1 of the Misrepresentation Act 1967.

The decision in *Inntrepreneur Pub Co.* v *East Crown Ltd* [2000] 2 Lloyd's Rep 611, for facts see *page 211*, makes it clear that the existence of an entire agreement clause does not affect the status of a statement as a misrepresentation. Of course, there may be both an entire agreement clause and a provision designed to exclude liability for misrepresentation (as was the case in *Inntrepreneur* but was found not to exist in *Thomas Witter*). Where this is the case, it was held in *Inntrepreneur* that s. 3 of the Misrepresentation Act 1967 will apply to the clause excluding the liability for misrepresentation but not the entire agreement clause (the purpose of which is to define where the contractual terms are to be found).

Does a non-reliance clause operate as an exclusion of liability to which s. 3 of the Misrepresentation Act 1967 applies?

The entire agreement clause may be in two parts and the second part may be a 'non-reliance' clause. In *Watford Electronics Ltd v Sanderson CFL Ltd* [2001] EWCA Civ 317, [2001] 1 All ER (Comm) 696, for facts see *page 315*, there was a clause stating that these terms and conditions represented the entire agreement between the parties and that 'no statement or representations by either party have been relied upon'. The judge had considered that the non-reliance clause fell within s. 3 as in substance it was excluding liability for misrepresentation since a clause could only exclude reliance on the basis that there was a statement that was capable of being relied upon. He held the non-reliance clause to be unreasonable in the context of the agreement as a whole. However, the Court of Appeal adopted a very different approach. Chadwick LJ, relying on his own unreported judgment in *EA Grimstead & Son Ltd v McGarrigan*, unrep. 27 October (1999), considered (*obiter*) that a non-reliance clause meant that the innocent party was estopped from asserting reliance on any misrepresentation so that s. 3 was inapplicable. He stated that he considered that for reasons of commercial certainty it was important for commercial parties to be able to make clear what matters had been relied upon in entering into any agreement.

CHADWICK LJ: . . .

39 The effect of an acknowledgement of non-reliance, in terms which were sufficiently similar to those in the second part of the entire agreement clause in the present case as to be indistinguishable, was considered in this court in *Grimstead (EA) & Son Ltd v McGarrigan* [1999] CA Transcript 1733. In a passage which was obiter dicta—but which followed full argument on the point—I said this (at p 32 of the transcript):

'In my view an acknowledgement of non-reliance . . . is capable of operating as an evidential estoppel. It is apt to prevent the party who has given the acknowledgement from asserting in subsequent litigation against the party to whom it has been given that it is not true. That seems to me to be a proper use of an acknowledgement of this nature, which, as Mr Justice Jacob pointed out in *Witter (Thomas) Ltd v TBP Industries Ltd* [1996] 2 All ER 573, has become a common feature of professionally drawn commercial contracts.'

I went on, at p 35, to say this:

'There are, as it seems to me, at least two good reasons why the courts should not refuse to give effect to an acknowledgement of non-reliance in a commercial contract between experienced parties of equal bargaining power—a fortiori, where those parties have the benefit of professional advice. First, it is reasonable to assume that the parties desire commercial certainty. They want to order their affairs on the basis that the bargain between them can be found within the document which they have signed. They want to avoid the uncertainty of litigation based on allegations as to the content of oral discussions at pre-contractual meetings. Second, it is reasonable to assume that the price to be paid reflects the commercial risk which each party—or, more usually, the purchaser—is willing to accept. The risk is determined, in part at least, by the warranties which the vendor is prepared to give. The tighter the warranties, the less the risk and (in principle, at least) the greater the price the vendor will require and which the purchaser will be prepared to pay. It is legitimate, and commercially desirable, that both parties should be able to measure the risk, and agree the price, on the basis of the warranties which have been given and accepted.'

40 Those passages were not cited to the judge. He held that Sanderson could not rely on the acknowledgement of non-reliance contained in the second part of the entire agreement clause. He said ([2000] 2 All ER (Comm) 984 at 1014 (para 107)):

'. . . the clause is, in substance, one that excludes liability rather than precludes liability from ever occurring. The clause states that no statement or representation has been relied on. It follows that the clause can only first bite once a statement or representation has been made that is capable of being relied on. The clause bites, therefore, on a potential misrepresentation that has been made. It is not preventing words that have been uttered from being a misrepresentation at all. Furthermore, the words that were used did, as a matter of fact, as I have found, induce the contract. Thus, this clause is one which is in substance an exclusion clause to which s 3 of the 1967 Act is applicable.'

I confess to some difficulty in following the reasoning in that passage. It is true that an acknowledgement of non-reliance does not purport to prevent a party from proving that a representation was made, nor that it was false. What the acknowledgement seeks to do is to prevent the person to whom the representation was made from asserting that he relied upon it. If it is to have that effect, it will be necessary—as I sought to point out in the *Grimstead* case—for the party who seeks to set up the acknowledgement as an evidential estoppel to plead and prove that the three requirements identified by this court in *Lowe v Lombank Ltd* [1960] 1 All ER 611, [1960] 1 WLR 196 are satisfied. That may present insuperable difficulties; not least because it may be impossible for a party who has made representations which he intended should be relied upon to satisfy the court that he entered into the contract in the belief that a statement by the other party that he had not relied upon those representations was true. But the fact that, on particular facts, the acknowledgement of non-reliance may not achieve its purpose does not lead to the conclusion that the acknowledgement is 'in substance an exclusion clause to which s 3 of the 1967 Act is applicable'. Nor does it lead to the conclusion that the entire agreement clause can be disregarded when construing the earlier limit of liability clause—cl 7.3 in the terms and conditions of sale and cl.10.6 in the terms and conditions of software licence.

41 The importance of the entire agreement clause in the present context—and, in particular, the importance of the acknowledgement of non-reliance which constitutes the second part of that clause—is that the first sentence in cl 7.3 (or cl 10.6, as the case may be) has to be construed on the basis that the parties intend that their whole agreement is to be contained or incorporated in the document which they have signed and on the basis that neither party has relied on any pre-contract representation when signing that document. On that basis, there is no reason why the parties should have intended, by the words which they have used in the first sentence of the limit of liability clause, to exclude liability for negligent pre-contract misrepresentation. Liability in damages under the 1967 Act can arise only where the party who has suffered the damage has relied upon the representation. Where both parties to the contract have acknowledged, in the document itself, that they have not relied upon any pre-contract representation, it would be bizarre (unless compelled to do so by the words which they have used) to attribute to them an intention to exclude a liability which they must have thought could never arise.

NOTE: Chadwick LJ considered that in the context of commercial negotiations conducted by parties of equal bargaining power who had the benefit of professional advisers, a court should be reluctant to refuse recognition to a non-reliance clause. However, the clause cannot fulfil its objective where there is a fraudulent misrepresentation since it cannot be claimed that there was no reliance on such a statement. Therefore, an acknowledgement of non-reliance will not operate to exclude liability for fraudulent misrepresentation and such clauses should be drafted to exclude their application to fraud.

It is questionable whether Chadwick LJ was correct in assuming that s. 3 did not apply to clauses which prevented liability in misrepresentation from arising and it would be very unfortunate if a non-reliance clause were to operate, as in *Watford*, so as to prevent an exclusion or limitation clause from applying to a misrepresentation. In *SAM Business Systems Ltd* v *Hedley & Co.* [2002] EWHC 2733, [2003] 1 All ER (Comm) 465, *page 317*, *Watford Electronics* was distinguished on the basis that, although there was an entire agreement clause, there was no non-reliance clause. In any event, the judge held that SAM had waived the entire agreement clause.

(iv) It is not possible to avoid the 1977 Act by a clause purporting to deny the existence of any representation by treating the statement as opinion

---

Cremdean Properties Ltd v Nash
(1977) 244 EG 547 (CA)

The plaintiffs claimed rescission of contracts for the sale of two properties, alleging misrepresentation in the particulars of the invitation to tender as to the area of lettable office space which was within the planning permission with which the property was sold. The defendants relied in their defence on a footnote clause in the conditions of sale by tender which provided that:

> (a) These particulars are prepared for the convenience of an intending purchaser or tenant and although they are believed to be correct their accuracy is not guaranteed and any error, omission or misdescription shall not annul the sale or be grounds on which compensation may be claimed and neither do they constitute any part of an offer of a contract.
>
> (b) Any intending purchaser or tenant must satisfy himself by inspection or otherwise as to the correctness of each of the statements contained in these particulars.

As a preliminary point it had to be decided whether this footnote could operate as a disclaimer.

BRIDGE LJ: . . . In effect what [counsel for the defendants] says is this. The terms of the footnote are not simply, if contractual at all, a contractual exclusion either of any liability to which the defendant would otherwise be subject for any misrepresentation in the document, or of any remedy otherwise available on that ground to the plaintiff. The footnote is effective, so the argument runs, to nullify any representation in the document altogether; it is effective, so it is said, to bring about a situation in law as if no representation at all had ever been made. For my part, I am quite unable to accept that argument. I reject it primarily on the simple basis that on no reading of the language of the footnote could it have the remarkable effect contended for. . . .

[After referring to *Overbrooke Estates Ltd* v *Glencombe Properties Ltd* [1974] 3 All ER 511, Bridge LJ continued:]

It is one thing to say that s. 3 does not inhibit a principal from publicly giving notice limiting the ostensible authority of his agents; it is quite another thing to say that a principal can circumvent the plainly intended effect of s. 3 by a clause excluding his own liability for a representation which he has undoubtedly made.

I am quite content to found my judgment in this case on the proposition that the language of the footnote relied upon . . . simply does not, on its true interpretation, have the effect contended for. But I would go further and say that if the ingenuity of a draftsman could devise language which would have that effect, I am extremely doubtful whether the court would allow it to operate so as to defeat s. 3. Supposing the vendor included a clause which the purchaser was required to, and did, agree to in some such terms as 'notwithstanding any statement of fact included in these particulars the vendor shall be conclusively deemed to have made no representation within the meaning of the Misrepresentation Act 1967,' I should have thought that that was only a form of words the intended and actual effect of which was to exclude or restrict liability, and I should not have thought that the courts would have been ready to allow such ingenuity in forms of language to defeat the plain purpose at which s. 3 is aimed.

I should add that on this part of the case we heard a further argument . . . purporting to draw a distinction between giving information or making a statement of opinion or belief on the one hand, and making a representation on the other. For my part, the distinction seems to be one without a difference. The word 'representation' is an extremely wide term; I cannot see why one should not be making a representation when giving information or when stating one's opinion or belief. To my mind it would be a retrograde step if the court were to give the word 'representation,' when it appears in the Misrepresentation Act 1967, any narrow or limited construction, less wide than the perfectly natural meaning of the word.

SCARMAN LJ: . . . [T]he case for the [defendants] does have an audacity and a simple logic which I confess I find attractive. It runs thus: a statement is not a representation unless it is also a statement that what is stated is true. If in context a statement contains no assertion, express or implied, that its content is accurate, there is no representation. *Ergo*, there can be no misrepresentation; *ergo*, the Misrepresentation Act 1967 cannot apply to it. Humpty Dumpty would have fallen for this argument. If we were to fall for it, the Misrepresentation Act would be dashed to pieces which not all the King's lawyers could put together again.

. . . [Counsel for the defendants] submits that a note, or postscript, to the special conditions of sale by tender qualify the statement by removing from it any representation that its content was accurate. According to his argument, the statement went no further than to imply that the defendant believed it to be accurate. In my judgement it is not possible so to read the statement or the note. The statement was a plain representation that under the outline planning consent approximately 17,900 sq ft would be available for offices. The note, fairly construed, was a warning to the would-be purchaser to check the facts; that is to say, not to rely on it. Such a warning does not destroy the representation; indeed, it is wholly consistent with the statement being a representation. It is because the statement contains the representation that the warning is given. Since the statement was false, there was a false representation; the Act therefore applies.

Reasonableness under s. 3

Howard Marine & Dredging Co. Ltd v *A. Ogden & Sons (Excavations) Ltd*
[1978] QB 574 (CA)

The facts of this case appear at *page 582*. The relevant clause stated: '. . . the charterers acceptance of handing over the vessel shall be conclusive that they have examined the vessel and found her in all respects seaworthy, in good order and condition and in all respects fit for the intended and contemplated use by the charterers and in every other way satisfactory to them.'

BRIDGE LJ: A clause of this kind is to be narrowly construed. It can only be relied on as conclusive evidence of the charterers' satisfaction in relation to such attributes of the vessel as would be apparent on an ordinary examination of the vessel. I do not think deadweight capacity is such an attribute. It can only be ascertained by an elaborate calculation or by an inspection of the ship's documents. But even if, contrary to this view, the clause can be read as apt to exclude liability for the earlier misrepresentation, Howards still have to surmount the restriction imposed by s. 3 of the Misrepresentation Act 1967. . . .

What the judge said in this matter was: 'If the wording of the clause is apt to exempt from responsibility for negligent misrepresentation as to carrying capacity, I hold that such exemption is not fair and reasonable.'. . .

NOTES
1. The factor influencing the majority (Bridge and Shaw LJJ) is that it cannot be reasonable to exclude liability for misrepresentation in respect of information to which the representor had access and the representee did not. In *South Western General Property Company Ltd* v *Marton* (1982) 263 EG 1090, Croom-Johnson J had to decide on the reasonableness of a clause where the representation related to planning permission. He stated that it was a question of judging the particular clause in the contract with the particular buyer. He found the clause to be unreasonable because the facts on which the representation was based were only within the knowledge of the vendor and related to matters which were central to the contract. In addition, the particular buyer was a householder, buying the site for his own residence, as opposed to a property speculator.

2. However, Lord Denning in *Howard Marine*, applying the original s. 3, considered that the question which had to be asked was whether 'reliance on the clause was fair and reasonable in the circumstances of the case', and on that basis he considered that it was reasonable. He said (at p. 594):

> If the clause itself is reasonable, that goes a long way towards showing that reliance on it is fair and reasonable. It seems to me that the clause was itself fair and reasonable. The parties here were commercial concerns and were of equal bargaining power. The clause was not foisted by one on the other in a standard printed form. It was contained in all the drafts which passed between them, and it was no doubt given close consideration by both sides, like all the other clauses, some of which were amended and others not. It was a clause common in charterparties of this kind: and is familiar in other commercial contracts, such as construction and engineering contracts, see, for instance, *S. Pearson & Son Ltd* v *Dublin Corporation* [1907] AC 351, 356, and the useful observations in *Hudson on Building Contracts*, 10th ed. (1970), pp. 39, 48. It is specially applicable in cases where the contractor has the opportunity of checking the position for himself. It tells him that he should do so: and that he should not rely on any information given beforehand, for it may be inaccurate. Thus it provides a valuable safeguard against the consequences of innocent misrepresentation.
>
> Even if the clause were somewhat too wide (I do not think it is), nevertheless this is, I think, a case where it would be fair and reasonable to allow reliance on it. Here is a clause by which Ogdens accepted that the barges were 'in all respects fit for the intended and contemplated use by the charterers.' Ogdens had had full inspection and examination of the barges. They had had an on-hire survey by their surveyors. Any expert could have given them a reliable estimate as to the deadweight capacity. Yet they seek to say that the barges were not fit for the use for which they intended them—in that they were of too low carrying capacity. And in support of this case they have no written representation to go upon. They only have two telephone conversations and one interview—as to which there is an acute conflict of evidence. It is just such conflicts which commercial men seek to avoid by such a clause as this. I would do nothing to impair its efficacy. I would allow Howards to rely on it.

Lord Denning considered that the representee should have checked the information he was given.

3. It is more difficult to conclude that a clause is reasonable when applying the amended s. 3 so that reasonableness is judged at the time the contract is made.

Walker v *Boyle*
[1982] 1 WLR 495

In answer to a preliminary inquiry before the sale of land, the vendor negligently stated that to the vendor's knowledge there were no boundary disputes. Contracts were exchanged using the National Conditions of Sale (19th edn). Condition 17(1) provided that 'no error, misstatement or omission in any preliminary answer concerning the property shall annul the sale'. When the purchaser discovered the boundary dispute he sought rescission, but the vendor claimed that this was precluded by condition 17(1). The purchaser argued, *inter alia*, that condition 17(1) was an exclusion clause that fell within s. 3 of the Misrepresentation Act 1967 and had to be shown to be reasonable. Held: this condition did not apply to misrepresentations where the true facts were within the vendor's knowledge and, in any event, it was an exclusion clause within s. 3 which the vendor had not established to be reasonable. The mere fact that it was a common clause in standard conditions of sale, or that both parties had experienced solicitors acting for them, did not make it reasonable.

NOTES
1. Again, the vital factor was that the vendor alone had the information and therefore could not exclude liability in misrepresentation in respect of that information.
2. In *Thomas Witter* v *TBP Industries* [1996] 2 All ER 573, *page 600*, Jacob J went on to consider that, in any event, the clause purporting to exclude liability for misrepresentation was unreasonable within s. 3 of the Misrepresentation Act 1967:

> . . . But I have to say that even if cl. 17.2 had exclusionary effect it would to my mind be neither fair nor reasonable. The problem is its scope. The 1967 Act calls for consideration of the *term* as such. And it refers to 'any liability' and 'any misrepresentation'. It does not call for consideration of the term so far as it applies to the misrepresentation in question or the kind of misrepresentation in question. The term is not severable: it is either reasonable as a whole or not. So one must consider its every potential effect. The clause does not distinguish between fraudulent, negligent, or innocent misrepresentation. If it excludes liability for one kind of misrepresentation it does so for all. I cannot think it reasonable to exclude liability for fraudulent misrepresentation—indeed [counsel for the defendants] accepted it would not work in the case of fraud. It may well be, with a different clause, reasonable to exclude liability for innocent misrepresentation or even negligent misrepresentation. But since the width of this clause is too great I would have held it failed the requirement of reasonableness and so was of no effect.
>
> A possible route around this latter objection would be to construe the clause so that it did not apply to a fraudulent misrepresentation. This approach is artificial. It is unnecessary now that the 1977 Act exists to destroy unreasonable exclusion clauses. The construction involves creating an implied exception in the case of fraud. What about an implied exclusion of negligence? Or gross negligence? It is not for the law to fudge a way for an exclusion clause to be valid. If a party wants to exclude liability for certain sorts of misrepresentations, it must spell those sorts out clearly.

In coming to this conclusion the judge expressly rejected the argument that the clause was reasonable because it was in common use.

If this is correct, it would seem to be important to draft such a clause so as to remove its potential to apply to fraudulent misrepresentations because it will not be possible to sever objectionable parts (which accords with the approach taken in *Stewart Gill Ltd* v *Horatio Myer & Co. Ltd* [1992] 1 QB 600, *page 288*). However, in *Government of Zanzibar* v *British Aerospace (Lancaster House) Ltd* [2000] 1 WLR 2333, Judge Raymond Jack QC in relation to a part of an entire agreement clause which expressly sought to exclude liability for misrepresentation, rejected the argument that the clause had to be unreasonable because it *could* extend to cover fraud even though no fraud was alleged on the facts. It was accepted only that no such clause could operate where there was an allegation of fraud.

13

Duress, Undue Influence, and Inequality of Bargaining Power

Although English law is not generally concerned with the fairness of the bargain reached by the parties and does not recognise any general duty of contractual fairness, there are recognised instances where it will intervene due to the circumstances surrounding the way in which the contract was made, or if its content infringes the statutory and common law rules designed to prevent onerous or unfair terms, e.g., Consumer Credit Act 1974, the Unfair Terms in Consumer Contracts Regulations 1999 (*pages 318–27*) and the penalty rule (*pages 414–26*).

In *Interfoto Picture Library Ltd* v *Stiletto Visual Programmes Ltd* [1989] 1 QB 433 (for facts see *page 219*), Bingham LJ made the following comment (at p. 439):

> . . . In many civil law systems, and perhaps in most legal systems outside the common law world, the law of obligations recognises and enforces an overriding principle that in making and carrying out contracts parties should act in good faith. This does not simply mean that they should not deceive each other, a principle which any legal system must recognise; its effect is perhaps most aptly conveyed by such metaphorical colloquialisms as 'playing fair,' 'coming clean' or 'putting one's cards face upwards on the table.' It is in essence a principle of fair and open dealing. In such a forum it might, I think, be held on the facts of this case that the plaintiffs were under a duty in all fairness to draw the defendants' attention specifically to the high price payable if the transparencies were not returned in time and, when the 14 days had expired, to point out to the defendants the high cost of continued failure to return them.
>
> English law has, characteristically, committed itself to no such overriding principle but has developed piecemeal solutions in response to demonstrated problems of unfairness. Many examples could be given. Thus equity has intervened to strike down unconscionable bargains. Parliament has stepped in to regulate the imposition of exemption clauses and the form of certain hire-purchase agreements. The common law also has made its contribution, by holding that certain classes of contract require the utmost good faith, by treating as irrecoverable what purport to be agreed estimates of damage but are in truth a disguised penalty for breach, and in many other ways.
>
> The well known cases on sufficiency of notice are in my view properly to be read in this context. At one level they are concerned with a question of pure contractual analysis, whether one party has done enough to give the other notice of the incorporation of a term in the contract. At another level they are concerned with a somewhat different question, whether it would in all the circumstances be fair (or reasonable) to hold a party bound by any conditions or by a particular condition of an unusual and stringent nature.

At common law and in equity the doctrines of duress and undue influence allow a contract to be set aside if one party has put unfair and improper pressure on the other in the negotiations leading up to the contract.

In *Royal Bank of Scotland plc* v *Etridge (No. 2)* [2001] UKHL 44, [2002] 2 AC 773, Lord Nicholls explained that such situations are difficult to identify with any precision:

6 . . . Undue influence is one of the grounds of relief developed by the courts of equity as a court of conscience. The objective is to ensure that the influence of one person over another is not abused. In everyday life people constantly seek to influence the decisions of others. They seek to persuade those with whom they are dealing to enter into transactions, whether great or small. The law has set limits to the means properly employable for this purpose. To this end the common law developed a principle of duress. Originally this was narrow in its scope, restricted to the more blatant forms of physical coercion, such as personal violence.

7 Here, as elsewhere in the law, equity supplemented the common law. Equity extended the reach of the law to other unacceptable forms of persuasion. The law will investigate the manner in which the intention to enter into the transaction was secured: 'how the intention was produced', in the oft repeated words of Lord Eldon LC, from as long ago as 1807 (*Huguenin v Baseley* 14 Ves 273, 300). If the intention was produced by an unacceptable means, the law will not permit the transaction to stand. The means used is regarded as an exercise of improper or 'undue' influence, and hence unacceptable, whenever the consent thus procured ought not fairly to be treated as the expression of a person's free will. It is impossible to be more precise or definitive. The circumstances in which one person acquires influence over another, and the manner in which influence may be exercised, vary too widely to permit of any more specific criterion.

SECTION 1: DURESS

A: Duress to the person

Barton v Armstrong
[1976] AC 104 (PC)

B, the managing director of a public company, resented the interference of the company's chairman, A. A was removed as chairman and B was informed by the company's principal lender that they would not advance further money. B believed that if the money owed to A was paid, the lender would agree to provide further finance. It was established that A had threatened to kill B and had made threatening telephone calls to B. B also genuinely believed that A had hired a criminal to kill him. B executed a deed, which was favourable to A, whereby the company agreed to pay $140,000 in cash to A and to purchase A's shares in the company for $180,000. The lender still refused to advance any money to the company which was soon in financial difficulties. B claimed that the deed was void as it had been executed under duress. The trial judge, Street J, had considered that the sole reason why B had executed the deed was commercial necessity. The Court of Appeal of the Supreme Court of New South Wales held that the onus was on B to show that, but for the threats, he would not have signed the agreement, and B had failed to discharge that onus. The Privy Council by a majority of 3:2 (Lord Wilberforce and Lord Simon of Glaisdale dissenting) overturned this decision. Held: duress had to be treated in the same way as fraudulent misrepresentation, so that as long as A's threats were *one* of the reasons why B executed the deed, B was entitled to relief (see *Edgington v Fitzmaurice* (1885) 29 ChD 459, *page 551*). Once unlawful pressure was established, it was for A to establish that the threats and unlawful pressure exerted on B had in no way affected B's decision to enter the agreement. The majority of the

Privy Council held that A had not established this, and therefore the deed was 'void' for duress.

LORD CROSS OF CHELSEA: . . . It is hardly surprising that there is no direct authority on the point, for if A threatens B with death if he does not execute some document and B, who takes A's threats seriously, executes the document it can be only in the most unusual circumstances that there can be any doubt whether the threats operated to induce him to execute the document. But this is a most unusual case and the findings of fact made below do undoubtedly raise the question whether it was necessary for Barton in order to obtain relief to establish that he would not have executed the deed in question but for the threats. . . . There is an obvious analogy between setting aside a disposition for duress or undue influence and setting it aside for fraud. . . . Had Armstrong made a fraudulent misrepresentation to Barton for the purpose of inducing him to execute the deed of January 17, 1967 the answer to the problem which has arisen would have been clear. If it were established that Barton did not allow the representation to affect his judgment then, he could not make it a ground for relief even though the representation was designed and known by Barton to be designed to affect his judgment. If on the other hand Barton relied on the misrepresentation Armstrong could not have defeated his claim to relief by showing that there were other more weighty causes which contributed to his decision to execute the deed, for in this field the court does not allow an examination into the relative importance of contributory causes.

'Once make out that there has been anything like deception, and no contract resting in any degree on that foundation can stand': per Lord Cranworth LJ in *Reynell* v *Sprye* (1852) 1 De GM & G 660, 708. . . . Their Lordships think that the same rule should apply in cases of duress and that if Armstrong's threats were 'a' reason for Barton's executing the deed he is entitled to relief even though he might well have entered into the contract if Armstrong had uttered no threats to induce him to do so. . . . If Barton had to establish that he would not have made the agreement but for Armstrong's threats, then their Lordships would not dissent from the view that he had not made out his case. But no such onus lay on him. On the contrary it was for Armstrong to establish, if he could, that the threats which he was making and the unlawful pressure which he was exerting for the purpose of inducing Barton to sign the agreement and which Barton knew were being made and exerted for this purpose in fact contributed nothing to Barton's decision to sign. The judge has found that during the 10 days or so before the documents were executed Barton was in genuine fear that Armstrong was planning to have him killed if the agreement was not signed. His state of mind was described by the judge as one of 'very real mental torment' and he believed that his fears would be at an end when once the documents were executed. . . . The proper inference to be drawn from the facts found is, their Lordships think, that though it may be that Barton would have executed the documents even if Armstrong had made no threats and exerted no unlawful pressure to induce him to do so the threats and unlawful pressure in fact contributed to his decision to sign the documents and to recommend their execution by Landmark and the other parties to them.

In the result therefore the appeal should be allowed and a declaration made that the deeds in question were executed by Barton under duress and are void so far as concerns him. . . .

The dissenting judgment of Lord Wilberforce and Lord Simon of Glaisdale does not differ from the majority on the law applicable to duress to the person. However, the minority considered that they could not overturn Street J's findings of fact and found the contract to be valid.

LORD WILBERFORCE and LORD SIMON OF GLAISDALE, *dissenting*: The action is one to set aside an apparently complete and valid agreement on the ground of duress. The basis of the plaintiff's claim is, thus, that though there was apparent consent there was no true consent to the agreement: that the agreement was not voluntary.

This involves consideration of what the law regards as voluntary, or its opposite; for in life, including the life of commerce and finance, many acts are done under pressure, sometimes overwhelming pressure, so that one can say that the actor had no choice but to act. Absence of choice in this sense does not negate consent in law: for this the pressure must be one of a kind which the law does not regard as legitimate. Thus, out of the various means by which consent may be obtained—advice, persuasion, influence, inducement, representation, commercial pressure—the law has come to select some which it will not accept as a reason for voluntary action: fraud, abuse of relation of confidence, undue influence, duress or coercion. In this the law, under the influence of equity, has developed from the old common law conception of duress—threat to life and limb—and it has arrived at the modern generalisation expressed by Holmes J—'subjected to an improper motive for action': *Fairbanks* v *Snow* (1887) 13 NE 596, 598.

In an action such as the present, then, the first step required of the plaintiff is to show that some illegitimate means of persuasion was used. That there were threats to Barton's life was found by the judge, though he did not accept Barton's evidence in important respects. . . .

The next necessary step would be to establish the relationship between the illegitimate means used and the action taken. For the purposes of the present case (reserving our opinion as to cases which may arise in other contexts) we are prepared to accept, as the formula most favourable to the appellant, the test proposed by the majority, namely that the illegitimate means used was *a* reason (not *the* reason, nor the *predominant* reason nor the *clinching* reason) why the complainant acted as he did. We are also prepared to accept that a decisive answer is not obtainable by asking the question whether the contract would have been made even if there had been no threats because, even if the answer to this question is affirmative, that does not prove that the contract was not made because of the threats.

Assuming therefore that what has to be decided is whether the illegitimate means used was a reason why the complainant acted as he did, it follows that his reason for acting must (unless the case is one of automatism which this is not) be a conscious reason so that the complainant can give evidence of it: 'I acted because I was forced'. If his evidence is honest and accepted, that will normally conclude the issue. . . .

We think it important to notice how little of Barton's case was accepted: how much of it—indeed almost the whole of his essential contentions—failed. In general the judge found that his case was reconstructed after the event; it was not until nearly a year after signing the agreement in January 1967 that he brought forward his claim of duress. . . .

Street J had found that Barton was motivated to enter into the agreement by sheer commercial necessity. By this he meant that the company would survive and be profitable without Armstrong, but not with him, and that the likelihood and extent of such profit justified the price to be paid to get rid of Armstrong. He meant also, as his judgment shows, that Barton was motivated by a desire for uncontested control over the business, rather than a sharing of it with Armstrong. . . .

The judge's findings were . . . accepted, after careful examination by Taylor A-JA—'. . . the conclusion', he finds, 'that Barton entered into this agreement because he wanted to and from commercial motives only is, I think undoubtedly correct.'

The appeal cannot succeed unless these most explicit findings are overturned. We consider that no basis exists for doing so. . . .

NOTES

1. Although Lord Cross refers to duress as rendering a contract void *ab initio*, it is only voidable. If Lord Cross was stating the consequence *after* avoidance, his statement can be reconciled with accepted principle. (As duress renders a contract voidable, the bars to rescission apply so that the remedy can, for example, be lost by affirmation, see *page 554*.)

2. The Privy Council held that absence of choice is not sufficient on its own to negate consent, since the pressure must be illegitimate, and *Barton* v *Armstrong* has clearly confirmed that threats to life are illegitimate. In other categories of duress the definition of 'illegitimate threats' is not as obvious.

3. The burden of proof is placed upon the pressurising party to establish that the threats in no way influenced the contract. This will be very difficult to establish.

4. In their dissenting judgment, Lords Wilberforce and Simon stress the delay of a year in bringing the claim of duress. This has proved to be a vital factor affecting the ability to set aside a contract for economic duress, *page 613*.

B: Duress to property

Duress to property occurs when there is a threat to seize the owner's property or to damage it. In *Occidental Worldwide Investment Corp* v *Skibs A/S Avanti, The Siboen and the Sibotre* [1976] 1 Lloyd's Rep 293, Kerr J considered that a contract could be avoided in such cases.

> . . . First, [counsel] submitted that English law only knows duress to the person and duress to goods, and that a case like the present falls into neither category, with the result that this defence must fail in limine. Secondly, he submitted that although money paid under duress to goods is recoverable, a contract can only be set aside for duress to the person but not in any other case of duress. He said that in every case in which a party enters into a contract otherwise than under duress to the person, any payment or forbearance pursuant to such contract is regarded as voluntary, whatever may have been the nature or degree of compulsion, short of violence to the person, which may have caused him to enter into the contract. He relied mainly on a line of authority in which *Skeate* v *Beale*, (1841) 11 Ad & E 983 is the leading case.
>
> I do not think that English law is as limited . . . though there are statements in some of the cases which support his submissions. For instance, if I should be compelled to sign a lease or some other contract for a nominal but legally sufficient consideration under an imminent threat of having my house burnt down or a valuable picture slashed, though without any threat of physical violence to anyone, I do not think that the law would uphold the agreement. I think that a plea of coercion or compulsion would be available in such cases. . . .

This is also confirmed by Lord Goff in *Dimskal Shipping Co. SA* v *International Transport Workers' Federation, The Evia Luck* [1991] 4 All ER 871, 878. See also *The 'Alev'* [1989] 1 Lloyd's Rep 138, *page 622*.

C: Economic duress

It is only comparatively recently that the courts have accepted that a contract can be set aside where illegitimate commercial pressure is exerted by one party on another. The previous mechanism to prevent such promises being enforceable was the doctrine of consideration (*Stilk* v *Myrick* (1809) 2 Camp 317, 6 Esp 129 (*page 133*) and *Atlas Express* v *Kafco Ltd* [1989] 1 All ER 641).

Following the Court of Appeal's decision in *Williams* v *Roffey Brothers & Nicholls (Contractors) Ltd* [1991] 1 QB 1 (*page 135*), the emphasis has shifted, so that economic duress will be vitally important in preventing extortion in the future. The limits of the doctrine therefore need to be clearly defined, and in the view of academic commentators it needs to be given a sounder conceptual basis.

(a) Coercion of the will which vitiates consent

Occidental Worldwide Investment Corporation v Skibs A/S Avanti, The Siboen and the Sibotre

[1976] 1 Lloyd's Rep 293

In 1970, the defendants agreed to let two tankers for three years to Concord, a subsidiary company of Occidental Petroleum, at a rate of hire of $4.40 per ton per month. In the autumn of 1971, Occidental had financial problems and sought to renegotiate the charter to reduce the rates of hire. The impression given was that Concord, the charterer, did not have any substantial assets and that it required the continuing support of its parent company. If the hire was not reduced the charterer threatened cancellation of the charter, and alleged that the parent company would allow the charterer to go bankrupt so that the owners would not even be able to seek a remedy for breach of the charter. This was a gross distortion of the truth. The defendants agreed to reduce the hire to $4.10 but later they withdrew both vessels. The charterer sought damages for wrongful repudiation, and the defendants counterclaimed arguing that they had only agreed to the alteration because of duress. Held: the duress argument failed, because although the defendants had acted under great pressure in agreeing to the altered rate, it could not be regarded in law as a coercion of their will so as to vitiate their consent.

KERR J: But even assuming, as I think, that our law is open to further development in relation to contracts concluded under some form of compulsion not amounting to duress to the person, the Court must in every case at least be satisfied that the consent of the other party was overborne by compulsion so as to deprive him of any animus contrahendi. This would depend on the facts of each case. One relevant factor would be whether the party relying on duress made any protest at the time or shortly thereafter. Another would be to consider whether or not he treated the settlement as closing the transaction in question and as binding upon him, or whether he made it clear that he regarded the position as still open. The question whether or not there was any intention to close the transaction is referred to in the judgments of Lord Reading, CJ, and Lord Justice Buckley in *Maskell* v *Horner*, [1915] 3 KB 106. But the facts of the present case fall a long way short of the test which would in law be required to make good a defence of compulsion or duress. Believing the statements about the charterers' financial state to be true, as must for this purpose be assumed, Captain Tschudi made no protest about having to conclude the addenda, either at the Paris meeting on Mar. 26, 1972, or at any time before the telex of Apr. 28, 1973. He repeatedly said in his evidence that he regarded the agreement then reached as binding and sought to uphold it in the subsequent arbitration. He was acting under great pressure, but only commercial pressure, and not under anything which could in law be regarded as a coercion of his will so as to vitiate his consent. I therefore hold that the plea of duress fails.

NOTES
1. A line was drawn on the facts between acceptable commercial pressure and illegitimate pressure, but there are no guidelines to assist in drawing that line in the future.
2. It is incorrect to argue that duress is based upon consent being vitiated so that the act is not voluntary since the victim of duress undoubtedly submits intentionally and knows what he is doing. The more extreme the pressure the more real the consent will be. Duress, it is argued, does not deprive a person of all choice; rather, it presents him with a choice between evils. Lord Scarman clearly accepts this in *The Universe Sentinel* [1983] 1 AC 366 (*page 619*), when he stresses that it is intentional submission by a victim of duress because the victim realises there is no other practical choice available. Similarly, in *The Evia Luck* [1991] 4 All ER 871, Lord Goff doubted whether it was helpful to speak of the plaintiff's will having been coerced.

   Atiyah severely criticised this concept of consent being vitiated by duress ((1982) 98 LQR 197) and considered that it was likely to lead to irrelevant inquiries into the psychological motivations of the party pleading duress. In reality it is not any absence of consent which determines duress but the nature of the threat which has been made. See also Smith (1997) 56 CLJ 343.
3. In *DSND Subsea Ltd* v *Petroleum Geo-Services ASA* [2000] BLR 530, Dyson J formulated the criteria as requiring that the pressure or threat being applied should have the effect of producing a feeling of compulsion or lack of practical choice.

DYSON J stated:

> The ingredients of actionable duress are that there must be pressure, (a) whose practical effect is that there is compulsion on, or a lack of practical choice for, the victim, (b) which is illegitimate, and (c) which is a significant cause inducing the claimant to enter into the contract: see *Universal Tankships of Monrovia* v *ITWF* [1983] AC 336, 400B–E, and *The Evia Luck* [1992] 2 AC 152, 165G.

North Ocean Shipping Co. Ltd v *Hyundai Construction Co. Ltd, The Atlantic Baron*
[1979] QB 705

The plaintiffs entered into a contract with the defendant shipbuilding company to build a tanker for a fixed price, payable in five instalments. The defendant agreed to open a letter of credit to provide security for the repayment of the instalments if there was any default in performance of the contract. After the plaintiffs had paid the first instalment, the US dollar was devalued by 10 per cent and the defendant claimed an increase of 10 per cent in the remaining instalments, threatening not to complete the contract if this increase was not paid. Since the plaintiffs were negotiating a very lucrative contract for the charter of the tanker, they agreed in June 1973 to make the additional payments 'without prejudice' to their rights and asked the company to make a corresponding increase in the letter of credit, which the company did. The tanker was delivered in November 1974 without protest, but in July 1975 the plaintiffs sought the return of the extra 10 per cent paid on the last four instalments. There were two issues in the case: first, had the defendant provided consideration for the plaintiffs' promise to pay more (*page 134*) and, secondly, if it had, was it nevertheless an agreement entered into under duress and so voidable? Held: this threat to breach the contract without any legal justification amounted to duress by means of economic pressure, and therefore the agreement was voidable. However, as a result of the delay between November 1974 and July 1975, the plaintiffs must be taken to have affirmed the contract so that the claim failed.

MOCATTA J: . . . First, I do not take the view that the recovery of money paid under duress other than to the person is necessarily limited to duress to goods falling within one of the categories hitherto established by the English cases . . . Secondly, from this it follows that the compulsion may take the form of 'economic duress' if the necessary facts are proved. A threat to break a contract may amount to such 'economic duress.' Thirdly, if there has been such a form of duress leading to a contract for consideration, I think that contract is a voidable one which can be avoided and the excess money paid under it recovered.

I think the facts found in this case do establish that the agreement to increase the price by 10 per cent reached at the end of June 1973 was caused by what may be called 'economic duress.' The Yard were adamant in insisting on the increased price without having any legal justification for so doing and the owners realised that the Yard would not accept anything other than an unqualified agreement to the increase. The owners might have claimed damages in arbitration against the Yard with all the inherent unavoidable uncertainties of litigation, but in view of the position of the Yard vis-à-vis their relations with Shell it would be unreasonable to hold that this is the course they should have taken: see *Astley* v *Reynolds* (1731) 2 Str. 915. The owners made a very reasonable offer of arbitration coupled with security for any award in the Yard's favour that might be made, but this was refused. They then made their agreement, which can truly I think be said to have been made under compulsion, by the telex of June 28 without prejudice to their rights. I do not consider the Yard's ignorance of the Shell charter material. It may well be that had they known of it they would have been even more exigent.

If I am right in the conclusion reached with some doubt earlier that there was consideration for the

10 per cent increase agreement reached at the end of June 1973, and it be right to regard this as having been reached under a kind of duress in the form of economic pressure, then what is said in *Chitty on Contracts*, 24th ed. (1977), vol. 1, para. 442, p. 207, to which both counsel referred me, is relevant, namely, that a contract entered into under duress is voidable and not void:

> . . . consequently a person who has entered into a contract under duress, may either affirm or avoid such contract after the duress has ceased; and if he has so voluntarily acted under it with a full knowledge of all the circumstances he may be held bound on the ground of ratification, or if, after escaping from the duress, he takes no steps to set aside the transaction, he may be found to have affirmed it.

. . . There was . . . a delay between November 27, 1974, when the *Atlantic Baron* was delivered and July 30, 1975, before the owners put forward their claim.

. . . I have come to the conclusion that the important points here are that since there was no danger at this time in registering a protest, the final payments were made without any qualification and were followed by a delay until July 31, 1975, before the owners put forward their claim, the correct inference to draw, taking an objective view of the facts, is that the action and inaction of the owners can only be regarded as an affirmation of the variation in June 1973 of the terms of the original contract by the agreement to pay the additional 10 per cent . . . I do not think that an intention on the part of the owners not to affirm the agreement for the extra payments not indicated to the Yard can avail them in the view of their overt acts. As was said in *Deacon* v *Transport Regulation Board* [1958] VR 458, 460 in considering whether a payment was made voluntarily or not: 'No secret mental reservation of the doer is material. The question is—what would his conduct indicate to a reasonable man as his mental state.' I think this test is equally applicable to the decision this court has to make whether a voidable contract has been affirmed or not, and I have applied this test in reaching the conclusion I have just expressed.

I think I should add very shortly that having considered the many authorities cited, even if I had come to a different conclusion on the issue about consideration, I would have come to the same decision adverse to the owners on the question whether the payments were made voluntarily in the sense of being made to close the transaction.

Pao On v *Lau Yiu Long*
[1980] AC 614 (PC)

(The full facts of this case appear at *page 125*.) The plaintiffs threatened not to perform their promise that they would not sell 60 per cent of their shares in the Fu Chip Company for one year unless the defendants, the majority shareholders in the company, agreed to indemnify them against a loss in the value of their shares in that period. The defendants agreed to this demand and signed a written indemnity to compensate the plaintiffs on 60 per cent of their holding if the market price fell below $2.50 a share. The share price dropped and the plaintiffs sought to rely on the indemnity, but the defendants refused to comply with its terms. One of the questions related to whether the defendants' consent was vitiated by duress. Held: although the defendants had been subjected to commercial pressure, their will had not been coerced because they had taken a commercial decision. They had considered that the risk of a loss of public confidence in the company if the sale of the shares by the plaintiffs to the company did not take place, was greater than the risk that the share price would fall and that they would have to pay under the indemnity.

LORD SCARMAN: Duress, whatever form it takes, is a coercion of the will so as to vitiate consent. Their Lordships agree with the observation of Kerr J in *Occidental Worldwide Investment Corporation* v *Skibs A/S Avanti* [1976] 1 Lloyd's Rep 293, 336 that in a contractual situation commercial pressure is not enough. There must be present some factor 'which could in law be regarded as a coercion of his will so as to vitiate his consent.' This conception is in line with what was said in this Board's decision in *Barton* v *Armstrong* [1976] AC 104, 121 by Lord Wilberforse [sic] and Lord Simon of Glaisdale— observations with which the majority judgment appears to be in agreement. In determining whether there was a coercion of will such that there was no true consent, it is material to inquire whether the person alleged to have been coerced did or did not protest; whether, at the time he was allegedly coerced into making the contract, he did or did not have an alternative course open to him such as an adequate legal remedy; whether he was independently advised; and whether after entering the contract he took steps to avoid it. All these matters are, as was recognised in *Maskell* v *Horner* [1915] 3 KB 106, relevant in determining whether he acted voluntarily or not.

In the present case there is unanimity amongst the judges below that there was no coercion of the first defendant's will. In the Court of Appeal the trial judge's finding . . . that the first defendant considered the matter thoroughly, chose to avoid litigation, and formed the opinion that the risk in giving the guarantee was more apparent than real was upheld. In short, there was commercial pressure, but no coercion. Even if this Board was disposed, which it is not, to take a different view, it would not substitute its opinion for that of the judges below on this question of fact.

It is, therefore, unnecessary for the Board to embark upon an inquiry into the question whether English law recognises a category of duress known as 'economic duress.' But, since the question has been fully argued in this appeal, their Lordships will indicate very briefly the view which they have formed. At common law money paid under economic compulsion could be recovered in an action for money had and received: *Astley* v *Reynolds* (1731) 2 Str 915. The compulsion had to be such that the party was deprived of 'his freedom of exercising his will' (see p. 916). It is doubtful, however, whether at common law any duress other than duress to the person sufficed to render a contract voidable: see *Blackstone's Commentaries*, Book 1, 12th ed. pp. 130–131 and *Skeate* v *Beale* (1841) 11 Ad & E 983. American law (*Williston on Contracts*, 3rd ed.) now recognises that a contract may be avoided on the ground of economic duress. The commercial pressure alleged to constitute such duress must, however, be such that the victim must have entered the contract against his will, must have had no alternative course open to him, and must have been confronted with coercive acts by the party exerting the pressure: *Williston on Contracts*, 3rd ed., vol. 13 (1970), section 1603. American judges pay great attention to such evidential matters as the effectiveness of the alternative remedy available, the fact or absence of protest, the availability of independent advice, the benefit received, and the speed with which the victim has sought to avoid the contract. Recently two English judges have recognised that commercial pressure may constitute duress the pressure of which can render a contract voidable: Kerr J in *Occidental Worldwide Investment Corporation* v *Skibs A/S Avanti* [1976] 1 Lloyd's Rep 293 and Mocatta J in *North Ocean Shipping Co. Ltd* v *Hyundai Construction Co. Ltd* [1979] QB 705. Both stressed that the pressure must be such that the victim's consent to the contract was not a voluntary act on his part. In their Lordship's view, there is nothing contrary to principle in recognising economic duress as a factor which may render a contract voidable provided always that the basis of such recognition is that it must amount to a coercion of will, which vitiates consent. It must be shown that the payment made or the contract entered into was not a voluntary act. . . .

NOTE: Emphasis is placed upon whether there was any realistic alternative choice open to the defendants (see Macdonald [1989] JBL 460). In *Pao On* v *Lau Yiu Long*, Fu Chip could have sued the plaintiffs for specific performance of the original sale contract, but this possibility might have been so damaging that it could not realistically be entertained.

B & S Contracts & Design Ltd v Victor Green Publications Ltd
[1984] ICR 419 (CA)

The plaintiffs had agreed to erect exhibition stands for the defendants at Olympia for an exhibition which was to begin on 23 April 1979. A week before this date the plaintiffs' workers refused to work until a demand for £9,000 severance pay had been met. They rejected an offer by the plaintiffs of £4,500, and the plaintiffs informed the defendants that the contract would be cancelled unless the defendants paid the other £4,500 to meet this demand. The defendants paid this sum to avoid serious losses and claims from exhibitors to whom they had let stands. However, the defendants then deducted £4,500 from the contract price that they paid to the plaintiffs. Held: that the cancellation of the contract would have caused such serious damage to the defendants' economic interests that they had no choice but to pay. Although they could have refused to pay this figure and sued the plaintiffs for breach of contract, it was felt that this action would be too damaging.

KERR LJ: . . . [T]he plaintiffs were clearly saying in effect, 'This contract will not be performed by us unless you pay an additional sum of £4,500.' This faced the defendants with a disastrous situation in which there was no way out for them, and in the face of this threat—which is what it was—they paid the £4,500. In the light of the authorities it is perhaps important to emphasise that there is no question in this case of the defendants having subsequently approbated this payment or failed to seek to avoid it, which in some cases (such as the *North Ocean Shipping Co. Ltd* v *Hyundai Construction Co. Ltd* [1979] QB 705) . . . would be fatal. In the present case the defendants took immediate action by deducting that £4,500 from the invoice price.

I also bear in mind that a threat to break a contract unless money is paid by the other party can, but by no means always will, constitute duress. It appears from the authorities that it will only constitute duress if the consequences of a refusal would be serious and immediate so that there is no reasonable alternative open, such as by legal redress, obtaining an injunction, etc. . . .

Causation

A tight causal link must be established between the pressure and the contract. *Huyton SA* v *Peter Cremer GmbH & Co.* [1999] 1 Lloyd's Rep 620 confirmed that *Barton* v *Armstrong* [1976] AC 104, *page 608*, does not represent the authority on causation in the context of economic duress. Instead, it was confirmed that the illegitimate pressure had to constitute a significant cause inducing the other party to act as it did. Mance J referred to the pressure as 'decisive or clinching' so that the contract would not otherwise have been made.

Huyton SA   v   Peter Cremer GmbH & Co
[1999] 1 Lloyd's Rep 620

For facts and the decision see *page 622*. Mance J considered that there were two requirements for a finding of duress, namely illegitimate pressure which had to be a significant cause inducing the making of the agreement. *Obiter* the judge considered the question of causation on the basis of a finding that there had been illegitimate pressure. In fact, he had held that there was no illegitimate pressure and therefore no duress. He also addressed the argument that there was a third ingredient of economic duress, namely that the illegitimate pressure must have left the innocent party with no reasonable alternative and that the concept of 'significant cause' required an objective assessment of causation, i.e., an assessment of whether a reasonable person could have acted as the actual innocent party did.

MANCE J: I start with the requirement that the illegitimate pressure must, in cases of economic duress, constitute 'a significant cause' (cf. per Lord Goff in *The Evia Luck* [[1992] 2 AC 152], at p. 165, . . .). This is contrasted in Goff and Jones on *Law of Restitution* (4th edn), p. 251, footnote 59 with the lesser requirement that it should be 'a' reason which applies in the context of duress to the person. The relevant authority in the latter context is *Barton* v *Armstrong* [1976] AC 104 (PC) (a case of threats to kill). . . .

The use of the phrase 'a significant cause' by Lord Goff in *The Evia Luck*, supported by the weighty observation in the footnote in *Goff & Jones*, suggests that this relaxed view of causation in the special context of duress to the person cannot prevail in the less serious context of economic duress. The minimum basic test of subjective causation in economic duress ought, it appears to me, to be a 'but for' test. The illegitimate pressure must have been such as actually caused the making of the agreement, in the sense that it would not otherwise have been made either at all or, at least, in the terms in which it was made. In that sense, the pressure must have been decisive or clinching. There may of course be cases where a common-sense relaxation, even of a but for requirement is necessary, for example in the event of an agreement induced by two concurrent causes, each otherwise sufficient to ground a claim of relief, in circumstances where each alone would have induced the agreement, so that it could not be said that, but for either, the agreement would not have been made. On the other hand, it also seems clear that the application of a simple 'but for' test of subjective causation in conjunction with a requirement of actual or threatened breach of duty could lead too readily to relief being granted. It would not, for example, cater for the obvious possibility that, although the innocent party would never have acted as he did, but for the illegitimate pressure, he nevertheless had a real choice and could, if he had wished, equally well have resisted the pressure and, for example, pursued alternative legal redress.

I turn therefore to consider other ingredients of economic duress. One possibility, harking back, for example, to a word used by the minority in *Barton*, is that the pressure should represent the 'predominant' cause. Professor Birks in *An Introduction to the Law of Restitution* (1985), pp. 182–183 has suggested that, in cases such as *Pao On* v *Lau Yiu Long* [1980] AC 614 where relief was refused on the ground that there had been commercial pressure but no coercion' (p. 635), the court was, in effect, insisting 'on a more severe test of the degree of compulsion than is found in *Barton* v *Armstrong*', securing what he describes as 'a concealed discretion to distinguish between reasonable and unreasonable, legitimate and illegitimate applications of this species of independently unlawful pressure'. His own preference, he indicated, was for 'the simplest and more open course . . . to restrict the right to restitution to cases in which one party sought, *mala fide* to exploit the weakness of the other'. These comments highlight the extent to which any consideration of causation in economic duress interacts with consideration of the concept of legitimacy. [Counsel for Huyton] adopts the same approach as Professor Birks in relation to apparent contractual compromises for good consideration, suggesting that here at least bad faith ought to be a pre-condition to relief. The law will of course be cautious about re-opening an apparent compromise made in good faith on both sides. But it seems, on the one hand, questionable whether a 'compromise' achieved by one party who does not believe that he had at least an arguable case is a compromise at all—though it may be upheld if there is other consideration (cf. *Occidental Worldwide Investment Corp.* v *Skibs A/S Avanti ('The Siboen' and 'The Sibotre')* [1976] 1 Ll Rep 293 at p. 334); and, on the other hand, difficult to accept that illegitimate pressure applied by a party who believes bona fide in his case could never give grounds for relief against an apparent compromise. Another commentator, Professor Burrows, in *Law of Duress* (1993), pp. 181–182, has suggested that the concept of legitimacy is open to some flexibility or at least qualification, so that a threatened or actual breach of contract may not represent illegitimate pressure if there was a reasonable commercial basis for the threat or breach, e.g. because circumstances had radically changed. This suggestion, too, is by no means uncontentious.

. . . [I]n *The Siboen and The Sibotre*, one of the early cases on economic duress, Kerr J indicated at p. 335—in rejecting a contrary submission by Mr Robert Goff QC—that he did not think that bad faith had any relevance at all. On the other hand, in McHugh JA's judgment in the Supreme Court of New South Wales in *Crescendo Management Pty Ltd* v *Westpac Banking Corp.* (1988) 19 NSWLR 40 at p. 46, referred to by Lord Goff in *The Evia Luck*, McHugh JA said that 'Pressure will be illegitimate if it consists of unlawful threats or amounts to unconscionable conduct'. It is also clear that illegitimate pressure may exist, although the threat is of action by itself lawful, if in conjunction with the nature of the demand, it involves potential blackmail: see *Thorne* v *Motor Trade Association* [1937] AC 797, esp. at pp. 806–807, cited in Lord Scarman's dissenting judgment in *Universe Tankships Inc. of Monrovia* v *International Transport Workers Federation* [1983] 1 AC 366 at p. 401, and *CTN Cash and Carry Ltd.* v *Gallagher Ltd* [1994] 4 All ER 714. And in this last case, Steyn LJ as he was contemplated the possibility that unconscionable conduct might have a yet wider ambit. He said (at p. 719C):

Outside the field of protected relationships, and in a purely commercial context, it might be a relatively rare case in which 'lawful act duress' can be established. And it might be particularly difficult to establish duress if the defendant bona fide considered that his demand was valid. In this complex and changing branch of the law I deliberately refrain from saying 'never'.

That good or bad faith may be particularly relevant when considering whether a case might represent a rare example of 'lawful act duress' is not difficult to accept. Even in cases where the pressure relied on is an actual or threatened breach of duty, it seems to me better not to exclude the possibility that the state of mind of the person applying such pressure may in some circumstances be significant, whether or not the other innocent party correctly appreciated such state of mind. 'Never' in this context also seems too strong a word.

In *The Evia Luck*, Lord Goff did not speak in absolute terms. He said (at p. 165G–H), with reference to the previous authorities, that:

> it is now accepted that economic pressure may be sufficient to amount to duress for this purpose, provided at least that the economic pressure may be characterised as illegitimate and has constituted a significant cause inducing the plaintiff to enter into the relevant contract.

This description itself leaves room for flexibility in the characterisation of illegitimate pressure and of the relevant causal link. Lord Goff was identifying minimum ingredients, not ingredients which, if present, would inevitably lead to liability. The recognition of some degree of flexibility is not, I think, fairly open to the reproach that it introduces a judicial 'discretion'. The law has frequently to form judgments regarding inequitability or unconscionability, giving effect in doing so to the reasonable expectations of honest persons. It is the law's function to discriminate, where discrimination is appropriate, between different factual situations—as it does, to take one example, when deciding whether or not to recognise a duty of care. The present context is intervention in relation to bargains or payments in relatively extreme situations. Steyn LJ in *CTN Cash and Carry* cited, albeit in the context of threats involving no unlawful act, an aphorism of Oliver Wendell Holmes 'that general propositions do not solve concrete cases' and went on (at p. 717H):

> It may only be a half-truth, but in my view the true part applies to this case. It is necessary to focus on the distinctive features of this case, and then to ask whether it amounts to a case of duress.

A similar approach appears to me to be appropriate in the present context.

In older authorities, relief against economic duress was said to require illegitimate pressure coercing the innocent party's will and vitiating consent (cf. *The Siboen and The Sibotre* at p. 336 and *Pao On* v *Lau Yiu Long* at p. 635). Lord Goff in *The Evia Luck* doubted whether it was helpful to speak in such terms, and referred to McHugh JA's comments to that effect in the *Crescendo* case. The approach there adopted by McHugh JA, at p. 45, was based on statements by the House of Lords in *Director of Public Prosecutions for Northern Ireland* v *Lynch* [1975] AC 653, to the effect that, in cases of duress, 'the will [is] deflected, not destroyed'. Even on this more generous formulation, a simple enquiry whether the innocent party would have acted as he did 'but for' an actual or threatened breach of contract cannot, I think, be the hallmark of deflection of will. Whether because the specific ingredients identified by Lord Goff should be interpreted widely or because it is implicit in the flexibility of Lord Goff's formulation and the underlying rationale of the law's intervention to prevent unconscionability, relief must, I think, depend on the court's assessment of the qualitative impact of the illegitimate pressure, objectively assessed. It is not necessary to go so far as to say that it is an inflexible third essential ingredient of economic duress that there should be no or no practical alternative course open to the innocent party. But it seems, as I have already indicated, self-evident that relief may not be appropriate, if an innocent party decides, as a matter of choice, not to pursue an alternative remedy which any and possibly some other reasonable persons in his circumstances would have pursued. Relief may perhaps also be refused, if he has made no protest and conducted himself in a way which showed that, for better or for worse, he was prepared to accept and live with the consequences, however unwelcome. Factors such as these are referred to as relevant to relief against duress in both *The Siboen and The Sibotre* and *Pao On*, although in some contexts it may also be possible to rationalise them by reference to other doctrines such as affirmation or estoppel. The emphasis, now to be discarded, in such cases on coercion of will does not, it seems to me, mean that such factors are no longer relevant. Taking, for example, *Pao On*, the complainant there was able, in the face of the illegitimate pressure, to consider its position, to take alternative steps if it wished, and to decide, as it apparently did (and however wrongly with hindsight), that the substitute arrangements proposed were of no real concern or risk to it and that it was preferable to agree to them, rather than become involved in litigation. Although there would have been no re-negotiation at all 'but for' illegitimate pressure, the relationship between the illegitimate pressure applied and the substitute arrangements made was not of a nature or quality, or sufficiently significant in objective terms in deflecting the will, to justify relief. Examination of the same relationship may also involve taking into account the extent to which the party applying illegitimate pressure intended or could reasonably foresee that pressure which he applied would lead to the agreement or payment made, or at least the extent to which factors extraneous to that party played any important role.

NOTE: This decision heightens the difficulties in defining the precise requirements for relief based on a claim of economic duress. References to discretion and flexibility do little to provide certainty. However, the decision is clear authority supporting the two requirements specified by Lord Goff in *The Evia Luck* (i.e. significant cause and illegitimate pressure). Unfortunately, there is still uncertainty over the meaning of 'illegitimate pressure'.

(b) There must be pressure which is illegitimate

(i) Pressure

In *Alec Lobb (Garages) Ltd* v *Total Oil GB Ltd* [1985] 1 WLR 173 (*page 681*), the Court of Appeal held that it was not sufficient that on the facts the plaintiffs were in serious financial difficulties and had no realistic alternative but to make the lease-back agreement with the defendant containing a 'tie' covenant. The defendant had exerted no pressure on them and was reluctant to enter into the transaction, and it was the plaintiffs who had sought the defendant's assistance to avert financial collapse.

In *Williams* v *Roffey Brothers & Nicholls (Contractors) Ltd* [1991] 1 QB 1 (*page 135*), it was the main contractors who had initiated the new arrangement rather than the subcontractor, so that there was no economic duress. This is likely to lead to fine distinctions between 'advising' a main contractor of factors likely to result in an impending breach and applying pressure by threatening breach (i.e., the difference between an implicit and an explicit threat). Such a distinction will be impossible to operate in practice.

(ii) Illegitimate

Universe Tankships Inc. of Monrovia v *International Transport Workers Federation, The Universe Sentinel*
[1983] 1 AC 366 (HL)

A ship had docked at Milford Haven on 17 July 1978, and had discharged its cargo, but had been 'blacked' by ITF (a trade union) so that it was unable to leave port. The owners agreed to comply with ITF's demands, which included a contribution of $6,480 to a general welfare fund for sailors, because they feared disastrous economic consequences if they refused since the ship was off-hire under a time charter while the blacking continued. The ship was able to sail on 29 July, and on 10 August the owners claimed the return of the $6,480 paid under duress. However, s. 13 of the Trade Union and Labour Relations Act 1974 granted immunity in tort to the trade union in relation to actions, which included blacking vessels, if their actions had been taken in furtherance of a 'trade dispute' within s. 29 of that Act (i.e., this would have technically legitimated their acts). A majority (Lord Scarman and Lord Brandon of Oakbrook dissenting) thought that the payment to the welfare fund was recoverable, since s. 29(1)(a) required the trade dispute to relate to 'terms and conditions of employment' of the crew members and therefore s. 13 did not protect the trade union in respect of this payment to a general welfare fund so that the action was illegitimate.

LORD DIPLOCK: . . . [I]t is conceded that the financial consequences to the shipowners of the *Universe Sentinel* continuing to be rendered off-hire under her time charter to Texaco, while the blacking continued, were so catastrophic as to amount to a coercion of the shipowners' will which vitiated their consent to those agreements and to the payments made by them to ITF. This concession makes it unnecessary for your Lordships to use the instant appeal as the occasion for a general consideration of the developing law of economic duress as a ground for treating contracts as voidable and obtaining restitution of money paid under economic duress as money had and received to the plaintiffs' use. That economic duress may constitute a ground for such redress was recognised, albeit obiter, by the Privy Council in *Pao On* v *Lau Yiu Long* [1980] AC 614. . . .

It is, however, in my view crucial to the decision of the instant appeal to identify the rationale of this development of the common law. It is not that the party seeking to avoid the contract which he has entered into with another party, or to recover money that he has paid to another party in response to a demand, did not know the nature or the precise terms of the contract at the time when he entered into it or did not understand the purpose for which the payment was demanded. The rationale is that his apparent consent was induced by pressure exercised upon him by that other party which the law does not regard as legitimate, with the consequence that the consent is treated in law as revocable unless approbated either expressly or by implication after the illegitimate pressure has ceased to operate on his mind. It is a rationale similar to that which underlies the avoidability of contracts entered into and the recovery of money exacted under colour of office, or under undue influence or in consequence of threats of physical duress.

Commercial pressure, in some degree, exists wherever one party to a commercial transaction is in a stronger bargaining position than the other party. It is not, however, in my view, necessary, nor would it be appropriate in the instant appeal, to enter into the general question of the kinds of circumstances, if any, in which commercial pressure, even though it amounts to a coercion of the will of a party in the weaker bargaining position, may be treated as legitimate and, accordingly, as not giving rise to any legal right of redress. In the instant appeal the economic duress complained of was exercised in the field of industrial relations to which very special considerations apply. . . .

Lord Scarman disagreed with the majority view of s. 29(1)(a). He considered that this was a legitimate exercise of pressure and did not constitute duress.

LORD SCARMAN: It is, I think, already established law that economic pressure can in law amount to duress; and that duress, if proved, not only renders voidable a transaction into which a person has entered under its compulsion but is actionable as a tort, if it causes damage or loss: *Barton* v *Armstrong* [1976] AC 104 and *Pao On* v *Lau Yiu Long* [1980] AC 614. The authorities upon which these two cases were based reveal two elements in the wrong of duress: (1) pressure amounting to compulsion of the will of the victim; and (2) the illegitimacy of the pressure exerted. There must be pressure, the practical effect of which is compulsion or the absence of choice. Compulsion is variously described in the authorities as coercion or the vitiation of consent. The classic case of duress is, however, not the lack of will to submit but the victim's intentional submission arising from the realisation that there is no other practical choice open to him. This is the thread of principle which links the early law of duress (threat to life or limb) with later developments when the law came also to recognise as duress first the threat to property and now the threat to a man's business or trade. The development is well traced in *Goff and Jones, The Law of Restitution*, 2nd ed. (1978), chapter 9.

The absence of choice can be proved in various ways, e.g. by protest, by the absence of independent advice, or by a declaration of intention to go to law to recover the money paid or the property transferred: see *Maskell* v *Horner* [1915] 3 KB 106. But none of these evidential matters goes to the essence of duress. The victim's silence will not assist the bully, if the lack of any practicable choice but to submit is proved. The present case is an excellent illustration. There was no protest at the time, but only a determination to do whatever was needed as rapidly as possible to release the ship. Yet nobody challenges the judge's finding that the owner acted under compulsion. He put it thus [1981] ICR 129, 143:

> It was a matter of the most urgent commercial necessity that the plaintiffs should regain the use of their vessel. They were advised that their prospects of obtaining an injunction were minimal, the vessel would not have been released unless the payment was made, and they sought recovery of the money with sufficient speed once the duress had terminated.

The real issue in the appeal is, therefore, as to the second element in the wrong duress: was the pressure applied by the ITF in the circumstances of this case one which the law recognises as legitimate? For, as Lord Wilberforce and Lord Simon of Glaisdale said in *Barton* v *Armstrong* [1976] AC 104, 121D: 'the pressure must be one of a kind which the law does not regard as legitimate.'

As the two noble and learned Lords remarked at p. 121D, in life, including the life of commerce and finance, many acts are done 'under pressure, sometimes overwhelming pressure': but they are not necessarily done under duress. That depends on whether the circumstances are such that the law regards the pressure as legitimate.

In determining what is legitimate two matters may have to be considered. The first is as to the nature of the pressure. In many cases this will be decisive, though not in every case. And so the second question may have to be considered, namely, the nature of the demand which the pressure is applied to support.

The origin of the doctrine of duress in threats to life or limb, or to property, suggests strongly that the law regards the threat of unlawful action as illegitimate, whatever the demand. Duress can, of course, exist even if the threat is one of lawful action: whether it does so depends upon the nature of the demand. Blackmail is often a demand supported by a threat to do what is lawful, e.g. to report criminal conduct to the police. In many cases, therefore, 'What [one] has to justify is not the threat, but the demand . . .': see *per* Lord Atkin in *Thorne* v *Motor Trade Association* [1937] AC 797, 806.

The present is a case in which the nature of the demand determines whether the pressure threatened or applied, i.e. the blacking, was lawful or unlawful. If it was unlawful, it is conceded that the owner acted under duress and can recover. If it was lawful, it is conceded that there was no duress and the sum sought by the owner is irrecoverable. The lawfulness or otherwise of the demand depends upon whether it was an act done in contemplation or furtherance of a trade dispute. If it was, it would not be actionable in tort: section 13(1) of the Act. Although no question of tortious liability arises in this case and section 13(1) is not, therefore, directly in point, it is not possible, in my view, to say of acts which are protected by statute from suit in tort that they nevertheless can amount to duress. Parliament having enacted that such acts are not actionable in tort, it would be inconsistent with legislative policy to say that, when the remedy sought is not damages for tort but recovery of money paid, they become unlawful.

NOTES

1. Lord Diplock avoids defining what is acceptable commercial pressure and what is illegitimate. Lord Scarman does provide some assistance by stating that pressure *may* be illegitimate if what is threatened is in itself unlawful, e.g., to injure the victim or to breach a contract. Pressure may also be illegitimate even though what is threatened is lawful if the way in which that pressure is exerted is illegitimate, e.g., if the advantage which the party is seeking to obtain is illegitimate. Lord Scarman used blackmail to illustrate this. A threat to disclose a particular fact about a person may be perfectly lawful and yet the demand of money is unlawful.

2. In *Vantage Navigation Corporation* v *Suhail and Saud Bahwan Building Materials LLC, The Alev* [1989] 1 Lloyd's Rep 138, the plaintiffs had time-chartered the vessel to the charterers who had loaded a cargo. The charterers defaulted in the payment of hire but the plaintiffs were contractually obliged to carry the cargo to its destination. They advised the defendants, cargo owners, that unless the defendants agreed to pay what the plaintiffs demanded they would not get their cargo. The defendants agreed to pay port expenses and discharging costs, and the plaintiffs agreed to refrain from arresting or detaining the vessel. The defendants pleaded duress. Hobhouse J held that the defendants' promise had clearly been made under duress. The pressure exerted by the plaintiffs was illegitimate since the plaintiffs had no rights over the goods and could not refuse to deliver the cargo.

3. In *Huyton SA* v *Peter Cremer GmbH & Co.* [1999] 1 Lloyd's Rep 620, Mance J concluded that there was no illegitimate pressure so that the agreement was enforceable. Huyton had agreed to buy wheat from Cremer on terms whereby Huyton was to arrange freight, which was to be paid for by Cremer, and payment for the goods was to be made against documents. The vessel engaged by Huyton had incurred considerable port demurrage (payable for delay under the charter). Although the vessel had discharged its cargo and the goods were in the possession of sub-buyers, due to various discrepancies on the documents Huyton had withheld payment for the goods. Cremer claimed that as the cargo had been accepted, Huyton had waived any right to reject the documents, whereas Huyton claimed that Cremer was in repudiatory breach by not presenting conforming documents.

    During the negotiations aimed at settling the dispute it had been agreed that Huyton would pay against the documents as long as further contractual documents were presented, if Cremer agreed to pay the demurrage and agreed not to submit the dispute to arbitration. Cremer had reluctantly agreed to do this, but having been paid had then claimed that it was not bound by this agreement alleging economic duress, namely that Huyton's threat, not to pay the purchase price properly due, amounted to illegitimate pressure. Held: there was no illegitimate pressure on Cremer because its presentation of non-conforming documents constituted a repudiatory breach which had been accepted by Huyton so that it was not possible thereafter to re-tender conforming documents or to claim the contractual price. In any event, even if the pressure had been illegitimate it had not been shown to be a significant cause in Cremer's decision to enter into the agreement (see *page 616* for discussion of causation).

4. In *'R'* v *H.M. Attorney-General of England and Wales* [2003] UKPC 22, [2003] EMLR 24, the Privy Council (with Lord Scott dissenting) held that a threat to return an SAS member to his unit if he did not sign a confidentiality agreement to cover the period when he left the service, although considered as a disgrace and a severe penalty by SAS members, was a lawful act as it was within the discretion granted to the Crown to make such a transfer. As a result, the agreement had not been signed under duress. The Privy Council cited the approach of Lord Scarman in *Universe Tankship*, namely that the legitimacy of pressure must be examined in two respects: (1) 'the nature of the pressure', and (2) 'the nature of the demand which the pressure is applied to support'. Whereas generally speaking the threat of any form of unlawful action would be regarded as illegitimate, the fact that the threat was lawful would not necessarily render the pressure legitimate, e.g., instances of blackmail using a lawful threat. On these facts it was held that the demand supported by the lawful threat could be justified since the MOD was reasonably entitled to regard anyone unwilling to accept the confidentiality agreement as unsuitable for the SAS. This was not a case where the individual soldier had been ordered to sign. He had been faced with a choice, albeit that he had faced 'overwhelming pressure' to sign.

■ QUESTION

Is a threat to breach a contract automatically illegitimate? Whereas in *Carillion Construction Ltd* v *Felix (UK) Ltd* [2001] BLR 1, a threat by a subcontractor to withhold deliveries until settlement of its final account was considered as an illegitimate threat to breach the contract, the same judge (Dyson J) in *DSND Subsea Ltd* v *Petroleum Geo-Services ASA* [2000] BLR 530, held that a threat to breach the contract by ceasing part of the work was not an illegitimate threat. It seems that the distinguishing feature in *DSND* was that the threat was made in an attempt to get the insurance arrangements clarified so that DSND was 'entirely justified in wanting to resolve this' and the threat was no more than a reasonable attempt to resolve the position. Does it follow that there is a distinction in terms of whether the threat was made in good or bad faith? See the judgment of Mance J in *Huyton SA* v *Peter Cremer GMbH & Co., page 616,* on the question of the effect of bad faith.

Is there a more general category of 'lawful act duress'?

CTN Cash and Carry Ltd v Gallaher Ltd
[1994] 4 All ER 714 (CA)

The plaintiffs purchased consignments of cigarettes from the defendants under individual contracts on the defendants' standard terms. The defendants had also arranged credit facilities for the plaintiffs which they could withdraw for any reason at any time. One consignment had been incorrectly delivered to the wrong warehouse, but before the defendants could deliver it to the correct warehouse it had been stolen from the plaintiffs' premises. The defendants genuinely believed that the goods were at the plaintiffs' risk at the time of the theft and accordingly invoiced them for the goods. The plaintiffs refused to pay and only did so after the defendants threatened to withdraw their credit facilities. They then claimed the return of the money paid on the basis that it had been obtained as a result of economic duress and that the pressure was illegitimate because the defendants had demanded money to which they were not entitled. Held: the defendants' conduct did not constitute duress.

STEYN LJ: . . . The present dispute does not concern a protected relationship. It also does not arise in the context of dealings between a supplier and a consumer. The dispute arises out of arm's length commercial dealings between two trading companies. It is true that the defendants were the sole distributors of the popular brands of cigarettes. In a sense the defendants were in a monopoly position. The control of monopolies is, however, a matter for Parliament. Moreover, the common law does not recognise the doctrine of inequality of bargaining power in commercial dealings (see *National Westminster Bank plc* v *Morgan* [1985] 1 All ER 821, [1985] AC 686). The fact that the defendants were in a monopoly position cannot therefore by itself convert what is not otherwise duress into duress.

A second characteristic of the case is that the defendants were in law entitled to refuse to enter into any future contracts with the plaintiffs for any reason whatever or for no reason at all. Such a decision not to deal with the plaintiffs would have been financially damaging to the defendants, but it would have been lawful. A fortiori, it was lawful for the defendants, for any reason or for no reason, to insist that they would no longer grant credit to the plaintiffs. The defendants' demand for payment of the invoice, coupled with the threat to withdraw credit, was neither a breach of contract nor a tort.

A third, and critically important, characteristic of the case is the fact that the defendants bona fide thought that the goods were at the risk of the plaintiffs and that the plaintiffs owed the defendants the sum in question. The defendants exerted commercial pressure on the plaintiffs in order to obtain payment of a sum which they bona fide considered due to them. The defendants' motive in threatening withdrawal of credit facilities was commercial self-interest in obtaining a sum that they considered due to them. . . .

I . . . readily accept that the fact that the defendants have used lawful means does not by itself remove the case from the scope of the doctrine of economic duress. Professor Birks, in *An Introduction to the Law of Restitution* (1989) p. 177, lucidly explains:

Can lawful pressures also count? This is a difficult question, because, if the answer is that they can, the only viable basis for discriminating between acceptable and unacceptable pressures is not positive law but social morality. In other words, the judges must say what pressures (though lawful outside the restitutionary context) are improper as contrary to prevailing standards. That makes the judges, not the law or the legislature, the arbiters of social evaluation. On the other hand, if the answer is that lawful pressures are always exempt, those who devise outrageous but technically lawful means of compulsion must always escape restitution until the legislature declares the abuse unlawful. It is tolerably clear that, at least where they can be confident of a general consensus in favour of their evaluation, the courts are willing to apply a standard of impropriety rather than technical unlawfulness.

And there are a number of cases where English courts have accepted that a threat may be illegitimate when coupled with a demand for payment even if the threat is one of lawful action (see *Thorne* v *Motor Trade Association* [1937] 3 All ER 157 at 160–161, [1937] AC 797 at 806–807, *Mutual Finance Ltd* v *John Wetton & Sons Ltd* [1937] 2 All ER 657, [1937] 2 KB 389 and *Universe Tankships Inc of Monrovia* v *International Transport Workers' Federation* [1982] 2 All ER 67 at 76, 89, [1983] 1 AC 366 at 384, 401). On the other hand, Goff and Jones *Law of Restitution* (3rd edn, 1986) p. 240 observed that English courts have wisely not accepted any general principle that a threat not to contract with another, except on certain terms, may amount to duress.

We are being asked to extend the categories of duress of which the law will take cognisance. That is not necessarily objectionable, but it seems to me that an extension capable of covering the present case, involving 'lawful act duress' in a commercial context in pursuit of a bona fide claim, would be a radical one with far-reaching implications. It would introduce a substantial and undesirable element of uncertainty in the commercial bargaining process. Moreover, it will often enable bona fide settled accounts to be reopened when parties to commercial dealings fall out. The aim of our commercial law ought to be to encourage fair dealing between parties. But it is a mistake for the law to set its sights too highly when the critical inquiry is not whether the conduct is lawful but whether it is morally or socially unacceptable. That is the inquiry in which we are engaged. In my view there are policy considerations which militate against ruling that the defendants obtained payment of the disputed invoice by duress.

Outside the field of protected relationships, and in a purely commercial context, it might be a relatively rare case in which 'lawful act duress' can be established. And it might be particularly difficult to establish duress if the defendant bona fide considered that his demand was valid. In this complex and changing branch of the law I deliberately refrain from saying 'never'. But as the law stands, I am satisfied that the defendants' conduct in this case did not amount to duress.

NOTES

1. Thus it is not duress to threaten *not* to contract.
2. This demonstrates that in future cases the nature of the pressure may be the significant factor.
3. The Court of Appeal rejected any general category of 'lawful act duress'. In so doing it is clear that the Court was not comfortable with the fact that the defendants were permitted to keep money to which they were not entitled. However, Sir Donald Nicholls considered that in such circumstances the money might be reclaimed in restitution on the basis that the defendant had been unjustly enriched.

■ QUESTIONS

1. There is a clear willingness to grant greater protection to consumers than to commercial concerns 'dealing at arm's length'. Do you consider that the plaintiffs were dealing at arm's length?

2. Does the good faith of the defendants make a difference here? (See *Huyton SA* v *Peter Cremer GmbH & Co.* [1999] 1 Lloyd's Rep 620, *page 616.*)

SECTION 2: UNDUE INFLUENCE

The doctrine of undue influence is an equitable doctrine allowing a contract to be set aside where there has been a wrongful (undue) exercise of influence by one party over the other. What sort of influence will the courts view as being wrongful?

The traditional classification of cases of undue influence was summarised by Lord Browne-Wilkinson in *Barclays Bank plc* v *O'Brien* [1994] 1 AC 180:

A person who has been induced to enter into a transaction by the undue influence of another (the wrongdoer) is entitled to set that transaction aside as against the wrongdoer. Such undue influence is either actual or presumed. In *Bank of Credit and Commerce International SA* v *Aboody* [1990] 1 QB 923, 953, the Court of Appeal helpfully adopted the following classification.

Class 1: Actual undue influence. In these cases it is necessary for the claimant to prove affirmatively that the wrongdoer exerted undue influence on the complainant to enter into the particular transaction which is impugned.

Class 2: Presumed undue influence. In these cases the complainant only has to show, in the first instance, that there was a relationship of trust and confidence between the complainant and the wrongdoer of such a nature that it is fair to presume that the wrongdoer abused that relationship in procuring the complainant to enter into the impugned transaction. In Class 2 cases therefore there is no need to produce evidence that actual undue influence was exerted in relation to the particular transaction impugned: once a confidential relationship has been proved, the burden then shifts to the wrongdoer to prove that the complainant entered into the impugned transaction freely, for example by showing that the complainant had independent advice. Such a confidential relationship can be established in two ways, viz:

Class 2(A). Certain relationships (for example solicitor and client, medical advisor and patient) as a matter of law raise the presumption that undue influence has been exercised.

Class 2(B). Even if there is no relationship falling within Class 2(A), if the complainant proves the de facto existence of a relationship under which the complainant generally reposed trust and confidence in the wrongdoer, the existence of such relationship raises the presumption of undue influence. In a Class 2(B) case therefore, in the absence of evidence disproving undue influence, the complainant will succeed in setting aside the impugned transaction merely by proof that the complainant reposed trust and confidence in the wrongdoer without having to prove that the wrongdoer exerted actual undue influence or otherwise abused such trust and confidence in relation to the particular transaction impugned. . . .

Although there is no Class 2(A) presumption of undue influence as between husband and wife, it should be emphasised that in any particular case a wife may well be able to demonstrate that de facto she did leave decisions on financial affairs to her husband thereby bringing herself within Class 2(B), i.e. that the relationship between husband and wife in the particular case was such that the wife reposed confidence and trust in her husband in relation to their financial affairs and therefore undue influence is to be presumed. Thus, in those cases which still occur where the wife relies in all financial matters on her husband and simply does what he suggests, a presumption of undue influence within Class 2(B) can be established solely from the proof of such trust and confidence without proof of actual undue influence. . . .

This classification distinguished cases where the undue influence was proved affirmatively and those where it is presumed, either because the parties' relationship falls within a class of protected relationships (class 2A) or because, on the facts, the particular relationship between these parties was of such a nature that undue influence could be presumed.

Whereas it remains important to distinguish these three factual scenarios, the House of Lords in *Royal Bank of Scotland plc* v *Etridge (No. 2)* [2001] UKHL 44, [2002]

2 AC 773 has confirmed that the law on so-called 'presumed undue influence' has not been accurately stated because there is no presumption of both influence and that the influence was undue. The 'presumption' is no more than an evidential presumption that influence has been exercised and does not become an evidential presumption of undue influence unless there is something suspicious, or which calls for an explanation, on the facts, e.g. the size or nature of the transfers. It is therefore not the case, as had previously been understood, that the 'presumption' enables that step to be skipped and the exercise of undue influence to be presumed.

LORD NICHOLLS (whose speech was supported by the other members of the House of Lords):

8 Equity identified broadly two forms of unacceptable conduct. The first comprises overt acts of improper pressure or coercion such as unlawful threats. Today there is much overlap with the principle of duress as this principle has subsequently developed. The second form arises out of a relationship between two persons where one has acquired over another a measure of influence, or ascendancy, of which the ascendant person then takes unfair advantage. An example from the 19th century, when much of this law developed, is a case where an impoverished father prevailed upon his inexperienced children to charge their reversionary interests under their parents' marriage settlement with payment of his mortgage debts: see *Bainbrigge* v *Browne* (1881) 18 Ch D 188.

9 In cases of this latter nature the influence one person has over another provides scope for misuse without any specific overt acts of persuasion. The relationship between two individuals may be such that, without more, one of them is disposed to agree a course of action proposed by the other. Typically this occurs when one person places trust in another to look after his affairs and interests, and the latter betrays this trust by preferring his own interests. He abuses the influence he has acquired. In *Allcard* v *Skinner* (1887) 36 Ch D 145, a case well known to every law student, Lindley LJ, at p 181, described this class of cases as those in which it was the duty of one party to advise the other or to manage his property for him. In *Zamet* v *Hyman* [1961] 1 WLR 1442, 1444–1445 Lord Evershed MR referred to relationships where one party owed the other an obligation of candour and protection.

10 The law has long recognised the need to prevent abuse of influence in these 'relationship' cases despite the absence of evidence of overt acts of persuasive conduct. The types of relationship, such as parent and child, in which this principle falls to be applied cannot be listed exhaustively. Relationships are infinitely various. Sir Guenter Treitel QC has rightly noted that the question is whether one party has reposed sufficient trust and confidence in the other, rather than whether the relationship between the parties belongs to a particular type: see Treitel, *The Law of Contract*, 10th ed (1999), pp 380–381. For example, the relation of banker and customer will not normally meet this criterion, but exceptionally it may: see *National Westminster Bank plc* v *Morgan* [1985] AC 686, 707–709.

11 Even this test is not comprehensive. The principle is not confined to cases of abuse of trust and confidence. It also includes, for instance, cases where a vulnerable person has been exploited. Indeed, there is no single touchstone for determining whether the principle is applicable. Several expressions have been used in an endeavour to encapsulate the essence: trust and confidence, reliance, dependence or vulnerability on the one hand and ascendancy, domination or control on the other. None of these descriptions is perfect. None is all embracing. Each has its proper place. . . .

Burden of proof and presumptions

13 Whether a transaction was brought about by the exercise of undue influence is a question of fact. Here, as elsewhere, the general principle is that he who asserts a wrong has been committed must prove it. The burden of proving an allegation of undue influence rests upon the person who claims to have been wronged. This is the general rule. The evidence required to discharge the burden of proof depends on the nature of the alleged undue influence, the personality of the parties, their relationship, the extent to which the transaction cannot readily be accounted for by the ordinary motives of ordinary persons in that relationship, and all the circumstances of the case.

14 Proof that the complainant placed trust and confidence in the other party in relation to the management of the complainant's financial affairs, coupled with a transaction which calls for, explanation, will normally be sufficient, failing satisfactory evidence to the contrary, to discharge the burden of proof. On proof of these two matters the stage is set for the court to infer that, in the absence of a satisfactory explanation, the transaction can only have been procured by undue influence. In other words, proof of these two facts is prima facie evidence that the defendant abused the influence he acquired in the parties' relationship. He preferred his own interests. He did not behave fairly to the other. So the evidential burden then shifts to him. It is for him to produce evidence to counter the inference which otherwise should be drawn.

15 *Bainbrigge* v *Browne* 18 Ch D 188, already mentioned, provides a good illustration of this commonplace type of forensic exercise. Fry J held, at p 196, that there was no direct evidence upon which he could rely as proving undue pressure by the father. But there existed circumstances 'from which the court will infer pressure and undue influence'. None of the children were entirely emancipated from their father's control. None seemed conversant with business. These circumstances were such as to cast the burden of proof upon the father. He had made no attempt to discharge that burden. He did not appear in court at all. So the children's claim succeeded. Again, more recently, in *National Westminster Bank plc* v *Morgan* [1985] AC 686, 707. Lord Scarman noted that a relationship of banker and customer may become one in which a banker acquires a dominating influence. If he does, and a manifestly disadvantageous transaction is proved, 'there would then be room' for a court to presume that it resulted from the exercise of undue influence.

16 Generations of equity lawyers have conventionally described this situation as one in which a presumption of undue influence arises. This use of the term 'presumption' is descriptive of a shift in the evidential onus on a question of fact. When a plaintiff succeeds by this route he does so because he has succeeded in establishing a case of undue influence. The court has drawn appropriate inferences of fact upon a balanced consideration of the whole of the evidence at the end of a trial in which the burden of proof rested upon the plaintiff. The use, in the course of the trial, of the forensic tool of a shift in the evidential burden of proof should not be permitted to obscure the overall position. These cases are the equitable counterpart of common law cases where the principle of res ipsa loquitur is invoked. There is a rebuttable evidential presumption of undue influence.

17 The availability of this forensic tool in cases founded on abuse of influence arising from the parties' relationship has led to this type of case sometimes being labelled 'presumed undue influence'. This is by way of contrast with cases involving actual pressure or the like, which are labelled 'actual undue influence': see *Bank of Credit and Commerce International SA* v *Aboody* [1990] 1 QB 923, 953, and *Royal Bank of Scotland plc* v *Etridge (No. 2)* [1998] 4 All ER 705, 711–712, paras 5–7. This usage can be a little confusing. In many cases where a plaintiff has claimed that the defendant abused the influence he acquired in a relationship of trust and confidence the plaintiff has succeeded by recourse to the rebuttable evidential presumption. But this need not be so. Such a plaintiff may succeed even where this presumption is not available to him; for instance, where the impugned transaction was not one which called for an explanation.

18 The evidential presumption discussed above is to be distinguished sharply from a different form of presumption which arises in some cases. The law has adopted a sternly protective attitude towards certain types of relationship in which one party acquires influence over another who is vulnerable and dependent and where, moreover, substantial gifts by the influenced or vulnerable person are not normally to be expected. Examples of relationships within this special class are parent and child, guardian and ward, trustee and beneficiary, solicitor and client, and medical adviser and patient. In these cases the law presumes, irrebuttably, that one party had influence over the other. The complainant need not prove he actually reposed trust and confidence in the other party. It is sufficient for him to prove the existence of the type of relationship.

19 It is now well established that husband and wife is not one of the relationships to which this latter principle applies. In *Yerkey* v *Jones* (1939) 63 CLR 649, 675 Dixon J explained the reason. The Court of Chancery was not blind to the opportunities of obtaining and unfairly using influence over a wife which a husband often possesses. But there is nothing unusual or strange in a wife, from motives of affection or for other reasons, conferring substantial financial benefits on her husband. Although there is no presumption, the court will nevertheless note, as a matter of fact, the opportunities for abuse which flow from a wife's confidence in her husband. The court will take this into account with all the other evidence in the case. Where there is evidence that a husband has taken unfair advantage of his influence over his wife, or her confidence in him, 'it is not difficult for the wife to establish her title to relief': see In re Lloyds Bank Ltd; *Bomze and Lederman* v *Bomze* [1931] 1 Ch 289, 302, per Maugham J.

Independent advice

20 Proof that the complainant received advice from a third party before entering into the impugned transaction is one of the matters a court takes into account when weighing all the evidence. The weight, or importance, to be attached to such advice depends on all the circumstances. In the normal course, advice from a solicitor or other outside adviser can be expected to bring home to a complainant a proper understanding of what he or she is about to do. But a person may understand fully the implications of a proposed transaction, for instance, a substantial gift, and yet still be acting under the undue influence of another. Proof of outside advice does not, of itself, necessarily show that the subsequent completion of the transaction was free from the exercise of undue influence. Whether it will be proper to infer that outside advice had an emancipating effect, so that the transaction was not brought about by the exercise of undue influence, is a question of fact to be decided having regard to all the evidence in the case.

NOTE: Lord Nicholls therefore accepted that the classification of types of undue influence depends upon how that undue influence is proved. Thus, in some cases (actual undue influence: class 1), both the influence and the fact that it is undue will be affirmatively proved since there is clear evidence to support this. In other cases, the influence will be presumed (in the absence of actual evidence of undue influence), either because of the existence of a protected relationship or because there is a relationship of trust and confidence between these individual parties.

Cases of presumed undue influence are of two types. The distinction is that in the first category of 'protected' relationships, the influence is automatically (and irrebuttably) presumed, whereas in those cases falling outside these 'protected relationships', such as husband and wife and banker and customer, the party alleging undue influence needs to establish that trust and confidence was placed in the other party in order for the presumption of influence to arise. Such influence is not automatically assumed. In the case of both types of presumed undue influence the presumption of *undue* influence can then arise only if there is something suspicious about the transaction which calls for an explanation.

However, once this presumption of undue influence has arisen the burden of proof shifts so that it is for the other party to seek to show that no undue influence was in fact exercised and that the transaction was the product of a 'free and informed consent'. One possible way to do this would be by showing that independent legal advice had been received. However, there is some residual uncertainty concerning the role and effect of independent legal advice in this context (although see the comment of Lord Nicholls at [20]). It may not be as significant as had been thought pre-*Etridge*.

In summary, therefore, *Etridge* establishes two important points: (i) that any presumption only operates to indicate the exercise of influence and not the existence of *undue* influence; and (ii) that whereas the presumption of influence in class 2A (protected relationship) classes is irrebuttable, the presumption of influence in other cases needs to be established on the facts.

Establishing that the influence was undue: that the transaction is not readily explicable by the parties' relationship

In *National Westminster Bank plc* v *Morgan* [1985] AC 686, *page 638*, the House of Lords considered that the party claiming undue influence needed to establish that the transaction was manifestly disadvantageous to him. The existence of such a requirement has proved controversial. However, Lord Nicholls in *Royal Bank of*

Scotland plc v *Etridge (No. 2)* [2001] UKHL 44, [2002] 2 AC 773 indicated that there is a link between the existence of manifest disadvantage and the ability to establish that the influence was 'undue', i.e., that advantage was taken of a position of trust and confidence.

> **12**   In *CIBC Mortgages plc* v *Pitt* [1994] 1 AC 200 your Lordships' House decided that in cases of undue influence disadvantage is not a necessary ingredient of the cause of action. It is not essential that the transaction should be disadvantageous to the pressurised or influenced person, either in financial terms or in any other way. However, in the nature of things, questions of undue influence will not usually arise, and the exercise of undue influence is unlikely to occur, where the transaction is innocuous. The issue is likely to arise only when, in some respect, the transaction was disadvantageous either from the outset or as matters turned out.

Of course, the non-existence of manifest disadvantage would not eliminate the possibility of undue influence and other evidence may establish that despite the apparent fairness of the transaction, advantage was taken of the party influenced to contract. In theoretical terms it is difficult to see that the position of the claimant should be relevant to an assessment of the undue nature of the influence exercised by the defendant so that it clearly cannot be the *only* factor.

Lord Nicholls went on to reformulate the manifest disadvantage requirement, although only it seems in relation to class 2 situations ([21]), as a test of whether the transaction is readily explicable by the relationship of the parties, i.e., a small gift between relatives might be readily explicable whereas a very large transfer might raise the suspicion that undue influence may have been exercised and so shift the burden of proof to the other party. This is a helpful explanation since much confusion had been generated in the case law concerning the meaning of 'manifestly disadvantageous' and, in particular, the relationship between this requirement and the requirement for a third party surety to be put on inquiry (that the transaction on its face was not to the financial advantage of the party alleging undue influence). The Court of Appeal in *Macklin* v *Dowsett* [2004] EWCA Civ 904, [2004] 2 EGLR 75, has since confirmed that there is no longer a manifest disadvantage requirement in the context of the evidential presumption of undue influence. The particular transaction was suspicious since it gave M an option to require D to surrender his life tenancy in property for a payment of only £5,000.

> LORD NICHOLLS:
>
> **21**   As already noted, there are two prerequisites to the evidential shift in the burden of proof from the complainant to the other party. First, that the complainant reposed trust and confidence in the other party, or the other party acquired ascendancy over the complainant. Second, that the transaction is not readily explicable by the relationship of the parties.
>
> **22**   Lindley LJ summarised this second prerequisite in the leading authority of *Allcard* v *Skinner* 36 Ch D 145, where the donor parted with almost all her property. Lindley LJ pointed out that where a gift of a small amount is made to a person standing in a confidential relationship to the donor, some proof of the exercise of the influence of the donee must be given. The mere existence of the influence is not enough. He continued, at p 185 'But if the gift is so large as not to be reasonably accounted for on the ground of friendship, relationship, charity, or other ordinary motives on which ordinary men act, the burden is upon the donee to support the gift.' In *Bank of Montreal* v *Stuart* [1911] AC 120, 137 Lord Macnaghten used the phrase 'immoderate and irrational' to describe this concept.
>
> **23**   The need for this second prerequisite has recently been questioned: see Nourse LJ in *Barclays Bank plc* v *Coleman* [2001] QB, 20, 30–32, one of the cases under appeal before your

Lordships' House. [Counsel] invited your Lordships to depart from the decision of the House on this point in *National Westminster Bank plc* v *Morgan* [1985] AC 686.

24 My Lords, this is not an invitation I would accept. The second prerequisite, as expressed by Lindley LJ, is good sense. It is a necessary limitation upon the width of the first prerequisite. It would be absurd for the law to presume that every gift by a child to a parent, or every transaction between a client and his solicitor or between a patient and his doctor, was brought about by undue influence unless the contrary is affirmatively proved. Such a presumption would be too far-reaching. The law would be out of touch with everyday life if the presumption were to apply to every Christmas or birthday gift by a child to a parent, or to an agreement whereby a client or patient agrees to be responsible for the reasonable fees of his legal or medical adviser. The law would be rightly open to ridicule, for transactions such as these are unexceptionable. They do not suggest that something may be amiss. So something more is needed before the law reverses the burden of proof, something which calls for an explanation. When that something more is present, the greater the disadvantage to the vulnerable person, the more cogent must be the explanation before the presumption will be regarded as rebutted.

25 This was the approach adopted by Lord Scarman in *National Westminster Bank plc* v *Morgan* [1985] AC 686, 703–707. He cited Lindley LJ's observations in *Allcard* v *Skinner* 36 Ch D 145, 185, which I have set out above. He noted that whatever the legal character of the transaction, it must constitute a disadvantage sufficiently serious to require evidence to rebut the presumption that in the circumstances of the parties' relationship, it was procured by the exercise of undue influence. Lord Scarman concluded, at p 704:

> 'the Court of Appeal erred in law in holding that the presumption of undue influence can arise from the evidence of the relationship of the parties without also evidence that the transaction itself was wrongful in that it constituted *an advantage taken of the person subjected to the influence which, failing proof to the contrary, was explicable only on the basis that undue influence had been exercised to procure it.*' (Emphasis added.)

26 Lord Scarman attached the label 'manifest disadvantage' to this second ingredient necessary to raise the presumption. This label has been causing difficulty. It may be apt enough when applied to straightforward transactions such as a substantial gift or a sale at an undervalue. But experience has now shown that this expression can give rise to misunderstanding. The label is being understood and applied in a way which does not accord with the meaning intended by Lord Scarman, its originator.

27 The problem has arisen in the context of wives guaranteeing payment of their husband's business debts. In recent years judge after judge has grappled with the baffling question whether a wife's guarantee of her husband's bank overdraft, together with a charge on her share of the matrimonial home, was a transaction manifestly to her disadvantage.

28 In a narrow sense, such a transaction plainly ('manifestly') is disadvantageous to the wife. She undertakes a serious financial obligation, and in return she personally receives nothing. But that would be to take an unrealistically blinkered view of such a transaction. Unlike the relationship of solicitor and client or medical adviser and patient, in the case of husband and wife there are inherent reasons why such a transaction may well be for her benefit. Ordinarily, the fortunes of husband and wife are bound up together. If the husband's business is the source of the family income, the wife has a lively interest in doing what she can to support the business. A wife's affection and self-interest run hand-in-hand in inclining her to join with her husband in charging the matrimonial home, usually a jointly-owned asset, to obtain the financial facilities needed by the business. The finance may be needed to start a new business, or expand a promising business, or rescue an ailing business.

29 Which, then, is the correct approach to adopt in deciding whether a transaction is disadvantageous to the wife: the narrow approach, or the wider approach? The answer is neither. The answer lies in discarding a label which gives rise to this sort of ambiguity. The better approach is to adhere more directly to the test outlined by Lindley LJ in *Allcard* v *Skinner* 36 Ch D 145, and adopted by Lord Scarman in *National Westminster Bank plc* v *Morgan* [1985] AC 686, in the passages I have cited.

30 I return to husband and wife cases. I do not think that, in the ordinary course, a guarantee of the character I have mentioned is to be regarded as a transaction which, failing proof to the contrary, is explicable only on the basis that it has been procured by the exercise of undue influence by the husband. Wives frequently enter into such transactions. There are good and sufficient reasons why they are willing to do so, despite the risks involved for them and their families. They may be enthusiastic. They may not. They may be less optimistic than their husbands about the prospects of the husbands' businesses. They may be anxious, perhaps exceedingly so. But this is a far cry from saying that such transactions as a class are to be regarded as prima facie evidence of the exercise of undue influence by husbands.

31 I have emphasised the phrase 'in the ordinary course'. There will be cases where a wife's signature of a guarantee or a charge of her share in the matrimonial home does call for explanation. Nothing I have said above is directed at such a case.

NOTE: This process can be seen in operation in *Dailey* v *Dailey* [2003] UKPC 65, [2003] 3 FCR 369, where the Privy Council held

(i) as the relationship was that of husband and wife, the wife needed to establish that an evidential presumption should arise because of the particular features of their relationship and she had failed to do so, and

(ii) in any event, since the case involved a transfer by the wife of her interest in land to her husband as part of proceedings for ancillary relief and in return for a fair value, this was not a transaction where the presumption of *undue* influence arose.

Accordingly, the wife could not succeed in setting aside the transaction unless she established actual undue influence. Lord Hope explained the applicable principle:

24. Care needs to be taken to distinguish between cases where the wife has entered into a transaction with her husband which is gratuitous and those where the agreement is for her to receive full value for the property or interest which she is to transfer to him. In the former case, as Lindley LJ explained in *Allcard* v *Skinner* (1887) 36 Ch D 145, 185, the burden is on the donee to support the gift if it is so large as not to be reasonably accounted for on the ground of the relationship. A transaction which is entered into for full value needs no such explanation. There is no presumption to rebut. That is not to say that a transaction of this type is immune from the exercise of undue influence. But if it is to be set aside on this ground it is for the party who makes the allegation to prove that undue influence was in fact exercised.

A: Actual undue influence

Slade LJ in *Bank of Credit and Commerce International SA* v *Aboody* [1990] 1 QB 923 stated:

. . . [W]e think that a person relying on a plea of actual undue influence must show that (a) the other party to the transaction (or someone who induced the transaction for his own benefit) had the capacity to influence the complainant; (b) the influence was exercised; (c) its exercise was undue; (d) its exercise brought about the transaction. . . .

As a result of the 'cautionary note' introduced by Lord Nicholls in *Royal Bank of Scotland plc* v *Etridge (No. 2)* [2001] UKHL 44, [2002] 2 AC 773, it will be more difficult than had previously been thought to establish actual undue influence in the context of husband and wife relationships. However, it is clear that misrepresentations of fact will suffice for this purpose, see *UCB Corporate Services Ltd* v *Williams, page 633.*

A cautionary note

32 I add a cautionary note, prompted by some of the first instance judgments in the cases currently being considered by the House. It concerns the general approach to be adopted by a court when considering whether a wife's guarantee of her husband's bank overdraft was procured by her husband's undue influence. Undue influence has a connotation of impropriety. In the eye of the law, undue influence means that influence has been misused. Statements or conduct by a husband which do not pass beyond the bounds of what may be expected of a reasonable husband in the circumstances should not, without more, be castigated as undue influence. Similarly, when a husband is forecasting the future of his business, and expressing his hopes or fears, a degree of hyperbole may be only natural. Courts should not too readily treat such exaggerations as misstatements.

33 Inaccurate explanations of a proposed transaction are a different matter. So are cases where a husband, in whom a wife has reposed trust and confidence for the management of their financial affairs, prefers his interests to hers and makes a choice for both of them on that footing. Such a husband abuses the influence he has. He fails to discharge the obligation of candour and fairness he owes a wife who is looking to him to make the major financial decisions.

NOTE: Although the Court of Appeal in *BCCI* v *Aboody* had held that a transaction could not be set aside for actual undue influence unless the transaction in question was manifestly disadvantageous to the party affected, the House of Lords in *CIBC Mortgages plc* v *Pitt* [1994] 1 AC 200 emphatically rejected this requirement in the context of actual undue influence.

Lord Browne-Wilkinson in *CIBC* v *Pitt* said:

> My Lords, I am unable to agree with the Court of Appeal's decision in *Aboody*. I have no doubt that the decision in *Morgan* does not extend to cases of actual undue influence. Despite two references in Lord Scarman's speech to cases of actual undue influence, as I read his speech he was primarily concerned to establish that disadvantage had to be shown, not as a constituent element of the cause of action for undue influence, but in order to raise a presumption of undue influence within class 2. That was the only subject matter before the House of Lords in *Morgan* and the passage I have already cited was directed solely to that point. With the exception of a passing reference to *Ormes* v *Beadel* (1860) 2 Gif 166, all the cases referred to by Lord Scarman were cases of presumed undue influence. In the circumstances, I do not think that this House can have been intending to lay down any general principle applicable to all claims of undue influence, whether actual or presumed.
>
> Whatever the merits of requiring a complainant to show manifest disadvantage in order to raise a Class 2 presumption of undue influence, in my judgment there is no logic in imposing such a requirement where actual undue influence has been exercised and proved. Actual undue influence is a species of fraud. Like any other victim of fraud, a person who has been induced by undue influence to carry out a transaction which he did not freely and knowingly enter into is entitled to have that transaction set aside as of right. No case decided before *Morgan* was cited (nor am I aware of any) in which a transaction proved to have been obtained by actual undue influence has been upheld nor is there any case in which a court has even considered whether the transaction was, or was not, advantageous. A man guilty of fraud is no more entitled to argue that the transaction was beneficial to the person defrauded than is a man who has procured a transaction by misrepresentation. The effect of the wrongdoer's conduct is to prevent the wronged party from bringing a free will and properly informed mind to bear on the proposed transaction which accordingly must be set aside in equity as a matter of justice.
>
> I therefore hold that a claimant who proves actual undue influence is not under the further burden of proving that the transaction induced by undue influence was manifestly disadvantageous: he is entitled as of right to have it set aside.

In cases of actual undue influence the exercise of undue influence is affirmatively established without the need to rely on any evidential presumptions. As such, the requirements specified by Lord Nicholls in *Royal Bank of Scotland plc v Etridge (No. 2)* [2001] UKHL 44, [2002] 2 AC 773, at [21] would appear to have no relevance. There can be no manifest disadvantage requirement (however formulated) in cases of actual undue influence since the undue influence does not rest upon establishing the existence of a protected relationship or a relationship of trust and confidence. Actual undue influence is 'a species of fraud' and although disadvantage may assist in establishing the existence of undue influence (see [12]), it cannot exist as a separate requirement.

Since actual undue influence is akin to fraud, it follows that it is not a defence where actual undue influence has been proved to claim that the person influenced would have entered into the transaction anyway.

UCB Corporate Services Ltd v Williams
[2002] EWCA Civ 555, [2003] 1 P & CR 12 (CA)

The defendant's husband had been a partner in a business to which the claimant had lent money, secured in part on the home jointly owned by the defendant. She alleged that she had executed this charge in favour of the claimant lender because of the undue influence of her husband. It was found as a fact that the defendant had been the victim of fraudulent misrepresentation and actual undue influence. However, the judge considered that the defendant would have signed the charge of her own free will even if she had known of the full facts and the risks involved. On appeal Held: The fraud had deprived the defendant of the opportunity to make a free and informed choice to contract and it was not relevant to ask whether she would have entered into the transaction in any event. The only relevant factor was that the actual undue influence was *a* factor inducing her to execute the charge. The claimant was fixed with constructive notice of the defendant's right to have the transaction set aside for undue influence and fraudulent misrepresentation.

JONATHAN PARKER LJ (with whom Peter Gibson and Kay LJJ agreed):

86 Undue influence is exerted when improper means of persuasion are used to procure the complainant's consent to participate in a transaction, such that 'the consent thus procured ought not fairly to be treated as the expression of [the complainant's] free will' (see *Etridge* at para 7 per Lord Nicholls). In such a case, equity proceeds on the basis that the complainant did not consent to the transaction. Is that enough to give rise to an equity in the complainant to set aside the transaction as against the wrongdoer? In my judgment, it is. That conclusion seems to me to follow clearly from what Lord Browne-Wilkinson said in *CIBC* v *Pitt*. . . .

> 'Actual undue influence is a species of fraud.' That being so, I cannot see any reason in principle why (for example) a husband who has fraudulently procured the consent of his wife to participate in a transaction should be able, in effect, to escape the consequences of his wrongdoing by establishing that had he not acted fraudulently, and had his wife had the opportunity to make a free and informed choice, she would have acted in the same way. The fact is that the husband's fraud deprived the wife of the opportunity to make such a choice, and, as I see it, it is that fact which founds the wife's equity (as against her husband) to set aside the transaction.

NOTE: This question might equally well have been decided by reliance on the principle in *Edgington v Fitzmaurice* (1885) 29 ChD 459 that a fraudulent misrepresentation need only be *one* of the reasons inducing the misrepresentee to contract. It need not be the only reason.

B: Presumed (or evidential) undue influence: protected relationships

There are two categories of presumed undue influence. Slade LJ defined them in *BCCI* v *Aboody*:

There are well established categories of relationship, such as a religious superior and inferior and doctor and patient where the relationship as such will give rise to the presumption (frequently referred to in argument before us as 'class 2A' cases). The relationship of husband and wife does not as such give rise to the presumption: see *National Westminster Bank Plc* v *Morgan* [1985] AC 686, 703b, and *Bank of Montreal* v *Stuart* [1911] AC 120. Nor does the normal relationship of banker and customer as such give rise to it. Nevertheless, on particular facts (frequently referred to in argument as 'class 2B' cases) relationships not falling within the class 2A category may be shown to have become such as to justify the court in applying the same presumption.

NOTES
1. The language used in *Aboody* (class 2A and 2B) has been abandoned as a result of the *Etridge* reformulation.
2. The presumption to which Slade LJ refers has since been interpreted to mean an evidential presumption of influence and not a presumption that the influence was undue (Lord Nicholls in *Royal Bank of Scotland plc* v *Etridge (No. 2)* [2001] UKHL 44, [2002] 2 AC 773, *page 626*).
3. The law recognises that there are certain 'protected relationships' which raise an irrebuttable presumption of influence. These relationships include religious adviser and disciple (*Allcard* v *Skinner* (1887) 36 ChD 145), parent and child (*Bainbrigge* v *Browne* (1881) ChD 188) and solicitor and client (*Wright* v *Carter* [1903] 1 Ch 27). The husband and wife relationship is not a protected relationship (*Bank of Montreal* v *Stuart* [1911] AC 120).
4. However, it is still necessary to prove that the influence was wrongful. If there is something suspicious about the transaction it will be evidence to support such an allegation. The fact that the transaction is manifestly disadvantageous to the person claiming that undue influence was exercised (i.e., is not readily explicable in view of the relationship between the parties), will be strong evidence of the existence of undue influence ([22] and [24] in the speech of Lord Nicholls in *Etridge (No. 2)*, extracted at *pages 629–30*) but has been rejected as a explicit requirement.

C: Presumed (or evidential) undue influence: other cases established on the facts

In instances where it is not possible to affirmatively prove the existence of undue influence and where the relationship between the parties is not within one of the categories of protected relationships, it may nevertheless be possible to establish undue influence on the particular facts. However, the requirement of proof is very different to that which had previously been considered to apply to such cases. As explained by Lord Nicholls in *Etridge (No. 2)* (especially at [14], see *page 627*), if it can be established that one party placed trust and confidence in the other party to deal with his affairs, that raises a rebuttable presumption that influence was in fact exercised. However, it is necessary to prove that on the facts the claimant placed trust and confidence in the defendant. Once influence has been presumed as a result of this evidence, this presumption is capable of being rebutted by evidence to the contrary, which might include evidence that the party received independent advice from another. However, the party alleging undue influence would also need to establish that such presumed influence was 'undue' by showing that the nature of the transaction is suspicious and so calls for an explanation from the other party, see the discussion at *page 628*. If the other party is unable to produce evidence to counter the inference of undue influence, the court will conclude that the transaction was the result of the exercise of undue influence.

These cases of undue influence would equate, in broad terms, with so-called class 2B cases. However, it is important to bear in mind that this language was considered 'not a useful forensic tool' in *Etridge* (*per* Lord Hobhouse [107]) in view of the misinterpretation of the presumption in previous case law. Thus, although such cases of undue influence still exist it may be preferable to avoid references to 'class 2B'.

Nevertheless, much of the case law remains relevant in terms of identifying relationships falling outside 'class 2A' (protected relationships) where it has been established that the necessary trust and confidence was placed in the other party and this trust was abused.

Lloyds Bank Ltd v Bundy
[1975] QB 326 (CA)

The defendant, an elderly farmer, and his son had been customers of the plaintiff bank for many years. The son's company account was held at the same branch. Previously, the defendant had given a guarantee and a charge for £7,500 over his farmhouse (his only asset) to secure this company's overdraft. On that occasion he had been advised by a solicitor that this was the most that he could afford to put into his son's business. In December 1969, the son and the assistant bank manager visited the defendant, and the assistant manager told the defendant that the bank could only allow the company's overdraft to increase if the defendant guaranteed the account up to £11,000 and gave a further charge on the farmhouse to bring the total charge up to that amount. The defendant signed that charge documentation. The evidence was that the assistant manager knew that the defendant relied on him as his bank manager for advice in the transaction and that he knew that the house was the defendant's only asset. Subsequently the bank enforced the charge and sought possession of the house. Held: the charge should be set aside for undue influence. The bank had a conflict of interest and the defendant had received no independent advice as to the wisdom of the transaction.

SIR ERIC SACHS (with whose judgment Cairns LJ concurred): The first and most troublesome issue which here falls for consideration is as to whether on the particular and somewhat unusual facts of the case, the bank was, when obtaining his signatures on December 17, 1969, in a relationship with Mr Bundy that entailed a duty on their part of what can for convenience be called fiduciary care.

. . . As was pointed out in *Tufton v Sperni* [1952] 2 TLR 516, the relationships which result in such a duty must not be circumscribed by reference to defined limits; it is necessary to

refute the suggestion that, to create the relationship of confidence, the person owing the duty must be found clothed in the recognisable garb of a guardian, trustee, solicitor, priest, doctor, manager, or the like. (Sir Raymond Evershed MR, at p. 522.)

Everything depends on the particular facts, and such a relationship has been held to exist in unusual circumstances as between purchaser and vendor, as between great uncle and adult nephew, and in other widely differing sets of circumstances. Moreover, it is neither feasible nor desirable to attempt closely to define the relationship, or its characteristics, or the demarcation line showing the exact transition point where a relationship that does not entail that duty passes into one that does.

On the other hand, whilst disclaiming any intention of seeking to catalogue the elements of such a special relationship, it is perhaps of a little assistance to note some of those which have in the past frequently been found to exist where the court has been led to decide that this relationship existed as between adults of sound mind. Such cases tend to arise where someone relies on the guidance or advice of another, where the other is aware of that reliance and where the person upon whom reliance is placed obtains, or may well obtain, a benefit from the transaction or has some other interest in it being concluded. In addition, there must, of course, be shown to exist a vital element which in this judgment will for convenience be referred to as confidentiality. It is this element which is so impossible to define and which is a matter for the judgment of the court on the facts of any particular case.

Confidentiality, a relatively little used word, is being here adopted, albeit with some hesitation, to avoid the possible confusion that can arise through referring to 'confidence.' Reliance on advice can in many circumstances be said to import that type of confidence which only results in a common law duty to take care—a duty which may co-exist with but is not coterminous with that of fiduciary care. 'Confidentiality' is intended to convey that extra quality in the relevant confidence that is implicit in the phrase 'confidential relationship', and may perhaps have something in common with 'confiding' and also 'confidant' when, for instance, referring to someone's 'man of affairs.' It imports some quality beyond that inherent in the confidence that can well exist between trustworthy persons who in business affairs deal with each other at arm's length. It is one of the features of this element that once it exists, influence naturally grows out of it (cf. Sir Raymond Evershed MR, *Tufton's* case [1952] 2 TLR 516, 523. . . .)

It was inevitably conceded on behalf of the bank that the relevant relationship can arise as between banker and customer. Equally, it was inevitably conceded on behalf of Mr Bundy that in the normal course of transactions by which a customer guarantees a third party's obligations, the relationship does not arise. The onus of proof lies on the customer who alleges that in any individual case the line has been crossed and the relationship has arisen.

Before proceeding to examine the position further, it is as well to dispose of some points on which confusion is apt to arise. Undue influence is a phrase which is commonly regarded—even in the eyes of a number of lawyers—as relating solely to occasions when the will of one person has become so dominated by that of another that, to use the county court judge's words, 'the person acts as the mere puppet of the dominator.' Such occasions, of course, fall within what Cotton LJ in *Allcard* v *Skinner*, 36 ChD 145, 171 described as the first class of cases to which the doctrine on undue influence applies. There is, however, a second class of such cases. This is referred to by Cotton LJ as follows:

> In the second class of cases the court interferes, not on the ground that any wrongful act has in fact been committed by the donee, but on the ground of public policy, and to prevent the relations which existed between the parties and the influence arising therefrom being abused.

It is thus to be emphasised that as regards the second class the exercise of the court's jurisdiction to set aside the relevant transaction does *not* depend on proof of one party being 'able to dominate the other as though a puppet' nor any wrongful intention on the part of the person who gains a benefit from it; but on the concept that once the special relationship has been shown to exist, no benefit can be retained from the transaction unless it has been positively established that the duty of fiduciary care has been entirely fulfilled. To this second class, however, the judge never adverted and plainly never directed his mind.

It is also to be noted that what constitutes fulfilment of that duty (the second issue in the case now under consideration) depends again on the facts before the court. It may in the particular circumstances entail that the person in whom confidence has been reposed should insist on independent advice being obtained or ensuring in one way or another that the person being asked to execute a document is not insufficiently informed of some factor which could affect his judgment. The duty has been well stated as being one to ensure that the person liable to be influenced has formed 'an independent *and informed* judgment', or, to use the phraseology of Lord Evershed MR in *Zamet* v *Hyman* [1961] 1 WLR 1442, 1446, 'after full, free *and informed* thought.' . . .

Having discussed the nature of the issues to which the county court judge should have directed his mind, it is now convenient to turn to the evidence relating to the first of them—whether the special relationship has here been shown to exist at the material time.

. . . what happened on December 17, 1969, has to be assessed in the light of the general background of the existence of the long-standing relations between the Bundy family and the bank. It not infrequently occurs in provincial and country branches of great banks that a relationship is built up over the years, and in due course the senior officials may become trusted counsellors of customers of whose affairs they have an intimate knowledge. Confidential trust is placed in them because of a combination of status, goodwill and knowledge. . . .

It is, of course, plain that when Mr Head was asking Mr Bundy to sign the documents, the bank would derive benefit from the signature, that there was a conflict of interest as between the bank and Mr Bundy, that the bank gave him advice, that he relied on that advice, and that the bank knew of the reliance. The further question is whether on the evidence concerning the matters already recited there was also established that element of confidentiality which has been discussed. In my judgment it is thus established. . . .

What was required to be done on the bank's behalf once the existence of that duty is shown to have been established? . . . .

The documents Mr Bundy was being asked to sign could result, if the company's troubles continued, in Mr Bundy's sole asset being sold, the proceeds all going to the bank, and his being left penniless in his old age. That he could thus be rendered penniless was known to the bank—and in particular to Mr Head. That the company might come to a bad end quite soon with these results was not exactly difficult to deduce (less than four months later, on April 3, 1970, the bank were insisting that Yew Tree Farm be sold).

The situation was thus one which to any reasonably sensible person, who gave it but a moment's thought, cried aloud Mr. Bundy's need for careful independent advice. Over and above the need any man has for counsel when asked to risk his last penny on even an apparently reasonable project, was the need here for informed advice as to whether there was any real chance of the company's affairs becoming viable if the documents were signed . . . without which Mr Bundy could not come to an informed judgment as to the wisdom of what he was doing.

No such advice to get an independant opinion was given; on the contrary, Mr Head chose to give his own views on the company's affairs and to take this course, though he had at trial to admit: 'I did not explain the company's affairs very fully as I had only just taken over.' . . .

There remains to mention that [counsel for the Bank], whilst conceding that the relevant special relationship could arise as between banker and customer, urged in somewhat doom-laden terms that a decision taken against the bank on the facts of this particular case would seriously affect banking practice. With all respect to that submission, it seems necessary to point out that nothing in this judgment affects the duties of a bank in the normal case where it is obtaining a guarantee, and in accordance with standard practice explains to the person about to sign its legal effect and the sums involved. When, however, a bank, as in the present case, goes further and advises on more general matters germane to the wisdom of the transaction, that indicates that it may—not necessarily must—be crossing the line into the area of confidentiality so that the court may then have to examine all the facts including, of course, the history leading up to the transaction, to ascertain whether or not that line has, as here, been crossed. It would indeed be rather odd if a bank which vis-à-vis a customer attained a special relationship in some ways akin to that of a 'man of affairs'—something which can be a matter of pride and enhance its local reputation—should not, where a conflict of interest has arisen as between itself and the person advised, be under the resulting duty now under discussion. Once, as was inevitably conceded, it is possible for a bank to be under that duty, it is, as in the present case, simply a question for 'meticulous examination' of the particular facts to see whether that duty has arisen. On the special facts here it did arise and it has been broken.

NOTES

1. The judgment of Lord Denning MR rested on there being a general principle of inequality of bargaining power and is discussed at *page 662*.

2. In the light of *Etridge*, this case can be interpreted as turning on the proof of the trust and confidence placed by Mr Bundy in the advice of the bank manager in relation to his financial affairs. This would raise a presumption of influence and the nature of the transaction and the circumstances (including the benefit to the bank in securing the transaction) would provide evidence to support the fact that 'undue' influence had been exercised. The bank manager was not able to show that Mr Bundy had received independent advice in order to counter the inference of undue influence and had known that Mr Bundy was relying solely on him for financial advice.

3. The relationship of bank and customer is not a protected relationship (i.e., not a class 2A) but there may be undue influence exercised on the particular facts, either by proof of actual undue influence or as a result of the evidential presumption of influence arising from proof of trust and confidence placed in the other party where the facts disclose that that trust has been abused.

National Westminster Bank plc v Morgan
[1985] AC 686 (HL)

A husband and wife had a building society mortgage, but in 1977 the building society had begun proceedings for repossession. The husband's business was also in difficulty. The plaintiff bank agreed to refinance the building society loan on the normal condition that they obtained a charge over the property. The husband signed the charge instrument and the bank manager visited the wife to obtain her signature. The wife was concerned about the effect of the charge. She did not possess much confidence in her husband's business and did not want any security to extend to borrowing by the business. The bank manager innocently misled her into thinking that the charge was only to cover the home debt when in fact it also covered lending to the husband's business. Later the bank brought proceedings for possession. The wife claimed undue influence by the bank in obtaining her signature to the charge. Held: the relationship between the wife and the bank had never gone beyond the normal business relationship of banker and customer, and therefore no presumption of undue influence arose on the facts. At this time the transaction had to be to the manifest disadvantage of the person seeking to avoid it and the wife had benefited from the transaction because, if the bank had not given the mortgage, her home would have been repossessed by the building society. Therefore, the bank was not under any duty to ensure that she received independent advice.

LORD SCARMAN: As to the facts, I am far from being persuaded that the trial judge fell into error when he concluded that the relationship between the bank and Mrs Morgan never went beyond the normal business relationship of banker and customer. Both Lords Justices saw the relationship between the bank and Mrs Morgan as one of confidence in which she was relying on the bank manager's advice. Each took the view that the confidentiality of the relationship was such as to impose upon him a 'fiduciary duty of care.' It was his duty, in their view, to ensure that Mrs Morgan had the opportunity to make an independent and informed decision: but he failed to give her any such opportunity. They, therefore, concluded that it was a case for the presumption of undue influence.

My Lords, I believe that the Lords Justices were led into a misinterpretation of the facts by their use, as is all too frequent in this branch of the law, of words and phrases such as 'confidence,' 'confidentiality,' 'fiduciary duty.' There are plenty of confidential relationships which do not give rise to the presumption of undue influence (a notable example is that of husband and wife, *Bank of Montreal v Stuart* [1911] AC 120); and there are plenty of non-confidential relationships in which one person relies upon the advice of another, e.g. many contracts for the sale of goods. Nor am I persuaded that the charge, limited as it was by [the bank manager's] declaration to securing the loan to pay off the Abbey National debt and interest during the bridging period, was disadvantageous to Mrs Morgan. It meant for her the rescue of her home upon the terms sought by her—a short-term loan at a commercial rate of interest. The Court of Appeal has not, therefore, persuaded me that the judge's understanding of the facts was incorrect.

But, further, the view of the law expressed by the Court of Appeal was, as I shall endeavour to show, mistaken. Dunn LJ, . . . while accepting that in all the reported cases to which the court was referred the transactions were disadvantageous to the person influenced, took the view that in cases where public policy requires the court to apply the presumption of undue influence there is no need to prove a disadvantageous transaction. Slade LJ also clearly held that it was not necessary to prove a disadvantageous transaction where the relationship of influence was proved to exist. . . . [However] the authorities show that [the transaction] must constitute a disadvantage sufficiently serious to require evidence to rebut the presumption that in the circumstances of the relationship between the parties it was procured by the exercise of undue influence. In my judgment, therefore, the Court of Appeal erred in law in holding that the presumption of undue influence can arise from the evidence of the relationship of the parties without also evidence that the transaction itself was wrongful in that it constituted an advantage taken of the person subjected to the influence which, failing proof to the contrary, was explicable only on the basis that undue influence has been exercised to procure it. . . .

The principle justifying the court in setting aside a transaction for undue influence can now be seen to have been established by Lindley LJ in *Allcard* v *Skinner*, 36 ChD 145. It is not vague 'public policy' but specifically the victimisation of one party by the other. It was stated by Lindley LJ in a famous passage, at pp. 182–183:

> The principle must be examined. What then is the principle? Is it that it is right and expedient to save persons from the consequences of their own folly? or is it that it is right and expedient to save them from being victimised by other people? In my opinion the doctrine of undue influence is founded upon the second of these two principles. Courts of equity have never set aside gifts on the ground of the folly, imprudence, or want of foresight on the part of donors. The courts have always repudiated any such jurisdiction. It would obviously be to encourage folly, recklessness, extravagance and vice if persons could get back property which they foolishly made away with, whether by giving it to charitable institutions or by bestowing it on less worthy objects. On the other hand, to protect people from being forced, tricked or misled in any way by others into parting with their property is one of the most legitimate objects of all laws; and the equitable doctrine of undue influence has grown out of and been developed by the necessity of grappling with insidious forms of spiritual tyranny and with the infinite varieties of fraud.

The wrongfulness of the transaction must, therefore, be shown: it must be one in which an unfair advantage has been taken of another. [A] relationship of banker and customer may become one in which the banker acquires a dominating influence. If he does and a manifestly disadvantageous transaction is proved, there would then be room for the court to presume that it resulted from the exercise of undue influence.

This brings me to *Lloyds Bank Ltd* v *Bundy* [1975] QB 326. It was, as one would expect, conceded by counsel for the respondent that the relationship between banker and customer is not one which ordinarily gives rise to a presumption of undue influence: and that in the ordinary course of banking business a banker can explain the nature of the proposed transaction without laying himself open to a charge of undue influence. This proposition has never been in doubt, though some, it would appear, have thought that the Court of Appeal held otherwise in *Lloyds Bank Ltd* v *Bundy*. If any such view has gained currency, let it be destroyed now once and for all time . . . I would prefer to avoid the term 'confidentiality' as a description of the relationship which has to be proved. In truth, as Sir Eric recognised, the relationships which may develop a dominating influence of one over another are infinitely various. There is no substitute in this branch of the law for a 'meticulous examination of the facts.'

A meticulous examination of the facts of the present case reveals that Mr Barrow never 'crossed the line.' Nor was the transaction unfair to Mrs Morgan. The bank was, therefore, under no duty to ensure that she had independent advice. It was an ordinary banking transaction whereby Mrs Morgan sought to save her home.

I would allow the appeal. In doing so, I would wish to give a warning. There is no precisely defined law setting limits to the equitable jurisdiction of a court to relieve against undue influence. This is the world of doctrine, not of neat and tidy rules. The courts of equity have developed a body of learning enabling relief to be granted where the law has to treat the transaction as unimpeachable unless it can be held to have been procured by undue influence. It is the unimpeachability at law of a disadvantageous transaction which is the starting-point from which the court advances to consider whether the transaction is the product merely of one's own folly or of the undue influence exercised by another. A court in the exercise of this equitable jurisdiction is a court of conscience. Definition is a poor instrument when used to determine whether a transaction is or is not unconscionable: this is a question which depends upon the particular facts of the case.

NOTES

1. Both *Lloyds Bank* v *Bundy* and *National Westminster Bank* v *Morgan* are cases involving alleged undue influence by the other contracting party, i.e., the bank.
2. Lord Scarman rejected the 'confidentiality' factor which had been used by Sir Eric Sachs in *Lloyds Bank* v *Bundy* as determining whether the relationship had 'crossed the line'. Instead he favoured the test of whether the banker has acquired a 'dominating influence' over the customer. However, 'dominating influence' was rejected by the Court of Appeal in *Goldsworthy* v *Brickell* [1987] 1 All ER 853, where Nourse LJ stated that all that was required was a relationship of trust and confidence which had been ceded by the making of an improvident gift or transaction. This is clearly also the position accepted in *Etridge*; see *page 627*.
3. In *Avon Finance Co. Ltd* v *Bridger* [1985] 2 All ER 281 (*page 117*), the majority of the Court of Appeal (Brandon and Brightman LJJ) stressed the important factor was being in a position to influence. They held that the presumption of undue influence had arisen because the relationship between the son and his elderly parents was such that he could be expected to have had some influence over them and the finance company should have known this. The transaction was set aside for undue influence since it was of such a nature as to suggest that the son had abused his position of trust and no independent advice had been given to the parents.

    Lord Denning based his decision on the grounds of inequality of bargaining power and undue pressure. The son had exercised undue pressure as he had misled his parents concerning the nature of the document they were signing. As a result, the parents' bargaining power was impaired by their ignorance of the true situation.

■ QUESTIONS

1. Could *Lloyds Bank* v *Bundy* ('old Mr Bundy'), *Goldsworthy* v *Brickell* (where the plaintiff was 85) and *Avon Finance Co. Ltd* v *Bridger* have been based on the age of the victims in these cases? (See the discussion on inequality of bargaining power, at *page 667*.)
2. Could *Avon Finance* v *Bridger* have been decided on the basis of a misrepresentation? Would it have helped Mrs Morgan in *National Westminster Bank* v *Morgan* if the transaction had been set aside for misrepresentation?

R v *Attorney General of England and Wales*
[2003] UKPC 22, [2003] EMLR 24 (PC)

For facts and discussion of the duress argument, see *page 622*.

It was argued, in the alternative, that the confidentiality agreement was the product of undue influence. However, the Privy Council applied *Etridge* and concluded (Lord Scott dissenting) that there was no undue influence. The Privy Council stressed the contradiction between the duress argument (i.e. that the defendant had signed only because of a threat) on the one hand, and the argument in the context of the allegation of undue influence, that this was a relationship of trust and confidence between the Army (via the commanding officer) and the defendant soldier. In any event, it was necessary to establish that signing this agreement was suspicious in the light of the underlying relationship between the Army and the defendant. If so, that would be prima facie evidence of undue influence. However, by drawing an analogy between duress and undue influence, the Privy Council concluded that since the conduct was not illegitimate pressure for the purposes of duress, it must follow that the nature of the transaction did not amount to unfair exploitation of the parties' relationship. Lord Scott (dissenting) focused on the broader context of the relationship rather than any actions on the part of the Army and concluded that undue influence should therefore be presumed.

LORD HOFFMANN:

21 . . . Like duress at common law, undue influence is based upon the principle that a transaction to which consent has been obtained by unacceptable means should not be allowed to stand. Undue influence has concentrated in particular upon the unfair exploitation by one party of a relationship which gives him ascendancy or influence over the other.

22 The burden of proving that consent was obtained by unacceptable means is upon the party who alleges it. Certain relationships—parent and child, trustee and beneficiary, etc.—give rise to a presumption that one party had influence over the other. That does not of course in itself involve a presumption that he unfairly exploited his influence. But if the transaction is one which cannot reasonably be explained by the relationship, that will be prima facie evidence of undue influence. Even if the relationship does not fall into one of the established categories, the evidence may show that one party did in fact have influence over the other. In such a case, the nature of the transaction may likewise give rise to a prima facie inference that it was obtained by undue influence. In the absence of contrary evidence, the court will be entitled to find that the burden of proving unfair exploitation of the relationship has been discharged.

23 The absence of independent legal advice may or may not be a relevant matter according to the circumstances. It is not necessarily an unfair exploitation of a relationship for one party to enter into a transaction with the other without ensuring that he has obtained independent legal advice. On the other hand, the transaction may be such as to give rise to an inference of undue influence even if the induced party was advised by an independent lawyer and understood the legal implications of what he was doing.

24 In the present case it is said that the military hierarchy, the strong regimental pride which R shared and his personal admiration for his commanding officer created a relationship in which the Army as an institution or the commanding officer as an individual were able to exercise influence over him. Their Lordships are content to assume that this was the case. But the question is whether the nature of the transaction was such as to give rise to an inference that it was obtained by an unfair exploitation of that relationship. Like the Court of Appeal, their Lordships do not think that the confidentiality agreement can be so described. As in the case of duress, their Lordships think that the finding that it was an agreement which anyone who wished to serve or continue serving in the SAS could reasonably have been required to sign is fatal to such a conclusion. The reason why R signed the agreement was because, at the time, he wished to continue to be a member of the SAS. If facing him with such a choice was not illegitimate for the purposes of duress, their Lordships do not think that it could have been an unfair exploitation of a relationship which consisted in his being a member of the SAS. There seems to their Lordships to be some degree of contradiction between R's claim, in the context of duress, that he signed only because he was threatened with return to his unit and his claim, for the purposes of undue influence, that he signed because of the trust and confidence which he reposed in the Army or his commanding officer.

25 The question which has troubled their Lordships is the absence of legal advice.

. . .

27 The legal question, however, is whether failing to provide an opportunity for obtaining legal advice made the transaction one in which the MOD had unfairly exploited its influence over R. Here it is important to note that R does not allege that he did not understand the implications of what he was being asked to do. The contract was in simple terms and the explanatory memorandum even plainer. He does say that he had originally thought that it would only prevent publication of matter which remained confidential. However, a moment's thought would have told him that this would not have prevented the publications to which he and other members of the SAS most objected, namely *The One That Got Away* and the film which followed. In any case, when he saw the actual contract he knew what it meant.

28 In these circumstances, their Lordships do not think that the absence of legal advice affected the fairness of the transaction. The most that R can say is that a lawyer might have advised him to reflect upon the matter and, as in fact he changed his mind within a fairly short time after signing, that might have led to his not signing at all. But that is a decision which he could have made without a lawyer's advice.

NOTE: Lord Hoffmann clarified the effect of *Etridge* on cases of presumed undue influence. In addition, he discussed the nature of undue influence. Whereas it is clear that actual undue influence involves the commission of a wrong, cases of presumed undue influence are more problematical and some courts have denied that there is any requirement to establish a 'wrong' where the undue influence is presumed. For example, in *Macklin* v *Dowsett* [2004] EWCA Civ 904, [2004] 2 EGLR 75, the Court of Appeal rejected any notion that it was necessary to establish any misconduct. Lord Hoffmann made it clear that undue influence is based on the conduct of the defendant. It would seem that in the context of presumed undue influence the 'wrong' is taking advantage of the position to prefer one's own interests whilst not ensuring that the other party was exercising a free and informed choice in agreeing to the transaction. In *National Commercial Bank (Jamaica) Ltd* v *Hew* [2003] UKPC 51, Lord Millett refers to the party in the position of influence acting 'unconscionably by exploiting the influence to direct the conduct of another' and to abuse of influence and the taking of unfair advantage. This position can also be seen quite clearly in *Lloyds Bank* v *Bundy* where the Court of Appeal stressed that it is not the case that the party concerned has to set out to deceive the other and in *Hammond* v *Osborn* [2002] EWCA Civ 885, [2002] WTLR 1125, where the Court of Appeal considered that a defendant could not avoid a finding of undue influence by establishing an absence of wrongdoing on her part, i.e. that her conduct had been unimpeachable.

Rebutting the presumption of undue influence

Thus, absence of bad faith will not be sufficient to rebut the presumption of undue influence. The case law establishes that consent needs to be 'full, free and informed' and therefore the obvious way to rebut the presumption might be to point to the fact that independent legal advice has been given. However in *R* v *Attorney General of England and Wales* the Privy Council indicated that the existence of independent legal advice may or may not be a factor. Despite this position, it was treated as the pivotal factor in *Hammond* v *Osborn* [2002] EWCA Civ 885, [2002] WLR 1125 (and also in *Randall* v *Randall* [2004] EWHC 2258 (Ch), following *Hammond* v *Osborn*). In *Hammond* v *Osborn* an elderly donor had made a number of sizeable gifts (nearly £300,000) to the defendant who was his neighbour and had been taking care of him when his health began to decline. These gifts represented over 90 per cent of the donor's liquid assets and exposed him to a considerable tax liability. A relationship of trust and confidence was shown to exist on the facts and there was clearly something suspicious about gifts of this size in these circumstances. The defendant had not been able to rebut this presumption since the donor had received no advice concerning the wisdom of his actions and the implications. Therefore the gifts could not be the result of full, free, and informed thought.

It seems that any such advice would need to be quite detailed and would need to include advice concerning the nature of the transaction and its potential implications. Thus it will be extremely difficult to rebut the evidential presumption of undue influence although this may be no bad thing since a rigorous requirement to rebut the presumption will not only protect donors after the event but, hopefully, improve the nature and quality of the advice given so that imprudent transactions might be avoided.

D: Undue influence exercised by a third party

Can a transaction be set aside on the ground that undue influence was exercised by a third party? For example, a wife gives a guarantee and charge over the matrimonial home to a bank and wishes to have that contract with the bank set aside on the basis that she entered into the contract only because of her husband's undue influence.

(i) Pre-Etridge law
The courts traditionally laid down very limited circumstances when such a transaction could be set aside. It first needed to be established that there was either actual undue influence by the husband, or that the presumption could be shown to arise on the facts (class 2B). (Husband and wife is not a class 2A case: *Bank of Montreal v Stuart* [1911] AC 120.)

In *Bank of Credit and Commerce International SA v Aboody* [1990] 1 QB 923 (*obiter*), Slade LJ explained the additional requirements before the bank could be affected by Mr Aboody's undue influence over his wife and the transaction set aside as against the bank:

There are two distinct grounds on which the bank could be affected by Mr Aboody's action: (i) agency; and (ii) notice; although in some of the authorities cited to us these two grounds appear to have become mixed.

(i) *Agency*
Some confusion may have been caused by the use of the word 'agent'. We are not concerned here with the question as to whether or not the bank is vicariously responsible for the acts of Mr Aboody. The issue is whether the bank can be in any better position than Mr Aboody if, when Mr Aboody was acting on its behalf, Mr Aboody exerted (or, if this had been a class 2 case, was presumed to have exerted) undue influence. As we have made clear . . ., the undue influence is required to have brought about the transaction, and it would be inconsistent with the equitable nature of the relief for the bank not to be affected by the undue influence exerted by its agent when the transaction would not exist but for the wrongful acts of its agent. As a matter of principle, the bank in such circumstances should not be entitled to rely on the transaction and this is the view which has been taken by a series of authorities going back to the beginning of this century. The clearest statement of the principle, which we would adopt, is to be found in the judgment of Dillon LJ in *Kings North Trust Ltd v Bell* [1986] 1 WLR 119, 123:

> if a creditor, or potential creditor, of a husband desires to obtain, by way of security for the husband's indebtedness, a guarantee from his wife or a charge on property of his wife and if the creditor entrusts to the husband himself the task of obtaining the execution of the relevant document by the wife, then the creditor can be in no better position than the husband himself, and the creditor cannot enforce the guarantee or the security against the wife if it is established that the execution of the document by the wife was procured by undue influence by the husband and the wife had no independent advice. . . .

(ii) Notice

If a creditor has actual or constructive notice, at the time of the execution of the charge or guarantee in question, that the guarantee or charge on which it relies has been procured by the exercise of undue influence, it cannot enforce the transaction; an equity is raised against the creditor irrespective of any question of agency. Examples of the application of this principle are to be found in *Kempson* v *Ashbee* (1874) LR 10 Ch App 15 and *Bainbrigge* v *Browne* (1881) 18 ChD 188. In the former case James LJ said, at p. 21:

> The first question, therefore, is, whether the bond of 1859 was obtained by the undue exercise of influence of the stepfather, and was it obtained under such exercise as that the knowledge of it can be imputed to [the creditor]?

What notice will be requisite will depend on the nature of the undue influence alleged. Thus, in a class 1 case (actual undue influence), the creditor must have notice of the circumstances alleged to constitute the actual exercise of the undue influence; in a class 2 case it must have notice of the circumstances from which the presumption of undue influence is alleged to arise.

In *Avon Finance Co. Ltd* v *Bridger* [1985] 2 All ER 281 the majority of the court (Brandon and Brightman LJJ) decided the case on a combination of the two grounds of agency and constructive notice.

NOTE: On the facts in *Aboody* there was no evidence that the bank had entrusted Mr Aboody with obtaining his wife's signature so as to have appointed him agent for the bank. However, the solicitor appointed and paid by the bank to give Mrs Aboody advice had witnessed the actual undue influence by the husband, and the Court of Appeal therefore considered that the solicitor's knowledge was to be imputed to his client, the bank.

Barclays Bank plc v O'Brien
[1994] 1 AC 180 (HL)

Mr O'Brien was a shareholder in a company and arranged an overdraft for the company with the company's bank on the basis that Mr O'Brien would guarantee the company's indebtedness and that it would be secured by a second charge over the matrimonial home which was jointly owned by husband and wife. Although the bank manager gave instructions that both husband and wife should be made aware of the nature and effect of the documents they were signing and should be advised to take independent advice, the bank staff had not followed those instructions. Mrs O'Brien had signed the charge document at the bank without reading it. When the company's indebtedness exceeded the agreed overdraft the bank brought proceedings to enforce the guarantee. Mrs O'Brien claimed that she had signed because of her husband's undue influence and that he had misrepresented the nature of the document so that she thought she was signing a charge up to only £60,000 to last only three weeks, when in fact the charge covered £135,000. The Court of Appeal ([1993] QB 109) held the husband had not exercised undue influence, but that as a matter of policy married women providing security for their husband's debts were to be treated as a specially protected class of surety so that the transaction could be set aside as against the bank even if it had no knowledge of any undue influence or misrepresentation and had not appointed the husband as its agent. Since the relationship giving rise to a likelihood of influence was known to the bank, the bank had a duty to take reasonable steps to ensure that the married woman understood the nature and effect of the transaction and that the consent given was true and informed. The bank had failed in that duty so that the charge was not enforceable beyond £60,000. Held: on appeal their Lordships affirmed the decision of the Court of Appeal but on other grounds.

LORD BROWNE-WILKINSON:

Undue influence, misrepresentation and third parties

Up to this point I have been considering the right of a claimant wife to set aside a transaction as against the wrongdoing husband when the transaction has been procured by his undue influence. But in surety cases the decisive question is whether the claimant wife can set aside the transaction, not against the wrongdoing husband, but against the creditor bank. Of course, if the wrongdoing husband is acting as agent for the creditor bank in obtaining the surety from the wife, the creditor will be fixed with the wrongdoing of its own agent and the surety contract can be set aside as against the creditor. Apart from this, if the creditor bank has notice, actual or constructive, of the undue influence exercised by the husband (and consequentially of the wife's equity to set aside the transaction) the creditor will take subject to that equity and the wife can set aside the transaction against the creditor (albeit a purchaser for value) as well as against the husband: see *Bainbrigge* v *Browne* (1881) 18 ChD 188 and *BCCI* v *Aboody* [1990] 1 QB 923, 973. Similarly, in cases such as the present where the wife has been induced to enter into the transaction by the husband's misrepresentation, her equity to set aside the transaction will be enforceable against the creditor if either the husband was acting as the creditor's agent or the creditor had actual or constructive notice.

. . . In my judgment your Lordships should seek to restate the law in a form which is principled, reflects the current requirements of society and provides as much certainty as possible.

Conclusions

(a) Wives

My starting point is to clarify the basis of the law. Should wives (and perhaps others) be accorded special rights in relation to surety transactions by the recognition of a special equity applicable only to such persons engaged in such transactions? Or should they enjoy only the same protection as they would enjoy in relation to their other dealings? In my judgment, the special equity theory should be rejected. First, I can find no basis in principle for affording special protection to a limited class in relation to one type of transaction only. Second, to require the creditor to prove knowledge and understanding by the wife in all cases is to reintroduce by the back door either a presumption of undue influence of Class 2(A) (which has been decisively rejected) or the Romilly heresy (which has long been treated as bad law). Third, although Scott LJ found that there were two lines of cases one of which supported the special equity theory, on analysis although many decisions are not inconsistent with that theory the only two cases which support it are *Yerkey* v *Jones* (1940) 63 CLR 649 and the decision of the Court of Appeal in the present case. Finally, it is not necessary to have recourse to a special equity theory for the proper protection of the legitimate interests of wives as I will seek to show.

In my judgment, if the doctrine of notice is properly applied, there is no need for the introduction of a special equity in these types of cases. A wife who has been induced to stand as a surety for her husband's debts by his undue influence, misrepresentation or some other legal wrong has an equity as against him to set aside that transaction. Under the ordinary principles of equity, her right to set aside that transaction will be enforceable against third parties (e.g. against a creditor) if either the husband was acting as the third party's agent or the third party had actual or constructive notice of the facts giving rise to her equity. Although there may be cases where, without artificiality, it can properly be held that the husband was acting as the agent of the creditor in procuring the wife to stand as surety, such cases will be of very rare occurrence. The key to the problem is to identify the circumstances in which the creditor will be taken to have had notice of the wife's equity to set aside the transaction.

The doctrine of notice lies at the heart of equity. Given that there are two innocent parties, each enjoying rights, the earlier right prevails against the later right if the acquirer of the later right knows of the earlier right (actual notice) or would have discovered it had he taken proper steps (constructive notice). In particular, if the party asserting that he takes free of the earlier rights of another knows of certain facts which put him on inquiry as to the possible existence of the rights of that other and he fails to make such inquiry or take such other steps as are reasonable to verify whether such earlier right does or does not exist, he will have constructive notice of the earlier right and take subject to it. Therefore where a wife has agreed to stand surety for her husband's debts as a result of undue influence or misrepresentation, the creditor will take subject to the wife's equity to set aside the transaction if the circumstances are such as to put the creditor on inquiry as to the circumstances in which she agreed to stand surety.

It is at this stage that, in my view, the 'invalidating tendency' or the law's 'tender treatment' of married women, becomes relevant. As I have said above in dealing with undue influence, this tenderness of the law towards married women is due to the fact that, even today, many wives repose confidence and trust in their husbands in relation to their financial affairs. This tenderness of the law is reflected by the fact that voluntary dispositions by the wife in favour of her husband are more likely to be set aside than other dispositions by her: a wife is more likely to establish presumed undue influence of Class 2(B) by her husband than by others because, in practice, many wives do repose in their husbands trust and confidence in relation to their financial affairs. Moreover the informality of business dealings between spouses raises a substantial risk that the husband has not accurately stated to the wife the nature of the liability she is undertaking, i.e. he has misrepresented the position, albeit negligently.

Therefore, in my judgment a creditor is put on inquiry when a wife offers to stand surety for her husband's debts by the combination of two factors: (a) the transaction is on its face not to the financial advantage of the wife; and (b) there is a substantial risk in transactions of that kind that, in procuring the wife to act as surety, the husband has committed a legal or equitable wrong that entitles the wife to set aside the transaction.

It follows that, unless the creditor who is put on inquiry takes reasonable steps to satisfy himself that the wife's agreement to stand surety has been properly obtained, the creditor will have constructive notice of the wife's rights.

What, then are the reasonable steps which the creditor should take to ensure that it does not have constructive notice of the wife's rights, if any? Normally the reasonable steps necessary to avoid being fixed with constructive notice consist of making inquiry of the person who may have the earlier right (i.e. the wife) to see whether such right is asserted. It is plainly impossible to require of banks and other financial institutions that they should inquire of one spouse whether he or she has been unduly influenced or misled by the other. But in my judgment the creditor, in order to avoid being fixed with constructive notice, can reasonably be expected to take steps to bring home to the wife the risk she is running by standing as surety and to advise her to take independent advice. As to past transactions, it will depend on the facts of each case whether the steps taken by the creditor satisfy this test. However for the future in my judgment a creditor will have satisfied these requirements if it insists that the wife attend a private meeting (in the absence of the husband) with a representative of the creditor at which she is told of the extent of her liability as surety, warned of the risk she is running and urged to take independent legal advice. If these steps are taken in my judgment the creditor will have taken such reasonable steps as are necessary to preclude a subsequent claim that it had constructive notice of the wife's rights. I should make it clear that I have been considering the ordinary case where the creditor knows only that the wife is to stand surety for her husband's debts. I would not exclude exceptional cases where a creditor has knowledge of further facts which render the presence of undue influence not only possible but probable. In such cases, the creditor to be safe will have to insist that the wife is separately advised.

I am conscious that in treating the creditor as having constructive notice because of the risk of Class 2(B) undue influence or misrepresentation by the husband I may be extending the law as stated by Fry J in *Bainbrigge* v *Browne* (1881) 18 ChD 188 at 197 and the Court of Appeal in the *Aboody* case [1990] 1 QB 923, 973. Those cases suggest that for a third party to be affected by constructive notice of presumed undue influence the third party must actually know of the circumstances which give rise to a presumption of undue influence. In contrast, my view is that the risk of Class 2(B) undue influence or misrepresentation is sufficient to put the creditor on inquiry. But my statement accords with the principles of notice: if the known facts are such as to indicate the possibility of an adverse claim that is sufficient to put a third party on inquiry.

If the law is established as I have suggested, it will hold the balance fairly between on the one hand the vulnerability of the wife who relies implicitly on her husband and, on the other hand, the practical problems of financial institutions asked to accept a secured or unsecured surety obligation from the wife for her husband's debts. In the context of suretyship, the wife will not have any right to disown her obligations just because subsequently she proves that she did not fully understand the transaction: she will, as in all other areas of her affairs, be bound by her obligations unless her husband has, by misrepresentation, undue influence or other wrong, committed an actionable wrong against her. In the normal case, a financial institution will be able to lend with confidence in reliance on the wife's surety obligation provided that it warns her (in the absence of the husband) of the amount of her potential liability and of the risk of standing surety and advises her to take independent advice. . . .

(b) *Other persons*

I have hitherto dealt only with the position where a wife stands surety for her husband's debts. But in my judgment the same principles are applicable to all other cases where there is an emotional relationship between cohabitees. The 'tenderness' shown by the law to married women is not based on the marriage ceremony but reflects the underlying risk of one cohabitee exploiting the emotional involvement and trust of the other. Now that unmarried cohabitation, whether heterosexual or homosexual, is widespread in our society, the law should recognise this. Legal wives are not the only group which are now exposed to the emotional pressure of cohabitation. Therefore if, but only if, the creditor is aware that the surety is cohabiting with the principal debtor, in my judgment the same principles should apply to them as apply to husband and wife.

In addition to the cases of cohabitees, the decision of the Court of Appeal in *Avon Finance Co. Ltd v Bridger* [1985] 2 All ER 281 shows (rightly in my view) that other relationships can give rise to a similar result. In that case a son, by means of misrepresentation, persuaded his elderly parents to stand surety for his debts. The surety obligation was held to be unenforceable by the creditor inter alia because to the bank's knowledge the parents trusted the son in their financial dealings. In my judgment that case was rightly decided: in a case where the creditor is aware that the surety reposes trust and confidence in the principal debtor in relation to his financial affairs, the creditor is put on inquiry in just the same way as it is in relation to husband and wife.

Summary

I can therefore summarise my views as follows. Where one cohabitee has entered into an obligation to stand as surety for the debts of the other cohabitee and the creditor is aware that they are cohabitees: (1) the surety obligation will be valid and enforceable by the creditor unless the suretyship was procured by the undue influence, misrepresentation or other legal wrong of the principal debtor; (2) if there has been undue influence, misrepresentation or other legal wrong by the principal debtor, unless the creditor has taken reasonable steps to satisfy himself that the surety entered into the obligation freely and in knowledge of the true facts, the creditor will be unable to enforce the surety obligation because he will be fixed with constructive notice of the surety's right to set aside the transaction; (3) unless there are special exceptional circumstances, a creditor will have taken such reasonable steps to avoid being fixed with constructive notice if the creditor warns the surety (at a meeting not attended by the principal debtor) of the amount of her potential liability and of the risks involved and advises the surety to take independent legal advice.

I should make it clear that in referring to the husband's debts I include the debts of a company in which the husband (but not the wife) has a direct financial interest.

The decision of this case

Applying those principles to this case, to the knowledge of the bank Mr and Mrs O'Brien were man and wife. The bank took a surety obligation from Mrs O'Brien, secured on the matrimonial home, to secure the debts of a company in which Mr O'Brien was interested but in which Mrs O'Brien had no direct pecuniary interest. The bank should therefore have been put on inquiry as to the circumstances in which Mrs O'Brien had agreed to stand as surety for the debt of her husband. If the Burnham branch had properly carried out the instructions from Mr Tucker of the Woolwich branch, Mrs O'Brien would have been informed that she and the matrimonial home were potentially liable for the debts of a company which had an existing liability of £107,000 and which was to be afforded an overdraft facility of £135,000. If she had been told this, it would have counteracted Mr O'Brien's misrepresentation that the liability was limited to £60,000 and would last for only three weeks. In addition according to the side letter she would have been recommended to take independent legal advice.

Unfortunately Mr Tucker's instructions were not followed and to the knowledge of the bank (through the clerk at the Burnham branch) Mrs O'Brien signed the documents without any warning of the risks or any recommendation to take legal advice. In the circumstances the bank (having failed to take reasonable steps) is fixed with constructive notice of the wrongful misrepresentation made by Mr O'Brien to Mrs O'Brien. Mrs O'Brien is therefore entitled as against the bank to set aside the legal charge on the matrimonial home securing her husband's liability to the bank.

NOTES

1. The decision of the Court of Appeal had been interpreted as suggesting that a married woman could avoid such a contract as against the bank simply by stating that she did not understand the nature and effect of what she had signed and that the bank had failed in its duty to advise her.

2. Lord Browne-Wilkinson stressed the policy considerations and the need to balance the desire to protect married women against losing their homes with the need to ensure that banks would be prepared to lend money on the security of a jointly owned home. The banks required some guidance on the steps they needed to take in order to protect themselves against the risk of losing their security because of the undue influence of a third party. This guidance was proved first by the House of Lords in *O'Brien* and was subsequently revised by the House of Lords in *Etridge* [2001] UKHL 44, [2002] 2 AC 773, *page 649*.

3. The House of Lords made it clear that there must first be a legal wrong, i.e. undue influence (actual or presumed) or misrepresentation by the third party. (*Banco Exterior Internacional SA v Thomas* [1997] 1 All ER 46, is an example of a case where there was no legal wrong and *O'Brien* did not apply.) The question of whether the bank would be affected by that wrong would in practice turn on the question of the bank's notice of that influence, actual or constructive. The bank dealing with a wife or other cohabitee would be put on inquiry because of the likelihood of undue influence resulting from the relationship of trust and confidence, where the transaction was not of obvious financial advantage to that party. The bank would then come under a duty to take the reasonable steps specified, and if it failed to do so would be affected by constructive notice of the third party's undue influence.

4. In *CIBC Mortgages plc* v *Pitt* [1994] 1 AC 200, the House of Lords applied these principles but concluded that the lender was not affected by constructive notice of the third party's undue influence.

   The husband had influenced his wife into agreeing to let him borrow money on the security of the matrimonial home in order to buy shares on the stock market. However, on the joint application form for a loan they had both expressed the loan to be for the purpose of paying off the outstanding mortgage and using the balance to purchase a holiday home. The wife did not read the relevant documents, did not know the amount being borrowed and did not receive any advice about the transaction. The husband used the money to speculate but when he became unable to repay the mortgage payments the lender sought possession of the matrimonial home. Held:

   > . . . Applying the decision of this House in *O'Brien*, Mrs Pitt has established actual undue influence by Mr Pitt. The plaintiff will not however be affected by such undue influence unless Mr Pitt was, in a real sense, acting as agent of the plaintiff in procuring Mrs Pitt's agreement or the plaintiff had actual or constructive notice of the undue influence. The judge has correctly held that Mr Pitt was not acting as agent for the plaintiff. The plaintiff had no actual notice of the undue influence. What, then, was known to the plaintiff that could put it on inquiry so as to fix it with constructive notice?
   >
   > So far as the plaintiff was aware, the transaction consisted of a joint loan to husband and wife to finance the discharge of an existing mortgage on 26 Alexander Avenue and, as to the balance, to be applied in buying a holiday home. The loan was advanced to both husband and wife jointly. There was nothing to indicate to the plaintiff that this was anything other than a normal advance to husband and wife for their joint benefit.
   >
   > [Counsel] for Mrs Pitt argued that the invalidating tendency which reflects the risk of there being class 2B undue influence was, in itself, sufficient to put the plaintiff on inquiry.

I reject this submission without hesitation. It accords neither with justice nor with practical common sense. If third parties were to be fixed with constructive notice of undue influence in relation to every transaction between husband and wife, such transactions would become almost impossible. On every purchase of a home in joint names, the building society or bank financing the purchase would have to insist on meeting the wife separately from her husband, advise her as to the nature of the transaction and recommend her to take legal advice separate from that of her husband. If that were not done, the financial institution would have to run the risk of a subsequent attempt by the wife to avoid her liabilities under the mortgage on the grounds of undue influence or misrepresentation. To establish the law in that sense would not benefit the average married couple and would discourage financial institutions from making the advance.

What distinguishes the case of the joint advance from the surety case is that, in the latter, there is not only the possibility of undue influence having been exercised but also the increased risk of it having in fact been exercised because, at least on its face, the guarantee by a wife of her husband's debts is not for her financial benefit. It is the combination of these two factors that puts the creditor on inquiry.

The husband had clearly exercised undue influence over the wife in relation to completion of the mortgage application form, but the decision in *O'Brien* makes it clear that, where the bank has no actual knowledge, it need not specifically inquire of the wife whether she was the victim of undue influence and can rely on what is stated in an application form.

5. In *Royal Bank of Scotland plc* v *Etridge (No. 2)* [2001] UKHL 44, [2002] 2 AC 773, Lord Nicholl, at [19] and [30]–[31], extract, *pages 627–8*, recognised that a wife might have a variety of motives for 'conferring substantial financial benefits' on her husband and entering into guarantee transactions which might not appear wholly or even partly for her benefit. There could be no blanket assumption of undue influence in such cases. It might be relatively easy to establish trust and confidence in the context of a relationship of husband and wife. However, it was still necessary to establish that a wrong had occurred, i.e., that the husband had abused his position and taken advantage of the trust placed in him. Thus, the notice question would be irrelevant if the husband's undue influence cannot be *presumed*.

6. In *O'Brien* Lord Browne-Wilkinson referred to other relationships (falling short of cohabitation) where the lender is put on inquiry because of its knowledge of the circumstances. In *Credit Lyonnais Bank Nederland BV* v *Burch* [1997] 1 All ER 144 the surety was a junior employee in a company and had done some baby-sitting and was a family friend of the plaintiff, the main shareholder in that company. The defendant had agreed to the plaintiff's request that she should give a second charge over her flat to secure the unlimited liabilities of the plaintiff's company although she had no financial interest in the company. The Court of Appeal held that the bank had notice of facts from which a relationship of trust and confidence could be inferred (i.e. notice of the relationship of employer and employee) and should have realised that there was a real risk that undue influence had occurred. Despite this, the bank had failed to follow the necessary steps and was therefore fixed with constructive notice of the plaintiff's undue influence. Millett LJ described it as 'an extreme case' and one which 'shocks the conscience of the court'. If anything, the absence of cohabitation or a sexual relationship between the parties made the transaction more inexplicable since there were no obvious indirect benefits to the junior employee in entering into the surety transaction, whereas a wife or partner might consider that the family's livelihood required that the family home be put at risk.

7. The wife (or other surety) has the burden of pleading and proving that the lender had the necessary constructive notice of the undue influence (*Barclays Bank plc* v *Boulter* [1999] 1 WLR 1919 (HL)).

(ii) The position post-Etridge

In *Royal Bank of Scotland plc* v *Etridge (No. 2)* [2001] UKHL 44, [2002] 2 AC 773, the House of Lords reformulated the principles applicable to surety transactions, i.e., the situation where the party alleging undue influence is seeking to have the transaction set aside against a third party. In so doing, their Lordships explained the context for the development of legal principles and the need to balance the interests of the lenders and those giving security.

LORD BINGHAM: . . .

2   The transactions which give rise to these appeals are commonplace but of great social and economic importance. It is important that a wife (or anyone in a like position) should not charge her interest in the matrimonial home to secure the borrowing of her husband (or anyone in a like position) without fully understanding the nature and effect of the proposed transaction and that the decision is hers, to agree or not to agree. It is important that lenders should feel able to advance money, in run-of-the-mill cases with no abnormal features, on the security of the wife's interest in the matrimonial home in reasonable confidence that, if appropriate procedures have been followed in obtaining the security, it will be enforceable if the need for enforcement arises. The law must afford both parties a measure of protection. It cannot prescribe a code which will be proof against error, misunderstanding or mishap. But it can indicate minimum requirements which, if met, will reduce the risk of error, misunderstanding or mishap to an acceptable level. The paramount need in this important field is that these minimum requirements should be clear, simple and practically operable.

LORD NICHOLLS:

The complainant and third parties: suretyship transactions

34   The problem considered in *O'Brien's* case and raised by the present appeals is of comparatively recent origin. It arises out of the substantial growth in home ownership over the last 30 or 40 years and, as part of that development, the great increase in the number of homes owned jointly by husbands and wives. More than two-thirds of householders in the United Kingdom now own their own homes. For most home-owning couples, their homes are their most valuable asset. They must surely be free, if they so wish, to use this asset as a means of raising money, whether for the purpose of the husband's business or for any other purpose. Their home is their property. The law should not restrict them in the use they may make of it. Bank finance is in fact by far the most important source of external capital for small businesses with fewer than ten employees. These businesses comprise about 95% of all businesses in the country, responsible for nearly one-third of all employment. Finance raised by second mortgages on the principal's home is a significant source of capital for the start-up of small businesses.

35   If the freedom of home-owners to make economic use of their homes is not to be frustrated, a bank must be able to have confidence that a wife's signature of the necessary guarantee and charge will be as binding upon her as is the signature of anyone else on documents which he or she may sign. Otherwise banks will not be willing to lend money on the security of a jointly owned house or flat.

36   At the same time, the high degree of trust and confidence and emotional interdependence which normally characterises a marriage relationship provides scope for abuse. One party may take advantage of the other's vulnerability. Unhappily, such abuse does occur. Further, it is all too easy for a husband, anxious or even desperate for bank finance, to misstate the position in some particular or to mislead the wife, wittingly or unwittingly, in some other way. The law would be seriously defective if it did not recognise these realities.

37   In *O'Brien's* case this House decided where the balance should be held between these competing interests. On the one side, there is the need to protect a wife against a husband's undue influence. On the other side, there is the need for the bank to be able to have reasonable confidence in the strength of its security. Otherwise it would not provide the required money. The problem lies in finding the course best designed to protect wives in a minority of cases without unreasonably hampering the giving and taking of security. The House produced a practical solution. The House decided what are the steps a bank should take to ensure it is not affected by any claim the wife may have that her signature of the documents was procured by the undue influence or other wrong of her husband. Like every compromise, the outcome falls short of achieving in full the objectives of either of the two competing interests. In particular, the steps required of banks will not guarantee

that, in future, wives will not be subjected to undue influence or misled when standing as sureties. Short of prohibiting this type of suretyship transaction altogether, there is no way of achieving that result, desirable although it is. What passes between a husband and wife in this regard in the privacy of their own home is not capable of regulation or investigation as a prelude to the wife entering into a suretyship transaction.

38   The jurisprudential route by which the House reached its conclusion in *O'Brien's* case has attracted criticism from some commentators. It has been said to involve artificiality and thereby create uncertainty in the law. I must first consider this criticism. In the ordinary course a bank which takes a guarantee security from the wife of its customer will be altogether ignorant of any undue influence the customer may have exercised in order to secure the wife's concurrence. In *O'Brien* Lord Browne-Wilkinson prayed in aid the doctrine of constructive notice. In circumstances he identified, a creditor is put on inquiry. When that is so, the creditor 'will have constructive notice of the wife's rights' unless the creditor takes reasonable steps to satisfy himself that the wife's agreement to stand surety has been properly obtained: see [1994] 1 AC 180, 196.

39   Lord Browne-Wilkinson would be the first to recognise this is not a conventional use of the equitable concept of constructive notice. The traditional use of this concept concerns the circumstances in which a transferee of property who acquires a legal estate from a transferor with a defective title may nonetheless obtain a good title, that is, a better title than the transferor had. That is not the present case. The bank acquires its charge from the wife, and there is nothing wrong with her title to her share of the matrimonial home. The transferor wife is seeking to resile from the very transaction she entered into with the bank, on the ground that her apparent consent was procured by the undue influence or other misconduct, such as misrepresentation, of a third party (her husband). She is seeking to set aside her contract of guarantee and, with it, the charge she gave to the bank.

40   The traditional view of equity in this tripartite situation seems to be that a person in the position of the wife will only be relieved of her bargain if the other party to the transaction (the bank, in the present instance) was privy to the conduct which led to the wife's entry into the transaction. Knowledge is required: see *Cobbett v Brock* (1855) 20 Beav 524, 528, 531, per Sir John Romilly MR, *Kempson v Ashbee* (1874) LR 10 Ch App 15, 21, per James LJ, and *Bainbrigge v Browne* 18 Ch D 188, 197, per Fry J. The law imposes no obligation on one party to a transaction to check whether the other party's concurrence was obtained by undue influence. But *O'Brien* has introduced into the law the concept that, in certain circumstances, a party to a contract may lose the benefit of his contract, entered into in good faith, if he ought to have known that the other's concurrence had been procured by the misconduct of a third party.

41   There is a further respect in which *O'Brien* departed from conventional concepts. Traditionally, a person is deemed to have notice (that is, he has 'constructive' notice) of a prior right when he does not actually know of it but would have learned of it had he made the requisite inquiries. A purchaser will be treated as having constructive notice of all that a reasonably prudent purchaser would have discovered. In the present type of case, the steps a bank is required to take, lest it have constructive notice that the wife's concurrence was procured improperly by her husband, do not consist of making inquiries. Rather, *O'Brien* envisages that the steps taken by the bank will reduce, or even eliminate, the risk of the wife entering into the transaction under any misapprehension or as a result of undue influence by her husband. The steps are not concerned to discover whether the wife has been wronged by her husband in this way. The steps are concerned to minimise the risk that such a wrong may be committed.

42   These novelties do not point to the conclusion that the decision of this House in *O'Brien* is leading the law astray. Lord Browne-Wilkinson acknowledged he might be extending the law: see [1994] 1 AC 180, 197. Some development was sorely needed. The law had to find a way of giving wives a reasonable measure of protection, without adding unreasonably to the expense involved in entering into guarantee transactions of the type under consideration. The protection had to extend also to any misrepresentations made by a husband to his wife. In a situation where there is a substantial risk the husband may exercise his influence improperly regarding the provision of security for his business debts, there is an increased risk that explanations of the transaction given by him to his wife may be misleadingly incomplete or even inaccurate.

43 The route selected in *O'Brien* ought not to have an unsettling effect on established principles of contract. *O'Brien* concerned suretyship transactions. These are tripartite transactions. They involve the debtor as well as the creditor and the guarantor. The guarantor enters into the transaction at the request of the debtor. The guarantor assumes obligations. On the face of the transaction the guarantor usually receives no benefit in return, unless the guarantee is being given on a commercial basis. Leaving aside cases where the relationship between the surety and the debtor is commercial, a guarantee transaction is one-sided so far as the guarantor is concerned. The creditor knows this. Thus the decision in *O'Brien* is directed at a class of contracts which has special features of its own. That said, I must at a later stage in this speech return to the question of the wider implications of the *O'Brien* decision.

The threshold: when the bank is put on inquiry

44 In *O'Brien* the House considered the circumstances in which a bank, or other creditor, is 'put on inquiry'. Strictly this is a misnomer. As already noted, a bank is not required to make inquiries. But it will be convenient to use the terminology which has now become accepted in this context. The House set a low level for the threshold which must be crossed before a bank is put on inquiry. For practical reasons the level is set much lower than is required to satisfy a court that, failing contrary evidence, the court may infer that the transaction was procured by undue influence. Lord Browne-Wilkinson said [1994] 1 AC 180, 196:

'Therefore in my judgment a creditor is put on inquiry when a wife offers to stand surety for her husband's debts by the combination of two factors: (a) the transaction is on its face not to the financial advantage of the wife; and (b) there is a substantial risk in transactions of that kind that, in procuring the wife to act as surety, the husband has committed a legal or equitable wrong that entitles the wife to set aside the transaction.'

In my view, this passage, read in context, is to be taken to mean, quite simply, that a bank is put on inquiry whenever a wife offers to stand surety for her husband's debts.

45 The Court of Appeal, comprising Stuart-Smith, Millett and Morritt LJJ, interpreted this passage more restrictively. The threshold, the court said, is somewhat higher. Where condition (a) is satisfied, the bank is put on inquiry if, but only if, the bank is aware that the parties are cohabiting or that the particular surety places implicit trust and confidence in the principal debtor in relation to her financial affairs: see *Royal Bank of Scotland plc* v *Etridge (No. 2)* [1998] 4 All ER 705, 719.

46 I respectfully disagree. I do not read (a) and (b) as factual conditions which must be proved in each case before a bank is put on inquiry. I do not understand Lord Browne-Wilkinson to have been saying that, in husband and wife cases, whether the bank is put on inquiry depends on its state of knowledge of the parties' marriage, or of the degree of trust and confidence the particular wife places in her husband in relation to her financial affairs. That would leave banks in a state of considerable uncertainty in a situation where it is important they should know clearly where they stand. The test should be simple and clear and easy to apply in a wide range of circumstances. I read (a) and (b) as Lord Browne-Wilkinson's broad explanation of the reason why a creditor is put on inquiry when a wife offers to stand surety for her husband's debts. These are the two factors which, taken together, constitute the underlying rationale.

47 The position is likewise if the husband stands surety for his wife's debts. Similarly, in the case of unmarried couples, whether heterosexual or homosexual, where the bank is aware of the relationship: see Lord Browne-Wilkinson in *O'Brien's* case, at p 198. Cohabitation is not essential. The Court of Appeal rightly so decided in *Massey* v *Midland Bank plc* [1995] 1 All ER 929: see Steyn LJ, at p 933.

48 As to the type of transactions where a bank is put on inquiry, the case where a wife becomes surety for her husband's debts is, in this context, a straightforward case. The bank is put on inquiry. On the other side of the line is the case where money is being advanced, or has been advanced, to husband and wife jointly. In such a case the bank is not put on inquiry, unless the bank is aware the loan is being made for the husband's purposes, as distinct from their joint purposes. That was decided in *CIBC Mortgages plc* v *Pitt* [1994] 1 AC 200.

49 Less clear cut is the case where the wife becomes surety for the debts of a company whose shares are held by her and her husband. Her shareholding may be nominal, or she may have a minority shareholding or an equal shareholding with her husband. In my view the bank is put on inquiry in such cases, even when the wife is a director or secretary of the company. Such cases cannot be equated with joint loans. The shareholding interests, and the identity of the directors, are not a reliable guide to the identity of the persons who actually have the conduct of the company's business.

NOTES

1. Lord Nicholl confirms that once undue influence by the husband has been affirmatively established, or been established on the evidential presumption in circumstances where the wife placed trust and confidence in her husband, the bank will be put on inquiry whenever a wife (and other persons falling within the scope of this principle) stands as surety *for her husband's debts or those of a company in which her husband is involved*. This is clear and important in terms of certainty as lenders will know that in all such situations they will need to follow the appropriate steps in order to avoid being fixed with constructive notice of the husband's undue influence. However, it will not avoid the uncertainties inherent in the *O'Brien* requirement whereby the lender needs to assess that the transaction was not to the financial advantage of the surety and therefore that it is put on inquiry. This is because, despite the broad principle, due to the link to security for the husband's debts, it will still be necessary to distinguish loans for joint purposes and other instances of possible benefit by a wife.

2. In relation to the comments at [49] relating to instances where a wife may have a shareholding in this company or even be listed as an officer of the company, the lender's knowledge of the reality of the situation within the company may be relevant to the question of whether it is required to take the necessary steps. A useful illustration of this type of scenario is provided by the facts of *Bank of Cyprus (London) Ltd v Markou* [1999] 2 All ER 707, although it might not always be the case that the lender will have the necessary knowledge of the realities underlying the operation of a family company. In *Markou* a husband and wife each held one share in the family company but the wife took no active role and the company was wholly controlled by the husband. The wife had given an unlimited guarantee for the company's debts and this guarantee had been secured on the matrimonial home. The judge considered that the wife had established undue influence by her husband since her shareholding had little significance. She was wholly at the mercy of her husband since he made all the decisions relating to the company. The judge also held that the bank was put on inquiry not because of its constructive knowledge but as a result of its imputed knowledge of these circumstances.

   This is necessarily uncertain and may not sit easily with the approach adopted in relation to what are referred to by Lord Nicholls as 'non-sexual relationships' in relation to which he stated 'there is no rational cut-off point, with certain types of relationship being susceptible to the *O'Brien* principle and others not. Further, if a bank is not to be required to evaluate the extent to which its customer has influence over a proposed guarantor, the only practical way forward is to regard banks as "put on inquiry" in every case where the relationship between the surety and the debtor is non-commercial.' He added that he regarded this as 'a modest burden for banks and other lenders' [87]. Thus, the safest course for the lender will be to assume that it is put on inquiry and to take the appropriate steps in any non-commercial relationship. To this extent, at least, *Etridge* extends the protection granted to sureties.

The steps the lender needs to take once it has been put on enquiry

In *Royal Bank of Scotland plc* v *Etridge (No. 2)* [2001] UKHL 44, [2002] 2 AC 773, the House of Lords explained, in precise terms, the steps required by a lender to avoid being fixed with constructive notice of the husband's undue influence. The balance between the competing interests has moved towards bank protection. In general terms, the bank only needs to take reasonable steps to satisfy itself that the practical implications of the proposed transaction have been explained to the wife and can rely on confirmation from the bank's solicitor that this advice has been given, unless the bank knows or ought to realise that the appropriate advice was not received.

LORD NICHOLLS: . . .

The steps a bank should take

50 The principal area of controversy on these appeals concerns the steps a bank should take when it has been put on inquiry. In *O'Brien* [1994] 1 AC 180, 196–197 Lord Browne-Wilkinson said that a bank can reasonably be expected to take steps to bring home to the wife the risk she is running by standing as surety and to advise her to take independent advice. That test is applicable to past transactions. All the cases now before your Lordships' House fall into this category. For the future a bank satisfies these requirements if it insists that the wife attend a private meeting with a representative of the bank at which she is told of the extent of her liability as surety, warned of the risk she is running and urged to take independent legal advice. In exceptional cases the bank, to be safe, has to insist that the wife is separately advised.

51 The practice of the banks involved in the present cases, and it seems reasonable to assume this is the practice of banks generally, is not to have a private meeting with the wife. Nor do the banks themselves take any other steps to bring home to the wife the risk she is running. This has continued to be the practice since the decision in *O'Brien's* case. Banks consider they would stand to lose more than they would gain by holding a private meeting with the wife. They are, apparently, unwilling to assume the responsibility of advising the wife at such a meeting. Instead, the banking practice remains, as before, that in general the bank requires a wife to seek legal advice. The bank seeks written confirmation from a solicitor that he has explained the nature and effect of the documents to the wife.

52 Many of the difficulties which have arisen in the present cases stem from serious deficiencies, or alleged deficiencies, in the quality of the legal advice given to the wives. . . . On behalf of the wives it has been submitted that under the current practice the legal advice is often perfunctory in the extreme and, further, that everyone, including the banks, knows this. Independent legal advice is a fiction. The system is a charade. In practice it provides little or no protection for a wife who is under a misapprehension about the risks involved or who is being coerced into signing. She may not even know the present state of her husband's indebtedness.

53 My Lords, it is plainly neither desirable nor practicable that banks should be required to attempt to discover for themselves whether a wife's consent is being procured by the exercise of undue influence of her husband. This is not a step the banks should be expected to take. Nor, further, is it desirable or practicable that banks should be expected to insist on confirmation from a solicitor that the solicitor has satisfied himself that the wife's consent has not been procured by undue influence. As already noted, the circumstances in which banks are put on inquiry are extremely wide. They embrace every case where a wife is entering into a suretyship transaction in respect of her husband's debts. Many, if not most, wives would be understandably outraged by having to respond to the sort of questioning which would be appropriate before a responsible solicitor could give such a confirmation. In any event, solicitors are not equipped to carry out such an exercise in any really worthwhile way, and they will usually lack the necessary materials. Moreover, the legal costs involved, which would inevitably fall on the husband who is seeking financial assistance from the bank, would be substantial. To require such an intrusive, inconclusive and expensive exercise in every case would be an altogether disproportionate response to the need to protect those cases, presumably a small minority, where a wife is being wronged.

54 The furthest a bank can be expected to go is to take reasonable steps to satisfy itself that the wife has had brought home to her, in a meaningful way, the practical implications of the proposed transaction. This does not wholly eliminate the risk of undue influence or misrepresentation. But it does mean that a wife enters into a transaction with her eyes open so far as the basic elements of the transaction are concerned.

55 This is the point at which, in the *O'Brien* case, the House decided that the balance between the competing interests should be held. A bank may itself provide the necessary information directly to the wife. Indeed, it is best equipped to do so. But banks are not following that course. Ought they to be obliged to do so in every case? I do not think Lord Browne-Wilkinson so stated in *O'Brien*. I do not understand him to have said that a personal meeting was the only way a bank could discharge its obligation to bring home to the wife the risks she is running. It seems to me that, provided a suitable alternative is available, banks ought not to be compelled to take this course. Their reasons for not wishing to hold a personal meeting are understandable. Commonly, when a bank seeks to enforce a security provided by a customer, it is met with a defence based on assurances alleged to have been given orally by a branch manager at an earlier stage: that the bank would continue to support the business, that the bank would not call in its loan, and so forth. Lengthy litigation ensues. Sometimes the allegations prove to be well founded, sometimes not. Banks are concerned to avoid the prospect of similar litigation which would arise in guarantee cases if they were to adopt a practice of holding a meeting with a wife at which the bank's representative would explain the proposed guarantee transaction. It is not unreasonable for the banks to prefer that this task should be undertaken by an independent legal adviser.

56   I shall return later to the steps a bank should take when it follows this course. Suffice to say, these steps, together with advice from a solicitor acting for the wife, ought to provide the substance of the protection which *O'Brien* intended a wife should have. Ordinarily it will be reasonable that a bank should be able to rely upon confirmation from a solicitor, acting for the wife, that he has advised the wife appropriately.

57   The position will be otherwise if the bank knows that the solicitor has not duly advised the wife or, I would add, if the bank knows facts from which it ought to have realised that the wife has not received the appropriate advice. In such circumstances the bank will proceed at its own risk.

. . .

The content of the legal advice

61   . . . in the present type of case it is not for the solicitor to veto the transaction by declining to confirm to the bank that he has explained the documents to the wife and the risks she is taking upon herself. If the solicitor considers the transaction is not in the wife's best interests, he will give reasoned advice to the wife to that effect. But at the end of the day the decision on whether to proceed is the decision of the client, not the solicitor. A wife is not to be precluded from entering into a financially unwise transaction if, for her own reasons, she wishes to do so.

62   That is the general rule. There may, of course, be exceptional circumstances where it is glaringly obvious that the wife is being grievously wronged. In such a case the solicitor should decline to act further. In *Wright* v *Carter* [1903] 1 Ch 27, 57–58. Stirling LJ approved Farwell J's observations in *Powell* v *Powell* [1900] 1 Ch 243, 247. But he did so by reference to the extreme example of a poor man divesting himself of all his property in favour of his solicitor.

63   In *Royal Bank of Scotland plc* v *Etridge (No. 2)* [1998] 4 All ER 705, 722, para 49, the Court of Appeal said that if the transaction is 'one into which no competent solicitor could properly advise the wife to enter', the availability of legal advice is insufficient to avoid the bank being fixed with constructive notice. It follows from the views expressed above that I am unable to agree with the Court of Appeal on this point.

[Lord Nicholls set out the advice a solicitor can be expected to give and continued]:

Independent advice

69   I turn next to the much-vexed question whether the solicitor advising the wife must act for the wife alone. Or, at the very least, the solicitor must not act for the husband or the bank in the current transaction save in a wholly ministerial capacity, such as carrying out conveyancing formalities or supervising the execution of documents and witnessing signatures. Commonly, in practice, the solicitor advising the wife will be the solicitor acting also for her husband either in the particular transaction or generally.

70   The first point to note is that this question cannot be answered by reference to reported decisions. The steps a bank must take once it is put on inquiry, if it is to avoid having constructive notice of the wife's rights, are not the subject of exposition in earlier authority. This is a novel situation, created by the *O'Brien* decision.

71   Next, a simple and clear rule is needed, preferably of well nigh universal application. In some cases a bank deals directly with a husband and wife and has to take the initiative in requiring the wife to obtain legal advice. In other cases, a bank may deal throughout with solicitors already acting for the husband and wife. *Bank of Baroda* v *Rayarel* [1995] 2 FLR 376 is an example of the latter type of case. It would not be satisfactory to attempt to draw a distinction along these lines. Any such distinction would lack a principled base. Inevitably, in practice, the distinction would disintegrate in confusion.

72   Thirdly, here again, a balancing exercise is called for. Some features point in one direction, others in the opposite direction. Factors favouring the need for the solicitor to act for the wife alone include the following. Sometimes a wife may be inhibited in discussion with a solicitor who is also acting for the husband or whose main client is the husband. This occurred in *Banco Exterior Internacional* v *Mann* [1995] 1 All ER 936: see the finding of the judge, at p 941f-g. Sometimes a solicitor whose main client is the husband may not, in practice, give the same single-minded attention to the wife's position as would a solicitor acting solely for the wife. Her interests may rank lower in the solicitor's scale of priorities, perhaps unconsciously, than the interests of the husband. Instances of incompetent advice, or worse, which have come before the court might perhaps be less likely to recur if a solicitor were instructed to act for the wife alone and gave advice solely to her. As a matter of general understanding, independent advice would suggest that the solicitor should not be acting in the same transaction for the person who, if there is any undue influence, is the source of that influence.

73   The contrary view is that the solicitor may also act for the husband or the bank, provided the solicitor is satisfied that this is in the wife's best interests and satisfied also that this will not give rise to any conflicts of duty or interest. The principal factors favouring this approach are as follows. A requirement that a wife should receive advice from a solicitor acting solely for her will frequently add significantly to the legal costs. Sometimes a wife will be happier to be advised by a family solicitor known to her than by a complete stranger. Sometimes a solicitor who knows both husband and wife and their histories will be better placed to advise than a solicitor who is a complete stranger.

74   In my view, overall the latter factors are more weighty than the former. The advantages attendant upon the employment of a solicitor acting solely for the wife do not justify the additional expense this would involve for the husband. When accepting instructions to advise the wife the solicitor assumes responsibilities directly to her, both at law and professionally. These duties, and this is central to the reasoning on this point, are owed to the wife alone. In advising the wife the solicitor is acting for the wife alone. He is concerned only with her interests. I emphasise, therefore, that in every case the solicitor must consider carefully whether there is any conflict of duty or interest and, more widely, whether it would be in the best interests of the wife for him to accept instructions from her. If he decides to accept instructions, his assumption of legal and professional responsibilities to her ought, in the ordinary course of things, to provide sufficient assurance that he will give the requisite advice fully, carefully and conscientiously. Especially so, now that the nature of the advice called for has been clarified. If at any stage the solicitor becomes concerned that there is a real risk that other interests or duties may inhibit his advice to the wife he must cease to act for her.

Agency

. . .

77   . . . Confirmation from the solicitor that he has advised the wife is one of the bank's preconditions for completion of the transaction. But it is central to this arrangement that in advising the wife the solicitor is acting for the wife and no one else. The bank does not have, and is intended not to have, any knowledge of or control over the advice the solicitor gives the wife. The solicitor is not accountable to the bank for the advice he gives to the wife. To impute to the bank knowledge of what passed between the solicitor and the wife would contradict this essential feature of the arrangement. The mere fact that, for its own purposes, the bank asked the solicitor to advise the wife does not make the solicitor the bank's agent in giving that advice.

78   In the ordinary case, therefore, deficiencies in the advice given are a matter between the wife and her solicitor. The bank is entitled to proceed on the assumption that a solicitor advising the wife has done his job properly. I have already mentioned what is the bank's position if it knows this is not so, or if it knows facts from which it ought to have realised this is not so.

79   I now return to the steps a bank should take when it has been put on inquiry and for its protection is looking to the fact that the wife has been advised independently by a solicitor.

(1) One of the unsatisfactory features in some of the cases is the late stage at which the wife first became involved in the transaction. In practice she had no opportunity to express a view on the identity of the solicitor who advised her. She did not even know that the purpose for which the solicitor was giving her advice was to enable him to send, on her behalf, the protective confirmation sought by the bank. Usually the solicitor acted for both husband and wife.

Since the bank is looking for its protection to legal advice given to the wife by a solicitor who, in this respect, is acting solely for her, I consider the bank should take steps to check directly with the wife the name of the solicitor she wishes to act for her. To this end, in future the bank should communicate directly with the wife, informing her that for its own protection it will require written confirmation from a solicitor, acting for her, to the effect that the solicitor has fully explained to her the nature of the documents and the practical implications they will have for her. She should be told that the purpose of this requirement is that thereafter she should not be able to dispute she is legally bound by the documents once she has signed them. She should be asked to nominate a solicitor whom she is willing to instruct to advise her, separately from her husband, and act for her in giving the necessary confirmation to the bank. She should be told that, if she wishes, the solicitor may be the same solicitor as is acting for her husband in the transaction. If a solicitor is already acting for the husband and the wife, she should be asked whether she would prefer that a different solicitor should act for her regarding the bank's requirement for confirmation from a solicitor.

The bank should not proceed with the transaction until it has received an appropriate response directly from the wife.

(2) Representatives of the bank are likely to have a much better picture of the husband's financial affairs than the solicitor. If the bank is not willing to undertake the task of explanation itself, the bank must provide the solicitor with the financial information he needs for this purpose. Accordingly it should become routine practice for banks, if relying on confirmation from a solicitor for their protection, to send to the solicitor the necessary financial information. What is required must depend on the facts of the case. Ordinarily this will include information on the purpose for which the proposed new facility has been requested, the current amount of the husband's indebtedness, the amount of his current overdraft facility, and the amount and terms of any new facility. If the bank's request for security arose from a written application by the husband for a facility, a copy of the application should be sent to the solicitor. The bank will, of course, need first to obtain the consent of its customer to this circulation of confidential information. If this consent is not forthcoming the transaction will not be able to proceed.

(3) Exceptionally there may be a case where the bank believes or suspects that the wife has been misled by her husband or is not entering into the transaction of her own free will. If such a case occurs the bank must inform the wife's solicitors of the facts giving rise to its belief or suspicion.

(4) The bank should in every case obtain from the wife's solicitor a written confirmation to the effect mentioned above.

80   These steps will be applicable to future transactions. In respect of past transactions, the bank will ordinarily be regarded as having discharged its obligations if a solicitor who was acting for the wife in the transaction gave the bank confirmation to the effect that he had brought home to the wife the risks she was running by standing as surety.

NOTES
1.   Prior to this decision solicitors had been placed in the unenviable position of having to decide whether, having explained the position to the wife, they should decline to act and veto the transaction on the basis that the transaction was so disadvantageous to the wife. In particular, if it was a transaction that 'no competent solicitor could properly advise the wife

to enter' the accepted view was that the solicitor should decline to act (*per* Stuart-Smith LJ in the Court of Appeal in *Royal Bank of Scotland* v *Etridge (No. 2)* [1998] 4 All ER 705). This statement was seized upon by counsel in subsequent cases to support an argument that the lender had failed to take the necessary steps. For example, in *Credit Lyonnais Bank NV* v *Burch* [1997] 1 All ER 144, the Court of Appeal held that the transaction was of such a nature that the solicitor should have refused to act for the employee when she persisted with it after being advised not to do so. The difficulty was that the vast majority of these surety cases appear to be unwise with hindsight and arguably the balance had swung too far against the solicitor, who can be sued for negligent advice where there is a causal link between the advice and the giving of the security. The House of Lords has redressed this by accepting that [62] in the absence of 'glaringly obvious' 'grievous wrong' and on the assumption that appropriate advice has been received, the onus is on the wife to decide whether to proceed with the transaction. It would be far too paternalistic to place a more onerous policing responsibility on solicitors.

2. Whilst the wife cannot be wholly protected from undue influence and its consequences, she will at least have received a warning and have received appropriate advice. If there are deficiencies in the advice given, she will have a claim against the solicitor, although the solicitor is protected by having the clear guidance of the House of Lords concerning the nature of the advice to be given and the circumstances in which that advice can be given, e.g., where there is a potential conflict of interest. The decision has therefore resolved many of the issues examined in the case law since *O'Brien*. One obvious negative is that what is required of solicitors is more demanding and will clearly take more time and therefore lead to increased costs.

    On the other hand, the lender is entitled to rely on the fact that the solicitor has properly advised the wife unless it is aware or ought to be aware that this is not the case.

    Overall, this would appear to be a more satisfactory attempt to strike the right balance. The only 'loser' would appear to be the wife who, as a result of the decision of the House of Lords in *Etridge*, has lost the benefit of the presumption of undue influence and must prove on the evidence that the husband has committed a wrong, albeit that this may not prove too problematical where the transaction is wholly in favour of the husband.

Of course, it is clear that in instances where a surety is not entirely independent of the party alleged to have exercised undue influence, their influence may extend to the process where the wife receives advice so that although the decision to enter the transaction should be informed, it may not be 'free'. This distinction was recognised by Lord Hobhouse at [111].

LORD HOBHOUSE: . . . The need to guard against lack of comprehension is important and applies in any event to a non-business surety. But it is not the same as guarding against undue influence. It may be a first step but it is a fallacy to confuse the two. Comprehension is essential for any legal documents of this complexity and obscurity. But for the purpose of negativing undue influence it is necessary to be satisfied that the agreement was, also, given freely in knowledge of the true facts. It must be remembered that the equitable doctrine of undue influence has been created for the protection of those who are sui juris and competent to undertake legal obligations but are nevertheless vulnerable and liable to have their will unduly influenced. It is their weakness which is being protected not their inability to comprehend.

In contrast Lord Nicholls stressed that absolute protection was impossible to achieve. The line had been drawn in such a way that protection against the risk of undue influence did not extend to all cases where sureties might not have exercised a free and informed choice. It is only 'exceptionally' that the bank will believe or suspect that the transaction is the product of misrepresentation or is not the product of the exercise of free will. In those cases the bank's duty is discharged by informing the wife's solicitors of these facts or suspicions. It is for the surety to establish any allegations based on actual undue influence or misrepresentation.

E: The effect of undue influence

The contract is voidable so that both parties are to be restored to their original positions. Partial rescission is not permissible, see the discussion of this at *page 558*.

However, in exceptional circumstances it may be possible to sever the objectionable parts of an instrument. In *Barclays Bank* v *Caplan* [1998] FLR 532, in relation to the original charge covering a home loan and guaranteeing a loan to one of Mr Caplan's companies, the bank had taken reasonable steps and accordingly was not fixed with constructive notice of any undue influence exercised by Mr Caplan over his wife. Nevertheless, the bank had later obtained Mrs Caplan's signature to a side-letter extending that charge to cover guarantees of Mr Caplan's debts in respect of a further three companies for an unlimited amount. In relation to the side-letter the bank had failed to ensure that the necessary steps were taken. The judge confirmed that only rarely would it be possible to sever objectionable parts of an instrument following a finding of undue influence since such a finding vitiated consent. On these facts, although it was clear that Mrs Caplan had freely consented to the first guarantee she had not been properly advised in relation to the other guarantees. In addition, unlike the position in *TSB Bank* v *Camfield* [1995] WLR 430, *page 558*, it was possible to sever these objectionable parts of the instrument without effectively rewriting it. Accordingly, the first loan was validly secured.

It is clear from *Dunbar Bank plc* v *Nadeem* [1998] 3 All ER 876, that if undue influence is established, the victim needs to make restitution of all that they have obtained from the transaction. The judge at first instance interpreted this to mean that Mrs Nadeem had to make restitution to the bank for the benefit she had received from the use of the money advanced for the purchase of a longer lease of the matrimonial home, namely one half of the money advanced with interest. However, the Court of Appeal held *obiter* (because of the finding that there was no undue influence) that if the wife had been entitled to have half the charge set aside then it was her beneficial interest in the lease for which she needed to make restitution. That would involve restoring her beneficial interest to her husband, which would have resulted in the bank enjoying the beneficial interest in the whole of the lease. Morritt LJ said:

> The appeal by the wife does not . . . arise. However, the matter was fully argued and as it gives rise to problems likely to arise in other cases it may assist if I indicate what appear to me to be the appropriate principles to apply.
>
> The applicant for an order for a transaction to be set aside on the ground of undue influence or for any other invalidating tendency, as they were described by Lord Browne-Wilkinson in *Barclays Bank plc* v *O'Brien* [1993] 4 All ER 417 at 424, [1994] 1 AC 180 at 190, must as a condition for relief give back all he obtained from the transaction (see *Erlanger* v *New Sombrero Phosphate Co.* (1878) 3 App Cas 1218 at 1278–1279, [1874–80] All ER Rep 271 at 286). . . . In this case the wife seeks only that the legal charge be set aside against her for that is the practical result she desires. In my view it would be to take too narrow a view to regard that as the only transaction she seeks to have set aside.
>
> In a case such as the present there were two relevant transactions. First, there was the agreement or arrangement between the husband and the wife that he would procure for her a half interest in the new lease to be granted by the landlord in respect of the matrimonial home if she would join with the husband in borrowing from the bank the sum needed for that and other purposes and charging the new lease to the bank to secure it. Second, and pursuant to the first agreement or arrangement, there was the agreement for the loan and the security made between the husband

and wife on the one hand and the bank on the other contained in the facility letter and the legal charge. On the footing, as found by the judge, that the bank had notice of the relevant undue influence, such influence had been exercised to procure both transactions, not just the legal charge, so that each of them was liable to be set aside as against both the husband and the bank.

In these circumstances it seems to me that the right or advantage acquired by the wife which she was bound to restore as a condition of rescission was the beneficial interest in the lease granted by the landlord and not a proportion of the debt secured by the legal charge. It was no part of the bargain made by any of the three parties involved that there should be a several loan to the wife of any proportion of the joint loan of £260,000. Further, the wife did not receive any part of that loan otherwise than pursuant to the obligation to apply it for the purposes set out in the facility letter. I accept the submissions for the wife that the judge erred in imposing a condition on the order to set aside the legal charge that she should repay that part of it which might be attributable to the acquisition of her beneficial interest. So to do was to impose a condition not warranted by the obligation to make restitution and, therefore, contrary to the decision of this court in *TSB Bank plc* v *Camfield* [1995] 1 All ER 951, [1995] 1 WLR 430.

It seems to me to follow from this analysis that the obligation of the wife to make restitution as a condition for the setting aside of the legal charge is to restore to the husband, if she can, the beneficial interest in the lease she acquired in consequence of the transactions as a whole. It is, in my view, plain that the wife cannot retain the beneficial interest in the lease if she is to escape from liability under the facility letter and legal charge. Her obligation to restore the beneficial interest in the lease cannot be regarded as an obligation to restore it to the bank for the bank did not provide it and no one ever intended the bank to be anything other than a legal chargee of it. In my view with regard to the wife the husband was the source of the beneficial interest in the lease now vested in his wife subject to the legal charge. If the beneficial interest were restored to him then it would come within his charge to the bank which is not impugned. The result would be that the bank would then enjoy a legal charge over the whole of the beneficial interest in the lease as security for the whole of the liability. In my view this would produce a just result. The wife's personal liability would be extinguished in exchange for the removal of her beneficial interest, being the two consequences to her of the two transactions I referred to earlier. But the further consequence would be that the wife could have no defence to the claim of the bank made against her for possession of the property comprised in the lease and charged to the bank. . . .

What is the position if restoration to the original positions cannot be achieved?

Cheese v Thomas
[1994] 1 WLR 129 (CA)

In 1990 the 86-year-old plaintiff and the defendant, his great nephew, had agreed to purchase a house. The purchase price was £83,000. The house was purchased in the sole name of the defendant, with the plaintiff contributing £43,000 and the defendant £40,000 by means of a building society mortgage on the property. It was agreed that the plaintiff would live in the property until his death and then the defendant would be solely entitled. The defendant failed to keep up the mortgage payments. The plaintiff claimed that the transaction should be set aside for undue influence and wanted the return of his £43,000. The house was sold for only £55,000. Held: where it was not possible to restore the parties to their exact original positions the court would look at the circumstances and do what was fair and just in practical terms. Since the purpose of the transaction had been to benefit both parties, it would not be just for the defendant to suffer the entire loss of market value. Each party should receive a proportionate share of the net proceeds (i.e. 43:40).

NOTES

1. This case involved an presumption of undue influence (class 2A—fiduciary relationship) which had not been rebutted since the nephew had not advised his uncle to obtain independent advice. However, the Court of Appeal clearly considered that it was relevant that the nephew had not behaved improperly or tricked his uncle although this cannot be relevant to the question of whether the presumption of undue influence can be rebutted, see discussion at *page 642*.

2. Since this was a presumed undue influence case, pre-*Etridge* the transaction had to be shown to be manifestly disadvantageous to the uncle, which the Court of Appeal held it to be because he could not compel a sale if he wished to move and because he was placed at considerable risk if the nephew failed to pay the mortgage instalments. Since *Etridge* the presumption is recognised as only being evidential and there is no manifest disadvantageous 'requirement'. Nevertheless, the fact that a transaction is disadvantageous can be used as evidence to support an allegation of *undue* influence.

Mahoney v Purnell
[1996] 3 All ER 61

Mahoney had been persuaded to sell his 50 per cent shareholding in a business to his son-in-law, who owned the other 50 per cent, for £200,000. Payment was to be made over a 10-year period. Although the company's solicitor had explained the proposed terms, he had stated that he could not advise Mahoney on the commercial reasonableness of the proposal because he was acting for the company. However, Mahoney was not explicitly advised to obtain independent legal advice. One year after this agreement was made the son-in-law sold the business for over £3 million. Mahoney sought rescission of the agreement and equitable relief of a money judgment on the basis of undue influence. However, the company went into liquidation at a time when Mahoney was still owed £80,000. The issue in the case related to the remedy for the undue influence since the parties could not be restored to their former positions. Held: the court had power to award compensation in equity where, as here, there was a relationship based on trust which was fiduciary in nature and this fiduciary relationship had been abused. Accordingly, May J made an award whereby the son-in-law was to compensate Mahoney in an amount equal to the value at the date of the agreement of what he had surrendered with credit being given for what he had received. This was calculated at approximately £202,000.

MAY J: . . . [W]here an agreement is made as a result of undue influence in circumstances where the court will in equity intervene, the normal remedy is for the agreement to be set aside and for the defendant to account for profits obtained from the improper agreements. The court is not deflected from this course because the parties cannot be restored to their former positions. The remedy is not to leave the agreement as it is and simply compensate the plaintiff for loss upon the principle in *Nocton v Lord Ashburton* [1914] AC 932, [1914–15] All ER Rep 45. Allowance must be made to the defendant for improvements or benefits which he has made and which accrue to the plaintiff upon the setting aside of the agreement. Where the facts do not fit neatly into this scheme, the court has to achieve practical justice between the parties. The question is what does the justice of the case require.

In this case, the commonsense and, if I may say so, fair remedy for Mr Mahoney is for him to receive in compensation the March 1988 value of what he surrendered under the agreements, appropriate credit being given for what he received under the agreements. The question is whether the law permits that result. . . . [T]aking an account in this case would not, in my view, do practical justice since, on the evidence, the value of what Mr Mahoney surrendered has been lost through no fault or action of his. The company is in liquidation and there is no presently quantifiable profit in the hands of Mr Purnell personally. The fact that at times between 1988 and now profits might have been calculated does not help, since there is no reason in principle for choosing any moment in time other than the present for the taking of an account. Practical justice in this case requires an award which is akin to damages. It might be said that the court cannot do that . . . But I am loath to reach that conclusion if the result would be, as I think it would be, that Mr Mahoney was denied commonsense and fair compensation.

In my view, the law is not so constrained. *O'Sullivan* [*O'Sullivan* v *Management Agency and Music Ltd* [1985] 3 All ER 351, [1985] QB 428] recognises that transactions may be set aside provided that the court can achieve practical justice by obliging the defendant to give up advantages while at the same time compensating him for value which he has contributed. No doubt that balance will usually be achieved by taking an account. But where that precise route will not achieve practical justice, an analogous permissible route to that end may be to balance the value which the plaintiff surrendered against any value which he has received and to award him the difference. That is not, I think to award him damages, but fair compensation in equity as an adjunct to setting aside the agreement.

I consider that *Nocton* v *Lord Ashburton* may be seen as authority supporting—or at least strongly encouraging—the conclusion that the court does have power to award fair compensation in equity where a plaintiff who has trusted a defendant succeeds in persuading the court to set aside an unfair agreement induced by reliance on that trust. . . . [A] plaintiff who suffers loss as a result of breach of a fiduciary duty by a defendant may claim relief in equity which need not be limited to the taking of an account of profit, and can take the form of compensation if the defendant has lost the property acquired from the plaintiff by a transaction which arose out of his confidential relationship with the man who had trusted him. . . .

The relationship which existed in this case between Mr Mahoney and Mr Purnell from which undue influence is presumed is based upon trust and may be described as fiduciary. Although Mr Mahoney's claim is not conventionally framed in the language of breach of duty, his ground for equitable relief is founded on abuse of trust. For present purposes the difference may be seen as semantic only. In *Nocton* v *Lord Ashburton* the breach of duty was that which lost the property. In this case, the abuse of the fiduciary relationship induced the agreements and the property was lost later. I do not consider that this is a distinction material to the search for a remedy, since in each case the plaintiff seeks equitable relief for an abuse of (or breach of) trust. . . .

NOTE: This case is only authority for the existence of jurisdiction to award monetary compensation where the undue influence involves a breach of fiduciary duty. It does not make this remedy available in instances of undue influence which do not involve a breach of fiduciary duty.

SECTION 3: INEQUALITY OF BARGAINING POWER

A: A general doctrine

See Waddams, 'Unconscionability in Contracts' (1976) 39 MLR 369.

Lord Denning MR in *Lloyds Bank Ltd* v *Bundy* considered that there was a general doctrine of inequality of bargaining power in English law.

Lloyds Bank v *Bundy*
[1975] QB 326 (CA)

The facts of this case appear at *page 635*.

LORD DENNING MR:

The general rule

Now let me say at once that in the vast majority of cases a customer who signs a bank guarantee or a charge cannot get out of it. No bargain will be upset which is the result of the ordinary interplay of forces. There are many hard cases which are caught by this rule. Take the case of a poor man who is homeless. He agrees to pay a high rent to a landlord just to get a roof over his head. The common law will not interfere. It is left to Parliament. Next take the case of a borrower in urgent need of money. He borrows it from the bank at high interest and it is guaranteed by a friend. The guarantor gives his bond and gets nothing in return. The common law will not interfere. Parliament has intervened to prevent moneylenders charging excessive interest. But it has never interfered with banks.

Yet there are exceptions to this general rule. There are cases in our books in which the courts will set aside a contract, or a transfer of property, when the parties have not met on equal terms—when the one is so strong in bargaining power and the other so weak—that, as a matter of common fairness, it is not right that the strong should be allowed to push the weak to the wall. Hitherto those exceptional cases have been treated each as a separate category in itself. But I think the time has come when we should seek to find a principle to unite them. I put on one side contracts or transactions which are voidable for fraud or misrepresentation or mistake. All those are governed by settled principles. I go only to those where there has been inequality of bargaining power, such as to merit the intervention of the court.

The categories

The first category is that of 'duress of goods.' A typical case is when a man is in a strong bargaining position by being in possession of the goods of another by virtue of a legal right, such as by way of pawn or pledge or taken in distress. The owner is in a weak position because he is in urgent need of the goods. The stronger demands of the weaker more than is justly due: and he pays it in order to get the goods. Such a transaction is voidable. He can recover the excess: see *Astley* v *Reynolds* (1731) 2 Stra 915. To which may be added the cases of 'colore officii,' where a man is in a strong bargaining position by virtue of his official position or public profession. He relies upon it so as to gain from the weaker—who is urgently in need—more than is justly due. In such cases the stronger may make his claim in good faith honestly believing that he is entitled to make his demand. He may not be guilty of any fraud or misrepresentation. The inequality of bargaining power—the strength of the one versus the urgent need of the other—renders the transaction voidable and the money paid to be recovered back: see *Maskell* v *Horner* [1915] 3 KB 106.

The second category is that of the 'unconscionable transaction.' A man is so placed as to be in need of special care and protection and yet his weakness is exploited by another far stronger than himself so as to get his property at a gross undervalue. The typical case is that of the 'expectant heir.' But it applies to all cases where a man comes into property, or is expected to come into it—and then being in urgent need—another gives him ready cash for it, greatly below its true worth, and so gets the property transferred to him. Even though there be no evidence of fraud or misrepresentation, nevertheless the transaction will be set aside: see *Fry* v *Lane* (1888) 40 ChD 312, 322 where Kay J said:

> The result of the decisions is that where a purchase is made from a poor and ignorant man at a considerable undervalue, *the vendor having no independent advice*, a court of equity will set aside the transaction.

This second category is said to extend to all cases where an unfair advantage has been gained by an unconscientious use of power by a stronger party against a weaker: see the cases cited in *Halsbury's Laws of England*, 3rd ed., vol. 17 (1956), p. 682. The third category is that of 'undue influence' usually so called. These are divided into two classes as stated by Cotton LJ in *Allcard* v *Skinner* (1887) 36 ChD 145, 171.

The fourth category is that of 'undue pressure.' The most apposite of that is *Williams* v *Bayley* (1866) LR 1 HL 200. Other instances of undue pressure are where one party stipulates for an unfair advantage to which the other has no option but to submit. As where an employer—the stronger party—has employed a builder—the weaker party—to do work for him. When the builder asked for payment of sums properly due (so as to pay his workmen) the employer refused to pay unless he was given some added advantage. Stuart V-C said: 'Where an agreement, hard and inequitable in itself, has been exacted under circumstances of pressure on the part of the person who exacts it, this court will set it aside': see *Ormes* v *Beadel* (1860) 2 Giff 166, 174 and *D & C Builders Ltd* v *Rees* [1966] 2 QB 617, 625.

The fifth category is that of salvage agreements. When a vessel is in danger of sinking and seeks help, the rescuer is in a strong bargaining position. The vessel in distress is in urgent need. The parties cannot be truly said to be on equal terms. The Court of Admiralty have always recognised that fact. The 'fundamental rule' is

> if the parties have made an agreement, the court will enforce it, unless it be manifestly unfair and unjust; but if it be manifestly unfair and unjust, the court will disregard it and decree what is fair and just. . . .

The general principles

Gathering all together, I would suggest that through all these instances there runs a single thread. They rest on 'inequality of bargaining power.' By virtue of it, the English law gives relief to one who, without independent advice, enters into a contract upon terms which are very unfair or transfers property for a consideration which is grossly inadequate, when his bargaining power is grievously impaired by reason of his own needs or desires, or by his own ignorance or infirmity, coupled with undue influences or pressures brought to bear on him by or for the benefit of the other. When I use the word 'undue' I do not mean to suggest that the principle depends on proof of any wrongdoing. The one who stipulates for an unfair advantage may be moved solely by his own self-interest, unconscious of the distress he is bringing to the other. I have also avoided any reference to the will of the one being 'dominated' or 'overcome' by the other. One who is in extreme need may knowingly consent to a most improvident bargain, solely to relieve the straits in which he finds himself. Again, I do not mean to suggest that every transaction is saved by independent advice. But the absence of it may be fatal. With these explanations, I hope this principle will be found to reconcile the cases. Applying it to the present case, I would notice these points:

(1) The consideration moving from the bank was grossly inadequate. The son's company was in serious difficulty. The overdraft was at its limit of £10,000. The bank considered that its existing security was insufficient. In order to get further security, it asked the father to charge the house—his sole asset—to the uttermost. It was worth £10,000. The charge was for £11,000. That was for the benefit of the bank. But not at all for the benefit of the father, or indeed for the company. The bank did not promise to continue the overdraft or to increase it. On the contrary, it required the overdraft to be reduced. All that the company gained was a short respite from impending doom.

(2) The relationship between the bank and the father was one of trust and confidence. The bank knew that the father relied on it implicitly to advise him about the transaction. The father trusted the bank. This gave the bank much influence on the father. Yet the bank failed in that trust. It allowed the father to charge the house to his ruin.

(3) The relationship between the father and the son was one where the father's natural affection had much influence on him. He would naturally desire to accede to his son's request. He trusted his son.

(4) There was a conflict of interest between the bank and the father. Yet the bank did not realise it. Nor did it suggest that the father should get independent advice. If the father had gone to his solicitor—or to any man of business—there is no doubt that any one of them would say: 'You must not enter into this transaction. You are giving up your house, your sole remaining asset, for no benefit to you. The company is in such a parlous state that you must not do it.'

These considerations seem to me to bring this case within the principles I have stated. But, in case that principle is wrong, I would also say that the case falls within the category of undue influence of the second class stated by Cotton LJ in *Allcard* v *Skinner*, 36 ChD 145, 171. I have no doubt that the assistant bank manager acted in the utmost good faith and was straightforward and genuine. Indeed the father said so. But beyond doubt he was acting in the interests of the bank—to get further security for a bad debt. There was such a relationship of trust and confidence between them that the bank ought not to have swept up his sole remaining asset into its hands—for nothing—without his having independent advice.

NOTE: Sir Eric Sachs expressed some sympathy with this view but did not commit himself to it.

■ QUESTIONS

1. If there is such a general doctrine, how will abuse of an unequal bargaining position be determined? Would it give rise to too much uncertainty when in general the sanctity of contract is paramount?

    See Thal, 'The Inequality of Bargaining Power Doctrine: The Problem of Defining Contractual Unfairness' (1988) OJLS 17.

2. Has the emergence of a doctrine of economic duress reduced the need for a separate principle of inequality of bargaining power?

NOTES

1. There is at least some recognition by the courts of the issue of contractual fairness (e.g., in the incorporation and interpretation of exemption clauses and in the penalty rule). (See Bingham LJ in *Interfoto Picture Library Ltd* v *Stiletto Visual Programmes Ltd* [1989] 1 QB 433, 439, *page 607*.)

    See P. S. Atiyah, 'Contract and fair exchange' in *Essays in Contract*, pp. 329–54; Tiplady, 'The judicial control of contractual unfairness' (1983) 46 MLR 601.

    In *Alec Lobb (Garages) Ltd* v *Total Oil GB Ltd* [1985] 1 WLR 173 (for full facts see *page 681*), Dillon LJ appeared to recognise that there might be limited circumstances when the court would step in to prevent 'the weak being pushed to the wall', but on these facts the conduct of the defendants was not unconscionable. Mr Lobb's bargaining position was weak because of his financial difficulties, but he did have clear legal advice throughout and rejected it in favour of entering into an unfavourable leaseback arrangement, which included a tie to purchase the defendants' petrol for 21 years. The price and rent charged were either at or below market price, the defendants had been reluctant and the initiative for financial assistance from them had come from Mr Lobb. The Court of Appeal held that a transaction would not be rendered harsh or unconscionable merely because the parties were of unequal bargaining power and the stronger party had not shown that it was fair, just, and reasonable in its terms. Dillon LJ said (at pp. 182–3):

    > The whole emphasis is on extortion, or undue advantage taken of weakness, an unconscientious use of the power arising out of the inequality of the parties' circumstances and on unconscientious use of power which the court might in certain circumstances be entitled to infer from a particular—and in these days notorious—relationship unless the contract is proved to have been in fact fair, just and reasonable. Nothing leads me to suppose that the course of the development of the law over the last 100 years has been such that the emphasis on unconscionable conduct or unconscientious use of power has gone and relief will now be granted in equity in a case such as the present if there has been unequal bargaining power, even if the stronger has not used his strength unconscionably. I agree with the judgment of Browne-Wilkinson J, in *Multiservice Bookbinding Ltd* v *Marden* [1979] Ch 84, which sets out that to establish that a term is unfair and unconscionable it is not enough to show that it is, objectively, unreasonable.

    > In the present case there are findings of fact by the deputy judge that the conduct of Total was not unconscionable, coercive or oppressive. There is ample evidence to support those findings and they are not challenged by the appellants. Their case is that the judge applied the wrong test; where there is unequal bargaining power, the test is, they say, whether its terms are fair, just and reasonable and it is unnecessary to consider whether the

conduct of the stronger party was oppressive or unconscionable. I do not accept the appellants' proposition of law. In my judgment the findings of the judge conclude this ground of appeal against the appellants.

Inequality of bargaining power must anyhow be a relative concept. It is seldom in any negotiation that the bargaining powers of the parties are absolutely equal. Any individual wanting to borrow money from a bank, building society or other financial institution in order to pay his liabilities or buy some property he urgently wants to acquire will have virtually no bargaining power; he will have to take or leave the terms offered to him. So, with house property in a seller's market, the purchaser will not have equal bargaining power with the vendor. But Lord Denning MR did not envisage that any contract entered into in such circumstances would, without more, be reviewed by the courts by the objective criterion of what was reasonable: see *Lloyds Bank Ltd v Bundy* [1975] QB 326, 336. The courts would only interfere in exceptional cases where as a matter of common fairness it was not right that the strong should be allowed to push the weak to the wall. The concepts of unconscionable conduct and of the exercise by the stronger of coercive power are thus brought in, and in the present case they are negatived by the deputy judge's findings.

2. Lord Denning's views in *Lloyds Bank* v *Bundy* were firmly rejected by Lord Scarman in two cases. First, in *Pao On* v *Lau Yiu Long* [1980] AC 614 (*page 125*), Lord Scarman held that there could be no relief based solely on an unfair use of a dominant bargaining position. He said (at pp. 634–5):

> . . . [The] question, their Lordships repeat is whether, in a case where duress is not established, public policy may nevertheless invalidate the consideration if there has been a threat to repudiate a pre-existing contractual obligation or an unfair use of a dominating bargaining position. Their Lordships' conclusion is that where businessmen are negotiating at arm's length it is unnecessary for the achievement of justice, and unhelpful in the development of the law, to invoke such a rule of public policy. It would also create unacceptable anomaly. It is unnecessary because justice requires that men, who have negotiated at arm's length, be held to their bargains unless it can be shown that their consent was vitiated by fraud, mistake or duress. If a promise is induced by coercion of a man's will, the doctrine of duress suffices to do justice. The party coerced, if he chooses and acts in time can avoid the contract. If there is no coercion, there can be no reason for avoiding the contract where there is shown to be a real consideration which is otherwise legal.
>
> Such a rule of public policy as is now being considered would be unhelpful because it would render the law uncertain. It would become a question of fact and degree to determine in each case whether there had been, short of duress, an unfair use of a strong bargaining position. It would create anomaly because, if public policy invalidates the consideration, the effect is to make the contract void. But unless the facts are such as to support a plea of 'non est factum,' which is not suggested in this case, duress does no more than confer upon the victim the opportunity, if taken in time, to avoid the contract. It would be strange if conduct less than duress could render a contract void, whereas duress does no more than render a contract voidable. Indeed, it is the defendants' case in this appeal that such an anomaly is the correct result. Their case is that the plaintiffs, having lost by cancellation the safeguard of the subsidiary agreement, are without the safeguard of the guarantee because its consideration is contrary to public policy, and that they are debarred from restoration to their position under the subsidiary agreement because the guarantee is void, not voidable. The logical consequence of [this] submission is that the safeguard which all were at all times agreed the plaintiffs should have—the safeguard against fall in value of the shares—has been lost by the application of a rule of public policy. The law is not, in their Lordship's judgment, reduced to countenancing such stark injustice: nor is it necessary, when one bears in mind the protection offered otherwise by the law to one who contracts in ignorance of what he is doing or under duress. Accordingly, the submission that the additional consideration established by the extrinisic evidence is invalid on the ground of public policy is rejected.

Second, in *National Westminster Bank* v *Morgan* [1985] AC 686 (*page 638*), Lord Scarman said (at pp. 707–8):

> Lord Denning MR [in *Lloyds Bank Ltd* v *Bundy*] believed that the doctrine of undue influence could be subsumed under a general principle that English courts will grant relief where there has been 'inequality of bargaining power'. He deliberately avoided reference to the will of one party being dominated or overcome by another. The majority of the court did not follow him; they based their decision on the orthodox view of the doctrine as expounded in *Allcard* v *Skinner*, 36 ChD 145. The opinion of the Master of the Rolls, therefore, was not the ground of the court's decision, which was to be found in the view of the majority, for whom Sir Eric Sachs delivered the leading judgment.
>
>   ... The doctrine of undue influence has been sufficiently developed not to need the support of a principle which by its formulation in the language of the law of contract is not appropriate to cover transactions of gift where there is no bargain. The fact of an unequal bargain will, of course, be a relevant feature in some cases of undue influence. But it can never become an appropriate basis of principle of an equitable doctrine which is concerned with transactions 'not to be reasonably accounted for on the ground of friendship, relationship, charity, or other ordinary motives on which ordinary men act' (Lindley LJ in *Allcard* v *Skinner*, at p. 185). And even in the field of contract I question whether there is any need in the modern law to erect a general principle of relief against inequality of bargaining power. Parliament has undertaken the task—and it is essentially a legislative task—of enacting such restrictions upon freedom of contract as are in its judgment necessary to relieve against the mischief: for example, the hire-purchase and consumer protection legislation, of which the Supply of Goods (Implied Terms) Act 1973, Consumer Credit Act 1974, Consumer Safety Act 1978, Supply of Goods and Services Act 1982 and Insurance Companies Act 1982 are examples. I doubt whether the courts should assume the burden of formulating further restrictions ...

NOTE: See also the Unfair Contract Terms Act 1977, *page 287*, and the Unfair Terms in Consumer Contracts Regulations 1999, *page 318*, as further legislative examples, and in particular the requirement of good faith in reg. 5(1) of the Regulations.

■ QUESTION

The statutory provision is necessarily piecemeal. Should the courts therefore do more to recognise abuse of a dominant position?

B: Protection for the 'poor and ignorant'

There is an ever-widening category where transactions can be set aside on the ground of characteristics possessed by a victim which necessarily mean that he requires protection, coupled with a taking advantage of the position by the other party.

Earl of Aylesford v *Morris*
(1873) 8 Ch App 484

As soon as he reached majority, Aylesford borrowed from Morris at a rate of over 60 per cent interest in order to pay off the large debts he had incurred in his minority. He had an allowance of less than £500 a year at that time but would have been entitled on his father's death to a large inheritance. Lord Selborne LC referred to a presumption of fraud arising from the circumstances or conditions of the parties, with weakness on one side and extortion or advantage taken of that weakness on the other side.

LORD SELBORNE LC: . . . Fraud does not here mean deceit or circumvention; it means an unconscientious use of the power arising out of these circumstances and conditions; and when the relative position of the parties is such as *prima facie* to raise this presumption, the transaction cannot stand unless the person claiming the benefit of it is able to repel the presumption by contrary evidence, proving it to have been in point of fact fair, just, and reasonable.

NOTES

1. *Fry* v *Lane* (1888) 40 ChD 312, involved sales by 'poor and ignorant' persons at considerable undervalues without independent advice. Kay J held that in those circumstances a court of equity could set aside the sales. He said (at p. 322):

    The result of the decisions is that where a purchase is made from a poor and ignorant man at a considerable undervalue, the vendor having no independent advice, a Court of Equity will set aside the transaction. . . .

    The circumstances of poverty and ignorance of the vendor, and absence of independent advice, throw upon the purchaser, when the transaction is impeached, the onus of proving, in Lord Selborne's words, that the purchase was 'fair, just, and reasonable.'

2. In *Cresswell* v *Potter* [1978] 1 WLR 255, Megarry J extended the scope of the principle in *Fry* v *Lane* by holding that a lady who was a Post Office telephonist and who sought to avoid a conveyance of her rights in the matrimonial home to her husband, was 'poor and ignorant'. He said (at pp. 257–9):

    The judge [Kay J in *Fry* v *Lane*] thus laid down three requirements. What has to be considered is, first, whether the plaintiff is poor and ignorant; second, whether the sale was at a considerable undervalue; and third, whether the vendor had independent advice. I am not, of course, suggesting that these are the only circumstances which will suffice; thus there may be circumstances of oppression or abuse of confidence which will invoke the aid of equity. But in the present case only these three requirements are in point. Abuse of confidence, though pleaded, is no longer relied on; and no circumstances of oppression or other matters are alleged. I must therefore consider whether the three requirements laid down in *Fry* v *Lane* are satisfied.

    I think that the plaintiff may fairly be described as falling within whatever is the modern equivalent of 'poor and ignorant.' Eighty years ago, when *Fry* v *Lane* was decided, social conditions were very different from those which exist today. I do not, however, think that the principle has changed, even though the euphemisms of the 20th century may require the word 'poor' to be replaced by 'a member of the lower income group' or the like, and the word 'ignorant' by 'less highly educated.' The plaintiff has been a van driver for a tobacconist, and is a Post Office telephonist. The evidence of her means is slender. The defendant told me that the plaintiff probably had a little saved, but not much; and there was evidence that her earnings were about the same as the defendant's, and that these were those of a carpenter. The plaintiff also has a legal aid certificate.

    In those circumstances I think the plaintiff may properly be described as 'poor' in the sense used in *Fry* v *Lane*, where it was applied to a laundryman who, in 1888, was earning £1 a week. In this context, as in others, I do not think that 'poverty' is confined to destitution. Further, although no doubt it requires considerable alertness and skill to be a good telephonist. I think that a telephonist can properly be described as 'ignorant' in the context of property transactions in general and the execution of conveyancing documents in particular. I have seen and heard the plaintiff giving evidence, and I have reached the conclusion that she satisfies the requirements of the first head. . . . [The second question was whether the sale was at a 'considerable undervalue'. Megarry J found that it was.]

    As for independent advice, from first to last there is no suggestion that the plaintiff had any. The defendant, his solicitor and the inquiry agent stood on one side: on the other the plaintiff stood alone. This was, of course, a conveyancing transaction, and English land law is notoriously complex. I am certainly not saying that other transactions, such as hire-purchase agreements, are free from all difficulty. But the authorities put before me on setting aside dealings at an undervalue all seem to relate to conveyancing transactions, and one may wonder whether the principle is confined to such transactions, and, if so, why. I doubt whether the principle is restricted in this way; and it may be that the explanation is that it is in conveyancing matters that, by long usage, it is regarded as usual, and, indeed, virtually essential, for the parties to have the services of a solicitor. The absence of the aid of a solicitor is thus, as it seems to me, of especial significance if a conveyancing matter is involved. The more usual it is to have a solicitor, the more striking will be his absence, and the more closely will the courts scrutinise what was done.

. . . [Counsel for the defendant] points out that the plaintiff was not bereft of possible legal assistance; for on or before July 28, 1959, when she was having difficulty in getting some furniture and effects from Slate Hall, she consulted a Colchester firm of solicitors . . . If she wanted legal advice, he said, this shows that she knew how to get it. However, what matters, I think, is not whether she could have obtained proper advice but whether in fact she had it; and she did not. Nobody, of course, can be compelled to obtain independent advice: but I do not think that someone who seeks to uphold what is, to him, an advantageous conveyancing transaction can do so merely by saying that the other party could have obtained independent advice, unless something has been done to bring to the notice of that other party the true nature of the transaction and the need for advice. . . .

At the end of the day, my conclusion is that this transaction cannot stand. In my judgment the plaintiff has made out her case, and so it is for the defendant to prove that the transaction was 'fair, just, and reasonable.' This he has not done. . . .

■ QUESTION

Is the crucial factor 'ignorance' rather than poverty, since considerable emphasis was placed on the fact that a conveyancing document is not easy for the layman to understand without legal advice?

NOTES

1. As in *Lloyds Bank* v *Bundy*, there was a positive duty imposed to advise the plaintiff of the need to seek legal advice. However, since there is no actual definition of 'poor and ignorant', situations covered by this principle are unclear.

2. In *Watkin* v *Watson-Smith*, *The Times*, 3 July 1986, Hirst J held *obiter* (because the contract was vitiated for mistake) that an old man of 80 who signed a contract to sell his bungalow for £2,950 instead of £29,500 could have relied on the principle in *Fry* v *Lane* even though he was not 'poor and ignorant'. The judge held that the desire for a quick sale and the old man's age, together with the accompanying diminution of his mental capacity and judgment, could suffice in place of 'poor and ignorant'.

   Thus *Fry* v *Lane* appears not to be restricted to the traditional three requirements, and it may be that, if this were desired, it could be extended to cover a general concept of 'unconscionable bargains'. However, the test of whether the terms of the transaction are fair, just, and reasonable in cases of inequality in bargaining power was rejected by Dillon LJ in *Alec Lobb* v *Total Oil GB Ltd* [1985] 1 WLR 173. He held that it had to be shown that the conduct of the stronger party was oppressive or unconscionable. (This was confirmed in *Hart* v *O'Connor* [1985] AC 1000, where it was stressed that there must be victimisation, i.e., the stronger party must take advantage of the weaker party.) On unconscionability, see the decision of the High Court of Australia in *Commercial Bank of Australia Ltd* v *Amadio* (1983) 151 CLR 447.

3. In *Boustany* v *Pigot* (1993) 69 P & CR 298 (noted Cartwright (1993) 109 LQR 530), the Privy Council set aside a transaction entered into by an ageing lady whose affairs were normally conducted by her cousin, and stressed that it is not sufficient that the transaction is unreasonable or unfair. What is required is unconscionable conduct in the sense of an 'abuse' of position. This suggests that in addition to the *Fry* v *Lane* requirements it is also necessary to prove unconscionability. Unconscionability cannot, it seems, simply be inferred from the existence of the *Fry* v *Lane* requirements.

4. In *Barclays Bank* v *Schwartz*, *The Times*, 2 August 1995, the Court of Appeal held that illiteracy

or unfamiliarity with the English language might found a claim in equity to set aside a transaction as a harsh and unconscionable bargain, but it would be necessary to establish more than weaker bargaining power. It would also need to be established that unfair advantage had been gained by the use of this bargaining power against the weaker party. This appears to be in line with the approach advocated in *Boustany* v *Pigot*.

5. In *Credit Lyonnais* v *Burch* [1997] 1 All ER 144, *page 649*, Nourse LJ considered that the principle in *Fry* v *Lane* was capable of being adapted 'to different transactions entered into in changing circumstances' and he considered it to be arguable that, applying this principle, Miss Burch could have had the legal charge set aside as an unconscionable bargain. However he did not decide the case on this basis because there had been no argument on this ground in the court below.

It is interesting, however, that Nourse LJ considered that unconscionability was directly material to the undue influence issue. But see Birks and Chin, 'On the Nature of Undue Influence' in *Good Faith and Fault in Contract Law*, Beatson and Friedmann (eds) (OUP, 1995). Millett LJ also appeared to consider that in both cases the impropriety by one party, e.g., taking advantage of the situation, could be inferred from the harshness of the terms of the transaction. He stated that:

> Miss Burch did not seek to have the transaction set aside as a harsh and unconscionable bargain. To do so she would have had to show not only that the terms of the transaction were harsh or oppressive, but that 'one of the parties to it has imposed the objectionable terms in a morally reprehensible manner, that is to say, in a way which affects his conscience' (see *Multiservice Bookbinding Ltd* v *Marden* [1978] 2 All ER 489 at 502, [1979] Ch 84 at 110 per Browne-Wilkinson J and *Alec Lobb (Garages) Ltd* v *Total Oil GB Ltd* [1983] 1 All ER 944 at 961, [1983] 1 WLR 87 at 95, where I pointed out that there must be some impropriety, both in the conduct of the stronger party and in the terms of the transaction itself, but added that 'the former may often be inferred from the latter in the absence of an innocent explanation').
>
> In the present case, the bank did not obtain the guarantee directly from Miss Burch. It was provided to the bank by Mr Pelosi, who obtained it from Miss Burch by the exercise of undue influence. In such a context, the two equitable jurisdictions to set aside harsh and unconscionable bargains and to set aside transactions obtained by undue influence have many similarities. In either case it is necessary to show that the conscience of the party who seeks to uphold the transaction was affected by notice, actual or constructive, of the impropriety by which it was obtained by the intermediary, and in either case the court may in a proper case infer the presence of the impropriety from the terms of the transaction itself.

In *Dunbar Bank plc* v *Nadeem* [1998] 3 All ER 876, *page 659*, Millett LJ appeared to recognise a link between unconscionability and undue influence. He stated (at p. 884):

> The court of equity is a court of conscience. It sets aside transactions obtained by the exercise of undue influence because such conduct is unconscionable. But however the present case is analysed, whether as a case of actual or presumed influence, the influence was not undue. It is impossible, in my judgment, to criticise Mr Nadeem's conduct as unconscionable.

Chen-Wishart argues ([1997] CLJ 60, at 62–3) that 'unconscionability should be recognised as the informing principle at the root of the *O'Brien* formulation' and that unconscionability would give *O'Brien* 'a sound theoretical basis'.

The link between undue influence and unconscionability was considered further in the following case.

Portman Building Society v Dusangh

[2000] 2 All ER (Comm) 221 (CA)

The defendant, then aged 72 and regarded as poor and illiterate, had been granted a 25 year mortgage on his property. The advance was to be used by the defendant's son in order to purchase a supermarket business. The son was the guarantor of the mortgage and had agreed to pay it off. The son defaulted and the building society sought possession. The defendant alleged, *inter alia*, that the transaction had been entered into as a result of undue influence and it was an unconscionable bargain (relying on *Credit Lyonnais* v *Burch*). These defences were rejected and the defendant appealed. On appeal held: the requirements to establish undue influence and unconscionability were similar but none had been established in this case.

WARD LJ:

Does Barclays Bank v O'Brien apply?

That was a case concerned with undue influence. A person who has been induced to enter into a transaction by undue influence of another (the wrongdoer) is entitled to set that transaction aside as against the wrongdoer. Where a person is unconscionably prevailed upon by the wrongdoer to enter into a transaction, then equity again allows rescission. There is some interesting argument for merging the two doctrines: see the article by David Capper 'Undue Influence and Unconscionability: A Rationalisation' (1998) 114 LQR 479, from which I gratefully acknowledge having drawn some of these ideas. Professors Birks and Chin in their article 'On the Nature of Undue Influence', in J Beatson and D Friedmann (eds) *Good Faith and Fault in Contract Law* (1995) would preserve the distinction. They see undue influence as being 'plaintiff-sided' and concerned with the weakness of the plaintiff's consent owing to an excessive dependence upon the defendant, and unconscionability as being 'defendant-sided' and concerned with the defendant's exploitation of the plaintiff's vulnerability. I do not find it necessary to resolve this debate. I am content to accept for present purposes the judgment of Mason J in the *Commercial Bank of Australia Ltd* case (1983) 151 CLR 447 at 461:

> Historically, courts have exercised jurisdiction to set aside contracts and other dealings on a variety of equitable grounds. They include fraud, misrepresentation, breach of fiduciary duty, undue influence and unconscionable conduct. In one sense they all constitute species of unconscionable conduct on the part of a party who stands to receive a benefit under a transaction which, in the eye of equity, cannot be enforced because to do so would be inconsistent with equity and good conscience. But relief on the ground of 'unconscionable conduct' is usually taken to refer to the class of case in which a party makes unconscientious use of his superior position or bargaining power to the detriment of a party who suffers from some special disability or is placed in some special situation of disadvantage, e.g. . . . an unfair contract made by taking advantage of a person who is seriously affected by intoxicating drink. Although unconscionable conduct in this narrow sense bears some resemblance to the doctrine of undue influence, there is a difference between the two. In the latter the will of the innocent party is not independent and voluntary because it is overborne. In the former the will of the innocent party, even if independent and voluntary, is the result of the disadvantageous position in which he is placed and of the other party unconscientiously taking advantage of that position.

In *Barclays Bank plc* v *O'Brien* [1993] 4 All ER 417 at 428, [1994] 1 AC 180 at 195 Lord Browne-Wilkinson said:

> A wife who has been induced to stand as a surety for her husband's debts by his undue influence, misrepresentation *or some other legal wrong* has an equity as against him to set aside that transaction. Under the ordinary principles of equity, her right to set aside her transaction will be enforceable against third parties (e.g. against a creditor) if . . . the third party had actual or constructive notice of the facts giving rise to her equity. (My emphasis.)

Unconscionable conduct is 'some other legal wrong'.

In *Burch's* case [1997] 1 All ER 144 at 153 Millett LJ said:

> . . . the two equitable jurisdictions to set aside harsh and unconscionable bargains and to set aside transactions obtained by undue influence have many similarities. In either case it is necessary to show that the conscience of the party who seeks to uphold the transaction was affected by notice, actual or constructive, of the impropriety by which it was obtained by the intermediary, and in either case the court may in a proper case infer the presence of the impropriety from the terms of the transaction itself. . . .

Unconscionable conduct by the building society itself

This became the primary basis of the appeal. The case was that the father was entitled to set aside the charge directly against the building society as an unconscionable bargain. It was submitted that the transaction was unconscionable in the light of knowledge possessed by the building society that the borrower was a retired man of 72 years who might well be dead before the expiry of the 25-year term of the borrowing, whose existing mortgage was only £4,000 and whose ability to repay the £33,750 lent on this occasion could not be supported by his income even when supplemented by his son. It was an improvident transaction which put the borrower's home at risk. Furthermore, had the society's own policies been followed, then the society would have learnt that the borrower was illiterate with a poor understanding of English, had no need to mortgage his own home and did so solely for his son's benefit. The case put was:

> In summary the advance was unconscionable in that [the father] by reason of his age, illiteracy, lack of education and poverty was under some serious disadvantage affecting his ability to protect himself. . . .

The first defendant's argument derives from an application of the judgment of Kay J in *Fry* v *Lane, re Fry, Whittet* v *Bush* (1888) 40 Ch D 312 at 322, as modernised by Megarry J in *Cresswell* v *Potter* [1978] 1 WLR 255n. The first defendant concentrates on the three elements there referred to: first, the 'poor and ignorant man'; second, the considerable undervalue/manifest disadvantage; and, third, the lack of independent advice.

It may be that the absence of legal advice is not so much an essential free-standing requirement, but rather a powerful factor confirming the suspicion of nefarious dealing which the presence of advice would serve to dispel. As Megarry J pointed out in *Cresswell's* case [1978] 1 WLR 255 at 258, the authorities seem to have related to conveyancing transactions where, by long usage, it was regarded as usual, and, indeed, virtually essential, for the parties to have the services of a solicitor. He added, and I agree: 'The more usual it is to have a solicitor, the more striking will be his absence, and the more closely will the courts scrutinise what was done.' Assuming, however, that all three elements are required and that they are all established then, as Millett LJ put it in *Burch*'s case [1997] 1 All ER 144 at 152: 'The transaction gives rise to grave suspicion. It cries out for an explanation.' The burden then falls on the beneficiary of the transaction to show, in Lord Selborne LC's words, that it was 'fair, just and reasonable'.

I venture to think, however, that when Kay J cast the onus on the purchaser, he had in mind no more than that the facts would give rise to an evidential presumption of wrongdoing. I tend to agree with Capper (p. 496) that that means that:

> . . . where a sufficiently bad case of relational inequality and transactional imbalance exists, one which almost speaks for itself that there has been unconscionability, then unconscionable conduct can be inferred unless the defendant can offer an explanation to displace it. To hold that a presumption arising upon the mere coincidence of the first two elements of the doctrine of unconscionability would be to deny the effect of high authority clearly stating that unconscionable conduct is an essential part of this doctrine.

That is the weakness of the first defendant's case. What the first defendant's approach on the facts of this case appears to me to miss is this: for the lending by the building society to be unconscionable, it must, as is implicit in the very word, be against the conscience of the lender—he must act with no conscience, with no moral sense that he is doing wrong. Making all the assumptions in the first defendant's favour of the frailties of the father, the lack of wisdom in taking on this large commitment with limited income, the real risk of foreclosure, the failure by the building society to follow its own rules, even an assumption that the building society in those heady days of rising property prices was lending money almost irresponsibly, none of that, in my judgment, gets near to establishing morally reprehensible conduct on its part. The family wanted to raise money: the building society was prepared to lend it. One shakes one's head, but with sadness and with incredulity at the folly of it all, alas not with moral outrage. I am afraid the moral conscience of the court has not been shocked. That is an end of the matter.

Accordingly the appeal should be dismissed.

NOTES

1. Unfortunately the Court of Appeal does not give an in-depth assessment of the relationship between undue influence and unconscionability but does accept that they are very similar in their requirements. Ward LJ is prepared to rely on the statement of Mason J in *Commercial Bank of Australia* v *Amadio* although this also identifies a fundamental distinction between the doctrines without resolving its effect, if any, in terms of outcome.

2. The reference to the manifest disadvantage requirement and to whether the transaction was one that 'no competent solicitor could have advised the defendant to enter into' must now be read in the light of the decision of the House of Lords in *Royal Bank of Scotland* v *Etridge (No. 2), pages 628 and 655.*

14

Illegality and Capacity to Contract

Contracts may be void by reason of a statutory provision or on grounds of public policy. Alternatively, contracts may be illegal.

An example of contracts which statute renders void and unenforceable is gaming and wagering contracts (s. 18 of the Gaming Act 1845).

SECTION 1: CONTRACTS VOID ON GROUNDS OF PUBLIC POLICY

A: Contracts in restraint of trade

A restraint of trade is a contractual undertaking whereby one party agrees to restrict his freedom to trade or to conduct his business in a particular area for a specified period of time. (See Smith, 'Reconstructing Restraint of Trade' (1995) 15 OJLS 565.)

(a) Basic principles

Nordenfelt v *Maxim Nordenfelt Guns & Ammunition Company Ltd*
[1894] AC 535 (HL)

The defendant, who owned patents and operated a business of manufacturing quick-firing guns and ammunition, sold the business and its goodwill to a company. The agreement contained a covenant on the part of the defendant that for 25 years the defendant would not, directly or indirectly, engage in the business of a manufacturer of guns or ammunition except on behalf of the company, and would not engage in any business competing or liable to compete in any way with the business being carried on by the company. The House of Lords was asked to consider only the first part of the covenant (relating to engaging in a gun manufacturing business). Held: it was valid because even though it was a worldwide restriction, there was only a limited number of customers (governments of this and other countries) so that the restriction was not wider than was necessary to protect the company and it was not injurious to the public interest. (The Court of Appeal had held that the second part was void because it went further than was necessary to protect the business acquired, *see below*.)

LORD MACNAGHTEN: In the age of Queen Elizabeth all restraints of trade, whatever they were, general or partial, were thought to be contrary to public policy, and therefore void. In time, however, it was found that a rule so rigid and far-reaching must seriously interfere with transactions of every-day occurrence. Traders could hardly venture to let their shops out of their own hands; the purchaser of a business was at the mercy of the seller; every apprentice was a possible rival. So the rule was relaxed. It was relaxed as far as the exigencies of trade for the time being required, gradually and not without difficulty, until it came to be recognised that all partial restraints might be good, though it was thought that general restraints, that is, restraints of general application extending throughout the kingdom, must be bad. Why was the relaxation supposed to be thus limited? Simply because nobody imagined in those days that a general restraint could be reasonable, not because there was any inherent or essential distinction between the two cases. 'Where the restraint is general,' says Lord Macclesfield, in *Mitchel* v *Reynolds* (1711) 1 P Wms 181, 'not to exercise a trade throughout the kingdom,' the restraint 'must be void, being of no benefit to either party and only oppressive. . . .' Later on he gives his reason. 'What does it signify,' he says, 'to a tradesman in London what another does at Newcastle; and surely it would be unreasonable to fix a certain loss on one side without any benefit to the other.' . . .

The true view at the present time I think, is this: The public have an interest in every person's carrying on his trade freely: so has the individual. All interference with individual liberty of action in trading, and all restraints of trade of themselves, if there is nothing more, are contrary to public policy, and therefore void. That is the general rule. But there are exceptions: restraints of trade and interference with individual liberty of action may be justified by the special circumstances of a particular case. It is a sufficient justification, and indeed it is the only justification, if the restriction is reasonable—reasonable, that is, in reference to the interests of the parties concerned and reasonable in reference to the interests of the public, so framed and so guarded as to afford adequate protection to the party in whose favour it is imposed, while at the same time it is in no way injurious to the public.

NOTES

1. The presumption that contracts in restraint of trade are void can be rebutted by a party seeking to rely on the restraint showing that the restraint is reasonable as between the parties. Once this is established, the restraint can be relied upon unless the party seeking to prevent its enforcement shows that it is contrary to the public interest.

2. *Nordenfelt* v *Maxim Nordenfelt* concerned a covenant on the sale of a business (i.e., that the vendor would not carry on a business competing with the business purchased). These covenants are more likely to be held to be reasonable and enforceable because a price will be paid for the goodwill of the business, and therefore the purchaser has a legitimate interest in protecting that goodwill and the business connections. It would be unfair to the purchaser if the vendor could then set up a competing business. (Compare with the position, as in *Dranez Anstalt* v *Hayek* [2002] EWCA Civ 1729, [2003] 1 BCLC 278, where the purchaser only receives shares in the business as the price for a financial investment and therefore does not have the same legitimate interest in protecting the goodwill of the business.) In any event, the restraint must be restricted to protecting only the goodwill of the business actually sold (see *British Reinforced Concrete Engineering Co. Ltd* v *Schelff* [1921] 2 Ch 563).

(b) Covenants between employer and employee

The restriction must seek to protect a *legitimate interest* of the employer (i.e., influence over customers or trade secrets) as opposed to protection against skills acquired by the employee which might render him a potential competitor. The restriction must be reasonable as between the parties and no wider than reasonably necessary to protect the business connections or confidential information of the employer. There are three factors: subject matter, area, and duration.

Herbert Morris Limited v *Saxelby*

[1916] 1 AC 688 (HL)

The plaintiff company, leading manufacturers of hoisting machinery in the UK, employed the defendant as a draftsman and then as an engineer on a two-year contract. The terms of this contract contained a covenant by the defendant that he would not, 'during a period of seven years from ceasing to be employed by the company, either in the United Kingdom of Great Britain or Ireland, carry on either as principal, agent, servant or otherwise, alone or jointly or in connection with any other person, firm or company, or be concerned or assist, directly or indirectly, whether for reward or otherwise, in the sale or manufacture of pulley blocks, hand overhead runways, electric overhead runways, or hand overhead travelling cranes'. The plaintiff company sought to enforce this covenant. Held: the covenant was wider than was required for the protection of the plaintiff company and was not enforceable.

LORD PARKER OF WADDINGTON: It will be observed that in Lord Macnaghten's opinion [in *Nordenfelt*] two conditions must be fulfilled if the restraint is to be held valid. First, it must be reasonable in the interests of the contracting parties, and, secondly, it must be reasonable in the interests of the public. In the case of each condition he lays down a test of reasonableness. To be reasonable in the interests of the parties the restraint must afford adequate protection to the party in whose favour it is imposed; to be reasonable in the interests of the public it must be in no way injurious to the public.

With regard to the former test, I think it clear that what is meant is that for a restraint to be reasonable in the interests of the parties it must afford *no more than* adequate protection to the party in whose favour it is imposed. So conceived the test appears to me to be valid both as regards the covenantor and covenantee, for though in one sense no doubt it is contrary to the interests of the covenantor to subject himself to any restraint, still it may be for his advantage to be able so to subject himself in cases where, if he could not do so, he would lose other advantages, such as the possibility of obtaining the best terms on the sale of an existing business or the possibility of obtaining employment or training under competent employers. As long as the restraint to which he subjects himself is no wider than is required for the adequate protection of the person in whose favour it is created, it is in his interest to be able to bind himself for the sake of the indirect advantages he may obtain by so doing. It was at one time thought that, in order to ascertain whether a restraint were reasonable in the interests of the covenantor, the Court ought to weigh the advantages accruing to the covenantor under the contract against the disadvantages imposed upon him by the restraint, but any such process has long since been rejected as impracticable. The Court no longer considers the adequacy of the consideration in any particular case. If it be reasonable that a covenantee should, for his own protection, ask for a restraint, it is in my opinion equally reasonable that the covenantor should be able to subject himself to this restraint. The test of reasonableness is the same in both cases.

It was suggested in argument that the interests of the public ought to be considered and weighed in determining whether a restraint is reasonable in the interests of the parties. I dissent from this view. It would, indeed, entirely destroy the value of Lord Macnaghten's tests of reasonableness. The first question in every case is whether the restraint is reasonable in the interests of the parties. If it is not, the restraint is bad. If it is, it may still be shown that it is injurious to the public, though . . . the onus of so showing would lie on the party alleging it.

My Lords, it appears to me that Lord Macnaghten's statement of the law requires amplification in another respect. If the restraint is to secure no more than 'adequate protection' to the party in whose favour it is imposed, it becomes necessary to consider in each particular case what it is for which and what it is against which protection is required. Otherwise it would be impossible to pass any opinion on the adequacy of the protection.

. . . It was argued before your Lordships that no distinction can be drawn between the position of the purchaser of the goodwill of a business taking a covenant from his vendor and the case of the owner of a business taking a covenant from his servant or apprentice. In both cases it was said that the property to be protected was the same and the dangers to be guarded against the same. I am of opinion that this argument cannot be accepted. The distinction between the two cases is, I think, quite clear, and is recognised both by Lord Macnaghten and Lord Herschell in the *Nordenfelt Case* [1894] AC 535. The goodwill of a business is immune from the danger of the owner exercising his personal knowledge and skill to its detriment, and if the purchaser is to take over such goodwill with all its advantages it must, in his hands, remain similarly immune. Without, therefore, a covenant on the part of the vendor against competition, a purchaser would not get what he is contracting to buy, nor could the vendor give what he is intending to sell. The covenant against competition is, therefore, reasonable if confined to the area within which it would in all probability enure to the injury of the purchaser.

It is quite different in the case of an employer taking such a covenant from his employee or apprentice. The goodwill of his business is, under the conditions in which we live, necessarily subject to the competition of all persons (including the servant or apprentice) who choose to engage in a similar trade. The employer in such a case is not endeavouring to protect what he has, but to gain a special advantage which he could not otherwise secure. I cannot find any case in which a covenant against competition by a servant or apprentice has, as such, ever been upheld by the Court. Wherever such covenants have been upheld it had been on the ground, not that the servant or apprentice would, by reason of his employment or training, obtain the skill and knowledge necessary to equip him as a possible competitor in the trade, but that he might obtain such personal knowledge of and influence over the customers of his employer, or such an acquaintance with his employer's trade secrets as would enable him, if competition were allowed, to take advantage of his employer's trade connection or utilise information confidentially obtained.

In *Mason v Provident Clothing and Supply Co.* [1913] AC 724 it was argued, . . . that an employer might reasonably say 'I will not have the skill and knowledge acquired in my employment imparted to my trade rivals,' and that the validity of the restraint did not depend upon personal contact with the employer's customers, but upon the fact that the employee gained that general knowledge which put him into a position to compete with his master and made him a source of danger, against which the master was entitled to protect himself.

This argument was rejected by your Lordships' House, and the restraint in question was held bad, as being wider than was necessary to protect the employer from injury by misuse of the employee's acquaintance with customers or knowledge of trade secrets. In fact the reason, and the only reason, for upholding such a restraint on the part of an employee is that the employer has some proprietary right, whether in the nature of trade connection or in the nature of trade secrets, for the protection of which such a restraint is—having regard to the duties of the employee—reasonably necessary. Such a restraint has, so far as I know, never been upheld, if directed only to the prevention of competition or against the use of the personal skill and knowledge acquired by the employee in his employer's business.

My Lords, it remains to apply what I have said to the particular circumstances of the present case. Mr Herbert Morris, the managing director of the plaintiff company, very candidly admitted that the real object of the plaintiff company in imposing the restraint was to preclude competition on the part of the defendant after he had left the company's employment. The company objected, he said, to skill and knowledge acquired in its service being put at the disposition of any trade rival, and the skill and knowledge he referred to was the general skill and knowledge which an employee of any ability must necessarily obtain as opposed to knowledge of any matter and skill in any process in which the company could be said to have any property at all. . . . As directed against competition or against the use of this skill and knowledge, I am clearly of opinion that the restraint was in no way required for the plaintiffs' protection, and therefore unreasonable and bad in law.

An attempt was, however, made in argument to justify the restraint on the ground that it was no more than adequate for the protection of the plaintiffs' trade connection and trade secrets. I am of opinion that this attempt completely failed. With regard to the plaintiffs' connection, there is little or no evidence that the defendant ever came into personal contact with the plaintiffs' customers. For a period, it is true, he was manager of the London branch of the plaintiffs' business, and for another period sales manager at Loughborough. With the exception of these periods he was employed entirely in the engineering department. Had the restraint been confined to London and Loughborough and a reasonable area round each of these centres, it might possibly have been supported as reasonably necessary to protect the plaintiffs' connection, but a restraint extending over the United Kingdom was obviously too wide in this respect.

With regard to trade secrets, I am not satisfied that the defendant was entrusted with any trade secret in the proper sense of the word at all. . . .

NOTE: A 'trade secret' can always be protected even where there is no express clause in the contract. In *Forster & Sons (Ltd)* v *Suggett* (1918) 35 TLR 87, the defendant was employed as the plaintiff's works manager and had been instructed in their confidential manufacturing processes for glass. The contract of employment contained a covenant whereby the defendant was not to divulge any trade secrets and was not to carry on or be interested in glass bottle manufacture or any other business connected with glass making carried on by the plaintiffs for five years after the termination of his employment. Sargant J granted an injunction to restrain the divulging of the trade secret, namely the confidential manufacturing processes, since this restriction was reasonable to protect the company's interests, even though it extended to the whole country and lasted for five years.

Mason v Provident Clothing & Supply Company Ltd
[1913] AC 724 (HL)

The defendant was employed as a canvasser by the plaintiffs for the district of Islington in London. The defendant covenanted not to work in any similar business for three years within 25 miles of London. Held: as the defendant's duties were confined to the district of Islington, the clause was wider than was reasonably necessary to protect the plaintiffs' interests.

LORD MOULTON: . . . Are the restrictions which the covenant imposes upon the freedom of action of the servant after he has left the service of the master greater than are reasonably necessary for the protection of the master in his business?

The first task of the Court, therefore, is to ascertain with due particularity the nature of the master's business and of the servant's employment therein. . . .

The nature of the employment of the appellant in this business was solely to obtain members and collect their instalments. A small district in London was assigned to him, which he canvassed and in which he collected the payments due, and outside that small district he had no duties. His employment was therefore that of a local canvasser and debt collector, and nothing more.

Such being the nature of the employment, it would be reasonable for the employer to protect himself against the danger of his former servant canvassing or collecting for a rival firm in the district in which he had been employed. If he were permitted to do so before the expiry of a reasonably long interval he would be in a position to give to his new employer all the advantages of that personal knowledge of the inhabitants of the locality, and more especially of his former customers, which he had acquired in the service of the respondents and at their expense. Against such a contingency the master might reasonably protect himself, but I can see no further or other protection which he could reasonably demand. If the servant is employed by a rival firm in some district which neither includes that in which he formerly worked for the respondents, nor is immediately adjoining thereto, there is no personal knowledge which he has acquired in his former master's service which can be used to that master's prejudice. The respondents would be in no different position from that in which they would be if the appellant had acquired his experience in the service of some other company carrying on a like business.

Considering the strictly local character of the employment, I have no hesitation in saying that I should be prepared to hold that [the] area [here] is very far greater than could be reasonably required for the protection of his former employers.

(c) Exclusive dealing agreements

Esso Petroleum Co. Ltd v *Harper's Garage (Stourport) Ltd*
[1968] AC 269 (HL)

The parties entered into agreements relating to the supply of Esso petrol to two garages belonging to Harper. By these agreements Harper agreed to purchase petrol only from Esso, and in return they obtained a small discount on the price. For the first garage the tie was to last for four years and five months, but for the second garage a loan of £7,000 was made and the tie was to last for 21 years while the mortgage repayments were made on this loan. An injunction was sought to prevent Harper from buying petrol from another supplier. Held: these exclusive dealing agreements were within the restraint of trade doctrine because Harper had given up a right to sell other petrol. Although the restraint which operated for four and a half years was not longer than was necessary to afford adequate protection to Esso's legitimate interests in maintaining a stable system of distribution, the tie of 21 years went beyond a reasonable period, and therefore that restraint agreement was void.

LORD REID: . . . It is true that it would be an innovation to hold that ordinary negative covenants preventing the use of a particular site for trading of all kinds or of a particular kind are within the scope of the doctrine of restraint of trade. I do not think they are. Restraint of trade appears to me to imply that a man contracts to give up some freedom which otherwise he would have had. A person buying or leasing land had no previous right to be there at all, let alone to trade there, and when he takes possession of that land subject to a negative restrictive covenant he gives up no right or freedom which he previously had. . . .

In my view this agreement is within the scope of the doctrine of restraint of trade as it had been developed in English law. Not only have the respondents agreed negatively not to sell other petrol but they have agreed positively to keep this garage open for the sale of the appellants' petrol at all reasonable hours throughout the period of the tie. It was argued that this was merely regulating the respondent's trading and rather promoting than restraining his trade. But regulating a person's existing trade may be a greater restraint than prohibiting him from engaging in a new trade. And a contract to take one's whole supply from one source may be much more hampering than a contract to sell one's whole output to one buyer. I would not attempt to define the dividing line between contracts which are and contracts which are not in restraint of trade, but in my view this contract must be held to be in restraint of trade. So it is necessary to consider whether its provisions can be justified.

[Lord Reid referred to Lord Macnaghten's statement in the *Nordenfelt* case, *page 674*, and continued:]

So in every case it is necessary to consider first whether the restraint went farther than to afford adequate protection to the party in whose favour it was granted, secondly whether it can be justified as being in the interests of the party restrained, and, thirdly, whether it must be held contrary to the public interest. I find it difficult to agree with the way in which the court has in some cases treated the interests of the party restrained. Surely it can never be in the interest of a person to agree to suffer a restraint unless he gets some compensating advantage, direct or indirect. And Lord Macnaghten said: '. . . of course the quantum of consideration may enter into the question of the reasonableness of the contract.'

Where two experienced traders are bargaining on equal terms and one has agreed to a restraint for reasons which seem good to him the court is in grave danger of stultifying itself if it says that it knows that trader's interest better than he does himself. But there may well be cases where, although the party to be restrained has deliberately accepted the main terms of the contract, he has been at a disadvantage as regards other terms: for example where a set of conditions has been incorporated which has not been the subject of negotiation—there the court may have greater freedom to hold them unreasonable.

. . . [W]hether or not a restraint is in the personal interests of the parties, it is I think well established that the court will not enforce a restraint which goes further than affording adequate protection to the legitimate interests of the party in whose favour it is granted. This must I think be because too wide a restraint is against the public interest. . . .

When petrol rationing came to an end in 1950 the large producers began to make agreements, now known as solus agreements, with garage owners under which the garage owner, in return for certain advantages, agreed to sell only the petrol of the producer with whom he made the agreement. Within a short time three-quarters of the filling stations in this country were tied in that way and by the dates of the agreements in this case over 90 per cent had agreed to ties. It appears that the garage owners were not at a disadvantage in bargaining with the large producing companies as there was intense competition between these companies to obtain these ties. So we can assume that both the garage owners and the companies thought that such ties were to their advantage. And it is not said in this case that all ties are either against the public interest or against the interests of the parties. The respondents' case is that the ties with which we are concerned are for too long periods.

The advantage to the garage owner is that he gets a rebate on the wholesale price of the petrol which he buys and also may get other benefits or financial assistance. The main advantages for the producing company appear to be that distribution is made easier and more economical and that it is assured of a steady outlet for its petrol over a period. As regards distribution, it appears that there were some 35,000 filling stations in this country at the relevant time, of which about a fifth were tied to the appellants. So they only have to distribute to some 7,000 filling stations instead of to a very much larger number if most filling stations sold several brands of petrol. But the main reason why the producing companies want ties for five years and more, instead of ties for one or two years only, seems to be that they can organise their business better if on the average only one-fifth or less of their ties come to an end in any one year. The appellants make a point of the fact that they have invested some £200 millions in refineries and other plant and that they could not have done that unless they could foresee a steady and assured level of sales of their petrol. Most of their ties appear to have been made for periods of between five and 20 years. But we have no evidence as to the precise additional advantage which they derive from a five-year tie as compared with a two-year tie or from a 20-year tie as compared with a five-year tie.

The Court of Appeal held that these ties were for unreasonably long periods. They thought that, if for any reason the respondents ceased to sell the appellants' petrol, the appellants could have found other suitable outlets in the neighbourhood within two or three years. I do not think that that is the right test. In the first place there was no evidence about this and I do not think that it would be practicable to apply this test in practice. It might happen that when the respondents ceased to sell their petrol, the appellants would find such an alternative outlet in a very short time. But, looking to the fact that well over 90 per cent of existing filling stations are tied and that there may be great difficulty in opening a new filling station, it might take a very long time to find an alternative. Any estimate of how long it might take to find suitable alternatives for the respondents' filling stations could be little better than guesswork.

I do not think that the appellants' interest can be regarded so narrowly. They are not so much concerned with any particular outlet as with maintaining a stable system of distribution throughout the country so as to enable their business to be run efficiently and economically. In my view there is sufficient material to justify a decision that ties of less than five years were insufficient, in the circumstances of the trade when these agreements were made, to afford adequate protection to the appellants' legitimate interests . . . A tie for 21 years stretches far beyond any period for which developments are reasonably foreseeable. Restrictions on the garage owner which might seem tolerable and reasonable in reasonably foreseeable conditions might come to have a very different effect in quite different conditions: the public interest comes in here more strongly. And, apart from a case where he gets a loan, a garage owner appears to get no greater advantage from a 20-year tie than he gets from a five-year tie. So I would think that there must at least be some clearly established advantage to the producing company—something to show that a shorter period would not be adequate—before so long a period could be justified. But in this case there is no evidence to prove anything of the kind. . . . I would add that the decision in this case—particularly in view of the paucity of evidence—ought not, in my view, to be regarded as laying down any general rule as to the length of tie permissible in a solus agreement . . . I must not be taken as expressing any opinion as to the validity of ties for periods mid-way between the two periods with which the present case is concerned.

NOTE: Lord Reid stated that the restraint of trade doctrine only applied where a person gave up a right that would otherwise have been enjoyed. Therefore, if an exclusive dealing transaction relating to land was inserted in a conveyance or lease of land, it would not be subject to the doctrine, since a person buying or leasing land has no previous right to trade there and would not be giving up any right previously held.

Potentially, this provides a method for petrol companies to avoid the operation of the restraint of trade doctrine in the context of exclusive dealing agreements. However, in the next case the Court of Appeal refused to allow this device to operate on the facts.

Alec Lobb (Garages) Ltd v Total Oil GB Ltd
[1985] 1 WLR 173 (CA)

In order to raise capital, the plaintiff company leased the land on which it carried on business as a garage and filling station to the defendant petrol company. The plaintiff company had earlier borrowed money from the defendant company and had an exclusive dealing agreement lasting for 18 years (the duration of the loan). The defendant company leased the land back to the proprietors of the plaintiff company (Mr and Mrs L) for an annual rental payment. The agreement contained a solus agreement to purchase the defendant's petrol exclusively for a 21-year period. Held: although technically the individual plaintiffs had no right to trade on the land before the leaseback arrangement, the reality was that the lease and leaseback should be treated as one transaction designed to enable the plaintiffs to continue to trade on the property. The defendant company should not be in a better position than if the leaseback had been granted to the plaintiff company. The tie for 21 years was reasonable because the arrangement was a rescue operation designed to benefit the plaintiffs, the leaseback had break clauses after seven and 14 years so that Mr and Mrs L were not locked in for the 21 years, and the consideration for the lease (and the tie) equated with the market value.

NOTE: It is important to be aware that restrictions on free competition are subject to detailed legislative regulation. See Competition Act 1998 and Articles 81 and 82 of the EC Treaty (as amended by the Treaty of Amsterdam). For a detailed discussion see M. Furse, *Competition Law of the EC & UK*, 4th edn, 2004: Oxford University Press; and for a briefer account, see J. Poole, *Textbook on Contract*, 7th edn, 2004: Oxford University Press, section 12.7.9.

In *Courage Ltd* v *Crehan* (C-453/99) [2002] QB 507, the European Court of Justice held that Article 81(1) permitted one party to an anti-competitive agreement to sue the other for damages resulting from the operation of that anti-competitive agreement. The matter arose in the factual context of an exclusive dealing agreement relating to the supply of beer. The ECJ went further and stated that an English national law, barring such a damages claim *on the sole ground* that the claimant was a party to an illegal contract, was precluded by Article 81 since it would impair the effectiveness of that provision. Such a national rule barring the recovery of damages would, however, be permissible where the claimant bore 'a significant responsibility for the distortion of competition'. This would depend upon factors such as the respective bargaining power of the parties and the economic and legal context of the agreement. In *Crehan* v *Inntrepreneur Pub Company CPC* [2004] EWCA Civ 637, [2004] UKCLR 1500, [2004] ECC 28, the Court of Appeal held that the claimant could recover such damages in respect of an agreement breaching the EU

Treaty. Further, in *Days Medical Aids Ltd* v *Pihsiang Machinery Manufacturing Co. Ltd* [2004] EWHC 44 (Comm), [2004] 1 All ER (Comm) 991, Langley J held where Community law (Article 81) did not invalidate an agreement because it did not have anti-competitive effects, the agreement could not be subject to the common law restraint of trade doctrine.

(d) Exclusive service agreements

A. *Schroeder Music Publishing Co. Ltd* v *Macaulay*
[1974] 1 WLR 1308 (HL)

M, an unknown 21-year-old song writer, entered into a contract with S Ltd, music publishers, whereby they engaged his exclusive services for five years. Under the contract, M assigned full copyright for all of his compositions during the contractual period. However, S Ltd were not obliged to publish anything composed by M. If M's royalties exceeded £5,000 during the five-year period the contract was to be automatically extended for another five years, but although S Ltd could terminate the agreement on one month's notice, M had no such rights. M alleged that the agreement was contrary to public policy. Held: the agreement fell within the restraint of trade doctrine. It was unreasonable as between the parties since it was one-sided.

LORD REID: . . . I think that in a case like the present case two questions must be considered. Are the terms of the agreement so restrictive that either they cannot be justified at all or they must be justified by the party seeking to enforce the agreement? Then, if there is room for justification, has that party proved justification—normally by showing that the restrictions were not more than what was reasonably required to protect his legitimate interests? . . .

The public interest requires in the interests both of the public and of the individual that everyone should be free so far as practicable to earn a livelihood and to give to the public the fruits of his particular abilities. The main question to be considered is whether and how far the operation of the terms of this agreement is likely to conflict with this objective. The respondent is bound to assign to the appellants during a long period the fruits of his musical talent. But what are the appellants bound to do with those fruits? Under the contract nothing. If they do use the songs which the respondent composes they must pay in terms of the contract. But they need not do so. As has been said they may put them in a drawer and leave them there.

No doubt the expectation was that if the songs were of value they would be published to the advantage of both parties. But if for any reason the appellants chose not to publish them the respondent would get no remuneration and he could not do anything. Inevitably the respondent must take the risk of misjudgment of the merits of his work by the appellants. But that is not the only reason which might cause the appellants not to publish. There is no evidence about this so we must do the best we can with common knowledge. It does not seem fanciful and it was not argued that it is fanciful to suppose that purely commercial consideration might cause a publisher to refrain from publishing and promoting promising material. He might think it likely to be more profitable to promote work by other composers with whom he had agreements and unwise or too expensive to try to publish and popularise the respondent's work in addition. And there is always the possibility that less legitimate reasons might influence a decision not to publish the respondent's work.

[I]t appears to me to be an unreasonable restraint to tie the composer for this period of years so that his work will be sterilised and he can earn nothing from his abilities as a composer if the publisher chooses not to publish. If there had been in clause 9 any provision entitling the composer to terminate the agreement in such an event the case might have had a very different appearance. But as the agreement stands not only is the composer tied but he cannot recover the copyright of work which the publisher refuses to publish.

It was strenuously argued that the agreement is in standard form, that it has stood the test of time, and that there is no indication that it ever causes injustice. Reference was made to passages in the speeches of Lord Pearce and Lord Wilberforce in *Esso Petroleum Co. Ltd* v *Harper's Garage (Stourport) Ltd* [1968] AC 269 with which I wholly agree. Lord Pearce said, at p. 323:

> It is important that the court, in weighing the question of reasonableness, should give full weight to commercial practices and to the generality of contracts made freely by parties bargaining on equal terms,

and Lord Wilberforce said, at pp. 332–333:

> But the development of the law does seem to show that judges have been able to dispense from the necessity of justification under a public policy test of reasonableness such contracts or provisions of contracts as, under contemporary conditions, may be found to have passed into the accepted and normal currency of commercial or contractual or conveyancing rela-tions. That such contracts have done so may be taken to show with at least strong prima force that, moulded under the pressures of negotiation, competition and public opinion, they have assumed a form which satisfies the test of public policy as understood by the courts at the time, or, regarding the matter from the point of view of the trade, that the trade in question has assumed such a form that for its health or expansion it requires a degree of regulation.

But those passages refer to contracts 'made freely by parties bargaining on equal terms' or 'moulded under the pressures of negotiation, competition and public opinion.' I do not find from any evidence in this case, nor does it seem probable, that this form of contract made between a publisher and an unknown composer has been moulded by any pressure of negotiation. Indeed, it appears that established composers who can bargain on equal terms can and do make their own contracts.

Any contract by which a person engages to give his exclusive services to another for a period necessarily involves extensive restriction during that period of the common law right to exercise any lawful activity he chooses in such manner as he thinks best. Normally the doctrine of restraint of trade has no application to such restrictions: they require no justification. But if contractual restric-tions appear to be unnecessary or to be reasonably capable of enforcement in an oppressive manner, then they must be justified before they can be enforced.

In the present case the respondent assigned to the appellants 'the full copyright for the whole world' in every musical composition 'composed created or conceived' by him alone or in collabor-ation with any other person during a period of five or, it might be 10 years. He received no payment (apart from an initial £50) unless his work was published and the appellants need not publish unless they chose to do so. And if they did not publish he had no right to terminate the agreement or to have copyrights re-assigned to him. I need not consider whether in any circumstances it would be possible to justify such a one-sided agreement. It is sufficient to say that such evidence as there is falls far short of justification. It must therefore follow that the agreement so far as unperformed is unenforceable.

NOTES
1. In *Watson* v *Prager* [1991] 1 WLR 726, the restraint required the boxer to accept and fulfil all commitments negotiated on his behalf by his manager, whereas the manager's duty to the boxer—namely to negotiate the highest possible boxing fees—was in conflict with the man-ager's interests as a boxing promoter.
2. In *Societa Esplosivi Industriali SpA* v *Ordnance Technologies (UK) Ltd* [2004] EWHC 48 (Ch), [2004] 1 All ER (Comm) 619, Lewison J noted that '[t]he lack of a reciprocal obligation may be an important feature in deciding whether a restraint on trade is reasonable'.

(e) Severance of the objectionable parts of covenants

(i) Striking out the objectionable part as it stands

Goldsoll v Goldman
[1915] 1 Ch 292 (CA)

The plaintiff and the defendant were both in business as dealers in imitation jewellery at Old Bond Street and New Bond Street in London. The defendant sold his business to the plaintiff and covenanted that for two years he would not:

... either solely or jointly with or as agent or employee for any person or persons or company directly or indirectly carry on or be engaged or concerned or interested in or render services (gratuitously or otherwise) to the business of a vendor of or dealer in real or imitation jewellery in the county of London, England, Scotland, Ireland, Wales, or any part of the United Kingdom of Great Britain and Ireland and the Isle of Man or in France, the United States of America, Russia, or Spain, or within twenty-five miles of Potsdamerstrasse, Berlin, or St. Stefans Kirche, Vienna.

Held: the covenant was too wide in terms of subject matter since it referred to real jewellery when the defendant had not traded in real jewellery. It was also too wide in geographical area since the defendant had not traded abroad. However, these restrictions were severable from the rest of the promise, leaving a covenant that the defendant would not carry on the business of dealing in imitation jewellery in the UK or the Isle of Man. This restriction was reasonably necessary for the plaintiff's protection, and hence was enforceable.

NOTES
1. This is an example of severance in a covenant relating to the sale of a business. It may be that the courts are less likely to sever in the case of covenants between employer and employee, where the bargaining power may be unequal.
2. *Nordenfelt* v *Maxim Nordenfelt Guns & Ammunition Company Ltd* [1894] AC 535 (*page 674*), is another example of severance in the context of a covenant on the sale of a business. The second part of the covenant, relating to engaging in any business competing with that of the company, was void because it went further than was reasonably necessary to protect the business acquired. However, it could be severed from the first part as the two were clearly separable promises.
3. In *Mason* v *Provident Clothing & Supply Company Ltd* [1913] AC 724 (*page 678*) (a covenant between employer and employee), the House of Lords refused to redraft a clause so as to render it reasonable. Therefore, the whole promise was void and unenforceable. Lord Moulton said (at pp. 745–6):

It would in my opinion be pessimi exempli if, when an employer had exacted a covenant deliberately framed in unreasonably wide terms, the Courts were to come to his assistance and, by applying their ingenuity and knowledge of the law, carve out of this void covenant the maximum of what he might validly have required. It must be remembered that the real sanction at the back of these covenants is the terror and expense of litigation, in which the servant is usually at a great disadvantage, in view of the longer purse of his master. It is sad to think that in this present case this appellant, whose employment is a comparatively humble one, should have had to go through four Courts before he could free himself from such unreasonable restraints as this covenant imposes, and the hardship imposed by the exaction of unreasonable covenants by employers would be greatly increased if they could continue the practice with the expectation that, having exposed the servant to the anxiety and expense of litigation, the Court would in the end enable them to obtain everything which they could have obtained by acting reasonably. It is evident that those who drafted this covenant aimed at making it a penal rather than a protective covenant, and that they hoped by means of it to paralyse the earning capabilities of the man if and when he left their service, and were not thinking of what would be a reasonable protection to their business, and having so acted they must take the consequences.

(ii) Severance must not alter the nature of the original covenant

Attwood v Lamont
[1920] 3 KB 571 (CA)

The plaintiff carried on business in Kidderminster as a draper, tailor, and general outfitter. The defendant, an employee in the tailoring department, covenanted that he would not at any time thereafter, 'either on his own account or on that of any wife of his or in partnership with or as assistant, servant or agent to any other person, persons or company carry on or be in any way directly or indirectly concerned in any of the following trades or businesses; that is to say, the trade or business of a tailor, dressmaker, general draper, milliner, hatter, haberdasher, gentlemen's, ladies' or children's outfitter at any place within a radius of 10 miles of' Kidderminster. The defendant set up business as a tailor at Worcester, outside the 10 miles' limit, but obtained and executed tailoring orders in Kidderminster. The covenant was held to be wider than was reasonably necessary for the protection of the plaintiff's business. The plaintiff argued that the covenant could be severed to leave only the restraint relating to tailoring. Held: the covenant was a single covenant for the protection of the plaintiff's entire business, and not several covenants for the protection of different businesses. Consequently, it could not be severed without altering the nature of the covenant.

YOUNGER LJ: . . . [T]his was not a case in which upon any principle this severance was permissible. The learned judges of the Divisional Court, I think, took the view that such severance always was permissible when it could be effectively accomplished by the action of a blue pencil. I do not agree. The doctrine of severance has not, I think, gone further than to make it permissible in a case where the covenant is not really a single covenant but is in effect a combination of several distinct covenants. In that case and where the severance can be carried out without the addition or alteration of a word, it is permissible. But in that case only.

Now, here, I think, there is in truth but one covenant for the protection of the respondent's entire business, and not several covenants for the protection of his several businesses. The respondent is, on the evidence, not carrying on several businesses but one business, and, in my opinion, this covenant must stand or fall in its unaltered form.

But, further, I am of opinion that even if this were not so this case is not one in which any severance, even if otherwise technically permissible, ought to be made. In my view the necessary effect of the application of the principle on which *Mason's Case* [1913] AC 724 and *Morris* v *Saxelby* [1916] 1 AC 688 have both been decided has been to render obsolete the cases in which the Courts have severed these restrictive covenants when acting on the view that being prima facie valid it was their duty to bind the covenantee to them as far as was permissible. It may well be that these cases are still applicable to covenants between vendor and purchaser, for upon such covenants the effect of Lord Macnaghten's test upon the law as previously understood has been little more than a matter of words, and Lord Moulton's observations have no direct application to such covenants. But these authorities do not seem to me to be any longer of assistance in the case of a covenant between employer and employee. To such a covenant I think the statement of Lord Moulton in *Mason's Case* [see *page 678*] necessarily applies.

SECTION 2: ILLEGAL CONTRACTS

In *Hall* v *Woolston Hall Leisure Ltd* [2001] 1 WLR 225 Peter Gibson LJ summarised the principles governing illegality in English law.

Illegality under English law

28. There can be no doubt but that under English law a claim, whether in contract or in tort, may be defeated on the ground of illegality or, in the Latin phrase, *ex turpi causa non oritur actio*. The classic statement of the principle was by Lord Mansfield in *Holman* v *Johnson* (1775) 1 Cowp. 341 at p. 343:

> No court will lend its aid to a man who founds his cause of action upon an immoral or illegal act. If, from the plaintiff's own stating or otherwise, the cause of action appears to arise *ex turpi causa*, or the transgression of a positive law of this country then the court says he has no right to be assisted.

29. . . . In contract the decision of the House of Lords in *Tinsley* v *Milligan* [1994] 1 A.C. 340 has reaffirmed that the claimant cannot found his claim on an unlawful act. But when the claimant is not seeking to enforce an unlawful contract but founds his case on collateral rights acquired under the contract the court is neither bound nor entitled to reject the claim unless the illegality of necessity forms part of the claimant's case (p. 377 per Lord Browne-Wilkinson).

30. In two types of case it is well-established that illegality renders a contract unenforceable from the outset. One is where the contract is entered into with the intention of committing an illegal act; the other is where the contract is expressly or implicitly prohibited by statute (*St. John Shipping Corp.* v *Joseph Rank Ltd.* [1957] 1 Q.B. 267 at p. 283 per Devlin J.).

31. In a third category of cases a party may be prevented from enforcing it. That is where a contract, lawful when made, is illegally performed and the party knowingly participated in that illegal performance. In *Ashmore, Benson Ltd.* v *Dawson Ltd.* [1973] 1 W.L.R. 828 Lord Denning M.R. (at p. 833) said:

> Not only did [the plaintiff's transport manager] know of the illegality. He participated in it by sanctioning the loading of the vehicle with a load in excess of the regulations. That participation in the illegal performance of the contract debars [the plaintiff] from suing [the defendant] on it or suing [the defendant] for negligence.

So too Scarman L.J. (at p. 836):

> But knowledge by itself is not enough. There must be knowledge plus participation. . . . For those reasons I think the performance was illegal.

A: Contracts prohibited by statute

(a) Express prohibition

Re Mahmoud & Ispahani

[1921] 2 KB 716 (CA)

In 1919, under the Defence of the Realm Regulations, an Order was made prohibiting the purchase or sale of linseed oil without a licence. The plaintiff, who had a licence, sold linseed oil to the defendant, having been incorrectly assured by the defendant that the defendant also had the required licence. The terms of the plaintiff's licence specified that delivery was only to be made to persons who held a licence. The defendant subsequently refused to accept delivery of the linseed oil, pleading that, due to his own absence of a licence, the contract was illegal. Held: since the defendant had no licence the contract of sale was prohibited by the Order. It was therefore illegal and unenforceable by the plaintiff.

ATKIN LJ: . . . When the Court has to deal with the question whether a particular contract or class of contract is prohibited by statute, it may find an express prohibition in the statute, or it may have to infer the prohibition from the fact that the statute imposes a penalty upon the person entering into that class of contract. In the latter case one has to examine very carefully the precise terms of the statute imposing the penalty upon the individual. One may find that the statute imposes a penalty upon an individual, and yet does not prohibit the contract if it is made with a party who is innocent of the offence which is created by the statute. . . . [H]ere it appears to me to be plain that this particular contract was expressly prohibited by the terms of the Order which imposes the necessity of a compliance with the licence. With great respect to the learned judge, I think the underlying fallacy in his judgment is that he has not directed his attention to the terms of the licence or to the terms of the Order which says that no sale shall be made unless it complies with the terms of the licence. When one looks at the licence one finds an express prohibition against the plaintiff selling to the defendant as the latter had not a licence.

NOTES
1. If a contract is illegal by statute, neither party can enforce it. The innocence of the plaintiff in *Re Mahmoud & Ispahani* did not allow him to recover damages under the illegal contract.
2. It was confirmed in *Mohamed* v *Alaga & Co. (A Firm)* [2000] 1 WLR 1815, that legislation for these purposes includes subordinate legislation.

   The plaintiff, a leading member of the Somali community in the UK, had sought payment under an alleged oral contract he claimed he had made with the defendant firm of solicitors. The plaintiff alleged that in return for his assistance in introducing Somali refugees whom the defendant would seek to represent, the defendant was to pay him half of the fees it received from the Legal Aid Board in connection with the refugees' applications for asylum. However, the Solicitors' Practice Rules, made under s. 31 of the Solicitors Act 1974, expressly prohibited solicitors from entering into such contracts and from making such payments. The defendant therefore claimed that even if there was any such agreement, it was illegal and unenforceable. The Court of Appeal held that such a contract was illegal as it was expressly prohibited by legislation. It made no difference that the plaintiff did not know of the prohibition. The court rejected a claim for recovery on a *quantum meruit* for the value of the services in introducing clients because this would be tainted with the same illegality affecting the alleged contract. However, the Court of Appeal did grant leave for the claim to be amended to allow recovery on a *quantum meruit* for the translation services provided by the plaintiff since he was blameless and, since this service could be separated from the illegal introduction fee, no public policy would be infringed by allowing him to recover for translation services.

   By contrast, *Mohamed* v *Alaga* was distinguished in *Awwad* v *Geraghty & Co. (A Firm)* [2000] 3 WLR 1041, where a claim for a *quantum meruit* failed. In *Awwad* v *Geraghty* a firm of solicitors was attempting to recover a fee charged under the terms of a contract which was prohibited by subordinate legislation and to have allowed recovery on a *quantum meruit* would have achieved the same purpose as enforcing that illegal contract.

An innocent party may have some remedy if he can establish the existence of a collateral undertaking by the other party to ensure that the contract is not illegal. However, this will be of use only in exceptional cases.

Strongman (1945) Ltd v *Sincock*
[1955] 2 QB 525 (CA)

Builders entered into a contract with the architect owner whereby they were to supply materials and carry out work at his premises. The architect owner orally promised to obtain all the licences required under the Defence (General) Regulations 1939. Licences were obtained for £2,150 of authorised costs, but the total value of the work carried out was £6,905. The architect had paid £2,900 and sought to avoid paying the balance by arguing that performance of the contract was illegal. The builders sought the unpaid sum or damages for breach of the warranty that the architect would obtain any necessary licences. Held: that although the builders could not recover the contract price, since the contract was prohibited by the regulations, the assurance amounted to a warranty or collateral promise by the architect that he would obtain any necessary licences, and they were entitled to damages for breach of that promise.

DENNING LJ: It is said that, if damages could be recovered, it would be an easy way of getting round the law about illegality. This does not alarm me at all. It is, of course, a settled principle that a man cannot recover for the consequences of his own unlawful act, but this has always been confined to cases where the doer of the act knows it to be unlawful or is himself in some way morally culpable. It does not apply when he is an entirely innocent party . . . [Counsel for the architect] referred us to the observations of this court in *In re Mahmoud & Ispahani* [1921] 2 KB 716. On a consideration of that case it seems to me that the court only decided that no action lay upon the contract for the purchase of goods. They did not decide whether there was an action for fraud or breach of promise or warranty: and I do not think that their observations were intended to express any view on the matter.

■ QUESTION

Can this case be distinguished from *Re Mahmoud & Ispahani, page 686*?

(b) Contracts impliedly illegal in formation

The courts are reluctant to hold that a statute impliedly prohibits the making of a contract.

Archbolds (Freightage) Ltd v *S. Spanglett Ltd*
[1961] 1 QB 374 (CA)

The defendants owned a number of vans with 'C' licences, enabling them, under the Road and Rail Traffic Act 1933, to carry their own goods, but not the goods of others, for payment. The plaintiffs, believing that the defendants had 'A' licences enabling them to carry goods for others for reward, employed the defendants to carry whisky from Leeds to London. The whisky was stolen en route owing to the driver's negligence, and the plaintiffs claimed damages for the loss. The defendants pleaded illegality, in that their van did not have an 'A' licence as required by statute. Held: this contract was not prohibited either expressly or impliedly by statute, and therefore was not illegal at its inception. Since the plaintiffs were unaware of the true facts and were innocent parties, they could recover damages for breach of contract.

PEARCE LJ: If a contract is expressly of by necessary implication forbidden by statute, or if it is ex facie illegal, or if both parties know that though ex facie legal it can only be performed by illegality or is intended to be performed illegally, the law will not help the plaintiffs in any way that is a direct or indirect enforcement of rights under the contract. And for this purpose both parties are presumed to know the law.

The first question, therefore, is whether this contract of carriage was forbidden by statute. The two cases on which the defendants mainly rely are *In re an Arbitration between Mahmoud and Ispahani* [1921] 2 KB 716 and *J. Dennis & Co. Ltd* v *Munn* [1949] 2 KB 327. In both those cases the plaintiffs were unable to enforce their rights under contracts forbidden by statute. . . . In neither case could the plaintiff bring his contract within the exception that alone would have made its subject-matter lawful, namely, by showing the existence of a licence. Therefore, the core of both contracts was the mischief expressly forbidden by the statutory order and the statutory regulation respectively.

In *Mahmoud's* case the object of the order was to prevent (except under licence) a person buying and a person selling, and both parties were liable to penalties. A contract of sale between those persons was therefore expressly forbidden. In *Dennis's* case the object of the regulation was to prevent (except under licence) owners from performing building operations, and builders from carrying out the work for them. Both parties were liable to penalties and a contract between these persons for carrying out an unlawful operation would be forbidden by implication.

The case before us is somewhat different. The carriage of the plaintiffs' whisky was not as such prohibited; the statute merely regulated the means by which carriers should carry goods. Therefore this contract was not expressly forbidden by the statute.

Was it then forbidden by implication? The Road and Rail Traffic Act, 1933, section 1, says: 'no person shall use a goods vehicle on a road for the carriage of goods . . . except under licence,' and provides that such use shall be an offence. Did the statute thereby intend to forbid by implication all contracts whose performance must on all the facts (whether known or not) result in a contravention of that section? . . .

The object of the Road and Rail Traffic Act, 1933, was not (in this connection) to interfere with the owner of goods or his facilities for transport, but to control those who provided the transport with a view to promoting its efficiency. Transport of goods was not made illegal but the various licence holders were prohibited from encroaching on one another's territory, the intention of the Act being to provide an orderly and comprehensive service. Penalties were provided for those licence holders who went outside the bounds of their allotted spheres. These penalties apply to those using the vehicle but not to the goods owner. Though the latter could be convicted of aiding and abetting any breach, the restrictions were not aimed at him. Thus a contract of carriage was not impliedly forbidden by the statute.

This view is supported by common sense and convenience. If the other view were held it would have far-reaching effects. For instance, if a carrier induces me (who am in fact ignorant of any illegality) to entrust goods to him and negligently destroys them, he would only have to show that (though unknown to me) his licence had expired, or did not properly cover the transportation, or that he was uninsured, and I should then be without a remedy against him. Or, again, if I ride in a taxicab and the driver leaves me stranded in some deserted spot, he would only have to show that he was (though unknown to me) unlicensed or uninsured, and I should be without remedy. This appears to me an undesirable extension of the implications of a statute.

■ QUESTION

What would the position have been in *Archbolds* v *Spanglett* if the plaintiffs had known that there was no 'A' licence?

NOTES

1. *Re Mahmoud & Ispahani* (*page 686*), was distinguished in *Archbolds* v *Spanglett* because the statute in that case expressly prohibited the sale to an unlicensed person. In *Archbolds* v *Spanglett* the carriage of the whisky was not prohibited but the statute did regulate the manner of the transportation. This contract was not illegal from the beginning but was performed by the defendants in an illegal way.

2. In the next case, Kerr LJ identified the factors relevant in deciding whether a statute (the Insurance Companies Act 1974) rendered contracts made by unauthorised insurers illegal.

Phoenix General Insurance Co. of Greece SA v Administratia Asigurarilor de Stat
[1988] 1 QB 216 (CA)

KERR LJ: . . . [I]t seems to me that the position can be summarised as follows:

(i) Where a statute prohibits both parties from concluding or performing a contract when both or either of them have no authority to do so, the contract is impliedly prohibited: see *In re Mahmoud and Ispahani* [1921] 2 KB 716 and its analysis by Pearce LJ in *Archbolds (Freightage) Ltd* v *S. Spanglett Ltd* [1961] 1 QB 374, with which Devlin LJ agreed. (ii) But where a statute merely prohibits one party from entering into a contract without authority, and/or imposes a penalty on him if he does so (i.e. a unilateral prohibition) it does not follow that the contract itself is impliedly prohibited so as to render it illegal and void. Whether or not the statute has this effect depends on considerations of public policy in the light of the mischief which the statute is designed to prevent, its language, scope and purpose, the consequences for the innocent party, and any other relevant considerations. . . . (iii) The Insurance Companies Act 1974 only imposes a unilateral prohibition on unauthorised insurers. If this were merely to prohibit them from carrying on 'the business of effecting contracts of insurance' of a class for which they have no authority, then it would clearly be open to the court to hold that considerations of public policy preclude the implication that such contracts are prohibited and void. But unfortunately the unilateral prohibition is not limited to the business of 'effecting contracts of insurance' but extends to the business of 'carrying out contracts of insurance'. This is a form of statutory prohibition, albeit only unilateral, which is not covered by any authority. However, in the same way as Parker J in the *Bedford* case [*Bedford Insurance Co Ltd* v *Instituto de Resseguros do Brasil*] [1985] QB 966, I can see no convincing escape from the conclusion that this extension of the prohibition has the unfortunate effect that contracts made without authorisation are prohibited by necessary implication and therefore void. Since the statute prohibits the insurer from carrying out the contract—of which the most obvious example is paying claims—how can the insured require the insurer to do an act which is expressly forbidden by statute? And how can a court enforce a contract against an unauthorised insurer when Parliament has expressly prohibited him from carrying it out? In that situation there is simply no room for the introduction of considerations of public policy. As Parker J said in the *Bedford* case, at p. 986A: 'once it is concluded that on its true construction the [Act] prohibited both contract and performance, that is the public policy.' (iv) It follows that, however reluctantly, I feel bound to agree with the analysis of Parker J in the *Bedford* case and his conclusion that contracts of insurance made by unauthorised insurers are prohibited by the Act of 1974 in the sense that they are illegal and void, and therefore unenforceable. In particular, I agree with the following passages which led him to this conclusion, at pp. 981–982:

> The express prohibition is on the carrying on of insurance business of a relevant class, but, as I have already mentioned, the definition in the case of each class begins, 'the effecting and carrying out of contracts of insurance'. What therefore is prohibited is the carrying on of the business of effecting and performing contracts of insurance of various descriptions in the absence of an authorisation. It is thus both the contracts themselves and the performance of them at which the statute is directed.

Hughes v Asset Managers plc
[1995] 3 All ER 669 (CA)

The argument advanced in this case was that since s. 1 of the Prevention of Fraud (Investments) Act 1958 required an individual who dealt with share purchases to have a licence to deal in securities under that Act, if at the relevant time the person dealing did not have such a licence then any purchase contract made by that person was void. Such a result would have avoided a loss consequent on the actual share purchase which had been made by the person giving the instruction to purchase. The trial judge held that the purchase contracts were not void. Held: on appeal, the purchase contracts were neither expressly nor impliedly prohibited by the Act. In addition, public policy considerations did not support the argument advanced because the aim of the Act was to protect the public by licensing professional dealers and this protection would be lost if contracts made by unlicensed dealers were void.

SAVILLE LJ: . . . I readily accept that the purpose of the 1958 Act was to protect the investing public by imposing criminal sanctions on those who, as principals or agents, engaged in the business of dealing in securities without being duly licensed. Parliament clearly intended to provide the investing public with the safeguard of the approval and licensing of professional dealers by the Board of Trade. However, I can see no basis in either the words the legislature has used or the type of prohibition under discussion, or in considerations of public policy (including the mischief against which this part of the 1958 Act was directed), for the assertion that Parliament must be taken to have intended that such protection required (over and above criminal sanctions) that any deals effected through the agency of unlicensed persons should automatically be struck down and rendered ineffective. On the contrary, it seems to me that not only is there really no good reason why Parliament should have taken up this stance, but good reason why Parliament should have held the contrary view.

In this connection it must be remembered as Kerr LJ pointed out in *Phoenix General Insurance Co. of Greece SA* v *Administratia Asigurarilor de Stat* [1987] 2 All ER 152 at 176–177, [1988] QB 216 at 273–275, that rendering transactions void affects both the guilty and the innocent parties. The latter, just as much as the former, cannot enforce a void bargain or obtain damages for its breach. In the context of the section under discussion this could well produce very great hardship and injustice on wholly innocent parties; for example, where the dealer fails to perform a bargain which would have resulted in a profit or saved the investor from a loss. In other words, the argument put forward by the appellants necessarily involves the proposition that Parliament has chosen to provide a defence against claims for breach of contract in favour of the very people who have ignored its licensing requirements. I repeat that I can find nothing to indicate that this is what Parliament did, or intended to do, when enacting this statute, nor anything to indicate any good reason or public need for such a result. . . .

HIRST LJ: . . . In my judgment, upon the proper construction of s. 1(1) of the Prevention of Fraud (Investments) Act 1958, the contracts between the appellants and the respondents which are at issue in this case are not expressly forbidden by the statute. What is forbidden by s. 1(1)(b) is the dealing by the servant or agent of one of the two parties to the contract, in this case the respondents.

The question therefore is whether these contracts are impliedly forbidden. On this issue I gain the greatest assistance from the judgment of Kerr LJ in *Phoenix General Insurance Co. of Greece SA* v *Administratia Asigurarilor de Stat* [1987] 2 All ER 152, [1988] QB 216. The ratio of the relevant part of this judgment, to which Saville LJ has already referred, is that, because of the express prohibition in the Insurance Companies Act 1974 of 'carrying out contracts of insurance' of the relevant kind, contracts made without the necessary authorisation were impliedly prohibited and therefore void (see [1987] 2 All ER 152 at 176, [1988] QB 216 at 273–274 per Kerr LJ) . . . Looking at that judgment as a whole, it is quite clear that, but for the embargo against carrying out contracts of insurance, the decision would have gone the other way. Although this part of that judgment is strictly obiter, it is of the greatest persuasive force and, indeed, was adopted and applied as the ratio of the decision in *Re Cavalier Insurance Co. Ltd, Re* [1989] 2 Lloyd's Rep 430 at 443 by Knox J, who also reached his conclusion with the greatest reluctance because, though undesirable, it was inescapable. If [counsel for the purchaser] were right and these contracts were void, the innocent client might well suffer loss which he could not recover in the circumstances already described by Saville LJ, which (as Pearce LJ stated in *Archbolds (Freightage) Ltd* v *S Spanglett Ltd (Randall, third party)* [1961] 1 All ER 417 at 424, [1961] 1 QB 374 at 387) would be a most unsatisfactory result, and one which, in my judgment, would be inimical to public policy, which is the ultimate test to be applied.

I would add that I think the public interest under this statute was fully met by the exaction, in appropriate cases, of the quite severe penalties prescribed by s. 1(2) of the 1958 Act. I would therefore hold that these contracts are not impliedly forbidden by the statute, and for these reasons I would also dismiss this appeal.

(Nourse LJ agreed with both judgments.)

B: Contracts that are illegal in their performance

St John Shipping Corporation v *Joseph Rank Ltd*
[1957] 1 QB 267

It was an offence under the Merchant Shipping (Safety and Load Line Conventions) Act 1932 to load a ship to such an extent that the load line was below water. The plaintiff charterers overloaded the ship and caused the load line to be submerged. The master was prosecuted and fined £1,200 for this offence. The defendants, who were the consignees of part of the cargo, withheld some of the freight due (equivalent to the amount due on the overloaded cargo) and argued that the plaintiffs had performed the charter in an illegal manner. Held: the plaintiffs could recover the freight due. Illegal performance of a contract did not render the contract illegal unless the contract as performed was one which the statute meant to prohibit. This Act merely punished infringements of the load line rules and did not prohibit the contract of carriage which was performed in breach of the rules.

DEVLIN J: . . . There are two general principles. The first is that a contract which is entered into with the object of commiting an illegal act is unenforceable. The application of this principle depends upon proof of the intent, at the time the contract was made, to break the law; if the intent is mutual the contract is not enforceable at all, and, if unilateral, it is enforceable at the suit of the party who is proved to have it. This principle is not involved here. Whether or not the overloading was deliberate when it was done, there is no proof that it was contemplated when the contract of carriage was made. The second principle is that the court will not enforce a contract which is expressly or impliedly prohibited by statute. If the contract is of this class it does not matter what the intent of the parties is; if the statute prohibits the contract, it is unenforceable whether the parties meant to break the law or not. A significant distinction between the two classes is this. In the former class you have only to look and see what acts the statute prohibits; it does not matter whether or not it prohibits a contract; if a contract is deliberately made to do a prohibited act, that contract will be unenforceable. In the latter class, you have to consider not what acts the statute prohibits, but what contracts it prohibits; but you are not concerned at all with the intent of the parties; if the parties enter into a prohibited contract, that contract is unenforceable.

Two questions are involved. The first—and the one which hitherto has usually settled the matter—is: does the statute mean to prohibit contracts at all? But if this be answered in the affirmative, then one must ask: does this contract belong to the class which the statute intends to prohibit? For example, a person is forbidden by statute from using an unlicensed vehicle on the highway. If one asks oneself whether there is in such an enactment an implied prohibition of all contracts for the use of unlicensed vehicles, the answer may well be that there is, and that contracts of hire would be unenforceable. But if one asks oneself whether there is an implied prohibition of contracts for the carriage of goods by unlicensed vehicles or for the repairing of unlicensed vehicles or for the garaging of unlicensed vehicles, the answer may well be different. The answer might be that collateral contracts of this sort are not within the ambit of the statute.

. . . [A]n implied prohibition of contracts of loading does not necessarily extend to contracts for the carriage of goods by improperly loaded vessels. Of course, if the parties knowingly agree to ship goods by an overloaded vessel, such a contract would be illegal; but its illegality does not depend on whether it is impliedly prohibited by the statute, since it falls within the first of the two general heads of illegality I noted above where there is an intent to break the law. The way to test the question whether a particular class of contract is prohibited by the statute is to test it in relation to a contract made in ignorance of its effect.

In my judgment, contracts for the carriage of goods are not within the ambit of this statute at all. A court should not hold that any contract or class of contracts is prohibited by statute unless there is a clear implication, or 'necessary inference,' that the statute so intended. If a contract has as its whole object the doing of the very act which the statute prohibits, it can be argued that you can hardly make sense of a statute which forbids an act and yet permits to be made a contract to do it; that is a clear implication. But unless you get a clear implication of that sort, I think that a court ought to be very slow to hold that a statute intends to interfere with the rights and remedies given by the ordinary law of contract. Caution in this respect is, I think, especially necessary in these times when so much of commercial life is governed by regulations of one sort or another, which may easily be broken without wicked intent. Persons who deliberately set out to break the law cannot expect to be aided in a court of justice, but it is a different matter when the law is unwittingly broken. To nullify a bargain in such circumstances frequently means that in a case—perhaps of such triviality that no authority would have felt it worth while to prosecute—a seller, because he cannot enforce his civil rights, may forfeit a sum vastly in excess of any penalty that a criminal court would impose; and the sum forfeited will not go into the public purse but into the pockets of someone who is lucky enough to pick up the windfall or astute enough to have contrived to get it. It is questionable how far this contributes to public morality. In *Vita Food Products Inc.* v *Unus Shipping Co.* [1939] AC 277, Lord Wright said: 'Nor must it be forgotten that the rule by which contracts not expressly forbidden by statute or declared to be void are in proper cases nullified for disobedience to a statute is a rule of public policy only, and public policy understood in a wider sense may at times be better served by refusing to nullify a bargain save on serious and sufficient grounds.' It may be questionable also whether public policy is well served by driving from the seat of judgment everyone who has been guilty of a minor transgression. Commercial men who have unwittingly offended against one of a multiplicity of regulations may nevertheless feel that they have not thereby forfeited all right to justice, and may go elsewhere for it if courts of law will not give it to them. In the last resort they will, if necessary, set up their own machinery for dealing with their own disputes in the way that those whom the law puts beyond the pale, such as gamblers, have done. I have said enough, and perhaps more than enough, to show how important it is that the courts should be slow to imply the statutory prohibition of contracts, and should do so only when the implication is quite clear. The Act of 1932 imposes a penalty which is itself designed to deprive the offender of the benefits of his crime. It would be a curious thing if the operation could be performed twice—once by the criminal law and then again by the civil. It would be curious, too, if in a case in which the magistrates had thought fit to impose only a nominal fine, their decision could, in effect, be overridden in a civil action. But the question whether the rule applies to statutory offences is an important one which I do not wish to decide in the present case. . . .

The rights which cannot be enforced must be those 'directly resulting' from the crime. That means, I think, that for a right to money or to property to be unenforceable the property or money must be identifiable as something to which, but for the crime, the plaintiff would have had no right or title. That cannot be said in this case. . . .

NOTES
1. In *Shaw* v *Groom* [1970] 2 QB 504, a rent book did not contain all the information required by statute, which was an offence punishable with a maximum fine of £50. When the plaintiff landlord claimed arrears of rent, the tenant relied on the failure to provide a proper rent book as prohibiting the plaintiff from recovering any rent. The Court of Appeal held that the contract was not illegal since this provision was not intended to prevent the recovery of rent.
2. In *Anderson Ltd* v *Daniel* [1924] 1 KB 138, it was an offence to sell artificial fertilisers without giving the buyer an invoice stating the percentages of certain chemicals in the fertilisers. No invoice was issued by the seller, and since the object of the statute in requiring the invoice was to protect purchasers, this could only be achieved by rendering the sale without an invoice illegal. Scrutton LJ said (at pp. 147–9):

> When the policy of the Act in question is to protect the general public or a class of persons by requiring that a contract shall be accompanied by certain formalities or conditions, and a penalty is imposed on the person omitting those formalities or conditions, the contract and its performance without those formalities or conditions is illegal, and cannot be sued upon by the person liable to the penalties. . . . Now here the provision as to the invoice is

clearly to protect a particular class of the public—namely, the people who buy artificial manures. The seller is required to give on or before or as soon as possible after delivery of the article an invoice stating the percentages of its ingredients. The vendors did not do so. It follows from the principle that I have stated that when they come to sue for the price they can be met with the defence that the way in which they performed the contract was illegal. . . . [T]he giving of the invoice is part of the performance of the contract. . . . [T]he vendors have committed an illegality in the performance of their contract, and that as the statutory provision was enacted for the protection of a class, including the purchaser who is now being sued, the vendors cannot recover the price.

The illegal performer of a contract which has become illegal because of the way in which it has been performed, cannot enforce that contract. Thus, in *Anderson Ltd* v *Daniel*, the seller could not claim the price of the fertilisers because his failure to present the invoice had rendered the contract illegal.

3. The contract in *Archbolds* v *Spanglett* (*page 688*) had become illegal because of the way in which it was performed, but the innocent party, who was ignorant of the unlawful perform-ance, could have sued upon it.

Thus, an innocent party can sue on a contract performed in an illegal manner unless that party 'participated' in the illegality.

Ashmore, Benson, Pease & Co. Ltd v A. V. Dawson Ltd
[1973] 1 WLR 828 (CA)

The plaintiff company had manufactured two 25 ton tube banks and had agreed with the defendants, a small road haulage firm, for the carriage of these tube banks to the port of shipment. The plaintiff company's transport manager was present when one of the tube banks was loaded onto the defendants' lorry in contravention of the Road Traffic Act 1960, s. 64(2), which specified that the maximum weight laden of the lorry was not to exceed 30 tons. The weight of the lorry with the tube bank was 35 tons, but the plaintiff company's transport manager raised no objec-tion and did not insist on the use of a low loader, although he knew that this was the appropriate vehicle for such a load. On the journey one of the lorries toppled over damaging the tube bank. The defendants claimed that the contract was void for illegality because the plaintiffs' servants knew that carriage of such loads on these lorries was in breach of the statute. Held: (Phillimore LJ dissenting) although this contract was lawful in its inception, it had been performed in an unlawful manner to the knowledge of, and with the participation of, the plaintiffs' servants. Therefore the plaintiff company could not recover in damages.

NOTE: Whereas in *Archbolds (Freightage) Ltd* v *S. Spanglett Ltd, page 688*, the plaintiffs did not need to rely on the illegality to support the claim for damages for theft of the whisky, in *Ashmore* the plaintiff company would have to plead the illegal act of overloading the lorry in order to establish how the loss occurred.

Marles v Philip Trant & Sons Ltd
[1954] 1 QB 29 (CA)

The defendants, seed merchants, bought wheat, described as spring wheat known as Fylgia, from a third party. The defendants resold it under the same description to the plaintiff farmers. In fact it was not spring wheat and was known as Vilmorin. The plaintiffs recovered damages against the defendants. The defendants then claimed an indemnity and damages from the third-party supplier. The third party alleged that the defendants had not delivered a statement to the plaintiffs as they should have done under s. 1 of the Seeds Act 1920, specifying particulars of the variety, purity, and germination of the seeds, so that the contract between the plaintiffs and the defendants was illegal. Held: the contract was not illegal in itself although it was illegal in the manner of its performance. That meant that the contract between the plaintiffs and the defendants was unenforceable by the defendants (they could not have sued for the price), but (Hodson LJ dissenting) the contract between the third-party supplier and the defendants was not unlawful and the defendants could recover from the supplier for their loss on the contract with the plaintiffs.

DENNING LJ: . . . There can be no doubt that the contract between the seed merchants and the farmer was not unlawful when it was made. If the farmer had repudiated it before the time for delivery arrived, the seed merchants could certainly have sued him for damages. Nor was the contract rendered unlawful simply because the seed was delivered without the prescribed particulars. If it were unlawful, the farmer himself could not have sued upon it as he has done. The truth is that it was not the contract itself which was unlawful, but only the performance of it. The seed merchants performed it in an illegal way in that they omitted to furnish the prescribed particulars. That renders the contract unenforceable by them, but it does not render the contract illegal. . . .

Once rid of the notion that the contract with the farmer was itself illegal, the question becomes: what is the effect of the admitted illegality in performance? It certainly prevents the seed merchants from suing the farmer for the price, but does it prevent them suing their supplier for damages? I think not. There was nothing unlawful in the contract between the seed merchants and their supplier, neither in the formation of it, nor in the performance of it. The seed merchants must therefore be entitled to damages for the breach of it. So far so good, but the difficulty comes when they seek to prove their damages. They want to be indemnified for the damages which they have been ordered to pay to the farmer. To prove those damages, they have to prove the contract with the farmer, and the circumstances under which the damages were awarded. It is said that once they begin to rely on their deliveries to the farmer, they seek aid from their own illegality; and that that is a thing which they are not allowed to do. The maxim is invoked: Ex turpi causa non oritur actio. That maxim must not, however, be carried too far. Lord Wright gave a warning about it 15 years ago in *Beresford* v *Royal Insurance Co. Ltd* [1938] AC 586 when he said: 'The maxim itself, notwithstanding the dignity of a learned language, is, like most maxims, lacking in precise definition. In these days there are many statutory offences which are the subject of the criminal law, and in that sense are crimes, but which would, it seems afford no moral justification for a court to apply the maxim. There are likewise some crimes of inadvertence which, it is true, involve mens rea in the legal sense but are not deliberate or, as people would say, intentional.' Those observations apply with especial force in this case. The omission by the seed merchants to deliver the prescribed particulars was an act of inadvertence. It was not a deliberate breach of the law. I venture to assert that there is no moral justification for the court to apply the maxim in this case. But is there any legal justification? A distinction must be drawn, I think, between an illegality which destroys the cause of action and an illegality which affects only the damages recoverable.

■ **QUESTION**

Can this case be distinguished from *Anderson Ltd* v *Daniel* (*page 693*)?

In *Anderson Ltd* v *Daniel* statute punished sellers who failed to issue the required invoice. As a result the seller could not sue on such a contract as it was illegal in performance. However, the other party to the contract is not deprived of his civil remedies.

C: Contracts that are unlawful, immoral, or prejudicial to the interests of the state

Alexander v *Rayson*
[1936] 1 KB 169 (CA)

The plaintiff let a flat to the defendant at a total rent of £1,200 p.a. This was achieved by means of two documents. The first was a lease for £450 p.a. providing for certain services to be rendered by the plaintiff, and the second services agreement provided for the plaintiff to render certain services (which were substantially the same as those in the lease) in consideration of a payment of £750 p.a. The defendant refused to pay an instalment due under the documents, and when the plaintiff sought to recover, argued that the object of the two documents was to deceive the local authority into reducing the rateable value of the flat by only disclosing the lease document to them. Held: since the plaintiff intended to use the lease and service agreement for an illegal purpose, the plaintiff could not enforce either the lease or the service agreement.

NOTES

1. In *Pearce* v *Brooks* (1866) LR 1 Exch 213, the plaintiffs, coach-builders, had sued the defendant, a prostitute, for hire payments due on a brougham they had supplied to her. Since they had supplied this brougham in the knowledge that she was a prostitute and knowing that the brougham was to be used for an immoral purpose, it was held that they could not recover. But see *Armhouse Lee Ltd* v *Chappell* (1996) *The Times*, 7 August where the Court of Appeal held that a contract for the advertising of telephone 'sex lines' was not contrary to public policy since such lines were subject to control by an independent body. The result was that the defendants could not avoid their liability to pay for this advertising. It is clear therefore that what is regarded as contrary to public policy may change over time, and this is confirmed by the Law Commission Consultation Paper No. 154, 1999, *Illegal Transactions: The Effect of Illegality on Contracts and Trusts*, para. 1.9. See also *Sutton* v *Mischon de Reya* [2003] EWHC 3166 (Ch), [2004] 1 FLR 837: deed of cohabitation between two people in a master/slave sexual relationship was not contrary to public policy.

2. Another example of a contract which is illegal under this head is a contract involving corruption in public life. In *Parkinson* v *College of Ambulance Ltd & Harrison* [1925] 2 KB 1, Lush J held that a contract whereby money was given on the assumption that the payer would be rewarded with a knighthood, was contrary to public policy and illegal.

3. It is also contrary to public policy to allow a criminal or his estate to benefit from his crime (*Beresford* v *Royal Insurance Co. Ltd* [1938] AC 586).

4. Compare with *21st Century Logistic Solutions Ltd (in Liquidation)* v *Madysen Ltd* [2004] EWHC 231 (QB), [2004] 2 Lloyd's Rep 92. Although the supplying company had been incorporated to evade the payment of VAT, it was able to enforce a contract for the supply of the relevant goods since that contract was lawful in itself and the fraudulent intent in relation to VAT was too remote from the contract for it to be held unenforceable on grounds of illegality. The fraud in relation to VAT would be committed only when the supplier failed to account to Customs for it at the end of the relevant accounting period. Thus, not every contract entered into with the intention of committing an illegal act will be illegal and unenforceable.

D: Money or property transferred under an illegal contract

(i) General rule: not recoverable

As a general principle, money or property transferred under an illegal contract cannot be recovered. For example, in *Parkinson* v *College of Ambulance Ltd & Harrison* [1925] 2 KB 1, *page 696*, it was not possible for the payer to recover the money paid in the belief that he was to receive a knighthood, even though he had been defrauded. The parties were equally at fault so that one could not get his property back from the other.

(ii) Recovery if not in pari delicto

However, if the parties are not *in pari delicto* (i.e., not equally guilty), then money paid by the wholly innocent party can be recovered.

Kiriri Cotton Co. Ltd v *Dewani*
[1960] AC 192 (PC)

KC Ltd let a flat in Uganda to Dewani, and Dewani paid a premium of Shs 10,000. This was a breach of the Uganda Rent Restriction Ordinance 1949, but neither party realised this. Dewani claimed the return of the premium. Held: Dewani could recover the premium since the parties were not *in pari delicto*. The purpose of the Ordinance was to protect tenants and the duty to observe it rested on the landlord.

(iii) Repentance before partial performance

If a party 'genuinely repents' entering into a contract whose purpose is illegal, it is possible for that party to recover what has been transferred unless the contract has already been partially performed ('the doctrine of *locus poenitentiae*'). However, see *Tribe* v *Tribe* [1996] Ch 107, *page 702*, where the Court of Appeal held that repentance was not necessary.

Kearley v *Thomson*
(1890) 24 QBD 742 (CA)

The defendants were solicitors who were acting on behalf of a creditor petitioning against a bankrupt. The plaintiff, a friend of the bankrupt, agreed to pay the defendants their costs if they did not appear at the public examination of the bankrupt and if they did not oppose the order of discharge against the bankrupt. The money was paid and the solicitors did not appear at the public examination. However, before the application to discharge the bankrupt, the plaintiff changed his mind and sought the return of his money from the defendants. Held: the plaintiff could not recover. The contract was illegal since it interfered with the administration of justice, and as the defendants had partially performed this contract, the plaintiff's repentance was too late.

FRY LJ: . . . [I]n the case of *Taylor* v *Bowers* (1876) 1 QBD 291 . . . Mellish LJ, in delivering judgment, says at p. 300: 'If money is paid, or goods delivered for an illegal purpose, the person who had so paid the money or delivered the goods may recover them back before the illegal purpose is carried out.' I cannot help saying for myself that I think the extent of the application of that principle, and even the principle itself, may, at some time hereafter, require consideration, if not in this Court, yet in a higher tribunal: and I am glad to find that in expressing that view I have the entire concurrence of the Lord Chief Justice. But even assuming the exception to exist, does it apply to the present case? What is the condition of things if the illegal purpose has been carried into effect in a material part, but remains unperformed in another material part? As I have already pointed out in the present case, the contract was that the defendants should not appear at the public examination of the bankrupt or at the application for an order of discharge. It was performed as regards the first; but the other application has not yet been made. Can it be contended that, if the illegal contract has been partly carried into effect and partly remains unperformed, the money can still be recovered? In my judgment it cannot be so contended with success. Let me put an illustration of the doctrine contended for, which was that partial performance did not prevent the recovery of the money. Suppose a payment of 100l. by A to B on a contract that the latter shall murder C and D. He has murdered C, but not D. Can the money be recovered back? In my opinion it cannot be. I think that case illustrates and determines the present one.

I hold, therefore, that where there has been a partial carrying into the effect of an illegal purpose in a substantial manner, it is impossible, though there remains something not performed, that the money paid under that illegal contract can be recovered back.

(iv) Recovery if no reliance on the illegal contract

Money paid can be recovered if there is an independent proprietary right to it, without having to rely on the illegal contract.

Bowmakers Ltd v Barnet Instruments Ltd
[1945] KB 65 (CA)

The plaintiffs had been supplied with machine tools and had let them to the defendants under three hire-purchase contracts. War-time regulations provided that no person was to pay or receive any price for any machine tool produced in the UK until a maximum price had been issued by the Ministry of Supply. All three contracts were assumed to contravene these regulations. The defendants failed to make hire-purchase payments due and sold the tools they had acquired under two of the contracts. They refused to return the tools held under the third contract. The defendants argued that the plaintiffs had no remedy because the contracts were in breach of the regulations and therefore illegal. The plaintiffs brought an action for conversion of the tools. Held: this action could succeed because it was not based on founding a claim on the contracts which were illegal but on the plaintiffs' proprietary right to their own goods.

DU PARCQ LJ: The question, then, is whether in the circumstances the plaintiffs are without a remedy. So far as their claim in conversion is concerned, they are not relying on the hiring agreements at all. On the contrary, they are willing to admit for this purpose that they cannot rely on them. They simply say that the machines were their property, and this, we think, cannot be denied.

Why then should not the plaintiffs have what is their own? No question of the defendants' rights arises. They do not, and cannot, pretend to have had any legal right to possession of the goods at the date of the conversion. [Counsel] is, we think, right in his submission that, if the sale by Smith to the plaintiffs was illegal, then the first and second hiring agreements were tainted with the illegality, since they were brought into being to make that illegal sale possible, but, as we have said, the plaintiffs are not now relying on these agreements or on the third hiring agreement. Prima facie, a man is entitled to his own property, and it is not a general principle of our law (as was suggested) that when one man's goods have got into another's possession in consequence of some unlawful dealings between them, the true owner can never be allowed to recover those goods by an action. It would, indeed, be astonishing if (to take one instance) a person in the position of the defendant in *Pearce v Brooks* (1866) LR 1 Exch 213, supposing that she had converted the plaintiff's brougham to her own use, were to be permitted, in the supposed interests of public policy, to keep it or the proceeds of its sale for her own benefit. The principle which is, in truth, followed by the court is that stated by Lord Mansfield, that no claim founded on an illegal contract will be enforced, and for this purpose the words 'illegal contract' must now be understood in the wide sense which we have already indicated and no technical meaning must be ascribed to the words 'founded on an illegal contract.' The form of the pleadings is by no means conclusive. More modern illustrations of the principle on which the courts act are *Scott* v *Brown, Doering, McNab & Co.* [1892] 2 QB 724 and *Alexander* v *Rayson* [1936] 1 KB 169, but, as Lindley LJ said in the former of the cases just cited: 'Any rights which [a plaintiff] may have irrespective of his illegal contract will, of course, be recognised and enforced.'

In our opinion, a man's right to possess his own chattels will as a general rule be enforced against one who, without any claim of right, is detaining them, or has converted them to his own use, even though it may appear either from the pleadings, or in the course of the trial, that the chattels in question came into the defendant's possession by reason of an illegal contract between himself and the plaintiff, provided that the plaintiff does not seek, and is not forced, either to found his claim on the illegal contract or to plead its illegality in order to support his claim.

■ QUESTION

To what extent can this decision be justified as allowing the plaintiffs to obtain a remedy against the defendants and preventing the defendants from benefiting from their misconduct?

NOTES
1. The defendants' rights to possession arose under a bailment contract. Although for two of the agreements the defendants' possession under the bailment had terminated on the sale of the tools, under the other contract the defendants were still in possession of the tool, and the plaintiffs only had the right to possession of the tool by establishing the breach of that agreement. They would therefore have had to rely on the illegality of that agreement. To this extent the decision can be criticised, since in relation to the tool that was not sold the Court of Appeal appears to have enforced an illegal contract.
2. The *Bowmakers* principle was applied by the Court of Appeal in *Skilton* v *Sullivan, The Times*, 25 March 1994. This case concerned a contract for the sale of koi carp (a fish). The plaintiff's subsequent invoice described the fish as 'trout', which was zero-rated for VAT purposes whereas koi carp was not. It was held that the contract itself was not illegal (it was illegal only in the way it was carried out), since the plaintiff had formed a dishonest intent to defer paying the VAT only after the contract had been made. The plaintiff could establish liability to pay by relying on the contract itself, which was lawful, and did not need to rely on the invoice, which constituted an unlawful act.

Although the decision on the facts in *Bowmakers* may be questioned, the principle has been recognised by the House of Lords in the next case.

Tinsley v *Milligan*
[1994] 1 AC 340 (HL)

The plaintiff and the defendant were lovers and both supplied money for the purchase of a house. However, the house was put in the sole name of the defendant in order to enable the plaintiff to make false social security claims. Later there was a disagreement and the plaintiff moved out. She then claimed that she was entitled to a share of the property since she had an equitable interest resulting from her contribution to the purchase price. The defendant argued that she was not so entitled since the whole arrangement had been entered into in order to further an illegal purpose. Held: the majority (Lords Browne-Wilkinson, Jauncey, and Lowry; Lords Keith and Goff dissenting) held that the plaintiff should succeed. She did not need to rely on the illegality in order to support her claim because the presumption of the resulting trust in her favour was raised by the fact that the house was held in the name of the defendant alone and by the fact that she had contributed to the purchase price. The reason why the house was in the sole name of the defendant did not need to be relied on to establish the claim. It was the defendant who had to raise the illegality in seeking to rebut the presumption of the resulting trust.

LORD BROWNE-WILKINSON: My Lords, I agree with the speech of my noble and learned friend Lord Goff of Chieveley, that the consequences of being a party to an illegal transaction cannot depend, as the majority in the Court of Appeal held, on such an imponderable factor as the extent to which the public conscience would be affronted by recognising rights created by illegal transactions. However, I have the misfortune to disagree with him as to the correct principle to be applied in a case where equitable property rights are acquired as a result of an illegal transaction.

Neither at law nor in equity will the court enforce an illegal contract which has been partially, but not fully, performed. However, it does not follow that all acts done under a partially performed contract are of no effect. In particular it is now clearly established that at law (as opposed to in equity), property in goods or land can pass under, or pursuant to, such a contract. If so, the rights of the owner of the legal title thereby acquired will be enforced, provided that the plaintiff can establish such title without pleading or leading evidence of the illegality. It is said that the property lies where it falls, even though legal title to the property was acquired as a result of the property passing under the illegal contract itself. I will first consider the modern authorities laying down the circumstances under which a legal proprietary interest acquired under an illegal transaction will be enforced by the courts. I will then consider whether the courts adopt a different attitude to equitable proprietary interests so acquired.

The position at law is well illustrated by the decision in *Bowmakers Ltd* v *Barnet Instruments Ltd* [1945] KB 65. . . . [T]he following propositions emerge: (1) property in chattels and land can pass under a contract which is illegal and therefore would have been unenforceable as a contract; (2) a plaintiff can at law enforce property rights so acquired provided that he does not need to rely on the illegal contract for any purpose other than providing the basis of his claim to a property right; (3) it is irrelevant that the illegality of the underlying agreement was either pleaded or emerged in evidence: if the plaintiff has acquired legal title under the illegal contract that is enough.

I have stressed the common law rules as to the impact of illegality on the acquisition and enforcement of property rights because it is the appellant's contention that different principles apply in equity. In particular it is said that equity will not aid Miss Milligan to assert, establish or enforce an equitable, as opposed to a legal, proprietary interest since she was a party to the fraud on the DSS. The house was put in the name of Miss Tinsley alone (instead of joint names) to facilitate the fraud. Therefore, it is said, Miss Milligan does not come to equity with clean hands: consequently, equity will not aid her. . . .

In my judgment to draw such distinctions between property rights enforceable at law and those which require the intervention of equity would be surprising. More than 100 years has elapsed since the administration of law and equity became fused. The reality of the matter is that, in 1993, English law has one single law of property made up of legal and equitable interests. Although for historical reasons legal estates and equitable estates have differing incidents, the person owning either type of estate has a right of property, a right in rem not merely a right in personam. If the law is that a party is entitled to enforce a property right acquired under an illegal transaction, in my judgment the same rule ought to apply to any property right so acquired, whether such right is legal or equitable.

In the present case, Miss Milligan claims under a resulting or implied trust. The courts below have found, and it is not now disputed, that apart from the question of illegality Miss Milligan would have been entitled in equity to a half share in the house in accordance with the principles exemplified in *Gissing* v *Gissing* [1971] AC 886; *Grant* v *Edwards* [1986] Ch 638 and *Lloyds Bank plc* v *Rosset* [1991] 1 AC 107. The creation of such an equitable interest does not depend upon a contractual obligation but on a common intention acted upon by the parties to their detriment. It is a development of the old law of resulting trust under which, where two parties have provided the purchase money to buy a property which is conveyed into the name of one of them alone, the latter is presumed to hold the property on a resulting trust for both parties in shares proportionate to their contributions to the purchase price. In argument, no distinction was drawn between strict resulting trusts and a *Gissing* v *Gissing* type of trust.

. . . '[D]oes a plaintiff claiming under a resulting trust have to rely on the underlying illegality?' Where the presumption of resulting trust applies, the plaintiff does not have to rely on the illegality. If he proves that the property is vested in the defendant alone but that the plaintiff provided part of the purchase money, or voluntarily transferred the property to the defendant, the plaintiff establishes his claim under a resulting trust unless either the contrary presumption of advancement displaces the presumption of resulting trust or the defendant leads evidence to rebut the presumption of resulting trust. Therefore, in cases where the presumption of advancement does not apply, a plaintiff can establish his equitable interest in the property without relying in any way on the underlying illegal transaction. In this case Miss Milligan as defendant simply pleaded the common intention that the property should belong to both of them and that she contributed to the purchase price: she claimed that in consequence the property belonged to them equally. To the same effect was her evidence in chief. Therefore Miss Milligan was not forced to rely on the illegality to prove her equitable interest. Only in the reply and the course of Miss Milligan's cross-examination did such illegality emerge: it was Miss Tinsley who had to rely on that illegality.

Although the presumption of advancement does not directly arise for consideration in this case, it is important when considering the decided cases to understand its operation. On a transfer from a man to his wife, children or others to whom he stands in loco parentis, equity presumes an intention to make a gift. Therefore in such a case, unlike the case where the presumption of resulting trust applies, in order to establish any claim the plaintiff has himself to lead evidence sufficient to rebut the presumption of gift and in so doing will normally have to plead, and give evidence of, the underlying illegal purpose.

. . . In my judgment the time has come to decide clearly that the rule is the same whether a plaintiff founds himself on a legal or equitable title: he is entitled to recover if he is not forced to plead or rely on the illegality, even if it emerges that the title on which he relied was acquired in the course of carrying through an illegal transaction.

As applied in the present case, that principle would operate as follows. Miss Milligan established a resulting trust by showing that she had contributed to the purchase price of the house and that there was a common understanding between her and Miss Tinsley that they owned the house equally. She had no need to allege or prove *why* the house was conveyed into the name of Miss Tinsley alone, since that fact was irrelevant to her claim: it was enough to show that the house was in fact vested in Miss Tinsley alone. The illegality only emerged at all because Miss Tinsley sought to raise it. Having proved these facts, Miss Milligan had raised a presumption of resulting trust. There was no evidence to rebut that presumption. Therefore Miss Milligan should succeed.

NOTES

1. While *Bowmakers* established that a person can enforce his right to money paid or property transferred if he can establish his legal title thereto without having to rely on the illegality, *Tinsley* establishes that founding an equitable interest in the property will also suffice.

   In *Mahonia Ltd* v *JP Morgan Chase Bank* [2003] EWHC 1927 (Comm), [2003] 2 Lloyd's Rep 911, Colman J clarified the scope of this principle. He stated (at [27]) that *Tinsley* v *Milligan* 'is concerned with enforcement of collateral rights, legal or equitable, acquired under an illegal contract or one having an illegal purpose but leaves untouched the principle that the English Courts will not enforce a contract lawful on its face which is entered into for an unlawful purpose. A collateral right in this context normally refers to a proprietary right and does not include a right of action on the contract itself.'

2. See Berg [1993] JBL 513 and Enonchong (1995) 111 LQR 135.

3. Lord Goff was in the minority in considering that the court could not give equitable assistance to a claimant who had not come with 'clean hands'. His judgment is also important in that (at pp. 363–4) he advocated reform of the law, possibly along the lines of the New Zealand Illegal Contracts Act 1970 which is based on discretionary relief, and stated that he

would welcome an investigation of this question by the Law Commission on the basis that the present rules are 'indiscriminate in their effect, and are capable therefore of producing injustice'.

4. In its 1999 Consultation Paper No. 154, *Illegal Transactions: The Effect of Illegality on Contracts and Trusts* (paras 7.27–7.57), the Law Commission proposed introducing such a discretion (in cases other than those where the contract is illegal as being contrary to public policy), enabling the courts to decide whether illegality should act as a defence to a claim to enforce a contract the formation, purpose, or performance of which is illegal. The Law Commission is, however, proposing that in exercising this discretion the courts should consider:

   (a) the seriousness of the illegality involved;
   (b) the knowledge and intention of the plaintiff;
   (c) whether denying relief will act as a deterrent;
   (d) whether denying relief will further the purpose of the rule which renders the contract illegal; and
   (e) whether denying relief is proportionate to the illegality involved.

   Inevitably such a proposed reform would introduce uncertainty, but it would give the courts the flexibility to examine the claimant's position on the individual facts of the case and ensure that the policy objectives lying behind the illegality rules are respected.

5. *Tinsley* v *Milligan* was applied by the Court of Appeal in *Mortgage Express* v *Robson* [2001] EWCA Civ 887, [2001] 2 All ER (Comm) 886. The appellant was held to be entitled to a share of the equity in a property purchased as a joint enterprise with her husband and brother but with monies representing the equity in previous properties purchased with mortgages obtained by the appellant's husband using false names. The brother had evicted the appellant and her husband and had fraudulently remortgaged the house to the claimant. When the brother defaulted, the claimant had started proceedings for possession and the appellant and her husband had sought recognition of their equitable interests on the basis of their contribution to the purchase price and other sums the appellant had spent on improvements. At first instance the judge had distinguished *Tinsley* v *Milligan* on the basis that it was concerned with property acquired for an unlawful purpose, whereas this case concerned money from an unlawful source (i.e., the equity resulting from the previous fraudulent mortgages). However, the Court of Appeal considered that this was not a distinction of any significance. Since the couple had founded their claim on the acquisition of a property right and were not seeking to enforce an illegal transaction, *Tinsley* v *Milligan* applied and enabled that equitable interest to be recognised. In addition, the property purchased as the joint purchase did not involve any new illegality on their part since it involved the use of the couple's own money, albeit it could be traced back to earlier frauds.

Lord Browne-Wilkinson indicated, however, that the principle in *Tinsley* v *Milligan* would have serious shortcomings in practice, since if the presumption of advancement (to make a gift) applied—e.g., a transfer from husband to wife or from a father to his child—in order to seek to rebut it a claimant might need to rely on the illegal purpose and could not therefore successfully claim rights in the property.

This result seems somewhat strange and the Court of Appeal has since held that a transferor could withdraw from a transaction to transfer property for an illegal purpose as long as he did so before any part of the illegal purpose had taken place. This is sometimes referred to as '*locus poenitentiae*', see *page 697 above*. In such circumstances the transferor could recover the property by relying on the illegality to rebut a presumption of advancement.

Tribe v *Tribe*
[1996] Ch 107 (CA)

The plaintiff owned 459 out of 500 shares in the family company. He was also the tenant of two leasehold premises which the company occupied as licensee. The landlords of these premises had required the plaintiff to carry out substantial repairs to these premises. The plaintiff had been advised that this would be costly and that he might be forced to sell the company or dispose of his shares. The plaintiff transferred his shares in the company to the defendant, one of his sons, and it was found that this had been done with the purpose of defrauding the plaintiff's creditors by making it appear that he did not own any shares in the company. Although the transfer was expressed to be for a consideration of £78,030, this was not paid.

In the end the plaintiff did not need to pay for repairs because the landlord of one of the properties accepted a surrender of the lease and the landlord of the other property sold the reversion to the plaintiff.

When the plaintiff asked the defendant to return the shares, the defendant refused. The plaintiff claimed that the defendant held the shares on trust and had agreed to redeliver them once the repairs issue was settled. The defendant denied any such agreement and argued that there was a presumption of advancement in his favour which the plaintiff could not rebut without revealing the illegal purpose behind the transfer. Held: there was an exception to the *in pari delicto* rule if the transferor had withdrawn from the transaction before any part of the illegal purpose had been carried into effect. No creditors had in fact been defrauded so no part of the illegal purpose had been achieved. Therefore the father could give evidence of the illegality to rebut the presumption of advancement to the son and recover the shares.

NOURSE LJ: . . . The rule that no court will lend its aid to man who founds his cause of action on an immoral or illegal act has often led to seemingly unjust results. That is because, as Lord Mansfield CJ made clear when stating the rule in regard to contracts in *Holman* v *Johnson* (1775) 1 Cowp 341, 343, it is not a principle of justice; it is a principle of policy, whose application is indiscriminate and so can lead to unfair consequences as between the parties to litigation: see per Lord Goff of Chieveley in *Tinsley* v *Milligan* [1994] 1 AC 340, 355B–C. But since such consequences are in general unacceptable to them, the courts have made exceptions to the rule. The exception here in point was recognised by Lord Goff, at p. 356:

In particular, an exception to the principle is to be found in cases in which the illegal purpose has not been carried into effect; but all those cases in which that exception has been recognised have proceeded on the basis that, absent those exceptional circumstances, the principle would have applied. It is not necessary to examine the nature of this exception for present purposes. It is often said to derive from *Taylor* v *Bowers* (1876) 1 QBD 291, which was in fact a case at law. However, the exception was foreshadowed in a number of earlier cases in equity, notably *Platamone* v *Staple* (1815) Coop 250; *Cecil* v *Butcher* (1821) 2 Jac & W 565 and *Symes* v *Hughes* (1870) LR 9 Eq 475; and it has since been applied in, for example, *Chetty* v *Muniandi Servai* (1908) LR 35 Ind App 98 and *Perpetual Executors and Trustees Association of Australia Ltd* v *Wright* (1917) 23 CLR 185.

The exception was also recognised by Lord Browne-Wilkinson, at p. 374:

There was originally a difference of view as to whether a transaction entered into for an illegal purpose would be enforced at law or in equity if the party had repented of his illegal purpose before it had been put into operation, i.e. the doctrine of locus poenitentiae. It was eventually recognised both at law and in equity that, if the plaintiff had repented before the illegal purpose was carried through, he could recover his property: see *Taylor* v *Bowers*, 1 QBD 291; *Symes* v *Hughes*, LR 9 Eq 475.

In both *Tinsley* v *Milligan* [1994] 1 AC 340 and the present case A transferred property into the name of B with the mutual intention of concealing A's interest in the property for a fraudulent or illegal purpose. Before *Tinsley* v *Milligan* the general rule that A could not recover the property was consistently applied irrespective of whether the presumption of advancement arose between A and B or not: see per Lord Goff, at p. 356B–F and the authorities there cited. But now the majority of their Lordships have made a clear distinction between the two cases. In holding that the general rule does not apply where there is no presumption of advancement, they have necessarily affirmed its application to cases where there is. Thus Lord Browne-Wilkinson pointed out, at p. 372B–C, that, in a case where the presumption of advancement applies, in order to establish any claim, the plaintiff has himself to lead evidence sufficient to rebut the presumption of gift and in so doing will normally have to plead, and give evidence of, the underlying illegal purpose: see also at p. 375C.

At the end of his judgment in the court below, Judge Weeks QC said:

Finally, it is not for me to criticise their Lordships' reasoning, but with the greatest respect I find it difficult to see why the outcome in cases such as the present one should depend to such a large extent on arbitrary factors, such as whether the claim is brought by a father against a son, or a mother against a son, or a grandfather against a grandson.

I see much force in those observations. If the defendant had been his brother, grandson, nephew or son-in-law, the plaintiff would have succeeded without further inquiry. Moreover, in times when the presumption of advancement has for other purposes fallen into disfavour (see, for example, the observations of Lord Reid, Lord Hodson and Lord Diplock in *Pettitt* v *Pettitt* [1970] AC 777, 793, 811, 824) there seems to be some perversity in its elevation to a decisive status in the context of illegality. Be that as it may, we are bound by *Tinsley* v *Milligan* [1994] 1 AC 340 for what it decided. It decided that where the presumption of advancement arises the general rule applies. It did not decide that there is no exception where the illegal purpose has not been carried into effect. If anything, it may be said to support the existence of the exception in such a case: see in particular Lord Goff's reference, at p. 356H, to *Perpetual Executors and Trustees Association of Australia Ltd* v *Wright* (1917) 23 CLR 185.

[Nourse LJ then reviewed the authorities and continued:]

On this state of the authorities I decline to hold that the exception does not apply to a case where the presumption of advancement arises but the illegal purpose has not been carried into effect in any way. *Wright's* case, 23 CLR 185, supported by the observations of the Privy Council in *Chettiar* v *Chettiar* [1962] AC 294, is clear authority for its application and no decision to the contrary has been cited. In the circumstances I do not propose to distinguish between law and equity, nor to become embroiled in the many irreconcilable authorities which deal with the exception in its application to executory contracts, nor even to speculate as to the significance, if any, of calling it a locus poenitentiae, a name I have avoided as tending to mislead. In a property transfer case the exception applies if the illegal purpose has not been carried into effect in any way.

I return to the facts of this case. The judge found that the illegal purpose was to deceive the plaintiff's creditors by creating an appearance that he no longer owned any shares in the company. He also found that it was not carried into effect in any way. [Counsel] for the defendant, attacked the latter finding on grounds which appeared to me to confuse the purpose with the transaction. Certainly the transaction was carried into effect by the execution and registration of the transfer. But *Wright's* case shows that that is immaterial. It is the purpose which has to be carried into effect and that would only have happened if and when a creditor or creditors of the plaintiff had been deceived by the transaction. The judge said there was no evidence of that and clearly he did not think it appropriate to infer it. Nor is it any objection to the plaintiff's right to recover the shares that he did not demand their return until after the danger had passed and it was no longer necessary to conceal the transfer from his creditors. All that matters is that no deception was practised on them. For these reasons the judge was right to hold that the exception applied. . . .

I desire to add two comments. First, as to the facts. The judge said that he would have been minded to exercise his discretion, had he had one, in favour of the plaintiff. He evidently thought that the defendant had acted basely by seeking to retain for himself assets which he knew the plaintiff had desired to protect for the benefit of the whole family. In a case of this kind a view of the general merits formed by the judge who has seen and heard the parties give their evidence deserves to be treated with the greatest possible respect. Second, as to the law. If Miss Milligan was able to recover against Miss Tinsley even though she had succeeded in defrauding the Department of Social Security over a period of years, it would indeed be a cause for concern if a plaintiff who had not defrauded his creditors in any way was prevented from recovering simply because the defendant was his son. For my part, I am glad to hold that that is not the law.

MILLETT LJ: . . . There are, in my opinion, two questions of some importance which fall for decision in the present case. The first is whether, once property has been transferred to a transferee for an illegal purpose in circumstances which give rise to the presumption of advancement, it is still open to the transferor to withdraw from the transaction before the purpose has been carried out and, having done so, give evidence of the illegal purpose in order to rebut the presumption of advancement. The second is whether, if so, it is sufficient for him to withdraw from the transaction because it is no longer necessary and without repenting of his illegal purpose. I shall deal with these two questions in turn.

The presumption of advancement and the locus poenitentiae

In *Tinsley* v *Milligan* [1994] 1 AC 340, 370 Lord Browne-Wilkinson summarised the common law rules which govern the effect of illegality on the acquisition and enforcement of property rights in three propositions:

> (1) property in chattels and land can pass under a contract which is illegal and would therefore have been unenforceable as a contract; (2) a plaintiff can at law enforce property rights so acquired provided that he does not need to rely on the illegal contract for any purpose other than providing the basis of his claim to a property right; and (3) it is irrelevant that the illegality of the underlying agreement was either pleaded or emerged in evidence: if the plaintiff has acquired legal title under the illegal contract that is enough.

The decision of the majority of their Lordships in that case was that the same principles applied in equity. It is, therefore, now settled that neither at law nor in equity may a party rely on his own fraud or illegality in order to found a claim or rebut a presumption, but that the common law and equity alike will assist him to protect and enforce his property rights if he can do so without relying on the fraud or illegality. This is the primary rule.

It is, however, also settled both at law and in equity that a person who has transferred property for an illegal purpose can nevertheless recover his property provided that he withdraws from the transaction before the illegal purpose has been wholly or partly performed. This is the doctrine of the locus poenitentiae and it applies in equity as well as at law: see *Symes* v *Hughes* (1870) LR 9 Eq 475 for the former and *Taylor* v *Bowers* (1876) 1 QBD 291, for the latter. The availability of the doctrine in a restitutionary context was expressly confirmed by Lord Browne-Wilkinson in *Tinsley* v *Milligan* [1994] 1 AC 340, 374.

While both principles are well established, the nature of the relationship between them is unclear. Is the doctrine of the locus poenitentiae coextensive with and by way of general exception to the primary rule? The question in the present case is whether a plaintiff who has made a gratuitous transfer of property to a person in whose favour the presumption of advancement arises can withdraw from the transaction before the illegal purpose has been carried into effect and then recover the property by leading evidence of his illegal purpose in order to rebut the presumption. Closely connected with this question is its converse: is a plaintiff who has made such a transfer in circumstances which give rise to a resulting trust so that he has no need to rely on the illegal purpose, as in *Tinsley* v *Milligan* itself, barred from recovering if the illegal purpose has been carried out? If both questions are answered in the negative, then either the locus poenitentiae is a common law doctrine which has no counterpart in equity or it is a contractual doctrine which has no place in the law of restitution.

. . . [In *Tinsley* v *Milligan*] Lord Browne-Wilkinson, at p. 374, expressly confirmed the existence of the doctrine of the locus poenitentiae and its application in a restitutionary context; indeed, he founded part of his reasoning upon it. Moreover, it is in accordance with ordinary restitutionary principles. The fact that title has passed is no bar to a claim for restitution; on the contrary, this is the normal case. But to succeed at law it is necessary for the transferor to repudiate the transaction which gave rise to its passing, and this is what the locus poenitentiae allows him to do.

The locus poenitentiae is not therefore an exclusively contractual doctrine with no place in the law of restitution. It follows that it cannot be excluded by the mere fact that the legal ownership of the property has become lawfully vested in the transferee. It would be unfortunate if the rule in equity were different. It would constitute a further obstacle to the development of a coherent and unified law of restitution. . . .

There is no modern case in which restitution has been denied in circumstances comparable to those of the present case where the illegal purpose has not been carried out. In *Tinsley* v *Milligan* Lord Browne-Wilkinson expressly recognised, at p. 374, the availability of the doctrine of the locus poenitentiae in a restitutionary context, and cited *Taylor* v *Bowers* . . . as well as *Symes* v *Hughes* . . . without disapproval. In my opinion the weight of the authorities supports the view that a person who seeks to recover property transferred by him for an illegal purpose can lead evidence of his dishonest intention whenever it is necessary for him to do so provided that he has withdrawn from the transaction before the illegal purpose has been carried out. It is not necessary if he can rely on an express or resulting trust in his favour; but it is necessary (i) if he brings an action at law and (ii) if he brings proceedings in equity and needs to rebut the presumption of advancement. The availability of the locus poenitentiae is well documented in the former case. I would not willingly adopt a rule which differentiated between the rule of the common law and that of equity in a restitutionary context. . . .

At heart the question for decision in the present case is one of legal policy. The primary rule which precludes the court from lending its assistance to a man who founds his cause of action on an illegal or immoral act often leads to a denial of justice. The justification for this is that the rule is not a principle of justice but a principle of policy: see the much-quoted statement of Lord Mansfield CJ in *Holman* v *Johnson* (1775) 1 Cowp 341, 343. The doctrine of the locus poenitentiae is an exception which operates to mitigate the harshness of the primary rule. It enables the court to do justice between the parties even though, in order to do so, it must allow a plaintiff to give evidence of his own dishonest intent. But he must have withdrawn from the transaction while his dishonesty still lay in intention only. The law draws the line once the intention has been wholly or partly carried into effect.

Seen in this light the doctrine of the locus poenitentiae, although an exception to the primary rule, is not inconsistent with the policy which underlies it. It is, of course, artificial to think that anyone would be dissuaded by the primary rule from entering into a proposed fraud, if only because such a person would be unlikely to be a studious reader of the law reports or to seek advice from a lawyer whom he has taken fully into his confidence. But, if the policy which underlies the primary rule is to discourage fraud, the policy which underlies the exception must be taken to be to encourage withdrawal from a proposed fraud before it is implemented, an end which is no less desirable. And if the former objective is of such overriding importance that the primary rule must be given effect even where it leads to a denial of justice, then in my opinion the latter objective justifies the adoption of the exception where this enables justice to be done.

To my mind these considerations are even more compelling since the decision in *Tinsley* v *Milligan* [1994] 1 AC 340. One might hesitate before allowing a novel exception to a rule of legal policy, particularly a rule based on moral principles. But the primary rule, as it has emerged from that decision, does not conform to any discernible moral principle. It is procedural in nature and depends on the adventitious location of the burden of proof in any given case. Had the plaintiff transferred the shares to a stranger or distant relative whom he trusted, albeit for the same dishonest purpose, it cannot be doubted that he would have succeeded in his claim. He would also have succeeded if he had given them to his son and procured him to sign a declaration of trust in his favour. But he chose to transfer them to a son whom he trusted to the extent of dispensing with the precaution of obtaining a declaration of trust. If that is fatal to his claim, then the greater the betrayal, the less the power of equity to give a remedy.

In my opinion the following propositions represent the present state of the law. (1) Title to property passes both at law and in equity even if the transfer is made for an illegal purpose. The fact that title has passed to the transferee does not preclude the transferor from bringing an action for restitution. (2) The transferor's action will fail if it would be illegal for him to retain any interest in the property. (3) Subject to (2) the transferor can recover the property if he can do so without relying on the illegal purpose. This will normally be the case where the property was transferred without consideration in circumstances where the transferor can rely on an express declaration of trust or a resulting trust in his favour. (4) It will almost invariably be so where the illegal purpose has not been carried out. It may be otherwise where the illegal purpose has been carried out and the transferee can rely on the transferor's conduct as inconsistent with his retention of a beneficial interest. (5) The transferor can lead evidence of the illegal purpose whenever it is necessary for him to do so provided that he has withdrawn from the transaction before the illegal purpose has been wholly or partly carried into effect. It will be necessary for him to do so (i) if he brings an action at law or (ii) if he brings proceedings in equity and needs to rebut the presumption of advancement. (6) The only way in which a man can protect his property from his creditors is by divesting himself of all beneficial interest in it. Evidence that he transferred the property in order to protect it from his creditors, therefore, does nothing by itself to rebut the presumption of advancement; it reinforces it. To rebut the presumption it is necessary to show that he intended to retain a beneficial interest and conceal it from his creditors. (7) The court should not conclude that this was his intention without compelling circumstantial evidence to this effect. The identity of the transferee and the circumstances in which the transfer was made would be highly relevant. It is unlikely that the court would reach such a conclusion where the transfer was made in the absence of an imminent and perceived threat from known creditors.

The doctrine of the locus poenitentiae
It is impossible to reconcile all the authorities on the circumstances in which a party to an illegal contract is permitted to withdraw from it. At one time he was allowed to withdraw so long as the contract had not been completely performed; but later it was held that recovery was barred once it had been partly performed: see *Kearley* v *Thompson* (1890) 24 QBD 742. It is clear that he must withdraw voluntarily, and that it is not sufficient that he is forced to do so because his plan has been discovered. In *Bigos* v *Bousted* [1951] 1 All ER 92 this was, perhaps dubiously, extended to prevent withdrawal where the scheme has been frustrated by the refusal of the other party to carry out his part.

The academic articles Grodecki 'In Pari Delicto Potior Est Conditio Defendentis' (1955) 71 LQR 254, Beatson 'Repudiation of Illegal Purpose as a Ground for Restitution' (1975) 91 LQR 313 and Merkin 'Restitution by Withdrawal from Executory Illegal Contracts' (1981) 97 LQR 420 are required reading for anyone who attempts the difficult task of defining the precise limits of the doctrine. I would draw back from any such attempt. But I would hold that genuine repentance is not required. Justice is not a reward for merit; restitution should not be confined to the penitent. I would also hold that voluntary withdrawal from an illegal transaction when it has ceased to be needed is sufficient. It is true that this is not necessary to encourage withdrawal, but a rule to the opposite effect could lead to bizarre results. Suppose, for example that in *Bigos* v *Bousted* . . . exchange control had been abolished before the foreign currency was made available: it is absurd to suppose that the plaintiff should have been denied restitution. I do not agree that it was correct in *Groves* v *Groves* (1829) 3 Y & J 163, 174 and similar cases for the court to withhold its assistance from the plaintiff because 'if the crime has not been completed, the merit was not his'.

NOTES
1. See Virgo [1996] CLJ 23 and Creighton (1997) 60 MLR 102.
2. This case further limits the availability of illegality as a defence to a proprietary claim. The area of operation of such a defence would appear to be restricted to instances where the presumption of advancement applies and the illegal purpose has been carried out at least to some extent. However, see the decision of the High Court of Australia in *Nelson* v *Nelson* (1995) 132 ALR 133, *page 708*.
3. In *Collier* v *Collier* [2002] EWCA Civ 1095, [2002] BPIR 1057, [2003] 1 P & CR D3, the Court of Appeal (*obiter*) considered the presumption of advancement to be applicable on the facts and

rejected an attempt to rely on the doctrine of *locus poenitentiae* in order to assist in the recovery of property transferred.

A father had granted leases of two business properties to his daughter. It was found that the intention was to defeat the claims of the revenue and the father's other creditors. The leases contained options to purchase, which the daughter had exercised on her father's instruction. They fell out and the father alleged that the daughter held the properties upon resulting trust for him. The Court of Appeal held that no resulting trust could have arisen on these facts because the transfers did not amount to a voluntary transfer of the properties; the leases appeared to have been granted for consideration from the daughter. If the transfers had been voluntary, the presumption of advancement would have applied to the transfer by a father to his child and the father would have been unable to establish his equitable interest without relying on the agreement. Counsel for the father attempted to rely on the doctrine of *locus poenitentiae* and the decision in *Tribe* v *Tribe*. However, the Court of Appeal considered that it was too late since the illegal purpose had been carried into effect. The father had given effect to his original dishonest intent by directing the daughter to exercise the option to acquire the freehold interest in the properties.

Mance LJ remarked that, given the daughter's involvement as a party to the illegal purpose, he had 'no great liking for the result', namely that the father could not establish a proprietary interest, but considered that result to be dictated by authority. He noted that the Law Commission's proposed reform, discussed at *pages 701–2*, would have permitted a more discretionary approach.

4. The decision in *Tribe* can be subjected to criticism. The plaintiff did not withdraw because he had second thoughts about the illegal purpose: he withdrew only because he no longer needed to make the transfer. It had previously been thought that in order to rely on this exception to *in pari delicto* it would be necessary for the transferor to 'repent'. However, the Court of Appeal in *Tribe* v *Tribe* considered that no evidence of contrition was necessary. The only test was whether the transferor had withdrawn before the illegal purpose was carried into effect in any way. This indicates a clear relaxation of the principles.

5. In *Tribe*, the Court of Appeal concluded that the plaintiff had withdrawn before the illegal purpose had been carried into effect because that purpose was the defrauding of creditors and no creditors had been deceived. However, it might be argued that the purpose was broader than that, namely to make it appear that the plaintiff did not own the shares. Clearly that purpose had been carried into effect.

6. Illegality and the presumption of advancement was also in issue before the High Court of Australia in *Nelson* v *Nelson* (1995) 132 ALR 133, (1995) 70 ALJR 47. However, the illegal purpose in this case had been achieved. Mrs Nelson had purchased a house and then transferred it into the names of her son and daughter so that she would not own that house and could obtain a statutory subsidy for the purchase of a second house. The son and daughter sold the first house and Mrs Nelson claimed that they held the proceeds on trust for her. It was held that the presumption of advancement (which applied between mother and child) was rebutted and that she was entitled to the proceeds of sale of the house provided she repaid the subsidy she had received. The reasoning of the majority was that the plaintiff would be prevented from recovering her property only where that result was required by the policy of the statute that had been infringed. That was not the position here and she could overcome the illegality by restoring the wrongly received benefit.

This decision represents a move away from technicalities and the artificial distinction drawn by the House of Lords in *Tinsley* v *Milligan* between resulting trusts and rebutting the presumption of advancement. (See Phang (1996) 11 JCL 53 and Creighton (1997) 60 MLR 102.)

7. Interestingly, the Law Commission's Consultation Paper, No. 154 (1999), *page 702*, paras 7.58–7.69, has provisionally proposed that the courts should have a discretion to allow a party to withdraw from an illegal contract and to have any property or benefits restored where this would reduce the likelihood of the illegal act being completed or the illegal purpose being accomplished. The court would first need to be satisfied that the contract could

not be enforced against that party, and in considering the exercise of this discretion it is proposed that the court should consider whether (i) the claimant genuinely repents of the illegality and (ii) the seriousness of the illegality in question.

8. For discussion of the provisional recommendations in the Law Commission's Consultation Paper of 1999, see Buckley, ' "Illegal Transaction": Chaos or Discretion' (2000) LS 155 and Enonchong, 'Illegal Transactions: The Future? (LCCP No. 154)' [2000] RLR 82.

SECTION 3: CAPACITY TO CONTRACT—MINORS' CONTRACTS

With some exceptions, a contract between a minor (under 18) and an adult is not binding on the minor unless, after attaining 18, the minor ratifies the contract.

A: Contracts involving continuing obligations

This category includes tenancy agreements, marriage settlements, partnership agreements, and agreements to take shares in a company which are only partly paid. The minor is at liberty to repudiate the obligations arising under these agreements as long as this is achieved during the minority or within a reasonable time of reaching majority (*Edwards* v *Carter* [1893] AC 360). However, in the absence of such repudiation, the contract will be binding on both parties.

If repudiation takes place, the minor can recover money paid or property transferred only if there has been a total failure of consideration.

Steinberg v *Scala (Leeds) Ltd*
[1923] 2 Ch 452 (CA)

The plaintiff, while a minor, applied for shares in a company and paid the amount due on allotment. She paid the amounts due on the first call but received no dividends and attended no company meetings. Eighteen months later, while still a minor, she repudiated the contract and requested repayment of the money she had paid to the company. Held: since she was a minor she was entitled to repudiate the contract, but as there had been no failure of consideration she could not recover the money paid to the company.

LORD STERNDALE MR: . . . I think the argument for the respondent has rather proceeded upon the assumption that the question whether she can rescind and the question whether she can recover her money back are the same. They are two quite different questions, as is pointed out by Turner LJ in his judgment in *Ex parte Taylor* (1856) 8 DM&G 254. He there says: 'It is clear that an infant cannot be absolutely bound by a contract entered into during his minority. He must have a right upon his attaining his majority to elect whether he will adopt the contract or not.' Then he proceeds: 'It is, however, a different question whether, if an infant pays money on the footing of a contract, he can afterwards recover it back. If an infant buys an article which is not a necessary, he cannot be compelled to pay for it, but if he does pay for it during his minority he cannot on attaining his majority recover the money back.' That seems to me to be only stating in other words the principle which is laid down in a number of other cases that, although the contract may be rescinded the money paid cannot be recovered back unless there has been an entire failure of the consideration for which the money has been paid. Therefore it seems to me that the question to which we have to address ourselves is: Has there here been a total failure of the consideration for which the money was paid?

> Now the plaintiff has had the shares allotted to her and there is evidence that they were of some value, that they had been dealt in at from 9s. to 10s. a share. . . .
>
> In those circumstances is it possible to say that there was a total failure of consideration? If the plaintiff were a person of full age suing to recover the money back on the ground, and the sole ground, that there had been a failure of consideration it seems to me it would have been impossible for her to succeed, because she would have got the very thing for which the money was paid and would have got a thing of tangible value.
>
> I cannot see any difference when you come to consider whether there has been consideration or not between the position of a person of full age and an infant. The question whether there has been consideration or not must, I think, be the same in the two cases. . . .

B: Contracts for necessaries

These contracts are binding on a minor to the extent that the minor must pay a reasonable price for necessaries sold and delivered to him.

SALE OF GOODS ACT 1979

3. Capacity to buy and sell

(2) Where necessaries are sold and delivered to a minor or to a person who by reason of mental incapacity or drunkenness is incompetent to contract, he must pay a reasonable price for them.

(3) . . . 'necessaries' means goods suitable to the condition in life of the minor or other person concerned and to his actual requirements at the time of the sale and delivery.

Nash v *Inman*
[1908] 2 KB 1 (CA)

The plaintiff supplied clothing to the defendant, a Cambridge undergraduate, to the value of £145 10s 3d. The clothing included 11 fancy waistcoats. The defendant argued that he was a minor at the time the goods were supplied and that they were not 'necessaries'. The defendant's father gave evidence that the son was already amply supplied with clothes. Held: the onus of proving that the goods supplied were suitable to the condition in life of the minor and that the defendant was not already adequately supplied with such goods, was on the plaintiff. The plaintiff had failed to establish this.

■ QUESTION

Why is the minor liable only for the reasonable price of necessaries and not their actual cost?

C: Beneficial contracts of service

A minor is bound by an employment contract if, on the whole, it is for his benefit.

Doyle v *White City Stadium*
[1935] 1 KB 110 (CA)

The plaintiff, a minor, applied to the British Boxing Board of Control for a licence as a boxer and agreed to be bound by the rules of the Board. He was issued with a boxer's licence. A few months later the rules were altered. Instead of a rule which provided that a boxer's money was only to be stopped if he was disqualified for a deliberate foul, the new rule was that in any case of disqualification the boxer was only to receive certain expenses. The plaintiff had arranged to box in return for £3,000 (win, lose, or draw) but he was disqualified for fouling. The Board withheld most of his £3,000. The plaintiff claimed the whole sum. Held: the contract as a whole between the plaintiff and the Board was beneficial to the plaintiff and therefore was binding on him.

LORD HANWORTH MR: I turn to *De Francesco* v *Barnum* (1890) 45 ChD 430, where Fry LJ says: 'I approach this subject with the observation that it appears to me that the question is this, Is the contract for the benefit of the infant? Not, Is any one particular stipulation for the benefit of the infant? Because it is obvious that the contract of apprenticeship or the contract of labour must, like any other contract, contain some stipulations for the benefit of the one contracting party, and some for the benefit of the other. It is not because you can lay your hand on a particular stipulation which you may say is against the infant's benefit, that therefore the whole contract is not for the benefit of the infant. The Court must look at the whole contract, having regard to the circumstances of the case, and determine, subject to any principles of law which may be ascertained by the cases, whether the contract is or is not beneficial. That appears to me to be in substance a question of fact.' . . .

The learned judge on the question of fact has held that the terms of the agreement in this case are favourable and to the advantage of the infant, and it seems therefore that the application of the rules cannot be held to be prevented by reason of the plaintiff's infancy.

D: Restitution by the minor

The court has a discretion to order the return of non necessaries which the minor has obtained under an unenforceable contract.

MINORS' CONTRACTS ACT 1987

3. Restitution

   (1) Where—
      (a) a person ('the plaintiff') has after the commencement of this Act entered into a contract with another ('the defendant') and
      (b) the contract is unenforceable against the defendant (or he repudiates it) because he was a minor when the contract was made, the court may, if it is just and equitable to do so, require the defendant to transfer to the plaintiff any property acquired by the defendant under the contract, or any property representing it.

E: Guarantees of minors' contracts

MINORS' CONTRACTS ACT 1987

2. Guarantees

Where—

(a) a guarantee is given in respect of an obligation of a party to a contract made after the commencement of this Act, and

(b) the obligation is unenforceable against him (or he repudiates the contract) because he was a minor when the contract was made, the guarantee shall not for that reason alone be unenforceable against the guarantor.

INDEX